Public Interest Group Profiles

Public Interest Group Profiles

2004–2005

CQ Press and
Foundation for Public Affairs

CQ PRESS

A Division of Congressional Quarterly Inc.
Washington, D.C.

CQ Press
1255 22nd Street, N.W., Suite 400
Washington, D.C. 20037

202-729-1900; toll-free, 1-866-4CQ-PRESS (1-866-427-7737)

www.cqpress.com

Printed and bound in the United States of America

08   07   06   05   04   5   4   3   2   1

Composition by Auburn Associates, Inc.
Cover designed by Joan Stephens

LIBRARY OF CONGRESS CATALOGING-IN-PUBLICATION DATA
Public interest group profiles, 2004–2005.
    p. cm.
  Includes index.
   ISBN 1-56802-886-5 (hardcover : alk. paper)
  1. Pressure Groups—United States—Directories.   I. Foundation for Public Affairs (Washington, D.C.)   II. Title.

 JK1118.P78 2004
 322.4′3′02573—dc22

2004017668

Contents

Topical Contents

Corporate Accountability/Responsibility

Environmental

Families/Children

International Affairs

Preface

Public Interest Group Profiles 2004–2005 is an in-depth guide to the most influential public affairs and advocacy groups in the United States. The 252 organizations profiled in this resource cover a wide range of views from across the spectrum of political orientations.

This updated, eleventh edition places at your fingertips all the information you need about a particular organization. Rather than searching through a dozen documents or Web sites, you can find contact information, mission statements, funding sources, leadership, publications, and press clippings for a given group in this one resource. A new layout for the organization entries makes finding the information you need quick and easy. Also for this edition, *Public Interest Group Profiles* provides extensive internship and employment contact information to assist readers looking for opportunities to be a part of the public advocacy process. The 2004–2005 volume surpasses previous editions in offering more in-depth information on organizational leadership and campaign contribution patterns.

This guide pinpoints the public affairs groups addressing areas of concern today, from business to the environment, from children and families to religion. The groups are organized alphabetically and a topical table of contents is provided to assist in finding groups by subject or function.

Public interest groups, whether they are lobbying a member of Congress or rallying their constituencies to engage in direct action, play a vital role in shaping the debate on public policy. The concentration of these groups in the nation's capital—more than 60 percent of the organizations profiled here are based in Washington, D.C.—testifies to their desire to affect policy on the national level.

Public interest group membership and activities, however, stretch beyond the Beltway. With access to high-speed communications technology, these groups can mobilize members around the country in a matter of minutes through e-mail alerts, Web site updates, faxes, and phone calls. Many of the organizations profiled in this resource regularly update their Web sites to enable users to join mailing lists, track legislation, contact elected representatives, and even make campaign contributions.

In researching these entries, CQ researchers and editors have focused on accuracy and relevancy. The meticulous and often arduous task of identifying and verifying information fell to an outstanding team of researchers. Diane Goldenberg-Hart led the team of researchers that included Denise Hersey, Emily Horning, Julie Linden, Gary Pattillo, Cory Stevens, and others, to whom I owe a debt of gratitude for their talent and tenacity. Thanks are also due to CQ Press development editor January Layman-Wood, who managed this project with patience and diligence, and who was always available to provide expert guidance and generous support. Sally Ryman did a remarkable job producing this title with its new user-friendly design. The three indexes for this volume were created by the skilled staff of Indexing Partners LLC.

Our goal for the eleventh edition of *Public Interest Group Profiles* is to provide our readers with an authoritative one-stop source for understanding the constellation of public interest groups. We hope you will find this reference a useful addition to your library. We welcome your comments and suggestions.

Doug Goldenberg-Hart
Acquisitions Editor

How to Use This Resource

RESEARCH METHOD

In compiling this new edition of *Public Interest Group Profiles,* CQ Press editors and researchers worked closely with the Foundation for Public Affairs (FPA) to draft the list of organizations for inclusion. The FPA, with its affiliate organization, the Public Affairs Council, maintains a national, nonpartisan clearinghouse of information on public interest groups and corporate affairs programs.

The organizations included in this book represent a wide range of political points of view, which in many cases reflect the diversity of their members or constituents. By using the term *public interest groups* we do not intend to imply that they represent the interest of the general public. These organizations are more commonly referred to by the media as *special interest groups, advocacy groups, pressure groups,* and *public policy organizations.*

Selection of Organizations

The Foundation for Public Affairs used the following criteria as a basis for selecting groups for inclusion in this edition:

- the extent of the group's influence on national policy,
- the number of inquiries about the group fielded by FPA staff,
- the volume of news coverage about the group, and
- the representative nature of the group in its field of interest and activity.

Research at CQ Press yielded a few modifications to the list, primarily to reflect the prominence of several newly formed organizations.

Contact with Organizations

In preparing the profiles, CQ Press compiled data from questionnaires sent to organizations. Further information was gleaned from follow-up telephone calls, e-mails, annual reports, publications catalogs, lists of current boards of directors, financial statements, the organization's official Web site, and other relevant literature. When information was not available directly from the organizations, researchers relied on other sources.

The phrase "Declined to comment" appearing under certain sections in some profiles indicates that the organization either did not respond to the questionnaire or did not provide all of the information requested. "None" indicates that a component does not apply to a group (for example, it does not have a PAC or a human resources director). "Information unavailable" is used for components for which CQ Press was unable to locate reliable information.

Balance of Coverage

It is important to note that *Public Interest Group Profiles* is not intended to act as a rating service. In compiling the section "Effectiveness and Political Orientation" of organizations, CQ Press editors have attempted to provide balance in terms of content and sources. The appearance of quotations that are critical of an organization do not imply agreement or an evaluation by the Foundation for Public Affairs or CQ Press.

Some organizations, by their very nature, generate more press coverage than others. Readers should consider the subjective sections of the profiles to be merely a representation of available commentary—nothing more, nothing less. Finally, the length of the profile does not reflect the relative influence of the organizations.

ORGANIZATION OF THE BOOK

Contents

The main body of the book is devoted to profiling 252 organizations. Previous editions of *Public Interest Group Profiles* organized these groups into issue (Environmental) or functional (Business/Economic) sectors, each sector comprising a chapter of the work. This approach required that readers know to which sector a group belonged. For this edition, all of the organization profiles are organized alphabetically throughout the work, rather than grouped into chapters by sector. To assist readers who may want to find groups by sector, the CQ Press editors provide a topical table of contents (p. viii) following the alphabetical table of contents (p. v).

Organization of the Components

For this edition, CQ Press has developed a new layout and organization for the components included in each group's entry. It is now easier for users to locate what they need by distinguishing quickly between directory information and the more substantive material about a group's purpose, concerns, method of operation, and effectiveness.

In the right column of each profile you will find the following components:

Year Established: The date under the organization's name indicates the year in which the group was established.

Contact Information: This information includes, whenever available, the organization's mailing address(es), telephone number(s), facsimile number, and general e-mail and Web site addresses. New to this edition is contact information for each group's communications director and human resources director.

Purpose: In most cases, the organizations provided the language for this section. In general, the text is a quotation from a mission statement.

Current Concerns: This component outlines the current interests of an organization.

Method of Operation: This section provides a standardized list of general methods of operation from "Advertising" and "Boycotts" to "Training" and "Technical Assistance."

Effectiveness and Political Orientation: Provides commentary from third-party sources on a group's efficiency and potency, as well as excerpt quotations on the political leanings of a group.

In the left column, you will find these components:

Director: When available, a brief biography of the executive director is provided.

Board of Directors: This component lists the organization's current governing body. CQ Press has made an extra effort for this edition to obtain the titles and outside affiliations of board members.

Scope: Details on an organization's membership, locations of branch or chapter offices, and affiliates are listed here. An organization's main office is not included in the total number of branch offices.

Staff: When possible, the number of staff members is subdivided into professional, support, part-time personnel, interns, and volunteers.

Tax Status: Most of the organizations described in this book are recognized as tax-exempt under section 501(c) of the Internal Revenue Code and fit into one of three categories:

501(c)(3): This designation is given to charitable, religious, scientific, literary, and educational nonprofits. This designation also includes groups that seek to prevent cruelty or abuse to children (Children's Defense Fund) and animals (People for the Ethical Treatment of Animals) and test products and services for public safety (Center for Auto Safety). Contributions to 501(c)(3) organizations are deductible as charitable donations for federal income tax purposes. Lobbying may not be a "substantial" part of the activities of a 501(c)(3) organization.

501(c)(4): Organizations ruled to be tax-exempt under this section of the Internal Revenue Code are civic leagues (League of United Latin American Citizens), social welfare organizations (Leadership Council on Civil Rights, Inc.), and local associations of employees. Contributions to 501(c)(4) organizations may be deductible as a business expense. There are fewer restrictions on lobbying by 501(c)(4) groups than by 501(c)(3) organizations.

501(c)(6): Organizations ruled to be tax-exempt under this section of the Internal Revenue Code include business leagues (Business Roundtable), chambers of commerce (U.S. Chamber of Commerce), real estate boards, and boards of trade. Contributions to 501(c)(6) organizations are not deductible as charitable donations for federal income tax purposes. If an individual or business supports a 501(c)(6) organization financially, that individual or business can deduct the amount as a business expense "if ordinary and necessary in the conduct of the taxpayer's business."

Finances: When available, information on an organization's most recent budget or revenue is provided.

Funding Sources: This component provides an analysis of an organization's income.

Political Action Committee (PAC): A political action committee is a legal vehicle for individuals to pool financial contributions to support political candidates. Affiliated PACs are presented in this section, as are pie charts of the political contributions made by the PACs to the two major parties during the 2002 elections, the most recent complete federal election cycle prior to this edition.

Employment: Included for the first time in this edition is information about types of positions available, job posting locations, application procedures, hiring practices, and contact persons.

Internships: Another useful feature presented for the first time in this edition is information about the availability of internships, including eligibility requirements, paid/unpaid opportunities, areas of service, application procedures, and contact persons.

Newsletters: This component lists current periodicals published by an organization.

Publications: This section lists recent books, directories, databases, and videos published or produced by an organization.

Conferences: This category provides details on conferences, seminars, and workshops sponsored by an organization.

Indexes

You can use the name index (p. 723) to locate any director or board member listed in this directory. The subject index (p. 767) allows you to look up a subject area or a specific organization. If you need information on a particular topic but do not know a particular source, the index has subject entries to help you find where that topic is covered. Use the state index (p. 719) to determine which organizations are located in a particular state or in the District of Columbia.

Public Interest Group Profiles

AARP

Established in 1958

DIRECTOR

William D. Novelli, chief executive officer. Novelli joined AARP in 2000 as associate executive director for public affairs. Prior to joining AARP, he was president of the Campaign for Tobacco-Free Kids. He has also served as executive vice president of CARE, the relief and development organization. He holds a B.A. from the University of Pennsylvania and an M.A. from the University of Pennsylvania's Annenberg School for Communication.

BOARD OF DIRECTORS

Yash Aggarwal, Ph.D., J.D., New York, NY
Nelda Barnett, Owensboro, KY
Rutherford "Jack" Brice, Decatur, GA
Cora L. Christian, M.D., M.P.H., Frederiksted, Virgin Islands
Bonnie M. Cramer, Raleigh, NC
Lavada E. DeSalles, Sacramento, CA
Joanne Disch, Minneapolis, MN
W. Lee Hammond, Salisbury, MD
Jennie Chin Hansen, San Francisco, CA
Douglas C. Holbrook, Fredericksburg, VA
Richard Johnson, Wilmington, DE
Chris Lamberti, Houston, TX
Charles Leven, Millbrook, NY
Culberto "Jose" Maldonado, Colorado Springs, CO
Charles J. Mendoza, Waverly Hall, GA
Mary Jane O'Gara, Omaha, NE
Erik D. Olsen, Mesa, AZ
N. Joyce Payne, Ed.D., Washington, DC
Clarence Pearson, New York, NY
Angel Rodolfo "A. R." Sales, Fort Myers, FL
Betty J. Severyn, Chattanooga, TN
Rev. Kenneth B. Smith, Sr., Chicago, IL
Thomas Byron Thames, M.D., Orlando, FL
Betty Noble Turner, Port Aransas, TX

SCOPE

Members: 35 million individuals
Branches/chapters: 53 state offices including Washington, DC, Puerto Rico, and the Virgin Islands; 3,700 chapters
Affiliates: AARP Foundation, a 501(c)(3) organization; AARP Andrus Foundation; AARP Services Inc.; National Retired Teachers Association, a tax-exempt organization

STAFF

1,824 total—1,099 professional; 725 support

TAX STATUS

501(c)(3)

FINANCES

Revenue: 2002—$62.63 million; 2001—$64.73 million; 2000—$64.90 million

CONTACT INFORMATION

601 E Street, NW, Washington, DC 20049
Phone: (202) 434-2277 • *Fax:* (202) 434-6484
Toll-free: (202) 434-3410
General E-mail: member@aarp.org • *Web site:* www.aarp.org

Communications Director: Lisa R. Davis
(202) 434-2560 • medioa@aarp.org
Human Resources Director: Richard Henry

PURPOSE: "AARP is a nonprofit, nonpartisan association dedicated to shaping and enriching the experience of aging for our members and for all Americans. We seek through education, advocacy and service to enhance the quality of life for all by promoting independence, dignity and purpose."

CURRENT CONCERNS: Economic security and work • Health and wellness • Long-term care and independent living • Personal enrichment

METHOD OF OPERATION: Advertisements • Awards program • Conferences/seminars • Congressional testimony • Films/video/audiotapes • Grantmaking (AARP Andrus Foundation [provides grants for applied research in gerontology at universities throughout the United States]) • Grassroots organizing • International activities • Internet AARP Webplace (Web site) • Legal assistance • Legislative/regulatory monitoring (federal, state, grassroots) • Library/information clearinghouse • Lobbying (federal, state, and grassroots) • Media outreach • Member services (AARP Motoring Plan; annuities program; credit card programs; insurance—group health, auto/homeowners, mobile home, and life, investment program—eight mutual funds, purchase privilege program; travel discounts) • Research • Speakers program • Telecommunications services (databases) • Television and radio production (Mature Broadcast News, Mature Focus, Prime Time Radio, production and distribution of video news releases) • Training and technical assistance (Experience for Hire promotes use of qualified, experienced professionals to meet changing staffing needs in business; Law Enforcement and Older Persons train law enforcement officers to help them communicate and deal more effectively with older persons; National Older Workers Information System provides a database for employers; Work Force Training Institute provides training programs and presentations to businesses and organizations on age diversity, intergenerational work teams, employment, and retirement planning) • Volunteer programs (55 Alive/Mature Driving retrains motorists age 50 and older; Grandparent Information Center provides grandparents raising their grandchildren with information and referrals to local support groups and other programs; Health Advocacy Services provides information about health promotion, disease prevention, and long-term care; Money After 50 helps lower-income adults develop money management skills; Senior Community Service Employment,

FUNDING SOURCES
Membership dues, 29.1%; programs and royalties, 20.8%; AARP Health Care Options, 20.4%; federal grant and other program revenue, 15.1%; advertising, 13.6%; investments and other income, 1%

PAC
None

EMPLOYMENT
Information on open positions is available at www.aarpjobs.com. Applicants should use the Web site's online form to submit resumes and cover letters. Applicants unable to use the online form should call 1-888-540-5627 for further instructions.

INTERNSHIPS
Information unavailable

NEWSLETTERS
AARP Connections (for volunteers; monthly)
AARP/NRTA Bulletin (monthly, except August)
Modern Maturity (bimonthly magazine)

PUBLICATIONS
AARP Grandparenting Survey
AARP National Survey on Consumer Preparedness and E-Commerce: A Survey of Computer Users Age 45 and Older
Accessory Dwelling Units: Model State Act and Local Ordinance
Acronyms in Aging: Organizations, Agencies, Programs, and Laws, 1999
Are Consumers Well Informed About Prescription Drugs? The Impact of Printed Direct-to-Consumer Advertising
Assisted Living in the United States
Beyond 50.03: A Report to the Nation on Independent Living and Disability
Final Details: A Guide for Survivors When Death Occurs
Fixing to Stay: A National Survey on Housing and Home Modification Issues
Funeral and Burial Planners Survey 1999
Independent Living: Adult Children's Perceptions of Their Parents' Needs
Making Medicare Choices
Medicare Basics
Midlife and Older Americans with Disabilities: Who Gets Help? A Chartbook
Money and the American Family
On Being Alone
Profile of Older Americans
Social Security Book: What Every Woman Absolutely Needs to Know
Social Security: Facts About the "Notch"
These Four Walls . . . Americans 45+ Talk About Home and Community
Also publishes how-to guides, reviews, and audiovisual materials on a variety of relevant subjects.

CONFERENCES
Convention (biennial)
National Retired Teachers Association (biennial)

administered through the AARP Foundation, trains economically disadvantaged older persons and helps place them in permanent jobs; Grief Loss Program, Tax Aide uses volunteer tax counselors trained by AARP Foundation in cooperation with the Internal Revenue Service; Widowed Persons Service provides organizational and training resources to local groups interested in community-wide programs to serve newly widowed men and women; Women's Financial Information Program gives training in financial decision-making; AARP/Vote uses volunteers to help educate and mobilize voters on issues concerning older persons-AARP/Vote does not endorse candidates for political office and does not contribute money to campaigns)

Effectiveness and Political Orientation

"Ann Lemley of South Point, Ohio, was 'shocked' last fall when the AARP threw its support behind the Medicare prescription-drug bill being pushed by President Bush and other Republicans. Lemley, a longtime AARP member and volunteer, initially was aghast that the organization, which has 35 million members, used its considerable clout to help pass legislation many Democrats and seniors viewed as bad medicine—more of a windfall for drug companies than for those saddled with expensive bills. She wasn't alone.

"AARP traditionally has been viewed as allied with Democrats on issues such as Medicare and Social Security. And with a presidential-election year approaching, support for the Medicare proposal was considered a coup for Republicans. Some AARP members who are devout Democrats decried giving the GOP a victory to brag about during the 2004 election, and others charged it was a sellout to pharmaceutical companies standing to gain millions of dollars under the bill. Some people burned membership cards in protest, and AARP Chief Executive William Novelli now says about 60,000 members dropped out.

"Despite the criticism, Novelli and AARP haven't backed away from the decision to support the measure, which GOP congressional leaders considered instrumental in getting the bill to Bush's desk. But AARP also says it's winning over skeptical members by campaigning to improve an imperfect law. Just last week, Novelli sent a letter to major pharmaceutical companies calling on them to voluntarily limit drug prices. The letter also urged the industry to 'cooperate with secure, reasonable drug importation legislation,' something the Bush administration and the pharmaceutical industry succeeded in keeping out of the final Medicare law. AARP also is running a national ad campaign designed to push the government into allowing drug importation from Canada and Mexico. . . .

"Indeed, Lemley, 76, hasn't given up on AARP. She says she's 'OK with AARP's role in it now. I can't say I think the law is 100 percent good. It isn't. . . . But I can say there is some good in it, especially for the people who need the most help.' That's a position that Rep. Deborah Pryce of Upper Arlington, chairwoman of the House Republican Conference, hopes most seniors will adopt as they weigh who to vote for this fall. 'The Medicare bill was a very good first step,' Pryce said. 'It was as far as we could go in the political climate we were working in. That's not to say it can't be better in the future."

(*Columbus Dispatch*, March 14, 2004)

"The Bush administration and Republican congressional leaders are being forced to take a hard new look at the idea of importing cheaper prescription drugs from foreign countries as an election-year clamor grows for removing prohibitions. Continuing increases in prescription drug prices and the pitched partisan battle over the new Medicare law have given the topic greater prominence in Congress and on the campaign trail.

"AARP, the 35-million-member seniors' group that gave Republican-backed Medicare legislation a critical endorsement last year, backs allowing imports. So do two Republican senators, former GOP leader Trent Lott of Mississippi and John Cornyn of Texas, both changing their position in recent days. And so do nearly two-thirds of Americans, according to a recent AP poll.

"Drug importation has become a proxy for talking about the high cost of prescription drugs in the United States. Spending on prescription drugs is the fastest-growing component of health care costs, rising 15.3 percent in 2002. Drug costs are expected to outstrip the overall growth in health care spending for the next 10 years, and that projection doesn't even take into account the new Medicare prescription drug benefit that begins in 2006. Many economists believe the change will lead to an additional increase in costs. . . .

"Lawmakers who supported the Medicare law said they believe the new prescription drug benefit will ease seniors' burden and act as a brake on price increases. But there also is a sense among opponents of importation both on Capitol Hill and in the administration that they can no longer simply cite concerns about the safety of imports. 'It's a very important issue and an issue that, as majority leader, I can tell you we will address. It deserves to be addressed,' Senate Majority Leader Bill Frist said Friday."

(*Chattanooga Times Free Press,* March 13, 2004)

"Judith Brown's message Monday to a roomful of people concerned about their aging parents was direct and succinct. 'Go home and tell your parents about your own financial situation, then ask for their information,' suggested Brown, a financial planner and former national chairwoman of AARP. 'Tell them, "Before you have a medical crisis, so we can plan ahead, we need to know if you can afford the extra help we might need in an emergency." Then go through the numbers.'

"Brown and other experts on a panel talked for 90 minutes to about 200 people at the forum at the Mall of America in Bloomington, and the thread linking all of their advice was that caregivers must get information to make good decisions. 'What's wrong with the long-term care system is that it offers choices that nobody wants,' said Dr. Robert Kane, who heads the Center on Aging at the University of Minnesota. 'The people who fare best are those who have a strong advocate, someone who is watching all the time and demanding information. . . .'

". . .Coping with caregiving starts with 'parents and children talking openly about your resources—financial, time, skills and other assets—about how you want to live, and sometimes about how you want to die,' said Michele Kimball, executive director of AARP Minnesota.

"Nearly a decade ago, Kimball took a leave from her job with AARP to care for her mother who was dying from brain cancer. 'We were lucky. We had a big Italian family who could help care for my mom,' she said. 'But I knew that the first thing we needed to do was talk about what resources we had, and how mom wanted to live.'"

(*Star Tribune,* [Minneapolis], September 23, 2003)

Accuracy in Media, Inc. (AIM)

Established in 1969

DIRECTOR

Don Irvine, chairman. In addition to handling the financial and investment decisions for AIM, Irvine is responsible for much of the day-to-day operations including personnel, internships, and online activities. He joined AIM in 1974, became operations manager in 1982, and was elected to the AIM board in 1984 as executive secretary.

BOARD OF DIRECTORS

Reed Irvine, chairman, Washington, D.C.
Donald Irvine, executive secretary, Washington, D.C.
Samuel Shepard Jones Jr., treasurer and general counsel
Trevor Armbrister, author, Pleasantville, NY
James Davis, financial consultant
Joan Hueter, former president, National Association of Pro-America, Washington, D.C.
Jerris Leonard, attorney, Bethesda, MD
Nancy Morgan, conservative activist, Los Angeles, CA
Malcolm E. Smith, retired advertising executive

SCOPE

Members: 3,000 individuals
Branches/chapters: None
Affiliates: None

STAFF

8 total—6 professional; 2 support; plus 2 interns, 1 volunteer

TAX STATUS

501(c)(3)

FINANCES

Budget: 2004—$1.2 million; 2003—$1.3 million; 2002—$1.3 million

FUNDING SOURCES

Foundation grants, 45 %; Individuals, 53%; Corporate donations, 1%; Publications, 1%

PAC

None

EMPLOYMENT

Information on open positions is available on the AIM Web site and through media postings. This organization offers positions in writing and administration.

Applicants should send resumes and other materials for employment to Dan Boden, Operations Manager, 4455 Connecticut Avenue, NW, Suite #330, Washington, DC 20008; phone: (202) 364-4401, ext. 105; fax: (202) 364-4098; e-mail address: dan.boden@aim.org.

CONTACT INFORMATION

4455 Connecticut Avenue, NW, Suite #330, Washington, DC 20008
Phone: (202) 364-4401 • *Fax:* (202) 364-4098
General E-mail: ar1@aim.org • *Web site:* www.aim.org

Communications Director: None
Human Resources Director: None

PURPOSE: Encourages members of the media to report the news fairly and objectively—without resorting to bias or partisanship.

CURRENT CONCERNS: News reporting of activities of governmental officials

METHOD OF OPERATION: Advertisements • Attendance at media trade association conventions • Conferences/seminars • Films/video/audiotapes • Internet (e-mail alerts) • Media outreach • Speakers program • Television and radio production

Effectiveness and Political Orientation

"U.S. Supreme Court justices reacted skeptically yesterday to a California lawyer's argument that the public should have access to 10 photographs of the body of Vincent Foster, a deputy White House counsel in the Clinton administration.

"The U.S. government has resisted the release of the photographs, and so have Foster's widow and sister, who fear that the graphic images will be published in supermarket tabloids and on the Internet. . . . But Allan J. Favish, who suspects that the unreleased death-scene photographs might cast doubt on the suicide explanation, filed a request for the photos under the Freedom of Information Act, as did the conservative group Accuracy in Media, or AIM.

"The Office of the Independent Counsel resisted disclosure of the photographs, citing an exception in the act for law-enforcement records that 'could reasonably be expected to constitute an unwarranted invasion of personal privacy.' Lower federal courts have supported the agency where some of the photos are concerned.

"Yesterday, Favish, representing himself, told the justices that in carving out a 'privacy' exception, Congress intended only to protect someone still living, not the sensitivities of survivors. Justice Antonin Scalia was sympathetic to this interpretation, saying, 'I wouldn't normally call [relatives' feelings] a privacy issue,' but other justices pounced on Favish. Justice David H. Souter complained that Favish was offering 'one narrow definition of privacy.'

"Justice Stephen Breyer cited ancient Greek tragedies and the tenets of 'every religion' for the proposition that 'respect for the dead and respect for survivors' are cherished values. 'Why isn't the word 'privacy' broad enough to cover that?' Breyer asked Favish."

(*Pittsburgh Post-Gazette*, December 4, 2003)

INTERNSHIPS
Internships are posted at http://www.aim.org/
join_us/internship.pdf. Resumes and cover
letters for intern positions can be e-mailed to
aimintern@yahoo.com. Internships last 6 to
12 weeks, and interns are required to work
40 hours per week. Internship areas include
marketing, journalism, and public relations.
Interns must be at least 16 years of age.
Interested individuals should contact Dan
Boden, operations manager, 4455 Connecticut
Avenue, NW, Suite #330, Washington, DC
20008; phone: (202) 364-4401, ext. 105; fax:
(202) 364-4098; e-mail address:
dan.boden@aim.org

NEWSLETTERS
AIM Report (bimonthly)

PUBLICATIONS
Media Monitor (daily 3-minute radio
    commentaries carried on about 150 radio
    stations)
Weekly column (distributed to 50 to 100 Web
sites [including that of AIM] and newspapers)

CONFERENCES
Usually one conference per year in
Washington, DC, covering issues regarding
media bias, inaccuracies, and underreporting.

"Bolstering the right's successful assault on mainstream news organizations are four well-financed institutions that "monitor" all major media, with special attention given to the television networks. The oldest is Accuracy in Media, created in the 70s by Reed Irvine, a former Treasury employee, as an instrument of Nixon's vendetta against the Washington Post. Irvine still thrives with subventions from Richard Mellon Scaife, the conspiracy-minded billionaire notorious for his determination to ruin the Clintons."

(*The Guardian* [London], September 18, 2003)

"Elaine D. Kaplan, the government's chief enforcer of Hatch Act and whistle-blower laws, announced her resignation yesterday. Kaplan, who has served as head of the Office of Special Counsel since May 1998 after being nominated by then-President Bill Clinton, sent a resignation letter to President Bush, and said she would leave June 2. Her term had expired last month and it seemed unlikely that Bush would keep a Democratic nominee in the post.

"During her time as special counsel, Kaplan turned around a small agency that had fallen into disfavor with some whistle-blower advocates. They contended that OSC should be abolished because it did little to protect federal employees who pointed out waste and fraud in their agencies. Kaplan obtained relief for several whistle-blowers who suffered retaliation, including an Immigration and Naturalization Service manager who, in testimony before Congress, criticized a Clinton administration citizenship program.

"Others defended by Kaplan included National Park Service rangers who had warned of unsafe tour boats, a Federal Aviation Administration employee who thought he had a clue to the Sept. 11 terrorist attacks and two Border Patrol agents who disclosed security risks along the Canadian border after the attacks. . . .

"Because of heightened concerns about national security, Kaplan said, 'it is very important that OSC be viewed as a credible, nonpartisan advocate on behalf of whistleblowers. . . .' Kaplan's supporters had urged Bush and congressional Republican leaders to keep her on the job for another term. Six Senate Democrats wrote Bush in March expressing their support . . .

"Leaders of advocacy groups and two union leaders had previously written to members of Congress to urge Kaplan's reappointment. Among those signing the letter were Reed Irvine, president of Accuracy in Media; Kris J. Kolesnik, executive director of the National Whistleblower Center; Danielle Brian, executive director of the Project on Government Oversight and Tom Devine, legal director of the Government Accountability Project. . . ."

(*The Washington Post,* May 13, 2003)

"After a military checkpoint tragedy in Iraq last week, a Pentagon statement noted that seven people died when their van's driver ignored orders and warning shots. A dispatch from an embedded Washington Post reporter gave a fuller account: Ten people died—five of them small children when frightened and confused soldiers blasted the van with high-explosive cannon fire. A week earlier, after a grenade exploded at an Army camp in Kuwait, reporters broadcast suspicions that terrorists had struck. The initial reports were wrong; an American soldier had turned on his troops.

"The episodes are in keeping with the inevitable fog of war. They also represent some of the best and worst of early war coverage under a new system of 'embedding' journalists near front lines of battle. . . .

"So far, the public has a mostly favorable view toward the coverage, polls have shown. But amid the praise for coverage, news analysts worry about the anecdotal and often fragmentary picture of war that is presented to Americans. Christopher Simpson, a journalism professor at American University in Washington, said television has given viewers 'hundreds, if not thousands of emotional and powerful stories that historically haven't been well-presented. But what is not well covered is what these little stories add up to.'

"The Pentagon's decision to embed about 600 journalists with the military during the war has helped the public to understand the risks endured by coalition forces in their drive toward Baghdad and their many episodes of bravery. . . .

"Reporters have also described the ugly side of the armed forces. A New York Times dispatch last weekend from an embedded reporter quoted a Marine summing up recent action. 'We had a great day. We killed a lot of people,' he said. . . .

". . . After analyzing several recent days of television coverage, the Project for Excellence in Journalism concluded last week that the vast amount (94 percent) aimed to report facts (rather than primarily providing analysis) and that the reporting was not overly graphic. . . ."

"Summing up the view of many anti-war protesters, activist Norman Solomon argued that television in particular has invested heavily in glorifying coalition troops and their weapons while treating deaths on the other side only in the abstract. . . .

"But Reed Irvine, founder of Accuracy in Media, a watchdog organization that often embraces conservative causes, believes the embedding system has been successful in letting the public see for themselves what is going on. He does not extend that praise to coverage of anti-war protests at home. 'We've got 70 percent of the people supporting the war, but if you want to go out and lie down in the street, you can get 70 percent of the coverage,' he said."

(*St. Louis Post-Dispatch,* April 6, 2003)

"A strong majority of Americans thinks the media have done a good or excellent job of covering the run-up to a war with Iraq, but several journalism experts disagree about the depth of the stories and the professionalism of some in [Washington]'s press corps. . . . A recent poll done by the Pew Research Center for the People and the Press showed 66 percent of the public thinks the media are doing a good or excellent job, with 73 percent of supporters of military action giving the media a favorable rating. But . . . others said that much of the media attention has focused on the military buildup and United Nations debates about resolutions on going to war.

"As a result, some important investigative stories have been crowded into late-hour television and into the inside pages in many newspapers. . . . Media critics from conservative think tanks were less critical of the media generally but faulted specific outlets such as ABC News and the New York Times for what these critics called their anti-war bias. Reed Irvine of Accuracy in Media and the Media Research Center said supposed liberal bias on the part of some editors is 'keeping Americans from getting the full story.' Irvine said the story about the French brokering prohibited missile fuel sales to Iraq, which was disclosed by New York Times columnist William Safire on Thursday, 'should have been on the Times' front page.'"

(*The Buffalo News,* March 17, 2003)

Action on Smoking and Health

Established in 1967

DIRECTOR
John F. Banzhaf III, executive director and chief counsel. Banzhaf founded Action on Smoking and Health in 1967. He is also a professor of law at George Washington University's National Law Center. Previously Banzhaf worked with the New York law firm of Watson, Leavonworth, Kelton, and Taggart. He has been a spokesperson on national news programs and has written for a number of publications worldwide. Banzhaf earned an undergraduate degree in electrical engineering at the Massachusetts Institute of Technology and a J.D. at Columbia University.

BOARD OF DIRECTORS
John F. Banzhaf III, professor of law, George Washington University
Chuck Crawford, Ph.D., president, Kimball Physics
Martin Adam Jacobs, New York Mercantile Exchange
Dr. Alfred Munzer, M.D., Washington Adventist Hospital
Ethel R. Wells, Dynamic Strategy Research Foundation

SCOPE
Members: None
Branches/chapters: None
Affiliates: None

STAFF
9 total

TAX STATUS
501(c)(3)

FINANCES
Revenue: 2002—$1.06 million; 2001—$965,000; 2000—$1.084 million

FUNDING SOURCES
Public subscription, 100%; "no government aid of any sort"

PAC
None

EMPLOYMENT
Declined to comment

INTERNSHIPS
Information unavailable

NEWSLETTERS
ASH Smoking and Health Review (bimonthly)

CONTACT INFORMATION
2013 H Street, NW, Washington, DC 20006
Phone: (202) 659-4310 • *Fax:* (202) 833-3921
Web site: www.ash.org

Communications Director: Information unavailable
Human Resources Director: Information unavailable

PURPOSE: "To act as the legal arm of the nonsmoking majority."

CURRENT CONCERNS: Protection of children from tobacco use • Protection of public property from abuse by tobacco advertising • Public education on dangers of environmental tobacco smoke • Restriction of tobacco advertising • Workplace smoking limitations or bans

METHOD OF OPERATION: Advertisements • Awards program • Conferences/seminars • Congressional testimony • Educational materials • Films/video/audiotapes • Grassroots organizing • International activities • Internet (Web site) • Legal assistance • Legislative/regulatory monitoring (federal and state) • Litigation • Lobbying (federal, state, and grassroots) • Media outreach • Participation in regulatory proceedings (federal and state) • Polling • Research

Effectiveness and Political Orientation

"Employees at New Jersey Manufacturers Insurance Co. don't walk through herds of smokers on break when entering or exiting company buildings. If workers want to smoke a cigarette, they're required to leave the property—no easy task at the company's 100-acre main site in West Trenton. . . .

"Anti-tobacco advocates say hospitals and insurance companies—particularly sensitive to the effects of secondhand smoke—traditionally have been among the first to ban smoking throughout their premises. And an increasing number of other private employers also are following suit. The West Deptford-based medical publisher Slack Inc., for example, recently banned smoking on its premises and provided employees with information on company-covered cessation programs. 'I think you're going to see far more total bans on smoking in workforces and in public places,' said John Banzhaf, executive director of Action on Smoking and Health in Washington, DC."

(*The Record* [Bergen County, New Jersey], November 20, 2003)

"When police Officer Wayne H. Jeffrey was dismissed from the force this spring for smoking cigarettes off-duty, he was a victim of compromise. In exchange for expanded disability pensions for police officers and firefighters who develop heart disease and high blood pressure, union officials agreed 15 years ago to make smoking—on and off the job—grounds for firing police and fire officials hired after 1988. Lawmakers didn't want to go give disability

PUBLICATIONS

Custody Information Package (information on child custody when one parent smokes and the other does not)
Taking Action to Protect You and Your Family from Tobacco Smoke
Taking Action to Protect Yourself from Tobacco Smoke in Public Places
Taking Action to Protect Yourself from Tobacco Smoke in the Workplace
Also publishes other individual papers and materials on tobacco-related health issues.

CONFERENCES

Sponsors conferences "on the occasion of landmark events"

payments to people debilitated by tobacco. The law served as the basis for Jeffrey's dismissal May 29—and provided days of fodder for talk radio.

"Although the law has been criticized by some as unfair, the Massachusetts Supreme Judicial Court ruled years ago that it is constitutional. The 'Heart Bill' passed in 1987 offers a disability pension to police officers and firefighters who enter their departments with a clean bill of health and are later diagnosed with heart disease or high blood pressure. . . .

"In November last year, Rep. Kathi-Anne Reinstein, D-Revere, filed legislation that would allow police officers and firefighters caught smoking to enter smoking-cessation programs. . . .

"Despite the proposed changes, there are some—even within law enforcement—who do not see a need for change. 'We support the law,' Jack Collins, general counsel for the Massachusetts Chiefs of Police Association, said in a telephone interview. 'Police officers and firefighters get really much better pension and retirement benefits than other employees,' Collins explained. Therefore, he said, the compromise between legislators and union leaders was a 'fair arrangement. . . .'

"Weakening the law might also make it more difficult to enforce, according to John Banzhaf, executive director of Action on Smoking and Health and professor of public interest law at George Washington University. 'I would be very strongly opposed to anything that would allow them to smoke,' Banzhaf said. 'Some people argue that it is discrimination, but the way I describe it to my students is that we allow employers discretion.' Banzhaf described discretion as a decision with a rational basis that does not differentiate among those with immutable differences such as race or gender.

"No other states have laws explicitly forbidding police officers from smoking, according to Kevin H. Watson, spokesman for the Law Enforcement Alliance of America, a Virginia-based nonprofit organization. However, some counties have ordinances that prohibit smoking, and some individual departments set nonsmoking policies, according to Banzhaf. . . ."
(*Providence Journal-Bulletin* [Rhode Island], July 27, 2003)

"The man who brought the threat of an anti-obesity lawsuit to the Seattle School Board works in a university office about 3,000 miles away, with a sign hanging outside the door that reads 'Torts R Us.' His 1989 white Ford van, once used to taxi his now-grown son around, has a vanity license plate reading 'SUEBAST'—short for 'Sue the Bastards,' a favorite credo. John Banzhaf III, a public-interest lawyer and law professor at George Washington University in Washington, DC, has a sense of humor his targets may not find amusing at all.

"The 63-year-old legal maverick who successfully took on the tobacco industry has turned his attention to the nation's obesity epidemic, and school districts that have exclusive contracts with soft-drink manufacturers are squarely in his crosshairs. The School Board is scheduled to vote tonight on whether to extend the district's exclusive five-year contract with Coca-Cola. Banzhaf recently sent a letter to board members, warning that they could be sued for allowing schools to sell soda to students, citing studies that suggest a link between soda consumption and obesity. . . .

"Banzhaf rose to prominence in 1967, when he first took on the tobacco industry. . . . The 26-year-old saw a cigarette commercial on television one day and 'something clicked.' He formed a non-profit lobbying organization, Action on Smoking and Health, and wrote a letter to the Federal Communications Commission that resulted in a ruling requiring anti-smoking announcements on radio and TV. . . .

"He and his protegees have helped establish smoke-free airplanes, prevented dry-cleaners and hairdressers from charging women more than men and brought about clearer warnings on birth control pills, among other initiatives. . . . Banzhaf has since moved on to obesity, providing advice in a class-action lawsuit filed last summer by Caesar Barber, a 270-pound Bronx man, who alleged that McDonald's, Burger King, Wendy's and KFC did not properly disclose the risks of eating too much of their fatty, salty fare. . . .

"Detractors of the high-profile lawyer see him as a money-hungry media hound who shifts responsibility away from irresponsible consumers. A Web site called Banzhaf Watch aims to debunk what it terms 'JB's Fuzzy Facts' and encourages people to report 'JB sightings.' The Center for Consumer Freedom, a Washington, DC, coalition that promotes personal responsibility and is backed by the food industry, is also critical of Banzhaf. Mike Burita, the center's communications director, accuses the attorney of championing frivolous lawsuits and said he's 'sunk to a new low' with his threat in Seattle. . . .

"Banzhaf doesn't see himself as an extremist. He admits he occasionally eats at McDonald's, eschewing fries and milkshakes in favor of salad and yogurt, and like many Americans, would like to drop a few pounds. He said he's not particularly fervent about the issues he pursues. If he had to make a list of his top 10 pet peeves, smoking wouldn't even be on it. . . .' "

(*The Seattle Post-Intelligencer,* July 17, 2003)

"Mayor Richard Daley is doing it in Chicago. So is Mayor Thomas Menino in Boston, as well as political leaders in Nassau, Suffolk and Westchester counties. All have followed Mayor Bloomberg's lead and are contemplating a ban on smoking in bars and restaurants, making New York a key battleground that could signal smoking policy changes across the country.

". . . Not that New York is the first place to propose such a ban. California and Delaware passed statewide bans in recent years. And New Jersey Gov. Jim McGreevey's staff recently sat down with the American Cancer Society to consider a ban there. But New York is New York—and if the anti-smoking forces can make it there, they might very well make it anywhere.

" 'When California did it,' said John Banzhaf, executive director of the Washington-based Action on Smoking and Health, 'I think a lot of people said, 'Oh, that's California, the land of the health nuts.' Nobody can say New York is full of health nuts.' The implications of New York going smoke-free also have registered with the National Restaurant Association, a lobbying group that has labeled Bloomberg 'persistently anti-tobacco' on its Web site."

(*Daily News* [New York], October 3, 2002)

Advocacy Institute

Established in 1985

DIRECTOR

Kathleen D. Sheekey, president and chief executive officer. Sheekey joined the Advocacy Institute as co-director in 1992. She oversees the objectives of a major leadership recognition awards program funded by the Ford Foundation, *Leadership for a Changing World.* She also has served as a principal Advocacy Institute facilitator for citizen leaders from the Untied States, Bangladesh, Bosnia, China, Croatia, Czech Republic, India, Macedonia, Namibia, Nepal, Russia, Serbia, Slovakia, South Africa, and Ukraine. She has more than 25 years of leadership experience in the public-interest sector. Prior to joining the institute, Sheekey served as legislative director from 1981–1991 for Common Cause, leading lobbying and coalition efforts in the areas of campaign finance reform, nuclear arms control, civil rights, and government accountability. She also served as director of congressional relations for the Federal Trade Commission and legislative director of the Consumer Federation of America.

BOARD OF DIRECTORS

David Cohen (co-chair), co-founder, Advocacy Institute

Michael Pertschuk (co-chair), co-founder, Advocacy Institute

Kathleen D. Sheekey, president; chief executive officer, Advocacy Institute

Sofía Quintero, secretary; co-founder, Chica-Luna Productions

Richard D. Paisner, treasurer; president, TEI Industries, Inc. and its affiliates (1976–2000)

Michael Armentrout, president, MEA Financial

Fernando Betancourt, executive director, State of Connecticut Latino and Puerto Rican Affairs Commission

Vincent DeMarco, executive director, Maryland Citizen's Health Initiative

Garrick C. Francis, spokesperson, Progress Energy

Peter Kovler, director, Marjorie Kovler Philanthropic Fund; founder, Kovler Center for Victims of Torture

Michael F. MacLeod, president and co-founder, Public Interest Data, Inc. (PIDI)

Lateefah Simon, executive director, Center for Young Women's Development

Linda Tarr-Whelan, partner, Tarr-Whelan & Associates

Rev. John Vaughn, former executive director, Peace Development Fund

Nondas Hurst Voll, executive director, Fund for Community Progress

Donna Red Wing, independent contractor, Dean Campaign; national field director, Human Rights Campaign (1996–1999)

CONTACT INFORMATION

1629 K St., NW, Suite 200, Washington, DC 20006-1629
Phone: (202) 777-7575 • *Fax:* (202) 777-7577
General E-mail: info@advocacy.org • *Web site:* www.advocacy.org

Communications Director: Jennifer Donaldson, communications manager (202) 777-7557 • jdonaldson@advocacy.org
Human Resources Director: Tika Junéja, administration manager (202) 777-7541 • jobs@advocacy.org

PURPOSE: Advocacy Institute works to make social justice leadership strategic, effective, and sustainable in pursuit of a just world. Founded in 1985, Advocacy Institute works to achieve a just society, in the United States and outside of it, grounded in the following core values: justice for those denied justice; economic equality for those denied sustenance and opportunity; public health and security for those at preventable risk; and access to political power for those who have been denied an equal voice in the policy-making process. In such a society, all people are able to participate fully in shaping public values and policies.

CURRENT CONCERNS: Economic/political justice issues (domestic and global) • Promoting public interest advocacy in a democratic society • Social justice issues (domestic and global) • Poverty • Public health • Affordable housing • Peace • Environment

Specific programs/initiatives include the following:

- Leadership for a Changing World: Through this program the institute recognizes and celebrates 20 extraordinary U.S. based community leaders and awards them $130,000 over 2 years to support their work and advance their learning. They also participate in institute-facilitated meetings that are designed for them to share their experiences, learn from and collaborate with each other, and enhance their leadership skills.
- Advocacy Leaders Program: Through reflection, networking with fellow advocates, and skill strengthening, the Advocacy Institute facilitates capacity building workshops and training programs that aim to strengthen social justice movements. Participants come from every state and more than 67 nations, from China to Indonesia to Poland and Zimbabwe.

METHOD OF OPERATION: Awards program • Coalition forming • Conferences/seminars • Information clearinghouse • International activities • Internet electronic bulletin boards • Internships • Library services for members only • Professional development services • Research • Training • Web site

SCOPE
Members: 4,800
Branches/chapters: None
Affiliates: None

STAFF
22 total—13 professional, 9 support; plus
2 part-time professionals, 1 part-time support,
and 1 intern

TAX STATUS
501(c)(3)

FINANCES
Budget: 2004—$6.6 million;
2001—$5.74 million; 2000—$7 million

FUNDING SOURCES
Foundation grants, 91%; Government contracts, 6.5%; Individuals, 1.3%; Publications,
.05%; other, 1.15%

PAC
None

EMPLOYMENT
Information on open positions is posted on the
Institute's Web site: www.advocacy.org, and
at www.idealist.org. This organization offers
positions in program development and administration, general administration, and fundraising and communications.

Cover letters, resumes and salary histories
can be mailed to Tika Junéja, administration
manager, Advocacy Institute, Human
Resources Dept., 1629 K Street, NW, Suite
200, Washington, DC 20006-1629; faxed to:
(202) 777-7577 or e-mailed to:
jobs@advocacy.org. No phone calls are
accepted for applications.

INTERNSHIPS
The Institute offers several paid summer
internships lasting 10 weeks, in the following
areas: advocacy leadership programs,
fundraising & development, and business
administration. Eligibility requirements are
dependent upon specific internship needs.
More information can be found at the organization's Web site.

Internship applications can be mailed to
Tika Junéja, administration manager,
Advocacy Institute, Human Resources Dept.,
1629 K Street, NW, Suite 200, Washington,
DC 20006-1629; faxed to: (202) 777-7577 or
e-mailed to: jobs@advocacy.org. No phone
calls are accepted for applications.

NEWSLETTERS
The Advocacy Institute will begin publishing
an e-Newsletter in 2004. Please see
www.advocacy.org for information on how to
subscribe.

PUBLICATIONS
*Advocacy for Social Justice: A Global Action
and Reflection Guide*
Advocacy Institute, Rosa de la Vega, Advocacy
Institute, and Gabrielle Watson
Become a Leader for Social Justice

Effectiveness and Political Orientation

"Chris Dennis smiled broadly as she surveyed the sea of hardhats, union wind-breakers and pro-John Kerry placards arrayed on a sunny midwinter day in front of the AFL-CIO headquarters here. The union movement, divided and ineffective in the opening round of Democratic presidential primaries, came together Thursday behind the front-runner, Sen. Kerry of Massachusetts. Dennis works for the International Association of Fire Fighters, which has been with Kerry from the outset.

" 'It's great that they're all coming on board now,' she said with a grin, 'maybe a little late.' Kerry stood under a 20-by-40-foot banner declaring, 'America Needs Good Jobs,' the top priority of the 13 million-member umbrella federation. . . . The union blessing gives Kerry added organizational strength, coast to coast, as the decisive Super Tuesday primaries approach. 'We are going to repeal every benefit, every tax loophole, every reward that entices any Benedict Arnold company to take jobs and ship them overseas,' Kerry vowed. . . .

"So what is a union endorsement worth in 2004? Is Big Labor a spent force? Not in Ohio, say labor advocates and critics alike. . . . Having the 'enthusiasm and effort' of union members working at the grassroots level will be critical next fall for a Democratic presidential candidate in places like Ohio, Michigan, Pennsylvania and Wisconsin, said David Cohen, co-director of the Advocacy Institute, which trains public interest lobbyists."

(*The Plain Dealer* [Cleveland], February 20, 2004)

"In an effort to burnish its tarnished image on Wall Street and Main Street, McDonald's has formed a partnership with the blue-eyed elder statesman of Hollywood and Broadway, Paul Newman. Mr. Newman will not be a spokes-man for the fast-food chain, though his picture will appear in its restaurants. Instead, he has agreed to sell McDonald's a line of salad dressing, similar to the bottled dressing made by his company, Newman's Own. Under the same philanthropic principle that guides Newman's Own, Mr. Newman said, all after-tax profits from the deal will be given to charity.

"Some see the partnership as a brilliant marketing move by McDonald's; others say it's too little too late. Mr. Newman said he is unconcerned. He has no problem with the chain's efforts to improve its image through association with his company. 'We get to give a lot more money to charity, and whatever we have to do with—the salads—are basically healthy products,' he said. 'If in any way that upgraded people's perception of McDonald's, what would be the problem with that?' The partnership might increase Newman's Own charita-ble giving by as much as 25 percent, he said. . . .

" 'All this is about buying the image of Paul Newman,' Mr. Pollan said. 'McDonald's is in the hole. It is trying to freshen and go upscale. It's redoing its flavor profile and making it more sophisticated and giving it an aura of health-consciousness and virtue, and this is a way to connect with virtue.' Or as Michael Pertschuk, a former Federal Trade Commission chairman and a co-director of the Advocacy Institute, which monitors public health issues, said: 'Innocence by association. It's really pushing the limits of public interest entrepreneurship.' "

(*The New York Times,* March 12, 2003)

CONFERENCES

None

"John O'Neal, artistic director of Junebug Productions, and Theresa R. Holden, project director of Junebug's Color Line Project, were the only artists to be selected among a field of 20 national recipients of the Ford Foundation's Leadership for a Changing World (LCW) awards. Each of the 20 awardees, chosen from 34 finalists and a pool of more than 1,400 nominations, will receive $100,000 to advance their work and $30,000 for supporting activities over the next two years.

"Launched two years ago by the Ford Foundation in partnership with the Advocacy Institute in Washington, D.C., and the Robert F. Wagner Graduate School of Public Service at New York University, the LCW program 'seeks to raise awareness that leadership comes in many forms and from diverse communities by recognizing the achievements of outstanding leaders who are not broadly known beyond their immediate communities or fields.'

" 'LCW awardees demonstrate the kinds of leadership that are particularly effective in addressing the complex social realities of contemporary communities,' according to Susan V. Beresford, president of the Ford Foundation. 'They share the ability to bring diverse groups together to overcome divisive issues and take action that will improve people's lives.' Junebug's Color Line Project is a national program that 'collects and archives remembrances of those who participated in or were influenced by the Civil Rights movement in the 1960s,' Holden said. 'Junebug brings together people to share their lives in the story circle process,' which Junebug has used for years to create its various storytelling presentations, which have toured internationally."

(*Times-Picayune* [New Orleans], October 10, 2002)

"The head of the Colorado Coalition for the Homeless was one of 20 activists nationwide to be awarded a $100,000 grant Tuesday for his work with the state's downtrodden population. John Parvensky, the coalition's executive director, was in New York Tuesday night to receive the 'Leadership for a Changing World' grant from the Ford Foundation, the Advocacy Institute and the Robert F. Wagner Graduate School of Public Service at New York University.

"In addition to the grant, Parvensky will receive $30,000 for support projects. Doug Wayland, director for the coalition's education and advocacy, said Parvensky was expected to use the $30,000 to continue his education to build his leadership skills. 'It's a very prestigious award' for Parvensky, Wayland said. 'It's an acknowledgment of John's dedication over a lot of years during very difficult times to this mission of overcoming homelessness. We're very proud of him.' Parvensky and the coalition have not decided how they will use the grant, Wayland said. However, Parvensky has been a major advocate of providing housing for homeless people."

(*Rocky Mountain News* [Denver], October 2, 2002)

Advocates for Highway and Auto Safety

Established in 1989

DIRECTOR

Judith Lee Stone, president. Stone has been with Advocates for Highway and Auto Safety since its inception in 1989. Previously she served as executive director of the National Association of Governors' Highway Safety Representatives, as director of federal affairs with the National Safety Council, and in the Transportation Department during the Carter administration. She was appointed to the Federal Motor Carrier Advisory in 1994 and elected to the board of directors of the National Insurance Crime Bureau in 1995. Stone is a graduate of Northwestern University.

BOARD OF DIRECTORS

Judith Lee Stone, president
Alliance of American Insurers
Allstate Insurance Co.
American College of Emergency
    Physicians
American Public Health Association
Center for Auto Safety
Consumer Federation of America, co-chair
Emergency Nurses Association
Independent Insurance Agents and
    Brokers of America
Kemper Auto and Home Group,
    Inc./Unitrin Co., co-chair
KIDS AND CARS
Liberty Mutual Group
Mothers Against Drunk Driving
National Association of Professional
    Insurance Agents
Police Foundation
Progressive Corp.
Prudential Property and Casualty
    Insurance Co.
Public Citizen
State Farm Insurance Co.
Trauma Foundation
USAA
Whirlwind Wheelchair International
Zurich North America

SCOPE

Members: 22 organizations ("Equal, shared leadership and membership. For each insurance company funder [dues $100,000 per year] there is a seat on the board for a consumer/safety organization. Each side selects/elects its own representatives. All decisions are by consensus of the group.")
Branches/chapters: Chapters in California, Connecticut, New York, and Florida
Affiliates: None

STAFF

10 total—8 professional, 2 support; plus 1 intern

CONTACT INFORMATION

750 First St. NE, Suite 901, Washington, DC 20002
Phone: (202) 408-1711 • *Fax:* (202) 408-1699
General E-mail: advocates@saferoads.org • *Web site:* www.saferoads.org

Communications Director: Lesley Steinhauser
(202) 408-1711 • lsteinhauser@saferoads.org
Human Resources Director: Judie Pasquini, director of administration
(202) 408-1711 • jpasquini@saferoads.org

PURPOSE: "Advocates for Highway and Auto Safety is an alliance of consumer, health and safety groups and insurance companies and agents working together to make America's roads safer. Advocates encourages the adoption of federal and state laws, policies and programs that save lives and reduce injuries. By joining its resources with others, Advocates helps build coalitions to increase participation of a wide array of groups in public policy initiatives which advance highway and auto safety."

CURRENT CONCERNS: Highway and auto safety laws and regulations

METHOD OF OPERATION: Advertisements (limited) • Awards program • Coalition forming • Congressional testimony • Grassroots organizing • Internet • Legislative/regulatory monitoring (federal and state) • Litigation • Lobbying (federal, state, grassroots) • Media outreach • Participation in regulatory proceedings (federal) • Polling

Effectiveness and Political Orientation

"One way to get a regulatory agenda moving is to get it attached to a piece of must-pass legislation. That's the goal of auto safety and consumer groups who want to see the National Highway Traffic Safety Administration address long-lingering issues, such as stronger vehicle roofs, safer power windows and design changes to make sport-utility vehicles less dangerous in crashes.

"So far, the strategy has worked. The $318 billion highway and transit funding bill the Senate passed last month includes more than a dozen regulatory initiatives that the NHTSA would have to complete over the next six years. The Bush administration is already on record criticizing the regulatory mandates in the bill, and the NHTSA provisions are expected to face opposition in the House. Many of the rulemakings directed by the Senate have been priorities for safety groups for years, and the safety agency has several of them on its to-do list as well. But consumer advocates believe a legislative directive that sets specific deadlines will mean safer vehicles sooner.

" 'We view this as an opportunity to direct the safety agenda for the next six years,' said Jacqueline Gillan, vice president of Advocates for Highway and Auto Safety. 'You give the agency specific directions with reasonable deadlines to implement specific actions.' Joan Claybrook, a former NHTSA administrator who is now president of Public Citizen, a consumer advocacy group,

TAX STATUS
501(c)(4)

FINANCES
Budget: 2000—$1.6 million; 1999—
$1.6 million

FUNDING SOURCES
100% private membership dues

PAC
None

EMPLOYMENT
Information on open positions can be
found on the organization's Web site:
http://www.saferoads.org/employment.htm.
Cover letters and resumes can be faxed to
Judie Pasquini, Director of Administration,
(202) 408-1699.

INTERNSHIPS
The organization offers both full- and part-time
internships. Hours are flexible. Internship
applications can be mailed to Judie Pasquini,
director of administration, Advocates for
Highway and Auto Safety, 750 First St. NE,
Suite 901, Washington, DC 20002; or faxed to:
(202) 408-1699.

NEWSLETTERS
None

PUBLICATIONS
Publishes informational brochures, fact sheets,
research reports, and policy statements.

CONFERENCES
None

said: 'NHTSA is aware of the need for all of these standards, but the public has no assurance that these rules will ever be issued in a final fashion. They have been on the docket for 20 years.' "

(*The Washington Post,* March 2, 2004)

"For nine months last year, state and Boston officials allowed heavy trucks to cross the ailing Charlestown Bridge between Charlestown and the North End, despite repeated warnings by engineers that the bridge's weight limit was outdated and too high, and warnings by the state's trucking industry that the situation was a potential disaster. During most of this time, the city-owned bridge was on Boston's designated hazardous cargo route, with drivers hauling anything from gasoline to medical waste. The trucks, weighing as much as 14 tons, rolled over a span that engineers in August said should be closed to vehicles weighing more than 4 tons—somewhat more than a large sport utility vehicle.

"The route was used for hazardous cargo beginning in March 2003, after the Big Dig's northbound tunnel opened. In response to the August inspection report from the engineering firm Purcell Associates, city officials promised to do more repairs and close the bridge's rusted and rotting two center lanes. With those closed, city officials said, engineers were confident the two outer lanes could handle truck traffic. But all lanes remained open from August, when the engineers issued their warning, until Sept. 27, when the center lanes were closed.

"The hazardous cargo route was changed later last year to avoid the bridge, a change the city said had nothing to do with the bridge's integrity. 'That's called cross your fingers and keep hoping,' said Gerald Donaldson, senior research director with Advocates for Highway and Auto Safety, a transportation safety lobbying group in Washington, DC. 'They seem to have just waved their hands over it and deemed it fit.' "

(*The Boston Globe,* February 9, 2004)

"Every year, it seems, there is a big debate in the Legislature about passing a primary seat belt enforcement law in Florida. Florida has long had secondary seat belt enforcement, but this requires that an officer or trooper pull over an offender for some other violation, such as speeding or reckless driving, before citing him for failure to use a seat belt.

"In other words, a driver can't be pulled over only because of a failure to use a seat belt. We were sent some statistics compiled by a group called Advocates for Highway and Auto Safety, of Washington, D.C., which bring home pretty graphically how big a difference it would make in Florida to have a primary seat belt enforcement law.

"For example, according to the National Highway Traffic Safety Administration [NHTSA], 20,425 people died in Florida in traffic accidents from 1996 to 2002. That's equal to the entire population of Lealman or Tarpon Springs. Of those 20,425 dead people, 9,623 weren't wearing seat belts. If everyone had been wearing seat belts, 4,330 of those people would have lived, according to the Meharry-State Farm Alliance Report. Scary, isn't it?

"Despite facts like these, the traffic safety administration found that seat belt use in Florida actually is declining, from 75.1 percent in 2002 to 72.6 percent in 2003. If Florida had a primary seat belt enforcement law, the NHTSA estimates that usage would have risen to 82.6 percent in 2002 and 87.6 percent in 2003. . . ."

(St. Petersburg Times, February 8, 2004)

"Transportation Secretary Norman Y. Mineta yesterday called on states to pass 'primary' seat-belt laws, which allow police to stop and cite motorists solely for failing to wear a seat belt. Twenty states . . . have primary seat-belt laws. Twenty-nine other states . . . allow officers to write a citation for not wearing a seat belt only if the motorist is stopped and cited for another infraction. Only New Hampshire has no seat-belt law. Primary seat-belt laws have been a hot-button issue for years in Virginia, where all efforts to enact a primary law have been beaten back.

"'Our nation simply cannot afford the more than $230 billion in economic losses each year by car crashes that devastate entire families,' Mineta said at the National Conference of State Legislatures' Fall Forum. 'The facts are clear. The most effective way to save lives is to enact primary safety-belt laws.' A total of 1,400 lives could be saved each year if all remaining states enacted primary laws, he said.

"The Advocates for Highway and Auto Safety commended Mineta's statement but said it does not go far enough. Advocates President Judith Lee Stone said in a statement that states are moving too slowly and that the federal government should require state action. Stone noted that Sens. John W. Warner (R-Va.) and Hillary Rodham Clinton (D-N.Y.) had introduced legislation on Tuesday that would put more pressure on the states to adopt primary laws."

(The Washington Post, December 11, 2003)

"Traffic deaths rose last year to the highest level since 1990, with more people dying in accidents involving drunken driving and motorcycles. In all, 42,850 people were killed, 1.7 percent more than the year before, the government said today. Alcohol-related deaths rose 3 percent to 17,970, the third straight increase after a decade of decline. Motorcycle fatalities rose for the fifth consecutive year, to 3,276, the most since 1990. That compares with a low of 2,116 in 1997.

"The statistics, released by the National Highway Traffic Safety Administration, showed that fewer young children died in car crashes. The number of those younger than 4 who were killed fell 5.7 percent, while there was an 8 percent decline for children 4 to 7. For the first time since the agency began keeping records in the 1970's, fewer than 500 children in each age category died in a year. There were 484 fatalities in the youngest age group and 496 for those age 4 to 7. Many states have passed laws requiring children to be belted or to ride in safety seats.

"'There's been a huge explosion of laws to expand the booster-seat laws so kids from 4 to 8 are required to be in booster seats,' said Judith Stone, president of Advocates for Highway and Auto Safety. 'If a law passes, people go out and buy booster seats, and they use them.' The government recommends that all children younger than 13 ride in the back. Infants less than 20 pounds should be in a rear-facing safety seat. Toddlers 20 pounds to 40 pounds should be in a forward-facing child seat. Children weighing more than 40 pounds but not yet 57 inches tall should be in a booster seat that helps the belt fit correctly across the lap and chest."

(The New York Times, April 23, 2003)

AIDS Action

Established in 1984

DIRECTOR

Marsha Martin, executive director. Martin joined AIDS Action in 2003. Previously she was executive director of the Interagency Council on the Homeless, Department of Housing and Urban Development. Martin is a graduate of the University of Iowa and Columbia University.

BOARD OF DIRECTORS

Ronald S. Johnson, chair; Gay Men's Health Crisis, NY
Craig Thompson, vice chair; AIDS Project Los Angeles, CA
Joseph Interrante, Ph.D., secretary; Nashville Cares, TN
Kenneth Malone, treasurer; The Assistance Fund, TX
Linda Frank, Ph.D., ACR, CRN, interim chair, Public Policy Committee;
National Association of AIDS Education & Training Centers, PA
Cornelius Baker, Whitman-Walker Clinic, Washington, DC
Irl Barefield, AIDS Research Alliance, CA
Yvonne Benson, MSW; AIDS Service Center, CA
Katy Caldwell, Montrose Clinic, TX
Craig Cobb, Harlem Directors Group, NY
Gunther Freehill, Los Angeles County Health Department, CA
Jeannie Gibbs, World AIDS Research Project, NY
Millicent Gorham, National Black Nurses Association, MD
Rebecca Haag, AIDS Action Committee, MA
Charles Henry, Los Angeles County Health Department, CA
Frank Oldham, New York City Office of AIDS Policy, NY
Ana Olivera, Gay Men's Health Crisis, NY
Thomas Peterson, AIDS Services Foundation, Orange County, CA
Kevin Pickett, The Palm Residential Care Facility, CA
Castulo de la Rocha, J.D., Altamen Health Services Organization, CA
Rev. Edwin Sanders, Metropolitan Interdenominational Church, TN
Pernessa Seele, The Balm in Gilead, Inc., NY
David Wexler, Rosenfeld, Meyer & Susman, LLP, CA
Phill Wilson, The Black AIDS Institute, CA

SCOPE

Members: 3,200 AIDS service members
Branches/chapters: None
Affiliates: None

STAFF

14 total—plus 4 interns

CONTACT INFORMATION

1906 Sunderland Place, NW, Washington, DC 20036
Phone: (202) 530-8030 • *Fax:* (202) 530-8031
General E-mail: aidsaction@aidsaction.org • *Web site:* www.aidsaction.org

Communications Director: Sarah Whitehead
Human Resources Director: George Ferguson

PURPOSE: "Dedicated to responsible federal policy for improved HIV/AIDS care and services, vigorous medical research and effective prevention."

CURRENT CONCERNS: HIV/AIDS issues • Managed care/Medicare

METHOD OF OPERATION: Awards program • Coalition forming • Conferences/seminars • Congressional testimony • Educational foundation • Internet (databases, e-mail alerts, Web site) • Internships • Legislative/regulatory monitoring (federal) • Lobbying (federal) • Media outreach • Research • Voting records

Effectiveness and Political Orientation

"The Bush administration sent Congress a five-year, $15 billion plan Monday to fight AIDS, calling it the 'largest and boldest assault on the global AIDS pandemic in history.' The 99-page 'President's Emergency Plan for AIDS Relief' details the tactics and objectives of the ambitious program President Bush first described in his 2003 State of the Union address.

"The administration also released the first installment for the plan, a $350 million down payment. A request of $2.7 billion for fiscal 2005 is pending in Congress. Over the next five years, the plan aims to pour $9 billion in new funding to AIDS programs in 14 of the hardest-hit countries, which combined account for half of the world's HIV infections. A country outside Africa and the Caribbean will be added to the list. The United States also will supply $5 billion through existing agreements to countries and $1 billion to the Global Fund to Fight AIDS, Tuberculosis and Malaria.

"Secretary of Health and Human Services Tommy Thompson said that no matter how much money the U.S. government commits to AIDS, the challenge is 'too big for any one country, and others must get involved.' AIDS advocates offered mixed reactions. Paul Zeitz of the Global AIDS Alliance said it has been more than a year since Bush said he would tackle the epidemic. 'Thirteen months after this great announcement, no new money has been dispersed,' Zeitz said. 'It's a go-slow, do-nothing approach.'

"Others were more positive. 'The money's now available, the teams are in place and the dollars are going to flow,' said Kate Carr, executive director of the Elizabeth Glaser Pediatric AIDS Foundation. Marsha Martin of AIDS Action praised Bush for 'unprecedented leadership,' but she added: 'Let's pay attention to where the money goes, how it's used and what impact it has.'"

(USA Today, February 24, 2004)

TAX STATUS
501(c)(3)

FINANCES
Revenue: 2001—$1.37 million; 2000—
$1.53 million; 1999—$1.61 million

FUNDING SOURCES
Declined to comment

PAC
Public Policy Committee

PAC CONTRIBUTIONS
Information unavailable

EMPLOYMENT
Information on open positions can be obtained
by contacting the Center at (202) 530-8030.

INTERNSHIPS
Information unavailable

NEWSLETTERS
Action News (quarterly)

PUBLICATIONS
Early Treatment for HIV Act
Faith-Based Response to HIV/AIDS
The Federal Budget Process and HIV/AIDS
Funding, A Guide to CBO Adherence
Programs
HIV Prevention and Care for Incarcerated
Populations
Medicare and HIV/AIDS
NORA AIDS Appropriations
Recommendations—Fiscal Year 2001
Ryan White CARE Act 2000 Reauthorization
The Ticket to Work and Work Improvement Act
of 1999
What Works in HIV Prevention For Gay Men
What Works in HIV Prevention For Incarcerated
Populations
What Works in HIV Prevention For Substance
Users
What Works in HIV Prevention For Women of
Color
What Works in HIV Prevention For Youth
Also publishes policy fact briefs and policy
recommendations.

CONFERENCES
None

"The budget President Bush is preparing to release early next month will contain $38 million in additional funds to slow the spread of AIDS in the United States and to help people already infected with the virus, federal health officials said yesterday. All but $3 million of the extra money would be devoted to a federal program that helps states pay for AIDS drugs for people who cannot afford them. The rest would enlarge a fund, overseen by the secretary of health and human services, intended to foster innovative ways to curb the human immunodeficiency virus (HIV) in minority communities.

"Administration officials announced the increases as a piece of good news. But in this instance, the 4.7 percent rise in funds to pay for drugs, known as the AIDS Drug Assistance Program (ADAP), would represent the smallest annual expansion of that program since Bush entered office. One administration official said the two increases in AIDS funds would be greater than those for most other social programs. . . .

"The announcement also is an effort to counteract criticism from AIDS activists. They complained last year that the president proposed—and Congress adopted—a large initiative to help curb the epidemic in African and Caribbean countries, without devoting equal attention to the disease domestically. The new funds did not immediately appease those activists. Ronald Johnson, board chairman for AIDS Action, an umbrella organization of local AIDS groups, said the increase 'is so well below what is needed.' Johnson praised the Global AIDS initiative but added: 'We also have to recognize that the domestic agenda should not be shortchanged.' "

(*The Washington Post,* January 17, 2004)

"Teary-eyed AIDS patients and playful orphans welcomed a delegation of U.S. senators to Soweto, South Africa, last week. The six-member Senate group, which is led by Majority Leader Bill Frist, R-Tenn., and includes Sen. Lamar Alexander, R-Tenn., will play an integral role in determining how to spend the billions of dollars pledged by the U.S. government to help African and Caribbean nations battle AIDS. 'I want to encourage the political leadership here to recognize the magnitude of the problem,' Sen. Frist told reporters in South Africa.

"A country almost twice the size of Texas, South Africa has the highest single caseload of HIV/AIDS patients in the world, with 600 people dying of the disease each day. . . . Paul Zeitz, executive director of the Global AIDS Alliance, said the virus accelerated rapidly in South Africa by migrant workers who practiced unsafe sex while following jobs across the country. . . . An unemployed, HIV-positive women wept as she told the senators about her struggles. 'I can't afford medicine; it's too expensive. I know with your help my dreams can come true,' said the 34-year-old women, who called herself Busi.

"Dr. Marsha Martin, executive director of AIDS Action, said antiretroviral is a 'miracle' treatment that started in 1996. She said the combination of drugs in the treatment helps sustain infected people's ability to participate in daily life for up to a decade or more. 'Before antiretroviral drugs became available, people were going to funerals every day,' she said. 'There were coffins for sale on the side of the road. What is important about antiretroviral drug treatment is that they get their health back, their stamina back and are able to take care of their children. People are living with HIV now, and not dying of AIDS.' "

(*Chattanooga Times Free Press,* August 25, 2003)

"For conspiracy buffs, it doesn't get much scarier than this. Boyd Graves, an Annapolis graduate who put himself through law school, is convinced the U.S. government created AIDS in a secret program aimed at killing African-Americans. Today, at San Diego's federal courthouse, he will get his day in court. Graves is suing the United States for allegedly failing to hand over documents under the Freedom of Information Act that he says prove the government is behind the AIDS pandemic.

"Legal experts say there is a place in the justice system for such unconventional lawsuits. 'This is a modern-day David vs. Goliath battle,' said Graves, 50, an AIDS activist who lives in Normal Heights and represents himself in the federal lawsuit. 'The paper trail does exist. These are official documents.' Graves contends that AIDS is the product of decades of ultra-classified government research into developing a race-specific virus that attacks and kills blacks. He compares the project to the eugenics movement early last century, when scientists and others advocated 'racial hygiene'—a practice that in Germany led to Nazis working to eliminate Jews. . . .

"George Bellinger Jr. of the Washington, D.C., advocacy group AIDS Action said lawsuits such as the one filed by Graves can cause more harm than good—as do rumors and unproven cure-alls. 'It prevents people from getting the real information and taking precautionary measures to enhance their lives or prevent them from getting HIV,' he said. Additionally, Bellinger said, bickering over the beginnings of AIDS at this point matters very little. Far more pressing, he said, are developing a vaccine and preventing new infections. "

(*The San Diego Union-Tribune,* July 3, 2003)

Alliance for Justice

Established in 1979

DIRECTOR

Nan Aron, president. Prior to founding the Alliance in 1979, Aron was a staff attorney for the ACLU's National Prison Project. She also served as a trial attorney for the Equal Employment Opportunity Commission. She received a B.A. from Oberlin College and a J.D. from Case Western Reserve University.

BOARD OF DIRECTORS

Nan Aron, president

Jim Weill, chair; president, Food Research and Action Center

Rita McLennon, vice chair; executive director, National Center on Poverty Law

Sally Greenberg, secretary; policy consultant

Greg Wetstone, treasurer; director of advocacy programs, Natural Resources Defense Council

David Alberswerth, director, Wilderness Society's Bureau of Land Management Program

Judith C. Appelbaum, vice president and legal director, National Women's Law Center

Betsy Cavendish, vice president of the NARAL Foundation

Jim Coleman, professor of the practice of law, Duke University School of Law

Marisa Demeo, regional counsel, Mexican American Legal Defense and Educational Fund (MALDEF)

Fred Gittes, president, National Employment Lawyers Association

Ronald L. Goldfarb, partner, Goldfarb & Associates

Clint Lyons, president and chief executive officer, National Legal Aid and Defender Association

Susanne Martinez, vice president for public policy of the Planned Parenthood Federation of America (PPFA)

Norman Rosenberg, president, I Am Your Child Foundation

Diane Shust, director of government relations, National Education Association

SCOPE

Members: 53 public interest, legal, and advocacy organizations

Branches/chapters: None

Affiliates: None

STAFF

26 total—plus interns and volunteers

TAX STATUS

501(c)(3)

FINANCES

Budget: 2002—$3.9 million; 2001—$3.6 million; 2000—$2.6 million

CONTACT INFORMATION

11 Dupont Circle, NW, 2nd Floor, Washington, DC 20036

Phone: (202) 822-6070 • *Fax:* (202) 822-6068

General E-mail: alliance@afj.org • *Web site:* www.afj.org

Communications Director: Julie Bernstein
(202) 822-6070 • julie@afj.org

Human Resources Director: Marissa Brown
(202) 822-6070 • marissa@afj.org

PURPOSE: "To advance the cause of justice for all Americans, strengthen the public interest community's ability to influence public policy, and foster the next generation of advocates."

CURRENT CONCERNS: Access to justice • Erosion of civil rights and civil liberties by the Supreme Court • Judicial selection • Promoting the expansion of public interest law

METHOD OF OPERATION: Coalition forming • Conferences/seminars • Congressional testimony • Films/video/audiotapes • Grassroots organizing • Internet (Web site) • Legislative/regulatory monitoring (federal and state) Lobbying (federal, state, and grassroots)

Effectiveness and Political Orientation

"As she edges closer to confirmation as a federal appeals judge, Wisconsin Supreme Court Justice Diane S. Sykes is sparring with an Illinois senator who has raised questions about her judicial independence and views on abortion rights, and with a liberal advocacy group that Sykes claims has distorted her record. In written questions sent last month, Sen. Dick Durbin (D-Ill.), a member of the Senate Judiciary Committee reviewing her nomination, asked Sykes about praise she gave two anti-abortion protesters at their sentencing in 1993 for obstructing access to a Milwaukee clinic. . . .

"At several points in her reply to Durbin, Sykes said she was forbidden from responding to theoretical questions because of the judicial code that prohibits commenting on cases that may come before a court. But Sykes has spoken at length about her judicial philosophies to members of the Federalist Society, a conservative judicial group to which she belongs that has been critical of the activist streak of liberal jurists such as Earl Warren, the former U.S. Supreme Court chief justice.

"'I think she's being evasive,' said Nan Aron. 'She's using the code to stonewall members of the Senate Judiciary Committee. Aron is president of the Alliance for Justice, a Washington-based umbrella organization that represents such members as the Humane Society, the Wilderness Society, the National Association for Women and the Children's Defense Fund. The alliance has opposed Sykes' nomination on the grounds that she could not rule fairly on various issues, including abortion and defendants' rights. Sykes, in

FUNDING SOURCES
Foundations, 61%; individuals, Combined Federal Campaign, and annual luncheon, 24%; membership dues, 7%; other, 8%

PAC
None

EMPLOYMENT
Information on open positions can be found on the AFJ Web site: http://www.alliancefor justice.org/about_AFJ/jobs/index.html. All inquiries, resumes and cover letters should be e-mailed to Marissa Brown at marissa @afj.org or faxed to (202) 822-6068.

INTERNSHIPS
The AFJ offers summer internships. The Goldfarb Public Interest Fellowship offers a stipend of $5,000; other internships are unpaid. More information is available at http://www.allianceforjustice.org/ about_AFJ/jobs/index.html.

Internship applications can be e-mailed to Marissa Brown at marissa@afj.org or faxed to (202) 822-6068.

NEWSLETTERS
Pipeline (2 times a year)

PUBLICATIONS
America: Up in Arms (video)
Annual Report of the Judicial Selection Project
Being a Player: A Guide to the IRS Lobbying Regulations for Advocacy Charities
Bringing Justice Home (video),
The Co-Motion Guide to Youth-Led Social Change
The Connection: Strategies for Creating and Operating 501(c)(3)s, 501(c)(4)s, and PACs
Deadly Business: How the Gun Industry and the NRA Market Mayhem to America (video)
Directory of Public Interest Law Centers
E-Advocacy for Nonprofits: The Law of Lobbying & Election-Related Activity on the Net
First Monday Video (video series)
Justice for Sale: Shortchanging the Public Interest for Private Gain
Justice in the Making: A Citizen's Handbook for Choosing Federal Judges
Liberty and Justice for All: Public Interest Law in the 1980s and Beyond
Myth vs. Fact-Foundation Support of Advocacy
National Service and Advocacy
Of Rights and Wrongs: The Threat to America's Freedoms (video)
Packing the Courts: The Battle Over President Bush's Judicial Appointments (video)
Worry-Free Lobbying for Nonprofits
Also publishes several advocacy guides.

CONFERENCES
Annual luncheon (Washington, DC)

turn, named the group in her letter to Durbin as one of those that 'distort records and attack reputations in order to defeat some judicial nominees.' She offered no specifics."

(*Milwaukee Journal Sentinel,* March 9, 2004)

"The Skyline and Oakland Tech high school basketball teams wore T-shirts emblazoned with 'No. 8' during the pregame warm-ups of Wednesday afternoon's basketball game. The shirts. . . .served as a memorial to the eight young people who die from gun violence every day in the United States, according to the nonprofit Alliance for Justice.

"Host team Skyline was one of three Oakland high schools that participated in the inaugural year of Coaches Against Gun Violence, a national campaign that calls attention to the problem as it affects the country's youth. The team called for an end to the violence during the ceremony that featured speeches from Skyline coach Curtis Webster, Golden State Warriors Vice President Al Attles and Oakland police officer Ja'Son Scott. Similar ceremonies were held prior to games last week at Fremont and Oakland Tech high schools.

"Webster said joining the campaign, which is sponsored by Washington, D.C.-based nonprofit Alliance for Justice, was a no-brainer. 'We support anything that's going to provide a positive solution to the troubles plaguing the community,' he said. According to the nonprofit, more than 20,000 people under the age of 20 are killed or injured by gun violence every year. Nineteen of Oakland's 114 homicide victims last year were 20 or younger, according to the Oakland Police Department. Sixteen were killed by guns. . . . Alliance for Justice worked with Youth Alive, an Oakland youth group, to bring the campaign to Oakland. The Warriors and the Oakland Police Department have joined as campaign partners."

(*San Francisco Chronicle,* February 26, 2004)

"Thwarting a Democratic filibuster in the Senate for the second time this year, President Bush on Friday appointed Alabama lawyer Bill Pryor to the federal appeals court in Atlanta. Pryor, 41, was thrust into the national spotlight last year when, as state attorney general, he prosecuted Alabama Chief Justice Roy Moore, ousting him from the state Supreme Court for refusing to remove a 5,300-pound Ten Commandments monument he had placed in the state judicial building.

"Pryor had earlier publicly supported displaying the Ten Commandments in a public courtroom, only to set aside those beliefs to enforce a federal court order in the Moore case. In a statement Friday, President Bush said he was proud to place 'this leading American lawyer' on the 11th U.S. Circuit Court of Appeals. . . . The president condemned the Democrats' filibuster of Pryor's nomination, saying the Alabamian had bipartisan support and would have been confirmed if given a vote on the floor of the Senate. Such stalling tactics directed at Pryor and other judicial nominees 'are inconsistent with the Senate's constitutional responsibility and are hurting our judicial system,' Bush said. . . .

"Nan Aron, president of Alliance for Justice, which monitors judicial nominations, accused Pryor of trying to dismantle abortion rights, environmental protections and the separation of church and state. 'There is something in Bill Pryor's record to offend nearly every constituency,' Aron said, 'except maybe the far right, whom the president needs to energize for his re-election effort.'. . ."

(*The Atlanta-Journal Constitution,* February 21, 2004)

"Laurence Silberman, a retired judge nominated by the Bush administration as the co-chairman of the commission investigating pre-war intelligence on Iraq, was involved in a major cover-up during the Reagan era, his critics alleged yesterday. Mr. Silberman sat on the Foreign Intelligence Surveillance Court of Review, which approved the expanded surveillance powers for the justice department under the controversial Patriot Act.

"President Bush named him as the senior Republican on a nine-member bipartisan commission examining how and why U.S. intelligence had been so wrong about Saddam Hussein's alleged weapons of mass destruction. It will report next spring—well after the November elections. Democrats are skeptical about Judge Silberman's presence. Nan Aron, head of the Alliance for Justice, a liberal pressure group, said: 'This is not a statesman of the sort the president should be seeking to preside over this crucial and sensitive investigation.'

"Judge Silberman is most notorious in American liberal circles for his 1990 judgment overturning the conviction of Colonel Oliver North, who admitted his central role in the Iran-Contra affair, in which proceeds from secret arms sales to Iran were diverted illegally to the Contra anti-communist rebels in Nicaragua. Col. North, who coordinated the payments from the White House, denied President Reagan knew what was going on. He became a martyr for the American far right and the dismissal of his conviction caused uproar. Judge Silberman cast one of the two votes in the appeals court that set him free. He is now a media commentator. The Republican-appointed special prosecutor in the case, Lawrence Walsh, later wrote that Mr. Silberman should have been disqualified for his bias and his sympathy for Col. North's cause."

(*The Guardian* [London], February 10, 2004)

"As voters head to caucuses today in this first large industrial state to weigh in on the Democratic presidential race, one might think that all eyes would be on Michigan. But with Sen. John Kerry riding a wave of momentum from victories in seven other states, and his rivals abandoning this Midwestern manufacturing base to campaign elsewhere, Michigan—a prime example of the nation's economic woes—now looks more like a pit stop on the road to the nomination.

"Kerry blazed through Michigan yesterday, picking up the endorsement of a one-time rival, Rep. Richard A. Gephardt of Missouri. Long a favorite of organized labor—a key Democratic constituency—Gephardt said he hoped his union backers would now side with the Massachusetts senator. 'This campaign is not about me, it's not about any of the candidates, it's about us,' said Gephardt, who quit the race after a weak finish in Iowa dashed his hopes for the nomination.

"At a rally with firefighters and veterans at the DeCarlo Banquet Hall and Convention Center in Warren, Gephardt said of Kerry: 'We need this man to be the next president.' Later, Gephardt, who had the backing of most of the major industrial and manufacturing unions, told reporters he had been lobbying labor leaders to throw their support to Kerry. 'They're moving in that direction,' Gephardt said. Word spread yesterday that the Alliance for Justice, the industrial unions' umbrella group, would likely endorse Kerry next week. . . ."

(*The Baltimore Sun,* February 7, 2004)

Alliance for Retired Americans

Established in 2001

DIRECTOR

Edward Coyle, executive director. Under Coyle, the Alliance has become a powerful voice for seniors, most notably in the advocacy for a prescription Medicare drug benefit. Prior to joining the Alliance, Coyle founded Radio Fair America, a nonpartisan, nonprofit organization, to monitor and report on the effect of talk radio on national politics and public policy. As the organization's national director, he also provided frequent on-air political analysis. Earlier, as founding partner of Coyle, McConnell & O'Brien, Coyle was responsible for planning direct mail advertising and fundraising campaigns and assisting nonprofit organizations and political candidates in strategic development. Coyle also founded and developed Independent Action, a successful, progressive political action committee. Coyle served the organization from 1980 through 1997, first as executive director, and then as chair of the board

BOARD OF DIRECTORS

Information unavailable

SCOPE

Members: More than 3 million individual members
Branches/chapters: Chapters in the following states: AZ, CA, CO, FL, IL, IN, MD, MO, NC, NE, NV, NY, OH, OR, RI, WA
Affiliates: None

STAFF

50 total—25 full-time professional; 25 full-time support; plus 3 volunteers

TAX STATUS

501 (c)(3)

FINANCES

Information unavailable

FUNDING SOURCES

Information unavailable

PAC

None

EMPLOYMENT

Job postings can be found in publications such as area newspapers. ARA offers positions in the following areas: administrative, field organizers, public relations, legislative, accounting, and member services. Applicants should send resumes and other materials for employment to Mary Kuhlman, Executive Secretary, 888 16th Street, NW, Washington, DC 20006. Phone: (202) 974-8224. Fax: (202) 974-8265. E-mail: mkuhlman@retiredamericans.org.

CONTACT INFORMATION

888 16th Street, NW, Washington, DC 20006
Phone: (202) 974-8222 or (888) 633-4435 • *Fax:* (202) 974-8256
General E-mail: webadmin@retiredamericans.org •
Web site: www.retiredamericans.org

Communications Director: Patti Reilly
(202) 974-8271 • preilly@retiredamericans.org
Human Resources Director: Mary Kuhlman, executive secretary
(202) 974-8224 • mkuhlman@retiredamericans.org

PURPOSE: "To ensure social and economic justice and full civil rights for all citizens, so they may enjoy lives of dignity, personal and family fulfillment and security. With the help of our members, the Alliance aims to influence government through action on retiree legislative and political issues at the federal, state and local levels."

CURRENT CONCERNS: Issues that affect older Americans and their families • Medicare • Medicaid • Nursing homes and long-term care • Pensions • Social Security

METHOD OF OPERATION: Advertisements • Coalition forming • Conferences/seminars • Congressional testimony • Congressional voting analysis • Demonstrations • Grassroots organizing • e-mail alerts • Web site • Internships • Legislative/regulatory monitoring (federal and state) • Lobbying (grassroots) • Media outreach • Polling • Research • Voter registration • Voting records

Effectiveness and Political Orientation

"In sharp contrast to the Bush administration's ad campaign touting the new Medicare law, a national health care advocacy group and other senior organizations have launched their own efforts to educate seniors about provisions in the controversial landmark measure. . . .

"Less than three months before Medicare's drug discount program is set to begin, opposing sides have launched intense campaigns to help seniors dissect the complicated measure. . . .

" 'This is a complicated bill. People don't know much about it,' said Trish Neuman, director of Kaiser's Medicare policy project. She said the educational efforts 'will raise awareness and confuse people. There's going to be an onslaught of ads, stories and brochures.'

"Michael Burgess of the New York Senior Action Council, an advocacy group, has found many seniors confused. 'The bad thing is the confusion is turned into anger, because when people finally get the details explained to them, they don't like it,' he said. . . .

"Bush officials have set aside $12.8 million for 30-second national ads that will run through the end of the month. The ads say that traditional Medicare

INTERNSHIPS

Both paid and unpaid internship positions are offered; postings can be found on the Internet. College students are preferred, and application deadlines are ongoing. Interns work a minimum of 8 hours per week, for at least 3 months or more. Internship areas include accounting, communications, legislative, and field mobilization. Applicants should demonstrate their interest in the department applied for, their ability to work well with others, and their experience or interest in working with nonprofits or elected officials.

The internship coordinator is David Blank, Congressional Liaison, 888 16th street, NW, Washington, DC 20006. Phone: (202) 974-8226. Fax: (202) 974-8222. E-mail: dblank@retiredamericans.org.

NEWSLETTERS
AgeWise (quarterly)

PUBLICATIONS
The Profit in Pills
The Failure of Medicare+Choice
Nursing Home Care: When Will We Get It Right?

CONFERENCES
Legislative Conference (biannual)

has not changed and that new benefits are available, but they don't include details. The administration plans to air more ads next month focusing on the discount card. . . .

"Democrats and some senior groups have called the ads taxpayer-funded political ads. An investigation by the General Accounting Office found that the ads have a partisan tone and leave out some information, but don't violate the law.

"'We are going to remain aggressive in our education efforts for seniors,' HHS Secretary Tommy Thompson said in a statement. 'We're going to keep providing seniors with fact-based information on the new benefits under Medicare and give them straight answers to their questions.'

"The Alliance for Retired Americans, a group of mostly retired union workers, questioned the timing of the ads. 'We wonder why the administration feels the need to do this six or seven months before an election,' said Edward Coyle, ARA's executive director.

"Coyle said the ARA plans mass mailings, phone calls and town hall meetings to educate seniors about 'flaws' in the Medicare law, and ensure they are election-year issues. . . ."

(*Newsday* [New York], March 15, 2004)

"A group that represents 3 million union retirees called on Congress on Wednesday to defeat legislation that would add a limited prescription drug benefit to Medicare and make other major changes in the program.

"'Seniors are angry because Medicare as we know it will cease to exist under this plan,' said George J. Kourpias, president of the Alliance for Retired Americans. 'The real beneficiaries of this bill will be the pharmaceutical and insurance industries. They stand to make a bundle at the expense of seniors.'

"Kourpias' call to defeat the legislation, which was drafted largely by Republicans, was backed by hundreds of seniors and by the Democratic leaders of the Senate and House who appeared at a noon rally on Capitol Hill. 'We're going to do everything we can to stop it,' said Senate Minority Leader Thomas A. Daschle, D-S.D.

"About two dozen alliance members then took a bus to the national headquarters of AARP, where they cut up their membership cards to protest AARP's support for the legislation. 'I am outraged they have not conferred with the seniors they represent,' said Shirley Ehrlickman, 75, of New York City. . . .

". . . experts predicted the House ultimately will approve the legislation by a slim margin. At the rally, House Minority Leader Nancy Pelosi, D-Calif., said that Democrats would not provide any help. 'Democrats will work day and night against this shameful bill,' she declared.

"In addition to the drug benefit, which would cover about 22 percent of Medicare beneficiaries' projected pharmaceutical costs over the next decade, the bill would begin to cover a number of preventive services that are not now part of Medicare. . . ."

(*Hartford Courant* [Connecticut], November 20, 2003)

"The Supreme Court has given senior citizens and the uninsured new hope in the fight to bring down skyrocketing drug prices.

"The high court ruled last week that federal law does not block Maine's plan to reduce drug prices for citizens without health insurance. The plan would use the state's leverage to negotiate massive drug purchases and pass the savings to the needy.

"Litigation has blocked the enactment of the prescription program since it was passed by state lawmakers.

"More struggles surely lie ahead, but the Supreme Court ruling should encourage other states to move forward with this practical approach to helping needy citizens obtain prescription drugs at affordable prices, the Alliance for Retired Americans said. . . ."

(*San Antonio Express-News,* May 25, 2003)

"SARS is on the decline north of the border, but seniors have nonetheless decided to delay what are becoming annual trips to Canada in search of more affordable prescription medicines.

"Local seniors working with the Alliance for Retired Americans had planned a three-day trip to buy medicines in Hamilton, Ontario for May 27–30.

"But with all the concern about severe acute respiratory syndrome, the local trip and 16 other "Rx Express" bus rides from at least 10 states have been delayed by the alliance, a Washington D.C.-based group of union retirees. . . .

"Jean Friday of Belle Vernon, the organizer of a bus group from Western Pennsylvania, said two seniors expressed concerns to her in recent weeks about making the trip while SARS cases were still being reported in Toronto. But the concerns weren't so great that the seniors wouldn't have gone, she said.

"The national organization got similar input from other regions. . . .

"Busing to Canada for medicines is an odd form of tourism, but one that persists as seniors struggle to pay for medicines and interest groups such as the Alliance for Retired Americans continue to push for legislation to make drugs more affordable. Rx Express trips carried more than 375 senior citizens to Canada last year.

"Those seniors realized a combined savings of $126,711, an average of more than $300 per person. Since those prescriptions could be refilled by mail for up to a year, the groups' total savings could have surpassed $500,000.

"Last year, seniors traveled an average of 277 miles while riding an average of 14 hours on Rx Express buses to purchase the medicines.

"There were so many people for the two-day trip last year that seniors struggled to get their prescriptions filled, said Friday, the local organizer.

"So, this year's trip—the third she has helped organize from Pittsburgh in four years—will be three days. . . ."

(*Pittsburgh Post-Gazette,* May 1, 2003)

"AARP, which represents 34.7 million older Americans, is in for some competition from the biggest labor organization in the country, the AFL-CIO. Labor's new Alliance for Retired Americans began sending union retirees membership information last month. . . .

"ARA, that's the union group, will represent about 135,000 retirees in Ohio, including close to 36,000 in Cleveland. They had been members of the Retirees' Council, which ARA will replace.

"ARA's Cleveland chapter president, John Gallo, says the group will fight for prescription drug coverage, preserving Social Security, and other issues that AARP has also pursued.

(*The Plain Dealer* [Cleveland], July 21, 2001)

American-Arab Anti-Discrimination Committee

Established in 1980

DIRECTOR

Mary Rose Oakar, president. Oakar has served on the American-Arab Anti-Discrimination Committee's (ADC) Advisory Board since the organization's beginning. She was named President of ADC in June 2003. Oakar received her B.A. in Fine Arts at Ursuline College in Cleveland, Ohio, and her M.A. at John Carroll University, also in Cleveland. She has received several honorary doctorate degrees from various institutions. From 1967 to 1975 she was a college professor at Cuyahoga Community College and other college institutions. She has served in all three legislative branches as member of the Cleveland City Council (1974–1976), as U.S. Representative (1977–1993), and as member of the Ohio House of Representatives (2001–2003). While in Congress, she worked on several pieces of legislation related to peace and justice in the Middle East and for those of Middle East ancestry.

BOARD OF DIRECTORS

Safa Rifka, chairman
Albert Mokhiber, vice chairman
Mohammad Oweis, treasurer
George Gorayeb, secretary
David Khairallah, at large
Mona Aboelnaga
Hon. James Abourezk
Thomas Tony George
Samer Khanachet
George Majeed Khoury
Linda Mansour
Ahmad Sbaiti

SCOPE

Members: 10,000 individuals
Branches/chapters: 2 regional offices/
   39 chapters (Web site)
Affiliates: ADC Research Institute, a 501(c)(3)
   organization

STAFF

14 total—12 professional; 2 support;
plus 9–10 interns

TAX STATUS

501(c)(3)

FINANCES

Information unavailable

FUNDING SOURCES

Individual contributions

PAC

None

CONTACT INFORMATION

4201 Connecticut Avenue, NW, Suite 300, Washington, DC 20008
Phone: (202) 244-2990 • *Fax:* (202) 244-3196
General E-mail: adc@adc.org • *Web site:* www.adc.org

Communications Director: Hussein Ibish
(202) 244-2990 • media@adc.org
Human Resources Director: Information unavailable

PURPOSE: "To protect the rights of people of Arab descent, promote and defend the Arab-American heritage, and serve the needs of the Arab-American community."

CURRENT CONCERNS: Airport profiling • Census data • Civil rights consequences of the counter-terrorism bill • Discrimination • Human rights • Immigration counseling • Promoting Arab heritage • U.S. policy in the Middle East

METHOD OF OPERATION: Awards program • Coalition forming • Conferences/seminars • Congressional testimony • Demonstrations • Films/video/audiotapes • Grassroots organizing • International activities • Internet • Legal assistance • Library/information clearinghouse • Lobbying (grassroots) • Local/municipal affairs • Media outreach • Research • Speakers program • Telecommunications services (databases, mailing lists)

Effectiveness and Political Orientation

"A leading Arab American civil rights organization has asked Merriam-Webster Inc. to publicly repudiate what the group calls a 'false and damaging' definition of anti-Semitism in the unabridged version of Webster's Third New International Dictionary.

"That dictionary lists, as one of the meanings . . . 'opposition to Zionism: sympathy with opponents of the state of Israel.'

". . . [T]he American-Arab Anti-Discrimination Committee also asked the company to delete the definition in future reprintings . . ."
(*The Washington Post*, March 13, 2004)

"With mounting concern that Arab and Muslim U.S. citizens returning from overseas trips may be facing broader and more frequent questioning by customs agents, a civil rights group spoke out Wednesday against what it views as increasingly intrusive tactics by the Department of Homeland Security.

"Linda Sherif, the legal director for the San Francisco chapter of the American-Arab Anti-Discrimination Committee, said at a news conference that she has noticed a disturbing pattern to accounts that have come to the organization's attention. . . .

EMPLOYMENT
Information unavailable

INTERNSHIPS
ADC Research Institute's (ADCRI) Internship Program: candidates must be currently enrolled in college and have completed at least one year of undergraduate study. This includes recent graduates, graduate students, and law students. Individual departments have their own requirements. Interns are expected to become regular ADC members. While the program is primarily oriented to Arab-American students, the ADC encourages applicants of all ethnic backgrounds.

Volunteer positions for work-study or college credit are available during the academic year at the ADC National Office and are arranged on a case-by-case basis. Internships carry a small stipend. Full-time interns receive $400 per month for undergraduates and $500 for graduate students. Interns receiving course credit do not receive a stipend. During the school year, applications are considered as they are received. Work hours can be accommodated to student's class schedules.

During the summer, up to 15 internships are available at the National Office. The internships are full-time positions and normally last from June 1 to July 31. There is a $750 stipend for undergraduate students, $1,000 for graduate students. Those who receive course credit for the internship do not receive a stipend.

Applicants must submit the following items: completed application form (available from the organization's Web site, or by fax by contacting Marvin Wingfield by phone at (202) 244-2990); resume; academic transcript; two letters of recommendation; and a two-page personal statement about the student's goals as an ADCRI intern and how the student's academic, professional, extracurricular activities, or career goals are related to the position requested. Applicants must be U.S. citizens or have a visa that permits them to work in the United States. Completed applications should be sent to Intern Coordinator, ADC Research Institute, 4201 Connecticut Avenue, NW, Suite 300, Washington, DC 20008.

NEWSLETTERS
ADC Times (monthly)
Arab Daily Chronicle (online news service)
Inter Perspective (annually)

PUBLICATIONS
Information unavailable

CONFERENCES
Annual national convention in Arlington, VA
Symposiums

"Sherif said a letter sent last week asking for a meeting with the director of the bureau's San Francisco office to address the committee's concerns had not received a response.

"Michael Fleming, a bureau spokesman in Los Angeles, said the agency intends to meet with committee members and that 'it is not the policy of the Bureau of Customs and Border Protections to discriminate against citizens or noncitizens arriving in the United States who are arriving home, regardless of race, creed or national origin.'"

(*The San Francisco Chronicle*, May 29, 2003)

"As Attorney General John Ashcroft defended his decision to invite 5,000 immigrants from predominantly Arab countries in for "consensual" interviews, Chicago lawyers volunteered Thursday to accompany the men on the interviews.

"'We're supporting their right to counsel,' Khaled Elkhatib, vice president of the American Arab Anti-Discrimination Committee said at a news conference at the Chicago office of the American Civil Liberties Union. 'For a lot of these people, English is not their first language.'"

(*Chicago Sun-Times*, December 7, 2001)

"Expecting to be interviewed and photographed, men arriving at the San Francisco office of the Bureau of Immigration and Customs Enforcement on Tuesday to reregister themselves as visa holders from Middle Eastern countries instead were handed a letter telling them that they were no longer required to do so.

"The letter, . . . explained that the government had immediately suspended the law mandating that men from predominantly Muslim and Arab countries register with immigration officials once a year. Immigration attorneys, advocates and activists regarded the decision as an important victory but said concerns and resentments still linger about how the program, known officially as the National Security Entry/Exit Registration System, had been handled.

"'This is definitely a step in the right direction, but the administration has a long way to go before it gains the trust of the Arab and Muslim community,' said Ramiz Rafeedie, an attorney and board member of the American-Arab Anti-Discrimination Committee chapter in San Francisco. 'There are still more than 13,000 people who face deportation as a result of the earlier special registration requirements. And even though this program has ended, we know there are other ways the government can unfairly target you and deport you . . . but it's always a positive development when a law that is founded on the concept of guilt by association or ethnicity is repealed.'"

(*The San Francisco Chronicle*, December 3, 2003)

"Arabs and others who appeared to be Muslim were threatened, beaten and generally discriminated against more last year than at any other time in the past, according to the FBI's annual survey of hate crimes released yesterday.

"Largely in the aftermath . . . of Sept. 11, 2001, the FBI counted 481 attacks against people of Middle Eastern descent, Muslims and South Asian Sikhs, who are often mistaken as Muslim. That number was up from 28 in 2000, an increase of more than 1,500 percent.

"Directors of Arab and Asian groups said the report validated surveys they had taken after the attacks . . .

" 'This absolutely validates what we were saying,' said Hussein Ibish, spokesman for the American-Arab Anti-Discrimination Committee. 'This data corresponds to our data, to Human Rights Watch, to all the available data.' "

(*The Washington Post,* November 26, 2002)

American Civil Liberties Union (ACLU)

Established in 1920

DIRECTOR

Anthony D. Romero, executive director. Romero has been executive director of the ACLU since 2001. Prior to coming to the ACLU he led the Ford Foundation's Human Rights and International Cooperation Program. He is a graduate of Stanford University Law School and Princeton University's Woodrow Wilson School of Public Policy and International Affairs.

BOARD OF DIRECTORS

Kenneth B. Clark, chair; psychologist, New York, NY
Nadine Strossen, president
Richard Zacks, treasurer
Julie Davis
Milton Estes
James Ferguson
Mary Ellen Gale
Diane Geraghty
Susan Herman
Marina Hsieh
Rosllyn Litman
Michael Meyers
Robert Remar

SCOPE

Members: 275,000 individuals
Branches/chapters: 53 affiliate offices, including one in each state
Affiliates: ACLU Foundation, a 501(c)(3) organization

STAFF

150 total—105 professional; 45 support (not including affiliates)

TAX STATUS

501(c)(4)

FINANCES

Revenue: 2001—$19.8 million; 2000—$15.8 million; 1999—$13.5 million

FUNDING SOURCES

Private organizations and individuals, 100%; no government funding

PAC

None

EMPLOYMENT

Information on open positions can be on the ACLU Web site: www.aclu.org/jobs/jobsmain.cfm. Letters of interest and resumes can be mailed to Human Resources, ACLU, 125 Broad Street, New York, NY 10004 or e-mailed to: hrjobs@aclu.org.

CONTACT INFORMATION

125 Broad Street, New York, NY 10004
Phone: (212) 549-2500

122 Maryland Avenue, NE, Washington, DC 20002
Phone: (202) 544-1681 • *Fax:* (202) 546-0738
General E-mail: aclu@aclu.org • *Web site:* www.aclu.org

Communications Director: Emily Tynes
(212) 549-2500
Human Resources Director: Information unavailable

PURPOSE: "To preserve, defend and expand application of the constitutional guarantees and freedoms set forth in the Bill of Rights."

CURRENT CONCERNS: Affirmative action • Civil rights • Criminal justice • Death penalty • Disability rights • Drug policy • Gay rights • Government regulation of the Internet • HIV/AIDS • Immigrants' rights • National security • Racial equality • Religious liberty • Reproductive rights • Rights to privacy of information • Students' rights • Voting rights • Women's rights • Workplace rights

METHOD OF OPERATION: Advertisements • Awards program • Coalition forming • Conferences/seminars • Congressional testimony • Congressional voting analysis • Demonstrations • Films/video/audiotapes • Grassroots organizing • Information clearinghouse • Internet (e-mail alerts, Web site) • Internships • Legal assistance • Legislative/regulatory monitoring (federal and state) • Litigation • Lobbying (federal, state, and grassroots) • Media outreach • Polling • Research •

Effectiveness and Political Orientation

"The American Civil Liberties Union is challenging the Glendale [Colorado] Police Department's training procedures as a result of the death of a man who was repeatedly shocked with a Taser while suffering drug-induced seizures last fall. In a letter sent to city officials Thursday, Legal Director Mark Silverstein said the officer used the Taser on Glenn Leyba on Sept. 29 because she was told there are 'no documented cases of permanent injury or death caused by Taser use.'

"Silverstein, in a letter earlier this month asking Denver police to curb their use of Tasers, cited several reports that raise questions about the weapons' safety. 'The training failed to inform officers of medical evidence indicating that electroshock weapons may be dangerous, or even lethal, to extremely agitated or psychotic persons; persons suffering from high levels of drug intoxication; and persons with heart disease,' Silverstein wrote.

"The ACLU's challenges come at a time when police agencies across the country are purchasing more and more Tasers in the hope of reducing suspect and officer fatalities. Tasers fire needle-like probes up to 21 feet. The probes are connected to a wire that delivers a 26-watt charge, causing a suspect's muscles to lock up for five seconds. The manufacturer says the weapon is safe. 'We stand by the safety of our product. It does not cause death,' Taser International co-founder and president Tom Smith said Thursday. 'We've done medical testing and field testing to support this. In fact, 14.6 percent of all of our documented uses involve suspects using dangerous narcotics.'"

(*Rocky Mountain News* [Denver], March 12, 2004)

"Tax-exempt bond financing for construction at Christian schools violates a California constitutional ban on public support of religious institutions, says a state appellate court. The 2–1 ruling by the Court of Appeal in Sacramento on Tuesday drew a bristling dissent from Justice George Nicholson, who accused the majority of 'hostility toward religion.' The ruling is another setback for advocates of public aid to religious education; the U.S. Supreme Court on Feb. 25 upheld a state's refusal to fund a scholarship for a theology student, under a constitutional provision similar to California's.

"Nationally, 'there is a massive effort to channel public funds to religious institutions that discriminate in hiring and that infuse their services with religious doctrine,' Margaret Crosby, an American Civil Liberties Union lawyer who took part in the bond case, said Wednesday. In light of U.S. Supreme Court rulings in recent years that have allowed increased public funding of religious schools, she said, state constitutions have become an important safeguard, and Tuesday's ruling 'shows that the California Constitution's protection for religious freedom is extremely powerful.' She said it was the first such ruling in the nation."

(*The San Francisco Chronicle*, March 11, 2004)

"Relatives of European citizens held by the United States at its Navy base at Guantanamo Bay in Cuba accused the Bush administration Tuesday of violating international law. They did not comment on the innocence or guilt of their loved ones, who were captured as part of the U.S. war on terrorism. But they accused Americans of holding the prisoners indefinitely 'like animals,' without charges or access to lawyers.

"Azmat Begg, a British citizen and retired banker, is among those trying to bring attention to the issue on Capitol Hill. His 36-year-old son Moazzam was taken from his home in Islamabad, Pakistan, by American soldiers and Pakistani policemen and eventually sent to Guantanamo Bay, he said. The family received a few heavily redacted letters from Moazzam, who Begg said was a humanitarian worker, but they stopped six months ago. 'If I can't take Moazzam with me no . . . at least let me see him,' Begg said at a press conference at the National Press Club in Washington. Begg said his son has been poorly fed, denied sleep and kept mostly in a dark cell for a year. He was joined by relatives of detainees from France and Germany and a member of the French parliament.

"Organizing the event was the American Civil Liberties Union, which has protested the detentions and other Bush administration policies in the war on terrorism. 'These fathers, mothers and siblings have come to the U.S. in search of the legal process. Instead, what are they finding? A separate and unequal system of justice for foreigners, immigrants and non-citizens,' said Anthony D. Romero, the ACLU's executive director. . . .'

"Romero said the proposed rules for the military commissions that will conduct the trials deny the prisoners protections required under international law. For example, they do not allow defendants to appeal outside of the mili-

CONFERENCES

Internet forums (America Online keyword: ACLU)

tary chain of command and they permit the government to continue holding defendants even if they are cleared of all charges, he said. . . ."

(*The Atlanta Journal-Constitution,* March 10, 2004)

"Ten Commandments-Georgia Inc. is trying to spread its wings and its message: Put replicas of the tablets from Mount Sinai on public buildings throughout the state. To do that, the group hopes to organize chapters in each of the state's 159 counties. Since the nonprofit organization was begun late last fall, Barrow, Baldwin, Glynn and Hart County chapters have formed. . . . Former Alabama Supreme Court Justice Roy Moore is the lightning rod for the movement. He refused a court order to remove a 2-ton replica of the Commandments from Alabama's main judicial building and was subsequently removed from the bench.

"The issue has cropped up in Georgia, where Habersham County recently dropped its appeal of an order to remove its Ten Commandments displays. The decision to drop the appeal was purely financial, said County Manager Bill Shanahan. In Barrow County, the American Civil Liberties Union, representing an anonymous plaintiff, is suing to have a Commandments display removed from the courthouse. While the suits are litigated in Georgia, the displays draw support and opposition elsewhere. Liberty Counsel, an Orlando-based group active in First Amendment religious issues, represented Habersham for free. Barrow turned to high-priced Virginia lawyer Herb Titus to argue its case. Titus had been involved on behalf of Moore.

(*The Atlanta Journal-Constitution,* March 7, 2004)

"The U.S. Justice Department yesterday joined the Boy Scouts in their court fight to continue leasing a Fiesta Island aquatics center from the city. The agency filed a brief in U.S. District Court in San Diego, saying the Scouts' lease of the half-acre Fiesta Island site is just as valid as the more than 100 leases the city has with other nonprofit groups to use public land. The American Civil Liberties Union filed a lawsuit in 2000 challenging the Scouts' lease of public land in Balboa Park and on Fiesta Island.

"The ACLU argues that the Boy Scout leases were invalid because the group discriminates by requiring members to profess a belief in God and doesn't allow homosexuals to join. The suit was brought on behalf of a lesbian couple and an agnostic couple, both of which have sons who want to become Scouts. In July, U.S. District Judge Napoleon Jones Jr. ruled that the Balboa Park lease violated the constitutional separation of church and state. He concluded there was 'overwhelming and uncontradicted evidence' showing that the Boy Scouts of America is a religious organization. . . .

"ACLU attorney M. Andrew Woodmansee said 'it is sadly ironic' that the Justice Department, which has fought for the civil rights of African Americans, 'has now chosen to align itself with an organization such as the Boy Scouts that proudly and openly discriminates against people on the basis of their religious non-belief and sexual orientation.' Woodmansee said the Justice Department action was meant to advance 'the right-wing political agenda' of the Bush administration. 'Thankfully, we have neutral, objective courts in this country, and I doubt very much that the federal government's political agenda will influence the court's opinion here,' Woodmansee said."

(*The San Diego Union-Tribune,* March 5, 2004)

American Conservative Union

Established in 1978

DIRECTOR

Richard Lessner, Ph.D., executive director. From 1981 to 1993 Lessner was a writer and editor at *The Arizona Republic*. After a brief turn as a political consultant and campaign worker, Lessner returned to journalism, as the director of the editorial page at *The Union-Leader* in Manchester, New Hampshire. The Associated Press named Lessner the best editorial writer in New England for 1999. He is a graduate of Pacific Christian College, the Southern Baptist Theological Seminary and Baylor University.

BOARD OF DIRECTORS

David A. Keene, chair; The Carmen Group, Washington, DC

Thomas S. Winter, first vice chair; Fund for Effective News Reporting, Washington, DC

Donald J. Devine, Ph.D., second vice chair; former director, Office of Personnel Management, Washington DC

Jameson Campaigne Jr., secretary, Ottawa, IL

Marc E. Rotterman, treasurer; senior fellow, John Locke Foundation, Raleigh, NC

Jeffrey Bell Manhattan Institute, Arlington, VA

Charles Black, Black, Kelly, Scruggs & Healey, Washington, DC

Morton Blackwell, founder, The Leadership Institute, Springfield, VA

Beau Boulter, Carmen Group, Arlington, VA

Floyd Brown, executive director, Reagan Ranch Program, Santa Barbara, CA

Al Cardenas, attorney, Miami, FL

Muriel Coleman, Madison,WI

Becky Norton Dunlop, The Heritage Foundation, Arlington VA

M. Stanton Evans, director, National Journalism Center,Washington, DC

Alan Gottlieb, Bellevue, WA

Sen. Jesse Helms, Washington, DC

Rep. Duncan Hunter, Washington, DC

James V. Lacy, attorney, Monarch Beach, CA

Wayne LaPierre, executive vice president, National Rifle Association, Fairfax, VA

Michael Long, chair, New York Conservative Party, Brooklyn, NY

Robert Luddy, founder and chief executive officer, Captive-Aire Systems, Raleigh, NC

State Senator Serphin Maltese, Glendale, NY

Cleta Mitchell, Foley & Lardner, LLP, Washington, DC

Steve Moore, Republican Club for Growth, Washington, DC

Joseph Morris, attorney, Morris & De La Roca, Chicago, IL

Grover Norquist, president, Americans for Tax Reform, Washington, DC

CONTACT INFORMATION

1007 Cameron Street, Alexandria, VA 22314
Phone: (703) 836-8602 • *Fax:* (703) 836-8606
General E-mail: acu@conservative.org • *Web site:* www.conservative.org

Communications Director: Ian Walters
(703) 836-8602 • iwalters@conservative.org
Human Resources Director: Diana Carr, administrative director
(703) 836-8602 • dcarr@conservative.org

PURPOSE: "To effectively communicate and advance the goals and principles of conservatism through one multi-issue, umbrella organization."

CURRENT CONCERNS: Advocating the need for near-term deployment of strategic defenses • Battling against higher taxes • Monitoring the influence of the Occupational and Safety Health Administration (OSHA) on small businesses • Opposing the Panama Canal giveaway • Opposing the SALT treaties • Promoting the confirmation of conservative justices to the Supreme Court • Supporting aid to freedom fighters in Marxist countries

METHOD OF OPERATION: Advertisements • Campaign contributions • Coalition forming • Congressional testimony • Congressional voting analysis • Films/video/ audiotapes • Grassroots organizing • Internet (databases, e-mail alerts, Web site) • Internships • Legislative/regulatory monitoring (federal) • Lobbying (federal) • Media outreach • Voting records

Effectiveness and Political Orientation

"Next week's congressional primary election might be called a sleeper. Facing nominal opposition within their parties, six Maryland congressman and one U.S. senator are expected to win nomination for re-election in the Super Tuesday contest. . . . Despite the odds, challengers of two of the highly favored incumbents are playing an angle. They're avidly portraying Republican Reps. Roscoe G. Bartlett of Western Maryland and Wayne T. Gilchrest of the Eastern Shore as being too liberal. They hope their message might sway the kind of Republicans who traditionally come out to vote in a primary even when their incumbent president doesn't have any major rivals—hard-core party loyalists, most of them conservative.

"That's the tack Frederick County State's Attorney Scott L. Rolle and state Sen. Richard Colburn, both conservative Republicans, are taking in their closely watched campaigns to unseat Bartlett and Gilchrest, respectively. . . .

"The ultraconservative Bartlett dismisses Rolle's notion that he is not conservative enough. Having earned near-perfect ratings from the American Conservative Union, Bartlett is anti-abortion, opposes gay marriage, favors lower taxes and has co-sponsored legislation to require that the Ten Com-

Tom Pauken, chairman, Texas Republican Party, Dallas, TX

James Arthur Pope, attorney, Raleigh, NC

Ron Robinson, president, Young America's Foundation, Reston, VA

Allen Roth, New York State Conservative Party, New York, NY

Craig Shirley, consultant, Alexandria, VA

Lewis Uhler, Council for National Policy, Roseville, CA

Kirby Wilbur, radio host, Duvall, WA

SCOPE
Members: 1 million individuals
Branches/chapters: None
Affiliates: ACU Foundation, a 501(c)(3) organization; American Conservative Network

STAFF
12 total—plus interns

TAX STATUS
501(c)(4)

FINANCES
Information unavailable

FUNDING SOURCES
Membership and donations from individuals, 97%; foundation grants, 2%; corporate donations, 1%

PAC
American Conservative Union Political Action Committee

EMPLOYMENT
Information on open positions can be found on the ACU Web site: www.conservative.org/about/jobs.asp. Cover letters and resumes can be e-mailed to Stacey Chamberlin, schamberlin@conservative.org.

INTERNSHIPS
The ACU actively recruits interns. Information on Internships can be found on the ACU Web site: www.conservative.org/about/jobs.asp. Cover letters and resumes can be e-mailed to Stacey Chamberlin, schamberlin @conservative.org.

NEWSLETTERS
Battleline (quarterly)

PUBLICATIONS
Annual Rating of Congress
Bad News for Bush in New York State
The Clinton Plan: More Power to Government
Conference Delivers the Right Agenda
Conventions Offer True Picture of Parties
Government Health Falling Down
Hitler's Pope?
Interim Ratings of Congress
Killing the Boom?
No Presidential Coattails for Congress Candidates
Only the Moral Need Apply
Pharmaceutical Price Controls
Right Unites to Push Conservative Platform
Setup of Microsoft Case

mandments be displayed in the House and Senate. 'There's not a whole lot of room to my right,' Bartlett, 77, said."

(*The Baltimore Sun,* February 28, 2004)

"It is a cardinal rule of politics, all the more so for a president who saw his father defeated largely because he failed to heed it fully: Pay attention to the party's base. In recent weeks, on a variety of fronts, President Bush has done just that, trying to allay the concerns and stoke the spirits of his restive conservative base. His impassioned endorsement on Tuesday of a constitutional amendment banning same-sex marriage, after weeks of intensive lobbying by social conservatives, was the culmination of this rapprochement.

"But will he pay a price with the centrist voters who so often decide presidential elections, as the Democrats hope? Or is the country at such an ideologically polarized point that the middle simply matters less? Almost no one suggests that Mr. Bush is operating solely on the basis of political calculations. In his remarks on Tuesday, he emphasized that 'an amendment to the Constitution is never to be undertaken lightly,' and closed his remarks with a plea to 'conduct this difficult debate in a manner worthy of our country, without bitterness or anger.'

"But as David A. Keene, chairman of the American Conservative Union, put it, 'neither is it fair to say that the politics of it aren't important.' The administration clearly recognized in recent weeks that it faced political unrest on its right, after what Mr. Keene described as 'a short period of denying the problem existed.' The soaring deficits, the growth in government, and most particularly the passage of a Medicare bill that amounted to the biggest expansion of that entitlement program in 38 years, all led to growing discontent among economic conservatives. Other conservatives were dismayed by the administration's immigration proposal, granting temporary work permits to illegal immigrants.

(*The New York Times,* February 25, 2004)

"Congress takes up several bills this week that may have little chance of becoming law but hold huge election-year potential for energizing each party's political base and stimulating special-interest donors. The Senate is expected to vote today on the 'Healthy Mothers, Healthy Babies Access to Care Act,' a GOP-backed bill that would curb medical malpractice judgments, but that neither party believes will pass. . . .

"The Republicans, who hold majorities in the House and the Senate, 'will highlight these [bills] in fundraising appeals and get-out-the-vote drives on how the party has worked hard for issues you care about,' Noble said. In this politically charged environment, he said, 'in one sense, it doesn't really matter whether the bill passes.' That is expected to hold true through much of the rest of what is scheduled to be a short and light session, with lawmakers recessing early to campaign.

" 'Both sides in even-numbered years find provisions that they know aren't going to go anywhere but will have a lot of meaning to their constituency groups,' said a senior Republican Senate aide, speaking on condition that he not be named. . . . 'Democrats are prepared to work constructively on important issues, but we will not stand by while the majority passes laws that reward their corporate benefactors at the expense of ordinary Americans,' said Todd Webster, a spokesman for Senate Minority Leader Tom Daschle (D-S.D.).

Shaming the Educational Bureaucracy
There Will Be a Conservative Platform
Voting Indices
What Million Mom March Was Really About
Why Taiwan's Independence Must Be Protected

CONFERENCES
Conservative Political Action Committee
Conference (annual)

"But Democratic filibusters, said Richard Lessner, executive director of the American Conservative Union, raise the question: 'Why are all the Democrats stopping so much good legislation from passing the Senate?' Republicans point out that they accomplished the key elements of their agenda last year: expanding Medicare benefits; boosting funding for the Pentagon to finance the Iraq war and reconstruction; restricting late-term abortions; cutting taxes; relaxing some clean air requirements; and allowing more logging in national forests.

(*Los Angeles Times,* February 24, 2004)

"Modern conservatism has always been skeptical of the role of government, and since Franklin Roosevelt's New Deal created the foundations of the modern welfare state, limiting the size of government has been a central tenet of American conservatism. For most of the past generation, conservative Republicans have come into office vowing to slash spending and eliminate entire Cabinet departments.

". . .But conditions changed dramatically during the latter part of the 1990s, as the economy expanded and the growth of government spending was relatively slow. Budgets were balanced and deficits turned to surpluses, and the idea of smaller government faded as an issue. In 2000, Bush ran as a 'compassionate conservative' who said government could do some good. He did not propose disbanding any Cabinet departments.

"'I don't think it is conservatism,' Donald Devine, a former Reagan administration official and vice chairman of the American Conservative Union, said of the Bush philosophy. 'He is a social conservative, but he is not an economic conservative. Traditional conservatism has been both economic and social conservatism, and this guy has only one of the two.' Devine said that discontent is growing among conservatives in the political community, and much grumbling was heard about spending and the drug bill at the recent Conservative Political Action Conference in Washington. Some also have complained about the federal government's reach in the No Child Left Behind Act, which imposes federal performance standards on local school districts."

(*Times-Picayune* [New Orleans], February 3, 2004)

"Conservatives are angry at George W. Bush for his big-spending ways, although they aren't going to do anything about it. And that tells the tale of the transformation of 'conservatism' in the 21st century, as it expands—and radicalizes—at home as well as abroad. To be sure, a few limited-government types have protested. Chuck Muth, former executive director of the American Conservative Union, calls Bush a 'compulsive spender.' And Steve Moore, of the government-shrinking Club for Growth, goes further, likening Bush budgeteers to 'drunken sailors.'"

(*Newsday* [New York], February 3, 2004)

American Conservative Union **33**

American Council for Capital Formation

Established in 1976

DIRECTOR

Mark Bloomfield, president. Bloomfield lectures, writes and comments widely on various economic and policy issues. Bloomfield is also president of the ACCF's economic policy think tank, the ACCF Center for Policy Research, and is a founding director of the International Council for Capital Formation. He also serves as co-chair of the Bulgarian Council for Capital Formation. He received his B.A. from Swarthmore College, an M.B.A. from the Wharton School of the University of Pennsylvania, and a J.D. from the University of Pennsylvania Law School.

BOARD OF DIRECTORS

Dr. Charles E. Walker, chair
Mark A. Bloomfield, president
Mari Lee Dunn, senior vice president, Washington, DC
Dr. Margo Thorning, executive vice president and director of research
Ernestine R. Johnson, assistant secretary and treasurer
Hon. Bill Archer, former chairman, House Ways and Means Committee, Washington DC
Hon. Lloyd M. Bentsen, former secretary of the Treasury, Houston, TX
Hon. William E. Brock, former U.S. senator, Annapolis, MD
John J. Byrne, chairman, White Mountains Insurance Group, Hanover, NH
Red Cavaney, president and chief executive officer, American Petroleum Institute, Washington, DC
Joe F. Colvin, president and chief executive officer, Nuclear Energy Institute, Washington, DC
Josephine S. Cooper, president and chief executive officer, Alliance of Automobile Manufacturers, Washington, DC
John M. Derrick Jr., chairman, Pepco Holdings Inc., Washington, DC
Hon. Kenneth M. Duberstein, former chief of staff to President Reagan, St. Paul, MN
Hon. Glenn English, chief executive officer, National Rural Electric Cooperative Association, Washington, DC
Matthew P. Fink, president, Investment Company Institute, Washington, DC
Robert W. Galvin, chairman emeritus, Motorola, Inc., Schaumburg, IL
Hon. William H. Gray III, former chairman, House Committee on the Budget, New York, NY
J. Barry Griswell, chairman, president and chief executive officer, Principal Financial Group, Des Moines, IA
Mark Heesen, president, National Venture Capital Assn., New York, NY

CONTACT INFORMATION

1750 K Street, NW, Suite 400, Washington, DC 20006-2302
Phone: (202) 293-5811 • *Fax:* (202) 785-8165
General E-mail: info@accf.org • *Web site:* www.accf.org

Communications Director: Robert L. Whiddon
(202) 293-5811
Human Resources Director: Mari Lee Dunn
(202) 293-5811

PURPOSE: "To help redefine and restructure U.S. tax, trade, and environmental policies so that this country can increase the pace of economic growth, provide high-quality jobs, and compete effectively in world markets."

CURRENT CONCERNS: Environmental policy • Regulatory policy • Tax policy • Trade policy and sanctions

METHOD OF OPERATION: Coalition forming • Conferences/seminars • Congressional testimony • Educational foundation • Internet (Web site) • Internships • Legislative/regulatory monitoring (federal) • Lobbying (federal) • Media outreach • Research • Speakers program

Effectiveness and Political Orientation

"One of the Senate's staunchest opponents of the estate tax has drafted an inheritance tax reform proposal that would keep it intact in a much modified version, breaking a long-held Republican taboo against any plan that does not fully abolish the 'death tax.' Sen. Jon Kyl (R-Ariz.) has taken pains to keep his efforts secret, but his proposal—detailed in internal e-mails and confirmed by business lobbyists—would raise the estate tax exemption to $15 million for individuals and $30 million for couples and lower the tax rate on inherited assets above that level to 15 percent, the current rate on capital gains and dividends. . . .

"Republicans succeeded in 2001 in enacting legislation that would repeal the estate tax in 2010 but would allow it to revive again the following year when the legislation expires. Since then, an effort has been underway to kill the estate tax permanently. . . .

"Indeed, the deal that lobbyists struck with Congress in 2001—with a long lag before meaningful estate tax changes and a one-year elimination—is viewed now by many as a 'debacle,' said Mark Bloomfield, president of the American Council for Capital Formation. Bloomfield, who also lobbies on the estate tax for a small but powerful group of affluent families, first floated what he called the 'cap tax' shortly after passage of the 2001 law. The plan would take the estate tax rate to the capital gains tax level immediately, but it was

SCOPE

Members: 200 corporate, foundation, association, and individual supporters
Branches/chapters: None
Affiliates: ACCF Center for Policy Research, a 501(c)(3) organization

STAFF

9 total—5 professional, 4 support; plus interns

TAX STATUS

501(c)(6)

FINANCES

Revenue: 2002—$1.4 million; 2001—$1.5 million; 2000—$1.4 million

FUNDING SOURCES

Corporate donations, 72%; associations, 19%; individuals, 5%; conferences, 3%; foundation grants, 1%

PAC

None

vehemently opposed by the small-business community, which has always provided the muscle behind the repeal movement."

(*The Washington Post*, October 22, 2003)

"When a coalition of wealthy families, small-business groups and farm interests won temporary repeal of the estate tax two years ago, they immediately resumed their campaign for permanent repeal. Now, even as the House is expected to vote today for just that, some in the alliance have second thoughts. It's not that they have backed off their vehement opposition to the tax on large inheritances. Rather, as the federal budget deficit grows and their patriarchs and matriarchs age, they are losing faith that permanent repeal will ever happen and are considering compromises that were unthinkable two years ago.

"The House is expected to vote today to permanently repeal the estate tax after 2010, when it is set to expire after being in effect for only one year. . . .

" 'There is some real concern that 2010 is not soon enough,' said a lobbyist working on the issue, referring to the deficit and the uncomfortable fact that some affluent benefactors may not live until 2010. Grover Connell of privately held Connell Co., for example, is 85. The matriarchs and patriarch of the Hallmark greeting-card fortune are in their seventies.

"With all those factors in mind, some of the biggest names in the estate tax coalition are looking to compromise. The candy-making Mars family of McLean gave more than $1 million to lobbying powerhouse Patton Boggs LLP last year, in part to explore 'estate and gift tax reform,' according to lobbying disclosure forms. . . . Stephen Moore, a conservative tax-cutting activist with the Club for Growth, and Mark A. Bloomfield, president of the business-backed American Council for Capital Formation, proposed taxing estates at the current capital gains rate of 15 percent. Taxable estates are subject to a 49 percent tax.

" 'There are Republicans who want this debate to last forever, keep the 'campaign' money flowing in, keep the Democrats off guard,' Moore said. 'Mark Bloomfield and I have been on crusade to get this done, to break the logjam.' "

(*The Washington Post*, June 18, 2003)

"ExxonMobil's continued refusal to accept the dangers of climate change may be getting through at last. Following Greenpeace's invasion of the world's biggest oil company's headquarters in Dallas last week, this message appeared on the Greenpeace US noticeboard: 'I work for Exxon, and while I don't like your tactics, your message ought to be heard. There are many of us working for this company who believe that current management is making a mistake by ignoring or, worse, challenging the science on climate change. Oil isn't going to go away tomorrow. But neither is global warming, and we ought to stop pretending it will. I'd prefer to work for a company that took that problem seriously, and did more to look after my children's future.' "

"ExxonMobil's board remains unmoved, however. The company has increased donations to Washington-based policy groups to pounds 1m. The five named by the New York Times—the Competitive Enterprise Institute, Frontiers of Freedom, the George C Marshall Institute, the American Council for Capital Formation Center for Policy Research and the American Legislative Exchange Council—all question the human role in global warm-

EMPLOYMENT
Information on open positions can be obtained by contacting the Center at (202) 293-5811. Cover letters and resumes can be mailed to Mari Lee Dunn, chief administrative officer, American Council for Capital Formation, 1750 K Street, NW, Suite 400, Washington, DC 20006-2302.

INTERNSHIPS
Information unavailable

NEWSLETTERS
Capital Formation (bimonthly)

PUBLICATIONS
Balancing Economic Growth & Environmental Goals
Business Taxes, Capital Costs, & Competitiveness
Climate Change Policy: Practical Strategies to Promote Economic Growth and Environmental Quality
Climate Change Policy, Risk Prioritization, and U.S. Economic Growth
The Consumption Tax: A Better Alternative?
Economic Effects of the Corporate Alternative Minimum Tax
An Economic Perspective on Climate Change Policies
Enhancing Environmental Quality Through Economic Growth
Environmental Policy and the Cost of Capital
Free Trade vs. Protectionism and Economic Sanctions: What Are the Issues?
The Impact of Climate Change Policy on Consumers: Can Tradable Permits Reduce the Cost?
The Impact of the U.S. Tax Code on the Competitiveness of Financial Service Firms
Intellectual Property Rights and Capital Formation in the Next Decade
The Kyoto Commitments: Can Nations Meet Them with the Help of Technology?
Strategies for Improving Environmental Quality and Increase Economic Growth
Tax Policy for Economic Growth in the 1990s
Tools for American Workers: The Role of Machinery and Equipment in Economic Growth
U.S. Environmental Policy and Economic Growth: How Do We Fare?
U.S. Investment Trends: Impact on Productivity, Competitiveness & Growth
The U.S. Savings Challenge: Policy Options for Productivity & Growth
U.S. Waste Management Policies: Impact on Economic Growth and Investment Strategies
Also publishes special reports, congressional testimonies by ACCF staff members, and issue briefs.

CONFERENCES
ACCF Economic Evenings (monthly)

ing and argue that even the proposed Bush policies to limit carbon dioxide emissions are too heavy-handed."

(*The Guardian* [London], June 4, 2003)

"Since January, President Bush has been pushing Congress to eliminate taxes paid by individuals on stock dividends by arguing that corporations already pay taxes on profits, so shareholders shouldn't pay again when those earnings are distributed as dividends. 'It's not fair to tax something twice,' Bush has said time after time in speeches around the country. But tax experts say earnings are routinely subjected to many layers of taxes. 'There is double taxation all around,' said Reuven Avi-Yonah, director of the International Tax Program at the University of Michigan. . . .

"But while many conservatives agree that examples of double taxation abound, they support Bush's focus on dividends because such tax relief would help clear away hindrances to business investment. If Congress were to cut dividend taxes, 'it would go part of the way we need to go to make it more attractive to save and invest,' said Margo Thorning, chief economist for the American Council for Capital Formation, a group that supports tax cuts to encourage investments. 'It's a good first step.' Thorning said that after securing a dividend tax reduction, Bush should push for the elimination of taxes on capital gains, the increase in the value of property."

(*The Atlanta Journal-Constitution,* May 18, 2003)

"The divide between Democrats and Republicans over how to recharge the nation's lagging economic recovery could hardly be more clear. On Monday, House Democratic leader Nancy Pelosi of San Francisco rolled out a $136 billion Democratic stimulus plan focused on a $300 rebate to each individual worker, $31 billion in federal aid to fiscally strapped states and faster write-offs for small businesses.

"Today in Chicago, President Bush is expected to propose a $600 billion plan, its centerpiece the elimination of the tax on corporate dividends aimed squarely at reviving the stock market. . . .

"Democrats framed their plan as being 'about the job market, rather than the stock market.' Previewing the huge fight about to ensue in Congress, Pelosi blasted the Bush proposal as nothing more than 'a Trojan horse to wheel in pet projects for their rich friends.' Republicans counter that reducing taxes on capital is essential to business investment and ultimately job growth. 'Nowhere more than in Northern California is the connection between job loss and slumping equity values more apparent,' said Rep. Chris Cox, a Newport Beach Republican who has pushed for the elimination of the dividend tax since 1992. . . .

" 'The elimination of the double taxation of dividends has been at the top of every tax policy's wish list,' said Mark Bloomfield, president of the American Council for Capital Formation. 'This is a very, very significant development.' Now that Republicans hold majority control of the House and Senate, they are expected to move quickly to achieve a long-sought goal that even White House officials concede resembles long-term tax reform more than short-term stimulus."

(*San Francisco Chronicle,* January 7, 2003)

American Council on Science and Health

Established in 1978

DIRECTOR

Elizabeth M. Whelan, president and founder. She holds master's and doctoral degrees in public health from the Yale School of Medicine and the Harvard School of Public Health. She is the author or co-author of over two dozen books, including *Panic in the Pantry* and *A Smoking Gun: How the Tobacco Industry Gets Away with Murder.*

BOARD OF DIRECTORS

Elizabeth M. Whelan, president and founder;
John H. Moore, Ph.D., chairman, Grove City College, Grove City, PA
Elissa P. Benedek, M.D., University of Michigan, Ann Arbor, MI
Norman E. Borlaug, Ph.D., Texas A&M University, College Station, TX
Michael B. Bracken, Ph.D., M.P.H., Yale University School of Medicine, New Haven, CT
Christine M. Bruhn, Ph.D., University of California, Davis, CA
Taiwo K. Danmola, C.P.A., Ernst & Young, New York, NY
Thomas R. DeGregori, Ph.D., University of Houston, TX
Henry I. Miller, M.D., Hoover Institution, Palo Alto, CA
A. Alan Moghissi, Ph.D., Institute for Regulatory Science, Columbia, MD
Albert G. Nickel, Lyons Lavey Nickel Swift, Inc., New York, NY
Kenneth M. Prager, M.D., Columbia College of Physicians and Surgeons, New York, NY
Stephen S. Sternberg, M.D., Memorial Sloan-Kettering Cancer Center, New York, NY
Mark C. Taylor, M.D., Physicians for a Smoke-Free Canada, Ottawa, Ontario, Canada
Lorraine Thelian, Ketchum Public Relations, New York, NY
Kimberly M. Thompson, Sc.D., Ketchum Public Relations, Cambridge, MA
Robert J. White, M.D., Ph.D., Metrohealth Medical Center, Cleveland, OH

SCOPE

Members: 5,000 companies and individuals
Branches/chapters: None
Affiliates: None

STAFF

10 total—plus interns

TAX STATUS

501(c)(3)

FINANCES

Budget: 2002—$1.6 million; 2001—$1.3 million; 2000—$1.8 million

CONTACT INFORMATION

1995 Broadway, 2nd Floor, New York, NY 10023-5860
Phone: (212) 362-7044 • *Fax:* (212) 362-4919
General E-mail: acsh@acsh.org • *Web site:* www.acsh.org

Communications Director: Jeff Stier
(212) 362-7044 • stier@acsh.org
Human Resources Director: Cheryl E. Martin
(212) 362-7044 • martin@acsh.org

PURPOSE: "The American Council on Science and Health, Inc. (ACSH) is a consumer education consortium concerned with issues related to food, nutrition, chemicals, pharmaceuticals, lifestyle, the environment and health."

CURRENT CONCERNS: Alcohol • AIDS • Biotechnology • Cigarette smoking • Food safety • Health-care reform • Health quackery • Low-level radiation • Medical screening • Nutrition • Pharmaceutical safety • Pesticides

METHOD OF OPERATION: Advertisements • Awards program • Coalition forming • Conferences/seminars • Congressional relations • Congressional testimony • Editorial fellowship program • Internet (Web site) • Media outreach • Participation in regulatory proceedings (federal) • Performance rating • Public television documentaries • Research • Speakers program

Effectiveness and Political Orientation

"Shoppers who would like to know where everything from their green onions to hamburger came from have been left whistling in an icy wind. The mandatory country-of-origin labeling passed in 2002 as part of the Farm Bill is effectively dead. A week ago the U.S. Senate passed a budget package that contains a provision to delay the September implementation until 2006, effectively killing the program. . . .

"With the Senate voting against country-of-origin labeling, consumers will continue to wonder how to differentiate between foreign and domestic products at the grocery store. 'This vote is a slap in the face to U.S. consumers, as well as family farmers and ranchers, all of whom would benefit from the labeling program because they could distinguish their products in the marketplace,' said Wenonah Hauter, director of Public Citizen, a nonprofit consumer advocacy group based in Washington, DC. . . .

" 'Why was the whole dairy herd destroyed when scientists theorize that mad cow disease (bovine spongiform encephalopathy, or BSE) does not spread from one animal to another? Ron DeHaven, the U.S. Department of Agriculture's chief veterinarian, said the decision was not wholly based on science, acknowledging the tremendous impact that public perception has had on the industry. Or, as Elizabeth Whelan, president of industry organization American Council on Science and Health, put it: 'Food is a highly emotionally charged issue. When it comes to scares, to paraphrase an old proverb, reports

FUNDING SOURCES
Foundation grants, 52%; corporate donations, 42%; individual memberships and publications sales, 6%

PAC
None

EMPLOYMENT
Information on open positions is available at http://www.acsh.org/about/employment.html. Cover letters and resumes can be mailed to Cheryl E. Martin, Associate Director, American Council on Science and Health, 1995 Broadway, 2nd Floor, New York, NY 10023-5860, faxed to: (212) 362-4919 or e-mailed to: martin@acsh.org.

INTERNSHIPS
Information unavailable

NEWSLETTERS
Inside ACSH (semiannual)
Media Update (semiannual)
Priorities (quarterly)

PUBLICATIONS
The ACSH Definitive Report on Smoking
Analysis of Alleged Health Risk from DBCP in Drinking Water
Anthrax: What You Need to Know
Aspirin and Health
The Beef Controversy
Biotech Pharmaceuticals and Biotherapy
Biotechnology and Food
The Breast Cancer Prevention Diet by Dr. Bob Arnot: Unscientific and Deceptive—A Disservice to American Women
Chronic Fatigue Syndrome: A Comparison of the Health Effects of Alcohol Consumption and Tobacco Use in America
Dietary Fiber
Does Moderate Alcohol Consumption Prolong Life?
Environmental Tobacco Smoke: Health Risk or Health Hype?
Estrogen and Health: How Popular Magazines Have Dealt with Hormone Replacement Therapy
Facts Versus Fears
Fat Replacers: The Cutting Edge of Cutting Calories
Global Climate Change and Human Health
The Irreversible Health Effects of Smoking
Is a Deal with the Cigarette Industry in the Interest of Public Health?
Kicking Butts in the Twenty-First Century: What Modern Science Has Learned About Smoking Cessation
Lead and Human Health
Low-Calorie Sweeteners
Making Sense of Over-the-Counter Pain Relievers
Moderate Alcohol: Consumption and Health
Much Ado about Milk
Multiple Chemical Sensitivity
Osteoarthritis and Its Treatment: What You Need to Know
Postmenopausal Hormone Replacement Therapy

of exaggerated risks can be halfway around the world before the truth gets its boots on.'"

(*Pittsburgh Post-Gazette,* January 29, 2004)

"After reports of mad cow disease hit the news more than two weeks ago, Raj Soundarrajan stopped eating beef. Now, the Valley Stream computer analyst, who dropped 15 pounds during the past two months following the Atkins diet, is considering cutting back on another food favorite: salmon. Soundarrajan, 30, who dines on salmon two or three times a week, said he was alarmed by a new study, published on Thursday, that found high levels of carcinogens in farm-raised salmon, the most common kind available. 'After this news, I think I will just reduce it,' he said, opting instead for 'more chicken and turkey than red meat.'

"He's not alone. Followers of the high-protein, low-carbohydrate diet regimen first promoted 30 years ago by the late diet guru Dr. Robert C. Atkins find themselves in a tizzy about how to feed their protein cravings. . . . But some experts say dieters shouldn't be worried. . . . A spokesman for the American Council on Science and Health said the recent food scares are distracting the public from such issues as nutrition and obesity.

" 'The beef is safe, the fish is safe, despite the allegations,' said Jeff Stier of the generally pro-business group of doctors and scientists, based in Manhattan, which issues position statements on science and the environment.

(*Newsday* [New York], January 11, 2004)

"Normandy Cleaners is a small shop, barely noticeable in the stretch of storefronts at the Potomac Promenade Shopping Center in Potomac. Even its new white neon 'Natural CO2 Cleaners' sign gets too washed out to read on bright days. 'It's hard to see,' says Gongsan Park, vowing to change the sign so customers will know this is now an environmentally safe, health-conscious 'alternative dry cleaners.' Two months ago, Gongsan and her husband, Jaeman Park, who have owned and operated Normandy Cleaners for nearly six years, invested in cutting-edge cleaning technology to replace the standard but controversial dry cleaning method. The Parks are among the first cleaners in the metropolitan area to offer the liquid carbon-dioxide cleaning method.

"The standard solvent used in dry cleaning is perchloroethylene, commonly known as 'perc.' More than 90 percent of the nation's 33,000 cleaners use the chemical, which the Environmental Protection Agency lists as a pollutant of air and groundwater. Cleaners are required to follow EPA regulations in handling perc and disposing of its byproducts at hazardous waste facilities. . . .

"Meanwhile, environmental and health advocates are pressing the dry-cleaning industry to rid itself of perc. Last week, environmental groups filed a suit asking a federal court to order the EPA to review the health risks from perc emissions from dry cleaners and to set new standards. Southern California became the first region in the country to ban perc by 2020. Other states have passed regulations imposing fees on dry cleaners to help pay for cleaning up perc-contaminated sites.

" 'We don't endorse one solvent over another,' says Nora Nealis, spokeswoman for the National Cleaners Association, a trade group that embraces a 2001 report by the American Council on Science and Health which concluded perc is not hazardous to humans when used according to regulations. Meanwhile, the Parks, who emigrated from Seoul in 1996, believe the CO2 system

CONFERENCES
Periodic media seminars on various public health issues.

will pay back their investment. 'We believe people will want to come here because of this,' Gongsan Park says.

(*The Washington Post,* November 25, 2003)

"For the past two weeks, ex-IBM workers Sammie Burch and Rose Rolike have attended hearings in a Santa Clara courtroom to support two former colleagues facing off with the technology giant. The plaintiffs, Alida Hernandez and Jim Moore, accuse IBM of negligently exposing them to toxic chemicals, which they claim led them to develop cancer. 'I know a lot of people who have died,' Rolike said during a break. Added Burch: 'In the past 15 years, I have been to 12 funerals of former IBM employees. . . . I feel very strongly that these injuries were work related . . . I worry everyday.'

"Across the country, in New York City, an attorney for the American Council on Science and Health is worried for a different reason. 'This could absolutely open the floodgates' to more lawsuits, said Jeff Stier. 'It's tremendously significant. If we begin to reward plaintiffs whose claims aren't supported by science, all employers are at risk of having to pay huge rewards.

"Among the potential future plaintiffs is Cora Loanzon, whose husband, Ron Loanzon, worked at IBM for 20 years before he suddenly died of brain cancer three years ago. . . . When her husband was at the hospital, she said co-workers who came to visit mentioned other IBM employees who had developed cancer. The Loanzons later decided to join the lawsuit [against IBM].

"But Stier, of the American Council on Science and Health, noted that fear of cancer and exposure to toxic chemicals has often been overblown. 'A lot of those scares are driven by ideology rather than science, by plaintiff's attorneys who are driven by potential profits, not by interest in promoting the public health,' he said."

(*San Francisco Chronicle,* November 17, 2003)

"Studies show that children begin asking for brand-name products as early as 18 months old. By age 2, half of all kids show a preference for specific brands. And by age 5, some of them are like David Rice of Hastings. 'He has parts of commercials memorized,' said his mother, Robin Rice. 'He sees a sign for Snickers and he says, "Snickers—don't let hunger happen to you." ' It's no wonder David can recite a candy-bar slogan. The food industry spends $15 billion a year making sure that he and millions of other kids remember its messages. . . .

"Critics charge that the food industry is preying on society's most vulnerable audience. Some of the best minds in the advertising business, they say, have created a marketing machine of awesome power and sophistication which has been aimed at a group of consumers still learning to tie their shoelaces. 'We have issued a free pass to the food industry to the hearts and minds of our children, with no regard at all to protecting our children from negative influence,' said Kelly Brownell, chairman of the philosophy [sic] department at Yale and director of the university's Center for Eating and Weight Disorders. . . .

"Defenders of the food business bristle at such comments. 'There's nothing wrong with a kid having four or six Oreos with his milk,' said Elizabeth Whelan, president of the American Council on Science and Health in New York, a nonprofit group of physicians and scientists funded by foundations, corporations and trade organizations. 'There's no reason these products should not be advertised, even intensively,' she said. 'Advertising is a part of life in a free society.' "

(*Star-Tribune* [Minneapolis], October 13, 2003)

American Enterprise Institute for Public Policy Research

Established in 1943

DIRECTOR

Christopher DeMuth, president. Prior to working for AEI, DeMuth was managing director of Lexecon Inc. from 1984–1986. He was administrator in the Office of Information and Regulatory Affairs, U.S. Office of Management and Budget from 1981–1984. DeMuth served as executive director of the Presidential Task Force on Regulatory Relief, the White House, 1981–1983. He also was director of the Harvard Faculty Project on Regulation; lecturer in public policy, Kennedy School of Government, 1977–1981; associate general counsel for Consolidated Rail Corp., 1976–1977; attorney for Sidley & Austin, 1973–1976; and staff assistant to the president, the White House, 1969–1970.

BOARD OF DIRECTORS

CONTACT INFORMATION

1150 17th Street, NW, Washington, DC 20036
Phone: (202) 862-5800 • *Fax:* (202) 862-7177
General E-mail: info@aei.org • *Web site:* www.aei.org

Communications Director: Veronique Rodman, director of public affairs
(202) 862-4871 • vrodman@aei.org
Human Resources Director: Michael Drueen
(202) 862-5913 • jobs@aei.org

PURPOSE: Dedicated to preserving and strengthening the foundations of freedom—limited government, private enterprise, vital cultural and political institutions, and a strong foreign policy and national defense—through scholarly research, open debate, and publications.

CURRENT CONCERNS: Economics and trade • International affairs • Social welfare • Government tax • Spending, regulatory, and legal policies • U.S. politics • U.S. defense and foreign policies

METHOD OF OPERATION: Conferences/seminars • Congressional testimony • International activities • Internet (Web site) • Library/information clearinghouse • Media outreach • Research

Effectiveness and Political Orientation

" 'There has been no progress in Iran on the issues the United States cares about,' said Danielle Pletka of the American Enterprise Institute for Public Policy Research, a think tank in Washington affiliated with the Bush administration. 'The Iranians have weapons of mass destruction and they support terrorist groups, and it's only getting worse.' "

(*The Boston Globe*, April 25, 2003)

"The Bush administration deserves credit for its long-term commitment to democracy in the Middle East. But even a good idea can be spoiled by clumsy execution. Worse still, the idea can backfire—particularly if people come to suspect that ulterior motives are at work.

"This is precisely what is happening with President Bush's 'Greater Middle East initiative,' which outlines steps the United States and its partners in the Group of 8 industrialized nations can take to promote political freedom, equality for women, access to education and greater openness in the Middle East. Elements of the proposal include the creation of free trade zones in the region, new financing for small businesses and help overseeing elections. . . .

"There is no question that the administration has its work cut out for it. For starters, the democracy initiative was unveiled by the president in a patronizing way: before an enthusiastic audience at the American Enterprise Institute, a Washington policy institution enamored of the war in Iraq and not particularly sympathetic toward the Arab world. The notion that America,

SCOPE

Members: None
Branches/chapters: None
Affiliates: None

STAFF

150 total

TAX STATUS

501(c)(3)

FINANCES

Revenue: 2004—$20.77 million; expenses
19.77 million
2003—$31.04 million; expenses $19.71
million
2002—$18.22 million; expenses 17.97 million

FUNDING SOURCES

Individuals, 36%; corporations, 23%; foundations, 22%; conferences, sales, and other revenues, 19% (Source: 2003 Annual Report)

PAC

None

EMPLOYMENT

Employment opportunities consist of research
and staff assistant positions in three program
areas: economic policy studies, foreign and
defense policy studies, and social and political
studies. In addition, staff vacancies also occur
in development, seminars and conferences,
publications marketing, accounting, public
relations, and publications departments.
Information on open positions is available on
the Web site. Cover letters and resumes can
be sent to: Director of Human Resources,
American Enterprise Institute, 1150 17th
Street, NW, Washington, DC 20036. Fax: (202)
862-7178. E-mail: jobs@aei.org.

INTERNSHIPS

AEI internships provide students with an
opportunity to work with some of America's
most renowned scholars, economists, legal
scholars, political scientists, and foreign policy
specialists doing research on current public
policy questions. Internship opportunities are
available to undergraduates, graduate students, and postgraduates. Additional information about internships is available on the
Web site.

with Europe's support and Israel's endorsement, will teach the Arab world
how to become modern and democratic elicits, at the very least, ambivalent
reactions. . . ."

(*The New York Times,* March 8, 2004)

"Wanting to know how a charity or foundation spends the millions it collects,
or, more important, whether the programs it runs do any good, would seem
reasonable, even necessary, to most people.

". . . There are millions of these groups—commonly referred to as non-
governmental organizations, or NGO's—worldwide, but few are subjected to
that kind of meaningful oversight, say the specialists studying NGO accountability. . . .

"Even activists like Ralph Nader and the anti-globalization firebrand
Naomi Klein, who have often been at the forefront of efforts demanding
accountability from corporations and governments, have lashed out at calls for
holding NGO's similarly responsible. Mr. Nader, for example, objected to a
new NGO Watch Web site (ngowatch.org) created this summer by the conservative American Enterprise Institute—itself an NGO—as a politically
motivated effort to 'go after liberal or progressive NGO's.' Ms. Klein likened
it to a 'McCarthyite blacklist.' So far the Web site lists more than 160 NGO's,
with links to information about their finances, support and programs.

" 'They should take a pill,' said Danielle Pletka, a vice president of the
American Enterprise Institute, referring to the Web site's critics. 'It is in all of
our interests to have NGO's, even NGO's we agree with, be accountable and
transparent and have a role in international institutions that is clear to everybody.' She added, 'I don't think there's any disagreement from the left or
the right.' "

(*The New York Times,* January 3, 2004)

"President Bush's speech at the American Enterprise Institute's annual black-
tie dinner last winter was a triumphant moment for many neoconservatives in
the audience. Mr. Bush had 'borrowed' a number of them from the institute
and put them in high places, he said. And he echoed the neocon belief that
reshaping key parts of the world in America's image was the surest way to protect U.S. security."

(*The Wall Street Journal,* September 19, 2003)

NEWSLETTERS

AEI Newsletter (monthly); *The American
    Enterprise* (bimonthly); *Economic Outlook*
    (monthly); *Environmental Policy Outlook*
    (bimonthly);
Federalist Outlook (periodic); *Latin American
    Outlook* (monthly); *Russian Outlook*
    (quarterly)

PUBLICATIONS

The Beginning of Wisdom: Reading Genesis
*Beyond Therapy: Biotechnology and the
    Pursuit of Happiness*
*Bias Against Guns: Why Almost Everything
    You've Heard about Gun Control Is Wrong*
*Boots on the Ground: A Month with the 82nd
    Airborne in the Battle for Iraq*
*Closing the Education Achievement Gap: Is
    Title I Working?*
*Coercing Virtue: The Worldwide Rule of
    Judges*
Congress Preserving Our Institutions
*Cuba the Morning After: Confronting Castro's
    Legacy*
*Democracy by Decree: What Happens When
    Courts Run Big Government*
*Diversity in America: Keeping Government at
    a Safe Distance*
Drug Treatment: The Case for Coercion
*Financial Privacy, Consumer Prosperity, and
    the Public Good*
*Health and the Income Inequality Hypothesis:
    A Doctrine in Search of Data*
High-Stakes Antitrust: The Last Hurrah?
*High-Tech Protectionism: The Irrationality of
    Antidumping Laws*
*Korea in Asia: Korea's Development, Asian
    Regionalism, and U.S.-Korea Economic
    Relations*
*Lessons from Deregulation: Telecommuni-
    cations and Airlines after the Crunch*
*Making Tort Law: What Should Be Done and
    Who Should Do It*
*No Child Left Behind? The Politics and
    Practice of School Accountability*
*No Way Back: Why Air Pollution Will Continue
    to Decline*
*The Real Environmental Crisis: Why Poverty,
    Not Affluence, Is the Environment's
    Number One Enemy*
Reconstructing Climate Policy: Beyond Kyoto
*The Right Man: The Surprise Presidency of
    George W. Bush*
*The Rule of Lawyers: How the New Litigation
    Elite Threatens America's Rule of Law*
Saving Lives and Saving Money
*Saving the Mail: How to Solve the Problems
    of the U.S. Postal Service*
*Sell Globally, Tax Locally: Sales Tax Reform
    for the New Economy*
Skepticism and Freedom
*Trade Liberalization in Aviation Services: Can
    the Doha Round Free Flight?*
Additional titles available on Web site.

CONFERENCES

Bradley Lecture Series (monthly)
Election Watch (monthly series during national
    election years)
Irving Kristol Lecture and Annual Dinner

American Family Association

Established in 1977

DIRECTOR
Donald E. Wildmon, president. Wildmon is an ordained United Methodist minister, having earned his M.Div. from Emory College in 1965. After serving in the U.S. Army's Special Services, he pastored churches from 1965 until he founded National Federation for Decency (NFD) in 1977. NFD became American Family Association in 1988.

BOARD OF DIRECTORS
Donald E. Wildmon, president
Timothy B. Wildmon, vice-president
Forrest Ann Daniels, secretary-treasurer
Dr. Gayle Alexander, director
Rev. Tim Fortner, director
Rev. Tim Lampley, director
Rev. Bobby Hankins, director
Rev. Bert Harper, director
Rev. Curtis Petrey, director
Dr. Forrest Sheffield, director
Rev. Jack Williams, director

SCOPE
Members: 1.9 million in 19 states
Branches/chapters: Information unavailable
Affiliates: Information unavailable

STAFF
105 total

TAX STATUS
501(c)(3)

FINANCES
Revenue: 2002—$14 million; 2001—$13.66 million

FUNDING SOURCES
"This organization is seeking funds from contributions and grants. These funds will be used for unrestricted operating expenses." In 2002, nearly all funding was from contributions ($12 million); $2.9 million were from investments; $25,000 came from other sources.

PAC
None

EMPLOYMENT
Information unavailable

INTERNSHIPS
Information unavailable

NEWSLETTERS
AFA Action Alert
AgapePress News Summary
AFA Journal (11 times a year)

CONTACT INFORMATION
P.O. Drawer 2440, Tupelo, MS 38803
Phone: (662) 844-5036 • *Fax:* (662) 842-7798
General E-mail: www.afa.net/contact.asp • *Web site:* http://www.afa.net/

Communications Director: Information unavailable
Human Resources Director: Information unavailable

PURPOSE: "Represents and stands for traditional family values, focusing primarily on the influence of television and other media—including pornography—on our society."

CURRENT CONCERNS: Abortion • Church in America • Culture and society • Education • Entertainment industry • Marriage and family • Gambling • Homosexuality • Library Internet filtering • Money and finance • Pornography • Preservation of the marriage and family • Decency and morality • Sanctity of human life • Media integrity

METHOD OF OPERATION: Advertisements • Boycotts • Coalition forming • Direct action • Film/video/audiotapes • Grassroots organizing • Legal assistance • Litigation • Local/municipal affairs • Media outreach • Radio production • Research • Speakers program • Telecommunications (American Family Radio) • Training and technical assistance

Effectiveness and Political Orientation

"Last spring, the Rev. Donald E. Wildmon of Tupelo, Miss., decided to hold a summit meeting of the Christian conservative movement.

"Mr. Wildmon felt the movement was losing the culture war, he recalled in an interview on Friday. Since plunging into political activism nearly 30 years ago, Christian conservatives had helped Republicans take control of Washington but did not have enough to show for it, Mr. Wildmon said. At the same time, the election of Republican politicians had drained some of the motivation out of its grass-roots constituents.

"So Mr. Wildmon, founder of the American Family Association and a crusader against sex and violence in the media, sent an e-mail message inviting about two dozen other prominent Christian conservatives to a meeting in Arlington, Va., last June. About 14 people turned up with no set agenda, Mr. Wildmon recalled.

"'All we knew was we were going to get together and see if there were some issues of concern that we could agree on and combine our efforts,' Mr. Wildmon said. 'The first thing that popped up,' he said, 'was the federal marriage amendment.'

"Mr. Wildmon's meeting gave birth to a concerted campaign for a constitutional amendment blocking gay marriage that some Christian conservative leaders say is helping revitalize their movement. It is giving them a rare opportunity to forge potential alliances with African-American and Hispanic

PUBLICATIONS
A Guide to What One Person Can Do About Channel One
Homosexuality: Current Thinking & Biblical Guidelines
Homosexuality: Exposing the Myths
Also publishes brochures, posters, and billboards.

CONFERENCES
Information unavailable

churchgoers. And it promises to reopen the flow of financial contributions to their advocacy groups that had slowed to a trickle when Republicans took over Washington. . . ."

(*The New York Times,* February 8, 2004)

"At the Nogaymarriage.com website, the conservative American Family Association is raising funds and has collected more than 728,000 signatures supporting the Federal Marriage Amendment. The website warns that 'homosexual marriage will soon be a reality' because the Massachusetts high court 'is expected' to rule in favor of the gay couples."

(*The Boston Globe,* November 7, 2003)

"The group that sued to stop the University of North Carolina from assigning freshmen a book on the Koran is taking aim at the school's plans to hold an Islamic awareness week. The American Family Association's Center for Law and Policy filed an amended court complaint last week to try to block UNC from hosting seminars and discussions on Islam on Nov. 11–15."

(*The Washington Post,* October 12, 2002)

"The full-time Defenders of Marriage also like to pretend that they are 'tolerant' of their misguided gay brethren, but their priorities give them away. You'd think they'd be most concerned about divorce, which ends half of all American marriages, or spousal abuse, but a study by the National Gay and Lesbian Task Force last fall discovered that 334 documents on the American Family Association's Web site contained the word 'homosexual' while 'divorce' and 'domestic violence' together merited fewer than 70 mentions. Such is the bent of the Family Research Council and the Traditional Values Coalition that they lobbied the Justice Department to deny 9/11 compensation to the domestic partners of those killed in the terrorists' attack, lest it further 'the gay agenda at the expense of marriage and family.'"

(*The New York Times,* February 29, 2004)

". . . a fashion line called French Connection UK is causing a stir where we shop. You may have seen its sex-charged perfume ads that scream 'FCUK Her' or its T-shirts blaring 'FCUK like a bunny.' You get it, right? Well, U.S. family groups have had it. One, the American Family Association, orchestrated such a successful e-mail campaign to outrage parents that Federated Department Stores' Bloomingdale's and Macy's stopped selling the products. No announcement was made, said a spokeswoman, because the chains didn't want to give more PR to FCUK. Now AFA and other family groups want the May Department Stores Co. and Target—which have curbed FCUK promotions aimed at teens—to follow Federated's lead and will boycott if they don't do it soon.

(*U.S. News & World Report,* October 27, 2003)

American Foundation for AIDS Research (amfAR)

Established in 1985

DIRECTOR

Mathilde Krim, founding chairman and chairman of the board American Foundation for AIDS Research. "Soon after the first cases of the acquired immunodeficiency syndrome (AIDS) were reported in 1981, Mathilde Krim recognized that this new disease raised grave scientific and medical questions and that it might have important socio-political consequences. She dedicated herself to increasing the public's awareness of AIDS and to a better understanding of its cause, its modes of transmission, and its epidemiologic pattern. Dr. Krim also became personally active in AIDS research through her work with interferons—natural substances now used in the treatment of certain viral and neoplastic diseases." (Source: amfAR Web site)

BOARD OF DIRECTORS

Mathilde Krim, Ph.D., founding chairman and chairman of the board
Dame Elizabeth Taylor, founding international chairman
Kenneth Cole, vice chairmen
Patricia J. Matson, vice chairmen
Wallace Sheft, treasurer
William D. Zabel, secretary
Governing Directors
Arlen H. Andelson
William M. Apfelbaum
David E. Bloom, Ph.D.
Zev Braun
Jonathan S. Canno
Donald Capoccia
Jane B. Eisner
Wafaa El-Sadr, M.D., M.P.H.
Beatrix Ann Hamburg, M.D.
Arnold W. Klein, M.D.
Michael J. Klingensmith
Arnold J. Levine, Ph.D.
Jay A. Levy, M.D.
Kenneth H. Mayer, M.D.
Michele V. McNeill, Pharm.D.
Bill Melamed
Richard H. Metzner
William E. Paul, M.D.
Allan Rosenfield, M.D.
Alan D. Schwartz
Mervyn F. Silverman, M.D., M.P.H.
John C. Simons
Peter R. Staley
Rev. William E. Swing
Directors
John F. Breglio
Robert L. Burkett
Sandra Hernández, M.D.
Sherry Lansing
Jane F. Nathanson
Michael D. Shriver
Kevin Wendle

CONTACT INFORMATION

120 Wall Street, 13th Floor, New York, NY 10005-3908
Phone: (212) 806-1600 • *Fax:* (212) 806-1601
Toll-free: (800) 392-6327 • *Web site:* www.amfAR.org

Communications Director: Information unavailable
Human Resources Director: Susan Kennedy, director, human resources
(212) 806-1625 • susan.kennedy@amfAR.org

PURPOSE: "Dedicated to the support of HIV/AIDS research, AIDS prevention, treatment education, and the advocacy of sound AIDS-related public policy."

CURRENT CONCERNS: Basic biomedical and clinical research on HIV/AIDS • Global initiatives • Prevention programs • Public and professional education • Public information • Public policy reforms • Treatment information services

METHOD OF OPERATION: Advertisements (donated) • Awards program • Coalition forming • Conferences/seminars • Congressional testimony • Films/video/audiotapes • Grantmaking • International activities • Internet (databases and Web site) • Internships • Legislative/regulatory monitoring (federal) • Library/information clearinghouse • Lobbying (federal) • Media outreach • Research • Scholarships • Technical assistance

Effectiveness and Political Orientation

". . . a model of 'abstinence-only' education. This approach encourages young people to avoid sex until marriage, while offering little information about contraception.

"Since 1998, abstinence-only instruction has proliferated, fueled by a huge increase in federal funding. Over that time, federal and state governments have given out almost $1 billion to programs such as the one at New Creation. . . .

"But many public health researchers say the programs remain, at best, unproven. While the method works well for some, they say, it has no effect on many others, who become sexually active with little knowledge of safe sex. At the same time, some 'comprehensive' approaches—which include information about condoms and contraception—have been proven, these scientists say. . . .

"Abstinence-only proponents say that providing contraceptive information undermines the no-sex message and encourages teen-agers to think that protected sex is without risk. . . .

"Until the late 1990s, the main approach to sex education was the comprehensive method, which encourages abstinence while also offering information on condoms and other contraception. This approach assumes that

SCOPE

Members: None
Branches/chapters: Office in Washington, DC
Affiliates: Concerned Parents for AIDS
   Research, a 501(c)(3) organization

STAFF

Information unavailable

TAX STATUS

501(c)(3)

FINANCES

Revenue: 2002—$18 million; 2001—
$21.2 million

FUNDING SOURCES

Contributions, 86.2%; government grants,
8.7%; program services, 2.7%; investments,
1.9%; sales and other, 0.5%

PAC

None

EMPLOYMENT

"Current openings are posted on the Web site.
Applicants should send resumes to the
Director of Human Resources. Referrals of
qualified applicants are also welcome. Only
those applicants who have experience and
qualifications most closely matching the job
profile will be contacted."

   Susan Kennedy, Director, Human
Resources, American Foundation for AIDS
Research, 120 Wall Street, 13th Floor, New
York, NY 10005-3908, e-mail: susan.kennedy@
amfAR.org, Fax: (212) 806-1606.

INTERNSHIPS

Information unavailable

NEWSLETTERS

Treatment Insider (eight times a year)
amfAR e-News (monthly E-mail newsletter)
amfAR News (three times a year E-mail
   newsletter)

PUBLICATIONS

HIV/AIDS Treatment Directory

CONFERENCES

Conference on Global Strategies for the
   Prevention of HIV Transmission from
   Mothers to Infants (biannual)
National HIV/AIDS Update Conference
   (annual)
World AIDS Day symposium (annual)
Also holds various community forums, physi-
cian update seminars, and continuing medical
education programs throughout the year.

many teen-agers will have sex regardless of what adults tell them and should know how to minimize their risk.

"From this perspective, abstinence-only seems illogical. 'It's an ideological position, not a public health strategy,' said sociologist Judy Auerbach, public policy director of the American Foundation for AIDS Research, which opposes increasing federal funds for abstinence-only programs. She says that it is unrealistic to expect people to stay abstinent until they are 26—the average age of marriage in the United States."

(*The Baltimore Sun,* February 29, 2004)

"About 200 gay men in Atlanta will be among the first 3,000 people in the world to test a promising but controversial new AIDS strategy: a pill to prevent HIV infection.

"Three studies to begin this spring, including one funded by the federal Centers for Disease Control and Prevention in Atlanta, will look at whether the drug tenofovir can stop HIV from causing infection. The drug, also known as Viread, is now used to treat people who have the virus that causes AIDS.

". . . The most anticipated approach, a vaccine, appears to be years or decades away.

"In the meantime, an HIV prevention pill could curb transmission of the virus. If the tenofovir studies prove successful, the drug—taken daily at a cost of about $4,600 a year, or $12.67 a day—could be used by people most at risk for HIV.

"'At this point in the epidemic, this is one of the key HIV prevention questions to ask. It could have a lot of benefits,' said Judy Auerbach, vice president for public policy at the American Foundation for AIDS Research.

(*The Atlanta Journal-Constitution,* February 5, 2004)

"Christians, with many Minnesotans in the lead, are putting aside their judgments and fears to wage a serious national campaign to rid the world of a major health crisis—the spread of HIV/AIDS.

"They are marshaling the resources of American churches to help ease the suffering and work on eliminating poverty and ignorance, called the underlying causes in developing countries where the deadly disease is virtually wiping out entire villages. They are joining the national, secular efforts of many organizations, including amfAR, the American Foundation for AIDS Research."

(*Star Tribune* [Minneapolis], April 19, 2003)

"Health experts have been warning for two years that the global Aids epidemic is spreading far beyond Africa.

"Now they have a new and powerful supporter in the form of the US Central Intelligence Agency, which says China, India and Russia are among five countries in a 'new wave' of HIV/Aids.

"According to a new report by the National Intelligence Council, a group of experts that advises the CIA, the number of infected people in these countries will rise from 14m–23m now to 50m–75m by 2010. . . .

"Many Aids experts believe insufficient attention is being paid to the countries that are likely to suffer from the spread of the epidemic.

"'There are parts of India and China with an infection rate higher than 5 percent, which is when an epidemic can really take off,' says Mathilde Krim, who runs the American Foundation for Aids Research and has been monitoring the disease for 20 years. 'It is almost pathetic to see countries that don't take advice from foreigners and don't take any action until people start dying in the streets.'

"According to the report, by 2010 India will have the highest number of HIV infected people—[20 to 25 million]. Heterosexual transmission of the virus will be the main driver, with between 30 and 60 percent of prostitutes infected.

"In China, the incidence of HIV/Aids has grown sharply because of the sale of infected blood plasma and is being aided by the '100 million rural migrants on the move in the country' "

(*Financial Times,* October 4, 2002)

"It's not a distinction that the nation's capital cares to trumpet, but Washington has the highest incidence of new AIDS cases of any big city in the country. . . .

"Dr. Judy Auerbach, the vice president of public policy for the American Foundation for AIDS Research, called AIDS in Washington 'an epidemic.'. . ."

(*The Houston Chronicle,* December 17, 2003)

American Israel Public Affairs Committee (AIPAC)

Established in 1954

DIRECTOR
Howard Kohr, executive director. Prior to joining AIPAC, Kohr held a number of distinguished posts, including management fellow at the Department of Defense, deputy director of the National Jewish Coalition, and assistant Washington representative of the American Jewish Committee. Over the past nine years, he has helped navigate congressional passage of the annual U.S. foreign aid bill and has played a key role in conceiving, developing, and passing groundbreaking sanctions aimed against rogue states.

BOARD OF DIRECTORS
None

SCOPE
Members: 85,000
Branches/chapters: 10 regional offices
Affiliates: N / A

STAFF
174 total

TAX STATUS
501(c)(4)

FINANCES
Budget: 2001—$16 million; 2000—$16 million

FUNDING SOURCES
100% membership dues

PAC
None

EMPLOYMENT
AIPAC offers a wide range of positions including, but not limited to, research, development, communications, and administration.
Send cover letter and resume to inquire about opportunities to Morris Edeson, director of administration and finance, 440 First St., NW, Suite 600, Washington, DC 20001. Fax: (202) 347-5036. E-mail: medeson@aipac.org.

INTERNSHIPS
Internship areas include the following: legislative, political, development, leadership development, communications, and research.
Summer positions are paid and school year positions are unpaid. Interns are required to work 9 a.m to 6 p.m. during the summer. School year hours are flexible.

Application deadlines:
Fall–September 1
Winter–December 15
Spring–February 15
Summer–March 26

CONTACT INFORMATION
440 First Street, NW, Suite 600, Washington, DC 20001
Phone: (202) 639-5200 • *Fax:* (202) 347-4889
General E-mail: update@aipac.org • *Web site:* www.aipac.org

Communications Director: Renee Rothstein, communications director
rrothstein@aipac.org
Human Resources Director: Morris Edeson, director of administration and finance • medeson@aipac.org

PURPOSE: To strengthen the U.S.–Israel relationship.

CURRENT CONCERNS: Standing by Israel to ensure the security of the only democracy in the Middle East • Stopping Iran from acquiring nuclear weapons • Educating Congress about the U.S.–Israel relationship • Defending Israel against tomorrow's threats • Preparing the next generation of pro-Israel leaders

METHOD OF OPERATION: Conferences/seminars • Congressional testimony • Congressional voting analysis • Educational foundation • Films/video/audiotapes • Grassroots organizing • Information clearinghouse • Internet (e-mail alerts, Web site) • Internships • Legislative/regulatory monitoring (federal) • Lobbying • (federal, state, grassroots) • Media outreach • Research • Speakers program • Voter registration • Voting records • Training

Effectiveness and Political Orientation

". . . American Israel Public Affairs Committee, the influential pro-Israel lobby. . . ."

(*The New York Times*, February 2, 2004)

"Yasser Arafat is rich, but his Palestinian Authority is going broke. And with foreign aid drying up, his economy chief has had to take out a bank loan to pay 125,000 workers. . . .

"The Palestinians, however, blame their fiscal woes on the Israelis, who have refused to turn over millions in tax revenues and have enforced travel bans to deter terrorist attacks. Now the Palestinian Authority is facing a $400 million shortfall, according to the World Bank, despite having received $6.5 billion in foreign aid over six years.

"Josh Block of the pro-Israel lobby group AIPAC said the Palestinian Authority is broke because Arafat and his cronies have been lining their pockets with aid money for years.

"'If Yasser Arafat and the thugs running the PA hadn't stolen their people's money and spent it on terrorism, not only would they be able to make payroll, they would have the money to invest in improving people's lives,' Block said. 'Clearly, terrorism is their priority.'"

(*New York Daily News*, January 14, 2004)

Internship applications should be sent to Havi Arbeter, campus communications coordinator, 440 First St., NW, Suite 600, Washington, DC 20001. Phone: (202) 639-6924. Fax: (202) 347-6760. E-mail: harbeter@aipac.org

Further information about internships can be found at http://www.aipac.org.

NEWSLETTERS

Near East Report (biweekly)

PUBLICATIONS

Publishes brochures, *The AIPAC Papers on U.S.-Israel Relations* and *The AIPAC Papers on the Mideast Peace Talks*

Also publishes the AIPAC E-mail Update, and issue briefs on topics of current concern.

CONFERENCES

Annual Policy Conference held in spring (Washington, DC)

"Targeting other 'rogue' states. Even as war continues in Iraq, Bush administration officials have made threatening statements about other countries the White House considers threats.

"Rumsfeld and Wolfowitz have suggested that Syria could be the next target if it does not end its support for the remnants of Saddam's regime and for anti-Israel terrorist groups.

"U.S. forces bombed Iraqi positions near Syria on Thursday, and special operations forces monitored the border to try to prevent Saddam supporters from escaping or new fighters from entering Iraq, U.S. officials said. 'The Syrians are behaving badly, they need to be reminded of that, and if they continue . . . we need to think about what our policy is,' Wolfowitz told the Senate Armed Services Committee on Thursday. Asked if there were plans to send U.S. forces into Syria, Wolfowitz replied said,: 'None I know of,' but said that it would be 'a decision for the president and the Congress.'

"Administration supporters also hope Saddam's fall will weaken Syria's economy. An influential lobby group, the American-Israel Public Affairs Committee (AIPAC), has been arguing that future Iraqi oil shipments should no longer be exported through Syria but through Turkey and Jordan instead. . . ."

(*USA Today*, April 11, 2003)

"Has AIPAC gone GOP?

"The powerful pro-Israel lobby, the American Israel Public Affairs Committee, has a long tradition of partisan neutrality. So some eyebrows were raised on Capitol Hill last week when Roll Call published an article titled 'GOP Turns to Israeli Lobby to Boost Iraq Support.'

" 'AIPAC's initiative is part of an intense public and private campaign by the White House,' the newspaper reported. Among the group's targets: none other than Sen. Joseph I. Lieberman (Conn.), an orthodox Jew who is a Democratic presidential candidate.

"The report came two weeks after AIPAC, in its newsletter, scolded another Democratic candidate, former Vermont governor Howard Dean, for his statement that the United States should 'not take sides' in the Israeli-Palestinian conflict.

"This was too much for Jeremy Rabinovitz, chief of staff to Rep. Lois Capps (D-Calif.) and an AIPAC research analyst in the mid-1980s. 'For years, AIPAC has distinguished itself as a strictly bipartisan advocate for strong U.S.-Israel relations,' he said on Friday. 'It's disheartening to see the organization become an increasingly partisan voice for the Republican agenda, and this approach will not help the pro-Israel cause in Washington.'

"AIPAC denies this. 'AIPAC is a nonpartisan organization,' said spokeswoman Rebecca Dinar. 'It's our job to make sure that it stays that way.' She said the group was not attacking Dean but 'the concept of evenhandedness.' The group has previously taken shots at Bill Clinton, Jesse L. Jackson and, of course, Pat Buchanan. Apparently no tough words yet for President Bush, who last week defended Israel's attack inside Syria. . . ."

(*The Washington Post*, October 12, 2003)

"President Bush's stalwart support of Israel is winning effusive praise from major organizations representing American Jews, who voted against Bush in overwhelming numbers 17 months ago.

"Several leading pro-Israel lobbyists said they have concluded that Bush is profoundly, personally sympathetic to Israel. They attributed that sympathy to the president's religious outlook, his inclination to think in terms of good and evil, and a trip he took to Israel in late 1998.

" 'Friends of Israel feel a sense of deep appreciation for the stance that the administration, led by the president, is taking at this moment of crisis,' said Howard Kohr, executive director of the American Israel Public Affairs Committee, or AIPAC, the linchpin of the pro-Israel lobby in Washington. 'If you back up and say, was this the expectation that most people in the Jewish community had for this administration at the time it took office, the answer would be: probably not,' he added. . . .

"In recent days, AIPAC and other Jewish groups have issued statements cheering the Bush administration's stand, especially its calls for Palestinian leader Yasser Arafat to do more to stop terrorism and the president's statement Saturday, 'I fully understand Israel's need to defend herself.' . . .

"In January, AIPAC praised the president's State of the Union address for his reference to Iraq and Iran as part of an 'axis of evil.' And, Kohr said, 'it is not lost on our community that the foreign leader who has been more times to the White House than any other' is Israeli Prime Minister Ariel Sharon, while Arafat has not been invited even once since Bush took office."

(*The Washington Post,* April 4, 2002)

". . .The 10 most influential interest groups the GOP listed were . . . the American Israel Public Affairs Committee (AIPAC). . . .

"The top 10 on the Democrats' list were . . . AIPAC. . . ."

(*The Washington Post,* July 5, 2001)

American Jewish Committee (AJC)

Established in 1906

DIRECTOR

David A. Harris, executive director. Executive director of the AJC since 1990, Harris has been described as one of the foremost American advocates for Israel's political and diplomatic standing, meeting frequently with world leaders to discuss issues affecting the Middle East. He has testified before Congress, as well as before the UN Commission on Human Rights. A graduate of the University of Pennsylvania, he pursued his graduate studies in international relations at the London School of Economics and then spent a year as a junior associate at Oxford University (St. Antony's College). In 2000–2002, he was a visiting scholar at the Johns Hopkins University School of Advanced International Studies. He is a member of the Council on Foreign Relations. He is the author of four books, and he has had a regular radio commentary on leading stations in New York, Washington, Los Angeles, and Boston since 2001.

BOARD OF DIRECTORS

Robert Goodkind, incoming president; attorney, New York, NY
Declined to comment on remaining members

SCOPE

Members: more than 125,000
Branches/chapters: 33 nationwide
Affiliates: None

STAFF

250 total

TAX STATUS

501(c)(3)

FINANCES

Budget: 2004—$29.4 million; 2003—$31 million

FUNDING SOURCES

Members (primary funding source), foundations, and individuals

PAC

None

EMPLOYMENT

Higher positions are advertised in *The New York Times;* for more information about openings contact Shifra Sharbat, (212) 891-1359, sharbats@ajc.org.

INTERNSHIPS

American Jewish Committee Fellows Program (summer): "designed to develop future leaders in the areas of international and domestic politics, diplomacy, public relations, and management. This selective paid Fellowship gives a

CONTACT INFORMATION

P.O. Box 705, New York, NY 10150
Phone: (212) 751-4000 • *Fax:* (212) 891-1492
General E-mail: PR@ajc.org • *Web site:* www.ajc.org

Communications Director: Kenneth Bandler, director of public relations
(212) 751-4000, ext. 271 • pr@ajc.org
Human Resources Director: Shifra Sharbat
(212) 891-1359 • sharbats@ajc.org

PURPOSE: "To safeguard the welfare and security of Jews in the United States, in Israel, and throughout the world; to strengthen the basic principles of pluralism around the world as the best defense against anti-Semitism and other forms of bigotry; to enhance the quality of American Jewish life by helping to insure Jewish continuity and deepen ties between American and Israeli Jews."

CURRENT CONCERNS: Combating bigotry and extremism • Democracy • Human rights • Israeli security • Jewish identity and continuity • Jewish security • Pluralism and positive intergroup relations

METHOD OF OPERATION: Advertisements • Coalition forming • Conferences/seminars • Congressional testimony • Demonstrations • Direct action • Films, video, audio tapes • Grassroots organizing • Information clearinghouse • International activities • E-mail alerts • Web sites in English, Spanish, Russian, and German • Internships • Library services open to the public • Lobbying (federal, state, & grassroots) • Local/municipal affairs • Media outreach • Polling • Research • Speakers program

Effectiveness and Political Orientation

"When the Supreme Court last weighed affirmative action in university admissions a quarter-century ago, American Jewish organizations were in the forefront of the opposition.

"Yet as the Supreme Court prepares to revisit the issue in a pair of 'reverse discrimination' cases brought by white students against the University of Michigan, leading Jewish organizations have kept a conspicuously low profile, and at least one, the 100,000-member American Jewish Committee, has decided to file a friend-of-the-court brief in support of the university."

(*The Washington Post,* December 22, 2002)

"An unusually broad coalition of religious groups is pushing a bill that would protect religious expression in the workplace, but civil liberties groups are concerned the bill could be used to advance on-the-job proselytizing.

"The Workplace Religious Freedom Act, introduced by Sens. Rick Santorum (R-Pa.) and John Kerry (D-Mass.), would force employers to 'reason-

group of young people the unique opportunity to work for a period of nine weeks full-time (or longer part-time) at offices throughout the world. . . . Fellows work closely with supervisors in a mentor relationship to learn about strategy, advocacy, and the development and implementation of programming. Fellows may also spend part of their time developing an independent project with the AJC office to which they are assigned." AJC Fellows receive $3,000 for the 9-week program plus major travel expenses.

The AJC Fellows Program is open to undergraduates in their junior or senior years and students in graduate and professional schools. There is no application form for the program, but the following items must be sent in one complete package: cover letter; résumé; college and graduate school transcript as applicable; essay of approximately 500–750 words describing the student's background and fields of interest for the fellowship; recent short (one to two-page) writing sample or excerpt of a larger paper, preferably on a topic of political, social, ethical, or specifically Jewish interest; and letter of recommendation from a faculty member or relevant previous employer.

Please send the above materials in one complete package to Rebecca Neuwirth, The American Jewish Committee, P.O. Box 705, New York, NY 10150. If application cannot be mailed, it can be sent via fax or E-mail. Fax: (212) 891-1450. E-mail: fellowship@ajc.org. More information is available at www.ajc.org, under Who We Are/Programs.

NEWSLETTERS
AJC Weekly News Update (E-mail newsletter, members only)

PUBLICATIONS
The following is a list of representative publications:
American Jewish Year Book
Annual Survey of American Jewish Opinion
Anti-Americanism and Anti-Semitism
Intergroup Relations in a Diverse America
Islamic Jihad Movement in Palestine (Terrorism briefings series)
Muslim anti-Semitism: A Clear and Present Danger
The Passion: A Resource Guide
A Primer on the American Jewish Community
The West, Christians and Jews in Saudi Arabian Schoolbooks
Additional publications listed on Web site.

CONFERENCES
Annual meeting, every May in Washington; periodic conferences, subject-specific.

ably accommodate' employees who want to wear religious articles or take time off for worship services. . . .

"The American Jewish Committee, one of the bill's primary backers, points to cases like that of Amric Singh Rathour, who was fired as a New York City traffic officer when he refused to shave his religiously mandated beard or remove his turban. Rathour's suit against the city, filed in March, is pending.

"The AJC also defended a New York Rastafarian who was fired from his job at FedEx when he refused to cut his dreadlocks, a part-time Methodist minister who was fired from a furniture store for taking time off to conduct a funeral and a Muslim woman who was fired from Alamo Rent A Car for insisting that she wear a headscarf. . . ."

(*The Washington Post,* May 10, 2003)

"The Bush administration today will launch a spirited defense of its plan to allow religious charities to administer government-funded programs, outlining a formula for such groups to separate their religious and secular works.

"The White House has received unexpected objections to its 'faith-based' program from some religious conservatives who believe that government will become entangled in the affairs of churches, diluting their ability to proselytize. On the other side, civil libertarians worry about too much religious influence in government programs. Both suggest the government should avoid direct grants to charities that proselytize.

". . . two other thorny areas: whether religious charities receiving government funds could discriminate in hiring based on religion, and whether controversial groups, such as the Nation of Islam, could compete for funds. In both cases, officials said, they probably could. Richard Foltin, director of legislative affairs for the American Jewish Committee, said the government would 'in effect subsidize discrimination' by allowing religious-based hiring."

(*The Washington Post,* March 7, 2001)

"Maryland lawmakers reluctant to turn over public money to private schools are rallying around a bit of legislation that would help the private institutions without giving them a penny of state money.

"Under the bill . . . public and private schools could unite to buy textbooks in bulk, a cost-saving measure that could inadvertently doom the $8 million proposal by Gov. Parris N. Glendening (D) to help private schools with textbooks.

"Morhaim said he offered the buying-consortium bill to save money. He predicts it would save about 10 percent of the $140 million that the state spends on books each year. At the same time, he and others say, the measure could help stem the contentious debates that have erupted between public and private school advocates increasingly at odds over public dollars. . . .

"'It's smart,' said David Bernstein, a regional director of the American Jewish Committee, which opposes state aid for private schools. 'It doesn't undermine [the separation of] church and state and doesn't set a further precedent with public dollars for private schools.'. . ."

(*The Washington Post,* March 4, 2001)

American Jewish Congress

Established in 1918

DIRECTOR

Neil B. Goldstein, executive director. Immediately prior to AJCongress, Goldstein served 4 years as the northeast director of American Israel Public Affairs Committee. He has also served 4 years as the chief of staff to a U.S. Representative. Goldstein has also served as the assistant executive director of AJCongress as well as the northeast director of the U.S. Holocaust Museum.

BOARD OF DIRECTORS

Richard Anderman, presidential appointment-governing council
Robert Asher, regional president
John Baer, regional president
Phillip Baum, executive director
Leonard Blavatnik, executive committee
Paul D. Breitner, regional president
Seth Buchwald, executive committee
Morton Bunis, executive committee
George T. Caplan, senior vice-president
Leona Chanin, senior vice-president
Beatrice Disman, executive committee
Belle Faber, associate executive director
Steven Fellman, ex officio
Joseph S. Geller, regional president
Neil Goldstein, director of national affairs
Richard Gordon, vice chair
Alvin Gray, executive committee
Barry Greenberg, regional president
Robert Guzzardi, executive committee
Jack Halpern, executive committee
John M. Heffer, presidential appointment-governing council
Chiae Herzig, executive committee
Jeffrey Horowitz, executive committee
Nancy Jacobson, presidential appointment-governing council
David V. Kahn, president
Jerome Kaplan, regional president
Munr Kazmir, executive committee
David A. Kipper, vice president policy
Dennis F. Klein, executive committee
Abe Krieger, ex officio
Janine Landow-Esser, regional president
Pinkas Lebovits, executive committee
Jacqueline Levine, president
Harley Lippman, president and chief executive
Trudy L. Mason, ex officio
Meir Melnicke, executive committee
Paul S. Miller, domestic public policy advocacy
Robert B. Millner, ex officio
David Mortman, vice president marketing
Irvin Nathan, executive committee
Michael Nussbaum, regional president
Abe Oster, executive committee
Jda Partners, vice president marketing
Doris Pechman, ex officio
David Perskie, executive committee

CONTACT INFORMATION

15 E. 84th Street, New York, NY 10028
Phone: (212) 879-4500 • *Fax:* (212) 249-3672
General E-mail: communications@ajcongress.org •
Web site: www.ajcongress.org

Communications Director: David Twersky, chief information officer
(212) 360-1586 • dtwersky@ajcongress.org
Human Resources Director: Mark Seal, director of operations
(212) 360-1505 • mseal@ajcongress.org

PURPOSE: Motivated by the need to ensure the creative survival of the Jewish people, deeply cognizant of the Jewish responsibility to participate fully in public life, inspired by Jewish teachings and values, informed by liberal principles, dedicated to an activist and independent role, and committed to making its decisions through democratic processes, AJCongress has its mission to:

- Protect fundamental constitutional freedoms and American democratic institutions, particularly the civil and religious rights and liberties of all Americans and the separation of church and state;
- Advance the security and prosperity of the State of Israel and its democratic institutions, and to support Israel's search for peaceful relations with its neighbors in the region;
- Advance social and economic justice, women's equality, and human rights at home and abroad;
- Remain vigilant against anti-Semitism, racism, and other forms of bigotry, and to celebrate cultural diversity and promote unity in American life; and
- Invigorate and enhance Jewish religious, institutional, communal and cultural life at home and abroad, and seek creative ways to express Jewish identity, ethics and values.

CURRENT CONCERNS: Abortion rights • Affirmative action • Church-state separation • Civil rights and voting rights • Global anti-Semitism • Energy independence • Intergroup relations • Israel and the Middle East • Prejudice, anti-Semitism, and racism • Religious freedom • Terrorism, bombings, violence • Threats to separation of church and state • Women's health and cancer Israel

SPECIFIC PROGRAMS/INITIATIVES: U.S. Israel Security • Council for World Jewry • Religious Freedom • Energy Task Force • Crisis on the Campus

METHOD OF OPERATION: Coalition forming • Conferences/seminars • Congressional testimony • Information clearinghouse • International activities • Internet databases • E-mail alerts • Legal assistance • Legislative/regulatory monitoring (federal and state) • Lobbying (federal,

Seymour Persky, senior vice-president
Alan J. Pines, executive committee
Bettina Plevan, commission chair
Arnold Pollard, presidential appointment-
    governing council
Gary Ratner, director of southwest region
Robert Raymar, presidential appointment-
    governing council
Norman Redlich, chair, governing council
Israel Roizman, presidential appointment-
    governing council
Jack Rosen, president
Joseph Rosen, executive committee
Lya Dym Rosenblum, regional president
Alan B. Slifka, senior vice-president
Henry Smith, regional president
Stephen J. Solarz, international affair
Marc Stern, co-director of CLSA
Lillian Steinberg, president
Stuart A. Sundlun, executive committee
Susan Jaffe Tane, senior vice-president
Roy Tanzman, regional president
Douglas P. Teitelbaum, vice president
    finance
Steven Teitelbaum, regional president
Gail Wechsler, ex officio
Edward Weinberg, regional president
Matthew Weinstein, ex officio
Stewart M. Weintraub, regional president
Melvyn I. Weiss, presidential appointment-
    governing council
Leonard A. Wilf, presidential appointment-
    governing council
Barry N. Winograd, treasurer
Wendy Zizmor, presidential appointment-
    governing council

SCOPE
Members: 50,000
Branches/chapters: 11
Affiliates: None

STAFF
Full-time—35; Part-time—5

TAX STATUS
501(c)(3)

FINANCES
Budget: 2004—approximately $6 million;
2003—approximately $5.5 million

FUNDING SOURCES
Individuals, 40%; membership dues, 20%; special events/projects, 25%; other sources, 15%

PAC
None

EMPLOYMENT
Inquiries about employment may be sent to:
Mark Seal, director of operations, 15 E. 84th
Street, New York, NY 10028; (212) 360-1505;
mseal@ajcongress.org.

INTERNSHIPS
Unpaid internships related to domestic issues
and foreign affairs are available in the
Washington office. For more information, con-
tact Sarah Stern, director of Washington
Office, 1001 Connecticut Avenue, STE 407,

state, and grassroots) • Media outreach • Research • Speakers program • Telecommunications services (mailing lists)

Effectiveness and Political Orientation

"Jews, on the other hand, are drifting toward the GOP. A poll by Steven Cohen of Hebrew University found that almost half the Jews who chose Gore over Bush are uncertain they would vote the same way today. Perhaps even more crucial, prominent Democratic donors have crossed party lines. Jack Rosen, president of the American Jewish Congress and a supporter of Democrats, wrote a $100,000 check last year to the Republican National Committee. 'It would be a mistake for the Jewish community not to show our appreciation to the president,' Rosen said. . . ."

(*The Washington Post*, December 7, 2003)

"A leading Jewish organization is urging Hollywood figures to reconsider their plans to attend the Cannes Film Festival this month, citing a recent series of anti-Semitic attacks in France.

"In full-page ads in trade newspapers this week, the West Coast chapter of the American Jewish Congress compared the situation in contemporary France to the climate 60 years ago, when the anti-Semitic Vichy government was in power and Hitler stalked the rest of Europe.

" 'France, 1942: Synagogues and Jewish schools set on fire, Jews beaten on the streets, Jewish cemeteries vandalized,' the ad reads. . . .

"The French reacted angrily to the advertisement, calling it a distortion of the situation in their country. . . .

"But Gary Ratner, executive director of the AJC, asserted, 'There has been a disgusting display of anti-Semitism in France, with over 440 incidents in April alone.' The purpose of the ad, he said, is to make Hollywood—where Jews constitute a large segment of the industry—think twice before heading to the festival, which runs May 15-26.

"If they do go, Ratner added, 'maybe they'll raise the issue of anti-Semitism in France while they're there. People in the entertainment industry who have been advocates on other world causes . . . haven't said a word about anti-Semitism.' "

(*The Washington Post*, May 9, 2002)

"Notre Dame may be looking good on the gridiron these days, but George W. Bush has to hope that the luck of the Irish holds in court. For if a new lawsuit targeting federal support for an innovative Notre Dame teacher-training program succeeds, it would put a major crimp in the president's plans to mobilize America's faith-based 'armies of compassion.'

"The federal suit was filed last month by the American Jewish Congress against the Corporation for National Community Service, which runs AmeriCorps. Specifically, it alleges that AmeriCorps' funding for Notre Dame's Alliance for Catholic Education (ACE) and two similar programs amounts to taxpayer-supported 'religious indoctrination' violating the Constitution."

(*The Wall Street Journal*, November 8, 2002)

"As President Bush prepares to host Ramadan feasts at the White House this week to bolster Muslim support for the war on terrorism, he is shadowed by

Washington, DC 20036. Phone: (202) 466-9661. E-mail: washrep@ajcongress.org.

NEWSLETTERS
Congress Monthly Magazine (monthly)
The Capital View (periodic)
Inside Israel (periodic)
Judaism (quarterly)

PUBLICATIONS
Ehud Barak, The National Tranquilizer
Faith in School: A Parent's Guide to Religion and Public Education
Public Schools & Religious Communities: A First Amendment Guide
Understanding the Genetics of Breast Cancer in Jewish Women

CONFERENCES
Energy Conference
Conference of Mayors

criticism of the administration's outreach efforts to American Muslims during the past two months.

"Jewish groups and some conservatives have been lobbying the president to stop courting certain Muslim leaders who, they say, have equivocated on terrorism by condemning the Sept. 11 attacks but praising Hamas and Hezbollah. Those two groups, which are fighting Israel, are on the State Department's list of terrorist organizations.

"'It's a very simple proposition,' said Phil Baum, executive director of the American Jewish Congress. 'The White House ought to be certain that the people they associate with don't defend, excuse or condone suicide bombing.'"

(*The Washington Post,* November 18, 2001)

"Leaders of some of the nation's largest Jewish organizations last night told the director of President Bush's plan to expand federal funding of social services provided by religious groups that the program could drastically undermine the constitutional separation of church and state with 'sinful and tyrannical' results. . . .

"'As a minority of 2 percent scattered increasingly throughout the countryside,' said Marc Stern, assistant executive director of the American Jewish Congress, the prospect that some communities might only have 'some Christian group running social services' and the danger 'of religious discrimination in government-funded employment scares Jews.'"

(*The Washington Post,* February 27, 2001)

American Legislative Exchange Council (ALEC)

Established in 1973

DIRECTOR

Duane Parde, executive director. Prior to serving as executive director, Parde was ALEC's chief of staff, responsible for the management of internal operations, including the development, implementation, and enforcement of financial, administrative, and personnel policies and procedures. He also served as liaison to the board of directors. From 1992 to 1995, Duane was the director of state affairs for the Council for Affordable Health Insurance, a national trade association representing the interests of small and medium-sized health insurance companies. Duane also served in the Kansas Attorney General's Office. He is a member of the American Society of Association Executives. He is the author of numerous papers and articles on state policy, and has testified many times before state legislative committees on a wide range of issues. (Source: ALEC Web site)

BOARD OF DIRECTORS

Donald Ray Kennard, chairman, Louisiana representative
Susan Wagle, first vice chair, Kansas senator
Billy Hewes III, second vice chairman, Mississippi senator
Earl Ehrhart, treasurer, Georgia representative
Delores Mertz, secretary, Iowa representative
Jim Dunlap, immediate past chair, Oklahoma senator
Private Enterprise Board
Kurt L. Malmgren, Ph.R.M.A., chairman
Jerry Watson, American Bail Coalition, first vice chairman
Scott Fisher, Altria Corporate Services, Inc., second vice chairman
Pete Poynter, BellSouth Corp., treasurer
Edward D. Failor Sr., Iowans for Tax Relief, secretary
Michael K. Morgan, Koch Industries, immediate past chairman
Allan E. Auger, Coors Brewing Co., chairman emeritus
Ronald F. Scheberle, Verizon Communications, Inc., chairman emeritus

SCOPE

Members: 2,400 individuals and 300 corporate and foundation members (Web site)
Branches/chapters: None
Affiliates: None

STAFF

25 total—plus 8 interns

TAX STATUS

501(c)(3)

CONTACT INFORMATION

1129 20th Street, NW, Suite 500, Washington, DC 20036
Phone: (202) 466-3800 • *Fax:* (202) 466-3801
General E-mail: info@alec.org • *Web site:* www.alec.org

Communications Director: Joe Rinzel, assistant director of public affairs/media relations • jrinzel@alec.org
Human Resources Director: Information unavailable

PURPOSE: "To develop dynamic partnerships between state legislators and the private sector in order to advance a public policy agenda based on the Jeffersonian principles of free markets, limited government, individual liberty, and traditional family values. . . . To help members create effective, innovative public policies that promote free enterprise, spur economic growth, encourage individual responsibility and independence, and enhance the nation's competitiveness in the global marketplace."

CURRENT CONCERNS: Homeland security • Air pollution and automobile emissions reduction • Air transportation • Automobile insurance • Biotechnology in agriculture • Broadband Internet services • Budget forecasting and taxation • Cellular phones and driving • Charter schools • Children and parents • Civic literacy • Class action reform • Digital divide • Digital signatures • Drunk drivers • Educators' liability • E-Government • Encryption • Environmental federalism • Federal lands • Fiscal responsibility • Free trade and sanctions • Government contracts with private attorneys • Health care professionals • Health insurance reform • Health insurance regulation • Health plan liability • Highway funding • Homeland security • Improving public education • Infectious disease control • Internet taxation • Junk science • Living wage • Long-term care • Medicaid reform • Model Emergency Health Powers Act (MEPHA) • Organ donation • Prescription drugs • Property and casualty insurance modernization • Public pension modernization • Public transit • Railroad labor issues • Red light cameras—automated enforcement • Right to appeal • School choice • Separation of powers • Social security modernization • Tax reform and taxpayers' rights • Urban growth • Welfare

METHOD OF OPERATION: Conferences/seminars • Internet (Web site) • Legislative/regulatory monitoring (state) • Library/information clearing house • Local/municipal affairs • Media outreach • Research • Speakers program • State model legislation

Effectiveness and Political Orientation

"A pile of bills at the Ohio Statehouse seeking to limit or cut taxes continues to grow, as Republicans seek to regain their conservative footing in an election year after approving a 20 percent sales-tax increase.

FINANCES
Revenue: 2002—$4.99 million; 2001—$5.83 million

FUNDING SOURCES
Corporate contributions, 55%; foundation grants, 30%; conferences, membership, other, 15%

PAC
None

EMPLOYMENT
Information unavailable

INTERNSHIPS
"ALEC offers internships to students in all years and all majors, including current undergraduate students, recent graduates, and graduate students. Preferred applicants will have demonstrated a strong interest in fields such as Government, History, Economics, Business, Information Technology, Marketing, or Finance, although no specific prior experience is required. Candidates should also have a strong interest in advancing the principles of individual liberty, limited government, and federalism.

"Fall and Spring semester internships are offered in the Office of Legislation and Policy and the Public Affairs Department, and Summer internships are available in all departments. Fall and spring semester interns often travel to ALEC policy summits, and fall semester interns are essential in ALEC's States and Nation Policy Summit, held each December in Washington, DC. Summer interns travel to ALEC's Annual Meetings, held across the country every August. Each department of the organization requires unique skills in its interns. Detailed information and the internship application, are available on the Web site."

NEWSLETTERS
Inside ALEC (six times per year)
Leadership Briefing (as needed)
Task Force News (six times per year)

PUBLICATIONS
2004 Guide to Health Insurance Solutions
Agenda for Liberty
ALEC Policy Forum
Crisis in State Spending:
    A Guide for State Legislators
Excuses Left Behind: The Truth About NCLB
Legislators and Consumers Guide to
    Prescription Drug Importation
Report Card on American Education: A State-
    by-State Analysis, 1980-2002
Second Hand Science: Revisiting Smoking
    Bans
Show me the Money: Budget Cutting
    Strategies for Cash Strapped State
    Legislatures

CONFERENCES
ALEC Annual Meeting
States & Nation Policy Summit

"The latest proposal came Wednesday, when state Rep. Jean Schmidt, a Cincinnati-area Republican, unveiled her 'Tax and Expenditure Limitation Act.' The bill—championed by the fiscally conservative American Legislative Exchange Council—would limit Ohio's spending through a constitutional amendment to the rate of increase in inflation and population."
(*The Plain Dealer* [Cleveland], February 6, 2004)

"The Supreme Court will hear arguments today in a case that could open the way to far greater public funding of religious education.

"The justices will consider a case that asks whether a state, in an effort to avoid using public money to train clergy, may deny scholarships to theology students. The court's decision in the case could resolve a broader legal question that touches hundreds of thousands of American schoolchildren and their families: whether federal, state and local governments can be required to fund the growing number of voucher programs that offer tuition payments to parents who send their children to religious schools.

"Last year, the court ruled that local governments could provide such funds, but it stopped short of saying that they were required to do so.

" 'This is very, very big,' says Mike Flynn, policy director for the American Legislative Exchange Council, a think tank in Washington, D.C., that advises state legislators. 'This is the last legal obstacle to vouchers.' "
(*USA Today,* December 2, 2003)

"A rise in ecoterrorism is prompting federal and state lawmakers to craft laws aimed specifically at radical environmental and animal-rights activists. . . .

"In Congress last month, a bill was introduced specifying ecoterrorism as a federal crime and providing stiff penalties for anyone who 'intentionally damages the property of another with the intent to influence the public with regard to conduct the offender considers harmful to the environment.' . . .

"Part of the problem is that 'most states make no legal distinction between a disgruntled youth vandalizing a public park and an organized ecoterrorist torching a family's home,' says Sandy Liddy Bourne of the American Legislative Exchange Council (ALEC), a conservative think tank.

"The ALEC, an organization of state and national lawmakers backed by corporate sponsors, has written model legislation that makes any property damage or destruction in the name of animal rights or environmental protection a category of domestic terrorism. The legislation would increase penalties and punish those who assist or finance such acts. It also would create a 'terrorist registry' where a photo and other personal information about anybody found guilty under the law would be posted on a website for at least three years—similar to registries of sex offenders.

" 'The legislation specifically addresses actions that are designed to intimidate, coerce, invoke fear or other forms of terror . . . So far, lawmakers in Oklahoma, Texas, New York, Arkansas, Missouri, Nebraska, Ohio, and Oregon have introduced laws patterned after the model."
(*Christian Science Monitor,* November 26, 2003)

"A proposed law that would double the chances of being called for jury duty and send no-shows to jail is being hammered as impractical and costly by a panel reviewing the legislation.

"The proposal 'will increase court caseload, increase workload, increase expenses related to court operations, impose numerous administrative burdens on judges . . . and undermine public confidence in the courts,' according to the Ohio Judicial Conference.

"The group reviews pending legislation in Ohio and reports on the impact it could have on the justice system.

"Senate Bill 71, introduced in April, is modeled after the Jury Patriot Act, legislation intended to increase the number of people who serve on juries. It's being promoted by the American Legislative Exchange Council, a nationwide group of conservative state legislators. . . . The bill has generated strident opposition from local judges and court officials.

" 'It radically revamps a system that isn't broken, and it would cost a horrendous amount of money in Franklin County,' said Common Pleas Judge Nodine Miller, who has been a judge for 10 years. 'It would be a tremendous logistical nightmare.' . . .

"But Kristin Armshaw, director of the Legislative Exchange Council, said most who are worried just fear change. 'In most of the states there is some concern initially, especially with the one-day, one-court system,' Armshaw said. 'I know that Ohio has expressed more concerns than other states have. But I don't feel that a lot of concerns they have are grounded in what the language of the bill is. I think they don't like the idea of change.' "

(*Columbus Dispatch* [Ohio], November 17, 2003)

"The often-cited rationale for giving higher benefits to public employees is that they earn less in salary than private—sector workers. A 1997 study by the Congressional Budget Office found that federal employees earned lower salaries on average and less total compensation than their private-sector counterparts.

"But some question such conclusions. The conservative American Legislative Exchange Council has argued that average salaries are actually higher in the public sector, while labor unions have called the comparison misleading.

"Figures from the federal Bureau of Labor Statistics, in fact, show all public employees earned an average of $22.68 an hour this year, compared with $16.08 for private-sector employees. But Norma Malcolm, a bureau economist, noted that the public sector has a higher percentage of white-collar and college-educated employees.

" 'There aren't many minimum-wage jobs in government,' Malcolm noted. 'You have retail and fast-food jobs in the private sector.' "

(*The Milwaukee Journal Sentinel,* November 16, 2003)

"If you were wondering where 29 Colorado legislators were last week, you needed only look to Washington, D.C., where the conservative American Legislative Exchange Council, or ALEC, was meeting.

"Gov. Bill Owens was also there, giving the luncheon keynote Friday, sponsored by drugmaker GlaxoSmithKline. Two of the group's three legislators of the year are from Colorado: Senate President John Andrews, R-Centennial, and Sen. Bob Hagedorn, D-Aurora.

"ALEC has been faulted by environmental groups for its open solicitation of corporate money and influence. ALEC responds that giving corporations a say brings balance. That balance was on display at the conference. R.J. Reynolds Tobacco Co. sponsored the golf tournament Saturday. Thursday's breakfast debate on global warming was sponsored by ExxonMobil.

"Owens, an avid ALEC member in his legislative days, said such partnerships are common among government associations."

(*The Denver Post,* August 3, 2003)

American Public Health Association (APHA)

Established in 1872

DIRECTOR

Georges C. Benjamin, executive director. Benjamin, a nationally renowned leader in public health, assumed leadership of the APHA in December 2002. He is a former secretary of health for Maryland, chief of emergency medicine at the Walter Reed Army Medical Center, and commissioner for public health for the District of Columbia. An expert in emergency medicine, Benjamin is an active participant in the national debate on how best to protect the American people against the risks of bioterrorism. A graduate of the Illinois Institute of Technology and the University of Illinois College of Medicine, Benjamin is board certified in internal medicine and is a fellow of the American College of Physicians. He is a past president of the Association of State and Territorial Health Officials and serves on several national advisory groups including the U.S. Department of Health and Human Service's Advisory Committee on Public Health Preparedness and the Centers for Disease Control and Prevention Director's Advisory Committee

BOARD OF DIRECTORS

Louise A. Anderson, M.S.N., Committee on Affiliates chairperson
Georges C. Benjamin, M.D., executive director
Jay M. Bernhardt, Ph.D., M.P.H., member
Virginia A. Caine, M.D., president
Jose F. Cordero, M.D., M.P.H., member
Ingrid Davis, M.P.A., Action Board chairperson
Linda C. Degutis, D.R.P.H., M.S.N., member
Cheryl E. Easley, Ph.D., R.N., Education Board chairperson
Oliver T. Fein, M.D., member
Jay H. Glasser, Ph.D., M.S., past president
Drew A. Harris, D.P.M., M.P.H., member
Alan R. Hinman, M.D., M.P.H., speaker of the governing council
Camara Phyllis Jones, M.D., M.P.H., Ph.D., member
Toni Rhodes Leeth, M.P.H., public health student caucus president
Patricia D. Mail, M.P.H., Ph.D., C.H.E.S., vice chairperson
Edwin Cochran Marshall, O.D., M.S., M.P.H., chairperson
Carmen Rita Nevarez, M.D., M.P.H., member
Larry K. Olsen, Dr.P.H., C.H.E.S., Intersectional Council chairperson
Harry Perlstadt, Ph.D., M.P.H., Science Board chairperson
Diane L. Rowley, M.D., member
Melvin D. Shipp, O.D., Dr.P.H., M.P.H., treasurer
Walter Tsou, M.D., M.P.H., president-elect

CONTACT INFORMATION

800 I Street, NW, Washington, DC 20001-3710
Phone: (202) 777-2742 • *Fax:* (202) 777-2534
General E-mail: comments@apha.org • *Web site:* www.apha.org

Communications Director: Information unavailable
Human Resources Director: Information unavailable

PURPOSE: Dedicated to improving the public's health. The APHA promotes the scientific and professional foundation of public health practice and policies, advocates the conditions for a healthy society, emphasizes prevention, and enhances the ability of members to promote and protect environmental and community health.

CURRENT CONCERNS: Federal and state funding for health programs • Gun control • Patient's bill of rights • Pollution control • Professional education in public health • Programs and policies related to chronic and infectious diseases • Racial and ethnic health disparities • Tobacco control

METHOD OF OPERATION: Advertisements • Coalition forming • Conferences/seminars • Congressional testimony • Educational foundation • Films/video/audiotapes • Grassroots organizing • Information clearinghouse • Initiative/referendum campaigns • Internet (Web site) • Internships • Lobbying (federal, state, and grassroots) • Media outreach • Participation in federal regulatory proceedings • Professional development services • Speakers program • Telecommunications services (fax-on-demand number: [703] 336-5552, mailing lists) • Technical assistance

Effectiveness and Political Orientation

"A number of leading researchers are mobilizing against a Bush administration plan that would require new health and environmental regulations to rely more solidly on science that has been peer-reviewed—an awkward situation in which scientists find themselves arguing against one of the universally accepted gold standards of good science.

"The administration proposal, which is open for comment from federal agencies through Friday and could take effect in the next few months, would block the adoption of new federal regulations unless the science being used to justify them passes muster with a centralized peer review process that would be overseen by the White House Office of Management and Budget.

"Administration officials say the approach reflects President Bush's commitment to 'sound science.'

"But a number of scientific organizations, citizen advocacy groups and even a cadre of former government regulators see a more sinister motivation: an effort to inject White House politics into the world of science and to use the uncertainty that inevitably surrounds science as an excuse to delay new rules that could cost regulated industries millions of dollars.

Karen L. Valenzuela, M.A., M.P.A., member
Terri D. Wright, M.P.H., member

SCOPE
Members: 50,000
Branches/chapters: 52
Affiliates: 20,000 state and local affiliates

STAFF
65 total—plus volunteers and interns

TAX STATUS
501(c)(3)

FINANCES
Revenue: 2002—$11.9 million

FUNDING SOURCES
Conventions, 31%; membership dues, 30%; publications, 28%; contracts and grants, 5%; other, 6%

PAC
None

EMPLOYMENT
Information on open positions can be obtained by going to the Web site and clicking on CareerMart at http://www.apha.org/career.

INTERNSHIPS
Information about internships is available through the CareerMart section at http://www.apha.org/career.

NEWSLETTERS
American Journal of Public Health (monthly)
The Nation's Health (monthly)

PUBLICATIONS
Caring for Our Children: National Health and Safety Performance Standards for Out-Of-Home Child Care
Children with Special Needs Applicable Standards from Caring for Our Children
Collaborative Research: University and Community Partnership
Collision on I-75
Communicating Public Health Information Effectively: A Guide for Practitioners
Confronting Violence
Exclusion and Inclusion of Ill Children in Child Care Facilities and Care of Ill Children in Child Care: Applicable Standards from Caring for Our Children
Promises to Keep: Public Health Policy for American Indians and Alaska Natives in the 21st Century
Public Health Management of Disasters: The Practice Guide
Race and Research: Perspectives on Minority Participation in Health Studies
Terrorism and Public Health
The Schools of Ground Zero: Early Lessons Learned In Children's Environmental Health

CONFERENCES
Annual meeting (fall)

" 'The way it's structured it allows for the political process to second-guess the experts,' said Georges Benjamin, executive director of the 50,000-member American Public Health Association, one of many groups that have spoken against the proposal. . . ."

(*The Washington Post,* January 15, 2004)

"Last month, the American Public Health Association announced its opposition to OMB's [Office of Management and Budget] proposal, arguing that 'public-health decisions must be made in the absence of scientific certainty, or in the absence of perfect information.' "

(*The Wall Street Journal,* December 5, 2003)

"In news certain to reinvigorate the longstanding does-so/does-not slapfight between those who believe salt raises blood pressure and those who don't, officials with the American Public Health Association (APHA) last week exhorted food producers to remove excessive sodium from processed foods. Stephen Havas of the University of Maryland School of Medicine estimated that by reducing the amount of salt in processed foods by 50 percent over 10 years, food processors would save 150,000 lives a year by lowering blood pressure in vulnerable individuals. The industry responded by airing fears that people wouldn't enjoy foods with less salt—and that diets high in fruit and vegetables have also been shown to reduce blood pressure. (Of course, the high fruit and vegetable diets most recently found to reduce blood pressure also controlled salt intake.) The government says people should eat less than 2,500 milligrams of salt a day; most people get 4,000. And the problem isn't with the salt shaker: 75 percent of a typical person's intake comes from processed foods, APHA says."

(*The Washington Post,* November 19, 2002)

"Sens. Bill Frist and Edward Kennedy are pushing the 'Bioterrorism Preparedness Act of 2001' which spends most of its $3.2 billion on fortifying the public health system. With anthrax scares, the possibility of smallpox outbreaks, and the specter of other terrifying chemical or biological weapons used against us, Sens. Frist and Kennedy are clearly on the right track. But how prepared for 'preparedness' is the public health profession? Not very if one looks to the American Public Health Association for guidance.

"At its 129th annual meeting in October in Atlanta, the very backyard of the Centers for Disease Control and Prevention, the APHA compiled its "Guiding Principles for a Public Health Response to Terrorism." Put together just a month or so after Sept. 11, one would think the APHA blueprint would be all over the anthrax and smallpox threats with plans to update labs and improve massive response to an epidemic. Not exactly. . . ."

(*The Wall Street Journal,* December 13, 2001)

American Rivers

Established in 1973

DIRECTOR

Rebecca Wodder, president. Wodder has been president of American Rivers since 1995. In 2004, she served as Chair of the "Green Group"—an informal association of the leaders of national environmental organizations. Previously she was vice president for organizational development at The Wilderness Society in Washington, DC. Educated at the University of Kansas and the University of Wisconsin, Madison, Wodder moved to Washington, DC, in 1978 to work as legislative aide to then U.S. Senator Gaylord Nelson, with responsibility for environmental and energy issues.

BOARD OF DIRECTORS

Martha C. Brand, chair, Minneapolis, MN
Donald B. Ayer, McLean, VA
Myer Berlow, New York, NY
Louis Capozzi, New York, NY
Raymond Cross, Missoula, MT
Sylvia Earle, Oakland, CA
Caroline D. Gabel, Chestertown, MD
David J. Hayes, Arlington, VA
Christian Hohenlohe, Washington, DC
Lotsie Hermann Holton, St. Louis, MO
Thomas D. Hughes, Seattle, WA
Landon Jones, St. Louis, MO
Linda Laird, Jackson, WY
Anthony A. Lapham, Washington, DC
Dee Leggett, Great Falls, VA
David M. Leuschen, New York, NY
George Lund, Sioux Falls, SD
Lee W. Mather Jr., Greenwich, CT
Susan McDowell, Jackson Hole, WY
Judy L. Meyer, Athens, GA
Z. Cartter Patten III, Chattanooga, TN
Nicholas G. Penniman IV, Naples, FL
Edward W. Pettigrew, Seattle, WA
Tom Skerritt, Seattle, WA
John I. Taylor Jr., Boulder, CO
Albert Wells, Belgrade, MT
Edward B. Whitney, New York, NY
Ted Williams, Grafton, MA

SCOPE

Members: 31,000 individuals
Branches/chapters: 2 regional offices;
    7 field offices
Affiliates: None

STAFF

50 total—40 professional; 10 support; plus 2–5 volunteers and 8–10 interns

TAX STATUS

501(c)(03)

FINANCES

Budget: 2004—$5 million; 2003—$5 million; 2002—$5 million

CONTACT INFORMATION

1025 Vermont Avenue, NW, Suite 720, Washington, DC 20005
Phone: (202) 347-7550 • *Fax:* (202) 347-9240
General E-mail: amrivers@americanrivers.org •
Web site: www.americanrivers.org

Communications Director: Peter Kelley
(202) 347-7550 • pkelley@americanrivers.org
Human Resources Director: Anne Hoffert
(202) 347-7550 • ahoffert@americanrivers.org

PURPOSE: "Dedicated to protecting and restoring healthy, natural rivers and the variety of life they sustain for people, fish and wildlife."

CURRENT CONCERNS: Hydropower policy reform • Imperiled aquatic species • Northwest salmon restoration • Protection of wild rivers • Reforming the Army Corps of Engineers • Removal of lower Snake River dams • Restoration of rivers in urban and rural communities • Restoring instream flow • Small dam removal

METHOD OF OPERATION: Coalition forming • Conferences/seminars • Congressional testimony • Grassroots organizing • Internet (Web site) • Internships • Litigation • Lobbying (federal, state, and grassroots) • Media outreach • Participation in regulatory proceedings (federal and state)

Effectiveness and Political Orientation

"Fish in the Anacostia River have cancerous tumor rates that are as high as ever documented in an American river, and a U.S. government-led study to be published next month links the tumors to pollution caused by vehicle emissions and runoff. Fifty to 68 percent of mature brown bullhead catfish collected in 2001 from three parts of the river in the city had liver tumors, most of which were cancerous, according to the study led by the U.S. Fish and Wildlife Service. In addition to the liver tumors, 13 to 23 percent of the bullheads had skin tumors, scientists found. . . .

"This isn't the first time the tumor rates in the Anacostia have been surveyed, and it's not the first time the results have been the cause for concern. A 1996 study of Anacostia fish, also organized by Pinkney, cited liver tumor rates ranging from 50 to 60 percent. After that study was published, the environmental advocacy group American Rivers deemed the Anacostia the nation's most polluted river."

(*The Washington Post,* February 11, 2004)

"For as long as anybody can remember, a dam has cleaved the Mill River in downtown Stamford, its shimmering, tinsel waterfall an attractive beacon to local residents strolling under cherry trees, international bankers commuting to work and, according to local legend, even George Washington.

FUNDING SOURCES

Individuals, 33%; foundation grants, 32%; membership dues, 11%; corporate donations, 9%; government contracts, 1%; other, 14% (all percentages are approximations)

PAC

None

EMPLOYMENT

Job postings for open positions are available at www.americanrivers.org. For more information contact Anne Hoffert at ahoffet@americanrivers.org, or by telephone at (202) 347-7550.

INTERNSHIPS

American Rivers offers "volunteer internships for both undergraduates and graduate students interested in various aspects of river conservation, public policy, public communications and online community development. We are seeking applicants with interest in the environment who are energetic, creative, and enthusiastic about river conservation. We strive to give our interns a relevant experience that will prepare them for employment in the environmental and/or non-profit field. . . . Internships are 25 hours per week and are unpaid. Most interns work three full days per week and have time to get a paying part-time job."

Brochure, available online at www. americanrivers.org, contains more information about various internship programs, as well as an application form. Internship application materials should be sent to Anne Hoffert, internship coordinator, American Rivers, 1025 Vermont Avenue, NW, Suite 720, Washington, DC 20005. Fax: (202) 347-9242. E-mail: ahoffert@americanrivers.org.

NEWSLETTERS

American Rivers (quarterly)
River Monitor (bimonthly)

PUBLICATIONS

Paving Our Way to Water Shortages: How Sprawl Aggravates the Effects of Drought
Voyage of Recovery—Fostering a Missouri River Renaissance
Where Rivers are Born: The Scientific Imperative for Defending Small Streams and Wetlands

CONFERENCES

Endangered Rivers News Conference (annually in April)
Other conferences held occasionally.

"Admirers of the dam may soon have to find inspiration elsewhere.

"A group of ecologists, sport fishermen, open space advocates, public housing directors, business leaders and the mayor has bonded together in an attempt to remove the dam and restore the Mill River to its unencumbered, pre-Colonial condition. . . .

" 'The removal of one dam may not seem like a lot, but restoration won't happen overnight, just like the fragmentation of the river system didn't happen overnight,' said Laura Wildman, regional coordinator for American Rivers, a conservation group in Washington working to remove dams around the country. 'We're just taking small steps in a positive direction.' "

(*The New York Times,* February 8, 2004)

"In the latest twist in a decades-old legal battle over water levels along the Missouri River, a federal judge in Minnesota has ordered the Army Corps of Engineers to lower the level to protect the habitat of two endangered species of birds and one species of fish.

"The Army Corps of Engineers and government lawyers are appealing the ruling, but the corps said yesterday it will comply with the court order by reducing water releases into the river. . . .

"Environmental groups and advocates hailed Judge Paul A. Magnuson's ruling but criticized the corps for taking a week to begin implementing the order and for lowering the river for only part of the month.

" 'The summer low flow period will not be as long or as beneficial as it should have been, but there are still gains to be had,' said Eric Eckl, a spokesman for American Rivers. 'We're very disappointed with the way the Army Corps has chosen to play this.'

" 'If they were serious about compliance, they would begin to ramp down [the water level] now,' said David Hayes, a lawyer for the group and an Interior Department deputy secretary in the Clinton administration. 'There are literally two tows in active transit on the river, yet they say they need a full week to clear the river.' "

(*The Washington Post,* August 7, 2003)

"The Army Corps of Engineers yesterday began lowering water levels along the Missouri River in response to a federal court order aimed at saving two endangered species of birds and one species of fish that have been caught up in a decades-old battle over the management of the sprawling waterway. . . .

"The conservation group American Rivers and several other environmental organizations had sought the order to protect the sandbar nesting grounds of the endangered birds—the least tern and Great Plains piping plover—and to help preserve the vanishing pallid sturgeon. . . .

"Conservation groups yesterday hailed Kessler's ruling as a major turning point in the long-standing struggle, and noted that for the first time a federal judge has indicated that the Army Corps' management plan for keeping river levels artificially high violated the Endangered Species Act. . . .

" 'We see this as a real breakthrough in this long-standing political logjam,' said Eric Eckl, a spokesman for American Rivers. 'The ruling was very affirmative and unambiguous that prevailing operations of the Missouri River are in clear violation of the Endangered Species Act.' "

(*The Washington Post,* July 14, 2003)

"With many of the nation's dams no longer making economic or environmental sense, old dams are being dismantled, in a slow-moving but remarkable reversal of fortune for rivers and fish. . . .

"The deconstructions in Oregon are unusual because they are fully functioning hydroelectric dams still producing power—a move that once upon a time would have been almost unimaginable.

" 'This is a major development in the environmental history of the West,' said Eric Eckl, a spokesman for American Rivers, an advocacy group. 'It is one of first removals of hydroelectric dams, and they are not only taking down the dams, but restoring habitat for threatened salmon and steelhead.'

"Conservationists hope it is the beginning of a long-term trend. Hundreds of dams are slated for possible demolition; more than 60 are scheduled to be removed this year alone, the highest number since American Rivers began keeping count five years ago. . . ."

(*The Washington Post,* November 20, 2002)

"The Army Corps of Engineers is suspending work on about 150 congressionally approved water projects to review the economics used to justify them, an unprecedented response to mounting criticism of Corps analyses inside and outside the Bush administration. . . .

"But some critics said the Corps could be creating the illusion of action to prevent a growing cadre of would-be reformers from taking real action. This year, President Bush's budget called for major cuts and changes at the Corps. In March, the day after Smith filed his bill, Bush budget director Mitchell E. Daniels Jr. helped engineer the ouster of Corps civilian chief Michael Parker, who had complained publicly about the budget cuts. . . .

" 'Acknowledging you have a problem is the first step toward solving it,' said Rebecca R. Wodder, president of the environmental advocacy group American Rivers, whose recent list of the nation's most endangered rivers blamed the Corps for most of them. 'But we remain convinced that Congress will have to intervene.' "

(*The Washington Post,* May 1, 2002)

"The National Academy of Sciences warned yesterday that the Missouri River and its ecosystem will continue to deteriorate unless its natural flow is significantly restored, calling for 'immediate and decisive management actions' to shatter a 14-year political stalemate.

"The academy's report is the latest milestone in a controversy that has taken nearly as many twists as the original Big Muddy itself. The report mostly echoed long-standing proposals by environmentalists and recreational interests that the channelized river be allowed to rise and fall and meander more freely, proposals bitterly opposed by farmers and the barge industry.

" 'This report is an affirmation of everything we've been saying,' said Chad Smith, Missouri River coordinator for the group American Rivers."

(*The Washington Post,* January 10, 2002)

American Society for the Prevention of Cruelty to Animals (ASPCA)

Established in 1866

DIRECTOR
Edwin Sayres, president.

BOARD OF DIRECTORS
Information unavailable

SCOPE
Members: 740,000 individuals
Branches/chapters: Regional offices in
  Urbana, IL, and Albany, NY
Affiliates: N / A

STAFF
300 in seven offices

TAX STATUS
501(c)(3)

FINANCES
Revenue: 2002—$41.26 million

FUNDING SOURCES
Individual donations, 70%; service fees,
16%; investment income, 5%; corporate donations, 5%; foundation grants, 2%; publications,
1%; special events/projects, 1%

PAC
None

EMPLOYMENT
Interested applicants please submit a cover
letter and resume to: The American Society for
the Prevention of Cruelty to Animals, Human
Resources, 424 East 92nd Street, New York,
NY 10128. Fax: (212) 876-0014. E-mail:
HR@aspca.org. No phone calls please.

INTERNSHIPS
The ASPCA provides fellowship opportunities.

NEWSLETTERS
Animal Watch (quarterly)

PUBLICATIONS
The following is a partial list of brochures:
About the ASPCA
Prevent Animal Cruelty
Spray and Neuter

CONFERENCES
None

CONTACT INFORMATION
424 East 92nd Street, New York, NY 10128-6804
Phone: (212) 876-7700 • *Fax:* (212) 423-0416
General E-mail: information@aspca.org • *Web site:* www.aspca.org

Communications Director: Patricia Jones, vice president, media relations
(212) 876-7700 ext. 4655 • press@aspca.org
Human Resources Director: Lee Murray, senior vice president, Human Resources
(212) 876-7700 ext. 4433

PURPOSE: To provide effective means for the prevention of cruelty to animals throughout the United States.

CURRENT CONCERNS: Hands-on animal care and placement • Overpopulation • Regulating pet breeding and selling • Responsible pet care • Strengthening and enforcing anticruelty laws • Studying the link between animal abuse and domestic abuse • Wildlife issues, especially hunting and trapping

METHOD OF OPERATION: Advertisements • Animal adoption and placement • Awards program • Coalition forming • Conferences/seminars • Congressional testimony • Direct action (law enforcement) • Grantmaking • Grassroots organizing • Information clearinghouse • Initiative/referendum campaigns • Internet (Web site) • Internships • Legal assistance • Legislative/regulatory monitoring (federal and state) • Litigation • Lobbying (federal, state, and grassroots) • Local/municipal affairs • Media outreach • Participation in regulatory proceedings (federal and state) • Product licensing • Research • Scholarships • Technical assistance and training • Telecommunications services (mailing lists)

Effectiveness and Political Orientation

"The Federal Aviation Administration has proposed regulations that would require airlines to report all pets, including fish and snakes, that die or are injured in transit.

"But airlines say the rule is so cumbersome and the term 'pets' is so vague they might stop shipping animals altogether, or at least make it more costly.

"That prospect has breeders and pet shop owners up in arms. . . .

"Animal-rights activists have a different take. They say they hope the FAA's proposed rules will force air carriers to compete for pet lovers' business. 'We were hoping airlines would want to stand out as pet friendly,' says Lisa Weisberg, senior vice-president government affairs for the American Society for the Prevention of Cruelty to Animals. . . .

"Concern for in-flight animal safety dates back decades. In 1956 the American Society for the Prevention of Cruelty to Animals opened Animal Port, a holding area for animals in transit, and oversaw the handling of live cargo. A 1976 amendment to the Animal Welfare Act allows the Animal and Plant Health Inspection Service to penalize airlines for inhumane treatment of animals . . ."

(*The Wall Street Journal,* December 20, 2002)

"Pet owners should 'think twice' about flying pets in the cargo holds of commercial airlines, the American Society for the Prevention of Cruelty to Animals says in a recent news release.

"Hogwash, responds the Air Transport Association. The trade organization for the airlines says cargo holds are safe for animals, with some exceptions—such as pug-nosed dogs—and with certain precautions, such as flying to hot places in the early morning or late evening.

"The debate is heated as the FAA prepares new regulations that would require the airlines to report incidents of pet injury or loss, to determine the cause, to rectify the problem and to make their safety records public. The ASPCA complains that the proposed regulations do not address the law's requirement that crews be trained in humane handling of animals. . . .

(*The Washington Post,* December 8, 2002)

"Finally, after more than four decades of public service, it's retirement time for Rita.

"The 47-year-old chimpanzee, brought to the United States from Africa by the Air Force in the 1950s, is a prime candidate for a new retirement home to be built near Shreveport, La. The facility is expected to cost at least $35 million, most of it federal money, to build and operate over a 10-year period.

"Under a $19 million contract awarded yesterday by the National Institutes of Health, Chimp Haven Inc., a nonprofit group based in Shreveport, will operate "a sanctuary system for all chimpanzees retired from federal biomedical facilities," the group announced. In addition, Chimp Haven said it plans to contribute $6 million in matching funds. . . .

" 'After these chimpanzees have endured years in medical research laboratories, society owes them a tremendous debt,' said Larry Hawk, president of the American Society for the Prevention of Cruelty to Animals. Proponents of the project said it will save taxpayers money in the long run because the cost of keeping chimpanzees in research labs is about double the cost per animal of harboring them in the sanctuary. According to chimpanzee advocates, there are 1,300 to 1,600 federally owned or supported chimpanzees in biomedical laboratories, including 600 to 900 who are eligible for retirement because they are no longer used for research.

(*The Washington Post,* October 1, 2002)

". . . Ms. Buchwald is a program director at the American Society for the Prevention of Cruelty to Animals in Manhattan, and after the terrorist attack she helped coordinate efforts to meet the needs of pets and their owners.

". . . the [ASPCA] helped rescue almost 200 animals. There were many cats, some dogs and a few reptiles and rabbits. The rescues were still going on weeks later because in some buildings, emergency workers looking for human victims had left doors open, allowing animals to escape into the streets.

"Getting animals out of the disaster zone was only the first step. Then came medical care—cleaning their eyes, rehydrating them—and making new living arrangements. For a few pets, that meant adoption because their owners had died. For most, it meant figuring out whether the owner was willing and able to resume care. . . .' "

(*The New York Times,* November 12, 2001)

Americans for Democratic Action, Inc. (ADA)

Established in 1947

DIRECTOR
Amy F. Isaacs, national director

BOARD OF DIRECTORS
Jim McDermott, president
Joel Cohen, executive committee chair
Chris Riddiough, treasurer
Maria Wilkinson, secretary
Jack Blum, counsel
Johanna Bucholz, NLDA/youth chair
Jim Jontz, president emeritus

SCOPE
Members: 65,000
Branches/chapters: 20 chapters
Affiliate: ADA Educational Fund, a 501(c)(3)
    organization; Youth Division

STAFF
10 total—plus interns

TAX STATUS
501(c)(4)

FINANCES
Information unavailable

FUNDING SOURCES
Membership, 75%; large contributions,
including unions, 25%

PAC
ADA Political Action Committee

PAC CONTRIBUTIONS 2002

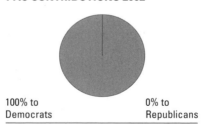

| 100% to | 0% to |
| Democrats | Republicans |

EMPLOYMENT
Information unavailable

INTERNSHIPS
ADA offers an unpaid internship that combines a variety of skills and talents. The summer internship program for ADA introduces interns to both the District and the Hill in an interesting, enjoyable, and educational way. It is an unpaid, individualized program in which the interns' input and action are both respected and required.

"In June, the office—interns included—prepares for ADA's annual convention at the end of the month. Interns primarily work on the

CONTACT INFORMATION
1625 K Street, NW, Suite 210, Washington, DC 20006
Phone: (202) 785-5980 • *Fax:* (202) 785-5969
General E-mail: adaction@ix.netcom.com • *Web site:* www.adaction.org

Communications Director: Don Kusler
(202) 785-5980
Human Resources Director: Information unavailable

PURPOSE: "Dedicated to individual liberty and economic and social justice at home and abroad."

CURRENT CONCERNS: Domestic policy • Economic policy • Environmental policy • Foreign policy • Military policy

METHOD OF OPERATION: Campaign contributions • Coalition forming • Conferences/seminars • Internet (Web site) • Legislative and political education • Legislative/regulatory monitoring (federal and state)

Effectiveness and Political Orientation

"Americans for Democratic Action, which promotes liberal causes. . . ."
                    (*Columbus Dispatch* [Ohio], January 12, 2004)

"Americans for Democratic Action, an activist group seen as a barometer of liberal thinking, already has blamed Democratic failures on an embrace of the 'mushy middle' in American politics. . . ."
                    (*The Plain Dealer* [Cleveland], November 8, 2002)

"The left-wing Americans for Democratic Action. . . ."
                    (*St. Louis Post-Dispatch,* October 27, 2002)

"One may say that the Bush administration is not out to liberalize Iranian society but to prevent terrorism and overcome the threat of weapons of mass destruction. Such a notion ignores the point that, unlike Iraq, where Saddam Hussein may well be replaced by another tyrant, if Iran were governed by reformers it would likely moderate its foreign policy. During a meeting I attended, a leading Iranian reformer called for cutting the defense budget to pay for domestic development. For a moment, I thought I was at a meeting of Americans for Democratic Action."
                    (*Christian Science Monitor,* June 4, 2002)

"In the recent past, activists on the left and right have fought the government's power to seize private assets in criminal investigations. They defended religious liberties. They lobbied against the anti-terrorism measures enacted under President Clinton after Oklahoma City. Led by the Free Congress Foundation, they helped defeat "know your customer" rules for tracking bank cus-

updating, amending, writing, etc. of ADA policy in the form of resolutions. In addition, interns get the chance to meet and network with many prominent progressive figures in areas ranging from international trade to elected officials to D.C. politics. . . . In May, July, and August, the program is much broader and interns are encouraged to explore both D.C. and the Hill. Each intern is assigned a policy area and most projects, assignments, and activities relate broadly to this area. Still, each intern decides his or her own daily agenda; thus, not all activities must connect to the assigned policy area.

Other potential intern activities include legislative lobbying; participating in the Campaign for a Fair Minimum Wage; ADA Web site construction; and media relations. To apply to ADA, send a resume, cover letter, likely starting and ending dates, along with a preference for one of the following policy areas: politics and government, social and domestic, foreign and military, or economic, environmental, and energy. The cover letter should include a couple of paragraphs discussing one's interest in interning with a liberal lobbying group, any personal background in working on grassroots liberal issues, what legislative interests one has, and what one would want to learn from the internship. Send materials to Valerie Dulk-Jacobs, special assistant to the director, 1625 K Street, NW, Suite 210, Washington, DC 20006. Phone: (202) 785-5980. Fax: (202) 785-5969. E-mail: valerie@adaction.com.

NEWSLETTERS

ADA Today (quarterly)
News and Notes (weekly when Congress is in session)

PUBLICATIONS

ADA Voting Record (annual)
Also publishes special reports and policy briefs.

CONFERENCES

Annual convention (every June)
Sponsors other conferences on selected issues

tomers and odd transactions. Jansen, the group's technology expert, calls it 'bank spying,' though others have stepped up calls for the measure to follow the terrorists' money trail.

"Jansen says conservatives who object to the Bush plan don't necessarily mistrust Attorney General John Ashcroft. . . .

"When the package reached the House Judiciary Committee last Monday, it was the panel's most conservative and liberal members who complained the loudest. California Democrat Maxine Waters agreed with Bob Barr, and could scarcely believe it.

"These incongruities are even starker among the interest groups involved. The coalition that opposes the bill has a Web site (indefenseoffreedom.org) that lists its members. One of them is the Americans for Democratic Action, which calls itself the 'nation's oldest independent liberal organization.' Another is the American Conservative Union, which calls itself the 'nation's oldest conservative lobbying organization.'"

(*The Milwaukee Journal Sentinel,* September 30, 2001)

"Washington Conservative Republicans lost another icon yesterday as Texas Sen. Phil Gramm announced he would not seek re-election to a fourth term next year. . . .

"Gramm joins an exodus of conservatives from the Senate, whose departures will change the body's complexion, if not the numerical balance between the parties. In the past month, North Carolina Sen. Jesse Helms and South Carolina Sen. Strom Thurmond announced their retirements. . . .

"To liberals, Gramm, Helms and Thurmond were the epitome of reactionary excess, and they often were used in fund-raising appeals for progressive causes.

"'They are, far away, in a class by themselves,' said Amy Isaacs, national director for the Washington-based Americans for Democratic Action.

"Isaacs described Gramm's announcement as an 'exceedingly pleasant surprise, especially when you put it together with Mr. Helms and Mr. Thurmond.'

(*The San Francisco Chronicle,* September 5, 2001)

Americans for Tax Reform

Established in 1985

DIRECTOR

Grover G. Norquist, president. He serves on the board of directors of the National Rifle Association of America and the American Conservative Union, serves as president of the American Society of Competitiveness, and writes the monthly politics column for the American Enterprise Institute Magazine. Prior to joining the ATR, Norquist served as a commissioner on the Advisory Commission on Electronic Commerce (ACEC), was economist and chief speech-writer for the U.S. Chamber of Commerce (1983–1984), worked on the campaign staff on the 1988, 1992, and 1996 Republican Platform Committees, was executive director of the National Taxpayers' Union, and was executive director of the College Republican National Committee. He wrote the book *Rock the House*—an analysis of the 1994 elections and served on the National Commission on Restructuring the Internal Revenue Service.

BOARD OF DIRECTORS

None

SCOPE

Declined to comment
Branches/chapters: None
Affiliates: Americans for Tax Reform
   Foundation, a 501(c)(3) organization

STAFF

45 total—20 professional, 15 support; plus 15 interns

TAX STATUS

501(c)(4)

FINANCES

Revenue: 2002—$950,573; Budget: 2000—$750,000

FUNDING SOURCES

Declined to comment

PAC

Anti-Tax PAC

PAC CONTRIBUTIONS

Information unavailable

EMPLOYMENT

Open positions at ATR and application instructions are posted at www.atr.org/aboutatr/jobs.html, www.townhall.com, and www.americasfuture.org. ATR hires staff who focus on organizing related groups in the states, as well as experts in policy who influence Congress and the administration on important issues. Applicants should send resumes and other materials to Damon Ansell,

CONTACT INFORMATION

1920 L Street, NW, Suite 200, Washington, DC 20036
Phone: (202) 785-0266 • *Fax:* (202) 785-0261
General E-mail: friends@atr.org • *Web site:* www.atr.org

Communications Director: Jonathan Collegio
(202) 785-0266 • jcollegio@atr.org
Human Resources Director: Damon Ansell
(202) 785-0266 • dansell@atr.org

PURPOSE: Americans for Tax Reform (ATR) opposes all tax increases as a matter of principle and believes in a system in which taxes are simpler, fairer, flatter, more visible, and lower than they are today. ATR leads the fight to stop new avenues of taxation, such as the Streamlined Sales Tax Proposal (SSTP) and Internet taxation. Americans for Tax Reform strongly supports the concept of a single rate, flat tax, and works to reduce the number of times the same money is taxed.

CURRENT CONCERNS: Campaign finance reform • Flat tax concept • Internet tax moratorium • Pension reform • Regulation initiatives and referenda • Size and scope of government • Social Security • Tax limitation amendment and supermajority • Taxpayer protection pledge • Value added tax

METHOD OF OPERATION: Advertisements • Awards Programs • Coalition forming • Congressional testimony • Congressional voting analysis • E-mail alerts • Grassroots organizing • Internships • Initiative/referendum campaigns • International activities • Legislative/regulatory monitoring (federal) • Legislative/regulatory monitoring (state) • Lobbying (federal) • Lobbying (state) • Lobbying (grassroots) • Media outreach • Web site

Effectiveness and Political Orientation

"Even as President Bush and his national Republican Party boast of record tax cuts and vow to hold the line against future tax increases, Republicans here and elsewhere are undercutting the election-year message: They are for raising taxes.

"Worried about declines in schools and basic services, many Republican leaders in the states say they have little choice. . . .

"The upshot is that taxes are creating a new divide between Republicans at the national level and those in the states, one that transcends the more familiar ideological rift between ascendant antitaxers and traditional budget-balancers. . . .

" 'At the national level, it's a settled question: Republicans don't raise taxes. Done,' says antitax activist Grover Norquist, head of the Washington-based Americans for Tax Reform and a close ally of senior Bush adviser Karl Rove. But the states, he says, are 'full of old-line Republicans' and, especially in the recently converted South, former Democrats. Both types, he says, favor bigger government and balanced budgets over lower taxes.

chief of staff at 1920 L Street, NW, Suite 200, Washington, DC 20036. Phone: (202) 785-0261. Fax: (202) 785-0261. E-mail: dansell@atr.org.

INTERNSHIPS

ATR has several internships available. ATR accepts applications from undergraduate and graduate students of all majors. However, applicants should have a strong interest in tax reform and economic policy. Part-time hours are available; full-time associates receive a $250/week stipend, with part-time scale varying. The deadline for spring applications is December 1; summer applications is April 1; fall applications is July 1. Interested applicants should send a resume, a short writing sample, a cover letter with interest in ATR outlined, and three references/letters of recommendation to Liz Grzych, Americans for Tax Reform, 1920 L Street, NW, Suite 200, Washington, DC 20036. Phone: (202) 785-0266. Fax: (202) 785-0261. E-mail: lgrzych@atr.org.

NEWSLETTERS

The Tax Reformer (quarterly)

PUBLICATIONS

Postal Alert
Tax Alert
Tax Update
Trade News

CONFERENCES

None

"Virginia is only the latest state in the past three years in which Republican-led state legislatures, Republican governors or both, amid much intraparty battling, have backed big tax and fee increases. The motivation is both to fill budget gaps left by the national economic downturn and the states' outdated tax codes, and the need to meet growing education, health and infrastructure costs. . . ."

(*The Wall Street Journal,* February 20, 2004)

"To many people, President Bush tax-cutter, born-again Christian, invader of Iraq—is the face of American conservatism. But here at the annual Conservative Political Action Conference, many of the assembled are questioning whether he is conservative enough.

"Conservatives complain about the administration's spending on Medicare and education and its proposed spending on space exploration, its expansion of law enforcement powers to fight terrorism and its proposed guest-worker program for immigrants. . . .

"Many conservatives attribute the 1992 electoral defeat of the first President Bush to disillusionment at the conservative grass roots over his failure to understand the movement and his willingness to raise taxes. " 'Bush Sr. jumped over the line and we had to whack him,' said Grover G. Norquist, president of Americans for Tax Reform and a strategist of the conservative movement.

"But the Conservative Political Action Conference has also been a significant component of the party's ascent in national politics. For 31 years, the conference has been where the Republican big tent is assembled, convening disparate groups like evangelical advocates, gun enthusiasts, antitax groups, antilabor groups, pro-business groups and libertarians."

(*The New York Times,* January 25, 2004)

"Norquist, 47, is known for his weekly strategy sessions of conservatives, a Washington institution. But quietly, for the past five years, he also has been building a network of 'mini-Grover' franchises. He has crisscrossed the country, hand-picking leaders, organizing meetings of right-wing advocates in 37 states. The network will meet its first test in the presidential race. . . . Norquist presented his master contact list . . . mapped out and bound in a book. . . .

"The binder was Norquist's gift to the presidential race. His aspirations, though, extend far beyond the White House. Congress, governorships, state legislatures, the media, the courts—Norquist has a programming plan, and it is all Republican, all the time. Norquist closes his letters, 'Onward.' He takes the mission so seriously, he has named a successor in his will. Socially, he is often introduced as the head of the vast right-wing conspiracy. He accepts the title with a faint blush. . . .

" 'He is an impresario of the center-right,' the president's strategist, Karl Rove, said in an interview. Rove said Norquist's activists helped President Bush push trade promotion, tax cuts, judicial nominees and tort reform, among other items. 'They've been out there slogging for us in the trenches.' "

(*The Washington Post,* January 12, 2004)

"Howard Dean said for the first time yesterday that he will propose cutting payroll taxes to provide middle-income tax relief. . . .

"But the idea of financing tax relief to the middle class through general revenues was promptly ridiculed by Grover Norquist of Americans for Tax

Reform, a conservative Republican strategist who has close ties to the White House. 'There is no money in the general fund. You are talking about bankrupting Social Security,' Norquist said.

"Norquist and the White House favor a plan under which workers could take a percentage of the payroll taxes they pay and instead invest it in the stock market. President Bush has not done much to push that idea, which some consider a partial privatization of Social Security."

(*The Boston Globe,* January 10, 2004)

"Congress is set to end its session next week with a vote on an $820 billion appropriations bill, capping two years of record-level spending economists say has raised the per-household outlay to its highest since World War II. . . .

"The Heritage Foundation and other conservative groups expressed concerns yesterday about the spending habits of a Republican Congress that had promised fiscal restraint. The foundation said this Congress's spending increases went well beyond outlays for defense and homeland security: Subtracting those, spending still went up 11 percent over the past two years.

"These spending patterns have angered conservatives, who expected a dominant GOP to tighten budgets and shrink government. . . .

" 'It's not good enough to say, "the other [Democratic] team would be worse," 'said Grover T. Norquist, president of Americans for Tax Reform and one of a group of economists who voiced their budget worries to officials at a private White House meeting yesterday. While Republicans are on the same page when it comes to cutting taxes, he said, there is a lack of consensus over how to limit spending. 'The Republican Party has not completely closed the deal on how to do it,' he said."

(*The Boston Globe,* December 4, 2003)

Americans United for Separation of Church and State

Established in 1947

DIRECTOR

Barry W. Lynn, executive director. Before joining Americans United, Lynn was legislative counsel for the American Civil Liberties Union and served in a variety of positions with the national offices of the United Church of Christ, including legislative counsel for its Office of Church in Society. An ordained minister, Lynn received his degree in theology from Boston University School of Theology, his law degree from Georgetown University Law Center, and his bachelor's degree from Dickinson College.

BOARD OF DIRECTORS

Barry W. Lynn, executive director
John W. Webster, president; business executive, Omaha, NE
Ralph Watkins, vice president; attorney, Washington, DC
Betty Evans Boone, secretary; attorney, San Diego, CA
Robert "Cam" McConnell, treasurer; minister, Manhattan, KS
Robert S. Alley, trustee; university professor, Richmond, VA
Charlotte H. Coffelt, trustee; retired public schoolteacher, Houston, TX
Ronald B. Flowers, trustee; university professor, Fort Worth, TX
Flynn T. Harrell, trustee; activist, Columbia, SC
James H. Hall Jr., trustee; attorney, Milwaukee, WI
Cynthia S. Holmes, trustee; attorney, Clayton, MO
Rev. Meg Riley, trustee; nonprofit executive, Washington, DC
Rabbi Merrill Shapiro, trustee; rabbi, Richmond, VA
Paul D. Simmons, trustee; medical school professor, Louisville, KY
John M. Suarez, trustee; retired medical doctor, Newbury Park, CA

SCOPE

Members: 75,000 individuals
Branches/chapters: 44 chapters in 25 states
Affiliates: None

STAFF

34 total—25 professionals; 9 support; plus approximately 10 interns.

TAX STATUS

501(c)(3)

FINANCES

Budget: 2004—$3.2 million
2003—approx. $3 million
Revenue: 2002—$4.2 million

CONTACT INFORMATION

518 C Street, NE, Washington, DC 20002
Phone: (202) 466-3234 • *Fax:* (202) 466-2587
General E-mail: americansunited@au.org • *Web site:* www.au.org

Communications Director: Joe Conn
(202) 466-3234 • conn@au.org
Human Resources Director: Chris Colburn
(202) 466-3234 • colburn@au.org

PURPOSE: "Americans United was founded in 1947 by a distinguished group of political, religious, and educational leaders seeking to defend the U. S. Constitution's guarantees of religious freedom. AU's primary task is educating the American public about the importance of religious liberty through the separation of church and state and defending that crucial constitutional principle against attacks by extremist Religious Right groups such as the Christian Coalition."

CURRENT CONCERNS: Charitable choice • Creationism in public school curriculum • Impact of the religious right • Religious liberty • School prayer • School vouchers

METHOD OF OPERATION: Advertisements • Awards program • Coalition forming • Conferences/seminars • Congressional testimony • Congressional voting analysis • Grassroots organizing • Information clearinghouse • Initiative/referendum campaigns • Internet (Web site) • Legal assistance • Legislative/regulatory monitoring (federal and state) • Litigation • Lobbying (federal, state, and grassroots) • Local/municipal affairs • Media outreach • Research • Speakers program

Effectiveness and Political Orientation

"Focus on the Family, one of the nation's largest Christian ministries, will not accept federal money from a faith-based program funded by the federal government.

" 'We believe that with federal dollars eventually comes strings,' said Tom Minnery, vice president of public policy for Focus. 'Our donations come in small amounts from a whole lot of people, and as long as we serve those people we'll be in existence, and if we stop serving those people we don't deserve to be in existence.'

". . . Minnery said Focus supports the president's faith-based initiative and believes it will work the way the president has proposed.

" 'It would work fine by setting up the income structure so that the money from the federal government clearly goes to the soup and the kitchen and the bed and the heating, and separate funding goes toward the preaching, if that's part of the offering, so there are separate funds,' Minnery said.

FUNDING SOURCES
Individuals/membership, 85%; foundation
grants, 15%

PAC
None

EMPLOYMENT
Job openings at Americans United appear on
the organization's Web site; for more information contact Chris Colburn. Phone: (202) 466-
3234. E-mail: colburn@au.org.

INTERNSHIPS
Americans United has a number of full- or half-
time internships available to individuals currently in college or graduate school (including
seminary). Individuals must have strong communication and organizational skills and
demonstrate interest in AU's mission.
Internships are available in several areas
including religious outreach and grassroots
outreach. A local public transportation subsidy
will be provided. Academic credit can be
arranged. Written performance evaluation provided on conclusion of the internship. Some
financial assistance is available. Internship
availability and contact information are available at http://www.au.org/fieldjobs.htm.

NEWSLETTERS
Church and State Magazine (11 times per year)

PUBLICATIONS
Charitable Choice
Close Encounters with the Religious Right
Education Vouchers
Eleven Myths about Church and State
*Eternal Hostility: The Struggle Between
    Theocracy and Democracy*
The First Freedom
*God and the Public Schools: Religion,
    Education and Your Rights*
The Godless Constitution
*A Matter of Conscience: Why Faith Groups
    Oppose Government-Sponsored Prayers in
    Public Schools*
*The Most Dangerous Man in America? Pat
    Robertson and the Rise of the Christian
    Coalition*
*Religion in the Public Schools: A Joint
    Statement of Current Law*
*The Right to Religious Liberty: The Basic ACLU
    Guide to Religious Rights*
*Should You Pay Taxes to Support Religious
    Schools?*
*Stars in the Constitutional Constellation:
    Federal and State Constitutional
    Provisions on Church and State*
We Hold These Truths
*Why the Religious Right Is Wrong about
    Separation of Church and State*

CONFERENCES
National Conference on Church and State
    (annual)

"Others disagree, saying they fear recipients might not receive services if they did not agree to listen to a sermon or gospel.

"Bush's faith-based initiative has been controversial since he introduced it early in his presidency, especially among groups such as Americans United for Separation of Church and State. . . .

"The Rev. Barry Lynn, executive director for Americans United for Separation of Church and State, said: 'This field hearing appears to be little more than a showcase for the extreme views of Focus on the Family. That's bad enough. But for Congress to provide a forum for the views of ex-gay ministries is beyond the pale and an insult to millions of Americans.' "

(*Denver Post*, January 25, 2004)

"By agreeing that the new owner must use more muted ground lights, the Ventura City Council on Thursday night took the final step toward averting a costly lawsuit backed by a national 1st Amendment watchdog group. "As part of their negotiation, prospective plaintiffs supported by Americans United for Separation of Church and State have dropped their threat to sue over the constitutionality of the 24-foot wooden cross. Similar litigation elsewhere has dragged on for more than a decade.

" 'We did everything we could to avoid a costly and ugly legal battle,' said Mayor Ray DiGuilio. 'A suit would have exacerbated the situation tremendously.'

"At a contentious hearing July 31, more than 40 speakers denounced demands that the city either take down the landmark cross or sell it to a private party. Convinced it almost certainly would lose in court, the council agreed to take sealed bids for the cross and an acre around it.

"Thursday night's action amended the deed a new owner would have to live by.

"The conflict was similar to many that have taken place around the United States over crosses, nativity scenes and other religious symbols placed on public property.

"Founded in 1947, Americans United for Separation of Church and State has been active in a number of those cases, as well as in the current bitter dispute over a monument to the Ten Commandments in the lobby of Alabama's Supreme Court."

(*Los Angeles Times*, August 23, 2003)

"Religious and advocacy groups filed suit Tuesday to block Colorado's new school voucher law, setting up a legal fight that could spill into the nation's classrooms.

"The suit . . . contends that giving taxpayer money to low-income families so their children can attend private school illegally enriches church-run schools.

" 'Colorado taxpayers should not be asked to subsidize religious indoctrination,' said Jeffrey Sinensky, general counsel of the American Jewish Committee.

"But voucher proponents say Colorado's voucher program gives poor families with children in struggling schools a chance to succeed. They say they are confident it will get legal backing in the state's courts. . . .

"Colorado's voucher law was the first passed since the U.S. Supreme Court declared that taxpayer-supported vouchers are constitutional.

"The decision set the stage for vouchers to be challenged on a state level to determine whether they violate state constitutions . . .

"The suit also is backed by teachers unions. . . .

"Also supporting it are other national organizations, including the American Civil Liberties Union, the American Jewish Committee and Americans United for Separation of Church and State, which see Colorado's experiment in school vouchers as a dangerous blurring of lines separating government and religion.

" 'The lawsuit in Colorado is an important battle in a larger conflict over the proper relationship between religion and government in America,' said the Rev. Barry W. Lynn, executive director for Americans United for Separation of Church and State."

(*The Denver Post,* May 21, 2003)

"The Army major general who commands Fort Bragg's training center for special operations forces has invited a group of predominantly Southern Baptist pastors to the base this month to participate in a military-themed motivational program for Christian evangelists.

"The unusual collaboration is the result of a friendship between Maj. Gen. William G. Boykin, commanding general of the John F. Kennedy Special Warfare Center and School at Fort Bragg, and the Rev. Bobby H. Welch, a Southern Baptist minister in Daytona Beach, Fla., who has started an evangelistic campaign called FAITH Force Multipliers.

"Hundreds of ministers received an invitation last month from Mr. Welch saying that participants would observe weapons demonstrations, sleep overnight on the base and 'go with General Boykin and Green Beret instructors to places where no civilians and few soldiers ever go!'

"But the marriage of military and ministry offended one Baptist pastor invited to attend. That minister, who said he did not want to be identified for fear of his colleagues' ire, informed Americans United for Separation of Church and State, an advocacy group in Washington.

"Lawyers with the group faxed a letter to General Boykin and the secretary of the Army on Friday warning that the event, planned for April 22 and 23, is unconstitutional because it amounts to government promotion of a religious event.

" 'It's completely inappropriate to have the Army put on a revival meeting at a military base, and that is the bottom line of this event,' said the Rev. Barry Lynn, executive director of Americans United.

" 'This is a particularly bad time to have the Army appear to be promoting Christianity,' he continued, 'in the middle of a war with a Muslim country.'

"The American military does not ban religion on bases. It offers chaplains, chapels and services for people of all faiths.

"The difference here, said Americans United, is government sponsorship of religion. . . ."

(*The New York Times,* April 6, 2003)

America's Promise—
The Alliance for Youth

Established in 1997

DIRECTOR
Peter Gallagher, president. Gallagher has been president and chief executive officer of America's Promise since 1997. Prior to joining America's Promise, Gallagher was chief executive officer of Source One Financial Services, Inc., from 1994 through 1996, and he was senior vice president and co-founder of the AT&T Universal Credit Card, from 1989 to 1993. He has served on the boards of private companies such as Retrieval Technologies, Inc.; MEDSTAR Healthcare Corp.; and the American Financial Services Association. He has also served on the U.S. Department of Commerce's Foreign and Commercial Service advisory board. He was appointed to the District of Columbia Financial Control Board and the Emergency Board of Trustees and served as trustee for Capitol Hill Hospital; the United Way of Jacksonville, Fla.; and Arena Stage. He is a board member of the Pew Partnership for Civic Change; VHA Health Foundation Inc.; and the National Assembly of Health and Human Service Organizations. He is also a director of Friedman, Billings, Ramsey Group, Inc.

BOARD OF DIRECTORS
Peter Gallagher, president and chief
    executive officer
Alma J. Powell, co-chair
Harris Wofford, co-chair
C. Gregg Petersmeyer, vice chair
Maya Babu, member; team member,
    Youth Partnership
Peter L. Benson, member; president,
    Search Institute
Jean Case, member; chief executive officer,
    Case Foundation
Raymond G. Chambers, member; chairman,
    Amelior Foundation
Robert M. Devlin, member; chairman,
    Curragh Capital Partners
Michelle Engler, member; former first lady of
    Michigan
Jamie Gorelick, member; partner,
    Wilmer, Cutler and Pickering
Daniel Horgan, member; Allegheny County's
    Promise
Michael Jordan, member; SFX
Kathryn Kendall, member; team member,
    Youth Partnerhsip
Cal Ripken Jr., member; founder, Ripken
    Baseball and Cal Ripken, Sr. Foundation
Jin Roy Ryu, member; chairman and chief
    executive officer, Poongsan Corp.
Robert B. Rogers, member; chairman
    emeritus, Ewing Marion Kauffman
    Foundation
Timothy J. Russert, member; moderator of
    "Meet the Press," NBC News

CONTACT INFORMATION
909 N. Washington Street, Suite 400, Alexandria, VA 22314-1556
Phone: (703) 684-4500 • *Fax:* (703) 535-3900
General E-mail: commit@americaspromise.org •
Web site: www.americaspromise.org

Communications Director: Information unavailable
Human Resources Director: Information unavailable

PURPOSE: "America's Promise—The Alliance for Youth is mobilizing people from every sector of American life to build the character and competence of America's youth by fulfilling Five Promises: caring adults; safe places; a healthy start; marketable skills; and opportunities to serve."

CURRENT CONCERNS: Community mobilization • Shared responsibility • Volunteerism • Youth development

METHOD OF OPERATION: Advertisements • Coalition forming • Conferences/seminars • Films/video/audiotapes • Grassroots organizing • Internet (databases, e-mail alerts, Web site) • Internships • Lobbying (grassroots) • Local/municipal affairs • Media outreach • Regional Training Forums

Effectiveness and Political Orientation

"Some local students will get special attention this year, thanks to a national organization that aims to improve the lives of America's youths. America's Promise—The Alliance for Youth chose Charleston's Promise as one of 13 community networks across the country to receive personnel support from the Washington, D.C.-based organization during the next year. The staff members are experts in getting federal grants, working with local elected officials, bringing in business partners, engaging more young people in leadership and decision-making, tracking the number of children who benefit from program efforts as well as other areas, according to Brittany Hoff, director of community communications for America's Promise. The staff also will help Charleston's Promise develop communication strategies, media campaigns and special events to raise public awareness and get parents more involved.

" 'Aside from helping the young people in Charleston, we're going to be looking to Charleston for case studies to develop best practices,' said Chad Tragakis, a spokesman with America's Promise. 'That's going to help us to teach other communities to replicate these efforts.' . . .

"America's Promise was founded by Colin Powell after the Presidents' Summit for America's Future in 1997. Since then, it has created a network of more than 400 national organizations called that make large-scale national commitments and more than 400 local efforts involving community and state organizations across the nation."

(*The Post and Courier* [Charleston, South Carolina], September 4, 2003)

Donald L. Staheli, elder; member; Church of
Christ and Latter-Day Saints
Lance Weaver, member; executive vice
chairman, MBNA America

SCOPE
Information unavailable
Branches: None
Affiliates: None

STAFF
Information unavailable

TAX STATUS
501(c)(3)

FINANCES
Revenue: 2002—$9.9 million; Budget: 2000—
$7.6 million

FUNDING SOURCES
Information unavailable

PAC
None

EMPLOYMENT
Open positions at America's Promise and
application instructions are posted at
http://www.americaspromise.org/about/
jobopps.cfm. Cover letters and resumes can be
mailed to Human Resources, 909 N.
Washington Street, Suite 400, Alexandria, VA
22314. Fax: (703) 535-3905. E-mail:
jobs@americaspromise.org.

INTERNSHIPS
Information unavailable

NEWSLETTERS
The America's Promise Bulletin (biweekly)
Promise Letter (quarterly)

PUBLICATIONS
America's Promise
The Promise Book
Report to the Nation

CONFERENCES
None

"As many as one in four school-age children have vision problems, according to a survey by the American Optometric Association. . . .

"Although pediatricians and schools do routine vision screening, Chou said, many children seem to fall through the cracks when it comes to getting the eye care or eyeglasses they need. That's why he recently signed on with the Vision Service Plan's Sight for Students program.

"Sight for Students provides free comprehensive eye exams, eye care and glasses to children whose parents work but are ineligible for government support and cannot afford the care and glasses their children need. . . .

"Sight for Students became a part of America's Promise—Alliance for Youth organization founded by Secretary of State Colin Powell in 1997, when Powell was an Army general. Since then, the program has provided more than 50,000 youngsters a year with eye care and glasses. Some 18,000 eye doctors across the nation participate in the program, which provided $9 million worth of free eye care last year and has provided $20 million in free eye care services since its inception in 1997.

"The program operates nationally through a network of partnerships with nonprofit organizations such as the YMCA, Boys & Girls Clubs of America, the Children's Health Fund, Head Start, National Council of La Raza and Prevent Blindness America."

(*The San Diego Union-Tribune*, April 6, 2002)

"As part of the industry's most ambitious charitable campaign ever, America's chain drugstores have joined as partners of America's Promise—The Alliance for Youth to develop 'Pharmacies of Promise' across the nation.

"Over a three-year period, the chain pharmacy industry will establish 'Pharmacies of Promise' in every state as part of a national campaign to help America's youth. Participating pharmacies will develop tutoring and mentoring programs, sponsor internships for students, provide health care services and information, and promote health insurance programs for uninsured children.

" 'Our nation's chain pharmacies are joining in this commitment as another way to give back to the communities they serve,' said NACDS President Craig Fuller, who today kicked-off the three-year partnership at an Osco pharmacy here. In addition to announcing the program's scope, Fuller also presented a check for $100,000 to America's Promise officials from the NACDS Charitable Foundation."

(*PR Newswire*, April 19, 2001)

Amnesty International USA (AIUSA)

Established in 1961

DIRECTOR

William F. Schulz, executive director. Schulz was appointed executive director of Amnesty International USA in March 1994. An ordained minister, he came to Amnesty after 15 years with the Unitarian Universalist Association of Congregations, the last 8 as president of the Association. He served on the council of the International Association for Religious Freedom from 1985 to 1993 and has served on the board of many organizations, including People for the American Way and the Planned Parenthood Federation of America. He is a graduate of Oberlin College, holds an M.A. in philosophy from the University of Chicago, and received both an M.A. in theology and a D.Min. degree from Meadville/Lombard Theological School.

BOARD OF DIRECTORS

William F. Schulz, executive director.

SCOPE

More than 1.5 million members, supporters and subscribers in more than 150 countries and territories in every region of the world.
Branches/chapters: 5 regional offices
Affiliates: N / A

STAFF

137 paid staff

TAX STATUS

501(c)(3)

FINANCES

Revenue: 2002—$29.5 million

FUNDING SOURCES

Individual donations, 77%; donated services, 20%; foundation grants, 1%; publications, 1%; other sources, 1%

PAC

None

EMPLOYMENT

Open positions and application instructions at AIUSA are posted at http://www.amnestyusa. org/contact/employment.do. Recruitment activities for regular paid positions in the United States are coordinated through the Human Resources Department in New York. Amnesty International is an Equal Opportunity Employer. Women and minorities encouraged to apply for opportunities that are available.

INTERNSHIPS

Information on internship opportunities is available at http://www.amnestyusa.org/ activist_toolkit/leadershipeducation/

CONTACT INFORMATION

322 8th Avenue, New York, NY 10001
Phone: (212) 807-8400 • *Fax:* (212) 627-1451
General E-mail: aimember@aiusa.org • *Web site:* www.amnesty-usa.org

Communications Director: Information unavailable
Human Resources Director: Information unavailable

PURPOSE: "Amnesty International's mission is to undertake research and action focused on preventing and ending grave abuses of the rights to physical and mental integrity, freedom of conscience and expression, and freedom from discrimination, within the context of our work to promote all human rights."

CURRENT CONCERNS: Death penalty • Detention without charge or trial • "Disappearances" • Extrajudicial executions • Human rights abuses by armed opposition groups • Prisoners of conscience • Torture and ill-treatment • Unfair trials

METHOD OF OPERATION: Congressional testimony • Demonstrations • federal, State, and Grassroots Lobbying • Films/video/audiotapes • Grassroots organizing • International activities • Internet (Web site) • Library/information clearinghouse • Lobbying (federal and grassroots) • Media outreach • Research • Speakers program

Effectiveness and Political Orientation

"Human rights watchdog Amnesty International Japan on Friday called on the Justice Ministry's Immigration Bureau to stop its recently launched service to receive e-mail tips on suspected illegal aliens, saying it promotes racism. The group said in a statement that the Immigration Bureau is 'encouraging reports without any concrete proof.'

"Immigration officials responded by saying the service for informants is 'simply part of measures to computerize' such information. . . .

"Amnesty said the preset options, such as 'causing anxiety' or 'causing a nuisance to the neighborhood,' are unrelated to the offense of staying in Japan illegally and will 'fan aversion and anxiety' toward non-Japanese."

(*Kyodo News,* February 20, 2004)

"The Midwest Regional Office of Amnesty International USA (AIUSA) will be hosting the visit of a human rights delegation from the United Kingdom on Thursday, Feb. 19 and Friday, Feb. 20. The purpose of the visit is to raise awareness about the case of death row inmate Kenny Richey and to focus attention on the arbitrary and unfair nature of the death penalty.

"Members of the delegation . . . Alistair Carmichael, Member of Parliament, who has introduced legislation that would call on the British Prime Minster and other British officials to intervene on the behalf of Mr.

leadershipeducation.html. To apply, send a cover letter and resume to the Amnesty office where you would like to intern.

AIUSA also offers the Ralph J. Bunche Human Rights Fellowship Program. Each year, 1–3 year fellowships are granted to applicants who have demonstrated involvement or leadership at the local level with a traditionally underserved community of color. U.S. fellows work with a program manager or unit manager in one of Amnesty's U.S. offices on projects that are designed by one or more of Amnesty's programs or units. The fellowships begin in September and end in August of every year. Ralph J. Bunche Human Rights fellows receive a stipend and comprehensive insurance benefits for the term of the fellowship. Interested applicants can contact humanresources @aiusa.org for more information.

The Patrick Stewart Scholarship offers a unique opportunity for students to gain practical experience in the field of human rights. To be eligible, students must arrange a summer internship with a human rights organization or design a short-term human rights project to be completed in the United States or abroad. Scholarships can be used for travel, materials, and other expenses and range from $300 to $1800. Applications are available in November and are due in February for the following summer.

For more information, an application, or details on how to set up a project or internship, contact the National Field Program in Amnesty's office in Washington, DC, or visit http://www.amnestyusa.org/patrickstewart/.

NEWSLETTERS
Amnesty Action (quarterly)
Amnesty International Newsletter (monthly)
Internet Dispatch (monthly)

PUBLICATIONS
A.I. Policy Manual
Amnesty International Handbook
Amnesty International Report 2000
Business and Human Rights in a Time of Change
Collateral Damage or Unlawful Killings?
The Crackdown on the Falun Gong
Crimes of War
Death Penalty and Torture
Enduring Spirit
Espanol
Failing the Future
Fair Trials Manual
Forsaken Cries: The Story of Rwanda
*Global Trade, Labour and Human Rights
   Healthy Professionals*
The Human Price of Oil
*Human Rights Abuses of Women Trafficked
   From Countries of the Former Soviet Union
   into Israel's Sex Industry*
Human Rights: Is It Any of Your Business?
A Justice System Without Justice
Kosovo: The Evidence
*The Legacy of Human Suffering in a Forgotten
   War*
*A Life in the Balance: The Case of Mumia
   Abu-Jamal*

Richey with Governor Taft and U.S. President George Bush . . . Kate Allen, Director, Amnesty International UK, has been actively campaigning on behalf of Mr. Richey and working to generate international attention for his case . . . Nancy Bothne, Director, Midwest Regional Office, represents Amnesty International USA's activities and programs . . ."

(*U.S. Newswire*, February 18, 2004)

"In the next couple of weeks, pineapples, mangos and grapes bearing 'Fair Trade Certified' stickers will start hitting scores of supermarkets nationwide, part of a broader movement to make shoppers feel good about themselves and the food they are buying. The labels mean that workers in poor countries received higher-than-usual wages and other benefits. Along with other new buzzwords such as 'certified sustainable' and 'responsibly traded,' Fair Trade Certified food products are being embraced with surprising speed by some of the nation's biggest food marketers . . .

"For years, that word, 'organic,' summed up everything politically correct in food. It became a catch phrase for all kinds of alternative cuisine—everything from carrots grown in a commune, to healthy granola. But now that the term organic is strictly defined and regulated by the government, alternative food producers are looking for new ways to express the difference in their products.

"Many initiatives got their start at nonprofit or specialized retailers. Amnesty International USA, the human-rights group, for example, has long sold in its catalogs only products it feels are 'fairly traded' and not produced in countries it feels are unfair to workers, like China. Morally pure marketing like this is also partly an outgrowth of the growing clamor about free trade and the effects of globalization on third-world workers. The growth of the grassroots movement, combined with the success of the Fair Trade movement in Europe . . . is now persuading mainstream companies to get on board."

(*The Wall Street Journal*, February 17, 2004)

"Terror suspects held at the military prison at Guantanamo Bay, Cuba, will be given the chance to appeal their detentions to a new panel to determine if they represent an ongoing threat to the United States, Defense Secretary Donald H. Rumsfeld said Friday. Rumsfeld said the panel would hear cases annually to decide whether the suspects remain a threat or could be released. . . .

" 'In most wars this country has fought, enemy combatants are detained through the duration of the conflict, as is recognized under the rights of the laws of war,' Rumsfeld said. 'There can be hardly any doubt that the conflict has not ended.'

"The Bush administration's policy involving the Guantanamo detainees has garnered criticism from human rights groups and some foreign governments who question the detainees' treatment and the lack of trials or access to lawyers. One human rights group called the panel proposal 'a sham.'

" 'It's not justice to jail a man without charge for years, then offer him a chance to protest his innocence tarred by a presumption of guilt,' said William F. Schulz, executive director of Amnesty International USA. 'No jerry-rigged procedures can justify the shredding of the Geneva Conventions and violations of fundamental due process rights.' "

(*Associated Press Newswires*, February 13, 2004)

Regularly publishes country reports and other documents on human rights issues around the world; also offers a selection of posters, videos, and calendars.

CONFERENCES

General Meeting (annual, in a city where AIUSA has a regional office)

"The U.S. military released its three youngest prisoners, boys thought to be between 13 and 15 years old, from Guantanamo Bay, Cuba.

"They were returned to their home country, which the U.S. Defense Department did not identify. All three were captured in Afghanistan and brought to the military's prison for terrorist suspects in February 2003, said Lt. Col. Pamela Hart, a military spokeswoman at Guantanamo. . . .

"Human rights groups have long criticized their detention, saying the long separation from their families would hurt the boys.

" 'The detention of children as "enemy combatants" and their interrogation without even the basic safeguards to which they were entitled was a significant violation of human rights,' William F. Schulz, executive director of Amnesty International USA, said in a statement. 'The release of these children is long overdue, but does not let the U.S. off the hook for continued violations of the rights of hundreds of other detainees.'

"Vienna Colucci, an international justice specialist with Amnesty, said the boys had the right to see their parents and attorneys."

(*Associated Press Newswires,* January 29, 2004)

ANSER Institute for Homeland Security

Established in 2001

DIRECTOR

Asha M. George, managing director. George directs planning and policy development, oversees technical and research activities, and implements global and domestic projects in support of the institute's mission to strengthen homeland security in the global community. George came to the institute from the Nuclear Threat Initiative (NTI), where she developed, monitored, and evaluated biological program activities in support of the NTI mission to reduce the threat of weapons of mass destruction. George was director of emergency preparedness and response at the Association of Public Health Laboratories and director of the National Coalition for Adult Immunization. She also worked with the Association of Schools of Public Health as an MPH program analyst, coordinated the Federal Employees Worksite Wellness program and the Community Epidemiology Work Group on Substance Abuse for the University of Hawaii, and supervised a nationwide health information services program for the Agency for Health Care Policy and Research. She had a distinguished career in the U.S. Army as a military intelligence officer and as a paratrooper. Her service in Saudi Arabia and Iraq during Operations Desert Shield and Storm earned her eight military decorations and official commendations. George holds a doctorate in public health from the University of Hawaii at Manoa, a master's of science in public health from the University of North Carolina at Chapel Hill, and an undergraduate degree from Johns Hopkins University.

BOARD OF DIRECTORS

Jay C. Davis, Ph.D., chair; former director, Defense Threat Reduction Agency
Ruth David, Ph.D., member; president and chief executive officer, ANSER
Harold W. Gehman, admiral, member; former commander-in-chief, Joint Forces Command
John Hamre, Ph.D., member; president and chief executive officer, Center for Strategic and International Studies
Phil E. Lacombe, member; president, Information Infrastructure Protection Center, Veridian
Joshua Lederberg, Ph.D., member; Nobel laureate, microbiology
Judith Miller, member; former general counsel to secretary of defense
Michael C. Moriarty, Ph.D., member; vice president of research, Auburn University

CONTACT INFORMATION

2900 South Quincy Street, Suite 800, Arlington, VA 22206
Phone: (703) 416-3597 • *Fax:* (703) 416-3343
General E-mail: Institute.Director@anser.org •
Web site: www.homelandsecurity.org

Communications Director: Alan Capps
(703) 416-4745 • alan.capps@anser.org
Human Resources Director: Robert Walls
(703) 416-3358 • robert.walls@anser.org

PURPOSE: "Build the intellectual foundation for homeland security in the global community."

CURRENT CONCERNS: Domestic and international security • Homeland security

METHOD OF OPERATION: Conferences/seminars • Congressional testimony • Congressional voting analysis • Educational foundation • International activities • Internet database • Internet electronic bulletin boards • Web site • Internships • Legislative/regulatory monitoring (federal and state) • Library services open to the public • Media outreach • Professional development services • Research • Speakers program • Technical assistance • Training

Effectiveness and Political Orientation

"British Airways yesterday canceled flights from London to the capitals of the United States and Saudi Arabia, the latest in a series of international flights disrupted over security concerns. . . .

"Washington has been vigilant since Homeland Security Secretary Tom Ridge declared a 'high alert' two weeks ago, citing intelligence that Al Qaeda might be planning to hijack foreign airlines and crash them into populated areas and high-risk industrial sites in the United States.

"A spokeswoman for the Department of Homeland Security, Rachael Sunbarger, said yesterday that the information the United States shared with the British government involved a specific threat to the Washington-bound flight from London. . . .

"Retired Army colonel David McIntyre, deputy director of the ANSER Institute for Homeland Security, said he thinks the recent security steps were based on 'some pretty strong evidence,' but officials need to offer a better explanation for their actions or risk undermining public confidence in the terror alert system.

'We should ask questions,' McIntyre said. 'How much did we know and when did we know it?'

"Still, McIntyre added: 'The government is in a terrible dilemma. If nothing happens, then it appears that they overreacted. If something does happen, they appear inept and incompetent. The bad news is you never know when you're successful.' "

(*The Boston Globe,* January 3, 2004)

"As the nation approaches the height of the holiday season under its fourth high alert for terrorism this year, recent studies question how prepared the government is to meet the continuing threat.

"A federal commission concluded last week that the momentum toward securing the nation 'appears to have waned' since the Sept. 11, 2001, terrorist attacks.

"Another report, by a national health advocacy group, warned that states 'are only modestly better prepared' to respond to bioterrorism and other major health emergencies, despite an infusion of nearly $2 billion in federal funds. . . .

"The Department of Homeland Security disputes those conclusions. 'Those who go to work every single day concerned about some aspect of homeland security have only since 9/11 gotten stronger and more focused on their mission,' Homeland Security Secretary Tom Ridge said Monday. . . .

"Independent terrorism experts say it is difficult to assess exactly how much the security situation has improved in the two years since the terrorist attacks on the World Trade Center and the Pentagon.

" 'I think we have certainly become better prepared. But the thing about preparedness is we have so many different elements, so many different factors, it's difficult to say how prepared is prepared enough,' said Asha M. George, managing director of the ANSER Institute for Homeland Security, a research group based in suburban Washington.

"Just days before the federal government raised the national terrorism alert level to orange, or high, an advisory panel established by Congress voiced 'serious concern about the current state of homeland security efforts.' "

(*The San Diego Union-Tribune,* December 24, 2003)

"Seattle witnessed the nation's homeland-security apparatus at work last week as police officers and firefighters responded to a pretend bomb blast, all under the scrutiny of federal officials who devised the terror game.

"But . . . a larger question looms: Who calls the shots when protecting the homeland?

"The real challenge in coming months, several experts say, will be ironing out the role of the federal government and how it relates to the cities and states that carry out the war on terrorism. . . .

" 'This will work effectively only if we understand that the federal government has no first responders,' said Homeland Security Secretary Tom Ridge in an interview Friday. 'We're never going to be in control.' . . .

" 'It can't all be decided by a czar in Washington, D.C.,' he said. 'People ought to make some of their own decisions, and if they make a mistake, they make a mistake.'

"Seattle Police Chief Gil Kerlikowske agrees. . . .

"In the coming months, Kerlikowske said, the national alert system will have to be worked out so law-enforcement officials really understand what the different levels mean to their jurisdictions. . . .

"There are legal considerations as well. The Homeland Security Department cannot constitutionally assume control over a local police department. . . .

"David McIntyre, deputy director of the Washington, D.C.-based Anser Institute for Homeland Security a nonprofit research organization established a few months before the Sept. 11 terrorist attacks offers a third option for negotiating between local control and federal mandates.

"He envisions a time when homeland security becomes like the federal highway program. Just as the U.S. Department of Transportation determines the freeway route and the thickness of the blacktop, the security agency would decide how to guard against a biological or chemical attack. Deterring smaller incidents, or fixing potholes, would fall to police and fire departments, he said.

"But it could be a decade before the relationship among the cities, states and federal government is finally sorted out. And even if the Homeland Security Department and its local partners are successful in preventing terrorism, someone is likely to grumble it wasn't done properly, McIntyre said.

"'Success in fighting the war against terrorism is someone standing in their garage and saying, 'What am I doing with all this duct tape? Nothing happened!'"

(*The Seattle Times,* May 18, 2003)

"Twenty months after the 2001 terrorist attacks, America's spy agencies still don't share troves of valuable threat information with each other, and rarely provide intelligence to state and local authorities on the front lines in the war on terrorism, according to government officials and private specialists.

". . . the Bush administration plans to open a new intelligence clearinghouse next week at CIA headquarters. But critics assert that the CIA's secretive agency culture will continue to leave federal law enforcement authorities and local first responders in the dark. . . .

"CIA officials acknowledge that gap but insist the new clearinghouse will provide 'actionable' intelligence quickly to those who can most effectively react to it. . . .

"The new clearinghouse, which will open May 1 with an initial staff of 60 analysts from across the government, is designed to provide a single point of contact for the amalgam of American intelligence and law enforcement agencies engaged in the war on terrorism.

"The clearinghouse is also intended to close a yawning information gap between Washington and local authorities, who said that they are kept out of the loop about terrorist threats. . . .

". . . many intelligence officers fear that by sharing sensitive information with local police, fire, and emergency response personnel, they will release too much information about intelligence gathering operations.

"Retired Colonel David McIntyre, deputy director of the ANSER Institute for Homeland Security and former dean of the National Defense University, said local law enforcement agencies are useful as 'reconnaissance troops, collecting information in accordance with indicators provided from the feds.' But he worried about local authorities securing too much intelligence information from Washington.

"Local law enforcement agencies 'solve murders, break robbery rings, . . . and they tend to see the new connection with federal intelligence people as a new source for their analysis,' he said. 'But that is not the way a national-level security issue is addressed.'"

(*The Boston Globe,* April 25, 2003)

Anti-Defamation League

Established in 1913

DIRECTOR

Abraham H. Foxman, national director. Foxman joined the Anti-Defamation League in 1965 and was named national director in 1987. Born in 1940, Foxman was saved from the Nazis by his Polish nanny who baptized him and raised him as a Catholic until the end of the war when his parents returned. He and his parents immigrated to New York in 1950 where he earned a B.A. from City College of the City University of New York and a J.D. from New York University School of Law. A world renowned leader in the fight against anti-Semitism, racism, bigotry, and discrimination, Foxman is the author of *Never Again? The Threat of the New Anti-Semitism.* He received the Townsend Harris Medal from the City College of New York Alumni Association (1994). He was co-recipient of the first Martin Luther King Jr. and Donald R. Mintz Freedom and Justice Award from Dillard University (1997). He also received Austria's highest honor, the Grand Decoration of Honor in Gold (2001).

BOARD OF DIRECTORS

Barbara B. Balser, national chair
Abraham H. Foxman, national director
Alvin J. Rockoff, vice chair
Gerald Stempler, vice chair
Robert H. Naftaly, treasurer
Murray Koppelman, assistant treasurer
I. Barry Mehler, secretary
Lesley Israel, assistant secretary
Meyer Eisenberg
James Grosfeld
Irwin Hochberg
Judith Krupp
Cynthia Marks
Lawrence J. Miller

SCOPE

Membership: nonmembership organization
Branches/chapters: 30 U.S. regional offices; international offices in Israel and Moscow
Affiliates: ADL: A World of Difference Institute; Anti-Defamation League Foundation; Braun Holocaust Institute; Hidden Child Foundation/ADL; Leon and Marilyn Klinghoffer Memorial Foundation of the Anti-Defamation League; William and Naomi Gorowitz Institute on Terrorism and Extremism

STAFF

400 total—200 professional; 200 support

TAX STATUS

501(c)(3)

CONTACT INFORMATION

823 United Nations Plaza, New York, NY 10017
Phone: (212) 885-7700 • *Fax:* (212) 885-5881
General E-mail: webmaster@adl.org • *Web site:* www.adl.org

Communications Director: Myrna Shinbaum
(212) 885-7700 • adlmedia@adl.org
Human Resources Director: Ronni Meltzer
(212) 885-7904 • rmeltzer@adl.org

PURPOSE: "The immediate object of the League is to stop, by appeals to reason and conscience and, if necessary, by appeals to law, the defamation of the Jewish people. Its ultimate purpose is to secure justice and fair treatment to all citizens alike and to put an end forever to unjust and unfair discrimination against and ridicule of any sect or body of citizens."

CURRENT CONCERNS: Anti-bias education & training • Anti-Semitism • Arab-Israeli relations • Civil liberties • Discrimination • Extremism • Hate crimes • Hate in cyberspace • Holocaust education • Interfaith relations • Israel • Separation of church and state • Terrorism

METHOD OF OPERATION: Advertisements • Awards program (Courage to Care Award, Distinguished Statesman Award, Hubert H. Humphrey First Amendment Freedoms Prize, Joseph Prize for Human Rights, Klinghoffer Award, Norman Newhouse Human Relations Communications Award) • Coalition forming • Conferences/seminars • Congressional testimony • Curriculum development • Exhibits • Films/videos • International activities • Internet (Web site) • Internships • Legislative/regulatory monitoring (federal and state) • Library/information clearinghouse • Litigation • Media outreach • Monitoring of extremist groups • Polling • Research • Speakers program • Training and technical assistance (A Campus of Difference, A Workplace of Difference, A World of Difference, A Community of Difference)

Effectiveness and Political Orientation

"The Anti- Defamation League (ADL) commends law enforcement and intervening parents for their immediate response to the potential horrifying incident at Laguna Creek High School on Tuesday.

"Education Director of the Sacramento ADL, Marielle Tsukamoto comments, 'This potential incident demonstrates the critical need to deal with bullying and hate crime issues in the Sacramento region.'

"The Anti-Defamation League has on-going programs for youth that deal with anti-bullying, hate crime and discrimination issues. These programs focus on making youth aware of the critical issues on campus, and focus on understanding the importance of speaking out against hate before it is allowed to foster.

FINANCES
Budget: 2004—$49 million; 2003—$53 million
Revenue: 2002—$51 million

FUNDING SOURCES
Private contributions

PAC
None

EMPLOYMENT
Job openings are posted on the ADL Web site, www.adl.org. ADL offers administrative, accounting, information technology, and printing positions. Resumes and other employment materials should be sent to Director, human resources, Anti-Defamation League, 823 United Nations Plaza, New York, NY 10017. Phone: (212) 885-7700. Fax: (212) 885-5862.

INTERNSHIPS
ADL offers various internships, both paid and unpaid, of varying durations, in the areas of marketing, civil rights/legal affairs, the Middle East, and education. Eligibility requirements vary. Internship opportunities are posted on the ADL Web site at www.adl.org.

NEWSLETTERS
ADL on the Frontline (periodic)
The Hidden Child Newspaper (periodic)
Interfaith Connections (periodic)
Law Enforcement Bulletin (biannual)
Terrorism Update (periodic)
Audit of Anti-Semitic Incidents (annual)
Also publishes regional newsletters

PUBLICATIONS
The following is a list of sample publications:
Anatomy of Anti-Israel Incitement: Jenin, World Opinion, and the Massacre That Wasn't
Audit of Anti-Semitic Incidents (annual)
Campus Kit: Countering Anti-Semitism, Racism and Extremist Propaganda
Combating Extremism in Cyberspace
Danger: Extremism—the Major Vehicles and Voices on America's Far-Right Fringe
Deafening Hate: The Revival Resistance Records
Explosion of Hate: The Growing Danger of the National Alliance
Extremism in America: A Guide
Feminism Perverted: Extremist Women on the World Wide Web
From the Prisons to the Streets: The Nazi Low Riders Emerge in California Hate Crime Laws
Global Anti-Semitism Source Book, Excerpts from the Global Anti-Semitism Conference, Oct 31–Nov 1, 2002, Countering Suicide Terrorism
Hitler's Apologists: The Anti-Semitic Propaganda of Holocaust "Revisionism"
A New Millennium: Christian and Jewish Reflections
A Parents' Guide to Hate on the Internet
Poisoning the Web: Hatred Online
The Prejudice Book
Prejudice, You Can Beat It: 101 Ways to Make Your Community a Prejudice Free Zone

"The Anti-Defamation League, founded in 1913, is the world's leading organization fighting anti-Semitism and discrimination through programs and services that counteract hatred, prejudice, and bigotry."
(*U.S. Newswire,* February 11, 2004)

"Rear Adm. John Crommelin was one of five Alabama brothers known as the 'Fightin Crommelins' for their World War II exploits, with a Navy ship now named in their honor.

"But Crommelin also was a fierce anti-Semite and segregationist—a fact critics were quick to remember when he was inducted posthumously into the Alabama Military Hall of Honor recently.

"Crommelin, once considered one of the Navy's top pilots, made claims that a 'communist-Jewish conspiracy' was behind racial integration and that segregationist Alabama Gov. George Wallace was too soft on blacks.

"Opponents say Crommelin's induction into the state-supported hall was an insult to those who remember his comments of the 1950s and '60s.

" 'This is not a man who you would just consider a sign of the times,' said Deborah Lauter, regional director of the Anti-Defamation League in Atlanta. 'He was a leader in the hate movement.' . . .

"In Alabama, Crommelin became known as an outspoken segregationist with anti-Semitic views. He charged that Jews wanted to create a 'copper-colored' race of slaves and wipe out Christianity so they could rule the world from Israel and the United Nations, according to material gathered by the Anti-Defamation League. 'He would use his Navy background to lend credence to what he was saying,' Lauter said. . . ."
(*Houston Chronicle,* February 8, 2004)

"Two Jewish organizations and the NAACP yesterday criticized Garfield High School and the Seattle School District for how they handled a drama teacher's concerns that she may be the target of hate crimes.

"The teacher, who is Jewish, told police she found a swastika drawn in the school's theater in late November and, later that day, a dead ferret hanging in the room. A week later, she found a noose hanging in the same area. . . .

"Garfield Principal Susan Ders would not discuss details of the case yesterday, saying it was under investigation. But she said she launched an investigation immediately after administrators learned about the incidents. . . .

"But the Seattle branch of the National Association for the Advancement of Colored People, the Anti-Defamation League, the American Jewish Committee and some Garfield parents contend school and district officials failed to treat the incidents as seriously as they should have.

" 'The school actually began to follow through with some of the actions we had requested,' said Sue Stengel, an attorney for the Anti-Defamation League. 'We appreciate what they did, and we recognize their good intentions, but we felt their actions fell a bit short.'

"The letter sent home to parents, she said, didn't explicitly say such behavior will not be tolerated and will be punished severely."
(*The Seattle Times,* January 17, 2004)

"Jewish advocacy groups led an avalanche of sharp criticism yesterday against two potential television ads that compare President Bush to Adolf Hitler and were posted on a Web site run by MoveOn.org.

Public Libraries: A New Forum for Extremists
Religion in the Public Schools: Guidelines for a
Growing and Changing Phenomenon
Also publishes videos, posters, and
educational materials.

CONFERENCES
National Commission (annual)
National Youth Leadership Mission (annual)
Washington Leadership Conference (annual)

"The Simon Wiesenthal Center, the Anti-Defamation League and the American Jewish Congress said the ads were beyond the pale of political discussion. Rep. Eric Cantor, Virginia Republican, called them 'hate-mongering.'

" 'Certainly myself, as an American and as a Jew, I'm disgusted by the casual use of Hitler by liberal Democrats and groups such as MoveOn.org,' said Mr. Cantor, the House chief deputy majority whip.

" 'To compare any American president, much less George W. Bush, to Adolf Hitler, cheapens the sacrifice of millions of lives that have been lost by this country over its history and really denigrates the efforts by the American military,' Mr. Cantor said."

(*The Washington Times,* January 6, 2004)

Arab American Institute

Established in 1985

DIRECTOR

James J. Zogby, president. A co-founder and chair of the Palestine Human Rights Campaign in the late 1970s, Zogby later co-founded and served as president of Save Lebanon, Inc. In 1984, Zogby was vice chair and deputy campaign manager for fundraising of the Jesse Jackson for President Campaign. In 1993, he was asked by Vice President Gore to lead Builders for Peace, an American private-sector committee to promote investment in the West Bank and Gaza. Zogby was appointed to the Democratic National Committee in 1994 and was elected a co-convener of the National Democratic Ethnic Coordinating Committee, an umbrella organization of Democratic Party leaders of European and Mediterranean descent. A lecturer and scholar on Middle East issues, he appears frequently on television and radio and writes a weekly column on politics for the major newspapers of the Arab world. Zogby received his doctorate from Temple University's department of religion.

BOARD OF DIRECTORS

James J. Zogby, director and president
John Zogby, director and vice president; president and chief executive officer, Zogby International, Utica, NY
Helen Samhan, director and secretary; executive director of the Arab American Institute Foundation, Washington, DC
Jean Abinader, director and treasurer; president and chief executive officer, IdeaCom, Bethesda, MD
George Salem, director; partner, Akin, Gump, Strauss, Hauer & Feld, Washington, DC

SCOPE

Information unavailable
Branches/chapters: 12 regional councils—Illinois, Michigan, Mid Atlantic, Midwest, National Capital Area, New England, Ohio, Pacific Northwest, Pennsylvania, Southeast, South Central, and Southwest
Affiliate: Arab American Leadership Council

STAFF

15 total—10 professional; 5 support; plus 5 interns and 4 part-time field organizers

TAX STATUS

501(c)(4)

FINANCES

Revenue: 2002—$870,000; 2001—$650,000
Budget: 2000—$1 million

FUNDING SOURCES

Individual contributions, 75%; conferences and meetings, 10%; grants, 10%; publications 5%

CONTACT INFORMATION

1600 K Street, NW, Suite 601, Washington, DC 20006
Phone: (202) 429-9210 • *Fax:* (202) 429-9214
General E-mail: aai@aaiusa.org • *Web site:* www.aaiusa.org

Communications Director: Jennifer Salan, media director
(202) 429-9210, ext. 21 • jsalan@aaiusa.org
Human Resources Director: Dianne Davidson
(202) 429-9210 • ddavidson@aaiusa.org

PURPOSE: "The Arab American Institute Foundation was formed to inform and educate the public about the role of the Arab American community in American society with a goal of promoting fuller and deeper public understanding of Arab American contributions and concerns. AAIF developed an educational and PSA campaign to challenge stereotypes and hate crimes following the Sept. 11 tragedy."

CURRENT CONCERNS: Arab American civil/political rights • Arab American electoral participation • Demographics and census 2000 • Ethnic/race relations in urban centers • Immigration reform • Middle East peace process

METHOD OF OPERATION: Coalition forming • Conferences/seminars • Congressional testimony • Congressional voting analysis • Direct action • Electoral politics (Arab American Democratic and Republican Clubs, Arab American Leadership Council) • Grassroots organizing • Initiative/referendum campaigns • International activities • Internet (Web site) • Library/information clearinghouse • Lobbying (state and grassroots) • Local/municipal affairs • Media outreach • Polling • Research • Speakers program • Telecommunications services (databases, mailing lists) • Training and technical assistance • Voter registration • Voting records

Effectiveness and Political Orientation

"Palestinian organizations are refusing to accept U.S. foreign aid this year, rather than sign a pledge promising that the money will not be used to support terrorism.

" 'This requirement is a worldwide requirement, not just for Palestinians,' said Portia Palmer, a spokesman for the U.S. Agency for International Development (USAID). 'The majority of the [nongovernmental organizations] worldwide have signed it.'

"The Palestinian Non-Governmental Organization's Network (PNGO), an umbrella organization comprised of 92 Palestinian aid groups, is urging its members to refuse to sign the pledge. . . .

"James Zogby, president of the Arab American Institute, said that the refusal to sign the pledge should not be seen as support for terrorism, rather that in Palestinian society it is politically expedient to reject the funds than endure the tremendous political pressure they will face for signing the pledge.

PAC
None

EMPLOYMENT
Information unavailable

INTERNSHIPS
The Arab American Institute offers paid internship positions to full- and part-time students, graduate students and recent college graduates. The internship program is active throughout the year, with openings during the spring, summer and fall semesters. Students must be able to work at least six consecutive weeks for a minimum of 20 hours per week.

Internship availability and contact information are available at http://www.aaiusa.org/for_students.htm#internships. Contact Dianne Davidson at Arab American Institute, 1600 K Street, NW, Suite 601, Washington, DC 20006. Phone: (202) 429-9210. Fax: (202) 429-9214. E-mail: ddavidson@aaiusa.org.

NEWSLETTERS
Countdown (electronic, weekly)
Issues (quarterly newsletter about Arab American political work)
Washington Watch (electronic, weekly)

PUBLICATIONS
American Voters and Mideast Peace
Arab Americans: Making a Difference (brochure)
Arab Americans Today: A Demographic Profile of the Arab American Community
The Department of Justice and the Civil Rights of Arab Americans
The Emerging Majority: American Voters and Palestinian Rights in the 1990s
Empowerment
The Financing of U.S. Congressional Elections by Pro-Israel PACs
Life, Liberty and the Pursuit of Happiness: A Three-Decade Journey in the Occupied Territories
New Thinking for Israeli-Palestinian Peace
The 105th Congress and Middle East Peace
A Plan That Works Well: A Political Blueprint for Arab Americans
Preserving America's Freedoms: The Omnibus Counterterrorism Act of 1995 vs. the Bill of Rights
Profiles on the Middle East Position of the 1992 Presidential Candidates
Roster of Arab Americans in Public Service and Political Life
The State of the Middle East Policy Debate: Changing Public Opinion, An Emerging Partisan Split, and the Positions of the Presidential Candidates of 2000
Statements of Major Churches and Religious Institutions on the Question of Jerusalem
Surveillance and Defamation
2000 Voter Guides from Key States

CONFERENCES
National Leadership Conference (annual), Statewide Leadership Meetings

" 'This is not clearly understood in the United States,' said Mr. Zogby. 'The idea of providing no 'material support' is such a broad brush stroke, it compromises the ability of the humanitarian organizations to function.'

"He said making Palestinian organizations judge who is and who is not a terrorist is a prescription for creating civil war in the Gaza Strip and West Bank."

(*The Washington Times,* January 8, 2004)

"Marking a historic change in how America will now treat foreign visitors, the United States on Monday began an unprecedented effort to track people coming here on visas in an aggressive move aimed at deterring terrorism.

"About 24 million international travelers each year will be fingerprinted and photographed—shaping their first impression of the United States—in the government's arduous struggle to nab potential terrorists before they strike. . . .

"Critics of the new program, called the U.S. Visit and Immigrant Status Indicator Technology, predicted it would not scare away terrorists. . . .

"Many leaders in the Arab-American community dismissed the new security regimen as ineffective.

" 'We don't know who the terrorists are, so getting fingerprints isn't going to help,' said James Zogby, president of the Arab American Institute in Washington. 'It won't pop up someone like (Sept. 11 hijacker) Mohammad Ata,' the leader of the terrorists who was in the U.S. legally.

" 'Osama bin Laden—we don't have a fingerprint of him,' Zogby added.

"Some Arab-Americans said ordinary visitors were the most likely to suffer.

"Opponents also feared the moves would mark the first step toward more protectionist measures aimed at safeguarding U.S. borders, resulting in unfair treatment of certain communities."

(*Chicago Tribune,* January 6, 2004)

"An Arab-American group is undertaking an effort to register new voters of Middle Eastern descent and organize a big turnout for the state's Feb. 7 Democratic presidential caucuses.

" 'Our votes are not going to have a free price,' said Imad Hamad, director of the Arab-American Anti-Discrimination Committee of Michigan. 'There is no free Arab-American vote. We see ourselves as part of the process.'

"The ADC plans to use education, storefront offices and door-to-door canvassing to get new voters on the rolls for next month and to turn out the vote in November. . . .

"Jean Abi-Nader, managing director of the Arab American Institute in Washington, said there now is a large enough number of Arab-Americans to demand that presidential candidates—especially Democrats—pay attention to their concerns. 'We had our national leadership conference in Dearborn in October,' Abi-Nader told The Detroit News for a story Friday. 'Eight of the nine presidential candidates were there. They have addressed our issues.' "

(*Associated Press Newswires,* January 2, 2004)

"The Department of Homeland Security said it will end a controversial requirement that men and boys visiting from 25 mostly Arab countries reregister yearly with the government while in the U.S.

"The program was the most contested element of a security initiative adopted after the Sept. 11, 2001, terror attacks. It affected thousands of people, mostly here as students, on business or visiting family members, forcing them to check in with the government for an interview 30 days after entering the U.S. and every year after that. . . .

"The program will continue to collect fingerprints and detailed information about the reason for a person's visit here at the port of entry. . . .

"James Zogby, president of the Arab American Institute, a nonprofit group in Washington, said the program has frightened Muslims, resulted in the deportation of thousands of law-abiding citizens for minor visa violations, deterred scholars from Arab countries from coming to the United States and damaged the U.S.'s standing in the Middle East. 'From the beginning, the program was a mess. It was poorly thought out, it was poorly executed and it put our communities in a terrible bind,' he said."

(*The Wall Street Journal,* December 2, 2003)

Asian American Legal Defense and Education Fund

Established in 1974

DIRECTOR

Margaret Fung, director. Fung is a graduate of New York University Law School, where she was a member of the NYU Law Review, a Root-Tilden Scholar, and an Arthur Garfield Hays Civil Liberties Fellow. She previously held a judicial clerkship in the U.S. Court of Appeals for the Second Circuit. Fung was appointed to serve on the New York State Commission on Constitutional Revision and the Mayor's Task Force on Police/Community Relations. She serves on the boards of directors of Common Cause, the New York Civil Liberties Union, and the National Committee for Responsive Philanthropy.

BOARD OF DIRECTORS

Harsha Murthy, president
Denley Chew, vice president and treasurer
Joan Washington, secretary
Karen Sauvigne, executive committee
    member
Sameer Ashar
Irene Chang
Nicholas V. Chen
Vivian Cheng-Khanna
Jack Greenberg
Grace Y. Hwang
Jinsoo H. Kim
Peter D. Lederer
Shirley Lung
Philip Tajitsu Nash
Ayaz R. Shaikh
Michael Shen
Sumantra Tito Sinha
Sung-Hee Suh
Ko-Yung Tung
Susan Chong Wong
Margaret Y. K. Woo
Gail J. Wright-Sirmans

SCOPE

Members: Declined to comment
Branches/chapters: None
Affiliates: Public Interest Law Center

STAFF

16 total—13 professional, 3 support;
approximately 5 interns

TAX STATUS

501(c)(3)

FINANCES

Revenue: 2004—$1.4 million; 2003—
$1.2 million; 2002—$1.7 million

FUNDING SOURCES

Foundation, 40%; corporate, 23%; individual
donors, 9%; special events, 28%

CONTACT INFORMATION

99 Hudson Street, 12th Floor, New York, NY 10013-2869
Phone: (212) 966-5932 • *Fax:* (212) 966-4303
General E-mail: info@aaldef.org • *Web site:* www.aaldef.org

Communications Director: None
Human Resources Director: None

PURPOSE: "AALDEF, founded in 1974, is the first nonprofit organization on the East Coast to protect and promote the civil rights of Asian Americans through litigation, advocacy and community education. AALDEF believes that all Americans should have equal access to the legal system, regardless of their race, ethnicity, immigration status or English language ability."

CURRENT CONCERNS: Affirmative action • Economic justice for workers • Elimination of Anti-Asian violence • Immigration and immigrants' rights • Language access to services • Youth rights • Educational equity • Police misconduct • Voting rights

METHOD OF OPERATION: Awards program • Coalition forming • Congressional testimony • Demonstrations • Direct action • Grassroots organizing • Information clearinghouse • Internet (E-mail alerts) • Internships • Legal assistance • Legislative/regulatory monitoring (federal and state) • Litigation • Lobbying (federal, state, and grassroots) • Local/municipal affairs • Mailing lists • Media outreach • Professional development services • Research • Speakers program • Telecommunications services (mailing lists) • Training and technical assistance • Training and technical assistance • Voter surveys

Effectiveness and Political Orientation

"For Belayet Hossain and his family, the promise of America will most likely end on Feb. 19.

"Like thousands of others, Mr. Hossain, a baker who lives in Kensington, Brooklyn, was picked up for violating his visa under a controversial aspect, now defunct, of a 'special registration' program. This program, started in November 2002, required men from North Korea and 24 mostly Muslim countries to register in person with the federal government. Mr. Hossain registered last April.

"Since then, his world has been a nightmarish combination of bad luck, bad timing and, to him, incomprehensible bureaucracy. As a result, barring a last-minute reprieve, he will soon be bound for Bangladesh, his homeland, even though his application for a green card is being processed. . . .

"LAST week, Sin Yen Ling, an attorney at the Asian American Legal Defense and Education Fund, agreed to take Mr. Hossain's case, and she plans to file the motion to reopen it tomorrow. The judge will decide whether Mr.

Hossain may remain in the country beyond Feb. 19, but Ms. Ling thinks Mr. Hossain has a good chance of getting a little more time."

(*The New York Times*, February 8, 2004)

"A coalition of legal advocacy groups said Wednesday that a federal program requiring males from 25 predominantly Muslim nations to register with the Immigration and Naturalization Service has resulted in the arrest and deportation of thousands of laborers, students and parents for what are characterized as minor, often technical violations.

The group studied 219 men, of whom about 110 faced deportation, and found that not one has been charged with having a connection to al Qaeda or other terrorist organizations. About 80 percent of the deportees had overstayed their visas or had pending applications for green cards and other papers. About half left behind wives and children in this country.

"Visitors from these 25 countries are required to re-register again this year, a process that begins Thursday. 'This program has resulted in the expulsion of working-class Muslim immigrant communities,' said Saurav Sarkar, an organizer with Asian American Legal Defense and Education Fund here. 'This program has set a very dangerous precedent for what happens when government decides that Muslims are suspect.'"

(*The Washington Post*, November 13, 2003)

"A national Asian-American civil rights group is calling on the city to print multilingual ballots, joining others who say it would help officials prevent the kind of voting irregularities that allegedly occurred in Chinatown during the September preliminary. In an Oct. 17 letter to Nancy Lo, chairwoman of the Boston Election Commission, the staff attorney for the Asian American Legal Defense and Education Fund said ballots in Chinese would help preserve the sanctity of the voting process, which has come under fire amid allegations of improprieties that stemmed from language difficulties during the Sept. 23 preliminary. 'Ideally, the ballots should be translated into Chinese,' wrote Glenn D. Magpantay of the New York- based organization, who also detailed such problems as a dearth of multilingual voting instructions that arose while he served as an election observer during Boston's preliminary.

" 'This will give the voters the ability to cast their vote free from improper influence and in private,' he wrote. Currently, the city provides ballots in English and Spanish, the two languages required under a federal formula based on the minority's population and their proficiency in English. City officials say that if they started voluntarily printing ballots in Chinese, they would have to do them in other languages as well, and that is too costly and cumbersome. 'It's a question about fairness,' Mayor Thomas M. Menino said in a phone interview. 'We have 140 different languages in the city of Boston.'

"As for the cost, Magpantay urged the city to work with the state to tap into federal funds earmarked for making the election process more accessible to voters. 'The ability to vote in private without influence really does outweigh the cost and the complications,' Magpantay said in a phone interview. . . ."

(*The Boston Globe*, November 2, 2003)

"For some citizens, casting a vote in last year's mayoral elections was harder than simply deciding between Mike Bloomberg and Mark Green. Asian-American voters throughout the city faced discrimination at the polls, according to a report issued by a civil rights group.

" 'We found in the last election there were improper demands for identification,' said Glenn Magpantay, staff attorney of the Asian- American Legal Defense and Education Fund. 'Poll workers were hostile towards Asian voters or would not allow Asian voters to get assistance,' he added.

"Instances of discrimination are increasing, Magpantay said, as Asian-Americans—often first-time voters with limited English-speaking ability—turn out in greater numbers on Election Day.

"The group's staff conducted exit polls at 35 voting sites, including locations in Flushing, Elmhurst, Floral Park and Richmond Hill in Queens; Sunset Park and Homecrest in Brooklyn, and Chinatown in Manhattan.

"They talked to voters during the primaries on Sept. 25, the runoffs on Oct. 11 and the general elections on Nov. 6.

"The group learned that Chinese-language ballots used were in tiny print that was impossible for many voters to read."

(*The New York Daily News,* August 18, 2002)

"The decision to add a written essay to the widely taken SAT college entrance exam has raised new questions.

"Can someone from a home where another language is spoken whip out polished prose in English in 25 minutes? If not, does that mean he or she doesn't deserve to go to a competitive college?

" 'The time limit is particularly difficult for kids who have to translate in their head,' says Robert Schaeffer of Fair Test, a Massachusetts-based group that advocates less reliance on standardized tests. In the real world of college, he argues, 'if you write slowly or need a dictionary or have to stay up all night, you can do it.'

"On the other hand, the writing test 'gets at real behavior,' and the ability to speak, read and write in English is key to undergraduate success, says Wayne Camara, vice president for research at the College Board, the New York-based nonprofit that owns the SAT.

". . . ACT is adding an essay for California students only; its officials are still working on the format.

"The point is not to keep English-learners out of college, but to measure their ability to write, says ACT spokesman Ken Gullette. 'They will need the skills, so to measure the skills and to give them information to help them improve their skills is a good thing.' . . .

"But at the Asian American Legal Defense and Education Fund, executive director Margaret Fung has heard from several concerned parents and students.

'It's clear that Asian families want to be sure their children speak English. It just seems as if that (essay requirement) may put people at a disadvantage,' she says."

(*Associated Press Newswires,* July 21, 2002)

Association of Community Organizations for Reform Now (ACORN)

Established in 1970

DIRECTOR
Steve Kest, executive director.

BOARD OF DIRECTORS
Made up of elected members from ACORN's membership

SCOPE
Members: 150,000 individual/family members
Branches/chapters: 750 neighborhood chapters in more than 60 cities
Affiliates: ACORN Housing Corp., ACORN Community Land Association, and the Montana Peoples Alliance

STAFF
Approximately 400

TAX STATUS
Nonprofit (not tax-exempt)

FINANCES
Information unavailable

FUNDING SOURCES
Membership dues, grassroots fundraising, and grants

PAC
ACORN Political Action Committee

EMPLOYMENT
Depends on position; postings appear in various publications depending on where position is located and what the job entails.

INTERNSHIPS
ACORN® regularly has openings for two types of internships. One is working on financial justice issues in its Baltimore office; the other working on communications and media out of its Washington, DC, office. In both cases, ACORN® pays its intern a stipend.

Financial Justice Internship: This internship in Baltimore involves work for ACORN's Financial Justice Center. The job involves learning to research problems related to community reinvestment, predatory mortgage lending, and such practices as rent-to-own deals and payday lending. Duties will include obtaining and sorting data, analyzing lending patterns, researching corporations' practices, and producing popular educational materials. The successful candidate must have good computer skills, good writing and speaking skills, be dependable, have an interest in community development and social justice, and be able to work independently. Familiarity with the Internet and with word processing programs is required. Knowledge of database programs is required. Knowledge of statistics or of Spanish would be an advantage. To

CONTACT INFORMATION
88 3rd Avenue, Brooklyn, NY 11217
Phone: (718) 246-7900 • *Fax:* (718) 246-7939
739 8th Street SE, Washington, DC 20003
Phone: (202) 547-2500 • *Fax:* (202) 546-2483
(ACORN National has offices in Boston, Dallas, Little Rock, New York, New Orleans, Phoenix, and Washington, DC, and local offices throughout the country.)
General E-mail: natexdirect@acorn.org • *Web site:* www.acorn.org

Communications Director: Allison Conyers, communications coordinator (Washington office) • aconyers@acorn.org
Human Resources Director: Branch offices handle their own hiring

PURPOSE: "To organize the unorganized, and to advance the interests of low- to moderate-income families."

CURRENT CONCERNS: Community media • Community reinvestment • Health and environmental justice • Housing development • Jobs and living wages • Neighborhood safety • School reform • Voter registration and participation

METHOD OF OPERATION: Coalition forming • Congressional testimony • Demonstrations • Direct action • Electoral politics • Grassroots organizing • Initiative/referendum campaigns • Internet (Web site) • Legislative/regulatory monitoring (federal) • Lobbying (federal, state, and grassroots) • Local/municipal affairs • Media outreach • Participation in regulatory proceedings (federal) • Research • Training and technical assistance • Voter registration

Effectiveness and Political Orientation

"A U.S. consumer group said on Tuesday it has launched a series of protests against H&R Block Inc., the nation's largest tax preparer, saying its tax refund loans are too expensive and hurt low-income families.

"The Association of Community Organizations for Reform Now (ACORN) said interest rates and fees on refund anticipation loans are too high, typically costing $150 or more to provide money only marginally faster.

"Low-income families, often cash-strapped, end up using a hefty part of their refunds from earned income tax credits, in some cases as much as half, to cover the cost of the loans, according to ACORN.

"Borrowers in many cases get their refund money only about a week sooner than if they waited to get it from the government. . . .

"ACORN members plan demonstrations at H&R Block offices in more than 30 cities around the country, including New York City, Washington, D.C., and Los Angeles, the group said."

(*Reuters News,* January 13, 2004)

apply, contact Valerie Coffin at (410) 752-4103. E-mail: natacornres@acorn.org.

Communications Internship: This internship in Washington, DC, involves work for ACORN's Communications department. The job involves learning to work with reporters. Duties include database research, assisting ACORN members in working with the media, writing short articles for internal publications, assisting local ACORN offices with press plans, making calls to media outlets, sending faxes and E-mails, organizing press clippings, producing press kits, and assisting at press events. As part of the job, it will be necessary to acquire a familiarity with a number of areas ACORN works in, including fighting predatory lending, campaigning for living wage laws, and promoting affordable housing. The successful candidate must have good writing and speaking skills, good computer skills, be dependable, have an interest in community development and social justice, and be able to work independently. Familiarity with the Internet and with word processing programs is required. Knowledge of database programs is desirable. Knowledge of statistics or of Spanish would be an advantage. To apply, E-mail a letter, resume, and short writing sample to Allison Conyers at aconyers@acorn.org.

NEWSLETTERS
ACORN Report (quarterly)
United States of Acorn (quarterly)

PUBLICATIONS
Capital and Communities
Documenting a Disaster
Giving No Credit Where Credit Is Due
No Silver Bullet
No Substitute—An Urgent Call for Trained, Permanent Teachers in Oakland Schools
One Step Forward, Two Steps Back
Secret Apartheid I-III
Stripping the Wealth: An Analysis of Predatory Lending

CONFERENCES
ACORN Leadership School (every summer)
ACORN Legislative and Political Conference (annual)
ACORN National Convention (June 2000)

"The political action group Association of Community Organizations for Reform Now, along with a group of parents and one teacher, is seeking an injunction against the Baltimore school system to stop the more than 700 employee layoffs school officials announced Tuesday.

"The request, filed in Circuit Court yesterday, says the layoffs pose a threat to the quality of education received by the city's 92,000 schoolchildren.

" 'The bottom line is the state has the obligation to fund these schools, and so does the city, and they need to start coming up with the money,' said Mitchell Klein, ACORN's chief organizer."

(*The Baltimore Sun*, November 27, 2003)

"ACORN is the nation's largest community organization of low- and moderate-income families, with more than 150,000 member families organized into 700 neighborhood chapters in 51 cities across the country."

(*Houston Chronicle*, November 27, 2003)

"A large subprime lender that borrowers claimed engaged in predatory lending tactics entered into a settlement yesterday with its borrowers and a large community-rights group.

"Household International Inc., a Prospect Park, Ill.-based subsidiary of HSBC Holding, announced a proposed settlement with a series of borrowers and the Association of Community Organizations for Reform Now (ACORN), a community activist group that filed the suit on behalf of the borrowers in October 2002. The settlement is worth about $100 million of which $72 million will be channeled to a foreclosure avoidance program. The company did not admit wrongdoing.

"The foreclosure avoidance program, which started Oct. 1, is administered by ACORN and Household and aims to help Household borrowers who are at least 60 days late on their mortgage payments.

"Angela Staron, a Chicago-based ACORN spokeswoman, said there are 35,000 borrowers who are 60 days late, with an additional 200 joining those ranks on a daily basis.

"Staron said the settlement means that Household will pay an additional $28 million to be spent on loan counseling and paying some borrower's claims. The terms of the settlement are awaiting the approval of U.S. District Court, Northern District of California."

(*Newsday* [New York City], November 25, 2003)

"ACORN, founded in Little Rock, Ark., in 1970 as an advocacy group for welfare recipients, has chapters in 51 cities. The group has been instrumental in passing local laws to rein in abusive lending, including statutes in Los Angeles and Oakland.

"The group also has had an effect on big national lenders, including Ameriquest Mortgage Co. and Household International Inc. . . .

"When Household International reached an unprecedented $484-million settlement of predatory lending charges last year with state regulators across the country, much of the language was taken from lawsuits filed by ACORN chapters, said Iowa Assistant Atty. Gen. Kathleen Keest, a longtime consumer-protection official involved in crafting the agreement."

(*Los Angeles Times*, May 5, 2003)

The Atlantic Council of the United States (ACUS)

Established in 1961

DIRECTOR

Henry E. Catto, chairman. Catto was elected chairman in January 1999. He has been director of the United States Information Agency (1991–1993); U.S. Ambassador to Great Britain (1989–1991); Assistant Secretary of Defense for Public Affairs and Pentagon Spokesman (1981–1983); U.S. Representative to the United Nations Offices in Geneva (1976–1977); Chief of Protocol, White House and Department of State (1974–1976); U.S. Ambassador to El Salvador (1971–1973); and Deputy Representative to the Organization of American States (1969–1971); He is presently a partner in the insurance firm Catto & Catto. From 1983 to 1989, he was vice chairman and president of Broadcast Group at H&C Communications. He is a graduate of Williams College.

BOARD OF DIRECTORS

Henry E. Catto, chair
Christopher J. Makins, president
Jan M. Lodal, treasurer
Walter B. Slocombe, secretary
Carol Adelman, vice chair
Chas. W. Freeman Jr., vice chair
Roger Kirk, vice chair
Geraldine S. Kunstadter, vice chair
Richard L. Lawson, vice chair
John D. Macomber, vice chair
Jack N. Merritt, vice chair
Virginia A. Mulberger, vice chair
W. DeVier Pierson, vice chair
Paula Stern, vice chair
Ronald P. Verdicchio, vice chair

SCOPE

Members: 2,000 individuals, including 400 academic associates
Branches/Chapters: None
Affiliate: ACUS is a member of Atlantic Treaty Association, an international group with institutions in each NATO and Partnership for Peace country.

STAFF

25 total—plus 12 nonresident senior fellows; 100 volunteers; 12–18 interns per semester

TAX STATUS

501(c)(3)

FINANCES

Budget: 2001—$3.1 million

FUNDING SOURCES

Foundation grants, corporate donations, government contracts, individuals, and publications.

CONTACT INFORMATION

910 17th Street, NW, Suite 1000, Washington, DC 20006
Phone: (202) 463-7226 • *Fax:* (202) 463-7241
General E-mail: info@acus.org • *Web site:* www.acus.org

Communications Director: None
Human Resources Director: None

PURPOSE: "The Atlantic Council promotes constructive U.S. leadership and engagement in international affairs based on the central role of the Atlantic community in meeting the international challenges of the 21st century."

CURRENT CONCERNS: Central Asia • China • Economics, energy and environment • Future role of NATO • Global future of nuclear energy • International security • Transatlantic trade and security issues • U.S.–EU relations and European integration • U.S.–Iranian relations • U.S. relations in the Middle East • U.S.–Russian relations

METHOD OF OPERATION: Conferences/seminars • Educational foundation • Fellowships (Partnership for Peace, Senior Fellows Seminars Series, Senior Fellows Publications Series) • Information clearinghouse • International activities • Internships • Speakers program • Web site

Effectiveness and Political Orientation

". . .(T)he Atlantic Council of the United States (is) a Washington, D.C., non-profit group that promotes U.S. leadership and engagement in international affairs.

"The council is a co-organizer of the Prague (Atlantic) Student Summit. Its goal is to bring students together with top NATO leaders and other experts for dialogue and questions."

(*Omaha World Herald,* November 20, 2002)

"A centuries-old legal concept called 'sovereign immunity' had prevented Americans from suing foreign countries in U.S. courts. Laws enacted in 1996 and 2000, however, have opened the way for a barrage of lawsuits against nations that the State Department says support terrorism: Cuba, Iran, Iraq, Libya, North Korea, Sudan and Syria. Last year's law authorizes the U.S. government to pay damages now—and then try to collect later. . . .

"According to the Treasury's Office of Foreign Assets Control, Iraq has $1.5 billion in assets frozen in the United States. Like Iran's assets, however, it is unlikely they would be tapped. 'If we set that precedent, then foreign governments can attach our assets overseas,' says Elaine Morton, a former State Department official. She wrote a report for the Atlantic Council of the United States, a bipartisan foreign policy group, that recommends repeal of the 1996

EMPLOYMENT
Employment opportunities are listed on the ACUS Web site as they are available.

INTERNSHIPS
The John A. Baker Internship Program offers 10 to 15 volunteer positions during the fall, spring, and summer academic terms. These positions require a strong interest in international affairs and U.S. foreign relations. Applicants should possess some experience in scholarly research, as well as administrative or office experience. Course credit may be arranged through the student's academic institution.

Resumes and academic transcripts, a brief writing sample, two letters of recommendation (either professional or academic), and a short cover letter (including your dates of availability) may be sent to: Internship Coordinator, Atlantic Council of the United States, 910 17th Street, NW, Suite 1000, Washington, DC 20006. Fax: (202) 463-7241. E-mail: Internships@acus.org. Application deadlines are: summer term—March 30, 2004; fall term—June 30, 2004; spring term—November 15, 2004.

NEWSLETTERS
Atlantic Council News (biennial)

PUBLICATIONS
Energy Technology Cooperation for Sustainable Economic Development
Taiwan 2020—Developments in Taiwan to 2020: Implications for Cross Strait Relations and U.S. Policy
United States and China Relations at a Crossroad
The United States and Japan: Cooperative Leadership for Peace and Global Prosperity
U.S. Energy Imperatives for the 1990s
Also publishes bulletins, occasional papers, policy papers, and speeches.

CONFERENCES
Sponsors conferences and seminars on various topics throughout the year; annual awards dinner.

law, 'which is in violation of widely recognized principles of international law' and makes normal relations with Iran even more difficult to achieve."

(*USA Today,* June 14, 2001)

"U.S. missile defense plans would not necessarily destabilize Asia if the United States handles the issue carefully and takes steps to avoid alienating China, according to a study released last week by the Atlantic Council of the United States.

"The nonpartisan Washington-based research institute believes well-developed missile defenses in Asia may prevent instability, though such a policy would require Washington to continue discussing plans in public and consulting closely with key states. Most missile defense systems under development will not be ready for several years, giving U.S. policymakers time to consider various options, according to the report's authors, who include former under secretaries of defense Walter Slocombe and Jacques Gansler as well, as retired Air Force Gen. Michael Carns and C. Richard Nelson, director of the Atlantic Council's program on international security. . .

"To avoid overreaction from Beijing over missile defense, the report recommends the United States engage in nonconfrontational dialogue with mainland authorities at all levels."

(*Inside the Pentagon,* July 17, 2003)

"U.S.-advocated missile defenses need not destabilize Asia, but may not protect South Korea or Taiwan in meaningful ways and could provoke a U.S.-China crisis, a new study released this week says. . . .

"In the study, the Atlantic Council of the United States, a research institute, said 'If it continues to be managed well, the development of missile defenses in Asia need not lead to instability. . . .'

"Most missile defense systems being developed will not be ready for several years and even when deployed, China, the main U.S. rival in Asia, 'should be confident they do not pose a threat to its deterrent capabilities,' the report said.

"Nevertheless, some negative Chinese reaction to U.S. missile defenses is 'unavoidable,' even though the capability of defensive systems under development 'will be very limited' against Chinese missiles, it said.

"Especially if the United States sells Taiwan a missile defense system, this 'would likely set off a major crisis in U.S.-Chinese relations,' the researchers concluded."

(*Reuters News,* July 10, 2003)

"The United States should maintain close contacts with Taiwan's military but should avoid making purely symbolic gestures to the island, such as allowing the Taiwanese president to visit America, a new policy paper says.

"Much of the report—published this month by the private Washington-based Atlantic Council of the United States—focuses on the potentially explosive relationship between Taiwan, China and America.

"Washington has long warned Beijing that it might help defend Taiwan if Chinese leaders act on their long-standing threat to invade the island. Taiwan and China split amid civil war in 1949, and Beijing says the Taiwanese must unify eventually or face war.

"The Atlantic Council paper—'Staying the Course: Opportunities and Limitations in U.S.-China Relations'—said a war in the Taiwan Strait would involve 'incalculable risks and costs to all parties.'

"But the report added, 'It is true that for the United States to stand aside if China launched an unprovoked attack on Taiwan would not only be the abandonment of a loyal, democratic friend, but a terrible blow to U.S. credibility and influence in Asia.'"

(*Associated Press Newswires,* September 11, 2002)

Atlantic Legal Foundation, Inc.

Established in 1977

DIRECTOR

William H. Slattery, president. "Following graduation from Stanford University in 1965, with distinction and Honors in Economics, Slattery received his J.D. degree from Yale Law School. His six-year stint with Simpson Thacher & Bartlett in New York City was interrupted by active duty in Vietnam and Okinawa as a Captain in the United States Army. He subsequently served as vice president and counsel of Irving Trust Co. and, from 1982 to 2000, was employed by Republic National Bank of New York, where he served as Senior vice President and General Counsel. He has been active in several professional groups, including the New York Bankers Association, the Financial Services Roundtable, the New York Clearing House Association, and the Association of the Bar of the City of New York."

BOARD OF DIRECTORS

Hayward D. Fisk, chair; vice president, and general counsel, Computer Sciences Corp., El Segundo, CA

Douglas Foster, vice chair; Atlantic Legal Foundation

William H. Slattery; president, Atlantic Legal Foundation

Stephen J. Harmelin, treasurer; managing partner, Dilworth Paxson Philadelphia, PA

Charles R. Work, secretary; partner, McDermott, Will & Emery, Washington, DC

Francis B. Burch Jr., member; co-chairman, Piper Rudnick LLP, Baltimore, MD

William J. Calise Jr., member; senior vice president, and general counsel, Rockwell Automation, Milwaukee, WI

George S. Frazza, member; Patterson, Belknap, Webb & Tyler, New York, NY

William H. Graham, member; partner, Connell Foley, Roseland, NJ

Henry H. Hopkins, member; vice president, and chief legal counsel, T. Rowe Price Associates, Baltimore, MD

Ernest B. Hueter, member; president, National Legal Center for the Public Interest, Washington, DC

Quentin J. Kennedy, member; executive vice president (retired), Federal Paper Board Co.

Jeffrey B. Kindler, member; senior vice president, and general counsel, Pfizer, Inc., New York, NY

Edwin L. Lewis, member; general counsel, Photronics, Inc., Brookfield, CT

Robert A. Lonergan, member; vice president & general counsel, Rohm and Haas Co., Philadelphia, PA

CONTACT INFORMATION

150 East 42nd Street, New York, NY 10017
Phone: (212) 573-1960 • *Fax:* (212) 857-3653
General E-mail: atlanticlaw@yahoo.com • *Web site:* www.atlanticlegal.org

Communications Director: None
Human Resources Director: None

PURPOSE: "Advocates the principles of limited and responsible government, the private enterprise system and the rights of individuals."

CURRENT CONCERNS: Civil rights • Excessive regulation • Proper use of science in litigation • Property rights

METHOD OF OPERATION: Awards program • Conferences/seminars • Web site • Internships • Legal assistance • Legislative/regulatory monitoring (federal and state) • Litigation • Participation in regulatory proceedings (federal)

Effectiveness and Political Orientation

". . . a number of [web]sites offer copies of briefs at no cost. Some provide briefs from a range of courts covering a variety of topics, others are more focused. . . .

"Atlantic Legal Foundation, www.atlanticlegal.org/briefs.html. [Prepares a]micus briefs on issues that include courtroom science, charter schools and reverse discrimination. . . ."

(*Law Technology News,* July 25, 2003)

"Atlantic Legal Foundation, a public interest law firm, for the past decade has advocated the application of sound scientific principles in legal and regulatory proceedings. ALF has represented many distinguished scientists as friends of the court in cases where testimony has been offered incorrectly purporting to be reliable science, including the Daubert trilogy before the Supreme Court.

"ALF has now marshaled the resources of its Advisory Council, both scientific and legal, to ensure that sound science is applied in determining the admissibility of expert testimony in cases involving indoor mold health claims. . . .

"ALF has reviewed the most often cited of the technical articles considering the connection between indoor mold and health effects for admissibility/cross-examination purposes. Abstracts are available on line at no charge on ALF's website, www.atlanticlegal.org. Leading articles and decisions discussing evidentiary and procedural issues arising in mold litigation are also available on the ALF website."

(*The Metropolitan Corporate Counsel,* December 10, 2002)

SCOPE

Members: Information unavailable
Branch/chapter: Information unavailable
Affiliates: Information unavailable

STAFF

5 total—3 full-time professional; 2 full-time support; plus 2 part-time support; 1–2 interns

TAX STATUS

501(c)(3)

FINANCES

Budget: 2004—$500,000 (proposed)
Revenue: 2002—$534,371

FUNDING SOURCES

Foundation grants, 55 percent; corporate donations, 40 percent; individual contributions, 5 percent

PAC

None

EMPLOYMENT

Information unavailable

INTERNSHIPS

Information unavailable

NEWSLETTERS

Atlantic Legal Foundation Bulletin (periodic) (Web site)

PUBLICATIONS

Atlantic Legal Foundation Report
Atlantic Legal Foundation Science in the Courtroom Review

CONFERENCES

None

"In its first decision on charter schools since giving public school districts the right to challenge a charter application, an appellate panel last week sent the bid of the Roosevelt Children's Academy back to State University of New York trustees.

"The Appellate Division . . . said the SUNY Board of Trustees neglected to make the mandatory statutory finding that the issuance of a charter was likely to improve student learning. However, the court also rejected arguments of the Roosevelt Union Free School District that the state trustees failed to appropriately consider the fiscal impact and community opinion. . . .

"In the Roosevelt matter, the local school board actively opposed the issuance of a charter. Roosevelt is a poor district that mainly serves minority students, and local officials were concerned that the operation of a charter school would exacerbate its financial problems. Regardless, the SUNY Board of Trustees approved the charter, resulting in this action. . . .

"Acting as amicus curiae were Briscoe R. Smith of the Atlantic Legal Foundation in Manhattan for the New York Charter Public Schools Association, and from Lawrence W. Reich of Ingerman & Smith LLP in Northport for the Uniondale Union Free School District."

(*New York Law Journal*, October 23, 2001)

"Leaders of an industry panel that advises White House officials on chemical trade have filed a lawsuit in the U.S. District Court in Washington, D.C., aiming to head off a planned settlement that would appoint environmental representatives to the panel—one of 16 Industry Sector Advisory Committees (ISAC). The suit was filed January 5 by the Atlantic Legal Foundation (ALF; New York) on behalf of the chemical ISAC's chairman, DuPont chief international counsel Geoffrey Gamble, and its vice chairman, Fanwood Chemical (Fanwood, NJ) president Vincent DeLisi.

"The suit charges that the Clinton Administration broke terms of the Trade Act of 1974 when it agreed last year to settle a lawsuit filed by Earthjustice Legal Defense Fund (San Francisco) (CW, July 14, 2000, p. 13). The suit demanded U.S. Trade Representative Charlene Barshefsky add an environmentalist to the chemical ISAC under terms of the Federal Advisory Committee Act of 1972. The U.S. District Court in Seattle, which is overseeing the settlement, earlier ruled in favor of a 1999 Earthjustice lawsuit that demanded environmentalists be a part of ISACs for wood and paper products. . . .

" 'We're asking the [Washington, D.C.] court to declare that the Trade Act has been violated,' says Briscoe Smith, senior v.p. and counsel at ALF, a business and trade advocacy group."

(*Chemical Week*, January 17, 2001)

Better Business Bureau Wise Giving Alliance

Established in 2001

DIRECTOR

H. Art Taylor, president and chief executive officer. Taylor graduate from Franklin & Marshall College in 1980, and from Temple University with a law degree in 1989. From 1990 to 1999, Taylor headed the Opportunities Industrialization Centers of America, Inc. (OICA).

BOARD OF DIRECTORS

Douglas Bauer, chair; philanthropic advisor, Rockefeller Philanthropy Advisors, New York, NY

Virginia M. Esposito, secretary; president, National Center for Family Philanthropy, Washington, DC

Paul Tschirhart, treasurer; attorney, Sher & Blackwell, Washington, DC

Ronna Brown, member; president, Better Business Bureau of Metropolitan New York, New York, NY

Nora Carpenter, member; executive director; Better Business Bureau of Southwest Idaho, Boise, ID

Emelda Cathcart, member; AOL Time Warner (retired), New York, NY

Deborah C. Foord, member; managing director, Credit Suisse Asset Management, New York, NY

Ernest R. Gutierrez Jr., member; senior program officer, Kresge Foundation, Tro, MI

Marcus Owens, member; attorney, Caplin & Drysdale, Washington, DC

George Penick, member; president, Foundation for the Mid South, Jackson, MS

Jill Darrow Seltzer, member; Lloyd A. Fry Foundation, Chicago, IL

Peter Shiras, member; senior vice president; Independent Sector, Washington, DC

H. Art Taylor, ex officio; president and chief executive officer, BBB Wise Giving Alliance, Arlington, VA

SCOPE

15,000 Members
Branch/chapter: None
Affiliates: Council of Better Business Bureaus

STAFF

10 total—in addition, staff members from the affiliated Council of Better Business Bureaus, Inc. provide administrative and office.services

TAX STATUS

501(c)(3)

FINANCES

Information unavailable

CONTACT INFORMATION

4200 Wilson Boulevard, Suite 800, Arlington, VA 22203
Phone: (703) 276-0100
General E-mail: give@cbbb.bbb.org • *Web site:* www.give.org

Communications Director: None
Human Resources Director: None

PURPOSE: "The BBB Wise Giving Alliance collects and distributes information on hundreds of nonprofit organizations that solicit nationally or have national or international program services."

CURRENT CONCERNS: ". . . to serve donors' information needs and also help donors to make their own decisions regarding charitable giving."

METHOD OF OPERATION: Information clearinghouse • Web site • Performance ratings/Report cards (companies, products, etc.)

Effectiveness and Political Orientation

"The Better Business Bureau's Wise Giving Alliance takes a strong stance on charity standards, setting benchmarks in several categories regarding how money is spent.

"But among other charity watchdogs, there is no standard set of standards—or even agreement that firm standards are a good idea.

"When the Alliance evaluates a nonprofit group, it uses 23 standards in several areas. For expenses, there are three main measures: At least 50 percent of income should be spent on programs; no more than 35 percent of fund-raising revenue should be spent on fund-raising costs; and fund-raising and administrative costs combined should not exceed 50 percent of income.

"Sometimes the Alliance considers a charity's special circumstances, said Bennett Weiner, the group's chief operating officer. But usually, a group must meet all 23 standards to pass in the Alliance's eyes."

(*Tulsa World,* December 29, 2002)

"Many charities raise money by selling or renting names of contributors to like-minded organizations. Charities that buy the lists use them to reach out to new donors. Some charities say the solicitations are key to their continued survival.

"Yet many Americans view the sale of their names and addresses as an invasion of privacy. A recent survey commissioned by the Better Business Bureau's Wise Giving Alliance found that 85% of adults believe charities shouldn't raise money by selling their personal information. Some 82% said charities should allow donors to block the sale of their personal information. Only 15% said such a policy would go too far in limiting charitable fundraising.

FUNDING SOURCES
Sales of consumer education publications,
100%

PAC
None

EMPLOYMENT
Information unavailable

INTERNSHIPS
Information unavailable

NEWSLETTERS
Better Business Bureau Wise Giving Guide
(quarterly)

PUBLICATIONS
*BBB Wise Giving Alliance Standards for Charity
Accountability Implementation Guide to the
BBB Wise Giving Alliance Standards for
Charity Accountability*
Charity reports: in response to inquiries from
the general public, businesses, and other
potential donors, the BBB Wise Giving Alliance
provides reports on organizations that conduct
national or international fund raising or program services.

CONFERENCES
None

"In response, the alliance plans to add a privacy provision to the standards it uses to evaluate charities. To comply, charities would have to withhold personal information if donors request it.

"For example, a charity could include a check box on the card donors return with their contributions, says Bennett Weiner, chief operating officer of the Wise Giving Alliance."

(*USA Today,* November 12, 2002)

"A leading charity watchdog group has stripped its top rating from the American Red Cross, already battered over its response to the Sept. 11 attacks.

"The Better Business Bureau's Wise Giving Alliance has taken down a favorable report on the Red Cross from its Web site, where donors are updated on whether a charity meets the watchdog's management standards. The alliance pulled the report while it awaits Red Cross's response to 35 detailed questions about the charity's Sept. 11 relief work, including its use of donated money and blood. . . .

"'We're not singling out the Red Cross,' Bennett Weiner, the alliance's chief operating officer, said yesterday. 'We're going through an appropriate procedure in a charity report situation here—in this case where there has been a lot of public inquiries and discussion.'

"The alliance updates its reports on the 350 charities it tracks about every 18 months. About three-quarters of the charities evaluated meet the alliance's standards. The previous alliance report on the Red Cross, Weiner said, was dated July 2000."

(*The Washington Post,* February 21, 2002)

Beyond Pesticides/National Coalition Against the Misuse of Pesticides

Established in 1981

DIRECTOR

Jay Feldman, executive director. Feldman previously was director of health programs for Rural America. An author of many publications and articles, he has been a member of several Environmental Protection Agency (EPA) advisory bodies. Feldman earned his B.A. at Grinnell College and his M.A. in urban and regional planning at Virginia Polytechnic Institute.

BOARD OF DIRECTORS

Jay Feldman, executive director; Beyond Pesticides, Washington, DC
Gregg Small, president; Washington Toxics Coalition, Seattle, WA
Ruth Berlin, vice president; Maryland Pesticide Network, Annapolis, MD
Terry Shistar, secretary; Kansas Chapter, Sierra Club, Lawrence, KS
Allen Spalt, treasurer; Education Project, Agricultural Resources Center, Carrboro, NC
Audrey Thier, at-large; Environmental Advocates, Albany, NY
Laura Caballero, member; Lideres Campesinas en California, Greenfield, CA
Alan Cohen, member; Bio-Logical Pest Management, Inc., Washington, DC
Shelley Davis, member; Farmworker Justice Fund, Washington, DC
Lorna Donaldson-McMahon, member; Donaldson-McMahon Family Farms, Tiptonville, TN
Tessa Hill, member; Kids for Saving Earth Worldwide, Plymouth, MN
Lani Lamming, member; Ecological Services Inc., Alpine, WY
Nina Powers, member; Sarasota County Government, Sarasota, FL
Paul Repetto, member; Horizon Organic Dairy, Inc., Boulder, CO

SCOPE

Members: 1,000
Branches/chapters: None
Affiliate: None

STAFF

6 total—plus 1 intern

TAX STATUS

501(c)(3)

FINANCES

Budget: 2000—$500,000

FUNDING SOURCES

Contributions, 62%; grant support, 26%; membership dues, 4%; other sources, including publication sales and interest income, 8%

CONTACT INFORMATION

701 E Street, SE, Suite 200, Washington, DC 20003
Phone: (202) 543-5450 • *Fax:* (202) 543-4791
General E-mail: info@beyondpesticides.org •
Web site: www.beyondpesticides.org

Communications Director: Meghan Taylor, public education coordinator (202) 543-5450, ext. 18 • mtaylor@beyondpesticides.org
Human Resources Director: Information unavailable

PURPOSE: "To serve as a national network committed to pesticide safety and the adoption of alternative pest management strategies which reduce or eliminate a dependency on toxic chemicals."

CURRENT CONCERNS: Children, schools and pesticides • Hazardous lawn pesticides • Human health effects of toxins • Pest management • Pesticides • Pesticides in hospitals • Public education on pesticide hazards and alternatives • West Nile virus pesticides • Wood preservatives

METHOD OF OPERATION: Coalition forming • Conferences/seminars • Congressional testimony • E-mail alerts • Films, video, audio tapes • Grassroots organizing • Information clearinghouse • Internships • Legislative/regulatory monitoring (federal) • Library services open to the public • Litigation • Media outreach • Research • Speakers program• Web site

Effectiveness and Political Orientation

"Pesticide use in hospitals was the subject of a first-of-its-kind survey designed to encourage health care facilities to rethink pest-control practices that may put patients and staff at risk.

"The report, 'Healthy Hospitals: Controlling Pests Without Harmful Pesticides,' found that 100 percent of hospitals responding to the survey reported using pesticides in or around their buildings.

"The survey's sponsors, Beyond Pesticide and Health Care Without Harm, offer resources for managing pests while protecting health."
(*St. Petersburg Times* [Florida], December 30, 2003)

"Environmental groups and a union asked a federal court to ban the use of several toxic materials in treated, pressurized wood products, saying the Environmental Protection Agency isn't moving quickly enough.

"Wood preservatives containing arsenic and dioxin have been increasingly targeted as unsafe by advocacy groups. Those preservatives have been commonly used in utility poles, wood decks and playgrounds.

"On Tuesday, Beyond Pesticides and the Communication Workers of America sued in U.S. District Court for the District of Columbia, saying the EPA has enough evidence about health and environmental dangers to ban the use of chromated copper arsenate, pentachlorophenol and creosote.

PAC

None

EMPLOYMENT

Information on administrative and public education positions is available at www.beyondpesticides.org and www.ecojobs.com. Resumes and other materials can be mailed to Kagan Owens, Project Director, 701 E Street, SE, Suite 200, Washington, DC 20003. Phone: (202) 543-5450. Fax is (202) 543-4791. E-mail: kowens@beyondpesticides.org.

INTERNSHIPS

Paid internships are available, lasting from 2 to 6 months. Application deadlines are rolling. Information about internship positions is available at www.beyondpesticides.org and www.ecojobs.com. The internship coordinator is Kagan Owens, project director, 701 E Street, SE, Washington, DC 20003. Phone: (202) 543-5450. Fax is (202) 543-4791. E-mail: kowens@beyondpesticides.org.

NEWSLETTERS

Pesticides and You (quarterly)
School Pesticide Monitor (bimonthly)
Technical Report (monthly)

PUBLICATIONS

Agriculture: Soil Erosion, Pesticides, Sustainability
Building Blocks for School IPM: A Least-Toxic Structural Pest Management Manual
Estrogenic Pesticides
A Failure to Protect
NCAMP's Pesticide Chemical FactSheets
Organic Gardening: Sowing the Seeds of Safety
Pest Control Without Toxic Chemicals
Pesticides and Schools: A Collection of Issues and Articles
Pesticides and You: Twentieth Anniversary Edition, 1981–2000
Pesticides and Your Fruits and Vegetables
Pesticides in Our Homes and Schools
Pesticides: Are You Being Poisoned Without Your Knowledge?
Poison Poles: A Report about Their Toxic Trail and the Safer Alternatives
Safer Schools: Achieving a Healthy School Environment
Safety at Home: A Guide to the Hazards of Lawn and Garden Pesticides and Safer Ways to Manage Pests
Taking Action to Control Pesticides and Promote Alternatives—"How-To" Series
Unnecessary Risks: The Benefit Side of the Risk-Benefit Equation
Voices for Pesticide Reform: The Case for Safe Practices and Sound Policy

CONFERENCES

National Pesticide Forum (annually in April)

"Jay Feldman, Beyond Pesticides's director, said the preservatives were left on the market for the past couple decades only because alternatives weren't available, but that is no longer the case with the advent of composite and recycled materials."

(*Associated Press Newswires,* December 10, 2002)

"Last week, a study in New England Journal of Medicine showed that mosquitoes avoid feasting on arms covered in DEET-based bug repellents. But at least one maker of alternative repellents, which fared less well in the tests, and a consumer advocacy group raised safety concerns about the synthetic pesticide.

"Avon Products, which objected to the study's approach of testing the products under lab conditions instead of in outdoor field tests, suggests its product is safer. And Jay Feldman, executive director of Beyond Pesticides, a consumer group that seeks to limit pesticide use, said the study minimized DEET's dangers. DEET, he said, is 'a neuotoxic agent' that has been shown to have subtle effects on muscle movement, learning, and memory and concentration."

(*The Washington Post,* July 9, 2002)

"A battle is brewing over legislation that would set the first federal standards on using pesticides in public schools. . . .

"The Senate included the pesticide legislation in its version of the education bill; the House did not. Although it is viewed as a 'side show' to the issue of school testing and major provisions of the education reform bill, the pesticide legislation has ignited a intense debate over the federal role in regulating pesticides in public schools.

" 'Because of the lack of federal involvement in this area, the level of protection afforded children is varied and uneven across the country,' said Jay Feldman, executive director of Beyond Pesticides, a Washington, D.C.-based environmental group.

" 'The passage of this legislation will provide all children across the country with a basic level of protection.' "

(*Pittsburgh Post-Gazette,* August 12, 2001)

B'nai B'rith International

Established in 1843

DIRECTOR
Joel S. Kaplan, international president.

BOARD OF DIRECTORS
Board of governors, 195 members elected by region

SCOPE
Members: 110,000 members
Branches/chapters: 540 active chapters
(lodges and units)
Affiliates: the Anti-Defamation League and Hillel are former branches of B'nai B'rith—but they are now different and separate organizations, although they have members on each other's boards

STAFF
77 total

TAX STATUS
501(c)(3)

FINANCES
Declined to comment

FUNDING SOURCES
Programs, 73%; fundraising, 13%; administrative, 12%; other, 2%

PAC
none

EMPLOYMENT
Depending on the position, postings may be advertised in any of the following Web sites and publications: JournalismJobs.com, craigslist (http://washingtondc.craigslist.org), mediabistro.com, *The Washington Post, Roll Call*, and *The Hill;* questions should be directed to Crystal Solomon, Manager of Human Resources, (202) 857-6510.

INTERNSHIPS
Internship opportunities available in B'nai B'rith Klutznick National Jewish Museum and in the B'nai B'rith Center for Public Policy; questions should be directed to Crystal Solomon, manager of human resources, (202) 857-6510

NEWSLETTERS
B'nai B'rith Magazine
Dor L' Dor—The B'nai B'rith Foundation Newsletter
YLAN Voice
The B'nai B'rith International Communications Department also publishes 17 regional B'nai B'rith Today bimonthly newspapers.

CONTACT INFORMATION
2020 K Street, NW, 7th Floor, Washington, DC 20006
Phone: (202) 857-6600 • *Fax:* (202) 857-2780
General E-mail: internet@bnaibrith.org • *Web site*: www.bnaibrith.org

Communications Director: Jay Garfinkel
(202) 857-6677 • jgarfinkel@bnaibrith.org
Human Resources Director: Crystal Solomon
(202) 857-6510

PURPOSE: "To unite persons of the Jewish faith and to enhance Jewish identity through strengthening Jewish family life and the education and training of youth, broad-based services for the benefit of senior citizens, and advocacy and action on behalf of Jews throughout the world."

CURRENT CONCERNS: Discrimination • Humanitarian and "good works," specifically in Latin America • Israel's relationship with the European Union • Legislation affecting seniors (Medicare, prescription drugs, concerned about proposed privatization of social security) • Monitoring the press • Monitoring UN activity concerning Israel (use of the International Court of Justice instead of bilateral negotiations; how UN agencies [especially the Human Rights Commission] adversely affect Israel) • Rise of anti-Semitism in Europe • Senior housing for Jewish community

METHOD OF OPERATION: Direct mail • International activities • Internships • Legislative/regulatory monitoring (federal) • Planned giving • Print advertisements • Special events • Web site

Effectiveness and Political Orientation

"The Rev. William Vanderbloemen knows Jesus, and he knows Jesus movies.

"The self-described film buff and senior minister of First Presbyterian Church of Houston has caught much of the Jesus movie multitude, often on late-night cable. Vanderbloemen said the Hollywood saviors have boiled down to 'nice people, bad wigs.'

"But at the screening of Mel Gibson's new film, The Passion of the Christ, held for church leaders in Los Angeles last month, Vanderbloemen watched in awe as one of the central stories of his faith vividly and emotionally unfolded on screen. . . .

"Rabbi Steven Gross of Congregation Beth Israel also had an emotional response to The Passion of the Christ when Gibson showed a early version of the film in Houston last summer.

"But on that August day at the Museum of Fine Arts, Houston, Gross did not see a story of love and forgiveness. He witnessed a violent film filled with caricatures of Jews consumed with a desire to crucify Jesus.

PUBLICATIONS
Jihad, Jews, and Anti-Semitism in Syrian School Texts

CONFERENCES
none

" 'From the Jewish perspective, it is very, very threatening and very scary,' he said. 'Historically, when Passion plays have been released, the rise of anti-Semitism has been exponential.'

"Long before opening day neared, Gibson's depiction of the last 12 hours of Jesus' life generated historic buzz as some church leaders praised it and scholars criticized it. . . . But they, and many Jewish and Christian leaders throughout the area, are preparing for different films.

" 'The experience of the film is completely different for a Jewish and Christian audience,' Gross said. . . .

" 'I think we see it as both a moment to be concerned and prepared and a moment to reach out and build on our ecumenical relations,' said Martin B. Cominsky, the Houston-based Southwest regional director for the Anti-Defamation League of B'nai B'rith."

(*The Houston Chronicle,* February 22, 2004)

"An international Jewish group has decided that Boston civil rights leader Paul Parks can keep his decoration for 'distinguished' World War II service, even though its inquiry into his war record found no proof that Parks helped liberate the Dachau concentration camp, as he often contended.

"B'nai B'rith International, which had said it would demand a rigorous standard of proof during its review of Parks's wartime claims, concluded there is insufficient evidence either to firmly support or conclusively dismiss Parks's contention that volunteer mine-clearing duties led him to the gates of the concentration camp outside Munich 57 years ago. . . .

"The Jewish organization's decision to honor Parks, and his decision to accept the award in the face of multiple contradictions about his wartime record, enraged some acknowledged liberators of Dachau. They have assailed him as a fraud and an affront to U.S. soldiers who marched into the camp that day."

(*Boston Globe,* August 27, 2002)

"B'nai B'rith International, the world's largest Jewish human rights, community action and humanitarian service organization."

(*Pittsburgh Post-Gazette,* June 26, 2002)

"The leaders of B'nai B'rith International—the nation's oldest and largest Jewish social service organization—are leaving behind their decades-old headquarters at 1640 Rhode Island Ave. NW, a building whose very address has become synonymous with Jewish identity and activism.

"B'nai B'rith officials said they could not afford to spend tens of millions of dollars on repairs to the structure. Come mid-July, they will begin renting the seventh floor of a newer, more corporate building at 2020 K St. NW.

"The move will force B'nai B'rith to close its Klutznick Museum and replace it with a smaller gallery accessible only by appointment. Open access is simply not feasible at an office building with many other tenants, the group's officials said. Also closing is the museum gift shop, which is holding a 'going out of business sale' and has already sold about half of its roughly 4,000 items."

(*The Washington Post,* June 15, 2002)

BoardSource

Established in 2002 (formerly National Center for Nonprofit Boards, established 1988)

DIRECTOR

Deborah S. Hechinger, president and chief executive officer. Hechinger joined BoardSource in October 2003, after serving as executive vice president of the World Wildlife Fund. Prior to joining the World Wildlife Fund in 1994, Hechinger was deputy comptroller and director of Securities and Corporate Practices Division at the U.S. Office of the Comptroller of the Currency and held senior executive positions in the Division of Enforcement at the U.S. Securities and Exchange Commission. Hechinger has served on the boards of Sidwell Friends School, the Children's National Medical Center, the Washington Scholarship Fund, and the Black Student Fund. Hechinger received a B.A. from Brown University and a J.D. from Georgetown University Law Center. She is currently a member in good standing of the District of Columbia Bar.

BOARD OF DIRECTORS

Lorie A. Slutsky, chair; president, The New York Community Trust

Phyllis J. Campbell, vice chair; president and chief executive officer, Seattle Foundation

Barry D. Gaberman, secretary; senior vice president, Ford Foundation

Peter A. Kirsch, treasurer; chief of staff, Office of James V. Kimsey

Audrey R. Alvarado, member; executive director, National Council of Nonprofit Associations

Jameson A. Baxter, member; president, Baxter Associates, Inc.

Richard P. Chait, member; professor, Harvard University Graduate School of Education

Rien van Gendt, member; executive director, Van Leer Group Foundation

Deborah S. Hechinger; president and chief executive officer, BoardSource

SCOPE

Members: 13,000 individuals and organizations
Branches/chapters: None
Affiliates: 32 collaborating organizations

STAFF

34 total—21 professional; 13 support

TAX STATUS

501(c)(3)

FINANCES

Revenue: 2001—$8,040,195

CONTACT INFORMATION

1828 L Street, NW, Suite 900, Washington DC 20036-5114
Phone: (202) 452-6262 • *Fax:* (202) 452-6299
Toll-free: (800) 883-6262
General E-mail: mail@boardsource.org • *Web site:* www.boardsource.org

Communications Director: Lynda F. Williams
(202) 452-6262 • lwilliams@boardsource.org
Human Resources Director: Marci Sunderland
(202) 452-6262 • msunderland@boardsource.org

PURPOSE: "BoardSource is dedicated to increasing the effectiveness of nonprofit organizations by strengthening their boards of directors."

CURRENT CONCERNS: Nonprofit board development programs • Nonprofit organizations and advocacy • Regulation of nonprofits • Volunteer liability

METHOD OF OPERATION: Conferences/seminars • Films/video/audiotapes • Information clearinghouse • International activities • Internet (Web site) • Library services open to the public • Media outreach • Professional development services • Research • Speakers program • Telecommunications services (Fax-on-demand) • Training

Effectiveness and Political Orientation

"A Globe review of giving by private foundations found numerous trustees directing foundation assets to causes that bring them personal prestige. Some have accepted naming rights and public honors in return for donations. Others have steered large sums to their own favored causes.

"Such decisions often go unchallenged. The world of foundations, despite the billions of dollars at stake, is virtually unregulated. And institutions seeking major gifts are quick to offer up flattering rewards, like naming rights. Of the benefits trustees reap from running foundations, building a personal legacy with another person's money may be one of the most tempting, and enduring. . . .

"Some experts in charitable practices find such transactions troubling. . . .

" 'It's highly unusual, and it would certainly be a transaction that would raise eyebrows and raise questions,' said Deborah S. Hechinger, of BoardSource, a national group that specializes in best practices for nonprofit boards.

"Taking personal credit for gifts does not violate IRS rules against self-dealing, Hechinger said, because the trustee receives no monetary gain. 'But it's still problematic,' she said. 'There is a sense that an individual is getting inappropriate credit . . . for something that the foundation is in fact doing.' "

(*The Boston Globe*, December 21, 2003)

"It used to be only an elite few sat on a charity's board. But with corporate scandals and tight donations, getting involved is getting easier—especially at the top.

FUNDING SOURCES
Contributions, 50%; program services, 18%; sales, 16%; investments, 10%; other, 6%

PAC
None

EMPLOYMENT
Information on open positions can be obtained at the Web site or by contacting BoardSource at (202) 452-6262. Cover letters and resumes can be mailed to Marci Sunderland, Manager, Human Resources, BoardSource, 1828 L Street, NW, Suite 900, Washington, DC 20036-5114. Fax: (202) 452-6299. E-mail: msunderland@boardsource.org.

INTERNSHIPS
Both paid and unpaid internship opportunities are available in the areas of Marketing/ Communications and Products & Services. Duration, application deadlines, eligibility requirements, and hours vary and are negotiable.

NEWSLETTERS
Board Member (6 issues per year)

PUBLICATIONS
Advisory Councils
The Board Meeting Rescue Kit
The Business Professional's Guide to Nonprofit Board Service
Chief Executive Succession Planning
Development Committee
Driving Strategic Planning
Executive Committee
Extraordinary Board Leadership
Fearless Fundraising for Nonprofit Boards
Financial Committees
Financial Responsibilities of Nonprofit Boards
Governance Committee
The Guide for Community Foundation Board Members
Hiring the Chief Executive
How to Help Your Board Govern More and Manage Less
The IRS Form 990: A Window into Nonprofits
Leadership Roles in Nonprofit Governance
Legal Responsibilities of Nonprofit Boards
Managing Change
Managing Conflicts of Interest
The Nonprofit Board's Guide to Bylaws
Presenting: Fund-Raising
Risk Oversight: Board Lessons for Turbulent Times
Step-by-Step: Recruitment and Orientation
Step-by-Step: Nonprofit Financials
Structures and Practices of Nonprofit Boards
Ten Basic Responsibilities of Nonprofit Boards
Transforming Board Structure
Understanding Nonprofit Financial Statements
Unlocking Profit Potential
Also publishes videotapes, audiotapes, and booklets.

CONFERENCES
BoardSource Leadership Forum (biennial), Washington, DC
Also sponsors various workshops and regional conferences.

"Charity watchers say more than 3 million board seats are unfilled. That's good news if you're interested in becoming a board member—especially if you're young, have a special expertise, or represent a minority.

"Many charities are anxious to fill those seats and, in the process, revamp their leadership. There are two major reasons: Donors are demanding that charities demonstrate a new and increased commitment to accountability, and that they reflect the communities they serve. That signifies a striking change for many.

"Board memberships have been typically doled out to individuals who contributed vast sums of money or celebrities who indirectly brought funds to the charity, experts say. Cash remains essential, but now the focus is on donating a 'personally significant amount' rather than set dollars. That clever change is unlocking the door for many who otherwise couldn't afford a seat at the table. And the hoped-for result is a more diverse board and access to a larger donor pool.

" 'Charities are looking to reflect the community and that means a push to diversify their boards,' says Lynda Williams, director of communications for BoardSource, a nonprofit industry consulting group. 'A diverse board will bring different perspectives, different ideas, and recommendations that are better informed and more representative of the community's needs. . . .'

"To fill and diversify their boards, charities now target "up and comers," typically rising stars in the corporate world and "functional experts" who bring specialized expertise. Public-relations executives, accountants, lobbyists, and legal experts are in the most demand, Ms. Williams adds. 'First [board members] need to believe in the charity's mission, but they also need to bring money, a special expertise, or connections to occupy a seat.' "

(*Christian Science Monitor,* November 24, 2003)

"This organization provides tips and training for nonprofit organizations. It's a great resource for someone who needs to learn how to run a board meeting or committee."

(*The Atlanta Journal-Constitution,* October 19, 2003)

"There are compelling signs that UK charities need to invest more heavily in training—not least, recent surveys showing staff turnover in the voluntary sector on the increase. The most recent shows a worrying 10.7 percent staff turnover rate in 2002, largely caused by staff resignations, and also highlighted skills shortages causing recruitment problems. . . .

"In an attempt to find solutions to the ongoing crisis, many experts are now looking across the Atlantic. There, management training, especially in fundraising, is well advanced and, according to Bernard Ross, director of The Management Centre, 'on a scale and sophistication that we haven't even begun to look at. . . .'

"The USA also offers much more formal and 'high-end training' such as masters in volunteer administration. The UK has at least begun to catch up with this. . . .

"The same cannot be said for volunteer training, a major area of failure for the UK. America boasts a huge network in BoardSource, providing training for trustees and has annual meetings attracting 900 members. There is nothing comparable here. But some charities are moving to address this transatlantic rift."

(*Charity Times,* March 2003)

Brady Campaign to Prevent Gun Violence United with the Million Mom March and the Brady Center to Prevent Gun Violence

DIRECTOR

Michael Barnes, president. Barnes became president of the Brady Campaign to Prevent Gun Violence (formerly Handgun Control) and the Brady Center to Prevent Gun Violence (formerly the Center to Prevent Handgun Violence) in 2000. From 1979 to 1987, Barnes served in the U.S. House of Representatives. After leaving Congress, he was a partner in the law firm of Hogan & Hartson and he served as counsel for the governments of Chile, Cyprus, Panama, and South Korea. He also served as chair of the Center for National Policy; as co-chair of the NAFTA Congressional Caucus and Forum; as co-chair of the U.S. Committee for the United Nations Development Programme; and as chair of the U.S.-Panama Business Council. A former Marine, Barnes graduated from the University of North Carolina and received his J.D. from George Washington University Law School.

BOARD OF DIRECTORS

Brady Campaign
Phyllis Segal, chair, Boston, MA
Sarah Brady, campaign chair, Rehoboth, DE
Steve Sposato, vice chair, Lafayette, CA
Mike Barnes, president, Silver Spring, MD
Mark Ingram, treasurer, Arlington, VA
Byrl Phillips-Taylor, secretary,
 Charles City, VA
Andrew Varney, general counsel, Fried,
 Frank, Harris, Shriver & Jacobson,
 Washington, DC
Other members
Douglas L. Bailey, Freedom's Answer,
 Washington, DC
Michael Berman, Duberstein Group, Inc.,
 Washington, DC
David Birenbaum, Fried, Frank, Harris,
 Shriver & Jacobson, Washington, DC
Peter Buttenwieser, Philadelphia, PA
Maria Cuomo Cole, New York, NY
Bill D'Elia, La Canada, CA
Shikha Hamilton, Detroit, MI
Bill Harwood, Verrill & Dana, Portland, ME
James Meeks, Salem Baptist Church of
 Chicago, Chicago, IL
Charles Moose, Silver Spring, MD
Richard North Patterson, West Tisbury, MA
Dr. Mark Rosenberg, Task Force for Child
 Survival and Development, Decatur, GA
John Rosenthal, Meredith Management,
 Newton, MA
Rachel Smith, Raleigh, NC
Margaret A. Williams, New York, NY
Michael Wolkowitz, MJM Creative Services,
 New York, NY
Brady Center: Brady Campaign
Phyllis Segal, chair, Boston, MA
Sarah Brady, campaign chair, Rehoboth, DE

Established in 1974 (The National Council to Control Handguns)

CONTACT INFORMATION

1225 Eye Street NW, Suite 1100, Washington, DC 20005
Phone: (202) 898-0792 • *Fax:* (202) 682-4462
General e-mail: info@bradymail.org • *Web sites:* www.bradycampaign.org and www.millionmommarch.org and www.stopthenra.com

Communications Director: Peter Hamm
(202) 898-0792 • phamm@bradymail.org
Human Resources Director: Jean LeTien, controller
(202) 898-0792 • info@bradymail.org

PURPOSE: "As the nation's largest national, non-partisan, chapter-based grassroots organization leading the fight to prevent gun violence, the Brady Campaign to Prevent Gun Violence united with the Million Mom March is dedicated to creating an America free from gun violence, where all Americans are safe at home, at school, at work, and in their communities."

CURRENT CONCERNS: Responsible gun safety laws

METHOD OF OPERATION: Advertisements • Campaign contributions • Congressional testimony • Congressional voting analysis • Electoral politics • E-mail alerts • Grassroots organizing • Internet databases • Internships • Legal assistance • Legislative/regulatory monitoring (federal and state) • Lobbying (federal, state, and grassroots) • Media outreach • Polling • Speakers program • Voting records • Web site

Effectiveness and Political Orientation

"With the 10-year federal ban on assault-style weapons scheduled to expire this year, state Rep. Dan Frankel, D-Squirrel Hill, and 22 of his colleagues are pushing for passage of a law that would outlaw Uzis, AK-47s and other similar firearms in Pennsylvania. . . . They want Pennsylvania to join seven other states that have their own version of a ban, including California, New York and Maryland.

"Frankel cited a study by the Brady Center to Prevent Gun Violence that showed a 66 percent reduction in the number of crimes traced to the specific weapons banned under the federal law since 1994. . . .

"Dave Mitchell, director of law enforcement relations for the Brady Center to Prevent Gun Violence, said the nation is safer because of the federal ban. He said law-abiding gun owners, such as hunters, have nothing to fear from a Pennsylvania ban.

"'There is no legitimate hunting purpose for an Uzi, for a MAC-10,' he said. 'They're there to kill people.'"

(Pittsburgh Post-Gazette, March 20, 2004)

SCOPE

Members: 50,000 individuals
Branches/chapters: 35 Million Mom March
chapters
Affiliates: None

STAFF

45 total full-time—35 professional, 10 support, plus 2 professional part-time; 100 volunteers plus 3 interns.

TAX STATUS

Brady Campaign to Prevent Gun Violence
united with the Million Mom March:
501(c)(4)
Brady Center to Prevent Gun Violence:
501(c)(3)

FINANCES

Budget: 2004—$14 million

FUNDING SOURCES

Individuals, 50%; membership dues,
40%; foundation grants: 5%; corporate
donations: 5%

PAC

Brady Voter Education Fund

EMPLOYMENT

Job openings are advertised in *The
Washington Post* and in *Roll Call*, the newspaper distributed on Capitol Hill. Types of jobs
advertised for are administrative, organizers,
legislative specialists, and attorneys. Cover
letters and resumes may be mailed to Jean
LeTien, Controller, 1225 Eye Street NW, Suite
1100, Washington, DC 20005. Fax: (202) 682-
4462. E-mailed to: info@bradymail.org.

"The nation's largest gun-control group accused the government Thursday of violating the federal law that bans assault weapons by allowing manufacturers to rebuild existing—and legally owned—assault weapons.

"The Brady Campaign to Prevent Gun Violence, along with the Million Mom March, made its allegation in a lawsuit against the Justice Department that probably will fuel the congressional debate over efforts to renew the assault-weapons ban, which expires in September."

(*USA Today*, March 19, 2004)

"Now, in the wake of their father's death, Pascal Charlot's children are trying to forge some of their own answers—in a federal courthouse in Washington. . . .

"Charlot's children declined to speak about the suit, saying that their father's death is too painful to discuss. Hogan & Hartson, the law firm representing the Charlot family, and the Brady Center to Prevent Gun Violence consider the Charlot case, filed in October, a crucial test of the District's law allowing courts to hold manufacturers responsible for 'abnormally' dangerous firearms.

"The Charlot suit was filed in a courthouse that is just steps away from Capitol Hill, where gun makers and the National Rifle Association have been pushing hard for legislation that would bar suits like the family's. A measure passed the House of Representatives but died in the Senate last week after it was amended with pro-gun control provisions that made it unpalatable to the National Rifle Association and others.

" 'We believe very strongly that victims of gun violence have a right to seek compensation in the courts, like victims of any other sort of misconduct or wrongdoing,' said Jonathan Lowy, a lead lawyer with the Brady Center, which helped file the suit for the Charlots. . . .

" 'The family has suffered a horrible tragedy,' he said. 'And District law entitles them to compensation for that loss.' "

(*The Washington Post*, March 11, 2004)

"The Senate on Tuesday overwhelmingly rejected a measure to shield gun manufacturers and dealers from lawsuits. The defeat came after a roller-coaster day in which Republicans abruptly withdrew their support for the bill because Democrats had tacked on amendments to renew the 10-year assault weapons ban and require background checks on customers at gun shows. . . .

"(John) Kerry took the occasion to deliver what amounted to an eight-minute stump speech on the Senate floor in support of the amendments, a talk that advocates of gun control credited with helping to pass them.

" 'This is a huge victory,' said Richard Aborn, former president of the Brady Center to Prevent Gun Violence. 'Kerry has placed the gun issue on assault weapons firmly back into the presidential debate.' "

(*The New York Times*, March 3, 2004)

"Pushed by pro-gun interests, a wave of states has passed legislation in recent years allowing citizens to carry concealed weapons—including neighboring Minnesota, which in May approved a law that is similar to what is being proposed in Wisconsin.

INTERNSHIPS
Some paid and some unpaid internships are available. Internships last 3 to 6 months in the area of legal, organizing, communications, and fundraising. Hours and application deadlines are flexible. Write to Gale Smith, operations manager, 1225 Eye Street NW, Suite 1100, Washington, DC 20005. Phone: (202) 898-0792. Fax: (202) 682-4462. E-mail: info@bradymail.org.

NEWSLETTERS
Legal Action Newsletter (quarterly)

PUBLICATIONS
None

CONFERENCES
None

"Nationwide, there are 33 states that allow citizens to carry concealed weapons without convincing authorities they have a compelling need to, according to the Brady Campaign to Prevent Gun Violence. . . .

"Advocates of Wisconsin's legislation to allow concealed carry, which comes up for a public hearing in the Capitol on Tuesday, say it will make citizens safer by deterring criminals who would otherwise assume law-abiding citizens are likely prey because they are unarmed.

"But opponents insist the current law has not been proven to be faulty and that putting more weapons on Wisconsin streets will imperil public safety. . . .

"Luis Tolley, state legislative director for the Brady Campaign to Prevent Gun Violence, predicted the issue will be hotly contested in Wisconsin because of the state's outright prohibition.

"Opponents fear that relaxing the law could endanger the lives of innocent people and put gun users at some risk, as well.

" 'How would you feel if you were at a Little League game, and the guy next to you is yelling, "Kill the ump!" and has a gun in his pocket?' Tolley asked.

"In addition, Eric Howard, a spokesman for the Brady Campaign, said those who obtain the permits—including some who may be unbalanced, short-tempered or exercising poor judgment—may feel empowered to use handguns on people committing property crimes, such as breaking into a car.

" 'It deputizes everybody. It makes them judge, jury and executioner on the spot,' Howard said."

(*Milwaukee Journal Sentinel,* September 8, 2003)

"Just as U.S. President George W. Bush tries to make post-Sept. 11 America safer, his administration is threatening to undermine the U.S. capital's long-standing ban on handguns.

"In fact, gun control advocates fear the Bush administration's radical new policy may soon jeopardize gun safety laws throughout the country.

"In line with the wishes of the National Rifle Association (NRA), which supported his Republican presidential campaign, Bush has reversed decades of federal government policy by boldly declaring that all Americans have the right to own a gun. . . .

" 'This will place strong gun laws at risk by making them more difficult to defend,' said Michael D. Barnes, president of the Brady Centre to Prevent Gun Violence, named after press secretary James Brady, seriously wounded in a 1981 assassination attempt on president Ronald Reagan.

" 'Indeed, the National Rifle Association has openly stated that it will use a changed U.S. position to challenge the constitutionality of common-sense gun laws. This is a step backward in the fight to defend against gun violence,' he said."

(*Toronto Star* [Canada], June 3, 2002)

The Brookings Institution

Established in 1916

DIRECTOR

Strobe Talbott, president. Talbott became president in July 2002 after a career in journalism, government, and academe. His immediate previous post was founding director of the Yale Center for the Study of Globalization. Talbott served in the State Department from 1993 to 2001, first as ambassador-at-large and special adviser to the secretary of state for the new independent states of the former Soviet Union, then as deputy secretary of state for 7 years. Previous to that, Talbott worked for 21 years with *Time* magazine. Talbott has been a fellow of the Yale Corporation; a trustee of the Hotchkiss School; and a director of the Council on Foreign Relations, the North American Executive Committee of the Trilateral Commission, the Aspen Strategy Group, and the American Association of Rhodes Scholars. He is currently a trustee of the Carnegie Endowment for International Peace and a member of the participating faculty of the World Economic Forum. Talbott earned degrees from Yale (B.A., 1968, M.A.Hon., 1976) and Oxford (M.Litt., 1971).

BOARD OF DIRECTORS

John L. Thornton, chair of the board
Strobe Talbott, president
Elizabeth E. Bailey
Zoe Baird
Alan R. Batkin
Richard C. Blum
James W. Cicconi
Arthur B. Culvahouse Jr.
Alan M. Dachs
Kenneth W. Dam
Robert A. Day
Thomas E. Donilon
Mario Draghi
Kenneth M. Duberstein
Lawrence K. Fish
Richard W. Fisher
Cyrus F. Freidheim Jr.
Bart Friedman
David Friend
Ann M. Fudge
Jeffrey W. Greenberg
Brian L. Greenspun
William A. Haseltine, Ph.D.
Teresa Heinz
Samuel Hellman, M.D.
Joel Z. Hyatt
Shirley Ann Jackson, Ph.D.
Ann Dibble Jordan
Michael H. Jordan
Marie L. Knowles
Mario M. Morino
William A. Owens
Frank H. Pearl
John Edward Porter
Steven Rattner

CONTACT INFORMATION

1775 Massachusetts Avenue, NW, Washington, DC 20036
Phone: (202) 797-6000 • *Fax:* (202) 797-6004
General E-mail: brookinfo@brookings.edu • *Web site:* www.brook.edu

Communications Director: Stephen Smith, vice president for communications
(202) 797-6105 • communications@brookings.edu
Human Resources Director: Information unavailable

PURPOSE: "The Brookings Institution is an independent, nonpartisan organization devoted to research, analysis, education, and publication focused on public policy issues in the areas of economics, foreign policy, and governance. The goal of Brookings activities is to improve the performance of American institutions and the quality of public policy by using social science to analyze emerging issues and to offer practical approaches to those issues in language aimed at the general public."

CURRENT CONCERNS: Antitrust and regulatory policy • Budget/fiscal policy • Campaign finance reform • Education • Federal budget • Foreign policy • Homeland Security • Humanitarian intervention • Immigration trends • Income distribution • International economics • Iraq • Macroeconomics • Nuclear weapons • Regulatory issues • Social security • Tax policy • Technology • Telecommunications • Terrorism • Trade policy • Transportation • Urban policy • Welfare reform

METHOD OF OPERATION: Advertisements • Conferences/seminars (offered through the Center for Public Policy Education • Congressional testimony • Congressional voting analysis • International activities • Legislative/regulatory monitoring (federal and state) • Library/information clearinghouse • Media outreach • Research • Speakers program • Web site

Effectiveness and Political Orientation

"The federal public finances in the U.S. are sliding towards record deficit. But a sense of urgency about the issue is curiously absent from everyday political discussion.

"Part of this may reflect the Bush administration's stonewalling on the subject. Its strategy of promising to halve the deficit in five years appears to be based on waiting for the revival of economic growth to feed through into higher tax revenues, and then proclaiming the problem is getting better.

"The budget in February is likely to be accompanied by ferocious rhetoric about clamping down on discretionary spending—that is, spending authorized each year rather than entitlements mandated by law—while deferring fundamental reform of Social Security and Medicare, the biggest fiscal challenges. But the authors of a report released today by the Brookings Institution, the liberal-leaning think-tank, say realistic forecasts of budget deficits—

SCOPE
Members: None
Branches/chapters: None
Affiliates: None

STAFF
280 total—plus nonresident scholars, fellows, and research assistants

TAX STATUS
501(c)(3)

FINANCES
Revenue: 2002—$31.9 million

FUNDING SOURCES
Endowment, 34%; Center for Public Policy revenue, 11%; publications, 8%; gifts and grants, 4%; government funding, 2%; other, 2%

PAC
None

EMPLOYMENT
Employment information is available on the Brookings Institution Web site. Resumes and cover letters may be mailed to: The Brookings Institution, Human Resources, 1775 Massachusetts Avenue, NW, Washington, DC 20036. Fax: (202) 797-2479. E-mail: hrjobs@brookings.edu.

INTERNSHIPS
Unpaid internships are available in a variety of areas of interest. Deadlines, duration, and contact information vary. Internship information is available on the Web site. Predoctoral and postdoctoral fellowships are also available.

NEWSLETTERS
Brookings Papers on Economic Activity (semiannual journal)
Brookings Papers on Education Policy
Brookings Trade Forum (annual)
Brookings-Wharton Papers on Financial Services
Brookings-Wharton Papers on Urban Affairs
Microeconomics (annual journal)

PUBLICATIONS
The following is a sample list of publications:
Agenda for the Nation
Andes 2020: A New Strategy for the Challenges of Colombia and the Region
Arab Economic Integration: Between Hope and Reality
Beyond Tiananmen: The Politics of U.S.-China relations, 1989–2000
Brazil's Second Chance: En route Toward the First World

assuming no drastic action on taxes or spending—show little prospect of the shortfall halving in the near future.

"The report adjusts the baseline forecast made by the non-partisan Congressional Budget Office to include the recent prescription drug benefit added to Medicare, the costs of making permanent tax cuts currently scheduled to expire, and to fix a looming problem with a little-known part of the tax code called the alternative minimum tax."

(*Financial Times* [London, England], January 13, 2004)

"Peppered by questions throughout the 2000 campaign about whether he was qualified to be president, George W. Bush often responded with humor.

"He joked that his critics complained 'this boy's never done anything. Just running on his daddy's name. And that's fine. That just means I'm going to be underestimated in the political arena. . . .'

"Bush took office under a cloud: He lost the popular vote but won the Electoral College after the U.S. Supreme Court ended a recount of the disputed Florida result.

"'He's been incredibly successful, although I certainly would not have been able to believe it or understand or predict that he would get it the way he got it,' said Stephen Hess, a presidential scholar at the Brookings Institution, a nonpartisan research organization in Washington. 'It's been sort of a circuitous trip to get where he wanted to go.

"'But certainly he is going to be the first president in a long time who can say, "OK, here are the commitments I've made, and here are the commitments I've kept."'"

(*Columbus Dispatch* [Ohio], January 4, 2004)

"Want to know how Americans will vote next election day? Watch what they do the weekend before.

"If they attend religious services regularly, they probably will vote Republican by a 2-1 margin. If they never go, they likely will vote Democratic by a 2-1 margin. . . .

"'It's the most powerful predictor of party ID and partisan voting intention,' said Thomas Mann, a political scholar at the Brookings Institution, a center-left Washington research center. 'And in a society that values religion as much as (this one), when there are high levels of religious belief and commitment and practice, that's significant.'"

(*Milwaukee Journal Sentinel,* December 14, 2003)

"In recent years, finance directors have been on the receiving end of a lot of advice telling them that what they report now is not good enough. What exactly the reformers want varies—but they have two powerful and recurring messages.

"First, they claim that the traditional financial reporting model is inadequate, especially in relation to intangibles, which the reformers argue are a modern company's most important assets. If this is true, it follows that both internal and external reporting based on the traditional model are misleading and must lead to poor decisions and misallocation of resources.

"Second, the reformers argue that businesses need to be more open in the public disclosure of internal data. They especially emphasize the importance of disclosing non-financial and forward-looking data—partly, but not solely,

Also publishes policy briefs, reports, articles, speeches and interviews.

CONFERENCES

Briefings and team presentations

Executive forums

Teleconferences

because they see information of this sort as a remedy for the alleged failings of financial reporting.

"Who are these reformers—a bunch of starry-eyed dreamers and eccentrics? I hope not. For they include professional bodies such as my own, the Institute of Chartered Accountants in England & Wales (ICAEW), big accountancy firms, significant think-tanks such as the Brookings Institution in Washington and leading consultants and academics.

(*Financial Times* [London, England], December 11, 2003)

"There was Bush, in gray Army windbreaker sporting the crest of the First Armored Division, ladling out turkey and stuffing for grateful US troops. The snap visit, the fruit of six weeks of secret planning, guaranteed the president prime campaign coverage and left his Democratic challengers locked in the headlights of an incumbent's juggernaut.

" 'The candidate who is president does things as the president, and his opponent is the politician who does things like a politician,' said Stephen Hess, a senior fellow at the centrist Brookings Institution. 'The Democrats now have to find a way to say, "Yes, it's the appropriate thing for the president to do, however . . .' "

(*The Boston Globe,* December 11, 2003)

"With a fund-raising gala and a possible address by the vice president of the United States, Rice University's James A. Baker III Institute for Public Policy this week will mark its 10th year of existence in the crowded and clamorous world of policy shapers. . . .

"But among those in the higher echelons—the Woodrow Wilson Institute, the Kennedy School of Government, the Hoover Institution, the Brookings Institution, the Cato Institute, to name just a few—the Baker is still a precocious, promising, new kid on the block."

(*The Houston Chronicle ,* October 12, 2003)

Business for Social Responsibility (BSR)

Established in 1992

DIRECTOR

Robert H. Dunn, chief executive officer. Prior to joining Business for Social Responsibility full time, Dunn was vice president for corporate affairs at Levi Strauss & Co. In that capacity Dunn developed and implemented the company's groundbreaking Global Code of Conduct. As the staff director of the company and its foundation's philanthropic activities, Dunn developed global programs addressing issues of economic development, AIDS, and racial discrimination. Dunn has also worked as a senior staff member in the Carter White House, a diplomat at the U.S. Embassy in Mexico, and as chief of staff and a cabinet member for the governor of Wisconsin. Earlier he served as a dean and faculty member at Wesleyan University in Middletown, CT. He has a B.A. from Brown University and a J.D. from Vanderbilt University and was admitted to the Bar in the State of Connecticut.

CONTACT INFORMATION

111 Sutter Street, 12th Floor, San Francisco, CA 94104
Phone: (415) 984-3200 • *Fax:* (415) 984-3201
General E-mail: marketing@bsr.org or joinbsr@bsr.org •
Web site: www.bsr.org

Communications Director: Information unavailable
Human Resources Director: Information unavailable

PURPOSE: "We work with member companies to help them achieve success while respecting ethical values, people, communities, and the environment."

CURRENT CONCERNS: Audits and accountability • Community involvement • Environment • Ethics • Governance • Human rights and the global economy • Marketplace • Workplace

METHOD OF OPERATION: Conferences/seminars • Educational foundation • Internet (Web site) • Research • Technical assistance • Training

Effectiveness and Political Orientation

"Fair or not, big business is being called to justify its approach to a growing array of social, environmental and ethical concerns. Despite the economic downturn, many companies are concluding that they cannot afford not to invest in being seen as responsible.

" 'We're facing the greatest demand for our assistance that we've seen in our nine-year history,' says Bob Dunn, chief executive of Business for Social Responsibility (BSR), a U.S. non-profit advisory organisation whose membership includes many top multinationals.

"Financial constraints have forced companies to think more carefully about where to put scarce resources, he says. Their priority is to embed social, environmental and ethical considerations in every operation, including their supply chain. This is a long-term task requiring sensitive antennae. . . .

"Microsoft, Lucent and United Technologies have joined BSR this year, as well as Altria, a more traditional target for pressure groups and litigation as the parent company of both Kraft Foods and Philip Morris."
(*Financial Times* [London, England], September 29, 2003)

"Still, whether for PR or out of a genuine desire to change, most big public companies have at least adopted the rhetoric of corporate social responsibility. Implausibly, corporate scandals have become a boon for the movement. 'Companies need to show that they are not just greedy institutions,' says Debra Dunn, senior vice president for corporate affairs at Hewlett-Packard. More U.S. companies have been publishing reports that measure their social and environmental impact. Big consulting firms are expanding their corporate social responsibility practices to include hundreds of professionals. Business

Jeff Zalla, member; vice president, treasurer, and corporate responsibility officer, Chiquita Brands International Inc.

Martin Zimmerman, member; group vice president, corporate affairs, Ford Motor Co.

SCOPE

Members: More than 1,400 members and affiliated member companies that collectively employ nearly 5 million workers

Branches/chapters: 11 regional networks: Arizona, Greater Boston, Colorado, Connecticut River Valley, New England, New Hampshire, Oregon/Washington, San Francisco Bay Area, Southern California, Upper Midwest, and Washington, DC

Affiliates: Business for Social Responsibility Education Fund, Business for Social Responsibility Maine, and Business for Social Responsibility Vermont, all 501(c)(3) organizations

STAFF

53 total

TAX STATUS

501(c)(3) and 501(c)(6) (PIP01-02)

FINANCES

Information unavailable

FUNDING SOURCES

Foundation grants, 34%; membership dues, 23%; conferences, 15%; government contracts, 9%; corporate donations, 3%; other, 16%

PAC

None

EMPLOYMENT

Information about open positions is available on BSR's Web site: www.bsr.org. Interested applicants can apply online at jobs@bsr.org or by mail at the following address: Business for Social Responsibility, 111 Sutter Street, 12th Floor, San Francisco, CA 94104.

INTERNSHIPS

BSR posts all available paid internship positions in the BSR Jobs section of its Web site. If you are interested in an unpaid internship with BSR, send your cover letter describing your area of interest and résumé to jobs@bsr.org.

NEWSLETTERS

BSR News Monitor (weekly)

PUBLICATIONS

Cause-Related Marketing: Partnership Guidelines & Case Studies
Comparison of Selected Corporate Social Responsibility-Related Standards
Corporate Social Responsibility Guidebook
Designing a CSR Structure
Designing Social and Environmental Reporting Processes for Verification
Green Building Design for Small/Mid-Sized Enterprises

for Social Responsibility, an industry group formed a decade ago, has about 450 corporate members including Wal-Mart, Microsoft, Sony, General Motors, Pfizer, and Shell."

(*Fortune,* June 23, 2003)

"In fact, many companies like Reebok, Gap and Levi Strauss & Co. of San Francisco have made concerted efforts in recent years to implement anti-sweatshop codes of conduct for their supply chains. This process has been spearheaded by Business for Social Responsibility, a corporate group in San Francisco that conducts training programs around the world for executives and factory floor managers in ethical labor practices.

"In the past few years, at least 250 U.S. companies, mostly in the apparel, footwear and toy industries, have created codes of conduct for their suppliers.

" 'Companies are starting to work more closely with their suppliers, developing management systems to make sure that factories take more ownership of the codes (of conduct) and that the changes are sustainable,' said Debbie O'Brien, director of the group's business and human rights program."

(*The San Francisco Chronicle,* September 29, 2002)

"Although no hard data are available, a recent study by Prudential Insurance of America estimates that a third of large U.S. companies now have formal policies to pay workers or give them time off for volunteer work.

"Experts say the practice grew in the 1990s, in part because of a growing cultural and corporate emphasis on volunteerism, nurtured through groups like The Points of Light Foundation, which has a special program to help corporations develop employee volunteer programs.

"In addition, says Dinah Waldsmith, senior manager of community investment with Business for Social Responsibility, many companies also began to think of employees as stakeholders during the last decade, and looked for ways to show their commitment to employee concerns.

" 'Companies are doing what they can to make sure employees are aware of the ways in which companies support things the employee cares about,' says Ms. Waldsmith. 'In the case of corporate-sponsored volunteering, or loaned executives, the company is kind of walking its talk.' "

(*Christian Science Monitor,* May 13, 2002)

"Business for Social Responsibility is a non-profit organization that was founded about 10 years ago by 50 companies—including Ben & Jerry's ice cream and Patagonia clothing—that were interested trying to balance a profitable business with social responsibility."

(*Seattle Post-Intelligencer,* November 8, 2001)

"Representatives from some of the largest multinational corporations in the world gather this week in Seattle to discuss issues such as globalization, environmental policy and labor practices.

". . . At the Business for Social Responsibility conference, Microsoft, Ford, Weyerhaeuser and Starbucks will be talking about how they can be better corporate citizens.

"Among the topics to be addressed at the three-day conference, starting Wednesday: socially responsible downsizing, improving human rights in third-world countries and making corporate social responsibility strategies pay off on Wall Street.

CONFERENCES
Annual conference

"Bob Dunn, BSR's chief executive officer, says the group's goal is to 'help people get their arms around social responsibility.'

". . . A nonprofit founded about 10 years ago by companies such as Patagonia, Ben & Jerry's and Stonyfield Farms, BSR has since grown considerably. At this year's annual BSR conference companies that are typically the target of social activists, such as Nike, Gap and Chevron, are scheduled to listen to speeches that address the agendas of their traditional foes.

"But very few of those activists will be on hand for the conference—about 75 percent of the participants represent businesses. An $800 to $1,500 admission fee left some activists feeling excluded, but Dunn defended the pricing.

" 'We need to put some cap on participation in order to preserve some of the community we want to create,' he says.

"The company does invite some activists, he says, but aims to build a community of corporations talking among themselves."

(*Associated Press,* November 5, 2001)

Business-Industry Political Action Committee (BIPAC)

Established in 1963

DIRECTOR

Gregory S. Casey, president and chief executive officer. Casey has held the position since 1999. He came to BIPAC after serving as transition director for the newly elected governor of Idaho. Until November 1998, Casey served for more than 2 years in the U.S. Senate as sergeant at arms and doorkeeper. Prior to that, Casey served as deputy chief of staff in the Office of the Senate Majority Leader in the spring of 1996. From 1990 to 1996 he was the chief of staff to U.S. Senator Larry E. Craig of Idaho. He served for 3 years as the executive vice president of the Homebuilders Association of Southwest Idaho, 2 years as a vice president of Pioneer Title Corporation, and 4 years as the president and chief executive officer of the Idaho Association of Commerce and Industry. Casey has a degree in political science and history from the University of Idaho and has completed graduate programs in legislative affairs through the Library of Congress.

BOARD OF DIRECTORS

Gregory S. Casey, president and chief executive officer
Diemer True, chair; partner, True Companies, Casper, WY
J. Larry Nichols, vice chair; chair, president, and chief executive officer, Devon Energy Corp., Oklahoma City, OK
Donald R. (Dee) Margo II, immediate past chair; chief executive officer, JDW Insurance El Paso, TX
Allan Cors, treasurer; McLean, VA
Jan W. Baran, general counsel; attorney-at-law, Wiley, Rein & Fielding, Washington, DC
Other members
Renee Amoore
Gregory W. Baise
Michael E. Baroody
Steve Bartlett
Edward W. Blessing
Linden Blue
Donald T. Bollinger
Peter R. Carney
John J. Castellani
Stephen E. Chaudet
Ken W. Cole
James E. Coles
Stan Crader
Gordon Crow
Michael B. Crutcher
Charles E. Dominy
Mark A. Dunn
Dwight H. Evans
William D. Fay
Harry S. Flemming
Walter L. Foxworth
Russell B. Hagen

CONTACT INFORMATION

888 16th Street, NW, Suite 305, Washington, DC 20006
Phone: (202) 833-1880 • *Fax:* (202) 833-2338
General E-mail: info@bipac.org • *Web site*: www.bipac.org

Communications Director: Lauren S. Yates
yates@bipac.org
Human Resources Director: None

PURPOSE: "To identify, endorse and elect to Congress champions of free enterprise." It was "founded to elect pro-business candidates to Congress."

CURRENT CONCERNS: Business competitiveness and profitability • Economic growth • Election of pro-business candidates to Congress

METHOD OF OPERATION: Awards program • Campaign contributions • Coalition forming • Conferences/seminars • Congressional voting analysis • Electoral politics • Grassroots organizing • Information clearinghouse • Internet (databases, Web site) • Internships • Professional development services • Research • Speakers program • Technical assistance and training • Voter registration • Voting records

Effectiveness and Political Orientation

"Republican donors, friends, family and a who's-who of Cabinet officials are among dozens of guests to stay overnight at Camp David, the longtime presidential retreat that has become one of President Bush's favorite weekend getaways.

"George W. and first lady Laura Bush have played host to more than 240 guests at the Catoctin Mountain retreat near Frederick, Md., since the president took office in January 2001, a list released Friday by the White House shows. . . .

"They include Secretary of State Colin Powell, Defense Secretary Donald Rumsfeld, national security adviser Condoleezza Rice, Homeland Security chief Tom Ridge, CIA Director George Tenet, Commerce Secretary Donald Evans and Treasury Secretary Paul O'Neill. . . .

"Other Bush supporters making the overnight list include Gerry Parsky, a Los Angeles venture capitalist who served as chair of Bush's 2000 election effort in California; and Dee Margo, a Bush donor, Texas insurance executive and leader of the Business Industry Political Action Committee whose wife, Adair, is a friend of Mrs. Bush's.

(*Associated Press State & Local Wire*, January 17, 2003)

". . .(T)he National Journal . . . surveyed the won-lost record of 20 interest groups in competitive House and Senate races this year. The six most successful were all conservative: United Seniors Association, National Rifle Association, Club for Growth, National Right to Life Association, BIPAC (the

Richard C. Hall
Derek C. Hathaway
Robert L. Healy
Andy Ireland
Micaela Isler
Isabel H. Jasinowski
Karen Kerrigan
William Russell King
Christopher M. Kinsey
Gregory S. Lashutka
Robert List
William G. Little
Pierce J. Lonergan
John R. McArthur
Norman P. McClelland
John Noble McConnell Jr.
Gerald T. McPhee
Edward Pease
Rodger D. Phelps
Conrad A. Plimpton
Chris A. Robbins
James J. Rouse
Daryl D. Smith
Burton H. Snyder
Steve R. Spencer
Michael R. Stanford
Thomas J. Tauke
Constance E. Tipton
William B. Trent Jr.
Jade West
Gerald Whitburn
Earle C. Williams
Michael M. Wilson
Robert L. Wright, O.D.
Henry B. Wehrle Jr.
George M. Yates

SCOPE
Members: 400 corporations and
     370 individuals
Branches/chapters: None
Affiliates: None

STAFF
10 total

TAX STATUS
BIPAC consists of two components: Action Fund is a Political Action Committee and the Business Institute for Political Analysis is a for-profit organization.

FINANCES
Budget: 2001—$2.5 million

FUNDING SOURCES
Corporate donations, 15%; individual contributions, 9%; special events/projects, 9%; membership dues, 6%; conferences, 3%; remaining 58% information unavailable

PAC
Action Fund

Business-Industry Political Action Committee) and the U.S. Chamber of Commerce.

(*Chicago Sun-Times,* November 14, 2002)

"Dirk Van Dongen, the well-connected president of an obscure but powerful business association, worked hard for Tuesday's Republican election victory.

"His National Association of Wholesaler Distributors endorsed 256 candidates in 44 states, just 13 of them Democrats. Member businesses advised their workers on candidates, stuffed paycheck envelopes with voter guides, whipped together political Web sites, got employees to the polls, even pushed absentee balloting and early voting when they could.

"Now it's payback time for the distributors and other business groups whose pent-up demands for policy changes, large and small, will soon burst into public.

"Around Washington, business lobbyists like Van Dongen are celebrating their victories and licking their chops. . . . Topping the list for large businesses is tax change for overseas operations and a permanent extension of tax breaks for investments that were approved last year as a temporary economic stimulus.

"The Business Roundtable, the American Petroleum Institute, and the American Chemistry Council and the Independent Petroleum Association of America contracted with the Business Industry Political Action Committee to exchange employee lists, tailor political Web sites and develop voter guides with politically pointed candidate voting records.

"In all, BIPAC set up such sites for 200 corporations and distributed political material to 1,700 other businesses, said Darrell Shull, BIPAC's vice president for political operations. He estimates the coordinated effort reached 11 million voters.

" 'We started this effort in the last election cycle. We started to show businesses there was a different way to be involved,' he said. 'This time, we had enough businesses involved for others to take notice.' "

(*The Washington Post,* November 8, 2002)

"Stan Greenberg, a Democratic pollster, frequently surveys voters on whether they care which party controls Congress, and mostly they don't, he said.

" 'You find out it ranks about 15th after a long list of specific issues,' Greenberg said. "When you try to introduce political process arguments, like balancing the president or helping one of the parties achieve or retain their majority, it usually falls flat for most voters.

" 'Real America wants to know taxes, the economy, corporate behavior, college savings accounts, prescription drugs and Social Security. Those are the issues that impact real voters.'

"Political strategist Gregory Casey, who runs the Business-Industry Political Action Committee, a Republican-leaning group, agrees with Greenberg.

" 'We are not in a nationalized election,' Casey said. 'Left-right appeals are increasingly irrelevant. Party is not as significant a determinant for many voters. They look for a message of relevance to their daily lives, delivered by a source with whom they have a relationship. To the party faithful, control means a great deal. But to voters who need to be motivated to make a difference in the outcome of all these elections, it just doesn't mean much.' "

(*The New Orleans Times-Picayune*, September 21, 2002)

PAC CONTRIBUTIONS 2002

95% to
Republicans

5% to
Democrats

EMPLOYMENT
Declined to comment

INTERNSHIPS
Unpaid internships are available for full or part-time work. Internship opportunities are available throughout the year. Flexible schedules are available. Internships are available in marketing or communications, and political operations. About 70–80 percent of a BIPAC intern's work is substantive; the rest involves the more traditional "intern duties."

NEWSLETTERS
Action Report
BIPAC Weekly Report (electronic)
Elections Insight (bimonthly, quarterly, and
    electronic)
Pro-Business Picks
Washington Political Briefing Series

PUBLICATIONS
Alcee Hastings: Business Role Model?
Censure, Plus-Plus
Pols Are from Mercury, Business Is from Jupiter
The Reluctant Democracy
A Senate Strategy for Business
Thinking Anew
The Trouble with Voting Records
Voting Records (annual)

CONFERENCES
BIPAC Adam Smith Award Dinner (annual)
Leadership breakfasts (twice per month)
National briefings (periodic)
PAC workshops (monthly)
Washington briefings (monthly)

"At a briefing Tuesday, veteran political operative Bernadette Budde observed, 'We have an electorate that, as far as we can see, are bored or at least not engaged in this election.'

"Budde is senior vice president of the Business Industry Political Action Committee, an influential, Republican-leaning group that was the first pro-business PAC. In Budde's view, harried Americans, juggling work and family, simply find it too early to pay much attention to politics."

(*USA Today,* September 18, 2002)

The Business Roundtable

Established in 1972

DIRECTOR

John J. Castellani, president. Castellani became president May 1, 2001. Previously, Castellani was with Tenneco, Inc., which he joined in 1992 as senior vice president, government relations. He was named executive vice president in 1997 with responsibility for investor relations, government relations, communications, environment, health and safety, security and risk management. He joined the Roundtable following a stint leading the corporate and financial practice at the public relations firm, Burson-Marsteller.

BOARD OF DIRECTORS

Henry A. McKinnell, chair; chair and chief executive officer, Pfizer Inc.
Franklin D. Raines, co-chair; chair and chief executive officer, Fannie Mae
Edward B. Rust Jr., co-chair; chair and chief executive officer, State Farm Insurance Companies
John J. Castellani; president, Business Roundtable
Patricia Hanahan Engman; executive director, Business Roundtable
Johanna I. Schneider; executive director, external relations, Business Roundtable
Other members
C. Michael Armstrong
Ramani Ayer
J. T. Battenberg III
Kenneth I. Chenault
Edward M. Liddy
Harold McGraw III
Michael G. Morris
Steve Odland
David J. O'Reilly
Stephen W. Sanger
Joseph M. Tucci
G. Richard Wagoner

SCOPE

Members: approximately 150 corporations represented by their chief executive officers
Branches/chapters: None
Affiliates: None

STAFF

21 total—10 professional; 11 support

TAX STATUS

501(c)(6)

FINANCES

Declined to comment

FUNDING SOURCES

Membership dues, 100%

CONTACT INFORMATION

1615 L Street, NW, Suite 1100, Washington, DC 20036-5610
Phone: (202) 872-1260 • *Fax:* (202) 466-3509
General E-mail: info@brt.org • *Web site*: www.brt.org

Communications Director: Patricia (Tita) Freeman
(202) 496-3269 • tfreeman@businessroundtable.org
Human Resources Director: None

PURPOSE: "The Business Roundtable is an association of chief executive officers of leading corporations with a combined workforce of more than 10 million employees in the United States. The Roundtable is committed to advocating public policies that ensure vigorous economic growth, a dynamic global economy, and the well-trained and productive U.S. workforce essential for future competitiveness. The Business Roundtable believes that its potential for effectiveness is based on the fact that it draws on chief executive officers directly and personally, and presents government with reasoned alternatives and positive suggestions."

CURRENT CONCERNS: Civil justice reform • Corporate governance • Education reform (K-12) • Fiscal policy • Health care and retirement income • International trade and investment (trade liberalization) • Small business partnerships • State tax simplification

METHOD OF OPERATION: Advertisements • Awards program • Coalition forming • Congressional testimony • Grant-making • Internships • Legislative/regulatory monitoring (federal and state) • Lobbying (federal and state) • Media outreach • Polling • Research • Web site

Effectiveness and Political Orientation

"The growing Boeing Co. tanker controversy that claimed its chief executive has also set an influential business lobby scrambling to replace its leader.

"Boeing's Philip M. Condit resigned Monday amid growing skepticism from Congress and the Pentagon over the company's activities in pursuing some government contracts, including an Air Force contract to lease and buy Boeing refueling tankers. Boeing fired its chief financial officer last week for what it said was unethical conduct in the hiring of an Air Force procurement official this year. Condit was not the target of an ethics investigation.

"At the same time, Condit stepped down as chairman of the Business Roundtable, an association of chief executives of Fortune 500 companies, less than six months after assuming the top post. The association, which says its members lead companies 'with a combined workforce of more than 10 million employees in the United States and $3.7 trillion in annual revenues,' was a major force in pushing the Medicare overhaul Congress enacted last week."
(*The Washington Post*, December 4, 2003)

"The law, the Sarbanes-Oxley Act, is an all-encompassing to-do list that ranges from requiring outside auditors to be rotated every five years to hotlines that let employees be anonymous whistle-blowers. It forces companies to document that they are tracking what's going on in every crevice of the company so as to make it all but impossible for rogue executives to secretly bring a company to its knees.

"The law was supported by major business organizations such as The Business Roundtable. But popularity among top executives is falling. Thirty percent of 136 chief financial officers of large global companies surveyed by PricewaterhouseCooper had a favorable opinion of the law in June, down from 42% in October 2002."

(*USA Today,* October 20, 2003)

"U.S. regulators yesterday sparked criticism from both business leaders and labour unions by proposing rules to give shareholders more power to press for boardroom changes.

"Some corporate leaders said the proposals from the Securities and Exchange Commission played into the hands of special interest groups, while unions said they did not go far enough.

"The proposals would allow shareholders to nominate their own directors for election at annual meetings, potentially over the wishes of board-nominating committees. . . .

"The Business Roundtable, a group of chief executives, criticised the plans.

"Hank McKinnell, the chairman of Pfizer and co-chairman of the Business Roundtable, said the plans 'will not enhance corporate governance. Instead, the proposals present the possibility of special interest groups hijacking the director election process.' "

(*Financial Times* [London, England], October 20, 2003)

"The widening learning gap between lower- and higher-income children before they enter kindergarten may be the most serious problem facing education in the United States. And it's only going to get worse unless high-quality and costly early-education programs are put in place.

"This is the essence of a statement issued jointly by the Business Roundtable and Corporate Voices for Working Families, two leading business groups. The principles and background document issued earlier this month provide useful information, including a cost-benefit analysis, but the groups concede that money for so ambitious an undertaking will be hard to come by."

(*Columbus Dispatch* [Ohio], May 17, 2003)

"If a member of the House got phone calls from the president's right-hand man and from the secretary of the Treasury, and then held a private meeting with the Speaker of the House, that would be a pretty good day around here.

"Ordinarily. But these men were not talking at Rep. Jack Quinn, R-Hamburg, to pat him on the back. They were not offering him a cushy deal.

"This was the gantlet the White House set up to force Quinn to go back on his word to other members of the House, and his district.

"Quinn was among 11 moderate Republicans who said in a letter to the House Republican leadership they would not vote for a GOP leadership tax cut bill and budget that slashed $189 billion in federal aid for New York State over 10 years.

"To pressure Quinn into caving in, the Bush administration sicced lobbyists on him—people representing the ominously powerful Business Roundtable and at least one telecommunications business back home."

(*Buffalo News* [New York], March 31, 2003)

"The Business Roundtable, an organization of chief executives from large corporations, startled many of its normal allies last week by arguing that tax breaks for individuals would be more helpful than tax breaks for business.

"Indeed, the Roundtable's top recommendation was one favored by many Democrats: bolstering tax relief for low- and middle-income families by temporarily cutting payroll tax contributions for Social Security and Medicare.

" 'There is substantial overcapacity in the economy, so we don't need more capacity right now,' said John J. Castellani, the president of the Business Roundtable. 'We felt it would be more prudent and effective to stimulate consumption.'

"Those words sent shivers through rival business groups—like the National Association of Manufacturers—which are pressing for big new write-offs on investments."

(*The New York Times,* November 29, 2002)

The Campaign For Tobacco-Free Kids

Established in 1996

DIRECTOR

Matthew L. Myers, president. Myers, a nationally recognized tobacco-control advocate, previously served as the center's executive vice president and general counsel. He holds a B.A. from Tufts University and a J.D. from the University of Michigan Law School, where he was awarded the Order of the Coif and served on the staff of the Journal of Law Reform. In 1996, he received the Smokefree America Award as the lawyer who had made the greatest contribution to tobacco-control efforts in the United States. In 1989, he was awarded the prestigious Surgeon General's Medallion from Dr. C. Everett Koop for contributions to the public health of the nation. Myers is published widely in health and medical publications, and he appears regularly on national news programs to discuss tobacco issues.

BOARD OF DIRECTORS

Christopher Conley, president, Nonprofit Capital
Ernest Fleishman, senior vice president, Scholastic, Inc.
William D. Novelli, chief executive officer, AARP
John Seffrin, chief executive officer, American Cancer Society
David R. Smith, chancellor, Texas Tech University
Randy Smoak, first past president, Board of Trustees, AMA
Dorothy Wilson, member, NEA Board of Directors
Walter Kerr, Youth Advocate of the Year
S. Epatha Merkerson, actress
Cass Wheeler, chief executive officer, American Heart Association
Dileep G. Bal, chief, Cancer Control Branch, California Dept of Health
Michael C. Moore, general counsel, Litigation, Phelps Dunbar

SCOPE

Members: Declined to comment
Branches/chapters: Declined to comment
Affiliates: Declined to comment

STAFF

53 total—40 full-time professional; 11 full-time support; 2 part-time professional; plus 3 interns

TAX STATUS

501(c)(3)

FINANCES

Budget: 2004—$15.19 million
2003—$14.88 million
2002—$14.24 million

CONTACT INFORMATION

1400 I Street, NW, Suite 1200, Washington, DC 20005
Phone: (202) 296-5469 • *Fax:* (202) 296-5427
General E-mail: info@tobaccofreekids.org •
Web site: www.tobaccofreekids.org

Communications Director: Vince Willmore
(202) 296-5469 • vwillmore@tobaccofreekids.org
Human Resources Director: Jacqueline Bolt, director of finance and administration
(202) 296-5469 • jbolt@tobaccofreekids.org

PURPOSE: The Campaign For Tobacco-Free Kids seeks to promote environmental and policy changes that will prevent and reduce tobacco use and exposure to secondhand smoke, especially among children and that will minimize the harms caused by tobacco products.

CURRENT CONCERNS: Full funding of state and federal tobacco prevention programs • International tobacco control efforts • State and federal excise taxes on tobacco products • State and local smoke-free laws • U.S. Food and Drug Administration authority to regulate tobacco

METHOD OF OPERATION: Advertisements • Awards program • Coalition forming • Conferences/seminars • Congressional testimony • Congressional voting analysis • Films/video/audio tapes • Grant-making • Grassroots organizing • Information clearinghouse • International activities • Internet (databases, electronic bulletin boards, E-mail alerts, and Web site) • Internships • Legislative/regulatory monitoring (federal) • Legislative/regulatory monitoring (state) • Lobbying (federal, state, and grassroots) • Local/municipal affairs • Media outreach • Participation in regulatory proceedings (federal) • Participation in regulatory proceedings (state) • Polling • Research • Scholarships • Speakers program • Technical assistance • Training • Voting records

SPECIFIC PROGRAMS/INITIATIVES: Accountability Project (holding the tobacco industry accountable for its actions) • Faith-Based Outreach to Religious Groups • Grassroots Outreach to anti-tobacco advocates ("E-Champions") • "Kick Butts Day" (national event) • Outreach to Women ("Girl Talk") • Youth Advocate of the Year Awards

Effectiveness and Political Orientation

"A television commercial that debuted in Florida in 1998 portrayed tobacco executives as the world's biggest killers—ahead of murderers, even Hitler.

"A newspaper ad the same year featured a flabby, bikini-clad man smoking a cigarette while stretched out near a pool.

FUNDING SOURCES
Foundation grants, 77%; corporate donations, 11%; individuals, 1%; special events/projects, 2%; other sources, 9%.

PAC
None

EMPLOYMENT
Potential applicants can learn about job openings with this organization from the organization's Web site at www.tobaccofreekids.org, or by consulting *Roll Call, The Hill,* or *The Washington Post.*

The organization offers positions in the areas of administration, communications, advocacy, grassroots, research, accounting, computer and development. Applicants send resumes and other materials for employment to Jacqueline Bolt, director of finance & administration, 1400 I Street, NW, Suite 1200, Washington, DC 20005. No phone calls please. Fax: (202) 296-5427. E-mail: jobs@tobaccofreekids.org.

INTERNSHIPS
Offers both paid and unpaid internships. Potential applicants can learn about internship opportunities at tobaccofreekids.org and MonsterTrak.com. Internships are typically 3–4 months on average. Application deadlines are ongoing. A minimum of 15 hours are required, and internship areas include communications, development, grassroots and advocacy. Successful candidates for internships must demonstrate attention to detail, strong writing skills, an ability to handle multiple tasks with aggressive deadlines, and professional attitude and demeanor.

The internship coordinator at this organization is Laura Thomas, associate, communications and special events, 1400 I Street, NW, Suite 1200, Washington, DC 20005. Phone: (202) 296-5469. Fax: (202) 296-5427. E-mail: lthomas@tobaccofreekids.org.

NEWSLETTERS
None

PUBLICATIONS
Show Us the Money (report on state tobacco settlement spending)
Saving Lives (Video)

CONFERENCES
None

"The caption read: 'No wonder tobacco executives have to hide behind sexy models.'

"Not everyone agreed with the messages but nearly all remember them. And most give the ads credit for helping reduce teen smoking.

"Smoking dropped 57 percent among middle school students and 36 percent among high schoolers in the five years since. Still, almost 18 percent of high school students smoke, and 35,900 kids take up the habit every year, according to the Campaign For Tobacco-Free Kids.

"That's why the national group wants the Legislature to increase funding for the state's tobacco prevention program. Funding was cut from $70 million in 1998, when it was created, to $1 million last year.

"Gov. Jeb Bush has recommended restoring funding to $16 million this session. House and Senate budgets contain no money for the initiative. . . ."

(*Tampa Tribune,* [Florida], March 31, 2004)

"A cigarette tax increase would be healthy for the Texas economy and its citizens, advocates said Friday.

"Danny McGoldrick, research director for the Washington, D.C.-based Campaign For Tobacco-Free Kids, said a $1-a-pack increase would raise $987 million in new tax revenues and save billions in long-term health care costs.

"'This is a tremendous opportunity for the state of Texas to address its budget problems relating to education as well as to address the leading health problem in Texas, (which) is tobacco use,' McGoldrick said.

"But Bill Orzechowski, an anti-cigarette tax consultant, said raising the tax would increase the demand for black-market cigarettes. . . .

"The testimony came on the second day of a hearing by a legislative committee trying to find new revenue options to fund public schools. . . .

"States that have raised their cigarette taxes have found that demand for tobacco decreased. McGoldrick said he believes an increase in Texas would result in 301,000 fewer youth smokers and 179,000 fewer adult smokers.

"Over time, the state also would save $5 billion in long-term health care costs, McGoldrick said. . . ."

(*The Houston Chronicle,* December 6, 2003)

"Tobacco giant Philip Morris (now known as the Altria Group) and public health advocates don't often sing the same tune. But yesterday Matthew Myers of the Campaign for Tobacco-Free Kids declared, regarding legislation to grant the Food and Drug Administration regulatory authority over tobacco: 'No major impediments remain to reaching an agreement that can win support from a broad bipartisan coalition in Congress.' Altria representative Mark Berlind said he 'fully endorses' Mr. Myers's words: 'There shouldn't be any impediment in terms of the substance of the bill.' But, alas, Mr. Myers and Mr. Berlind agree about something else too: There remains a big nonsubstantive impediment to what would otherwise become landmark legislation that both the nation's leading cigarette manufacturer and its key public-health adversaries could support. That impediment is an effort by Sens. Elizabeth Dole (R-N.C.) and Mitch McConnell (R-Ky.), along with tobacco-state members of the House of Representatives, to stick into the omnibus appropriations bill a provision to buy out struggling tobacco farmers. If this effort succeeds, Mr. Berlind stresses, 'it will unquestionably be harder to get the FDA effort through. . . .' "

(*The Washington Post,* November 21, 2003)

"Antismoking groups say they are concerned that the city's new law banning smoking in bars and restaurants is getting a bum rap, so they are planning a campaign to publicize a poll, which they commissioned, showing that the ban enjoys wide support.

"The poll, which was taken for a consortium of antismoking groups including the Campaign for Tobacco-Free Kids and the American Cancer Society, found that 70 percent of city voters surveyed said they supported the ban, while 27 percent oppose it.

"The antismoking groups hope to use the findings to dispel media reports suggesting that the ban is unpopular and could hurt the elected officials who supported it. They are planning a million-dollar advertising campaign to boost the ban, along with an Internet campaign and a lobbying effort to show local officials that the law is popular. . . ."

(*The New York Times,* September 22, 2003)

"Chris Christensen, manager of Marquard's Smoke Shop in downtown San Francisco, isn't too worried that 192 nations have unanimously adopted a global treaty aimed at curbing tobacco use.

"Nor is he terribly concerned about a provision of the treaty banning all 'tobacco advertising, promotion and sponsorship,' even though his shop, which has been in business for almost half a century, is festooned with cigarette ads and promotions.

"Christensen has been following the issue and he knows that even though the United States was among the nations adopting the treaty last week, it still must be first signed by President Bush and then ratified by the U.S. Senate.

"As we've seen with the Kyoto global-warming treaty, not all accords adopted internationally end up being embraced by this administration.

"So will Bush sign the tobacco treaty?

"Christensen smiled. 'Probably not,' he said.

"Indeed, while anti-smoking advocates hailed passage of the tobacco treaty as a milestone in protecting global public health, they know chances remain slim that the United States will join the party.

"Enactment of key treaty provisions will be bitterly opposed by the tobacco industry, which, according to regulatory filings, has doled out more than $26 million in political contributions since 1997. Eighty percent of that sum went to Republican interests.

" 'Nearly every nation at the ceremony in Geneva stood up and said they not only support the treaty but look forward to signing and ratifying it,' observed Matt Myers, president of the Campaign for Tobacco-Free Kids, an anti-smoking lobbying group.

" 'The United States was the only nation that stood up and said, "We support it but our president is still reviewing the text and hasn't decided what he'll do.' "

(*The San Francisco Chronicle,* May 25, 2003)

Capital Research Center

Established in 1984

DIRECTOR

Terrence Scanlon, president. Scanlon was named Capital Research Center president and chair of its board of trustees in 1994. Earlier, he was vice president for corporate relations at The Heritage Foundation. His public career includes an appointment by President Ronald Reagan to the U.S. Consumer Product Safety Commission where he served seven years, including service as chair. He holds a B.S. in economics from Villanova University in Pennsylvania. He serves on several nonprofit boards and is a frequent contributor for various newspapers, cable news networks, and radio stations.

BOARD OF DIRECTORS

Terrence Scanlon, chair and president; Capital Research Center

Beverly Danielson, trustee; Institute of World Politics

Constance C. Larcher, president and executive director; Washington Legal Foundation

Edwin Meese III, Ronald Reagan distinguished fellow; The Heritage Foundation

Daniel J. Popeo, chair and general counsel; Washington Legal Foundation

Dean Webster, retired chief executive officer; Blue Seal Foods, Inc.

Marion G. Wells, secretary; Lillian Wells Foundation

SCOPE

Members: None
Branches/chapters: One
Affiliates: None

STAFF

14 total—10 professional; 4 support

TAX STATUS

501(c)(3)

FINANCES

Revenue: 2002—$1.5 million

FUNDING SOURCES

Declined to comment

PAC

None

EMPLOYMENT

Those interested in obtaining a career with Capital Research Center should contact the organization by e-mail at contact@capitalresearch.org. The center employs research fellows, research assistants, and editors. Cover letters and resumes can be mailed

CONTACT INFORMATION

1513 16th Street, NW, Washington, DC 20036-1480
Phone: (202) 483-6900 • *Fax:* (202) 483-6902
General E-mail: contact@capitalresearch.org •
Web site: www.capitalresearch.org

Communications Director: Robert Volmer
(202) 232-6575 • rvolmer@crosbyvolmer.com
Human Resources Director: Chris Morris
(202) 483-6900 • cmorris@capitalresearch.org

PURPOSE: "To increase public awareness of the leadership, activities, and sources of funding for advocacy groups."

CURRENT CONCERNS: Free market economy • Individual liberty • Limited constitutional government • Nonprofit sector's involvement in the environment, education, healthcare, economic development, social policy, and foreign policy • Personal responsibility • Philanthropy • Tax-exempt status rulings

METHOD OF OPERATION: Educational foundation • Electoral politics • Grant-making • Informational clearinghouse • International activities • Internet (databases, E-mail alerts, and Web site) • Internships • Legislative/regulatory monitoring (federal) • Legislative/regulatory monitoring (state) • Media outreach • Performance ratings • Research

Effectiveness and Political Orientation

"In its role as a conservative watchdog of the philanthropic community, the Capital Research Center of Washington, D.C., has detailed the clout of advocacy NGOs at international meetings."

(*National Review,* January 26, 2004)

"According to Daniel Oliver, a research associate with the Capital Research Center, which studies nonprofit organizations in the U.S., animal rights groups 'routinely use false and unsubstantiated allegations of animal abuse to raise funds, attract media attention, and bring supporters into the movement.'

"As well, they 'have imposed significant costs on the individuals, businesses, and concerns they have targeted.'"

(*The Toronto Sun* [Canada], December 2, 2001)

"Terrence Scanlon, president of Capital Research Center, an organization critical of the political activities of liberal foundations, said conservatives 'fear that the Office of Faith-Based Initiatives is going to be churning out government grants and tempting charities with federal dollars. . . .'

"'The administration must avoid the pitfalls that have caused so many charities to become wards of the federal government and advocates for bigger

to Robert Huberty, director of research, 1513 16th Street, NW, Washington, DC 20036-1480. Fax: (202) 232-6535. E-mail: contact@ capitalresearch.org.

INTERNSHIPS

Unpaid semester-long internships are available in the areas of research, communications, and fundraising. There are no application deadlines. Working hours are 15–40 hours per week. Applicants must be pursuing a college degree and have an interest in free market principles and charity. Internship applications can be sent to Chris Morris, editor, Capital Research Center, 1513 16th Street, NW, Washington, DC 20036-1480. E-mail: cmorris@capitalresearch.org.

NEWSLETTERS

Compassion and Culture (monthly)
Foundation Watch (monthly)
Labor Watch (monthly)
Organization Trends (monthly)

PUBLICATIONS

Capital Research Center 20001 Donor's Guide to Philanthropy Advisory Services
Classical Education
Frightening America's Elderly
The Fulbright Program after 50 Years
Global Greens
The Great Philanthropists and the Problem of "Donor Intent"
Guide to Feminist Organizations
Loving Your Neighbor
Mandate for Charity
Patterns of Corporate Philanthropy
Return to Charity?
The Rise of the Nanny State
Should Foundations Live Forever?

CONFERENCES

Conferences vary greatly and are announced as needed.

government,' Scanlon said at a news conference to release a report entitled 'Mandate for Charity.' Scanlon was joined by Robert L. Woodson Sr., a conservative advocate of neighborhood-based programs.

"Woodson and Scanlon, while not rejecting the idea of government grants to faith-based groups, placed more emphasis on expanding tax breaks—including eliminating the estate tax and relaxing rules for taxpayers who take charitable deductions—and lifting state, federal and city regulation of religious charities. . . .

"There has been some division within conservative ranks over the proposed elimination of the estate tax. Yesterday, Scanlon came down firmly in favor of abolition."

(*The Washington Post*, February 17, 2001)

"According to a March 2000 report by (Ted) Turner's United Nations Foundation, a grant of $2.5 million was directed to Honduras . . . for 'social licensing of reproductive health clinics.'

"Said Terrence Scanlon, president of the Capital Research Center, a conservative, Washington-based, charity watchdog: 'I don't think that should be any American tycoon's mission. Many times, this money is going into countries where a majority of the people, whether Muslim or Christian, oppose this family planning.'"

(*The San Francisco Chronicle*, January 21, 2001)

Carnegie Endowment
for International Peace

Established in 1910

DIRECTOR

Jessica Tuchman Mathews was appointed president of the Endowment in 1997. Her career includes posts in the executive and legislative branches of government, in management and research in the nonprofit arena, and in journalism.

BOARD OF DIRECTORS

Bill Bradley; managing director, Allen & Company, New York, NY

Robert Carswell; counsel, Shearman & Sterling, New York, NY

Jerome A. Cohen; counsel, Paul, Weiss, Rifkind, Wharton & Garrison, New York, NY

Gregory B. Craig, vice chairman; partner, Williams & Connolly, Washington, DC

Richard A. Debs; advisory director, Morgan Stanley, New York, NY

Susan Eisenhower; president, The Eisenhower World Affairs Institute, Washington, DC

Donald V. Fites; chairman of the board, retired, Caterpillar, Inc., Peoria, IL

James C. Gaither, chairman; managing director, Sutter Hill Ventures, Palo Alto, CA; special counsel, Cooley Godward, Palo Alto, CA

Leslie H. Gelb; president emeritus, Council on Foreign Relations, Washington, DC

William W. George; former chairman and chief executive officer, Medtronic, Inc., Minneapolis, MN

Richard Giordano; chairman, retired, BG Group, United Kingdom

Jamie Gorelick; partner, Wilmer, Cutler & Pickering, Washington, DC

Stephen D. Harlan; partner, Harlan Enterprises LLC

Donald Kennedy; president emeritus and Bing Professor of Environmental Science Emeritus, Stanford University, Institute for International Studies, Stanford, CA

Robert Legvold; professor of political science, The Harrison Institute, Columbia University, New York, NY

Stephen R. Lewis Jr.; president emeritus, Carleton College, Northfield, MN

Jessica T. Mathews; president, Carnegie Endowment for International Peace, Washington, DC

Zanny Minton Beddoes; economics correspondent, *The Economist,* United Kingdom

Olara A. Otunnu; special representative of the Secretary General for Children and Armed Conflict, United Nations, New York, NY

William J. Perry; professor, Stanford University, Institute for International Studies, Stanford, CA

CONTACT INFORMATION

1779 Massachusetts Avenue, NW, Washington, DC 20036-2103
Phone: (202) 483-7600 • *Fax:* (202) 483-1840
General E-mail: info@CarnegieEndowment.org •
Web site: www.CarnegieEndowment.org

Communications Director: Carmen MacDougall, vice president for communications
(202) 939-2319 • cmacdougall@CarnegieEndowment.org
Human Resources Director: Lynne Sport, director, human resources and administration
(202) 939-2221 • lsport@CarnegieEndowment.org

PURPOSE: The Carnegie Endowment for International Peace is a private, nonprofit organization dedicated to advancing cooperation between nations and promoting active international engagement by the United States. Founded in 1910, its work is nonpartisan and dedicated to achieving practical results.

CURRENT CONCERNS: Russia • Eurasia • China • Middle East • South Asia • Global policy (nonproliferation, democracy, rule of law, U.S. role in the world, international trade)

METHOD OF OPERATION: Advertisements • Conferences/seminars • Congressional testimony • Films, video, audiotapes • International activities • Internet (databases, e-mail alerts, and Web site) • Internships • Media outreach • Research • Telecommunications services (mailing lists)

Effectiveness and Political Orientation

"The search for weapons of mass destruction in Iraq grows ever less likely to produce results. But the futility of the hunt should produce something just as important: lessons for Americans.

"The Pentagon is withdrawing much of the team looking for chemical, biological or nuclear weapons and delivery systems. That's a strong signal.

"A new report from the Carnegie Endowment for International Peace suggests Iraq destroyed its weapons after the Gulf War. The think tank said that pressure on U.S. intelligence analysts contributed to the faulty information given the public about an imminent threat.

"As Secretary of State Colin Powell on Thursday defended pre-war assessments, Saddam Hussein obviously hoped to revive his weapons programs. Indeed, the pre-war concern extended to the Clinton administration and many leading congressional Democrats.

"Yet, unless Pentagon inspectors are missing huge stockpiles, the United States launched a war without an immediate threat to national security. In doing so, we aborted an effective United Nations inspection program.

W. Taylor Reveley III; dean, William & Mary School of Law, Williamsburg, VA

Strobe Talbott; president, Brookings Institution, Washington, DC

SCOPE

Members: None
Branches/chapters: None
Affiliates: None

STAFF

97, plus 37 at Carnegie Moscow Center

TAX STATUS

501(c)(3)

FINANCES

Budget: 2004—$19.5 million (estimated); 2003—$18.6 million; 2002—$18.3 million

FUNDING SOURCES

Endowment operating funds, 60%; foundation grants, corporate and individual support grants, 19%; publications, 11%; other, 10%

PAC

None

EMPLOYMENT

A range of research and administrative positions are available. Current employment opportunities are posted at www.CarnegieEndowment.org and at www.foreignpolicy.com. Resumes should be sent to the address listed on the position announcement. The Carnegie Endowment accepts resumes for posted positions only. Unsolicited resumes are not retained. The Carnegie Endowment is an equal opportunity employer.

General contact information for the human resources department: e-mail: hr@CarnegieEndowment.org; fax: (202) 939-2392.

INTERNSHIPS

Internships are offered through the Endowment's Junior Fellows Program. Each year the Endowment offers 8–10 one-year fellowships to qualified graduating seniors and individuals who have graduated during the past academic year. Carnegie Junior Fellows work as research assistants to the Endowment's senior associates. The Endowment's nomination deadline is January 15 of each year. Colleges generally set an earlier application deadline. Interested persons should consult their career services/placement office to learn more about the college internship application process.

For additional information contact Julia McElderry, administrator of the Carnegie Junior Fellows Program, at jrfellowinfo@carnegieendowment.org.

NEWSLETTERS

Foreign Policy (six times a year)
Arab Reform Bulletin (monthly)

"The Carnegie report calls for reconsideration of the administration's sweeping doctrine of pre-emptive attack. And we need to rely first on what was working, namely cooperative action through the United Nations."

(*Seattle Post-Intelligencer,* January 11, 2004)

"A 400-strong American team, tasked with searching Iraq for military equipment, has been withdrawn, senior US government officials said yesterday.

"According to some officials, the withdrawal of the Joint Captured Material Exploitation Group was a sign that the Bush administration has lowered its expectations of finding hidden weapons of mass destruction in Iraq.

"It comes as an independent report by a Washington think tank suggested that US intelligence officials came under political pressure to make a stronger case for war against Iraq.

"The Carnegie Endowment for International Peace concluded that intelligence assessments on Iraq were 'broken.'

"Report author Joseph Cirincione said: 'We looked at the intelligence assessment process and we have come to the conclusion that it is broken.

" 'It has now become deeply politicized . . . it is very likely that intelligence officials were pressured by senior administration officials to conform to the threat assessment of pre-existing policies.'

"He said Iraqi weapons programmes were 'crippled' by years of sanctions and US air strikes.

(*Birmingham Post* [England], January 9, 2004)

"As the North American Free Trade Agreement nears its 10th anniversary, a study has concluded that the pact has failed to generate substantial job growth in Mexico, hurt hundreds of thousands of subsistence farmers there and had ''minuscule'' net effects on jobs in the United States.

"The study by the Carnegie Endowment for International Peace, an independent Washington-based research institute, was released Tuesday to coincide with a new round of trade talks aimed at the adoption of a Nafta-like pact for the entire Western Hemisphere. Trade ministers from 34 countries in the Americas are gathering now in Miami. The report seeks to debunk the fears of U.S. labor that Nafta would lure large numbers of jobs to low-wage Mexico. It also damps the hopes of the trade deal's proponents that it would lead to rising wages in Mexico and declines in income inequality and illegal immigration. Though sorting out the exact causes is complicated, wages in Mexico, adjusted for inflation, are lower now than they were when the agreement was adopted, despite higher productivity. In addition, income inequality is greater there and immigration has continued to soar.

" 'On balance, Nafta's been rough for rural Mexicans,' said John Audley, who edited the report. 'For the country, it's probably a wash. It takes more than just trade liberalization to improve the quality of life for poor people around the world.' "

(*International Herald Tribune,* November 20, 2003)

"As American and British troops in Iraq deal with ambushes and sabotage, Iraqi citizens continue to deal with a lack of electricity, water, food and civil infrastructure—let alone order. Vastly more manpower—and the right kind of manpower—is needed.

Proliferation News (biweekly e-mail
newsletter with links to news stories on
weapons of mass destruction and periodic
issues briefs on breaking news)
Pro et Contra (published in Russian by
Carnegie Moscow Center, with online
English summaries)
Carnegie e-News (twice-monthly e-mail alert)

PUBLICATIONS

Carnegie produces 30–40 publications per
year, ranging from books and reports to working papers to electric content. Staff also publish extensively in newspapers, magazines,
and journals. Visit www.CarnegieEndowment
.org/pubs for more details. Recent publications
include the following:

*Ambivalent Neighbors: The EU, NATO and the
Price of Membership*
*Between Dictatorship and Democracy:
Russian Post-Communist Political Reform*
*Democracy Challenged: The Rise of Semi-
Authoritarianism*
Islam and Democracy in the Middle East
*Of Paradise and Power: America and Europe in
the New World Order*
*Open Networks, Closed Regimes: The Impact
of the Internet on Authoritarian Rule*
Putin's Russia
*Russia's Restless Frontier: The Chechnya
Factor in Post-Soviet Russia*

CONFERENCES

The Carnegie Endowment hosts more than
100 events per year, ranging from small,
private meetings to larger gatherings. The
Endowment hosts the biannual Carnegie
Endowment Non-Proliferation Conference
every 18 months. All events are by invitation
only. Many events are presented as "Live at
Carnegie" with audio or video on the web.

"Paul Bremer, the American in charge of civil authority, believes Baathist elements are largely to blame for assaults on U.S. troops—who are acutely aware that the war isn't over. After visiting Iraq, Sens. Joe Biden and Chuck Hagel, the ranking Democrat and Republican on the Foreign Relations Committee, called for international forces—including NATO—to be recruited to help. . . .

"As for nation-building, Biden described American efforts as 'vastly underfunded and vastly undermanned.' And Jessica Mathews, president of the Carnegie Endowment for Peace, wrote in *Foreign Policy:* 'Iraq clearly proves again . . . that the United States chronically underestimates the difficulties of nonmilitary aspects of foreign interventions and wildly inflates nonmilitary goals without committing the resources required to achieve them.' . . .

"Minxin Pei of Carnegie Endowment studied successes and failures of all U.S. attempts at nation-building in America's history. What he found is fascinating: 'A key aspect of nation-building failures,' he writes, 'has been a unilateral approach. . . . Multilateralism has its limitations, such as poor coordination and burdensome bureaucracy. Yet history suggests that multilateralism manages risk, while unilateralism invites it.' "

(*Star Tribune* [Minneapolis, Minn.], June 30, 2003)

Catalyst

Established in 1962

DIRECTOR

Ilene H. Lang, president. Lang has been president since September 2003. She was formerly president and chief executive officer of Individual.com Inc. and chief executive officer of Essential.com, an energy and communications marketplace serving small business and residential customers. She was founding chief executive officer of AltaVista Internet Software Inc., a subsidiary of Digital Equipment Corporation. Lang was also senior vice president of the Desktop Business Group at Lotus Development Corporation; interim chief operating officer of the Industrial Technology Institute; president of Adelie Corporation; and an executive of Ontos. Lang also served in management positions at Symbolics. Lang earned an A.B. degree in history and literature from Radcliffe College and an M.B.A. from Harvard Business School.

BOARD OF DIRECTORS

Lord Browne of Madingley
Tony Comper
Michael J. Critelli
Douglas N. Daft
Thomas J. Engibous
Christopher B. Galvin
Cinda A. Hallman
William B. Harrison Jr.
Charles O. Holliday Jr.
Jeffrey R. Immelt
Ann Dibble Jordan
Andrea Jung
Karen Katen
Ilene H. Lang
Dawn Gould Lepore
Edward M. Liddy
John J. Mack
Reuben Mark
C. Steven McMillan
Anne M. Mulcahy
Joseph Neubauer
Katherine Ortega
Henry M. Paulson Jr.
Joseph A. Pichler
Barbara Paul Robinson, Esq.
Judith Rodin
Stephen W. Sanger
Martha R. Seger
Cam Starrett
James S. Turley
G. Richard Wagoner Jr.
Lawrence A. Weinbach
John D. Zeglis

CONTACT INFORMATION

120 Wall Street, 5th Floor, New York, NY 10005
Phone: (212) 514-7600 • *Fax:* (212) 514-8470
General E-mail: info@catalystwomen.org • *Web site:* www.catalystwomen.org

Communications Director: Nancy Guida, vice president, marketing and public affairs
nguida@catalystwomen.org
Human Resources Director: Jennifer Daniel-Davidson, vice president, finance/administration
jdaniel@catalystwomen.org

PURPOSE: "To enable women to achieve their full professional potential and to help employers capitalize fully on women's talents and abilities. Catalyst conducts research on all aspects of women's career advancement and provides . . . consulting services on a global basis to help companies and firms advance women and build inclusive work environments."

CURRENT CONCERNS: Flexibility in the workplace (child care, part-time work, telecommuting) • Glass ceiling components • Glass wall • Leadership issues—individual strategies • Managing diversity • Sexual harassment • Women of color in corporate management • Women on corporate boards • Women's workplace networks • Work/family issues

METHOD OF OPERATION: Awards program • Conferences/seminars • Corporate and professional advisory services • Corporate board placement • Information clearinghouse • Library services (members only) • Media outreach • Research • Speakers bureau

Effectiveness and Political Orientation

"At a time when women comprise close to half the work force and hold more than half the managerial and professional jobs, their arrival in corporate boardrooms progresses at glacial speed.

"As of March, women held just 13.6 percent of board seats at Fortune 500 companies, up from 12.4 percent two years ago and 9.6 percent in 1995, according to a report released today by Catalyst, a Manhattan-based research and advisory group. 'The numbers are directionally correct but it's disappointing we haven't seen more progress,' said Ilene H. Lang, Catalyst's new president. That 13.6 percent figure 'does not adequately reflect the influence and impact women have on the economy. . . .'

"Indeed, Lang points to some positives. The Catalyst 'honor roll' of 54 firms with boards comprised of 25 percent or more women. That's up from 30 firms in 2001 and 11 in 1995, when Catalyst first started keeping track.

"She pointed, too, to the opening up of the board selection process being brought about by the Sarbanes-Oxley Act. Women will benefit, she said, as com-

SCOPE
Members: 299 corporate members
Branches/chapters: Western Region office:
2825 North First Street, Suite 200,
San Jose, CA 95134; Toronto office:
8 King Street East, Suite 505, Toronto,
Ontario M5C-1B5
Affiliates: None

STAFF
55 total—plus student interns and volunteers

TAX STATUS
501(c)(3)

FINANCES
Revenue: 2002—$7.4 million

FUNDING SOURCES
A nationwide consortium of corporations, professional firms, and foundations

PAC
None

EMPLOYMENT
Currently open staff positions listed on the Catalyst Web site. Resumes and a cover letter may be e-mailed to: jobs@catalystwomen.org. Information on open positions can be obtained by contacting Rukshana Mazagonwalla at (212) 514-7600, ext. 388. E-mail: rmazagonwalla@catalystwomen.org.

INTERNSHIPS
Internships are available in the advisory services, marketing, public affairs, research, and technical services departments. Internships are available in the New York, San Jose, and Toronto locations. Information on internships can be obtained by contacting Rukshana Mazagonwalla at (212) 514-7600, ext. 388. E-mail: rmazagonwalla@catalystwomen.org.

NEWSLETTERS
Perspective (monthly)

PUBLICATIONS
The following is a sample list of publications:
Advancing Asian Women in the Workplace
Advancing Latinas in the Workplace
Be Your Own Mentor
Census of Women Directors of the Fortune 500 (annual)
Cracking the Glass Ceiling: Strategies for Success
Flexible Work Arrangements III: A Ten-Year Perspective
Going Global: Passport to Opportunity
Human Resources Professionals' Desk Set
A New Approach to Flexibility: Managing the Work/Time Equation
Women and the MBA: Gateway to Opportunity
Women of Color in Corporate Management: Opportunities and Barriers

CONFERENCES
Annual awards dinner, conference, and pre-conference luncheon (every March, New York City).

panies cast a wider net, especially in finance and compensation, two areas where she says women have done well. 'We are encouraged by the possibilities.' "

(*Newsday* [New York], December 4, 2003)

"The United States leads the world in technological advances, but women are still denied many of the high-tech industry's leadership roles, according to a new study by Catalyst, a nonprofit research and advisory group dedicated to advancing women in business.

"The obstacles women face while climbing the corporate ladder—a male-dominated business culture, poor recruitment and professional development, and work-life balance issues—hold them back regardless of the industry, the report said.

" 'The barriers and demands of the high-tech industry are very similar to those of traditional industries,' Catalyst President Ilene Lang said. 'What is surprising is that in an industry that thinks of itself as a meritocracy, women and men both perceive a lack of acceptance of women.'

"The study, released Wednesday, revealed that nearly a third of men and women participants agreed that women have a difficult time getting ahead. Among Fortune 500 high-tech companies, women make up 11.1 percent of corporate officers. That's lower than the 15.7 percent of corporate officers women account for in Fortune 500 firms overall, according to Catalyst. . . .

"The report suggests that in order to change, companies should address the barriers to women's advancement by including women in career development programs, providing opportunities for mentoring and networking with other successful women, and fostering flexibility."

(*The Houston Chronicle*, November 13, 2003)

"Ever since we launched Fortune's Most Powerful Women list in 1998, we've noticed that many top-performing companies . . . have an above-average population of women at the top. Now there's some hard evidence that gender diversity and financial performance are linked. A just-released study of FORTUNE 500 companies by Catalyst, the research firm that tracks corporate women, shows that companies with the highest representation of senior women had a 35% higher return on equity and a 34% higher return to shareholders than companies with the fewest women near the top. . . .

"Catalyst's researchers hazard that gender-balanced companies fish the entire talent pool and manage to avoid the sort of herd mentality that can stunt creativity. . . . 'Good companies manage well in multiple areas,' figures Catalyst president Ilene Lang. 'If you're doing a good job with your talent, you're probably doing a good job around marketing and sales and product development too.' "

(*Fortune*, February 9, 2004)

"A pioneer in the high-tech industry, Ilene Lang is preparing for another challenge. The former chief executive officer of Individual.com, and the founding chief executive officer of AltaVista Internet Software Inc., Lang is leaving Boston for New York to become president of Catalyst, the nation's leading nonprofit organization focused on advancing women in business. A venture partner in the Boston-based First Light Capital, Lang, a Radcliffe graduate, will take the reins of the $8.5 million Catalyst organization Sept. 8. . . . "

(*The Boston Globe*, August 23, 2003)

Cato Institute

Established in 1977

DIRECTOR

Edward H. Crane, president. Crane has been president of the Cato Institute since its founding. Crane is a chartered financial analyst and former vice president at Alliance Capital Management Corp. Crane serves on the Board of U.S. Term Limits and is a member of the Mont Pèlerin Society. Crane is a graduate of the University of California at Berkeley and the University of Southern California Graduate School of Business Administration.

BOARD OF DIRECTORS

William A. Niskanen, chair; Cato Institute
Edward H. Crane, president; Cato Institute
Peter Ackerman, managing director; Rockport Financial Ltd.
K. Tucker Andersen, senior consultant; Cumberland Associates
Frank Bond, chair; Foundation Group
Richard J. Dennis, president; Dennis Trading Group
Theodore J. Forstmann, principal; Forstmann Little & Company
Ethelmae C. Humphreys, chair; Tamko Roofing Products, Inc.
David H. Koch, executive vice president; Koch Industries, Inc.
John C. Malone, chair; Liberty Media Corporation
David H. Padden, president; Padden & Company
Lewis E. Randall, board member; E*Trade Financial
Howard S. Rich, president; U.S. Term Limits
Frederick W. Smith, chair & chief executive officer; FedEx Corp.
Jeffrey S. Yass, managing director; Susquehanna International Group

SCOPE

Members: 13,000 individual sponsors, 75 corporate sponsors, 50 foundation sponsors
Branches/chapters: None
Affiliates: None

STAFF

98 total—76 professional; 22 support; 22 interns; plus adjunct scholars and fellows

TAX STATUS

501(c)(3)

FINANCES

Budget: 2004—$14.5 million
2003—$14.8 million
2002—$17.75 million

FUNDING SOURCES

Foundation grants, 14%; corporate donations, 7%; individuals, 72%; publications, 1%; conferences/special events/projects, 6%

CONTACT INFORMATION

1000 Massachusetts Avenue, NW, Washington, DC 20001-5403
Phone: (202) 842-0200 • *Fax:* (202) 842-3490
General E-mail: cato@cato.org • *Web site:* www.cato.org

Communications Director: Richard Pollock, vice president for communications
(202) 218-4628 • rpollock@cato.org
Human Resources Director: William Erickson, vice president for finance and administration
(202) 842-0200 • erickson@cato.org

PURPOSE: "To broaden the parameters of public policy debate to allow consideration of the traditional American principles of limited government, individual liberty, free markets and peace. Toward that goal, the Institute strives to achieve greater involvement of the intelligent, concerned lay public in questions of policy and the proper role of government."

CURRENT CONCERNS: Civil liberties • Constitutional studies • Defense policy • Economics • Education • Environment and natural resource studies • Energy policy • Fiscal policy • Foreign policy • International economic development • Health and welfare • Monetary and banking policy • Privatization • Regulation • Social issues • Social Security • Technology

METHOD OF OPERATION: Advertisements • Awards program • Conferences/seminars • Congressional testimony • Educational foundation • Fax-on-demand • Films/video/audiotapes • Information clearinghouse • International activities • Internet (databases, E-mail alerts, and Web site) • Internships • Legislative/regulatory monitoring (federal and state) • Local/municipal affairs • Mailing lists • Media outreach • Performance ratings/Report cards (companies, products, etc.) • Research • Speakers program

Effectiveness and Political Orientation

"Mike Tanner is director of the Project on Social Security Choice at the Cato Institute, a Washington think tank that advocates limited government and free markets."

(*USA Today,* February 24, 2004)

"Conservatives and other limited-government types are furious at President George W. Bush for his big-spending ways. One group said the Republican-controlled government is dispensing cash like a 'drunken sailor.' But in fact, there's nothing spontaneous or accidental about the spending spree. What we're seeing is the sober logic of a changing Republican Party, as well as a changing American psyche, post-9/11—from peacetime consumerism to wartime welfarism. Those seeking to measure such changes might dip into

EMPLOYMENT
Potential applicants can learn about job openings with the Cato Institute at their Web site. The organization employs policy directors, policy analysts, and research assistants in the areas of development, marketing, administration and human resources, technical and web support, media relations, accounting and finance. Cover letters and resumes can be sent to Janette Stout, director of administration, 1000 Massachusetts Avenue, NW, Washington, DC 20001-5403. Fax: (202) 842-3490. E-mail: jstout@cato.org.

INTERNSHIPS
Semester-long paid internships are available, including during the summer. Internship information is available on the Web site. Application deadlines are March 1 for summer session; July 1 for fall session; and November 1 for spring session. Both full-time and part-time internships are available in the areas of constitutional studies, economics, education, environment and natural resource studies, government affairs, energy policy, fiscal policy, foreign policy, defense policy, international economic development, health and welfare, monetary and banking policy, privatization, regulation, social issues, social security, technology, and media relations.

College students, graduate students, recent college graduates, law school students, and recent law school graduates are eligible. Internship applications can be sent to Justin Logan, intern coordinator, 1000 Massachusetts Avenue, NW, Washington, DC 20001-5403. E-mail: jlogan@cato.org.

NEWSLETTERS
Cato Audio Series (monthly)
Cato Journal (3 times a year)
Cato Policy Report (bimonthly)
Cato's Letter (quarterly)
Regulation (quarterly)

PUBLICATIONS
Antidumping Exposed
Bad Neighbor Policy: Washington's Futile War on Drugs in Latin America
Cato Handbook for Congress (108th)
Cato Supreme Court Review: 2002–2003
Corporate Aftershock
Economic Freedom of the World: 2003 Annual Report
Eco-nomics
The Half-Life of Policy Rationales: How New Technology Affects Old Policy Issues
In Defense of Global Capitalism
Just Get Out of the Way
Mugged by the State
The Pocket Constitution
The Poverty of Welfare
Restoring the Lost Constitution
Space: The Free-Market Frontier
Voucher Wars: Waging the Legal Battle Over School Choice
What's Yours Is Mine
Who Rules the Net?

Bush's newly released Fiscal Year 2005 budget; its pages offer proof that the era of big government is back again.

"Those who dislike the trend have been vocal in their opposition. On Jan. 15, six right-leaning groups—including the Club for Growth, the National Taxpayers Union and Citizens Against Government Waste—announced that they had made a 'major break' with the Bush White House and the Republican-controlled Congress in response to budgeting that had driven discretionary spending up 27 percent in Bush's first three years in office. The Cato Institute calculates that Bush has presided over the largest increases in discretionary spending since President Lyndon B. Johnson's budgets of the late '60s."

(*The Washington Post*, February 8, 2004)

"No sooner had the Bush administration heralded its initiative last week to spend $1.5 billion to promote marriage, particularly among low-income couples, than some social and religious conservatives began to worry. The gesture, they said, was a weak substitute for their larger goal: support from the White House for a constitutional amendment banning gay marriage. . . .

"Part of the concern stems from the language chosen by the administration—'promoting marriage'—which for the critics conjures everything from a draconian social experiment to simple big-government meddling. Kim Gandy, president of the National Organization for Women, has called the initiative 'thinly disguised social engineering.' Michael Tanner of the libertarian Cato Institute refers to it as '1965-style Great Society liberalism.'"

(*The New York Times*, January 18, 2004)

"After three straight years of double-digit increases in federal spending, President Bush and the Republican Congress say they have the situation under control. But a number of conservatives say the actual spending this year will be triple the figures cited by the White House. . . .

"The debate over federal spending has become politically charged, with both sides tossing out markedly divergent numbers. On Dec. 15, Bush said at a news conference that his administration and the GOP-controlled Congress had held spending not related to the military or homeland security to a 6 percent increase in fiscal year 2002, with a 5 percent increase last fiscal year and a 3 percent increase for the 2004 fiscal year, which began Oct. 1. . . .

"Tad DeHaven, a budget researcher at the libertarian Cato Institute, published his version of the numbers a few days later. He found a 6.8 percent increase in the same categories in 2002, an 8.3 percent increase last fiscal year, and a 6.3 percent increase this year—more than double Bush's 2004 number.

"The president's figures 'amount to a spin job,' DeHaven wrote on the Web site of the conservative National Review. 'Many people who support the president's tax cuts and his conduct of the war can no longer stomach his expansion of big government via big spending.'"

(*The Boston Globe*, December 27, 2003)

"Federal Reserve Chairman Alan Greenspan warned Thursday that 'creeping protectionism' could worsen the U.S. trade deficit, tightening the pressure on President Bush to relax trade protections.

"'Some clouds of emerging protectionism have become increasingly evident on today's horizon,' Greenspan told a monetary conference sponsored by

You Can't Say That! The Growing Threat to Civil Liberties from Antidiscrimination Laws

CONFERENCES
Benefactor Summit (annual)
Book Forums (twice each month)
Monetary Conference (annual)
Policy Forums (weekly)
Capitol Hill Briefings (twice each month)
Technology and Society Conference (annual)
Cato University (twice each year)
Cato Club 200 (annual)

the Cato Institute and the British publication *The Economist,* two organizations that support free trade."

(*The Atlanta Journal-Constitution,* November 21, 2003)

". . . according to a study by the National Committee for Responsive Philanthropy, Heritage and other conservative think tanks—the best known being the libertarian Cato Institute and the neoconservative American Enterprise Institute—spent an estimated $1 billion promoting conservative ideas in the 1990's. From their ranks sprang some credible academics whose think-tank writings spawned powerful careers, including Jeane Kirkpatrick, the former U.N. ambassador, and Antonin Scalia, the Supreme Court associate justice. There also came a flood of conservative theorists—like Charles Murray, whose book 'The Bell Curve' attacked assumptions about racial equality, and John Lott, who proposed that we would be safer if everyone carried a gun—whose arguments, however dubious, bled indelibly into the public debate."

(*The New York Times Magazine,* October 12, 2003)

Center for American Progress

Established in 2003

DIRECTOR

John Podesta, president and chief executive officer. Podesta served as chief of staff to President Bill Clinton from October 1998 until January 2001. He also served in the White House as assistant to the president, staff secretary, and senior policy advisor on government information, privacy, telecommunications security, and regulatory policy. Before serving at the White House, he held a number of positions on Capitol Hill and worked as a trial attorney in the U.S. Justice Department's Honors Program in the Land and Natural Resources Division. He has served as a member of the Council of the Administrative Conference of the United States, and the U.S. Commission on Protecting and Reducing Government Secrecy. Podesta received his B.A. from Knox College in 1971 and earned his J.D. from Georgetown University Law Center in 1976. Podesta is also a visiting professor of law at Georgetown University Law Center.

BOARD OF DIRECTORS

John Podesta, president and chief executive officer

Carol Browner, member; principal, Albright Group LLC; former administrator for the Environmental Protection Agency

Richard Leone, member; president, Century Foundation

Peter Lewis, member; chair, chief executive officer, and president, Progressive Corp.

Cheryl Mills, member; senior vice president and counselor for operations and administration, New York University

Aryeh Neier, member; president, Open Society Institute; former executive director, Human Rights Watch

Marion Sandler, member; chair of the board and chief executive officer, Golden West Financial Corp.

SCOPE

Members: not a membership organization
Branches/chapters: none
Affiliates: American Progress Action Fund

TAX STATUS

501(c)(3)

FINANCES

Budget: 2004—$10.9 million

FUNDING SOURCES

"Dozens of large contributions from individuals and some foundations; numerous donations from small donors."

PAC

None

CONTACT INFORMATION

805 15th Street, NW, Suite 400, Washington, DC 20005
Phone: (202) 682-1611
General E-mail: progress@americanprogress.org •
Web site: www.centerforamericanprogress.org

Communications Director: Laura Nichols, senior vice president for communications and strategy
(202) 682-1611
Human Resources Director: Brad Kiley, director of finance and administration
(202) 682-1611

PURPOSE: "Progressive ideas for a strong, just, and free America." Policy and communications objects focus on four areas: developing a long-term vision of a progressive America; providing a forum to generate new progressive ideas and policy proposals; responding effectively and rapidly to conservative proposals and rhetoric with a thoughtful critique and clear alternatives; and communicating progressive messages to the American public.

CURRENT CONCERNS: Domestic issues (access to justice; civil rights and civil liberties; education; energy; environment; health care; Medicare) • Economy (economic outlook; economic policy; labor market; manufacturing; private pensions; retiree health care; social security) • National security (environment; foreign policy; homeland security; military; terrorism; war in Iraq: the intelligence story; nations/regions)

METHOD OF OPERATION: Conferences/seminars • Congressional testimony • Experts directory • Internships • Legislative/regulatory monitoring (federal) • Media outreach • Research • Web site

Effectiveness and Political Orientation

"To defeat President Bush in the fall elections, a number of well-heeled liberal organizations and wealthy Democrats are pouring millions of dollars into special nonprofit groups that will campaign separately from the Democratic Party.

"This flow of political money—some $300 million is expected to be pumped into these shadow organizations in this election cycle—is the latest attempt to get around the federal laws on campaign finance. . . .

"[T]he Federal Election Commission plans to discuss possibly regulating these groups (known as 527s, for their tax status), by broadening its interpretation of the 2002 Bipartisan Campaign Reform Act.

"That act curbed the flow of 'soft money'—unlimited donations from corporations, unions, and wealthy individuals—to political parties. Now such money is finding its way into groups like the Center for American Progress and the Partnership for America's Families, which plan TV ads and get-out-the-vote drives. . . . "

(*The Christian Science Monitor* [Boston], February 4, 2004)

"Al Franken was becoming agitated. The comedian and conservative-basher was at a Washington party for the new liberal think tank, the Center for American Progress, when he was asked to say a few words to the crowd. As he often does, Franken began riffing on the subject of the Fox News Channel, and in no time at all had worked himself into a fit of anger. . . .

"The crowd, made up mostly of left-leaning activist, political, and media types, loved it. 'We have to fight back,' Franken exhorted them. Looking at John Podesta, the former Clinton White House chief of staff who is heading the new think tank, Franken said, 'Thank God you're doing this. We have to fight back.'

"Sen. Hillary Rodham Clinton, standing nearby with former Clinton national security adviser Sandy Berger, applauded and nodded her head in approval. Earlier, she too had lamented the 'great void of positive energy on the left and urged the crowd to fight back in the 'idea game and war that we're engaged in with the other side.'

"Fighting back could well be the theme of the Center for American Progress. Supporters of the project seem to sincerely believe that they are up against a pervasive conservative bias in the nation's media that can only be answered by an aggressive public-relations counter-offensive, which they call "pushback." And although it bills itself as a traditional think tank—scholarship and all—for now, at least, the Center appears to be all about pushback."

(*The National Review,* November 24, 2003)

"At a little before 6 each morning, a wiry, 27-year-old political operative fires up his computer in his Washington, D.C., apartment. While other Democratic spinners are still in bed, . . . David Sirota is already at the keyboard, hacking out a daily barrage of anti-Bush media clips, commentary and snappy quotes. . . .

"Though young, Sirota is well schooled in the art of Washington warfare. After college at Northwestern, Sirota . . . worked for Rep. Bernie Sanders, the vocal independent congressman from Vermont, and then David Obey, the senior Democrat on the powerful House Appropriations Committee. There he started E-mailing his attacks on Bush, giving Democrats neatly packaged sound bites and journalists irresistible quotes.

"One of those buried under Sirota's E-mails earlier this year was John Podesta, the former Clinton White House chief of staff, who was just then setting up the Center for American Progress. 'I didn't know him,' says Podesta. 'I just saw he had an eye for critique and the instinct for the jugular.' Podesta's dream is to replicate the success of the Heritage Foundation and other conservative think tanks, which act as incubators for Republican ideas. He gave Sirota a job, and a bigger platform—a new daily Web log called the Progress Report."

(*Newsweek,* October 27, 2003)

"[Center for American Progress founder John Podesta's] goal is to build an organization to rethink the very idea of liberalism, a reproduction in mirror image of the conservative think tanks that have dominated the country's political dialogue for a generation.

"Many such left-leaning ventures have been tried over the years and have failed to wield much influence, but Podesta's effort seems different, not only because of his considerable personal stature within the party but also because rage at the Bush administration has galvanized Democrats."

(The New York Times, October 12, 2003)

Center for Auto Safety

Established in 1970

DIRECTOR

Clarence M. Ditlow III, executive director. Ditlow has held this position since 1975. He was formerly a patent examiner at the U.S. Patent and Trademark Office as well as a staff attorney for the Public Interest Research Group. Ditlow has a degree in chemical engineering from Lehigh University and law degrees from Georgetown University Law Center and Harvard Law School.

BOARD OF DIRECTORS

Clarence M. Ditlow III, executive director
Katherine A. Meyer, secretary/treasurer; attorney at law, Meyer & Glitzenstein, Washington, DC
Nicholas Ashford, member; professor, Massachusetts Institute of Technology, Cambridge, MA
James Fitzpatrick, member; attorney at law, Arnold & Porter, Washington, DC
A. Benjamin Kelley, member; executive director, Public Health Advocacy Institute, Boston, MA
Jon S. Vernick, member; assistant professor, Johns Hopkins University School of Hygiene and Public Health, Baltimore, MD

SCOPE

Members: 20,000 individuals
Branches/chapters: None
Affiliates: None

STAFF

6 total—plus 2 interns and 1 volunteer

TAX STATUS

501(c)(3)

FINANCES

Budget: 2004—$503,133
2003—$485,201
2002—$600,754

FUNDING SOURCES

Membership dues, 54%; foundation grants, 24%; individuals, 11%; publications, 11%

PAC

None

EMPLOYMENT

Information on open positions can be obtained by contacting the Center at (202) 328-7700. Cover letters and resumes can be sent to Clarence Ditlow, executive director, Center for Auto Safety, 1825 Connecticut Avenue, NW, Suite 330, Washington, DC 20009. Fax: (202) 387-0140. E-mail: webmaster@autosafety.org.

CONTACT INFORMATION

1825 Connecticut Avenue, NW, Suite 330, Washington, DC 20009
Phone: (202) 328-7700 • *Fax:* (202) 387-0140
General E-mail: webmaster@autosafety.org • *Web site:* www.autosafety.org

Communications Director: None
Human Resources Director: None

PURPOSE: "Dedicated to reducing deaths and injuries from unsafe vehicle design and defects, improving vehicle reliability and quality, reducing the adverse environmental impact of vehicles, and improving fuel efficiency." The center is a research and advocacy organization founded by Consumers Union and Ralph Nader. It is a nationally recognized leader in the areas of automotive safety and consumer protection.

CURRENT CONCERNS: Automotive fuel economy • Ending unfair geographic recalls • Increasing federal fuel economy standards • Rollover/roof crush prevention • State lemon laws • Upgrading federal fuel integrity standard • Vehicle safety

METHOD OF OPERATION: Direct action • Grassroots organizing • Internet (databases and Web site) • Legislative/regulatory monitoring (federal and state) • Library services (for members) • Litigation • Media outreach • Participation in regulatory proceedings (federal) • Performance ratings/report cards • Research

Effectiveness and Political Orientation

"Ralph Nader may be considering yet another run for presidency in 2004, but many groups that supported him in controversial 2000 election—consumer groups Nader was once affiliated with, such as Center For Auto Safety—say they won't support him, blaming him for taking votes away from Al Gore and giving President Bush election."

(*The Wall Street Journal Abstracts,* January 14, 2004)

"A consumer group accused the National Highway Traffic Safety Administration [(NHTSA)] . . . of delaying the release of crash-test scores to help the auto industry, but the federal agency denied any impropriety.

"'NHTSA has placed sales over safety by withholding new crash test results for 2004 models from the American buying public for months,' Clarence Ditlow, head of the Center for Auto Safety, wrote in a letter to NHTSA administrator Jeffrey Runge.

"Ditlow said NHTSA has yet to release the first crash-test scores of 2004 models, which should have been available to the public months ago, but has shared the results with the automakers.

INTERNSHIPS

Internships for researchers lasting 3 months are available. Fall/winter positions are unpaid; summer positions include a stipend. There are no application deadlines and the hours are flexible. Applicants must be graduate or post-graduate students with an interest and/or background in consumer advocacy and public interest work. Information on internships can be obtained through college and university career development offices.

Internship applications can be mailed to Michael Brooks, staff attorney, Center for Auto Safety, 1825 Connecticut Avenue, NW, Suite 330, Washington, DC 20009. Faxed to: (202) 387-0140. E-mailed to: webmaster@ autosafety.org.

NEWSLETTERS

IMPACT (quarterly)
The Lemon Times (quarterly)

PUBLICATIONS

Automobile Design Liability
The Car Book
The Lemon Book
Little Secrets of the Auto Industry
Also publishes safety research reports and vehicle-specific consumer packets.

CONFERENCES

None

"To restore the agency's credibility, Ditlow said, it should start releasing crash information more quickly and not provide information to automakers unless it is also available to the public.

"But NHTSA spokesman Rae Tyson said the only reason for the delay was that the agency wanted to release a group of scores all at once, which is customary, and wanted to include several minivans, which it thought would be most helpful to consumers if done at the same time.

"Tyson said that the last 2004 vehicle was tested late in November and that the results would be released in the next few days.

"There has been no attempt to help the auto industry, Tyson said. It is routine to provide automakers with the results of the crash tests so that their crash experts can review them and comment.

"The Center for Auto Safety, based in Washington, D.C., was founded by Ralph Nader."

(*The Plain Dealer* [Cleveland], January 6, 2004)

"It could be the perfect SUV, getting a fuel-efficient 36 miles to the gallon and sporting enough safety devices to cut driving fatalities nationwide by 2,900 a year.

"There's just one drawback to the Guardian XSE—it can't be found in showrooms anywhere.

"The concept car design was unveiled yesterday by the Union of Concerned Scientists and the Center for Auto Safety at press conferences in Baltimore, Philadelphia and Los Angeles. Their engineers call the Guardian a blueprint to show auto manufacturers how to produce sport utility vehicles that are less dangerous and friendlier to the environment.

" 'This represents a comprehensive approach to an SUV that is safer and more fuel efficient,' said David Friedman, the organization's clean vehicles program research director and co-designer of the Guardian. 'Families deserve a better SUV, one that is safer, with improved fuel economy, but has the same size, same power and same performance as they have now.' "

(*The Baltimore Sun,* September 17, 2003)

"Five consumer and safety organizations are protesting a decision by federal safety regulators to halt publication of monthly status reports on vehicle defect investigations. . . .

"Last year, the agency eliminated the monthly reports. [National Highway Traffic Safety Administration (NHTSA)] officials explained that the reports were incompatible with a new computer system. They also said that safety investigations are constantly updated on the agency Web site. . . .

"But Clarence Ditlow, executive director of the Center for Auto Safety, says the reports were the means by which NHTSA was 'held accountable' for its decisions on safety recalls.

"The Center for Auto Safety is one of the organizations protesting the elimination of monthly reports. Ditlow says the quality of the agency's online information is spotty. As for the agency's explanation that an upgraded computer system forced the change, Ditlow says, 'You're supposed to get better,' not worse."

(*Automotive News,* April 28, 2003)

"Consumers filed 57 claims, from 1989 to 1995, against Bridgestone-Firestone. There were 367 complaints in 1998, and 353 filed in 1999.

"The National Highway Traffic Safety Administration (NHTSA), an arm of the U.S. Department of Transportation, came under fire when the agency dragged its feet before responding to a 1998 complaint from a State Farm Insurance researcher's warning about an alarming number of claims against Firestone tires. This was a year before news reports about Firestone tires sparked hundreds of complaints to the agency. It took public outcry from groups such as Public Citizen, individual lawsuits, as well as a suit filed by the Center for Auto Safety, to get a bill passed giving the NHTSA more authority to investigate and hold automobile makers accountable."

(*Black Enterprise,* April 2002)

Center for Business Ethics

Established in 1976

DIRECTOR

W. Michael Hoffman, executive director. Hoffman founded CBE in 1976. He has written or edited 16 books and more than 60 articles on business ethics. He is contacted frequently by news media for analysis and comment in connection with ethical issues of the day. For more than 20 years he has been consulting on business ethics for universities, government agencies, and corporations. He is the advisor to the board of the Ethics Officer Association (EOA), which he co-founded in 1991. He is the past president of the Society for Business Ethics and is also the senior ethics consultant for LRN, the Legal Knowledge Company, head-quartered in Los Angeles.

BOARD OF DIRECTORS

W. Michael Hoffman, executive director
William E. Davis; former chair, National Grid USA
John J. Desmond III; senior vice president, legal and compliance officer (retired) Boston Edison Co.
Dawn-Marie Driscoll; former vice president of corporate affairs and general counsel, Filene's
William M. Egan; executive vice president (retired), Stone & Webster, Inc.
Jacquelyn B. Gates; former ethics officer, World Bank
Robert Holland; president and chief executive officer, WorkPlace Integrators; former president and chief executive officer, Ben & Jerry's
Ira A. Lipman; chair and president of Guardsmark
William K. O'Brien; Global Human Capital Leader (retired) PricewaterhouseCoopers
Howard D. Putnam; president, Howard D. Putnam Enterprises, Inc. former chief executive officer, Southwest Airlines
William T. Redgate; former vice president for business practices, Dun & Bradstreet Corp.
Donald B. Reed; chief executive officer, Global Services Cable and Wireless
Anthony J. Rucci; executive vice president and chief administrative officer, Cardinal Health, Inc.
Alison Taunton-Rigby; president, forester Biotech; former president and chief executive officer, Aquila Biopharmaceuticals
Jean C. Tempel; managing director, First Light Capital
Nancy Thomas-Moore; chair, board of directors, Ethics Officer Association; director, ethics and business conduct, Weyerhaeuser Co.

CONTACT INFORMATION

Bentley College, 175 Forest Street, Waltham, MA 02452
Phone: (781) 891-2981 • *Fax:* (781) 891-2988.
General E-mail: cbeinfo@bentley.edu •
Web site: ecampus.bentley.edu/dept/cbe/

Communications Director: Janet Mendelsohn, director of public affairs
(781) 891-2070 • jmendelsohn@bentley.edu
Human Resources Director: Barbara Addison Reid
(781) 891-2640 • breid@bentley.edu

PURPOSE: A 25-year-old center dedicated to promoting ethical business conduct in contemporary society. "The center provides an international forum for benchmarking and research in business ethics. The center helps corporations and other organizations strengthen their ethical cultures through educational programming and consulting."

CURRENT CONCERNS: Business values and social justice • Corporate governance and institutionalizing ethics • Ethics and the multinational enterprise • Ethics in banking and finance • Ethics of the management of computer technology • International perspectives in business ethics • Power and responsibility in American business • Work ethic

METHOD OF OPERATION: Awards program • Conferences/seminars • Educational foundation • Executive Fellows Program • Films/video/audiotapes • International activities • Internet (library databases, Web site) • Library (open to the public) • Media outreach • Research • Scholarships • Speakers program

Effectiveness and Political Orientation

"From that online shopping site you discretely browse at work to the E-mails sent from your private Web-based account, there's a very good chance your company knows exactly what you're up to.

"A whopping 92 percent of companies surveyed said they monitor their employees' E-mail and Internet use while at work, according to a new poll from the Center for Business Ethics at Bentley College in Waltham.

"A quarter of those employers said they are watching 'all the time' and 17 percent indicated they monitored 'regularly.' Just 34 percent indicated they do it 'only for good reason.'

"'It surprised us,' said study co-author Mark Rowe. 'We would certainly advocate for a more judicious approach to monitoring, perhaps more selective.'

"Even more surprising, Rowe said, was the fact that nearly half the companies surveyed had no written guidelines or policies for monitoring their monitors—the folks who can track electronically everything employees are doing at their computers."

(*Boston Herald,* October 19, 2003)

SCOPE
Members: 100 associate members
Branches/chapters: None
Affiliate: Bentley College; often co-sponsors events and seminar with the Ethics Officer Association (EOA), an organization of "practicing ethics officers from hundreds of major corporations," which promotes ethical business practices, and continues to partner with the EOA and other ethics-related organizations.

STAFF
4 total—4 professional; plus executive and research fellows and numerous student workers

TAX STATUS
501(c)(3)

FINANCES
Declined to comment

FUNDING SOURCES
Most of the funding for the Center for Business Ethics comes from Bentley College, although the center receives corporate and private foundation contributions.

PAC
None

EMPLOYMENT
Positions at the Center for Business Ethics at posted on the Bentley College Web site at http://www.bentley.edu/jobs/. The college encourages applicants to use the online electronic application form when applying for positions and actively discourages the use of faxed applications. Applicants may call (781) 891-3427 for assistance.

INTERNSHIPS
There are several positions available annually for executive and research fellows. Full information can be found at http://ecampus.bentley.edu/dept/cbe/about/fellows.html.

NEWSLETTERS
Business and Society Review (quarterly)
Ethics Matters (online quarterly)

PUBLICATIONS
Business, Ethics, and the Environment: the Public Policy Debate
Corporate Monitoring of Employee E-mail and Internet Usage ,
Ethics Matters: How to Implement Values-Driven Management
Raytheon Lectureship in Business Ethics Monographs
Sears Lectureship in Business Ethics Monographs

CONFERENCES
Graduate Certificate in Business Ethics (four course program)
Raytheon Lectureship in Business Ethics
Sears Lectureship in Business Ethics

"Many of the people who spend their time thinking about business ethics for a living devote a large chunk to thinking about forced ranking. They have to. What businesspeople call forced ranking is known as 'grading on the curve' in academia—and professors and students grapple with that slippery statistical slope every day.

"'Grading on a strict bell curve means that if you give someone an A, you have to give someone else an F,' says W. Michael Hoffman, executive director of the Center for Business Ethics at Bentley College in Waltham, Massachusetts. 'But perhaps—and maybe a lot more than perhaps—the people at the low end of the bell curve don't deserve to flunk or be kicked out of school. Or in the case of a corporation, fired.' Hoffman personally finds grading on the curve (and its corporate sibling, forced ranking) distasteful, but not unethical. It's distasteful, he says, because it doesn't recognize students who aren't good test-takers (or employees who lack champions upstairs at evaluation time) but who demonstrate unquantifiable qualities like loyalty, dependability, determination and persistence. It's not quite unethical, he says, because it's often unavoidable. In the classroom, as in the workplace, a laissez-faire attitude toward grading may lead to grade inflation, the Lake Wobegon Effect, where just about everybody is judged to be above average. And that makes the grades meaningless to students, teachers and prospective employers alike.

"Hoffman adds that forced ranking remains ethical 'as long as there are certain transparent and clearly communicated criteria that employees are aware of when they take and while they're working on the job.'"

(*Workforce Management,* July 1, 2003)

Center for Community Change

Established 1968

DIRECTOR

Deepak Bhargava, executive director. Before becoming executive director of the center in 2002, Bhargava served as its director of public policy of the center for 8 years. He also directed the National Campaign for Jobs and Income Support, one of the center's projects. In this capacity he helped groups of low-income people engage in the reauthorization of welfare law. Prior to joining the center, he worked as legislative director of ACORN. Bhargava received his bachelor's degree from Harvard College.

BOARD OF DIRECTORS

Deepak Bhargava, executive director
Edwin Booth, chair; president and chief executive officer, IdeaS Revenue Management, Minneapolis, MN
Henry J. Fernandez, co-vice chair; economic development administrator, City of New Haven, CT
Mary M. Lassen, co-vice chair; president and chief executive officer, Women's Educational & Industrial Union, Boston, MA
Sandra L. Ferniza, chair of finance committee; director, Governor's Office for Excellence in Government, Tempe, AZ
Jane Fox-Johnson, chair of development committee; consultant, Jane Fox & Associates
John Carr, member; secretary, Department of Social Development, U.S. Conference of Catholic Bishops, Washington, DC
Roger A. Clay Jr., member; president, the National Economic Development & Law Center, Oakland, CA
Ronald V. Dellums, member; partner, Dellums, Brauer, Halterman & Associates, Oakland, CA
Maria Elena Durazo, member; president, Hotel Employees & Restaurant Employees Union, Local 11, Los Angeles, CA
Peter Edelman, member; professor, Georgetown University Law School, Washington, DC
Irma Flores Gonzales, member
Ronald Grzywinski, member; chairman, ShoreBank Corporation, Chicago, IL
Jean Hardisty, member; president, Political Research Associates, Somerville, MA
Marie Kirkley-Bey, member; special project coordinator, Youth Opportunities Hartford, CT
Winona LaDuke, member; founding director, White Earth Land Recovery Project, Ponsford, MN
Madeline Lee, member

CONTACT INFORMATION

1000 Wisconsin Avenue, NW, Washington, DC 20007
Phone: (202) 342-0519 • *Fax:* (202) 333-5462
General E-mail: info@communitychange.org •
Web site: www.communitychange.org

Communications Director: Leila McDowell
(202) 339-9329 • lmcdowell@communitychange.org
Human Resources Director: George Walker, deputy operations director
(202) 339-9324 • gwalker@communitychange.org

PURPOSE: "The Center for Community Change is a national nonprofit organization whose mission is to develop the power and capacity of low-income people, especially low-income people of color, to have a significant impact on the policies and institutions, which impact them and their communities." The center has two units: the Field Unit, which works on grassroots organizing throughout the United States; and the Policy Unit, which monitors Capital Hill, researches issues, and provides access to legislators.

CURRENT CONCERNS: Budget and tax policy work • California partnership • Community voting • Day labor • Education • Health care • Higher education and youth organizing • Housing • Immigration • Income supports for low-income families • Low wage worker organizing • Native American concerns • New organizers • Parenting & families • Southern organizing • Transportation • Welfare reform

METHOD OF OPERATION: Coalition forming • Conferences/seminars • Grassroots organizing • Internet (Web site) • Internships • Legislative/regulatory monitoring (federal) • Lobbying (federal) • Research

Effectiveness and Political Orientation

"COLUMBIA, S.C.—Democratic presidential candidates showcased their economic plans during a forum yesterday before thousands who have been affected by the exodus of textile jobs here. . . .

"Thousands packed the Columbia Township Auditorium downtown for a 'Dialogue with America's Families,' an event sponsored by the Center for Community Change. The event was moderated by popular radio personality Tom Joyner.

"The center has partnered with numerous organizations to register 2 million voters in 30 states. Later, some families in attendance went door-to-door to register Columbia residents.

"Mr. Edwards addressed the downfall of free-trade agreements such as the North American Free Trade Agreement, passed under President Clinton. All of the candidates agreed that the policy has allowed many companies to close U.S. manufacturing plants and move their shops overseas.

Aleyamma Mathews, member; director of programs, National Coalition for Asian Pacific American Community, Washington, DC

Paulette J. Meyer, member; consultant

Lawrence Parks, member; senior vice president, Federal Home Loan Bank of San Francisco, CA

Benson F. Roberts, member; vice president for policy, Local Initiative Support Corporation, New York, NY

Phil Tom, executive board committee; associate, Urban Ministry Office for the Presbyterian Church USA, Louisville, KY

SCOPE

Members: Works onsite with more than 200 community groups a year

Branches/chapters: Southern California office (near Los Angeles); staff outstationed in Chicago; San Francisco; Hartford, CT; Boise, ID; Richmond, VA; and Portland, ME

Affiliates: Member of numerous coalitions

STAFF

65 total—65 professional; plus 3 summer interns

TAX STATUS

501(c)(3) (public charity)

FINANCES

Budget: 2004—$12 million
2003—$12 million
2002—$10.2 million

FUNDING SOURCES

Foundations, 80 %; individuals, 15 %; endowment, 5 %

PAC

None

EMPLOYMENT

Open positions at the center are posted at http://communitychange.org/positions/. Cover letters and resumes can be mailed to Center for Community Change, George Walker, deputy operations director, 1000 Wisconsin Avenue, NW, Washington, DC 20007. Fax: (202) 342-1132. The center pursues an aggressive program of affirmative action. Women and people of color are encouraged to apply.

INTERNSHIPS

Various types of internships are available, including summer internships, which are filled on a rolling application basis. Applications procedures vary based on the type of internship. Information on internships is posted at http://www.communitychange.org/positions/.

NEWSLETTERS

Community Change (3–4 times a year)
Housing Organizing
Organizing (6 times a year)

PUBLICATIONS

The following is a list of sample publications:
HOPE Unseen: Voices from the Other Side
Immigration Storybook

"The practice has grown under President Bush with new incentives for companies to move jobs to other continents to expand trade, Mr. Edwards said. And he said he would look to alter trade deals without adequate protections against the loss of American jobs.

"We should create a full employment economy with new jobs aimed at rebuilding our infrastructure—roads, bridges, highways and firehouses in our cities and nationwide," said Rep. Dennis J. Kucinich of Ohio.

" 'When I'm president, there won't be one Benedict Arnold company getting incentives to take our jobs overseas and sticking the American people with the bill,' " Mr. Kerry said.

"Mr. Kucinich, Mr. Edwards, the Rev. Al Sharpton, former Vermont Gov. Howard Dean and Wesley Clark took part in the event. Sen. Joe Lieberman of Connecticut withdrew at the last minute. Sen. John Kerry of Massachusetts held a similar event at South Carolina University, which involved Vietnam War veterans."

(*The Washington Times*, January 31, 2004)

"For the unveiling Wednesday of a new grass-roots effort aimed at registering low-income Americans to vote, the setting was incongruous: a private dining room in the Occidental Grill, a luxurious restaurant adjacent to the Willard Hotel and a favorite of high-priced Washington lobbyists.

" 'It's no accident that we're here,' said Deepak Bhargava, director of the event's sponsor, a low-income advocacy group called the Center for Community Change. 'We're sending the signal that low-income voters will be the new power brokers in the politics of 2004.'

"The initiative targets 30 states, including Missouri and Illinois, for intensive effort. The goal is to use $15 million in foundation grants to finance registration campaigns by existing grass-roots organizations to mobilize as many as 2 million low-income voters by November. . . .

"The Center for Community Change will work with two existing community organizing efforts, a religious outreach effort led by the Gamaliel Foundation and ACORN, the national community-action network. One-third of the $15 million budget has been raised so far. Included are grants from George Soros' Open Society Institute and the ARCA and Tides foundations. . . .

"The national initiative is described as nonpartisan. But a study released Wednesday suggests that mobilizing low-income voters is especially significant for the Democratic Party. On average, households with incomes of less than $30,000 gave Democrats a 9-percentage-point advantage in the 2000 election, while every other income group favored Republicans, according to the analysis by the Campaign for Community Change."

(*St. Louis Post-Dispatch*, January 15, 2004)

". . . a liberal advocacy group. . . ."

(*Business Week*, October 20, 2003)

"City officials across the country are rallying behind federal legislation that would create a dedicated funding stream to help alleviate the nation's affordable housing crunch. The National Affordable Housing Trust Fund Act of 2003 was introduced by Rep. Bernie Sanders, I-VT, in March and has attracted the tri-partisan support of 186 co-sponsors. The bill would 'provide for the development, rehabilitation and preservation of decent, safe and affordable housing for low-income families. . . .'

CONFERENCES

Sponsors periodic conferences and workshops.

"Sanders offered the legislation at the same time that Congress is negotiating the 2004 budget and President Bush's economic stimulus plan. City officials argue that establishing the housing trust fund would help jumpstart the economy by providing jobs and shelter for people. In fact, the Washington, D.C.-based Center for Community Change estimates that more than 180,000 jobs would be created if the federal government spent $5 billion to build affordable housing units. . . .

"More than 4,000 organizations and individuals have endorsed the creation of a dedicated national housing fund, according to the Washington, D.C.-based National Housing Trust Fund Campaign. The organizations supporting the fund range from NLC and USCM to the Baltimore-based National Association for the Advancement of Colored People and the Washington, D.C.-based United States Conference of Catholic Bishops."

(*American City & Country,* May 1, 2003)

"Texas has quietly become a hotbed of subprime lending activity—at least according to the findings in a recent study on the subject.

"Texas cities have the highest percentage of subprime mortgage refinance loans in the nation. And five Texas metropolitan statistical areas lead the list of 331 areas with the highest rate of subprime refinance loans, according to a study by the Center for Community Change, an advocacy group based in Washington, D.C. . . .

"The study, titled Risk or Race? Racial Disparities and the Subprime Refinance Market, raised concerns among public policy experts and consumer groups about the state of subprime lending.

"Subprime loans have higher interest rates and fees than prime loans. And policy experts argue that the predominance of subprime lenders in the market opens up the possibility for predatory lending."

(*The Dallas Morning News,* June 12, 2002)

Center for Defense Information (CDI)

Established in 1972

DIRECTOR

Bruce G. Blair, president. Blair was named president in 2000 after 13 years as a senior fellow at the Brookings Institution. He is an expert on the security policies of the United States and the former Soviet Union, specializing in nuclear forces and command-control systems. Blair is the author of a number of books and articles on security issues, including Strategic Command and Control. He was awarded a MacArthur Fellowship Prize in 1999. He is a 1970 graduate of the University of Illinois, after which he entered the U.S. Air Force. He earned a Ph.D. in operations research from Yale University in 1984.

BOARD OF ADVISORS

Bruce G. Blair, president

James D. Head, chair of the board; president, Strategy Development Company, Freeland, MI

Doris Z. Bato, member; Santa Fe, NM

Barbara Berger, member; Aspen, CO

Bruce Berger, member; Aspen, CO

Arthur D. Berliss Jr., member; Captain, U.S. Naval Reserve (Retired); former vice president, Allen-Hollander, Co., New York, NY

Edward H. R. Blitzer, member; former chair, Lightolier Inc., New York, NY

Dick Bruckenfeld, member; Dobbs Ferry, NY

Ben Cohen, member; chair, Ben & Jerry's Homemade, Inc., South Burlington, VT

James R. Compton, member; president, J. R. Compton Developments; chair, Fund for Peace Board, Los Gatos, CA

Joseph N. Deblinger, member; president, Deblinger Sales & Marketing Corp., Manhasset, NY

Gay Dillingham, member; CNS Communications, Santa Fe, NM

James A. Donovan, member; Colonel, U.S. Marine Corps (Retired); author, former publisher, Journal of the Armed Forces, Atlanta, GA

Raymond Frankel, member; Los Angeles, CA

Robert L. Frome, member; senior partner, Olshan, Grundman and Frome, Attorneys, New York, NY

Seth M. Glickenhaus, member; Investment Banker, New York, NY

Eva Haller, member; Santa Barbara, CA

Yoel Haller, member; Santa Barbara, CA

David H. Horowitz, member; New York, NY

Robert G. James, member; Rear Admiral, U.S. Naval Reserve (Retired); president, Enterprise Development Associates, New York, NY

Alan F. Kay, member; businessman, St. Augustine, FL

CONTACT INFORMATION

1779 Massachusetts Avenue, NW, Washington, DC 20036
Phone: (202) 332-0600 • *Fax:* (202) 462-4559
General E-mail: info@cdi.org • *Web site:* www.cdi.org

Communications Director: Declined to comment
Human Resources Director: Declined to comment

PURPOSE: "[D]edicated to strengthening security through: international cooperation; reduced reliance on unilateral military power to resolve conflict; reduced reliance on nuclear weapons; a transformed and reformed military establishment; and, prudent oversight of, and spending on, defense programs.

"CDI seeks to contribute alternative views on security to promote wide-ranging discourse and debate. CDI educates the public and informs policy-makers about issues of security policy, strategy, operations, weapon systems and defense budgeting, and pursues creative solutions to the problems of today and tomorrow.

"CDI aims to improve understanding between the United States and key nations on security matters through new media initiatives that inform and educate opinion-makers, policy-makers, and general public."

CURRENT CONCERNS: Conventional arms issues (arms trade; children and armed conflict; landmines; small arms & light weapons) • Defense and foreign policy (failed states; intelligence community; missile defense; preventative diplomacy; security strategy; United Nations; weapons testing/acquisition issues) • International peacekeeping (humanitarian relief; peacekeeping; United Nations) • Military forces, strategy, and spending (Air Force issues; Army issues; aviation; base realignment and closure; Navy/ Marine Corps issues; personnel/flag officers/statistics; U.S. military budge; U.S. military deployments; weapon systems; world military expenditures) • Nuclear, biological, and chemical weapons issues (arms control and disarmament; chemical and biological warfare; nuclear issues) • Regional/ country affairs (Asia; Central Asia, and Caucuses; China; Europe; regional security issues; Russia; the Americas) • Special projects

METHOD OF OPERATION: Audiotapes • Conferences/seminars • Congressional testimony • Films/video • International activities • Internet (databases, E-mail alerts, electronic newsletters, and Web site) • Internships • Legislative/regulatory monitoring (federal) • Library/information clearinghouse (open to public) • Media outreach • Research • Speakers program • Television and radio production

Effectiveness and Political Orientation

"From 'shock and awe' to the capture of Saddam Hussein, news of the Iraq war and subsequent occupation dominated headlines around the world much of the year, and that isn't likely to change in 2004. . . .

SCOPE

Members: Declined to comment
Branches/chapters: Additional offices in Los Angeles, Moscow, Brussels
Affiliates: Washington ProFile, an independent international news and analysis agency focused on providing information in Russian on American politics, business and culture. Washington ProFile also liaises with government officials, nongovernmental organizations and academia.
Washington Observer, a Chinese-language partner of Washington ProFile.
Azimuth Media

STAFF

29 total, including research fellows

TAX STATUS

501(c)(3)

FINANCES

Revenue: 2001—$4.1 million; 2000—$4.1 million

FUNDING SOURCES

Declined to comment. The center does not accept government or defense industry funding.

PAC

None

" 'I think the administration got a nice blip up in its effort [with the capture of Saddam Hussein] at the end of the year,' said Marcus Corbin, senior analyst at the Center for Defense Information in Washington, D.C. 'They appear to be making a lot of arrests now that Saddam has been captured, which is a good sign for the effort.'

" 'I think the outlook for the new year is rather unsettled. It remains to be seen if the capture of Saddam will really deflate the morale of the attackers,' Corbin said. 'A lot of them were reported to be saying they were never fighting for Saddam in the first place but to get rid of the U.S. forces.'

" 'I think the big question for the new year,' he added, 'is what happens in the summer by the time some form of Iraqi government takes the reins. Then, in theory, it's not our war anymore. It remains to be seen if that's the case.' "

(*Boston Herald*, December 28, 2003)

"It was Cuba's $1 billion gamble to train an army of scientists, develop a sprawling biotech industry and tackle every disease from cancer to AIDS. . . .

"But some U.S. officials aren't quite ready to applaud. They remain suspicious of Cuba's intentions and reiterate their charge that the socialist nation is running a secret germ-warfare program.

"Cuba 'has at least a limited, developmental, offensive biological-weapons research-and-development effort and is providing dual-use biotechnology to other rogue states,' Roger Noriega, assistant secretary of state for the Western hemisphere, told a Senate committee in October.

"Cuban officials contend that the Bush administration, which has not found evidence to back its charge that Iraq had weapons of mass destruction, lacks credibility to make such an inflammatory claim.

"Some others agree.

"The Center for Defense Information, or CDI, a private research group based in Washington, toured nine of Cuba's 53 biotech centers and could not find any signs the country was researching or making biological weapons. . . .

"The CDI, founded in 1972, is a watchdog organization that has exposed wasteful defense spending, questioned the deployment of the MX mobile missile system and exposed the Pentagon's so-called black projects, considered so secret that their budgets are often hidden from public view.

"The group's delegates to Cuba included retired four-star Gen. Charles Wilhelm, former commander of the U.S. Southern Command; bioweapons policy experts; former U.S. assistant secretaries of state and defense; a leading infectious-disease specialist and senior research scientists.

"In May, delegation members published a 50-page report on their visit to Cuba. In it, they said that while the germ-warfare accusations were difficult to prove or disprove, they didn't believe the socialist government was hiding anything."

(*Seattle Times*, November 28, 2003)

". . . an independent Washington think tank."

(*New York Daily News*, October 19, 2003)

"There was supposed to be a new missile-defense test [of the IFT-9] on Saturday, but the Pentagon scrubbed it because of a technical glitch. . . .

"What's interesting, however, is that the Pentagon's announcement flies in the face of what missile-defense critics were saying earlier this year, when

EMPLOYMENT
Declined to comment

INTERNSHIPS
Full-time paid internships at the Los Angeles and Washington, DC, offices in the areas of research, television, and computers/Web editing are available. First priority is given to filling full-time paid internships. Full information on internships is available at http://www.cdi.org/about/internships.cfm. Application procedures and deadlines vary by the type of internship, but all pay $1,000 per month. Writing samples, university-level transcripts, and two letters of recommendation must in included in all applications. College graduates, graduate students, and highly qualified undergraduates with a strong interest in military policy, national security, foreign affairs and related public policy issues and/or and interest in broadcast communications or information technology are eligible to apply.

Completed internship applications can be sent to Victoria Sampson, internship coordinator, Center for Defense Information, 1779 Massachusetts Avenue, NW, Washington, DC 20036-2109. Fax: (202) 462-4559. E-mail: internships@cdi.org.

NEWSLETTERS
CDI Russia Weekly (E-mail)
CDI Space Security Updates (online)
The Defense Monitor (10 issues per year)
The e-Defense Monitor (online)

PUBLICATIONS
Arms Control Chronology
Assessing the Threats
C3: Nuclear Command, Control Cooperation
Challenging Conventional Wisdom: Debunking the Myths and Exposing Risks of Arms Export Reform
Homeland Security: A Competitive Strategies Approach
Honing the Sword: "Lessons Learned" from 9/11 and Afghanistan
How Little Is Enough? U.S. End-Use Monitoring and Oversight of the Weapons Trade
Imperial America: The Bush Assault on the World Order
Less Talk, More Walk: Strengthening Homeland Security Now
Mr. Smith Is Dead: No One Stands in the Way as Congress Laces Post-Sept. 11 Defense Bills with Pork
Security after 9/11: Strategy Choices and Budget Tradeoffs
A Swift, Elusive Sword, 2nd edition
The Week of Shame: Congress Wilts as the President Demands an Unclogged Road to War
Women on War: An International Anthology of Writings from Antiquity to the Present
World Military DataBase 2002
Also publishes reports, positions papers and strategy analyses (available online).

CONFERENCES
Regularly hosts seminars with visiting military, educational, and other public interest groups.

they blasted the Missile Defense Agency for excessive secrecy. In May, MDA said it would begin to classify some of its testing information. 'The Pentagon has made a decision that threatens to keep the American public and Congress in the dark about how things are going with the Bush administration's high-priority missile-defense program,' declared Philip E. Coyle III, a Clinton-administration official now with the Center for Defense Information. 'Defense Department press releases on missile-defense tests might become undependable, revealing the good news on successes but using classification to skirt the bad news in failures.'

". . . [The Pentagon press release] describe[s] how the problem was identified and how it will be fixed. . . . In other words, it's an honest effort of relate what's going on with the program—and hardly an attempt to 'skirt the bad news.'

"Yet Coyle would have us believe the Missile Defense Agency is engaged in an effort to make it 'practically impossible for Congress, the popular press, defense trade journals, and the American public to evaluate missile-defense development. . . .'"

(*National Review,* August 26, 2002)

". . . a think tank critical of missile defense. . . ."

(*Aviation Week & Space Technology,* July 7, 2003)

Center for Democracy and Technology

Established in 1994

DIRECTOR

James X. Dempsey, executive director. Dempsey joined CDT at the beginning of 1997 and became executive director in 2003. Prior to joining CDT. Dempsey was deputy director of the Center for National Security Studies. From 1995 to 1996, he also served as special counsel to the National Security Archive, a nongovernmental organization that uses the Freedom of Information Act to gain the declassification of documents on the U.S. foreign policy. From 1985 to 1994, Dempsey was assistant counsel to the House Judiciary Subcommittee on Civil and Constitutional Rights. From 1980 to 1984, he was an associate with the Washington, DC, law firm of Arnold & Porter, where he practiced in areas of government and commercial contracts, energy law, and antitrust.

BOARD OF DIRECTORS

Jerry Berman; president, CDT
Toni Carbo; dean and professor, University of Pittsburgh, School of Information Sciences
Carol A. Fukunaga; state senator, Hawaii
Judith Krug; director, Office for Intellectual Freedom, American Library Association
Mark Lloyd; executive director, Civil Rights Forum on Communications Policy
Daniel Weitzner; technology and society domain leader, World Wide Web Consortium
Tracy Westen; president, Center for Governmental Studies

SCOPE

Members: None
Branches/chapters: None
Affiliates: None

STAFF

11–20 total—plus 1–5 volunteers

TAX STATUS

501(c)(03)

FINANCES

Revenue: 2001—$1.95 million

FUNDING SOURCES

Corporate donations, 64%; foundation grants, 35%

PAC

None

EMPLOYMENT

Information on employment opportunities is available from the organization's Web site.

CONTACT INFORMATION

1634 Eye Street NW, Suite 1100, Washington, DC 20006
Phone: (202) 637-9800 • *Fax:* (202) 637-0968
General E-mail: info@cdt.org • *Web site:* www.cdt.org

Communications Director: None
Human Resources Director: None

PURPOSE: Dedicated to advocating "for democratic values and constitutional liberties in the digital age. CDT seeks practical solutions to enhance free expression and privacy in global communications technologies."

CURRENT CONCERNS: Access to the Internet • Electronic surveillance and cryptography • Free expression on the Internet • Information privacy • Online democracy • Terrorism

METHOD OF OPERATION: Coalition forming • Conferences/seminars • Congressional testimony • Congressional voting analysis • Demonstrations • Direct action • Educational foundation • Grassroots organizing • Information clearinghouse • International activities • Internet (databases, e-mail alerts, and Web site) • Internships • Legislative/regulatory monitoring (federal) • Litigation • Lobbying (federal and grassroots) • Media outreach • Participation in regulatory proceedings (federal) • Research • Scholarships • Voting records

Effectiveness and Political Orientation

"Should every agency in the federal government have a chief privacy officer sitting alongside other senior executives? Or should a privacy officer be appointed at the White House Office of Management and Budget to oversee the entire federal government's compliance with privacy regulations?

"Those questions were posed this week at a congressional hearing that was convened to review the performance to date of the Department of Homeland Security's privacy officer, the only such mandated position in the government.

"Federal Computer Week reported that University of Michigan Law School professor Sally Katzen urged the committee members "to create a statutory privacy officer at OMB, an office headed by the chief counselor for privacy." The OMB position would be preferable to agency-by-agency posts, she said. Katzen, who served in the Clinton administration, said such previously existed at OMB. "We had such an office and it served us well. It's unfortunate that the current administration has chosen not to fill that position," she said.

"The Center for Democracy Technology witness at the hearing tried to split the difference, supporting an OMB-level officer along with a few agency-specific privacy chiefs. CDT Executive Director James Dempsey testified: 'One way to strike the right balance is to have a designated chief privacy officer in OMB, and then to go agency by agency where it is particularly necessary,' he said, according to FCW's coverage. . . ."

(*Washingtonpost.com,* February 12, 2004)

"Bribery and poor security at motor vehicle offices across the country allowed thousands of fraudulent driver's licenses to change hands last year, for as little as $350 each, a report to be released today says.

"The report, by the Center for Democracy and Technology, a Washington policy group, focuses on internal fraud at the motor vehicle offices—a development that the center says has been overlooked as a national problem. The group relied on information culled from local news reports. . . .

" 'Even if we make this ID as strong as possible, even if we make this a national system, bribery is still an issue at the local level,' said Ari Schwartz, associate director for the Center for Democracy and Technology. 'The problem we're pointing out has not gotten as much attention as it deserves because it has been seen as a local problem.' "

(*The New York Times,* February 2, 2004)

"LARRY ABRAMSON reporting:
"Seventy-year-old Johnny Thomas(ph) often gets grilled when she goes to the airport because her name is similar to those of a couple of suspected bad guys. Her travails have garnered lots of media stories and the attention of law enforcement officials who promise to clear her. But Thomas says thanks to the government's inscrutable system of watch lists, she still gets stopped.

"Ms. JOHNNY THOMAS (Traveler): They are looking for a man; I am not a man. They're looking for a Caucasian man; I am not Caucasian. They're looking for a young man; I am not young.

"ABRAMSON: When they're not annoying, government watch lists can be downright dangerous. Congressman Jim Turner of Texas points out that the CIA had placed two of the 9/11 hijackers on a terrorist watch list, but that information was not shared with other agencies, so the two slipped into the country. . . .

"ABRAMSON: Turner wants to know exactly how the new terrorist screening center will address these problems, but so far the details of the operation remain secret. Jim Dempsey, of the Center for Democracy and Technology, says the FBI may be lying low because it hasn't figured out answers to some very tough questions, like. . .

"Mr. JIM DEMPSEY (Center for Democracy and Technology): What are the consequences that flow from the watch-listing of a person? . . . However inaccurate or unreliable or limited that list may be, if there's any opening to the private sector to that list, it will be used.

"ABRAMSON: Dempsey says citizens currently have no clear legal redress for false information on these lists. It's intelligence and can't really be challenged. . . ."

(*National Public Radio, "All Things Considered,"* November 28, 2003)

"Last summer, the Internet civil liberties group Center for Democracy and Technology set out to get to the bottom of the online scourge known as spam. It set up hundreds of dummy E-mail accounts to measure how and why they attracted unsolicited messages.

"The project led to a report, released last month, with recommendations on how to protect your IN box. . . ."

(*Newsweek,* May 12, 2003)

"The Washington, D.C.-based Center for Democracy and Technology said it will try to compel Pennsylvania's attorney general to disclose details about efforts in that state to force Internet providers to block visits to Web sites containing child pornography. Lawyers for the group compared the technique to disrupting mail delivery to an entire apartment complex over one tenant's illegal actions. Pennsylvania's attorney general has so far instructed Internet providers with customers in the state to block subscribers from at least 423 Web sites around the world."

(*The San Diego Union-Tribune,* February 24, 2003)

Center for Democratic Renewal

Established in 1979

DIRECTOR

Beni Ivey, executive director. Ivey has been executive director of the CDR since 1993. She graduated from California State University at San Jose with a degree in criminology. Ivey worked for a time as a probation officer, and she was an organizer of the first black conference of the "Black Power" era held in San Francisco in 1966. A former Atlanta restaurateur, her initiation in the social justice arena began as a member of the Student Non Violent Coordinating Committee.

BOARD OF DIRECTORS

Beni Ivey, executive director
C. T. Vivian, chair; minister, activist
Tom Turnipseed, president; former state senator, founder of Turnipseed & Associates
Joann Watson, vice president; member, Detroit City Council
Joe Agne, secretary; pastor, Memorial United Methodist Church, White Plains, NY
Leah Wise, treasurer; executive director, Southeast Regional Economic Justice Network, Durham, NC
Julian Bond; professor, American University, Washington, DC, and University of Virginia
Anne Braden; activist, founder of Progress in Education and the Kentucky branch of the Alliance Against Racist and Political Repression
Marilyn Clement; director, Center for Constitutional Rights
Ron Daniels; columnist, Vantage Point
Lois Dauway; executive, Women's Division of the Board of Global Ministries
Judy Hanenkrat; owner, JSH Building Services
Martin Luther King
Ralph Paige; executive director, Federation of Southern Cooperatives
Suzanne Pharr; founding member, Woman's Project, Arkansas
Othello Poulard, director, Center for Community Change
Mab Segrest; writer, social activist
Hilary Shelton; director, Washington Bureau of the NAACP
Lucius Walker; executive director, Interreligious Foundation for Community Organization

SCOPE

Members: 2,000 contributing members; 500 organizational members
Branches/chapters: None
Affiliates: 60 organizations

CONTACT INFORMATION

P.O. Box 50469, Atlanta, GA 30303
Phone: (404) 221-0025 • *Fax:* (404) 221-0045
General E-mail: info@thecdr.org • *Web site:* www.thecdr.org

Communications Director: Information unavailable
Human Resources Director: Information unavailable

PURPOSE: To "advance the vision of a democratic, diverse and just society, free of racism and bigotry."

CURRENT CONCERNS: Antigay violence • Immigration • Minority issues • White supremacy ideologies' effects on mainstream America

METHOD OF OPERATION: Capacity building • Coalition forming • Conferences/ seminars • Congressional testimony • Direct action • Grassroots organizing • International activities • Internet • Legal assistance • Library/information clearinghouse • Research • Technical assistance • Training

Effectiveness and Political Orientation

"Americans can't set up individual offices of homeland security, but each person can do things to make America safer, experts on hate groups said Saturday.

"Individuals can take action by supporting school prejudice reduction programs and objecting when immigrants and citizens of foreign origin are targets of bigotry. . . .

"'You don't have to march in the streets,' said Center for Democratic Renewal community organizer Dexter Wimbish. 'You can collect newspaper clippings of stories about bigotry and talk about them with your children and grandchildren.'"

(*The Atlanta Journal-Constitution*, January 12, 2003)

"Remember the 'backlash' of widespread discrimination against Arab Americans and Muslims following Sept. 11? It made you ashamed to be an American, didn't it? It showed that we were no better than Osama bin Laden. It gave us an all-too-brief glimpse into the dark heart of American patriotism.

"Well, here's a quiz for concerned citizens: What does that backlash have in common with the Jenin massacre in the West Bank and the 1996 'epidemic' of black church burnings by white supremacists in the United States? . . .

"They never happened. . . .

"In 1996 the racist 'epidemic' of black church burnings was for a month or so the hottest political story in the nation. Newspapers across the nation ran headlines such as 'Flames of Hate: Racism Blamed in a Shock Wave of Church Burnings.'

"Some intrepid journalists decided to find out what exactly had happened. Writing in the New Yorker, Michael Kelly pointed out that fires at both black

STAFF
6 total—5 full-time professional; 1 full-time support; plus 1 part-time professional; 3 consultants; 2 interns

TAX STATUS
501(c)(3)

FINANCES
Revenue: 2002—$383,197

FUNDING SOURCES
Foundation grants, 83%; individual donations, sales, special events, and other, 10%; membership dues, 7%

PAC
None

EMPLOYMENT
Information unavailable

INTERNSHIPS
Information unavailable

NEWSLETTERS
Activist Update
The Monitor (3 times a year)
The Right Unmasked

PUBLICATIONS
Ballot Box Bigotry: David Duke and the Populist Party
Bitter Harvest: Gordon Kahl and the Posse Comitatus-Murder in the Heartland
Blacks, Jews, and White Supremacy: Redirecting the Fight
Blood in the Face: The KKK, Aryan Nations, Nazi Skinheads and the Rise of a New White Culture
The Changing Faces of White Supremacy
The Christian Identity Movement
The Electronic Connection: White Supremacists and the Information Superhighway
Fundraising for Community-Based Groups
Hiding Behind Righteousness: Decoding the Language of the Radical Right
Lyndon LaRouche & the New American Fascism
Memoirs of a Race Traitor
Neo-Nazi Skinheads & Youth Information Packets
Quarantines and Death: The Far Right's Homophobic Agenda
Standing Toe to Toe: Fighting Racism in Georgia
They Don't All Wear Sheets: A Chronology of Racists and Far-Right Violence, 1980 to 1986
Verbal Violence: Free Speech vs. Hate Speech
When Hate Groups Come to Town: A Handbook of Effective Community Responses
Women's Watch: Violence in the Anti-Abortion Movement

CONFERENCES
Schedule varies

and white churches had been declining since 1980, and the evidence was that most fires at black churches had causes other than racism. Fred Bayles of the Associated Press reviewed federal, state and local records and found that of 409 church fires since 1990, two-thirds had been at white churches, and that 'only random links to racism' could be found in black church burnings.

Michael Fumento in the Wall Street Journal traced the 2,200 stories written on the epidemic to a single press conference alleging a massive rise in church burnings held by a left-wing radical group, the Center for Democratic Renewal, which, in Fumento's dry description, was almost never identified as such in the stories that uncritically repeated its allegations. . . ."

(*Chicago Sun-Times*, June 18, 2002)

"As the count down to the historical State of the Black World Conference (SOBWC) in Atlanta November 28–December 2 begins, one thing is certain-the burning issue of reparations for Africans in America, the continent of Africa and the Caribbean will be a main focal point of the deliberations. As the Rev. Jesse L. Jackson remarked during the World Conference on Racism (WCR), which recently concluded in Durban, South Africa, 'Reparations is an idea whose time has come.'. . .

"Dr. Raymond Winbush, director of the influential Race Relations Institute at Fisk University in Nashville and Beni Ivey, Executive Director of the Center for Democratic Renewal in Atlanta, have been asked to organize a briefing on WCR. The panel of presenters will include Viola Plummer of the December 12 Movement and Dr. Conrad Worrill, National Chairman of the Black United Front, among other organizational representatives who went to Durban. . . ."

(*Atlanta Inquirer*, November 10, 2001)

"The rough spoken local leader of the Ku Klux Klan claims he is 'tired of being ostracized' and is 'retiring.'

"Civil rights watchers disagree over whether Barry Black's quitting as Imperial Wizard of the International Keystone Knights of the Ku Klux Klan is a blow to white supremacist organizations in western Pennsylvania.

"Chris Freeman, a researcher for Center for Democratic Renewal, an anti-Klan group in Atlanta, suggested Black's decision will do little to slow the group down.

" 'There's just not much to him,' Freeman said. 'He's been active, but I don't think he's very much respected as far as Klan leaders go.'

"Freeman also has his doubts about Black's 'retirement.'

" 'I'll believe it when I see it. He may go on to form his own gang, something a little different,' Freeman said. 'A lot of people with the Klan are getting fed up with it. They're not doing anything. There's a lot of infighting, a lot of backstabbing. There's not a unified ideology.' "

(*The Associated Press State & Local Wire*, May 28, 2001)

"In what civil rights leaders called a testament to the success of the movement, an aging former Ku Klux Klansman was convicted Tuesday in Alabama of planting a bomb that killed four black girls at a Birmingham church.

"Thomas Blanton Jr., 62, is the second of four suspects convicted in the fatal blast that ripped through the Sixteenth Street Baptist Church during a packed Sunday school service in 1963. . . .

" 'This tells us that the movement that brought total voter reform also is paying off in every other area of life,' said the Rev. C. T. Vivian, 76, chairman of the Center for Democratic Renewal in Atlanta. 'It does not mean that everybody wants civil rights, but it says we have slowly come around to where a man who did one of the most horrendous bombings in the nation can be put in prison.' "

(*Ventura County Star* [California], May 2, 2001)

Center for Education Reform

Established in 1993

DIRECTOR

Jeanne Allen, president. Allen has held this position since 1993, when she founded the center. She is a frequent commentator in print and broadcast media, and her writings and editorials appear in more than 200 publications yearly. Allen received a bachelor's degree in political science from Dickinson College and went on to work on Capitol Hill and for the U.S. Department of Education.

BOARD OF DIRECTORS

Jeanne Allen, president
Chris White, chair, Global Events Partner, Washington, DC
William J. Hume, chair emeritus, Basic American Foods, Inc.
Gisele Huff, vice chair, Jaquelin Hume Foundation, San Francisco, CA
Other members
Leslye A. Arsht, senior advisor, Education Ministry, Baghdad, Iraq
John Chubb, Edison Schools, Inc., New York, NY
Donald Hense, Friendship House Association, Washington, DC
Robert Johnston, Johnston Associates Inc., Princeton, NJ
Lewis C. Solmon, Milken Family Foundation, Santa Monica, CA
Rev. William R. Steinbrook Jr., Challenge Foundation, Plano, TX
Alexander Troy, Greenwich, CT

SCOPE

Members: 20,000 individuals
Branches/chapters: None
Affiliates: 50 organizations, all 501(c)(3)

STAFF

20 total—plus interns

TAX STATUS

501(h)

FINANCES

Budget: 2004—$3.1 million; 2003—$2.4 million; 2002—$2.1 million

FUNDING SOURCES

Foundation grants, 71%; government contracts, 20%; individuals, 5%; publications, 1%; special events and projects, 3%

PAC

None

EMPLOYMENT

Information on open positions can be found on the Center's Web site, http://www.edreform.com. Cover letters and resumes can be mailed to the director of administration, Center for

CONTACT INFORMATION

1001 Connecticut Avenue, NW, Suite 204, Washington, DC 20036
Phone: (202) 822-9000 • *Fax:* (202) 822-5077
General E-mail: cer@edreform.com • *Web site:* www.edreform.com

Communications Director: Drew Helene
(202) 822-9000 • drew@edreform.com
Human Resources Director: Shawn Sussin
(202) 822-9000 • shawn@edreform.com

PURPOSE: "The Center for Education Reform is a national voice for more choices in education and more rigor in education programs, both of which are key to more effective schooling. It delivers practical, research-based information and assistance to engage a diverse audience—including parents, policymakers, and education reform groups—in taking actions to ensure that U.S. schools are delivering a high quality education for all children in grades K–12."

CURRENT CONCERNS: Building national awareness of education reform • Charter schools • Grassroots and special interests • Parents • Parents Network-Southeast • Partners Program • School governance • School choice • Standards and accountability • State charter school development

METHOD OF OPERATION: Coalition forming • Conferences/seminars • Congressional testimony • Grassroots organizing • Information clearinghouse • Internet (e-mail alerts and Web site) • Internships • Legislative/regulatory monitoring (federal and state) • Media outreach • Polling • Research • Speakers program • Technical assistance • Telecommunications services (mailing lists) • Training • Voting records

Effectiveness and Political Orientation

"Driver's education teachers in Illinois are among the longest tenured and highest paid in the state, with more than one in 10 earning at least $100,000 a year, according to an analysis of statewide data conducted by the Chicago Tribune. Full-time driver's education instructors earned an average of $64,503 and over 11 percent took home six-figure salaries. Both figures were among the highest in the state, the Tribune reported in a story published Sunday. The average pay for all teachers in the 2002–03 school year was $50,537.

"All teachers' earnings are driven largely by experience and level of education, though compensation for coaching sports and overtime for working weekends also was a factor in the salaries of driver's education teachers. According to the data, driver's education teachers average about 21 years of experience—more than instructors who taught physics (15), biology (13) and civics (12). The data includes only teachers whose main assignment is driver's education.

" 'There is something seriously wrong with driver's ed teachers making so much money, based mainly on the fact that they've been around for so long,'

Education Reform, 1001 Connecticut Avenue, NW, Suite 204, Washington, DC 20036. Fax: (202) 822-5077. E-mail: shawn@edreform.com.

INTERNSHIPS

Internship opportunities are available for college and university students. A written essay is required for consideration. Stipends are provided for housing and meals. Interns normally work 40 hours per week. Information on internships can be obtained at http://www.edreform.com.

Internship applications can be sent to Kate Hickok, associate director, External Affairs, Center for Education Reform, 1001 Connecticut Avenue, NW, Suite 204, Washington, DC 20036. Fax: (202) 822-5077. E-mail: kate@edreform.com.

NEWSLETTERS

Parent Power! (8 times a year)
Monthly Letter to Friends (6–8 times a year)
Also publishes brochures, info-packs, and publicity materials on a variety of subjects.

PUBLICATIONS

The American Education Diet: Can U.S. Students Survive on Junk Food?
Beyond Brick and Mortar: Cyber Charters Revolutionizing Education
Charter Closures: The Opportunity for Accountability
Charter School Laws Across the States: Ranking Score Card and Legislative Profiles
Charter Schools: Results from CER's Annual Survey of America's Charter Schools
Charter Schools Today: Changing the Face of American Education
Finishing College: The Facts That Most Influence Success
History Failure: Doomed to Repeat Itself?
The National Charter School Directory
The New ESEA: A Primer for Policy Makers
Nine Lies About School Choice: Answering the Critics
School Choice Today
The School Reform Handbook: How to Improve Your Schools
Sizing Up What Matters: The Importance of Small Schools
Solving the Charter School Financing Conundrum
What the Research Reveals About Charter Schools

CONFERENCES

None

said Jeanne Allen, president of the Center for Education Reform in Washington. 'We should be looking at the areas with the most need, the areas where it's hard to attract good teachers, and pay them gobs of money. No one can tell me that a driver's ed teacher is as valuable to a school as a good math or science teacher.' "

(*Associated Press State & Local Wire,* January 26, 2004)

"A battle over whether to give hundreds of District of Columbia students federal money to attend private schools could be resolved this week in Congress. Opponents view the stakes as enormous, saying approval of the first federal funding of private school vouchers could set a national precedent. 'Once you open that floodgate, what is to say that any state couldn't use their federal dollars for a voucher program?' said Nancy Keenan, education policy director of People for the American Way, one of the groups leading the opposition. 'We just believe it is bad public policy.'

"Jeanne Allen, president of the Center for Education Reform, a nonprofit organization that advocates school choice, said voucher opponents are using 'deliberate scare tactics. The unions have made it a flash point,' Allen said, referring to the National Education Association and the American Federation of Teachers AFL-CIO. 'If the NEA and the AFT weren't out in droves convincing some legislators . . . that this is going to spell the death of public schools as they know them,' she said, 'it would not be an issue.'

"She argued that federally funding vouchers in the district would not be a precedent because the federal government has a different obligation to district schools than schools in the states. Both the House and Senate versions of the legislation would provide vouchers of up to $7,500 per student, with the House providing enough for about 1,300 and the Senate enough for about 1,700 of the city's 66,000 students. Both versions of the legislation would make the vouchers available to students from families earning less than about $34,000 for a family of four. Both would require private schools participating in the program to admit students selected by lottery."

(*Austin American-Statesman* [Texas], November 16, 2003)

"Congress took a step Friday toward turning the nation's capital city into the home of the first federally supported school voucher plan, an idea with implications across the country. The House narrowly endorsed private-school vouchers for poor District of Columbia students Friday, a plan likely to win final approval when the city's budget comes to a vote next week. The Senate, too, will soon consider a plan to let district students attend private school at public expense. The last time proponents got this far, in 1997, the voucher proposal stalled in the Senate after a veto threat from then-President Clinton. This time, proponents say the idea may have enough support in the Senate, and the White House isn't an obstacle: President Bush backs school choice.

"If Congress adopts vouchers for one of the nation's most troubled districts, it could influence the choices of state leaders and further energize those on both sides of the issue. Six states offer some form of vouchers, but voters in other states have rejected them. 'Sometimes vouchers don't get traction because they're not in places anyone pays attention to. But for Washington, D.C., to house a program of choices, that could have tremendous traction,' said Jeanne Allen, president of the Center for Education Reform. 'We're closer than we've ever been.' "

(*Desert Morning News* [Salt Lake City], September 6, 2003)

"Increasing scores on both math and verbal SAT college admission tests provided encouraging signs Tuesday that the overall results of the American education system are getting better. The math scores were the highest they have been since at least 1967, the College Board, which runs the SAT program, said in releasing new results for the nation's most widely used admission tests. But the gap between haves and have-nots remained large, and in some instances grew. Verbal scores, while up, were still substantially below the levels of the late 1960s and early 1970s.

" . . .'Higher SAT scores, a record number of test-takers, and more diversity add up a brighter picture for American education,' said Gaston Caperton, president of the College Board. 'While we certainly need to make more progress, the fact remains that we are clearly headed in the right direction.'

"Reacting to the national scores, Johnny Lott, president of the National Council of Teachers of Mathematics, said, 'The focused efforts to improve the mathematics education of our students are clearly bearing fruit. He said the results also reflected the fact that more high school students are taking higher-level math courses. 'These scores show the value of more students taking a challenging curriculum,' Lott said.

"But the Center for Education Reform, a Washington-based non-profit group that has often criticized the status quo in public schooling, dismissed the improved SAT results. 'This once venerable test . . . is a shell of what it used to be,' the organization said in a statement. It said changes in the tests meant that scores had been inflated in recent years and some types of challenging questions had been dropped. Students are now given more time to take the math tests and are allowed to use calculators on some questions, the group pointed out."

(*Milwaukee Journal Sentinel,* August 27, 2003)

"Charter schools were designed to shake up public education by fostering innovation that would benefit students and pressure traditional public schools to improve.

But have charter schools—the most significant education reform movement in the last decade—also fostered segregation? Yes, according to a report by the Civil Rights Project at Harvard University. The report, written by Gary Orfield, concludes that the publicly funded, privately run schools are places of isolation, especially for minority students.

"Orfield found that 70 percent of black charter-school students attend intensely segregated schools compared with 34 percent of black public school students. In almost every state studied, the average black charter school student attends school with a higher percentage of black students and a lower percentage of white students, Orfield says. . . .

"Pro-charter groups have already labeled Orfield's study misleading. The Washington, D.C.-based Center for Education Reform, for instance, says that while charters do have a disproportionate number of minority students, the ratio among races is almost always better than in public school districts. Besides, the fact that parents of black and Latino youngsters are choosing charter schools is a good thing, not a bad one. But because charter schools have the flexibility to transcend school district boundary lines, many find their failure to integrate surprising."

(*The Plain Dealer* [Cleveland], July 15, 2003)

Center for Health, Environment, and Justice

Established in 1981

DIRECTOR

Lois Marie Gibbs, executive director. Prior to starting the center in 1981, Gibbs founded the Love Canal Homeowners' Association. She has also been active in the Citizens' Clearinghouse for Hazardous Wastes.

BOARD OF DIRECTORS

Dave Beckwith, capacity builder/trainer, Needmor Fund, Toledo, OH

Clyde Foster, grassroots leader and former mayor, Triana, AL

Vilma Hunt, retired environmental researcher, EPA Health Assessment Group, Magnolia, MA

Luella Kenny, grassroots leader, Love Canal Homeowners Association, Buffalo, NY

Pame Kingfisher, grassroots leader, Indigenous Women's Network, Austin, TX

Murray Levine, professor of psychology, State University of New York, Buffalo, NY

Esperanza Maya, grassroots leader, People for Clean Air and Water, Hanford, CA

Maria Pellerano, researcher, Environmental Research Foundation, New Brunswick, NJ

Suzi Ruhl, attorney, Tallahassee, FL

Alonzo Spencer, grassroots leader, Save Our County, East Liverpool, OH

Holly Gibson, corporate secretary, Richardsville, VA

Ron Simon, general counsel, Washington, DC

SCOPE

Members: 8,000 grassroots organizations; approximately 24,000 individuals
Branches/chapters: None
Affiliates: None

STAFF

9 total—plus interns

TAX STATUS

501(c)(3)

FINANCES

Revenue: 2002—$1.39 million; 2001—$2.45 million; 2002—$2.01 million

FUNDING SOURCES

Church and private foundation grants, 67%; members, 33%

PAC

None

EMPLOYMENT

Information on open positions can be obtained by contacting the Center at chej@chej.org. Cover letters and resumes can be mailed to Sharon Franklin, finance/administration director, Center for Health, Environment and

CONTACT INFORMATION

150 S. Washington Street, Suite 300, Falls Church, VA 22046
Mailing address: P.O. Box 6806, Falls Church, VA 22040-6806
Phone: (703) 237-2249 • *Fax:* (703) 237-8389
General E-mail: chej@chej.org • *Web site:* www.chej.org

Communications Director: Information unavailable
Human Resources Director: Sharon Franklin, finance/administration director
sfranklin@chej.org

PURPOSE: "To assist grassroots leaders in creating and maintaining local community organizations which fight toxic polluters and environmental hazards."

CURRENT CONCERNS: Dioxin exposure • Hazardous waste • Medical waste • Plant emissions and discharges • Solid waste • Waste reduction/toxics prevention/recycling

METHOD OF OPERATION: Coalition forming • Conferences/seminars • Demonstrations • Direct action • Grantmaking (Community Leadership Training Program provides small grants of $500–$5,000 to grassroots groups for education and training programs) • Grassroots organizing • Internet (Web site) • Library/information clearinghouse (open to public) • Media outreach • Research • Speakers program • Special projects (Citizens Alliance Program, Stop Dioxin Exposure Campaign) • Training and technical assistance

Effectiveness and Political Orientation

"Herndon High School's environmental group, Students Against Global Abuse, has earned one of the first Green Flag awards for its recycling efforts, which have gathered an average of more than 100 tons of paper and other waste annually since the group was founded more than a decade ago. The group's work to recycle waste from the school and from 150 businesses in the Herndon area has raised $250,000 for college scholarships and environmental programs.

"The recognition comes from the Green Flag program, an initiative of the Center for Health, Environment and Justice's 'Child Proofing Our Communities' campaign, which works to reduce environmental health hazards in schools. The center, based in Falls Church, was founded by Lois Marie Gibbs, a community leader at the toxic Love Canal in New York."

(*The Washington Post,* January 1, 2004)

"Love Canal was a disaster spawned of ignorance and carelessness. For decades, Hooker Chemical & Plastics dumped barrels of toxic waste, including the carcinogen dioxin, into a 18-metre-wide ditch by the banks of the Niagara River, the remains of a failed power-generating project launched by industrialist

Justice, P.O. Box 6806, Falls Church, VA 22040-6806. E-mail: sfranklin@chej.org.

INTERNSHIPS
Information on internships is available at http://www.chej.org/interns.html. Applications can be sent to the internship coordinator, P.O. Box 6806, Falls Church, VA 22040-6806. E-mail: sfranklin@chej.org.

NEWSLETTERS
Dioxin Digest (quarterly)
Everyone's Backyard (quarterly)

PUBLICATIONS
The following is a sample list of publications:
Asthma: Breathtaking Facts
Bad Boy Laws
Best of Science
Brownfields
The Buried Truth: Landfill Failures
Burning Rubber: Tire Incineration
Cancer Clusters
Cellular Phone Towers
Civics for Democracy
Community Health Surveys
*Detoxifying Your Home: Protecting Your
    Family and Community*
Drinking Water: An Endangered Resource
*Dying From Dioxin: A Citizen's Guide to
    Reclaiming Our Health and Rebuilding
    Democracy*
*Empowering Ourselves: Women and Toxics
    Organizing*
Environmental Testing
Everyone's Backyard
How to Deal with a Proposed Facility
How to Win in Public Hearings
Love Canal Guidebook
Mold: A Public Health Threat
Organizing Toolbox
Pesticides in Your Community
Powerlines
*Recycling: The Answer to Our Garbage
    Problem*
*Reducing Children's Environmental Health: A
    Parents' Guide*
Ruling the Roost: Poultry Waste
Safety Plans: What You Need to Know
Superfund
Toxic Waste Site Lists
User's Guide to Lawyers
*Using Your Right-To-Know: A Guide to the
    Community Right to Know Act*
Water Filters
*Women Activists: Challenging the Abuse of
    Power*

CONFERENCES
CHEJ cosponsors: CEOs-Continuing Education
    for Organizers
Grassroots Convention; Leadership
    Development Conferences

William Love in the 1890s. In 1953 the landfill was covered over and sold to the Niagara Falls Board of Education for $1. In the 1960s, residents, many of whom worked for Hooker, began noticing odors in their basements and sludge coming out of the ground.

"A barrel would emerge from the ground surrounded by black gunk and someone would complain their child was playing in the hole, so the city would dump some dirt over it," said Lois Gibbs, who led the fight to force the government to respond to the crisis. By the late 1970s, children were coming down with strange illnesses, women were suffering from a high rate of miscarriages and stillbirths. And during a four-year period at that time, an alarming 56 percent of children were born with birth defects. . . . 'Because of Love Canal, polluters can no longer bury waste and walk away from it and assume there is no harm,' Gibbs said. . . .

" 'A black cloud lays over the top of our heads, like the daughter whose mother had breast cancer,' said Gibbs, who is 51 and runs the Center for Health, Environment and Justice, an advocacy group based in Virginia. 'You wonder each time you go to the doctor, or your children do, (if) something terrible will happen. This is the first time an administration has abandoned the 'polluter pays' philosophy.'

" 'For years people called it "the annoyances," ' said Lois Gibbs, who led the fight to force the government to respond to the crisis. 'We were mom and apple pie and we were being harmed,' Gibbs said. 'We represented the American dream and the dream had broken.' "

(*The Gazette* [Montreal, Canada], August 3, 2003)

"Love Canal activist Lois Gibbs stood in front of Mayor Anthony M. Masiello's West Side home Saturday and urged Hickory Woods residents to 'get in the mayor's face.' Gibbs and about 30 protesters, most of them homeowners from Hickory Woods, showed up unannounced at Masiello's doorstep to protest what they claim are two years of broken promises by the mayor. 'This is wrong,' Gibbs said during a news conference in front of the house. 'It's unfair, and the mayor should be ashamed of himself.'

"Homeowners from the contaminated neighborhood in South Buffalo chose Saturday, the two-year anniversary of Masiello's pledge to make them 'whole,' to demonstrate outside his house near the Albright-Knox Art Gallery. They carried signs that said 'Pinocchio for Mayor' and 'Masiello's biological weapon: Hickory Woods' and chanted slogans demanding the relocation of residents. As they marched up and down Masiello's street, they carried a huge clock with the phrase 'Time's Up,' a reference to the mayor's 2-year-old pledge of assistance. Hickory Woods, a subdivision of about 60 homes, was built during the 1990s on land bought and developed by City Hall. . . .

"Masiello said the city is working with the state to increase the pool of money being offered to the neighborhood. 'They're waiting for people to tire of this or die,' Richard Ammerman, president of Hickory Woods Residents for a Clean Environment, said of the city's efforts. Christina Schrader, a Hickory Woods resident and the pregnant mother of two young children, recalled her first meeting with Masiello and his claim that he, too, had young kids and 'knew how she felt.' 'You don't know how I feel,' Schrader said of Masiello on Saturday, her voice trembling with emotion. 'I don't know if they're going to grow up healthy or grow up sick.'

"Ammerman said residents, at Gibbs' urging, plan to turn up the heat on Masiello. 'Politicians are insulated,' said Gibbs, executive director of the

Center for Health, Environment and Justice in Falls Church, Va. 'The mayor needs to know how difficult it is for these people.' "

(Buffalo News [New York], February 23, 2003)

"It was chosen over two other sites as the better location for a Gwinnett County school—a stretch of land a half mile away from two landfills where buzzards fly overhead and a pungent odor pierces the air. A study by Gwinnett County Public Schools engineers concluded that the 30-acre site in Buford was fit for construction. That there would be no reason to suspect contamination from either of the landfills would ever reach the property at 5695 Sycamore Road.

"Meanwhile, Sycamore Elementary School is slated to open in August with an estimated enrollment of 869 students. Parents of some of those students have called upon an environmental activist group, the Center for Health, Environment and Justice, to help them compel the school system to perform scientific tests at Sycamore. At the very least, parents would like to see air monitoring devices installed. . . . School officials maintain the Sycamore school site is safe for children. 'The site was in the right area and was determined to be the best site in terms of location, size, availability, land features, and ease of development,' said Sloan Roach, spokeswoman for Gwinnett Schools. . . .

"Paul Ruther, of the Center for Health, Environment and Justice, has . . . worked with a community in Ohio facing similar issues with a school built between two landfills. 'This community has alarms installed in the school set up to monitor hydrogen sulfide emissions from the landfill,' said Ruther. 'Some of the health effects they have seen have been burning eyes, runny noses and rashes to the much more serious, like sudden onset of asthma.' Gwinnett administrators do not plan to install any monitors at Sycamore. Engineers who conducted the system's Phase I Environmental Site Assessment said the school is on a separate watershed from the landfills and should not be exposed to contaminants."

(The Atlanta Journal-Constitution, February 3, 2003)

Center for Justice & Democracy

Established in 1998

DIRECTOR

Joanne Doroshow, executive director. The founder of the Center for Justice & Democracy (CJ&D), Doroshow is an attorney who has worked on civil justice issues since 1986, when she first directed a project for Ralph Nader on liability and the insurance industry. In that capacity, she developed some of the first educational materials used to fight tort reform around the country. Doroshow was a member of the Steering Committee of the Brookings Institute/American Bar Association's Advisory Committee on the Future of the Civil Jury. In 1997, she was the staff attorney and lobbyist on civil justice issues for Public Citizen. Doroshow was selected by the Stern Family Fund as a 1999 Public Interest Pioneer.

BOARD OF ADVISORS

Erin Brockovich; director of research, Law Offices of Masry & Vititoe

Richard Dysart; actor

Lucinda M. Finley; professor of law, University of Buffalo Law School

Ben Franklin; editor, *The Washington Spectator*, former *The New York Times* national correspondent

Marc Galanter; professor of law, University of Wisconsin Law School, Madison

Joseph D. Harbaugh; dean, Nova Southeastern University Law Center

J. Robert Hunter; director of insurance, Consumer Federation of America

Thomas H. Koenig; professor of sociology, Northeastern University

Andrew McGuire; executive director, Trauma Foundation

Michael Moore; filmmaker and author

Joan Mulhern; Earthjustice Legal Defense Fund

Henry Myers; former science advisor, U.S. House Committee on Interior and Insular Affairs

Willard P. Ogburn; executive director, National Consumer Law Center

Joseph A. Page; professor of law, Georgetown University Law Center

Annie King Philips; juror representative, Council for Court Excellence, Washington, DC

Jerry Phillips; professor of law, University of Tennessee College of Law

Andrew F. Popper; professor of law, Washington College of Law, American University

Michael Rustad; professor of law and director of High Technology Law Program, Suffolk University Law School

CONTACT INFORMATION

80 Broad Street, 17th Floor, New York, NY 10004
Phone: (212) 267-2801 • *Fax:* (212) 764-4298
General E-mail: centerjd@centerjd.org • *Web site:* http://centerjd.org

Communications Director: None
Human Resources Director: None

PURPOSE: "The Center for Justice & Democracy is a national consumer organization working to fight the so-called 'tort reform' movement, engaging in battles around the country to protect the civil justice system. "We are working full-time to expose unscrupulous attacks by special interests on judges, juries, injured consumers and the attorneys who represent them. We are dedicated to raising public awareness of the value of our civil justice system and the dangerous campaign behind the so-called 'tort reform' movement."

CURRENT CONCERNS: Insurance industry • Judiciary • Juries • Lawsuits • Lawyers • Legislative issues • Tort reform • Tort reform groups

METHOD OF OPERATION: Advertisements • Coalition forming • Congressional testimony • Direct action • Films/video/audiotapes • Grassroots organizing • Internet (databases, e-mail alerts, and Web site) • Internships • Legislative/regulatory monitoring (federal and state) • Library services open to the public • Library services for members only • Lobbying (federal, state, and grassroots) • Local/municipal affairs • Media Outreach • Research • Technical assistance • Training

Effectiveness and Political Orientation

"Doctors from around the state, many wearing white lab coats over winter jackets, rallied in Annapolis yesterday against rising medical malpractice premiums, saying the costs have forced some to stop offering services such as delivering babies and have jeopardized access to other health care. . . .

"Others at the gathering included Mark and Mindell Cohen of Owings Mills, whose 34-month-old daughter Brianna died after receiving five times the prescribed amount of potassium from a Johns Hopkins Hospital pharmacy.

"The Cohens and other victims said they wanted the money to punish the medical professionals or, in some cases, to care for themselves for the rest of their lives. . . .

"Gene Stilp, a field organizer for the Center for Justice & Democracy, a national consumer group that organized the counter-gathering, said that in addition to policing 'bad' doctors, an evaluation of the insurance industry's recent premium increases is needed.

"The increases might be the result of a bad economy and insurers' stock market losses, some victim advocates said.

Michael J. Saks; professor of law, Arizona State University

SCOPE
Members: Declined to comment
Branches/chapters: None
Affiliates: None

STAFF
4 total—3 full-time professional; 1 full-time support; plus 2 part-time professional, 2 part-time support; and 1–4 interns

TAX STATUS
501(c)(3)

FINANCES
Revenue: 2002—$435,257

FUNDING SOURCES
Declined to comment (20% from membership [from tax form])

PAC
None

EMPLOYMENT
Potential applicants can learn about job openings with this organization from centerjd.org, postings to idealist.org, ads in newspapers such as the *The New York Times* and *The Washington Post*, and at the Web site pslawnet.org. This organization offers employment opportunities in advocacy, policy, legal, administrative, and development. Applicants should send resumes to James Freedland, administrative director, 80 Broad Street, 17th Floor, New York, NY 10004. Phone: (212) 267-2801. Fax: (212) 764-4298. E-mail: centerjd@centerjd.org.

INTERNSHIPS
CJ&D offers various internship opportunities, paid and unpaid, in the following the areas of advocacy, policy, legal, and development. Individuals interested in applying for internship opportunities should send resumes to Geoff Boehm, legal director, 80 Broad Street, 17th Floor, New York, NY 10004. Phone: (212) 267-2801. Fax: (212) 764-4298. E-mail: centerjd@centerjd.org.

NEWSLETTERS
Impact (quarterly)

PUBLICATIONS
Average Medical Malpractice Payments Only $30,000; Payouts Virtually Flat for a Decade
The CALA Files: The Secret Campaign by Big Tobacco and Other Major Industries to Take Away Your Rights
The Eight Biggest Myths about Medical Malpractice—and How to Respond
Lifesavers: CJ&D's Guide to Lawsuits that Protect Us All
Premium Deceit: The Failure of "Tort Reform" to Cut Insurance Prices

" 'Let's not make this doctors vs. patients,' Stilp said. 'Let's figure out what the real problem is.' "

(*The Baltimore Sun,* January 22, 2004)

"The caller to Joanne Doroshow's office last month described himself as working for Sky Radio Network, a company that produces programming for Forbes Radio, one of the audio channels available to passengers on American Airlines.

"As the executive director of the Center for Justice and Democracy, a nonprofit organization that casts itself as a champion of consumer rights, Ms. Doroshow was asked if she would be interviewed for a talk show examining the issue of tort reform. When Ms. Doroshow agreed, she said, the caller informed her that it would cost her organization $5,900 to have its point of view heard. When Ms. Doroshow balked, she said, the caller offered to see if it could be reduced to $3,500.

" 'I was furious,' Ms. Doroshow said. 'I thought this was another way corporations are dominating what people hear, and are getting only their side presented because they're willing to pay for it.'

"Ms. Doroshow was so angry that she directed lawyers for the center, whose board includes Erin Brockovich and Ralph Nader, to draft a complaint letter to the Federal Trade Commission, which the center intends to submit today. It asks that Sky Radio, which also produces programming for United, Delta, Northwest and several other airlines, be required to disclose prominently that its news-style programs are actually little more than paid advertisements. . . ."

(*The New York Times,* October 27, 2003)

"There is little evidence that patients are losing access to health care because doctors are paying more for medical malpractice insurance, according to a study by the investigative arm of Congress.

"The General Accounting Office report issued last week appear to contradict one of the main arguments used by supporters of Proposition 12, a proposed constitutional amendment that would limit the amount of damages Texas juries can award in medical malpractice cases.

"Proposition 12 supporters, including the Texas Medical Association and the state's Republican leadership, contend that lawsuit limits are needed to lower malpractice premiums. Without the caps, they say, Texas patients will suffer as doctors close or curtail their practices because they cannot afford the insurance rate increases.

"But after studying nine states—Texas not among them—the accounting office found that increased premiums are causing no "widespread" loss of health care, including in five states that the American Medical Association have said are in 'crisis.'. . .

"A coalition of national consumer groups, including Public Citizen, the Center for Justice and Democracy and the U.S. Public Interest Research Group, said in a letter that the report shows that AMA officials have 'misled, fabricated evidence or, at the very least, wildly overstated their case about how these medical malpractice insurance problems have limited access to health care.' "

(*Austin American-Statesman* [Texas], September 5, 2003)

"Linda McDougal, whose breasts were removed in an unnecessary surgery at a St. Paul hospital, came to Capitol Hill on Thursday to say that President Bush 'intends to harm me and other victims' by seeking to put a $250,000

Restoring Shattered Lives: A Primer on War, Terrorism and the U.S. Civil Justice System
Also publishes bimonthly White Papers.

CONFERENCES
None

limit on jury awards for victims of medical errors.

" 'I have lived with the horror of this for over 7½ months . . . I will never have what I had before,' McDougal said at a news conference.

"McDougal, who went public with her story last week, has found allies in Washington. They include the Association of Trial Lawyers of America and the Center for Justice and Democracy, two groups that are publicizing her case as they fight the president's plan.

"Bush argues that too many doctors can't afford malpractice insurance and that jury awards are driving up health costs. With unlimited awards, Bush says, doctors can be pressured into settling cases, 'and the system looks like a giant lottery.'. . .

"[McDougal] came to Washington to help the Center for Justice and Democracy—which got its seed money from filmmaker Michael Moore—kick off its 'Medical Rights Bus Tour.' A white school bus will tour at least 13 states, with victims of medical malpractice telling their stories along the way."

(*Star Tribune* [Minneapolis], January 24, 2003)

"The upcoming legislative battle over medical malpractice reform primarily centers on this question:

"Will capping the dollar amount juries can award victims of medical negligence stop soaring costs physicians pay for malpractice insurance?

"For every special interest group that says 'yes,' just as many say 'not so fast.'

"Both sides are rolling out studies, surveys and reams of statistics that bolster their own positions and contradict the others.

"And whether the Legislature and Gov. Jeb Bush ultimately cap damages in the legislative session that opens March 4 will depend on whose statistics lawmakers believe. . . .

"The Center for Justice and Democracy, a Ralph Nader consumer group that concentrates on fighting tort reform, says injured victims win jury awards in only 23 percent of their cases. That's a decrease from 1992 when 30.5 percent of claimants won awards, according to the center."

(*Tampa Tribune,* November 24, 2002)

Center for Media and Public Affairs

Established in 1985

DIRECTOR

S. Robert Lichter, president. Lichter is the author of a dozen books and numerous scholarly and popular articles on the role of media in society. His studies are frequently cited in academic venues as well as the popular press, and he has appeared on all major network news shows and many other media outlets. Lichter has worked with such groups as the Alliance for Better Campaigns, the Digital Promise Project, and the Global Interdependence Initiative. He has also testified before Congress and served as an expert witness on media content and effects. He holds a Ph.D. in government from Harvard University and a B.A., summa cum laude, from the University of Minnesota. He has taught at Harvard, Princeton, Georgetown, and George Washington Universities.

BOARD OF DIRECTORS

S. Robert Lichter, president
Linda S. Lichter, vice president
David Gergen; commentator, journalist
Paul Mongerson; engineer, businessman and author
Paul McCracken
Honorable Robert D. Stuart Jr.

SCOPE

Members: None
Branches/chapters: None
Affiliates: None

STAFF

9 total—7.5 professional; 1.5 support

TAX STATUS

501(c)(3)

FINANCES

Revenue: 2002—$659,859

FUNDING SOURCES

Declined to comment

PAC

None

EMPLOYMENT

Potential applicants can learn about job openings from www.cmpa.com; types of positions include research and administrative. Application materials should be sent to Keith Bundy, director of administration and publications, 2100 L Street, NW, Suite 300, Washington, DC 20037-1525. Phone: (202) 223-2942. Fax: (202) 872-4014. E-mail: employment@cmpa.com.

CONTACT INFORMATION

2100 L Street, NW, Suite 300, Washington, DC 20037-1525
Phone: (202) 223-2942 • *Fax:* (202) 872-4014
General E-mail: info@cmpa.com • *Web site:* www.cmpa.com

Communications Director: Matthew Felling, media director
(202) 223-2942 • mfelling@cmpa.com
Human Resources Director: Keith Bundy, director of administration and publications
(202) 223-2942 • kbundy@cmpa.com

PURPOSE: "To provide an empirical basis for ongoing debates over media fairness and impact through well-documented, timely, and readable studies of media content."

CURRENT CONCERNS: Cable television programming • Divergence between expert opinions and media coverage • Election coverage • Media balance • Portrayal of minorities on television • Violence on television

METHOD OF OPERATION: Congressional testimony • Web site • Internships • Media monitoring • Research

SPECIFIC PROGRAMS/INITIATIVES: Content analysis of print/broadcast news and/or entertainment media. Timely commentary on media-related issues.

Effectiveness and Political Orientation

"As Jayson Blair begins his book-selling blitz Friday with the first of a string of high-profile television appearances, newspapers are weighing how much ink to spill on the former New York Times reporter whose serial plagiarism and fabrication triggered a massive journalism scandal last year.

"'This presents something of a conundrum,' said Eric Gibson, the Wall Street Journal's leisure and arts features editor. 'On the one hand, you don't want to give somebody like that any more free publicity and implicitly thereby credit them or honor them.

"'On the other hand,' Gibson said, 'it's news.'. . .

"But Blair's questionable fame will continue to grow, whether or not he gets the newspaper exposure he wants to sell his books, predicts Matthew Felling of the Center for Media and Public Affairs.

"'In an America where outrage is the ultimate marketing tool, he's riding the wave of celebrity, cashing in on journalistic sin,' Felling said. 'Today's media embraces fame, no matter how shamefully it was acquired.'"

(Hartford Courant [Connecticut], March 4, 2004)

". . . Black visibility dips on network news

"African-American correspondents were seen less last year on the network news than in any year since 1994, and women and minorities overall were less visible on the evening news, a new study finds. But Hispanics saw a record amount of story assignments.

"A study by the Center for Media and Public Affairs examined 11,834 news stories broadcast on the ABC, CBS and NBC evening news programs during 2003.

"Among findings: African-American story assignments dropped steeply, from 9.4% in 2002 to 7.1% in 2003. This is the lowest assignment rate since the non-profit organization began tracking the race and sex of network correspondents in 1994. (African-Americans comprise 12.3% of the population.) Most visible black reporters: ABC's Pierre Thomas and CBS' Byron Pitts, each with 65 stories. . . .

"Says Matthew Felling, the center's media director: 'It reminds me of the glass ceiling we used to discuss for women in professional life, except in this case the minority correspondents are working against a 'white ceiling.' "

(*USA Today*, February 26, 2004)

"The White House is moving swiftly to establish the administration's place in history as the Friday Night Presidency.

"Last Friday afternoon, President Bush announced that he was circumventing the Senate confirmation process and appointing controversial judicial nominee William H. Pryor Jr. to the federal bench. It was the second such recess appointment to be made late on a Friday, following last month's appointment of Charles W. Pickering Sr. . . .

"It is an old political tradition to dump unpopular news on Friday, because fewer people are reading newspapers or watching television news over the weekend. But the Bush administration has been using the trick so routinely that it is losing effectiveness. 'They're not as successful now in hiding these Friday stories,' said Robert Lichter of the nonpartisan Center for Media and Public Affairs. 'Everybody does it, but this administration has done it too much for their own good.'

"Indeed, Friday has become a Bush favorite both for dropping bad news and for making announcements that appeal to the president's conservative base, not necessarily the general public. . . ."

(*The Washington Post*, February 24, 2004)

"President Bush got such negative TV coverage during January—and Democrats got so much favorable attention—that one wonders why Bush's polls aren't worse than they are.

"Bush's approval ratings are now down to the low 50s and he loses in head-to-head matchups with both the Democratic frontrunner, Sen. John Kerry (D-Mass.), and his only rival, Sen. John Edwards (D-N.C.). . . .

"Bush's depressed polls can be explained by what the public has heard over the past month. A study by the Center for Media and Public Affairs shows that references to Bush in January were more than two-thirds negative on the three broadcast network evening newscasts, while references to Democratic presidential candidates were 71 percent positive.

"A negative press isn't new for Bush, according to the center's director, Robert Lichter. 'Except after Sept. 11 and during the Iraq war, he's had a terrible press,' Lichter said. 'The fact is that all presidents do. Presidential coverage is overwhelmingly negative, a little less for Democrats, more for Republicans.'

"A large-scale study by the center before Bush became president showed that Ronald Reagan got only 30 percent positive notices in the network newscasts and in the New York Times and Washington Post during his first year in office. . . ."

(*Chicago Sun-Times,* February 22, 2004)

"In the final days before the Iowa caucuses, Howard Dean has targeted another institution that he says is aligned against his insurgent candidacy, assailing the 'established press' and complaining of attacks in 'newspaper column after newspaper column.'

"Dean's criticism of the mainstream media—which has showered him with more attention than any other Democratic candidate—looks like a tactic for rallying his outsider base, according to political and media analysts. But they also say it reflects the reality that sooner or later, the relationship between an anointed front-runner and the media is bound to sour. . . .

"But it's also hard to overstate just how much Dean and his Internet-driven campaign have dominated coverage to date. He easily wins the battle of the glossies, having appeared on the covers of Time and Newsweek four times since the summer. (The only other Democrat to make a newsweekly cover was Wesley K. Clark.) Andrew Tyndall, who monitors the ABC, CBS, and NBC nightly newscasts, said that in the final quarter of 2003 Dean got more minutes of airtime than the rest of his Democratic rivals combined. The Center for Media and Public Affairs, a nonpartisan research organization based in Washington, evaluated network news coverage of the campaign for all of 2003 and found that Dean was the subject of more than twice as many stories as his nearest Democratic competitor for airtime, John F. Kerry.

"Not all the coverage was positive. Some stories raised doubts about Dean, and the CMPA study noted that there were a large number of negative on-air evaluations offered up by partisan sources and rivals. Still, this avalanche of early attention helped lift Dean to the top of the field. 'A lot of his momentum was built over the summer through major coverage' in the print press, said CMPA media director Matthew Felling. . . ."

(*The Boston Globe,* January 18, 2004)

Center for National Policy

Established in 1981

DIRECTOR

Tim Roemer, president. Roemer represented the 3rd District of Indiana for six terms, from 1991 until 2003. After leaving Congress he became a partner in the Washington-based consulting firm of Johnston and Associates. He has served on the National Commission on Terrorist Attacks Upon the United States and was a distinguished scholar at George Mason University.

BOARD OF DIRECTORS

Peter B. Kovler, chair (CNP); The Marjorie Kovler Fund, Washington, DC

Leon E. Panetta, national advisory board chair (CNP); Panetta Institute, CSU Monterey Bay, CA

Tim Roemer; president, Center for National Policy, Washington, DC

Maureen S. Steinbruner; vice president and senior policy advisor, Center for National Policy, Washington, DC

Terrence D. Straub, vice chair (CNP); US Steel Corp., Washington, DC

David Geanacopoulos, counsel (CNP); Akin, Gump, Strauss, Hauer & Feld, Washington, DC

James L. Tanner Jr., secretary (CNP); Williams & Connolly, Washington, DC

Stephanie Matthews O'Keefe, treasurer (CNP)

Michael D. Barnes; Center to Prevent Handgun Violence, Washington, DC

John Brademas; New York University, New York, NY

Canon Robert J. Brooks; Washington, DC

Jack W. Buechner; Manatt, Phelps, & Phillips, Washington, DC

Sandra Feldman; American Federation of Teachers, Washington, DC

John Freidenrich; Bay Partners, Cupertino, CA

Dan Glickman; Akin, Gump, Strauss, Hauer & Feld, LLP, Washington, DC

Marcia Hale; Democratic National Committee, Washington, DC

Benjamin W. Heineman Jr.; General Electric Co., Fairfield, CT

Lester S. Hyman; Swidler & Berlin, Washington, DC

Sara S. Morgan; Houston, TX

Andrea S. Panaritis; Christopher Reynolds Foundation, New York, NY

Deborah M. Sale; Hospital for Special Surgery, New York, NY

J. Anthony Smith; Schmeltzer, Aptaker & Shepard, Washington, DC

Maurice Tempelsman; Leon Tempelsman & Son, New York, NY

Samuel J. Tenenbaum; Lexington, SC

CONTACT INFORMATION

1 Massachusetts Avenue, NW, Suite 333, Washington, DC 20001
Phone: (202) 682-1800 • *Fax:* (202) 682-1818
General E-mail: thecenter@cnponline.org • *Web site:* www.cnponline.org

Communications Director: Kevin Lawlor, public affairs coordinator klawlor@cnponline.org
Human Resources Director: None

PURPOSE: "To advance the public policy process and determine how government can best serve American interests both at home and abroad."

CURRENT CONCERNS: Affirmative action • Domestic and foreign policy • Health insurance • Retirement security • Social security • Trade policy

METHOD OF OPERATION: Awards program • Conferences/seminars • Congressional testimony • Focus groups • International activities • Internet (Web site) • Internships • Media outreach • Policy analysis • Polling • Promoting debate on public policy issues • Research • Speakers program

Effectiveness and Political Orientation

"The Democratic voter who wants to pick a presidential candidate on the basis of issues faces a big challenge this year.

"The problem, said several Washington policy wonks, is that the contradictions in the records of individual candidates outnumber the differences among the leading contenders remaining in the race.

" 'If you clip off the people on the fringe,' said Maureen Steinbrunner of the Democratic-leaning Center for National Policy, 'there's a pretty strong agreement on what should be done. . . . They are past the point of wanting to fight with each other on ideological questions.' "

(*The Washington Post*, February 9, 2004)

"Former Secretary of State Madeleine Albright is the latest favorite to fill the empty New York Stock Exchange board seat and save face for Dick Grasso.

"Grasso, head of the NYSE, is looking to tap Albright's international contacts and end a string of embarrassments with the selection, Bloomberg News reported yesterday. . . .

" 'I think it's a terrific idea,' said Maureen Steinbruner, president of the Center for National Policy, a progressive Washington think tank formerly led by Albright.

" 'For a long time she has had a really clear view of the important interactions between the global economy and global society,' Steinbruner said. 'I think she would bring just a really important perspective to a discussion that might otherwise tend to be fairly narrow.'

"But other Wall Street watchers were more tentative. . . ."

(*New York Daily News*, April 26, 2003)

SCOPE
Members: 400
Branches/chapters: None
Affiliates: None

STAFF
10 total

TAX STATUS
501(c)(3)

FINANCES
Revenue: 2002—$831,783

FUNDING SOURCES
Corporate donations, 40%; individuals, 2%; government contracts, 15%; membership dues, 10%; foundation grants, 10%; publications, 5%

PAC
None

EMPLOYMENT
Information about employment opportunities can be found at http://www.cnponline.org/employment.htm.

INTERNSHIPS
The Center for National Policy offers full-time internships for talented undergraduate students and recent graduates. An intern's work involves general program support for CNP's Foreign and Domestic Policy Programs. Duties include background research, news updates, project and office support, and other tasks as assigned. Information about internships is available at http://www.cnponline.org/employment.htm.

Candidates should have strong analytical ability in addition to excellent writing, computer, and organizational skills. Background preferred in political science, economics, history, international relations or similar field. CNP prefers a five-day, full-time work schedule, but four workdays a week is an acceptable schedule. Internships are available on a for-credit basis during the academic year.

Please fax resume, cover letter, most recent transcript and 2- to 3-page writing sample to Alex Sunshine at (202) 682-1818. Applications are also accepted by e-mail, at asunshine@cnponline.org. For e-mailed applications, all relevant information should be attached as Microsoft Word documents. Incomplete applications will not be considered.

NEWSLETTERS
Stateline (monthly)

PUBLICATIONS
In Brief (series of issue papers linking population pressures and U.S. foreign policy interests)
Common Ground in a Changing World: An American Perspective
Diagnosing Voter Discontent: Politics, Identity, and the Search for Common Ground

"Sharpening his attack on President Bush's energy policy, Senator John F. Kerry today is calling for tax incentives and a change in government philosophy to replace the nation's dependence on imported oil with an emphasis on creating domestic renewable sources. . . .

" 'Old thinking passed through the doors of 1600 Pennsylvania Avenue far more often and easily than new thinking,' said the text of a speech Kerry is giving this morning at the Center for National Policy, a nonpartisan group that promotes issue discussions. . . ."

(*The Boston Globe,* January 22, 2002)

"U.S. workers are less likely to be offered health insurance than they were in 1979 if they work for manufacturers or in low-wage jobs, according to a study that suggests benefits could erode further.

"The share of workers with health insurance through their jobs fell to 54 percent in 1998 from 66 percent in 1979, the study by the Center for National Policy found, with the biggest decline in manufacturing. . . .

"The study tracked private-sector employees only, said Howard Shapiro, a Washington, D.C., health policy consultant and one of the report's authors. The Center for National Policy compiled the report based on the U.S. Census Bureau's Current Population Survey.

" 'Employers are looking at the cost of benefits and saying, 'Uh-oh,' and trying to control costs. Employees are looking at things and saying, 'Uh-oh, what can I do to protect my family?" said Maureen Steinbrunner, president of the nonpartisan center in Washington.

"The study doesn't suggest any policy solutions."

(*The Denver Post,* June 14, 2001)

"In preparing his new budget, President Bush focused his attention on a particular type of spending, the sort subject to annual appropriations by Congress.

"Such so-called 'discretionary spending,' which includes everything from biomedical research to warships and public works, accounts for about one-third of the federal budget: $692 billion of the $1.96 trillion proposed for next year.

"That's a lot of money, enough for members of the House and Senate Appropriations Committees to boast of their ability to direct federal money to projects in their districts or their states. But a study issued last week by the Center for National Policy suggests that the amount of 'bacon' brought home by members of Congress is relatively small, compared with the big benefit programs, also known as entitlements. Of these, the dominant ones are Social Security, Medicare and Medicaid. . . ."

(*The New York Times,* April 15, 2001)

"It is conventional wisdom in Washington these days that Congress is turning more protectionist, and that this protectionism could complicate prospects for passage this election year of the already negotiated Central American Free Trade Agreement and a free-trade deal with Australia, the details of which the Bush administration hopes to nail down soon. As with most conventional political wisdom, it is only partly true.

"Congress's voting record is clear. Over the past three decades, passing trade legislation has undeniably become much harder. And based on this trend

Job Quality Index (quarterly review of the economy's changing job mix and compensation)
Life in the City: A Status Report on the Revival of Urban Communities in America
Passing the Test: The National Interest in Good Schools for All
Policywires (series of issue papers on domestic economic issues)

CONFERENCES
Economic Policy Forums
Edmund S. Muskie Distinguished Public Service Award Dinner
Newsmaker breakfasts, lunches, and squaretable debates (monthly)

line, economist Howard F. Rosen concludes in a recent study for the Democratic Party's Center for National Policy, the next major trade bill would probably pass the Senate, but not the House.

"But why trade votes are closer today is harder to explain. It is far too simplistic to presume that a possible protectionist outcome—the rejection of trade legislation—is attributable solely to rising protectionist sentiments on Capitol Hill. In fact, the coarsening, increasingly partisan nature of Congress is at least as much to blame for the recent undermining of traditionally broad congressional support for trade. More important, the misdiagnosis of congressional behavior has already led the GOP leadership in Congress and the Bush administration to pursue strategies-aiming for narrow, partisan victories and focusing on politically 'winnable' trade agreements-that further divide Congress on trade.

"The erosion of congressional support for trade has been steady, especially in the House. The Trade Agreements Act of 1979 passed in that chamber by 388 votes. . . . Fast-track trade-negotiating authority, which gives the White House more flexibility to conclude trade pacts, passed the House in 2002 by just three votes."

(*National Journal,* January 24, 2004)

Center for Policy Alternatives

Established in 1975

DIRECTOR

Tim McFeeley, executive director. A lawyer, writer, manager, and strategic consultant, McFeeley received his bachelor's degree from Princeton University and his J.D. from Harvard Law School. McFeeley practiced law in Boston for 17 years, first as an associate at a midsized law firm and later as corporate counsel for National Medical Care, Inc. From 1989–1995, he served as executive director of the Human Rights Campaign Fund (HRCF), a federal political action committee and lobbying organization that advances the cause of civil rights for gay and lesbian Americans. Following his departure from HRCF in January 1995, McFeeley provided consulting services to a variety of for-profit and nonprofit organizations, including the National Senior Citizens Law Center, Common Cause, the National Association of Commissions for Women, and the National Stonewall Democrats. McFeeley served as political director for the National Gay and Lesbian Task Force, directing its efforts in policy research, field organizing and leadership development.

BOARD OF DIRECTORS

Donna Callejon, co-chair/executive committee member

Sen. Rodney Ellis, co-chair/executive committee member; Texas State Senate

Miles Rapoport, secretary/executive committee member; president, Demos

Representative Antonio Riley, treasurer/ executive committee member; executive director, Wisconsin Housing & Economic Development Authority

Sen. G. Spencer Coggs; Wisconsin State Senate

Sen. Scott Dibble; Minnesota Senate

Connie Evans; president, WSEP Ventures, Inc.

Rep. Jessica Farrar; Texas House of Representatives

Spencer Hathaway; president, Hathaway & Associates

Rep. Phyllis Gutierrez Kenney; Washington House of Representatives

William Lucy; international secretary/ treasurer, AFSCME

Rep. Kendrick Meek; U.S. House of Representatives

Rep. Nan Grogan Orrock, executive committee member; Georgia House of Representatives

Donna Parson; consultant

Chellie Pingree; president and chief executive officer, Common Cause

Delba Riddick; executive vice president, Eureka Communities

CONTACT INFORMATION

1875 Connecticut Avenue, NW, Suite 710, Washington, DC 20009-5728
Phone: (202) 387-6030 • *Fax:* (202) 387-8529
General E-mail: info@cfpa.org • *Web site:* www.stateaction.org

Communications Director: Bernie Horn, senior director of policy and communications
(202) 956-5135 • bhorn@cfpa.org
Human Resources Director: Jane Gruenebaum, deputy executive director
(202) 956-5139 • jgruenebaum@cfpa.org

PURPOSE: "Working to strengthen the capacity of state legislators to lead and achieve progressive change."

CURRENT CONCERNS: More than 100 proactive state policies across all issue categories, including health care, criminal justice, housing, education, reproductive rights, and workforce investments

METHOD OF OPERATION: Awards program • Coalition forming • Conferences/seminars • Education foundation • Information clearinghouse • Internet (databases, E-mail alerts, and Web site) • Internships • Legislative/regulatory monitoring (state) • Media outreach • Professional development services • Research • Speakers program • Technical assistance • Training

Effectiveness and Political Orientation

"Pfizer Inc. and Gov. Jeb Bush of Florida announced yesterday that they were extending a program for Pfizer to pay for health counseling for poor patients, saying that millions of dollars were saved and that patients' health had improved. . . .

" 'We've had very positive results in the first year of partnership with Pfizer,' Governor Bush said in a statement. 'Florida is seeing cost savings and our most vulnerable citizens are benefiting from personalized counseling and health education. . . .'

"Even so, a recent study by the state's Office of Program Policy Analysis and Government Accountability found that the state would have saved an extra $64.2 million if the drug companies had paid cash rebates instead of providing health counseling. . . .

"Bernard P. Horn, policy director at the Center for Policy Alternatives, a liberal group that specializes in state issues, said that Florida "is losing a remarkable amount of money" through the Pfizer program. The state would be better off, Mr. Horn said, if it hired independent companies to provide health counseling for Medicaid recipients and forced Pfizer and other drug companies to provide rebates for its drugs. . . ."

(The New York Times, September 24, 2003)

Juan Sepulveda, executive committee member; executive director, Common Enterprise
John Sweeney; president, AFL-CIO
Rep. Dale Swenson; Kansas House of Representatives
Rep. Roy Takumi; Hawaii House of Representatives
Reg Weaver; president, National Education Association
Designate: Peter Arum; senior policy advisor, National Education Association
Designate: Rich Walsh; field mobilization director, AFL-CIO
Designate: Vernon Watkins; executive assistant, AFSCME

SCOPE
CPA has no formal membership; CPA has partners: more than 1,200 state legislators working with CPA at the state level
Branches/chapters: None
Affiliate: Flemming Fellows Leadership Institute

STAFF
13 total—13 full-time professional; plus 3–4 interns

TAX STATUS
501(c)(3)

FINANCES
Budget: 2004—$2 million
2003—$2.4 million
2002—$2.8 million

FUNDING SOURCES
Foundation grants, 79%; special events/projects, 7%; rent/subcontracting, 6%; corporate donations, 3%; individuals, 2%; membership dues, 1%; conferences, 1%; labor, 1%

PAC
None

EMPLOYMENT
Open positions are posted at http://www.stateaction.org, www.idealist.org, and www.movingideas.org. Cover letters and resumes can be mailed to Jane Gruenebaum, deputy executive director, Center for Policy Alternatives, 1875 Connecticut Ave, NW, Suite 710, Washington, DC 20009. E-mail: jgruenebaum@cfpa.org.

INTERNSHIPS
Unpaid internships are available in several areas, including policy and communications, state action (networking), leadership, and development. Undergraduate and graduate students are eligible for internships. Internships are 3 to 6 months in duration; candidates must be able to work a minimum of 20 hours per week. Application deadlines: spring—Jan 15; summer—April 15; winter—August 15.
   Information about internship opportunities is available at www.stateaction.org, www.idealist.org, and www.movingideas.org. CPA's internship coordinator is Sarada Peri,

"From her office in Arlington, Va., [Linda] Tarr-Whelan chuckles about *Ladies Home Journal* naming her one of the 50 most powerful women in Washington, D.C. . . . Now a business partner with her husband, Keith, in an international consulting firm, she had jobs in the administrations of Jimmy Carter and Bill Clinton, the latter as U.S. ambassador to the U.N. Commission on the Status of Women. She's been a lobbyist and policy director for labor groups like the National Education Association, AFSCME and AFL-CIO. As head of the Center for Policy Alternatives, she helped build it into a leading progressive policy group nationally."

(*Capital Times* [Madison, Wisc.], March 6, 2003)

"Massachusetts ranked third and Connecticut sixth in dollars spent on lobbying state legislatures in 2000, the Washington-based Center for Public Integrity announced last week, but other New England states stood out for other reasons. New Hampshire and Rhode Island don't calculate lobbying spending; Vermont doesn't require legislators to disclose potential conflicts of interest. One problem is that many New England lawmakers are part time— overworked and underpaid, says Liz Cattaneo of the Center for Policy Alternatives, a group that works on state-level issues. Another, says Cattaneo, is new tactics like "astroturf lobbying," in which lobbyists masquerade as grassroots citizens groups."

(*The Boston Globe*, May 5, 2002)

"[State Rep. Patti Bellock (R-Hinsdale)] was in New York at a conference held by the progressive, non-partisan group Center for Policy Alternatives. The group chose Bellock as one of 12 state legislators from across the U.S. to sit on a panel examining global issues and their impact on local and state government policies. . . .
   "Leaders with the Washington-based group said the panel is important because of the increasing significance of globalization, especially as free trade and human rights issues continue to be raised.
   " 'We're hearing more and more from our state legislators that they need more resources and contacts to be effective policymakers,' said Kristina Wilfore, a spokeswoman for the group. . . .
   "Although the center is non-partisan, Bellock said its views are more liberal than hers. She noted that most of the other 11 legislators on the panel, including fellow state Rep. Julie Hamos (D- Evanston), are Democrats. But Bellock said she felt she was chosen because, though she may be politically conservative, she works well across party lines."

(*Chicago Tribune*, April 27, 2001)

" 'In 1992 the economy was rotten, but women were optimistic,' says Linda Tarr-Whelan, president of the Center for Policy Alternatives. But nearly a decade of good times later, the female outlook has clouded. The center, with Lifetime Television, co-sponsored a study, 'Women's Voices 2000,' asking women how they felt about the way America was going. They responded with words like 'angry,' 'awful,' 'sick' and 'fed up.' As the survey summed it up: 'Women are asking, 'Is this as good as it gets?' "

(*Newsweek*, January 8, 2001)

manager, policy and communications, 1875 Connecticut Ave, NW, Suite 710, Washington, DC 20009. Phone: (202) 956-5133. Fax: (202) 387-8529. E-mail: speri@cfpa.org.

NEWSLETTERS

CPA News (monthly)

PUBLICATIONS

Progress in the States Report
Progressive Agenda
Progressive Platform

CONFERENCES

Annual Summit on the States (Washington, DC)
Various other issue-specific conferences that vary annually—2004 includes Criminal Justice and Reproductive Health conferences.

"Prescription drugmakers give doctors billions of dollars in gifts each year, a practice that an Illinois legislator says gives the companies too much influence over which medicines doctors prescribe.

"State Rep. Jack Franks, D-Woodstock, introduced a bill this week that would force drugmakers to disclose how much they are giving to doctors. He said gifts can influence many doctors into prescribing more-expensive drugs.

" 'It's all about money. They are the most profitable industry on the planet,' Franks said. 'Doctors, I think, will admit that one of the reasons they meet with the representatives is because of the goodies.'

"Pharmaceutical companies spent more than $15 billion in 2001 on promotions to doctors, according to the U.S. General Accounting Office. That's about 80 percent of the companies' advertising.

" 'The most frequent thing (doctors) get is lunch or dinner. The most expensive thing they get is trips to exotic places,' said Bernie Horn, policy director for the Center for Policy Alternatives in Washington.

"But Wanda Moebius, spokeswoman for the Pharmaceutical Research and Manufacturers of America, said that most of the $15 billion spent on promotions to doctors is for free samples of medicines. She said the pharmaceutical industry considers the samples a service to patients. Dr. Stephen Lefrak, a professor of medicine at the Washington University School of Medicine, said the relationship among doctors, patients and the drug companies is complicated because doctors answer to patients while the drug companies answer to the bottom line.

" 'The drug companies will tell you a lot of things, but when push comes to shove, they have a responsibility to the stockholders,' Lefrak said.

"Lefrak said doctors shouldn't accept gifts such as pens, dinner and trips because of the ethical complications, but added that most medical research funding comes from pharmaceutical companies, so it is difficult for doctors to distance themselves from it.

" 'I think the future is very bleak,' Lefrak said. 'They're going to run the medical community.' "

(St. Louis Post-Dispatch, January 30, 2004)

Center for Public Integrity

Established in 1989

DIRECTOR

Charles Lewis, executive director and founder. The center has published more than 200 investigative reports, and Lewis has been the author of several of them, including *The Cheating of America, The Buying of the President, The Buying of the Congress* and *The Buying of the President 2000*. Since 1992, Lewis has spoken on corruption or journalism internationally. In early 1997, he traveled to the troubled Ferghana Valley region of Tajikistan, Uzbekistan, and Kyrgystan in Central Asia as part of a Council on Foreign Relations conflict-prevention delegation. From 1977 to 1988, he did investigative reporting at ABC News and CBS News, most recently as a producer for "60 Minutes" assigned to correspondent Mike Wallace. In 1998, the John D. and Catherine T. MacArthur Foundation awarded Lewis a MacArthur Fellowship. He holds a master's degree from Johns Hopkins University School of Advanced International Studies and a B.A. in political science with honors and distinction from the University of Delaware.

BOARD OF DIRECTORS

Charles Lewis, executive director and founder, CPI

Susan Loewenberg; founder, producing director, L.A. Theatre Works

Paula Madison; president, general manager, NBC4 (Los Angeles)

Charles Piller, co-founding member and chairman

Allen Pusey; special projects editor, Washington Bureau, *The Dallas Morning News* and Belo Broadcasting

Ben Sherwood; former senior broadcast producer, *NBC Nightly News with Tom Brokaw*

Marianne Szegedy-Maszak; senior editor, *U.S. News & World Report*

Isabel Wilkerson; on leave from *The New York Times*

SCOPE

Members: 9,390 individuals
Branches/chapters: None
Affiliates: None

STAFF

35.5 total—29 full-time professional; 3 full-time support; 6 part-time professional; 1 part-time support; plus 12 interns

TAX STATUS

501(c)(3)

FINANCES

Revenue: 2002—$2.9 million

CONTACT INFORMATION

910 17th Street, NW, 7th Floor, Washington, DC 20006
Phone: (202) 466-1300 • *Fax:* (202) 466-1101
General E-mail: contact@publicintegrity.org •
Web site: www.publicintegrity.org

Communications Director: Ann Pincus, director of communications and outreach • apincus@publicintegrity.org
Human Resources Director: None

PURPOSE: "To provide the American people with the findings of our investigations and analyses of public-service, government-accountability, and ethics related issues. To produce high-quality, well-documented, investigative research that will result in an informed citizenry; a citizenry that is in a position to demand a higher level of accountability for its government and elected leaders."

CURRENT CONCERNS: Conflicts of interest in state legislatures • Government programs and policies affecting low-income children • International investigative reporting • Issue ad watch • Political activities of news media companies • Use of the Internet for political education • Wrongful convictions and prosecutorial misconduct

METHOD OF OPERATION: Awards program • Conferences/seminars • Congressional testimony • Congressional voting analysis • International activities • Internet (databases and Web site) • Internships • Media outreach • Research • Training

Effectiveness and Political Orientation

"The major contenders in this year's presidential election, which is on track to become by far the most expensive in history, have all done public policy favors for their big contributors during their time in office, the Center for Public Integrity reported Thursday.

" 'This is the inside skinny about the candidates that you won't see in their campaign ads or on their Web sites,' Executive Director Charles Lewis said as the Washington-based research group released 'The Buying of the President 2004,' a 510-page book of investigative candidate profiles compiled by 53 researchers, writers and editors. . . .

"All the candidates refused the center's request to be interviewed about its findings.

"Lewis said voters can use the paperback book, and updates to be posted every other week on the center's Web site (www.publicintegrity.org), to find out who has been underwriting each hopeful's political career. The profiles track all contributions ever given by individuals, businesses or groups to cam-

FUNDING SOURCES
Foundations, 81%; membership dues, 8%; consulting, investment income, 4%; individuals, 4%; publications, 2%; other, 1%

PAC
None

EMPLOYMENT
Information is available on the center's Web site.

INTERNSHIPS
Information is available on organization's Web site. The summer internship program lasts ten weeks; the application deadline is March 1. Additionally, during the academic year, the center occasionally hires interns who attend schools in the Washington, DC, area.

The center encourages applications from people regardless of their sex, race, color, religion, age, national origin, socioeconomic background, political affiliation, veteran status, physical disability, sexual preference or marital status.

Application materials should be sent to Nathan Kommers, The Center for Public Integrity, 910 17th Street, NW, Suite 700, Washington, DC 20006. Phone: (202) 466-1300.

NEWSLETTERS
The Public i (online weekly; 6 issues per year)

PUBLICATIONS
The following is a sample list of publications:
Animal Underworld
The Buying of the Congress
The Buying of the President 2000
The Buying of the President 2004
Canned Hunts Exposed
The Cheating of America
Citizen Muckraking
Fat Cat Hotel
Global Access
Nothing Sacred
Off the Record
Power & Money in Indiana
State Secrets
State Projects
Toxic Deception
Unreasonable Risk

CONFERENCES
Annual Conference for International Consortium of Investigative Journalists

paigns or political committees controlled by a candidate, unless the money was to or from a political party."

(The Atlanta Journal-Constitution, January 9, 2004)

"Space.com, Salon.com and the Center for Public Integrity (http://www.publicintegrity.org/dtaweb/home.asp) were among the award winners announced at the Online News Association awards recently. Space.com was cited for its breaking news coverage of the Columbia shuttle disaster. Salon.com was cited for reporting on mysterious deaths of hundreds of women in a Texas border town. The Center for Public Integrity's coverage of the relationship between the broadcast industry and the federal Communications Commission was also an award winner. . . ."

(The San Diego Union-Tribune, November 24, 2003)

"Many of the companies that have received government contracts to rebuild Iraq and Afghanistan have collectively contributed more money to President Bush's election campaigns than to any other candidate in more than a decade, according to a study released yesterday.

In one of the most detailed studies of postwar contracts, the Center for Public Integrity, a nonprofit government watchdog, found that at least 70 companies have been awarded a total of $8 billion in contracts in the past two years. . . ."

(The Boston Globe, October 31, 2003)

"Wireless phone companies have collected $629 million in fees since January 2002 for installing number-portability technology, according to a study by the Center for Public Integrity, a nonprofit group in Washington that studies ethics-related issues.

"The fees are legal, but they rankle consumers who can't yet take their numbers with them when they change wireless providers. That's about to change; the Federal Communications Commission's deadline for number portability is Nov. 24.

"The fees, often lumped with charges for enhanced 911 service and telephone-number pooling, ranged from nothing to $1.75 a month at 10 companies surveyed by the center. The study included all the companies that provide service here, but some declined to give the information.

"Bob Williams, a staff member with the group in Washington, said it found 'no rhyme or reason' for how the fees or the cost estimates for installing the technology were determined. The Ford Foundation paid for the study. . . ."

(St. Louis Post-Dispatch, October 21, 2003)

"Maryland individual and corporate donors gave $4.8 million in the past three years to a type of 'soft money' political committee that critics say can be used to legally skirt state and federal campaign finance restrictions, a new study shows.

"The analysis by the Center for Public Integrity in Washington examined political committees similar to the one that Maryland Senate President Thomas V. Mike Miller heads to raise money for Democratic candidates running for state offices around the country.

"Miller's work for the Democratic Leadership Campaign Committee has drawn critical scrutiny—and prompted a federal inquiry—because $225,000 in contributions were obtained from racing interests seeking to legalize slot machine gambling in Maryland.

"The report by the Center for Public Integrity, a nonprofit, nonpartisan research group, says both major political parties and their special-interest allies have been using the same type of tax-exempt committees to raise big sums around the country. . . ."

(*The Baltimore Sun,* September 25, 2003)

Center for Responsive Politics

Established in 1983

DIRECTOR

Larry Noble, executive director. Noble joined the center as executive director and general counsel in January 2001. Prior to that, he served as general counsel of the Federal Election Commission from October 1987 through December 2000. Noble also served as the president of the Council on Governmental Ethics Laws from 1997 to 1998 and received the 2000 COGEL Award for his "efforts to promote the highest level of ethical conduct amongst governmental officials and candidates." He has testified before Congress on problems with the existing campaign finance laws and has served as an official observer and consultant with respect to elections held in the former Soviet Union, Benin, Senegal, Mexico, the Dominican Republic, Cambodia and Bangladesh. He also teaches Campaign Finance Law at George Washington University Law School.

BOARD OF DIRECTORS

Paul S. Hoff, chair; attorney, Garvey, Schubert & Barer

Sonia Jarvis; professor, George Washington University School of Media and Public Affairs

Charles McC. Mathias; retired partner, Jones, Day, Reavis & Pogue

Abner J. Mikva; visiting professor, University of Chicago

Ellen S. Miller; publisher, TomPaine.com

John G. Murphy; professor, Georgetown University

Frank P. Reiche; attorney, Archer & Greiner, Princeton, NJ

Whitney North Seymour; attorney, Landy & Seymour

Robert A. Weinberger; vice president for government relations, H&R Block

SCOPE

Members: None
Branches/chapters: None
Affiliates: None

STAFF

12 total—11 professionals; 1 part-time; plus 1 intern

TAX STATUS

501(c)(3)

FINANCES

Budget: 2004—$1.2 million; 2003—$1.2 million; 2002—$1.2 million

FUNDING SOURCES

Foundation grants, 95%; individuals, 3%; conferences, 1%

CONTACT INFORMATION

1101 14th Street, NW, Suite 1030, Washington, DC 20005
Phone: (202) 857-0044 • *Fax:* (202) 857-7809
General E-mail: info@crp.org • *Web site:* www.opensecrets.org

Communications Director: Steven Weiss
(202) 354-0111 • sweiss@crp.org
Human Resources Director: None

PURPOSE: Dedicated to tracking money in politics and its effect on elections and public policy by conducting computer-based research on campaign finance issues for the news media, academics, activists, and the public at large. The goal is to create a more educated voter, an involved citizenry, and a more responsive government.

CURRENT CONCERNS: Enforcement of the campaign finance law; specific programs and initiatives include: tracking the money being raised and spent for federal elections; examining money's effects on elections, legislation, and public policy.

METHOD OF OPERATION: Congressional voting analysis • Internet (databases, e-mail alerts, and Web site) • Internships • Legislative/regulatory monitoring (federal) • Media outreach • Participation in regulatory proceedings (federal) • Research • Training

Effectiveness and Political Orientation

"A campaign finance watchdog group on Thursday called on North Carolina Sen. John Edwards to release the names of his top presidential fundraisers before Super Tuesday—a request the Edwards campaign said it would decline.

"The nonpartisan Center for Responsive Politics said it sent a letter to Edwards after he and his staff declined to respond to repeated phone calls and e-mails seeking the names of those supporters who have collected the most donations for his presidential campaign.

" 'We're not releasing any names. That's our policy,' said Edwards' campaign spokesperson Kim Rubey.

"Campaign disclosure laws do not require candidates to reveal the names of their top fundraisers. . . .

"Larry Noble, executive director of the Center for Responsive Politics, said he thought the names of top fundraisers should be made public in the presidential race because of their potential influence in the White House. He calls them 'the new power brokers.'

" 'These are people who are going to be wielding a certain amount of influence if Sen. Edwards becomes president. We feel the public has a right to know who these people are,' Noble said.

" '. . . As you and others have said during the presidential campaign, special interests have enormous clout in Washington,' the letter stated. 'One mea-

PAC
None

EMPLOYMENT
Potential applicants can learn about job openings with this organization by consulting www.opensecrets.org, *The Washington Post,* or *Roll Call.* This organization offers positions in the areas of research, database, information technology, and reporting/writing. Applicants should send resumes and other materials for employment to Larry Noble, executive director, Center for Responsive Politics, 1101 14th Street, NW, Suite 1030, Washington, DC 20005. E-mail: info@crp.org.

INTERNSHIPS
This organization offers unpaid internships, 3 months in duration; interns are required to work 25 hours per week. Application deadlines: fall—September 30; spring—January 15; and summer—March 15.

The center accepts interns from all majors, undergraduate and graduate students. Interns should have an interest in and be willing to learn about politics in general and money in politics issues in particular. Relevant majors include: government, political science, communications, law, and journalism. Applicants should have some familiarity with computers, though no specific experience is necessary. Internship areas include computer-assisted research and writing.

Information about internships is available at www.opensecrets.org. Internship applications can be sent to Doug Weber, researcher, Center for Responsive Politics, 1101 14th Street, NW, Suite 1030, Washington, DC 20005. Fax: (202) 857-7809. E-mail: info@crp.org.

NEWSLETTERS
Money in Politics Alerts (2–3 per months)

PUBLICATIONS/WEB SITES
The Big Picture
CapitalEye.org
FECWatch.org
OpenSecrets.org
Speaking Freely: Washington Insiders Talk About Money in Politics

CONFERENCES
None

sure of that clout is the amount of money individuals associated with a particular interest group contribute to campaigns.'

"The Edwards campaign said it did not plan to release the names of its top fundraisers because it didn't raise money the way the Bush campaign did. . . ."

(*Los Angeles Times,* February 27, 2004)

"A valuable patch of common ground has unexpectedly surfaced in the first phase of the presidential election. In their early skirmishes over who's pandering most to special interests, both Democrats and Republicans have begun citing the same authority—the Center for Responsive Politics, a research group dedicatedly nonpartisan in publicizing the power of money in politics. Imagine, in lieu of mud, the slinging of accurate information.

"Denouncing the Democratic front-runner, Senator John Kerry, the Bush campaign cited the center's count that the Massachusetts Democrat has collected nearly $640,000 in donations from lobbyists in the past 15 years. In quick reply, the Kerry campaign also used the center to point out that in the last year alone the president raised that much and more—$960,000 from lobbyists—while reigning as 'the king of special interests,' attracting $3.2 million from the gas and oil industry. . . ."

(*The New York Times,* February 23, 2004)

"As footage of Osama bin Laden played across the screen, an announcer warned about the dire consequences of electing Howard Dean, a presidential candidate with no military or foreign policy experience.

"The message of the 30-second ad was abundantly clear. The messenger wasn't.

"The spot, which ran in two early Democratic primary states, included a tag that said it was paid for by 'Americans for Jobs, Health Care and Progressive Values,' but gave no hint about who financed the group or what its agenda is beyond attacking the then-Democratic front-runner.

"The 2002 campaign finance law may have shut off an important avenue of special interest 'soft money'—unlimited cash to the political parties for party-building activities—but it has given rise to a host of new, well-financed special interest groups that lately have been taking their message directly to voters. And like the bin Laden-Dean ad, those messages tend to be sharp-edged and stealthy.

"The groups, known as 527s for their designation in Section 527 of the federal tax code, are not bound by the ban on unregulated soft money placed on political parties. In fact, some are attracting fat donations from people and special interest groups who used to give directly to the parties but can't anymore.

"The law requires 527s to periodically report their donors to the Internal Revenue Service or the Federal Election Commission, but deciphering the role of the players behind the ads—and their agendas—can be tricky.

" 'At the moment they watch the ad, the real identity of the group running it could be a mystery,' said Steve Weiss of the Center for Responsive Politics, a campaign watchdog group that monitors 527s. 'The voters don't realize who is paying for the ad, and the agenda of the financier is very important to know. Those paying for the ad may be trying to accomplish something that may not be at all obvious.' "

(*The Times-Picayune* [New Orleans, La.], February 23, 2004)

"The Ohio utility holding company at the center of investigations into last week's blackout is no stranger to Washington politics, having given more than $1 million to Republicans and Democrats in the last election cycle and with a top executive who was among President Bush's fund-raisers.

"Roughly 70 percent of the federally reported donations from FirstEnergy and its workers went to Republicans, the nonpartisan Center for Responsive Politics reported. FirstEnergy spent $2.25 million last year lobbying Congress on such issues as clean-air regulations and oversight of power markets and nuclear plants, the nonpartisan Political Money Line Internet site reported. . . ."

(*The Boston Herald,* August 20, 2003)

"A new study by the nonpartisan Center for Responsive Politics confirms Democrats' worst fears: They rely far more on fat cats than the Republicans. Despite Democratic claims that the GOP is the party of the rich, the analysis of more than 1.4 million contributors in the 2002 election cycle shows Dems got 92% of million-dollar-plus checks—the kind now banned (unless the Supreme Court invalidates campaign-finance reform later this year). Small, hard-money donors gave 64% of their money to Republicans. . . ."

(*Business Week,* July 14, 2003)

Center for Science in the Public Interest

Established in 1971

DIRECTOR
Michael F. Jacobson, executive director.

BOARD OF DIRECTORS
Michael F. Jacobson; executive director, CSPI

Anne Bancroft; actor

William V. Corr; executive vice-president, National Center for Tobacco-Free Kids

David J. Hensler; attorney, Hogan and Hartson, Washington, DC

Mark Ingram, treasurer; president, Ingram CPA Review

Diane MacEachern; founder, Vanguard Communications, Washington, DC

Kathleen O'Reilly; writer

James Sullivan, founding member; meteorologist

Deborah Szekely; president, Szekely Family Foundation, San Diego, CA

SCOPE
Members: 900,000 individuals
Branches/chapters: None
Affiliates: None

STAFF
57 total—45 full-time professional;
12 full-time support; plus 13 part-time;
4 interns

TAX STATUS
501(c)(3)

FINANCES
Revenue: 2002—$13.9 million

FUNDING SOURCES
Publication sales, 7%; individuals, 15%; private foundations, 7%; royalties, list rentals, investments, 6%

PAC
None

EMPLOYMENT
Employment information is available at http://cspinet.org/about/jobs.html.

INTERNSHIPS
Internship information is available at http://cspinet.org/about/jobs.html.

NEWSLETTERS
Nutrition Action Healthletter (10 times a year)

PUBLICATIONS
Diet, ADHD, & Behavior: A Quarter Century Review
Healthwise Quantity Cookbook

CONTACT INFORMATION
1875 Connecticut Avenue, NW, Suite 300, Washington, DC 20009-5728
Phone: (202) 332-9110 • *Fax:* (202) 265-4954
General E-mail: cspi@cspinet.org • *Web site:* www.cspinet.org

Communications Director: Information unavailable
Human Resources Director: Information unavailable

PURPOSE: "To conduct innovative research and advocacy programs in health and nutrition, and to provide consumers with current, useful information about their health and well-being."

CURRENT CONCERNS: Alcohol • Food safety • Nutrition

METHOD OF OPERATION: Coalition forming • Congressional testimony • Films/video/audiotapes • Legislative/regulatory monitoring (federal) • Litigation • Media outreach • Participate in regulatory proceedings (federal) • Performance ratings • Product merchandising • Research • Telecommunications services

Effectiveness and Political Orientation

"Hey parents, always on the lookout for eateries with kids' menus? Beware. A new study says they're recipes for fat, unhealthy children. According to the Center for Science in the Public Interest, kids' menus at 20 of the nation's biggest table-service restaurant chains offer megaportions of greasy fries, chicken fingers, burgers, and pizza that are chock full of calories, salt, and heart-harmful fats. . . ."

(*U.S. News & World Report,* March 8, 2004)

"The world's largest restaurant chain, under attack from critics for abetting obesity, is phasing out its super-size french fries and soft drinks later this year. McDonald's said it wants to simplify the menu and operations at its 18,000 restaurants.

"Michael Jacobson, executive director of the Center for Science in the Public Interest and a critic of McDonald's menu, applauded the change and said rivals should follow suit.

"But, he added, 'If McDonald's truly cared about its customers' hearts and arteries, it would reformulate its cooking oil to eliminate trans fat.'

"McDonald's and its rivals have begun offering an array of foods that diverge from traditional fast-food fare. . . ."

(*The Houston Chronicle,* March 4, 2004)

"The dispute over whether advertising for alcoholic beverages is being aimed at teenagers is taking a new twist, as an advocacy organization questions a campaign from Allied Domecq Spirits North America to promote its Malibu rum brand featuring the reggae singer Shaggy.

Kitchen Fun for Kids (video)
The Real Scoop about Diet and Exercise
(video)
Also offers informational posters.

CONFERENCES
None

"In letters to the Federal Trade Commission and the Distilled Spirits Council of the United States, the organization, the Center for Science in the Public Interest in Washington, said that Shaggy should not have promoted Malibu because he had a large fan base among teenagers. The organization cited Shaggy's two Teen Choice awards, based on voting in Seventeen magazine and online, and performances with youthful musical acts like the Backstreet Boys, Bow Wow and Mandy Moore. . . ."

(*The New York Times,* January 21, 2004)

"Federal agencies have more power to recall defective toys and auto parts than they do tainted beef, according to consumer groups opposed to a federal rule that forbids state health departments from disclosing where beef products from the Washington state mad cow case were sold.

"A 10,000 pound batch of beef that included cuts and bones from a single infected dairy cow was distributed last month in six states, including California.

"Officials with the federal Department of Agriculture said Monday they knew where nearly all the recalled meat and bones had been sold but maintained that information was considered proprietary and not available to the public.

"Consumer groups said that the argument was both familiar and outrageous.

"'It is inexcusable that the USDA forbids California from informing consumers where the meat is,' said Caroline Smith Dewaal, director of food safety for the Center for Science in the Public Interest, a Washington, D.C., advocacy group.

"'This policy is proof positive that the USDA voluntary recall system is more concerned about protecting the beef industry than protecting the public health,' she added. . . ."

(*The San Francisco Chronicle,* January 6, 2004)

"First they came for the beef and cheese nachos. Now they have come for Cold Stone Creamery's Mud Pie Mojo. In a development that was as predictable as it is absurd, the killjoy cranks over at CSPI, the Center for Science in the Public Interest, have issued a report denouncing ice-cream shops for hawking 'coronaries in cones.' Well, no surprise there. Writing in the July issue of Reason magazine, Jacob Sullum describes how the center (despite its name, it has nothing do with either science or the public interest) has a menu of menaces that must not be allowed anywhere near a dining room. These include fried mozzarella sticks ('just say no'), double cheeseburgers ('a coronary bypass special'), and even fettuccine Alfredo ('a heart attack on a plate').

". . . CSPI immodestly describes its researchers (even that seems too generous a word) as 'food sleuths,' but for now, these self-appointed calorie cops have no warrant. This does not mean that their critics can relax. The center may peddle hysteria, half-truths, and the guilty pleasures of self-denial, but they have a way with the media and in the lunatic world of the gathering 'war against obesity' theirs is likely to be an influential voice. For that reason, if no other, their crusade against cones is worth a closer look. . . .

"CSPI's ice-cream screed is a reminder that the center is a master of hyperbole, if not of science. . . ."

(*National Review,* August 28, 2003)

Center for Security Policy

Established in 1988

DIRECTOR

Frank J. Gaffney Jr., president. Gaffney was assistant secretary of defense for international security policy during the Reagan administration, following four years of service as the deputy assistant secretary of defense for nuclear forces and arms control policy. Previously, he was a professional staff member on the Senate Armed Services Committee under the chairmanship of the late Sen. John Tower, and a national security legislative aide to the late Sen. Henry M. Jackson.

BOARD OF DIRECTORS

James deGraffenreid, chair; president, First Service Networks

M. D. B. Carlisle; former assistant secretary of defense for legislative affairs, and former chief of staff, Sen. Thad Cochran

Frank J. Gaffney Jr, president, Center for Security Policy

Charles M. Kupperman; vice president, Space and Strategic Missiles Sector, Lockheed Martin Corp.

Dominic J. Monetta; president, Resource Alternatives, Inc.

Roger W. Robinson Jr.; president, RWR, Inc.

David P. Steinmann; managing director, American Securities

SCOPE

Members: No information on Web site or annual report
Branches/chapters: None
Affiliates: None

STAFF

9 total—plus fellows

TAX STATUS

501(c)(3)

FINANCES

Revenue: 2001—$1.35 million

FUNDING SOURCES

Foundations, 70%; corporations (defense), 16%; individuals, 10%; corporations (nondefense) 4%

PAC

Information unavailable

EMPLOYMENT

Information unavailable

INTERNSHIPS

Volunteer interns are needed year-round. Although there is occasional clerical work, interns are primarily responsible for performing substantive research and analysis and for writing reports geared toward the center's

CONTACT INFORMATION

1920 L Street, NW Suite 210, Washington, DC 20036
Phone: (202) 835-9077 • *Fax:* (202) 835-9066
General E-mail: info@centerforsecuritypolicy.org •
Web site: www.centerforsecuritypolicy.org

Communications Director: None
Human Resources Director: None

PURPOSE: A nonprofit, nonpartisan organization "committed to the time-tested philosophy of promoting international peace through American strength. It accomplishes this goal by stimulating and informing national and international policy debates, in particular, those involving regional, defense, economic, financial and technology developments that bear upon the security of the United States."

CURRENT CONCERNS: Defense (including homeland security, missile defense, military readiness, weapon systems, arms control, proliferation, nuclear weapons, space, and information warfare) • Economic security • Foreign Policy (including NATO) • Security & Intelligence • Terrorism

METHOD OF OPERATION: Awards programs • Conferences/seminars • Internships • Performance ratings/Report cards • Research • Web site

Effectiveness and Political Orientation

"Reality is always a hard concept to pin down, especially in Washington. Here, reality changes hourly according to perceptions, and according to the money and connections of the people peddling those perceptions.

"The folks behind a gala tribute to the 'Liberators of Iraq' one recent Washington evening had no shortage of cash and influence. The elegant dinner was put on by an outfit called the Centre for Security Policy (CSP)—the perch from which many of the Bush administration's uber-hawks flew in—while the medallion of beef and ginger orange halibut were paid for by a near-exhaustive list of premier league defence contractors. The list, printed inside the programme, included such titans as Bechtel and Halliburton (both continuations of the Republican party by commercial means) which are currently accumulating multi-billion dollar reconstruction deals in Iraq. . . ."

(*The Observer*, October 16, 2003)

"So who is Mr. Abbas? Since the 1960s, he's been the No. 2 man in the militant Fatah wing of the PLO. Last year, Fatah was the leading initiator of suicide-bombing attacks against Israeli citizens. Even now, the Israelis estimate they are thwarting 40 to 50 attacks a week. 'Abu Mazen has been working hand in glove with Arafat for 40 years,' warns Frank Gaffney of the Washington, DC-based Center for Security Policy. Mr. Gaffney also calls Mr. Abbas 'a Holocaust denier'; he points to a 1982 doctoral dissertation and a

timely publications concerning national security affairs. Opportunities are available for students, both undergraduate and graduate, and recent graduates. Interns need to have formidable writing and communications skills, familiarity with computers, and the ability to perform Internet-based research. A minimum commitment of 15–20 hours per week is required, but hours are flexible, as are start dates and duration of internship. Internship are not paid.

Those interested should submit a cover letter and resume; a 300–500 word essay explaining the candidate's interest in the Center for Security Policy; and a sample paper in the style and form of the center's "Decision Briefs," discussing a major current issue or event in the center's area of interest. "Decision Briefs" are located in the "Center Publications" section of our Web site.

Incomplete applications will not be considered. For more information regarding internships, see http://www.centerforsecuritypolicy.org, under "About Us." All materials should be sent to the internship coordinator, Center for Security Policy, 1920 L Street, NW, Suite 210, Washington, DC 20036. E-mail: cannon@centerforsecuritypolicy.org.

NEWSLETTERS
None

PUBLICATIONS
Active Measures
Deep-Six This Treaty
Hemispheric Insecurity
A Fateful Choice
Misleadership
Privatizing Counterproliferation
Reykjavic Redux?
The Right Questions
Unhelpful Freelancing
The Vision Thing
Other publications listed on organization Web site.

CONFERENCES
High-Level Roundtable Discussions and Symposia

book, both written by Mr. Abbas, suggesting the Jews exaggerate the horror of the Holocaust. . . ."

(*World Magazine,* June 7, 2003)

"A public controversy broke out in Washington late last week between two prominent Republican conservatives with close ties to the Bush administration. The spat centers around the administration's outreach to Islamic fundamentalist organizations and, according to Washington insiders, could have implications on proposed measures to enhance U.S. homeland security in the fight against global terrorism.

"The two warring parties are Grover Norquist, a prominent political organizer who is closely allied with President George W. Bush's chief political adviser, Karl Rove, and Frank Gaffney, president of the Center for Security Policy think tank in Washington.

"Gaffney, an assistant secretary of defense in the Reagan administration, is closely allied with Pentagon and National Security Council officials.

"Norquist, president of the conservative political action committee Americans for Tax Reform, is also the founder and first president of the Islamic Institute in Washington. . . ."

(*The Jerusalem Post* [Israel], February 11, 2003)

"President Bush on Friday cited the need for continuity in case of attack for setting up a backup operation of government officials working out of secret locations.

"White House officials confirmed that they had set up an alternative government that could be activated to take care of basic needs in case the nation's capital was destroyed or had to be evacuated. . . .

" 'It is a program that thoughtful people realized was necessary during an era when enemy power might try to decapitate our government,' said Gaffney, who now works at the Center for Security Policy, a Washington think tank.

"Gaffney said the backup government plan languished during the terms of Bush's father and Clinton. . . ."

(*The Houston Chronicle,* March 2, 2002)

"Atlanta Maj. Michael Ouzts of the Marine Corps has been selected to participate in the Corps' Year Out Fellowship, a program that establishes links with corporate, private and nongovernmental organizations with a reputation for leadership and innovation.

"Ouzts, who recently completed a tour at the U.S. Space Command in Colorado Springs, has earned a Defense Meritorious Service Medal. He will complete his one-year fellowship at the Center for Security Policy in Washington. The center is a nonprofit organization dedicated to stimulating debate on all aspects of security policies. . . ."

(*The Atlanta Journal-Constitution,* October 25, 2001)

Center for Strategic and International Studies (CSIS)

Established in 1962

DIRECTOR

John J. Hamre, president and chief executive officer. Hamre was elected CSIS president and chief executive officer in January 2000. Before joining CSIS, he served as U.S. deputy secretary of defense (1997–1999) and under secretary of defense (comptroller) (1993–1997). Before serving in the Department of Defense, Hamre worked for 10 years as a professional staff member of the Senate Armed Services Committee. He received a B.A. from Augustana College in Sioux Falls, SD, in 1972. He also studied as a Rockefeller fellow at the Harvard Divinity School.

BOARD OF DIRECTORS

Sam Nunn, chair; chair and chief executive officer, Nuclear Threat Initiative

David M. Abshire; vice chair and cofounder of CSIS; president, Center for the Study of the Presidency

Anne Armstrong; chair, executive committee; former U.S. ambassador to Great Britain

Betty Stanley Beene; resident scholar, Wesley Theological Seminary

Reginald K. Brack; chair emeritus, Time Inc.

William E. Brock; chair, Bridges Learning Systems, Inc.

Harold Brown; former chair, Foreign Policy Institute, Johns Hopkins University

Zbigniew Brzezinski; professor, School of Advanced International Studies, Johns Hopkins University

William S. Cohen; chair and chief executive officer, Cohen Group

Ralph Cossa; president, Pacific Forum/CSIS

Douglas N. Daft; chair of the board and chief executive officer, Coca-Cola Co.

Richard Fairbanks; former president, CSIS

Michael P. Galvin; president, Galvin Enterprises

John J. Hamre; president and chief executive officer, CSIS

Benjamin W. Heineman Jr.; senior vice president, general counsel, and secretary, General Electric Co.

Carla A. Hills; char and chief executive officer, Hills & Co.

Ray L. Hunt; chair and chief executive officer, Hunt Oil Co.

Henry A. Kissinger; chair and chief executive officer, Kissinger & Associates, Inc.

Kenneth G. Langone; president and chief executive officer, Invemed Associates

Donald B. Marron; chair, Lightyear Capital

E. Stanley O'Neal; chair, chief executive officer, and president, Merrill Lynch & Co., Inc.

Felix G. Rohatyn; president, Rohatyn Associates

Charles A. Sanders; former chair and chief executive officer, Glaxo Inc.

CONTACT INFORMATION

1800 K Street, NW, Suite 400, Washington, DC 20006
Phone: (202) 887-0200 • *Fax:* (202) 775-3199
General E-mail: webmaster@csis.org • *Web site:* www.csis.org

Communications Director: Jay C. Farrar, vice president, external affairs
(202) 775-3141 • jfarrar@csis.org
Human Resources Director: Greg Broaddus, vice president for operations and treasurer
(202) 775-3221 • gbroaddu@csis.org

PURPOSE: "Policy impact is the basic mission of CSIS. Our goal is to inform and shape policy decisions in government and the private sector by providing long-range, anticipatory, and integrated thinking over a wide range of policy issues."

CURRENT CONCERNS: Agriculture • Banking and capital formation • Economic competitiveness and business conditions • Energy and national security • Enterprise for the environment • Global aging initiative • Global organized crime • International communications • International finance and economics • Security and foreign policy • Strategic energy initiative • Telecommunications and information technology • Transportation

METHOD OF OPERATION: Action commissions • Awards program • Conferences and seminars • Congressional study groups • Congressional testimony • Consultation with and advice to businesses and governments • Distinguished speakers • Educational foundations • International activities • Internet (Web site) • Internships • Library/information clearinghouse (for employees only) • Media outreach • Research • Telecommunications services (mailing lists)

Effectiveness and Political Orientation

"It is a perverse law. The world's population, which is about 6.33 billion now, is projected to grow to 7.8 billion by 2025. Most of the growth will take place in the developing world, that is, in many of those countries that are least equipped to support the new numbers. By contrast, the populations of many developed countries are expected to shrink over the next two decades, threatening their ability to maintain labour forces, raise sufficient taxes from the working population and, ultimately, preserve their standard of living. Combine that prospect with an ageing population, and the conclusion is a frightening one. Just how frightening was suggested by Mr. Erik R. Peterson and Mr. Jay C. Farrar of the Washington-based Center for Strategic and International Studies. Today, they told a conference here recently, there are 30 pension-eligible elders in the developed world for every 100 working-age adults. By the year 2040, there will be 70. . . .

SCOPE

Members: None
Branches/chapters: Pacific Forum/CSIS, a
Honolulu-based nonprofit policy institute
that merged with CSIS in 1981, researches
political, economic, and security interests
and trends in the Asia-Pacific region
Affiliates: None

STAFF

170 total—90 research specialists; 80 support;
plus 15 fellows; 70 interns

TAX STATUS

501(c)(3)

FINANCES

Revenue: 2002—$18.94 million; 2001—
$16.89 million; 2000—$16.36 million

FUNDING SOURCES

Foundation grants, corporate contributions,
and individuals, 85%; endowment, publications, and government contracts, 15%

PAC

None

EMPLOYMENT

Postings are listed at http://csis.org/employ-
ment/. Resumes, letters of interest, and salary
requirements should be mailed to CSIS, 1800 K
Street, NW, Suite 400, Washington, DC 20006.
Fax: (202) 466-5141. E-mail:
employment@csis.org.

INTERNSHIPS

CSIS offers both full and part-time internships
in the fall, spring, and summer for undergraduate, advanced students, and recent graduates
interested in gaining practical experience in
public policy at an institution dedicated to
analysis and policy impact. Applicants must be
at least a college junior in standing, an
advanced student, or a recent graduate; must
have a GPA of at least 3.0; and must be eligible to work in the United States.

Internship applications can be mailed to
Shavshigeh Howard, internship coordinator,
CSIS, 1800 K Street, NW, Suite 400,
Washington, DC 20006.

"Given these stark realities, it should be logical for those in poorer countries to opt to have fewer children—to preserve the little that they have—and
for those in richer countries to produce more children to sustain what they
have. But the reality is very different. All around the world, people live as if
there is no tomorrow. The poor, accustomed to scarcity, do not appear to care
what happens to the next generation. The rich, anxious to protect their living
standards, do not seem to understand that their children would not enjoy the
same if their numbers fell sharply. . . ."
(*The Straits Times* [Singapore], January 26, 2004)

"If the six-way talks on the North Korean nuclear arms issue fail, the possible
consequences include a shift in the balance of power and an arms race in Asia,
according to Patrick Cronin, senior vice president of the Center for Strategic
and International Studies, a foreign policy think tank in Washington. In an
interview Friday, Cronin told The Daily Yomiuri that a verifiable dismantle-
ment of North Korean weapons would be impossible, so the United States
would need a way of stopping the proliferation of North Korea's weapons as
the risks would be intolerable.

"First, an expanded North Korean nuclear program could start an irreversible arms race in Northeast Asia. Second, there would be too many
weapons for U.S. intelligence to track, according to Cronin. 'Our intelligence
has already proved inept. We can't allow these weapons to become loose
nukes. In the longer term, can we live with Kim Jong Il? There is evidence that
he isn't willing to negotiate a serious deal,' he said. 'The (George W.) Bush
administration would like to deal with a post-Kim Jong Il regime, but that's
the longer term.'

"Earlier this month, North Korea offered what it called a 'bold concession' to stop its nuclear program to get negotiations going again with six concerned countries. Last week, South Korea, Japan and the United States held
preliminary talks in an effort to restart talks. Cronin and other experts have
expressed skepticism about the North Korean gesture. 'Kim has never made a
bold concession,' Cronin said. Instead, Kim would like to legitimize his
weapons program, according to Cronin. 'He's talking about a freeze plus:
Freeze the weapons that he now has in place, which is a better deal than he had
under the Agreed Framework (to end North Korea's nuclear weapons program
in exchange for two light-water nuclear reactors),' Cronin said."
(*The Daily Yomiuri* [Tokyo, Japan], January 25, 2004)

"Pledges by the world's richest nations to secure nuclear, biological and chemical materials are falling 'far short' of what is needed 'to prevent terrorists from
obtaining weapons of mass destruction,' an international coalition of 21 security organisations has warned. The Global Partnership Update, released yesterday by a consortium of research institutes in 16 countries, and led by the
Washington-based Center for Strategic and International Studies (CSIS),
paints a worrying picture more than a year after G8 leaders agreed to spend
Dollars 20bn . . . over 10 years against WMD proliferation.

"Sam Nunn, former chairman of the U.S. Senate's armed services committee, said: 'There is a dangerous gap between the pace of progress and the
scope and urgency of the threat. The Dollars 20bn has only been pledged, not
allocated, and it falls far short of what's needed.' Only a small number of new
projects had started, and only a 'tiny fraction' of funds disbursed, since G8
leaders launched the Global Partnership in June 2002, the consortium said.

NEWSLETTERS

Calendar of Events (6 times per year)
Chronicle (twice a month)
CSIS Briefing Notes on Islam, Society, and Politics (bimonthly)
CSIS Euro-Focus (bimonthly)
CSIS Hong Kong Update (monthly),
CSIS Press Catalog (spring and fall)
CSIS Watch (weekly)
CSIS Western Hemisphere Election Study (periodic)
NEWS@CSIS (quarterly)
Post-Soviet Prospects (bimonthly)
Summary of Current Events (quarterly)
The Washington Quarterly (journal)

PUBLICATIONS

The following is a sample list of publications:
Altering U.S. Sanctions Policy
Averting the Defense Train Wreck in the New Millennium
Beyond Unilateral Economic Sanctions
Building the Global Information Economy
Charting a Path for U.S. Missile Defenses
China's New Journey to the West
Commentaries on International Political Economy
The Convergence of Ideas on Improving the Environmental Protection System
Cybercrime . . . Cyberterrorism . . . Cyberwarfare . . .
Data Mining and Data Analysis for Counterterrorism
Defending the U.S. Homeland
The Future of Islam and the West Clash of Civilizations or Peaceful Coexistence?
Improving the Practice of National Security Strategy
The Information Revolution and National Security
The Iraq War
The Lessons of Afghanistan
Managing the Global Nuclear Materials Threat
The Role of Sea Power in U.S. National Security in the Twenty-First Century
Technology and Security in the Twenty-First Century
Virtual Nuclear Arsenals
Visions of America and Europe

CONFERENCES

Albania Forum
European Congressional Forum
Germany 2007
Japan Chair Forum
South America 2005
South East Europe Reconstruction
Statesmen's Forum
WTO Ministerial

Among other problems, 'Russian security forces continue to stymie co-operation at sensitive sites,' leading to 'suspicion and ill will on both sides'

"The warning comes as the UN awaits details on a call by President George W. Bush to bring a non-proliferation resolution to the Security Council."

(*Financial Times* [London, England], November 19, 2003)

"The effects of HIV and AIDS on African society, home-grown terrorism and increasing dependence on African oil will dominate American policy toward African countries in the coming years, an expert on African affairs said yesterday. 'There is a newfound recognition of the power of three issues that slowly crept up on us in the 1990s,' said Stephen Morrison, African program director at the Center for Strategic and International Studies, a nonpartisan Washington think tank.

"President Bush's trip to Africa this summer was a signal that the continent is taking a more prominent place in American foreign policy, Morrison told an audience at the City Club. Morrison is also the executive director of the center's HIV/AIDS task force, created in 2001 to look at the ways American foreign policy can affect the course of the disease in African countries, where 30 million of the world's 42 million HIV-positive people live. 'We're at an early point in the pandemic,' Morrison said. 'It will probably not climax for another 30 or 40 years.'

"American AIDS assistance is motivated by two factors, he said: a rational desire to stabilize the situation and a compassionate desire to help the people affected by the disease. 'It is an interesting merger of religious, moral and security concerns,' Morrison said. Terrorism in Africa has gained a higher profile since the 1998 bombing of U.S. embassies in Kenya and Tanzania shocked the government, Morrison said. In recent years African terrorism and the threats posed by anarchic, failed states have become another important influence on American foreign policy in Africa."

(*The Plain Dealer* [Cleveland], September 6, 2003)

Center for Study of Responsive Law

Established in 1968

DIRECTOR
John Richard, administrator.

BOARD OF DIRECTORS
Layman Allen
Laura Milleron
Ralph Nader
Edmund Shaker

SCOPE
Members: None
Branches/chapters: None
Affiliates: None

STAFF
15 total

TAX STATUS
501(c)(3)

FINANCES
Budget: 2002—$1.21 million; 2001—$1.53 million; 2000—$1.02 million

FUNDING SOURCES
Declined to comment

PAC
None

EMPLOYMENT
Information unavailable

INTERNSHIPS
Information unavailable

NEWSLETTERS
Nader Letter on Banks and Consumers (monthly)

PUBLICATIONS
The Frugal Shopper Checklist Book
Getting the Best from Your Doctor
It Happened in the Kitchen
Spices of Life
Why Women Pay More

CONFERENCES
None

CONTACT INFORMATION
1530 P Street, NW, Washington, DC 20005
Mailing address: P.O. Box 19367, Washington, DC 20036
Phone: (202) 387-8030 • *Fax:* (202) (202) 234-5176
General E-mail: csrl@csrl.org • *Web site:* www.csrl.org

Communications Director: Information unavailable
Human Resources Director: Information unavailable

PURPOSE: "Seeks to raise the public's awareness of consumer issues and encourage public and private institutions to be more responsive to the needs of citizens and consumers."

CURRENT CONCERNS: Banking regulations • Computerized access to government information • Drug pricing • Political process • Rights of consumers

METHOD OF OPERATION: Coalition forming • Conferences/seminars • Freedom of Information Clearinghouse) • Initiative/referendum campaigns • Grassroots organizing • Legislative/regulatory monitoring (federal and state) • Participation in regulatory proceedings (state) • Research • Web site

Effectiveness and Political Orientation

"Tom Grey wakes up in a strange bed in suburban Baltimore, where he's spent the night lying next to a bunch of antique dolls and a stuffed white whale. He's been on the road for weeks, sleeping on couches and in spare rooms in places like Fargo, N.D., and Pocatello, Idaho—towns poised to become new outposts of legalized gambling. Grey is working feverishly to stop that from happening, just as he has throughout his decade-long, bare-bones, one-man crusade against the country's casino giants. . . .

"The industry is already facing a legal challenge from David Williams, a . . . frugal man who clipped grocery coupons and had paid off his house in Evansville, a small city on the Ohio River. Then the company that owns the Tropicana Resort and Casino in Las Vegas opened a riverboat casino and mailed Williams a coupon redeemable for $20 in tokens. On his first visit, he lost $20. On his second, he lost $800. 'He called it electronic morphine,' says his attorney, Terry Noffsinger.

"The casino issued Williams a Fun Card, enabling the pit bosses to keep track of his gambling activity. During two days in 1997, they watched Williams lose $21,000 on one slot machine. During the month of March 1998, they tracked him as he lost an additional $34,000. Finally, after a worried friend wrote to ask the riverboat executives to intervene, they agreed to ban Williams from the casino. He was admitted to an Evansville treatment center, where he stayed temporarily in a suicide ward. For a time, the intervention worked. But in 1999, Williams went back. And not only did the casino renew action on his Fun Card, but it began sending him promotions to get him to come more often.

"... When the casino banned Williams, Grey says, it acknowledged that he was a gambling addict, potentially exposing the whole industry to liability. This idea is exciting to John Richard, the director of the Center for Study of Responsive Law, an organization founded by Ralph Nader. During a meeting with Grey at the center, Richard offers to research a 'friend of the court' brief. But he also reminds Grey that a legal battle of this magnitude is not won overnight. It could involve a long series of losses before anything resembling a victory."

(*The Washington Post,* February 2, 2003)

"Philip Howard is resigned that he can't avoid sensational cases when arguing that America's biggest legal problem is its out-of-control litigious culture, in which anybody can sue anyone for just about anything. He knows that those off-the-wall claims and headline verdicts are the focus of the public's love-hate relationship with lawsuit mania. . . .

"Among them are farcical cases, like the disabled man who sued a West Palm Beach strip club because his seat didn't provide an 'equal access' view of the stage. Outrageous cases, like the families of 11 illegal immigrants, who died trying to cross 800,000 acres of desert from Mexico this summer, suing the United States for not providing water. . . .

In his latest book, 'The Collapse of the Common Good: How America's Lawsuit Culture Undermines Our Freedom,' Howard makes his anecdote-loaded case: Fear of being sued infects the daily decisions of every American. 'Anytime you are dealing with other people, there is clearly a cloud hanging overhead,' he says. . . .

"Meanwhile, in April, hoping to spark a national movement, Howard launched Common Good, a nonprofit organization dedicated to restoring common sense to settling differences. Looking for nonpartisan consensus on its advisory board, Howard recruited leaders from across the political spectrum—liberals such as former Democratic presidential candidate George McGovern and former Democratic senator Paul Simon, and conservatives such as the American Enterprise Institute's Christopher DeMuth and former Republican congressman Gingrich. . . .

"Consumer activist Ralph Nader, at the Center for Study of Responsive Law, calls Howard 'an empty vessel' and says the lawsuit crisis Howard carps about doesn't really exist. 'His books are a complete mythology,' he says, pointing out statistics from the Justice Department and various think tanks that show the number of tort lawsuits has dropped steadily since 1996 in state and federal courts. 'Quite a crisis, huh?' says Nader. 'In other words, he doesn't have a factual foundation. He's into psychiatry, not facts. He relies solely on this fear factor. You know what a frivolous suit is? It's any lawsuit against 'us.' '"

(*The Washington Post,* October 1, 2002)

"A portrait of bygone Yankees first baseman 'Iron Horse' Lou Gehrig adorns the office of gadfly turned presidential spoiler Ralph Nader. The consumer activist still savors his hero's long-standing record for playing in the most games in a row: 2,130. 'That is what taught me stamina when I was a kid,' Nader said wistfully. . . .

"Forming a group called League of Fans in January as an offshoot of his Center for Study of Responsive Law, Nader and his Ohio-born executive director, Shawn McCarthy, picked taxpayer funding of new sports stadiums for their first battle. The two dismiss new stadiums like those in Cleveland, Baltimore and Nashville as sellouts to grasping team owners and monopoly leagues. 'More pressing needs were neglected in Cleveland while the taxpayers were forced to finance wealthy owners that could afford these sports places themselves,' said McCarthy, a Milan, Ohio, native who grew up making regular 40-minute jaunts to Browns, Indians and Cavaliers games. 'Why did they call it Jacobs Field when the public footed the bill? It should be called 'Taxpayer Field.' "

(The Plain Dealer [Cleveland], March 11, 2001)

"The vice president is worried about Green Party presidential candidate Ralph Nader. Environmentalist Robert Kennedy Jr. summed up his concern nicely: 'Nader's candidacy could siphon votes from Al Gore—the environment's most visible champion since Theodore Roosevelt—and lead to the election of George W. Bush.' Looking at the Web sites of Gore and the Democrats and Nader and the Green Party, it is clear that both parties and individuals rate the environment and the poor as high domestic and international priorities.

"But there is no mention on Nader's election site of the one project he should be most proud of: the funding of the Malaria Project from his Center for the Study of Responsive Law in Washington, D.C. The Malaria Project has almost single-handedly fought, in the face of massive environmentalists' opposition, for the continued use of DDT for mosquito control in poor countries. Since DDT is such a totemic baddie for the Greens, it is politically dangerous for Nader to support (even tacitly) its use, especially as he is running as the Green candidate."

(Milwaukee Journal Sentinel, September 17, 2000)

Center for Voting and Democracy

Established in 1992

DIRECTOR

Robert Richie, executive director. Richie has addressed a wide range of groups, including the annual conventions of the American Political Science Association, National Association of Counties, and National Conference of State Legislatures; testified in special sessions before charter commissions in several cities and before state legislative committees in Alaska, Vermont, Virginia and Washington; helped organize six well-attended national conferences on electoral system reform; published commentary in the *Wall Street Journal, Roll Call, Washington Post, National Civic Review, Boston Review, Christian Science Monitor* and *Legal Times;* written essays that have appeared in seven books; and been a guest on many radio and television programs. Richie graduated from Haverford College with a B.A. in philosophy. Before becoming the center's director in 1992, he worked for three winning congressional campaigns in Washington state and for non-profit organizations in Washington and the District of Columbia.

BOARD OF DIRECTORS

John B. Anderson, chair; former Illinois representative, Washington, DC/FL
Faye Park, vice chair; associate director, CALPIRG, Santa Barbara, CA
Cynthia Terrell, secretary; political consultant, MD
William Redpath, treasurer; CPA, VA
Hendrik Hertzberg; senior editor, New Yorker magazine, NY
Malia Lazu; former executive director, Mass Vote, MA
Nina Moseley; former executive director, Democracy South, NC

SCOPE

Members: 650 members
Branches/chapters: 6
Affiliates: None

STAFF

5 total—4 full-time professional; 1 full-time support; plus 2 part-time professional, 25 national volunteers, and 3 interns

TAX STATUS

501(c)(3)

FINANCES

Budget: 2004—$474,000; 2003—$395,000; 2002—$575,000

FUNDING SOURCES

Foundation grants, 64%; individuals, 29%; publications, 0.5%; membership dues, 5%;

CONTACT INFORMATION

6930 Carroll Avenue, Suite 610, Takoma Park, MD 20912
Phone: (301) 270-4616 • *Fax:* (301) 270-4133
General E-mail: info@fairvote.org • *Web site:* www.fairvote.org

Communications Director: Steven Hill, senior analyst
(415) 665-5044 • shil@fairvote.org
Human Resources Director: Robert Richie, executive director
(301) 270-4616 • rr@fairvote.org

PURPOSE: "Founded in 1992, the Center for Voting and Democracy advances fair elections where the right to vote is protected and exercised, where every vote counts and where all voters have a fair opportunity to be represented. We build understanding of and support for democratic voting systems. Specifically, we promote instant runoff voting to elect executive offices and replace traditional runoff elections, and forms of full representation to replace exclusionary winner-take-all elections. We support effective implementation of these systems, particularly among communities of color, language minorities and low-income communities."

CURRENT CONCERNS: Election reform • Voting rights

METHOD OF OPERATION: Awards program • Coalition formation • Conferences/seminars • Congressional voting analysis • Films/video/audiotapes • Grassroots organizing • Information clearinghouse • Initiative/referendum campaigns • Internet (e-mail alerts and Web site) Internships • Legal assistance • Legislative/regulatory monitoring (state) • Library services for members only • Local/municipal affairs • Media outreach • Performance ratings/Report cards (companies, products, etc.) • Polling • Research • Speakers program

SPECIFIC PROGRAMS/INITIATIVES: Election services • Fair Vote America • IRV for America • Election Services USA • Your Right to Vote • Redistricting.Org

Effectiveness and Political Orientation

"Berkeley voters will decide next month whether to follow San Francisco by pursuing an 'instant runoff' system that has not yet been used in California. While Berkeley has not decided exactly how the system would work, it would ask voters to elect mayors, city council members and auditors by ranking them by preference on the ballot. Voters whose first-choice candidates do poorly would see their second-place choice applied if necessary. . . .

"The system, which is used in Cambridge, Mass., and Australia, has been supported in concept in a handful of Bay Area cities and is being pushed in 20 states, according to the Center for Voting and Democracy. But it is complex and has several variations, and election officials have mixed feelings about it.

conferences, 1%; special events/projects, 0.5%

PAC
None

EMPLOYMENT
Job postings are available at http://www.fair-vote.org/about_us/job_listings.htm. This organization offers positions primarily in program work. Cover letters, resumes, writing samples, and references can be sent to Robert Richie, 6930 Carroll Ave, Suite 610, Takoma Park, MD 20912. E-mail: rr@fairvote.org.

INTERNSHIPS
Internship opportunities are posted at www.fairvote.org/about_us/interns.htm. Positions are generally unpaid in the summer, but paid with a 6-month commitment. Internships last 8–12 weeks for unpaid internships, six months minimum for paid program associate positions. Internship areas include the following: outreach assistants, voting rights/civil rights assistant, materials and products coordinator, press assistant, development assistant, Web site assistant, election reform on campus, legislation and lobbying, demonstration elections assistant, membership assistant, federal elections research assistant, elections research assistant, and legal interns.

The center accepts resumes and writing samples at any point during the year. Eligibility requirements are flexible, although generally college graduates are accepted for paid internships. Materials should be mailed to Center for Voting and Democracy, 6930 Carroll Avenue, Suite 610, Takoma Park, MD 20912. Phone: (301) 270-4616. Fax: (301) 270-4133. E-mail: rr@fairvote.org.

NEWSLETTERS
Fair Elections Report (8–10 email newsletters per year)
Voting and Democracy Review (2–3 postal newsletters per year)

PUBLICATIONS
Dubious Democracy
Monopoly Politics (both are regular, biannual reports)

CONFERENCES
Periodic conferences such as major "Claim Democracy" conference in November 2003 in Washington, DC (see www.democracyusa.org).

In San Francisco, where voters mandated instant runoffs in 2002, officials plan to launch the state's first instant-runoff voting program in November. The program, which must be certified by the California secretary of State, costs $1.6 million in technology upgrades, said John Arntz, director of the city Elections Department. Last year's traditional runoff for mayor and district attorney cost the city $2 million, he said."

(*The San Francisco Chronicle*, February 7, 2004)

"This is what the cutting edge of American democracy has come down to: a 'supine seahorse' and an 'upside-down Chinese dragon.' They are descriptions of the approximate shape of congressional voting districts drawn in Pennsylvania to maximize the political clout of the Republican Party. Such attempts by statehouse politicians to rig election boundaries to benefit favored candidates or punish political enemies are nothing new, nor are they activities reserved exclusively for Republicans. But experts say political gerrymandering has never been so prevalent or so effective.

"Now, for the first time in 17 years, the U.S. Supreme Court has taken up a case to determine whether at some point political gerrymandering becomes so egregious as to violate safeguards in the Constitution. The nation's highest court has set aside an hour Wednesday to hear oral argument about gerrymandering in Pennsylvania. The case has national implications because if the justices find a violation, it could invalidate the vast majority of the nation's heavily gerrymandered congressional districts.

"Political leaders have the power to change the system themselves. But neither major party is willing to disarm unilaterally. Instead, as exemplified in legislative walkouts in Colorado and Texas over unprecedented attempts at mid-decade redistricting, the nation is spiraling toward all-out gerrymandering warfare. 'There has got to be a better way,' says Robert Richie of the Center for Voting and Democracy in Tacoma Park, Md. 'We are just completely outside the international norm in the way we allow legislators to draw their own districts.'"

(*Christian Science Monitor*, December 10, 2003)

"The bill was introduced on a Monday, passed on Wednesday and signed into law on Friday. There was minimal debate and no time for public comment. Still, Colorado statute SB-352 could be a political milestone: the first successful application of a new tactic being pushed by Republican leaders in Washington. The Colorado law redraws the borders of all of the state's congressional districts—just two years after the redistricting that followed the 2000 Census. The sole purpose, as leaders of the Republican-controlled legislature confirm, was to strengthen the party's majority in the state's congressional delegation.

"A similar effort at re-redistricting failed in May in Texas, when Democratic legislators decamped to Oklahoma, making a quorum impossible in the state House of Representatives. But on Monday, Texas Republicans started to try again; Gov. Rick Perry (R) has called a special session to redraw that state's 2001 congressional map. The session is to run for 30 days, making it harder for Democrats to thwart action. If Texas this time follows the Colorado model, Democrats have warned that they might retaliate, redrawing congressional district maps to strengthen their party in New Mexico and Oklahoma, where Democrats control both the legislature and the governor's office. . . .

" 'Redistricting is almost always a corrupt business,' notes Robert Richie, executive director of the Takoma Park-based Center for Voting and Democracy. 'But what just happened in Colorado is really disgusting, because what they had before was one of the best districts in the country in terms of being responsive to the voters.' "

(*The Washington Post*, July 7, 2003)

"Two weeks ago, the Texas Legislature made national news when Democrats absconded to Oklahoma to block a Republican plan that would have created more safe GOP congressional seats. They succeeded, for now, but the tale won't die. This week, Democrats in Washington, led by presidential candidate Sen. Joseph Lieberman, D-Conn., asked the Bush administration to reveal any help the federal government provided in trying to locate the Democrats so that Texas Republicans could try to rig the state's electoral system. . . .

"The broader outrage, though, is the redistricting system behind the Texas saga—along with similar wrangles over the shape of congressional or legislative districts in seven other states, from Colorado to Maine. Unlike other major democracies, the U.S. lets politicians design electoral districts that serve their interests, not the public's. Legislatures routinely set bizarre boundaries to maximize the number of seats the party in power can claim. The Center for Voting and Democracy, a group that promotes electoral reform, says that when Democrats ruled Texas in the 1990s, they played the same games, creating eight of the nation's 50 'most twisted' congressional districts."

(*USA Today*, May 28, 2003)

"Perhaps last week you saw a video capturing some 235 Haitians jumping off a boat near Key Biscayne and swimming madly to shore. I didn't have the audio up, so I just figured they had come to monitor our elections. . . .

"Since the disgraceful national 'election' of 2000, Florida has spent $50 million trying to redeem its voting process. . . . The federal government will spend $4 billion in the next three years, according to a bill signed this week by President Bush, but most of its provisions don't apply to this election.

"Funny how Bush got around to it this week after making barely a peep about the problem since a two-fisted political atrocity delivered him to Washington in December 2000. A national election in 2002 America is essentially an open sore, festering from fundamental centuries-old design flaws, misunderstood and misapplied technologies and advanced cheating. There is no elixir for all that. There are merely ideas that have to be aired by people without agendas, people who can make sense of it. I spoke with one such person this week, Rob Richie, executive director at the Center for Voting and Democracy in Takoma Park, Md.

" 'We're in a climate right now where we're seeing a lot of changes,' Richie said. 'All a runoff system needs is a sensible ballot design. In Ireland, for example, they've just gone to a touch-screen system, and there are very low rates of error in Ireland, even though rates of literacy are about the same as ours.' The current project and the hoped-for partial fix offered by the Center for Voting and Democracy support the instant runoff system. Voters make a first choice and a second choice in a framework that allows third- and fourth party candidates to compete without becoming spoilers."

(*Pittsburgh Post-Gazette*, November 3, 2002)

Center on Budget and Policy Priorities

Established in 1981

DIRECTOR

Robert Greenstein, executive director. Prior to founding the center in 1981, Greenstein was administrator of the Food and Nutrition Service at the U.S. Department of Agriculture. He has appeared on national television news and public affairs programs and has been called to testify on Capitol Hill several times. In 1996, Greenstein was awarded a MacArthur Fellowship. He has a B.A. from Harvard University.

BOARD OF DIRECTORS

David De Ferranti, chair; vice president for Latin America and the Caribbean, World Bank

John R. Kramer, vice chair; professor, Tulane University Law School

Henry J. Aaron; senior fellow, Brookings Institution

Kenneth Apfel; professor, LBJ School of Public Affairs, University of Texas at Austin

Barbara Blum; senior fellow for Child and Family Policy, National Center for Children in Poverty, Columbia University

Marian Wright Edelman; president, Children's Defense Fund

James O. Gibson; senior fellow, Center for the Study of Social Policy

Beatrix Hamburg; visiting scholar, Cornell Medical College

Frank Mankiewicz; vice chair, Hill and Knowlton

Richard P. Nathan; distinguished professor of political science and public policy and director, Nelson A. Rockefeller Institute of Government

Marion Pines; senior fellow, Johns Hopkins University Institute for Policy Studies

Sol Price; founder and chair, Price Co.

Robert D. Reischauer; president, Urban Institute

Audrey Rowe; senior vice president of Public Affairs, ACS, Inc.

Susan Sechler; senior advisor, Rockefeller Foundation

Juan Sepulveda Jr.; executive director, Common Enterprise/San Antonio Research Associate

William Julius Wilson; Lewis P. and Linda L. Geyser University Professor and director of the Joblessness and Urban Poverty Research Program, Harvard University

SCOPE

Members: None
Branches/chapters: None
Affiliates: None

STAFF

59 total

CONTACT INFORMATION

820 1st Street, NE, Suite 510, Washington, DC 20002
Phone: (202) 408-1080 • *Fax:* (202) 408-1056
General E-mail: center@cbpp.org • *Web site:* www.cbpp.org

Communications Director: Henry Griggs
(202) 408-1080 • egriggs@cbpp.org
Human Resources Director: Bill Walton, personnel and office manager
walton@cbpp.org

PURPOSE: "To inform public debates over proposed budget and tax policies and to help ensure that the needs of low-income families and individuals are considered in these debates."

CURRENT CONCERNS: Federal budget issues • Federal tax policies • Food and nutrition programs • Jobs creation • Minimum wage • Poverty and income • Unemployment insurance • State fiscal policies • State welfare and low-income issues

METHOD OF OPERATION: Congressional testimony • International activities • Internet • Internships • Media outreach • Research • Telecommunications services (mailing lists)

Effectiveness and Political Orientation

"The Bush administration's justification for America's dramatic plunge from huge federal surpluses to record federal deficits hangs from a single thread: stimulus for the economy. Tax cuts spur investment, consumer spending and recovery, the argument goes. It's getting increasingly hard to swallow. While there are indications earlier rounds of tax cuts may have shortened the recession and started a painfully slow recovery, the price has been a drastic drop in federal revenues and huge projected deficits that will hamper the economy in years to come. Now President Bush wants to add tax cuts and make the current ones permanent, while pledging spending cuts that will halve the projected deficits his administration has created.

"The Congressional Budget Office, though, sees little of the continued economic stimulus predicted by the White House. Its annual fiscal analysis for lawmakers foresees only a 'minimal impact' from the cuts in the president's proposed $2.4 trillion budget. In light of the revenue needed to support valuable domestic programs, pay for wars and rebuilding in Iraq and Afghanistan, shore up Social Security and Medicaid and make much-needed reforms in the Alternative Minimum Tax program, enacting additional cuts and making the current ones permanent will result in major pain for little gain.

"When this administration proposed its initial tax cuts, many analysts were quick to note that as large as they were, they were small in comparison with a $12 trillion annual economy that moves more in concert with business cycles than government action. The tax cuts were like trying to turn an ocean

TAX STATUS
501(c)(3)

FINANCES
Budget: 2002—$8.2 million; 2001—
$7.7 million; 2000—$6.1 million

FUNDING SOURCES
Supported primarily by major foundation grants.

PAC
None

EMPLOYMENT
Job postings are listed at www.cbpp.org/jobs.html. Cover letters and resumes can be sent to The Center on Budget and Policy Priorities, 820 1st Street, NE, Suite 510, Washington, DC 20002. Fax: (202) 408-1056. E-mail: center@cbpp.org.

INTERNSHIPS
Internships are available for the fall, spring, and summer semesters. Students with a master's degree receive $10.00 per hour. Graduate students receive $9.00 for a first internship and up to $9.50 per hour for succeeding internships. Students with an undergraduate degree receive $8.00 for a first internship and up to $8.50 per hour for succeeding internships. Current undergraduate students receive $7.50 for a first internship and up to $8.00 per hour for succeeding internships. Interns receive three days of paid sick leave per each semester-length internship, but do not receive health or other benefits.

Internship applications are available online at http://www.cbpp.org/intern-app.htm. Applications and resumes should be sent to: Internship Coordinator, Center on Budget and Policy Priorities, 820 First Street, NE, Suite 510, Washington, DC 20002. Fax: (202) 408-1056.

NEWSLETTERS
WIC (9 times a year)

PUBLICATIONS
The following is a sample of recent publications:
Aligning Policies and Procedures in Benefit Programs
Assessing the Impact of State Estate Taxes
Budget Priorities Gone Awry
Capping Appropriations
Decline in Federal Grants Will Put Additional Squeeze on State and Local Budgets
Emerging Pay-As-You-Go Proposal Severe Weaknesses
Improving Children's Health
Large Tax Cuts But Little Else: Administration Proposes Tax Cuts That Cost Vastly More Than Other Domestic Initiatives Combined
Many States Are Decoupling from the Federal Estate Tax Cut
Out in the Cold: Enrollment Freezes in Six State Children's Health Insurance Programs Withhold Coverage from Eligible Children
State of the Union Primer: Selected Analyses

liner with an outboard motor, some said. That analogy would almost certainly hold for a new round of tax cuts. What's more, the president's proposals include measures that, according to the liberal-leaning Center on Budget and Policy Priorities, would increase rather than reduce deficits, by about $1.4 trillion over the already-high projections for the next 10 years."

(*The Buffalo News,* March 14, 2004)

"The number of unemployed workers in the United States who have exhausted regular jobless benefits without qualifying for more will reach a record 760,000 by the end of the month, and that number could swell to more than 1 million by midyear, the Center on Budget and Policy Priorities said yesterday. The research group's findings are based on US Labor Department data, and suggest that the job market remains weak despite some signs of economic recovery, said Isaac Shapiro, a senior fellow at the Washington think tank.

" 'By all indications, the number of people who have exhausted benefits but are ineligible for a federal extension is at a record high,' Shapiro said. 'In 1991 and 1992, when we had high levels of unemployment, there was a program in place that qualified just about everybody for extended benefits. This time the exhaustion level is very high, but there is nothing in place.' "

(*The Boston Globe,* February 26, 2004)

"A record-high 375,000 jobless workers will exhaust their unemployment insurance this month and an estimated 2 million workers will find themselves in the same predicament during the first half of the year, according to an analysis of Labor Department statistics by the Center on Budget and Policy Priorities. The report from the center, a liberal research and policy group, found that in the first six months of the year, about 5,800 jobless workers in the District of Columbia, 20,200 in Maryland and 29,600 in Virginia will run out of unemployment benefits unless they find new jobs or get additional government help.

"The jobless recovery has become an issue in this presidential election year, and the report shows the jobless benefits will run out for large numbers of workers in several key states, including Michigan, Pennsylvania, Indiana, North Carolina and South Carolina. While the unemployment rate dropped to 5.7 percent in December, down from 6.3 percent in June, businesses added only 1,000 jobs that month. The country has lost more than 2.8 million manufacturing jobs in a steady erosion over the past 41 months."

(*The Washington Post,* January 30, 2004)

"During a year of budget deficits, 34 states, including Alabama, have cut either children's health insurance, Medicaid or both, according to a study by the Washington D.C.-based Center on Budget and Policy Priorities. 'Cuts of this magnitude in health coverage for low-income families are unprecedented,' said Leighton Ku, a senior fellow at the center.

The study estimated that up to 1.6 million people, including 500,000 children, were affected by the reductions nationwide."

(*Birmingham News* [Alabama], December 23, 2003)

"Cash-strapped state governments still aren't out of the financial woods. A new report suggests most state legislatures will be forced into yet another round of budget cuts or tax increases next year that could approach $40 billion nation-

CONFERENCES

Annual state services conference

ally. That's on top of $200 billion worth of budget-balancing adjustments made in the previous three years, according to an analysis by the Center on Budget and Policy Priorities.

"Beyond that, the report said, states such as Indiana, Kentucky, Michigan and Ohio are likely to confront deficits already occurring in the current, 2004 fiscal year. 'The fiscal crisis is by no means over,' said Iris Lav, the report's author. Lav said the new cuts that will confront state legislatures when they convene next year will be some of the most painful yet because most of the easy reductions have been approved. . . .

"Initially, states reacted by dipping into their rainy-day funds and making other mild adjustments. But as the deficit projections persisted and rose, legislatures increasingly were forced into difficult cuts. Last year, 18 states reduced eligibility for public health-insurance programs, according to the Center on Budget and Policy Priorities. At least 32 have trimmed child-care subsidies."

(*Fresno Bee* [California], October 26, 2003)

Children's Defense Fund

Established in 1973

DIRECTOR

Marian Wright Edelman, president. Before founding CDF in 1973, Edelman directed the NAACP Legal Defense and Education Fund in Jackson, Mississippi. Later she moved to Washington, DC, to become counsel for Dr. Martin Luther King's Poor People's Campaign. Edelman is a graduate of Spelman College and the Yale University Law School.

BOARD OF DIRECTORS

David W. Hornbeck, chair; president and chief executive officer, International Youth Foundation, Baltimore, MD

Carol Oughton Biondi; child advocate/ commissioner, Los Angeles County Commission for Children and Families; CA

Angela Glover Blackwell, vice chair; president, PolicyLink, Oakland, CA

Rev. Kirbyjon Caldwell; senior pastor, Windsor Village, St. John's United Methodist Churches, Houston, TX

Geoffrey Canada, vice chair; president and chief executive officer, Harlem Children's Zone, Inc., New York, NY

Maureen A. Cogan, vice chair; child advocate, New York, NY

Leonard Coleman; Cendant Corp., New York, NY

Leslie Cornfeld, Esq.; child advocate, New York, NY

Leslee Dart; president, PMK/HBH Public Relations, New York, NY

John Deardourff; director, E.V.A., Inc., McLean, VA

Marian Wright Edelman; president, Children's Defense Fund

Winifred Green; president, Southern Coalition for Educational Equity, Jackson, MS

Dorothy Height; president emerita and chair of board, National Council of Negro Women, Washington, DC

Michael Klein; chief executive officer, Citigroup Europe, Middle East, and Africa Global Corporate and Investment Banking Group, New York, NY

William Lynch Jr.; president, Bill Lynch Associates, New York, NY

Leonard Riggio; founder and chair, Barnes & Noble, Inc., New York, NY

Dennis Rivera; president, 1199 SEIU New York's Health & Human Service Union, SEIU, AFL-CIO, New York, NY

J. Michael Solar, Esq.; Solar & Associates, LLP, Houston, TX

Thomas A. Troyer, Esq.; partner, Caplin & Drysdale, Washington, DC

Robert F. Vagt; president, Davidson College, Davidson, NC

CONTACT INFORMATION

25 E Street, NW, Washington, DC 20001
Phone: (202) 628-8787 • *Fax:* (202) 662-3510
General E-mail: cdfinfo@childrensdefense.org •
Web site: www.childrensdefense.org

Communications Director: Patricia Williams
(202) 662-3613 • pwilliams@childrensdefense.org
Human Resources Director: Mamie Robertson
(202) 662-3697 • mrobertson@childrensdefense.org

PURPOSE: "The mission of the Children's Defense Fund is to Leave No Child Behind® and to ensure every child a Healthy Start, a Head Start, a Fair Start, a Safe Start, and a Moral Start in life and successful passage to adulthood with the help of caring families and communities. CDF provides a strong, effective voice for all the children of America who cannot vote, lobby, or speak for themselves. We pay particular attention to the needs of poor and minority children and those with disabilities. CDF educates the nation about the needs of children and encourages preventive investment before they get sick, into trouble, drop out of school, or suffer family breakdown."

CURRENT CONCERNS: Child care (Head Start) • Child health (Healthy Start) • Child welfare and mental health (Safe Start) • Family income (Fair Start) • Violence prevention and youth development (Safe Start)

METHOD OF OPERATION: Advertisements • Awards program • Coalition forming • Conferences/ seminars • Congressional testimony • Congressional voting analysis • Demonstrations • Direct action • Educational foundation • Films/videos/audiotapes • Grassroots organizing • Information clearinghouse • Internet (e-mail alerts and Web site) • Internships • Legislative/regulatory monitoring (federal and state) • Lobbying (federal and grassroots) • Local/municipal affairs • Media outreach • Polling • Research • Telecommunica-tion services (mailing lists) • Training • Voting records

SPECIFIC PROGRAMS: The Black Community Crusade • CDF Action Council • CDF Legislative Take Action • Children's Health Insurance Program • Child Watch Visitation Program • Freedom Schools • SHOUT • SPROUT

Effectiveness and Political Orientation

"Every so often, two or three radical ideas converge from different directions with a force sufficient to burst through a stubborn barrier and create a measurably better Minnesota. That's exactly what happened this month when the Children's Defense Fund came forward with a plan to create universal health insurance for Minnesota's children. . . .

SCOPE
Members: None
Branches/chapters: MN, TX, CA, MS, TN, SC, NY, OH, LA, and DC (headquarters)
Affiliates: CDF Action Council, a 501(c)(4) organization

STAFF
190 total—plus 16 interns and volunteers

TAX STATUS
501(c)(3)

FINANCES
Budget: 2004—$20 million; 2003—$20 million; 2002—$18.5 million

FUNDING SOURCES
Foundation grants, 65%; individuals, 10%; special events/projects, 7%; corporate donations, 1%; publications, 1%; conferences, 1%

PAC
None

EMPLOYMENT
Information on open positions can be obtained by contacting the CDF Jobline at (202) 662-3680, or checking the CDF Web site at http://www.childrensdefense.org/jobs/default.asp. Cover letters and resumes can be sent to Mamie Robertson, director of administrator and human resources, Children's Defense Fund, 25 E Street, NW, Washington, DC 20001-1591. Fax: (202) 662-3510. E-mail: mrobertson@childrensdefense.org.

INTERNSHIPS
Information on internships is available at http://www.childrensdefense.org/internships/default.asp. Internships last 10–12 weeks and are unpaid. Interns for legal positions must have attended or be attending law school. Internship applications can be sent to Warren Bufford, intern coordinator, CDF, 25 E Street, NW, Washington, DC 20001. Fax: (202) 662-3570. E-mail: wbufford@childrensdefense.org.

NEWSLETTERS
None

PUBLICATIONS
Bringing It Together: State-Driven Community Early Childhood Initiatives
Child Care Subsidy Policy: An Introduction
Children in the States
A Fragile Foundation: State Child Care Assistance Policies
Freedom Schools Curriculum Guide
Healing the Whole Family: A Look at Family Care Programs
Helping Children by Strengthening Families
The High Cost of Child Care Puts Quality Care Out of Reach for Many Families
Incarcerated Youths
Insuring Children's Health: A Community Guide to Enrolling Children in Free and Low-Cost Health Insurance Programs

". . . The bill, sponsored by Rep. Paul Thissen of Minneapolis and Sen. Yvonne Prettner Solon of Duluth, would expand children's health insurance in two steps. Phase One would consolidate four or five existing public programs into one pool covering every child under 300 percent of the federal poverty level. Lawmakers would finance it with an increase in the cigarette tax, although the state already pays for many of these children through Medical Assistance and other programs.

"Phase Two would reach the state's remaining children—most of them now covered by their parents' work-based policies. This second phase would require a substantial, and so far unspecified, state tax increase. But it wouldn't raise overall health-care outlays, because Minnesota businesses and their employees are already footing the bill—a very considerable bill, as any employer will tell you. In fact, the Children's Defense Fund estimates that one big plan, operating as efficiently as the state's admired MinnesotaCare program, could cover every child in the state for 20 percent less than Minnesotans now pay through their fragmented and inadequate system."

(*Minneapolis Star-Tribune,* March 14, 2004)

"Students and activists will retrace the path of 1960s civil rights workers through the South on Freedom Ride 2004, an effort to encourage African-American youths to vote, organizers said Tuesday. Beginning June 10, a bus caravan will carry participants to Georgia, Alabama, Mississippi, Virginia, North Carolina, South Carolina, Tennessee, New York, Washington and Pennsylvania, where they will conduct door-to-door voter education and registration drives.

"Stops will include:
- Southern Christian Leadership Conference offices and the King Center in Atlanta.
- The Southern Poverty Law Center and the Civil Rights Memorial in Montgomery.
- Money, Miss., where black teenager Emmett Till was kidnapped and murdered.
- Memphis, where the Rev. Martin Luther King Jr. was assassinated.

"The caravan will start in New York City and end in Washington, where participants plan to present proposed civil rights legislation to Congress. Young black people 'are not taking advantage of opportunities,' said Ben Chaney, national director of the Chaney Goodman Schwerner Justice Coalition.

"The tour also will commemorate the deaths of James Chaney, Andrew Goodman and Michael Schwerner, who were murdered in Mississippi during the Freedom Summer of 1964 as they worked to register black voters. Chaney was 10 years old when his brother James was killed. About 30 percent of the more than 1 million registered African-American voters did not go to the polls during the 2000 elections, resulting in a 64 percent loss in voting power among youths aged 18 to 24, according to figures from the Children's Defense Fund, a Washington-based advocacy group.

"'We've got a very real crisis of long-term disempowerment of our community,' said Marian Wright Edelman, founder of the Children's Defense Fund. 'If you don't use your power to vote, you don't have any credit in the political bank.'"

(*The Atlanta Journal-Constitution,* February 25, 2004)

CONFERENCES
Annual Conference

"Black children in Ohio are more than twice as likely to die before age 1 as children of other races, according to a report released today by Children's Defense Fund-Ohio. The report, 'Everybody's Child,' documents the gap in several social indicators between black children and other kids but notes there have been improvements over the last decade. Between 1991 and 2001, births to teen moms dropped from 26 percent to 21 percent of births to all black women. Head Start enrollment for preschool-age children jumped from 47 percent of eligible children to 75 percent. The number of black children getting immunized shot up from 52 percent to 76 percent. . . .

"The report found that 372 black infants died before turning 1 in 2001, a rate of 16 out of every 1,000 births. The rate was six infant deaths per 1,000 births for children of all other races. The findings update a 1993 report by Children's Defense Fund-Ohio, a child advocacy group, which set goals for black children in the state. Researchers selected benchmarks that seemed attainable, yet would represent a significant improvement for black children. . . .

"Everyone will feel the effect of the successes and failures, not just black families, said Eileen Cooper Reed, director of Children's Defense Fund-Ohio. 'If we put the money in up front and made sure kids were educated and got the health care they needed, we won't have to pay $30,000 down the road for a jail cell,' Reed said. 'It doesn't take a lot.'. . ."

(*The Plain Dealer* [Cleveland], December 10, 2003)

"Health care advocates charged Gov. Arnold Schwarzenegger yesterday with reneging on a campaign pledge by capping enrollment in the Healthy Families program, which provides health care for low-income children. If his proposal is enacted, up to 300,000 children covered by the joint state-federal program could wind up on a waiting list, a coalition of health care groups warned at a Capitol news conference.

" 'We're very disappointed because during the governor's campaign, he shared our goal of making sure that all the children in the state have health insurance,' said Deena Lahn of the Children's Defense Fund. During the recall campaign, Schwarzenegger praised the program and repeatedly stated that he was 'passionate' about children's issues.

" 'We have to make sure that every child in California is insured,' he proclaimed in his only debate appearance, where he criticized then-Gov. Gray Davis for not enrolling more children in Healthy Families. The government, Schwarzenegger said during the debate, has 'not done a good job in reaching out and finding the people and letting them know to sign up . . . It is really terrible.'

"But last week, as part of a plan to cut $1.9 billion from the current budget, the governor proposed capping caseloads in health and social service programs, including Healthy Families. Enrollment in Healthy Families increased from about 100,000 to 700,000 under Davis. The growth in health and social services accounted for the largest chunk of new spending under Davis—43 percent of all the dollars added—and contributed to the budget crisis that led to his recall.

"H. D. Palmer, a spokesman for the state Department of Finance, said the governor was unaware of the extent of the state's budget shortfall until his finance director, Donna Arduin, reviewed state finances shortly before the Nov. 17 inauguration."

(*The San Diego Union-Tribune,* December 2, 2003)

Christian Coalition of America

Established in 1989

DIRECTOR
Roberta Combs, executive vice president

BOARD OF DIRECTORS
Roberta Combs, executive director, executive vice president
M. G. "Pat" Robertson, chair
Marshall Staunton, secretary
Billy McCormack

SCOPE
Members: 2 million individuals
Branches/chapters: More than 2,000 state chapters
Affiliates: All 50 states; Christian Coalition International

STAFF
Declined to comment

TAX STATUS
501(c)(4)

FINANCES
Declined to comment

FUNDING SOURCES
Individual contributions, 95%; other, 5%

PAC
None

EMPLOYMENT
Declined to comment

INTERNSHIPS
Declined to comment

NEWSLETTERS
Action Alert (weekly)
Christian Coalition Congressional Scorecard (semiannual)
Christian Coalition Insider (bimonthly)
Religious Rights Watch (monthly)

PUBLICATIONS
Answering the Call: Ten Ways Christian Citizens Can Shape America's Future
Contract with the American Family
Also publishes voter guides.

CONFERENCES
Grassroots Activist Training Seminars (weekly)
Road to Victory (annual convention in Washington, DC)

CONTACT INFORMATION
P.O. Box 37030, Washington, DC 20013-7030
Phone: (202) 479-6900 • *Fax:* (202) 479-4260
General E-mail: Coalition@cc.org • *Web site:* www.cc.org

Communications Director: Michele Ammons
(202) 479-6900, ext. 201 • michele@cc.org
Human Resources Director: None

PURPOSE: "To educate and mobilize people of faith on issues that impact families."

CURRENT CONCERNS: Abortion • Choice in education • Foreign policy • Gambling • Homosexuality • National defense • Pornography • Religious freedom

METHOD OF OPERATION: Advertisements • Awards program • Coalition forming • Conferences/seminars • Congressional testimony • Congressional voting analysis • Direct action • Films/video/audiotapes • Grassroots organizing • Initiative/referendum campaigns • Internet (databases, E-mail alerts, and Web site) • Internships • Legislative/regulatory monitoring (federal and state) • Lobbying (federal, state, and grassroots) • Media outreach • Participation in regulatory proceedings (federal and state) • Prayer • Product merchandising • Professional development services • Research • Speakers program • Telecommunications services • Television and radio production (monthly satellite broadcast to 250 downlink centers nationwide) • Training and technical assistance • Voter registration • Voting records

Effectiveness and Political Orientation

"Alabama is one of four states that allow state taxpayers to deduct all the federal income taxes they pay. But that will end—wiping away billions in deductions—if voters approve the governor's tax plan Tuesday. Gov. Bob Riley says the federal income tax deduction favors big taxpayers. He said his plan makes Alabama's tax structure friendlier toward lower-income taxpayers and toward families by raising the standard deduction and the exemptions for the taxpayers and their dependents.

" 'This plan was designed to help that mom and dad who are each earning $18,000 to $20,000 a year, and they've got a combined income of $40,000, three kids and trying to put them in college,' Riley said. The governor says two-thirds of Alabama taxpayers would see their state income tax drop or stay the same, while one-third would pay more. 'This is very pro-family,' said Roberta Combs, president of the Christian Coalition of America.

"Opponents, like state Christian Coalition President John Giles, say any savings on income taxes would be offset by Riley's new taxes on repairs, cars, cigarettes, deeds and mortgages, and some utility services. 'The whole story is that everyone in this state is going to feel the burden of new taxes regardless of your income level,' Giles said."

(Chattanooga Times Free Press [Tennessee], September 4, 2003)

"The Christian Coalition of America on Wednesday endorsed Gov. Bob Riley's $1.2 billion tax plan, a strange twist since its Alabama chapter has been campaigning against it. Christian Coalition of America President Roberta Combs, who succeeded Pat Robertson as leader of the group, flew around the state Wednesday to champion the plan in a series of press conferences. The endorsement was a coup for Riley, who has been trying to sell his tax plan as a morality issue.

" 'The Christian Coalition of America supports Gov. Bob Riley's plan for tax reform because it is clearly and unquestionably designed to help the least among us and asks those who are most able to pay their fair share of the taxes,' she said. 'We believe the governor's proposal is both visionary and courageous.' For weeks, the Christian Coalition of Alabama had been opposing Riley's plan in radio ads and public debates. Combs said she was disappointed in the local chapter because she feels Riley's proposal is pro-family.

"But state coalition leaders called the national group's endorsement a 'mystery' and a policy flip-flop. Bob Russell, chairman emeritus of the Christian Coalition of Alabama, and John Giles, the group's president, said the endorsement was a radical departure from the group's usual beliefs. 'This is as much a shock to me as it is to all of you,' Giles said. He and Russell were caught off guard by Combs' visit and hastily called a press conference to retort."

(Birmingham News [Alabama], August 7, 2003)

"Sen. Charles Schumer has reached far across the ideological divide to enlist the support of the Christian Coalition in his campaign to protect children from pornographic e-mail messages. Schumer, D-N.Y., stood Thursday with Roberta Combs, president of the Christian Coalition of America, and Sen. Lindsey Graham, R-S.C., to promote legislation designed to slow the waves of unwanted electronic messages finding their way into computer mailboxes.

" 'The political model of the past will not address the problems of this century,' said Graham. 'Chuck and I do disagree on a lot philosophically, but we can come together to address the dark side of the Internet.' Schumer's legislation—the Stop Pornography and Abusive Marketing (SPAM) Act—would create a voluntary 'do-not-spam' registry for families that want to block unwanted e-mails. The registry would be modeled on the 'do-not-call' models that have been successful against telemarketers."

(The Post-Standard [Syracuse, N.Y.], June 13, 2003)

"Conservative Christian groups are fighting to get back into the political game. Years after its political influence waned, the Christian Coalition of America is spearheading a movement to register voters and encourage ministers to speak out on political issues. A bill in Congress would give preachers more freedom to back political causes while preserving their tax-exempt status.

"And yet, even with President Bush, a born-again Christian, in the White House and Republicans in control of Congress, religious conservatives are finding difficulty motivating the faithful. The coalition combined with Priests for Life, a Catholic antiabortion group, and the National Pro-Life Religious Council to announce Monday a voter registration drive at conservative Christian churches on four Sundays leading up to the 2004 primaries. . . .

"The Christian Coalition drew strength by opposing President Clinton. In the 2000 election, the coalition said, it distributed 70 million voter guides, mostly at churches. While the coalition claimed the guides were nonpartisan, critics complained that they were skewed toward Republican candidates. Many Christian Coalition members have become GOP activists. But since 2000, conservative religious political groups have fallen on hard times, with many of them disintegrating and laying off staff, said Jim Guth, a political analyst who studies the movement at Furman University in Greenville, S.C."

(*Tampa Tribune,* June 6, 2003)

"The Christian Coalition of America is raising money by encouraging members to sign up and make their calls using an anti-abortion phone company that will send its profits back to the coalition. The two-million-member coalition, long a force in Republican politics, recently sent out a solicitation encouraging its members to sign up for the local or long-distance services of Pro Life Communications. 'For the first time ever, with Pro Life Communications we have a local phone company that desires to honour God, uphold family values and save the 3,500 innocent babies that are killed each day in the name of "choice," ' coalition president Roberta Combs wrote in the e-mail appeal. . . ."

(*The Gazette* [Montreal, Quebec], March 27, 2003)

"A day after masses of Americans took to the streets to protest the war in Iraq, a group of demonstrators gathered in Times Square Sunday in a rare show of public support for U.S. troops. Among the thousands who waved American flags, sang 'God Bless America,' and criticized antiwar protesters with signs proclaiming 'Pacifism kills' were Arab-Americans. Several said they support the Bush administration's efforts to liberate Iraq from decades of suffering under Saddam Hussein.

. . .The demonstration was organized by the New York chapter of Free Republic, and several Jewish groups, including the Zionist Organization of America, the Coalition for Jewish Concerns-Amcha, and the Jewish Action Alliance were among the dozen cosponsors.

". . . The State of Israel received blessings and support from several speakers, including the president of the Christian Coalition of America, Roberta Combs, who noted that the fall of Saddam means an end to the $25,000 rewards funneled by his government to the families of Palestinian suicide bombers. 'Anti-war protesters are anti-Bush and anti-American,' she said. 'How can you not stand up for your troops when they're giving their lives for our freedom?'

"Wahid E., an Egyptian immigrant who turned out for the rally, said he hopes that after the war, the U.S. will help bring human rights to minority communities throughout the Middle East. 'I admire the American spirit that is reaching out to the Iraqis as people,' said Wahid, 39, a Christian, who said he was shot at by Islamic fundamentalists in 1992. 'I appreciate the message that this is not a war about petroleum, but removing a worldwide threat of weapons of mass destruction.' "

(*The Jerusalem Post* [Jerusalem, Israel], March 25, 2003)

Citizens for a Sound Economy

Established in 1984

DIRECTOR

Paul Beckner, president. Beckner joined CSE in 1987, serving as vice president for membership, director of public policy and director of development. He previously worked for Bantam Books and the Tribune Co. Beckner received a B.A. from Northwestern University and an M.B.A. from the Wharton School.

BOARD OF DIRECTORS

Dick Armey, co-chair of CSE, Dallas, TX
C. Boyden Gray, co-chair of CSE, Washington, DC
J. Clyde Ballard, Olympia, WA
Jim Burnley, Washington, DC
Charles Hilton, Panama City, FL
Thomas Knudsen, New York, NY
David H. Padden, Chicago, IL
Richard Stephenson, St. Thomas, U.S. Virgin Islands

SCOPE

Members: 250,000 individuals, corporations, and foundations
Branches/chapters: State chapters in Alabama, Florida, Illinois, Louisiana
Affiliates: Citizens for a Sound Economy Educational Foundation, a 501(c)(3) organization

STAFF

93 total

TAX STATUS

501(c)(4)

FINANCES

Revenue: 2002—$3.6 million

FUNDING SOURCES

Corporate donations, 68%; individuals, 15%; trade associations, 12%; other, 5%

PAC

None

EMPLOYMENT

Information on open positions is posted at http://www.cse.org/know/employment.php. Application materials should be mailed to Human Resources Department, Citizens for a Sound Economy, 1523 16th Street, NW, 2nd Floor, Washington, DC 20036.

INTERNSHIPS

CSE offers several internships; details are posted at http://www.cse.org/know/intern.php. Applicants should be "interested in and have a strong commitment to free-market ideas and public policy." Internships are unpaid, but transportation expenses are covered. Applications, resumes, writing samples,

CONTACT INFORMATION

1523 16th Street, NW, 2nd Floor, Washington, DC 20036
Phone: (202) 783-3870 • *Fax:* (202) 232-8356
Toll-free: (888) 564-6273
General E-mail: cse@cse.org • *Web site:* www.cse.org

Communications Director: Chris Kinnan, director of public affairs
(202) 942-7616 • ckinnan@cse.org
Human Resources Director: Judy Mulcahy, director of human resources
jmulcahy@cse.org

PURPOSE: "To promote economic freedom and opportunity for all citizens by mobilizing people who can change public policy."

CURRENT CONCERNS: Electricity deregulation • Environment regulation • FDA reform • Health care reform • Insurance reform • International trade • Natural resources • Regulatory reform • Social Security • Tax and budget reform • Telecommunications reform • Tort reform

METHOD OF OPERATION: Advertisements • Awards program • Coalition forming • Conferences/seminars • Congressional testimony • Educational foundation • Grassroots organizing • Internet (Web site) • Internships • Lobbying (federal, state, and grassroots) • Media outreach • Polling • Research

Effectiveness and Political Orientation

"Oregon voters' resounding rejection of an $800 million revenue measure has burnished this state's reputation as a bastion for the national movement to limit taxes. The measure's failure, which was defeated Tuesday by a 59 to 41 percent vote, is expected to trigger cuts in education, public safety and knock many more people off the Oregon Health Plan, which offers medical coverage to tens of thousands of residents.

"The Oregon revenue proposal known as Measure 30 was crafted by the state Legislature in August after the longest session in history. Grappling with one of the worst fiscal crises in state history, Republican and Democratic legislators narrowly approved increases in the state personal income tax, as well as corporate and other taxes. Defeat of the legislative compromise could have long-term effects on representative government, some lawmakers say.

". . . The initiative campaign to put the tax measure on the ballot was led by the Oregon chapter of Citizens for a Sound Economy, a national tax-limit group. Russ Walker, the group's Oregon director, says voters in a state with some of the highest unemployment in the nation wanted a slimmer government not new taxes.

" 'It's pretty arrogant for the legislators to say they know better how to balance a budget than the people who have to pay for it,' Walker said. The Citizens for a Sound Economy has also fought at the national level for federal

and transcripts can be mailed to: Michelle Perillo, Citizens for a Sound Economy, 1523 16th Street, NW, 2nd Floor, Washington, DC 20036.

NEWSLETTERS

Citizen Alert (bimonthly; produced by Citizens for a Sound Economy Foundation)
Sentinel (bimonthly)

PUBLICATIONS

The following is a sample list of publications:
Breaking the Regulatory Stranglehold
Bring in the Prognosticators
Bureaucratic Insecurity vs. Homeland Security
The Competition Is in the Mail
Convention Hotel Subsidies Hurt Private Businesses
Is Regulatory Reform Next?
It's Raining Special Interest Politics
Media Bias on Campaign Finance
Moral Character and Proper Incentives
Regulators to the Rescue?
Searching for a Legislative Compass
Seeing Straight on Contact Lens Regulations
Washington vs. Wall Street: Will New Rules Boost the Market?
When Government Grows
Where Have All the Conservatives Gone?
Who Is Nancy Pelosi?
Win, Lose or Draw: The Elections and Consumers
Also publishes impact statements on trade, the federal budget, and regulation; Capitol comments; economic and regulatory perspectives; fact sheets; and "issues and answers." Most publications are available on CSE's Web site.

CONFERENCES

Scrap the Code (a tax debate that tours cities across America)
Also issue-related conferences (not regularly scheduled)

tax cuts, and in September waged a successful campaign to defeat an Alabama tax measure."

(*The Seattle Times,* February 6, 2004)

"As voters and pundits focus on the inexorable winnowing to select a president, another national political effort could determine the ability of governors and state lawmakers to manage their finances. In the end, this could have as much impact on individual Americans as whoever occupies the White House next year. Secure in the knowledge that President Bush and the Republican-led Congress are unlikely to raise federal taxes, antitax groups now are focusing on states. Such Washington groups as Americans for Tax Reform, the National Taxpayers Union, and Citizens for a Sound Economy are fanning out around the country, building local support and providing financial backing and political muscle to limit state taxes.

"The focus now is on Oregon, where a ballot measure Tuesday asks voters to decide between an $800 million revenue package and what some analysts warn could be dramatic cuts in education, health care, and other services if the measure—trailing in the polls—fails. National antitax groups see the vote as a key test of their ability to influence public policy and politics beyond the Capital Beltway. And they bring to the battle considerable political clout. Citizens for a Sound Economy is headed by former House majority leader Dick Armey (R) of Texas. Grover Norquist, president of Americans for Tax Reform and one of the most influential activists in Washington, has been described as 'the field marshal' of Mr. Bush's tax-cutting plan.

"They've already proved their ability to influence events in Alabama, where Mr. Armey's group played an important role in the overwhelming ballot-box defeat of Republican Gov. Bob Riley's $1.2 billion tax package."

(*Christian Science Monitor,* February 2, 2004)

"Logging in to your personal home Internet account with broadband Internet access could help pump $14 billion into the Virginia economy as well as 32,000 new jobs, a new study finds. The study by Citizens for a Sound Economy Freedom Works Foundation, an educational and lobbying organization, said that a complete broadband deployment would help boost jobs for the state in the high-tech sector, which saw a loss of about 19,000 jobs in 2002.

"The figures nationwide for broadband stimulus would be 1.2 million jobs and $531 billion. Corresponding figures for North Carolina are 34,000 jobs and $13.4 billion in economic activity. 'There's a couple stages,' said Wayne T. Brough, the report's author and chief economist with the CSE. 'The first is the direct effect of actually building and maintaining the infrastructure or Internet.'

"That work, which Brough said would make up about 14,000 of the possible new jobs, involves building new lines in the ground and getting wires in people's homes. The next stages involve a ripple effect in which 'people are demanding those services in their communities, which makes up the rest. And that gets you up to the 32,000 jobs,' Brough said. Unfortunately, the future of broadband is clouded by regulatory and legal uncertainty, including issues from tax jurisdictions to intellectual property, the report said.

" 'There are a lot of companies looking at this market but are a little nervous about it,' Brough said. Once their fears are cleared, 'I'm sure a lot of companies are willing to play.' The report calls on policymakers to eliminate regulatory and legal uncertainties that inhibit the capital expenditures necessary to encourage full broadband deployment."

(*The Virginian-Pilot* [Norfolk], December 23, 2003)

"Conservatives are cutting President George W. Bush 'a lot of slack' on his education initiative and other increases in government spending, former U.S. House Majority Leader Dick Armey said yesterday. Armey, co-chair of the Citizens for a Sound Economy advocacy group, was in New Hampshire as part of his 'Freedom Works' tour promoting CSE's conservative principles and his new book, 'Armey's Axioms: 40 Hard-Earned Truths from Politics, Faith and Life.'

"CSE cannot endorse candidates for office, said Armey, but he said that by framing issues, the group has helped many Republican congressmen win election, including, he said, Sen. Elizabeth Dole in North Carolina. Armey served in the House for 18 years and said he 'walked out on top of my game on my own terms.' He said he will not seek political office again. CSE has 3,500 members in New Hampshire, said chapter executive director Chuck McGee.

"In an interview with Union Leader editors and a reporter, Armey criticized Bush for allowing expensive 'pork' to be included in post-9/11 emergency spending for New York City. He said Republicans in Washington had been doing a fair job controlling spending until 9/11, when, he said, 'the dam broke.' He also blasted the USA Patriot Act as an 'appalling' invasion of privacy."

(*The Union Leader* [Manchester, N.H.], October 30, 2003)

"Alabama voters yesterday overwhelmingly rejected Gov. Bob Riley's $1.2 billion tax package. With 82 percent of precincts reporting last night, 742,446, or 68 percent, opposed the plan while 345,811, or 32 percent, voted for it. The margin of more than 2-to-1 was a repudiation of the Republican governor, who had promoted the largest tax increase in the state's history as the way to raise Alabama from the bottom of national education rankings.

"'It's an irrefutable message,' said former House Majority Leader Dick Armey, now co-chairman of Citizens for a Sound Economy, who campaigned against the tax increase. David Lanoue, chairman of the political science department at the University of Alabama, told the Associated Press: 'The opponents were able to play on the voters' cynicism about politicians in Alabama, that the tax increase wasn't necessary, and that even if it did pass the money wouldn't go to education.'

"The Alabama Legislature is expected to be called into special session in about a week to deal with a $675 budget deficit. The next fiscal year begins Oct. 1. Mr. Riley, a Southern Baptist in a Bible Belt state, suggested that Christian voters ought to help the poor by reforming a state tax structure that he called immoral."

(*The Washington Times,* September 10, 2003)

Citizens for Tax Justice

Established in 1979

DIRECTOR

Robert S. McIntyre, director. McIntyre has been with Citizens for Tax Justice since 1980, and he was formerly director of federal tax policy for CTJ. Prior to joining CTJ, McIntyre was director of Public Citizen's Tax Reform Research Group. A graduate of both Providence College and the University of Pennsylvania Law School, he also holds an LL.M. from the Georgetown University Law Center.

BOARD OF DIRECTORS

Robert S. McIntyre, director

SCOPE

Members: 2,200 individuals and 25 organizations
Branches/chapters: None
Affiliates: None

STAFF

9 total—8 full-time professional; 1 full-time support; plus 4 interns

TAX STATUS

501(c)(4)

FINANCES

Declined to comment

FUNDING SOURCES

Foundation grants, 50%; labor unions, 40%; membership dues, 10%

PAC

None

EMPLOYMENT

Job postings are available at http://www.ctj.org/html/jobmenu.htm.

INTERNSHIPS

Internship information is posted at http://www.ctj.org/html/intern.htm. Materials can be mailed to: Intern Coordinator, Citizens for Tax Justice, 1311 L Street, NW, Suite 400, Washington, DC 20005.

NEWSLETTERS

CTJ Update (9 times per year)

PUBLICATIONS

Analysis of McCain Tax Proposal
Bush Tax Plan Takes Giant Bite Out of Social Security
CTJ Analysis of Senate Minimum Wage Bill
CTJ's Guide to Fair State and Local Tax Policy
Distributional Analysis of House GOP and Democratic Marriage Penalty Bills
Flat Tax Proposals: An Introduction to Recent Legislation

CONTACT INFORMATION

1311 L Street, NW, Suite 400, Washington, DC 20005
Phone: (202) 626-3780 • *Fax:* (202) 638-3486
General E-mail: mattg@ctj.org • *Web site:* www.ctj.org

Communications Director: Information unavailable
Human Resources Director: Information unavailable

PURPOSE: "To give middle- and low-income families a greater voice in the development of tax laws at the national, state, and local levels."

CURRENT CONCERNS: Adequately funding important government services • Marriage penalty tax • Opposing flat tax and national sales tax • Opposing further reductions in capital gains tax • Reducing the federal debt • Support greater progressivity • Tax fairness

METHOD OF OPERATION: Coalition forming • Conferences/seminars • Congressional testimony • Educational foundation • Internet (e-mail alerts and Web site) • Internships • Lobbying (federal) • Local/municipal affairs • Media outreach • Performance ratings • Polling • Research

Effectiveness and Political Orientation

"Gov. Mark Warner's tax-reform plan is under fire not only from hard-core anti-taxers, but also from analysts who say it neither goes far enough toward meeting Virginia's revenue needs nor on balance makes the system fairer. In an article in the January 2004 issue of 'The American Prospect,' for example, the director of Citizens for Tax Justice says that modest income-tax increases for the wealthy under Warner's plan would be offset by his proposed increase in sales and cigarette taxes (which take a greater percentage of poorer people's incomes) and his proposed relaxation of Virginia's estate tax on millionaires.

"'When all the dust clears,' Robert S. McIntyre writes, 'the poorest fifth of Virginians would pay slightly more in taxes. . . , the richest Virginians would pay a bit less, and every other income group would pay virtually the same amount.' Moreover, he notes, the $1 billion biennial revenue boost projected by Warner amounts to only 4 percent of discretionary spending in a budget that already had been cut by 11 percent over the last three years. And even that small increase would diminish as local car-tax subsidies are fully phased in by 2008.

"McIntyre, though, fails to mention the political context in which Warner must work. Nor does he factor in the impact on poorer Virginians of the continuing slide in public services if Warner's plan fails. Realistically, the choice is not between the governor's plan and a plan more to McIntyre's (or our) liking. Nor, for that matter, is it between Warner's plan and the status quo. Realistically, the choice is between some improvement in state finances, however modest, and their further degradation."

(Roanoke Times & World News [Virginia], January 4, 2004)

CONFERENCES
None

"Policy analysts across the political spectrum yesterday denounced the energy bill that Republicans in Congress hope to push to approval this week, saying it represented micromanagement of the economy and would open vast new opportunities for tax cheating. Many experts said they were taken aback by the size of the proposed breaks, estimated by Capitol Hill staff members at $25.7 billion over 10 years. That is more than three times the $8 billion in tax incentives that the Bush administration said last year in a letter to Congress that it wanted for energy producers.

"The measure would give individuals tax breaks for buying energy-efficient appliances. But it specifies, for example, that refrigerator-freezers would have to be frost-free models with at least 16.5 cubic feet of space for food storage. A homeowner who installs a solar water heating system would receive a $1,000 tax credit, but not if the system heats a swimming pool. Energy companies would receive three-fourths of the incentives, or $17 billion, with provisions intended to encourage developing oil, gas, coal and nuclear power. Many of the credits would involve complex formulas and require installing specified equipment, rather than leaving industry free to use any equipment that achieved the same energy savings. . . .

"Terming the bill stupid, Robert McIntyre, director of Citizens for Tax Justice, a group with labor backing, questioned the logic of the legislation. 'Don't we believe in markets anymore?' Mr. McIntyre asked. 'What are we doing with this bill? Are we cutting prices for energy so we use more of it? Do we need to cut taxes for oil companies because oilmen are inherently lethargic and can't work to pay taxes? No. This bill is just political payoffs to people who make contributions.'"

(*The New York Times,* November 19, 2003)

"Minnesota could lose as much as $280 million over the next two years if tax cuts proposed by President Bush are passed, according to a coalition of groups led by the Minnesota AFL-CIO. The tax cut bill being debated in Congress would diminish state tax revenues by $220 million during fiscal years 2004–05, said Wayne Cox, executive director of Minnesota Citizens for Tax Justice, a think tank funded by the AFL-CIO. Any reductions in state revenue as a result of the tax cuts would come on top of the deficit of $4.23 billion already projected for the same period, which begins July 1.

"There is a relatively simple way to recoup the money. Typically, Minnesota adheres to federal tax practice, meaning that whatever tax breaks the U.S. government gives, Minnesota gives, too. But because of the deficit, the state is far likelier to reject a state version of the Bush tax cuts. That would complicate the state's income tax form slightly but would recoup the money. More problematic is a possible sizable reduction in federal aid to states built into the 10-year budget resolution passed by Congress this month.

"Minnesota's share of that comes out to $300 million, Cox said. The cuts could amount to an average of $30 million a year, he said. . . .

" 'Health care, affordable housing, child care, job training—these are fundamental needs that, both morally and socially, should take precedence over the desires of the rich for more tax cuts,' he said. Bush has sought tax cuts totaling $726 billion over the next 10 years, but a group of moderate Republicans is working to limit the cuts to $350 billion. A key element of the Bush plan is to eliminate income taxes on most stock dividends."

(*Minneapolis Star Tribune,* April 30, 2003)

"Even before Congress begins debating President Bush's tax cut plan, Republican tax-writing aides have inserted a generous new provision for major corporations and their shareholders that some fear could open the legislation to a tidal wave of loopholes. The provision would be of tremendous benefit to such blue-chip giants as International Business Machines Corp., Ford Motor Co. and General Electric Co., which otherwise would have had the value of billions of dollars in tax credits radically reduced by the president's plan to end the 'double taxation' of dividends. . . .

"The cost to the Treasury may be minimal—$2 billion a year or less—said Robert S. McIntyre, director of Citizens for Tax Justice, a liberal tax watchdog group. But, he said, it could open the floodgates to lobbyists already seeking to protect their favorite tax credits from the impact of the president's plan. 'This is sort of the camel's nose in the tent,' said William G. Gale, an economist at the Brookings Institution. 'They just blew the barn door off this bill,' a Republican tax lobbyist said. . . .

"McIntyre said the proposal is unfair because it would in effect make the Bush dividend tax cut retroactive. Because companies are allowed to carry AMT credits indefinitely, shareholders could benefit from taxes paid as far back as 1987, when the corporate AMT went into effect. For some companies' shareholders, the provision would be a windfall. A 2001 Congressional Research Service report said companies held more than $26 billion in AMT credits."

(*The Washington Post,* March 1, 2003)

"For years, some of the wealthiest people in America avoided paying federal income taxes—thanks to deductions, credits, business losses, and loopholes. In response to public anger, Congress enacted the alternative minimum tax during the 1980s to shut down most tax shelters. But the same tax, designed to collect taxes from those who earn more than $200,000, could soon affect working families. Unless Congress acts by the end of this year, the AMT by 2010 could sock 35 million families with incomes starting at $75,000 with bigger tax bills.

"The AMT, a tax that's figured separately, eliminates many deductions and credits and results in a bigger tax liability for anyone who would otherwise pay less tax. The tentative minimum tax rates on ordinary income are 26 percent and 28 percent. . . . Since Congress never indexed the AMT for inflation, a growing number of taxpayers are being forced to pay it. In 1990, 132,103 taxpayers footed the bill, according to the Internal Revenue Service. In 2000, more than 1.3 million paid the tax, with an average payment of $3,614. . . .

"This month, Treasury Secretary John Snow said the problem should be addressed by Congress and the administration. But Snow declined to provide details about what a tax package should include or how the ATM would be amended. So far, Democrats and Republics can't agree on what action to take. 'Everyone agrees that we have to fix the AMT problem this year, but there's a big disagreement on what to do,' said Robert McIntyre, director of Citizens for Tax Justice, a Washington-based public interest research group.

" 'Republicans want to do away with the AMT completely,' he said, 'while Democrats are asking how we will make up the $400 billion in lost revenues if we do.' "

(*The Boston Globe,* February 23, 2003)

Coalition for Environmentally Responsible Economies (CERES)

Established in 1989

DIRECTOR

Mindy S. Lubber, executive director. Lubber has held leadership positions in government as the regional administrator of the U.S. Environmental Protection Agency, in the financial services sector as founder, president, and chief executive officer of Green Century Capital Management. She is an attorney and holds an M.B.A.

BOARD OF DIRECTORS

Norman Dean, chair; executive director, Friends of the Earth

Stuart Auchincloss; member of the Corporate Responsibility Committee of the Sierra Club

Joan Bavaria; founding chair, president and chief executive officer, Trillium Asset Management

Leslie Fields; Esq., enforcement co-chair, Interim Black Environmental and Economic Justice Coordinating Committee

Paul Freundlich; president, Fair Trade Foundation

Michel Gelobter; executive director, Redefining Progress

Neva Goodwin; co-director, Global Development and Environment Institute, Fletcher School, Tufts University

Julie Fox Gorte; director of Social Research, Social Research Department, Calvert Group

Alisa Gravitz; vice president, Social Investment Forum

Ashok Gupta; senior energy director, Natural Resources Defense Council

Paul L. Joffe; senior director, International Affairs, National Wildlife Federation

Kevin Knobloch; executive director, Union of Concerned Scientists

Robert Kinloch Massie; senior fellow, CERES

Vidette Bullock Mixon; director of Corporate Relations and Social Concerns, General Board of Pension and Health Benefits of the United Methodist Church

Rev. William Somplatsky-Jarman; Associate for Mission Responsibility Through Investment and Environmental Justice, Presbyterian Church

Ken Sylvester; assistant comptroller for pension policy, City of New York

Betsy Taylor; executive director, Center for a New American Dream

Joe Uehlein; director of strategic campaigns, AFL-CIO

Brooks B. Yeager; vice president, Global Threats Program, World Wildlife Fund

CONTACT INFORMATION

99 Chauncy Street, 6th Floor, Boston, MA 02111
Phone: (617) 247-0700 • *Fax:* (617) 267-5400
Web site: www.ceres.org

Communications Director: Nicole St. Clair
(617) 247-0700 • stclair@ceres.org
Human Resources Director: Elizabeth Boyle, manager of finance and administration • boyle@ceres.org

PURPOSE: "To encourage companies . . . to endorse and practice the CERES Principles. Endorsing the CERES Principles represents a commitment for business to make continuous environmental improvement and to become publicly accountable for the environmental impact of all its activities."

CURRENT CONCERNS: Corporate environmental reporting • Global reporting initiative 5-year reviews • Shareholder relations

METHOD OF OPERATION: Coalition forming • Media outreach • Mediation • Publicly disclosed corporate environmental reporting • Research • Shareholder resolutions

Effectiveness and Political Orientation

"The midsummer week that saw Geraldo Rivera marry for the fifth time (he's 60, she's 28) also saw a California company introduce the world's first disposable digital camera. Coincidence? Maybe.

"On the other hand, what percentage of guests at Geraldo's nuptials felt confident they'd be toasting the bride and groom on their 10th anniversary? Indeed, it's not hard to imagine them examining the throwaway cameras commonly handed out as party favors and instinctively looking for the erase button. As a monument to modern matrimony, after all, Rivera is about as durable as a $10 Kodak. In a consumer society built on disposable income, if not marriage vows, it's safe to say anything goes. But a throwaway digital camera? Now, that's amazing. . . .

"'If you look at the big picture, in a sense everything is becoming disposable,' says Tim Brennan, director of development for the Coalition for Environmentally Responsible Economies, a Boston-based organization made up of business, environmental, and investor groups. On three recent occasions, Brennan reports, he took a malfunctioning appliance to a repair shop. Stereo receiver, humidifier, 35mm camera—didn't matter. Each time he was told he'd be better off buying a new one. 'They all said, "Why would you want to fix that?" ' says Brennan, rather disconsolately. Lately, he's heard General Motors is developing a hydrogen-powered car with a replaceable, snap-on body. 'I guess you just throw the old one away,' Brennan muses, conjuring up

SCOPE
SCOPE
Members: Approximately 70 organizations and 50 endorsing companies
Branches/chapters: None
Affiliates: None

STAFF
18 total—plus interns

TAX STATUS
501(c)(3)

FINANCES
Declined to comment

FUNDING SOURCES
Grant revenue, 56%; endorser and coalition fees, 21%; conference fees and program revenue, 20%; gifts and bequests, 3%

PAC
None

EMPLOYMENT
Information on open positions is posted at www.ceres.org/about/careers.htm.
Application materials should be sent to: CERES Search Committee, 99 Chauncy Street, 6th Floor, Boston, MA 02111. Fax: (617) 267-5400. E-mail: careers@ceres.org.

INTERNSHIPS
Internships of one or two semesters are available. Interns work 8–16 hours per week. More information is available at www.ceres.org/about/careers.htm.

NEWSLETTERS
CERES (electronic, monthly)

PUBLICATIONS
CERES Five-Year Review of Sunoco, Inc.: A Collaborative Road to Progress
CERES Report (annual)
Corporate CERES Report
Corporate Governance and Climate Change: Making the Connection
Electric Power, Investors, and Climate Change: A Call to Action
Guide to the CERES Principles
Sleeping Tiger, Hidden Liabilities: Amid Growing Risk and Industry Movement on Climate Change ExxonMobil Falls Farther Behind
Touchstone: Issues in Sustainability Reporting
Value at Risk: Climate Change and the Future of Governance
Also publishes company performance reviews.

CONFERENCES
Annual conference (April)

a time in the not-so-distant future when the guy at the auto-body shop smiles and asks: 'Paper or plastic?' "

(*The Boston Globe,* August 27, 2003)

"Many of the world's largest companies are doing a poor job of preparing for the business impact of global warming, a report issued yesterday by investor, environmental and public interest groups said. Most of the 20 corporate giants discussed, including leaders in the oil, auto and utility industries, are also failing to disclose to investors enough about the financial risks they face from climate change, according to the report, which was prepared by the Investor Responsibility Research Center in Washington.

"None of the companies have produced dollar estimates of the potential costs or benefits of climate change, like more extreme weather, or of the financial impact of changing regulations on carbon emissions, the report said. And eight companies, including General Electric, General Motors and Exxon Mobil, made no mention of climate change in filings last year with the Securities and Exchange Commission. 'We are not talking about issues that are 50 years out,' said Mindy Lubber, executive director of the Coalition for Environmentally Responsible Economies, which commissioned the study. 'We are seeing inadequate board reviews in many, many companies.'

"The study rated the companies in 14 categories covering the oversight of climate-change issues by corporate boards and progress in setting performance goals as well as disclosure. Two foreign oil companies, BP and Royal Dutch/Shell, were the only ones credited with activity in all 14 categories. The worst performers, including Exxon, G.E. and TXU, an energy services concern, have reported just four of the practices the report identified as prudent."

(*The New York Times,* July 10, 2003)

"International non-governmental organisations (NGOs) must become more accountable if they are to retain their influence and position of trust, according to a United Nations report. The study says many NGOs are moving from confrontation to engagement with business but most lack the accountability they demand from companies. John Elkington, chairman of international consultancy SustainAbility and co-author of the report, said: 'Unless they recognise and address growing financial, competitive and accountability pressures, their impact will be significantly reduced.'

"The report, commissioned by the United Nations Environment Programme and the UN Global Compact, is based on interviews with 200 NGOs and opinion-formers. It is likely to be controversial with those who argue that transparency limits NGOs' ability to run nimble and flexible campaigns. The study, published today, says some NGOs already produce detailed reports to demonstrate their accountability, the best practitioners being the US-based Coalition for Environmentally Responsible Economies (Ceres) and Oxfam, WWF and Save the Children in the UK."

(*Financial Times* [London, England], June 26, 2003)

"Corporate scandal has done wonders to motivate shareholder activists. They've already proposed more corporate governance votes for this year's proxy season than for all of last year. The proposals range from limits on executive compensation to calls to expense the cost of options, to linking pay more closely to company performance. 'The crisis in confidence is an unprecedented opportunity for reform,' said Tim Smith, president of Social Investment Forum. . . .

" 'Shareholder resolutions, if nothing else, wave a very large red flag,' said Sister Pat Wolf, executive director of the Interfaith Center on Corporate Responsibility. About a quarter of such resolutions are withdrawn because the sponsors and the company reach an agreement on the issue or agree to discuss it, said Smith. Accounting scandals at Enron and other companies came to light too late to affect the nature of shareholder proposals last year.

"But this year the focus clearly has switched. Last year, proposals on anti-takeover provisions and concurrent terms for directors dominated corporate governance voting. This year, executive compensation issues represent 44 percent of the 625 governance proposals. Some 529 corporate governance proposals were made last year. Other issues that shareholders bring up each year commonly deal with environmental and social matters. A slight increase is expected in those categories, according to four organizations that either sponsor resolutions or advise investors on proxy votes.

" 'We hope these resolutions will increase awareness among corporate directors, institutional investors and others about how responsible behavior on climate change builds shareholder value,' said Mindy Lubber. She heads the Coalition for Environmentally Responsible Economies."

(*The Atlanta Journal-Constitution,* February 13, 2003)

"A group of shareholders said Thursday that it has filed resolutions aimed at forcing five large electric utility companies, including Minneapolis-based Xcel Energy, to disclose their potential financial risk from emissions of carbon dioxide and air pollutants. The shareholder group was led by the Coalition for Environmentally Responsible Economies (CERES), a Boston-based organization that represents environmental, investor and advocacy groups.

"The resolutions were filed against the nation's five biggest utility emitters of carbon dioxide, which results from burning coal and other fossil fuels and has been linked to global warming. The utilities, which the group called the 'filthy five,' also included American Electric Power of Columbus, Ohio; Southern Co. of Atlanta; Cinergy Corp. of Cincinnati, and TXU Corp. of Dallas. . . .

"In a conference call with reporters, the shareholder group said that electric utilities face costs related to compliance with future regulation of carbon dioxide levels and potential liability for air pollution, and that investors are entitled to know the extent of that risk. CERES spokeswoman Nicole St. Clair said the target companies were chosen based on the amount of their carbon dioxide emissions, without considering what actions the utilities might be taking to reduce emissions. 'The point is to have disclosure of the full financial picture to shareholders,' she said.

"Bill Grant, Midwest director of the Izaak Walton League in St. Paul, said that he 'probably agrees that [disclosure] ought to be done' but that the resolutions 'don't seem to be a terribly useful approach.' Determining each company's financial risk would be difficult 'when we don't know what those future regulations might be,' he said. 'It would be quite the guessing game.' "

(*Minneapolis Star Tribune,* January 17, 2003)

Committee for
a Responsible Federal Budget

Established in 1981

DIRECTOR

Maya MacGuineas, executive director. Before coming to the Committee for a Responsible Federal Budget, MacGuineas served as a Social Security advisor to the McCain for President campaign. She has also worked at the Brookings Institution, the Concord Coalition, and on Wall Street. She received her masters' in public policy from the John F. Kennedy School of Government at Harvard University.

BOARD OF DIRECTORS

Maya MacGuineas, executive director
Leon Panetta, co-chair
Bill Frenzel, co-chair
Roy L. Ash
Thomas L. Ashley
Charles Bowsher
Dan L. Crippen
Willis Gradison
William H. Gray III
Ted Halstead
Jim Jones
James T. Lynn
James T. McIntyre Jr.
David Minge
June O'Neill
Marne Obernauer Jr.
Rudolph G. Penner
Timothy Penny
Peter G. Peterson
Robert Reischauer
Alice M. Rivlin
James Slattery
David A. Stockman
Paul A. Volcker
Carol Cox Wait
Joseph R. Wright Jr.

SCOPE

Members: Members: 200 individuals and 50 corporations
Branches/chapters: None
Affiliates: None

STAFF

3 total

TAX STATUS

501(c)(3)

FINANCES

Budget: 2001—$600,000

FUNDING SOURCES

Corporate donations, 68%; foundation grants, 15%; individuals, 15%; publications, 2%

PAC

None

CONTACT INFORMATION

1630 Connecticut Avenue, NW, 7th Floor, Washington, DC 20009
Phone: (202) 986-6599 • *Fax:* (202) 986-3696
General E-mail: crfb@newamerica.net • *Web site:* www.crfb.org

Communications Director: Declined to comment
Human Resources Director: Declined to comment

PURPOSE: To "educate the public about the federal budget, the budget process and related issues that have major macro-economic impacts." The committee has become part of the New America Foundation.

CURRENT CONCERNS: Budget process reform • Federal fiscal policy • Impact of changing demographics on the economy and the budget when the baby-boom generation retires

METHOD OF OPERATION: Coalition forming • Conferences/seminars • Congressional testimony • Information clearinghouse • Legislative/regulatory monitoring (federal) • Media outreach • Research • Speakers program • Technical assistance • Telecommunications Services (fax-on-demand and mailing lists) • Training

Effectiveness and Political Orientation

"As Congress rushes to conclude its 2003 session, Republican leaders are trying to garner votes for controversial legislation by loading the bills with billions of dollars in added costs that analysts said would expand the budget deficit for years to come. The year-end binge has alarmed analysts in Washington and on Wall Street, coming as it does after three years of presidential and congressional initiatives that have both substantially boosted government spending and shrunk its tax base. . . .

"Former Treasury secretary Robert E. Rubin said, 'Our political system has simply lost its willingness to take the very difficult path of maintaining fiscal discipline.' Some rank-and-file GOP lawmakers expressed concern that the burgeoning deficit is happening under the watch of the Republican Party, which came to power in Washington preaching fiscal restraint and less government. 'I'm very troubled by the possibility that the party of Ronald Reagan, the party that came to Washington to change the welfare state, could fall into that 75-year parade of entitlement makers,' said Rep. Mike Pence (R-Ind.), citing the new Medicare bill. 'This will be the third time in history, first with the New Deal, then in Great Society, and now 2003, that Congress created a massive new entitlement.'. . .

"Maya MacGuineas, executive director of the Committee for a Responsible Federal Budget, said the biggest impact . . . will come toward the end of the decade, when baby boomers begin to retire. The true cost of the Medicare bill, for instance, would not begin until 2007, but it would escalate rapidly from there. In 2007, the Congressional Budget Office estimated, the bill would cost

EMPLOYMENT
Openings are posted on the New America
Foundation Web site: http://www
.newamerica.net.

INTERNSHIPS
Internships are posted at the New
America Foundation Web site:
http://www.newamerica.net.

NEWSLETTERS
Budget Issue Update (irregular)

PUBLICATIONS
*Annual and biennial compendia of results
    from Exercises in Hard Choices*
*Building a Better Future: An Exercise in Hard
    Choices* (annual/biennial reports)
Building a Better Future: Chart Book (CD-ROM)
*Building a Better Future: The Graying of
    America*
*The Federal Budget Process:
    Recommendations for Reform*
Policymaking & Scorekeeping
*Social Security Reform: Economic and Budget
    Concepts, Enforcement and Scorekeeping
    Perspectives*

CONFERENCES
Annual meeting (location and time varies)

$40.2 billion. By 2013, that price tag would be $65.2 billion. CBO Director Douglas Holtz-Eakin has told members of Congress that the bill's cost in its second 10 years could reach between $1.7 trillion and $2 trillion. . . ."

(*The Washington Post,* November 24, 2003)

"Using excess payroll taxes for unintended purposes masks the true size of the operating deficit. The budget office predicts that the net deficit will shrink from $475 billion in fiscal 2004 to $226 billion, or 1.7 percent of gross domestic product, in 2008. Take away the ever-larger Social Security surpluses used in each of those years, however, and the on-budget deficit will stand at $464 billion in 2008. The reality will likely be far worse, especially if you factor in costs that the White House doesn't include in its projections—like the $87 billion recently appropriated for the war, or the extension of recently enacted tax cuts. . . .

"The figures show that the personal and corporate income taxes that are supposed to fund government operations no longer come within shouting distance of doing so. And the refusal of the administration or its Congressional allies to acknowledge this reality has left normally mild-mannered deficit hawks on the verge of apoplexy. 'The last time the situation reached this point, in the early 1990's, we had bipartisan agreement that we were reaching a fiscal crisis,' said Maya MacGuineas, executive director of the Committee for a Responsible Federal Budget in Washington.

"The response then was an unpalatable, but ultimately successful, mix of spending restraints and tax increases. But in the last few years—with the sums involved far greater than they were in the early 1990's, and with the baby boomers nearing retirement—Washington has raised spending sharply and cut taxes even more sharply. It's a fiscal Bizarro world."

(*The New York Times,* November 23, 2003)

"Here's wishing a pleasant retirement to Carol Cox Wait, a frustrated departing president of the Committee for a Responsible Federal Budget. 'After 22 years as president, I am leaving the committee . . . and ask your indulgence,' says Mrs. Wait, sharing some final thoughts on the federal budget. She first observes that the committee opened its doors in 1981, for once a group outside of government that was committed to a sound budget process.

" 'Not to specific spending or tax initiatives or programs, but rational, transparent, disciplined budget decision-making rules,' she says. 'Almost immediately, the committee was overwhelmed by the specter of historically large, seemingly endless, structural budget deficits.' But the committee, under her leadership, buckled down. And 17 years later, on Feb. 2, 1998, President Clinton released a $1.7 trillion balanced budget that he said marked 'the end of an era.' . . .

" 'It is very unfortunate, to say the least, that the budget enforcement rules expired just as huge unanticipated surpluses emerged,' Mrs. Wait says. 'Budget balance proved to be a fragile hothouse flower. Huge surpluses evaporated just as quickly as they emerged. Here we are, 22 years later, and it is deja vu all over again.' Mrs. Wait hopes her successors urge political leaders to act sooner rather than later to address medium- to long-term challenges, and remind them what did and did not work the last time around.

" 'But as my children say, I have been there and done that, and it is time for me to go,' she says."

(*The Washington Times,* July 21, 2003)

"Who knew a federal budget document could evoke feelings of passion? That's what happened Saturday when participants in 'An Exercise in Hard Choices' stripped away the stark numbers—the surplus dollar estimates, spending trend data and revenue charts—and considered the impact on people. The conference, put on by the Committee for a Responsible Federal Budget and held at the Adam's Mark Hotel downtown, put about 200 Coloradans in the shoes of their members of Congress. . . .

"Carol Cox Wait, president of the Committee for a Responsible Federal Budget, said she has learned there are few in Washington who want to save surplus dollars to reduce the federal debt. On three separate occasions when surplus dollars were found, legislators found ways to spend them, rather than bring down the nation's debt, said Wait, who has served on federal budget committees.

"Few members of Congress want to tell their constituents that they voted down a local project to save money to reduce the national debt, she said. 'That does not have very much political appeal,' Wait said. Participants did manage to have fun with their roles as politicians, even if it was at the expense of their elected officials. Roger Dowd, a Denver educator, found a way to win the vote of Dennis Elrud, a member of his group, when a decision on the domestic discretionary budget reached a stalemate. 'You give us your vote and we'll make sure you get your airport factory (in your district),' Dowd told Elrud, who held the swing vote. Elrud gave in."

(*The Denver Post,* February 23, 2003)

"With his economic program's outlines charted, President Bush was looking for a secretary of the Treasury and national economic adviser who would energetically sell his tax cuts. In tapping John Snow and Stephen Friedman, he picked two sometime deficit hawks to culminate an absent-minded selection process. . . .

. . .On Nov. 14, I wrote that Paul O'Neill and Lawrence Lindsey both were on their way out, a decision that had been made weeks earlier. The president had the time to build a new economic team totally in tune with his supply-side economics proposals, but he clearly did not. Snow does hold some conservative credentials. He and CSX were early financial supporters of the free-market Competitive Enterprise Institute, though recently he said he was too busy to address CEI's anniversary celebration. He served on the 1996 tax advisory commission headed by supply-sider Jack Kemp, who this week expressed 'great enthusiasm' for Snow as a 'terrific guy' and tax reformer.

"However, Snow was a member of the Committee for a Responsible Federal Budget, which opposes tax reduction. It includes such stalwart anti-supply-siders as Leon Panetta, Bill Frenzel, Alice Rivlin, Peter Peterson and David Stockman. In the early 1990s, Snow headed the Business Roundtable, which then was notorious for its opposition to all tax reduction and its tilt in political contributions to Democrats. Representing big business, he worked with the Clinton administration in 1993-94 for deficit reduction—achieved by tax increases."

(*Chicago Sun-Times,* December 12, 2002)

Committee for Economic Development

Established in 1942

DIRECTOR

Charles M. Kolb, president. Kolb became CED's president in 1997. Prior to joining CED, he was general counsel and secretary of United Way of America. He was also deputy assistant for domestic policy to President George Bush. In the Reagan and Bush administrations he also served as assistant general counsel for regulations and legislation, and as deputy undersecretary for planning, budget and evaluation at the Department of Education. A 1973 Princeton graduate, Kolb holds a master's degree in philosophy, politics, and economics from Oxford University and a law degree from the University of Virginia.

BOARD OF DIRECTORS

Roy J. Bostock, chair; chair, Bcom3 Group, Inc.

George H. Conrades, vice chair; chair and chief executive officer, Akamai Technologies, Inc.

James A. Johnson, vice chair; chair and chief executive officer, Johnson Capital Partners

Arthur F. Ryan, vice chair; chair and chief executive officer, Prudential Insurance Co. of America

Frederick W. Telling, vice chair; vice president for Corporate Strategic Planning and Policy Division, Pfizer, Inc.

Plus 240 other trustees

SCOPE

Members: 250 trustees ("mostly heads of major corporations and university presidents")
Branches/chapters: None
Affiliates: None

STAFF

31 total—22 professional; 9 support

TAX STATUS

501(c)(3)

FINANCES

Budget: 2002—$4.57 million; 2001—$4.38 million; 2000—$4.34 million

FUNDING SOURCES

Foundation grants, 20%; corporate donations, 7%; special events/projects, 5%; other (unspecified), 68%

PAC

None

EMPLOYMENT

Information on open positions is posted at http://www.ced.org/join/employment.shtml. Application materials should be sent to Human

CONTACT INFORMATION

2000 L Street, NW, Suite 700, Washington, DC 20036
Phone (202) 296-5860 • *Fax:* (202) 223-0776
General E-mail: info@ced.org • *Web site:* www.ced.org

Communications Director: Morgan Broman
(202) 296-5860 • morgan.broman@ced.org,
Human Resources Director: Laura Lee, vice president for finance and administration
(202) 296-5860 • laura.lee@ced.org

PURPOSE: "Dedicated to policy research on the major economic and social issues of our time and the implementation of its recommendations by the public and private sectors."

CURRENT CONCERNS: E-Commerce • Education • Finance reform • Health care • Immigration • Trade

METHOD OF OPERATION: Awards program • Coalition forming • Conferences/seminars • Congressional testimony • Internet (Web site) • Internships • Media outreach • Research • Speakers program

Effectiveness and Political Orientation

"The entertainment industry's pursuit of tough new laws to protect copyrighted materials from online piracy is bad for business and for the economy, according to a report being released today by the Committee for Economic Development, a Washington policy group that has its roots in the business world. Record companies and movie and television studios have fought copyright infringement on many fronts, hoping to find ways to prevent their products from being distributed free on the Internet. But critics warn that many of the new restrictions that the entertainment industry proposes—like enforcing technological requirements for digital television programming that would prevent it from being transmitted online—would upset the balance between the rights of the content creators and the rights of the public.

"'We are sympathetic to the problems confronting the content distribution industry,' said the report, 'Promoting Innovation and Economic Growth: The Special Problem of Digital Intellectual Property.' 'But these problems—perfect copies of high-value digital works being transmitted instantly around the world at almost no cost—require clear, concentrated thinking, rather than quick legislative or regulatory action.' Until recently, those who opposed strong copyright protections have been characterized by the entertainment industry as a leftist fringe with no respect for the value of intellectual property. . . .

"The entry of the Committee for Economic Development into the copyright wars, some say, is surprising given its long history as a policy-setter in the world of economics and business. The 60-year-old organization left its

Resources, Committee for Economic Development, 2000 L Street, NW, Suite 700, Washington, DC 20036. Fax: (202) 223-0776. E-mail: hr@ced.org.

INTERNSHIPS

Research internships are available year-round. Stipends up to $1,000 are available. Successful applicants will have a major or minor in economics or related social science, as well as strong analytical skills (for example, introductory statistics). Knowledge of public policy issues is strongly recommended. International students are welcome to apply but are required to possess an appropriate F-1 or J-1 visa.

Internship applications can be sent to Tracy Kornblatt, research associate, Center for Economic Development, 2000 L Street, NW, Suite 700, Washington, DC 20036. Fax: (202) 223-0776. E-mail: tracy.kornblatt@ced.org.

NEWSLETTERS

CED (twice per year)

PUBLICATIONS

Breaking the Litigation Habit: Economic Incentives for Legal Reform
The Case for Permanent Normal Trade Relations with China
Dialogue on Diversity
The Digital Economy: Promoting Competition, Innovation, and Opportunity
Economic Policy in a New Environment: Five Principles
Engaging the Global Enterprise
Exploding Deficits, Declining Growth: The Federal Budget and the Aging of America
Fixing Social Security
How Economies Grow: The CED Perspective on Raising the Long-Term Standard of Living
Improving Global Financial Stability
Investing in Learning: School Funding Policies to Foster High Performance
Investing in the People's Business: A Business Proposal for Campaign Finance Reform
Justice for Hire: Improving Judicial Selection
Learning for the Future: Changing the Culture of Math and Science Education to Ensure a Competitive Workforce
Measuring What Matters
New Opportunities for Older Workers
A New Vision for Health Care: A Leadership Role for Business
Preschool for All: Investing in a Productive and Just Society
Promoting Innovation and Economic Growth: The Special Problem of Digital Intellectual Property
Promoting U.S. Economic Growth and Security Through Expanding World Trade: A Call for Bold American Leadership
From Protest to Progress: Addressing Labor and Environmental Conditions Through Freer Trade
Reforming Immigration: Helping Meet America's Need for a Skilled Workforce
The Role of Women in Development
A Shared Future: Reducing Global Poverty
U.S. Trade Policy Beyond the Uruguay Round

intellectual mark on initiatives like the Marshall Plan and the Bretton Woods agreement, which created the World Bank and the International Monetary Fund. In more recent years, the committee's policy papers have had a measure of influence on issues like campaign finance reform and the movement to set standards for public schools through testing."

(*The New York Times,* March 1, 2004)

"In 1989, then-President Bush vowed at an education summit that 'by the year 2000, all children will start school ready to learn.' President Clinton signed on to that goal in 1992. And in 2001 the younger President Bush vowed to 'leave no child behind.' Yet three years after the deadline, the nation still falls abysmally short of providing the resources to make children 'school-ready.' New York's 'universal' pre-school initiative covers barely one-quarter of pre-schoolers.

"This month, a delegation of pre-K advocates came to Syracuse to promote school-readiness again. Why Syracuse? "This is a bright and shining example of educational possibilities,' said a proud city schools Superintendent Stephen Jones. He also noted that percentage-wise, Syracuse has more children in poverty than New York City. And Syracuse is the home base of Donna DeSiato, a former principal and now Dr. Jones' assistant superintendent for curriculum and instruction. DeSiato's ongoing doctoral research focuses precisely on the value of pre-K education. 'Donna has some of the best data available,' said Roy J. Bostock, a former advertising executive who chairs the Washington-based Committee for Economic Development, which is leading the charge for pre-K.

"CED President Charlie Kolb said the business leaders in his group are a relatively 'new voice' in the education debate. 'We're consumers of the education system; we understand change; and we're somewhat impatient.' CED stresses that universal pre-K won't be cheap: It will require at least a doubling of the current $25 billion investment. But that investment can lower costs for remedial education, boost graduation rates, improve worker productivity and reduce crime. 'When you have a problem, you fix it up front,' said Kolb. 'Not in fourth grade or eighth grade.' "

(*The Post-Standard* [Syracuse, N.Y.], December 22, 2003)

"When the White House reported Monday that the federal deficit for 2003 came in below expectations—a mere $374 billion—President Bush's aides were quick to celebrate. 'We can put the deficit on a reasonable downward path if we continue progrowth economic policies and exercise responsible spending restraint,' budget director Joshua Bolten told the Wall Street Journal. This outlandish spin is an insult to the nation's taxpayers and suggests that the White House is reading its own budget documents as badly as it read the prewar intelligence on Iraq. A new report by two respected budget watchdogs—the probusiness Committee for Economic Development and the hawkish Concord Coalition—shows that the federal budget outlook is now the worst in the nation's history and that the Bush administration is doing absolutely nothing to fix it."

(*Minneapolis Star Tribune,* October 23, 2003)

"The chief justice of the Texas Supreme Court took his election reform campaign to the national stage Friday, endorsing a list of innovations for reducing the influence of money and partisan politics on the judiciary. Chief Justice

Tom Phillips applauded ending elections based on party affiliation and a host of other suggestions contained in a 53-page report from the nonpartisan Committee for Economic Development.

" 'These races in our own lifetimes have gone from being rather sleepy backwater affairs . . . to some really nasty political fights,' said Phillips, a persistent critic of Texas' election system, which allows judges to solicit contributions from lawyers and others who appear in their courtrooms. Money, special interests and the act of campaigning conspire to undermine a judge's impartiality, according to the report, 'Justice for Hire,' which was unveiled Friday at a luncheon where Phillips gave the keynote address.

"The report offered a radical solution: Take the decision out of voters' hands by appointing judges, said Derek Bok, former president of Harvard University and co-chairman of the study committee. Bok suggested that states create nonpartisan committees to recommend a list of nominees for governors or lawmakers to choose from. A separate panel would review each judge's performance when it came time to reappoint. . . .

". . . the Committee for Economic Development, a nonprofit business policy organization that recently criticized the role of soft money (political contributions not subject to federal campaign limits), listed interim solutions to improve judicial elections that take place in Texas and 30 other states: End partisan elections, which portray judges as party advocates; Lengthen terms to six to 10 years to reduce political pressure and the need for frequent fund raising. Texas judges serve four- to six- year terms; Use tax money to finance judicial campaigns; Strengthen disclosure laws to better identify donors, particularly special-interest groups."

(*Austin American-Statesman* [Texas], August 10, 2002)

"The future of the U.S. health-care system will be shaped by rising costs, limited access, and poor quality if large private employers fail to confront these issues, says a report published by the Washington-based Committee for Economic Development (CED). The report, titled 'A New Vision for Health Care: A Leadership Role for Business,' found that the system is broken because of erroneous incentives awarded to providers and users of the system.

"Meanwhile, the policy debate centers on managed care. 'The problem is not a lack of good intentions, but a series of structural flaws,' said Charles Kolb, president of CED, a non-profit, non-partisan group of more than 200 business and education leaders. The report was produced by a subcommittee of CED trustees led by Peter Benoliel, chairman of the executive committee, Quaker Chemical Corp.; Jerome Grossman, M.D., chief executive officer, Lion Gate Management Corp.; and Steffen Palko, vice chairman and president, XTO Energy Inc.

"The report urges employers to improve the system by becoming more educated and more demanding purchasers of health care, or risk harm to their businesses and employees and the nation. 'There is no easy overnight solution, but we as business leaders, we must step up to the challenge,' said Grossman, also the director of the Health Care Delivery Program at Harvard University. All the major stakeholders—small business, labor, government, managed care organizations, physicians, and hospitals—should work to resolve the problem by aligning their incentives and practices to promote competition and liability, the CED says."

(*The Record* [Bergen County, New Jersey], May 24, 2002)

Common Cause

Established in 1942

DIRECTOR
Chellie Pingree, president and chief executive officer. Pingree served as a state senator in Maine from 1992 to 2000. In 2002, she ran as a candidate for the U.S. Senate on the Democratic ticket.

BOARD OF DIRECTORS
Derek Bok, chair; Cambridge, MA
Richard North Patterson, vice chair; San Francisco, CA
Jocelyn Larkin, treasurer; Berkeley, CA
Chellie Pingree, president; Washington, DC
Barbara Arnwine, Washington, DC
Rebecca Avila, Whittier, CA
Margery Bronster, Honolulu, HI
Michele Demers, New York, NY
Paul Duke, Washington, DC
Thaddeus "Tad" Foote II, Miami, FL
Margaret Fung, New York, NY
Fred Harris, Albuquerque, NM
Charles Kolb, Washington, DC
Bill Kraus, Madison, WI
Eric Liu, Seattle WA
Harold McDougall, Silver Spring, MD
Spencer Overton, Washington, DC
William Parsons, Denver, CO
Robert A. Pastor, Atlanta, GA
Bradley Phillips, Los Angeles, CA
Martha Phillips, Litchfield, CT
Wendy Marcus Raymont, Washington, DC
Nancy Rhodes, Providence, RI
Philip R. Rotner, New York, NY
John Shattuck, Cambridge, MA
Don Stewart, Chicago, IL
Daniel Tokaji, Los Angeles, CA
Adam Werbach, San Francisco, CA

SCOPE
Members: 250,000 members and supporters
Branches/chapters: 37 state chapters
Affiliates: Common Cause Education Fund, a 501(c)(3) organization

STAFF
47 total at national office—42 professional; 5 support

TAX STATUS
501(c)(4)

FINANCES
Revenue: 2002—$10.77 million

FUNDING SOURCES
Membership contributions and dues, 89%; other income, 11%

PAC
None

CONTACT INFORMATION
1250 Connecticut Avenue, NW, Suite 600, Washington, DC 20036
Phone: (202) 833-1200 • *Fax:* (202) 659-3716
Toll-free: (800) 926-1064
General E-mail: grassroots@commoncause.org •
Web site: www.commoncause.org

Communications Director: Mary Boyle
(202) 736-5770 • mboyle@commoncause.org
Human Resources Director: Colleen O'Day
(202) 736-5772 • coday@commoncause.org

PURPOSE: "A citizen's lobby that advocates for honest, open and accountable government, as well as citizens' participation in the democratic process."

CURRENT CONCERNS: Campaign finance and strong ethics reform laws • Government accountability • Limiting the influence of PACs and banning soft money • Protect civil rights of all citizens

METHOD OF OPERATION: Advertisements • Awards program • Coalition forming • Computerized listing of Federal Election Commission records • Conferences/seminars • Congressional testimony • Congressional voting analysis • Demonstrations • Grassroots organizing • Initiative/referendum campaigns • Internet (e-mail alerts and Web site) • Legislative/regulatory monitoring (federal and state) • Litigation • Lobbying (federal, state, and grassroots) • Local/municipal affairs • Media outreach • Research • Shareholder resolutions • Voting records

Effectiveness and Political Orientation

"The nation's leading government watchdog group is calling for U.S. Rep. Billy Tauzin, R-Chackbay, to step down from his House leadership post while he negotiates a job with one of the nation's leading medical lobbies. Common Cause said Monday that it intends to send a letter to House Speaker Dennis Hastert asking him to remove Tauzin from his slot as chairman of the powerful House Energy and Commerce Committee.

"Tauzin is considering an offer to be the next president of the Pharmaceutical Research and Manufacturers of America. Remaining on the committee that governs American business while negotiating for a position to represent some of the nation's largest pharmaceutical companies is a clear conflict of interest, the group said. 'It's a clear conflict for (Tauzin) to be there any longer,' said Common Cause spokeswoman Mary Boyle. 'It doesn't look good.'

"A spokesman from Hastert's office said Tauzin has agreed to recuse himself from any committee matters involving PhRMA. 'That would meet with the approval of the speaker,' Hastert spokesman John Feehery said. News of Tauzin's interest in the PhRMA job leaked out two weeks ago when he turned down an offer to become the chief lobbyist for the Major Motion Picture

Association of America. The PhRMA deal reportedly is worth more than $2 million in salary and other compensation."

(*The Advocate* [Baton Rouge, La.], February 3, 2004)

"The state government is in serious need of an ethics overhaul, watchdog groups urged Monday in calling on Gov. George E. Pataki and legislators to enact stronger oversight of the ways lobbying and political campaigns are conducted in New York. 'We need to know the public can have confidence in our system,' said Rachel Leon, executive director of New York Common Cause.

"Common Cause, along with the New York League of Women Voters and the New York Public Interest Research Group, outlined a package of proposed reforms that would: Broaden the state's Freedom of Information Law; Expand the definition of 'lobbying' to include the multibillion-dollar business of companies' trying to win procurement contracts from state agencies; Ban all gifts and junkets to lawmakers and top policymakers. The groups also urged the creation of an independent ethics office to oversee the State Legislature and the Pataki administration; the two ethics agencies now in place are controlled by lawmakers and the governor."

(*Buffalo News,* January 6, 2004)

"Government watchdog group Common Cause added its voice Thursday to the debate over phone rate hikes. Common Cause, which has 9,000 members in Florida, has joined Florida Attorney General Charlie Crist and the AARP in asking state regulators to throw out a proposed rate increase by the state's three largest local phone providers. 'They aren't interested in having their phone rates increased,' said Mike Twomey, an attorney representing Common Cause and the AARP.

"Twomey, who said he is filing Common Cause's petition to intervene with the Florida Public Service Commission today, has drawn up letters to state legislators about the rate hikes that also express the group's concern over how PSC members, as well as the state public counsel, are chosen. Crist, Common Cause and the AARP are opposing an increase in basic phone rates proposed by BellSouth Corp., Verizon Communications and Sprint-Florida.

"The companies have asked the PSC to tack on an additional $3 to $7.25 a month to phone bills over the next four years in exchange for lowering the amount they charge long-distance carriers to use their phone lines. The companies, which must prove to the PSC that their rate increases are revenue-neutral, say that the changes will foster competition in the local-phone market. 'The local companies haven't even attempted to offer proof that local customers might 'break even' or 'win' on their total monthly bills by savings on reduced in-state toll calls,' Twomey wrote in the letters.

"The PSC has held more than a dozen public hearings statewide on the proposed rate hikes and is preparing for a series of technical hearings in December. Intervenors such as Common Cause and the AARP are allowed to cross-examine witnesses and file briefs, said Kevin Bloom, PSC spokesman. 'It moves one into the realm of participation as opposed to spectating,' Bloom said."

(*Palm Beach Post* [Florida], November 21, 2003)

"Ten companies and four people in Anne Arundel County—many with ties to development—exceeded the state's limits for campaign contributions over the past four years, the public interest group Common Cause/Maryland said in a report issued yesterday. 'This goes to the issue of, "How much influence do wealthy voters have?" and "How much should they have?" ' said James Browning, the nonprofit group's executive director. Development is a commonly debated issue in a county where political leaders regularly must weigh land preservation against growth.

"Several donors listed on the report said they are investigating, but many also said they question its accuracy. State law prohibits individuals or companies from giving more than $10,000 in contributions during a four-year election cycle. Donors are responsible for monitoring their contributions. Koch Realty of Annapolis topped the report distributed by Common Cause, which pulled its information from state election records. According to the group, Koch Realty made $27,175 in contributions in the cycle that ended Dec. 31. . . .

"Common Cause gathered the information from the state Board of Elections Web site, Browning said. The group issued a similar report on Montgomery County earlier this year. 'They weren't all violations,' said State Prosecutor Stephen Montanarelli, who investigated the Montgomery findings. '(Common Cause) had valid criticism, though. They were correct in most of them, I would say.' "

(*The Baltimore Sun,* October 7, 2003)

"This spring the new president of Common Cause took a quick trip to Chicago to participate in a discussion about the media business. . . . The experience convinced Chellie Pingree (a state senator, chronic reformer, and activist as well as last year's Democratic challenger of Senator Susan Collins of Maine) to make joining the crusade against the Federal Communications Commission a Common Cause issue.

"Back in Washington she began speaking out, joining other groups that were already trying to stop the FCC from helping Big Media get bigger. . . . Nationally, the fact that a few people and citizens' groups were willing to stick their necks out elicited a torrent of public reaction. With no organization whatsoever, the FCC was inundated with nearly a million messages—the largest public reaction ever to a pending matter before the typically insider-dominated agency. Virtually all opposed the attempt to expand media concentration in the alleged interest of efficiency.

"Under the haughty but politically challenged leadership of chairman Michael Powell, the FCC went ahead and on a 3-2 partisan vote approved the regulatory relaxation, but the public outcry has been so loud and sustained that last week the Senate Commerce Committee voted by a wide, bipartisan margin to reinstate the media ownership restrictions. . . .

"What happened nationally had its counterpart for Common Cause, the 33-year-old citizens' group, which is looking to an experienced state legislator with a solid record of accomplishment in health care and election reform for fresh energy. No sooner had the anti-media concentration ads been published than Common Cause got some 60,000 direct inquiries from the public, and half of those people ended up becoming new members; in one week the group raised more money off the Internet than it ever had before. For a group with 200,000 members and 35 active state chapters around the country, this is not hay."

(*The Boston Globe,* June 24, 2003)

Common Good

Established in 2002

DIRECTOR

Jeffrey D. Pariser, executive director. A lawyer with 10 years' experience in courts around the nation, Pariser most recently was a partner with the Washington, DC-based firm Hogan & Hartson, where he worked extensively on health care issues and represented a number of nonprofit organizations. Pariser was a law clerk to Hon. Stewart Pollock of the New Jersey Supreme Court and has served on the adjunct writing faculty at Brooklyn Law School. He is a graduate of the New York University School of Law and the University of Virginia, and a member of the bars of New York, New Jersey, Maryland, and the District of Columbia. Pariser is located in the Washington, DC, office of Common Good.

BOARD OF DIRECTORS

Board of Trustees

Philip K. Howard, chair of the board; vice chair, Covington & Burling

Eric Holder; partner, Covington & Burling, former deputy United States attorney general

Anthony C. M. Kiser; president, William & Mary Greve Foundation

Judyth Pendell; fellow, AEI-Brookings Joint Center for Regulatory Studies

J. Michael Shepherd; executive vice president and general counsel, Bank of New York

Scott F. Smith; partner, Covington & Burling

Missie Rennie Taylor; media consultant

SCOPE

Members: None
Branches/chapters: None
Affiliates: None

STAFF

9.5 total: 6.5 full-time professional; 3 full-time support; plus 2 volunteers/interns

TAX STATUS

501(c)(3)

FINANCES

Revenue: 2002—$285,060

FUNDING SOURCES

Information unavailable

PAC

None

EMPLOYMENT

Apply to Jeffrey Pariser, executive director. Send e-mail or regular mail. Enclose resume and cover letter. Job openings are typically posted on popular Internet sites, such as PSLaw.net.

CONTACT INFORMATION

675 Third Avenue, 32nd Floor, New York, NY 10017
Phone: (212) 681-8199 • *Fax:* (212) 681-8221
Washington Office
1424 16th Street, NW, Suite 210, Washington, DC 20036
Phone: (202) 483-3760 • Fax: (202) 483-3365
General E-mail: hg@cgood.org • *Web site:* http://cgood.org/

Communications Director: Danielle Rhoades
c/o Goodman Media at danielle@goodmanmedia.com
Human Resources Director: Jeffrey Pariser, executive director
(202) 483-3760, ext. 15 • jpariser@cgood.org

PURPOSE: "A bipartisan initiative to overhaul America's lawsuit culture."

CURRENT CONCERNS: Educating and promoting awareness on the need for legal reform (guidestar)

METHOD OF OPERATION: Awards program • Coalition forming • Conferences/seminars • Information clearinghouse • Internet (E-mail alerts and Web site) • Internships • Litigation (amicus briefs) • Lobbying (federal) • Media Outreach • Performance ratings/report cards (companies, products, etc.) • Polling • Research

Effectiveness and Political Orientation

"Congressman Ric Keller (Republican-Florida) has introduced a bill that would deal a body blow to our litigation madness: the Personal Responsibility in Food Consumption Act. His legislation would prohibit frivolous lawsuits concerning obesity-related claims against the food industry. Keller's proposal doesn't preclude people from suing for false advertising, mis-labeling of food, adulterated food or injuries sustained from eating tainted food. As this sensible legislator points out, 'There should be common sense in the food court, not blaming other people in the legal court whenever there is an excessive consumption of food. . . . Nobody is forced to supersize their fast-food meals or choose less healthy options on the menu.'

"Not surprisingly, Keller's bill is giving indigestion to much of the plaintiff bar. If these vultures can do to the food industry what they did to tobacco, they could rake in more than $40 billion in fees.

"The Keller act would be a major step in addressing a growing affliction in this country—fear of lawsuits. Almost instinctively, before doing anything these days, we ask ourselves what our liability might be. Want to coach the local Little League team? You'd better find out what your liability could be. Before a teacher disciplines an unruly student, he'd better be aware of the potential liability. What Philip K. Howard, a lawyer leading the charge for restoring common sense to our courts, labels 'legal fear' is corroding our daily

INTERNSHIPS
Common Good offers only unpaid internships and is very flexible as to length. Typically people intern for a semester of law school, or over the summer. Inquiries should be directed to Jeffrey Pariser, executive director.

NEWSLETTERS
Common Good Wire (press releases and issue briefs by e-mail.)

PUBLICATIONS
The Effects of Law on Health Care
Elements of a System of Medical Justice

CONFERENCES
Common Good regularly holds forums with leading experts on medical liability reform and education reform. For further information, contact Jeffrey Pariser or visit Web site.

life. Congressman Keller's bill would take a good-size bite out of that fear. We should all push hard for its passage."

(*Forbes,* March 29, 2004)

"But judges cannot be sued. If it were allowed, our already contorted and costly justice system would be even more so. It would be like, well, our medical system. . . .

"Today, a combination of runaway juries, pro-plaintiff judges and greedy trial lawyers who sue at the drop of a stethoscope has forced the medical profession to rewrite its rules. Doctors now practice defensive medicine, using unnecessary tests and procedures to avoid being sued. Obstetricians, who are sued more than just about any other type of doctor, have had to embrace defensive medicine big time. . . .

"Many young doctors won't specialize in obstetrics. They fear the threat of suits and wince at malpractice insurance costs, which run around $200,000 a year. Last summer, Manhattan's Elizabeth Seton Childbearing Center, which practiced natural childbirth, had to close when its malpractice premiums rocketed to $2 million.

"Litigation reformer Philip Howard has a solution: Create a special medical court. Replace sympathy-prone juries with experienced judges well-versed in medical procedures who would limit the size of pain-and-suffering awards and compensate plaintiffs according to a preestablished formula, depending on the injury.

"Lotto-size jury awards would be supplanted by settlements that are fair to patients and doctors. Incompetent doctors would be sanctioned but honest mistakes would not end a career. "Such a system would relieve obstetricians and all doctors of enormous stress and let them make decisions in the best interests of patients. It would end the wasteful practice of defensive medicine, which costs our economy an estimated $50 billion to $100 billion a year. It would allow doctors to do what they think is right. . . ."

(*New York Daily News,* February 12, 2004)

" 'The trial lawyers are under siege for a good reason,' says New York corporate lawyer Philip Howard, leader of Common Good, a bipartisan group that he says seeks to change America's lawsuit culture. 'They have been a divisive and exploitative force in society for the last decade or two, and their interest is not in protecting victims, it's in getting rich themselves.' Common Good has petitioned 12 state courts to consider changes that would cut the contingency fees trial lawyers receive when parties settle early in personal injury cases."

(*Christian Science Monitor,* June 10, 2003)

"A group seeking to lower legal costs has filed petitions in 12 states calling for a limit to contingency fees paid to lawyers in some personal-injury claims.

"Common Good is proposing an amendment to the rules of professional conduct, which would reduce the fees paid to attorneys in 'early offer' settlements to 10% of settlement from the average of 20% to 30% today. The goal is to 'clear some of the cases that shouldn't be in litigation and get compensation to injured people early on,' said Nancy Udell, director of policy and general counsel at Common Good, a New York bipartisan group seeking to overhaul the legal system.

"Contingency fees were established to ensure legal representation for people unable to pay upfront legal costs and entitle the lawyers payment in exchange for taking on risky suits. Currently, plaintiff lawyers are paid a portion of the amount recovered.

"The proposed amendment falls short, critics say, because instead of putting more money in the plaintiffs' pockets, it would lower the overall amount recovered in settlements."

(*The Wall Street Journal,* May 8, 2003)

"Opinions inside the legal system and out are mixed on [Philip] Howard's initiative. CNN's Dobbs thinks his weekly guest has struck a nerve with viewers.

" 'He has created an initiative that is important in the public debate,' says Dobbs. 'How far will we let punitive damages take us? And what are the proper limits of the courtroom? Phil and Common Good are the most important representatives of this side of the argument.' "

(*The Washington Post,* October 1, 2002)

Competitive Enterprise Institute

Established in 1984

DIRECTOR

Fred L. Smith Jr., president and founder. Before founding Competitive Enterprise Institute, Smith served as director of government relations for the Council for a Competitive Economy, as a senior economist for the Association of American Railroads, and for five years as a senior policy analyst at the Environmental Protection Agency. He is a frequent guest on national television and radio programs and has written numerous articles for newspapers and magazines. Smith received his undergraduate degree from Tulane University and his graduate training in economics and research at the University of Pennsylvania.

BOARD OF DIRECTORS

William A. Dunn; president, Dunn Capital Management

Scott Fallon; vice president of developer relations, BEA Systems, Inc.

Michael S. Greve; resident scholar, American Enterprise Institute

Leonard Liggio; vice president, Atlas Economic Research Foundation

Thomas Gale Moore; senior fellow, Hoover Institution

William O'Keefe; president and founder, Solutions Consulting

Frances B. Smith; executive director, Consumer Alert

Fred L. Smith Jr.; president and founder, Competitive Enterprise Institute

SCOPE

Members: None
Branches/chapters: None
Affiliates: Center for Private Conservation

STAFF

30 total

TAX STATUS

501(c)(3)

FINANCES

Revenue:2002—$2.95 million
2001—$3.17 million

FUNDING SOURCES

Individual donations, 16%; corporate contributions, 31%; foundation grants, 52%

PAC

None

EMPLOYMENT

See Jobs@CEI:
http://www.cei.org/pages/jobs.cfm for information about employment and fellowship opportunities.

CONTACT INFORMATION

1001 Connecticut Avenue, NW, Suite 1250, Washington, DC 20036
Phone: (202) 331-1010 • *Fax:* (202) 331-0640
General E-mail: info@cei.org • *Web site:* www.cei.org

Communications Director: Jody Clarke
(202) 331-1010 • jclarke@cei.org
Human Resources Director: Kym McLaughlin
(202) 331-1010 • kmclaughlin@cei.org

PURPOSE: "A pro-market, public policy group committed to advancing the principles of free enterprise and limited government."

CURRENT CONCERNS: Agricultural biotechnology • Air pollution • Airline deregulation • Antitrust reform • Banking reform • Budget and tax reform • Corporate Average Fuel Economy (CAFE) standards • Corporate welfare • Drug and medical device regulation • Energy and electricity • Environmental policy • FDA reform • Financial services and deposit insurance reform • Food and safety labeling • Free speech • Gasoline taxes • Global warming and global climate changes • Health care • Intellectual property • International trade • Internet policy • Litigation on economic and constitutional issues • Private conservation • Property rights • Risk and insurance • Social Security • Tobacco and smoking • Trade and international environment • Transportation • Wildlife and marine resources

METHOD OF OPERATION: Advertisements • Coalition forming • Conferences/seminars • Congressional testimony • Congressional voting analysis • Direct action • Fellowships (Warren T. Brookes Fellowships in Environmental Journalism, "yearly appointments granted to journalists to enable them to research, study, and write about private and public approaches to environmental protection") • Films/video/audiotapes • Grassroots organizing • Information clearinghouse • Internet (e-mail alerts and Web site) • Legislative/regulatory • Monitoring (federal and state) • Litigation • Media outreach • Participation in regulatory proceedings (federal and state) • Polling • Research

Effectiveness and Political Orientation

"The 10th anniversary of the world's first treaty on global warming is today, its main provisions ignored by the United States and most other countries.

"Although it is an obscure document, the U.N. Framework Convention on Climate Change contains specific requirements for reduction in greenhouse gases.

". . . adamant opponents of action on global warming remain. Fred Smith, who heads the Competitive Enterprise Institute, called the framework 'the first misstep on the road to global poverty.'

" 'There's no real threat from climate per se to a wealthy, technologically adroit world,' Smith said, adding that restrictions like the framework convention and the Kyoto Protocol would stand in the way of economic development that could enable poor countries to cope with climate change."

(*The Atlanta Journal-Constitution*, March 21, 2004)

"The Bush administration and some big companies are at odds over the terms of a voluntary system for cutting greenhouse-gas emissions amid concerns that too aggressive an approach could open the door to mandatory emission rules down the road. At issue is whether companies should be rewarded for past cleanup efforts with credits that could be traded with other companies. Opponents of mandatory emissions rules have warned that such a system would lead inexorably to limits under future administrations.

"Two years ago, the Bush administration promised the system of credits to reward companies for past and present efforts to curb their emissions of carbon dioxide, the chief suspected global-warming gas. But now the administration appears to be retreating from that position, saying it no longer believes it has the legal authority to create the system of credits. Companies that had been counting on receiving tradable credits are irate. . . .

"Those opposed to credits argue that companies that could most easily reduce their emissions, and generate extra credits, would start lobbying for mandatory limits that would boost the market value of their credits. Tradable credits would 'divide and conquer the business community,' said Marlo Lewis, senior fellow in environmental policy for the Competitive Enterprise Institute, a conservative Washington think tank."

(*The Wall Street Journal*, March 5, 2004)

"How likely is your SUV to roll over in traffic? After decades of research and bitter debate, the federal government unveiled a new test yesterday that may provide the answer.

"The test is the first to be based on a vehicle's actual performance, instead of a mathematical formula. It is expected to increase pressure on car makers to speed up technological changes that are intended to reduce rollover accidents. . . .

"Auto makers acknowledge that SUVs handle differently than cars, because they are designed to travel off-road, but they note that rollover accidents involving all vehicles account for only 2.5% of all crashes, and that most of those who die in such accidents neglect to wear seat belts.

"Even before yesterday's test at a NHTSA facility in East Liberty, Ohio, a conservative Washington think tank, the Competitive Enterprise Institute, assailed the agency for portraying SUVs in a negative light. The institute noted that the nation's highway fatality rate has continued to decline in recent years as millions of SUVs have entered the U.S. fleet. A spokesman for the Alliance of Automobile Manufacturers said the group won't pass judgement on the new test until it has had a chance to review test data, which will take several days. . . ."

(*The Wall Street Journal*, October 8, 2003)

"The proposal to allow U.S.-made prescription drugs to be reimported from foreign countries sparked a fierce debate among conservatives in Republican activist Grover Norquist's weekly meeting on Wednesday. Rep. Gil Gutknecht (R-Minn.) outlined his bill before representatives from several think tanks. The attendees—including Steve Moore from the Club for Growth and Fred Smith from the Competitive Enterprise Institute—blasted the proposal, according to participants. Pharmaceutical companies oppose the reimportation idea, but consumer groups support it.

"At one point, Smith accused Gutknecht of trying to stifle pharmaceutical innovation. The bill, he said, would prevent U.S. companies from speeding lifesaving drugs to the commercial market. 'Your bill's going to kill people,' Smith said."

(*The Washington Post,* July 21, 2003)

"Given that Christine Todd Whitman was not corrupt or dogged by scandal, it is striking that her resignation yesterday as head of the Environmental Protection Agency provoked so much rejoicing. . . . The Competitive Enterprise Institute, a group that bitterly opposes the environmental movement, declared that her resignation offered the EPA a chance to choose a leader who can 'bring the agency into the 21st century.' "

(*The Washington Post,* May 22, 2003)

Concerned Women for America

Established in 1979

DIRECTOR

Beverly LaHaye, chair. LaHaye founded Concerned Women for America (CWA) in 1979 to protect and promote biblical values for women and families. LaHaye has been frequently recognized for her leadership in the political and Christian community. In 1984, she was named Christian Woman of the Year. She has authored or co-authored 15 books and pioneered the award-winning radio show Beverly LaHaye Live as a daily outreach to influence women and men to take political action, build strong families, and take leadership in their communities.

BOARD OF DIRECTORS

Beverly LaHaye, chair
Anne Ball, director
Barrie Lyons, director
Norma Seifert, director
Barbara Fanara, director
Betty Lou Martin, director
Lee LaHaye, chief financial officer
Peg Bishop, director
Judy Smith, secretary
James Woodall, treasurer
Barbara Towne, director
Lori Scheck, director
Maxine Sieleman, director
Jenny Larson, director

STAFF

33 total—13 full-time professional; 20 full-time support; plus 1 part-time professional; 1 part-time support; 900 volunteers and 5 interns

TAX STATUS

501(c)(3)

FINANCES

Revenue: 2002—$11.99 million
2001—$11.03 million

FUNDING SOURCES

Information unavailable.

SCOPE

Members: 558,495 individuals
Branches/chapters: 500 prayer/action chapters
Affiliates: Culture and Family Institute, Beverly LaHaye Institute

PAC

None

EMPLOYMENT

Information unavailable

INTERNSHIPS

Internships are available in the following areas: press and media relations, radio broad-

CONTACT INFORMATION

1015 15th Street, NW, Suite 1100, Washington, DC 20005
Phone: (202) 488-7000 • *Fax:* (202) 488-0806
General E-mail: Web form at www.cwfa.org • *Web site:* www.cwfa.org

Communications Director: Information unavailable
Human Resources Director: Information unavailable.

PURPOSE: "The mission of CWA is to protect and promote Biblical values among all citizens—first through prayer, then education, and finally by influencing our society—thereby reversing the decline in moral values in our nation."

CURRENT CONCERNS: Definition of the Family • Education • National Sovereignty • Pornography • Religious Liberty • Sanctity of Human Life

METHOD OF OPERATION: Boycotts • Coalition forming • Conferences/seminars • Congressional testimony • Congressional voting analysis • Films/video/audiotapes • Grassroots organizing • Internet (e-mail alerts and Web site) • Internships • Legislative/regulatory monitoring (federal and state) • Lobbying (federal, state, grassroots) • Media outreach • Research • Scholarships • Voting records

Effectiveness and Political Orientation

"Concerned Women for America, a conservative Christian group that has been a leading opponent of gay marriage and civil unions. . . ."
(*The Washington Post,* March 13, 2004)

"If 2004 is shaping up as the culture war's second coming, last week saw the fiercest fighting yet on its main battlefront: gay marriage. After months of keeping his distance, President Bush threw his weight behind a constitutional amendment that would ban same-sex matrimony. . . .

"While Bush's announcement was widely seen as a valentine to some of his party's restive conservative backers, it wasn't a slam-dunk for the cultural right. Bush also said that states were free to allow gay couples to enter civil unions (which endow many of the legal benefits of marriage). . . .

"Presidential aides say that Bush insisted on the civil union language, telling them: 'That way, people can still live the life they choose.' The gesture irked religious conservatives. 'The White House should be sounding a clear trumpet on this cultural issue,' says Robert Knight, director of Concerned Women for America's Culture and Family Institute, 'instead of trying to have it both ways.'"
(*U.S. News & World Report,* March 8, 2004)

"If a Food and Drug Administration advisory committee has its way, drugs that prevent or terminate pregnancy after unprotected sex could soon be on

casting, lobbying and government relations, grassroots development (state and local affairs), publications (writing and research: all CWA issues), and legal studies. Applications are available on the Web site. For more information, contact the national office: (202) 488-7000.

NEWSLETTERS
Family Voice (bimonthly magazine)

PUBLICATIONS
A Pledge to End Judicial Tyranny
Hidden Truth: What You Deserve to Know About Abortion

CONFERENCES
National convention (biannual)

your grocery store shelf—with huge social implications.

"Here's one reason why this is crazy: The morning-after pill is essentially an extra-strong version of a regular oral contraceptive. Those regular oral contraceptives themselves require a doctor's prescription and supervision because they sometimes create health problems. But now the FDA committee—finishing a process begun under the Clinton administration—wants companies to take that same prescription medication, increase its strength, make it more complex to administer and offer it on the shelf to any teenage girl who was already irresponsible enough not to protect herself before sex. . . .

"Three years ago, Great Britain made the morning-after pill available without a prescription, and the country is now facing a staggering public health crisis. Some sexually transmitted disease rates have doubled in the last year. The drug is now used by one out of every five girls under 16, and the amount of casual, unprotected sex is skyrocketing. And so, of course, are life-wrecking diseases.

"The same devastating trend could easily cross the pond if we remove the prescription requirement. Wendy Wright, Concerned Women for America's senior policy director, points out: 'Publicly, the Women's Capital Corporation claims the medication would only be used in emergency circumstances—but their Web site says they want it on shelves so it can be used as "frequently as needed." And one of their major advertising campaigns is targeted to teens. This is a huge public health risk.' "

(*The Atlanta Journal-Constitution,* February 11, 2004)

"The Supreme Court's rejection of state anti-sodomy laws is a decisive endorsement of gay rights that is likely to become a milestone in U.S. law and culture. . . .

"Jan LaRue, chief counsel for the Concerned Women for America, added that the court 'magically discovered a right of privacy that includes sexual perversion.' "

(*USA Today,* June 27, 2003)

"The idea of shutting women out of certain military jobs offends some mothers. People recoil at women in danger, 'but this just throws a mirror up to what we've always done to boys. Why is it all right to endanger them and not girls?' asks Sheryl Rudie, a Los Angeles hospital administrator and mother of two girls.

"Such sentiments ignore the reality that women are different from men, and they still play different roles in the family, argues Janice Shaw Crouse of Concerned Women for America, a conservative public-policy group. 'It's a matter of respecting the important role women play. Can a woman do this dangerous military work? Yes, she can do it. But is it a good thing for her to do? No.' "

(*USA Today,* April 8, 2003)

Concord Coalition

Established in 1992

DIRECTOR

Robert L. Bixby, executive director. Bixby has been executive director since 1999, after serving as the coalition's policy director, national field director, and in other capacities since 1992. He frequently represents Concord's views on budget and entitlement reform policy at congressional hearings and in the national media. Bixby holds a bachelor's degree in political science from American University in Washington, DC, a juris doctorate from George Mason University School of Law in Arlington, VA, and a master's degree in public administration from the John F. Kennedy School of Government at Harvard University.

BOARD OF DIRECTORS

Warren B. Rudman, co-chair
Bob Kerrey, co-chair
Paul E. Tsongas (1941–1997), co-chair
Peter G. Peterson, president
Lloyd N. Cutler, secretary-treasurer
Harvey M. Meyerhoff, budget chair
Eugene M. Freedman, finance chair
Paul A. Allaire, vice chair
Roger E. Brinner, vice chair
Charles A. Bowsher, vice chair
James E. Burke, vice chair
John C. Danforth, vice chair
Hanna Holborn Gray, vice chair
William H. Gray III, vice chair
J. Alex McMillan, vice chair
Sam Nunn, vice chair
Timothy J. Penny, vice chair
Martha Phillips, vice chair
Steven Rattner, vice chair
Charles S. Robb, vice chair
Robert E. Rubin, vice chair
Niki Tsongas, vice chair
John G. Turner, vice chair
Paul A. Volcker, vice chair
John P. White, vice chair
Daniel Yankelovich, vice chair

SCOPE

Members: Approximately 200,000
Branches/chapters: Members in almost every congressional district
Affiliates: None

STAFF

15 total

TAX STATUS

501(c)(3)

FINANCES

Budget: 2004—$1.5 million; 2003—$1.5 million; 2002—$1.5 million

CONTACT INFORMATION

1011 Arlington Boulevard, Suite 300, Arlington, VA 22209
Phone: (703) 894-6222 • *Fax:* (703) 894-6231
General E-mail: concordcoalition@concordcoalition.org •
Web site: www.concordcoalition.org

Communications Director: John Labeaume
(703) 894-6222 • communications@concordcoalition.org
Human Resources Director: Harry Zeeve, operations director;
(703) 894-6222 • hzeeve@concordcoalition.org

PURPOSE: The Concord Coalition is a nonpartisan, grassroots organization advocating fiscal responsibility and generationally responsible entitlement policy.

CURRENT CONCERNS: Creating a sound economy for future generations • Eliminating federal budget deficits • Reforming Social Security, Medicaid, and Medicare to make these programs sustainable

METHOD OF OPERATION: Advertisements • Awards program • Coalition forming • Conferences/seminars • Congressional testimony • Congressional voting analysis • Films/video/audiotapes • Grassroots organizing • Internet (e-mail alerts and Web site) • Internships • Lobbying (grassroots) • Media outreach • Research • Speakers program • Telecommunications (mailing lists)

Effectiveness and Political Orientation

"President Bush and the Republican-led Congress are spending money at a rate not seen since World War II—and America's expanding war on terrorism isn't the main reason.

"Spending for national security, it is true, has surged due to the military effort in Iraq and stepped-up homeland security.

"But judging by a bill that Congress is taking up Monday, the lasting fiscal legacy of the Bush administration will also include a historic rise in domestic spending that could affect everything from consumer interest rates to a fiscal landscape that could force epic tax increases in future.

"The spending growth is punctuated this week by a single vote in the House that wraps in all the spending leftovers—not all the money for troops, not the big Medicare expansion—and totals $820 billion. That's as big as the annual economic output of Sweden and Spain combined. . . .

"Much of the $2.2 trillion that Washington is expected to spend in fiscal year 2004 is for mandatory spending on Social Security and Medicare. But so-called discretionary spending has also increased some 22 percent during the Bush presidency, from $734 billion in 2002 to $873 billion in 2004.

"The Concord Coalition, a bipartisan watchdog, calls this the 'most irresponsible year ever.'"

(*Christian Science Monitor,* December 8, 2003)

FUNDING SOURCES
Individual contributions, 69%; foundation grants, 17.1%; corporate donations, 13.9%

PAC
None

EMPLOYMENT
For more imformation, contact Harry Zeeve, operations director, 1011 Arlington Boulevard, Suite 300, Arlington, VA 22209. Phone: (703) 894-6222. Fax: (703) 894-6231. E-mail: hzeeve@concordcoalition.org.

INTERNSHIPS
A small stipend is provided for internship opportunities; duration, application deadlines and hours required are flexible. Internship areas include policy and administrative support. To apply or for more information, contact Harry Zeeve, Operations Director, 1011 Arlington Boulevard, Suite 300, Arlington, VA 22209. Phone: (703) 894-6222. Fax: (703) 894-6231. E-mail: hzeeve@concordcoalition.org.

NEWSLETTERS
The Concord Courier (quarterly)

PUBLICATIONS
Financing Retirement Security for an Aging America: Background Information about Population Change, Social Security and Medicare
Key Questions Voters Should Ask Their Candidates
106th Congress Legislative Scorecard-First Session
A Primer on Medicare
Saving Social Security: A Framework for Reform
Saving Social Security: Options for Reform
Will America Grow Up Before It Grows Old?
The Zero Deficit Plan

CONFERENCES
National Policy Forum (annually in Washington, DC)
Forums and interactive exercises are held throughout the year around the country.

"Tsongas died in 1997, but the former U.S. senator from Massachusetts, a Democrat, left behind the Concord Coalition, the bipartisan deficit watchdog group he founded with former New Hampshire senator Warren Rudman, a Republican. That organization continues to row bravely against the tide of red ink. Earlier this fall the coalition and its allies issued a credible warning that if the federal government stays on its present course, the budget will run a deficit of $5 trillion over the next 10 years rather than the $1.4 trillion the Congressional Budget Office projects. . . .

" 'There is no sense of a budget, there is no sense of trade-offs or restraints,' Robert Bixby, executive director of the Concord Coalition, says of the current atmosphere. 'It is anything goes. What is really missing is any remaining sense of long-term fiscal discipline, the whole generational aspect that Paul Tsongas stressed.' "

(*The Boston Globe*, December 5, 2003)

"Where is Ross Perot now that we need him?

"That was the thought that crossed my mind when the Bush administration announced last week that the budget deficit for the current year would hit a record $455 billion and grow next year to $475 billion.

"Josh Bolten, the new budget director, pronounced the deficits 'manageable,' but almost everyone who is not directly engaged in defending them found the long-term implications of the massive borrowing scary as hell. The Concord Coalition, a bipartisan budgetary watchdog group, gave Congress and the administration an 'F' on fiscal policy, saying it was characterized by 'deficits, deception and denial.' "

(*The Washington Post*, July 23, 2003)

"At the White House, Doug Badger has taken over the health-care portfolio. He's a former administrative assistant to Sen. Don Nickles and knows the politics of the Senate inside out. He'll report to Stephen Friedman, the new economic adviser who came under fire for being involved with the Concord Coalition, a deficit-reduction group. Supply-side conservatives worried Mr. Friedman's Concord Coalition ties might make him insufficiently enthusiastic about tax cuts. But in fact, the Concord Coalition's top priority in recent years has been fixing Social Security and Medicare. If Mr. Friedman tackles that tough task, he could end up pleasing both the free-market skeptics and his Concord Coalition colleagues. . . ."

(*The Wall Street Journal*, December 17, 2002)

"Remember the old days of budget surpluses? That's good, because you won't see them again for a long time: President Bush's fiscal 2003 budget could well kick off a tax-cutting and spending spree the likes of which we haven't seen since the days of Ronald Reagan. Even as Bush is proposing nearly $2 trillion in new initiatives and tax breaks over the next decade, Congress is ready to trump his ideas with costly ideas of its own.

"Bush's budget calls for a deficit for at least the next three years. After that, the budget would be back in the black, but only because he would use Social Security payroll taxes to fund other programs. 'This budget will open the floodgates,' says Robert Bixby, executive director of the Concord Coalition, a Washington group that backs fiscal discipline. . . ."

(*Business Week*, February 18, 2002)

The Conference Board, Inc.

Established in 1916

CONTACT INFORMATION

845 Third Avenue, New York, NY 10022-6679
Phone: (212) 339-0345 • *Fax;* (212) 836-9740
General E-mail: None • *Web site:* www.tcb.org

Communications Director: Randall Poe
(212) 339-0234
Human Resources Director: Doreen Massaroni
(212) 339-0237

PURPOSE: "The Conference Board creates and disseminates knowledge about management and the marketplace to help businesses strengthen their performance and better serve society. Working as a global independent membership organization in the public interest, The Conference Board conducts conferences, makes forecasts and assesses trends, publishes information and analysis, and brings executives together to learn from one another."

CURRENT CONCERNS: Corporate governance • Corporate performance • Economic indicators • Global corporate citizenship • Human resources management • Institutional investment trends

METHOD OF OPERATION: Conferences/seminars • International activities • Library services for members only • Research • Web site

Effectiveness and Political Orientation

"Last year, the Conference Board, a New York group that represents large businesses, convened a blue-ribbon commission to study possible corporate reforms.

"The commission included such luminaries as Paul Volcker, former chairman of the Federal Reserve; John Snow, former chairman of railroad company CSX Corp., who subsequently became U.S. Treasury secretary; Arthur Levitt Jr., former chairman of the Securities and Exchange Commission; and Intel's Grove.

"The commission strongly recommended that companies split the chair and Chief Executive Officer roles. Alternatively, the commission said, companies should name an outside lead director to run board meetings without management being present.

"The goal is to 'make boards more independent and more effective,' said panel member Charles Bowsher, former U.S. comptroller general."

(*The San Francisco Chronicle,* March 5, 2004)

"Government in the U.S. may keep its fingers out of religion—witness the sacking last year of Roy Moore, Alabama's chief justice, for refusing to remove a monument of the Ten Commandments from the state court—but many businesses do not.

Sir Martin Sorrell, WPP Group
Anton van Rossum, Fortis NV/SA
Heinrich von Pierer, Siemens AG
Ronald A. Williams, Aetna Inc.
Marjorie Yang, Esquel Group of Cos.

SCOPE

Members: Nearly 2000 companies in
60 nations
Branches/chapters: regional offices in Berlin;
Brussels (The Conference Board Europe);
Chicago; Skanderborg, Denmark ; London;
Madrid; New Delhi, Hong Kong; India;
Mexico City; Paris; Singapore; Warsaw,
Poland; Zurich, Switzerland
Affiliates: None

STAFF

240 total

TAX STATUS

501(c)(3)

FINANCES

Declined to comment

FUNDING SOURCES

Declined to comment

PAC

None

EMPLOYMENT

Job openings and information are listed on
The Conference Board's Web site:
www.tcb.org. Cover letters and resumes
should be sent to Doreen Massaroni, director,
human resources, The Conference Board, 845
Third Avenue, New York, NY 10022-6679.
Phone: (212) 759-0900. Fax: (212) 980-7014.

INTERNSHIPS

Doreen Massaroni is the internship coordinator. She may be contacted at The Conference
Board, 845 Third Avenue, New York, NY
10022-6679. Phone: (212) 759-0900.
Fax: (212) 980-7014.

NEWSLETTERS

Straight Talk (10 issues per year)
Across the Board Magazine (6 issues per year)

PUBLICATIONS

The following is a sample list of publications:
*Aligning Performance Measures and
Incentives in European Companies*
Are Bigger Banks Better?
Asia-Pacific Regional Design
*Chief Executive Officer Challenge: Top
Marketplace and Management Issues*
Change Management
Changing Global Role of Marketing
Communicating in the Future
Consumer Confidence Survey (monthly)
*Corporate Volunteerism: How Families Make a
Difference*
Determining Board Effectiveness
Diversity: An Imperative for Business Success
Environmental Policy-Making
Evolving Role of Ethics in Business

"An article in the November-December issue of Across the Board, the excellent magazine of the Conference Board, the New York-based business policy organisation, reports a 'growing religiosity' that 'is bubbling up into the corporate mainstream.' "

(*Financial Times* [London, England], February 18, 2004)

"The recession of 2001 wasn't severe in terms of consumer spending, but it was horrendous for corporate finances: The operating earnings of the blue-chip Standard & Poor's 500 index companies suffered their deepest plunge in more than 50 years.

"Mindful of that slump, and of the resulting surge in business bankrupt-cies, many companies feel continuing heavy pressure to bolster their finances, said Gail Fosler, chief economist at the New York-based Conference Board, a business-sponsored research group."

(*The Los Angeles Times,* February 8, 2004)

"The well-respected Conference Board predicts that 2004 will see the creation of 2 million new jobs and it expects the new year to be—from an economic standpoint—the best in the last 20."

(*The Boston Herald,* December 31, 2003)

"A financial writer for the online magazine Slate, sifting through the flurry of numbers, decided to search for unusual indicators that illuminate the U.S. and global economies, even if they are unfamiliar to most people. . . .

"Ken Goldstein, who oversees the Conference Board's Help-Wanted Advertising Index, says it remains a key barometer of America's job market.

"The ad index usually follows what's called the Beveridge Curve, after the British economist who noted that periods of low ad volume correspond to rel-atively high unemployment. True to form, the index fell after 2001 as the job-less rate climbed. . . .

"On the confidence side, the mainstays are the Conference Board's Consumer Confidence Index and the University of Michigan's Index of Con-sumer Sentiment. ABC News/Money magazine puts out a third, the Con-sumer Comfort Index.

"The Conference Board and Michigan surveys are based on answers to five questions correlated to baseline years set at 100 (1985 for the Conference Board, 1966 for the Michigan survey). The ABC/Money poll has three ques-tions and no base year. The ABC index can take on any value from minus-100 to plus-100. Each survey is computed according to a different scale, so the magnitude of the point changes among them is not directly comparable.

"Retailers give great attention to all three in gauging how Americans will spend some $4 trillion a year."

(*The Plain Dealer* [Cleveland], November 12, 2003)

"(A) board's effectiveness can be compromised when a Chief Executive Officer is chairman, backers of corporate reform argue. Every major corporate fraud in recent years has included a controlled or uninvolved board of directors. . . .

"Even The Conference Board, not known as a liberal bastion, has ques-tioned the combination of executive duties and favors the dismantling of what critics call the 'imperial Chief Executive Officer.'

CONFERENCES

Holds more than 110 conferences annually on topics that include: corporate citizenship, corporate communications, diversity, electronic procurement, environmental concerns, ethics, human resources, governance, leadership, marketing, and work and family issues.

"A dual chairman-Chief Executive Officer opens the potential for a conflict of interest, and The Conference Board recommends a separation of duties, or at least the creation of a 'lead' director position."

(*The Denver Post,* August 10, 2003)

"The number of companies cutting jobs has spiked since November, with AOL Time Warner, Boeing, Dow Jones, Eastman Kodak, Goodyear, J. C. Penney, McDonald's, Merrill Lynch, Sara Lee, and Verizon all announcing new layoffs. Barring a sustained rise in oil prices, however, the cuts appear likely to taper off in the coming months as the economy continues its slow recovery, most forecasters say.

"The bigger problem seems to be the unwillingness of companies to hire new workers. In December, the number of help-wanted advertisements in newspapers across the country fell to the lowest level in almost 40 years, according to the Conference Board, a research group in New York."

(*The New York Times,* February 6, 2003)

Congressional Management Foundation

Established in 1977

DIRECTOR

Rick Shapiro, executive director. Shapiro joined CMF as program director in 1988 and became executive director in 1990. He is involved in CMF's programs by leading confidential management assessments for congressional clients and by delivering management workshops for senior congressional staff. He is the author of *Frontline Management*, a guidebook for running district and state offices. Shapiro is also the author of several chapters in CMF's management guidebook, *Setting Course: A Congressional Management Guide*, and co-author of *Working in Congress: The Staff Perspective*. He has appeared on the television and cable news shows to discuss congressional management issues and is frequently cited in newspaper articles. Before coming to CMF, Shapiro held senior staff positions in both the Senate and House and worked as a management consultant for Coopers & Lybrand and the State of Arizona. He received his M.A. in Public Administration from Princeton University.

BOARD OF DIRECTORS

Ira Cha, president of Executive Coaching and Consulting Associates
Kelly Johnston, vice president of government affairs at the Campbell Soup Co.
Gary Serota, senior vice president of Business Development Memberdrive
David Strauss
Diane Thompson, Environment Program Officer with The Pew Charitable Trusts

SCOPE

Members: None
Branches/chapters: None
Affiliates: None

STAFF

7 total

TAX STATUS

501(c)(3)

FINANCES

Revenue: 2002—$6.49 million; 2001—$6.49 million

FUNDING SOURCES

Corporate donations and foundation grants, 75%; publications, 5%; other income: consulting, 20%

PAC

None

EMPLOYMENT

Information unavailable

CONTACT INFORMATION

513 Capitol Court, NE, Suite 300, Washington, DC 20002
Phone: (202) 546-0100 • *Fax:* (202) 547-0936
General E-mail: cmf@cmfweb.org • *Web site:* www.cmfweb.org

Communications Director: Information unavailable
Human Resources Director: Information unavailable

PURPOSE: Dedicated to "helping Congress become a more productive and effective institution through better management. CMF does not seek to change Congress by lobbying for institutional reform but chooses to work internally with Member offices, committees, and the leadership to foster management practices and systems."

CURRENT CONCERNS: Better use of technology in Congress • Congressional ethics • Employment trends of congressional staff • Management training of top congressional staff • Orientation of freshman members of Congress • Strategic planning for congressional offices

METHOD OF OPERATION: Films/video/audiotapes • Group facilitation • Internet (Web site) • Leadership management training • Management consulting • Publication of books and reports • Seminars/workshops • Survey research

Effectiveness and Political Orientation

"Members' Web sites lack the necessary information to meet their constituents' wartime needs, according to the Congress Online Project, which advises Members to add several features to their online offices.

"The Congress Online Project—through a joint venture between the Congressional Management Foundation and George Washington University—recently reviewed 200 House and Senate Web sites to assess how well lawmakers are responding to Operation Iraqi Freedom.

" 'We learned that while most Web sites had current statements from the Representative or Senator about the war, the overwhelming majority lacked the critical information and guidance that the public most needs,' stated the report, 'Responding to War . . . Online: 10 Ways to Use Your Congressional Web Site in War.' "

(*Roll Call* [Washington, DC], March 31, 2003)

"A lot of Americans are concerned that technological advancements have enabled the government to keep a closer eye on us.

"But they also enable us to keep a better eye on our government.

"Two years ago, the Congress Online Project was launched. This research program, funded by The Pew Charitable Trusts and conducted jointly by the George Washington University and the Congressional Management Founda-

INTERNSHIPS
Information unavailable

NEWSLETTERS
None

PUBLICATIONS
Congress Online 2003: Turning the Corner on the Information Age
Congress Online: Assessing and Improving Capitol Hill Web Sites
Congressional Intern Handbook
Developing Job Descriptions
E-mail Overload in Congress: Managing a Communications Crisis
Frontline Management: A Guide for Congressional District/State Offices
Management Guidance on Closing a Congressional Office
Senate Salary, Tenure, and Demographic Data: 1991–2001
Setting Course: A Congressional Management Guide
2001 Senate Staff Employment Study
2002 House Staff Employment Study
Working in Congress: The Staff Perspective

CONFERENCES
Assessing Your Management Skills
Conducting Performance Reviews
Creating an Effective Human Resources System for Your Office
Crisis Management: Handling the Workload Crunch in a Campaign Year
Establishing the Management Structure for the Office
First-Term Strategic Planning & Budgeting
Hiring Staff
How to Run More Productive Meetings
Information Technology Management
Management 101 for AAs: Management and Leadership Fundamentals
Management 101 for LDs: Basic Supervisory Skills
Managing Ethics
Managing for Motivation
Managing the Mail System
Quality Tools for Maximizing Staff Efficiency
Strategic Planning
Surviving January: Managing with Limited Resources
Understanding and Improving Your Management Style

tion, examined our representatives' Web sites and other forms of online communications.

"Its goal was to assess the Internet dialogue between members of Congress and the public. . . ."

(*Pittsburgh Post-Gazette,* March 5, 2003)

"E-mail has supplanted traditional mail and phone calls as the preferred method for constituents to contact their members, especially since the 2001 anthrax scare on Capitol Hill, and congressional Web sites have become a main source of information for constituents.

" 'The best Web sites show that the members anticipate the needs of their constituents. They anticipate the questions in advance and answer them,' said Brad Fitch, deputy director of the online project, which is a nonpartisan joint venture of the Congressional Management Foundation and George Washington University and is funded by the Pew Charitable Trust."

(*The San Francisco Chronicle,* March 4, 2003)

"Congressional Management Foundation—a nonprofit, nonpartisan think tank."

(*The Washington Post,* December 29, 2002)

"Help may be on the way for cash-strapped congressional offices.

"Riding along with the $5.5 billion defense supplemental bill that the House Appropriations Committee will take up on Thursday is a $47.2 million item for 'members' representational allowances.' That would cover such expenses as staff salaries, travel, utility bills and the purchase of computer software.

"The extra funding was promised last December by the House Administration Committee and was recently requested by President Bush. It would ease what some say are intolerable financial pressures on many congressional offices.

"To convince voters of its abiding concern for the taxpayers' money, Congress has regularly cut its budget. But the frugality is making it hard to retain good staff and keep up with advances in office technology, said Brad Fitch, deputy director of the nonprofit Congressional Management Foundation.

"With a new Republican administration taking over the White House, GOP leaders feared there would be an exodus of top staffers taking advantage of higher salaries in the executive branch unless a gesture was made.

"Indeed, some key staffers did defect. Data compiled by the Congressional Management Foundation shows that House staffers in 2000 were earning 39 percent less than Washington-based executive branch workers with comparable education, experience and responsibilities. Moreover, the gap has been widening since 1990."

(*The Washington Post,* June 11, 2001)

Conservation Fund

Established in 1985

DIRECTOR

Lawrence A. Selzer, president and chief executive officer. Before being named president in December 2001, Selzer served as senior vice president of sustainable programs for the organization. Prior to joining The Conservation Fund, Selzer directed marine research programs out of Woods Hole, MA. He currently serves as vice chair of the Sustainable Forestry Board and is on the board of directors of the Wildlife Habitat Council and the Natural Resources Council of America. Selzer holds a M.A. in business administration from the University of Virginia and a B.S. in environmental science from Wesleyan University.

BOARD OF DIRECTORS

Charles R. Jordan, chair
Lawrence A. Selzer, president and chief
    executive officer
J. Rutherford Seydel II, vice president and
    treasurer; partner, Lawson, Davis, Pickren
    & Seydel
Riley P. Bechtel, member; chair and chief
    executive officer, Bechtel Group
Jessica H. Catto, member; president,
    Crockett Street Management
Norman L. Christensen Jr., member;
    Nicholas School of the Environment, Duke
    University, Durham, NC
Sylvia A. Earle, member; chair, Deep Ocean
    Exploration and Research
Gilbert M. Grosvenor, member; chair of the
    board, National Geographic Society
KiKu H. Hanes, member; director,
    Conservation Fund Montana office
Hadlai A. Hull, member; conservationist,
    Washington, DC
Ann McLaughlin Korologos, member;
    former U.S. Secretary of Labor
John W. Patten, member; president emeritus,
    Business Week Magazine
George A. Ranney Jr., member; president
    and chief executive officer, Chicago
    Metropolis 2020
Nelson A. Rockefeller Jr., member;
    executive vice president, Intrepid Learning
    Systems
B. Francis Saul III, member; vice chair, Chevy
    Chase Bank
Patrick F. Noonan, chair emeritus
Hubert W. Vogelmann, chair emeritus;
    Botany Department, University of Vermont

SCOPE

Members: None
Branches/chapters: Regional offices in Alaska,
    California, Colorado, Florida, Georgia,
    Idaho, Illinois, Maryland, Michigan,
    Montana, Nevada, New Mexico, North

CONTACT INFORMATION

1800 N. Kent Street, Suite 1120, Arlington, VA 22209-2156
Phone: (703) 525-6300 • *Fax:* (703) 525-4610
General E-mail: postmaster@conservationfund.org •
Web site: www.conservationfund.org

Communications Director: Christine Fanning, director of marketing and communications
(703) 908-5800 • cfanning@conservationfund.org
Human Resources: Lori Withers
(703) 525-6300 • lwithers@conservationfund.org

PURPOSE: The Fund "forges partnerships to protect America's legacy of land and water resources. Through land acquisition, sustainable programs, and leadership training, the Fund and its partners demonstrate effective conservation solutions emphasizing the integration of economic and environmental goals." The Fund has protected more than 3.5 million acres since 1985.

CURRENT CONCERNS: Land conservation • Leadership training • Sustainable programs

METHOD OF OPERATION: Direct action

Effectiveness and Political Orientation

"A coal company has agreed to sell 800 acres for a memorial on behalf of those who died aboard United Airlines Flight 93, the San Francisco-bound jet that crashed during the Sept. 11, 2002, terrorist attacks.

"PBS Coals Inc. of Somerset County, Pa., intends to sell the land to the Conservation Fund of Arlington, Va., which is working to preserve land for a memorial to honor the 40 passengers and crew who died.

"Earlier in the week, the company said it would donate 29 acres of land to the fund, including part of the site where the Boeing 757 crashed into the countryside during a cockpit struggle.

"And earlier this month, Consol Energy of Pittsburgh announced it had donated 140 acres of land. . . .

"Patrick Noonan, founder of the Conservation Fund, said of the Consol donation, 'This gift to the nation will forever honor the heroes aboard Flight 93 and serve as a lasting tribute to their extraordinary courage and bravery.' "
(*The San Francisco Chronicle*, December 14, 2003)

"The DuPont Company announced it would donate to the Conservation Fund 16,000 acres of land in the Okefenokee Swamp that it had intended to strip mine for titanium dioxide. The mining plan was halted by a nationwide

Carolina, Pennsylvania, Texas, Vermont, and West Virginia
Affiliates: None

STAFF
125 total—100 full-time professional; 25 full-time support; plus 23 part-time professional; 4 part-time support/contractual; 10 interns; 60 volunteers

TAX STATUS
501(c)(3)

FINANCES
Revenue: 2002—$60 million; 2001—$64 million

FUNDING SOURCES
Corporations, 25%; foundations, 25%; individuals, 25%; public agencies, 25%

PAC
None

EMPLOYMENT
Positions are posted online at http://conservationfund.org. Cover letters and resumes can be mailed to a variety of locations; refer to the online posting for complete information. The Fund is an equal opportunity employer.

INTERNSHIPS
The Fund offers a variety of intern positions for students in the areas of protecting wildlife habitat, working landscapes, community open space and historic sites throughout the country. Most internships are available in full-time and part-time positions. Some are paid. A full listing of available internships is available at http://www.conservationfund.org. Students applying for fall internships should apply June 15–August 15; students applying for spring internships should apply October 15–December 15; students applying for summer internships should apply February 15–April 15.

NEWSLETTERS
Common Ground (quarterly)
Conservation Fund's (online)

PUBLICATIONS
Atlanta Campaign Guide
Balancing Nature and Commerce in Gateway Communities
Better Models for Commercial Development
The Civil War Battlefield Guide
Community of Choices
The Dollars and Sense of Preserving Community Character
Greenways: America's Natural Connection: a Video Primer
Land Conservation Financing
Land Use in America
Voices from the Environmental Movement: Perspectives for a New Era

CONFERENCES
None

opposition in 1997. International Paper will continue to exercise its rights to harvest timber on parts of the land until 2080."

(*The New York Times*, August 28, 2003)

"Anheuser-Busch flags a partnership between Natural Light and Natural Ice beers, and The Conservation Fund, with a 'Keep It Natural' campaign. Print, radio and [point of purchase] hop on the centennial of the National Wildlife Refuge System, created by Pres. Teddy Roosevelt, and will tell consumers that proceeds from beer purchases will be donated to help the [the Conservation Fund] buy and preserve one million acres of land. Proceeds will be supplemented by a grant from [Anheuser-Busch]. The [Conservation Fund] will roll a traveling exhibit from [Anheuser-Busch's] headquarters on Earth Day, April 26, that commemorates the centennial and credits the brewer as a sponsor of the One Million Acres program."

(*Brandweek*, April 21, 2003)

"The Sprawl Watch Clearinghouse today released a new report calling for states and communities to make green infrastructure an integral part of local, regional and state plans and policies. 'Green Infrastructure: Smart Conservation for the 21st Century' highlights the critical roles trails and greenways play in a strategic approach to land conservation: 'links' between open space, alternative transportation routes, preservers of valuable corridors of land and facilitator of coalition-building across jurisdictional boundaries. . . .

"Edward McMahon, vice president of The Conservation Fund and co-author of the report, said 'just as growing communities need to upgrade and expand their built infrastructure (roads, sewers, utilities, etc), so too they need to upgrade and expand their green infrastructure—the network of open space, woodlands, wildlife habitat, parks and other natural areas that sustains clean air, water and natural resources and enriches our quality of life.'

"According to the report, one-third of weekday trail users on major metropolitan trail systems in Washington, D.C., and Seattle, Wash., are commuters. Mark Benedict, director of the Conservation Leadership Network for The Conservation Fund and report co-author, said trails and greenways 'are the links that tie the (open space) together and allow it to function.'"

(*US Newswire*, February 14, 2002)

"An agreement between a federal agency and a nonprofit group may boost cleanup of abandoned mines, sparking an increase in economic development in poor neighborhoods.

"The Department of Interior's Office of Surface Mining (OSM) and the Conservation Fund have signed a memorandum of understanding to work together to restore mined lands and water resources to beneficial uses.

"OSM offers grants to states to reclaim land and water resources harmed by coal mining. The fund develops and improves innovative and cost-effective technologies for acid and wastewater treatment that can be applied to abandoned mines."

(*Hazardous Waste Superfund Week*, February 5, 2001)

Conservation International

Established in 1987

DIRECTOR

Russell A. Mittermeier, president. Before joining Conservation International in 1990, Mittermeier was vice president for science at the World Wildlife Fund (WWF) from 1987 to 1989, and a director of four different WWF programs between 1979 and 1989. He has served as chair of the Primate Specialist Group of the International Union for Conservation of Nature's Species Survival Commission (SSC), as SSC's vice chair for international programs, and as chair of the World Bank's Task Force on Biological Diversity. A prominent primatologist and wildlife conservationist, Mittermeier is the author of six books and more than 250 papers and articles. He received his B.A. from Dartmouth and his Ph.D. in biological anthropology from Harvard.

BOARD OF DIRECTORS

Peter A. Seligmann, chair and chief executive officer, Conservation International
Gordon E. Moore, chair of the executive committee; co-founder and chair emeritus, Intel Corp.
Meredith Auld Brokaw, vice chair; conservationist
Lewis W. Coleman, vice chair; president, Gordon and Betty Moore Foundation
Harrison Ford, vice chair; actor
Story Clark Resor, vice chair; conservationist
Henry H. Arnhold; co-chair, Arnhold & S. Bleichroeder, Inc.
Skip Brittenham; senior partner, Ziffren, Brittenham, Branca & Fischer
Lord Browne of Madingley; group chief executive, BP
Louis W. Cabot; chair, Cabot-Wellington
Barry Diller; chair and chief executive officer, USA Interactive, Inc.
Mark L. Feldman; president and chief executive officer, L&L Manufacturing Co.
Robert J. Fisher; Pisces, Inc.
Ann Friedman; teacher, Bethesda, MD
Michael H. Glawe; director emeritus, UAL Corp.
Judson Green; president and chief executive officer, Navigation Technologies Corp.
Charles J. Hedlund; chair emeritus, Conservation International
H. Fisk Johnson, Ph.D.; chair of the board, S.C. Johnson & Son, Inc.
S. K. I. Khama; lieutenant general, vice president, Republic of Botswana
Joel Korn; president, WKI Brasil Servicos
Oscar M. Lopez; chair and chief executive officer, First Philippine Holdings Corp.
John E. McCaw Jr.; chair, Orca Bay Capital Corp.
Peter McPherson; president, Michigan State University, East Lansing

CONTACT INFORMATION

1919 M Street, NW, Suite 600, Washington, DC 20036
Phone: (202) 912-1000 or (800) 406-2306 • *Fax:* (202) 912-1030
General E-mail: Web form at www.conservation.org •
Web site: www.conservation.org

Communications Director: Karen A. Ziffer, senior vice president, resources and communications
Human Resources Director: Information unavailable

PURPOSE: "To conserve the earth's heritage, our global diversity, and to demonstrate that human societies are able to live harmoniously with nature."

CURRENT CONCERNS: Research science • Business & environment • Protected areas • Conservation enterprise • Policy and economics • Ecotourism • Education & awareness • Population & environment • Climate change

METHOD OF OPERATION: Advertisements • Awards program • Conferences/seminars • Direct action • Films/video/audiotapes • Grassroots organizing • International activities • Internet (databases, Web site) • Internships • Media outreach • Product merchandising • Research • Training and technical assistance

Effectiveness and Political Orientation

"Your recent article 'So Much Shrimp' [Food, Feb. 25] failed to mention the tremendous environmental costs associated with shrimp fishing. Each pound of wild shrimp caught causes the death of 10 or more pounds of other marine life. This 'by-catch' is simply tossed back into the ocean. Shrimp fisheries are responsible for more than 11 million tons of by-catch deaths annually. When shrimp trawlers drag their heavy nets across the ocean floor, they destroy coral reefs, sea grasses and other marine life; flatten terrain; and kill numerous fish, turtles, starfish and crabs, among other creatures.

"New techniques for farming shrimp are beginning to resolve issues relating to pollution, genetic contamination, disease, and destruction of natural coastal mangroves and wetlands that have long plagued aquaculture operations. Consumers can help by learning about the economic and environmental costs of destructive fishing and fish farming.

Sylvia Earle, Executive Director, Global Marine Program, Conservation International"

(*The Washington Post,* March 3, 2004)

"Some of the world's poorest countries are hot spots for tourists interested in nature and indigenous cultures, but the influx of resort developers, affluent travelers, and their money has its pitfalls, according to a new report.

"The report on 'Tourism and Biodiversity' from Conservation International, a Washington, D.C.-based nonprofit environmental organization, calls

SCOPE
Members: 4,000 individuals and corporations
Branches/chapters: 2
Affiliates: None

STAFF
450 total—391 full-time professional; 59 full-time support; plus 2 part-time; 4 volunteers; and 30 interns

TAX STATUS
501(c)(3)

FINANCES
Revenue: 2003—$240 million; 2002—$279.7 million

FUNDING SOURCES
Government contracts, 45%; individuals, 27%; corporate donations, 16%; foundation grants, 10%; membership dues, 2%

PAC
None

EMPLOYMENT
Open positions are listed on the Web site. Submit resume online at the www. conservation.org/xp/CIWEB/about/jobs/jobapp.xml.

INTERNSHIPS
Internship opportunities are listed on the Web site: www.conservation.org/xp/CIWEB/about/jobs.

NEWSLETTERS
Conservation Frontlines (quarterly)

PUBLICATIONS
Africa
Atlantic Forest
Bats of Papua New Guinea Field Guide
Between Two Futures
Biosphere Reserves in Tropical America
Caratinga
Chalalán
Directory of Information Resources for Non-Timber Forest Products
A Dream for Guyana's Natural Heritage
Fanamby

global tourism 'the world's largest industry' and points out that ecotourism more than doubled between 1990 and 2000. . . .

"The report, released last month, warns that without proper planning, tourism in fragile ecosystems could kill 'the very things that attract tourists in the first place.' Hazards include the depletion of scarce freshwater resources, introduction of nonnative species, and threats to local culture.

"The report, which was prepared with the help of the United Nations Environment Programme, advocates better planning by governments to, among other things, protect sensitive ecosystems from construction, to give tourists an opportunity to donate directly to the maintenance of nature preserves, and to enforce laws against polluters."

(*The Boston Globe*, October 1, 2003)

"Africa's gorillas and chimpanzees are dying off at a startling rate despite their protected status, even in the more remote parts of the continent that have long been considered their strongholds, according to newly collected survey data.

"Surveys conducted from 1998 to 2000 found that ape populations have shrunk by more than half since 1983 in Gabon and the Republic of Congo, two nations where forests remain largely undisturbed and most of Africa's apes live today. The main causes are hunting for bushmeat and an epidemic of Ebola hemorrhagic fever, which has left thousands of dead primates in its bloody wake.

"With hunters venturing ever deeper into the forest along newly cut logging roads, and the Ebola virus poised to sweep into parks where many of the world's remaining gorillas and chimpanzees have taken refuge, disaster is close at hand, researchers said. . . .

"In the longer term, governments need to consider setting aside more protected areas, said Rebecca Kormos, a research fellow with the Center for Applied Biodiversity Science at Conservation International in Washington. 'We're learning that you can't have just one area where you're protecting the apes. Not just because of diseases like Ebola, which can wipe out an area, but also because of things like civil unrest and conflict.'"

(*The Washington Post*, April 7, 2003)

"Are the Greens getting in bed with the greenbacks—or is it the other way around?" Ford Motor Co. has given $25 million to Conservation International to establish the Center for Environmental Leadership in Business, which opened recently at CI's offices on M Street.

"'CI's idea here is that corporations and the environmental sector can work together; environmentalists should harness the private sector's ingenuity to make a difference,' said CELB spokesman Jason Anderson.

"The new center will identify environmentally friendly business practices, get specific companies to adopt them and then publicize any resulting environmental and economic benefits.

"Center officials have identified a Ford manufacturing plant in Sonora, Mexico, as a partner in improving water conservation practices. CI has worked with Starbucks to change the way its coffee is grown in Chiapas, Mexico, to help protect that haven of biodiversity. They also hope to work with the travel industry to lighten the burden tourists place on the environment.

"'It's our goal to make sure it's not just what we call 'greenwashing,' that there are actual, tangible results' on the environmental side and on the companies' ledgers, Anderson said.

*A Field Guide to the Families and Genera of
   Woody Plants of Northwest South
   America*
Hotspots
Langoué: A Treasure in Gabon
Megadiversity
Mikiaka Manantena: A Cry of Hope
Odzala
Redesigning the Landscape
Return to Tambopata
Say NO to Bushmeat
The Strategic Management Approach
Treasures Without Borders
Voices of the Pantanal
Wilderness: Earth's Last Wild Places
Wilderness
Wildlife Spectacles
Yepi (Help)
Also publishes policy papers and briefs and
project profiles.

CONFERENCES
None

"The center's dozen employees will work as a division of CI. They are governed by an executive board of heavy hitters—including the head of BP and the executive director of the Natural Resources Defense Council—and will operate independently from the environmental group and Ford."

(*The Washington Post,* July 3, 2001)

Consumer Alert

Established in 1977

DIRECTOR

Frances B. Smith, executive director. Before joining Consumer Alert in 1994, Smith was a senior executive with a financial services trade group, founder of a financial education foundation, and producer of two documentary videos. Smith also was the founder of an award-winning academic journal, the *Journal of Retail Banking.*

BOARD OF DIRECTORS

William C. MacLeod, chair, Collier Shannon, Scott, Washington, DC

Barbara Keating-Edh, founder and president Ex-Officio, Modesto, CA

Carol G. Dawson, Morattico, VA

Terry Neese, Women Impacting Public Policy, Oklahoma City, OK

Roger Meiners, University of Texas at Arlington, Arlington, TX

Frances B. Smith, executive director, Consumer Alert, Washington, DC

SCOPE

Members: 2,000 individuals
Branches/chapters: None
Affiliates: International Consumers for Civil Society, founded by Consumer Alert, a coalition of promarket nonprofits located in nine different countries; National Consumer Coalition, founded by Consumer Alert, which is a coalition of more than 27 public policy organizations with a combined membership of more than 3.9 million

STAFF

4 total—3 full-time professional; 1 full-time support; plus 1 part-time professional; 1–3 interns

TAX STATUS

501(c)(3)

FINANCES

Revenue: 2001—$277,147

FUNDING SOURCES

Foundations, 40%; corporations, 30%; individuals and membership dues, 20%; publications, 5%; royalties and other, 5%

PAC

None

EMPLOYMENT

Information unavailable

INTERNSHIPS

Information unavailable

CONTACT INFORMATION

1001 Connecticut Avenue, NW, Suite 1128, Washington, DC 20036
Phone: (202) 467-5809 • *Fax:* (202) 467-5814
General E-mail: consumer@consumeralert.org •
Web site: www.consumeralert.org

Communications Director: Information unavailable
Human Resources Director: Information unavailable

PURPOSE: "To educate policy makers, media, and the public about the value of consumer choice, competition, and sound science in advancing consumers' interests."

CURRENT CONCERNS: Agriculture subsidies • Benefits of new technology on food production and food safety • Biotechnology • Environmental issues • Federal fuel economy standards (CAFE) • International trade • Privacy on the Internet • Regulatory reform • Risk assessment • Taxation

METHOD OF OPERATION: Advertisements • Awards program • Coalition forming • Conferences/seminars • Congressional testimony • Internet • Internships • Legislative/regulatory monitoring (federal) • Litigation • Media outreach • Participate in regulatory proceedings (federal and state) • Research

Effectiveness and Political Orientation

"People in this country consider themselves fairly knowledgeable about food and food issues, but there are still are lot of contradictions and fads in the American diet," said Frances Smith, executive director of the Washington, DC-based anti-regulatory group Consumer Alert. "We're used to conventionally grown food that gives us a wide variety of inexpensive food, and I don't think people will easily give that up, despite these scares."

(The San Francisco Chronicle, January 4, 2004)

"Consumer Alert reacted today to the White House's National Energy Policy with a mix of applause and caution. Consumers can only benefit from expanded energy supplies and their attendant lower prices after a decade of energy-suppression policies. But mandatory conservation measures in the plan could harm consumers with higher prices.

" 'After years of anti-energy policies, it's good to see a serious effort to open up the marketplace and allow consumers the opportunity to buy abundant, affordable energy,' said Executive Director Frances Smith. 'New technologies allow for cleaner and safer oil and gas exploration over greater areas with greater yields—and there's no reason why consumers shouldn't benefit from that.'

NEWSLETTERS
Commonsense Consumer (monthly)
Consumer Comments (bimonthly)
CPSC Monitor (monthly)
On the Plate (monthly)

PUBLICATIONS
Produces monographs and issues briefs. Has a monthly column published in *Consumers' Research*.

CONFERENCES
Various topical seminars. Also participates as NGO at international meetings.

"Consumer Alert also applauded the Administration's continued resistance to price controls on electricity, which create shortages (like rolling blackouts) and discourage investment in new power generation, exacerbating the problem over the long term."

(The Washington Post, October 20, 2001)

Consumer Federation of America

Established in 1968

DIRECTOR
Stephen Brobeck, executive director. Brobeck has served as executive director since 1980. From 1976 to 1979 he was a board member and vice president. During the 1970s, Brobeck held the position of assistant professor of American Studies at Case Western Reserve University. Since then, he has served as a visiting associate professor of consumer economics at Cornell University and as an adjunct associate professor of consumer economics at the University of Maryland. Brobeck graduated from Wheaton College with high honors and earned a Ph.D. in American Studies from the University of Pennsylvania. From 1990 to 1996, he served as a director of the Federal Reserve Bank of Richmond.

BOARD OF DIRECTORS
Information unavailable

SCOPE
Members: 300 consumer organizations including: cooperatives, credit unions, unions, national consumer organizations, state and local consumer organizations, public power associations, rural electric cooperatives.
Branches/chapters: Information unavailable
Affiliates: Information unavailable

STAFF
27 total—14 full-time professional; 4 full-time support; 9 part-time professional; plus 2 interns

TAX STATUS
501(c)(3)

FINANCES
Budget: 2004—$4.0 million; 2003—$4.0 million

FUNDING SOURCES
Foundation grants, 30%; corporate donations, 25%; government contracts, 17%; publications, 1%; membership dues, 4%; conferences, 12%; special events/projects, 3%; other sources: 9% (awards, interest, honoraria)

PAC
None

EMPLOYMENT
Job openings are posted at www.monstertrak .monster.com. This organization offers positions in public policy. Applicants should send resumes and other materials for employment to Betty Leppin, director of administration, 1424 16th Street, NW, Suite 604, Washington, DC 20036. Phone: (202) 387-6121. Fax: (202) 265-7989. E-mail: bleppin@consumerfed.org.

CONTACT INFORMATION
1424 16th Street, NW, Suite 604, Washington, DC 20036
Phone: (202) 387-6121 • *Fax:* (202) 265-7989
General E-mail: cfa@consumerfed.org • *Web site:* www.consumerfed.org

Communications Director: Jack Gillis, public affairs director
(202) 737-0766 • jack@jagillis.com
Human Resources Director: Betty Leppin, director of administration
(202) 387-6121 • bleppin@consumerfed.org

PURPOSE: The Consumer Federation of America is a nonprofit association of 300 consumer groups that was established in 1968 to "advance pro-consumer policy on a variety of issues before Congress, regulatory agencies, and the courts; to disseminate information on consumer issues to the public and the media, as well as to policymakers and other public interest advocates; and to provide support to national, state, and local organizations committed to the goals of consumer advocacy and education."

CURRENT CONCERNS: Banking/financial services • Consumer cooperatives/public power • Electricity/gas deregulation • Firearms • Food safety • Insurance • Investor protection • Mortgage lending/housing • Product safety • Structure and ownership of media and telecommunications industry

METHOD OF OPERATION: Coalition forming • Conferences/seminars • Congressional testimony • Educational foundation • Grassroots organizing • Information clearinghouse • Internships • Legislative/regulatory monitoring (federal) • Legislative/regulatory monitoring (state) • Lobbying (federal and state) • Lobbying (grassroots) • Media Outreach • Participation in regulatory proceedings (federal) • Participation in regulatory proceedings (state) • Research • Web site

SPECIFIC PROGRAMS/INITIATIVES: America Saves (nationwide campaign in which a broad coalition of nonprofit, corporate, and government groups helps individuals and families save and build wealth) • SafeChild.net (the most comprehensive child safety site on the Internet) • Buy Energy Efficient Web site provides information on buying energy efficient products for the home • Radon Fix-It Program provides advice to consumers on lowering radon levels in homes • Regulateguns.org provides information to advocates, policy makers, and press about a national campaign to regulate guns as consumer products

Effectiveness and Political Orientation

"The Consumer Federation of America and allied consumer groups around the country sharply criticized Ernie Csiszar, the president of the national association of insurance regulators yesterday, accusing him of paving the way for a weakening of protections for insurance customers.

INTERNSHIPS

This organization offers internship opportunities in fields such as affordable housing, financial services, food safety, product safety, America Saves, and child safety. Interns are paid a small stipend. Internships are available in all seasons; there are no application deadlines, and hours are not specified. Eligibility requirements include possessing strong research and writing skills and the ability to work independently. Graduate students interested in public policy, health policy, and law are encouraged to apply. Positions can be designed for course credit.

Interested applicants should contact Susan Peschin, firearms project director, 1424 16th Street, NW, Suite 604, Washington, DC 20036. Phone: (202) 387-6121. Fax: (202) 265-7989. E-mail: speschin@consumerfed.org.

NEWSLETTERS

CFA News (6 times per year)
American Saver (4 times per year)

PUBLICATIONS

The following is a sample list of publications:
A Buyer's Guide to Insurance
Buying A Home: What Buyers and Sellers Need to Know About Real Estate Agents
Clean Cars, Clean Air: A Consumer Guide to Auto Emission Inspection and Maintenance Programs
Congress Online: Assessing and Improving Capitol Hill Web Sites
Congressional Intern Handbook
Developing Job Descriptions
Frontline Management: A Guide for Congressional District/State Offices
Hidden Hazards Number One
Home Play Equipment: Safety Tips for Buying and Using
Households with Low Income: Wealth and Financial Behaviors
How Healthy Is the Air in Your Home? A Room by Room Checklist
How Safe Is Your Local Playground? A Parent's Checklist
Keeping Secrets About You . . . On the Internet!: A Kid's Guide to Internet Privacy
Know Your Score: Think Your Grade Point Average Is Your Only Score That Matters?
Lowering Radon Levels: Help for Consumers
Managing Your Debts: How to Regain Financial Health
Setting Course: A Congressional Management Guide
Spring Break in the U.S. Oil Industry: Price Spikes, Excess Profits and Excuses
Working in Congress: The Staff Perspective

CONFERENCES

Consumer Assembly, Annual Conference, Washington, DC
National Food Policy Conference, annual, Washington, DC
Financial Services Conference, annual, Washington, DC

"In a letter to chief insurance regulators in the 50 states and the District of Columbia, the consumer groups expressed 'grave concern about damage to insurance regulation being done' by Mr. Csiszar, who is also the director of insurance in South Carolina.

"Mr. Csiszar, who became president of the National Association of Insurance Commissioners late last year, was quoted in a statement issued from the association's headquarters in Kansas City, Mo., as saying that the comments by the consumer groups were inaccurate. . . .

"The consumer groups said that Mr. Csiszar was using his position to further his views rather than those of the association and suggested that he consider resigning. They said he had abandoned some of the association's regulatory projects and did not appear to fully support state regulation of insurance. The association, whose members are state officials, propose insurance laws that are generally adopted by state legislatures.

"'I have absolutely not abandoned state regulation nor any N.A.I.C. established policies,' Mr. Csiszar said in his statement. He did not respond to the suggestion that he resign.

"In their letter, the consumer groups wrote that, 'As you know, Csiszar favors broad deregulation of many aspects of insurance.'

"'His views,' the groups added, 'are on the extreme of the spectrum of views' and, if put in place, could hurt consumers and deprive state regulators of the 'authority to help consumers.'

"The clash between the consumer groups and Mr. Csiszar comes as debate is intensifying over the effectiveness of state regulation of insurance. . . ."
(*The New York Times,* March 4, 2004)

"It's a common come-on: You buy a car and the dealer offers to handle the financing. But is there a catch?

"One in 4 Americans who finances a new or used car through a dealership ends up paying a higher interest rate than their credit record calls for, according to the Consumer Federation of America (CFA). Those most frequently tagged with the markups: Hispanics and African-Americans, the group says.

"That charge—fiercely contested by auto dealers and finance companies—highlights a little-known area of the car-purchase process. When consumers finance their purchase through a dealer, the dealer typically makes additional money.

"'These hidden finance kickbacks typically add at least $1,000 to the cost of an auto loan, and are costing consumers as much as $1 billion annually,' says Steve Browbeck, CFA executive director. 'We consider it an unfair practice. And I think any consumer would be against this.'"
(*Christian Science Monitor,* February 2, 2004)

"Comcast inadvertently swatted a hornets' nest when it recently raised high-speed Internet rates by about 33% for some customers it picked up from its merger with AT&T Broadband.

"The Consumers Union and the Consumer Federation of America have asked the Justice Department and Federal Trade Commission to investigate whether Comcast violated antitrust laws by raising Internet fees only for customers who don't also subscribe to cable TV. They'll pay about $57 per month, $14 more than subscribers who also order TV service. . . ."
(*USA Today,* April 2, 2003)

"How long should a consumer recall hot line remain hot?

"Consumer Federation of America officials said yesterday that federal safety regulators should require numbers for recalled children's products to operate indefinitely. The group reached that conclusion after finding that nearly one out of five recall hot lines created over the past decade was inoperative.

"The federation's general counsel, Mary Ellen Fise, said the large number of unused hot-line numbers is 'genuinely disturbing' and represents a 'startling disconnect' in the recall process. She said the problems could be particularly acute with children's products, where the potential risks are high and the products tend to remain in use long after they are made, recycled to other families or sold in yard sales.

"Makers of children's products countered that keeping a permanent hot line might be an inefficient use of resources, particularly if the product had been recalled several years before.

"Frederick Locker, general counsel for the Juvenile Products Manufacturers Association, said, 'I don't think it's necessarily effective to keep an exclusive number set up for a company for people to contact on a particular recall 10 to 15 to 20 years later.' With the growth of the Internet, he said, it's easier than ever to get recall information and get in touch with companies.

"The consumer federation estimates that only 18 percent of recalled products are actually repaired or returned. To improve that rate, the group decided to create a Web site, SafeChild.net, to help alert parents about recalled products. . . ."

(*The Washington Post,* June 22, 2001)

"A consumer group that blames credit card marketing tactics for pushing many Americans over their heads in debt says the industry greatly increased mail solicitations and lines of credit last year, even as it sought legislation to make it harder for consumers to wipe out debt through bankruptcy.

"Credit card issuers are brazenly lobbying for new bankruptcy restrictions at the same time their aggressive marketing and lending practices are pushing many families closer to the financial brink," Consumer Federation of America lobbyist Travis Plunkett said at a news conference yesterday. . . .

"The nonprofit consumer group released a report showing that in addition to shipping an estimated 3.3 billion mail offers last year, up from 2.87 billion in 1999, the credit card industry expanded available credit beyond consumer demand.

"Lines of credit card debt increased 15 percent, to $2.43 trillion, in the first nine months of 2000, the latest numbers available, compared with $2.11 trillion for all of 1999, according to the report. Outstanding consumer debt for the same period of 2000 grew to $531 billion, a 4 percent increase over all of 1999.

"The group says that aggressive sales tactics, coupled with a decline in consumer bankruptcies and uncollected debt last year, were key reasons credit card profits have soared nearly 50 percent in two years and are at a five-year high. . . .

"The Consumer Federation and other consumer groups that oppose the bill say it is too hard on debtors who face financial hardship because of divorce, illness or job loss."

(*The Washington Post,* February 28, 2001)

Consumers International

Established in 1960

DIRECTOR

Julian Edwards, director general. "Edwards has long acted as a leading figure in the United Kingdom and international consumer movement."

BOARD OF DIRECTORS

Executive members

Marilena Lazzarini, president; Instituto Brasileiro de Defesa do Consumidor, Sao-Paulo, Brazil

Felix Cohen, vice president; Consumentenbond, The Hague, Netherlands

Breda Kutin, treasurer; ZPS- Slovene Consumers Association, Ljubljana, Slovenia

Samuel Ochieng, honorary secretary; Consumer Information Network, Nairobi, Kenya

Pamela Chan; Hong Kong Consumers Council, Hong Kong SAR, China

Jim Guest; Consumers Union of United States Inc., New York, NY

Kim Lavely; Consumers' Association (CA), London, England

Indrani Thuraisingham; Federation of Malaysian Consumer Association, Selangor Darul Ehsan, Malaysia

Nonexecutive members

Saree Aongsonwang, Foundation for Consumers, Bangkok, Thailand

Rosemary Chikarakara, Consumer Council of Zimbabwe, Harare, Zimbabwe

Salimata Diarra Coulibaly, Association des Consommateurs du Mali, Bamako, Mali

Armand de Wasch, Association des Consommateurs/Verbruikersunie Test Achats, Brussels, Belgium

Benedicte Federspiel, Forbrugerrådet, Copenhagen, Denmark

Armando Flores, Centro para la Defensa del Consumidor, San Salvador, El Salvador

Sri Ram Khanna, Voluntary Organisation in the Interest of Consumer Education, New Delhi, India

Kim Jai Ok, Citizens' Alliance for Consumer Protection Korea, Seoul, Republic of Korea

Maria Rodriguez, Confederación de Consumidores y Usuarios, Madrid, Spain

Maria Jose Troya, Tribuna Ecuatoriana de Consumidores y Usuarios, Quito, Ecuador

Dimitry Yanin, KonfOP-Inter-Republican Confederation of Consumer Societies, Moscow, Russia

SCOPE

Members: 250 organizations in 115 countries
Branches/chapters: Regional offices in Santiago, Chile; Kuala Lumpur, Malaysia; Harare, Zimbabwe
Affiliates: None

CONTACT INFORMATION

24 Highbury Crescent, London, N5 1RX, United Kingdom
Phone: 44-207-226-6663 • *Fax:* 44-207-354-0607
General E-mail: consint@consint.org •
Web site: www.consumersinternational.org

Communications Director: Information unavailable
Human Resources Director: Information unavailable

PURPOSE: "To promote consumer policy internationally and assist with institution building."

CURRENT CONCERNS: Electric commerce • Environment • Food • Health • Public utilities • Technical standards • Trade and foreign direct investment

METHOD OF OPERATION: Coalition forming • Conferences/seminars • International activities • Internet (Web site) • Legislative/regulatory monitoring (international) • Library/information clearinghouse (open to public) • Lobbying (regional and international) • Media outreach • Research • Training and technical assistance

Effectiveness and Political Orientation

"The World Health Organisation yesterday agreed to allow further revision of its plans to combat obesity worldwide after pressure from the U.S.

"Health officials predicted yesterday there would be a huge battle over the draft in the coming weeks but noted that the final version would be left to the WHO secretariat, which will issue it in mid-March. The strategy will be submitted to the WHO's annual assembly for endorsement in May. . . .

"Health campaigners have accused the U.S. of trying to sabotage WHO efforts to combat obesity under the influence of the food industry, especially the powerful sugar lobby. . . .

"Though the U.S. yesterday received support in the 32-member executive board from some developing countries, including sugar producers such as Mauritius, the WHO position was strongly backed by European governments, Canada, South Africa and New Zealand.

"The 18-page 'global strategy on diet, physical activity and health' aims to guide member states in drawing up national plans to curb an explosion of diseases such as heart disease, diabetes and cancer. These now account for about 60 per cent of deaths worldwide, a figure that is expected to rise to 73 per cent by 2020.

"Separately, a drafting group will meet today to consider U.S. and other proposed changes to the draft resolution for the May assembly. The U.S. amendments again emphasise individual responsibility and the need to involve 'all concerned stakeholders' including the food industry.

"Activist groups urged the WHO to stand firm against any watering down of the strategy and the resolution, saying the emphasis on personal responsi-

STAFF
70 total

TAX STATUS
Tax-exempt

FINANCES
Information unavailable

FUNDING SOURCES
membership fees, about 35%; and project grants, about 65%

PAC
None

EMPLOYMENT
Information unavailable

INTERNSHIPS
Consumers International offers unpaid internships for periods of six weeks up to a year at a time. Interns usually provide support for projects and carry out research on a range of policy issues such as trade, food, health, environment, and e-commerce as well as capacity building and fundraising. Applicants should send a resume and a letter of application to the appropriate office explaining what they would like to do during their internship and the dates they are available. Applicants can use mail, fax, or e-mail.

NEWSLETTERS
African Consumer
Asia Pacific Consumer

PUBLICATIONS
The Consumer Guide to Competition: A Practical Handbook
Cultivating a Crisis: The Global Impact of the Common Agricultural Policy
Genetically Modified Crops: A Resource Guide for the Asia Pacific
GM Foods: The Facts and the Fiction
Corporate Citizenship in the Global Market: Accountability and the Consumer Perspective

CONFERENCES
Triennial World Congress

bility made no sense in an environment where the food industry spends billions of dollars on marketing and advertising, much of it aimed at children.

" 'The (U.S.) policy emphasising individual responsibility has been tried and has failed,' Consumers International said. 'Is it right to export this failed policy to the rest of the world?' "

(*Financial Times* [London, England], January 21 2004)

"Once again, Europe and the U.S. are at loggerheads. This time, they're fighting over food, not foreign policy. On July 2, the European Parliament passed legislation calling for detailed labeling of genetically modified (GM) food products.

"You'd think Washington would be pleased. After all, the new laws will pave the way for American GM products to be sold within the European Union, ending a five-year ban. . . .

"Certainly, U.S. companies have a lot riding on European acceptance of GM products. Monsanto and DuPont alone have invested billions in bio-engineered seed technology and are determined not to be shut out of Europe, one of the world's biggest agricultural markets. American farmers are losing out, too. The U.S. produces two-thirds of the world's GM crops. U.S. soy exports to the EU have declined by half over the past five years, to $1.6 billion, reflecting that 80% of the U.S. soybean harvest is now GM. U.S. agribusiness believes the EU's new rules will only make a bad situation worse by sending Europeans fleeing from anything with a GM label. Might as well slap a skull and crossbones sign on boxes of American cereal.

"But why shouldn't European consumers have a right to know exactly what they are eating? By next year, 35 countries covering half of the world's population, including China, Japan, India, and Australia, will require mandatory government safety assessments before GM products are allowed into the market. 'The main reason big companies are against labeling is because they realize that there is a huge potential that consumers may then choose not to buy GM products,' says Nita Pillai, senior coordinator of the global food program at Consumers International. . . ."

(*Business Week,* July 21, 2003)

"As the federation of consumer organisations in 115 countries, Consumers International has long lobbied for reductions in trade barriers. Agriculture in the developing world directly supports hundreds of millions of people. Expanding their markets would contribute hugely to economic development and poverty reduction."

(*The Guardian,* June 25, 2003)

"President George W. Bush yesterday stepped up the pressure on the European Union to overturn its ban on genetically modified organisms.

"Speaking at the annual conference of the Biotechnology Industry Organisation (Bio) in Washington, Mr Bush said European governments had blocked the import of biotechnology crops 'based on unfounded and unscientific fears.'

"As a result, many African nations were afraid to use GM crops for fear that they would not get access to European markets. 'For the sake of a continent threatened by famine, I urge European nations to end their opposition to biotechnology,' he added. . . .

"Last year, several southern African countries rejected GM food aid from the US despite suffering severe food crises. . . .

"However, speaking at a conference in Washington last week, Amadou Kanoute, regional director of the African office of Consumers International, said the spread of US biotechnology crops would put small-scale African farmers at a disadvantage."

(*Financial Times* [London, England], June 24, 2003)

Consumers Union of the United States, Inc.

Established in 1936

DIRECTOR
James A. Guest, president.

BOARD OF DIRECTORS
James A. Guest, president
Paul Hoffman, director
David Kesster, director
Eileen Hemphill, director
Conrad Harris, chief financial officer
Joel J. Nobel, director
Joan L. Chambers, director
Clarence M. Ditlow, treasurer
Bumele Venable Powell, secretary
Christine A. Bjorklund, director
Edward Skloot, director
William F. Baker, director
Bamard E. Brooks, director
Robert Adler, director
Karen Heln, director
Jean Ann Fox, vice president (board)
Joan B. Claybrook, director
Sharon L. Nelson, president (board)
Barbara S. Friedman, director
Norman I. Silber, director
Joel L. Gunn, executive vice president

SCOPE
Members: 4.5 million *Consumer Reports*
    subscribers (*Consumer Reports* subscribers
    can become members by voting in the
    annual election for CU's board of directors)
Branches/chapters: Offices in Austin, TX; San
    Francisco, CA; and Washington, DC
Affiliates: None

STAFF
494 total—including Auto Test Center and
advocacy offices

TAX STATUS
501(c)(3)

FINANCES
Revenue: 2003—$156.66 million;
2002—$151.42 million

FUNDING SOURCES
Publications, 92%; individuals, 7%; foundation
grants, 1%

PAC
None

EMPLOYMENT
Information about job opportunities is
available on its Web site: www.
consumersunion.org/aboutcu/jobs.html

INTERNSHIPS
Information unavailable

CONTACT INFORMATION
101 Truman Avenue, Yonkers, NY 10703
Phone: (914) 378-2000 • *Fax:* (914) 378-2905
Web site: www.consumersunion.org

Communications Director: Information unavailable
Human Resources Director: Information unavailable

PURPOSE: "Advances the interests of consumers by providing information and advice about products and services and about issues affecting their welfare, and by advocating a consumer point of view."

CURRENT CONCERNS: Bank fees • Chemical residues • Electronic banking • Electronic deregulation • Genetically engineered food • Health insurance reform • Identity theft • Long-term and managed health care • Product liability • Student loan conversions

METHOD OF OPERATION: Coalition forming • Conferences/seminars • Congressional testimony • Electronic publishing • Films/video/audiotapes • International activities • Internet (Web sites: www.ConsumerReports.org • www.consumersunion.org • www.zillions.org) • Internships • Legislative/regulatory monitoring (federal and state) • Litigation • Lobbying (federal and state) • Media outreach ("From *Consumer Reports*" newspaper column) • Participation in regulatory proceedings (federal and state) • Participation in regulatory proceedings (federal and state) • Polling • Product merchandising • Product testing/reporting • Publishing • Research • Speakers program • Telecommunications services (Consumer Reports Books: (800) 272-0722, Consumer Reports by Request: (800) 896-7788, New Car Price Service: (303) 745-1700, Used Car Price Service: (900) 446-0500) • Television and radio production ("Report to Consumers" daily radio feature, Consumer Reports TV News service to local television)

Effectiveness and Political Orientation

"The blockbuster merger of Cingular Wireless and AT&T Wireless—and the consolidation of the wireless industry to five major competitors from six—may not lead to higher consumer prices for mobile phone service anytime soon, according to industry analysts. And the merger could spur better quality of service, they said.

"Nonetheless, consumer groups plan to challenge the $41 billion merger on the grounds that it could reduce competition in the South and Southwest United States, where BellSouth and SBC, Cingular's parents, are dominant. Consumers Union, an advocacy group, said it thought the acquisition of AT&T Wireless and its 22 million customers could give those two telephone giants excessive power in their local markets.

"SBC and Bell South are 'buying up the most likely competition against their own telephone monopoly,' said Gene Kimmelman, the policy director for Consumers Union, who added that the group intends to lobby the Federal Communications Commission and the Department of Justice to reject the deal as currently constructed. 'This needs to be restricted or rejected to continue to provide lower prices and better service to both wireless and wireline consumers,' Mr. Kimmelman said. . . .

"Some consumer advocates are not convinced that Cingular's purchase of AT&T Wireless would lead to better service. A survey published this month in Consumer Reports magazine found that both Cingular and AT&T Wireless fared less well than the competition in most of a dozen markets where customers were asked to rate their mobile phone provider.

" 'Two companies that have never been good at customer service are merging,' said David Heim, deputy director for special sections at Consumer Reports, which is published by Consumers Union. 'I'm not optimistic that their service will improve.' "

(*The New York Times,* February 18, 2004)

"Of all of the new automotive technologies, none presents a more complex set of benefits and risks than the 'black box' sensors that have already been placed in millions of cars nationwide. The latest models capture the last few seconds of data—like vehicle speed, seatbelt use and whether the driver applied the brakes—before a collision.

"Such detailed reporting of accidents raises privacy concerns, said experts at Consumers Union, which has filed comments with the federal government warning about possible violations of privacy. Sally Greenberg, senior product safety counsel at Consumers Union, said her group recognized the potential safety benefits of the reporting but wanted the government to 'proceed with caution.'

"People's cars have already started turning their owners in. Scott E. Knight, a California man, was convicted last year for the killing of a Merced, Calif., resident in a March 2001 hit-and-run accident; police tracked him down because the OnStar system in his Chevy Tahoe alerted OnStar when the airbag was set off. . . ."

(*The New York Times,* December 29, 2003)

"In a long-awaited victory for cellphone users, a federal appeals court ruling Friday paved the way for consumers to keep their telephone numbers when they change phone companies. While Congress could still stall or kill the move, further legal action is deemed unlikely and the ruling deals a huge blow to the already slowing wireless-telecommunications industry.

" 'Today's decision is an enormous victory for consumers, who will be better able to shop around on price and quality of service rather than being stuck with a carrier because you can't afford to lose your number,' said Chris Murray, legislative counsel for Consumers Union, a consumer-advocacy group in Washington, D.C."

(*The Wall Street Journal,* June 9, 2003)

"Comcast inadvertently swatted a hornets' nest when it recently raised high-speed Internet rates by about 33% for some customers it picked up from its merger with AT&T Broadband.

"The Consumers Union and the Consumer Federation of America have asked the Justice Department and Federal Trade Commission to investigate whether Comcast violated antitrust laws by raising Internet fees only for customers who don't also subscribe to cable TV. They'll pay about $57 per month, $14 more than subscribers who also order TV service.

" 'My fear is that this is the first salvo in an effort to drive satellite broadcasting out of business in the urban and suburban markets,' says Consumers Union's Gene Kimmelman."

(*USA Today,* April 2, 2003)

"It seemed like Washington at its backroom-dealing worst. With no debate, congressional conferees in November quietly inserted language into the Homeland Security Act that prevents parents from suing Eli Lilly & Co. and other makers of the mercury-containing preservative, thimerosal—an ingredient once used in infant vaccines that some believe is responsible for mushrooming rates of autism in young children. Parents and some consumer advocates have been complaining about the provisions ever since. 'The legislation gives Lilly a get-out-of-court-free card,' says Janell M. Duncan, legislative counsel at Consumers Union."

(*Business Week,* January 13, 2003)

Co-op America

Established in 1982

DIRECTOR

Alisa Gravitz, executive director. For more than 15 years, Gravitz has helped pioneer and lead the national agenda to create a socially and environmentally responsible economy. Gravitz co-authored Co-op America's acclaimed guide to social investing and helped launch Businesses for Social Responsibility, Coalition for Environmentally Responsible Economies (CERES), and the Social Investment Forum, a national nonprofit investment industry association. She is currently vice president of the Social Investment Forum. She travels across the U.S. speaking on socially responsible investing issues and appears regularly on cable and radio shows and in print. Gravitz also serves on the boards of directors of the Coalition for Environmentally Responsible Economies (CERES), the Social Venture Network, the Positive Futures Network, and the Anacostia Watershed Society. She is the 1995 recipient of the Socially Responsible Investing Service. Prior to Co-op America, Gravitz worked on the development of energy efficient technology for the Carter administration. Gravitz earned her B.A. in economics and environmental science from Brandeis University and an M.B.A. from Harvard University.

BOARD OF DIRECTORS

Diane Keefe, president
Elizabeth Glenshaw, vice-president
Denise Hamler, secretary-treasurer
Alisa Gravitz, executive director

SCOPE

Members: 50,000 individual members 2,500 business members
Branches/chapters: Chapters in all 50 states
Affiliates: Concord Coalition Citizens' Council, a 501(c)(4) organization

STAFF

37 total—35 full-time; 2 part-time; plus 3 interns

TAX STATUS

501(c)(3)

FINANCES

Revenue: 2001—$3.53 million; 2000—$3.18 million

FUNDING SOURCES

Individual contributions, 69%; foundation grants, 17.1%; corporate donations, 13.9%

PAC

None

CONTACT INFORMATION

1612 K Street, NW, Suite 600, Washington, DC 20006
Phone: (202) 872-5307 • *Fax:* (202) 331-8166
General E-mail: info@coopamerica.org • *Web site:* www.coopamerica.org

Communications Director: Information unavailable
Human Resources Director: Information unavailable

PURPOSE: Co-op America's mission is to harness economic power—the strength of consumers, businesses and the marketplace—to create a socially just and environmentally sustainable society.

CURRENT CONCERNS: Fair trade coffee • Recycled paper for magazines • Responsible shopper • Sweatshops • Shareholder action • Community investing • Socially responsible investing

METHOD OF OPERATION: Coalition forming • Conferences/seminars • Direct action • Grassroots organizing • Internet (e-mail alerts and Web site) • Internships • Media outreach • Research • Speakers program

Effectiveness and Political Orientation

"Let us save the planet, Co-op lobbyists say. And stop sending jobs over the border, where workers are paid a frightful fraction of what they would earn in the United States. And if jobs must be exported, let us ensure a fair wage for every employee everywhere.

" 'We approach it from the perspective that consumers and businesses have an obligation to use their economic clout to create a sustainable environment and to be committed to fair-trade practices,' [Chris] O'Brien [associate director of Co-op America] said. 'Workers deserve a job that gives them an empowered lifestyle and a living wage.' "

(*Newsday,* [New York], November 18, 2003)

"The founders of Shorebank Pacific started the bank to help local businesses improve their social and environmental practices. But the bank's greatest success has come from providing a safe place for socially driven investors to put their money. . . .

"Deposits are soaring as people across the nation find the bank a place to save money while helping the environment. . . .

" 'Shorebank Pacific is one of 10 companies across the country that we have featured in our media events, and our Web site as a leader in environmental lending,' said Todd Larsen, media director for Co-op America, a Washington, DC, nonprofit that helps investors find companies with good social and environmental practices. 'They have a very interesting portfolio of borrowers that are really making environmental progress,' Larsen said. . . ."

(*The Oregonian* [Portland], August 7, 2003)

EMPLOYMENT

Employment opportunities are listed on the Web site: www.coopamerica.org/positions/index.cfm.

INTERNSHIPS

Offers paid internships of various lengths to college students, college graduates, and graduate students. See Web site for detailed information: http://www.coopamerica.org/positions/index.cfm. Amanda Johnson is the intern coordinator.

NEWSLETTERS

Co-op America Quarterly (quarterly)
Real Money (bimonthly)

PUBLICATIONS

National Green Pages (annually)
Connections (bimonthly)
Financial Planning Handbook for Responsible Investors

CONFERENCES

National Green Festival in San Francisco, CA; Washington, DC; Austin, TX (annually)
Green Business Conference in San Francisco (annually)

"Investors vote with their pocketbooks, and many are voting for better ethical, environmental, and financial behavior by corporations.

"While domestic equity mutual funds posted outflows of more than $27 billion during 2002, socially responsible investing (SRI) mutual funds benefited from net inflows of more than $1.5 billion, according to Lipper Inc. And the trend continues during the first months of 2003.

" 'Due to the wave of recent corporate scandals, we're seeing more and more investors concerned about the companies in which they invest,' says Alisa Gravitz, executive director of Co-op America, a nonprofit investor-education organization. . . ."

(*Christian Science Monitor,* April 7, 2003)

". . .Though new for some this season, shopping with a conscience was already a growing trend. Internet shopping has been getting greener for several years, and Earth-friendly products show up in mainstream markets as well as in pounds of catalogs. It doesn't mean just saving a tree here and there; it can have a profound effect on a worker in an impoverished nation.

"Feeling good can mean seeking out fairly traded goods from vendors committed to providing fair wages and safe and healthy employment to economically disadvantaged artisans and farmers around the world.

" 'At Co-op America, we try to show consumers how their economic power can be better used to promote social environmental justice and sustainability,' said Todd Larsen, managing director of the company that is best known for its Green Pages, a listing of 2,500 companies carefully selected for their high standards on social issues.

"Larsen agrees that many consumers want to do the right thing when it comes to giving. . . ."

(*The Atlanta Journal-Constitution,* November 22, 2001)

CorpWatch

Established in 1999

DIRECTOR

The organization is guided by a five-member Executive Committee.

ADVISORY BOARD OF DIRECTORS

Executive Committee

China Brotsky; director, Special Projects, Tides Foundation and Tides Center.

Antonio Diaz; project director, PODER (People Organizing to Demand Environmental Rights)

Joshua Karliner; founder and executive director from 1996–2002

Mele Lau Smith; San Francisco Tobacco Free Project

Other Board Members

Nikki Fortunato Bas, Sweatshop Watch

Andre Carothers, journalist

John Cavanagh, Institute for Policy Studies

Anna Couey, DataCenter

Michael Dorsey, Sierra Club National Board

Jeanne Gauna, South West Organizing Project—*In memoriam*

Tom Goldtooth, Indigenous Environmental Network

Richard Grossman, Program on Corporations, Law and Democracy

Nicholas Hildyard, Corner House, England

Lisa Hoyos, South Bay AFL-CIO Central Labor Council

Allan Hunt-Badiner, Rainforest Action Network

Martin Khor, Third World Network, Malaysia

Yoichi Kuroda, Institute for Global Environmental Strategies, Japan

Sara Larrain, Chilean National Environmental Network, Chile

Joshua Mailman, Social Venture Network

Richard Moore, Southwest Network for Environmental and Economic Justice

Medha Patkar, National Alliance of People's Movements, India

S. (Bobby) Peek, groundWork, South Africa

Atila Roque, Brazilian Institute for Social and Economic Action, Brazil

Satinath Sarangi, Bhopal Committee for Information and Action, India

Ted Smith, Silicon Valley Toxics Coalition

Michael Stein, Nonprofit Internet Strategist

Francesca Vietor, International Rivers Network

SCOPE

Members: Information unavailable

Branches/chapters: Information unavailable

Affiliates: CorpWatch.org has developed formal "affiliate" relationships with organizations that serve as resource centers for corporate campaigners. Affiliation reflects reciprocal relationships where CW provides activists with access to affiliate organizations and vice versa.

CONTACT INFORMATION

1611 Telegraph Avenue, #702, Oakland, CA 94612

Phone: (510) 271-8080 • *Web site:* www.corpwatch.org

General E-mail: Web form at http://www.corpwatch.org/about/PFB.jsp

Communications Director: Information unavailable

Human Resources Director: Information unavailable

PURPOSE: "CorpWatch counters corporate-led globalization through education, network-building and activism. We work to foster democratic control over corporations by building grassroots globalization a diverse movement for human rights and dignity, labor rights and environmental justice."

CURRENT CONCERNS: Beyond 9-11 • Biotechnology • Corporate globalization • Campaigns • Corporate-free UN • Climate justice initiative • Corporate Japan • Education industry • Enron • Globalization • Grassroots globalization • Human rights • Internet Politics • Military industrial complex • Mining • Money and politics • Oil, gas, and coal • Pesticides • Pharmaceuticals • Prison industry • Sweatshops • Corporate planet • Tobacco • Trade agreements • Utility deregulation • Water wars • World Bank/IMF • WTO

METHOD OF OPERATION: Coalition forming • Conferences/seminars • Grassroots organizing • International activities • Media outreach • Research • Web site

Effectiveness and Political Orientation

". . . .What we ended up with [in the polling of companies on corporate philanthropy] is a snapshot of the biggest players in corporate philanthropy. Their survey responses, taken together with interviews of corporate foundation heads, nonprofit chief executive officers, and academic scholars, reflect the degree to which philanthropy is still an integral component of corporate cultures. . . .

". . . New Orleans' Freeport-McMoRan Copper & Gold Inc.. . . had the highest ratio of cash philanthropy to revenues on our list. There's a reason for that: In the idyllic Indonesian island province of Papua, Freeport operates the mammoth Grasberg mine—an engineering marvel that encompasses the largest gold reserve in the world. The mine also sits directly atop a mountain sacred to the indigenous Amungme tribe, which has inhabited the island for thousands of years. Tensions between Papuans and Freeport grew so fierce in 1996 that Freeport stopped mining operations for several days in reaction to a series of riots. To improve their standing with the people of Papua, Freeport and its local subsidiary vowed to start donating 1% of local annual revenues, to be disbursed by a board composed of local and company officials. That sum

The affiliates are: Corporate Agriculture
Research Project; Corporate Europe
Observatory; DataCenter; Environmental
Research Foundation; IBON Data Bank;
Multinationals Resource Center; Project
Underground; Public Information Network

STAFF
5 total

TAX STATUS
501(c)(3)

FINANCES
Information unavailable

FUNDING SOURCES
Information unavailable

PAC
None

EMPLOYMENT
Employment opportunities are listed on the
Web site as they become available.

INTERNSHIPS
Information unavailable

NEWSLETTERS
None

PUBLICATIONS
*Tangled Up in Blue: Corporate Partnerships at
the United Nations*
Greenhouse Gangsters vs. Climate Justice
Bromide Barons
Setting the Record Straight (documentary)

CONFERENCES
Information unavailable

totaled $14.8 million last year alone. Paired with Freeport's domestic donations, the company's total gifts reached $16.8 million.

"Today, the Amungme have new hospitals, scholarships for local children to study domestically and abroad, new community centers, and clean drinking water. But critics say they also have to live with Freeport's pollution, alleged human-rights abuses, and close relationship with the Indonesian government, whose paramilitaries provide the mine with its security forces. 'What we are talking about is greenwash,' says Pratap Chatterjee, program director of CorpWatch, a watchdog group in Oakland, Calif. 'The company is attempting to improve its image by giving people baubles, trinkets, and beads. It doesn't mean that it is going to change the environmental impact. Pollution can last centuries.' "

(*Business Week,* December 1, 2003)

"It's not that people here have anything against Starbucks. Most of them have tried a latte or Frappuccino. Many of them even enjoyed it.

"But the 2,400 residents of this historic town on Lake Minnetonka are trying to battle what Mayor Lynn Johnson calls 'corporate sameness.' They don't want the big chain stores that have cropped up across America, such as Starbucks, Home Depot and Wal-Mart. . . .

"To make that point, the town hired a Minneapolis advertising agency to craft a campaign for Excelsior's image. The firm, Andrews/Birt, developed advertisements in the form of cheeky letters to Starbucks, Home Depot and the Hard Rock Cafe. The letters bluntly say no thanks to corporate franchises. . . .

"Starbucks remains a bit perplexed by the ads.

" 'I don't know if I understand what they mean,' spokeswoman Lara Wyss says. 'We don't have a store in Excelsior. We weren't looking to put one there.'

"Still, the first-of-a-kind ads resonate with many young adults who might have a skeptical view of corporations in the aftermath of Enron and other business scandals. Some observers call it part of a backlash rooted in the protests at the World Trade Organization meetings in Seattle in December 1999. A concern about corporate globalism—and the idea that bigger is better—has begun to seep into mainstream American towns.

" 'People are beginning to realize, especially in small towns, that while they can pimp themselves for corporate dollars, that's not going to keep the economy going 30 years from now. It's not sustainable,' says Pratap Chatterjee of CorpWatch.org, a group that opposes globalization. 'And it's definitely young people at the forefront of this movement.' "

(*USA Today,* October 1, 2003)

"It is the world's biggest car-maker, boasting a turnover of pounds 120 billion last year. Sales of Vauxhall and Pontiac cars have propelled General Motors to the top of the auto industry.

"So when executives heard a song called 'Pass it Along,' they immediately wanted to use it as the sort of 'youthful and hip' tune that perfectly suited the image their new adverts sought to reinforce.

"But what they didn't know was that the British band in question—Chumbawamba—were lifelong anarchists opposed to big corporations like GM. . . .

"GM thought nothing more after handing over a cheque for pounds 70,000 to the band for the use of the song. But behind the scenes, Chumbawamba were negotiating with anti-corporate activists to see if they would take the fee and put it to use. The band contacted CorpWatch, a US campaign group aimed at 'holding corporations accountable,' to see if it would 'put the money to good anti-capitalist use if we accepted the ad'.

"CorpWatch had no trouble in agreeing. Chumbawamba vocalist Alice Nutter then sent an email 'in solidarity' to IndyMedia, a radical global network, to enquire if it would accept half of the money. 'We're offering this money to you because the work you do and information you supply is invaluable,' she wrote. . . .

" 'We're planning on using some of the money to document some of the social and environmental impacts of General Motors itself,' Joshua Karliner, executive director of CorpWatch, told The Observer

" 'It's known for resisting the kinds of change in production that would assist in reducing climate change, and for helping debunk the science of global warming. If the company knew how its fee was being used, I'd imagine it would make executives squirm in their big comfortable leather chairs.' "

(*The Observer* [London, England], January 27, 2002)

Council for Excellence in Government

Established in 1983

CONTACT INFORMATION

1301 K Street, NW, Suite 450 West, Washington, DC 20005
Phone: (202) 728-0418 • *Fax:* (202) 728-0422
General E-mail: ceg@excelgov.org • *Web site:* www.excelgov.org

Communications Director: Information unavailable
Human Resources Director: Information unavailable

PURPOSE: To improve "the performance of government at all levels and government's place in the lives and esteem of American citizens."

CURRENT CONCERNS: Increased citizen confidence and participation in government and governance, achieved through better understanding of government and its role • Strong public-sector leadership and management, driven by innovation and focused on results

METHOD OF OPERATION: Awards program • Coalition forming • Conferences/ seminars • Information clearinghouse • Internships • Performance ratings • Polling • Professional development services • Speakers program • Training • Web sites

Effectiveness and Political Orientation

" 'There is a tremendous communications gap in the homeland security arena,' said Patricia McGinnis, president and chief executive of the Council for Excellence in Government. 'The people [who government serves] don't know much, if anything, of what is going on.'

"McGinnis said her group is preparing a report this spring on 'homeland security from the citizen's perspective,' drawing findings and recommendations from six other national town hall meetings with Ridge and from national polling. . . ."

(*The Washington Post*, February 24, 2004)

". . . the Council for Excellence in Government, a 20-year-old nonprofit organization dedicated to improving the performance of government."

(*The Atlanta Journal-Constitution*, February 5, 2004)

"Media coverage of the federal government is growing increasingly scarce, and what news there is isn't very uplifting, according to a survey released yesterday by the Council for Excellence in Government.

" 'In terms of news about government, [people] are getting twice as much negative news as positive news,' said Patricia McGinnis, president and chief executive officer of the nonpartisan, nonprofit organization focused on improving government performance. 'I think people are turned off by government. I think they're turned off by the media and they're connected.'

"The study examined almost 30,000 stories from a sample that included the three nightly network newscasts, *The Washington Post*, *The New York*

Lee H. Hamilton; Woodrow Wilson International Center for Scholars
Edwin L. Harper; American Security Group
Gail Harrison; Shandwick Public Affairs
James F. Hinchman; National Research Council
Arthur H. House; Meridian Worldwide
Gwendolyn S. King; Prodium Prose
Susan R. King; Carnegie Corp. of New York
Mel Levine Gibson; Dunn & Crutcher
Robert G. Liberatore; DaimlerChrysler Corp.
Paul C. Light; Brookings Institution
Kenneth Lipper; Lipper & Co. Inc.
Homer E. Moyer Jr.; Miller & Chevalier
Joseph S. Nye Jr.; John F. Kennedy School of Government, Harvard University
Isabel V. Sawhill; The Brookings Institution
Susan C. Schwab; University of Maryland School of Public Affairs
George P. Shultz; Hoover Institution
Les Silverman; McKinsey & Co.
Rodney E. Slater; Patton Boggs, LLP
John P. White; Global Technology Partners, LLC
John C. Whitehead
James Lee Witt; James Lee Witt Associates, LLC

SCOPE
Members: 600 individuals and 30 corporate partners
Branches/chapters: None
Affiliates: None

STAFF
25 total—22 full-time professional; 3 full-time support; plus 4 part-time professional; 6 interns

TAX STATUS
501(c)(3)

FINANCES
Revenue: 2002—$7.425 million

FUNDING SOURCES
Government contracts, 47%; foundation grants, 8%; corporate donations, 6%; conferences, 6%; membership dues, 4%; interest, 5%; corporate/foundation support, 24%

PAC
None

EMPLOYMENT
Information unavailable

INTERNSHIPS
The council's internship program provides undergraduate and graduate students the unique opportunity to contribute to programs that focus on practical public-sector reform at all levels. Internships for the fall, spring, and summer semesters are available on an ongoing basis. Interested candidates should review the various council programs and send a resume, a 2–3 page writing sample, and a cover letter indicating program interest. Applications can also be sent to: Council for Excellence in Government, 1301 K Street, NW, Suite 450 West, Washington, DC 20005.

Times, the *Austin American-Statesman, The Des Moines Register*, the *San Jose Mercury News*, and the *St. Petersburg Times*. The stories were aired or published during the first year of Ronald Reagan's administration (1981), Bill Clinton's presidency (1993), and George W. Bush's term (2001). . . .

"One bit of good news for the media was the finding that the use of anonymous sources—a practice that can breed public distrust—has been decreasing in newspapers and TV newscasts. But the level of opinion and analysis creeping into television coverage of government jumped by a whopping 138 percent from 1981 to 2001.

"One other result likely to raise eyebrows is that the Clinton administration received more favorable overall coverage than the Bush and Reagan presidencies. While the study was careful not to label this as liberal bias, McGinnis said, 'We are just looking at three snapshots [but] we did see a couple of interesting patterns there.'"

(*The Boston Globe*, July 24, 2003)

"No kings, no dictators, no high priests. Under our democratic system of government, the leaders who run things are the people we elect by a popular vote.

"America is pretty proud of being the birthplace of the modern democracy and of having fixed the system to make it more fair: At first, only white men who owned land could vote. People struggled, fought and died to change that.

"But now one big problem remains with U.S. elections: Fewer and fewer people are showing up to vote in them. In recent years, a lot of young people have been blowing off elections. A group called the Council for Excellence in Government is trying to do something about it.

"'Democracy is not a spectator sport. All of us—even the kids—must get in the game,' said Patricia McGinnis, who heads the council. The group is pushing a campaign called Take Your Kids to Vote.

"Its purpose is to get parents to teach their kids to be voters by taking them along to the polling place and—if possible—into the voting booth.

"'We want to make voting a family affair and a family tradition,' McGinnis said. 'We want voting to be a habit that lasts a lifetime.' . . .

"So, the council has been spreading the word, at schools, on the Internet (www.takeyourkidstovote.org) and with brochures. . . ."

(*The Washington Post*, November 4, 2002)

"There are 30 million missing voters ages 18 to 24 out there, and the Center for Democracy and Citizenship is looking for them.

"'It is my personal belief that it would be a threat to democracy if young adults didn't vote,' says David Skaggs, who started the center in 1998. The center is part of the Council for Excellence in Government, whose mission is to identify ways to improve democracy.

"As a part of a campaign targeted to these young voters, the center has distributed to 8,000 state and federal candidates a 2002 'toolkit'—what Skaggs calls an easy step-by-step guide to understanding this age group.

"The toolkit contains research-based data to help design a campaign plan to win the young adult vote, including information on how young adults decide their vote, what values they are most concerned with and what they like—even where they are. It also offers suggestions on how to communicate with them through the Internet or by direct mail.

"Adam Anthony, project director for the Center for Democracy and Citizenship, said that one key to being successful with the '30 Million Missing

For interest in the Center for Democracy and Citizenship and Government from the Inside: Workshops for Journalists, send materials to Caryn Marks; for interest in improving government performance, send materials to Andria Cantu; for interest in innovations in American government/partnership for trust in government, send materials to Amy Edwards; for interest in e-government, send materials to Sarah Principe; for interest in the John C. Whitehead Forum/Principal & Corporate Programs, send materials to Cheri Griffin; and for interest in leadership development, send materials to Andria Cantu. Materials can also be faxed: (202) 728-0422.

NEWSLETTERS
E-News
Partnership (three times a year)
Scotty Campbell Senior Fellow

PUBLICATIONS
The Council publishes opinion polls, books, reports, newsletters, and Web sites that disseminate information, stimulate the exchange of ideas, and broaden understanding in support of excellence in government.

CONFERENCES
Excellence in Government Conference
Government from the Inside Workshops for
    Journalists
Government Performance Conference

Voters' campaign is to get candidates to increase their activity level toward young adults. . . ."

(*The Washington Post*, October 15, 2002)

Council of Institutional Investors

Established in 1985

DIRECTOR
Sarah Teslik, executive director

BOARD OF DIRECTORS
Sarah Teslik, executive director
Gary Findlay, chair; Missouri State
Employee's Retirement System
William Boarman, co-chair; CWA/ITU
Negotiated Pension Plan
Peggy Foran, co-chair; Pfizer Retirement
Annuity Plan
Peter Gilbert, co-chair; Pennsylvania State
Employee's Retirement System
Shelia Beckett, treasurer; Texas Employees
Retirement System
Sarah Palmer-Amos, secretary; UFCW
International Union Staff Trust Fund
Steve Abrecht; Service Employees
International Union
Mary Collins; District of Columbia Retirement
Board
Ed Durkin; United Brotherhood of Carpenters
Jack Ehnes; California State Teachers'
Retirement System
Shelley Smith; Los Angeles City Employees'
Retirement System
Coleman Stipanovich; Florida State Board of
Administration
Gail Stone; Arkansas Public Employees
Retirement System
Meredith Williams; Colorado Public
Employees Retirement Association
Susan Wolf; Schering-Plough Employees'
Savings Plan

TAX STATUS
501(c)(6)

FINANCES
Information unavailable

FUNDING SOURCES
Membership dues, 100%

SCOPE
Members: 278 public, union, and corporate
pension funds
Branches/chapters: None
Affiliates: None

PAC
None

STAFF
Information unavailable

EMPLOYMENT
Information unavailable

INTERNSHIPS
Information unavailable

CONTACT INFORMATION
1730 Rhode Island Avenue, NW, Suite 512, Washington, DC 20036
Phone: (202) 822-0800 • *Fax:* (202) 822-0801
General E-mail: info@cii.org • *Web site:* www.cii.org

Communications Director: Information unavailable
Human Resources Director: Information unavailable

PURPOSE: "The Council of Institutional Investors is an organization of large public, labor funds and corporate pension funds which seeks to address investment issues that affect the size or security of plan assets. Its objectives are to encourage member funds, as major shareholders, to take an active role in protecting plan assets and to help members increase return on their investments as part of their fiduciary obligations."

CURRENT CONCERNS: Broker voting • Corporate governance • Director independence • Executive compensation disclosure • Furthering good pension fund governance • Shareholder approval of stock option plans • Soft dollars

METHOD OF OPERATION: Coalition forming • Conferences/seminars • Direct action • International activities • Legislative/regulatory monitoring (federal and state) • Litigation • Lobbying (federal and state) • Research • Web site

Effectiveness and Political Orientation

"Even as Comcast Corp. keeps its hands publicly clean of the boardroom skirmish at Walt Disney Co., analysts and investors said yesterday that the outcome of the Disney conflict may help determine how aggressively Comcast proceeds with its takeover bid.

"While Michael D. Eisner's status as Disney's chief executive officer is in no imminent danger, his influence could be affected if enough investors support a move against him led by dissident former board member Roy E. Disney. The drama is likely to play out at Disney's March 3 shareholder meeting in Philadelphia.

"Eisner staunchly opposes Comcast's merger proposal, which Disney's board rejected unanimously on Monday. Comcast proposed last week to buy Disney in a deal valued at $49.2 billion in stock and $11.9 billion in debt at the close of stock market trading yesterday.

"But how much of a negative vote against Eisner would it take to seriously weaken Eisner—and perhaps advance Comcast's cause?

"The Council of Institutional Investors, which represents more than 130 pension funds, said yesterday that it would be a significant blow to Eisner's stature if Disney shareholders withheld 20 percent or more of votes for Eisner and the three other board members targeted by the dissident Disney shareholders.

" 'This is an important vote,' Ann Yerger, a council spokeswoman, said. 'But these votes to withhold are largely symbolic. It depends on how the company interprets the signal.' "

(*The Philadelphia Inquirer,* February 19, 2004)

"Amid the hand-wringing over corporate scandals, the Business Roundtable has unveiled an initiative to train the nation's CEOs in the finer points of ethics. But experts wonder if these old dogs can be taught new tricks.

"The Roundtable's plan is certainly ambitious: The association of top CEOs will start an ethics institute at the Darden Graduate School of Business Administration at the University of Virginia to conduct research, develop a B-school ethics program, and lead seminars. 'As the chief ethics officers at our companies, we know setting and maintaining the highest ethical standards starts at the top,' says Henry A. McKinnell, the group's chairman and Pfizer Inc.'s CEO. 'This effort will support business leaders to maintain a cutting-edge culture of ethical business practices.'

"Maybe, maybe not. The institute will tap some of the best minds in the U.S.—professors from Harvard Business School, Wharton, and other top B-schools. But governance experts say teaching corporate ethics is a tough assignment. They suggest case studies exploring the consequences of real-life behavior. Says Sarah B. Teslik, executive director of the Council of Institutional Investors: 'If packaged right, it could create the conditions for a "there but for the grace of God go I" epiphany.'

"The problem: By the time most CEOs become CEOs, they're pretty set in their ways. Says B. Espen Eckbo, founding director of the Center for Corporate Governance at Dartmouth College: 'You cannot teach ethics to a 55-year-old CEO with a big ego.' Let's hope he's wrong."

(*BusinessWeek,* January 26, 2004)

" 'I think I have made one thing crystal clear—99 senators with no accounting degree, and one senator with an accounting degree, have no business trying to rewrite the accounting methods of publicly listed companies.' That was Sen. Mike Enzi (R-Wyo.), the one with the accounting degree, speaking last year during the debate over the Sarbanes-Oxley corporate reform legislation. Mr. Enzi was fighting an amendment that would have required companies to treat the cost of stock options granted to employees as expenses on the corporate books. He argued that Congress should leave such green-eyeshade decisions to the green-eyeshade types, namely the Financial Accounting Standards Board (FASB), the private entity that writes rules for the profession. So Congress did, and now FASB is moving to require expensing of stock options—as it has been attempting to do for nearly two decades now, over the opposition of high-tech companies and their allies in Congress.

"You might think, then, that Mr. Enzi would be standing in the way of any move by lawmakers to undermine FASB's independence. Not exactly. Instead, Mr. Enzi has introduced legislation to short-circuit FASB and any new expensing rules. It would require expensing of options—but only those granted to the chief executive officer and the next four most highly paid executives. . . .

"Moreover, the bill instructs companies that in calculating the value of even that small set of options for top executives, they should set the 'expected volatility' of the stock at zero. In other words, companies should assume that their stock price won't go up, thereby minimizing the value of the options they've granted. Thus only a small portion of a company's options would be reflected in its bottom line, and even those would likely be undervalued. As the Council of Institutional Investors, which represents pension funds holding more than $3 trillion in assets, noted, this less-than-half-measure 'appears to reflect an interest rooted more in attractive numbers than comprehensive information.' "

(The Washington Post, January 2, 2004)

"When General Electric Co.'s chief executive officer, Jeffrey Immelt, needed advice on a thorny pay problem a few months back, he got it at Gorat's Steak House in Omaha, Nebraska.

"That is where Warren Buffett likes to hold court, usually over his standard meal of a rare T-bone steak, double order of hash browns and a cherry Coke. Mr. Immelt had sought out the 73-year-old billionaire investor for feedback on a new CEO pay plan. With steak sauce dripping on his papers, Mr. Immelt says he suggested an alternative to stock options—a new stock award based on performance. 'How would the average investor view this?' Mr. Immelt says he asked.

"In recent months, prominent CEOs including Xerox Corp.'s Anne Mulcahy and Walt Disney Co.'s Michael Eisner, have made the pilgrimage to Omaha, seeking Mr. Buffett not for stock tips, but for folksy wisdom and straight business advice. Microsoft Corp. chairman Bill Gates came to Omaha to discuss options changes over T-bones and hot-fudge sundaes.

" 'It's very telling that CEOs are insecure enough to need validation, and Buffett's the closest thing to God in the corporate world,' says Sarah Teslik, executive director of the Council of Institutional Investors, a Washington group that represents more than 130 pension funds with about $3 trillion (2.579 trillion euros) in assets. 'But there's a big risk when a large percentage of American capital is following one person's view. They better pray Buffett doesn't have a blind spot or lose his marbles.' "

(The Wall Street Journal, November 14, 2003)

"John Reed's plan to overhaul regulation at the New York Stock Exchange . . . may be just the first step in efforts to overhaul how all the nation's stock markets are regulated, say people familiar with the situation.

"While there's no clear consensus at the Securities and Exchange Commission, various parties believe changes in regulation at the exchange should go further than Reed's proposals.

"That may mean that the responsibility for regulating NYSE traders will remain the jurisdiction of the Big Board itself—a decision that SEC Chairman William Donaldson is believed to support. . . .

"Reed's plan is a reaction to the growing criticism the NYSE is getting for keeping its market business and the business' regulation under the same roof.

"That attack continued yesterday when the influential Council of Institutional Investors (CII) called on SEC Chairman William Donaldson to separate the NYSE's two main functions.

" 'The council continues to believe that a business such as the New York Stock Exchange should not act as a self-regulator and should not be charged with protecting the interests of the public,' wrote Sarah Teslik, the executive director of the CII."

(New York Post, November 5, 2003)

Council of State Governments

Established 1933

DIRECTOR

Daniel M. Sprague, executive director. Appointed executive director of the Council of State Governments (CSG) in 1989, Sprague previously was director of the Western Legislative Conference, CSG's western office, and president of WESTRENDS, a CSG project. Prior to joining CSG in 1980, he worked with county and federal organizations and with the Peace Corps in South America. Sprague holds a master's degree in public policy from the University of California-Berkeley and a doctorate in public administration from the University of Southern California.

BOARD OF DIRECTORS

Information unavailable

SCOPE

Members: Information unavailable
Branches/chapters: 4 regional offices in Sacramento, CA; Atlanta, GA: Lombard, IL; and New York City, NY, plus a Washington, DC office
Affiliates: American Probation and Parole Assoc.; Council on Licensure, Enforcement and Regulation; Midwestern Governors' Conference; National Assoc. of Attorneys General; National Assoc. of Government Labor Officials; National Assoc. of State Election Directors; National Assoc. of State Facilities Administrators; National Assoc. of State Personnel Executives; National Assoc. of Secretaries of State; National Assoc. of State Telecommunication; National Assoc. of State Treasurers; National Assoc. of Unclaimed Property Administrators of NAST; National Hispanic Caucus of State Legislators; National Emergency Management Assoc.; National Lieutenant Governors Association; State Debt Management Network of NAST; State International Development Organizations; College Savings Plan Network of NAST

STAFF

140 total

TAX STATUS

501(c)(3)

FINANCES

Revenue: 2001—$17.5 million; 2000—$15 million; 1999—$16 million

FUNDING SOURCES

State appropriations, 43%; entrepreneurial efforts (publication sales, conference revenue, CSG associates, contributions, and investment income), 29%; grants, 28%

CONTACT INFORMATION

2760 Research Park Drive, Lexington, KY 40511
Phone: (859) 244-8000 • *Fax:* (859) 244-8001
General E-mail: csg-dc@csg.org • *Web site:* www.csg.org

Communications Director: Laura Williams, director of membership, marketing and communications
lwilliams@csg.org
Human Resources Director: Sarah S. Pitt
spitt@csg.org

PURPOSE: "To champion excellence in state government and works with state leaders across the nation and through its regions to put the best ideas and solutions into practice."

CURRENT CONCERNS: Corrections and public safety • Environmental management • Health care • Internet taxation • Workforce development

METHOD OF OPERATION: Awards program • Conferences/seminars • Congressional testimony • Information clearinghouse • International activities • Internet (databases, e-mail alerts, and Web site) • Internships • Legislative/regulatory monitoring (federal and state) • Library services for members only • Media outreach • Mediation • Professional development services • Research • Technical assistance and training

Effectiveness and Political Orientation

"Many legislative leaders on Beacon Hill, citing reasons ranging from illness to travel to other Statehouse duties, missed dozens—in some cases, hundreds—of roll-call votes this year, a survey showed.

"According to the Boston Herald survey published Wednesday, Senate President Robert E. Travaglini missed 266 of the Senate's 416 roll-call votes this year—including issues such as bilingual education, domestic violence protection, open space and school breakfasts.

"Travaglini spokeswoman Ann Dufresne said the Senate president traditionally does not cast many votes. House Speaker Thomas M. Finneran ranked 129th among House Democrats for voting attendance, missing 47 of the lower chamber's 476 roll-call votes in 2003.

" 'Legislators' busy schedules frequently force them to choose between meetings with the executive, committee hearings or constituent demands, and chamber activity,' said Finneran's legal counsel, John Stefanini.

"According to the Herald, House Post Audit Chairman James H. Fagan (Taunton) missed 195 roll-call votes; House Criminal Justice Chairman James E. Vallee (Franklin) missed 183; House Ethics Chairman Arthur J. Broadhurst (Methuen) missed 110; and House Government Regulations Chairman Daniel E. Bosley (North Adams) missed 44.

PAC
None

EMPLOYMENT
Information on open positions can be found at www.csg.org/CSG/About+CSG/jobs/default. htm. CSG, an equal opportunity employer, has opportunities in its regional offices in the major cities of New York; Washington, DC; Chicago; Atlanta; and Sacramento, CA. CSG has opportunities in the areas of research, public policy, sales, publications, editing, finance, and administration. To apply for a position, applicants should mail, fax, or e-mail their resume and cover letter to the Council of State Governments, Human Resources, P.O. Box 11910, Lexington, KY 40578. Fax: (859) 244-8201. E-mail: Sarah Pitt at spitt@csg.org.

INTERNSHIPS
The Council of State Governments has positions in the winter, summer, and spring—coordinating with most college semesters. CSG DC Office interns are considered "pool staff" and will work on projects for all of the groups within the office. Information on internships can be obtained by sending inquiries to cnwachukwu@csg.org.

NEWSLETTERS
Nor'easter (quarterly)
Spectrum (quarterly)
State News (monthly magazine)
State Trends (quarterly)
Stateline (monthly)

PUBLICATIONS
Book of the States
CSG State Directory I: Elective Officials
CSG State Directory II: Legislative Leadership Committees & Staff
CSG State Directory III: Administrative Officials
Earthquake Insurance: Public Policy Perspectives from the Western United States
Earthquake Insurance Summit
Expenditures and Investments: Teen Pregnancy in Selected States
Getting in Step: A Guide to Effective Outreach in Your Watershed
Interstate Compacts & Agencies 1998
Investor's Research Guide to the Recycling Industry
Legislative Guide to Genetic Privacy and Discrimination
Merger and Acquisition Activity in the Recycling Industry
Mitigation Mutual Aid Handbook
Model Toxics in Packaging Legislation
1998 NAST Corporate Affiliate Handbook
The Quality of Medicaid Managed Care
Recycling Economic Information Project: Final Report
Resource Guide to State Environmental Management
Resource Guide to State Facilities Management
Sound Science vs. Pseudoscience: A Guide for Elected Officials

"Broadhurst missed most of his roll-call votes on one day in July when he took his family on a pleasure trip to New Hampshire.

"Bosley said he missed 44 votes partly because of a three-week bout with pneumonia, but mostly because of his duties as national chairman of the Council of State Governments required him to travel extensively."

(*Associated Press Newswires,* December 31, 2003)

"DuPage County officials soon will begin operating the state's first mental-health court, an increasingly popular option for dealing with a growing number of mentally ill people who get caught in the criminal-justice system without proper treatment.

"Based on the success of a one-year pilot program, DuPage County Board officials recently approved funds to establish a permanent mental-health court. It will start in January and will focus on finding treatment for mostly non-violent offenders instead of jail time. . . .

" 'People with mental illness are falling through the cracks of this country's social safety net and are landing in the criminal justice system at an alarming rate,' concluded another major national report released by the Council of State Governments in 2002. "Each year, 10 million people are booked into U.S. jails; studies indicate that rates of serious mental illness among these individuals are at least three to four times higher than the rates of serous mental illness in the general population."

(*Chicago Tribune,* December 19, 2003)

"The Midwest has a lot going for it: affordable housing, top universities and a quality work force. With those assets, why can't the region attract high-tech, good-paying jobs?

"Governors from four Midwestern states sought an answer to that question Thursday from panels of experts from businesses, academia and government.

"Gov. Bob Holden had called the specialists together for a brainstorming session sponsored by the Midwestern Governors' Association. The group is supposed to come up with recommendations for the governors of all 13 member states to consider early next year.

"The governors said they wanted to cooperate more with one another for the success of the region rather than compete with one another for existing jobs.

"The group's meetings usually coincide with semiannual National Governor's Association meetings. Holden called this meeting in St. Louis to formulate policies that will be put before the governors who are members when they meet again in regular session in February. The group's activities are organized through the Council of State Governments. Big businesses pay the costs of the conference."

(*St. Louis Post-Dispatch,* November 7, 2003)

"Officials at the Public Employees Insurance Agency hope that by mid-2004 they'll be able to extend health insurance coverage to small businesses that have been doing without it or are facing significant premium increases. The plan is to bring them into an insurance pool PEIA already has for entities that are not state agencies, including local governments, public service districts, senior centers and non-profit organizations.

"PEIA is using a three-year, $1.4 million State Government Initiatives grant funded by the Robert Wood Johnson Foundation to study and develop the program. If it seems to be financially sound, as Susman expects it to be, PEIA would go to the Legislature next year for permission to implement it.

"The Legislature authorized a similar program about 12 years ago, he said, but there were too many constraints on it and it was never implemented.

"The state is also a semi-finalist for a national Innovations Award from the Council of State Governments for the multi-state prescription drug purchasing pool that PEIA led the way in forming. Programs in the competition are judged on their creativity, effectiveness and transferability to other states.

"Susman said West Virginia will make a presentation in August that will determine whether the program is selected as one of two finalists from the South. It's competing against three programs from Florida, two from Arkansas and one each from Louisiana, Missouri, North Carolina and Texas.

"Eight finalists, two from each of the nation's four regions, will be honored at a Council of State Governments forum in Pittsburgh in October."

(*Charleston Gazette* [South Carolina], June 26, 2003)

"Members of The Council of State Governments gathered this past weekend to discuss all sorts of topics that are important for making state government work.

"The spring committee and task force meetings included sessions on 'Renewable energy initiatives,' 'The medical malpractice crisis,' and 'The future of Medicaid.'

"On Saturday, from 9 a.m. to noon, attendees took part in a session titled 'Surviving Tough Times: The State Fiscal Budget Crisis.'

" 'This panel discussion will highlight ways the federal and state governments can work together to close the significant gap that exists between state revenues and state spending.' The goal: 'To restore the fiscal health of all 50 states.'

"The meeting took place in Harbour Room I at the Marriott Frenchman's Reef, St. Thomas, Virgin Islands.

"Now, it might strike you as strange that government officials would need to spend a weekend in the Virgin Islands discussing ways to help fix our state budgets. Couldn't this brainstorming have been done someplace closer to home?

"Washington Post reporter Lori Montgomery put that question to Maryland Senate President Thomas V. Mike Miller Jr., who authorized airfare and $205 a day for eight of his state's lawmakers to attend the conference.

"Miller was quick to justify the trips, saying that even as the state scales back out-of-Maryland travel, it's important for key lawmakers to meet with policy experts and stay abreast of model legislation. The trip is not a junket, Miller said. Even if it is to the Virgin Islands.

" 'I'm sure the reason they scheduled it in the Virgin Islands is because nobody would go to Pittsburgh,' he said."

(*Pittsburgh Post-Gazette,* May 20, 2003)

Council on American Islamic Relations

Established in 1994

DIRECTOR

Nihad Awad, executive director. Awad was a former public relations director for the Islamic Association of Palestine. In addition to helping found CAIR in 1994. Awad joined the Civil Rights Advisory Panel to the White House Commission on Aviation Safety and Security in 1997. He received a B.S. from Al-Najah National University in Palestine in 1996 and an M.B.A. at Birzeit University in 2000.

BOARD OF DIRECTORS
Information unavailable

SCOPE
Information unavailable
Branches/chapters: 22 regional and state chapters.
Affiliates: Information unavailable

STAFF
Information unavailable

TAX STATUS
501(c)(03)

FINANCES
Information unavailable

FUNDING SOURCES
Information unavailable

PAC
None

EMPLOYMENT
Information unavailable

INTERNSHIPS
Interns receive practical training in the fields of community outreach and chapter development; public and media relations; legal and civil rights; and research and leadership training. Interns assist in research, organizing grassroots activities, writing information guides and pamphlets, and learning the art of media and public relations. Candidates must be a high school graduate, or pursuing a bachelor's degree or an advanced degree. (Exceptions will be made for highly qualified applicants.)

Interns can apply for summer, fall, or spring sessions. A flexible 1–3 month session can also be arranged. More information is available from the CAIR internship department. Phone: (202) 488-8787, ext. 6060. E-mail: internship@cair-net.org or www.cair-net.org /asp/internship.asp.

NEWSLETTERS
None

CONTACT INFORMATION
453 New Jersey Avenue, SE, Washington, DC 20003
Phone: (202)-488-8787 • *Fax:* (202)-488-0883
General E-mail: cair@cair-net.org • *Web site:* www.cair-net.org

Communications Director: Ibrahim Hooper
(202) 489-5108
Human Resources Director: Information unavailable

PURPOSE: CAIR is dedicated to presenting an Islamic perspective on issues of importance to the American public. In offering that perspective, CAIR seeks to empower the Muslim community in America through political and social activism.

CURRENT CONCERNS: Civil Rights for Muslims • Discrimination against Muslims • Islam in America

METHOD OF OPERATION: Advertisements • Conferences/seminars • Grassroots organizing • Internships • Media outreach • Web Site

Effectiveness and Political Orientation

"Embattled Jefferson Parish public school teacher Wes Mix has been removed from the classroom amid an investigation into allegations that he used religious slurs against a Muslim student and pulled off her head scarf.

"After first transferring Mix from West Jefferson High School in Harvey to Helen Cox Junior High School, the district decided to put him on an indefinite paid suspension, Assistant Superintendent of Personnel Ronald Ceruti said Wednesday.

"'We just thought that was in the best interest of the school district at this time,' Ceruti said. "No final decisions have been made regarding his employment status. . . .'

"Last week, Maryam Motar, a sophomore at West Jefferson, went public with claims that Mix had pulled off her religiously mandated head scarf, or hijab, during history class on Jan. 30, and told her: 'I hope God punishes you. No, I'm sorry, I hope Allah punishes you. . . .'

"Mix, a six-year veteran of the system and a professional musician, dismissed the student's allegations last week. He called the situation a 'nonissue' and a 'bunch of craziness.'

"'I'm not worried at all,' he said at the time, adding that 'all of this has been resolved.' He could not be reached for comment Wednesday.

"As word of the incident spread throughout the local Muslim community, friends encouraged the Motar family to contact the Council on American-Islamic Relations, a civil rights and advocacy group based in Washington, D.C.

PUBLICATIONS
Law Enforcement Official's Guide to the
Muslim Community
U.S. Congress Handbook
Publishes an annual civil rights report.

CONFERENCES
Information unavailable

"Its spokesman, Ibrahim Hooper, applauded the school system's decision Wednesday. "Definitely, we would see this as a step in the right direction," he said, adding that the group will continue to monitor the case."

(*The New Orleans Times-Picayune,* February 12, 2004)

"Those expecting prayer got a dose of politics as well Sunday morning as thousands of Muslims gathered downtown for one of their largest holiday celebrations of the year.

"'Are you a citizen? Are you registered to vote?' Umer Farouq, a volunteer, called out to people entering the Millennium Hotel ballroom being used as a prayer hall. The St. Louis chapter of the Council on American Islamic Relations set up the booth as part of a nationwide effort to register Muslim-American voters for the coming presidential election. A steady stream of people filled out the voter registration cards.

"'We want to get as many Muslims involved as we can,' said James Hacking, executive director of the St. Louis chapter of the council. 'We're really trying to encourage greater participation in the political process.'"

(*St. Louis Post-Dispatch,* February 2, 2004)

"The Senate Finance Committee said Wednesday that it had called on the Internal Revenue Service to turn over private tax and fund-raising records for major Muslim charities as part of an investigation into possible links between the charities and terrorist groups.

"The committee released a copy of a letter sent to the I.R.S. last month requesting 'all I.R.S. materials,' including donor records, for 27 Muslim charities, including several that have been under scrutiny by the Justice Department and the Treasury Department for possible ties to Al Qaeda and Palestinian terrorists.

"The I.R.S. had no immediate comment on the request, although Bush administration and Senate aides agreed that it was almost certain to comply because of the Finance Committee's broad jurisdiction to review otherwise confidential tax records.

"The request, first reported by *The Washington Post*, drew criticism from . . . Muslim and Arab-American organizations.

"The Council on American-Islamic Relations, an advocacy group for American Muslims, said in a statement that the 'Finance Committee's investigative net has been cast so wide that it seems to target all American Muslims as terrorism suspects—its indiscriminate scope smacks of a McCarthyite witch hunt.'"

(*The New York Times,* January 15, 2004)

"A federal immigration program targeting men from Middle Eastern countries for mandatory registration was abruptly ended yesterday by the Homeland Security Department.

"The National Security Entry-Exit Registration System (NSEERS) had been criticized by Muslims and Arabs for singling out such a limited group, despite the fact that all the hijackers involved in the September 11 attacks were Muslim. . . .

"The Council on American-Islamic Relations (CAIR) last December sued the government, claiming immigration authorities unlawfully arrested large numbers of people in Los Angeles as they came forward to comply with the registration requirements.

" 'Today's announcement will no doubt bring relief to thousands of people who are anxious about being singled out and discriminated against when visiting the United States,' said Nihad Awad, CAIR executive director. . . .

"David Ray, spokesman for the Federation for American Immigration Reform, said the registration program used by Homeland Security was only 'piecemeal,' as terrorists can come from any country."

(*The Washington Times,* December 2, 2003)

"Dokhi Fassihian is passionate about Iran, and her résumé reflects it. The policy analyst has written articles on Iran, helped with a book about the country and even worked there. So she was stunned when the Monster online service informed her recently that it would remove the word "Iran" from her résumé to comply with U.S. sanctions against that country. . . .

"In recent weeks, national Islamic groups have expressed alarm about reports of Muslims in New York, New Jersey, Massachusetts and other states facing demands by banks and credit-card companies for extra information or finding their accounts closed without explanation. The customers had been asked to provide tax and banking records, residency documentation and proof of identity, the organizations said. And some immigrants say they have been distressed by extra questioning they have faced at money-transferring institutions.

"National Muslim groups are trying to put together a registry of incidents to gauge the extent of the situation.

" 'We see evidence that the wolf has been in the neighborhood, but we want to confirm it,' said Khurrum Wahid, legal adviser to the Council on American-Islamic Relations. 'We want to see if this is truly a systemic problem or just one or two banks that might have gone about it the wrong way.' "

(*The Seattle Times,* July 10, 2003)

"The California office of the Council on American-Islamic Relations (CAIR-CA) today called on GOP leaders to repudiate recent Islamophobic remarks made by the former chairman of that state's Republican Party.

"At a pro-war rally on Friday sponsored by the University of Southern California (USC) College Republicans, Shawn Steel said: 'The Islamic community has a cancer growing inside it, which hates Jews, hates freedom and hates western society. . . . The disease of Islam must be rectified. It's kill or be killed.' He also blamed peace activists and the Democratic Party for the Holocaust, the Ku Klux Klan and slavery. During an April 8 rally at Loyola Marymount University, Steel referred to Islam as a 'dangerous' and 'diseased religion. . . .'

" 'The Republican Party can no longer remain silent in the face of the anti-Muslim bigotry spewed by a minority of hate-mongers within its ranks. Republican leaders and elected officials must repudiate this latest smear of Islam and reassure Muslims in California that Steel's Islamophobic views do not reflect those of the party. Such incidents can only serve to divide our nation along religious lines, increase discrimination against ordinary Muslims and harm America's image worldwide,' said CAIR-Southern California Executive Director Hussam Ayloush. He added that other Republicans officials have recently been involved in similar incidents around the nation. . . .

"CAIR is America's largest Islamic civil liberties group. It is headquartered in Washington, D.C., and has 16 regional offices nationwide and in Canada. Since its founding in 1994, CAIR has defended the civil and religious rights of all Americans."

(*U.S. Newswire,* April 15, 2003)

Council on Competitiveness

Established in 1986

DIRECTOR

Deborah Wince-Smith, president. Wince-Smith has been president of the Council on Competitiveness since December 2001. She is an internationally recognized expert on science and technology policy, innovation strategy, technology commercialization, and global competition, and is a frequent speaker and author on these topics. Wince-Smith serves on boards, committees, and policy councils of the Woodrow Wilson Center, the University of California President's Council on National Laboratories, the University of Pennsylvania Museum of Archaeology and Anthropology, the National Inventors Hall of Fame, the Pilgrims of the United States, and the International Women's Forum. Most recently, she was appointed to the U.S. Department of Energy's Task Force on the Future of Science Programs. Prior to joining the council as a senior fellow in 1993, Wince-Smith was the first assistant secretary for technology policy in the U.S. Department of Commerce, assistant director for international affairs and competitiveness in the White House Office of Science and Technology Policy, program manager at the National Science Foundation. Trained as a classical archaeologist, Wince-Smith graduated from Vassar College, received her master's degree from King's College, Cambridge University, and conducted fieldwork in Greece.

BOARD OF DIRECTORS

Deborah Wince-Smith, president
F. Duane Ackerman, chair; BellSouth Corp.
Raymond V. Gilmartin, immediate past chair; Merck & Co., Inc.
Sandra Feldman, labor vice chair; American Federation of Teachers, AFL-CIO
Charles M. Vest, university vice chair; Massachusetts Institute of Technology
John A. Young, founder; Hewlett-Packard Co.
David Baltimore; California Institute of Technology
Aflred R. Berkeley III; Community of Science
Robert R. Bishop; Silicon Graphics, Inc.
Molly Corbett Broad; University of North Carolina
William R. Brody; Johns Hopkins University
G. Wayne Clough; Georgia Institute of Technology
Vance D. Coffman; Lockheed Martin Corp.
Jared L. Cohon; Carnegie Mellon University
John J. De Gioia; Georgetown University
Gary T. DiCamillo; TAC Worldwide Cos.
Robert C. Dynes; University of California
John Edwardson; CDW Corp.
William R. Hambrecht; W.R. Hambrecht & Co., LLC
John L. Hennessy; Stanford University
Charles O. Holliday Jr.; E.I. DuPont de Nemours & Co.

CONTACT INFORMATION

1500 K Street, NW, Suite 850, Washington, DC 20005
Phone: (202) 682-4292 • *Fax:* (202) 682-5150
General E-mail: council@compete.org • *Web site:* www.compete.org

Communications Director: Information unavailable
Human Resources Director: Information unavailable

PURPOSE: "The Council sets an action agenda to drive U.S. economic competitiveness and leadership in world markets in order to raise the standard of living for all Americans. We focus on strengthening U.S. innovation, upgrading the workforce, and benchmarking national economic performance."

CURRENT CONCERNS: Company security • Benchmarking • Technology and innovation

METHOD OF OPERATION: Conferences/seminars • Congressional testimony • Legislative/regulatory monitoring (federal) • Media outreach • Research • Web site

Effectiveness and Political Orientation

"The Council on Competitiveness today announced the launch of a new initiative on National Innovation as the organization opened its annual meeting, 'Challenges in Globalization: National Innovation and Security.' The 200-plus corporate CEO's, university presidents and labor leaders were also given the details of a newly-completed survey of corporate recognition of the importance of security and competitiveness. Council Chairman, F. Duane Ackerman (Chairman and CEO of BellSouth Corp.) presided at the daylong session, which featured three panels highlighting the issues of: Strategies for National Innovation, Competitiveness and Security, and Global Economic Growth.

"Samuel J. Palmisano, Chairman and CEO of IBM Corporation, and G. Wayne Clough, President of the Georgia Institute of Technology, launched a 12–18 month National Innovation Initiative. According to Mr. Palmisano, who, along with Dr. Clough, will co-chair the initiative, the Council's efforts in the coming year will culminate in a National Innovation Summit to discuss the findings and recommendations of a broad-based steering committee to forge a national innovation strategy.

"In announcing the initiative, Mr. Palmisano said, 'To unleash the next wave of innovation, we need a definition of innovation for the 21st century. How can we go beyond traditional notions of "R&D" and identify and nurture the intersections that lead to innovation? Are there ways to drive innovation at the intersection of services and manufacturing—an imperative in a services- driven global economy?' He continued by pointing out, . . . 'the 42 industries represented on the Council of Competitiveness alone will create

SCOPE
Members: More than 150 chief executives
    from corporations, labor unions, and
    academia
Branches/chapters: None
Affiliates: More than 40 prominent research
    institutions, professional societies, and
    trade associations serve as national
    affiliates

STAFF
20 total

TAX STATUS
501(c)(3)

FINANCES
Budget: 2000—$3 million

FUNDING SOURCES
Information unavailable

PAC
None

EMPLOYMENT
Information unavailable

INTERNSHIPS
Information unavailable

NEWSLETTERS
Challenges (quarterly)

PUBLICATIONS
*Building on Baldrige: American Quality for the
    21st Century*
*Competing Through Innovation: A Report of
    the National Innovation Summit*
*Endless Frontier, Limited Resources: U.S. R&D
    Policy for Competitiveness*
*Going Global: The New Shape of American
    Innovation*
*Highway to Health: Transforming U.S. Health
    Care in the Information Age*
*The New Challenge to America's Prosperity:
    Findings from the Innovation Index*
Winning the Skills Race
Also publishes a policy studies series.

CONFERENCES
Sponsors meetings for members only.

nearly 13 million jobs worldwide over the next two years . . . And nearly 100 million jobs worldwide over the next decade. We believe that the preponderance of those jobs will be created as a result of innovations that are occurring, and will occur with increasing frequency, around the world.'"

(*PR Newswire*, October 30, 2003)

"It was just a few years ago that a top Mexican official boasted to an audience in Ottawa that his country was about to displace Canada as the largest exporter to the United States. That could still happen at some point in the future. But today, Mexico is struggling to hang on to second place in the United States as the massive Chinese export machine continues to generate big gains in the U.S. market. . . .

"What this means is that Mexico has to develop a new economic strategy, one that is similar to that followed earlier by South Korea and Taiwan, and now adopted by China—to invest heavily in education and training, technology transfer, transportation and energy infrastructure, science and technology and a financing system that enables its huge numbers of small and midsize companies to grow. One of Mexico's goals is to play a much bigger role in the North American automotive industry. . . .

"Mexico is getting help from the United States. Last month, the two countries held a Partnership for Prosperity Entrepreneurial Workshop in San Francisco to boost the competitiveness of the Mexican economy through cross-border collaboration between businesses, universities and research institutes.

"The U.S. Council on Competitiveness, for example, signed a partnership with the newly created Mexican Institute for Competitiveness. The two countries agreed to create a new kind of Peace Corps in which volunteers from the U.S. high-tech sector would work with Mexico's National Council on Science and Technology. The University of California announced plans to open a branch campus in Mexico. Other agreements were also announced on research, education and co-operation on building the skills of Mexico's smaller businesses."

(*The Toronto Star* [Canada], July 23, 2003)

"Gov. John Engler will join the Washington-based Council on Competitiveness as a distinguished fellow in late January, the council said Thursday.

"The council is a nonpartisan, nonprofit organization whose membership includes about 150,000 corporate chief executives, university presidents and labor leaders.

"The council has five fellows, spokeswoman Lea Kleinschmidt said. Engler will have an office at the council's headquarters but Kleinschmidt doesn't know how often Engler will be there.

" 'We haven't actually gotten a sense from Governor Engler how much time he'll spend in the office,' she said. . . .

" 'He sees this as an excellent way for him to continue to be part of the debate on education to legal reform and economic development,' she said. . . .

"Engler worked with the Council on Competitiveness while head of the National Governors Association from August 2001 to this past July. The NGA and the council held a daylong forum in Denver this past April at Engler's behest to help governors look at economic development in a different light.

"The council gave governors insights into ways to coordinate jobs and education, develop science and technology to respond to industry needs, reduce legislative blocks to development and promote global trade.

"Kleinschmidt did not know how much Engler will make working for the council. Former NASA administrator Dan Golden is among the fellows Engler will be joining at the council.

"Engler, a Republican who served 20 years in the Legislature before winning the governorship in 1990, will be succeeded by Democrat Jennifer Granholm on Jan. 1."

(*The Grand Rapids Press* [Michigan], December 20, 2002)

"Recently, Pittsburgh hosted a number of government and business leaders to discuss how American companies can compete in a safer and more secure environment as we all work to defend the freedom and values embraced by our nation.

"The National Symposium on Competitiveness and Security was led by Director of Homeland Security Tom Ridge and Carnegie Mellon University President Dr. Jared Cohon, and co-sponsored by the Council on Competitiveness and Security. It also featured speakers that included Commerce Secretary Donald Evans and chief executives of seven Fortune 500 companies."

(*Pittsburgh Post-Gazette,* November 5, 2002)

"The national Council on Competitiveness is developing an Atlanta flavor. Duane Ackerman, chief executive of BellSouth Corp., is chairman-elect of the council and will take the lead of the organization early next year for either a two- or three-year term.

"Georgia Tech President Wayne Clough also serves on the council's executive committee, helping set the agenda of what the United States needs to do to remain competitive in a global economy. 'Atlanta needs a policy base to exert our influence in Washington, D.C.,' said Clough, following a speech to the Atlanta Rotary Club this week.

"Deborah Wince-Smith, the new president of the council, was in Atlanta this week meeting with her executive committee members, saying that Georgia has already become a model in public-private cooperation. The Georgia Research Alliance, which incidentally is chaired by Ackerman, has become a national model of how research universities, government and industry can collaborate on the development of technology.

" 'I think Atlanta as a city and a region is a place of tremendous innovation,' " Wince-Smith said. 'The Georgia Research Alliance is one of the best networks in the country.'

"Ackerman said Atlanta can be a good example for the rest of the nation as it tries to keep its economy strong through research and technology.

" 'Atlanta is a microcosm of the national scene in many, many ways, whether it's technology or telecommunications policy,' Ackerman said, adding that the Council on Competitiveness 'serves not as a think tank but as a policy thought group.' "

(*The Atlanta Journal-Constitution,* March 21, 2002)

Council on Foreign Relations

Established in 1921

DIRECTOR

Richard N. Haass, president. Previously, Haass served as the director of policy planning at the Department of State, where he was a principal adviser to Secretary of State Colin Powell on a broad range of foreign policy concerns. Confirmed by the U.S. Senate to hold the rank of ambassador, Haass served as U.S. coordinator for policy toward the future of Afghanistan and was the lead U.S. government official in support of the Northern Ireland peace process. In 2003, he received the State Department's Distinguished Honor Award for his work supporting peace in Northern Ireland. Haass also held the position of director of foreign policy studies at the Brookings Institution. He earned a B.A. from Oberlin College in 1973, and a M.A. and Ph.D. from Oxford University in 1975 and 1982 respectively.

BOARD OF DIRECTORS

Peter G. Peterson, chair
Carla A. Hills, vice chair
Robert E. Rubin, vice chair
Richard N. Haass, president
Michael P. Peters, executive president, chief operating officer
David Kellogg, senior vice president, corporate affairs, and publisher
Janice L. Murray, senior vice president and treasurer
Irina Faskianos, vice president, national program and academic outreach
Elise Carlson Lewis, vice president, membership and fellowship affairs
James M. Lindsay, vice president, Maurice R. Greenberg chair, director of studies
Abraham Lowenthal, vice president
Anne. R. Luzzatto, vice president, meetings
Lisa Shields, vice president, communications
Lilita Gusts, secretary of the corporation
Fouad Ajami, member
Jeffrey Bewkes, member
Henry S. Bienen, member
Lee Cullum, member
John Deutch, member
Kenneth M. Duberstein, member
Jessica P. Einhorn, member
Martin S. Feldstein, member
Helene D. Gayle, member
Louis V. Gerstner Jr., member
Richard C. Holbrooke, member
Robert D. Hormats, member
Karen Elliott House, member
William J. McDonough, member
George J. Mitchell, member
Michael H. Moskow, member
Ronald L. Olson, member
Thomas R. Pickering, member
Warren B. Rudman, member
Richard E. Salomon, member
Anne-Marie Slaughter, member

CONTACT INFORMATION

58 E. 68th Street, New York, NY 10021
Phone: (212) 434-9400 • *Fax:* (212) 434-9800
General E-mail: • *Web site:* www.cfr.org

Communications Director: Lisa Shields
(212) 434-9888 • lshields@cfr.org
Human Resources Director: Information unavailable

PURPOSE: "An independent, national membership organization and a nonpartisan center for scholars dedicated to producing and disseminating ideas so that individual and corporate members, as well as policymakers, journalists, students, and interested citizens in the United States and other countries, can better understand the world and the foreign policy choices facing the United States and other governments."

CURRENT CONCERNS: Asia • International economics • National security

METHOD OF OPERATION: Conferences/seminars • International activities • Internet (Web sites) • Library/information clearinghouse • Media projects and video conferencing • Research • Speakers program

Effectiveness and Political Orientation

"Pressed to estimate the cost of future operations in Iraq, the Pentagon repeatedly has said it's just too hard to do.

"Now the ranks of disbelievers are growing—in Congress and among private defense analysts. Some say the Bush administration's refusal to estimate costs could erode American support for the Iraq campaign, as well as the credibility of the White House and lawmakers. . . .

"And it's not just Democrats who disagree with the administration's approach.

"Republican chairmen of the House and Senate budget committees penciled in tens of billions of dollars for the two military campaigns in spending plans they began pushing through Congress this week. . . .

"The Council on Foreign Relations, citing polls that show American support for the mission slipping, urged leaders of both parties this week to publicly commit to a multibillion dollar program over at least the next several years, outlining 'the magnitude of resources that will be necessary, even if they cannot identify all of the specific requirements.'"

(*Charleston Gazette* [South Carolina], March 11, 2004)

"Ten years ago, former President Jimmy Carter, Sen. Sam Nunn of Georgia and Colin Powell restored Haitian President Jean-Bertrand Aristide to power in a risky diplomatic mission followed by the arrival of 20,000 U.S. troops.

"Since then, Aristide has failed to fight corruption and encourage democracy and economic growth and now faces the possibility of being deposed, said

SCOPE
Members: 4,192 individuals
Branches/chapters: None
Affiliate: Pacific Council on International
   Policy, a 501(c)(3) organization

STAFF
226 total—plus about 12 visiting fellows

TAX STATUS
501(c)(3)

FINANCES
Revenue: 2002—$18.5 million

FUNDING SOURCES
Information unavailable

PAC
None

EMPLOYMENT
Information on open positions can be obtained
by contacting the Human Resources Office, 58
East 68th Street, New York, NY 10021. Fax
(212) 434-9893. E-mail: humanresources@cfr.
org. Or by visiting the Web site: www.cfr.org
/about/jobs.php.

INTERNSHIPS
Internships are available in either the spring or
summer in both the New York and Washington
offices. Information can be obtained at
www.cfr.org/about/jobs.php. In addition, the Council offers various fellowships.
The Office of Membership and Fellowship
Affairs administers the Intelligence Fellowship, the Edward R. Murrow Fellowship, the
Military Fellowships, the Department of State
Fellowship. Information can be found at
www.cfr.org/about/fellowship.php.

NEWSLETTERS
Foreign Affairs (bimonthly journal)
Correspondence: An International Review of
   Culture and Society (semiannual
   newsletter)

PUBLICATIONS
Cases and Strategies for Preventive Action
The City and the World: New York's Global
   Future
Digital Dragon: High-Technology Enterprises
   in China
The End of the American Era: U.S. Foreign
   Policy and the Geopolitics of the Twenty-
   First Century
The Expanding Role of State and Local
   Governments in U.S. Foreign Affairs
The Ideas That Conquered the World: Peace
   Democracy, and Free Markets in the
   Twenty-First Century
India, Pakistan, and the United States:
   Breaking with the Past

Robert Pastor, an expert in Latin America and the Caribbean who advised Carter, Nunn and Powell on the 1994 trip to Haiti. . . .

"Aristide was elected president in 1990, in the first democratic election in Haiti's history, but the military deposed him in 1991. President Bill Clinton sent troops to Haiti to restore Aristide in 1994, but President Bush is unlikely to dispatch troops in response to the current rebellion, which has gained strength since beginning Feb. 5, Pastor and other experts said.

"For one thing, U.S. military attention is focused on Iraq and Afghanistan. Also, Bush said during the 2000 election that he would not have sent troops to Haiti in 1994. Finally, sending troops to Haiti could be a polit-ical liability to Bush in the fall election, said Robert Fatton Jr., a native of Haiti and professor of political science at the University of Virginia. . . .

"Fatton agreed that the crisis is at least partly one of Aristide's own mak-ing, but he said opposition groups have written off negotiations with Aristide because they do not respect his legitimacy. In 2000, after several years out of office, Aristide was re-elected in a vote that most opposition groups boycotted. Michael McCarthy, a research associate at the Council on Foreign Relations in Washington, said the U.S. government has lately neglected the Caribbean and Latin America, deferring to the Organization of American States and Caribbean leaders in its approach to Haiti.

" 'There is no coherent policy toward Haiti,' he said."
(*The Atlanta Journal-Constitution*, February 19, 2004)

"Democracy is supposed to arrive in Afghanistan this June, by design of the United States and its allies.

"It should be a buoyant occasion, planting a free and representative gov-ernment in a terribly repressed country that has been hobbled for decades by armed conflict, oppressive regimes or government-by-warlord.

"Few, however, are smiling. Not yet. There are too many questions and too many competing forces to give anybody confidence that the grand demo-cratic future envisioned by the United States and incubated by the United Nations will come to pass. . . .

"Afghanistan is still a divided and dangerous place. Warlords control vast reaches of territory. The economy is in a shambles. Heroin is its most lucra-tive export. Remnants of the Taliban, the former ruling party that was thrown out of power by U.S. forces, continues to pose a problem. And although the country achieved a milestone in December when it adopted a new constitu-tion, the basic tools for a successful—and free—election are nowhere in sight. . . .

" 'Unless the present disturbing trends are arrested, the success of Operation Enduring Freedom will be in jeopardy. Afghanistan could again slide back into near anarchy and the United States could suffer a serious defeat in the war on terrorism,' concluded an independent report sponsored by the Council on Foreign Relations.

"The report, which was published last summer, pointed out what every-body knew. Afghanistan's history of stable self-governance is uneven at best. The country has had nine constitutions over the past 80 years, including the newest one adopted last December."
(*Seattle Post-Intelligencer*, February 17, 2004)

"One of the strengths of the American Foreign Policy is its private sector—the think tanks and university centers where the nature of American power

CONFERENCES

Numerous conferences and seminars throughout the year.

and how it should be project is under constant scrutiny. One recent and startlingly prescient position paper from this nongovernment sector was called 'New Priorities in South Asia: US Policy Towards India, Pakistan, and Afghanistan.' It came out late last year, the product of two years' work sponsored by the Council on Foreign Relations and the Asia Society in New York.

" 'Given the dangers inherent in the festering India-Pakistan rivalry, the United States should be more active in trying to help the two nuclear-armed enemies manage their differences, including the Kashmir dispute,' the report suggested. 'In addition, and in the light of the nuclear proliferation risks in South Asia, the executive branch should be searching for ways to integrate nuclear India and Pakistan within the global nonproliferation framework. Meanwhile, it should be working to ensure tighter controls against leakage of sensitive nuclear technology and material.'

"What a difference a few months can make. When the report came out, the extent to which nuclear technology and material were leaking out of Pakistan was not fully known. It is now clear that the Bush administration's worst nightmares about Iraq—that weapons of mass destruction could fall into the wrong hands—was actually taking place in Pakistan."

(*The Boston Globe,* February 13, 2004)

Council on Foundations

Established in 1949 as The National Committee on Foundations and Trusts for Community Welfare

DIRECTOR

Dorothy Ridings, president and chief executive officer. From 1988 until joining the Council in March 1996, Ridings served as publisher and president of Knight-Ridder's *Bradenton Herald* in Bradenton, Florida. She also served as a Knight-Ridder general executive while based in Charlotte, NC, and held editorial and reporting positions at *The Kentucky Business Ledger, The Washington Post,* and *The Charlotte Observer.* Ridings served the League of Women Voters of the United States as president from 1982 to 1986 and as a member of its board of directors from 1976 to 1986. She has been a trustee of the Ford Foundation and a director of the Benton Foundation and Independent Sector. She currently serves as board chair of the National Civic League and Louisville Presbyterian Theological Seminary, is a member of the boards of the Foundation Center and the Commission on Presidential Debates, and is a member of the councils that accredit journalism schools and law schools. Internationally, she has made speaking tours for the U.S. Department of State and led two fact-finding delegations sponsored by NATO. Ridings taught journalism at the University of Louisville and the University of North Carolina. She holds a B.A. in journalism from Northwestern University's Medill School of Journalism and a M.A. from the University of North Carolina.

BOARD OF DIRECTORS

Dorothy Ridings, president and chief executive officer

Mary Mountcastle, chair; president, Z. Smith Reynolds Foundation

Emmett D. Carson, vice chair; president and chief executive officer, Minneapolis Foundation

Lyn Wallin Ziegenbein, vice chair; executive director, Peter Kiewit Foundation

Gary Yates, treasurer; president and chief executive officer, California Wellness Foundation

Paul Spivey, secretary; president and chief operation officer, Edwin Gould Foundation for Children

Susan V. Berresford, member; president, Ford Foundation

John P. Binsted, member; vice president and chief operation officer, Vancouver Foundation

Sherry Salway Black, member; senior vice president, First Nations Development Institute

Caroline O. Boitano, member; trustee, Giannini Family Foundation

Sanford R. Cardin, member; executive director, Charles and Lynn Schusterman Family Foundation

CONTACT INFORMATION

1828 L Street, NW, Suite 300, Washington, DC 20036
Phone: (202) 466-6512 • *Fax:* (202) 785-3926
General E-mail: • *Web site:* www.cof.org

Communications Director: Ellen Dadisman, vice-president for government and media relations
(202) 467-0470 • dadie@cof.org
Human Resources Director: Debbie Vinson
(202) 467-0440 • vinsd@cof.org

PURPOSE: "To serve the public good by promoting and enhancing responsible and effective philanthropy."

CURRENT CONCERNS: Charitable contributions legislation • Corporate community involvement • Current research on grantmaking • Education and development of foundation trustees • Future of philanthropy • Long-term planning as a tool for grantmakers • Media outreach • Post-grant evaluation • Role of trustees in foundation administration • Strengthening community foundations as a vehicle for local giving

METHOD OF OPERATION: Awards program • Conferences/seminars • Congressional testimony • Films/video • International activities • International networking • Legislative/regulatory monitoring (federal) • Library/ • information clearinghouse • Media outreach • Research • Training and technical assistance • Web site

Effectiveness and Political Orientation

"Citing an array of financial abuses at charitable foundations, federal officials and the Massachusetts attorney general's office plan to push new legislation and tougher regulations designed to curtail excessive salaries, lavish spending, and conflicts of interest by some foundation directors.

"U.S. Senator Charles E. Grassley, an Iowa Republican and chairman of the Senate Finance Committee, called the improprieties at foundations detailed in a recent Globe series 'wrong and outrageous,' and said new laws and more stringent rules are needed to ensure that the billions of dollars in foundation assets are used for charitable purposes and not to enrich insiders. . . .

"The need for increased self-policing was . . . a central theme at a conference in Boston last week on accountability among foundations and public charities. At the conference, the head of a leading organization representing foundations announced the details of a two- year initiative to improve ethics and governance standards in the foundation world and to work with state and federal regulators to stop abuses.

"Dorothy S. Ridings, president of the Council on Foundations, a Washington, D.C., association of 2,000 grant-making organizations, said at the conference that 'the government's oversight and enforcement capacity . . .

SCOPE

Members: More than 2,000 independent, community, operating, and public foundations; corporate grantmakers; and trust companies
Branches/chapters: None
Affiliates: 38 affiliated groups

STAFF

80 total—all full time

TAX STATUS

501(c)(3)

FINANCES

Budget: 2003—$14.6; 2002—$16 million

have lagged far behind the astronomical growth our sector experienced in the 1990s.' As a consequence, she said, abuses have resulted, and 'grant-making foundations face the threat of eroding public trust and, for the first time in 35 years, stricter government regulation.'

"Calling IRS enforcement activity 'woefully scarce,' Ridings said her organization will focus on raising ethical awareness among foundation professionals and will continue to advocate for increased funding for IRS oversight of the sector."

(*The Boston Globe*, March 1, 2004)

"To stave off regulators and appease increasingly suspicious donors, a growing number of public charities are voluntarily implementing some of the provisions required by the Sarbanes-Oxley Act.

"Some not-for-profit companies are adopting the mandates requiring certification of financial reports and the creation of an independent audit committee. . . .

"Financial advisers, who often play a role in helping clients direct their charitable dollars, say any move by charities to improve corporate governance is likely to be welcomed by donors. . . .

"Still, simply adopting the requirements of Sarbanes-Oxley may not be the best way to raise the bar for corporate governance in the not-for-profit world, critics say.

"That's because for-profit and not-for-profit companies are two very different animals. Many of the provisions of Sarbanes-Oxley could have unintended consequences for charities.

"For example, the cost of independent auditing could severely hamper the ability of some charities to achieve their missions. Also, as a result of being shouldered by more responsibilities, some charities are likely to find it more difficult to recruit qualified outside directors—many of whom are not paid for their services.

" 'I think there's a lot to be learned from Sarbanes-Oxley for charitable organizations,' says Janne G. Gallagher, vice president and general counsel for the Council on Foundations in Washington, which represents some 450 community foundations nationwide. 'But I am not at all convinced that the right analysis is simply to take pieces of Sarbanes-Oxley and import them.'

"Instead, she says, charities should focus on taking steps to improve internal controls. In other words, an audit committee is likely to prove useless unless the information studied by that committee is completely accurate.

" 'If you haven't analytically thought through what you are trying to accomplish, I'm not sure you are adding much value,' says Ms. Gallagher."

(*Investment News*, December 1, 2003)

"Your recent editorial 'Giving a Full 5%' (Review & Outlook, Aug. 4) does a tremendous disservice to foundations and charities by stating that administrative expenses are an 'abuse' and amount to 'spending on themselves.'

"Counting administrative costs as a charitable expense is a perfectly legal and ethical practice. In fact, Congress has repeatedly said these costs are acceptable and even necessary to ensure charitable dollars are spent with the integrity the public expects.

"Foundations have been extremely effective at building strong communities specifically because their trustees and staff members conduct research, assist grantees, and evaluate the grants they make. In addition to funding a

FUNDING SOURCES

Membership dues, 61%; conference, seminar and professional development income, 21%; additional member contributions for projects, 7%; investment and other income, 6%; publications sales, 5%

PAC

None

EMPLOYMENT

For information on current employment opportunities, interested applicants should contact the director of human resources, Debbie Vinson. Phone: (202) 467-0440. E-mail: vinsd@cof.org.

INTERNSHIPS

Internships are offered on occasion. To find out if any are available and what the application criteria are, contact the director of human resources, Debbie Vinson. Phone: (202) 467-0440. E-mail: vinsd@cof.org.

NEWSLETTERS

Council Columns (biweekly)
Council on Foundations Annual Report
Corporate Update
Foundation News and Commentary (bimonthly)
Family Matters (quarterly)
International Dateline (quarterly)
Principles and Practices for Effective Grantmaking
Washington Update

PUBLICATIONS

The following is a list of sample publications:
Community Foundation Training Manuals
Creating Smaller Corporate Giving Programs: Positions, Roles and Strategies
Donors of Color: A Promising New Frontier for Community Foundations
First Steps in Starting a Foundation
Foundation Management Series
Grantmaking Basics: A Field Guide for Funders
International Grantmaking Fundamentals Package
Legal Compendium for Community Foundation
Organizing Corporate Contributions: Options and Strategies
Philanthropic Foundations in the United States: An Introduction
Rules of the Road: A Guide to the Law of Charities in the United States
Social Investment and Community Foundations
Understanding Multiculturalism: Corporate Response & Innovation
When Corporate Foundations Make Sense
Working with Investment Firms: A Guide for Community Foundations
A full listing of Council publications can be found at http://www.cof.org/Publications/Results.cfm.

CONFERENCES

Annual conference
Corporate Community Involvement Conference
Fall Conference for Community Foundations
Family Foundations Conference

community child-care center, foundations evaluate their operations, assist them in crafting marketing plans to get the word out about the center, and help them seek out other sources of income.

"To show how foundations can increase their spending, you also use a calculation that assumes a rate of return that has not been achievable during the past two years. Any analysis of foundation spending must take current economic conditions into consideration.

"Administrative expenses help make good grantmaking possible. —Dorothy Ridings, President and CEO, Council on Foundations, Washington" (*The Wall Street Journal*, August 10, 2003)

"Record bankruptcies. Plunging stocks. Surging deficits. The nation's economic downturn is leading many companies to rethink their corporate giving programs. But a new study commissioned by the Council on Foundations should encourage corporations to think twice before reducing or eliminating their philanthropy.

"According to the study, stockholders are more likely to keep their shares and buy even more stock if they believe in a company's philanthropic efforts. The survey of 426 investors revealed that 63 percent of shareholders who thought highly of a company's charitable giving said they would remain 'truly loyal' and continue to invest in a firm.

"The research also showed a positive link between corporate giving and customer loyalty, with 46 percent of all customers saying they would be more likely to stay with a particular product or brand if they felt good about the company's corporate giving policy.

"Great news for corporate giving? Yes, but only if customers and shareholders are actually aware of a company's philanthropy. And most are not, chiefly because most companies fail to focus their giving approach and to communicate their focus to stakeholders."
(*Seattle Post-Intelligencer*, October 3, 2002)

"The Ford Foundation today announced the launch of GrantCraft, a project designed to promote discussion about strategic and tactical lessons in philanthropy.

"The recent growth in the number of foundations has triggered increased demand for resources that address how best to do philanthropic work. Grant-Craft offers a range of publications and videos about practical issues in grant making. Some of the materials have been used in the Ford Foundation's orientation program for new grant makers. Others draw on the experiences not only of Ford but also of a wide range of other funders and grantees. . . .

"The project joins other recent efforts to meet the growing need for thoughtful materials on effective philanthropy. The Kauffman, Robert Wood Johnson, Packard, and John F. and James L. Knight Foundations are among the organizations supporting the development of publications on the practice of grant making. The Council on Foundations and the Regional Associations of Grantmakers offer workshops for people new to philanthropy and other specialized sessions on grant making."
(*U.S. Newswire*, April 24, 2002)

DataCenter

Established in 1977

DIRECTOR
Carol Cantwell, co-director
Ryan Pintado-Vertner, co-director.

BOARD OF DIRECTORS
Max Blanchet, chair
Robin Levi, vice-chair
LaVarn Williams, treasurer
Jesus Solorio, secretary
Judith Barish
Tim Christoffersen
Fred Goff
Pronita Gupta
Harry Strharsky

SCOPE
Members: Information unavailable
Branches/chapters: None
Affiliates: None

STAFF
Information unavailable

TAX STATUS
501(c)(3)

FINANCES
Budget: 2000—$685,895

FUNDING SOURCES
Information unavailable

PAC
None

EMPLOYMENT
Information unavailable

INTERNSHIPS
Information unavailable

NEWSLETTERS
CultureWatch (monthly)
Information Services Latin America
   (monthly service)
NewsNotes (4 times per year)

PUBLICATIONS
None

CONFERENCES
None

CONTACT INFORMATION
1904 Franklin St., Suite 900, Oakland, CA 94612
Phone: (510) 835-4692 • *Fax:* (510) 835-3017
General E-mail: datacenter@datacenter.org • *Web site:* www.datacenter.org

Communications Director: Not available
Human Resources Director: Not available

PURPOSE: "To promote human rights, social and economic justice, and peace by providing research and information services in support of domestic and international progressive organizing, advocacy, policy development, and educational efforts."

CURRENT CONCERNS: Foreign and domestic economic, political, and social issues

METHOD OF OPERATION: Information clearinghouse • Internet (Web site) • Online searches • Research • Training and technical assistance

Effectiveness and Political Orientation

"The Community Technology Foundation of California (CTFC) approved grants totaling $1.89 million to address the digital, economic, and cultural divides in underserved communities in the state.

"With these funds California nonprofits will:
- Expand civic engagement, advocacy, and policy advancement;
- Increase knowledge of and access to assistive technology and disability resources;
- Increase the use of multi-media tools by community-based organizations to serve underserved communities; and
- Preserve culture through digital storytelling.

"These grants create opportunities for underserved communities in California to leverage technology to transform information into social justice action," said CTFC President and CEO Tessie Guillermo. . . .2003 Grants . . . [include] The DataCenter, $15,000. . . .

"To provide customized training and online research tools to help organizations based in low-income communities of color do strategic research, gather and use information to educate communities, gather allies, overcome opponents, and change policy—using technology to create effective solutions to quality-of-life challenges, over six months. . . ."

(Associated Press Newswires, July 23, 2003)

"Irrespective of ideological proclivities, many Americans are highly critical of the media. Their discontent is not only concerned with what they have read, heard or seen, but also with those issues which have failed to make it into print or broadcasting. . . .

"Recent conferences attempted both to examine the root causes of public discontent as well as to stimulate action which would address their findings. . . .

"Following are a few of the score of groups represented at the two assemblies. . . .

"The DataCenter is a social justice research center 'dedicated to providing information to those working for progressive social change.' The Center collects information on political, social and economic issues from over 500 periodicals and specialized reports."

(*St. Louis Journalism Review*, April 1, 1996)

Defenders of Wildlife

Established 1947

DIRECTOR

Rodger O. Schlickeisen, president. Schlickeisen joined the Defenders of Wildlife in 1991. Previously he was chief of staff to Sen. Max Baucus (D-Mont.) and chief executive officer of Craver, Mathews, Smith & Co. Schlickeisen was the associate director of economics and administration in the Office of Management and Budget during the Carter administration. He earned an undergraduate degree in economics from the University of Washington, a master's degree in business administration from Harvard University, and a doctorate from George Washington University.

BOARD OF DIRECTORS

Winsome Dunn McIntosh, chair; president, Philanthropic Strategies, Inc.

Caroline Gabel, vice-chair; president and chief executive officer, Shared Earth Foundation, Maryland

Edward Asner, secretary; actor, CA

Alan W. Steinberg, treasurer; Alan W. Steinberg Ltd., FL

Ann Franks Boren, member; environmental advocate, CA

Gloria E. Flora, member; public lands management consultant, MT

David H. Getches, member; professor of law, University of Colorado-Boulder, CO

Adelaide P. Gomer, member; director and vice president, Park Foundation, NY

Katherine A. Meyer, member; founding partner, Meyer & Glitzenstein, DC

Ira New Breast, member; executive director, Native America Fish and Wildlife Society, CO

Barry R. Noon, member; professor of biology, Colorado State University, CO

Bryan G. Norton, member; professor of philosophy, Georgia Institute of Technology, GA

Brian B. O'Neill, member; attorney, Faegre & Benson, MN

Terry C. Pelster, member; corporate counsel, attorney, NY

Steward T. A. Pickett, member; scientist, Institute of Ecosystem Studies, NY

Alan R. Pilkington, member; retired chair, DDB Needham (Chicago), IL

H. Ronald Pulliam, member; professor of environment and ecology, University of Georgia, GA

George Rabb, member; director, Brookfield Zoo, IL

Rodger O. Schlickeisen, member; president, Defenders of Wildlife, VA

Andrew F. Sharpless, member; consultant, MD

Karin P. Sheldon, member; professor of environmental law, Vermont Law School, VT

CONTACT INFORMATION

1101 14th St. NW, Suite 1400, Washington, DC 20005
Phone: (202) 682-9400 • *Fax:* (202) 682-1331
General E-mail: info@defenders.org • *Web site:* www.defenders.org

Communications Director: William Lutz
(202) 772-0269 • wlutz@defenders.org
Human Resources Director: Not available

PURPOSE: "Defenders of Wildlife is a national, nonprofit membership organization dedicated to the protection of all native wild animals and plants in their natural communities."

CURRENT CONCERNS: Arctic National Wildlife Refuge • Biological diversity • Endangered Species Act • Federal lands • Habitat destruction • Protection of environmental laws • Reintroduction of wolves to their former habitat • Wildlife

METHOD OF OPERATION: Advertisements • Coalition forming • Congressional testimony • Direct action • Internet (e-mail alerts and Web site) • Internships • Legislative/regulatory monitoring (federal) • Litigation • Lobbying (federal) • Media outreach

Effectiveness and Political Orientation

"To the Bush campaign, newly announced independent presidential candidate Ralph Nader is a slow, dark horse in the race for the White House.

"But to environmentalists, who generally back Democrats for president, Nader is unsafe at any speed.

"Regarded by Democrats as a spoiler in the 2000 race, Nader's candidacy is considered more troubling this time around because environmentalists consider President Bush a greater threat to the nation's air, land and water than they imagined possible four years ago.

"The official announcement of Nader's candidacy was barely an hour old Sunday when one environmental advocacy group condemned the move.

"'It is monumentally irresponsible for Ralph Nader, who professes a reverence for our natural environment, to take any step that aids [Bush's] re-election bid,' said Rodger Schlickeisen, director of the newly formed Defenders of Wildlife Action Fund."

(*The Salt Lake Tribune*, February 24, 2004)

"A national wildlife group is asking Interior Secretary Gale Norton to turn her legal eye on Alaska's aerial wolf control program and find that it violates federal law.

"Defenders of Wildlife submitted a 15-page petition Monday requesting that Norton find that the Airborne Hunting Act of 1971 does not allow the use of aircraft to kill wolves to boost game populations.

SCOPE

Members: Information unavailable
Branches/chapters: 14 regional offices in AK,
AZ, CA, FA, ID, MT, NM, OR, VT, and DC.
International offices in Mexico and
Canada.
Affiliates: Information unavailable

STAFF

Information unavailable

TAX STATUS

501(c)(3)

FINANCES

Budget: 2002—$28 million; 2001—
$20 million; 2000—$12.6 million

FUNDING SOURCES

Contributions, 87%; legacy gifts, 8%; interest
and dividends, 2%; other, 3%

PAC

None

EMPLOYMENT

Information on employment opportunities can
be found at http://www.defenders.org/
employ.html. Job applicants should forward a
cover letter and resume to the address listed
in the job description.

INTERNSHIPS

Internship information can be obtained at
http://www.defenders.org/about/interns.html.
Defenders of Wildlife does offer both paid and
unpaid internships throughout the year. To
apply, send a resume and cover letter explaining why you are interested and when you will
be available. Please enclose a short writing
sample to: internship coordinator, Defenders
of Wildlife, 1101 14th Street, NW, Suite 1400,
Washington, DC 20005.

NEWSLETTERS

Defenders (quarterly magazine)
Florida Bear
Wolf Action
WolfLines (electronic)
Rural Updates (electronic)

PUBLICATIONS

Amber Waves of Gain
Integrating Land Use Planning and Biodiversity
Oregon's Living Landscape
Second Nature
*Weakening the National Environmental Policy
Act*

CONFERENCES

Information unavailable

"The Washington, D.C.-based group also is asking that Norton amend the federal law to say: 'A state may not issue permits, or engage in any other-wise prohibited activity under the Airborne Hunting Act, for the purpose of manipulating any wildlife populations.'

"Alaska currently has a state-sponsored aerial wolf kill program under way in two areas of the state. The game board will consider expanding the program to other parts of the state at a meeting in several weeks.

" 'Because the programs are for the purpose of enhancing hunting and other recreational opportunities, unrelated to protecting wildlife, they violate the Airborne Hunting Act,' the group said in its petition.

"The group is turning to the federal government for relief after another animal rights group, Friends of Animals, failed in state court to put a stop to the program in the McGrath area in the Interior and around Glennallen in Southcentral.

" 'Our efforts to address this issue with Alaska's leaders have fallen on deaf ears, leaving us no choice but to turn to the federal government for help,' Defenders of Wildlife spokesman Joel Bennett said in a statement."

(*Associated Press Newswires,* February 10, 2004)

"Jamie Rappaport Clark, former director of the U.S. Fish and Wildlife Service during the Clinton administration, is joining Defenders of Wildlife as execu-tive vice president. More recently, she's been senior vice president for conser-vation programs at the National Wildlife Federation.

" 'Threats to our natural resources heritage are now at levels unsurpassed in recent memory. I am excited to be joining an amazing team of dedicated professionals at Defenders of Wildlife committed to protecting our wild places and wild creatures for my son's generation and those beyond,' Clark said in a statement. She starts Feb. 9."

(*The Washington Post,* January 29, 2004)

"The U.S. Bureau of Land Management answers about 100 Freedom of Information Act requests a year in California, usually without charging for ser-vices rendered.

"So it came as a shock to Sierra Club representative Edie Harmon, of San Diego, to recently learn it would cost her group $25,280 for the BLM to pro-vide the information she sought in seven FOIA inquiries about off-road vehi-cle activity in California desert land managed by the agency. . . .

"The Sierra Club plans to appeal the bureau's denial of a fee waiver in Harmon's case, and incorporate it in a lawsuit filed in March against the U.S. Department of the Interior that oversees the BLM.

"In that lawsuit, the Sierra Club, Defenders of Wildlife, The Wilderness Society and the Alaska Wilderness League accuse the Interior Department of illegally denying FOIA requests by environmental groups."

(*The Grand Rapids Press* [Michigan], January 11, 2004)

"Some of Colorado's newest and most-famous residents are slinking about the state's rugged southern quarter on oversized paws, thanks to a 30-year-old law that Westerners love to hate.

"Radio collars placed on Colorado's reintroduced lynx have revealed crit-ical new information on the secretive species. And the 16 kittens produced by the reintroduced snow cats are being hailed worldwide as a conservation first.

"But as the Endangered Species Act marks its 30th anniversary in December, the country's most powerful environmental law finds itself under attack from all sides. . . .

"The waiting list of species that federal biologists agree need protection has climbed to 256, including Colorado's boreal toad, lesser prairie chicken and Gunnison sage grouse.

" 'What's happening is we are building up a huge conservation deficit in this country,' said Rodger Schlickeisen, president of Defenders of Wildlife. 'There is just not the political will to fund the important work this act requires.'

"Big, photogenic species such as the lynx have done well under the Endangered Species Act, largely because they capture the public's imagination and support. Biologists say the law has stopped the decline or extinction of most of the 1,263 species protected under its arm.

"But when the animals live on land coveted by people, the law has been less effective."

(*Denver Post,* November 30, 2003)

Eagle Forum

Established 1972

DIRECTOR
Phyllis Schlafly, president. The founder of Eagle Forum, Schlafly is the author of 20 books and is a syndicated columnist and radio commentator. She holds a J.D. from Washington University Law School.

BOARD OF DIRECTORS
Information unavailable

SCOPE
Members: 80,000
Branches/chapters: 50 state chapters
Affiliate: Eagle Forum Education and Legal Defense Fund (EFELDF), a 501(c)(3) organization headquartered in Alton, IL.

STAFF
Information unavailable

TAX STATUS
501(c)(4)

FINANCES
Information unavailable

FUNDING SOURCES
Voluntary contributions from members

PAC
Eagle Forum Political Action Committee

PAC CONTRIBUTIONS 2002

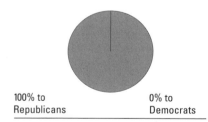

100% to Republicans   0% to Democrats

EMPLOYMENT
Information unavailable

INTERNSHIPS
There are internship opportunities in both their Washington and St. Louis offices. For an application and additional information contact: info@EFCollegians.org, Eagle Forum Collegians, 316 Pennsylvania Avenue, SE, Suite 203, Washington, DC 20003, (800) 504-6332 or (202) 544-0353. Fax: (202) 547-6996. Contact information is available at http://www.efcollegians.org/intern/index.shtml.

NEWSLETTERS
Education Reporter (monthly by EFELDF)
The Phyllis Schlafly Report (monthly)

CONTACT INFORMATION
P.O. Box 618, Alton, IL 62002
Phone: (618) 462-5415 • *Fax:* (618) 462-8909
Washington office
316 Pennsylvania Avenue, SE, Suite 203, Washington, DC 20003
Phone: (202) 544-0353 • *Fax:* (202) 547-6996
General E-mail: eagle@eagleforum.org • *Web site:* www.eagleforum.org

Communications Director: Information unavailable
Human Resources Director: Information unavailable

PURPOSE: "[T]o enable conservative and profamily men and women to participate in the process of self-government and public policy making so that America will continue to be a land of individual liberty, respect for family integrity, public and private virtue, and private enterprise."

CURRENT CONCERNS: Antiabortion • Constitutional convention (opposed) • Health care reform • Parents' rights in education • Tax reduction for families

METHOD OF OPERATION: Award program (EFELDF, Annual Fulltime Homemaker Award, Eagle Awards) • Coalition forming • Conferences/seminars • Congressional testimony • Electoral politics • Films/video/audiotapes • Grassroots organizing • International activities • Internet (e-mail alerts and Web site) • Legislative/regulatory monitoring (federal and state) • Library/information clearinghouse • Lobbying (federal, state, and grassroots) • Local/municipal affairs • Media outreach • Ratings on congressional votes • Research • Speakers program • Special projects for EFELDF (Phonics reading course, Parents Advisory Center) • Television and radio production (EFELDF, "The Phyllis Schlafly Report," and "Radio Live with Phyllis Schlafly") • Training and technical assistance

Effectiveness and Political Orientation

"The longest and furthest-reaching of the many child-welfare reform bills proposed this session had its first debate Tuesday with backers hailing it as a rebalancing in favor of 'families.'

"Rep. Wayne Harper's 109-page House Bill 226 would, among other things, require the state's Division of Child and Family Services (DCFS) to demonstrate protection is needed 'beyond a reasonable doubt' when a child has a shelter hearing, which occurs within three days of a child coming into division custody.

"Harper also proposes to redefine when the division may initiate a child welfare case.

" 'We need to take a look at how we are protecting children and the rights of families,' said Harper, R-West Jordan. 'It's a fine line. . . .'

CONFERENCES

Annual leadership conference
The Eagle Forum Education and Legal Defense
Fund sponsors and participates in various
educational conferences and seminars on child
care, school curricula, parental rights, and
national defense.

"Meanwhile, some state officials are hoping to keep HB226—which would change more than 50 areas of child welfare law—from returning or advancing.

"They argue the measure would leave too many abused children unprotected.

"Mark May, the chief of the state's Attorney General's Child Protection Division, said Harper's bill would allow a child to be chained to 'a cinder block in the basement' and caseworkers would need a warrant before removing the child. . . .

"Tuesday's debate pitted advocates for child protection against factions of the parental rights movement.

"'Children have rights and they are not property,' said Barbara Feaster, who suffered years of sexual abuse by her father before she was taken into state custody as a teenager. As lawmakers prepped to vote on the issue, Feaster stood in the back of the room crying.

"But Eagle Forum leader Gayle Ruzika praised the measure. "We need to protect families from abuse," she said."

(*The Salt Lake Tribune,* February 18, 2004)

"The Massachusetts Supreme Court started a scramble last week that could force an election-year face-off on whether to ban gay marriage in the Constitution.

"On Tuesday, the court declared unconstitutional a state ban on same-sex marriage, an issue that promises to add to the awkwardness of the positions of Democratic presidential front-runners. All have split the difference on gay rights' issues: Civil unions yes, gay marriage no. . . .

"Conservative groups that long pushed for a constitutional amendment to make laws banning gay marriage court-proof now believe the Massachusetts ruling will stir up supporters for their cause. It happened once already this year, right after the U.S. Supreme Court, on June 26, overturned a Texas law banning sodomy among same-sex couples.

"Phyllis Schlafly of the conservative advocacy group Eagle Forum said she believes the Massachusetts decision will sharpen support for an amendment.

"'It goes to the heart of what people believe and they don't see why they should be pushed around by these pressure groups or activist judges,' Schlafly said. 'I think every candidate will have to declare themselves one way or another on the constitutional amendment.'

"If Schlafly's wish comes true for a congressional vote next year on an amendment banning gay marriage, Gallup Poll editor-in-chief Frank Newport believes opposition to the measure could hurt Democrats in the general election."

(*St. Louis Post-Dispatch,* November 23, 2003)

"If religious conservatives ever had reason to be optimistic about advancing their legislative agenda, it was this year.

"With a conservative president, popular for his handling of the 2001 terrorist attacks, augmented by a bigger Republican majority in the House and a new, albeit slim, majority in the Senate, some conservatives were predicting unprecedented success.

"But eight months into the 108th Congress, the movement is still waiting for the payoff. . . .

"While conservatives applaud the three tax cuts Bush has pushed through Congress, some are unhappy with administration-backed increases in non-military, nonterrorism-related spending.

" 'He's proposed expenditures at record high levels far exceeding what Bill Clinton ever conceived of,' said Howard Phillips, chairman of the Conservative Caucus. Phillips is especially unhappy that Bush has advocated a $400 billion prescription drug benefit for senior citizens that Phillips said the nation can't afford.

"Other conservatives are more supportive.

" 'I think we've seen some progress and we need to realize it's only the first session of the 108th Congress, so there is a year and several months to work on legislation,' said Lori Waters, executive director of Eagle Forum, a conservative lobbying group. 'That doesn't mean we are not somewhat frustrated. For example, the grass roots can't understand why we can't get greater control of our borders' especially after the terrorist attacks of Sept. 11."

(*The New Orleans Times-Picayune,* August 8, 2003)

"Fewer than 50 people have been detained as material witnesses in the investigation of the Sept. 11, 2001, terrorist attacks, the Justice Department says in its most detailed public accounting yet of some of the more controversial tactics employed in the war on terrorism.

"The House Judiciary Committee, which asked the Bush administration to outline its use of sweeping law enforcement powers granted by Congress after Sept. 11, released a 60-page status report yesterday from the Justice Department.

"The document hits amid rising complaints from librarians, booksellers and civil libertarians, ranging from the ACLU to the Eagle Forum, that the USA Patriot Act encroaches on Americans' privacy rights."

(*Pittsburgh Post-Gazette,* May 21, 2003)

"Now that Republicans will control the House, Senate and White House, everyone from religious conservatives to anti-tax activists to business leaders has begun urging the GOP to push ahead on their pet causes, demanding results as a reward for their loyalty.

"But some conservative activists and Republicans are worried that the pressure to satisfy important but narrow GOP constituencies quickly could result in political harm to their party and ultimately their cause.

"The last thing the party needs looking toward the next election in 2004 is an extremist image that could prompt voters to turn back to Democrats, they said.

"The key question for the re-empowered Republicans is whether they can avoid the overreaching that so often seems to afflict a party that controls the levers of government, analysts said.

"Still, across the Republican spectrum, special-interest groups are making lists and beginning to agitate for attention to their causes.

" 'We are going to continue to push our agenda, and the leadership can either take it up or not,' said Lori Waters, executive director of the Eagle Forum, a conservative group advocating a ban on late-term abortions and human cloning and an end to amnesty for illegal aliens."

(*The Seattle Times,* November 10, 2002)

Earth First!

Established in 1979

DIRECTOR
None

BOARD OF DIRECTORS
None

SCOPE
Members: None
Branches/chapters: 250 contact groups
Affiliates: Cascadia Fire Ecology Education Project; Coastwatch; Cold Mountain; Cold Rivers Video Project; Earth Liberation Prisoners, EF! Action Update; End Corporate Dominance; Ranching Task Force; Warrior Poets Society; Zero BLOCKction for Public Lands

STAFF
5 total

TAX STATUS
501(c)(4)

FINANCES
Information unavailable

FUNDING SOURCES
Publications, 60%; merchandising, 25%; donations, 15%

PAC
None

EMPLOYMENT
Job openings at *Earth First! Journal* are listed at www.earthfirstjournal.org.

INTERNSHIPS
Information unavailable

NEWSLETTERS
Earth First! Journal (6 times a year)

PUBLICATIONS
None

CONFERENCES
Round River Rendezvous (annual)
Earth First! Organizers' Conference (annual)
Other rendezvous conferences are held throughout the world each year.

CONTACT INFORMATION
P.O. Box 3023, Tucson, AZ 85702
Phone: (520) 620-6900 • *Fax:* (413) 254-0057
General E-mail: collective@earthfirstjournal.org

Communications Director: None
Human Resources Director: None

PURPOSE: "To inform, educate, and inspire citizens to take action in defense of wilderness. The Journal articulates the philosophical basis of biocentrism and provides a forum for analysis, criticism, and debate over strategy, tactics, and goals of environmentalism."

CURRENT CONCERNS: Alternative energy • Ancient forest destruction • Commodification of wilderness • Fair trade for farmers • Genetically modified foods and organisms • Industrial fishing • Recycling • Vegetarianism

METHOD OF OPERATION: Advertisements • Boycotts • Campaign contributions • Coalition forming • Demonstrations • Direct action • Grassroots organizing • International activities • Legislative/regulatory monitoring (federal and state) • Lobbying (grassroots) • Local/municipal affairs • Media outreach • Product merchandising • Web site

Effectiveness and Political Orientation

"A pair of protesters who have lived atop trees on Wachusett Mountain for six weeks watched helplessly yesterday as loggers began cutting down nearly 2,000 northern red oaks around them to make way for two court-approved ski trails that they have been fighting.

"By the end of today, Wachusett Mountain Ski Area officials expect crews to have chopped down nearly 8 acres of trees, leaving only the six oaks inhabited by the Earth First! protesters. Yesterday, loggers cut trees within 40 feet of the protesters, the protesters said.

"Though workers made no effort to remove the tree sitters yesterday, the tree clearing is exactly what the protesters had hoped to prevent through what is believed to be the first major tree-sitting protest in New England history."
(*The Boston Globe,* September 16, 2003)

"During its last memorable visit to northeastern Minnesota, the environmental activist group Earth First! protested the cutting of 6,000 red pines at the Little Alfie timber site, blocked logging roads and sparked a 15-month controversy that had to be settled in federal court.

"So when area lumber companies learned that Earth First! was holding its annual Summer Rendezvous this week along the Caribou Trail, some contractors and loggers virtually boarded up shop—hiring BLOCK security, meeting with law enforcement officers and, in at least one case, purposely scaling down business to stay as anonymous as possible.

"Some of the tension may stem from a message on the Earth First! Web site that implores its members to 'stay for a rousing action on the final day of the rendezvous. Bring an affinity group, EF! banners, signmaking materials, lockdown devices and spirit!'

" 'It's disrupted our business,' said one lumber owner, who has met with the Cook County Sheriff's Office. The owner, who asked that he and his business not be identified, called the mere presence of Earth First! a 'threat.'

" 'Earth First! has in the past . . . used rhetoric that has supported direct action,' said Jackie Andrew, district ranger from the Superior National Forest office in Tofte."

(*Star Tribune* [Minneapolis], July 3, 2003)

"Founded in Arizona two decades ago, Earth First! is a collection of local chapters that operate autonomously, eschewing membership rolls and hierarchy. Their logo, a raised fist superimposed on the sun, speaks to their approach, as does their slogan: 'No compromise in defense of Mother Earth.' "

(*The San Diego Union-Tribune,* January 26, 2003)

"One of Northern California's most colorful, in-your-face environmental groups is searching for its soul after a death in the family and increasing jitters over eco-terrorism.

"The Santa Cruz chapter of Earth First is best known for its $2^1/_2$-year-old war with Redwood Empire, a San Jose-based lumber company, amid the majestic redwoods of the Santa Cruz Mountains. But in October one of its newest members fell to his death shortly after taking up residence in a tree named Esperanza, the Spanish word for hope.

"The death of Robert 'Naya' Bryan, 25, of Utah, was the first such fatality in California, a state where Julia 'Butterfly' Hill helped turned tree-sitting into environmental lore.

"But unlike Hill, who managed to save some redwoods in Humboldt County after living in one for nearly two years in the late '90s, Earth First Santa Cruz faces the sobering realization that its heralded 'direct action' saved no trees and cost a life.

"Activists abandoned the last of four 'tree-sit villages' after Bryan fell 100 feet after detaching his safety harness. The trees they fought so hard to rescue were later harvested by Redwood Empire.

" 'Naya's death was heartbreaking for all of us,' said Earth Firster Donna Beavers of Boulder Creek. The death of Bryan, along with the loss of the trees, 'makes us feel that we're losing the battle. We've been torn.'

"Also tearing at the group are accusations from law enforcement officials and groups battling eco-terror that some Earth First activists support the Earth Liberation Front, which the FBI has classified as a leading domestic terrorist organization. . . .

"Local Earth First members scoff at the notion that they support or condone terrorism.

"Indeed, many central coast environmentalists from mainstream groups like the Sierra Club have generally backed Earth First's tactics, as long as they stay peaceful. They say the tree-sits call attention to problems caused by logging such as sedimentation in streams and the threat to birds and fish spawning grounds."

(*San Jose Mercury News*, January 19, 2003)

"It took 12 years for Darryl Cherney to get another 15 minutes of fame. . . .

"On Tuesday, Cherney topped the news when a federal jury awarded him $1.5 million after finding that FBI agents and Oakland police violated his constitutional rights to free speech and protection from unlawful search.

"His only other big day in the news was May 24, 1990, when TV cameras showed him being led into an ambulance after a pipe bomb exploded in a Subaru station wagon as he and Judi Bari, Earth First organizers working to preserve old-growth redwoods, drove along Park Boulevard. He and Bari sued investigators who accused them of carrying the bomb. . . .

"The $4.4 million jury award he shares with the estate of Bari, who died of cancer in 1997, is believed to be the largest civil rights award ever in an FBI investigation of a political group.

"The jury agreed that six investigators from the FBI and Oakland police violated the civil rights of Bari and Cherney by arresting them and naming them as suspects."

(*The San Francisco Chronicle*, June 14, 2002)

Earth Island Institute

Established in 1982

DIRECTOR
David Phillips, co-executive director; and John A. Knox, co-executive director.

BOARD OF DIRECTORS
Robert Wilkinson, president
Lisa Faithorn, vice president
Michael Hathaway, vice president
John Goggin, secretary
Tim Rands, treasurer
Peter Winkler, counsel
Angana P. Chatterji
Carole Combs
Andrea Cousins
Martha Davis
Veronica Eady
Dorothy Green
Maria Moyer-Angus
Susan Marie Reid
Humphrey Wou

SCOPE
Members: 10,000 individuals, libraries, and organizations
Branches/chapters: None
Affiliates: None

STAFF
70 total—plus 20 part-time; 10 volunteers and interns

TAX STATUS
501(c)(3)

FINANCES
Budget: 2002—$4.9 million

FUNDING SOURCES
Foundation grants, 51.9%; individuals, 30.2%; service revenue, 8.9%; and other, 9%

PAC
None

EMPLOYMENT
Job openings are posted at www.earthisland.org. Resumes should be sent to Steven Zimmerman, associate director, Earth Island Institute, 300 Broadway, Suite 28, San Francisco, CA 94133-3312. E-mail: stevez@earthisland.org.

INTERNSHIPS
Internship positions are available on many of Earth Island Institute's projects. Responsibilities, qualifications, and application procedures vary by project. Detailed information on internships is available at www.earthisland.org.

CONTACT INFORMATION
300 Broadway, Suite 28, San Francisco, CA 94133-3312
Phone: (415) 788-3666 • *Fax:* (415) 788-7324
General E-mail: Web form on www.earthisland.org •
Web site: www.earthisland.org

Communications Director: None
Human Resources Director: Yvette Hash, administrative director
(415) 788-3666 • yvette@earthisland.org

PURPOSE: "Life on Earth is imperiled by human degradation of the atmosphere. Earth Island Institute develops and supports projects that counteract threats to the biological and cultural diversity that sustain the environment. Through education and activism, these projects promote the conservation, preservation, and the restoration of the Earth."

CURRENT CONCERNS: Alternative paper products • Environmental and social justice • Environmental education • Habitat preservation and restoration • International cooperative efforts • Marine mammal and sea turtle protection • Organic and sustainable agriculture • Protection of indigenous cultures and sacred sites • Rainforest protection • Sustainable development • Urban multicultural environmental leadership • Water pollution • Wilderness preservation

METHOD OF OPERATION: Advertisements • Awards program • Boycotts • Coalition forming • Conferences/seminars • Congressional testimony • Congressional voting analysis • Demonstrations • Direct action • Films/video/audiotapes • Grantmaking • Grassroots organizing • Information clearinghouse • International activities • Internet (e-mail alerts and Web site) • Internships • Legislative/regulatory monitoring (federal and state) • Library services open to the public • Lobbying (federal, state, and grassroots) • Local/municipal affairs • Media outreach • Participation in regulatory proceedings (federal and state) • Product merchandising • Research • Speakers program • Training

Effectiveness and Political Orientation

"Conservationists are accusing the American government of ignoring its own scientific advisers over a decision to import tuna fish from Mexico. In 2002, the U.S. Commerce Department agreed that tuna from Mexico could be labeled 'dolphin safe' and so be imported and sold in American shops. Conservationists last week revealed documents that suggest this decision was taken against scientific advice.

"The papers were circulated by the Earth Island Institute, a conservation group among plaintiffs suing the government over the issue. They are a 'smoking gun,' according to David Phillips, the institute's director."

(*The Guardian* [Manchester, England], February 12, 2004)

NEWSLETTERS
Earth Island Journal (quarterly)
IslandWire (online monthly)
Many of Earth Island's education and
advocacy projects publish periodic print and
electronic newsletters.

PUBLICATIONS
In the Light of Reverence (DVD)
*On Nature's Terms: Predators and People
    Co-existing in Harmony* (video)

CONFERENCES
None

"A federal appeals court ruled yesterday that a forest ravaged by fire in 2001 near Lake Tahoe cannot be logged despite government fears of renewed fire danger.

"A three-judge panel of the 9th U.S. Circuit Court of Appeals faulted federal forest officials for approving the cutting plan, an effort to prevent another fire, without adequately considering the plight of the California spotted owl and other environmental concerns.

"Environmental group Earth Island Institute sued to block the project alleging, among other things, there were owls in the area."

(*The San Diego Union-Tribune,* December 12, 2003)

"Environmental groups asked a federal court Tuesday to halt a rule that they say would weaken the 'dolphin safe' label on canned tuna and dramatically increase the number of deaths among the ocean mammals.

"For 12 years, the label had guaranteed consumers that the tuna was caught by nets that did not surround and harm dolphins. But in December, a new rule by the National Oceanic and Atmospheric Administration applied the label to tuna captured in encircling nets.

"The Earth Island Institute and six other groups asked the U.S. District Court in San Francisco for an injunction to the new rule, arguing that science—and not trade concerns—should guide environmental policy."

(*The San Francisco Chronicle,* February 12, 2003)

"Over the last decade, the Earth Island Institute has become a de facto global regulator of the $2 billion-a-year canned-tuna industry. Its 14 monitors track tuna fishermen worldwide for 'dolphin safe' practices, and woe to those who are caught with so much as one dolphin in their nets. Falling off the Earth Island list of 'certified' companies can kill a tuna business. First, however, may come a warning from a top Earth Island official, Mark Berman, whose e-mails sometimes begin, 'From: The Bermanator.' 'If one of these major companies cheated, all we would have to do is run a couple of full-page ads, and sales would fall,' says Berman.

"So powerful has Earth Island become that tuna companies live in fear of being blacklisted, and help fund its efforts to track their fishing habits. To say this is a rare turn in the growing global battles between activists and corporations is an understatement. . . . At least 97 percent of tuna on the world's supermarket shelves now meets Earth Island rules on what is dolphin safe, a standard so rigid that many other wildlife activists consider it too radical."

(*Newsweek,* May 6, 2002)

"The Bush administration has decided to review bans on jet-powered skis and similar watercraft at four national parks in Eastern and Midwestern states.

"The action provoked concern among conservation groups that the bans will be weakened or overturned. But critics of the bans cheered the move, saying that some park officials had acted precipitously in prohibiting the use of popular jet-powered skis and other small motorized craft. . . .

"Such watercraft are being banned in many national parks, and a recent court settlement requires the remaining 21 parks to conduct environmental reviews to see if bans are needed. The settlement came in a lawsuit brought by the Bluewater Network, part of Earth Island Institute, an environmental group."

(*The Los Angeles Times,* April 26, 2001)

Electronic Frontier Foundation

Established in 1990

DIRECTOR

Shari Steele, executive director. Prior to becoming EFF's executive director in 2000, Steele served as EFF's legal director for eight years. She is also co-founder of Bridges.org, a nonprofit working to ensure sound technology policy in developing nations. She has appeared widely on radio and television to speak on civil liberties law in newly emerging technologies. As EFF's legal director, she advised the NTIA on hate crimes in telecommunications, the U.S. Sentencing Commission on sentencing guidelines for the Computer Fraud and Abuse Act and the No Electronic Theft Act, and the National Research Council on U.S. encryption policy. She has spoken about Internet law as part of the Smithsonian Institution's lecture series on the Internet, the ABA's TechWorld Conference, the National Law Journal's annual Computer Law Conference, and the National Forum for Women Corporate Counsel. A graduate of Widener University School of Law, Steele later served as a teaching fellow at Georgetown University Law Center, where she earned an L.L.M. degree in advocacy. Steele also holds a M.S. in Instructional Media from West Chester University.

BOARD OF DIRECTORS

Brad Templeton, chair; entrepreneur, technologist
John Perry Barlow, vice chair and co-founder; entrepreneur, writer, lyricist
John Gilmore, co-founder; entrepreneur, technologist
David Farber; professor of telecommunications, University of Pennsylvania
Brewster Kahle; director and co-founder, Internet Archive
Lawrence Lessig; attorney, professor of law at Stanford Law School, columnist and author
Pamela Samuelson; professor of law and information management, co-director of Center for Law and Technology, University of California at Berkeley

SCOPE

Members: More than 12,000
Branches/chapters: None
Affiliates: Internet Free Expression Alliance (IFEA), the Global Internet Liberty Campaign (GILC), the Digital Future Coalition (DFC), and the Free Expression Network (FEN).

STAFF

24 total—17 full-time professional; 6 full-time support; plus 1 part-time; 6 active volunteers (more are signed up on the remote volunteers mailing list); 3 or more interns

CONTACT INFORMATION

454 Shotwell Street, San Francisco, CA 94110
Phone: (415) 436-9333 • *Fax:* (415) 436-9993
General E-mail: eff@eff.org • *Web site:* www.eff.org

Communications Director: Will Doherty, media relations director
(415) 436-9333, ext. 111 • press@eff.org
Human Resources Director: Shari Steele, executive director
(415) 436-9333, ext. 103 • ssteele@eff.org

PURPOSE: The Electronic Frontier Foundation is the leading civil liberties organization working to protect rights in the digital world. Founded in 1990, EFF actively encourages and challenges industry and government to support free expression and privacy online. EFF is a member-supported organization and maintains one of the most linked-to Web sites in the world at www.eff.org/.

CURRENT CONCERNS: Anonymity • Anti-terrorism • Biometrics • CAPPS II • Censorship • Copyright law • Digital rights management • Domain names • E-voting • File-sharing • Filtering • FTAA • Internet governance • ISP legalities • Licensing/UCITA • Linking • Patents • Privacy • Public records/FOIA • Reverse engineering • RFID • Spam • Surveillance • USA PATRIOT Act • Wireless

METHOD OF OPERATION: Advertisements • Awards program • Coalition forming • Direct action • Educational foundation • Grassroots organizing • Information clearinghouse • Initiative/referendum campaigns • International activities • Internet (databases, e-mail alerts, and Web site) • Internships • Legal assistance • Legislative/regulatory monitoring (federal and state) • Litigation • Lobbying (grassroots) • Local/municipal affairs • Media outreach • Mediation • Participation in regulatory proceedings (federal and state) • Speakers program • Technical assistance • Training

SPECIFIC PROGRAMS/INITIATIVES: Let the Music Play Campaign (campaign to help end the war against peer-to-peer file-sharing programs) • Chilling Effects (aims to educate recipients of cease-and-desist letters about their legal rights) • Subpoena Defense (resource for individuals seeking information on how to defend themselves if their identity has been subpoenaed to enforce their copyrights on the Internet) • DirectTV Defense (provides scientists, researchers, innovators and their lawyers with the resources necessary to fight legal threats from DirecTV) • EFF Action Center (allows EFF to create action alerts on technology and civil liberties issues and pending legislation)

Effectiveness and Political Orientation

". . . the Electronic Frontier Foundation, an advocacy group concerned with civil liberties in the digital age. . . ."

(*The New York Times*, September 25, 2003)

TAX STATUS
501(c)(3)

FINANCES
2004—$2.3 million; 2003—$2.3 million;
2002—$1.7 million

FUNDING SOURCES
Foundation grants, 34.2%; individuals, 32.3%;
membership dues, 29%; corporate donations,
0.8%; special events/projects, 0.4%; matching
gifts, 1.8%; interest income and other, 1.5%

PAC
None

EMPLOYMENT
Information about technical, administrative,
and attorney positions is available at
www.eff.org/opportunities. Applicants should
send resumes and other materials for employment to Shari Steele, executive director, 454
Shotwell Street, San Francisco, CA 94110.
Phone: (415) 436-9333. Fax: (415) 436-9993.
E-mail: ssteele@eff.org.

INTERNSHIPS
Information about internships is available at
eff.org/opportunities. Application deadlines
are rolling. Positions are for 3 months, 20
hours per week, and are unpaid. Internships
are available in the following areas: programming, electronic privacy, Blue Ribbon
Campaign Project, media, legal, and envelope
stuffing. Desired qualities include strong written and oral communication skills, strong personal computer skills (word processors,
spreadsheets, database tools, e-mail, Web
browsers), basic HTML experience preferred,
dedication and willingness to work hard,
attention to detail and ability to meet deadlines, and excellent knowledge of the assigned
field with at least a working understanding of
the issues EFF is devoted to. Preferred fields
are law and prelaw, communications, public
relations, journalism, English, computer science, information systems, political science,
and/or business. The internship coordinator is:
Katie Lucas, executive assistant, 454 Shotwell
Street, San Francisco, CA 94110. Phone: (415)
436-9333, ext. 104. Fax: (415) 436-9993.E-mail:
katie@eff.org.

NEWSLETTERS
EFFector (online weekly)

PUBLICATIONS
EFF produces white papers and analyses to
educate government policymakers and the
public about the civil liberties implications of
their actions and decisions, including, but not
limited to the following publications:
*A Better Way Forward: Voluntary Collective
    Licensing of Music File Sharing*
"Let the Music Play" (white paper)
*Unintended Consequences: Five Years under
    the DMCA*
*EFF Analysis of the Provisions of the USA
    PATRIOT Act that Relate to Online
    Activities*

"The Recording Industry Association of America just hired a new CEO, at a salary of $1 million a year.

"The Electronic Frontier Foundation, its legal nemesis, exists on a total annual budget of $2 million, doled out in small checks to fight the govern-ment and industry in battles over online song swapping, privacy, computer hacking and other Internet-related questions.

" 'We are defending the Constitution,' says John Perry Barlow, 55, a for-mer Grateful Dead lyricist, cattle rancher and writer who co-founded EFF in 1990. . . .

"EFF, located on a rundown street in San Francisco's Mission district, is the leading advocate for consumer rights in the RIAA's plans to sue hundreds of song swappers. The non-profit EFF, which has 23 staff members, has a data-base on its eff.org Web site to let users of pirate file-sharing services check to see whether their screen names are listed on the more than 1,000 subpoenas that have been filed by the RIAA for possible lawsuits. EFF also has launched a 'Let the Music Play' ad campaign promoting alternatives to litigation.

"Even while sounding the alarm, executive director Shari Steele concedes that the RIAA's action is the best thing that has ever happened to the EFF.

" 'In the past, we were getting five to 10 new members a day,' she says. 'Now we're up to 60 to 70. Our site almost went down the other day due to its popularity. This is the busiest we've ever been, by far.' "

(*USA Today*, August 5, 2003)

"Three weeks ago, technology groups and digital rights advocates were star-tled to discover that the motion picture industry had successfully pushed leg-islation in several states that strengthened cable TV piracy laws.

"Groups such as the Electronic Frontier Foundation and the Consumer Electronics Association claimed the new laws could potentially turn con-sumers into criminals. But just as alarming for these groups—which are nor-mally on top of such developments—was the fact that they hadn't noticed that Hollywood had been pushing the bills since 2001.

"Even critics had to begrudgingly tip their caps to the Motion Picture Association of America, the film industry's powerful trade group, for its sophisticated, multifaceted approach to protecting Hollywood from the kind of digital piracy that has put the recording industry on the ropes.

" 'These guys are everywhere,' said Fred von Lohmann, senior intellectual property attorney for the Electronic Frontier Foundation (EFF), a digital rights advocacy group in San Francisco. 'They're pushing their agenda in places we haven't even begun to look at.'

" 'Everywhere I turn over a stone, there's been a bevy of MPAA people who have been working that area for years,' he added. 'I almost never encoun-tered that with the RIAA (Recording Industry Association of America).' "

(*The San Francisco Chronicle*, April 28, 2003)

"Civil-liberties groups, energized by Congress's rebuke of a vast Pentagon antiterror-surveillance program, are gearing up to curtail a second system in the works to keep closer tabs on airline passengers.

"Following a little-noticed Federal Register announcement revealing new details about the government's plans, a coalition of privacy advocacy groups submitted comments late last week saying the profiling system 'raises major constitutional issues regarding the right to travel.' Among the issues: propos-als to keep sensitive personal records on people 'deemed to pose a possible risk'

CONFERENCES
None currently, but EFF staff speak at many conferences and seminars—for instance, EFF usually has a large presence at the Computers, Freedom and Privacy (CFP) conference. The EFF Pioneer Awards ceremony is held each year at CFP. See http://www.eff.org/awards/pioneer/ for more information.

to aviation or national security for as long as 50 years, and to make such data available to law-enforcement or regulatory authorities. . . .

"The aviation program, overseen by the Transportation Security Administration and known as the Computer Assisted Passenger Pre-screening II System, had been out of the public eye for several months while companies competed for contracts to build the system. It would rely on databases sifting through mounds of sensitive data on individuals traveling to, from, or within the U.S. TSA is expected to award a contract for the system, known as CAPPS II, as early as this week. . . .

"Civil-liberties groups say the aviation proposal appears overly intrusive. In its comments last week, the coalition led by the Electronic Frontier Foundation complained that TSA is proposing to gather 'a virtually unlimited amount of information about every air traveler.'

" 'They're not telling us how they'll decide people are risks,' said Lee Tien, an attorney for the San Francisco-based Electronic Frontier Foundation, a nonprofit civil-liberties group."

(*The Wall Street Journal,* February 24, 2003)

"While shoppers clamor for CD burners, MP3 players and digital video recorders, movie studios and record labels have been urging consumer electronics makers and software developers to alter these devices to keep movies, TV shows and records from being duplicated across the Internet. Studios and labels have also asked Congress to pass laws requiring manufacturers to put locks on these and other gadgets that would stop unauthorized copies.

"This conflict is shaping up to be one of the tech-policy battlegrounds of the year, as consumers, manufacturers and entertainment companies keep butting heads, sometimes winding up in court as a result.

"Yesterday, the Electronic Frontier Foundation filed suit on behalf of five owners of ReplayTV personal video recorders against a lineup of entertainment companies in U.S. District Court in Los Angeles. The suit asks the court to rule that owners of these digital recorders, which store TV broadcasts on internal hard drives, have the right to record shows, skip commercials and move recorded content to other devices. It also asks the court to forbid SonicBlue Inc. from downgrading the capability of ReplayTV boxes it has already sold."

(*The Washington Post,* June 7, 2002)

Electronic Privacy Information Center (EPIC)

Established in 1994

DIRECTOR

Marc Rotenberg, executive director. Rotenberg teaches information privacy law at Georgetown University Law Center and has testified before Congress on many issues, including access to information, encryption policy, consumer protection, computer security, and communications privacy. He has served on several national and international advisory panels, including the expert panels on Cryptography Policy and Computer Security for the OECD and the Legal Experts on Cyberspace Law for UNESCO. He currently chairs the ABA Committee on Privacy and Information Protection and is Secretary of the Public Interest Registry. He is editor of The Privacy Law Sourcebook and co-editor of Information Privacy Law. He is a graduate of Harvard College and Stanford Law School and served as counsel to Sen. Patrick J. Leahy on the Senate Judiciary Committee. He is the winner of the 2002 World Technology Award in Law.

BOARD OF DIRECTORS

Marc Rotenberg, president; executive director, Electronic Privacy Information Center

Peter Neumann, secretary; principal scientist, SRI International Computer Science Laboratory

Barbara Simons, treasurer; co-chair, U.S. Public Policy Committee of the Association for Computing Machinery

Whitfield Diffie; distinguished engineer, Sun Microsystems Laboratories

Oscar Gandy; Herbert I. Schiller Information and society professor, Annenberg School for Communication at the University of Pennsylvania

Deborah Hurley; senior research associate at the Kennedy School of Government, Harvard University

SCOPE

Members: None
Branches/Chapters: None
Affiliate: Fund for Constitutional Government, a 501(c)(3) organization

TAX STATUS

501(c)(3)

FINANCES

Budget: 2002—$1.1 million

FUNDING SOURCES

Foundation grants, 40%; individual contributions, 40%; corporate donations, 10%; publications, 10%

PAC

None

CONTACT INFORMATION

1718 Connecticut Avenue, NW, Suite 200, Washington, DC 20009
Phone: (202) 483-1140 • *Fax:* (202) 483-1248
General E-mail: info@epic.org • *Web site:* www.epic.org

Communications Director: None
Human Resources Director: None

PURPOSE: "To focus public attention on emerging civil liberties issues and to protect privacy, freedom of expression and constitutional values in the information age."

CURRENT CONCERNS: Air passenger profiling • Consumer privacy • Digital rights management • Encryption • Free speech on the Internet • Government surveillance • Individual privacy and technology • Medical privacy • NGO participation • Open government • Privacy of diplomatic communications • RFID • Spam • USA PATRIOT Act

METHOD OF OPERATION: Coalition forming • Conferences/seminars • Congressional testimony • Direct action • Grassroots organizing • Information clearinghouse • International activities • Internet (e-mail alerts and Web site) • Internships • Legislative/regulatory monitoring (federal and state) • Litigation • Media outreach • Participation in regulatory proceedings (federal and state) • Performance ratings • Research

Effectiveness and Political Orientation

"A federal appellate court in Denver upheld on Tuesday a national do-not-call list that helps more than 51 million Americans avoid unwanted telemarketing sales pitches.

"The national do-not-call registry is a reasonable attempt by the government to protect consumers' privacy and to prevent 'the risk of fraud or abuse,' the U.S. Court of Appeals for the 10th Circuit ruled. The court also dismissed the telemarketing industry's claims that the registry violates the free-speech rights of business. . . .

" 'This is a slam dunk, and a big win for anyone who values their privacy,' said Chris Hoofnagle, associate director of the Electronic Privacy Information Center in Washington. 'The vast bulk of calls come from commercial sources, and the court clearly recognizes that consumers need help stopping them.' "

(*Denver Post,* February 18, 2004)

"Northwest Airlines provided information on millions of passengers for a secret U.S. government air-security project soon after the Sept. 11, 2001, terrorist attacks, raising more concerns among some privacy advocates about the airlines' use of confidential customer data. . . .

"The Northwest and NASA documents were released in response to a Freedom of Information Act request filed by the Electronic Privacy Informa-

STAFF
11 total

EMPLOYMENT

The National Association of Public Interest Law (NAPIL) Fellowships for Equal Justice are awarded to graduating law students or recent graduates who, usually in cooperation with a sponsoring nonprofit organization, developed special projects designed to address and remedy civil injustices. NAPIL provides each fellow with salary, loan repayment assistance, a national training program, support and assistance throughout the fellowship, and the chance to gain high-quality, public interest legal experience.

Every year, EPIC is eager to find an outstanding recent law school graduate for a two-year Equal Justice fellowship focusing on Internet issues. Consult the Web site for further information: www.equaljusticeworks.org. Information about other job openings is available at www.epic.org.

INTERNSHIPS

The EPIC Internet Public Interest Opportunities Program (IPIOP) is an intensive, paid legal internship held during the summer, fall, and spring terms. The program gives law students the opportunity to actively participate in valuable programs in Internet law, policy, and legislation. IPIOP clerks also attend weekly seminars led by eminent scholars and practitioners in the field of Internet policy. Qualifications include energy, enthusiasm, and creativity; being currently enrolled in law school (non-U.S. schools are okay); excellent writing and communication skills; and strong interest in civil liberties issues relating to the Internet, particularly free speech, privacy, open government, and democratic governance.

Applicants should submit a letter of interest, a writing sample, a resume, and a recommendation letter. Indicate which semester or summer. Students are accepted on a rolling basis. Contact Chris Hoofnagle, Electronic Privacy Information Center, 1718 Connecticut Avenue, NW, Suite 200, Washington, DC 20009. Phone: (202) 483-1140. Fax: (202) 483-1248. E-mail: ipiop@epic.org.

NEWSLETTERS

EPIC Alert (online biweekly)

PUBLICATIONS

The Consumer Law Sourcebook 2000: Electronic Commerce and the Global Economy
Cryptography and Liberty 2000: An International Survey of Encryption Policy
Filters and Freedom 2.0: Free Speech Perspectives on Internet Content Controls
Litigation Under the Federal Open Government Laws (FOIA) 2002
Privacy and Human Rights 2003: An International Survey of Privacy Laws and Developments (2002, 2001, 2000 editions also available)

tion Center, a nonprofit organization that advocates privacy rights and open government. The organization, which provided the documents to *The Washington Post*, said it plans to take legal action this week in an effort to force the government to disclose more information about NASA's secret security project and to investigate Northwest's actions.

" 'We strongly believe aviation security programs should be developed publicly,' said David L. Sobel, general counsel for the group. 'While the airline in this case might have thought the action appropriate, the public at large sees it as a serious violation of personal privacy.' "

(*The Washington Post*, January 18, 2004)

"A researcher in Pakistan uncovered a flaw in Microsoft Corp.'s online purchasing system, called Passport, that left information from 200 million users vulnerable to hackers and which could, theoretically, trigger a $2.2 trillion fine against the software giant.

"Microsoft said yesterday that it had fixed the problem. The Redmond, Wash., company said it knew of no Passport accounts that were hacked.

"The glitch underscored problems pointed out nearly two years ago by consumer groups. Activists had complained to the Federal Trade Commission that Microsoft was making overblown claims about Passport's security.

" 'It's amazing,' said Marc Rotenberg, president of the Electronic Privacy Information Center. EPIC took the lead in complaining about Passport's security to the FTC.

"Rotenberg said the latest flaw shows 'how serious online security is, especially in these big, centralized systems. If it's a bad idea to put all your eggs in one basket, how bad an idea is it to put 200 million eggs in one basket?'

"With Passport, consumers can let Microsoft or others keep personal information, such as credit card numbers, and make it available as needed.

"It is used by dozens of retail Web sites, and also controls access for Windows users to Hotmail and instant-messaging accounts.

"Under the terms of a settlement between the FTC and Microsoft on Passport last year, Microsoft said it would take steps to protect personal consumer information or face fines up to $11,000 per violation."

(*The Boston Herald*, May 9, 2003)

"The Pentagon has released a study that recommends the government pursue specific technologies as potential safeguards against the misuse of data-mining systems similar to those now being considered by the government to track civilian activities electronically in the United States and abroad.

"The study, 'Security and Privacy,' was commissioned in late 2001 before the advent of the Pentagon's Total Information Awareness system, which is under the leadership of Dr. John M. Poindexter, national security adviser in the Reagan administration. The study was conducted by a group of civilian and military researchers, the Information Sciences and Technologies Study Group, or ISAT, which meets annually to review technology problems.

"A Washington privacy group, the Electronic Privacy Information Center, filed a Freedom of Information request last month with the Pentagon's Defense Advanced Research Projects Agency, or Darpa, and made the report available yesterday.

"The privacy group had asked the military to release documents relating to any review of the privacy implications of the Total Information Awareness system. Yesterday a group official said the study did not appear to be a com-

The Privacy Law Sourcebook 2003: United States Law, International Law, and Recent Developments (2002, 2001, 2000 editions also available)

Reports:

Critical Infrastructure Protection and the Endangerment of Civil Liberties: An Assessment of the Report of the President's Commission on Critical Infrastructure Protection

Network Advertising Initiative: Principles Not Privacy

Paying for Big Brother: A Review of the Proposed FY2003 Budget for the Department of Justice

Pretty Poor Privacy: An Assessment of P3P and Internet Privacy

The Public Voice and the Digital Divide: A Report to the DOT Force

Surfer Beware: Personal Privacy and the Internet

Surfer Beware II: Notice Is Not Enough

Surfer Beware III: Privacy Policies Without Privacy Protection

Your Papers, Please: From the State Driver's License to a National Identification System

CONFERENCES

EPIC frequently hosts and participates in various events and policy briefings on important privacy and First Amendment-related issues.

plete response to its request. 'They seem to be saying they have made no assessment of the privacy issues raised by the Total Information Awareness system,' said David Sobel, general counsel for the group. 'It's disturbing.'"

(The New York Times, December 19, 2002)

"The Bush Administration is developing a computer system to monitor every American's credit card transactions, phone calls and even borrowed library books in an anti-terrorist measure denounced as the country's most intrusive domestic spying network so far.

"Critics of the Total Information Awareness System, development of which was confirmed yesterday, say it will give the Government unprecedented powers to spy on citizens' personal habits. Marc Rotenberg, executive director of the Electronic Privacy Information Centre, a civil liberties group, called it 'the most sweeping plan to conduct surveillance on the public since at least the 1960s'.

"'It's probably one of the most significant public profiling proposals in modern US history,' he said. 'There's a very fine line between protecting homeland security and building a police state, and we are teetering on that line.'"

(The Times [London, England], November 22, 2002)

EMILY's List

Established in 1985

DIRECTOR

Ellen Malcolm, president. Malcolm, founder and president of EMILY's List, has been active in public service in Washington, DC, for 30 years. She worked at Common Cause in the early 1970s and later served as press secretary for the National Women's Political Caucus. She continued her career in politics by joining the White House staff in 1980 as press secretary for Esther Peterson, President Jimmy Carter's special assistant for consumer affairs.

BOARD OF DIRECTORS
None

SCOPE
Members: 73,000
Branches/chapters: None
Affiliates: None

STAFF
70 total—plus 12 interns

TAX STATUS
Declined to comment

FINANCES
Revenue: 2002—$22.7 million; 2003—$16.9 million

FUNDING SOURCES
Individuals, 81%; nonfederal transfers, 14%; contributions from other committees, 3%; other, 2%

PAC
EMILY's List

PAC CONTRIBUTIONS 2002

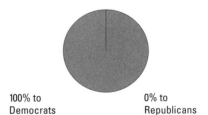

100% to	0% to
Democrats	Republicans

EMPLOYMENT
Political, development, administrative, and research positions are posted at www.emilyslist.org, Idealist.org, and WIN List. Resumes can be mailed to Kim Mathis, administrative director, 1120 Connecticut Avenue, NW, Suite 1100, Washington, DC, 20036. Phone: (202) 326-1400. Fax: (202) 326-1415.

CONTACT INFORMATION

1120 Connecticut Avenue, NW, Suite 1100, Washington, DC, 20036
Phone: (202) 326-1400 • *Fax:* (202) 326-1415
General E-mail: info@emilyslist.org • *Web site:* www.emilyslist.org

Communications Director: Ramona Oliver
(202) 326-1400 • roliver@emilyslist.org
Human Resources Director: Kim Mathis
(202) 326-1400

PURPOSE: An acronym for "Early Money Is Like Yeast" (it helps the "dough" rise), EMILY's List is the nation's largest grassroots political network, raising campaign contributions for prochoice Democratic women candidates running for the House, the Senate and for governor; helping women candidates build strong, winning campaigns; and helping mobilize women voters.

CURRENT CONCERNS: Educating women voters • Fundraising for Democratic prochoice women candidates • Get out the vote • Training for campaign workers and candidates • Women's rights

METHOD OF OPERATION: Campaign contributions • Electoral politics • Grassroots organizing • Internet (e-mail alerts and Web site) • Internships • Media outreach • Polling • Research • Training • Voter registration

Effectiveness and Political Orientation

"Labor, environmental and women's organizations, with strong backing from international financier George Soros, have joined forces behind a new political group that plans to spend an unprecedented $75 million to mobilize voters to defeat President Bush in 2004.

"The organization, Americans Coming Together (ACT), will conduct 'a massive get-out-the-vote operation that we think will defeat George W. Bush in 2004,' said Ellen Malcolm, the president of EMILY's List, who will become ACT's president."

(The Washington Post, August 8, 2003)

"Just one day after joining the governor's race, Christine Gregoire on Thursday celebrated an early pre-primary endorsement from the nation's largest women's campaign group.

"The nod from EMILY's List is expected to carry donations of hundreds of thousands of dollars over the next few months. . . .

"EMILY's List—the acronym means Early Money is Like Yeast—will include Gregoire in its next roster of endorsed candidates. The estimated 73,000 members send in money for the candidates they wish to finance. The per-person limit is $1,250 for the primary and $1,250 for the general election.

INTERNSHIPS

Internships in development, research, and political areas are posted at www.emilyslist.org. Internships last a semester and may be part-time or full-time hours. Application deadlines vary according to semester. The internship offers a $500 monthly stipend. The internship coordinator is Jill Wohrle, 1120 Connecticut Avenue, NW, Suite 1100, Washington, DC, 20036. Phone: (202) 326-1400. Fax: (202) 326-1415.

PUBLICATIONS

None

NEWSLETTERS

None

CONFERENCES

Majority Council Conference (annual)

"The group, which boosts the campaigns of Democratic women who support abortion rights, contributed nearly $10 million to candidates in 2002. During its 18-year history, recipients included seven women governors, 11 senators and 55 House members."

(*Associated Press Newswires,* July 31, 2003)

". . . . EMILY's List, a political action committee dedicated to electing Democratic women who support abortion rights."

(*Boston Globe,* May 21, 2003)

"Will women be big losers in the midterm elections? EMILY's List, a political-action committee that backs pro-choice, women Dems, has a losing record so far this cycle. The most notable defeat came on Aug. 6 in Michigan when Representative John D. Dingell trounced fellow Dem Representative Lynn N. Rivers.

"When redistricting threw both into the same district, Rivers mounted a scrappy campaign with the help of liberal groups. EMILY's List gave her $350,000. With Rivers' defeat, EMILY's has lost five out of nine, including bids in Illinois, West Virginia, and Tennessee. Certainly, the PAC can expect to lose a few, since it often backs women candidates despite long odds. And it wasn't all bad news in Michigan: Attorney General Jennifer Granholm overpowered two other Democratic candidates for governor, thanks in part to $450,000 from EMILY's List. But it's not shaping up as a banner year."

(*BusinessWeek,* August 26, 2002)

"A Washington-based group that raises money for pro-choice, female Democratic candidates is being criticized for turning its guns on Democratic men in recent primary elections.

"EMILY's List President Ellen Malcolm says the criticism is a sign that a double standard exists. It's fine for groups to pour in lots of money and support to elect men, she says, but when groups do the same to elect women, watch out.

"'EMILY's List now can make a tremendous difference in the elections. And the result of that is our political opponents are attacking us and trying to stop us,' she said.

"But many of the group's tactics haven't go over well, even with some EMILY's List supporters.

"U.S. Rep. Maxine Waters of California held a Detroit news conference earlier this month to denounce EMILY's List mailings in Michigan.

"The slick campaign literature criticized U.S. Rep. David Bonior and former Gov. James Blanchard, both vying in a heated race for the Democratic gubernatorial nomination against Attorney General Jennifer Granholm, an EMILY's List's endorsee.

"'I am absolutely disappointed that EMILY's List would use the money it collects from women across the country to distort the record of David Bonior in the interest of electing a woman,' said Waters, a Bonior backer who has been supported by EMILY's List since she was first elected in 1990."

(*Associated Press Newswires,* August 29, 2002)

"EMILY's List doesn't just give money to candidates. It mobilizes 68,000 supporters to send individual checks; it does more polling than the Democratic

National Committee; it runs TV ads for and against candidates; it staffs campaigns; it provides strategic advice.

"Already a major player, EMILY's List will only gain in stature with the enactment of the McCain-Feingold campaign finance reform act. While the national parties are struggling to figure out how to survive without 'soft money'—large donations often exceeding $100,000 from corporations, unions and individuals—EMILY's List is free to continue to raise both hard and soft money, and to pursue its true specialty: the bundling of small contributions into large packets of cash for favored candidates.

" 'We are the essence of campaign finance reform,' Malcolm recently told supporters. The new legislation 'does absolutely nothing to change the way we support our candidates. . . . It actually makes us even more powerful.'

"A candidate must meet three qualifications to be considered for an EMILY's List endorsement: back abortion rights, including the right to late-term (or 'partial birth') abortions; be a Democrat; and, in primary elections, be a woman.

"In many respects, EMILY's List is the Democratic counterpart to the National Rifle Association, a major Republican Party ally. The NRA was the top political action committee fundraiser in the 1999–2000 election cycle, at $17.9 million. Emily's List was second, at $14.6 million, although Malcolm pointed out that her group raised an additional $3.3 million for Democratic parties in 13 battleground states, making them virtually equal.

"The Democratic Party views EMILY's List as crucial in general elections. In 2000, the Democratic Congressional Campaign Committee gave the group $1.3 million in soft money. With the emergence in 1980 of a 'gender gap,' with women favoring Democrats and male Republicans, the ability of EMILY's List to mobilize women's voters has been viewed as essential to victory in close contests."

(*The Washington Post*, April 21, 2002)

Empower America

Established in 1993

DIRECTOR

James R. Taylor, president and chief executive officer. Prior to his appointment as president and chief executive officer of Empower America, Taylor was vice president for corporate communications for the U.S. Chamber of Commerce. Taylor's extensive legislative experience includes serving as chief of staff to Rep. Sue Myrick (R-NC) and as Jack Kemp's chief aide during the 1996 Dole-Kemp presidential campaign.

BOARD OF DIRECTORS

E. Floyd Kvamme, chair; partner, Kleiner Perkins Caulfield & Byers, Menlo Park, CA
William J. Bennett, co-director
William S. Cohen, co-director
Jack F. Kemp, co-director
Jeane J. Kirkpatrick, co-director
Vin Weber, co-director
James R. Taylor, president
Joseph G. Fogg III, chair of the advisory board; president, J.G. Fogg & Co., Inc., Westbury, NY
Theodore J. Forstmann, founding chair; senior partner, Forstmann Little & Co., New York, NY
Tim Blixseth; president, Blixseth Cos., Rancho Mirage, CA
Jamie B. Coulter; chair and chief executive officer, Lone Star Steakhouse & Saloon, Inc., Dallas, TX
Ronald E. Eibensteiner; president, Wyncrest Capital, Minneapolis, MN
Raul Fernandez; chair emeritus, Dimension Data, Reston, VA
James L. Gilmore III; partner, Kelley Drye & Warren LLP, Washington, DC
David W. Hanna; chair, Hanna Capital Management, Newport Beach, CA
Lisa Graham Keegan; chief executive officer, Education Leaders Council, Washington, DC
Michael Novak; George Fredrick Jewett scholar, American Enterprise Institute, Washington, DC
Joseph Schmuckler; chief operating officer, Nomura Holding America, Inc., New York, NY
Judy Shelton; economist, professor and author, Marshall, VA
Jack Thompson; co-founder (retired), J.E. Edwards, Larkspur, CO
Thomas W. Weisel; chief executive officer, Thomas Weisel Partners, San Francisco, CA

STAFF

25 total

TAX STATUS

501(c)(4)

CONTACT INFORMATION

1775 Pennsylvania Avenue, NW, 11th Floor, Washington, DC 20006-5805
Phone: (202) 452-8200 • *Fax:* (202) 833-0388
General E-mail: webmaster@empower.org • *Web site:* www.empower.org

Communications Director: Andrew Porter, press secretary
(202) 452-8200 • aporter@empower.org
Human Resources Director: Information unavailable

PURPOSE: "To promote progressive conservative public policies at both the state and national level, based on the principles of economic growth, international leadership, and cultural renewal."

CURRENT CONCERNS: Education reform • National security • Social security reform • Tax reform • Technology policy

METHOD OF OPERATION: Conferences/seminars • Internships • Lobbying (federal and grassroots) • Media outreach • Research • Web site

Effectiveness and Political Orientation

"A broad array of religious groups and conservative political activists has united behind the idea of a constitutional amendment against gay marriage. But the fledgling coalition is deeply divided about what, exactly, the amendment should say.

"At issue are not merely the fine details of legislative wording but the amendment's very purpose: Should it ban only same-sex marriage, or also take aim at Vermont-style civil unions and California-style partnerships that some opponents say amount to marriage in all but name? . . .

"At least three versions of the amendment are circulating in Washington, D.C. The leading text, and the only one introduced in Congress, has two sentences: 'Marriage in the United States shall consist only of the union of a man and a woman. Neither this constitution or the constitution of any state, nor state or federal law, shall be construed to require that marital status or the legal incidents thereof be conferred upon unmarried couples or groups.'

"Matt Daniels, president of the Alliance for Marriage, a bipartisan coalition of religious and political leaders backing that language, said the first sentence would ban gay marriage and the second is designed to stop courts from finding a constitutional right to same-sex unions. . . .

"Meanwhile, another powerful coalition of religious leaders is pushing for language that clearly would block Vermont-style civil unions. Known as the Arlington Group, because it first met in July in the Washington suburb of Arlington, Va., it unites the heads of almost every major political advocacy organization on the Christian right, including James Dobson of Focus on the Family, Gary Bauer of American Values, Bill Bennett of Empower America,

FINANCES
Information unavailable

FUNDING SOURCES
Declined to comment

SCOPE
Members: 165,000 individuals
Branches/chapters: None
Affiliates: None

PAC
None

EMPLOYMENT
Information unavailable

INTERNSHIPS
Summer internships last from early June to mid-August; the schedule is four full days a week. Internships at other times of the year are available; those schedules are flexible. Interns receive a $200 monthly stipend. Interns may work with the policy team, communications department, or development staff.
An application may be downloaded from www.empoweramerica.org; applicants must also submit a resume, cover letter explaining particular interest in Empower America, 3–5 page writing sample on a current event or a paper written for a relevant class, and a faculty recommendation in a sealed envelope (alternatively, the faculty member may send the recommendation directly to Empower America). Materials should be sent to the internship coordinator, Shaun Small, 1775 Pennsylvania Avenue, NW, 11th Floor, Washington, DC 20006-5805.

NEWSLETTERS
Empower America (for members who donate
      $1,000 or more)

PUBLICATIONS
None

CONFERENCES
Candidate schools (for federal, state, and local
      candidates)
Regional conferences
Congress Freshman Orientation (with Heritage
      Foundation)
Leadership Council Forums
Summer Western Retreat

Tony Perkins of the Family Research Council, Sandy Rios of Concerned Women for America and Paul Weyrich of the Free Congress Foundation."
(*The Seattle Times,* November 29, 2003)

". . . Empower America, a Washington conservative think tank. . . ."
(*The San Francisco Chronicle,* July 25, 2003)

"Emboldened by Monday's Supreme Court decisions upholding race-conscious college admissions, state legislators and education activists on both sides of the debate are scrambling for a position in the legal landscape created by the rulings.

"As supporters looked for ways to expand affirmative action's reach, opponents examined the feasibility of promoting ballot initiatives to outlaw affirmative action in states across the country. They also said they will file new lawsuits challenging affirmative action programs that they feel go beyond the limits the Supreme Court set. . . .

"Jack F. Kemp, the former Republican congressman who is now a director of Empower America, a Washington research organization, called the efforts to find new ways to oppose affirmative action in the wake of the court's ruling shortsighted.

" 'While I agree that ultimately a colorblind society should be our goal, we certainly are not there yet. Blacks were removed from the mainstream economy, denied access to education, job opportunities and access to capital and ownership,' he said. 'Thus, African Americans have long been denied their full measure of justice under the law, and while great progress has been made, we have a long way to go.' "
(*The Washington Post,* June 25, 2003)

"One of America's most prominent moral crusaders, the former 'drug tsar' Bill Bennett, has admitted a gambling habit that allegedly cost him millions of pounds over the past decade.

"Mr Bennett, the author of works such as *The Book of Virtues* and *The Death of Outrage,* rejected accusations of hypocrisy when reports emerged over the weekend that he was a favoured 'high roller' at casinos in Las Vegas and Atlantic City.

"He was said to have wagered hundreds of thousands of dollars at a time in a single night.

"Mr Bennett, a former education secretary under Ronald Reagan, is a leading critic of what he sees as America's moral decline.

"He helped found the Index of Leading Cultural Indicators, tracking the personal failings of Americans. Compulsive gambling was one of those indicators.

"Mr Bennett's pressure group, Empower America, also opposes the spread of legalised gaming.

"After *Newsweek* magazine reported that Mr Bennett had lost up to pounds 5 million over his gambling career, he initially protested that he had largely broken even and never spent his family's 'milk money.'

"He later said: 'It is true that I have gambled large sums of money . . . and this is not an example I wish to set.' He added that his gambling days were 'over.' "
(*The Daily Telegraph* [London, England], May 7, 2003)

"Earlier this month, William J. Bennett, a former education secretary and the conservative co-director of Empower America, sent Bush a memo outlining what he said was a 'true civil rights agenda.'

"It included ending racial preferences in college admissions; reauthorizing the 1996 welfare legislation with a greater emphasis on work and marriage; and extending school vouchers and creating a model school-choice program in the District of Columbia.

"Last week, Bush followed two of three recommendations, proposing to reauthorize the 1996 welfare law and siding with white students who brought a Supreme Court challenge against the University of Michigan over admissions policies that give an edge to minority applicants.

" 'I argued as loudly as I could that the consistent principle is color blindness and race neutrality,' Bennett said. 'Race shouldn't matter.' "

(*The Boston Globe,* January 19, 2003)

Environmental and Energy Study Institute

Established in 1984

DIRECTOR
Carol Werner, executive director.

BOARD OF DIRECTORS
Richard L. Ottinger, chair; professor emeritus and former dean, Pace University School of Law; former member of Congress (D-NY)

John J. Sheehan, vice chair; retired legislative director, United Steelworkers of America

Nancy Bacon; senior vice president, Energy Conversion Devices, Inc.

Anthony Beilenson; former member of Congress (D-CA) and former California state senator

Ambassador Richard E. Benedick; senior advisor, Joint Global Change Research Institute, Battelle Pacific Northwest National Laboratory (PNL); former deputy assistant secretary of state

Rosina M. Bierbaum; dean, School of Natural Resources and Environment, University of Michigan; former acting director, White House Office of Science and Technology Policy

Jared Blum; president, Polyisocyanurate Insulation Manufacturers Association

Frances S. Buchholzer; former director, Ohio Department of Natural Resources

Quincalee Brown; former executive director, Water Environment Federation

Mortimer M. Caplin; founder and partner, Caplin and Drysdale; former commissioner, Internal Revenue Service

Gerald Decker; chair, Decker Energy International Development, Inc.; chair, Competitive Power Forum

Roger Duncan; vice president, Austin Energy Services

Robert W. Edgar; general secretary of the National Council of the Churches of Christ in the USA; ordained minister; former Member of Congress (D-PA)

Christopher Flavin; president, World Watch Institute

Gilbert Gude; writer and lecturer; former member of Congress (R-MD); former director, Congressional Research Service

Ruth Patrick; senior curator, Academy of Natural Sciences of Philadelphia

Chris Schepis; government relations representative, National Farmers Union; former House and Senate staffer

Jeff Seabright; vice president, Environment and Water, Coca Cola Co.; former director of Energy, Environment & Technology, Agency for International Development; former executive director of the White House Climate Change Task Force

CONTACT INFORMATION
122 C Street, NW, Suite 630, Washington, DC 20001-2109
Phone: (202) 628-1400 • *Fax:* (202) 628-1825
General E-mail: eesi@eesi.org • *Web site:* www.eesi.org

Communications Director: None
Human Resources Director: None

PURPOSE: "Dedicated to promoting environmentally sustainable societies."

CURRENT CONCERNS: Agriculture and energy • Alternative environmental strategies • Biofuels and bioenergy • Clean bus fleets • Energy efficiency and renewable energy • Fiscal policy • Global climate change • Sustainable community development • Transportation

METHOD OF OPERATION: Conferences/seminars • Congressional testimony • Information clearinghouse • Internet (e-mail alerts and Web site) • Internships • Legislative/regulatory monitoring (federal) • Media outreach • Participation in regulatory proceedings (federal) • Telecommunications services

Effectiveness and Political Orientation

"Supporters of a plan to open the Arctic National Wildlife Refuge to oil and gas drilling seemed perfectly positioned this week as the Senate debated the issue in the midst of U.S. military action against Iraq and heightened concerns about the nation's domestic oil supply.

"The measure, inserted in a budget bill, needed only a simple majority, as opposed to the 60 votes required in previous attempts, but it failed Wednesday, 52–48, on a vote to strip it from the budget bill. Defeat came even though it was a priority of President Bush, whose party controls the Senate. . . .

"Carol Werner, executive director of the Environmental and Energy Study Institute, said many senators considered sympathetic to the drilling arguments were reluctant to vote for it because they had promised environmentalists that they would not."

(The New Orleans Times-Picayune, March 21, 2003)

"Mr. Bush proposed a plan yesterday that he said would bring climate change by encouraging businesses to cut their pollution levels and develop more energy-efficient technology.

"Mr. Bush said he would cut the growth rate in greenhouse gases by giving companies incentives to cut emissions, find alternative forms of energy, improving conservation and developing technology to reduce pollution.

"Mr. Bush said he was offering 'a new environmental approach that will clean our skies, bring greater health to our citizens and encourage environmentally responsible development in America and around the world.'. . .

SCOPE

Members: None
Branches/chapters: None
Affiliates: None

STAFF

7 total—plus 2 interns

TAX STATUS

501(c)(3)

FINANCES

Revenue: 2002—$783,507

FUNDING SOURCES

Primarily foundation grants. Other support comes from individuals, corporations, and government.

PAC

None

EMPLOYMENT

Information about open positions is available at www.eesi.org. To apply, send cover letter, resume, and a writing sample to: Jan Couch, director, finance and administration, EESI, 122 C Street, NW, Suite 630, Washington, DC 20001. Fax: (202) 628-1825. E-mail: jcouch@eesi.org. No calls, please.

INTERNSHIPS

Information about internship positions is available at www.eesi.org. Fall, spring, and summer policy program internships are offered. Internships are unpaid but may be used for undergraduate, graduate, or postgraduate credit. EESI also provides some metro transportation benefits. Program areas include climate change, energy efficiency, and renewable energy technologies; transportation-related environmental problems and vehicle technologies; water pollution and water resources; fundraising and development; and nonprofit administration and management. Applicants should send a resume, a writing sample of about two pages, an unofficial transcript, and a cover letter explaining what they hope to gain through an internship with EESI.

Apply to Claire Suen, intern coordinator, Environmental & Energy Study Institute, 122 C Street, NW, Suite 700, Washington, DC 20001-2109. Phone: (202) 662-1893. Fax: (202) 628-1825. E-mail:csuen@eesi.org.

NEWSLETTERS

Clean Bus Update (online monthly)
Climate Change News (online weekly)
BCO (online irregular)

PUBLICATIONS

Air Conditioner Efficiency Standards: SEER 12 vs. SEER 13
Analysis of Clean Bus Provisions in SAFETEA
EESI Bus Rapid Transit Memorandum
EESI 2001 Report: Alternative Fuel Projects Funded Through CMAQ
Fact Sheet on Cleaner Bus Technologies, Fuels and Deployment Status
Fuel Cell Fact Sheet

"Unlike the 1997 Kyoto accord, the plan unveiled by Mr. Bush does not require the U.S. to reduce its emissions of greenhouse gases. Instead, greenhouse gases could continue to rise as the American economy grows, although at a slower pace.

"Under the Bush plan, if the U.S. gross domestic product grows at the rate predicted by the American government, the country's greenhouse gas emissions will rise to 2,027 million tonnes by 2012, up from 1,677 million tonnes in 1990.

" 'It short-changes the environment,' said Carol Werner, executive director of the Washington-based Environmental and Energy Study Institute, a nonpartisan think-tank. 'It also totally short-changes the opportunities and capabilities of U.S. industries to reduce emissions.' "

(*The Ottawa Citizen* [Canada], February 15, 2002)

"The ads show behemoth sport-utility vehicles rumbling through the wilderness and hauling cargo to mountain peaks.

"Those gas-swigging giants with powerful engines might also have enough oomph to drag the Senate's energy bill into the muck of stalemate.

"The bill, to be introduced later this week, will feature several heated arguments that focus on oil demand, which has steadily increased in the 1990s largely because of the popularity of SUVs. . . .

"The Senate commerce committee has been discussing how to raise fuel-efficiency standards for SUVs and other light trucks. Currently, SUVs must get 20.7 miles per gallon. Cars, meanwhile, are required to get 27.5 mpg.

"Carol Werner, executive director of the Environmental and Energy Study Institute that briefs Congress on such issues, said raising the minimum level for miles per gallon is a logical short-term step to stem oil use.

" 'The longer we wait to raise standards and use oil more efficiently, the more we waste the oil already here,' she said."

(*The San Diego Union-Tribune*, February 12, 2002)

"The farm lobby could have the upper hand when products such as corn-based fuel compete for the federal government's purchasing power under a little-noticed proposal advancing in Congress.

"Federal agencies—which now spend more than $200 billion a year on a vast array of products and are the nation's largest consumer—would be required to buy 'biobased' products whenever they're found to be comparable in price, performance and availability to traditional products. . . .

"Carol Warner [sic], executive director of the Environmental and Energy Study Institute, a Washington-based think tank, said the bill would take the government further than President Clinton's 1999 executive order that merely made it U.S. policy to develop and promote biobased products.

" 'We see this as a very important step forward,' she said. 'It's really important to kick-start this whole thing.' "

(*Associated Press Newswires*, November 25, 2001)

"As President Bush prepares to release his energy plan today, the solar, biomass and other 'green' energy industries are cautiously optimistic about what it will contain.

"Despite the advance thrashing Bush has taken for his pro-nuclear, pro-drilling approach, producers of renewable fuels are expecting a host of tax credits to make their products more competitive with fossil fuels.

In addition, summaries of EESI's Congressional briefings are published at www.eesi.org.

CONFERENCES
Briefings on various environmental issues often regarding pending legislation (1–2 per month on Capitol Hill).

"Still, alternative-fuel lobbyists briefed on the report by Vice President Dick Cheney said the plan will be quite vague. They were told to expect no numeric goals on how much of U.S. energy needs should be supplied by renewables or any other source, and few specific legislative guidelines. . . .

"Cheney told renewable-fuels lobbyists that almost all the report's financial incentives will be for energy efficiency and renewables, not fossil fuels.

"But reliance on fossil fuels and nuclear power will still be the thrust of the report, giving short-shrift to conservation and renewables, advocates said.

" 'There are going to be some things we're going to support,' said Carol Werner, executive director of the Environmental and Energy Study Institute, a nonprofit policy group. 'We're just very concerned that the balance is going to be tilted in the other direction.' "

(*The San Francisco Chronicle,* May 17, 2001)

Environmental Defense

Established in 1967

DIRECTOR

Fred Krupp, president. In addition to working with Environmental Defense's experts, Krupp has represented environmental concerns worldwide, including at the Buenos Aries Climate meeting and the Kyoto Protocol. He is credited with leading the environmental community in the use of Internet technology, most notably with the zip code specific information site. Krupp has served as a member of several boards and advisory panels, including President Clinton's Commission on Sustainable Development and Advisory Committee for Trade Policy and Negotiations; the H. John Heinz III Center for Science, Economics and the Environment; the Kennedy School Environmental Council; and the Leadership Council of the Yale School of Forestry and Environmental Studies. Before joining Environmental Defense Krupp was a law partner at Cooper, Whitney, Cochran & Krupp (1984); law partner at Albis & Krupp (1978–1984); and founder/general counsel, Connecticut Fund for the Environment (19781984). He earned his J.D. from the University of Michigan.

BOARD OF TRUSTEES

CONTACT INFORMATION

257 Park Avenue South, New York, NY 10010
Phone: (212) 505-2100 • *Fax:* (212) 505-0892
General E-mail: members@environmentaldefense.org •
Web site: www.environmentaldefense.org

Communications Director: Tom Belford, vice president for marketing and communications
(202) 387-3500 • tbelford@environmentaldefense.org
Human Resources: Mark Priest
(212) 505-2100 • mpriest@environmentaldefense.org

PURPOSE: "[D]edicated to protecting the environmental rights of all people, including future generations. Among these rights are clean air and water, healthy and nourishing food, and a flourishing ecosystem. . . . Environmental Defense helped launch the modern environmental movement by winning a ban on the pesticide DDT. . . . Guided by science, Environmental Defense evaluates environmental problems and works to create and advocate solutions that win lasting political, economic, and social support because they are nonpartisan, cost-efficient and fair."

CURRENT CONCERNS: Biodiversity • Climate change • Health • Oceans • Environmental science

METHOD OF OPERATION: Coalition forming • Congressional testimony • Fellowships • Initiative/referendum campaigns • Internet (databases [www. scorecard.org], e-mail alerts, and Web site) • Internships • Legislative/regulatory monitoring (federal and state) • Media outreach

Effectiveness and Political Orientation

"Mainstream scientists around the world agree that climate change is real and that human activity is the primary culprit. Global warming is already impacting Connecticut and, if ignored, the problem will begin to fundamentally change the state's public health, coastlines, commercial fisheries and economy. And not for the better.

"A new study by Environmental Defense shows temperatures around Connecticut increased noticeably during the 20th century. If the warming continues unchecked, by 2050 the state is projected to have an additional 10 more high-heat-stress days a year than it did in the 1990s. . . .

"A warmer climate is also more hospitable to vector-borne diseases, such as Lyme disease and West Nile virus. Connecticut saw 26 human cases of West Nile since 1999; more than 520 birds from every county in the state tested positive for the virus in 2002. . . .

"Connecticut residents are literally driving toward this hot and dangerous future. Transportation produces 39 percent of Connecticut's greenhouse gas

SCOPE

Members: More than 400,000
Branches/chapters: Regional offices in Boston; Washington, DC; Raleigh, NC; Austin, TX; Boulder, CO; Oakland, CA; Los Angeles
Affiliates: None

STAFF

250 total

TAX STATUS

501(c)(3)

FINANCES

Budget: 2002—$43.8 million

FUNDING SOURCES

Membership and contributions, 67%; foundation grants, 22%; investment and other revenue, 6%; bequests, 4%; government and other grants, 1%

PAC

None

EMPLOYMENT

Information on open positions for the national office and all branch offices can be obtained online at www.environmentaldefense.org/careers.cfm. Cover letters, resumes, and salary requirements can be mailed directly to the branch posting the position; refer to the job posting online for full information. The organization is an equal opportunity employer. Women, minorities, veterans, and the physically challenged are encouraged to apply.

pollution, and as a whole, the state produces more heat-trapping greenhouse gases than Venezuela and Chile combined.

"Acting early to cut down on greenhouse pollution will be better for the environment, better for our health and better for our pocketbooks than denial and delay. As a longtime Connecticut resident [and president of Environmental Defense] and a founder of the Connecticut Fund for the Environment, I'm proud that the state is poised to help secure the future for our children. People have stopped just talking about the weather and have started to do something about it."

(*Hartford Courant* [Connecticut], February 6, 2004)

"Federal regulators can trump more permissive state officials in some disputes over costly measures to limit air pollution, the Supreme Court said Wednesday in a ruling that departed from its trend toward granting state governments more power.

"Alaska's governor wanted to allow the world's largest zinc mine to use cheaper, less effective antipollution equipment, but the federal Environmental Protection Agency said no. The Supreme Court's 5–4 ruling upholds EPA's veto power in such cases.

"'The highest court in the land has made it eminently clear that the EPA has ample authority to protect the public health and the environment from the harmful effects of air pollution,' said Vickie Patton, a lawyer with the interest group Environmental Defense.

"The victory for environmentalists may be more symbolic than substantive. The portion of the Clean Air Act at issue has not been front and center in court fights over pollution, and the court majority kept its ruling narrow."

(*St. Petersburg Times* [Florida], January 22, 2004)

"Most of the billions of chickens, pigs, and other animals raised for food each year receive antibiotics in their feed. They grow faster and stay healthier, but there's a huge potential cost: the creation of drug-resistant germs that may also attack people. The European Union has largely banned in animals four antibiotics commonly used by humans, but U.S. agencies have been slower to act. So the activist group Environmental Defense (ED) has been urging restaurant chains, caterers, and others to dissuade their suppliers from using antibiotics—and the strategy is working. In June, McDonald's said it would require meat suppliers to stop one routine use of the drugs, to promote growth. Now, Bon Appétit is going further. The caterer, which prepares 300,000 meals a day for companies such as Oracle Corp, universities, and others, announced on Dec. 4 that by next summer, its suppliers would stop dosing whole flocks of chickens to prevent disease. The drugs will be used only to treat sick animals. Such moves show that reducing drug use is 'both feasible and affordable,' says ED's Rebecca Goldburg."

(*Business Week*, December 22, 2003)

". . . a clean-air advocacy group. . . ."

(*The Los Angeles Times*, December 21, 2003)

"Jaws may have been bad PR for sharks, but Hawaii fishermen did a lot more damage. By the late 1990s, 50,000 Pacific sharks were being killed each year in a practice known as shark finning. Fishing crews would catch the sharks, amputate their fins, and toss the fish back in the ocean. The fins would be used to make a soup that's considered a delicacy in some Asian countries. . . ."The practice is described in gruesome detail on many Web sites. But just getting the word out wasn't enough for Environmental Defense (until recently, Environment Defense Fund), the New York-based nonprofit organization that helped ban the pesticide DDT and convinced McDonald's to drop the polystyrene-foam Big Mac boxes. 'We wanted action. We wanted shark finning to stop,' says Daniel Freedman, the group's chief Internet officer

"That's why last year Environmental Defense's online activism effort, Action Network, not only described the horrifying practice but also provided visitors the means to fax a prewritten letter of protest to officials. With the help of KAHEA, the Hawaiian Environmental Alliance, hundreds of messages were sent to Hawaiian authorities, which subsequently barred shark finning in state waters.

"Buoyed by that victory, Environmental Defense spearheaded a broader campaign for a nationwide ban. Nearly 10,000 faxes were sent to Congress, and in December 2000, a bill outlawing shark finning was signed into law by President Clinton. 'It's hard to say definitively what tipped the balance, but [the site] had an impact,' says Freedman. The Action Network also made a difference for the Texas sea turtles, which were perishing in shrimp nets.

"'The Internet is the ultimate expression of "think global, act local,"' says Environmental Defense's executive director, Fred Krupp. . . . With 300,000-plus dues-paying members, the organization lobbies legislators the old-fashioned way—with lobbyists—and publishes reports and op-ed pieces. But the sheer and instant breadth of the possible network with Web-based activism enables it to reach more people and be more effective in a shorter time period than ever before."

(*PC Magazine,* September 4, 2001)

Environmental Law Institute

Established in 1971

DIRECTOR

Leslie Carothers, president. Carothers has been a professional environmentalist for more than 30 years. Before her election as ELI president in June 2003, she served for 11 years as vice president for environment, health and safety at United Technologies Corp. in Hartford. She also served as commissioner of the Connecticut Department of Environmental Protection from 1987–1991 and senior environmental counsel for PPG Industries from 1982–1987. She began her environmental career with the U.S. Environmental Protection Agency in 1971 and later served as enforcement director, deputy regional administrator, and acting regional administrator of EPA's New England Region in Boston. Carothers is a past member and chair of the board of directors of the Connecticut Audubon Society and the Environmental Law Institute. She currently serves on the board of directors of Strategies for the Global Environment (Pew Center on Global Climate Change). She is a graduate of Smith College and Harvard Law School and also holds a Masters Degree in environmental law from George Washington University.

BOARD OF DIRECTORS

Leslie Carothers, president
Kenneth Berlin, chair; partner, Skadden, Arps, Slate, Meagher & Flom LLP, Washington, DC
Elliott Laws, secretary-treasurer; office counsel, Campbell George & Strong, L.L.C., Vienna, VA
Lynn L. Bergeson, executive committee member; partner, Bergeson & Campbell, P.C, Washington, DC
Christopher H. Buckley Jr., executive committee member; partner, Gibson, Dunn & Crutcher LLP, Washington, DC
David C. Cannon Jr., executive committee member; vice president, Environment, Health and Safety, PPG Industries, Inc., Pittsburgh, PA
Frank B. Friedman, executive committee member; president, Frank B. Friedman and Associates, LLC, Chevy Chase, MD
Paul E. Hagen, executive committee member; director, Beveridge & Diamond, P.C., Washington, DC
Howard A. Learner, executive committee member; executive director, Environmental Law & Policy Center, Chicago, IL
Gustavo Alanis-Ortega; president, Mexican Environmental Law Center, Colonia Condesa, Mexico
Sherwood L. Boehlert; U.S. representative, Washington, DC
Joseph L. Boren; president & CEO, AIG Environmental, New York, NY

CONTACT INFORMATION

1616 P Street, NW, Suite 200, Washington, DC 20036
Phone: (202) 939-3800 • *Fax:* (202) 939-3868
General E-mail: law@eli.org • *Web site:* www.eli.org

Communications Director: John Thompson, director, marketing and communications
(202) 939-3800 • thompson@eli.org
Human Resources Director: Laura Van Wyk
(202) 939-3800 • vanwyk@eli.org

PURPOSE: The Environmental Law Institute is "an independent, active, non-profit center conducting policy studies on the environment and sustainability and reaching out with educational programs, publications and technical assistance across the U.S. and abroad."

CURRENT CONCERNS: Drinking water • Endangered environmental laws • Environmental law and policy • Environmental management • Harmful invasive species • Homeland security • Nanotechnology • Public and private land conservation and use • Wetlands protection

METHOD OF OPERATION: Awards program • Conferences/seminars • International activities • Internet (e-mail alerts and Web site) • Internships • Legislative/regulatory monitoring (federal and state) • Mailing list • Media outreach • Research • Speakers program • Training and technical assistance

Effectiveness and Political Orientation

"The safety of America's drinking water has never been a more serious issue. The Environmental Law Institute (ELI) report *Homeland Security and Drinking Water: An Opportunity for Comprehensive Protection of a Vital Natural Resource* released today outlines the complex layers of federal and state laws and regulations established to promote homeland security and drinking water safety.

"Most notably, the ELI report demonstrates in a post 9-11 era of limited financial resources, the urgent need to integrate responses to drinking water challenges stemming from security, infrastructure, and contamination threats. In recent history our nation's drinking water has never been as vulnerable as it is today. It faces the threat of potential terrorist attacks, continued stress of growing urban populations on the existing drinking water resources and infrastructure, and potential contamination by mutating pathogens (e.g., antibiotic resistant bacteria) and other emerging contaminants (e.g., pharmaceuticals).

" 'The current drinking water debate focuses on supply for future generations but fails to consider challenges based on current exigencies. Rather than ask, "where do we get water to sustain future growth," we should be asking "how are we going to deliver safe water today and tomorrow" ' explains B. Suzi Ruhl, Director of the Public Health and Law Program at ELI. 'Now we must expand our focus and confront threats to our water supply from terrorism,

Carol A. Casazza Herman; assistant general counsel; senior director, Corporate EH&S-Legal, Pfizer Inc, New York, NY

Gail Charnley Elliott; HealthRisk Strategies, Washington, DC

Eileen Claussen; president, Pew Center on Global Climate Change, Arlington, VA

John H. Claussen; president, TRC Environmental Corp., Windsor, CT

William M. Eichbaum; vice president, Endangered Spaces Program, World Wildlife Fund, Washington, DC

Linda Fisher; Washington, DC

Howard M. Holtzmann; judge, New York, NY

John E. Huerta; general counsel, The Smithsonian Institution, Washington, DC

William H. Hyatt Jr.; partner, Kirkpatrick & Lockhart LLP, Newark, NJ

Clair E. Krizov; executive director, Environment and Social Responsibility, AT&T, Atlanta, GA

R. Christopher Locke; chair, Environmental Law Department, Farella Braun & Martel LLP, San Francisco, CA

Felicia Marcus; executive vice president and chief executive officer, Trust for Public Land, San Francisco, CA

Langdon Marsh; fellow, National Policy Consensus Center, Portland State University, Portland, OR

Susan Moore; vice president, Environmental Affairs, Georgia-Pacific Corp., Atlanta, GA

Ernie Rosenberg; president and chief executive officer, Soap and Detergent Assn., Washington, DC

Robert Stang; managing member, ReNEWal Realty, LLC, Willingboro, NJ

Robert Stanton; consultant, Resource Conservation Policy, Planning and Management, Fairfax Station, VA

Herbert H. Tate Jr.; counsel, Wolff & Samson PC, West Orange, NJ

Michael Traynor; partner, Cooley Godward LLP, San Francisco, CA

Thomas Udall; U.S. representative, Washington, DC

Robert A. Wyman; partner, Latham & Watkins LLP, Los Angeles, CA

SCOPE

Members: 3,000 total (894 individuals; approximately 100 firms and corporations)

Branches/chapters: None

Affiliates: Center for Pubic Health and Law; Environmental Management and Capacity Building; Sustainability and Resource Protection. Regional programs: Inter-American Program; Africa Program; India Program; Central and Eastern Europe

International programs: Environmental Consequences of War; Center for Native Lands.

TAX STATUS

501(c)(3)

FINANCES

Budget: 2003—$6.06 million; 2002—$4.95 million; 2001—$5.23 million

aging infrastructure, and other emerging biological and chemical contaminants and mutating pathogens.'"

(*U.S. Newswire*, December 15, 2003)

"Long time conservation leader William K. Reilly, currently the President and Chief Executive Officer for Aqua International Partners and Chairman of the World Wildlife Fund-US Board of directors, will receive the Environmental Law Institute's top honor, the 2003 Environmental Law Institute Award, in a ceremony at the Omni Shoreham Hotel in Washington, D.C. on October 8, 2003. Reilly was U.S. Environmental Protection Agency Administrator from 1989–1993. U.S. Congressman Christopher Shays (R-CT) will deliver the keynote address.

"The award cites Reilly for his effective leadership in a series of prominent positions in the private sector and in government. 'The ELI Award is given annually to honor an individual who has demonstrated a lifetime commitment to environmental protection and exemplary public service,' states ELI President, Leslie Carothers. 'We are very pleased to honor Bill Reilly this year. He is a true champion of the environment and an innovator in forging better ways to protect it around the world.' . .

"ELI is an independent, non-profit research and educational organization based in Washington, D.C. The Institute serves the environmental profession in business, government, the private bar, public interest organizations, academia, and the press."

(*AScribe Law News Service*, October 6, 2003)

"Formal environmental management systems (EMS) can improve the environmental performance of government units and businesses as well as their operating and management efficiencies and, sometimes, compliance with regulations, a major new study concludes.

" 'These results are more likely for facilities that are subsidiaries of publicly traded corporations, owing to their greater resources, but they occur in privately held and government facilities as well,' said Dr. Richard N.L. Andrews of the University of North Carolina at Chapel Hill.

"Andrews and colleagues conducted the first-of-its-kind study for the EPA's Office of Wastewater Management, with support from EPA's Office of Policy, Economics and Innovation. Also involved in the five-year project were ten state environmental agencies, the Environmental Law Institute, the Multi-State Working Group on Environmental Management Systems, the Star Track Program of the EPA's Region I and the Global Environmental Technology Foundation. . . .

"Generally, EMSs had positive effects on facilities' environmental performance, which although it makes sense had never been confirmed before. . . ."

(*Industrial Safety & Hygiene News*, May 2003)

FUNDING SOURCES
Foundation grants and contracts, 55%;
publications, 15%; associates, 14%;
royalties, 6%; other, 10%

PAC
None

STAFF
65 total—plus visiting scholars, fellows, and
interns

EMPLOYMENT
Information on current job openings is posted
online at www.eli.org. The staff consists of
attorneys, economists, scientists, management specialists, and editors plus administrative corps, fellows, and interns. The Environmental Law Institute is strongly committed to
advancing equal opportunity in recruitment,
employment, and promotion and to achieving
diversity.

INTERNSHIPS
Positions for legal and research interns are
posted online at www.eli.org. Completed
applications can be mailed to: Intern
Coordinator, Environmental Law Institute, 1616
P Street, NW, Suite 200, Washington, DC
20036. Applications in Microsoft Word or
WordPerfect format can be e-mailed to:
internsearch@eli.org. Fax: (202) 939-3868.

NEWSLETTERS
ELR: Environmental Law Reporter (online
    monthly)
ELR News & Analysis (online monthly)
ELR Update (online 3 times per month)
The Environmental Forum (bimonthly)
The National Wetlands (six times per year)

PUBLICATIONS
*Building Healthy, High Performance Schools: A
    Review of Selected State and School
    District Initiatives*
Endangered Species Deskbook
Harmful Invasive Species: Legal Responses
*Jurisdynamics of Environmental Protection:
    Change and the Pragmatic Voice in
    Environmental Law*
*Legal Tools and Incentives for Private Lands
    Conservation in Latin America: Building
    Models for Success*
*New Ground: The Advent of Local
    Environmental Law*
*Open Ground: Effective Local Strategies for
    Protecting Natural Resources*
*Reporting on Climate Change: Understanding
    the Science,* 3rd edition
Also publishes monographs and research
briefs.

CONFERENCES
ELI Associates Seminars
ELI Advanced Courses of Study
Miriam Hamilton Keare Policy Forum
National Wetlands Awards Ceremony
Also, numerous conferences worldwide.

Environmental Working Group

Established in 1993

DIRECTOR

Ken A. Cook, president. Cook co-founded the Group with Richard Wiles in 1993. In the decade since its founding, the Environmental Working Group has earned renown for its innovative, headline-making computer investigations of environmental problems. Both Cook and the Group have been the subject of profiles in numerous publications. Cook was recognized as one of Washington's top nonprofit lobbyists by *The Hill,* and he was also named one of "Agriculture's 100 Most Influential Leaders" by *Progressive Farmer.* He is a board member of Environmental Media Services, Earth Day Network, and the Amazon Conservation Team. Cook earned B.A., B.S., and M.S. degrees from the University of Missouri-Columbia.

BOARD OF DIRECTORS

Ken A. Cook, president
Kelsey Wirth, chair; former president, Align Technology, San Francisco, CA
Sandy Buchanan, secretary; Ohio Citizen Action, Cleveland, OH
Drummond Pike, treasurer; Tides Foundation/Tides Center, San Francisco, CA
David Baker; Community Against Pollution, Anniston, AL
Charlotte Brody, RN; Health Care Without Harm, Washington, DC
David Fenton; Fenton Communications, Washington, DC
Cari Rudd; Strategic Communications Consultant, Arlington, VA

SCOPE

Members: None
Branch/chapter: Regional offices in Oakland, CA
Affiliate: None

STAFF

19 total—18 full-time professional; 1 full-time support; plus 2 part-time support; 1 intern

TAX STATUS

501(c)(3), EWG Action Fund is 501(c)(4)

FINANCES

Budget: 2004—$2.7 million; 2003—$2.3 million; 2002—$2.3 million

FUNDING SOURCES

Foundation grants and private individuals, 93%; corporate donations, 2.5%; individuals, 2.5%; special events/projects, 2%

PAC

None

CONTACT INFORMATION

1436 U Street, NW, Suite 100, Washington, DC 20009
Phone: (202) 667-6982 • *Fax:* (202) 232-2592
General E-mail: info@ewg.org • *Web site:* www.ewg.org

Communications Director: Mike Casey, vice president for public affairs (202) 667-6982
Human Resources Director: Matt Rochkind, office manager (202) 667-6982

PURPOSE: The Environmental Working Group (EWG) uses the power of information to protect public health and the environment. Through original policy research, data analysis, and innovative public education campaigns, EWG seeks urgent, fundamental government reforms in order to protect the most vulnerable segments of the human population from health problems attributed to a wide array of environmental toxins. EWG seeks to replace federal policies, including government subsidies, that damage the environment and natural resources with policies that invest in conservation and sustainable development. EWG also seeks to harness the power of the marketplace by providing citizens and the private sector with practical information for reducing the health and environmental effects of toxic chemicals and unsustainable business practices.

CURRENT CONCERNS: Agriculture subsidies • Public lands • Toxic substances • Transportation • Water quality

METHOD OF OPERATION: Advertisements • Coalition forming • Congressional testimony • Information clearinghouse • Internet (databases, electronic bulletin boards, e-mail alerts, and Web site) • Internships • Legislative/regulatory monitoring (federal and state) • Litigation • Lobbying (federal and grassroots) • Media outreach • Participation in regulatory proceedings (federal) • Performance ratings/Report cards • Research

Effectiveness and Political Orientation

"What is it with fish these days? First mercury and now this: A new report in science says farm-raised Atlantic salmon contains dramatically higher concentrations of PCBs and other suspected cancer-causing agents than wild salmon. A likely reason, says the study: Farm varieties are fed meal made from fish plucked from contaminated waters. Worried? You should be, say researchers, who warn that the health risks of farm-raised salmon may even outweigh the benefits of eating it. So should you give it up? 'Absolutely not,' says Alex Trent of industry group Salmon of the Americas. 'It would do more harm than good,' because salmon is full of heart-healthy omega-3 fatty acids. He says the contaminants are within Food and Drug Administration safety limits, and that the industry has been reducing PCB levels by shifting from fish to vegetable-based feed. Others aren't so sure; while levels are within FDA regs, they exceed

more stringent Environmental Protection Agency guidelines. 'Limit consumption to [an 8-ounce serving] once a month,' says Jane Houlihan of the
Environmental Working Group. And be sure to trim PCB-laden fat—and
grill, bake, or broil the fish to cook off the fat. Or, if you're feeling flush, spring
for more expensive wild salmon. Researchers say their findings make the case
for labeling fish as farm-raised or wild.

"Just FYI: If it's not labeled, says Houlihan, assume it's farm-raised—
including restaurant fare. So much for that très pricey salmon du jour."

(*U.S. News & World Report*, January 19, 2004)

"Federal regulators should be allowed to use controversial studies in which
people are deliberately dosed with pesticides, an expert panel has decided. The
National Research Council (NRC) report concludes that such tests may be
acceptable if they meet scientific and ethical standards. Environmental groups
blasted the report as full of loopholes and urged the Environmental Protection
Agency (EPA) to put a moratorium on the pesticide tests, which they maintain are unethical.

"The issue arose because of a 1996 law that requires EPA to tighten limits on pesticide exposures to protect children. To offset this change, companies began sending EPA human studies to get around a fudge factor used in
standards based on rat data. This so-called safety factor is applied to results
from animals in case people are more sensitive than rats. But EPA put a hold
on the human tests after the Environmental Working Group (EWG), an
advocacy group based in Washington, D.C., issued a report slamming several
such studies in the United Kingdom. Later, the agency asked NRC to take a
look at all human dosing studies, including those exposing volunteers to air
and water pollutants. Meanwhile, last year a court ordered EPA to consider
the pesticide tests on a case-by-base basis."

(*Science Now,* February 19, 2004)

". . . a nonprofit organization that had pushed for a ban on CCA-treated
[chromated copper arsenate-treated] wood."

(*USA Today,* December 29, 2003)

"If you like juicy, ripe peaches—and who doesn't?—the nonprofit Environmental Working Group [EWG] in Washington has some bad news for you.
This succulent fruit tops the list of foods most contaminated with pesticide
residues. Last week the EWG released a report ranking pesticide levels in the
46 most common fruits and vegetables. The tally is based on more than
100,000 USDA and FDA studies conducted between 1992 and 2001, covering 192 different pesticides. Among the 'dirty dozen' at the top of the list are
delicate fruits like strawberries and cherries, but also less obvious suspects like
potatoes and spinach, which is routinely touted as one of the most healthful
foods. So what are we supposed to eat?

"Pesticide makers say there's no cause for alarm; their chemicals go
through more than 120 government-mandated safety tests before being
approved. And nutritionists insist that the benefits of eating produce far outweigh the risks. If you're still concerned, then buy organic versions of the most
contaminated foods, which also include apples, celery, pears, bell peppers and
imported grapes. 'Or substitute the foods with the fewest residues—like

bananas and kiwis—for those at the top of the list,' says Richard Wiles, senior vice president of EWG."

(Newsweek, November 3, 2003)

"A study by the Environmental Working Group (EWG: Washington) has found that U.S. women have up to 75 times higher levels of the flame retardants polybrominated diphenyl ethers (PBDEs) in their breast milk than the average levels present in European women. The European Union (EU) has enacted a ban on two PBDEs, penta-BDE and octa-BDE, that will take effect next year. California recently passed a bill that would ban the same two chemicals starting in 2008 (CW, Sept. 10, p. 42). A third PBDE, deca-BDE, has not been banned by either California or the EU, although EU officials say they will decide in the next several years whether deca-BDE needs to be phased out as well. . . .

"PBDEs, used in electronics, foams, plastics, and textiles, are persistent bioaccumulative chemicals and can have several adverse health effects, EWG says.

" 'Brominated fire retardants impair attention, learning, memory, and behavior in laboratory animals at surprisingly low levels,' EWG says. 'Research on animals shows that fetal exposure to minute doses of brominated fire retardants at critical points in development can cause deficits in sensory and motor skills, learning, memory, and hearing.' EWG says PBDEs could be the 'next polychlorinated biphenyls (PCBs).' PCBs are present in humans and the environment more than 25 years after they were banned.

"The study recommends that mothers continue to breastfeed their infants, however, because the health benefits of breast feeding outweigh the risks of exposure to chemicals such as PBDEs. But the group recommends the U.S. phase out the chemicals as soon as possible, and to label products containing PBDEs in the interim. . . ."

(Chemical Week, October 1, 2003)

"Farmers' self-esteem took another blow last fall, when an environmental group launched a Web site showing exactly how much federal largesse each producer was receiving. The Environmental Working Group wanted to publicize how unequal the system was, since the top 10 percent of producers were getting two-thirds of the subsidies. Farmers and rural businessmen flocked to the site to find out exactly how much money their neighbors were getting.

" 'You just couldn't avoid checking,' says Mr. Gay [a Rockport, IL farmer], who admits he was embarrassed at the publication of his own subsidies. But 'in some respects, they are helping us to reevaluate where we are.'

"The prognosis: Not good. As families have seen farm income fall, some have taken jobs in town. Others have expanded their agricultural operations in the hope that more volume would make ends meet.

"But the work has taken an emotional toll. There's 'less time for family, less time to enjoy the intrinsic values of farming,' says Paul Lasley, a sociology professor at Iowa State University in Ames. . . ."

(Christian Science Monitor, April 29, 2002)

Ethics and Public Policy Center

Established in 1976

DIRECTOR

M. Edward Whelan III, president. Whelan has served in positions of responsibility in all three branches of the federal government. Until March 2004, he served for more than 2 years as principal deputy assistant attorney general for the Office of Legal Counsel at the U.S. Department of Justice. He formerly served as general counsel to the U.S. Senate Committee on the Judiciary. Before that he was a law clerk to Supreme Court Justice Antonin Scalia and to Judge J. Clifford Wallace of the U.S. Court of Appeals for the Ninth Circuit. Whelan graduated with honors in 1981 from Harvard College and received his J.D. from Harvard Law School in 1985.

BOARD OF DIRECTORS

William R. Burleigh; chair, E.W. Scripps Co.
Robert P. George; McCormick Professor of Jurisprudence, Princeton University
Mary Ann Glendon; Learned Hand Professor of Law, Harvard University
Frederick W. Hill; chair, McCallum Hill Ltd.
Jeane J. Kirkpatrick; director of foreign & defense policy and senior fellow, American Enterprise Institute; former U.S. representative to the United Nations
Paul J. Klaassens; founder, chair, and chief executive officer, Sunrise Assisted Living
Father Richard John Neuhaus; president, Institute on Religion and Public Life; editor-in-chief, *First Things: a Monthly Journal of Religion and Public Life*

SCOPE

Members: None
Branches/chapters: None
Affiliates: None

STAFF

16 total—including research fellows

TAX STATUS

501(c)(3)

FINANCES

Budget: 2003—$2.5 million; 2002—$2.3 million

FUNDING SOURCES

Information unavailable

PAC

None

EMPLOYMENT

No information provided; please see www.eppc.org for information.

CONTACT INFORMATION

1015 15th Street, NW, Suite 900, Washington, DC 20005
Phone: (202) 682-1200 • *Fax:* (202) 408-0632
General E-mail: ethics@eppc.org • *Web site:* www.eppc.org

Communications Director: J. Scott Bond, office director
(202) 682-1200 • ethics@eppc.org
Human Resources Director: Information unavailable

PURPOSE: "To clarify and reinforce the bond between the Judeo-Christian moral tradition and the public debate over domestic and foreign policy issues."

CURRENT CONCERNS: Biotechnology and American democracy • Catholic studies • Evangelicals in civic life • Foreign policy • Islam and American democracy • Jewish studies • Religion and the media • South Asian studies

METHOD OF OPERATION: Initiative/referendum campaigns • International activities • Internships • Library (for members only) • Research • Mailing lists • Web site

Effectiveness and Political Orientation

"Christian books on the best-seller lists. Christian hip-hop in the Top 10. Christian computer games for the kids, Christian movies at the multiplex, Christian greeting cards in Hallmark stores, Christian clothing—from poke-bonnet modest to baggy-pants X-treme—on the Web.

"It's as if somebody looked around and asked, 'What would Jesus buy?'

"Christianity hasn't just entered the mainstream, it is swimming to the lead.

"Bill Anderson, head of the Colorado Springs-based Christian Book-sellers Association, says that's because more people are 'looking to root themselves in a world full of turbulence and instability.'

"Here's another possibility: More companies are looking to make money.

"The Christian retail industry accounts for $4.2 billion in annual sales, up from $1 billion in 1980, according to the CBA. 'Mainstream culture has discovered them as a huge profit-making potential,' says Michael Cromartie, director of the Evangelical Studies Project at the Ethics and Public Policy Center. . . ."

(*The Denver Post,* December 23, 2003)

"In the annals of U.S. history, the eugenics movement stands out, both for its virulence and weirdness. People at all levels—including scientists, lawmakers, clergymen and U.S. Supreme Court justices—firmly believed theories of heredity that were simplistic and silly.

"Today, eugenics has been discredited as a shameful pseudo-science. Yet modern research into genetics and heredity touches some of the same controversial issues.

"Cloning, genetic testing, embryo selection and other technologies are reigniting ethical debates about social engineering, genetic tampering and human worth.

" 'The question is no longer whether we will practise eugenics. We already do,' Christine Rosen, of the Ethics and Public Policy Center in Washington wrote recently in *New Atlantis* magazine.

" 'The question is: Which forms of eugenics will we tolerate and how much will we allow the practice of eugenics to expand?' "

(*The Toronto Star* [Canada], November 9, 2003)

"From every corner of the earth, tens of thousands of pilgrims have descended on Rome to honor the woman they have always considered a saint, the Albanian nun in the blue-striped white sari who ministered to the poorest of the poor, first in India and then throughout the world.

"Mother Teresa of Calcutta, who is to be beatified today by Pope John Paul II, is poised to become the first truly modern Roman Catholic saint—a 20th century woman who, thanks to television, was known throughout the world during her lifetime and was acclaimed as saintly long before she will formally be granted that designation. She died in 1997 at age 87.

" 'This 85-pound Albanian nun is the most recognizable icon of holiness in recent decades, and I think the pope is really speaking for the entire church in lifting her up as an example,' said George Weigel, a papal biographer and a senior fellow at the Ethics and Public Policy Center in Washington, D.C. 'In a sense, this is a return to the traditional pattern of doing these things by acclamation.' "

(*The Boston Globe,* October 19, 2003)

"The most critical battle in the war against terrorism may be the battle for hearts and minds. The real foe isn't al Qaeda but the virulent strain of Islam referred to as Wahhabism or Salafism. Spread throughout the world—intentionally and not—by the oil wealth of the Saudi kingdom, the radical message appeals to those who believe that modernity is a western game played at the expense of Islam's followers. While a relative few have followed the ideology to its violent jihadist conclusion, more and more of the world's 1 billion Muslims are being drawn to the music.

"How successfully has the United States government countered radical Islam's beguiling but deceitful airs? The answer, say both friends and critics of the Bush administration, is unevenly, at best. . . .

"Critics say Americans seem to have forgotten what worked during the Cold War: serious engagement with the arguments of communism. 'That's what we're not doing now,' says Hillel Fradkin, a scholar of Islam and president of the Ethics and Public Policy Center. 'We are not really engaging the Islamists.' The head of the State Department's public diplomacy programs until her retirement last spring was former advertising executive Charlotte Beers; her effort to 'brand' the United States as a warm and friendly nation had little effect. Most Arabs weren't overly impressed, an administration official admits, to learn 'that Muslims could run a pita bread store in Dearborn, Michigan.' A State Department-appointed committee headed by former diplomat Edward Djerejian is now compiling recommendations to help Margaret Tutwiler chart a different strategy when she takes over the public diplomacy division at State later this fall. . . ."

(*U.S. News & World Report,* September 15, 2003)

"The Bush administration is well aware that the Muslim world regards the liberation of Iraq as a war on Islam. Someone within the administration needs to convince the president that allowing evangelists into Iraq to push Christianity as well as humanitarian aid on a divided and defeated Muslim population will only deepen this conviction. This is one faith-based initiative the government cannot afford to support.

"So far, the only comment from the White House has come from press spokesman Ari Fleischer, who said the government has no control over privately funded religious charities like Samaritan's Purse, the agency headed by Franklin Graham, Billy's son and Bush family friend. . . .

"Many conservative evangelicals insist that they are different from other Christians—and in this instance, unfortunately, they are right. They proselytize as naturally as salesmen sell, salmon spawn, and pots cook pot roast. . . . Indeed, according to a poll released last month by Beliefnet and the Ethics and Public Policy Center, a think tank in Washington, DC, 81 percent of evangelical Protestants consider it 'very important' to evangelize Muslims abroad, and another 16 percent consider it at least 'somewhat important.' The same survey also reports that of 350 evangelical leaders queried, 77 percent hold a negative view of Islam, and seven out of ten agree that it is a 'religion of violence'—a view the president has sought to discourage. . . ."

(*Commonwealth,* June 6, 2003)

"By being out front on a number of issues, [the National Council of Churches] has become a lightning rod of criticism for conservative theologians. 'The NCC is in the pocket of a lot of those environmental groups' says Michael Cromartie, vice president of the Washington, D.C.-based Ethics and Public Policy Center. Because he signed the Oxford Declaration on global warming, Reverend Cizik of the National Association of Evangelicals (NAE) worries that 'friends at the Heritage Foundation and on the political [right]' will now think him a candidate for NCC membership. But Cizik isn't going that far. 'The NAE is the conservative alternative to the National Council of Churches,' he says. 'We represent mainline Christianity today, which the NCC does not. . . .'"

(*E Magazine: the Environmental Magazine,* November/December 2002)

Ethics Resource Center

Established as American Viewpoint in 1922, changed name 1977

DIRECTOR

Stuart C. Gilman, president. Gilman assumed this post in February 2002 after a 17-year career in the federal government. Prior to joining the ERC, he served as the director of strategic development at the Office of the U.S. Treasury Inspector General for Tax Administration. Gilman has overall responsibility for the ERC Fellows Program, a corporate membership group that brings together corporate, government, nonprofit and academic leaders who share an expertise and strong practical interest in business ethics. He has a bachelor's degree from the University of New Orleans and a master's and Ph.D. in political science from Miami University.

BOARD OF DIRECTORS

Kenneth C. Frazier, chair; senior vice president, and general counsel, Merck & Co.

Al DeLeon; treasurer; DeLeon & Stang

Stephen D. Potts, chair, ERC Fellows Program; former director, U.S. Office of Government Ethics

Robin Aram; vice president for external relations and policy development, Shell International

Irving W. Bailey II; managing director, Chrysalis Ventures, LLC

Jose A. Berrios; vice president for staffing and diversity, Gannett Corp.

Fred F. Fielding; senior partner, Wiley, Rein & Fielding

James Hamilton; partner, Swidler Berlin Shereff Friedman, LLP

Theodore M. Hester; partner, King & Spalding

Barbara H. Kipp; partner and global leader of ethics and business conduct, PricewaterhouseCoopers, LLP

Charles E. M. Kold; president, Committee for Economic Development

John Kuhnle; managing director of education practice, Korn Ferry International

Susan R. Meisinger; chief executive officer, Society for Human Resource Management

Sara E. Melendez; president, Independent Sector

Norma Pace; president, Paper Analytics Associates

Brent Snowcroft; lieutenant general (retired), U.S. Air Force; president, Forum for International Policy

Sheila Tate; vice chair, Powell Tate

Frank Vogl; president, Vogl Communications, Inc.; vice chair, Transparency International

SCOPE

Members: not a membership organization
Branches/chapters: Office in the Middle East, the UAE

CONTACT INFORMATION

1747 Pennsylvania Avenue, NW, Suite 400, Washington, DC 20006
Phone: (202) 737-2258 • *Fax:* (202) 737-2227
General E-mail: ethics@ethics.org • *Web site:* www.ethics.org

Communications Director: Nicole Germain
(202) 872-4768 • nicole@ethics.org,
Human Resources Director: Patricia Jones, director of operations
(202) 872-4782 • patricia@ethics.org,

PURPOSE: "To strengthen ethical leadership worldwide by providing leading-edge expertise and services through research, education and partnerships. The Ethics Resource Center strives to: inspire individuals to act ethically towards one another; inspire institutions to act ethically, recognizing their role as transmitters of values; inspire individuals and institutions to join together in fostering ethical communities."

CURRENT CONCERNS: Character development • Consulting and technical assistance • Education & advocacy • Global ethics and integrity • Institution and coalitional development • Organizational ethics • Research & knowledge building

METHOD OF OPERATION: Coalition forming • Conferences/seminars • Consulting • Educational foundation • Information clearinghouse (online) • International activities • Internet (database and Web site) • Professional development services • Research • Speakers program • Surveys • Training and technical assistance

Effectiveness and Political Orientation

"Fairness is as American as apple pie. We make rules to help us play fair. We have laws that punish us when we don't. . . .

"And then along comes change. The voting age gets lowered, the retirement age gets raised, and what used to be illegal becomes fair game.

"President Bush wants to change the country's immigration rules so illegal workers who are now here moonlighting could get legal status—at least temporarily. Under this plan, renewable, three-year visas would be made available for these men and women, as well as other foreigners interested in working here.

"To help sell it, Bush invoked the fairness word.

" 'Out of common sense and fairness, our laws should allow willing workers to enter our country and fill jobs that Americans are not filling,' the president said.

"But how do we know when change is fair?

"And just what is fairness, anyway?

Affiliates: Columbian Ethics Center, Ethics
Institute of South Africa, Gulf Centre for
Excellence in Ethics, and the Integrity
Alliance

STAFF
23 total

TAX STATUS
501(c)(3)

FINANCES
Information unavailable

FUNDING SOURCES
Fees for service, 35%; corporate
donations, 30%; foundation grants, 20%;
individuals, 15%

PAC
None

EMPLOYMENT
The center posts research and consulting
openings online at http://www.ethics.org
/employment.html.

INTERNSHIPS
At various times, the Center offers college students the opportunity to work in one of its
departments. Interested parties should e-mail
Patricia Jones, director of operations at
patricia@ethics.org

NEWSLETTERS
Ethics Today Online (monthly)
MAXIMize the Moment (weekly, for high
schools)

PUBLICATIONS
2003 National Business Ethics Survey
Character Way (video)
Code Construction and Content (online article)
Common Ethics Code Provisions (online article)
*Creating a Workable Company Code: a
Practical Guide to Identifying and
Developing Organizational Standards*
Ethics at Work (video series)
Insights 2000 (online)
*Not for Sale: Ethics in the American
Workplace* (video for high school students)
Truth and Trust
Also publishes research summaries, reports,
and *ERC Fellows Publications.*

CONFERENCES
ERC Fellows Program

" 'One of the key things about fairness is that notion that you treat every-one the same,' says Lawrence Hinman, a philosophy professor and director of the Values Institute at the University of San Diego.

"Stuart Gilman, president of the Ethics Resource Center in Washington, DC, offers a like definition of fairness as equity. Fairness, he says, is 'treating similar situations and similar people in the same manner. . . .'

" 'You really need to think about the greatest good for the greatest num-ber of people,' says Gilman. 'We have in the past created laws that created far more problems than they were worth, and we have modified those laws. . . .'

"So how do we know if change is fair?. . .

"Gilman says he loves what he calls 'the smell test.' 'Would you be embar-rassed to read it above the fold on the front page of the newspaper or to explain it to a 12-year-old child?' he asks.

"Or, he suggests you ask yourself if it would be good if everybody could do that. For example, would it be good if everybody could drink and drive? 'Suddenly, those laws make sense,' Gilman adds.

"Which brings us to the question of whether Bush's temporary worker proposal, which still must be approved by Congress, is a fair one."
(*The San Diego Union-Tribune,* February 5, 2004)

"In 'Glengarry Glen Ross,' David Mamet's play about cutthroat salesmen try-ing to move less-than-alluring residential real estate, the overarching mantra was 'always be closing.' The message was this: Do what it takes to sell prop-erty to the unsuspecting, even if that means being selective in what you dis-close about the houses you want to unload.

"The characters in the play may be extreme examples, but the practice of businesses selectively using information to sell products is widespread. 'Selec-tive marketing is basically emphasizing the positive elements of whatever goods you have,' said Stuart C. Gilman, president of the Ethics Resource Center in Washington.

" 'You can say that it's unfair, but it's absolutely reasonable. In a market-place you expect people to make sensible decisions.' "
(*The New York Times,* August 17, 2003)

"In the wake of stock market and corporate governance scandals, it's no sur-prise if human resources officials, those keepers of company rules, wonder where all the ethical people have gone.

"A survey released by the Ethics Resource Center and the Society for Human Resource Management in late April said nearly half of HR profes-sionals believe ethical conduct is not rewarded in business today. Perhaps more disturbing, 24 percent of HR pros feel pressured to compromise ethical stan-dards either all the time, fairly often or periodically. Only 13 percent felt that way in 1997.

"But the survey results may have an explanation that's more benign than a real increase in lapsed standards. Susan Meisinger, president of one of the sponsoring groups, the Society for Human Resource Management, thinks that the ethical breaches that have bubbled up in the past couple of years have heightened our awareness. People notice ethical—or unethical—behavior more now than in years when corporate responsibility was a back-page issue, she thinks. So they report it more, and, perhaps, feel more pressured to act unethically in previous years. . . .

"But 49 percent of the 462 survey respondents said that ethical conduct is not rewarded in business today. The belief that sometimes cutting corners really does get employees somewhere seems widespread. . . .

"Although the pressure that employees feel to compromise ethical standards has increased since the 1997 survey, actual misconduct has dropped, according to the survey, from 53 percent in 1997 to 35 percent today. But again, it could be that more people are thinking about ethics now than six years ago. . . .

" 'One of the main themes is that sense that in general there is a positive perception about what employees think of ethics,' said Joshua Joseph, the research manager with the Ethics Resource Center, the other survey sponsor. 'That kind of suggests to me that when ethics issues arise, chances are they are being dealt with.' "

(*The Washington Post,* May 4, 2003)

"Admit it. We sit back, horrified by unethical actions at big corporations such as Enron and WorldCom—which is understandable, considering the circumstances. But what about you? Have you ever falsified records and then justified your action because 'it'll help all parties involved'? When your immediate superior tells you to take the gift a client sent you, despite company policy against accepting gifts, is your boss in the wrong? Or are you wrong for listening to the boss?

"What about the tiny things, such as taking office stationery home for your children to use when they play 'teacher. . . .'

"Companies and employees are breaking rules all over the place. The 2001 National Business Ethics Survey, conducted by Lee WanVeer, director of advisory services at the Ethics Resource Center organization, found that 30 percent of employees observe others violating the law or their organization's standards. Twelve percent of respondents see co-workers who break rules, steal, commit fraud and lie to employers.

"Although 'they aren't always the huge headline types of things,' WanVeer said, 'it is the small things that can become commonplace that create a culture of acceptance in the name of expediency or customer service. But that can lead to larger infractions, which was the case at WorldCom and Enron.' "

(*The Washington Post,* November 10, 2002)

Fairness & Accuracy in Reporting (FAIR)

Established in 1986

DIRECTOR
None

BOARD OF DIRECTORS
Declined to comment

SCOPE
Members: 20,000 subscribers; 50,000-member
  e-mail list
Branches/chapters: None
Affiliates: None

STAFF
6 total—6 full-time professional; plus 1 part-
time support and 3 interns

TAX STATUS
501(c)(3)

FINANCES
Budget: 2004—$784,500; 2003—$836,992;
2002—$821,539

FUNDING SOURCES
Publications, 66%; foundation grants, 15%;
individuals; sales, 8%; radio show, 1%; list
rental, 1%

PAC
None

EMPLOYMENT
Potential applicants can learn about job open-
ings with this organization by consulting the
Web site: www.fair.org.

INTERNSHIPS
Potential applicants can learn about internship
opportunities at www.fair.org/internships
.html. Interns are given a small stipend for
12–15 hours per week. Positions are available
for a semester or summer/intersession.
Responsibilities vary according to position, but
many positions involve research, Web support,
media-monitoring, and administrative work; or
assistance on *BLOCK! Magazine* and the
nationally syndicated radio program
CounterSpin.
  Interested applicants should contact Peter
Hart, media activism and administration director, 112 West 27th Street, New York, NY,
10001. Phone: (212) 633-6700. Fax: (212) 727-
7668. E-mail: phart@fair.org.

PUBLICATIONS
*The Oh Really? Factor: Unspinning Fox News
  Channel's Bill O'Reilly* (Seven Stories
  Press)

CONTACT INFORMATION
112 West 27th Street, New York, NY 10001
Phone: (212) 633-6700 • *Fax:* (212) 727-7668
General E-mail: fair@fair.org • *Web site:* www.fair.org

Communications Director: Julie Hollar, communications director
(212) 633-6700 • jhollar@fair.org
Human Resources Director: None

PURPOSE: To invigorate the First Amendment by advocating for greater diversity in the press and by scrutinizing media practices that marginalize public interest, minority and dissenting viewpoints.

CURRENT CONCERNS: Advertiser influence • Censorship • Corporate ownership • Narrow range of debate • Public relations industry • Sensationalism • Telecommunications policy

METHOD OF OPERATION: Information clearinghouse • Internet (e-mail alerts and Web site) • Internships • Media outreach • Research • Syndicated radio show

Effectiveness and Political Orientation

"Talk host Michael Savage, who rose fast in the business by throwing a lot of shots, is about to catch another round of incoming.

  "The left-leaning media watchdog group Fairness and Accuracy in Reporting (FAIR) adds the latest charge in its July/August issue: that Savage 'is virtually the only national talk jock targeting progressive Jews with ugly ethnic slurs and stereotypes.'

  "In an article by Steve Rendall, FAIR says that last Dec. 6, Savage made this remark about Jerry Springer: 'He invites the lowest white trash he can dig his hands on and he makes a mockery of them and makes a living on it with his hooked nose.'

  "FAIR reports Savage has said of the grave markers in military cemeteries: 'I like seeing crosses on our war memorials. You know why? Because 99.9 percent of those who died are Christians!'

  "Savage, who could not be reached for comment, was born into a Jewish family. He is also a strong supporter of Israel and its military policy. . . ."
  (*New York Daily News*, July 15, 2003)

"When comedian Ellen DeGeneres decided in 1997 to craft an episode of her ABC series in which her character would mirror her 'coming out' as a lesbian, the Media Research Center, a conservative watchdog group, took out a full-page ad in Daily Variety declaring 'America's Families Deserve Better.'

  "And when MSNBC decided this year to hand talk-radio firebrand Michael Savage a TV show, liberal advocacy group Fairness and Accuracy in Reporting criticized the move, saying 'misogyny and homophobia are staples

NEWSLETTERS
BLOCK! Magazine (6 times a year)
BLOCK! Update (6 times a year)

CONFERENCES
None

of Savage's show,' noting his disparaging comments on a 'homosexualized America.'

"But even though FAIR and the Media Research Center rarely agree on anything, elements of their organizations have come together on one issue: the need to slow the Federal Communication Commission's drive to revamp rules on media ownership. . . ."

(St. Petersburg Times [Florida], April 29, 2003)

". . . the liberal media watchdog group FAIR (Fairness and Accuracy in Reporting) has just issued a report accusing the major networks of silencing voices of dissent.

"While most Americans will follow news from Iraq through the lens of the mainstream news outlets, some alternative media organizations are gearing up to provide a very different view of the conflict.

"Often ideological, with minimal budgets and small staffs, these organizations give voice to nontraditional or far-left perspectives that don't usually make it onto the Sunday morning talk shows or into the op-ed columns. . . .

"One organization that focuses on voices ignored by the media is the New York-based FAIR, which has an annual budget of about $700,000. In a recent survey that examined sources in stories about Iraq on the ABC, CBS, NBC, and PBS nightly newscasts during a two-week period, FAIR concluded that coverage was dominated by a lineup of US officials who rarely uttered a discouraging word about White House invasion plans.

"FAIR will continue to monitor the US press for knee-jerk jingoism, says a FAIR analyst, Rachel Coen, who accuses the media of a 'lack of critical distance' from the Bush administration.

" 'The problems we see in peacetime,' Coen says, 'become exacerbated in wartime.' "

(The Boston Globe, March 19, 2003)

"Even before the likely onset of war in Iraq, the major television networks have come under increasing scrutiny by media watchdogs on the left and the right, looking for subtle and overt signs of journalistic bias. . . .

"A liberal group, Fairness and Accuracy in Reporting, said the broadcast and cable networks were paying inadequate attention to the potential civilian casualties that United States action in Iraq could cause, as well as failing to ask tough questions of the administration. The group released a study Monday night saying people who were skeptical of President Bush's plans had been underrepresented. . . ."

(The New York Times, March 19, 2003)

Families and Work Institute

Established in 1989

DIRECTOR

Ellen Galinsky, president. A popular keynote speaker, Galinsky appears regularly at national conferences, on television and in the media. Galinsky is the author of more than 25 books and reports, including *The Six Stages of Parenthood, The Preschool Years,* and *Ask the Children: The Breakthrough Study That Reveals How to Succeed at Work and Parenting.* She has published more than 100 articles in academic journals, books, and magazines. A leading authority on work-family issues, she was a presenter at the 2000 White House Conference on Teenagers and the 1997 White House Conference on Child Care. She is the recipient of the 2004 Distinguished Achievement Award from Vassar College. Before co-founding FWI, Galinsky was on the faculty of Bank Street College of Education for 25 years, where she helped establish the field of work and family life.

SCOPE

Members: Friend of FWI membership (for individuals and organizations) and Corporate Leadership Circle members (companies for providing annual donations for general operating support of the Institute)

CONTACT INFORMATION

267 Fifth Avenue, 2nd Floor, New York, NY 10016
Phone: (212) 465-2044 • *Fax:* (212) 465-8637
General E-mail: Web form at www.familiesandwork.org/contact.html
Web site: www.familiesandwork.org

Communications Director: Erin Brownfield
(212) 465-2044, ext. 210 • ebrownfield@familiesandwork.org
Human Resources Director: Information unavailable

PURPOSE: "To provide data to inform decision-making on the changing workplace, changing family and changing community."

CURRENT CONCERNS: Community • Early childhood development • Employee benefits • Family • Generational and teen issues • Low wage workers • Quality and availability of child and elder care • Support for men's involvement in child rearing • Work-life

METHOD OF OPERATION: Conferences/seminars • Films/videos/audio tapes • Information clearinghouse • International activities • Internships • Media outreach • Research • Speakers program • Technical assistance • Web site

Effectiveness and Political Orientation

"While the average dual-income couple with children is spending considerably more time at work than 25 years ago, Mom and Dad also are spending more time with their children during the workweek, according to a new survey of more than 3,000 workers nationwide.

"The 2002 National Study of the Changing Workforce, released recently by the Families and Work Institute in Washington, reports that time spent at work by dual-earner parents averaged 91 hours a week, up from 81 hours in 1977.

"But despite working 10 more hours a week, working couples have managed to spend an additional hour a day with their children, from a combined 5.2 hours in 1977 to 6.2 hours in 2002. . . ."

(*St. Petersburg Times* [Florida], October 19, 2003)

"It happens to almost every working parent: The kids are sick. School, or a local park program, is canceled for the day. The regular baby sitter is out of town. . . .

"In fact, parents miss work because of a breakdown in child care an average of seven days a year, according to one study. The problem peaks as schools close, affecting many working parents, not to mention employers already operating with small staffs.

"In one three-month period during 1997, 29 percent of employed parents nationwide experienced some type of child-care breakdown that resulted in

Branches/chapters: None
Affiliates: None

STAFF
13 total—6 full-time professional; 7 full-time support; plus 3 part-time professional; 3 part-time support; 1 to 2 interns

TAX STATUS
501(c)(3)

FINANCES
Revenue: 2001—$4.1 million; 2000—$3.72 million

FUNDING SOURCES
Foundation grants, 35%; government contracts, 20%; publications, 18%; corporate donations, 11%; corporate grants, 7%; conferences, 3%; special events/projects, 2%; foundation donations, 2%; speaking fees, 2%

PAC
None

EMPLOYMENT
Information unavailable

INTERNSHIPS
Information unavailable

NEWSLETTERS
None

PUBLICATIONS
The following is a sample of recent publications:
Sparking Connections: Community-Based Strategies for Helping Family, Friend and Neighbor Caregivers Meet the Needs of Employees, Their Children and Employers
The Impact of Job and Workplace Conditions on Low-Wage and -Income Employees and Their Employers
Promising Practices: How Employers Improve Their Bottom Lines by Addressing the Needs of Lower-Wage Workers
Information for Employers about Low-Wage Employees from Low-Income Families
A publications list is available at www.familiesandwork.org/index.asp.

CONFERENCES
Annual Work-Life Conference (co-sponsored with The Conference Board)

absenteeism, tardiness, and reduced concentration at work, according to a study of nearly 1,000 families by the Families and Work Institute in New York.

"The institute also found that only 20 percent of working parents rely on day-care centers, where a corps of teachers make individual absences relatively insignificant. The remainder depend upon relatives and friends, which usually means they depend upon the health and availability of one person.

"As a result, corporate backup care has become a hot item, even if a sluggish economy has slowed its growth, according to Judith Presser, senior consultant for WFD Consulting, which specializes in work and family issues. . . ."
(*Christian Science Monitor,* June 16, 2003)

"For decades, mothers have been the target of reams of guilt-inducing child-development studies dissecting their every move, right down to how their moods will shape their babies as adults.

"Now, researchers are training their microscopes on fathers at last, with some compelling results. Not only do dads' interactions with their infants and toddlers influence the way kids relate later to other people and the world at large, but fathers' influence in some realms is even more powerful than moms'.

"The research is fueled by mounting worldwide interest in the contribution fathers make when they are present in the home, says James Levine, director of the Fatherhood Project at the Families & Work Institute, New York. It's also aided by $6.1 million in Bush administration funding for studies on promoting healthy marriages and responsible fatherhood; another $200 million is proposed for research and pilot projects in pending welfare-reform legislation. . . ."
(*Pittsburgh Post-Gazette,* June 15, 2003)

"Since 1993, young girls have been getting a glimpse of the working world courtesy of the Ms. Foundation's Take Our Daughters to Work Day—but starting this year, boys are an official part of the annual event, too.

"While the Ms. Foundation is not lessening its commitment to empowering the next generation of women by opening their eyes to future careers, the inclusion of boys is meant to get both sexes thinking about how they might better balance work and life when their turn comes.

" 'Most of today's kids know firsthand what it's like to live in a household where the adults are struggling to deal with work and home responsibilities,' said Carrie Fernandez, of the Ms. Foundation. 'And they don't necessarily want to face those same challenges when they grow up.'

"Fernandez cited a national study by the Families and Work Institute in which 81 percent of girls, and 60 percent of boys said they hope to reduce their work hours when they have children. . . ."
(*Buffalo News,* April 21, 2003)

"If every afternoon from work, your call to check in with the home front goes something like this . . .

"Hi, how was school?
"Fine.
"What are you doing?
"Nothin.'
"Have you started your homework?
"Yeah.

"... then the experts would say you need a different teleparenting approach. As Susan Ginsberg, of the Work & Family Life newsletter, explained, you should 'ask questions that don't have a monosyllabic answer. . . .'

"Make sure you concentrate as much on the conversation, however brief, as you want your children to. 'The worst thing is to be clicking on your computer as you talk,' said Ellen Galinsky, president of the Families and Work Institute in New York. 'They know you're not really focusing on them.'"

(*The Washington Post,* February 23, 2002)

Families USA Foundation

Established in 1981

DIRECTOR

Ronald F. Pollack, executive director. Pollack was the founding executive director of Families USA Foundation. In 1997–1998, Pollack was appointed the sole consumer organizational representative on the Presidential Advisory Commission on Consumer Protection and Quality in the Health Care Industry. In that capacity, Pollack helped prepare the Patients' Bill of Rights. Prior to his current position, Pollack was dean of the Antioch University School of Law. He was also the founding executive director of the Food Research and Action Center (FRAC), a leading national organization focused on the elimination of hunger in the United States. In that capacity, Pollack brought litigation that resulted in the creation of the so-called "WIC" Program for malnourished mothers and infants, and he argued many cases in the federal courts—including two successful cases argued on the same day in the U.S. Supreme Court—to improve food aid for low-income Americans.

BOARD OF DIRECTORS

Gordon Bonnyman; Tennessee Justice Center
Robert A. Crittenden; chief of family medicine service, University of Washington School of Medicine
Jack Ebeler; president and chief executive officer, Alliance of Community Health Plans
Douglas A. Fraser; former president, United Auto Workers Union
Angela Monson; Oklahoma state senator
Murray Saltzman; rabbi
Fernando Torres-Gil; associate dean, School of Public Policy and Social Research, UCLA
Philippe Villers; founder and president, Families USA Foundation

SCOPE

Members: None
Branch/chapter: None
Affiliates: Office in Concord, MA

STAFF

33 total—24 full-time professional; 9 full-time support; plus 1 part-time professional; 2 part-time support; and 3 interns

TAX STATUS

501(c)(3)

FINANCES

Budget: 2004—$8.73 million; 2003—$6.66 million; 2002—$6.125 million

CONTACT INFORMATION

1334 G Street, NW, Washington, DC 20005
Phone: (202) 628-3030 • *Fax:* (202) 347-2417
General E-mail: info@familiesusa.org • *Web site:* www.familiesusa.org

Communications Director: Jennifer Laudano
(202) 628-3030 • jlaudano@familiesusa.org
Human Resources Director: Delma Dawkins, director of finance & administration
(202) 628-3030 • ddawkins@familiesusa.org

PURPOSE: "To secure high-quality, affordable health care for all Americans."

CURRENT CONCERNS: Health care costs • Medicaid • Medicare • Prescription drugs • State Children's Health Insurance Program (SCHIP) • Uninsured individuals

METHOD OF OPERATION: Coalition forming • Conferences/seminars • Congressional testimony • Films/video/audiotapes • Grassroots organizing • Information clearinghouse • Internet (database, e-mail alerts, and Web site) • Internships • Legislative/regulatory monitoring (federal and state) • Lobbying (federal) • Media outreach • Research • Technical assistance

SPECIFIC PROGRAMS/INITIATIVES: *The Medicare Road Show,* a campaign to educate seniors about new Medicare prescription drug law

Effectiveness and Political Orientation

"A group of about 50 retirees at the Elizabeth Seton Center in Brookline alternately groaned, grumbled and applauded yesterday as Families USA, a Washington-based foundation and lobbying organization, delivered a broadside against the Medicare reform legislation enacted last year.

"Groans and grumbles came as speakers, live and on video, described gaps in coverage and projected increases in out-of-pocket costs for the prescription benefits that were the law's most widely discussed aspect.

"Applause broke out as the speakers sounded a rallying cry to reform the reform legislation.

"'A good number of you are still going to be facing significant costs,' even after the law's main benefits come into effect two years from now, said Dee Mahan, Families USA's senior health policy analyst. 'If you don't have affordable medicines, you don't have affordable health care.' . . .

"The big question on seniors' minds yesterday seemed to be what they needed to do about drug discount cards that will be marketed beginning May 1 and issued in June as a temporary measure to ease costs until prescription coverage benefits are rolled out in 2006. . . .

FUNDING SOURCES
Foundation grants, 67%; endowment, 24%; individuals, 4%; conferences, 4%; publications, 1%

PAC
None

EMPLOYMENT
Potential applicants can learn about job openings through the organization's Web site, *The Washington Post,* and *Roll Call.* This organization offers administrative and program (communications, policy, government affairs) positions. Job postings contain contact information for individual openings.

INTERNSHIPS
Potential applicants learn about internship opportunities at www.familiesusa.org, regular postings on www.monstertrak.com and idealist.com, and through college career centers. Interns are paid $6.15 per hour. The duration of an internship varies with the schedules of each intern, but they usually run about 3–4 months. There are no application deadlines, and interns usually work 40 hours per week. Internship areas include health policy research and communications. Requirements vary by internship. In general, interns must have a commitment to social justice and low-income issues and a strong interest in health care. Interns should also possess good oral and written communication skills. Health policy research positions prefer that interns be in a graduate or law school program.

For more information, or to submit internship materials, contact Melissa Rosenblatt, director of internship and fellow program, Families USA, 1334 G Street, NW, Washington, DC 20005. Phone: (202) 628-3030. Fax: (202) 347-2417. E-mail: mrosenblatt@familiesusa.org

NEWSLETTERS
Health Action (6 times a year)
New on the Web (e-newsletter 8 times a year)
ImPRESSive: A Media Tip Sheet for Advocates (4 times a year).

PUBLICATIONS
For policy reports, special reports, issue briefs, fact sheets, and other publications, see Web site: www.familiesusa.org.

CONFERENCES
Health Action conference held each January in Washington, DC.

"What should consumers look for? Seniors should pay attention to which pharmacies accept any card they're considering to make sure the one they choose will be good at the drugstore they frequent.

"In addition, anyone considering a card can check to see if the prescriptions they take are offered and how much their discounts are. But doing so won't ensure the best choice because card sponsors are permitted to change the drugs and discounts, according to information Families USA distributed. Earlier this month, the U.S. Department of Health and Human Services said 71 corporate sponsors had been approved to issue the drug discount cards, which will cost consumers up to $30 annually. . . ."

(*Pittsburgh Post-Gazette*, March 30, 2004)

"In sharp contrast to the Bush administration's ad campaign touting the new Medicare law, a national health care advocacy group and other senior organizations have launched their own efforts to educate seniors about provisions in the controversial landmark measure.

" 'We want to make sure seniors understand this law and make good decisions,' said Ron Pollack, executive director of Families USA, a health-care consumer group. 'We're providing real details for people. This is complex stuff. I haven't seen anything educational from the Bush administration. It's all politics.'

"Less than three months before Medicare's drug discount program is set to begin, opposing sides have launched intense campaigns to help seniors dissect the complicated measure. . . .

"Bush officials have set aside $12.8 million for 30-second national ads that will run through the end of the month. The ads say that traditional Medicare has not changed and that new benefits are available, but they don't include details. The administration plans to air more ads next month focusing on the discount card.

"The Department of Health and Human Services plans to spend $21 million this year to help state and local groups educate seniors about Medicare changes, which include the drug benefit, preventive care and new health care plans. . . .

"The Alliance for Retired Americans, a group of mostly retired union workers, questioned the timing of the ads. 'We wonder why the administration feels the need to do this six or seven months before an election,' said Edward Coyle, ARA's executive director.

"Coyle said the ARA plans mass mailings, phone calls and town hall meetings to educate seniors about 'flaws' in the Medicare law, and ensure they are election-year issues.

"Meanwhile, Families USA kicked off its $500,000 campaign this month with forums and a 13-minute video featuring journalist Walter Cronkite and seniors facing high drug costs. The group plans to distribute 10,000 copies of the video and conduct forums in 20 cities, including Albany, on May 3. . . ."

(*Newsday* [New York], March 15, 2004)

"A new report on the rising cost of prescription drugs yesterday provided fresh ammunition to members of Congress seeking ways to make medicines more affordable for senior citizens.

"The report, compiled by Families USA, a non-profit consumer group, showed that the prices of the top 50 medicines most commonly prescribed to seniors rose on average at 3.4 times the rate of inflation last year.

"Senate Democrats, led by Ted Kennedy, seized on the report as evidence of the need for a more generous prescription drug benefit than is currently supported by House Republicans. . . .

"Ron Pollack, the head of Families USA, said: 'Year after year, as drug prices rise much faster than inflation, more and more seniors are forced to go without much-needed medications.' "

(*Financial Times* [London, England], July 10, 2003)

"Nearly 75 million Americans under the age of 65—nearly one-third of the total—were uninsured for at least one month during 2001–2002. . . .

"The numbers released yesterday by the Washington, D.C., consumer group Families USA give a better sense of just how many Americans deal with the loss of health insurance, said Ron Pollack, executive director of Families USA.

"Annual reports from the U.S. Census Bureau, by contrast, gauge how many people were uninsured throughout the previous year, Pollack said.

"The most recent of these reports was issued in September and put the national uninsured number for 2001 at 41.2 million, or 14.6 percent of the population. In Pennsylvania, the uninsured number was 1.1 million or 9.2 percent of the state.

" 'Now that almost one out of three non-elderly Americans experience significant periods without health insurance, the uninsured problem is no longer simply an issue of altruism about other people,' Pollack said. 'Now it's one of self-interest for all of us.'

"Pollack said that of the 74.7 million Americans under 65 who were temporarily uninsured during the two-year period, most lacked health insurance for more than six months.

"The Families USA report was released by the Robert Wood Johnson Foundation in advance of next week's Cover the Uninsured Week events across the country. . . ."

(*Pittsburgh Post-Gazette,* March 6, 2003)

"An analysis by Families USA, a nonprofit advocacy group for health care consumers, found that U.S. drug companies spent almost one-and-a-half times as much on administration and marketing as they do on developing new drugs.

" 'The result is a skyrocketing cost spiral that is making drugs increasingly unaffordable for America's seniors,' said Families USA executive director Ron Pollack. . . ."

(*St. Petersburg Times* [Florida], July 23, 2002)

Family Research Council

Established in 1980

DIRECTOR

Tony Perkins, president. Perkins joined Family Research Council as the organization's fourth president in September 2003. He has established himself as a prolife and profamily leader throughout his active career in public policy. Perkins served two terms as a Louisiana state representative and has been the main opponent to the state's gambling law. In addition to the covenant marriage law, he has authored numerous other initiatives including a State Family Impact Statement; legislation to provide comprehensive regulation of abortion clinics; a law requiring public schools to install Internet filtering software on all student computers; and legislation that lowered the recidivism rate by increasing the participation of faith-based organizations with the Louisiana Department of Corrections. A veteran of the U.S. Marine Corps and a former police officer, Perkins oversaw the training of hundreds of international police officers as the general manager for a Washington, DC-based firm contracted to provide the training and services in antiterrorism to the U.S. State Department. Perkins is a graduate of Liberty University.

BOARD OF DIRECTORS

Thomas R. Anderson
Kim C. Bengard
Ronald Blue
Elsa Prince Broekhuizen
Kenneth L. Connor
Jack Dewitt
James C. Dobson
Lee Eaton
Robert P. George
Stephen W. Reed
Colin Stewart

SCOPE

Members: None
Branch/chapter: None
Affiliates: Family Policy Councils (FPCs)—
"independent entities with no corporate or financial relationship to each other or to Family Research Council. However, they share common core beliefs in the sanctity of human life and in the institution of marriage": Alabama Policy Institute, Center for Arizona Policy, California Family Council, Rocky Mountain Family Council, Family Institute of Connecticut, Georgia Family Council, Hawaii Family Forum, Iowa Family Policy Center, Cornerstone Institute of Idaho, Illinois Family Institute, Indiana Family Institute, The Family Foundation (KY), Louisiana Family Forum, Massachusetts Family Institute, Association of Maryland Families, Christian Civic League of Maine, Michigan

CONTACT INFORMATION

801 G Street, NW, Washington, DC 20001
Phone: (202) 393-2100 • *Fax:* (202) 393-2134 • *Web site:* www.frc.org

Communications Director: Genevieve Wood
(202) 393-2100
Human Resources Director: Angela Palmore
(202) 393-2100

PURPOSE: The Family Research Council (FRC) champions marriage and family as the foundation of civilization, the seedbed of virtue, and the wellspring of society. FRC shapes public debate and formulates public policy that values human life and upholds the institutions of marriage and the family. Believing that God is the author of life, liberty, and the family, FRC promotes the Judeo-Christian worldview as the basis for a just, free, and stable society.

CURRENT CONCERNS: Human life and bioethics • Pornography awareness • Sanctity of marriage

METHOD OF OPERATION: Coalition forming • Conferences/seminars • Congressional testimony • Congressional voting analysis • Demonstrations • Films/video/audio tapes • Grassroots organizing • Initiative/referendum campaigns • International activities • Internet (databases, e-mail alerts, and Web site) • Internships • Legislative/regulatory monitoring (federal and state) • Lobbying (federal and state) • Media outreach • Research • Voter registration • Voting records

Effectiveness and Political Orientation

"As recently as late January, the same-sex marriage fight was something people could track on a calendar, a matter of court dockets, legislative schedules and months between major developments.

But then, in quick succession . . .

The Massachusetts Supreme Judicial Court refused to accept a 'civil unions' alternative in that state, which prodded President Bush to mention the issue in his State of the Union speech, which inspired the mayor of San Francisco to allow same-sex weddings for thousands of couples, which pushed Bush to endorse a constitutional ban.

Now the terrain shifts weekly, daily, hourly. . . .

The issue is now 'six months further down the road than we anticipated,' said Family Research Council President Tony Perkins, a leading opponent of same-sex marriage. 'We did not think we would be at the point of licenses being issued this early. So we had to accelerate our plans.'. . .

Half a dozen Focus on the Family staff members—as well as Family Research Council's Perkins, Concerned Women for America President Sandy

Family Forum, Minnesota Family Institute, Mississippi Center for Public Policy, Montana Family Foundation, North Carolina Family Policy Council, North Dakota Family Alliance, Family First (NE), Cornerstone Policy Research (NH), New Jersey Family Policy Council, Nevada Concerned Citizens, New York Family Policy Council, Citizens For Community Values (OH), Ohio Roundtable, Oklahoma Family Policy Council, Stronger Families for Oregon, Pennsylvania Family Institute, Palmetto Family Council (SC), South Dakota Family Policy Council, Free Market Foundation (TX), The Family Foundation (VA), Families Northwest (WA), Family Research Institute of Wisconsin

STAFF
65 total

TAX STATUS
501(c)(3)

FINANCES
Revenue: 2003—$9.1 million; 2002—$9.73 million; 2000—$10.32 million

FUNDING SOURCES
Direct public support 97.9%; program services, 1.5%; interest on savings and temporary cash investments 0.4%; other, 0.2%

PAC
None

EMPLOYMENT
Applicants can find more information on job openings on the FRC Web site: www.frc.org. Applicants should send resumes and other materials for employment to Angela Palmore, human resources manager, 801 G Street, NW, Washington, DC 20001. Phone: (202) 393-2100.

INTERNSHIPS
The Witherspoon Fellowship is a civic and cultural leadership development program of the Family Research Council. Designed as a semester-long academic fellowship and professional fraternity, the fellowship seeks to inspire a Christian vision for the calling and obligation of citizenship in college-age students. More information is available at http://www.witherspoonfellowship.org/. Housing is provided for fellows, as well as an $1,800 stipend in the spring and fall terms, and $1,200 in the summer. Spring and fall positions last 15 weeks; the summer program lasts 11 weeks.

Internship areas include the following: public policy research and development; government relations; press and media relations; cultural studies; legal studies; academic programs; publications; executive leadership/management; nonprofit business administration; information systems; fundraising and marketing, and events management. College student or recent college graduates in good academic standing are eligible. Applicants must submit an application, and 3 letters of

Rios and many other activists—had been in Boston [the week of the first San Francisco same-sex wedding] trying to build support for a state constitutional amendment to trump the Massachusetts high court's decision that said all adults, including gays, have a right to marry their chosen partner. They failed to make any real headway, but Perkins said they believed they had fought gay-rights groups to an 'inconclusive draw.'. . . ."

(*The Washington Post,* March 8, 2004)

". . . Jerry Regier, founder of the conservative Christian Family Research Council. . . ."

(*Pittsburgh Post-Gazette,* February 22, 2004)

"A fight within the Republican Party over whether to push for a constitutional amendment banning gay marriage turned yesterday to a debate over the meaning of President Bush's open-ended comments on the subject in his State of the Union speech.

"Some evangelical groups celebrated what they called a presidential endorsement of an amendment, while other major groups, including the Family Research Council, said the president had failed to act fast enough on the issue . . . ."

(*The New York Times,* January 22, 2004)

"Lawmakers urged to go 'on the record'

"Pledges are popular in an election year. Groups whose goals range from lowering taxes to preserving the environment all want lawmakers 'on the record' on their issues.

"Rep. David Schultheis, R-Colorado Springs, had promised to ask lawmakers on the first day of the session last Wednesday to sign the 'Marriage Protection Pledge.' It's a national effort by the conservative Family Research Council to put elected officials on record as supporting the idea that marriage is between 'one man and one woman.' "

(*Rocky Mountain News* [Denver], January 13, 2004)

"Former gubernatorial candidate Dan Kyle has jumped into the race for state insurance commissioner to fill the Republican shoes of state Rep. Tony Perkins, who announced Wednesday he will take the leadership position of a major conservative political group in Washington. . . .

"Perkins was filming a television commercial for his campaign Monday when he got the call offering him the job as president of the Family Research Council, a nonprofit lobbying and think-tank organization with a $10 million annual budget that is considered one of the nation's most influential groups advocating conservative social values and public policy.

"The job will catapult Perkins into the national spotlight as a high-profile opponent of abortion, euthanasia and gay marriage. On education issues, the group backs home schooling, vouchers and freedom of religion in schools.

" 'There's no doubt that it gives him a national platform,' said Peter Montgomery, communications director for the People for the American Way, a nonprofit group that opposes most of the Family Research Council's positions. 'He is a sort of fit for who they look for.'

"As a state lawmaker, Perkins wrote the nation's first covenant marriage law as well as legislation regulating abortion clinics, installing filters on school

reference. For more information, contact Grimes Williams, director of admissions and student life, 801 G Street, NW, Washington, DC 20001. Phone: (202) 637-4605. Fax: (202) 393-2134. E-mail bgw@frc.org.

NEWSLETTERS
Washington Update (daily email update)
Washington Watch (monthly)
Culture Facts (monthly)

PUBLICATIONS
Family Policy Review
Family Portrait

CONFERENCES
Washington Briefing, FRC's annual conference

computers to protect students from sexually graphic material and encouraging faith-based organizations to work with prisoners."

(*The New Orleans Times-Picayune*, August 14, 2003)

FARM (Farm Animal Reform Movement)

Established in 1981

DIRECTOR

Alex Hershaft, president. In 1981, Hershaft organized 'Action For Life,' a national conference that launched the U.S. animal rights movement. Shortly thereafter, he gave up a successful career in environmental management to establish FARM, which has become a major force in the struggle for vegetarianism and improved treatment of farm animals. Previously, Hershaft had founded a regional environmental organization (1969), a national organization for religious freedom (1962), and several local organizations. He has been active in a number of organizations advocating social justice. His 25-year professional career has included teaching, materials and operations research, and environmental management for academic, aerospace, and consulting institutions. Hershaft holds a Ph.D. in chemistry from Iowa State University and a B.A. from University of Connecticut. Hershaft was born in Warsaw and is a survivor of the Warsaw Ghetto.

BOARD OF DIRECTORS

Alex Hershaft, president
Elliot Katz; president, In Defense of Animals
Howard Lyman; author *Mad Cowboy*
Laurelee Blanchard

SCOPE

Members: 15,000+
Branches/chapters: None
Affiliates: None

STAFF

9 total—4 full-time professional; 5 full-time support

TAX STATUS

501(c)(3)

FINANCES

Budget: 2003—$300,000
Revenue: 2002—$369,349; 2001—$469,754

FUNDING SOURCES

Individuals, 80%; foundation grants, 10%; conferences, 10%

PAC

None

EMPLOYMENT

Job opportunities are listed on the organization's Web site, at www.farmusa.org/jobs.htm and at www.idealist.org/. Applicants should send resumes and other materials for employment to Alex Hershaft, president, 10101 Ashburton Lane, Bethesda, MD 20817. Phone: (301) 530-1737. Fax: (301) 530-5747. E-mail: staffing@farmusa.org.

CONTACT INFORMATION

P.O. Box 30654, Bethesda, MD 20824
Phone: (888) ASK-FARM • *Fax:* (301) 530-5747
General E-mail: info@farmusa.org • *Web site:* www.farmusa.org

Communications Director: Dawn Moncrief, director of programs and operations
(301) 530-1737 • dawn@farmusa.org
Human Resources Director: None

PURPOSE: "To promote plant-based eating and to eliminate animal abuse and other destructive impacts of animal agriculture on human health, food resources, and environmental integrity."

CURRENT CONCERNS: Effect of animal agriculture on world food supplies and on agricultural resources and environmental quality • Effect of animal products on consumer health • Mistreatment of animals in "factory farms," auction yards, and slaughterhouses

METHOD OF OPERATION: Advertisements • Awards program • Children's education • Coalition forming • Conferences/seminars • Demonstrations • Education foundation • Grant-making • Grassroots organizing • Hotline • Information clearinghouse • International activities • Internet (e-mail alerts and Web site) • Internships • Mailing lists • Product merchandising • Professional development services • Research • Speakers program • Training

SPECIFIC PROGRAMS/INITIATIVES: Great American Meatout • World Farm Animals Day • Gentle Thanksgiving • CHOICE (Consumers for Healthy Options in Children's Education) • Plant-Based Hunger Solutions • Animal Rights National Conference.

Effectiveness and Political Orientation

"Ever sit down to eat a scrumptious ham and egg breakfast and pause to wonder how the pig and chicken were treated before they met their end?

"Probably not, but the people behind World Farm Animals Day 2003 hope to get Americans thinking about it.

"Contrary to popular belief, farm animals seldom frolic in plush green meadows or bask in the sun. Instead, rights activists say, animals spend most of their lives confined to tiny cages, never given the freedom to graze or interact with other animals.

"'So many people have this false image of farmers and their animals living happily together on a farm,' says Dawn Moncrief, national coordinator of World Farm Animals Day.

"Observed every Oct. 2 since 1983, the day also marks the birthday of Mahatma Gandhi, an advocate of humane farming. . . .

INTERNSHIPS

This organization offers both paid and unpaid internships, which vary in duration, subject area, and requirements; application deadlines and hours are flexible. To find out about internship opportunities send an E-mail to staffing@ farmusa.org. The internship coordinator is Dawn Moncrief, director of programs and operations, 10101 Ashburton Lane, Bethesda, MD 20817. Phone: (301) 530-1737. Fax: (301) 530-5747. E-mail: dawn@farmusa.org.

NEWSLETTERS

Meatout Mondays (weekly e-newsletter)
Campaign Updates (monthly e-newsletter)
FARM Alerts (random electronic alerts)

PUBLICATIONS

None

CONFERENCES

Animal Rights National Conference

"Since its inception 20 years ago, organizers of World Farm Animals Day say they have seen changes, albeit slowly.

"'There's a great deal more awareness now of how animals are treated in factory farms,' says Alex Hershaft, president and founder of the Farm Animal Reform Movement, a national public interest organization that promotes plant-based eating and humane treatment of animals. 'Many more people are aware of where their meat comes from and many industries are instituting animal welfare standards.'"

(*San Antonio Express-News* [Texas], September 29, 2003)

"... Animal Rights 2003, a national conference put together by groups including the Farm Animal Reform Movement. The Bethesda, Md., organization sports the motto, 'Saving our planet—one bite at a time.'"

(*Ventura County Star* [California], August 16, 2003)

"Once upon a time there was grass-roots politics. Now there's astroturf.

"With due acknowledgement to the holder of that trademark for a product used in landscaping, among journalists the term is used to refer to a political product—fake grass-roots activity.

"For instance, the kind that's generated by slick Web sites promising 'Click here, and we'll send your message to everybody in Congress' or to a long list of newspapers. . . .

"No one knows how much of this stuff actually gets published. Editors see so much of it that they get pretty good at weeding it out. But in any case, they have help. Several hundred people belong to an e-mail list maintained by the National Conference of Editorial Writers. Anyone who suspects a letter didn't originate with the person who claims to have written it posts the text of the letter to the list. If another paper has received the same letter, bingo! That's all she wrote.

"In some cases, literally. A good many papers refuse to print further letters from people who've been caught putting their names to astroturf. . . .

"There's little doubt about the intent to deceive. The Farm Animal Reform Movement, one of the worst offenders, enrolls people it calls 'FARM reps' who give permission for their names to be used.

"A site dedicated to consumer activism describes FARM's scheme as follows.

"The group faxes letters to local papers, each one 'signed' by the FARM rep in that area. 'Each time we fax letters to the editors,' new reps are told, 'we simultaneously e-mail a copy to you, so you can anticipate receiving a call from your editor confirming that you wrote/sent the letter.'

"That is, when your local paper asks you whether you wrote the letter, you are instructed to lie about it. . . ."

(*Rocky Mountain News* [Denver], March 22, 2003)

"If animals could talk, they'd wake up singing tomorrow—not just because it's the first day of spring.

"No, for those who would be grilled, the 18th annual Great American Meatout is really something to bellow about.

"On Wednesday, herbivorous Americans will encourage their carnivorous counterparts to sample a 'wholesome, nonviolent diet' of grains, vegetables and fruits.

"It's a health thing, the vegetarians say. Healthy for you, healthy for the animals.

" 'Vegetarians have about one-third the risk of meat eaters [of developing] killer diseases,' says Lucy Goodrum, research director for the Meatout, which is promoted each year by FARM (formerly Farm Animal Reform Movement), a national, nonprofit public interest organization based in Washington, DC . . ."

(*Tampa Tribune,* March 19, 2002)

"The same area where shoppers hunt for sales and gobble burgers is hosting hundreds who refuse to eat meat, wear leather or drink milk.

A few miles from posh shops and fast-food outlets, participants in the Animal Rights 2001 National Conference at the McLean Hilton at Tysons Corner this week are wrestling with questions that pop up in seminars on subjects such as 'Animal Spirituality' and 'How to Relate to Animals.'

"Some at the conference—which ends today and is sponsored by People for the Ethical Treatment of Animals and Farm Animal Reform Movement, among others—do legal work for corporations, and others earn their livings ranting against the evils of corporations. Some grew up on farms and some grew up as hippies. . . ."

(*The Washington Post,* July 5, 2001)

Federation for American Immigration Reform (FAIR)

Established in 1979

DIRECTOR

Daniel A. Stein, executive director. Prior to joining FAIR in 1982, Stein was executive director of the Immigration Reform Law Institute. His legal experience includes private practice and as congressional staff. He has testified more than 50 time before Congress. Cited in the media as "America's best known immigration reformer," he has appeared on major TV and radio news/talk programs in America and has contributed commentaries to a vast number of print media outlets.

BOARD OF DIRECTORS

Sharon Barnes, chair; business owner
Nancy S. Anthony; president, Fernwood Advisors, Inc.
Henry M. Buhl; founder, Association of Community Employment for the Homeless
Gen. Douglas E. Caton; chief executive officer, Management Services Corp., Charlottesville, VA
Donald A. Collins; program and financial consultant, nonprofit and charitable institutions
Sarah G. Epstein; art lecturer and volunteer
Peter Gadiel; attorney, real estate investor
Stephen B. Swensrud; chair, Fernwood Advisors, Inc., Boston; chair, RPP Corp., Lawrence, MA; director or trustee, various Merrill Lynch-Sponsored Mutual funds
John Tanton; founder; editor and publisher, *The Social Contract*
Alan Weeden; president, Weeden Foundation
John Rohe

SCOPE

Members: more than 70,000
Branch: FAIR-California, Los Angeles
Affiliates: FAIR Congressional Task Force

STAFF

22 total—15 full-time professional; 7 full-time support; plus 3 interns; 2 part-time

TAX STATUS

501(c)(3)

FINANCES

Revenue: 2002—$3.6 million

FUNDING SOURCES

Foundation grants, 60%; membership dues and contributions, 40%

PAC

None

CONTACT INFORMATION

1666 Connecticut Avenue, NW, Suite 400, Washington, DC 20009
Phone: (202) 328-7004 • *Fax:* (202) 387-3447
General E-mail: Web form at www.fairus.org • *Web site:* www.fairus.org

Communications Director: Dave Ray, associate director
(202) 328-7004 • dsray@fairus.org
Human Resources Director: Carla Rodgers, contact person
(202) 328-7004

PURPOSE: "To end illegal immigration and reduce legal immigration to numbers consistent with the national interest."

CURRENT CONCERNS: Combat foreign worker programs that undermine American high-tech workers and others • Elimination of immigration entitlements for extended family members to end chain of migration • Fraud-resistant worker eligibility documentation • Immigration moratorium for all but essential immigration • Research and public education on the relationship between mass immigration and suburban sprawl

METHOD OF OPERATION: Advertisements • Conferences/seminars • Congressional testimony • Demonstrations • Grassroots organizing • Immigration Internship Program • International activities • Internet (databases, electronic bulletin boards, and Web site) • Internships • Legislative/regulatory monitoring (federal) • Library/Information clearinghouse • Litigation • Lobbying (federal, state, and grassroots) • Local/municipal affairs • Media outreach • Polling • Research • Speakers program • Training

Effectiveness and Political Orientation

"Long, long ago, in a decade that now seems far away, terrorists were a non-issue and illegal immigrants were the brown peril of choice, particularly in Pete Wilson's California. In 1994, Californians voted into law Proposition 187, a measure to deny basic healthcare and educational access to undocumented immigrants, and a whole host of demagogues ran around blaming various social and economic woes on immigrants.

"In 1998, anti-immigrant activists forced the Sierra Club to put a referendum on immigration on the annual membership ballot. Having been blamed for every other sin under the sun, immigrants were now to be scapegoated for our environmental problems as well. The club's membership quickly voted the measure down.

"But today the issue has returned, with anti-immigration activists attempting an openly hostile takeover of the Sierra Club. Three candidates for the March board elections are looking to form a majority with some of the more dubious current board members in an effort to take control of the organization and use the issue of overpopulation to push for far-reaching curbs on immigration.

"The three are Frank Morris, David Pimentel and Richard Lamm, all of whom have links to the anti-immigration Diversity Alliance for a Sustainable America. Lamm, the former Colorado governor, is also a longtime board member of the Federation for American Immigration Reform, which gets funding from the pro-eugenics and 'race betterment' Pioneer Fund. . . ."

(*The Los Angeles Times,* March 12, 2004)

"Bruce DeCell left his New York home at 5:30 on a February morning recently so that he could make it to Annapolis in time to testify on a bill that would crack down on the issuance of Maryland driver's licenses.

"A retired New York cop and father-in-law to a Wall Street trader killed on Sept. 11, DeCell makes a powerful witness as he travels across the country testifying on similar legislation.

" 'We received my son-in-law in five different increments. We buried him five different times,' said DeCell, adding that terrorists today could use legally obtained licenses to board planes. 'No one in the country can understand how hard it was for us.'

"Clutching a poster with the faces of attack victims, DeCell gave a passionate plea to Maryland lawmakers to pass the new restrictions. But he conceded his travel expenses were paid for by FAIR, a large national lobbying group whose involvement in the immigration debate goes back to the 1970s.

"Coordinating state lobbying with media campaigns on local drive-time radio, FAIR helped derail an in-state tuition bill in Maryland last year and helped pass new restrictions on driver's licenses this year in North Carolina.

"The group has sent lawyers and lobbyists to Virginia, Maryland, North Carolina, New Jersey, California and Tennessee this year.

" 'The anti-immigrant movement is dramatically media driven. Whether it's FAIR, the Center for Immigration Studies or Numbers USA, those groups have real media operations, and they deploy them more effectively than the other side,' said Rick Swartz, a Washington political strategist allied with the pro-immigrant movement. . . ."

(*The Denver Post,* February 29, 2004)

"Finally, there is a Duncan Doctrine.

"At least that's the opinion of the Federation for American Immigration Reform, a national advocacy group that seeks to close the gates on immigrants so that levels are 'consistent with the national interest.'

"In a press release issued this week, Dan Stein, the federation's executive director, accused Montgomery County Executive Douglas M. Duncan of 'espousing a policy regarding illegal immigrants that is both legally questionable and intellectually dishonest.'

" 'The Duncan Doctrine is that enforcing immigration laws is strictly a federal matter, but helping illegal aliens get away with violating immigration laws is a county matter,' Stein said. 'It is a doctrine that amounts to "Heads: Illegal aliens win. Tails: The law-abiding residents of Montgomery County lose." '

"The broadside was triggered by Duncan's decision to headline a rally in Annapolis last week to speak out against six bills before the Maryland General Assembly that he says target immigrants.

"One of the measures attempts to outlaw acceptance of consular identification cards, which Duncan has said will help immigrants avoid exploitation by predatory lenders, check cashing outlets and unscrupulous landlords. . . ."

(*The Washington Post,* February 26, 2004)

"President Bush announced a sweeping new immigration reform proposal this week that could become a hot-button issue in the November election.

"For months, insiders have hinted that the president would propose a new guest worker program aimed at allowing more foreign workers into the country on a temporary basis.

"Widely favored by the American business community, a guest worker program would allow employers to fill jobs in industries that routinely experience shortages of workers willing to do the often difficult, dangerous jobs Americans shun—at least at wages that allow employers to remain in business.

"But the guest worker provisions won't be the most controversial part of the administration's new proposal. Although some groups that want to limit immigration altogether—such as the Federation for American Immigration Reform (FAIR)—oppose guest worker plans, even such staunch restrictionists as Republican Rep. Tom Tancredo of Colorado are on record as supporting the idea of guest workers. The real battle will be over what to do with those millions of illegal aliens who are already here. . . ."

(*The Baltimore Sun,* January 8, 2004)

"Pvt. Juan Escalante took a secret with him from Fort Stewart to Iraq.

"Although he wore the same uniform and faced the same dangers as other U.S. soldiers, Escalante is an illegal immigrant. He enlisted by showing a fake green card he bought for $50.

"The Army sees him as a 'valuable soldier' who risked his life to serve the United States, said Richard Olson, a Fort Stewart spokesman. 'He's just like any American kid who joined the Army,' Olson said.

"The Army has helped Escalante apply for citizenship but could still discharge him for misleading a recruiter.

"Some Americans worry about illegal immigrants joining the military in hopes of becoming citizens. They say the government needs to do a better job creating secure identity documents.

" 'This guy may be a stand-up guy—but suppose he was an agent of al-Qaida,' said Dan Stein, executive director of the Federation for American Immigration Reform in Washington, which favors tighter immigration controls. 'If the government [cared] about enforcing its immigration laws, this kid wouldn't have been able to enlist. . . ."

(*The Atlanta Journal-Constitution,* November 7, 2003)

Focus on the Family

Established in 1977

DIRECTOR
James C. Dobson, founder and chair. Dobson, author of 17 best-selling books, had previously served on the faculty of the University of Southern California and on the attending staff of Children's Hospital of Los Angeles. From a two-room suite in Arcadia, CA, Dobson began with radio—a weekly half-hour program heard on only a few dozen stations. Focus on the Family has since become an international organization with 82 different ministries and a staff of more than 1,200 employees.

BOARD OF DIRECTORS
James C. Dobson, chair
Ted Engstrom, vice chair; president emeritus of World Vision
Lee Eaton, secretary; president, Eaton Farms, Inc., Lexington, KY
Bobb Biehl, treasurer; president of Masterplanning Group International, Orlando, FL
Elsa D. Prince Broekhuizen; chair, Edgar and Elsa Prince Foundation and E.O.P.
Patrick P. Caruana; Northrop Grumman
Shirley M. Dobson; chair of the National Day of Prayer Committee
Robert E. Hamby Jr.; former senior vice president and CFO, Multimedia, Inc.
Don Hodel; president; founder and managing director, Summit Group International, Ltd.
Steve Largent; executive director, Wheelchair Foundation
Daniel L. Villanueva; president, Villanueva Cos.
Anthony Wauterlek; founder, Wauterlek and Brown, IL

SCOPE
Members: "There are no members, but rather constituents."
Branches/chapters: "We have autonomous associate offices, licensed with the Focus on the Family name. There are international Focus offices located in Australia, Belgium, Canada, Costa Rica, East Africa, Egypt, Indonesia, Japan, Korea, Malaysia, the Netherlands, New Zealand, Nigeria, Philippines, Singapore, South Africa, Taiwan and the United Kingdom"
Affiliates: None

STAFF
1,271 full-time professional; 75 total part-time professional; 150–170 active volunteers and 12 summer interns

TAX STATUS
501(c)(3)

CONTACT INFORMATION
8605 Explorer Drive, Colorado Springs, CO 80920
Phone: (719) 531-3400 or (800) 232-6459 • *Fax:* (719) 531-3424
General E-mail: mail@fotf.org • *Web site:* www.family.org

Communications Director: Paul Hetrick, vice president of media relations
(719) 531-3336 • hetrickp@fotf.org
Human Resources Director: David Bervig
(719) 548-4616 • bervigdj@fotf.org

PURPOSE: "To cooperate with the Holy Spirit in disseminating the Gospel of Jesus Christ to as many people as possible, and, specifically, to accomplish that objective by helping to preserve traditional values and the institution of the family."

CURRENT CONCERNS: Permanence of marriage • Preeminence of evangelism • Pro-life issues • Relationship of Church, family, and government • Sanctity of human life • Value of children

METHOD OF OPERATION: Conferences/seminars • Films/video/audiotapes • International activities • Internet (databases, e-mail alerts, and Web site) • Media outreach • Research • Radio broadcasting • Printed resources

SPECIFIC PROGRAMS: African American Outreach • Focus on the Family Institute • Focus Over Fifty • Focus on Your Child • Heritage Builders • Internet Ministries • National Day of Prayer • Pastoral Ministries • Physicians Outreach

Effectiveness and Political Orientation

"The conservative activists who traveled to Loveland, Colo., last summer to meet Rep. Marilyn N. Musgrave had their doubts that the soft-spoken one-time housewife was the ideal flag carrier for the national campaign against gay marriage.

"A Republican from rural eastern Colorado, Musgrave had proposed a constitutional amendment banning same-sex marriage just six months into her first term in Washington. It was an issue that social conservatives hoped might become key in the presidential campaign, and they fretted that the woman whose name was on the bill was untested in the national culture wars. But the group came away reassured.

"'We left the meeting very encouraged that this could not be in better hands—more experienced hands, to be sure, but not better,' said Glenn Stanton, the nonprofit Christian group Focus on the Family's senior analyst for marriage. . . ."

(*The Los Angeles Times*, March 14, 2004)

FINANCES
Budget: 2004—$128.69 million; 2003—
$122.43 million; 2002—$124.69 million

FUNDING SOURCES
Foundation grants, 6.4%; individuals, 77.9%;
publications, 5.8%; conferences, 0.8%; product sales and licensing, 5.5%; miscellaneous
income, 3.6%

PAC
None

EMPLOYMENT
Potential applicants can learn about job openings with this organization from the Focus on the Family Web site: www.family.org; the jobing.com Web site, monster.com, *Colorado Springs Gazette*, KGFT Radio (& their affiliate), and various trade papers for specific jobs. This organization offers positions in the following areas: administrative, marketing, accounting, customer service, call center, food services, international reps, public policy, distribution/warehouse, MIS, internet, and human resources. Applicants should send resumes and other materials for employment to Focus on the Family, Human Resources, 8605 Explorer Drive, Colorado Springs, CO 80920. Phone: (719) 531-3400. Fax: (719) 531-3359. E-mail address: hrmail@fotf.org.

INTERNSHIPS
This organization offers unpaid internship opportunities. Contact the volunteer department. Internship areas dependent on department needs. Applicants must complete a volunteer application, which includes references and Christian testimony. An interview is conducted to determine qualified candidates. For more information, or to apply, contact Arlys Smid, volunteer coordinator, 8605 Explorer Drive, Colorado Springs, CO 80920. Phone: (719) 268-4827 or (800)-531-1626. Fax: (719) 531-3303. E-mail: smidaa@fotf.org.

NEWSLETTERS
Breakaway (monthly)
Brio (monthly)
Brio and Beyond (monthly)
Citizen (monthly)
Clubhouse (monthly)
Clubhouse, Jr. (monthly)
Focus on the Family (monthly)
Pastor's Weekly Briefing (weekly)
Physician's (bimonthly)
Plugged In (monthly)

PUBLICATIONS
Produces films, videos, and radio and television programs. Videos include:
Adventures in Odyssey
Last Chance Detective
McGee and Me
No Apologies
Ribbits
Sex, Lies and the Truth
That the World May Know

"Justice Martha B. Sosman of the state Supreme Judicial Court raised the research flag first.

"In her dissent to the court's controversial ruling in support of gay marriage in November, she criticized her fellow justices for ignoring the scientific research on the subject of children, declaring. . . . 'Studies to date reveal that there are still some observable differences between children raised by opposite-sex couples and children raised by same-sex couples.'

"Two months later, Focus on The Family, a nonprofit family education group with close ties to evangelical Christianity, responded to the court's ruling with a full-page newspaper advertisement stating that studies show that children are more likely to be suspended from school, have emotional problems and take drugs when raised by a single parent instead of both biological ones.

"Now, with the state Legislature planning to reconvene a constitutional convention on gay marriage Thursday, others also are turning to science for answers.

"They are not likely to find them. Virtually all the nearly 50 studies on the children of gay and lesbian parents—who number between 6 and 14 million in the United States, according to various studies—have found no significant differences between children raised by heterosexual or homosexual parents.

"But most of the studies have been small and some of them solicited families through gay literature or participant referrals, rather than a more representative process. Critics, mostly opponents of gay marriage, charge they are methodologically flawed and, in some cases, politically biased.

" 'Those current studies that appear to indicate neutral to favorable results from homosexual parenting have critical flaws,' according to the American College of Pediatricians, an advocacy group that opposes gay marriage.

"Even veteran researchers concede that the field is in its infancy. . . ."
(*The Boston Globe*, March 9, 2004)

"Peter van Breda, senior pastor of Bellevue's The Gathering Place, strongly believes kids shouldn't see the violent, R-rated 'The Passion of the Christ.'. . .

"Perhaps more than any recent R-rated movie, 'The Passion of the Christ' is attracting questions about its appropriateness for children. . . .

"Movie critics and church representatives uniformly agree the movie is not for children and preteens. But opinions vary on whether young teens should view the detailed depiction of Jesus' last 12 hours, which includes brutal beatings and whippings.

"The influential conservative Christian group Focus on the Family endorsed the movie and recommends it for ages 13 and older.

" 'Is it gory? Yes. Is it gruesome? Yes. Is it raw? Yes,' said Bob Waliszewski, entertainment specialist for Focus on the Family, which usually condemns violent movies. 'But in this particular case, it's worth it.' "
(*The Seattle Times*, February 28, 2004)

"In Tuesday's Calendar, 'The Big Picture' columnist Patrick Goldstein, writing about 'The Passion of the Christ,' incorrectly stated that James Dobson of Focus on the Family was 'urging churches to buy tickets for every kid in Sunday school, even though the film is rated R.' While Dobson does indeed endorse the movie, he has specifically warned parents that 'it is wholly inappropriate for young children.' "
(*The Los Angeles Times*, February 26, 2004)

CONFERENCES

Clergy conference—every other year
Senior/Focus Over Fifty conference—yearly
Crisis Pregnancy Center conference—every
    other year
Physicians conference—every two years
Women's Leadership conference—yearly
International Directors conference—yearly.

"Focus on the Family, one of the nation's largest Christian ministries, will not accept federal money from a faith-based program funded by the federal government.

"'We believe that with federal dollars eventually comes strings,' said Tom Minnery, vice president of public policy for Focus. 'Our donations come in small amounts from a whole lot of people, and as long as we serve those people we'll be in existence, and if we stop serving those people we don't deserve to be in existence.'

"Minnery and four other Focus representatives—including Mike Haley, who tries to convert gays from homosexuality—and eight other faith-based social-services providers met in Colorado Springs on Friday to talk about President Bush's faith-based initiatives, which funnel federal dollars to religious-sponsored social services. . . ."

(*The Denver Post,* January 25, 2004)

Food Research and Action Center (FRAC)

Established in 1970

DIRECTOR

James D. Weill, president. Weill began his public interest career in 1969 at the Legal Assistance Foundation of Chicago. From there he went to the Children's Defense where he served from 1982 to 1997 as program director and then as general counsel.

BOARD OF DIRECTORS

Matthew E. Melmed, chair; Zero to Three
George L. Blackburn; Harvard Medical School
Elliot Bloom; Cendant Corp.
Dagmar Farr; Food Marketing Institute
Carol Tucker Foreman; Consumer Federation of America
Dan Glickman; Harvard University; former U.S. representative
Louise Hilsen; Nestle USA
Jerry Klepner; Black, Kelly, Scruggs & Healey
Clinton Lyons; National Legal Aid & Defender Association
Marshall L. Matz; Olsson, Frank and Weeda
John G. Polk; Polk Consulting
Ronald F. Pollack; Families U.S.A.
Patricia Scarcelli; United Food & Commercial Workers International Union
Marion Standish; California Endowment
Alan J. Stone; Harvard University
Susan Stout; Grocery Manufacturers of America
Judith H. Whittlesey; Susan Davis International
Maggie Williams; formerly of the office of President Bill Clinton

SCOPE

Members: None
Branches/chapters: None
Affiliate: Campaign to End Childhood Hunger

STAFF

19 total—plus 11–20 volunteers

TAX STATUS

501(c)(3)

FINANCES

Revenue: 2002—1.83 million; 2001—$1.56 million

FUNDING SOURCES

Contributions, 84.7%; program services, 5.6%; investments, 1.3%; special events, 7.9%; other, 0.5%

PAC

None

CONTACT INFORMATION

1875 Connecticut Avenue, NW, Suite 540, Washington, DC 20009-5728
Phone: (202) 986-2200 • *Fax:* (202) 986-2525
General E-mail: webmaster@frac.org • *Web site:* www.frac.org

Communications Director: Ellen Vollinger
(202) 986-2200, ext. 3016 • evollinger@frac.org
Human Resources Director: Information unavailable

PURPOSE: "To improve public policies to eradicate hunger and undernutrition in the United States."

CURRENT CONCERNS: Hunger and undernutrition in the United States, with emphasis on childhood hunger

METHOD OF OPERATION: Coalition forming • Conferences/seminars • Congressional testimony • Grassroots organizing • Legislative/regulatory monitoring (federal and state) • Library/information clearinghouse • Lobbying (federal, state, and grassroots) • Media outreach • Participation in regulatory proceedings (federal) • Research • Training and technical assistance • Web site

SPECIFIC PROGRAMS: Building Blocks Project: Promoting Education and Child Development with Nutrition Resources • The Campaign to End Childhood Hunger

Effectiveness and Political Orientation

"Many low-income children eligible for free or discount breakfasts are not getting them, according to the Food Research and Action Center.

"Only 6.7 million of the 16 million children eligible for the program are getting them.

"States that enrolled the most low-income kids last year for breakfasts were Oregon and West Virginia, the report said.

"The research center ranked Wisconsin last and New Jersey 49th. They enrolled about 34 low-income students in school breakfast for every 100 in the school lunch program. . . ."

(*Rocky Mountain News* [Denver], November 7, 2003)

"Going to bed without a single meal all day is not unusual for Andrea Gonzales.

"When her meager pay as a housekeeper for a small South Side motel doesn't stretch far enough, Gonzales, 30, frequently goes hungry to ensure that her 4-year-old son, Alex, has plenty to eat. She won't allow Alex to experience the pain and indignity of hunger. . . .

"Gonzales is among the 14.8 percent of Texans who must regularly search out emergency food from government centers and church pantries, according to a study recently released by the Food Research & Action Center.

EMPLOYMENT

Job openings are posted at www.frac.org /html/all_about_frac/jobs.html. Individual postings specify to whom applications should be submitted.

INTERNSHIPS

Information about internship opportunities is available at http://www.frac.org/html/ all_about_frac/internships.html. FRAC offers a variety of internship possibilities throughout the year. FRAC interns work as volunteers or with the support of third-party funding sources, such as work study programs. Interns work directly with policy and development staff and are assigned to specific projects. Our staff considers mentoring an important part of any internship program. Students with a strong commitment to public interest and antipoverty issues are encouraged to apply. Other requirements include solid research, writing and communications skills, computer literacy and interest in/knowledge of the political process.

To apply, send a cover letter and resume to Internship Coordinator, Food Research and Action Center, 1875 Connecticut Avenue, NW, Suite 540, Washington, DC 20009-5728. Fax: (202) 986-2525.

NEWSLETTERS

FRAC News Digest (weekly E-mail newsletter)

PUBLICATIONS

Community Childhood Hunger Identification Project (CCHIP): A Survey of Childhood Hunger in the United States
Feeding the Other Half: Mothers and Children Left Out of WIC
FRAC Releases State-by-State Rates of Household Hunger and Food Insecurity, 1997–1999
FRAC'S Guide to the Food Stamp Program
Fuel for Excellence: FRAC's Guide to School Breakfast Expansion
Get Ready for Food Stamp Reauthorization Changes in Your State
Good Choices in Hard Times: Fifteen Ideas for States to Reduce Hunger and Stimulate the Economy
Hunger Doesn't Take a Vacation
The Relationship Between Nutrition and Learning
School Breakfast Scorecard
School's Out, Let's Eat: FRAC's Guide to Using the Child and Adult Care Food Program (CACFP) to Expand Afterschool Opportunities for Children
State Government Responses to the Food Assistance Gap
State of the States: A Profile of Food and Nutrition Programs Across the Nation
WIC: A Success Story
WIC in Native American Communities: Building a Healthier America
WIC in the States: Twenty-Five Years of Building a Healthier America
WIC Works: Let's Make it Work for Everyone

CONFERENCES

National Anti-Hunger Policy Conference

"The study concluded that Texas has the second-highest rate of hunger in the nation, behind only Utah, which has 15.2 percent. . . ."

(*San Antonio Express-News*, November 5, 2003)

"As they celebrated another summer of fun at the neighborhood pool, Janna Benston's three children also were thinking about American kids who are far less fortunate.

"The Dunwoody woman decided to get her children involved when she saw a Parade magazine article about the Great American Bake Sale, a national drive to raise money to combat childhood hunger in the United States. . . .

"Proceeds from the national fund-raising drive go to Share Our Strength, which helps fund anti-hunger programs across the country. Seventy-five percent of the money raised in Georgia will stay in the state. Twenty percent goes to high-risk areas, and 5 percent to the Food Research and Action Center—a public policy organization. . . ."

(*The Atlanta Journal-Constitution*, July 10, 2003)

"For the American Kennel Club, the question is whether the government can decide when dogs will be allowed to breed. For big rice and cotton farmers, the issue is a provision that would limit each farmer's annual subsidy to $275,000. For advocates of the poor, the goal is to add legal immigrants to the food stamp program without undercutting hungry school children or their mothers.

"After three weeks of closed-door negotiations over the $171 billion farm bill, lobbyists for agribusiness and the poor are claiming victory, while environmentalists are complaining.

" 'This represents a very important investment for the needy,' said Ellen Vollinger of the Food Research and Action Center, which lobbies for nutrition programs for the poor. . . ."

(*The New York Times*, March 24, 2002)

"Fearing overload at food pantries, soup kitchens and shelters, representatives from more than 1,200 city food programs gathered yesterday to discuss the five-year welfare deadline, which will cut federal benefits to 40,000 New Yorkers in December. . . .

"The emergency food network is at capacity," said Lucy Cabrera, the food bank's president. 'As demand increases at street level, so does demand at the bank.'. . .

" 'They're telling people, "What are you going to do when welfare ends?" ' said Henry Freedman, executive director of the Welfare Law Center. 'A lot of people are going to be discouraged, confused, and be forced to drop off the welfare rolls.'

"James Weill, president of the Food Research and Action Center, also slammed the reform, citing increased demand for emergency food since 1996, despite a 32% drop in food stamp requests. . . ."

(*New York Daily News*, September 5, 2001)

The Foundation Center

Established in 1956

DIRECTOR

Sara L. Engelhardt, president. Engelhardt joined the staff as executive vice president in 1987, having served on the Center's Board of Trustees from 1984. For more than 20 years, she was on the staff of Carnegie Corporation of New York. During 1975–1987, she served as secretary of the corporation and managed the foundation's grants. In addition, she was program officer in the areas of philanthropy and nonprofit organizations and of women in higher education and public life. Engelhardt serves on the boards of the National Council for Research on Women and the Education & Research Foundation of the Metro New York Better Business Bureau. She also serves as the center's liaison to the board of directors of the Council on Foundations. She chairs the Foundations and Corporations Committee of the Wesleyan University National Campaign and the Annals Committee of the New York Academy of Sciences. A 1965 graduate of Wellesley College, Engelhardt holds a master's degree in administration of higher education from Teachers College, Columbia University.

BOARD OF DIRECTORS

Sarah L. Engelhardt, president
Barry D. Gaberman, chair; senior vice president, Ford Foundation
Loretta Ferrari, secretary and controller
Maureen Mackey, treasurer and chief operating officer
Audrey R. Alvarado; executive director, National Council of Nonprofit Associations
M. Christine DeVita; president, Wallace Foundation
Susan Lajoie Eagan; executive director, Mandel Center for Nonprofit Organizations, Case Western Reserve University
Robert C. Elliott; senior executive vice president, Bessemer Trust Co.
Nancy S. Kami; executive director, Lisa and Douglas Goldman Fund
Douglas W. Nelson; president, Annie E. Casey Foundation
Jerry A. O'Neil; partner-in-charge, Not-for-Profit Services, PricewaterhouseCoopers LLP
Elizabeth C. Reveal; management consultant, Trios Consulting Partners
Dorothy S. Ridings; president and chief executive officer, Council on Foundations
Nancy Roberts; president, Connecticut Council for Philanthropy
Robert K. Ross; president and chief executive officer, California Endowment
Thomas E. Wilcox; president, Baltimore Community Foundation

CONTACT INFORMATION

79 Fifth Avenue, 2nd Floor, New York, NY 10003
Phone: (212) 620-4230; (800) 424-9836 • *Fax:* (212) 807-3677
General E-mail: feedback@fdncenter.org • *Web site:* fdncenter.org

Communications Director: Cheryl Loe
(212) 807-2486 • cl@fdncenter.org
Human Resources Director: Juan Brito
(212) 807-3615

PURPOSE: "The Foundation Center's mission is to strengthen the nonprofit sector by advancing knowledge about U.S. philanthropy. To achieve our mission, we collect, organize, and communicate information on U.S. philanthropy; conduct and facilitate research on trends in the field; provide education and training on the grantseeking process; and ensure public access to information and services through our Web site, print and electronic publications, five library/learning centers, and a national network of Cooperating Collections. Founded in 1956, the Center is the nation's leading authority on philanthropy and is dedicated to serving grantseekers, grantmakers, researchers, policymakers, the media, and the general public."

CURRENT CONCERNS: Facilitating wide and efficient distribution of the most current information about private foundations and their grantmaking programs.

METHOD OF OPERATION: Information clearinghouse • Internet (databases, electronic bulletin boards, e-mail alerts, and Web site) • Library services open to the public • Product merchandising • Professional development services • Research • Training

Effectiveness and Political Orientation

"Academic information about nonprofits can also be found through a variety of online indexes. The Literature of the Nonprofit Sector (http://lnps .fdncenter.org/) is a large, searchable database on the literature of philanthropy compiled by the Foundation Center's five libraries. The search engine provided is very sophisticated and allows searching by author, title, subject, publisher, journal title, type of record, year, or keyword. . . . Abstracts are very lengthy and give a good summary of research."

(*Searcher,* February 2004)

"Fundraisers have had a tough job in recent years as both personal and corporate giving has tanked, along with the rest of the economy. Grants to foundations were down substantially in the U.S. in 2002, the first decline since 1983, reports The Foundation Yearbook, an annual philanthropic review published by The Foundation Center. Overall, foundations raised $200 million less in 2002, down from $30.5 billion to $30.3 billion for the year.

Patricia L. Willis; *Voices of Georgia's Children*, Atlanta, GA

SCOPE
Members: not a membership organization
Branches/chapters: 4
Affiliates: Field offices in Washington, DC; Atlanta; Cleveland; and San Francisco

STAFF
120 total

TAX STATUS
501(c)(3)

FINANCES
Budget: 2002—$15.5 million

FUNDING SOURCES
Publications sales, online services, educational programs, 60%; foundation and corporate grants, 40%

PAC
None

EMPLOYMENT
Current openings are posted online at www.fdncenter.org/about/careers/index.html. The center hires in the areas of editorial/publishing; fundraising; administrative; marketing; accounting; information technology; print production; communications; research; librarian; and educational trainer. Resumes and applications can be mailed to Juan Brito, director of human resources, The Foundation Center, 79 Fifth Avenue, 2nd Floor, New York, NY 10003.

INTERNSHIPS
Information unavailable

NEWSLETTERS
Associates Program News (members only)
Philanthropy News Digest (online)

PUBLICATIONS
The following is a sample of recent publications:
Associate Program Service
Effective Economic Decision-Making by Nonprofit Organizations
Foundation Directory 2004 edition
Foundation Giving Trends: Update on Funding Priorities
Foundation Grants to Individuals
Guía Para Escribir Propuestas
Guide to Grantseeking on the Web
Guide to Funding for International & Foreign Programs
Guide to Proposal Writing
Guide to Winning Proposals
Handbook Private Foundations
National Directory of Corporate Giving
National Guide to Funding in Arts & Culture
National Guide to Funding for the Environment & Animal Welfare
National Guide to Funding in Health
Philanthropy's Challenge: Building Nonprofit Capacity Through Venture Grantmaking

"Looking ahead, 'Continuing losses in endowment values, especially among the largest U.S. foundations, will take a toll on overall levels of giving,' says Sarah Engelhardt, president of the Foundation Center, in a recently published statement.

"At the same time, charities couldn't fail to notice the buckets of money being raised by various political campaigns in advance of the 2004 presidential elections. In particular, the "Dean Machine" behind Democratic candidate Howard Dean has become famous even notorious for the success it has had raising funds online via its 'Blog for America' site.

"Blog? What's a blog? Short for 'Web log,' it is an interactive online journal, with news and other information supplied by various constituents. With startup software costing as little as $200, it is also quickly becoming one of the more effective ways to enlist an audience, build loyalty with that group and— almost incidentally—raise substantial money for a cause.

"Why the rebounded interest in online fundraising? As Willie Sutton is alleged to have said when asked why he robbed banks, 'Because that's where the money is.' "

(*Promo Magazine*, February 1, 2004)

"In 2001 alone, private foundations gave $28.7 billion to charities. Such a wellspring of good works was made possible by the enormous federal tax benefits that for generations have flowed to those wealthy Americans who create, through their foundations, enduring philanthropic legacies.

"What does the country receive in return for these billions of dollars in subsidies?

"In large part, the biggest beneficiaries of foundation giving are the nation's wealthiest nonprofit institutions.

"To be sure, some charitable foundations focus their philanthropy on programs to help the disadvantaged. But the largest foundations parcel out a surprisingly high proportion of their grants to already well-endowed colleges and universities and other elite institutions.

"Indeed, the most prestigious universities on each coast, Harvard and Stanford, attracted hundreds of millions of dollars more than other recipients between 1992 and 2001, according to a study of foundation grantmaking patterns done for the Globe by the Foundation Center, a research and education organization based in New York.

"The study, which examined giving by 1,000 of the country's largest foundations, found that another 14 of that decade's top 20 grant recipients were also elite universities, among them Columbia, Yale, the University of Pennsylvania, the University of Chicago, and Duke. . . .

"The study by the Foundation Center examined grants of $10,000 or more given or committed between 1992 and 2001 by about 800 of the nation's 1,000 largest foundations, including almost all of the top 500. In addition to the 800 largest, the study also includes 200 other foundations of varying sizes. The sample accounts for more than half of all foundation giving."

(*The Boston Globe*, January 11, 2004)

"Two years after Sept. 11, $2.9 billion has been given to and more than $2.2 billion has been spent by Sept. 11 charities, said the Foundation Center, which will soon issue an update. Donations have slowed, and charities have begun to consider phasing out programs that delivered urgent support. The September

Securing Your Organization's Future
Also publishes CD-ROM products.

CONFERENCES
Sponsors seminars and workshops.

11 Fund, the second largest of the 350 funds created after the attacks, will cut off enrollment for some programs on Jan. 31 and close its office in 2004.

"Still, the Foundation Center estimates that more than $600 million remains unspent, and the focus has turned to administering programs over the long term. As money for emergency aid, employment assistance and cash grants to survivors is spent, at least two charitable efforts will live on for years—delivery of mental health services and college scholarships. . . ."

(The New York Times, November 17, 2003)

"A bill recently introduced into the U.S. House of Representatives—the 'Charitable Giving Act of 2003'—will increase the federally mandated level of annual giving a foundation must disperse as a percentage of assets. The bill, H.R. 7, will achieve this by making the inclusion of administrative expenses in the current figure—5% of assets—no longer allowable. If it becomes law, the entire 5% of yearly giving would have to be directed to charity, making the total disbursement level approximately 5.4%.

"According to stories in *Philanthropy News Digest,* a project of the Foundation Center, and the May 19 edition of *The New York Times,* the bill, sponsored by Rep. Roy Blunt (R-Mo.), the majority whip, and Rep. Harold E. Ford, Jr. (D-Tenn.), aims to encourage charitable giving at a time when not-for-profit groups are feeling the funding crunch. 'I'm told that [foundations'] average cost of administration is four-tenths of one percent, so all this bill does is increase the amount they would have to spend to 5.4%,' Blunt is quoted as saying.

"In a statement provided to Back Stage, however, the Foundation Center questions this figure. While stating that it 'does not take a position on pending legislation,' the organization's 'analyses of foundation data shed light on some of the issues raised by the legislation.'

"For example, Foundation Center data shows that 'over the past few years, independent foundations on average were paying out in grants alone close to 6% of their asset value.' This figure is expected to stay at this level because most foundation's 'assets have declined faster than their giving has.'

"The Foundation Center statement goes on to state that because 'administrative expenses comprise a small percentage of most foundations' spending, removing them from the payout calculation is not likely to yield substantial increases in giving.' Should this provision of the bill become law—it's the House version of a Senate bill that also provides tax breaks for charitable giving—the opposite could well happen, with foundation assets being eroded 'and thus their giving capacity in the long term.'"

(BackStage, May 30, 2003)

Foundation on Economic Trends

Established in 1977

DIRECTOR

Jeremy Rifkin, president. Rifkin is an advisor to heads of state and government officials around the world and speaks frequently before business, labor, and civic forums. He has also lectured at more than 500 universities in some 20 countries in the past 30 years. Since 1994, Rifkin has been a fellow at the Wharton School's Executive Education Program, where he lectures to CEOs and senior corporate management from around the world on new trends in science and technology and their impacts on the global economy, society and the environment. His monthly column on global issues appears in many of the world's leading newspapers and magazines. He holds a degree in economics from the Wharton School of the University of Pennsylvania, and a degree in international affairs from the Fletcher School of Law and Diplomacy at Tufts University.

BOARD OF DIRECTORS

Jeremy Rifkin, president
Alexia Robinson, secretary
Michelle Baker, treasurer
Richard Deutsch, director
Michael Uhl, director
Elliot Stein, director

SCOPE

Members: None
Branches/chapters: None
Affiliates: Global Days of Action, National Coalition Against Surrogacy, Pure Food Campaign, Save Organic Standards Campaign

STAFF

5 total

TAX STATUS

501(c)(3)

FINANCES

Revenue: 2002—$261,337; 2001—$616,932

FUNDING SOURCES

Contributions, 91.9%; program services, 5.6%; investments, 2.5%

PAC

None

EMPLOYMENT

Information unavailable

INTERNSHIPS

FET offers internships in Washington, DC, for individuals with interest in emerging trends in science and technology and their impacts on the environment, the economy, culture, and

CONTACT INFORMATION

1660 L Street, NW, Suite 216, Washington, DC 20036
Phone: (202) 466-2823 • *Fax:* (202) 429-9602
General E-mail: office@foet.org • *Web site:* www.foet.org

Communications Director: Michelle Baker, office manager and media relations
(202) 466-2823 • mbaker@foet.org
Human Resources Director: None

PURPOSE: "To examine emerging trends in science and technology and the impacts on the environment, the economy, culture and society."

CURRENT CONCERNS: Antitrust lawsuit against Monsanto • Gene therapy • Labeling of genetically engineered foods • Patents on life

METHOD OF OPERATION: Boycott • Coalition forming • Congressional testimony • Education • Grassroots organizing • International activities • Legislative/regulatory monitoring (federal and state) • Litigation • Media outreach • Participation in regulatory proceedings (federal and state) • Research

Effectiveness and Political Orientation

"Hold on to your wallets.

"Those record gasoline prices are expected to climb even higher just as the summer driving season gets under way. . . .

"That said, no one thinks the price spike will prompt families to sit home in the summer heat or suddenly switch to solar energy, although some may choose a cabin in the woods closer to home.

"Yet some economists are predicting an uptick in the cost of consumer goods from shoes to strawberries, as truckers' pricey trips to the pump are passed on to retailers and then on to you. Indeed, some believe gasoline prices are already putting a drag on the so-called jobless recovery. Come Memorial Day, they predict gas costs could put a damper on consumer spending, slowing the pace of recovery even further.

"But others contend the price spike will have little impact, other than a touch of personal frustration when drivers reach for their credit cards. They note that inflation so far has remained fairly low—in part because the high price of gas is being offset by other deflationary factors, such as the low cost of housing, thanks to the refinancing boom.

"The two competing camps do tend to agree on one thing: Gas prices will have to spike far higher than $2 a gallon for them to derail the current recovery.

" 'As shocking as the oil prices are, they're not shocking enough to knock us into a new downturn,' says Lakshman Achuthan, managing director of the Economic Cycle Research Institute in New York. 'The window of vulnerability that was open a year or two ago in this economy has slammed shut.'

society. FET generally admits 1 to 2 individuals for unpaid internships lasting approximately 4 months, beginning in January, May, and September. Internships may be part-time or full-time. Duties include research (Library of Congress and online); preparing and editing print material; handling media articles and correspondence; maintaining campaign files and database; answering calls; preparing and distributing campaign mailings; and responding to requests for general and campaign information. Requirements include excellent communication skills; ability to write and edit; organizational skills; and ability to work independently or with direction. Applicants must also be computer-literate college students (grad or under-grad) with a commitment to public interest.

Submit resumes to Sarah Mann, research coordinator, approximately 6 weeks prior to applicable term. Information regarding internships is available at http://www.foet.org/Internship-Volunteers.htm. Fax: (202) 429-9602. E-mail: smann@foet.org.

NEWSLETTERS
None

PUBLICATIONS
The Age of Access
The Biotech Century: Playing Ecological Roulette with Mother Nature's Designs
Cloning: What Hath Genomics Wrought?
Consider the Costs of Each Path to the "Biotech Century"
Cradle to Grave, You're a Customer First
Entropy: Into the Greenhouse World, Education in the Biotech Age
For the Experiences of a Lifetime, Sign on the Dotted Line
Genetic Blueprints Aren't Mere Utilities
God in a Labcoat
It's Death of a Salesman as Shared-Savings Catches On
Patent Pending
The Second Genesis
The Ultimate Therapy

CONFERENCES
None

"But even optimists say there could be a few dark clouds on the horizon. If crude oil prices stay high—which most analysts think they will, barring a sudden change—that could put a crimp in consumer spending and the pace of recovery.

" 'My expectation is that the higher oil and electricity prices are going to take a serious bite out of consumer budgets in the second or third quarter, and we're going to see unexpected shortfalls in economic growth by the third or fourth quarter,' says economist Philip Verleger, a visiting fellow at the Institute for International Economics in Washington. . . .

"Jeremy Rifkin, president of the Foundation on Economic Trends in Washington, says this could produce 'a perfect storm' that could plunge the economy into a deep recession by Election Day. That's if everything lines up: Gasoline prices spike to $2.50 to $3 a gallon, which impacts consumer spending and companies' willingness to invest, which drags down the economy. To stimulate it, the government either gives another tax break or increases spending. Either way, it increases the record deficit, which already is making foreign investors nervous. So in order to finance the debt and attract those investors, the government raises interest rates, which again will have a negative impact on the economy.

" 'It could have a tsunami effect,' says Dr. Rifkin, 'which could bring the economy to a screeching halt, plunging it into a deep recession by the November election.' "

(*Christian Science Monitor,* March 26, 2004)

"The long-lasting, environmentally friendly fuel cell is one of the most hotly pursued technologies of the decade, one in which the world's largest companies-from auto giants to computer makers-are investing heavily. If successful, fuel cells could not only hasten a shift in our energy infrastructure but also power mobile computers all day on a single charge.

" 'There is an energy revolution happening that is similar to what we saw with the PC revolution,' says Jeremy Rifkin, president of the Foundation on Economic Trends and author of The Hydrogen Economy. 'Moore's Law has set in with fuel cells,' he says, referring to the falling cost and increased efficiency of fuel cell technology.

"The first wave of fuel cell adoption is likely to happen with miniature, methanol-based fuel cells for laptops, tablet computers, handhelds, and cell phones. Such fuel cells promise longer life and ultimately lower expenses, because methanol costs next to nothing. . . ."

(*PC Magazine,* July 1, 2003)

"Canada's dependency on Alberta's tar sands oil and its lack of an alternative energy policy will leave it as the pariah of the world, a leading U.S. environmental scientist said yesterday.

"Canada's commitment to the fossil fuel era—'the dirty fuel from the tar sands'—is upping the ante for global warming in a very serious way, said Jeremy Rifkin, best-selling author and president of the Foundation on Economic Trends in Washington, D.C.

"Global warming, said Mr. Rifkin, is the 'greatest threat to ever cross the human family. . . .

"Mr. Rifkin was in Ottawa to promote his novel, *The Hydrogen Economy*, subtitled 'The Creation of the Worldwide Energy Web and the Redistribution of Power on Earth.' Later this month he is a guest speaker at an APEC (Asia Pacific Economic Cooperation) conference in Baja, Mexico, that Prime Minister Jean Chretien will be attending.

"Mr. Rifkin had some advice for him: 'Canada has the possibility to be a cutting-edge leader. If I were the prime minister I'd develop a road map saying that this country is going to make a transition over the next 20-25 years to become a hydrogen superpower for the Americas.

" 'Europe has made a written commitment that all energy for electricity has to be renewable by 2010. Hydrogen is the centrepiece of that, and that's what Canada should be doing.'. . .

"Hydrogen offers the most abundant and cleanest alternative fuel source available. Mr. Rifkin said that Dutch Shell and BP are forecasting the end of the hydrocarbon era within the next 50 years. Exxon Mobil, though, is sticking with oil. 'Dutch Shell and BP are buying up every renewable technology in sight and they're patenting it. They're going to control the future.'

"Mr. Rifkin said Iraq's oil reserves could well be motivating U.S. President George W. Bush's desire to remove Iraqi leader Saddam Hussein. . . ."

(*Ottawa Citizen* [Canada], October 12, 2002)

"A reason for world poverty was given me by a passenger on the Saga Rose cruise: 'They're lazy and have too many children.' There was an article in the national *Guardian* by Jeremy Rifkin, president of the Foundation on Economic Trends in Washington. He points to some of the blame closer to home and at something over which we all have personal control: what is on our plates.

"Meat production is making the rich ill and the poor hungry.

"He said: 'Hundreds of millions of people are going hungry all over the world because much of the arable land is being used to grow feed grain for animals rather than for people.

" 'The irony of the present system is that millions of wealthy consumers in the first world are dying from diseases of affluence brought about by gorging on fatty meats, while the poor in the third world are dying of diseases brought on by the denial of access to land to grow food for their families.' "

(*UK Newsquest Regional Press* [London, England], May 30, 2002)

"Biotechnology critics from more than 50 nations have proposed a ban on patents on living things and on parts of living things like genes and cells. The proposal would prevent countries from charging for access to their genetic resources but also prevent companies from patenting products made from them. Jeremy Rifkin, president of the Foundation on Economic Trends and a longtime critic of the biotechnology industry who is the main organizer of the effort, predicted that patents would become 'the rallying point for the second stage of biotech activism,' with the first stage having been opposition to genetically modified food."

(*The New York Times,* February 2, 2002)

Free Congress Research and Education Foundation (FCF)

Established in 1977

DIRECTOR
Paul M. Weyrich, chair and chief executive officer. From 1989 to 1996, Weyrich served as president of the Kreible Institute of the Free Congress Foundation, responsible for training democracy movements in the states comprising the former Soviet Empire. He is a founder and past director of the American Legislative Exchange Council, the founding president of the Heritage Foundation, and the current national chair of Coalitions for America. A former reporter and radio news director, Weyrich is a regular guest on daily radio and television talk shows. A sought-after writer, Weyrich has published policy reports and journals on a variety of conservative issues and has contributed editorials to major newspapers. He has been described by *The Economist* as "one of the conservative movement's more vigorous thinkers." He serves as a deacon in his church.

BOARD OF DIRECTORS
Paul M. Weyrich, president
Ralph M. Hall, chair
William L. Armstrong, vice chair
William G. Batchelder
Morton Blackwell
Howard H. Callaway
Jeffrey H. Coors
Michael P. Farris
Ralph E. Hostetter
Daniel R. McMichael

SCOPE
Members: 3500 subscribers to *Notable News Now*
Branches/chapters: 1
Affiliates: Declined to comment

STAFF
15 total—10 full-time professional; 5 full-time support; plus 2 interns

TAX STATUS
501(c)(3)

FINANCES
Budget: 2001—$3.5 million

FUNDING SOURCES
Foundation grants, 68%; individual contributions, 22%; special events/projects, 5%; other, 5%

PAC
Free Congress Political Action Committee

CONTACT INFORMATION
717 Second Street, NE, Washington, DC 20002-4368
Phone: (202) 546-3000 • *Fax:* (202) 544-2819
General E-mail: aoliver@freecongress.org • *Web site:* www.freecongress.org

Communications Director: Jill S. Farrell
(202) 204 5304 • jfarrell@freecongress.org
Human Resources Director: Marion Edwyn Harrison, president and counsel
(202) 546 3000

PURPOSE: Teaches people how to be effective in the political process, advocates judicial reform, promotes cultural conservatism, and works against the government encroachment of individual liberties.

CURRENT CONCERNS: Constitutional Marriage Amendment • First Amendment conflicts within McCain Feingold • Privacy rights infringement potential of PATRIOT Act and CAPPS II • Right to Life from conception to natural death • Runaway deficit/debt • Rail Transit • Various social conservatism issues

METHOD OF OPERATION: Coalition forming • Conferences/seminars • Congressional testimony • Educational foundation • Internet databases • E-mail alerts • Internships • Legislative/regulatory monitoring (federal and state) • Mailing lists • Media outreach • Research • Web site

Effectiveness and Political Orientation

"President Bush is cutting quick deals with Congress on high-stakes domestic issues to showcase his shift in emphasis from wartime commander in chief to a chief executive devoted to the day-to-day concerns of ordinary Americans.

"Bush's readiness to compromise on Medicare, tax cuts and a child tax credit for the poor, coupled with a renewed emphasis on economic issues, are speeding legislation to White House bill signing ceremonies in a development that could bolster his image of domestic leadership heading into the 2004 re-election campaign. The approach contrasts sharply with his willingness to go it alone on some foreign policy issues.

" 'Listen, I'm interested in one thing—I'm interested in helping people find work,' Bush told business leaders during a visit last week to Fridley, Minn. 'I want people who want to work to be able to find a job.'

"The shift in emphasis appears designed to avoid the mistake his father made in 1992, when President George H.W. Bush saw a 91% approval rating after victory in the Persian Gulf War plummet in the face of Democrat Bill Clinton's relentless attacks on the troubled economy.

"His son 'does not want to be seen preoccupied with foreign matters rather than the plight of the average American,' says Paul M. Weyrich, president of the Free Congress Research and Education Foundation, a conservative think

PAC CONTRIBUTIONS 2002

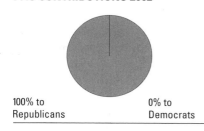

100% to
Republicans

0% to
Democrats

EMPLOYMENT
This organization offers the following types of positions: policy analysis staff and editorial staff (print and radio). Applicants should send resumes and other materials for employment to Marion Edwyn Harrison, president and counsel, 717 Second Street, NE, Washington, DC 20002, Phone: (202) 546-3000. Fax: (202) 544-5304.

INTERNSHIPS
Internships are unpaid, of varying duration, and require a minimum of 20 hours a week. Internship areas include communications (editing print and radio); database management; fundraising (database management); letter writing; and policy research (contacting other think tanks, working online, and working directly with Hill staff to gather information on various projects). Applicants must be dedicated conservatives—college juniors preferably—in the fields of communications; public policy or political science; or development or fundraising.

To apply, or for more information, contact Jill S. Farrell, director of communications, 717 Second Street, NE, Washington, DC 20002. Phone: (202) 204-5304. Fax: (202) 544-2819. E-mail: jfarrell@freecongress.org.

NEWSLETTERS
Notable News Now (daily E-mail)

PUBLICATIONS
None

CONFERENCES
Various—as needed

tank in Washington. 'His father's seeming disinterest in the American economy and people's suffering killed his re-election chances in 1992.'"

(*Milwaukee Journal Sentinel,* June 22, 2003)

"Gov. Tim Pawlenty invested two hours last week in an extended briefing on the proposed Northstar commuter-rail line. . . .

"As House majority leader, Pawlenty had steered the Republican majority away from funding the project. But he left the briefing saying that the numbers were impressive and that he would study them further.

"The session centered on the governor's request for proof that the 82-mile commuter line between downtown Minneapolis and the St. Cloud area would make economic sense and would be the best choice for moving people, compared with roads and buses. . . .

"Here's a look at the briefing, with some of the voices of support for the line. . . .

"The first plug for the project came from Keith Howe, vice president and general manager of United Defense, who told the governor that more than half of his 1,450 employees live between Fridley and Elk River along the Northstar Corridor. 'United Defense can use the benefits of such a rail line to attract and keep employees,' he said. . . .

"Next came Paul Weyrich by speakerphone from Washington, D.C. He is president of the conservative Free Congress Research and Education Foundation and author of a well-known 1999 position paper titled: 'Does Transit Work? A Conservative Reappraisal.'

"Weyrich vouched for the Northstar project, saying: 'It's as sound a piece of work as I have seen in many years of examining projects.'

"The connection to the Hiawatha light-rail line in downtown Minneapolis would be especially beneficial to get Northstar riders directly to their destinations, he said.

"Commuter-rail lines started in the past 10 years have all had ridership beyond projections, Weyrich reported."

(*Star Tribune* [Minneapolis], February 23, 2003)

"Civil-liberties groups are scrutinizing a far-reaching law aimed at uprooting foreign terrorists and their sympathizers.

"The administration has detained hundreds of foreigners and put some into deportation proceedings in the three months since President Bush signed the anti-terrorism measure. But most of the charges are for technical violations of immigration laws, such as overstaying visas.

"Still to be tested are such controversial provisions of the new law as the power to deport both suspected terrorists and foreigners who associate with groups on the government's terrorist list.

"Supporters of the law, known as the USA Patriot Act, argue that excluding and removing immigrants who promote or finance terrorist causes will help close off supply lines for terrorists.

"Critics of the new law counter that foreigners should have the right of free political expression, so long as they are not participating in violent or illegal acts.

" 'The new law gives the government a great deal of power to go after people on the basis of their political beliefs and associations,' American Civil Liberties Union legislative counsel Tim Edgar said. 'I think the courts are going to have to decide on that.'

"Edgars said his group is monitoring the Justice Department's use of the new anti-terrorism law. 'If the government goes too far, we would certainly challenge it,' he said.

"The liberal ACLU has been joined by others, including the conservative Free Congress Research and Education Foundation, in a line-by-line critique of the act. The analysis is scheduled to be released next month. . . ."

(*The Atlanta Journal-Constitution,* January 24, 2002)

"Traffic, everyone knows, is one of the bigger hassles of modern life. But just in time for Memorial Day, a blizzard of brand-new data confirms just how bad congestion has become. Since 1982, while the U.S. population has grown nearly 20 percent, the time Americans spend in traffic has jumped an amazing 236 percent. In major American cities, the length of the combined morning-evening rush hour has doubled, from under three hours in 1982 to almost six hours today. The result? The average driver now spends the equivalent of nearly a full workweek each year stuck in traffic. . . .

"So bad have the nation's traffic woes become that they are changing the politics of transportation—to the point that even some doctrinaire, free-market conservatives now support mass transit. Two years ago, Paul Weyrich and William Lind of the Free Congress Research and Education Foundation called for more public investment in trolley services and commuter trains. Such investment, Weyrich and Lind said, 'serves some important conservative goals, including economic development, which can be both spurred and shaped by rail-transit systems; helping the poor move off welfare and into jobs (which they have to get to somehow); and strengthening the bonds of community. . . .' Taking issue with traditional conservative objections to mass-transit subsidies, the two men noted that automobile drivers consume far more public resources than do subway riders. 'The dominance of automobiles and highways,' they wrote, 'is a product of massive government intervention in the marketplace, intervention stretching back to World War I.' "

(*U.S. News & World Report,* May 28, 2001)

"Despite his invitations to the White House and drop-bys at their meetings, the president's relationships with Senate Democrats have been prickly, because, they complain, he treats them like a minority party. Democrats believe they should have co-governing status in the Senate—beyond the existing arrangement that divides committee seats, funding, office space and so forth evenly between the two parties (though leaving all committee chairmanships in Republican hands).

"In addition to not consulting with them and fast-tracking his tax cut, Bush made another unilateral move that ignited the Democrats' partisan fires. That was his decision to deny the American Bar Association its quasi-official role in vetting judicial nominees, as it has done for the past 50 years. This move allowed Bush to hand a huge victory to conservatives—without expending much political capital with the public. 'We're thrilled,' said Thomas L. Jipping, vice president for legal policy at the conservative Free Congress Research & Education Foundation. To conservatives, the ABA—which takes stands on such controversial social issues as abortion and affirmative action—is a 'liberal interest group with a veto over judges,' as Jipping put it. Conservatives well remember how the ABA slighted two of their heroes—Robert Bork and Clarence Thomas—by raising questions about their qualifications to sit on the Supreme Court. . . ."

(*The Washington Post,* April 15, 2001)

Freedom Forum

Established in 1991

DIRECTOR

Charles L. Overby, chair and chief executive officer. In addition to heading the Freedom Forum, Overby also is chair and chief executive officer of two affiliate organizations: The Newseum, the interactive museum of news in Washington, DC, and the First Amendment Center, with offices at Vanderbilt University in Nashville, Tenn., and Arlington, VA. Overby is a former editor of *The Clarion-Ledger* in Jackson, Miss. He worked for 16 years as reporter, editor, and corporate executive for Gannett Co., the nation's largest newspaper company. He was vice president for news and communications for Gannett and served on the management committees of Gannett and *USA Today.* He was named president and chief executive officer of the Gannett Foundation in 1989. The foundation was renamed the Freedom Forum in 1991. He became chair as well as chief executive officer in 1997. Overby was also press assistant to Sen. John Stennis, D-Miss., chair of the Senate Armed Services Committee, and special assistant for administration to Gov. Lamar Alexander, R-Tenn. He serves on the board of the Committee to Protect Journalists, the Board of Regents of Baylor University, the board of the National Collegiate Athletic Association Foundation, and the board of FreedomChannel.com. He is a member of the foundation board of the University of Mississippi, his alma mater.

BOARD OF TRUSTEES

Charles L. Overby; chair and chief executive officer, Freedom Forum

Peter S. Prichard; president, Freedom Forum and Newseum

Alberto Ibargüen; publisher, *The Miami Herald*

Madelyn P. Jennings; former senior vice president/personnel, Gannett Co.

Malcolm R. Kirschenbaum; lawyer and civic leader

Bette Bao Lord; author

Jan Neuharth; president, Paper Chase Farms

H. Wilbert Norton Jr.; dean of the College of Journalism and Mass Communications, University of Nebraska

Mark Trahant; editorial page editor, *Seattle Post-Intelligencer*

Judy C. Woodruff; senior correspondent, CNN

SCOPE

Members: None

Branches/chapters: The Freedom Forum funds the Newseum, the First Amendment Center, and the Diversity Institute. The First Amendment Center and the Diversity

CONTACT INFORMATION

1101 Wilson Boulevard, Arlington, VA 22209

Phone: (703) 528-0800 • *Fax:* (703) 284-3770

General E-mail: news@freedomforum.org • *Web site:* www.freedomforum.org

Communications Director: Mike Fetters, director/marketing and communications, Newseum

(703) 284-2895 • mfetters@freedomforum.org

Human Resources Director: Constance Aguayo

(703) 284-3500 • caguayo@freedomforum.org

PURPOSE: The Freedom Forum is a nonpartisan foundation dedicated to free press, free speech and free spirit for all people. The foundation focuses on three priorities: the Newseum, First Amendment, and newsroom diversity.

CURRENT CONCERNS: First Amendment issues • Journalism • Newsroom diversity

METHOD OF OPERATION: Advertisements • Awards program • Conferences/ seminars • Films/video/audio tapes • Internships • Media outreach • Polling • Professional development services • Research • Scholarships • Training • Web site

SPECIFIC PROGRAMS/INITIATIVES: Al Neuharth Media Center at the University of South Dakota • American Indian Journalism Institute • Annual State of the First Amendment survey • ASNE/APME Fellows program • Chips Quinn Scholars program • Courage in Student Journalism Award • Diversity Institute • Diversity Leadership Awards • First Amendment Schools program • First Amendment Center Online (www.firstamendmentcenter.org) • Freedom Forum Journalists Memorial • Newseum in downtown Washington, DC • Newseum Web site (www.newseum.org) • "Speaking Freely" weekly television program • "Inside the First Amendment" weekly syndicated newspaper column • First Amendment Moot Court Competition • "Freedom Sings" multimedia experience

Effectiveness and Political Orientation

"Some of the nation's largest foundations pay their governing boards many thousands of dollars in fees and other compensation, according to a Georgetown University study whose authors argue that the foundations should spend the money on charitable causes.

"The study, which looked at the 1998 tax returns of 238 charitable foundations in the United States, calculated that the foundations paid their predominantly wealthy directors a total of almost $45 million that year. Fourteen of the largest foundations studied paid their trustees more than $100,000 each, the two-year study said. . . .

Institute are housed in the John Seigenthaler Center at Vanderbilt University in Nashville, TN.
Affiliates: The Freedom Forum Newseum, Inc.—501 (c)(3)
The Freedom Forum First Amendment Center, Inc.—501 (c)(3)

STAFF
154 total—plus 12 part-time

TAX STATUS
501(c)(3)

FINANCES
Budget: 2003—$36.5 million; 2002—$40.2 million

FUNDING SOURCES
The Freedom Forum's work is supported by income from an endowment of diversified assets.

PAC
None

EMPLOYMENT
Information on open positions can be obtained by consulting the organization's Web site at www.freedomforum.org. This organization offers various types of positions. Cover letters and resumes can be mailed to Constance Aguayo, vice president/human resources, Freedom Forum, 1101 Wilson Boulevard, Arlington, VA 22209. Phone: (703) 284-3500. Fax: (202) 284-3509. E-mail: news@ freedomforum.org.

INTERNSHIPS
Paid and unpaid internships are available. Application deadlines and hours vary. Information on internships can be obtained at www.freedomforum.org. Internship applications can be mailed to Constance Aguayo, vice president/human resources, Freedom Forum, 1101 Wilson Boulevard, Arlington, VA, 22209. Phone: (703) 284-3500. Fax: (202) 284-3509. E-mail: news@freedomforum.org.

PUBLICATIONS
Freedom Forum Annual Report

NEWSLETTERS
Newseum News (various times each year)

CONFERENCES
None

"Among Washington-based foundations, the study noted the 'generous compensation' provided Allen H. Neuharth, founding trustee of the Freedom Forum in Rosslyn. Neuharth received $504,254 in 1998, the report said. The Freedom Forum had assets of $1.05 billion at the time.

"Ten other board members that year each received fees ranging from $18,169 to $100,000, the report said. The Freedom Forum's offices were closed yesterday, and Neuharth did not return telephone calls. . . ."

(*The Washington Post*, August 30, 2003)

"The occasion: an exclusive blue-ribbon dinner in honor of the senators of the new 108th Congress. And their spouses. No lobbyists. No pressure groups. No other press.

"It was hosted by the Supreme Court Historical Society and sponsored by the Freedom Forum, a non-partisan foundation that promotes First Amendment freedoms. . . ."

(*USA Today*, January 10, 2003)

"The design of the new Newseum, to be unveiled formally at a news conference this morning, is a brash study of contrasts with the august architecture surrounding its prominent Pennsylvania Avenue address.

"It is almost all glass where its neighbors are almost all stone. It's transparent where they are opaque, light where they're heavy, breezily informal where they are attired for a decorous sit-down dinner.

"And, oh, it comes with a large LED media screen to project up-to-the-minute breaking news and other news-related images—the equivalent of a giant television set facing the 'nation's Main Street.'

"Designed by Polshek Partnership Architects of New York, the Washington incarnation of the interactive 'museum of news' will have three times the amount of exhibition space as the Newseum's first home in Rosslyn, which was closed in March after a successful five-year run.

"At least equally important as the added space, however, is the location: Front and center on the inaugural parade route, close by major federal buildings and the cultural institutions of the Mall, the plot of land at Sixth Street, NW, and Pennsylvania Avenue is of immense symbolic impact.

" 'This site on Pennsylvania Avenue really opens the door to educating millions of people over the next century about the importance of the First Amendment and a free press,' says Charles L. Overby, chairman and CEO of the Freedom Forum, the nonprofit parent to the Newseum.

"To emphasize the point, the design features a 60-foot-high plane of stone engraved with the 45 words of the First Amendment—a sober billboard, in effect, reminding all who pass of the crucial building blocks of the democracy. . . ."

(*The Washington Post*, October 29, 2002)

"US media watchdogs yesterday expressed dismay upon hearing that a little-known Pentagon office was considering influencing international opinion on the war on terrorism—which might include planting untrue stories in foreign media.

"If the proposals from the cloistered and well-funded Office of Strategic Influence were approved by Defence Secretary Donald Rumsfeld, it boded ill for both US journalists and perception of US operations abroad, experts said.

" 'Setting out to deliberately lie or "spread misinformation" can't have anything but a terrible impact . . . for any nation that claims to be an open and democratic society,' said Freedom Forum analyst Paul McMasters. 'The only thing more dangerous than reacting in panic is to set out on a deliberate policy of lying and deception, where it is next to impossible for ordinary people, Americans or otherwise, to know what is the truth and what is a lie.'

"Defence officials yesterday confirmed a *New York Times* report that Air Force general Simon Worden was quietly installed as the head of the OSI, formed after the September 11 terror attacks, to wage a campaign to shape international opinion. They said the office saw its mission as ranging from overt public diplomacy to the covert use of disinformation such as false stories to wage a secret propaganda war. . . ."

(*Courier Mail* [Queensland, Australia], February 21, 2002)

"Governors and state legislators are considering whether to clamp down on the public's access to government documents and meetings, driven by worries that terrorists could use the information to plan attacks or escape capture.

"Those proposals have dismayed open-government advocates and the media. They warn that a sweeping approach would block a key element of democratic society.

"Florida closed public records about security plans and drug stockpiles in December. New proposals are under debate or just being drafted there and in several other states.

"In Ohio, a bill proposed in the name of security would shield from the public architectural plans for private single-family dwellings.

"The bill, sponsored by Rep. James Trakas, Republican of Independence, was prompted by an attempt by *The Plain Dealer* to obtain plans under Ohio's public-records law for a Hunting Valley mansion being built by Cleveland Browns owner Al Lerner. . . .

"Some states would close the doors on talks about water supplies and sewer systems. Others would limit information about ongoing criminal investigations, evacuation plans and bioterrorism response assessments. . . .

"The Freedom Forum, a nonpartisan foundation dedicated to press and speech freedoms, is posting articles about the proposals on its Web site.

" 'We're just seeing the first wave. Everybody's going to see the potential for closing down meetings and for closing access to a variety of records,' said Paul McMasters, ombudsman at the Freedom Forum.

"But he said some of government's worries are legitimate. . . ."

(*The Plain Dealer* [Cleveland], February 6, 2002)

Friends of the Earth (FoE)

Established in 1990

DIRECTOR

Norman Dean, executive director. Immediately prior to joining FoE, Dean worked as the chief business officer for Co-op America. From late in 1998 until early 2000, Dean was executive director of the Center for Y2K and Society, a nonprofit organization he co-founded. The center was created to work with nonprofit organizations and foundations to respond to the societal impacts of the Y2K computer problem. Prior to joining the Y2K Center, he served as senior vice president for Conservation Programs of the National Wildlife Federation, the nation's largest membership-based environmental group. From 1990 until 1996 he served as chief operating officer and then president and CEO of Green Seal, the nation's first nonprofit environmental product testing and labeling organization. Dean has authored or co-authored several books and numerous articles on environmental and energy policy. He currently is chair of the board of directors of the Coalition on Environmentally Responsible Economies. Dean has also held positions at the Environmental Law Institute, practiced environmental law at the law offices of Bruce J. Terris, and taught environmental policy at Johns Hopkins University.

BOARD OF DIRECTORS

Avis Ogilvy Moore, chair
Dan Gabel, vice chair
Marion Hunt-Badiner, secretary
David Zwick, treasurer
Ed Begley Jr.
Jayni Chase
Harriett Crosby
Clarence Ditlow
Michael Herz
Ann Hoffman
Doug Legum
Patricia Matthews
Charles Moore
Edwardo Lao Rhodes
Arlie Shardt
Doria Steedman
Rick Taketa
Alicia Wittink

SCOPE

Members: 30,000 individuals
Branches/chapters: Friends of the Earth Northeast Office
Affiliate: Friends of the Earth International, a network of 66 international organizations

STAFF

24 total—21 full-time professional; 3 full-time support; plus 8 interns

TAX STATUS

501(c)(3)

CONTACT INFORMATION

1717 Massachusetts Avenue, NW, Suite 600, Washington, DC 20036-2002
Phone: (202) 783-7400 • *Fax:* (202) 783-0444
General E-mail: foe@foe.org • *Web site:* www.foe.org

Communications Director: Keira Costic, temporary publications and Web manager
(202) 222-0731 • kcostic@foe.org
Human Resources Director: Sherri Owens
(202) 222-0714 • sowens@foe.org

PURPOSE: Friends of the Earth defends the environment and champions a healthy and just world.

CURRENT CONCERNS: Bush administration • Clean air act • Clean water act • Climate change • Congress • Corporate accountability • Cosmetics • DC environmental network • Energy • Environmental justice • Environmental tax reform • Export-Import Bank • Factory farms • Genetically engineered food • Government subsidies • Interior Department • International Monetary Fund • International right to know • Mad cow disease • Mountaintop coal removal • Overseas Private Investment Corporation • Public lands • Road projects • Shareholder resolutions • SUVs • Transportation • Wall Street • World Bank • World Trade Organization *

METHOD OF OPERATION: Boycotts • Coalition forming • Congressional testimony • Demonstrations • Grassroots organizing • International activities • Internet (E-mail alerts and Web site) • Internships • Legislative/regulatory monitoring (federal) • Litigation • Lobbying (federal) • Local/municipal affairs • Media outreach • Participation in regulatory proceedings (federal) • Performance ratings/Report cards (companies, products, etc.) • Product merchandising • Shareholder resolutions

Effectiveness and Political Orientation

"Biotech company Bayer CropScience has ended its attempt to commercialise the GM forage maize variety Chardon LL in the UK.

"It blamed the UK government's constraints on conditional approval of the maize variety which it said created an 'open-ended' period of delay before commercial cultivation could start.

" 'This variety is already five years old and, with the additional constraints from the government, we estimate that it would be at least two more years before commercial growing could take place,' said Bayer spokesman Julian Little. 'The product would then be eight years old, whereas the average seed variety nowadays lasts for about five years. Under these circumstances, we came to the conclusion that the crop would not be economically viable.'. . .

"Friends of the Earth's GM campaigner Pete Riley said: 'This GM maize had serious question marks about its safety and performance and should never have been given UK approval.

FINANCES
Budget: 2003—$4 million; 2002—$4 million

FUNDING SOURCES
Foundation grants, 45%; membership dues, 52%; other, 3%

PAC
Friends of the Earth Action

PAC CONTRIBUTIONS 2002

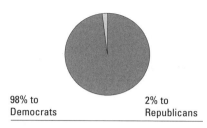

98% to Democrats   2% to Republicans

EMPLOYMENT
Potential applicants can learn about job openings with this organization at www.foe.org/about/jobs/index.html. This organization offers positions in the following areas: administration, accounting, fundraising, issue work. Resumes and other materials for employment can be sent to David Hirsch, program director, 1717 Massachusetts Avenue, NW, Suite 600, Washington, DC 20036-2002. Phone: (202) 222-0741. Fax: (202) 783-0444. E-mail: dhirsch@foe.org.

INTERNSHIPS
Information about internship opportunities is available at www.foe.org/about/jobs/fellows.html. Positions are unpaid, the duration is flexible, and application deadlines are flexible. 20 hours per week are required. Internship are available in the areas of environmental campaigners, administration, and communications. To be eligible, applicants must be in college, or be a recent college graduate. Application materials can be sent to Yasmeen Hossain, program associate, 1717 Massachusetts Avenue, NW, Suite 600, Washington, DC 20036-2002. Phone: (202) 222-0745. Fax: (202) 783-0444. E-mail: yhossain@foe.org.

NEWSLETTERS
Friends of the Earth (quarterly)

PUBLICATIONS
Climate Footprint
ExxonMobil
Green Scissors
Greening the Budget: 11 Ideas for Protecting the Environment and Easing Maryland's Fiscal Crisis
Taxations and Timber: An Inventory of State Tax Provisions in Maine, New Hampshire and Vermont

CONFERENCES
None

" 'But this was ignored by Bayer and the government in their blind rush to push GM on the public. This episode will be acutely embarrassing to ministers and of deep concern to Bayer's shareholders,' Mr Riley said, arguing that the government should now concentrate on protecting food, farming and the environment in the UK from GM contamination and put real effort into sustainable agriculture. . . ."

(*Farmers Weekly,* April 2, 2004)

"The Government is to be challenged today to back a new law prohibiting the planting of GM crops until the House of Commons has approved rules on economic and environmental liability and co-existence with other crops. New rules would be required to prevent contamination and to determine who pays if GM crops contaminate other areas.

"The second reading of the Genetically Modified Organisms Bill, introduced by Tory MP Gregory Barker, takes place today in the Commons. It is backed by a cross-party group of MPs, including former Conservative party leader William Hague and ex-Environment Minister Michael Meacher. It also has the backing of Friends of the Earth and the Five Year Freeze campaign. . . ."

(*Farmers Guardian,* March 26, 2004)

"Clients might not specify environmentally friendly materials, but it's the duty of interior designers to enlighten them and suggest innovative new processes and materials that also have sustainable characteristics, argues Pamela Buxton

"Specifying sustainable contract interiors is still a niche activity, despite 20 years of mainstream debate on environmental issues. 'My clients aren't really into that' or 'Can't help you there' are typical responses from designers who, while maybe willing in theory, don't feel empowered to challenge client attitudes and promote sustainable materials and approaches. . . .

"Designers have to put in the time and effort to find out about sustainable options, says interior designer and Changing Rooms presenter Oliver Heath, who writes for the *Friends of the Earth* magazine and believes that recycled materials are one of the most exciting areas in design today.

" 'It's up to everyone to do their bit—a conscious effort by the client saying, 'I care about the environment' and if the client isn't asking the questions, it's up to the designer to inform them,' he notes. . . ."

(*Design Week,* March 25, 2004)

"African mining companies, governments of developing countries and international banks have expressed concern over a proposal that the World Bank restrict oil and coal projects to protect the environment.

" 'We don't like it at all,' said South Africa's minister of minerals and energy, Phumzile Mlambo-Ngcuka, after meeting with African mineral and energy ministers last month in Cape Town. 'We think it takes an ideological approach rather than a practical one.'

"African governments that are heavily dependent on oil and mineral BLOCKction fear that the new environmental proposals, like more stringent waste disposal, as well as a possible ban on financing for new oil and coal projects, could harm future investment.

"The proposal came in the form of a report drafted by Emil Salim, a former environmental minister from Indonesia who was appointed to prepare it in 2001 by James D. Wolfensohn, the World Bank's president. The study was commissioned in response to criticism that the oil and coal projects contributed little to the bank's stated goal of alleviating poverty. . . .

" 'These oil and coals projects are not proven to alleviate poverty," said Jon Sohn, a senior policy analyst for Friends of the Earth in Washington, which also favors adoption of the review's findings.

" 'There's a misconception or misinformation campaign inside the bank that this is really just about some environmental groups that are trying to push an agenda,' Mr. Sohn said. 'With people like Desmond Tutu speaking out, they're finding this is a global issue.'

"In his report, Dr. Salim found that mining and oil projects could contribute to development but only if certain environmental and social conditions were met. . . ."

(*The New York Times,* March 24, 2004)

"The Household Waste Recycling Act was passed at the end of 2003 after extensive lobbying by Friends of the Earth (FoE) and the Act's sponsor, Labour MP for Lewisham and Deptford Joan Ruddock. The law now requires each local authority to make separate collections of at least two types of recyclable waste by 2010.

"FoE waste campaigner Georgina Bloomfield says: 'The aim of the Act is to get everyone involved in recycling and working towards universal recycling collections, so it is not limited to those with cars or those that have services on the street.'

"However, one industry source brands the initiative 'crap,' as many councils are already offering such a service. Bloomfield agrees that it does not equate to a 'comprehensive doorstep collection service, and is simply a minimum standard'.

"But it is a step in the right direction. 'Paper will be the first material that is collected, as it is a large part of the waste stream. The infrastructure is in place to reprocess it, and it is easy to collect,' states Bloomfield. . . ."

(*Precision Marketing,* March 5, 2004)

The Fund for Animals

Established in 1967

DIRECTOR

Michael Markarian, president. Markarian has lectured on animal protection issues across the United States and Brazil, has written feature articles on animal issues for numerous magazines, and has appeared on numerous television and radio shows nationwide to discuss sport hunting, commercial trapping, and other issues that affect wildlife. He also contributes op-ed columns to many major U.S. newspapers. He has an M.A. in English language and literature from the University of Maryland, and is a graduate of the University of Missouri's National Animal Cruelty Investigations School.

BOARD OF DIRECTORS

Marian Probst, chair
Michael Markarian, president
Barbara Brack; private philanthropist
Del Donati; private philanthropist
Neil B. Fang; Attorney at Law
Mary Max; private philanthropist
Judith Ney; private philanthropist
Edgar O. Smith; entrepreneur
Kathryn Walker; actress

SCOPE

Members: 200,000 individuals
Branches/chapters: None
Affiliates: None

STAFF

50 total—plus interns

TAX STATUS

501(c)(3)

FINANCES

Budget: 2004—$6.4 million; 2003—$7 million; 2002—$6.2 million

FUNDING SOURCES

Bequests, 47%; individuals, 47%; foundation grants, 6%

PAC

None

EMPLOYMENT

Open positions are posted at www.fund.org/about/n4_employment.asp. Cover letters and resumes can be mailed to Tashee Meadows, assistant to the president and national director, 8121 Georgia Avenue, Suite 301, Silver Spring, MD 20910. Fax: (301) 585-2595. E-mail: tmeadows@fund.org.

CONTACT INFORMATION

200 West 57th Street, New York, NY 10019
Phone: (888) 405-3863
National Campaign Office:
8121 Georgia Avenue, Suite 301, Silver Spring, MD 20910
Phone: (301) 585-2591 • *Fax:* (301) 585-2595.
General E-mail: fundinfo@fund.org • *Web site:* www.fund.org

Communications Director: Tracey McIntire
(301) 585-2591, ext. 314 • tmcintire@fund.org
Human Resources Director: None

PURPOSE: To speak for those who can't.

CURRENT CONCERNS: Animal protection

METHOD OF OPERATION: Advertisements • Awards program • Boycotts • Coalition forming • Congressional testimony • Congressional voting analysis • Demonstrations • Films/video/audiotapes • Grassroots organizing • Information clearinghouse • Initiative/referendum campaigns • International activities • Internet (databases, electronic bulletin boards, e-mail alerts, Web site) • Internships • Legislative/regulatory monitoring (federal and state) • Litigation • Lobbying (federal, state, and grassroots) • Local/municipal affairs • Media outreach • Participation in regulatory proceedings (federal and state) • Polling • Product merchandising • Research • Shareholder resolutions • Training • Voting records

Effectiveness and Political Orientation

"The anti-hunting movement is in turmoil this winter. For a change, animal rights groups are in power struggles instead of challenging a sportsman's right to fish or hunt. . . .

"The Fund for Animals wants a piece of the Audubon Society's hide. . . .

"The Fund for Animals, which reported $8.5 million in revenue last year, is trying to steal a little limelight by going after the venerable Audubon Society. They obviously didn't know that John J. Audubon, the group's founder, hunted many animals in order to illustrate them.

"The Audubon Society recently opened a 285-acre piece of property it owns in Greenwich, Conn., to bowhunters. Too many deer is a common problem all over America and the Audubon Society should be praised for allowing hunters to help solve its problem."

(*The Plain Dealer* [Cleveland], January 29, 2004)

"The Fund for Animals has issued a report with a decidedly gleeful message: The number of hunters is down—again—and so is the number of animals being killed.

INTERNSHIPS

Paid internships with flexible hours are available. Anyone 18 years or older may apply. Applications may be submitted year-round and internships are typically for 2–3 months. Information on internships is posted at www.fund.org/about/n4_employment.asp.

Internship inquiries and applications can be mailed to Jennifer Allen, program coordinator, 8121 Georgia Avenue, Suite 301, Silver Spring, MD 20910. Fax: (301) 585-2595. E-mail: jallen@fund.org.

NEWSLETTERS

Animal Crusaders (quarterly for elementary school teachers)
Animal Free Press (quarterly)
Fund for Animals Magazine (semi-annual)

PUBLICATIONS

El Caballo
Killing Coyote
Gunblast: Culture Clash
What's Wrong with Hunting
Solving Wildlife Problems
Also produces television public service announcements

CONFERENCES

None

"Using U.S. Fish and Wildlife figures along with state wildlife statistics, the organization said the number of hunters has declined from 14 million to 13 million since 1991.

"Doves and squirrels were killed in the largest numbers, accounting for more than 45 million of the total. On another tally, the report underscored that wildlife watchers outspend hunters by a considerable margin—almost 2 to 1—on their outings."

(*The Los Angeles Times,* January 27, 2004)

"With Yellowstone National Park's bison population at its highest in years, some environmentalists fear that many of the animals will wander into Montana this winter and be killed in the name of controlling disease.

"Fueling their concerns is a recent spell of harsh weather—hard winters often result in more bison leaving the park in search of food—and fears that officials will take a hard line against bison after a Wyoming cattle herd was found infected with brucellosis, a disease also present in the Yellowstone bison herd.

" 'We're in for yet another winter of tragic and unnecessary killing by state and federal agencies mismanaging bison over a perceived risk of the transmission of brucellosis to cattle,' said D. J. Schubert, a wildlife biologist for the Fund for Animals.

"Wandering bison concern ranchers and state livestock officials, who worry that the animals will infect cattle herds with brucellosis, a disease that causes cows to abort their calves and can cause fever in people. The bison defenders say there has never been a documented case of bison transmitting brucellosis to cattle in the wild. . . .

"Under a state-federal plan, bison that cannot be lured back into the park are captured and tested for brucellosis. Those testing positive will be sent to slaughter. If the park's population exceeds 3,000 by late winter and early spring each year, bison that stray into Montana can be killed without being tested first, said Rick Wallen, a wildlife biologist.

"More than 4,200 bison are now in the park, the most in nearly a decade, park officials say. One has been killed this winter, according to the Montana Department of Livestock."

(*The New York Times,* January 11, 2004)

"The U.S. Fish and Wildlife Service said yesterday that it is prepared to halt the killing of thousands of mute swans along the East Coast if an animal rights group drops its lawsuit to protect the birds in Maryland.

"The agency, which granted 50 state and local governments the go-ahead to reduce their swan populations, made the announcement one day after a federal judge issued a temporary injunction halting Maryland's plan to kill the swans.

"Environmentalists and wildlife biologists have argued that mute swans, a nonnative species, threaten ecosystems, including the Chesapeake Bay, because they scare away other birds and consume large amounts of underwater grasses, pushing out native species.

"The Fund for Animals filed suit in May to stop Maryland from killing 525 birds this year. In his ruling, U.S. District Court Judge Emmet G. Sullivan questioned whether the Fish and Wildlife Service adequately studied the swan's impact on the environment before it began issuing permits to harvest them two years ago.

"Nicholas Throckmorton, a spokesman for the Fish and Wildlife Service, said Sullivan's ruling left the agency little choice but to suspend efforts to control the swan population. . . .

"Attorneys for Fish and Wildlife and the Fund for Animals are scheduled to meet Oct. 6 to discuss the possible settlement, which would also halt planned swan killings in New York, Connecticut and other states. Federal authorities could begin revoking the permits within two weeks.

" 'This is a monumental victory for tens of thousands of majestic swans,' said Michael Markarian, president of the Fund for Animals. 'These animals will now be given a stay of execution.' "

(*The Washington Post,* September 18, 2003)

Gay and Lesbian Alliance Against Defamation (GLAAD)

Established in 1985

DIRECTOR

Joan M. Garry, executive director. Garry assumed leadership of GLAAD in 1997 after serving as vice president of Showtime Networks. Previously, Garry helped launch MTV, and as director of business development for MTV Networks, she developed new channels, helped to create the worldwide annual MTV Video Music Awards and the network's innovative merchandising program.

BOARD OF DIRECTORS

Phil Kleweno, co-chair
Karen Magee, co-chair
William Weinberger, treasurer
John McGill, secretary
Scott Barretto
Angela Betasso
Betsy Billard
Jack Calhoun
Bob Chase
Timothy Corrigan
Rafael Fantauzzi
Judy Gluckstern
John Hadity
Janet M. Haire
Nancy Kokolj
Mihail S. Lari
Maria Lescano
Joe Lupariello
Liz Page
Gabriel Reyes
Gregory Reynolds
Matt Riklin
Carol Rosenfeld
Steve Seidmon
Jeff Soukup
Paula Tighe
Tanya Wexler

SCOPE

Members: Information unavailable
Branches/chapters: None
Affiliates: None

STAFF

41 total—plus volunteers

TAX STATUS

501(c)(3)

FINANCES

Revenue: 2002—$5 million; 2001—$4 million

FUNDING SOURCES

Contributions, 89%; special events, 10.6%; investments, 0.4%

PAC

None

CONTACT INFORMATION

248 West 35th Street, 8th Floor, New York, NY 10001
Phone: (212) 629-3322 • *Fax:* (212) 629-3225
General E-mail: www.glaad.org/contact.php • *Web site:* www.glaad.org

Communications Director: John Sonego
sonego@glaad.org
Human Resources Director: Rossella Guardascione
guardascione@glaad.org

PURPOSE: GLAAD is "dedicated to promoting and ensuring fair, accurate and inclusive representation of people and events in the media as a means of eliminating homophobia and discrimination based on gender identity and sexual orientation."

CURRENT CONCERNS: Anti-lesbian, gay, bisexual, transgender (LGBT) ad campaigns, legislation, policy, and slurs in the media • Arbitrary infant gender assignment • Boy Scouts of America discrimination • Censorship • Digital media issues • Domestic partnership • Education/safe schools • ENDA/federal equal rights legislation • Hate violence • Hate crime prevention • Health • Immigration • LGBT in the military • LGBT Pride coverage • Local equal rights legislation • Parenting/adoption/foster • Prisoner abuse • Public-sex coverage • Reparative therapy • Same-gender marriage • Scientific research on sexual orientation • Sodomy laws • Straight spouses • Workplace issues • Youth abandonment • Youth suicide

METHOD OF OPERATION: Information unavailable

Effectiveness and Political Orientation

"The first true blizzard of the first public editor's first season began Sunday, Dec. 21. The lead headline on the front page of *The Times* declared, 'Strong Support Is Found for Ban on Gay Marriage.' Reading the article over my morning coffee, I wondered why a single poll—*The Times*'s own, co-sponsored by CBS—was itself considered news (at least one other released around the same time showed substantially different results). But for the next two weeks, rising drifts of e-mail provoked by the piece made me realize my attention belonged elsewhere.

"Most correspondents felt that the 55 percent of those polled favoring a constitutional amendment against same-sex marriage did not constitute 'strong support.' Many others, called to arms by the Gay and Lesbian Alliance Against Defamation, objected to the phrasing of the poll questions, and to the unequal number of pro- and anti-amendment respondents quoted in the article (three to one). Additionally, read the complaint posted on Glaad's Web site, 'the story sensationalized and misrepresented poll results, failing to ask

EMPLOYMENT
Information on open positions can be obtained by consulting the organization's Web site at www.glaad.org/about/work_opps.php. For a Web site posting, GLAAD prefers those wishing to apply to send their resumes and cover letters as an attached Microsoft Word or Simple Text document to jobs@glaad.org. Please do not send zip files. Resumes can be sent to GLAAD Human Resources, 248 West 35th Street, 8th Floor, New York, NY 10001. Fax: (212) 629-3225.

INTERNSHIPS
Information unavailable

NEWSLETTERS
Offers numerous GLAAD E-Newsletters:
Central Call to Action
GLAAD Alert
GLAAD Digital Events
GLAAD Stories to Watch
GLAAD's E-Activism Network
GLAADJobs
Media Focus: People of Color
Northeastern Call to Action
Northwestern Call to Action
Southeastern Call to Action
Southwestern Call to Action

PUBLICATIONS
GLAAD Media Reference Guide
How Youth Media Can Help Combat Homophobia Among American Teenagers
It's a Queer World After All: Studying the Sims and Sexuality
Complete title list available on Web site, at www.glaad.org/publications.

CONFERENCES
National Gay & Lesbian Athletics Conference
GLAAD Media Awards

basic poll questions that would have allowed respondents to consider the full range of issues at play.' "

(*The New York Times,* January 4, 2004)

"Out of the 674 leading or supporting actors on prime-time broadcast sitcoms and dramas, 11 are gay characters, according to statistics from the Gay and Lesbian Alliance Against Defamation (GLAAD).

"That number is slightly down from two years ago, but the bigger picture proves that there has been a slow and steady rise in the number of gay characters on both network and cable TV.

"Scott Seomin, GLAAD's Entertainment Media Director, said the portrayals are 'overwhelmingly good because they're popular.'

"That popularity is one reason gay characters draw attention even though there are fewer now than in recent years.

"Most TV viewers have heard of Bravo's 'Queer Eye for the Straight Guy;' NBC's 'Will & Grace,' featuring two gay characters, is one of the highest rated shows of recent seasons. . . .

"GLAAD's Communication Director, John Sonego said: 'The challenge is that it's not a complete picture. It would be like saying if I'm watching the Miss America pageant, that tells me all I need to know about American women. I should never make an assumption that that tells me everything that would be important for me to understand women in this country. We're as diverse as everyone else.'

"Seomin said there are more white, male gay characters on TV than any other gay demographic because there are more white, male writers.

" 'Lesbians are hitting the glass ceiling, just like their straight counterparts,' he said. 'When a lesbian is included, particularly in sitcom format, it's written by a straight white male. We don't have more lesbian characters because we don't have more lesbian writers and creators knowing how to make them real.'. . ."

(*The Washington Post,* November 30, 2003)

"Was there ever a show more ripe for parody than Bravo's Queer Eye for the Straight Guy? Apparently not. Bravo is creating Straight Eye for the Queer Guy, a campy hourlong special in 2004. 'Queer guys will finally learn that a screwdriver is not just a drink,' said Scott Seomin of the Gay & Lesbian Alliance Against Defamation. 'And they'll gain an appreciation for pork rinds and beer nuts.' "

(*Columbus Dispatch* [Ohio], November 14, 2003)

"In what the Gay & Lesbian Alliance Against Defamation (GLAAD) is calling a 'stand against the divisive, intolerant diatribes of Michael Savage,' all six national sponsors of Savage's debut show last Saturday on MSNBC have decided not to advertise on the TV program again. GLAAD had lobbied the companies—Procter & Gamble, Dell Computer, Casual Male, Idea Village, Cole Media Group, and Sharper Image—to withdraw support from Savage, a conservative talkmaster known for attacks on groups ranging from gays and lesbians to immigrants. . . ."

(*The Boston Globe,* March 13, 2003)

"*The Boston Globe* announced yesterday that it will begin publishing announcements of same-sex commitment ceremonies and civil unions, adding another name to a growing list of newspapers opening their wedding pages to gays. . . .

"The new policies bring the number of newspapers that publish and plan to publish same-sex union announcements to 139, according to the Gay & Lesbian Alliance Against Defamation. . . ."

(*The San Diego Union-Tribune,* September 30, 2002)

Greenpeace USA

Established in 1971

DIRECTOR

John Passacantando, executive director. Passacantando came to Greenpeace after co-founding Ozone Action, a grassroots organization dedicated to stopping global warming. Prior to founding Ozone Action. He was executive director of the Florence and John Schumann Foundation, helping focus its grant making programs on the grassroots renewal of democracy. Passacantando worked to support the foundation's efforts on campaign finance reform and environmental issues.

BOARD OF DIRECTORS

Greenpeace Fund, Inc.
David Chatfield, chair
Ellen McPeake, treasurer; Washington, DC
Leslie Allen, secretary; Hyattsville, MD
Sebia Hawkins; Santa Fe, NM
John Passacantando, executive director
Karen Topakian; San Francisco, CA
Greenpeace, Inc.
John Willis, chair; Toronto, Canada
Kenny Bruno; Brookly, NY
Peggy Burks; San Francisco, CA
Michael Clark; Bozeman, MT
Carmen Gonzalez; Seattle, WA
Terri Swearingen; Chester, WV

SCOPE

Members: 250,000 individuals in the United States and 2.5 million members worldwide
Branches/chapters: has an office in San Francisco, CA
Affiliates: Greenpeace International, formed in 1971, has branches in 30 countries in Asia, Australia, Europe, the Middle East, New Zealand, North America, South America, and the former Soviet Union with a total membership of approximately 4 million individuals

STAFF

90 total

TAX STATUS

Greenpeace Fund: 501(c)(3)
Greenpeace, Inc.: 501(c)(4)

FINANCES

Revenue: 2002—$21.79 million

FUNDING SOURCES

Individual donations, sale of merchandise, and foundation grants

PAC

None

CONTACT INFORMATION

702 H Street, NW, Suite 300, Washington, DC 20001
Phone: (202) 462-1177 or (800) 326-0959 • *Fax:* (202) 462-4507
General E-mail: info@wdc.greenpeace.org • *Web site:* www.greenpeaceusa.org

Communications Director: Melanie Janin
(202) 462-1177 • Melanie.Janin@wdc.greenpeace.org
Human Resources Director: Toni Wright, contact person
resumes@wdc.greenpeace.org

PURPOSE: "Independent campaigning organization that uses non-violent, creative confrontation to expose global environmental problems, and to force solutions that are essential to a green and peaceful future."

CURRENT CONCERNS: Eliminate persistent organic pollutants (POPs) • Eliminate the threat of genetic engineering • End the nuclear age • Protect the oceans • Save ancient forests • Stop global warming

METHOD OF OPERATION: Coalition forming • Congressional testimony • Direct action (nonviolent) • Grassroots organizing • International treaties and conventions • Legislative/regulatory monitoring (federal) • Litigation • Lobbying (federal) • Media outreach • Photo/video • Research • Training and technical assistance • Web site

Effectiveness and Political Orientation

"The security of parliament was the subject of urgent talks between top level political and security figures that took place just days before two protesters scaled Big Ben.

"Peter Hain, leader of the House of Commons, admitted yesterday that the subsequent security breach by the Greenpeace anti-war campaigners was a huge embarrassment.

"Mr Hain, who attended last week's meeting, demanded an urgent report into the breach on Saturday and said it raised serious questions about security at parliament.

" 'Twenty or 30 years ago an audacious protest like that by Greenpeace would have been seen for exactly that. But what if these had been suicide bombers? . . .

"The Greenpeace protesters said in a statement: 'People say the police are embarrassed. But they shouldn't be.

" 'Personally I just hope people recognised we just wanted to make a statement about the war and not security. Blair should be embarrassed for misleading us, not the police.'

"Ben Stewart, Greenpeace spokesman, said police had been told immediately that the pressure group was behind yesterday's protest.

EMPLOYMENT
Job postings are available at www.
greenpeaceusa.org at the "About Us" section
of the site. From Web site: "While passion for
protecting the environment is a key requirement for getting a job with Greenpeace, we
look for diverse people with solid work
experience for our administration, finance,
communications, development and campaigns
departments." Job postings contain
instructions for applying, including contact
information.

INTERNSHIPS
Information unavailable

NEWSLETTERS
Greenpeace Magazine (quarterly)

PUBLICATIONS
The following is a sample of recent
publications:
Endangered Forests
Endangered Freedoms
*Monsanto & Genetic Engineering: Risks for
Investors*
*117 Chemical Facilities Putting One Million or
More People At Risk*
Also produces reports and fact sheets;
complete publication list available on
Web site.

CONFERENCES
None

"He said: 'If our actions have exposed a security flaw, and we are not really convinced that they have, then that has got to be a good thing for everyone concerned.'

"Last night, the two protesters were bailed by police after being arrested on suspicion of causing criminal damage. The men were ordered to return to a central London police station next month. . . ."

(*The Herald,* [Glasgow, Scotland], March 22, 2004)

"One of the world's leading charities is to abandon 'chugging,' the controversial method of accosting people in the street and asking for money, because the public find it so irritating.

"The chairman of Greenpeace, Martyn Day, said that what the industry calls 'face to face' campaigning was having a negative effect on the group's profile and fundraising efforts. Chugging—short for 'charity mugging'—gained a bad name after initial successes led a flood of charities to use young people to ask passerbys to donate by direct debit. . . .

"The move by Greenpeace is particularly significant as the organisation is believed to have been the first to introduce chugging to Britain in 1996. The idea originated from Austria, where small charities had remarkable returns by signing up people for direct debits on the street rather than simply rattling collecting tins.

"Greenpeace said it would still use some face-to-face methods but in strictly controlled environments. Chuggers would still be used in small towns where the technique was less well known.

"The charity also called for the Government to bring in regulations to control the trade and stop illegal operators raising money. . . .

"Charities are beginning to distance themselves from chugging after new research released last month revealed that more discreet methods, such as personalised mailshots and door-to-door collection, were much more successful. . . ."

(*The Observer* [London, England], March 7, 2004)

"The Chinese government announced Monday that it had approved the import of genetically modified crops, a victory for the American biotech industry that will make it easier for the United States to export more food to China.

"But the decision is also a setback for environmentalist groups like Greenpeace, which describe such crops as 'frankenfoods,' and had sought to dissuade China to restrict their use in the world's largest market for soybeans and one of the largest for other crops. . . ."

(*The New York Times,* February 24, 2004)

"Greenpeace and the Sierra Youth Coalition have launched a campaign for more "socially responsible" investment practices at the Ontario Teachers' Pension Plan.

"The fund, to which all of Ontario's 154,000 public school teachers contribute, is Canada's largest investor in coal and has holdings in other fossil fuel companies and tobacco, the environmental groups say.

"'At the moment, the teachers as contributors into the pension have no say into where the funds are spent and that's a problem,' said Rob Milling, executive director of Greenpeace Canada. . . ."

(*The Toronto Star* [Canada], February 12, 2004)

"A top nuclear-safety official has said he wasn't aware that any American nuclear power plant diagrams were found in Afghanistan, despite a terrorist threat cited by President Bush in his State of the Union address two years ago.

"Edward McGaffigan Jr., a member of the US Nuclear Regulatory Commission, responding to an environmental group's query, said this month that he testified in 2002 after the speech in at least one closed congressional hearing that he was not aware of any evidence that ' "diagrams of American nuclear power plants" had been found in Afghanistan.'

"McGaffigan's statement has led some groups to assert that Bush either misled the country or mishandled the intelligence about the threat, because the NRC would be expected to play a pivotal role in safeguarding America's nuclear facilities.

"If plans of US nuclear plants had been discovered, then the NRC should have been alerted to help prepare a security response, said James P. Riccio, a Greenpeace policy analyst who exchanged correspondence with McGaffigan.

" 'The Bush administration has once again failed to place the intelligence in the appropriate hands. The NRC needs to be able to take action against appropriate threats,' Riccio said in a telephone interview yesterday. . . ."

(*The Boston Globe,* February 10, 2004)

Henry L. Stimson Center

Established in 1989

DIRECTOR

Ellen Laipson, president and chief executive officer. Laipson joined the center after nearly 25 years of government service. Previously, she was vice chair of the National Intelligence Council (NIC) (1997–2002); special assistant to the U.S. Permanent Representative to the UN (1995–1997); director for Near East and South Asian Affairs for the National Security Council (1993–1995); national intelligence officer for Near and South Asia (1990–1993); a member of the State Department's policy planning staff (1986–1987); and a specialist in Middle East Affairs for the Congressional Research Service. Laipson is a member of the Council on Foreign Relations, the International Institute of Strategic Studies, the Middle East Institute, and the Middle East Studies Association. In 2003, she joined the boards of the Asia Foundation and the Education and Employment Foundation. Laipson has an M.A. from the School of Advanced International Studies, Johns Hopkins University and an A.B. from Cornell University.

BOARD OF DIRECTORS

Barry M. Blechman; chair; DFI International
Charles W. Bailey II; journalist
Linda W. Banton; Russell Reynolds Associates
Barbara Davis Blum; BDB Investment Partnership
Richard M. Clarke; nash_elmo industries
Alton Frye; Council on Foreign Relations
William C. Harrop; retired diplomat
Arnold Kanter; Forum for International Policy
Farooq Kathwari; Ethan Allen, Inc.
Michael Krepon; founding president, Henry L. Stimson Center
Roger Leeds; Johns Hopkins University School of Advanced International Studies
Frank E. Loy; former under secretary of state for global affairs
Philip A. Odeen; retired TRW executive
Thomas R. Pickering; Boeing Co.
Enid C.B. Schoettle; consultant in international affairs
Jeffrey H. Smith; Arnold & Porter
Larry D. Welch; general, (retired) Institute for Defense Analyses
Carroll R. Wetzel Jr.; retired investment banker

SCOPE

Members: None
Branches/chapters: None
Affiliates: None

STAFF

27 total—20 professional; 7 support; plus 5 interns

CONTACT INFORMATION

11 Dupont Circle, NW, Suite 900, Washington, DC 20036
Phone: (202) 223-5956 • *Fax:* (202) 238-9604
General E-mail: info@stimson.org • *Web site:* www.stimson.org

Communications Director: Nicole Sallee, associate director of development
nsallee@stimson.org
Human Resources Director: Elizabeth Wallish, controller; accounting, human resources
ewallish@stimson.org

PURPOSE: "The Henry L. Stimson Center is a community of analysts devoted to offering practical, creative, non-partisan solutions to many of the most enduring and challenging problems of national and international security. Through our work, we seek to foster a world in which collaborative instruments of security, cooperation, and peace overtake humanity's historic tendencies toward conflict and war."

CURRENT CONCERNS: Examining links between technology, trade, and global security • Multilateralism • Promoting sustainable regional security • Reducing the threat of weapons of mass destruction • Strengthening national and international capacity for peace and security

METHOD OF OPERATION: Congressional testimony • Congressional voting analysis • Information clearinghouse • International activities • Internships • Legislative/regulatory monitoring (federal) • Media Outreach • Research • Web site

Effectiveness and Political Orientation

"A series of hopeful signs of a thaw in U.S.-Iran relations was capped by a massive U.S. response to the earthquake that killed at least 30,000 Iranians last month. In October, Iran agreed to intrusive inspections by the International Atomic Energy Agency to show it is not making nuclear weapons. Critics say relentless efforts by European and United Nations diplomats forged that deal, not U.S. efforts. Iran also turned down an administration bid to send an official U.S. aid mission headed by Sen. Elizabeth Dole, R-N.C.

" . . . . Libya pledged last month to scrap its banned weapons programs and allow inspections of its weapons sites after months of secret negotiations with U.S. and British officials. White House officials say at least one motivation for Libyan leader Moammar Gadhafi might have been watching the easy success of the U.S. invasion of Iraq. Critics say that British diplomats did the heavy lifting and that Gadhafi was motivated by the allure of U.S. economic sanctions being lifted.

" 'The Bush administration got lucky at year's end. Progress with Iran's and Libya's weapons programs is probably more due to hard negotiating work by the international community . . . than to the Bush administration's

TAX STATUS
501(c)(3)

FINANCES
Budget: 2004—$3.2 million; 2003—
$4.4 million; 2002—$2.85 million

FUNDING SOURCES
Foundation grants, 75%; corporate donations, 4%; government contracts, 18%; individual donations, 3%

PAC
None

EMPLOYMENT
Information on open positions can be obtained on the center's Web site. Positions offered are in the areas of administration and research. Cover letters and resumes can be sent to Elizabeth Wallish, controller, 11 Dupont Circle, NW, 9th Floor, Washington, DC 20036. Fax: (202) 223-5956. E-mail: resume@stimson.org.

INTERNSHIPS
Paid, semester-long internships are advertised on the center's Web site. Application deadlines vary. Work hours are 32–40 hours per week for full-time interns; part-time internships are occasionally available for a reduced stipend. Internships are offered in the areas of regional security projects (South Asia, Southwest Asia, East Asia); congressional study group project; chemical and biological weapons nonproliferation; human security and domestic preparedness; fundraising; UN peacekeeping; technology and security project; and military space policy. Interested parties may contact Erin Carmody, program coordinator, 11 Dupont Circle, NW, 9th Floor, Washington, DC 20036. Phone: (202) 223-5956. Fax: (202) 238-9604. E-mail: ecarmody@stimson.org.

NEWSLETTERS
The Stimson Quarterly Update on East Asian Security (SQUEAS)

PUBLICATIONS
The following is a sample list of publications:
Air Power and Escalation Control
An Alliance for Engagement: Building Cooperation in Security Relations with China
The Brahimi Report and the Future of UN Peace Operations
China and Missile Defense: Managing U.S.-PRC Strategic Relations
Dilemma of Deterrence: U.S. Strategic Ambiguity Policy and its Implications for the Taiwan Strait
Following the Money: The Bush Administration FY03 Budget Request and Current Funding for Selected Defense, State, and Energy Department Programs
Foreign High-Tech R&D in China: Risks, Rewards, and Implications for US-China Relations
Japan's Nuclear Option: Security Politics, and Policy in the 21st Century

approach,' says Ellen Laipson, an intelligence official in the Clinton administration and president of the Stimson Center, a Washington think tank."

(*USA Today*, January 9, 2004)

" 'When it comes to the grand idea of America's role in the world you have these two competing concepts in the Bush administration: The true conservative view that is focused on interests but not on trying to do too much, and the neoconservative ambition to use American power to make others more like us,' says Ellen Laipson, president of the Stimson Center, a Washington foreign-policy think tank. 'Even without Sept. 11, we would have had this struggle over how to use American power.' "

(*Christian Science Monitor*, September 10, 2003)

"The Bush administration dispatched a high-level team to Beijing yesterday for talks involving the United States, China and North Korea that will seek to break a six-month diplomatic impasse over North Korea's nuclear ambitions. . . .

"In any event, the meetings signify a face-saving compromise for both sides. Washington has insisted that only multilateral talks can resolve the nuclear crisis, while Pyongyang has demanded direct bilateral talks with the United States. . . .

" 'What the North Koreans need to leave an impression about is that they have not gone beyond the point of no return' in their quest for nuclear weapons, said Alan Romberg, director of the China program at the Henry L. Stimson Center, a Washington institute that seeks international peace and security. 'The U.S. needs to satisfy North Korea that, whatever the rhetoric, we are open to a new relationship.' "

(*Pittsburgh Post-Gazette*, April 22, 2003)

"What lies ahead in Iraq may well mark the biggest test of winning the peace since World War II. . . .

"Washington is implementing a plan that has a civilian American administration moving soon into pacified sections of Iraq. Its goal is to put the country back on its feet while an interim authority 'emerges' from the Iraqi people. . . .

" 'The end vision is fine, but the administration has not clearly mapped out a path for Iraq—how the country will get from one point to the next, what the benchmarks will be along the way,' says Victoria Holt, a former State Department official and now nation-building expert at the Henry L. Stimson Center in Washington."

(*Christian Science Monitor*, April 11, 2003)

"The U.S. military's plan to establish eight to 10 relatively small regional bases across Afghanistan reflects a belief that security is improving and is good enough in those areas to warrant a transition from combat sweeps to 'stability' operations, senior defense officials said last week.

"But the decision to create 'joint regional teams' that will each include about 60 U.S. troops, as well as Special Forces civil affairs troops, USAID officials and diplomatic personnel, also shows the Pentagon still thinks that the overall security situation in Afghanistan remains fragile and that new efforts must be made to bolster the fledgling government of Afghan President Hamid Karzai. . . .

Also publishes reports, occasional papers, and issue briefs; many of the center's publications are available online.

CONFERENCES
None

"William J. Durch, a peacekeeping specialist at the Henry L. Stimson Center, a Washington think tank, . . . questioned whether the regional teams will be large enough to do much more than protect themselves against possible attack.

" 'It's a step in the right direction,' Durch said. 'My concern is that it's not going to have enough muscle to make it work. And our policy in the Persian Gulf is undercutting this thing big time—it's sucking the air and the policy attention out of Afghanistan, and it's a half-finished job.' "

(*The Washington Post,* December 23, 2002)

"The Bush administration has abandoned an international effort to strengthen the Biological Weapons Convention against germ warfare, advising its allies that the United States wants to delay further discussions until 2006. A review conference on new verification measures for the treaty had been scheduled for November. . . .

"The 1972 Biological Weapons Convention, which has been ratified by the United States and 143 other countries, bans the development, stockpiling and production of germ warfare agents, but has no enforcement mechanism. Negotiations on legally binding measures to enforce compliance have been underway in Geneva for seven years. . . .

"Amy Smithson, a biological and chemical weapons specialist, said the administration is making a mistake by halting collaborative work to strengthen the convention. 'It sounds to me as though they've thrown the baby out with the bath water,' said Smithson, an analyst at the Henry L. Stimson Center. 'The contradiction between the rhetoric and what the administration is actually doing—the gulf is huge. Not a day goes by when they don't mention the Iraq threat.'

"The Stimson Center is releasing a report today that criticizes the U.S. approach to the convention. Drawn from a review by 10 pharmaceutical companies and biotechnology experts, the document argues that bioweapons inspections can be effective with the right amount of time and the right science and urges the administration to develop stronger measures. "

(*The Washington Post,* September 19, 2002)

The Heritage Foundation

Established in 1973

DIRECTOR
Edwin J. Feulner, president.

BOARD OF TRUSTEES

SCOPE
Members: More than 200,000
Branches chapters: Offices in Hong Kong and Moscow
Affiliates: None

STAFF
134 total

TAX STATUS
501(c)(3)

FINANCES
Budget: 2000—$30 million

CONTACT INFORMATION
214 Massachusetts Avenue, NE, Washington, DC 20002-4999
Phone: (202) 546-4400 • *Fax:* (202) 546-8328
General E-mail: info@heritage.org • *Web site:* www.heritage.org

Communications Director: Communications & Marketing Department (202) 546-4400
Human Resources Director: Wes Dyck, director of personnel (202) 546-4400

PURPOSE: A research and education think tank whose mission is "to formulate and promote conservative public policies based on the principles of free enterprises, limited government, individual freedom, traditional American values, and a strong national defense."

CURRENT CONCERNS: Budget and taxation • Crime, violence, and law • Economic and political theory • Education reform • Environment • Family, culture, and community • Federal spending • Foreign policy • Governing • Health care, social security, and welfare • National security • Regulations and infrastructures • Telecommunications • Trade and commerce

METHOD OF OPERATION: Coalition forming • Conferences/seminars • Congressional testimony • Films/video/audiotapes • International activities • Internet (electronic bulletin boards and Web sites) • Internships • Legislative/regulatory monitoring (federal) • Library/information clearinghouse • Media outreach • Product merchandising • Professional development services • Research • Speakers program

Effectiveness and Political Orientation

"To put it another way, Washington will be arguing over a mere $10 billion in domestic programs. By contrast, Medicare spending will increase by more than twice that next year—even before a costly new drug benefit kicks in. 'Spending will not be brought under control until entitlements are seriously reformed,' says Heritage Foundation budget expert Brian M. Reidl. 'You can't nickel-and-dime your way to balancing the budget.'"

(*Business Week,* February 16, 2004)

"Brian Riedl of the Heritage Foundation has been examining how much of the budget growth in recent years is due to national-security spending. Riedl finds that when you tease out all the anti-terrorism spending, it's still true that 'domestic non-security programs are growing at their fastest rate in a decade.' Even obsolete agencies that Republicans have long wanted to disconnect from life support are thriving in the hands-of Republican appropriators. Says John Berthoud, president of the National Taxpayers Union: 'For the first time in many years we are seeing that Republicans are outspending the Democrats.'"

(*National Review,* February 9, 2004)

FUNDING SOURCES
Individuals, 47%; foundation grants, 21%; investment income, 24%; publications, 4%; corporate donations, 4%

PAC
None

EMPLOYMENT
Information on current job openings is posted online at www.heritage.org/About/Careers/index.cfm. The Heritage Foundation does not keep resumes on file, nor does it accept resumes for positions that are not open or are currently filled. Individuals who would like to be considered for future openings with conservative organizations, congressional offices, and faith-based organizations may complete a Job Bank questionnaire, available online at www.heritage.org/About/JobBank/JobBankApp.cfm.

INTERNSHIPS
Students may apply for internships in the following departments: accounting, Asian studies, Center for American Studies, Center for Data Analysis, Center for Legal and Judicial Studies, coalition relations, communications and marketing, development, domestic policy, the executive offices, external relations, foreign policy, government relations, information systems, lectures and seminars, online communications, personnel, publishing services, special events, and townhall.com. Complete information is posted online at www.heritage.org/About/Internships/index.cf.

Applications are taken on a rolling basis and can be sent via e-mail to Dan Szy, intern coordinator, internships@heritage.org. Applications should demonstrate strong research and writing abilities, excellent communication skills, and the inquisitiveness to undertake various research, writing, administrative, and computer projects. Most internships require a commitment of at least 24 hours per week. Twenty to twenty-five interns are accepted during the fall and spring terms. Summer interns must be rising college juniors or older. Recent college graduates and masters-level students are encouraged to apply. In addition to the online application, applicants should have two letters of reference from college professors or employers sent to: The Heritage Foundation, ATTN: Intern Coordinator, 214 Massachusetts Avenue, NE, Washington, DC 20002-4999.

NEWSLETTERS
Heritage Members News (bimonthly)
Heritage Today (bimonthly)
Policy Review (bimonthly magazine)
The Windsor Newsletter (periodic)

PUBLICATIONS
The following is a list of sample publications:
Agenda 2003
March of Freedom
108th Congressional Directory
Pocket Guide to Declaration and Constitution
Policy Experts 2003

"... a leading conservative think tank. ..."

(*Education Week*, February 4, 2004)

"... whatever may be said of Bush's critics on the Right, they do present a more reasoned set of contentions. Last summer, the columnist George E. Will suggested that, under Bush, American conservatism was undergoing an identity crisis, one that might well end by rendering it incoherent. The crisis, according to Will, was being caused by the policies of the administration and a series of decisions by the purportedly conservative Supreme Court; jointly, these were gnawing at the very foundations of limited government and the preference for market forces over governmental intrusion in economic affairs. In the months since Will raised these doubts about the conservative bona fides of the administration, the murmurs of discontent have turned into a din.

".... it was Bush's decision to sign the Medicare-reform law passed by Congress just before Thanksgiving that pushed even quietly skeptical conservatives into open opposition. The new law, projected to cost as much as $2 trillion over the next two decades, is surely the greatest expansion of entitlement spending ever endorsed by a Republican President. The Wall Street Journal, in a harsh criticism, called the bill 'too expensive a gamble for principled conservatives to support. The supply-side economist Bruce Bartlett described himself as 'apoplectic.' Major conservative think tanks from the Heritage Foundation to the Cato Institute and the National Center for Policy Analysis all vigorously lobbied against the bill's passage. ...."

(*Commentary*, February 2004)

"The new Medicare drug benefit will cost about 35 percent more than Congress anticipated, helping to kick the federal budget deficit up to a record $500 billion next year, according to officials familiar with the fiscal 2005 budget that President Bush is to release Monday.

"The prescription drug plan, which will not be fully in effect until 2006, will cost about $540 billion over 10 years, instead of the $396 billion projected in the law that Congress approved late last year, said a government official and private-sector economists who have been briefed on the budget. This spring, the first phase of implementing the law will provide 40 million Medicare beneficiaries with discount cards for their prescriptions.

"The revised estimate angered deficit hawks, who had argued that the $396 billion was too costly. Democrats, meanwhile, said they will redouble their efforts to change the Medicare bill to allow the government to negotiate directly with drug companies to lower pharmaceutical prices.

"'This does not surprise us,' said Bill Beech, a budget analyst with the Heritage Foundation. 'I'm frankly a little bit surprised the number isn't larger.' The foundation opposed the Medicare drug law because of the cost, which the conservative research organization estimates will reach $625 billion over 10 years. ...."

(*The Boston Globe*, January 30, 2004)

"For Democrats suffering from Scarecrow Syndrome ('if we only had a brain'), John Podesta, the man behind the curtain at the Center for American Progress, thinks he has the cure: a $10-million-a-year think tank now taking shape in Washington. In a city heavy with well-funded right-wing think tanks (Heritage Foundation, Cato Institute, American Enterprise Institute, Hudson Institute, Federalist Society), the center is designed to provide some ballast for the

2004 Index of Economic Freedom
2003 U.S. and Asia Statistical Handbook
Scholl Choice 2003
Also publishes policy papers.

CONFERENCES
Third Generation discussion group (monthly gathering of young conservatives)
Variety of lectures, conferences, seminars, roundtables, and regional meetings

other side. Starting in the 1970s, the conservative tanks have forged the ideas that built Fortress GOP. Podesta believes that what the Democrats need to 'balance the national debate' is a Heritage Foundation of their own. Finally, the Democratic Party will have a 'brain.'. . .

"Podesta, who has gotten people up and running on white papers and policy initiatives on everything from homeland security to public education, relishes comparisons between his center and Heritage. 'I'm a policy wonk at heart,' he says. In its first few months, the center has organized a two-day conference on national security, issued a detailed critique of President Bush's record on antiterrorism and civil liberties, prepared a thoughtful analysis of the just-passed Medicare prescription drug bill and sponsored a foreign policy address by Senator Edward Kennedy."

(*The Nation,* March 1, 2004)

Hoover Institution
on War, Revolution, and Peace

Established in 1919

DIRECTOR

John Raisian, director. Raisian joined the Hoover Institution in 1986 and was appointed director in 1989. He also holds an appointment as a senior fellow at the Hoover Institution. Raisian was a consultant to the Rand Corporation from 1974 to 1975, after which he was a visiting professor of economics at the University of Washington from 1975 to 1976. From 1976 to 1980, he was an assistant professor of economics at the University of Houston. Raisian worked for the U.S. Labor Department for six years. He was president of Unicon Research Corporation, an economic consulting firm in Los Angeles, before joining the Hoover Institution. He received a B.A. in economics and mathematics from Ohio University and a Ph.D. in economics from the University of California at Los Angeles.

BOARD OF DIRECTORS

W. Kurt Hauser, chair
Peter B. Bedford, vice chair
W. Kurt Hauser, executive committee chair
Peter B. Bedford, executive committee vice chair
Martin Anderson
Wendy Borcherdt
Paul Lewis Davies III
William C. Edwards
Everett Hauck
Heather Higgins
Herbert Hoover III
Peyton M. Lake
Bowen H. McCoy
Robert J. Rishwain
Richard M. Scaife
Tad Taube
Thomas J. Tierney
David T. Traitel
Walter E. Williams

SCOPE

Members: None
Branches/chapters: None
Affiliates: None

STAFF

250 total—including scholars and support staff

TAX STATUS

501(c)(3)

FINANCES

Budget: 2004—$31.6 million; 2003—$31.6 million; 2002—$30.6 million

FUNDING SOURCES

Individuals, 44%; endowment, 41%; encumbered funds, 9%; Stanford University, 3%; publications, 3%.

CONTACT INFORMATION

Stanford University, 434 Galvez Mall, Stanford, CA 94305-6010
Phone: (650) 723-1754 • *Fax:* (650) 723-1687
General E-mail: info@hoover.stanford.edu • *Web site:* www.hoover.org

Communications Director: Jeffrey Bliss
(650) 725-3076 • bliss@hoover.stanford.edu
Human Resources Director: Helen M. Corrales
(650) 723-2052 • corrales@hoover.stanford.edu

PURPOSE: "To recall the voice of experience against the making of war, and to recall man's endeavors to make and preserve peace, and to sustain for America the safeguards of the American way of life."

CURRENT CONCERNS: Democracy and free markets • Education reform • The end of Communism • National security • Property rights • Tax policy

METHOD OF OPERATION: Advertisements • Conferences/seminars • Congressional testimony • Films/video/audiotapes • Information clearinghouse • International activities • Internet (e-mail alerts and Web site) • Library services open to the public • Media outreach • Research • Speakers program

Effectiveness and Political Orientation

" 'This gay wedding craze is starting to spread around the country. Today a guy in Utah married five other guys.'—Jay Leno

"Leno's joke isn't too far off the mark, says Stanley Kurtz, a scholar at the Hoover Institution, a conservative think tank at Stanford University. In Utah, lawsuits to overturn the state's ban on polygamy are already winding through the courts. Although legal experts question the merits of those cases, polygamy may be losing some of its taboo status."

(*The Los Angeles Times,* March 12, 2004)

"As unrest continues to rock the Middle East, U.S. officials are holding to a policy of hard-line confrontation against 'axis of evil' adversary Iran.

" 'We have to have carrots as well as sticks' to deal with Iran, said physicist Sidney Drell, longtime presidential adviser and senior fellow at Stanford University's conservative Hoover Institution. Drell recently co-authored 'The Gravest Danger: Nuclear Weapons.'

" 'We should say, "What are your sources of insecurity? What are the ways that it's to your advantage to be part of the world economically and politically?" '

(*The Denver Post,* March 9, 2004)

"Victor Hanson, a fruit grower and expert on ancient Greek warfare, has won fans in the Bush White House by likening the U.S. to Athens. . . .

EMPLOYMENT

The Hoover Institution hires for positions in research, administration, and clerical support. Jobs are advertised on the Stanford University Web site under "employment." Cover letters and resumes can be sent to Christina Ansel, employment specialist, Hoover Institution, 434 Galvez Mall, Stanford University, Stanford, CA 94305-6010. Fax: (650) 723-1687. E-mail: Ansel@hoover.stanford.edu.

INTERNSHIPS

Does not provide internship opportunities.

NEWSLETTERS

China Leadership Monitor (quarterly and online only)
Education Next (quarterly)
Hoover Digest (quarterly)
The Hoover Newsletter (monthly online and printed quarterly)
Policy Review (quarterly)

PUBLICATIONS

Anti Americanism in Europe: A Cultural Problem
Doing It Wrong and Doing It Right: Education in Latin America and Asia
Education and Capitalism: How Overcoming Our Fear of Markets and Economics Can Improve America's Schools
The Future of School Choice
The Gravest Danger: Nuclear Weapons
Neither Left nor Right: Selected Columns
Never a Matter of Indifference: Sustaining Virtue in a Free Republic
Our Schools and Our Future: Are We Still at Risk?
Politicizing Science
The Right to Private Property
Russia's Oil in America's Future: Policy, Pipelines, and Prospects
School Figures: The Data Behind the Debate
Some Implications of the Turnover of Political Power in Taiwan
The Soviet Gulag

CONFERENCES

Hoover Forum, at Hoover and in Washington, DC, periodically
Koret Task Force on K-12 Education, at Hoover and in Washington, DC, periodically
Democracy in Iran, at Hoover, periodically
Media Fellows presentations, weekly

"Hanson's moral parallels between the ancient Greeks' fight for democracy and our own struggles in Afghanistan and Iraq have endeared him to the Bush administration and changed his life. . . .

"Hanson will leave Cal State Fresno next summer as one of America's leading conservative writers, most prominently showcased in his weekly online column in the like-minded National Review.

"In April, amid the early stages of the U.S. invasion of Iraq, Hanson used his column to hail the American advance on Baghdad as 'unprecedented in its speed and daring' and predicted that its 'logistics will be studied for decades.' Vice President Dick Cheney enthusiastically quoted Hanson in a speech before the American Society of Newspaper Editors.

"Hanson's absolute, unflinching belief in the cause and its ultimate success made him a favorite of Cheney, who urges Hanson's books on his staff and on reporters traveling with him for foreign trips.

"Hanson is also a regular consultant to the influential Pentagon Office of Net Assessment, which has emerged as a key administration intelligence gathering and planning agency under Secretary of Defense Donald H. Rumsfeld and his senior deputy, Paul D. Wolfowitz. This week, Hanson was back in Washington to speak before the Board of Overseers of the Hoover Institution, the conservative Palo Alto think tank where Hanson is a resident fellow. . . . Sharing the podium were Secretary of State Colin L. Powell and Karl Rove, President Bush's main political advisor."

(*The Los Angeles Times,* February 25, 2004)

"(Arnold) Schwarzenegger . . . seems to be listening to advisers such as George Shultz and John Cogan, conservative economists at Stanford University's Hoover Institution who say the budget can be balanced and outstanding debt paid down without tax increases."

(*The San Francisco Chronicle,* October 9, 2003)

"(David) Horowitz charges that 'the political bias against conservatives in the hiring process amounts to an illegal political patronage operation, which provides huge advantages to the Democratic Party and to the political left.' An interesting point, when the White House and Congress are controlled by conservative Republicans. Perhaps he doesn't know of Stanford's conservative Hoover Institution or the University of Chicago's renowned and conservative economics department, which both have strong influence in setting our foreign, social and economic policies."

(*The Denver Post,* September 14, 2003)

Hudson Institute

Established in 1961

DIRECTOR

Herbert I. London, president. London became president of Hudson Institute in September 1997. He has been a member of the Hudson Institute Board of Trustees since 1974 and has been a senior fellow for more than 30 years, founding Hudson's Center for Education and Employment Policy. He is the John M. Olin University Professor of Humanities at New York University and was responsible for creating in 1972 the Gallatin School, where he served as dean until 1992. Herbert London graduated from Columbia University in 1960 and received his Ph.D. from New York University in 1966. He is a tenured professor of social studies at New York University.

BOARD OF DIRECTORS

Jeffrey T. Bergner; senior fellow, German Marshall Fund of the United States, Washington, DC

Lord Black; PCc, OC, KCSG, Toronto, Canada

Linden S. Blue, executive committee member; vice chair, General Atomics, San Diego, CA

Rudy Boschwitz; chair, Home Valu Interiors, Minneapolis, MN

Charles H. Brunie; chair, Brunie Associates, New York, NY

Joseph Epstein; lecturer, Northwestern University, Evanston, IL

Joseph M. Giglio, executive committee member; executive professor for strategic management, Northeastern University, Boston, MA

Roy Innis; national chair, Congress of Racial Equality, New York, NY

Deborah Kahn Cunningham; Chappaqua, NY

Paul J. Klaassen; chair of the board and chief executive officer, Sunrise Assisted Living, Fairfax, VA

Marie-Josée Kravis, executive committee member; Senior Fellow, Hudson Institute, New York, NY

Andre B. Lacy; chair and chief executive officer, LDI, Ltd., Indianapolis, IN

Herbert I. London, executive committee member; J. M. Olin Professor of Humanities, New York University, and president, Hudson Institute, Inc., Indianapolis, IN

Robert Mankin; Independent Management Consultant, Financial Services, New York, NY

Robert H. McKinney, executive committee member; chair and chief executive officer, First Indiana Corp., Indianapolis,

John M. Mutz; former Indiana lieutenant governor, Indianapolis

Neil H. Offen; president, Direct Selling Association, Washington, DC

CONTACT INFORMATION

1015 18th Street, NW, Suite 300, Washington, DC 20036
Phone: (202) 223-7770 • *Fax:* (202) 223-8537
General E-mail: info@hudson.org • *Web site:* www.hudson.org

Communications Director: Jennifer A. Butsch
(317) 549-4115 • jennifer@hudson.org
Human Resources Director: Mary Rahe
(317) 549-4148 • mary@hudson.org

PURPOSE: "As a public policy think tank, Hudson Institute forecasts long-term trends and designs near-term solutions for government, business, and the nonprofit world. We share optimism about the future and a willingness to question conventional wisdom. We believe in free markets, individual responsibility, the power of technology, and a determination to preserve America's national security."

CURRENT CONCERNS: American common culture • Central Europe and Eurasia • East Asia and the Pacific • Economic and regulatory studies • Global food issues and Biotechnology • Health care • Human rights and legal policy • The Middle East • National security studies • Philanthropy and Civic Renewal • Transportation • Workforce development

METHOD OF OPERATION: Awards program • Conferences/seminars • Congressional testimony • Information clearinghouse • International activities • Internet (e-mail alerts and Web site) • Internships • Legislative/regulatory monitoring (federal) • Media outreach • Performance ratings/Report cards (companies, products, etc.) • Research • Speakers program

SPECIFIC PROGRAMS/INITIATIVES: Declaration in Support of Protecting Nature with High-yield Farming and Forestry

Effectiveness and Political Orientation

"For more than a year, President Bush has connected the use of military force to topple Saddam Hussein with the broader war on terrorism he launched after the Sept. 11, 2001, attacks.

"For nearly as long, Democratic presidential candidates have criticized the Iraq war as a distraction and a resource drain from the fight against Al-Qaida and affiliated radical Islamic groups.

"Now, two key events—the Madrid train bombings and subsequent election ouster of Spain's pro-U.S. government, as well as new attacks by insurgents in Baghdad—could move that dispute beyond the domestic political arena.

"A number of military and foreign-policy analysts . . . express concern that those events—especially if followed by more attacks in Europe—could begin

SCOPE

Members: 650 individual members and 200 corporations
Branches/chapters: None
Affiliates: None

STAFF

63 total—39 full-time professional; 24 full-time support; plus 8 part-time professional; 11 part-time support; and 5 interns

TAX STATUS

501(c)(3)

FINANCES

Budget: 2003—$10.45 million; 2002—$6.387 million

FUNDING SOURCES

Foundation grants, 46%; corporate donations, 18%; government contracts, 23%; individuals, 13%

PAC

None

EMPLOYMENT

Job postings are available at www.hudson .org, in professional publications, on www.monster.com, in *Not-for-Profit News*, and through internal postings. The organization offers positions as research assistants, research fellows, and senior fellows. Standard administrative positions—such as in marketing and accounting—also are available. Contact information is included with a posted position.

INTERNSHIPS

Unpaid internship positions are available during the spring, fall, and summer semesters; deadlines vary according to position and semester. At least 15 hours are required per week. Internship areas include the following: research, editorial, and nonprofit administra-

to erode the anti-terrorism coalition that, despite fierce disagreement over Iraq, has held together reasonably well. . . .

"Retired Gen. William E. Odom, director of national security studies at the Hudson Institute in Washington, said the Iraq war has already weakened the international unity that Bush commanded after Sept. 11. . . .

" 'Everybody was with us,' Odom said. 'Today, a remarkable number of people have left us. The question is when and why. It starts with the president's 2002 State of the Union message, when he announced the axis of evil. The Europeans were absolutely shocked. They said, "We didn't sign up to fight Iraq, Iran and North Korea. We signed up to fight Al-Qaida.'

" 'That was the fork in the road,' Odom said. 'By waging war in Iraq, the president has managed to essentially erode the anti-terrorism coalition.'

"Odom, a former senior White House military adviser who served under Democratic President Jimmy Carter and Republican President Ronald Reagan, said he voted for Bush in 2000 but now regrets the decision."

(*Star Tribune* [Minneapolis], March 21, 2004)

"David Horowitz, a senior fellow at the conservative Hudson Institute, said Bush 'has allowed himself to focus on the wrong target,' which is a constitutional amendment defining marriage, rather than an amendment that prevents judges from making laws.

" 'Things are getting out of control when every mayor and public official feels free to interpret the constitution and issue rules that run pretty clearly contrary to state law,' Horowitz said. . . ."

(*The San Francisco Chronicle*, March 5, 2004)

"The Modern Red SchoolHouse Institute is a nonprofit organization that helps schools strengthen teaching and learning and measure their progress against rigorous standards.

"The organization was founded in 1991 by the Hudson Institute and was among the first 'break the mold' school improvement models selected by the U.S. Department of Education and the New American Schools Development Corp. to improve public education nationwide.

"Today, the school improvement organization collaborates with more than 100 school districts in 30 states to break down barriers that hinder student success. . . ."

(*The Atlanta Journal-Constitution*, February 12, 2004)

"Early every morning in the District of Columbia, hundreds of journalists from around the world check out websites that give the day's schedule for President George W. Bush and Vice-President Dick Cheney.

"The President's itinerary is given in some detail, stating the time and place of functions he will attend that day. Reporters can then make suitable arrangements to cover them.

"The same is true for Secretary of State Colin Powell and other American leaders.

"Except Mr Cheney. Aside from rare occasions, the Vice-President's schedule is summarised in one word: 'Unavailable.'. . .

"Said Ms Amy Kauffman, an expert on US politics at the Hudson Institute in Washington: 'Cheney's inaccessibility has always been a problem and a big mistake. Leaders need to talk to the media directly.'

tion. Undergraduate and graduate students are considered. Potential applicants can learn about opportunities at www.hudson.org.

For more information, contact Kim Bowling, intern coordinator, 1015 18th Street, NW, Suite 300, Washington, DC 20036. Phone: (202) 223-7770. Fax: (202) 223-8537. E-mail: info@hudsondc.org.

NEWSLETTERS
Newsletter (quarterly)
Hudson Headlines (weekly electronic
  newsletter)

PUBLICATIONS
Produces books, white papers, research reports, op-eds, and an annual report.

CONFERENCES
Discourses on Democracy (Washington, DC,
  bimonthly)
Program on Transitions to Democracy
  (Washington, DC, monthly)
Campaign Finance Reform Lunches
  (Washington, DC, bimonthly)
New York Speakers Series (New York City,
  monthly)
Ideology and Foreign Policy Conference Series
  (Washington, DC, bimonthly)

"But after 9/11, Mr Cheney became not so much inaccessible as virtually invisible.

"For weeks on end, sometimes even months, no one outside the administration had any idea where he was. People surmised that he was holed up in his mountain redoubt in his home state of Wyoming, but no one knew for sure.

"But now, with an election approaching that threatens to be very close, there are signs that the Vice-President is attempting to be, well, if not a regular guy, at least more visible and approachable.

"Last month, he took a highly publicised trip to Switzerland and Italy that included an audience with the Pope. It was only the second time he had travelled abroad in three years.

"He has also become more media-friendly and granted interviews to selected journalists.

"Said Ms Kauffman: 'With an election looming, the administration wants to remind people that Mr Cheney, whom we haven't seen in quite some time, is still there. And that he remains a very strong voice within the administration.'"
                                        (*The Straits Times* [Singapore], February 7, 2004)

"Something seemed terribly wrong on the 27th floor of the Vinson & Elkins law firm. Employees kept getting diagnosed with cancer.

"In three years, at least nine employees on the floor developed cancer—about one of 10 workers there—and many feared something in the workplace, perhaps the air or water, was to blame.

"About two years ago, the law firm brought in a slew of specialists to evaluate the building, but what they discovered surprised many staffers: The office was safe. And despite perceptions, employees' cancer rates weren't abnormally high.

" 'We were just at that age when people start getting breast cancer,' says Marilyn Roberts, 56, a legal assistant in the Houston office who was diagnosed with the disease. 'It was very comforting to know the company took all the steps to investigate.'

"From small law offices to corporate giants such as IBM, companies are facing employee concerns that their workplace is causing cancer. But despite the anxiety and headline-grabbing cases, medical researchers rarely find the workplace to blame. Instead, years of costly research often yield inconclusive findings or winds up proving that the number of cancers were not unusually high at all. . . .

" 'It used to be that the philosophy was, "It's God's will." Now, there's got to be a reason,' says Michael Fumento, a senior fellow at the Hudson Institute in Washington, D.C., who has researched environmental health issues. 'People want an answer. They're very uncomfortable with the laws of probability.'"
                                        (*USA Today,* February 2, 2004)

Human Rights Campaign (HRC)

Established in 1980

DIRECTOR

Cheryl Jacques, president. Jacques began as president and executive director of the Human Rights Campaign in January 2004 after serving nearly a dozen years in the Massachusetts state senate. Jacques was the first freshman legislator and first woman to chair the Judiciary Committee when she was elected to the state senate in 1992. Jacques also served as assistant district attorney in Middlesex County; assistant attorney general in the Trial Bureau of the Attorney General's Office; counsel to the law firm of Brody, Hardoon, Perkins and Kesten; and adjunct professor of law at Suffolk University Law School. She also has served on several state and local boards. Jacques is a graduate of the Boston College School of Business Administration and Suffolk University Law School.

BOARD OF DIRECTORS

Gwen Baba, Los Angeles, CA
Joe Barrows, Denver, CO
Bruce Bastian, Salt Lake City, UT
Terry Bean, Portland, OR
Michael Berman, Washington, DC
Tammara Billik, Studio City, CA
Timothy Boggs, Washington, DC
Mary Breslauer, Boston, MA
Tom Buche, Denver, CO
Philip Burgess, Chicago, IL
Dennis Coleman, Dallas, TX
Stampp Corbin, Columbus, OH
Rebecca Covell, Dallas, TX
Lawrie Demorest, Atlanta, GA
Timothy Downing, Cleveland, OH
Ingrid Duran, Washington, DC
Amy Errett, San Francisco, CA
Julia Fitz-Randolph, Denver, CO (ex-officio)
Emily Giske, New York, NY
Mitchell Gold, Conover, NC
Carolyn Hall, Dallas, TX
Stephanie Hart, New York, NY
Mary Jo Hudson, Columbus, OH
Barry Karas, Los Angeles, CA
Marty Lieberman, Seattle, WA
Andy Linsky, Palm Springs, CA
Candy Marcum, Dallas, TX
David Medina, Washington, DC
David Muck, Houston, TX
Lucilo Peña, Dallas, TX
Dana Perlman, Beverly Hills, CA
Trevor Potter, Washington, DC
Victoria Raymont, Chicago, IL
Karla Rikansrud, Boulder, CO (ex-officio)
Henry Robin, New York, NY
Henry Rosales, Denver, CO (ex-officio)
Abby Rubenfeld, Nashville, TN
Judy Shepard, Casper, WY
Mary Snider, Washington, DC
John Sullivan, Minneapolis, MN

CONTACT INFORMATION

1640 Rhode Island Avenue, NW, Washington, DC 20036-3278
Phone: (202) 216-1500 • *Fax:* (202) 347-5323
General E-mail: hrc@hrc.org • *Web site:* www.hrc.org

Communications Director (interim): Mark Shields, deputy director of media relations
(202) 216-1564 • mark.shields@hrc.org
Human Resources Director: Julian J. High

PURPOSE: "HRC is a bipartisan organization that works to advance equality based on sexual orientation and gender expression and identity, to ensure that gay, lesbian, bisexual and transgender Americans can be open, honest and safe at home, at work and in the community."

CURRENT CONCERNS: Advancing sound public policy on HIV/AIDS and lesbian health • Equal marriage rights • Fair-minded judiciary and "friend of the court" advocacy • Hate violence • Job discrimination • State and local advocacy • Working to elect fair-minded candidates

METHOD OF OPERATION: Advertisements • Awards program • Boycotts • Campaign contributions • Coalition forming • Conferences/seminars • Congressional testimony • Congressional voting analysis • Direct action • Educational foundation • Electoral politics • Fax-on-demand • Films/video/audio tapes • Grant-making • Grassroots organizing (Field Action Network, Speak Out Action Grams) • Information clearinghouse • Initiative/referendum campaigns • Internet (databases, e-mail alerts, and Web site) • Internships • Legislative/regulatory monitoring (federal and state) • Lobbying (federal, state, and grass roots) • Media outreach • Participation in regulatory proceedings (federal) • Polling • Product merchandising • Research • Shareholder resolutions • Training • Voter registration • Voting records

Effectiveness and Political Orientation

"(L)ast month . . . Bush endorsed a constitutional ban on same-sex marriage. . . .

"The raw emotion kicked up by the issue is affecting the presidential campaign in ways that no one anticipated. Ever since Bush endorsed a ban on same-sex unions, money has been pouring in to gay rights groups in record amounts. . . .

"'There is a huge energy created that I've never seen before,' said Winnie Stachelberg, political director of the Human Rights Campaign, which promotes gay rights. 'Will it translate into ground troops? It's a little too early to tell. But there is a kind of focused sense within the gay community on the election.'"

(*The Los Angeles Times*, March 18, 2004)

Andrew Tobias, Miami, FL
Tony Varona, New York, NY

SCOPE
Members: More than 500,000 individuals
Branches/chapters: None
Affiliates: None

STAFF
110 total—4 professional; 106 support; plus
15 interns and a nationwide network of
volunteers

TAX STATUS
501(c)(3) and 501(c)(4)

FINANCES
Budget: 2003—$22.4 million; 2002—$20.5
million; 2001—$22.3 million

FUNDING SOURCES
Membership dues, 34%; individuals, 28%;
special events/projects, 24%; merchandising,
bequests, earned income and in-kind contributions, 10%; foundation grants, 2%; corporate
donations, 2%

PAC
Human Rights Campaign PAC

PAC CONTRIBUTIONS 2002

83% to
Democrats

17% to
Republicans

EMPLOYMENT
Job openings are advertised on the HRC Web
site at www.hrc.org and in *The Washington
Post, Washington Blade*, www.washington-
jobs.com, and www.monster.com. Positions
are in the areas of administrative support;
graphic design/Web site; accounting; fund-
raising; public policy; and direct marketing.
Cover letters and resumes can be sent to
Career Opportunities, 1640 Rhode Island
Avenue, NW, Washington, DC 20036-3278.
Fax: (202) 216-1579. E-mail: careers@hrc.org.

INTERNSHIPS
Semester-long, paid internships are available.
Application deadlines are: summer semester—March 19; fall semester—July 28; spring
semester—November 1. However, application
deadlines are flexible depending on college
and university schedules. Both full and part-
time positions are available. Internships are
available in every department and all academic majors are invited to apply. All internships
require some general administrative tasks.
General qualifications required for all positions
include strong research, writing, and communication skills; enthusiasm and an interest in the
role of policy advocacy and gay, lesbian, bisex-

"Igniting a political powder keg, President Bush yesterday strode into the White House Roosevelt Room and insisted that traditional marriage between one man and one woman is in danger and must be defended by changing the U.S. Constitution. . . .

"The Human Rights Campaign, the nation's largest gay and lesbian polit-ical organization, said Bush's proposal would be discriminatory as well as 'un-American, shameful and divisive.'"

(*Pittsburgh Post-Gazette*, February 25, 2004)

"When the Massachusetts Supreme Court affirmed this week that gay men and lesbians have a constitutional right to marriage, victory seemed unequivocal. . . .

"But by Thursday afternoon, their victory seemed less certain. Several of the state's most powerful politicians—Gov. Mitt Romney (R) and House Speaker Thomas M. Finneran (D)—pledged to explore every legal avenue to block the court's order from taking effect in mid-May. The Catholic arch-bishop authorized mailings to 1 million households and instructed his flock to lobby every legislator to pass an amendment defining marriage as only between a man and a woman. . . .

"Catholic Archbishop Sean P. O'Malley called the court's stance 'overly activist' and said that marriage is about procreation and the education of chil-dren. 'Catholic citizens and all men and women of good will who value such a traditional, positive and forthright understanding of marriage must unite to take action,' he said in a statement. . . .

"'Lawmakers are nervous,' said Cheryl Jacques, who directs the Human Rights Campaign, one of the nation's largest gay and lesbian advocacy orga-nizations. 'But a lot of us were raised Catholic, and a lot of us disagree with the church on a lot of issues. I think that they're aware that history will judge them harshly if they vote for the amendment.'"

(*The Washington Post*, February 6, 2004)

"In a decision heralded by gay rights groups, Wal-Mart Stores, with 1.1 mil-lion domestic workers the nation's largest private employer, has amended its employment policies to expressly prohibit discrimination based on sexual orientation. . . .

"'For a company like Wal-Mart to say this, which is based in middle America and caters to middle America, it shows that these kind of policies are mainstream and should be standard policy,' said Kim Mills, education direc-tor for the Human Rights Campaign, a gay rights group based in Washington that monitors discrimination policy."

(*The Washington Post*, July 3, 2003)

"Attorney General John Ashcroft ignited a new controversy over his agency's treatment of gays and lesbians Friday after he refused to allow Justice Department employees to hold an annual event celebrating "gay pride month" at the agency's headquarters. . . .

"'It's shocking that the agency in charge of protecting the civil rights of all Americans is singling out one group of people for unequal treatment,' said David Smith, spokesman for the Human Rights Campaign, the nation's largest gay and lesbian advocacy group. 'It sends a very chilling message to gay and lesbian employees that says, "You are not welcome.'"

(*The San Francisco Chronicle*, June 7, 2003)

ual, and transgender issues; ability to work in a fast-paced, dynamic work environment; experience with Microsoft Office applications (Word, Excel, Access); as well as skills specifically tailored to a particular position.

Internships are advertised on the Web site. Interested individuals may contact Julian J. High, human resources and diversity director, 1640 Rhode Island Avenue, NW, Washington, DC 20036-3278. Phone: (202) 216-1521. Fax: (202) 216-1579. E-mail: careers@hrc.org.

NEWSLETTERS
Equality Magazine (quarterly)
LAWBriefs (quarterly)

PUBLICATIONS
Corporate Equality Index
A Decade of Violence: Hate Crimes Based on Sexual Orientation
Finally Free: How Love and Self-Acceptance Saved Us from the "Ex-Gay" Ministries
Mission Impossible: Why Reparative Therapy and Ex-Gay Ministries Fail
Mixed Blessings: Mainstream Religion and Gay and Lesbian Americans
The State of the Family for Lesbian, Gay, Bisexual and Transgender Americans
The State of the Workplace for Lesbian, Gay, Bisexual and Transgendered Americans (annual)

CONFERENCES
National Coming Out Project; also sponsors events nationwide.

"The growing importance of gays in politics will be evident this weekend, with the Log Cabin Republicans meeting in Washington and Democratic presidential candidate John Edwards addressing a Human Rights Campaign dinner Saturday in Atlanta.

"The events, involving two of the most recognized organizations of gay and lesbian activists, underscore how mainstream gay politics has become in recent years—so much so that the recent disparaging comments about same-sex relationships by a Republican congressional leader, Sen. Rick Santorum of Pennsylvania, were widely condemned. . . .

" 'We've made progress, but there's a lot of progress to be made,' said Winnie Stachelberg, political director of the nonpartisan Human Rights Campaign."

(*The Atlanta Journal-Constitution,* May 9, 2003)

"Bush's handpicked party chairman, Marc Racicot, spoke last month to 300 leaders of the bipartisan Human Rights Campaign, a 500,000-member group that promotes legal recognition of gay relationships and protection against job discrimination. The conservative Family Research Council calls the group 'a key player on the political left' and says of Republicans, 'a political party divided against itself cannot endure.' Bush chose Racicot to head the party, Republican strategist Matthew Dowd says, in part because Racicot believes in 'tolerance, acceptance, openness. That's who he is.' "

(*USA Today,* April 24, 2003)

Human Rights Watch

Established in 1978

DIRECTOR

Kenneth Roth, executive director. Roth has held the post since 1993. From 1987 to 1993, Roth served as deputy director. Previously, he was a federal prosecutor for the U.S. Attorney's Office for the Southern District of New York and the Iran-Contra investigation in Washington. He also worked in private practice as a litigator. Roth is a graduate of Yale Law School and Brown University.

BOARD OF DIRECTORS

Information unavailable

SCOPE

Members: Declined to state
Branches/chapters: Offices in Brussels, Belgium; Bujumbura, Burundi; Freetown, Sierra Leone; Geneva, Switzerland; Hong Kong; Kigali, Rwanda; London, England; Los Angeles; Moscow; Rio de Janeiro, Brazil; San Francisco; Santiago, Chile; Sierra Leone; Tashkent, Uzbekistan; Tbilisi, Republic of Georgia; Washington, DC
Affiliates: International Freedom of Expression Exchange

STAFF

190 total—plus short-term fellows, consultants, interns, and volunteers

TAX STATUS

501(c)(3)

FINANCES

Budget: 2003—$21.7 million; Revenue: 2002—$20.37 million

FUNDING SOURCES

Individual and foundation contributions

PAC

None

EMPLOYMENT

All full-time staff vacancies are posted on the Web site. Interested applicants should follow the application instructions posted.

INTERNSHIPS

Human Rights Watch offers academic semester and summer internships for undergraduate and graduate students in the New York, Washington, and Los Angeles offices. Internships are generally unpaid, although work-study funds are available. Academic credit can usually be arranged. Shorter restricted internships are also available. Refer to the Web site for full details. Interested students should submit resume, writing sample, references, and cover letter directly to the internship coordinator in the department of

CONTACT INFORMATION

350 Fifth Avenue, 34th Floor, New York, NY 10118-3299
Phone: (212) 290-4700 • *Fax:* (212) 736-1300
General E-mail: hrwnyc@hrw.org • *Web site:* www.hrw.org

Communications Director: Kay Seok
(212) 216-1832 • HRWpress@hrw.org
Human Resources Director: Maria Pignataro Nielsen

PURPOSE: "Dedicated to protecting the human rights of people around the world . . . to prevent discrimination, to uphold political freedom, to protect people from inhumane conduct in wartime, and to bring offenders to justice. We investigate and expose human rights violations and hold abusers accountable."

CURRENT CONCERNS: Abuses by governments worldwide • Academic freedom and freedom of expression • AIDS • Arms • Corporations and human rights • Death penalty • Drugs and human rights • Forced trafficking of women and girls • Police abuse • Prison conditions • Refugees • Women's and children's rights

METHOD OF OPERATION: Awards program • Coalition forming • Fellowships • Films/audiotapes • International activities • International film festival • Internships • Legislative/regulatory monitoring (international, federal, and state) • Library/information clearinghouse • Litigation • Media outreach • Research • Web site

Effectiveness and Political Orientation

"U.S. operations in Afghanistan are marred by needless civilian casualties and the alleged torture of prisoners, Human Rights Watch said in a report issued today.

"The U.S. military rejected the group's findings, saying it 'confused the situation' in strife-torn Afghanistan for one where peacetime methods could be used.

" 'The behavior of the United States sends the message that the U.S. operates on a set of double standards,' the New York-based rights group said, referring to U.S. criticism of other countries' human-rights records.

"The 50-page report said the military used excessive force to capture or kill suspects in residential areas. In one attack, six children were killed; nine children died in another.

"The military says it modified its procedures after the deaths of the children. 'We're not perfect,' U.S. military spokesman Lt. Col. Bryan Hilferty said. "But we work hard to improve.

"The report also criticized U.S. treatment of some of the estimated 1,000 Afghans and other nationals arrested in Afghanistan since 2002, saying there

their choice. New York: Human Rights Watch, 350 Fifth Avenue, 34th Floor, New York, NY 10118-3299. Phone: (212) 290-4700. Fax: (212) 736-1300. E-mail: hrwnyc@hrw.org. Washington: Human Rights Watch, 1630 Connecticut Ave, NW, Suite 500, Washington DC, 20009. Phone: (202) 612-4321. Fax: (202) 612-4333. E-mail: hrwdc@hrw.org. Los Angeles: Human Rights Watch, 11500 W. Olympic Boulevard, Suite 445, Los Angeles, CA 90064. Phone: (310) 477-5540. Fax: (310) 477-4622. E-mail: hrwla@hrw.org.

NEWSLETTERS

Human Rights Watch Update (monthly)

PUBLICATIONS

The following is a sample list of publications:
Azerbaijan: Crushing Dissent
Burmese Refugees in Bangladesh: Still No Durable Solution
Civilian Deaths in the NATO Air Campaign
Confessions at Any Cost: Police Torture in Russia
Crime or Custom: Violence Against Women in Pakistan
Cuba's Repressive Machinery: Human Rights Forty Years After the Revolution
Egypt: In a Time of Torture
"Enduring Freedom": Abuses by U.S. Forces in Afghanistan
Freedom of Expression Still Threatened
Genocide, War Crimes and Crimes Against Humanity
Getting Away with Murder, Mutilation, and Rape
Human Rights Watch World Report
Killing Civilians and Silencing Protest
Liberia: How to Fight, How to Kill
New U.S. Landmine Policy: Questions and Answers
Nobody's Children
Punishments and Prejudice: Racial Disparities in the War on Drugs
Rape As a Weapon of "Ethnic Cleansing"
The Silencing of Dissent
Thailand: Out of Sight, Out of Mind
Tibet Since 1950: Silence Prison or Exile
Torture, Trumped-up Charges and a Tainted Trial
Also publishes films.

CONFERENCES

Annual dinner
Human Rights Watch International Film Festival

were 'credible and consistent' allegations that prisoners were beaten, deprived of sleep and shackled for long periods."

(*The Seattle Times*, March 8, 2004)

"The (U.K.) government has been accused of undermining the international criminal court in the Hague by bowing to American pressure for a new extradition treaty.

"The British decision has caused dismay among rights groups. It means anyone extradited from the US to Britain will not be handed over to the international criminal court. . . .

"Richard Dicker, counsel to Human Rights Watch, the respected New York-based international group, said: 'Britain played a leading role in setting up the court and it was in the Labour manifesto.

" 'The international criminal court is not another state, and the perverse result of this could mean that a person extradited from the US for one offence could use Britain as a safe haven if they are being sought for horrific crimes against human rights.' "

(*The Guardian* [London, England], March 2, 2004)

"President Bush will bar the U.S. military from using certain types of land mines after 2010 but will allow forces to continue to employ more sophisticated mines that the administration argues pose little threat to civilians, officials said yesterday.

"The new policy, due to be announced today, represents a departure from the previous U.S. goal of banning all land mines designed to kill troops. That plan, established by President Bill Clinton, set a target of 2006 for giving up antipersonnel mines, depending on the success of Pentagon efforts to develop alternatives.

"Bush, however, has decided to impose no limits on the use of 'smart' land mines, which have timing devices to automatically defuse the explosives within hours or days, officials said. . . .

"Bush's decision drew expressions of outrage and surprise from representatives of humanitarian organizations that have pressed for a more comprehensive U.S. ban on land mines. They say the danger to civilians and allied soldiers during and after a war outweighs the benefits of such weapons. They also dispute the contention that unexploded smart mines are safe, saying there isn't enough evidence to know.

" 'We expected we wouldn't be pleased by the president's decision, but we hadn't expected a complete rejection of what has been U.S. policy for the past 10 years,' said Steve Goose, who heads the arms division of Human Rights Watch.

" 'It looks like a victory for those in the Pentagon who want to cling to outmoded weapons, and a failure of political leadership on the part of the White House. And it is stunningly at odds with what's happening in the rest of the world, where governments and armies are giving up these weapons.' "

(*The Washington Post*, February 27, 2004)

"Demographics of the black community affect both turnout and voter agendas, said David Bositis, a researcher with the Joint Center for Political and Economic Studies.

"One reason for higher participation among black women than black men is that a greater percentage of black men—more than 20 percent in some

Southern states—are convicted felons and have lost their right to vote, he said. His claim is supported by a 1998 study by the Sentencing Project, an advocacy organization for prisoners' rights, and Human Rights Watch, an organization that monitors human rights internationally."

(*The Atlanta Journal-Constitution,* February 15, 2004)

"Wend Patten is the type of brief you want on your side when you get into trouble. Fast-talking, clever and determined to win, the advocacy director of the civil-liberties group, Human Rights Watch, is one of scores of American lawyers fighting to extend the rule of law to Guantanamo Bay. Before she took her campaign to Britain last week, she reasoned there were two means of helping the detainees: either America's allies could put pressure on the Bush administration to soften its policies, or the US Supreme Court could intervene."

(*The Observer* [London, England], February 8, 2004)

"It should be cause for satisfaction, even catharsis, if not celebration. A special tribunal is being set up to try top people in Saddam Hussein's regime for genocide, torture, mass slaughter, and other atrocities. Human Rights Watch, a respected international lobby group, reckons that at least 290,000 Iraqis were murdered in the last two decades of Mr Hussein's rule; that figure excludes those—probably many more—who died as a result of wars started by Mr Hussein. Nor does it include the millions of Iraqis who suffered in other ways. Bringing the chief perpetrators to book and creating a new system of law must surely be applauded."

(*The Economist* [London, England], December 13, 2003)

"Liberians have fought for both government forces and rebels in Ivory Coast during the civil conflict triggered by an attempted coup last year, a report published today by a respected human rights group will claim.

"The report by Human Rights Watch, the US-based campaigning group, acknowledges that the Ivory Coast conflict was 'mainly spurred by internal grievances and movements' but says the neighbouring states of Liberia, Burkina Faso and Guinea all played roles in its evolution.

"The document highlights the close links between the civil war in Liberia and other conflicts in a troubled region of west Africa characterised by mass poverty, a breakdown in the rule of law and youths with access to arms and the ability to roam freely across porous borders. . . .

"Human Rights Watch details abuses by loyalist and rebel forces, including executions, sexual violence against women and looting of property. The report calls for an international commission of inquiry."

(*Financial Times* [London, England], August 5, 2003)

The Humane Society of the United States

Established in 1954

DIRECTOR

Wayne Pacelle, chief executive officer. Pacelle, appointed chief executive officer in April 2004, is the organization's leading spokesperson. He joined HSUS in 1994 as vice president for government affairs and media and was promoted to senior vice president for communications and government affairs in 1998. Pacelle has been instrumental in helping pass more than a dozen new federal laws to protect animals, more than 15 statewide ballot initiatives, and countless laws at the state level. He has helped to secure millions in federal dollars for enforcement of federal laws to protect animals in the United States and abroad. Pacelle previously served as executive director of The Fund for Animals, the national advocacy group founded by author Cleveland Amory. He graduated from Yale University in 1987.

BOARD OF DIRECTORS

Patricia Mares Asip
Peter A. Bender
Donald W. Cashen
Anita W. Coupe
Judi Friedman
Alice R. Garey
David John Jhirad
Jennifer Leaning
Amy Freeman Lee
Eugene W. Lorenz
Jack W. Lydman
William F. Mancuso
Patrick L. McDonnell
Judy J. Peil
Joe Ramsey
Jeffrey O. Rose
James D. Ross
Marilyn G. Seyler
Walter J. Stewart
Maurice F. Strong
John E. Taft
David O. Wiebers
Marilyn E. Wilhelm
K. William Wiseman

SCOPE

Members: More than 8 million members and constituents
Branches/chapters: Central States Regional Office (IL, KY, NC, TN, WI); Great Lakes Regional Office (IN, MI, OH, WV); Mid-Atlantic Regional Office (DE, NJ, NY, PA); Midwest Regional Office (IA, KS, MN, MO, NE); New England Regional Office (CT, MA, ME, NH, RI, VT); Northern Rockies Regional Office (CO, MT, ND, SD, UT, WY); Pacific Northwest Regional Office (AK, ID, OR, WA); Southeast Regional Office (AL, FL, GA, MS, SC); Southwest Regional Office (AZ, AR, LA, NM, OK, TX); West

CONTACT INFORMATION

2100 L Street, NW, Washington, DC 20037
Phone: (202) 452-1100 • *Fax:* (202) 778-6132
General E-mail: membership@hsus.org • *Web site:* www.hsus.org

Communications Director: Nicholas Braden
(301) 258-3072 • nbraden@hsus.org
Human Resources Director: Robert Roop, vice president of human resources and education
(301) 548-7715 • broop@hsus.org

PURPOSE: The mission of The Humane Society of the Unites States is to create a humane and sustainable world for all animals, including people, through education, advocacy, and the promotion of respect and compassion.

CURRENT CONCERNS: Animal cruelty • Animal fighting • Animal protection issues • Canned hunting • Factory farming • Fur and trapping • International trade • Pain and distress in research animals • Pet overpopulation • Puppy mills • Urban wildlife

METHOD OF OPERATION: Advertisements • Awards program • Coalition forming • Conferences/seminars • Congressional testimony • Congressional voting analysis • Demonstrations • Films/video/audio tapes • Grant-making • Grassroots organizing • Information clearinghouse • Initiative/referendum campaigns • International activities • Internet (e-mail alerts and Web site) • Internships • Legal assistance • Legislative/regulatory monitoring (federal) • Legislative/regulatory monitoring (state) • Litigation • Lobbying (federal) • Lobbying (state and grassroots) • Local/municipal affairs • Media outreach • Participation in regulatory proceedings (federal and state) • Professional development services • Research • Scholarships • Training

SPECIFIC PROGRAMS/INITIATIVES: Animals in research • Companion animals and equine protection • Farm animals and sustainable agriculture • Field and disaster services • Government affairs • Investigative services • Marine mammal protection • Wildlife and habitat protection

Effectiveness and Political Orientation

"In a few weeks, the spring flood will begin at animal shelters across the Washington area—an annual incoming tide of unwanted puppies and kittens.

"Some animal advocates, though, see signs of hope that their increasingly aggressive campaign to persuade people to spay and neuter their pets—a push that began in the mid-1970s—is having an impact. Nationally, even as pet ownership has increased, the number of cats and dogs euthanized each year has dropped to an estimated 3 million or 4 million a year, according to the Humane Society of the United States. . . ."

(The Washington Post, February 22, 2004)

Coast Regional Office (CA, NV, HA); Hollywood Office (formerly know as Ark Trust, this office produces the yearly Genesis Awards)
Affiliates: EarthVoice; National Association for Humane and Environmental Education; The Center for Respect of Life and Environment; The Wildlife Land Trust; Humane Society International (Serving Australia and Europe); Cape Wildlife Center

STAFF
292 total—259 full-time professional; 33 full-time support; plus 2 volunteers; 2 interns

TAX STATUS
501(c)(3)

FINANCES
Budget: 2004—$80.8 million; 2003—$72.1 million; 2002—$67.5 million

FUNDING SOURCES
Foundation grants, 5%; corporate/individual donations, 86%; publications, 1%; conferences, 1%; investment income, 4%; marketing/other, 3%

PAC
None

EMPLOYMENT
Employment opportunities at HSUS are available on the Web site, www.hsus.org, in various animal related publications, and in local newspapers and media sources. HSUS hires animal cruelty investigators, attorneys, wildlife biologists, marketing and communications experts, accountants, program experts, animal scientists, animal sheltering professionals, and veterinarians. Interest applicants should send a cover letter and resume to Nancy Allen, employment manager, 2100 L Street, NW, Washington, DC 20037. Phone: (301) 548-7757. Fax: (301) 548-7767. E-mail: nallen@hsus.org.

INTERNSHIPS
HSUS offers paid and unpaid internships that are typically 8 weeks in length. The application deadline varies. Hours are based on specific internship. Internship areas include animal research issues, government affairs, wildlife, the cape wildlife center, communications, and human resources. Additional information is available on the Web site. The internship coordinator is Nancy Allen, employment manager, 2100 L Street, NW, Washington, DC 20037. Phone: (301) 548-7757. Fax: (301) 548-7767. E-mail: nallen@hsus.org.

NEWSLETTERS
All Animals (quarterly)
Animal Sheltering Magazine (bimonthly)
Humane Living E-Newsletter (weekly)
HUMANElines (weekly)
KIND News™ (monthly September–May)
Pain & Distress Report (quarterly)
The Rural Area Veterinary Services (RAVS)
     E-Newsletter (monthly)

"Fraternity brothers have dropped a puppy off a Mississippi River bridge, beaten a goose to death with a golf club and abandoned an unconscious, intoxicated pig in a park. . . .

"These and other acts on campuses across the country have drawn the furor of animal lovers and others who say such abuse has grown into a dangerous trend because it is too often treated as college high jinks.

"'Animal cruelty is a crime and certainly can't be accepted. Years ago, it had to be made clear that rape is a crime,' said Ann Chynoweth, counsel to investigative services for the Humane Society of the United States.

"She recently wrote to the North-American Interfraternity Conference, asking it to educate its 350,000 undergraduate members about animal cruelty and its connection to human violence.

"But Pete Smithhisler, spokesman for the Indianapolis-based fraternity organization, dismissed the idea that animals are in any more danger at fraternity houses than anywhere else.

"'No, we don't believe it's a trend,' he said. 'I'm sure it came to light because it was a fraternity. Do we think that incidents like these happen everywhere? Yeah.'

"The Humane Society said the puppy's death at Quincy University in Illinois, the goose beating at Davidson College in North Carolina and the pig incident at Wake Forest back up its claims. . . .

"The Humane Society has asked the North-American Interfraternity Conference to add to its expectations for fraternity members recognition that the humane treatment of animals is part of living with respect for others. Academic integrity, drug and alcohol use, and abuse to human beings and property are already addressed. . . ."

(The Washington Post, February 8, 2004)

"The Bush administration took sweeping action Tuesday to rebuild public confidence in the nation's beef supply by banning the use of meat from all sick or lame animals—including so-called downer animals . . . —those that cannot walk to slaughter. . . .

"In acting exactly one week after the nation's first case of mad cow disease surfaced in a 6½-year-old Holstein dairy cow in Washington state, Agriculture Secretary Ann Veneman went well beyond previous Bush administration policy and adopted a position that food safety campaigners and animal rights activists had been pushing in Congress.

"Veneman's order will block an estimated 150,000 to 200,000 out of the 35 million cows and cattle slaughtered in the U.S. annually. Downer animals, which currently are used for ground beef, often come from dairies, which need to remove low milk producers from their herds. In all, the country has about 105 million head of cattle.

"Veneman's action was praised by Wayne Pacelle of the Humane Society of the United States, a group that has been campaigning for the downer ban for years, mainly on animal rights grounds. Such animals generally have to be dragged, lifted or pushed to slaughter.

"'We're enormously pleased that the government has reconsidered its position and agrees with our position,' Pacelle said. 'This will provide better assurances to the American people that the beef supply is safe and will eliminate one of the worst cruelties in the food production system.'"

(The San Francisco Chronicle, December 31, 2003)

PUBLICATIONS

CONFERENCES

National Conference of Animal in Disaster,
    location varies, every two years
Animal Care Expo, location varies, annually
First Strike Workshops, location and frequency
    vary
Wild Neighbors Workshops, location and
    frequency vary

"Nationally, as many as 40,000 people participate in organized dogfighting, says the Humane Society of the United States. And at least tens of thousands more are 'street fighters,' says Eric Sakach, director of the West Coast regional office of the Humane Society. He's also an expert on dogfighting. 'Street fighters' are people whose dogs may occasionally fight for small wagers or neighborhood bragging rights. The dogs are often shown off and fought by gang members. . . ."

"Dogfighting is hard to investigate because of the secretiveness of the dog owners.

"The appearance of a single unfamiliar face at a fight will cause the organizers to call it off, said Curt Ransom, the chief of investigations for the Humane Society of Missouri, but fights just go on somewhere else. . . .

"Enforcement of dogfighting laws often falls into a gray area. Flowers, the animal control officer, believes police should make it a priority to arrest people for dogfighting and seize the animals. But Doyle said gaining control over dangerous dogs is an animal control responsibility.

"The problem is compounded by the fact that Humane Society officers are often first on the scene of animal abuse cases but have no law enforcement powers.

" 'There is no other criminal activity where you have non-law enforcement officers assigned to investigate it,' Brownstein said. "If people are not getting arrested and having their dogs seized, there is little disincentive to just keep on doing it.

"Arrests for dogfighting are on the rise around the nation, said Sakach, of the Humane Society."

(*St. Louis Post-Dispatch,* November 16, 2003)

"Before a cheering crowd, the two combatants—hopped up on stimulants and trained in the martial arts—rush to the attack. Blood flows freely as they stab each other repeatedly with curved steel spikes known as gaffs. The match often ends when one is carried lifeless from the ring.

"It sounds like a scene from "Gladiator," but the reality is more mundane: The fighters are chickens, and the sport is cockfighting, a traditional if gory pastime with thousands of devoted followers in the three states—Louisiana, Oklahoma and New Mexico—where it is not yet against the law.

"Congress may finally take a step toward ending the practice. After several failed efforts over the last two years, animal protection groups and their congressional allies—led by Sen. Wayne Allard (R-Colo.), a veterinarian—have succeeded in including a ban on the interstate transport of fighting birds in the farm legislation that passed the House earlier this year and is now being debated in the Senate.

"The ban would close a loophole in the 1976 Animal Welfare Act that permits 'gamecock' breeders to ship their birds to states and countries where cockfighting is still legal. In the absence of such a ban, proponents of the measure say, cockfighting has continued to thrive even in states where it is supposedly against the law, because enthusiasts have an excuse for owning the birds and associated gear.

" 'It gives them a rationale for possessing the birds,' said Wayne Pacelle of the Humane Society of the United States. 'It's like having a drug law that says you can't smoke cocaine but you can grow it, possess it and ship it elsewhere.' "

(*The Washington Post,* December 17, 2001)

IFAW (International Fund for Animal Welfare)

Established in 1969

DIRECTOR

Frederick "Fred" O'Regan, president. Before becoming president of IFAW, O'Regan was Peace Corps regional director for Europe, Central Asia, and the Mediterranean. Prior to his work for the Peace Corps, O'Regan was program director with the Aspen Institute and head of the Community Economics Corporation, a policy and consulting organization specialized in developing local-level economic and development programs in the United States and the Third World. During the 1992–1993 academic year, O'Regan was visiting professor of public and international affairs at the Woodrow Wilson School, Princeton University, where he taught community-based economic development. From 1984–1989, he headed the Kenya Rural Enterprise Program, an intermediary finance and training organization for small- and micro-enterprise development. He founded and co-directed the Development GAP (1977–1984), an advocacy and consulting organization in international development. O'Regan was program director of the Community Action Program in Cambridge, MA, from 1974–1977, and he began his career as a Peace Corps volunteer in Swaziland (1969–1972).

BOARD OF DIRECTORS

Angelica Argon; actress, environmentalist
Manilal Premchand Chandaria; chair, Mabati Rolling Mills, Ltd.
John Garamendi; insurance commissioner, State of California
Brian Hutchinson; business consultant, Corporate Affairs, Community and Charitable Giving Specialist
Margaret A. Kennedy; finance manager, See Forever Foundation
Christopher J. Matthews; journalist and talk show host, MSNBC and CNBC
Thomas P. O'Neill III; chief executive officer, O'Neill and Associates
Thomas C. Ramey; executive vice president, Liberty Mutual Insurance Co. and president, Liberty International
Gary M. Tabor; program officer, Wilburforce Foundation
Carol A. Wolfson; president, Wolfson and Associates

SCOPE

Members: 3.1 million individuals and others
Branches/chapters: International Fund for Animal Welfare (Australia); International Fund for Animal Welfare Inc./Fonds International Pour La Protection des Animaux, Inc.; International Marine Mammal Association, Inc.; International Fund for Animal Welfare (France); IFAW Internationaler Tierschutz-Fonds gGmbH;

CONTACT INFORMATION

75 Attucks Lane, Hyannis, MA 02601
Phone: (508) 744-2000 • *Fax:* (508) 744-2009
General E-mail: info@ifaw.org • *Web site:* www.ifaw.org

Communications Director: Patrick Ramage, director of public affairs
(508) 744-2071 • pramage@ifaw.org
Human Resources Director: Melanie Powers, chief financial officer
(508) 744-2141 • mpowers@ifaw.org

PURPOSE: "IFAW . . . works to improve the welfare of wild and domestic animals throughout the world by reducing commercial exploitation of animals, protecting wildlife habitats and assisting animals in distress. IFAW seeks to motivate the public to prevent cruelty to animals and to promote animal welfare and conservation policies that advance the well being of both animals and people."

CURRENT CONCERNS: Assisting animals in distress • Commercial exploitation of animals • Protecting wildlife habitats

METHOD OF OPERATION: Advertisements • Awards program • Conferences/seminars • Congressional testimony • Demonstrations • Direct action • Films/video/audiotapes • Grant-making • Grassroots organizing • International activities • Internet (databases, e-mail alerts, and Web site) • Internships • Legal assistance • Legislative/regulatory monitoring (federal and state) • Media outreach • Polling • Product merchandising • Research • Speakers program • Technical assistance • Training

Effectiveness and Political Orientation

"One of Russia's best orphanages is thriving thanks to British fundraisers.

"But this exceptional home in remote Bubonitsy village is not for children—it cares for young bears orphaned when hunters kill or disturb their mothers.

"The pioneering work is made possible by the not-for-profit organisation, International Fund for Animal Welfare, and a remarkable Russian family who have dedicated their lives to saving the cubs. . . .

"Since the IFAW started backing their work in 1996, more than 100 cubs have been saved and returned to the wild."

(*The Express on Sunday* [London, England], April 4, 2004)

"The lobster industry is in the process of replacing floating ground lines—the rope that connects a chain of lobster pots—with sinking ones in hopes that the ropes will be closer to the seafloor and out of the path of whales.

"It's too early to say if these and proposed changes will reduce the number of right whale entanglements, said Jennifer Ferguson-Mitchell of the International Fund for Animal Welfare.

IFAW European Union; Stichting IFAW-Internationaal Dierenfonds (Nederland); International Fund for Animal Welfare (association incorporated under Section 21); IFAW Charitable Trust; IFAW Promotions Ltd.; IFAW Trading Ltd.; IFAW Japan; IFAW Russia; IFAW China; IFAW East Africa, Kenya; IFAW Latin America
Affiliates: None

STAFF
268 total—70 full-time professional; 183 full-time support staff; and 15 part-time support staff; plus 5 interns

TAX STATUS
501(c)(3)

FINANCES
Revenue: 2004—$60,694,624; 2003—$55,125,429; 2002—$52,566,708

FUNDING SOURCES
Individuals, 97%; foundation grants, 1%; in-kind donations and list rental income, 1%; corporate donations, less than 1%

PAC
None

EMPLOYMENT
Employment openings are advertised at www.ifaw.org/employment, *The Boston Globe, Cape Cod Times, Chronicle of Philanthropy*, ECO.com, Hotjobs.com, and Monster.com. Positions are in the areas of administration, marketing, development, finance/accounting, public relations, customer service, information technology, and campaigning. Cover letters and resumes can be mailed to Vikki Morris, Human Resources, 411 Main Street, Yarmouth Port, MA 02675. Fax: (508) 744-2119. E-mail: recruitus@ifaw.org.

INTERNSHIPS
Paid internships are advertised at www.ifaw.org/employment. Hours, application deadlines, and duration of internships vary by project and department. Internships are available in these program areas: wildlife and habitat, animals in crisis and distress, public affairs, and finance. For information, contact Lisa Milligan, chief executive officer special assistant, 75 Attucks Lane, Hyannis, MA 02601. Fax: (508) 744-2129. E-mail: recruitus@ifaw.org.

NEWSLETTERS
Our Shared World (quarterly)

PUBLICATIONS
The following is a sample list of publications:
Building Marine Awareness in the Caribbean
Creating a Better World for Animals and People
Disaster Preparation Tips for You and Your Animal Companions
Elephants on the High Street. An Investigation into Ivory Trade in the UK
Fighting Against Commercial Whale Slaughter
General IFAW Brochure

"Based in Cape Cod, Mass., the group recently joined with Massachusetts lobstermen and federal lawmakers to launch a pilot gear-exchange program to help fishermen absorb the higher cost of whale-safe fishing gear.

" 'It will be several years before there's enough gear in the water to evaluate the success of it,' Ferguson-Mitchell said."
(*The Post and Courier* [Charleston, S.C.], April 2, 2004)

"An international coalition has launched another campaign against Canada's seal hunt, saying the ocean mammals deserve the same protection as whales and African elephants.

"But a top independent marine scientist and the federal Fisheries Department say the group's argument is not based on science. . . .

"The harp seal population was estimated at 5.2 million in 1999, said Ken Jones, a senior fish management official in Ottawa. That was up from 1.8 million in the early 1970s and 4.8 million in 1994.

"Nevertheless, over 300 groups on six continents support the anti-sealing campaign, the International Fund for Animal Welfare said Monday.

"The fund has coordinated several anti-sealing offensives over the years but IFAW spokesman Rick Smith warned this one would be particularly aggressive.

" 'Animal welfare advocates and conservationists are serving notice that they will not sit idly by while the Canadian government embarks on a truly historic attack on these defenseless animals,' Smith said in a statement."
(*The Associated Press State & Local Wire*, November 25, 2002)

"A bizarre, nearly five-year struggle between the state of New Jersey and an Ocean County woman who loves and raises tigers is due to end Tuesday when the two dozen big cats at her private compound are shipped to a preserve in Texas.

" 'This is not as uncommon as people think,' said Chris Cutter, a spokesman for the International Fund for Animal Welfare, a relief agency campaigning to end private ownership of big cats. 'There are at least 10,000 tigers being kept as pets in the U.S., and there are only 5,000 in the wild in Asia.

" 'Tigers breed really well in captivity, and there are not a lot of laws that prohibit people from doing this,' he said."
(*Associated Press Newswires*, November 10, 2003)

"The big-game hunter raised a stainless-steel rifle and peered through its scope. He shifted the cross hairs from one bull to the other. In a lifetime of travel and trekking, the hunter, Pete Studwell, had killed 11 bears, 10 elk, 6 caribou, 3 moose, 2 musk oxen, 2 boars, a bison, a cougar and roughly 300 deer, part of a personal list of bagged animals that includes 45 categories of big game. He had never killed a walrus. Until a half-hour earlier, when the boat began threading through Arctic ice, he had never seen one in the wild. . . .

"Standing to Studwell's left, Caleb Iqqaqsaq, an Inuit guide, watched his father, Cain, who worked the wheel in silence as the boat shrunk the range. 'Get ready,' Caleb said. 'I will tell you when the time is.'

"The bulls rocked and grunted, more curious than afraid. The boat passed inside 15 yards, just beyond the distance a man might spit. The old Inuk nodded. His son whispered into Studwell's ear: "Shoot."....

"It is precisely this behavior that confounds antihunting sensibilities. Many elements of this sport hunt, including the hunter's motivation and the species' limited range, are rich material for animal-rights activism. Yet the Inuit, by merging modern markets with tradition, have largely escaped criticism. 'The public makes a clear distinction between subsistence and nonsubsistence hunting,' says Rick Smith of the International Fund for Animal Welfare, the organization whose protests from the 1960's to 1980's restricted markets for seal skins. 'Although I think the Inuit kind of weaken the ground they are on when they start mixing it up with these list hunters.' "

(The New York Times, August 25, 2002)

In Defense of Animals

Established in 1983

DIRECTOR
Elliot M. Katz, president. Katz founded In Defense of Animals (IDA) in 1983. A graduate of the Cornell University School of Veterinary Medicine, he is a practicing veterinarian and a community outreach coordinator.

BOARD OF DIRECTORS
Elliot Katz, DVM, president
Alex Hershaft, treasurer/secretary
Vicky Ho Lynn
Theresa Macellaro
Betsy Swart

SCOPE
Members: 80,000
Branches/chapters: None
Affiliates: None

STAFF
32 total

TAX STATUS
501(c)(3)

FINANCES
Revenue: 2002—$3.42 million; 2001—$3.09 million

FUNDING SOURCES
Donations and grants, 85%; interest, royalties, and other income, 7%; bequests, 6%; other, 2%

PAC
None

EMPLOYMENT
Open positions are posted on the Web site. For more information about jobs, contact Elliot Katz, In Defense of Animals, 131 Camino Alto, Suite E, Mill Valley, CA 94941. Phone: (415) 388-9641. Fax: (415) 388-0388. E-mail: ek@idausa.org.

INTERNSHIPS
Available internships are posted on the Web site. For more information about intern positions, contact Elliot Katz, In Defense of Animals, 131 Camino Alto, Ste. E, Mill Valley, CA 94941. Phone: (415) 388-9641. Fax: (415) 388-0388. E-mail: ek@idausa.org.

NEWSLETTERS
In Defense of Animals (quarterly)
In Defense of Animals: News Alert (weekly E-newsletter)

CONTACT INFORMATION
131 Camino Alto, Suite E, Mill Valley, CA 94941
Phone: (415) 388-9641 • *Fax:* (415) 388-0388
General E-mail: ida@idausa.org • *Web site:* www.idausa.org

Communications Director: Information unavailable
Human Resources Director: Information unavailable

PURPOSE: "To end the abuse and exploitation of animals by defending their rights, welfare, and habitat."

CURRENT CONCERNS: Animal experimentation • Animals for sport • Antifur campaign • Antipet theft campaign • Boycott Petland • Campaign to end cruel animal experimentation • Circuses • Dissection • Dog abuse in Korea • Elephant campaign • Elevating the status of animals • Eliminating marine mammal captivity • Foie gras • Marine mammals • Pet theft • Promoting plant-based diet • Puppy mills • Unwanted animals • Veganism

METHOD OF OPERATION: Advertisements • Awards programs • Boycotts (Boycott Procter & Gamble campaign) • Coalition forming • Congressional testimony • Demonstrations • Direct action • Films/video/audiotapes • Grantmaking • Grassroots organizing • Internet (e-mail alerts and Web site) • Internships • Legal assistance • Legislative/regulatory monitoring (federal and state) • Litigation • Lobbying (federal) • Local/municipal affairs • Media outreach • Product merchandising • Research • Shareholder resolutions • Speakers program

Effectiveness and Political Orientation

"Oregon trappers working to clear areas of animals that kill livestock or damage crops will have to inspect their traps every 76 hours under new regulations adopted Friday by the state Fish and Wildlife Commission.

"The commission's 4–2 vote provides specific guidance on the 2001 Legislature's vague and open-ended requirement that so-called restraining traps for "nuisance animals" such as coyotes, rabbits and rodents be checked "on a regular basis." Killing traps already had to be checked monthly under state rules.

"State law already requires traps to be checked every 48 hours when the quarry is "fur animals," such as mink. Animal-rights activists lobbied the commission to apply the same requirement to all traps.

" 'The message that the Oregon Department of Fish and Wildlife sends is that convenience for the trapper outweighs being humane,' Connie Durkee, a member of In Defense of Animals, said following the Friday vote. 'No wild animal should have to suffer needlessly.' "

(*The Oregonian* [Portland], February 7, 2004)

PUBLICATIONS
Offers a catalogue of publications on animal rights, including reports, brochures, and fact sheets.

CONFERENCES
Information unavailable

"Bowing to pressure from cat lovers, Harbor-UCLA Medical Center executives have agreed to a temporary ban on the roundup, removal and possible killing of feral cats as they consider other ways to control the felines, officials said Wednesday.

"The moratorium has raised the cat advocates' hopes that medical center executives will formally adopt a trap, sterilize and return approach to reduce the number of feral cats roaming the Torrance campus. . . .

"Dismayed by the possibility that feral felines could be euthanized if deemed unadoptable, cat caregivers pushed for a meeting to discuss their preferred method of trap-sterilize-return. . . .'I wanted to go right to the top,' said Bill Dyer, regional director of In Defense of Animals, an international animal protection group with headquarters in the San Francisco Bay Area.

"Persistent calls to Medical Director Gail Anderson's office resulted in a meeting Friday with Anderson, assistant administrator Calvin Kwan. . . .

" 'I think they realize that the trap-neuter-return is the only method that is practical and realistic,' Dyer said. 'Death to the cats is not a solution to the problem.'. . ."

(*The Los Angeles Times,* February 5, 2004)

"Michael Bilger, chef at the chic Restaurant Caneros, has it on his Christmas menu: 'Seared foie gras with persimmon bread pudding and pomegranate gastrique.'

"Carlo-Alessandro Cavallo, owner and chef at the celebrated Sonoma Meritage restaurant, likes to serve his foie gras northern Italian-style, wrapped in ravioli and drenched in a white truffle, butter and sage sauce.

"Needless to say, both chefs were a bit steamed last week when animal rights advocates presented the Sonoma City Council with a petition to ban the sale of foie gras in this California capital of wine and haute cuisine.

"Drafted by In Defense of Animals, an organization based in Marin County, the petition contends that the centuries-old process of force-feeding ducks and geese to produce the fattened-liver delicacy constitutes cruelty to animals.

"After hearing from both sides, the City Council took no action on the proposal. 'We are neither going to debate or vote on the foie gras issue,' said a testy Mayor Dick Ashford, who was surrounded by television cameras in the cramped council meeting space. City attorneys have even questioned the town's authority to ban a food product legally produced in the state.

"But, like it or not, this quaint wine-and-cheese tourist town has become the front line in the ongoing foie gras war. . . ."

(*The Los Angeles Times,* November 29, 2003)

"Trendy cuisine is the raison d'etre in Sonoma, but these days some activists want to halt what is served at white-linen restaurants.

"A petition signed by about 500 people will be presented tonight to the Sonoma City Council, asking for a ban on the sale of foie gras—fattened goose or duck liver—anywhere inside the city limits.

"Animal-rights activists call foie gras the "delicacy of despair," claiming that the fowl suffer horribly from the forced feedings that swell the livers to 12 times the normal size just days before slaughter. They hope their non-binding petition will enlighten Sonoma residents about how foie gras is made.

" 'Due to national media coverage of the inherent suffering involved in foie gras, Sonoma has become synonymous with animal cruelty,' reads the petition. 'I urge you to support an ordinance banning the sale of foie gras in the town of Sonoma. Doing so would restore Sonoma's image as well as promote the humane treatment of animals in our society.'

"Foie gras has become a flashpoint in the Sonoma Valley, where organic and hormone-free food and the conditions under which animals are raised have long been part of the food culture. The French delicacy already has prompted two lawsuits and thousands of dollars in vandalism. . . .

" 'I think the petition is an important way to help stop this perverse cruelty to animals,' said Dr. Elliot Katz of In Defense of Animals in Mill Valley. . . ."

(*The San Francisco Chronicle*, November 19, 2003)

"File it under the category of Sounds Good—well, at first anyway. The San Francisco Board of Supervisors voted last week to designate pet owners as pet 'owners or guardians.'

"Elliot Katz—president of In Defense of Animals, an animal rights organization in Mill Valley, and supporter of the measure—says that the term 'guardian' reminds the public that pets are not possessions that can be neglected, or discarded when inconvenient. 'Rather than thinking of themselves as an owner of disposable property,' Katz noted, pet guardians should be 'less likely to chain up the animal all alone in the backyard,' and more likely to treat the family dog as 'a member of their household.' . . .

"Katz assures me that the new language won't prompt lawsuits from neighbors who think it's pet neglect when 'guardians' leave the dog out all night. . . .

"Katz argues that animals should have the same legal rights as children. He doesn't mean dogs should be able to drive or vote, (kids either), he explained, but they should have 'rights that protect them from abuse.'

"The problem is, if animals' rights mirror children's rights, euthanizing a dog is abuse. When you look at it through the eyes of an animal, as Katz tells me he likes to do, raising animals for food is abuse. First owners become 'guardians,' then pets become near-human. Next, the line between pets and livestock blurs.

"I asked Katz point-blank if he thinks it should be illegal to kill animals, as in livestock. 'I think under certain circumstances there should be times when it is OK, and times when it's not OK,' Katz replied. 'Just like in times of war, it's OK to kill people.'. . ."

(*The San Francisco Chronicle*, January 19, 2003)

The Independent Institute

Established in 1986

DIRECTOR
David Theroux, president.

BOARD OF DIRECTORS
David J. Theroux, founder, president, and chief executive officer

Robert L. Erwin; chair and chief executive officer, Large Scale Biology Corp.

James D. Fair III; chair, Algonquin Petroleum Corp.

John S. Fay; president, Piney Woods Corp.

Peter A. Howley; co-founder, IP Wireless, Inc.

Bruce Jacobs; president, Grede Foundries, Inc.

Willard A. Speakman III; president and chief executive officer, Speakman Co.

W. Dieter Tede; president, Audubon Cellars & Winery

Mary L. G. Theroux; former chair, Garvey International, Inc.

Peter A. Thiel; founder, former chair and chief executive officer, PayPal, Inc.

SCOPE
Members: Information unavailable
Branches chapters: None
Affiliates: OnPower.org, FDAReview.org, EntrepreneurialEconmics.org, iFeminists.com

STAFF
12 total—7 professional; 5 support; plus 134 research fellows; 2 interns

TAX STATUS
501(c)(3)

FINANCES
Revenue: 2002—$1.66 million; 2001—$1.9 million

FUNDING SOURCES
Foundations, 30%; business, 23%; sales, 21%; individuals, 20%; other, 6%

PAC
None

EMPLOYMENT
Job postings are available online at www.independent.org and are also published in the Institute's quarterly journal, *The Independent Review*. Resumes and cover letters can be sent to Martin Buerger, chief operating officer, The Independent Institute, 100 Swan Way, Oakland, CA 94621. E-mail: MBuerger@independent.org.

CONTACT INFORMATION
100 Swan Way, Oakland, CA 94621
Phone: (510) 632-1366 • *Fax:* (510) 568-6040
Toll-free: (800) 927-8733
General E-mail: info@independent.org • *Web site:* www.independent.org

Communications Director: Pat Rose, director of public affairs
(510) 632-1366 • prose@independent.org
Human Resources Director: Ken Barnes
(510) 632-1366

PURPOSE: The Independent Institute is a nonprofit, nonpartisan, scholarly public policy research, and educational organization that sponsors comprehensive studies (including articles, books, and policy papers) of critical social and economic issues.

CURRENT CONCERNS: Public policy debates about social and economic issues

METHOD OF OPERATION: Advertisements • Awards program • Conferences/seminars • Congressional testimony • Films/videos/audiotapes • International activities • Internet (database, e-mail alerts, and Web site) • Internships • Library/information for members only • Local/municipal affairs • Media outreach • Research • Scholarships • Speakers program • Student fellowships (Olive W. Garvey Fellowships) • Television programs • Training

Effectiveness and Political Orientation

"For years, Pentagon officials planned around the 'one-and-a-half war' scenario—one major war (in central Europe, for example) and another smaller simultaneous conflict somewhere else in the world. . . .

"Now, it appears, Pentagon planners have to worry about how to handle the aftermath of even 'half' a war—particularly as it affects the hundreds of thousands of troops rotated in and out of peacekeeping and nationbuilding duty.

"And most of the challenge involves the numbers of soldiers, sailors, airmen, and marines that can be counted on.

" 'Avoiding a personnel crisis in the all-volunteer military has become the chief force management challenge for Secretary Rumsfeld and his successor,' says Michael O'Hanlon of the Brookings Institution in Washington, 'much more so than transforming the armed forces or relocating overseas bases.'

"To compensate, Army troops from Germany and marines from Okinawa are being rotated into Iraq.

" 'Rumsfeld already had tendencies to pull troops out of existing deployments—Europe and maybe even Korea,' says defense analyst Ivan Eland of the

Internships of negotiable duration (some for pay) are occasionally available. Interested applicants should contact the Institute by phone at (510) 632-1366. The Institute also has year-round, eight-week internships for college students. These internships pay $700 per month. Interns in this program work under the direction of institute fellows and conduct policy research on topics such as high technology and antitrust, environmental policy, crime and security, money and finance, or health and welfare. Interns write policy-related newspaper op-eds or magazine articles and by giving radio interviews related to their research.

Students studying economics, law, public policy, political science, or related social sciences are preferred. Interested students may send college transcript(s), two writing samples (term papers are adequate), cover letter outlining academic and career goals, and available dates to Carl Close, academic affairs director, The Independent Institute, 100 Swan Way, Oakland, CA 94621. Fax: (510) 568-6040. E-mail: cclose@independent.org.

NEWSLETTERS

The Independent Newsletter (quarterly)
The Independent Review: A Journal of Political Economy (quarterly)
The Lighthouse (online weekly)

PUBLICATIONS

Changing the Guard: Private Prisons and the Control of Crime
Drug War Crimes: The Consequences of Prohibition
Faulty Towers: Tenure and the Structure of Higher Education
Market Failure or Success: The New Debate
Reclaiming the American Revolution: The Kentucky and Virginia Resolutions and Their Legacy
Strange Brew: Alcohol and Government Monopoly
Also publishes policy reports, commentary, and transcripts and tapes of Independent Policy Forums.

CONFERENCES

Monthly policy forums, occasional conferences
Annual week-long summer seminar in political economy (June).

Independent Institute in Oakland, Calif. 'The stretch because of Iraq has likely strengthened those tendencies.'"

(*The Christian Science Monitor,* March 18, 2004)

"Trust traditionally is invested in the president when the nation goes to war, but recent polls indicate support for President Bush may be eroding, according to Ivan Eland, senior fellow and director of the Center on Peace & Liberty at The Independent Institute, a public policy group.

"As long as the war is going well, Americans support the president, said Eland, who heads the center founded earlier this year. It is a resource for research and information on the war and on its impact on civil liberties, economic welfare, national security and peace. The Independent Institute is based in Oakland, Calif. . . .

"While the majority of this week's Think Tank panelists are behind President Bush on Iraq, Eland said, polls show support is shifting on whether the nation should have gone to war. Bush's general popularity is declining as the public begins to focus on the issues.

"Support is slipping for a number of reasons. Among them, he said, is the recently released investigation into Sept. 11, 2001. Among other findings, it revealed U.S. intelligence bungled clues that could have led the FBI to some of the terrorists.

"Furthermore, Eland said, the United States waged war in Afghanistan on the basis of finding Osama bin Laden. U.S. forces are still there trying to rebuild the country, and bin Laden remains at large.

"Likewise, it is unknown how long soldiers will be in Iraq as the U.S. seeks to rebuild it. The longer the U.S. is there and the more soldiers die, Eland said, the more questions will be raised about why Iraq was attacked."

(*Pittsburgh Post-Gazette,* August 3, 2003)

"The Independent Institute has announced that national security expert Dr. Ivan Eland has joined the Oakland, Calif.-based think tank. Eland will to head the organization's new Center on Peace and Liberty.

"'At this moment of looming crisis from a pre-emptive war by the United States in Iraq, we are fortunate to have such a highly regarded authority on domestic security, defense, and foreign policy joining us as senior fellow and director of our new Center,' said David J. Theroux, founder and president of the institute. . . .

"Eland's widely published commentaries on these topics have appeared in national newspapers and periodicals, and he has provided analysis for both radio and television news programs. Eland has also testified on related issues before committees of the U.S. Senate and House of Representatives. He is also the author of a new book, *Putting 'Defense' Back into U.S. Defense Policy: Rethinking U.S. Security in the Post-Cold War World.*

"Theroux said that II's new Center for Peace and Liberty will 'enhance and deepen II's role as an independent, non-partisan voice in the ongoing dialog and debate on public policy.' In the polarized world of policy think tanks, where politically biased organizations routinely characterize themselves as nonpartisan, the Independent Institute is almost universally regarded as perhaps the only truly unbiased think tank.

"The board of advisors for the Center on Peace and Liberty includes scholars and policy experts such as former Assistant Defense Secretary Lawrence

Korb, Bruce Russett of Yale, Harvey Sapolsky of MIT and Monica Toft of Harvard.

"Eland has been director of defense policy studies at the Cato Institute, the principal defense analyst at the Congressional Budget Office, the evaluator-in-charge for the U.S. General Accounting Office in the area of national security and intelligence, and investigator for the House Foreign Affairs Committee."

(*United Press International,* March 6, 2003)

"While then Governor George W. Bush was campaigning for president, he proposed a $45 billion increase in annual spending over the next decade. By comparison, then Vice President Al Gore proposed a $100 billion increase over the same period.

"After the events of Sept. 11, 2001, it appears that President Bush will be keeping his campaign promise.

"But given that the current enemy facing the U.S. is a decentralized network of terrorist organizations, has the Bush administration made the case that military spending should continue at Cold War levels?

"No, says economist Robert Higgs, Senior Fellow at The Independent Institute. Among his books are *Arms, Politics and the Economy* and *Crisis and Leviathan: Critical Episodes in the Growth of American Government* (Oxford University Press).

" 'The Pentagon's business-as-usual defense policy—obviously—failed to defend the American people on Sept. 11. Nor will it defend them in the future,' writes Higgs in a forthcoming article.

" 'Just possibly, what's good for Lockheed-Martin, the top brass at the Pentagon, and the congressman in cahoots with them is not necessarily good for national security.'

"Higgs' *Etceteras* column, 'The Cold War Is Over, but U.S. Preparation for It Continues' appeared in the quarterly journal he edits, *The Independent Review,* before the events of Sept. 11.

"In his study, Higgs notes that in 1999, 'the U.S. accounted for 36 percent of world military expenditure.' By comparison, 'U.S. allies Japan, France, Germany, the United Kingdom, and Italy ranked second through sixth, respectively, and as a group accounted for 26 percent. Russia ranked seventh.'

"Higgs also points out that during the Cold War years (1955-65 and 1974-80), defense spending averaged $281 billion (dollars in 1999 purchasing power). That trend continued, as the average level of annual defense spending from 1995 through 2000 was $278 billion (dollars in 1999 purchasing power). . . ."

(*U.S. Newswire,* January 29, 2002)

Independent Sector

Established in 1980

DIRECTOR

Diana Aviv, president and chief executive officer. Aviv "joined Independent Sector in 2003 after spending nine years at United Jewish Communities as vice president for public policy and director of the Washington Action Office. She was formerly associate executive vice chair at the Jewish Council of Public Affairs, director of programs for the National Council of Jewish Women, and director of a comprehensive program to serve battered women and their families. She has had a private psychotherapy practice in New York and New Jersey and served as expert witness in capital cases in New Jersey. She currently serves as chair of the National Immigration Forum, is an advisory board member of the Stanford Social Innovation Review, and is a member of the Board of Governors for the Partnership for Public Service. A native of South Africa, Diana graduated with a B.S.W. from the University of Witwatersrand in Johannesburg and received her Master of Social Work degree at Columbia University."

BOARD OF DIRECTORS

John R. Seffrin, chair; chief executive officer, American Cancer Society

Paula Van Ness, treasurer; president and chief executive officer, Make-A-Wish Foundation of America

Diana Aviv, president; president and chief executive officer, Independent Sector

Gary L. Yates, vice chair; president and chief executive officer, California Wellness Foundation

Christopher Gates, secretary; president, National Civic League

Board Members

Edward H. Able Jr.; president and chief executive officer, American Association of Museums

Angela Glover Blackwell; president, PolicyLink

Kathleen W. Buechel; president, Alcoa Foundation

Hodding Carter III; president and chief executive officer, John S. & James L. Knight Foundation

Robert W. Edgar; general secretary, National Council of Churches of Christ in the USA

Lewis M. Feldstein; president, New Hampshire Charitable Foundation

David Ford; chief executive officer, Richard and Susan Smith Family Foundation

Barry D. Gaberman; senior vice president, Ford Foundation

Brian Gallagher; president and chief executive officer, United Way of America

Marilda Gándara; president and executive director, Aetna Foundation

CONTACT INFORMATION

1200 18th Street, NW, Suite 200, Washington, DC 20036
Phone: (202) 467-6100 • *Fax:* (202) 467-6101
General E-mail: info@independentsector.org •
Web site: www.independentsector.org

Communications Director: Patricia Nash, vice president for communications and marketing
patricia@independentsector.org
Human Resources Director: Keith Greenidge, assistant director, human resources and administration
keith@independentsector.org

PURPOSE: A nonpartisan coalition of national organizations, foundations, and corporate giving programs, collectively representing charitable groups in every state. IS's mission is to promote strengthen, and advance the nonprofit and philanthropic community to foster private initiative for the public good.

CURRENT CONCERNS: Communication among nonprofit organizations • Develop and maintain relations with the federal government • Develop and promote policies to enhance the sector's effectiveness-increase public awareness of the nonprofit sector • Develop leadership to promote the common good • Increase giving and volunteer service • Research on the nonprofit sector-promote accountability in the sector

METHOD OF OPERATION: Advertisements • Awards program • Coalition forming • Conferences/seminars • Congressional testimony • Internet (e-mail alerts and Web site) • Internships • Legislative/regulatory monitoring (federal) • Media outreach • Research • Telecommunications services (fax-on-demand)

Effectiveness and Political Orientation

"During the search for a new president three years ago, Dana-Farber Cancer Institute was so impressed with Dr. Edward J. Benz Jr. that 'we were going to do everything in our power to get him,' the board chairman said.

"So when Benz said Boston's extravagant home prices were a potential obstacle, trustees offered an incentive: a $600,000 no-interest loan for a house. . . .

"Diana Aviv, president of the Independent Sector based in Washington, D.C., the nation's largest coalition of charities and foundations, said she doesn't believe nonprofit organizations should loan employees money—except in rare cases.

"The practice, she said, puts charitable assets at risk because nonprofits don't have the expertise to know whether the borrower is a good risk or a bad risk. It can also lead to conflicts of interest because an organization may be

SCOPE

Members: 650 organizations
Branches/chapters: None
Affiliates: None

STAFF

36 total

TAX STATUS

501(c)(3)

FINANCES

Budget: 2004—exceeds $6 million; 2002—
exceeds $6 million

FUNDING SOURCES

Foundation grants, 60%; membership dues,
35%; conference, 3%; publications sales, 1%;
corporate donations, 1%

PAC

None

EMPLOYMENT

The Web site lists current openings and information on how to apply.

reluctant to fire or discipline an employee who owes it money. There's also the 'opportunity cost'—services the money could have been used for instead.

"But she said housing help may be an exception when done as part of a recruitment package.

" 'With the housing market being as high as it is in Boston, New York, and San Francisco, they may have to offer extra help,' she said. If the recruit is a 'key' employee, the hospital must report the loan or bonus on its annual tax filings . . .

"Aviv said public disclosure is crucial. If trustees know what similar organizations pay, they can better determine if they are offering a reasonable amount. . . ."

(*The Boston Globe*, February 29, 2004)

"It's known in some circles as the 'death tax.' But for many charities and other nonprofit groups it has proved a lifeline.

"By taxing estates of wealthy people who plan to leave assets to their heirs, the United States encourages them to instead give their money away, tax free, to foundations, churches, museums, and a host of other nonprofit organizations.

"Now, the estate tax is slated to disappear for a single year—in 2010—and some legislators and economists are pushing for permanent repeal. They say taxing estates of the richest Americans takes away funds likely to create new businesses and wealth.

"But the federal budget's burgeoning deficit makes permanent repeal less likely. Philanthropies are breathing a sigh of relief. They are disappointed, however, at the failure of Congress to pass proposed new incentives for charitable giving.

" 'We are very discouraged,' says Diana Aviv, president of the Independent Sector, a group representing more than 700 national organizations, foundations, and corporate philanthropy programs."

(*Christian Science Monitor*, November 24, 2003)

"Washington—The House voted overwhelmingly yesterday to expand tax breaks for donations to charity, giving President Bush a long-delayed victory on the least controversial part of his faith-based initiative.

"The House bill, like one adopted earlier this year by the Senate, would allow an estimated 86 million people who don't itemize deductions on their tax returns to deduct part of their donations to charity.

"The 408–13 vote was immediately hailed by charitable groups.

" 'The Charitable Giving Act will provide a lifeline to nonprofits struggling to meet increasing demands with diminished resources,' said Diana Aviv, president of Independent Sector, a coalition that represents thousands of charities."

(*The Plain Dealer* [Cleveland], September 18, 2003)

"A prospective change in postal regulations soon could open the door to mail solicitations that enrich commercial fundraisers operating under the guise of raising money for charitable groups, nonprofit advocates said last week.

"The U.S. Postal Service is expected to publish in the *Federal Register* this week changes to the cooperative mailing rule, which governs the use of less expensive postal rates for fundraising appeals by nonprofits. . . .

"Patricia Read, a spokeswoman for Independent Sector . . . said the change could dramatically increase the flow of unwanted mail and undercut the credibility of all nonprofit fundraising appeals.

"The change would give rise to fundraising arrangements similar to those common in telemarketing, in which a commercial fundraiser calls to solicit money on behalf of a charity, such as a local police benevolent fund, Read said. Donors often believe their entire contribution goes to the charity, but only a fraction does and the rest is kept by the fundraising company.

" 'This now opens the door to those situations where 90 percent or more, or a high percentage of the donation, is being retained by the for-profit entity.'. . ."

(*The Washington Post,* September 2, 2003)

"A major trade association for nonprofit organizations here said today that it did not support legislation in the House that would compel foundations to give more money to charity.

"The decision by the association, Independent Sector, which represents 700 nonprofit and philanthropic institutions, lends significant support to the foundation world, much of which vehemently opposes the proposal. Some people see the stance as awkward for the association, because it opposes a proposal aimed at increasing the charity money. The decision follows a similar announcement on Monday by the National Council of Nonprofit Associations, also in Washington.

"The president of Independent Sector, Diana Aviv, said it had polled its members before making its decision. About 20 percent of the members are foundations, and $1.98 million of its $5.4 million budget last year was from private and corporate foundations. Foundation representatives sit on its board.

" 'We just can't support it at this time,' Ms. Aviv said. 'We don't believe the data is clear as to whether this is a good or a bad thing. Our own staff collected all the studies, and at best, the picture is mixed.' "

(*The New York Times,* June 18, 2003)

INFACT

Established in 1977

DIRECTOR
Kathryn Mulvey, director. Mulvey became an organizer for INFACT in 1989. She studied English and French at the University of North Carolina and taught in China after graduation.

BOARD OF DIRECTORS
Jeffrey L Richardson, director
Wendy Fassett, chair
Michael Ho, treasurer
T. J. Boisseau, director
Mark Schultz, director
Nancy Cole, secretary
Karla Capers, director
Kathy Mulvey, assistant secretary
Patti Lynn, director
Greg Akili, vice chair

SCOPE
Members: 30,000 individuals
Branches/chapters: None
Affiliates: None

STAFF
20 total

TAX STATUS
501(c)(3)

FINANCES
Revenue: 2002—$1.82 million; 2001—$1.32 million

FUNDING SOURCES
Membership dues

PAC
None

EMPLOYMENT
Current openings are available on the INFACT Web site. Resumes and cover letters may be e-mailed to jobs@infact.org to apply for current openings.

INTERNSHIPS
Applicants should have highly effective written and verbal communication skills; excellent computer skills; good organizational skills and the ability to juggle several tasks while meeting deadlines; some experience in a high-energy, campaign, and nonprofit setting, and a commitment to corporate accountability and progressive social change. Opportunities are available throughout the year. Information is available on the Web site. To apply for an internship, send a letter of interest and resume to Internship Coordinator, INFACT Campaign Headquarters, 46 Plympton Street, Boston, MA 02118. Phone: (617) 695-2525. Fax: (617) 695-2626. E-mail: info@infact.org.

CONTACT INFORMATION
46 Plympton Street, Boston, MA 02118
Phone: (617) 695-2525 • *Fax:* (617) 695-2626
General E-mail: info@infact.org • *Web site:* www.infact.org

Communications Director: Information unavailable
Human Resources Director: Information unavailable

PURPOSE: "To stop life threatening abuses of transnational corporations and increase their accountability to people around the world."

CURRENT CONCERNS: INFACT's Hall of Shame documents how corporations have "harmed the environment and public health" • Stopping the tobacco industry from marketing its products to children and young people around the world

METHOD OF OPERATION: Boycotts (tobacco industry boycott, Kraft and Nabisco boycott) • Coalition forming • Demonstrations • Grassroots organizing • Media outreach • Research

Effectiveness and Political Orientation

"Kathy Mulvey has attended every annual meeting of Philip Morris USA for the past 10 years, but she's not a shareholder interested in the dividends of the world's most profitable tobacco company. In 1995, she helped unfurl a 200-foot banner with photos of people whose illnesses or deaths were smoking related. She then used her two minutes at the mike to memorialize 11 such victims. . . .

"Mulvey does not own Altria stock. She borrows the proxies of two convents—one in Kentucky, another in Texas—that own a few shares of stock in order to attend annual meetings where the nuns or their fellow activists lodge protests. Once there, Mulvey challenges Altria's 'deadly practices.'

"Mulvey is the executive director of Infact, a 26-year-old Boston nonprofit that targets what it calls corporate abuse. Infact has had a couple of big successes—notably, the Nestle boycott that brought about reforms in the marketing of infant formula in developing countries, and a boycott of General Electric that forced the industry leader out of the nuclear weapons business.

"Today Infact is poised to score its biggest coup: the ratification of the world's first public health treaty. The treaty would ban tobacco advertising, promotion, and sponsorship, meaning Altria would have to do away with its iconic Marlboro Man and stop sponsoring athletic and cultural events in the countries that ratify it. Cigarette brands would no longer appear on billboards, hats, bags, cafe umbrellas, and other merchandise. . . ."

(*The Boston Globe,* December 23, 2003)

". . . an anti-smoking activist group is criticizing Kraft, a unit of cigarette maker Philip Morris Cos., for holding its shareholders' meeting Monday in East Hanover, N.J.

" 'Philip Morris thinks it can have it both ways—using Kraft Foods to buy goodwill for its tobacco business while trying to convince investors that Kraft is free from the taint of tobacco,' said Kathryn Mulvey, executive director of Infact, a corporate accountability activist group based in Boston.

" 'Philip Morris's decision to hold the Kraft annual meeting in an out-of-the-way location in New Jersey with little fanfare is telling," Mulvey said.

"Kraft spokeswoman Kathy Knuth said the annual meeting is being held at a former Nabisco business headquarters 25 miles from Manhattan that is large enough to seat several hundred people. . . ."

(*Chicago Sun-Times,* April 18, 2002)

"If you see the Marlboro Man taking the L some day, don't be surprised. Chicago is a vital region of Marlboro Country, despite our lack of mountains and horses.

"We're home to Kraft Foods, an important subsidiary of Philip Morris, as well as the Marlboro Man's creator, the Leo Burnett advertising agency. The Marlboro Man might as well be a Bleacher Bum with an unusually big hat.

"That's why protesters were crowding around the steps of the Leo Burnett building last week, calling for the Marlboro Man's retirement. It was part of a national campaign by Infact, a group working for corporate accountability, also promoting its seven-year-old boycott of Kraft products.

"Infact was joined by local organizations including the Chicago Southside Branch of the NAACP and the National Black United Front. The Rev. Michael Pfleger of St. Sabina and the Rev. Paul Jakes of Old St. Paul Baptist Church were part of a delegation that tried to deliver 2,000 anti-Man messages to Burnett executives. They settled for giving the thick stack to an anonymous employee outside the front door.

"Why pick on the Marlboro Man? Because Advertising Age named him the most powerful brand image of the century, and anti-tobacco groups consider him the foremost marketing tool attracting children to smoking. A Centers for Disease Control study found that 60 percent of smokers ages 12 to 18 smoked Marlboros, and that teens favor brands that advertise most heavily. . . ."

(*Chicago Sun-Times,* April 27, 2001)

Institute for American Values

Established in 1987

DIRECTOR

David Blankenhorn, president. Prior to founding the Institute for American Values, Blankenhorn worked as a community organizer in Virginia and Massachusetts. In 1994, Blackenhorn also helped found the National Fatherhood Institute. He served two years as a VISTA volunteer. Blankenhorn has co-edited four books of scholarly essays. He graduated from Harvard University in 1977 and received an M.A. from the University of Warwick in Coventry, England, in 1978.

BOARD OF DIRECTORS

Enola G. Aird; activist mother
David Blankenhorn; president of the board, president of the Institute
Robert P. George; McCormick Professor of Jurisprudence, Princeton University
Sylvia Ann Hewlett; senior scholar, School of International and Public Affairs, Columbia University
Paul J. Klaassen; chair and chief executive officer, Sunrise Assisted Living
JoAnn Luehring; treasurer of the board; partner, Roberts & Holland
Arthur E. Rasmussen; former chair and chief executive officer, Household International
Ivan A. Sacks; attorney, Withers Bergman LLP
Emily D. Smucker; community volunteer
Donald M. Sykes Jr.; educational consultant
William K. Tell Jr.; retired senior vice president, Texaco, Inc.
Kenneth Von Kohorn; founder and president, Von Kohorn Research and Advisory

SCOPE

Members: None
Branches/chapters: None
Affiliates: None

STAFF

6 total

TAX STATUS

501(c)(3)

FINANCES

Revenue: 2003—$1.53 million; 2002—$1.05 million; 2001—$1.11 million

FUNDING SOURCES

Foundation grants, 63%; individual contributions, 32%; publications, 2.5%; other, 2.5%

PAC

None

EMPLOYMENT

Open positions are posted on the Web site.

CONTACT INFORMATION

1841 Broadway, Suite 211, New York, NY 10023
Phone: (212) 246-3942 • *Fax:* (212) 541-6665
General E-mail: info@americanvalues.org • *Web site:* www.americanvalues.org

Communications director: Mary Schwarz
mschwarz@americanvalues.org
Human Resources Director: None

PURPOSE: "To provide research, publication, and public education on major issues of family well-being and civil society."

CURRENT CONCERNS: Children of Divorce • Civil society in the United States • Definition of the human person • Family as a social institution • Fatherhood • Marriage • Motherhood

METHOD OF OPERATION: Conferences/seminars • Congressional testimony • Internet (e-mail alerts and Web site) • Media outreach • Research • Speakers program

Effectiveness and Political Orientation

"It's all over the news: gay and lesbian couples lining up for marriage licenses; jubilant celebrations that homosexuals have shed another unfair disadvantage; opponents fearing the diminishing of the very concept of marriage and proposing to amend the Constitution to make same-sex marriages unlawful.

"And this wry observation from David Blankenhorn: 'The only way anybody is talking about marriage these days is in the context of same-sex marriage.'

"Blankenhorn heads the Institute for American Values, whose all-encompassing theme for the past decade has been the importance of marriage to the well-being of children. The irony of the present situation, he says from his Manhattan headquarters, is that most of the current debate hasn't really been about marriage at all.

" 'The debate is mostly between those who want [to legalize same-sex marriage] because they see it as part of their demand for equal dignity for gays, and those who don't for a host of philosophical and religious reasons,' he said. 'But for all the intensity of the debate, it doesn't take you very far down the road of discussing marriage.'

"So, does Blankenhorn favor gay marriage or oppose it?

" 'I don't have a dog in that fight,' he said. 'What got me into this whole field some 15 years ago was the disturbing phenomenon of father absence. Thirty-five percent of our children are living without their fathers, a fact that exacerbates a whole range of social problems—and almost the entire problem of father absence is due to heterosexual behavior. But that doesn't make the opponents of gay marriage wrong.' "

(The Washington Post, February 23, 2004)

INTERNSHIPS
Information unavailable

NEWSLETTERS
American Values Reporter
Propositions (quarterly)

PUBLICATIONS
*Does Divorce Make People Happy? Findings
    from a Study of Unhappy Marriages*
The Experts' Story of Courtship
*The Family "Rebound" that Wasn't, and the
    Census Report that Failed*
*Hardwired to Connect: The New Scientific
    Case for Authoritative Communities*
*The Marriage Movement: A Statement of
    Principles*
*Watch Out for Children: A Mothers' Statement
    to Advertisers*
*What We're Fighting for: A Letter from
    America*
*Why Marriage Matters: Twenty-One
    Conclusions from the Social Sciences*
Also publishes working papers.

CONFERENCES
Seminars and conferences are held throughout
the year (attendance is by invitation only).

"The divorce wars are heating up. Not those between divorcing parents, but among those who study what happens to the children.

"With more than 1 million children a year experiencing the divorce of parents, the futures of these youngsters are of concern from the halls of Congress, where spending for marriage programs is debated, to the homes of parents. . . .

"The latest researcher with bad news for divorcing parents is Elizabeth Marquardt, a scholar with the Institute for American Values, a think tank on family issues. She presented preliminary findings at the recent 'Smart Marriages' conference in Reno, a gathering of experts who promote healthy marriages. Her full study, which shows that children often grow up torn between two households, will be published in a book in 2004.

"Growing bodies of research are emerging on at least two sides of the debate on the effects of divorce. Marquardt is among those who believe that even under the best of circumstances, children often suffer emotional scars that last a lifetime and have trouble with their own intimate relationships as adults.

"Another camp believes that by and large, the effects of divorce on kids have been overblown. Most emerge as competent, fairly happy adults if the divorced parents can avoid open warfare involving the child. This second camp refers to 'the good divorce' that reduces conflict and puts the welfare of the child first.

"Marquardt hates the term 'the good divorce.' Just because parents don't continue to argue doesn't mean the kids do well, she says.

"The 'good' divorce, Marquardt says, is an 'adult-centered vision. . . . No matter what the level of conflict, a divided family often requires children to confront a whole set of challenges that children in married-parent, intact families do not have to face.'"

(*USA Today,* July 14, 2003)

"A conservative women's group will issue a report today contending that while most college women embrace marriage as a life goal, their pursuit of that objective is undermined by the prevalence of relationships on college campuses that feature sex without commitment.

"The college dating scene leaves many women with two choices when it comes to men: launch intense but vague relationships, or 'hook up' for casual physical encounters, according to the report conducted for the Independent Women's Forum, which has gained attention in recent years with its critique of contemporary feminism.

" 'The social scene on college campuses does not support the aspirations for long-term relationships and marriage that these women say they have,' said Elizabeth Marquardt, co-author of the report and an affiliate scholar at the Institute for American Values. 'Women say they wish there was something in the middle. . . . They wish they could really get to know a guy without necessarily having a sexual relationship.'

"The New York-based Institute, a non-profit group that promotes the importance of family and fatherhood, conducted the report for the women's forum by surveying 1,000 women enrolled at secular four-year colleges. The report's authors said the telephone survey was aimed at filling a void in the national debate about marriage. . . ."

(*The Washington Post,* July 26, 2001)

"Flowers adorned the makeshift altar at the old Town Hall in Boca Raton, Fla. Flanked by their witnesses, Laura Kay and Anthony Scott lit candles and recited their vows. Teary-eyed, the couple exchanged rings.

And then it was done: They were divorced. 'We wanted to end the relationship in a positive way,' says Ms. Kay, a writer and photographer, who with her husband chose to commemorate their breakup with a formal ceremony. . . .

Of course, the idea strikes some people as more than a little off-kilter. David Blankenhorn, president of the Institute for American Values, a New York think tank, says the ceremonies wrongly suggest that divorce is simply part of life rather than a failure. 'I just find that to be a fundamentally misguided notion,' he says."

(*The Wall Street Journal,* May 4, 2001)

"The American family is not 'going to hell,' says gerontologist Vern Bengtson, who wants to ratchet up the debate on the future of the family.

"Based on his new study in the *Journal of Marriage and Family,* Bengtson says America has worked with a definition of family that is too narrow when trying to explain the support divorced parents have. Researchers don't look beyond the couple. But if social scientists pull back to include a bigger picture, to include grandparents, 'we see a lot of hidden linkages between generations that become activated in times of need and crisis.'

" 'We see grandparents who have enormous reservoirs of support to supply when it is needed, as it often is after divorce,' Bengtson says. They give generously of their time and their finances, he says, providing the glue binding families. . . .

"Because grandparents support their grandchildren after parental divorce doesn't mean today's families are healthy, says David Blankenhorn, founder of the Institute for American Values, a think tank that supports keeping families together. 'Sure, you have grandparents who step in after their children divorce, and we admire them. But that is not a socially desirable trend.' "

(*Chicago Sun-Times,* April 12, 2001)

Institute for International Economics

Established in 1981

DIRECTOR

C. Fred Bergsten, director. "Bergsten has been director of the Institute for International Economics (IIE) since its founding. He was previously assistant secretary of the treasury for international affairs, assistant for international economic affairs at the National Security Council, and a senior fellow at the Carnegie Endowment for International Peace, the Brookings Institution, and the Council on Foreign Relations. Bergsten co-chairs the G-8 Preparatory Conference, a gathering of distinguished private citizens from G-8 countries who develop proposals for consideration by the G-8 at their annual summits. He serves on many public policy councils and boards and is the author of numerous books."

BOARD OF DIRECTORS

Peter G. Peterson, chair of the board; chair, Blackstone Group

Anthony M. Solomon, chair of the executive committee; former president and chief executive officer, Federal Reserve Bank of New York; former under secretary of the treasury for monetary affairs

Leszek Balcerowicz, deputy prime minister, Poland

Conrad Black; chair and chief executive officer, Hollinger Inc. and chair, Telegraph Group Limited W.

Bill Bradley; managing director, Allen & Co.

Chen Yuan; governor, China Development Bank

George David; president and chief executive officer, United Technologies Corp..

Jessica Einhorn; dean, SAIS, John Hopkins University

Stanley Fischer; senior vice chair, Citigroup

Jacob A. Frenkel; former governor of the Bank of Israel and former IMF economic counselor and director of research

Maurice R. Greenberg; chair, American International Group

Carla A. Hills; chair, Hills & Co.

Nobuyuki Idei; chair and chief executive officer, Sony Corp.

Karen Katen; president, Pfizer Global Pharmaceuticals

W. M. Keck II; president, Coalinga Corp.

Lee Kuan Yew; senior minister and former prime minister of the Republic of Singapore

Donald F. McHenry; University Research Professor of Diplomacy and International Affairs, Georgetown University

Minoru "Jack" Murofushi; chair, ITOCHU Corp.

Hutham Olayan; president and chief executive officer, Olayan America Corp.

Paul O'Neill; former secretary of the Treasury

CONTACT INFORMATION

1750 Massachusetts Avenue, NW, Washington, DC 20036-1903
Phone: (202) 328-9000 • *Fax:* (202) 659-3225
General E-mail: Helen Hillebrand, administrative assistant, hillebrand@iie. com • *Web site:* www.iie.com

Communications Director: Ed Tureen, director of marketing
etureen@iie.com
Human Resources Director: Information unavailable

PURPOSE: "Devoted to analyzing important international economic issues and developing and communicating potential new approaches for dealing with them. The Institute's studies generally look ahead one to three years; they do not address long-term, theoretical problems."

CURRENT CONCERNS: Chinese exchange rate • Country and regional studies • Debt and development (corruption and governance, debt relief, foreign aid/technical assistance, transition economies, technology and developing countries, World Bank and regional development banks) • Dollar and other key currencies • EU and transatlantic relations • Failure at Cancún • Globalization • International finance/macroeconomics • International trade and investment • Outsourcing in the new economy • Trade and jobs • Trade and labor standards • U.S. economic policy • U.S. steel policy

METHOD OF OPERATION: Book publishing • Conferences/seminars • Congressional testimony • International activities • Media outreach • Research • Speakers program • Web site

Effectiveness and Political Orientation

"Led by bustling business activity in the US and Asia, the global economy has finally begun a strong revival—one that some see turning into a sustainable boom.

"Worldwide economic growth could hit 4 percent or higher this year, well above what was forecast just months ago. A key reason: Low interest rates, set by many nations' central banks after America's stock market meltdown rippled around the world in 2000 and 2001, are bearing fruit in consumer demand.

"A US recovery is now matched by signs of health in Japan. China and India, meanwhile, are roaring ahead so speedily that the talk is about when, not if, they become economic superpowers. . . .

"An underlying factor in this recovery: The balance of economic power in the world is shifting. When 10 more nations and their 70 million people join the European Community May 1, the EC's economy will be about the same size as that of the US.

"The US remains the world's only military superpower. But it has company in the economic sphere. That means the Bush administration may need

SCOPE

Members: None
Branches/chapters: None
Affiliates: None

STAFF

50 total—plus 30 research

TAX STATUS

501(c)(3)

to be less unilateral in economic policies, says C. Fred Bergsten, director of the Institute for International Economics. It can't ignore market forces. So the U.S. has 'no other option' than to be cooperative on trade and similar issues. . . ."

(*Christian Science Monitor,* April 16, 2004)

"Senator John Kerry, the presumptive Democratic nominee for president, says he is opposed to Cafta [Central American Free Trade Agreement] because it fails to protect workers in Central America as well as American workers, 'who are forced to compete hopelessly against companies that abide by no rules whatsoever.'

"To the Bush administration, that sounds like political showboating. Robert B. Zoellick, the United States trade representative, argues that Cafta, with its enforcement clauses to improve labor rights and fines for offenders, has the best labor provisions ever negotiated in a trade agreement. 'No country is doing more than the United States to push for strong labor and environmental provisions in international trade agreements,' Mr. Zoellick said. 'While some other countries talk about labor and the environment in the context of trade, only the United States is actually doing something to integrate these topics as an active part of its trade agenda.'

"The Institute for International Economics, a centrist research group in Washington, recently published a policy brief on labor standards and Cafta, arguing that 'globalization and workers rights are complementary' and that greater respect for the core international labor standards could help spread trade benefits more broadly."

(*The New York Times,* April 6, 2004)

"What could be a more modern dilemma? High-speed data links allow employers to ship white-collar jobs from rich countries to India, China and other nations where workers earn far less.

"Yet losing skilled jobs to low-wage foreign competition is as old as the Industrial Revolution. In the 1830s, the British textile industry became so efficient that Indian cloth makers couldn't compete. The work was outsourced to England, with disastrous consequences for Indian workers. 'The misery hardly finds parallel in the history of commerce,' India's governor general, William Bentinck, wrote to his superiors in London in 1834. . . .

"Wages in India and China, even if rising, are still far from U.S. levels. For instance, Intel Corp., the Silicon Valley semiconductor giant, estimates that its labor rates in India are one-third U.S. levels. This cost advantage will likely last for decades. The history of immigrations suggests that if outsourcing spreads, the wages of U.S. workers who compete with Indians and Chinese will suffer.

"Salaries of U.S. computer programmers, whose work has been outsourced abroad for more than a decade, were flat between 2000 and 2002, after inflation, according to Jacob Kirkegaard, a researcher at the Institute for International Economics, a Washington think tank. The number of U.S. programming jobs declined about 14%, he says. However, he adds that it's hard to distinguish between the effect of outsourcing and the burst of the high-tech bubble of the late 1990s."

(*The Wall Street Journal,* March 29 2004)

FINANCES
Revenue: 2002—$7.23 million; 2001—$7.15 million

FUNDING SOURCES
Foundation, corporation, and individual contributions; program services; investments; sales; and other

PAC
None

EMPLOYMENT
Information about employment opportunities is available on the Web site: http://www.iie.com/institute/jobs.htm.

INTERNSHIPS
Information unavailable

NEWSLETTERS
None

PUBLICATIONS
Debt Sustainability, Brazil, and the IMF
Economic Leverage and the North Korean Nuclear Crisis
Famine and Reform in North Korea
Global Economic Prospects: Through the Fog of Uncertainty
Globalization of IT Services and White Collar Jobs: The Next Wave of Productivity Growth
Is Germany Turning Japanese?
Labor Standards and the Free Trade Area of the Americas
More Pain, More Gain: Politics and Economics of Eliminating Tariffs
Religion, Culture, And Economic Performance
Senator Kerry on Corporate Tax Reform: Right Diagnosis, Wrong Prescription
Steel Policy: The Good, the Bad, and the Ugly
This Far and No Farther? Nudging Agricultural Reform Forward

CONFERENCES
One or more seminars, meetings, or conferences are held almost every week to discuss topical international economical issues.

"Many American computer programmers complain that they're losing their jobs to lower-paid workers in India. The trend toward foreign 'outsourcing' has become a political flashpoint.

"But the trend is less frightening and more promising than you'd think from either the angry talk from unemployed programmers or the scary estimates from consulting firms, argues Catherine L. Mann, an economist at the Institute for International Economics in Washington.

"First, the end of the technology boom, the general economic slump, and the downturn in manufacturing—not foreign programming competition—account for most job losses. Most estimates, Dr. Mann notes, compare the peak of the business cycle and technology boom with today's sluggish economy. That's not a valid comparison.

"Compared with the end of 1999, which was still a good time for programmers, December 2003 data show a 14 percent increase in business and financial occupations, a 6 percent increase in computer and mathematical jobs, and a 2 percent drop in architecture and engineering jobs. New programming jobs may be springing up in India, but they aren't canceling out job growth in the United States.

"The problem for white-collar professionals, as for line workers, is that manufacturing is still in a slump. 'When the production floor doesn't produce any more, the people in the window offices around the building also start to lose their jobs,' Dr. Mann says.

"Over the long run, she argues, the globalization of software and computer services will enhance American productivity growth and create new higher-value, higher-paid technical jobs. . . ."

(*The New York Times*, January 29, 2004)

Institute for Justice

Established in 1991

DIRECTOR

William H. Mellor III, president and general council. From 1986 until 1991, Mellor served as president of the Pacific Research Institute for Public Policy, a nationally recognized think tank located in San Francisco. Under his leadership, the institute commissioned and published the path-breaking books on civil rights, property rights, and technology and the First Amendment that serve as the Institute for Justice's long-term, strategic litigation blueprint. Prior to Pacific Research Institute, Mellor served in the Reagan administration as deputy general counsel for legislation and regulations in the Department of Energy. From 1979–1983, Mellor practiced public interest law with Mountain States Legal Foundation in Denver. Mellor received his J.D. from the University of Denver School of Law in 1977. He graduated from Ohio State University in 1973.

BOARD OF DIRECTORS

David B. Kennedy, chair; president of the Earhart Foundation

Mark Babunovic; vice president, Bank of New York

Arthur Dantchik; Partner at Susquehanna Investment Group

Robert Levy; Senior Fellow in Constitutional Studies at Cato Institute

James Lintott; chair of Sterling Foundation Management

William H. Mellor III, president and general counsel, Institute for Justice

Steven Modzelewski; president of Watermark Management Corp.

Abigail M. Thernstrom; commissioner on U.S. Commission on Civil Rights; senior fellow, Manhattan Institute

Gerrit H. Wormhoudt; attorney, Fleeson, Gooing, Coulson and Kitch

SCOPE

Members: Declined to comment
Branches/chapters: 3
Affiliates: Declined to comment

STAFF

37 total—19 full-time professional; 18 full-time support; plus 1 part-time professional; 5 volunteers and 8 interns

TAX STATUS

501(c)(3)

FINANCES

Budget: 2004—$6.47 million; 2003—$5.8 million; 2002—$4.93 million

FUNDING SOURCES

Individuals, 70%; foundation grants, 30%

CONTACT INFORMATION

1717 Pennsylvania Avenue, NW, Suite 200, Washington, DC 20006
Phone: (202) 955-1300 • *Fax:* (202) 955-1329
General E-mail: general@ij.org • *Web site:* www.ij.org

Communications Director: John E. Kramer
(202) 955-1300 • jkramer@ij.org
Human Resources Director: Brian Montgomery, director of finance & administration
(202) 955-1300 • bmontgomery@ij.org

PURPOSE: Through strategic litigation, training, communication and outreach, the Institute for Justice advances a rule of law under which individuals can control their own destinies as free and responsible members of society. It litigates to secure economic liberty, school choice, private property rights, freedom of speech and other vital individual liberties, and to restore constitutional limits on the power of government. In addition, it trains law students, lawyers and policy activists in the tactics of public interest litigation to advance individual rights. Through these activities, it challenges the ideology of the welfare state and illustrates and extends the benefits of freedom to those whose full enjoyment of liberty is denied by government.

CURRENT CONCERNS: Economic liberty • Entrepreneurship • First Amendment • Freedom of speech • Private property rights • School choice

METHOD OF OPERATION: Advertisements • Conferences/seminars • Congressional testimony • Demonstrations • Grassroots organizing • Information clearinghouse • E-mail alerts • Web site • Internships • Legal assistance • Litigation • Media Outreach • Media Outreach

SPECIFIC PROGRAMS/INITIATIVES: Castle Coalition (grassroots group of small property owners and activists dedicated to ending eminent domain abuse)

Effectiveness and Political Orientation

"Proponents of school vouchers struck against a lawsuit Thursday that's aimed at killing Colorado's plan to pay for low-income students to attend private schools.

"The Institute for Justice, a Washington, D.C.-based advocacy group that has fought for school voucher programs in several states, filed a motion in Denver District Court on Thursday to join the state's defense of the program.

"The motion was filed on behalf of several families who should be given a chance to get their children out of low-performing public schools, said Chip Mellor, the group's president and general counsel.

" 'Nothing in Colorado's constitution or legal history justifies denying educational opportunity to low-income children in failing schools,' Mellor

PAC
None

EMPLOYMENT
Information about employment opportunities is available on the Web site. For more information write or send an email message to: Administrator, Institute for Justice, 1717 Pennsylvania Avenue, NW, Suite 200, Washington, DC 20006. Phone: (202) 955-1300. Fax: (202) 955-1329. E-mail: general@ij.org.

INTERNSHIPS
This organization offers unpaid internships for undergraduates and paid positions for law students. Positions vary in duration, and application deadlines are rotating (early January for summer positions). During the summer, 40 hours are required. Internship areas include litigation support and communications. Eligible, candidates must demonstrate a dedication to free market ideals. More information can be obtained by contacting the Institute for Justice, 1717 Pennsylvania Avenue, NW, Suite 200, Washington, DC 20006. Phone: (202) 955-1300. Fax: (202) 955-1329. E-mail: general@ij.org.

NEWSLETTERS
Liberty & Law (newsletter)
Ize (clipbook)
Carry the Torch (occasional president's message)

PUBLICATIONS
Public Power, Private Gain (first-ever national survey of eminent domain abuse)

CONFERENCES
Annual law student conference training in the tactics of public interest litigation
Castle Coalition (grassroots group of small property owners and activists dedicated to ending eminent domain abuse)

said. 'Parents deserve a voice in this lawsuit and a choice for their children's education.' "

(*The Denver Post,* May 30, 2003)

"The constitutional challenge to the Texas 'homosexual conduct' law that the Supreme Court will take up next week has galvanized not only traditional gay rights and civil rights organizations, but also libertarian groups that see the case as a chance to deliver their own message to the justices. . . .

"Dana Berliner, a lawyer for the Institute for Justice, another prominent libertarian group here that also filed a brief, said, 'Most people may see this as a case purely about homosexuality, but we don't look at it that way at all.' The Institute for Justice usually litigates against government regulation of small business and in favor of 'school choice' tuition voucher programs for non-public schools.

" 'If the government can regulate private sexual behavior, it's hard to imagine what the government couldn't regulate,' Ms. Berliner said. 'That's almost so basic that it's easy to miss the forest for the trees.' "

(*The New York Times,* March 19, 2003)

"The Institute for Justice, the legal organization that successfully helped parents in Cleveland defend their school-choice program before the U.S. Supreme Court, is now turning its focus to the laws that many states use to deny public funding to religious schools for any reason.

"The Supreme Court's 5–4 decision in June bolstered the institute's belief that these state laws are 19th-century relics of anti-Catholic bigotry. The ruling held that under the U.S. Constitution, low-income parents in Ohio could receive public money to pay for tuition at parochial schools since the primary goal of the money was education, not religion. Attorneys for the organization believe it is illegal for states to interpret their constitutions in such a way as to overrule the highest court and discriminate against religious schools. . . ."

(*Tampa Tribune,* November 29, 2002)

"The Dom Perignon started to flow just hours after staffers at the Institute for Justice learned that the Supreme Court had upheld the constitutionality of school vouchers, a ruling leaders of the conservative legal foundation and other leading school choice advocates say will define the future of public education.

" 'This is the most important education case to come out of the Supreme Court since Brown v. Board of Education,' said Clint Bolick, the group's vice president, as supporters joined the champagne party at the organization's Pennsylvania Avenue offices.

While few may agree that the high court's school voucher ruling compares with the landmark 1954 case that outlawed segregation in public schools, there is little doubt the ruling will bolster a broader school choice movement that is already redefining public education.

" 'A court decision like this, if it had gone the other way, it really would have slammed the door shut to a lot of possibilities,' Bolick said. 'I think it would have slowed the inevitable trend toward making education more child-centered.' "

(*The Washington Post,* June 30, 2002)

Institute for Policy Studies

Established in 1963

DIRECTOR

John Cavanagh, director. As director, Cavanagh oversees programs, outreach, and organizational development. Prior to his tenure at the institute, he worked as an international economist for the United Nations Conference on Trade and Development (1978–1981) and the World Health Organization (1981–1982). He also directed IPS's Global Economy Project from 1983–1997. He is the co-author of 10 books and numerous articles on the global economy. Cavanagh received a B.A. from Dartmouth College and an M.A. from Princeton University.

BOARD OF DIRECTORS

Ruth Adams; former director of the Peace and International Cooperation Program, John T. and Catherine D. MacArthur Foundation

Harry Belafonte; singer, actor, producer, and activist

Elsbeth Bothe; retired Baltimore circuit court judge

Robert Borosage; founder and co-director of the Campaign for America's Future, former director of IPS

James Early; director of cultural studies and communication at the Center for Folklife Programs and Cultural Studies at the Smithsonian Institution

Barbara Ehrenreich; political essayist and columnist

Ralph Estes; executive director of Stakeholder's Alliance and senior scholar at the Institute for Policy Studies

Frances Farenthold; attorney

Lisa Fuentes; activist on Latin American and Israeli-Palestinian issues

Nancy Lewis; social activist

Clarence Lusane; assistant professor, School of International Service, American University

E. Ethelbert Miller; chair, Washington DC Humanities Council, core faculty member of the Bennington Writing Seminars at Bennington College, director of the African American Resource Center at Howard University

Lewis Steel; attorney, Steel, Bellman, Ritz & Clark, P.C., New York City

Katrina vanden Heuvel; editor, *The Nation*

SCOPE

Members: 4,200 contributors
Branches/chapters: None
Affiliates: Letelier-Moffitt Memorial Fund for Human Rights, Transnational Institute, Amsterdam

STAFF

30 total

CONTACT INFORMATION

733 15th Street, NW, Suite 1020, Washington, DC 20005
Phone: (202) 234-9382 • *Fax:* (202) 387-7915
General E-mail: Not available • *Web site:* www.ips-dc.org

Communications Director: Scott Williams, co-director of development for membership, communication, and foundations
scott@ips-dc.org
Human Resources Director: Robin Weiss-Castro, director of finance and human resources
robin@ips-dc.org

PURPOSE: "At a time when other think tanks celebrate the virtues of unrestrained greed, unlimited wealth, and unregulated markets, IPS is striving to create a more responsible society—one built around the values of justice, nonviolence, sustainability, and decency."

CURRENT CONCERNS: Democracy action • Drug policy • Economic conversion • Ecotourism and sustainable development • Electoral reform • Foreign policy in focus • Global economy • Migrant domestic workers rights • New internationalism—UN and the Middle East • Nuclear policy • Paths to the 21st century • Peace and security • Progressive challenge • Social action and leadership school • Sustainable energy and economy network

METHOD OF OPERATION: Awards program • Coalition forming • Conference/seminars • Films/video/audiotapes • International activities • Internship program • Media outreach • Research (reports and books) • Speakers program • Television and radio production • Training and technical assistance (Social Action and Leadership School for Activists; co-sponsored with the Fund for New Priorities)

Effectiveness and Political Orientation

"The preferred slogan of those opposed to war with Iraq is 'No blood for oil'—an explicit assumption that the Bush administration, dominated by former oilmen, is going to war primarily to secure Iraq's copious reserves for U.S. oil companies. 'Regime change' to a pro-U.S. government would permit the privatization of Iraq's state-controlled oil resources—and a bonanza for U.S. oil companies,' warns Miriam Pemberton of Washington's left-wing Institute for Policy Studies. Administration officials, on the other hand, reject any oil connection whatsoever. When asked, on CBS radio, whether the likely war is over oil, Secretary of Defense Donald Rumsfeld replied, 'It just isn't. There are certain things like that, myths that are floating around. I'm glad you asked. It has nothing to do with oil, literally nothing to do with oil.'

"Both views are half right. . . . If the Bush administration were gearing its foreign policy to the wishes of the oil industry, in fact, it would have taken an almost exactly opposite course. (Since the Gulf war, U.S. oil companies, eager

TAX STATUS
501(c)(3)

FINANCES
Budget: 2002—$1.7 million

FUNDING SOURCES
Foundation grants, individual donations, investment interest, publications and fees

PAC
None

EMPLOYMENT
Information unavailable

INTERNSHIPS
The internship Web site www.ips-dc.org/projects/internship.htm includes a list of IPS projects and their respective directors. Applicants must submit a completed application form (available on the Web site), resume, cover letter, two letters of recommendation, brief writing sample (no more than three pages), and a transcript (unofficial transcript is okay). Send completed application attention to Dorian Lipscombe, internship program director, via mail or fax; electronically submitted applications will not be considered, nor will incomplete applications. Dorian Lipscombe, Institute for Policy Studies, 733 15th Street, NW, Suite 1020, Washington, DC 20005. Fax: (202) 387-7915.

NEWSLETTERS
PS News (quarterly)

PUBLICATIONS
Protecting Paradise: Certification Programs for Sustainable Tourism and Ecotourism
A Tale of Two Markets: Trade in Arms and Environmental Technology
U.S. Foreign Military Training: Global Reach, Global Power, and Oversight Issues

CONFERENCES
Annual Letelier-Moffitt Human Rights Awards

to exploit Iraqi resources, have lobbied that U.S. sanctions on Saddam Hussein be reduced or even lifted.) On the other hand, even if oil played little or no role in the administration's war plans, it looms large in the restructuring of a post-Saddam Iraq. By my count—based on interviews with White House officials—at least three studies or administration reports have already been issued on this subject, and at least two others have been published by think tanks with close ties to the administration. The State Department has begun a Future of Iraq project, which, during the week before Christmas, hosted a two-day meeting of Iraqi-born oil and gas experts to discuss the country's energy future. . . ."

(*The New Republic,* January 20, 2003)

"Washington's thinking class has gone to war, offering context to the crisis in Iraq and directing smart verbal bombs at the administration, the administration's critics and sometimes at each other on television, radio and in news stories and op-ed columns. . . .

"Meanwhile, at the liberal Institute for Policy Studies, director John Cavanagh said the media was paying more attention to experts from the left than many expected.

" 'Large numbers of Americans have doubts about the war, [so] any story that's written and most TV formats require someone who is critical of the policy. So there is no doubt that has created much more space for IPS, as opposed to the first Gulf War,' he said. . . ."

(*The Washington Post,* March 25, 2003)

"The protest movement is looking to build global campaigns around more corporate targets as well as international financial institutions as it seeks to regain momentum after September 11.

"Campaign leaders gathering in Porto Alegre, Brazil, for the World Social Forum this weekend said that protesters looking for 'wins' should—and would—increasingly focus on large corporations.

"John Cavanagh, director of the Washington-based Institute for Policy Studies and one of the critics of global capitalism who sits on the board of the International Forum on Globalisation, said: 'We need to shift some of our energy away from the key public institutions—the International Monetary Fund, World Bank and the World Trade Organisation—to the drivers of corporate-led globalisation: the corporations.' "

(*Financial Times* [London, England], February 4, 2002)

"Next month, international financial and trade officials will gather in two important meetings—one in Doha, Qatar, and the other in Ottawa—to resume a series of talks that were scheduled before, but questioned after, the attacks on Sept. 11. As they meet, anti-globalization groups will be holding some type of protests, perhaps candle vigils, perhaps marches, in cities around the world.

"Their message, protesters say, warns about the ill effects of globalism, capitalism and world trade on poor nations. But how they express that message, even some leaders of the movement say, will probably bear little resemblance to the marches—often erupting in violence—that put them on the map in recent years.

"Strident demonstrations against globalization may occur in Europe, but protesters in the United States are scrambling to see if they can hold together a movement now that their most effective way of getting attention is out of sync with the national mood. . . .

"While the administration says one way to fight terrorism is by promoting a global policy that is pro-business, protesters say this approach will only make the world less stable. In addition, the administration has used the attacks to justify a new push for 'fast track' authority, which would allow trade agreements to be enacted with little Congressional oversight—another measure long opposed by protesters

"The activists say they are upset with the administration's effort to use the terrorist attacks as a way to push a pro-business agenda and fast-track negotiating authority.

"John Cavanagh, director of the Institute for Policy Studies, said that while Sept. 11 'stopped our movement,' it was beginning to come back. 'The fight has come back in the form of fast track,' he said. 'Groups are already gearing up for a big fight.'"

(*The New York Times,* October 28, 2001)

". . . a labor-oriented progressive think tank. . . ."

(*Chicago Sun-Times,* April 20, 2001)

Institute on Money in State Politics

Established in 1999

DIRECTOR

Edwin Bender, executive director. Bender has been executive director since August 2003. He served as the institute's research director since its creation in 1999. In that role, he led the research functions of the institute, directing both the development of campaign finance databases and analyses of those databases.

BOARD OF DIRECTORS

Larry Makinson; senior fellow, Center for Public Integrity
Adelaide Elm; communications director, Project Vote Smart
Jeff Malachowsky; consultant to foundations and grassroots programs
Geri Palast; executive director, Justice at State Campaign
Dan Petegorsky; executive director, Western States Center
Samantha Sanchez; senior research fellow, Institute on Money in State Politics
Dennis Swibold; associate professor, University of Montana

SCOPE

Members: None
Branches/chapters: None
Affiliates: None

STAFF

19 total

TAX STATUS

501(c)(3)

FINANCES

Revenue: 2002—$1.02 million

FUNDING SOURCES

Foundations

PAC

None

EMPLOYMENT

Information unavailable

INTERNSHIPS

Information unavailable

NEWSLETTERS

Information unavailable

PUBLICATIONS

Campaign Contributions and the Alabama Supreme Court
Campaign Contributions and the Louisiana Supreme Court
Campaign Contributions and the Michigan Court of Appeals

CONTACT INFORMATION

833 N. Main Street, 2nd Floor, Helena, MT 59601
Phone: (406) 449-2480 • *Fax:* (406) 457-2091
General E-mail: Web form: http://www.followthemoney.org/Contact/index.phtml • *Web site:* www.followthemoney.org

Communications Director: Sue O'Connell
(406) 449-2480 • sueo@statemoney.org
Human Resources Director: Information unavailable

PURPOSE: "National nonpartisan, nonprofit organization dedicated to accurate, comprehensive and unbiased documentation and research on campaign finance at the state level. The Institute develops searchable databases, makes them available to the public online, and analyzes the information to determine the role campaign money plays in public policy debates in the states. The Institute also publishes studies and provides technical assistance and resources to reporters, academic researchers and state groups that work on campaign-finance issues."

CURRENT CONCERNS: Campaign finance • Examine how contributions drive public policy debates • Special interests influence across state lines

METHOD OF OPERATION: Conferences/seminars • Information clearinghouse • Internet (databases and Web site) • Media outreach • Research

Effectiveness and Political Orientation

"It used to be simple. An election approached, and local Democratic and Republican parties ran phone banks, pounded doors, and sent mailings urging people to vote for their party slate. . . .

"Much of the national attention on the 2002 law widely known as McCain-Feingold has focused on its effect on the national parties, which no longer can accept unlimited "soft money" contributions. But the law also includes new restrictions and requirements that apply to state and local party committees.

"What if a county party chairman finds a benefactor willing to write a check to the local party? Then the chairman better quiz that donor about other political contributions. Otherwise the donor could wind up violating the new federal law, which caps the total amount they can give to assorted political organizations. . . .

"The sweeping 2002 campaign finance reforms . . . include a host of restrictions on how state and local political committees can participate in federal campaign activity.

"But with basic activities like mobilizing voters, the lines between federal activity and state and local political efforts can be blurry. Party officials have scant legal precedence or experience to guide them, even as they face the prospect of civil or criminal penalties for violations. . . .

CONFERENCES

Information unavailable

"Edwin Bender, executive director of the Institute on Money in State Politics, said it is unclear how strictly the law will be enforced. But he predicted varying troubles nationwide as states with different campaign finance laws grapple with the new federal rules.

" 'You're going to have some serious implementation issues coming up, and you're going (to see) some controversies and it will be different in every state,' Bender said. . . ."

(*St. Petersburg Times* [Florida], March 1, 2004)

"Public interest groups have long criticized the corrosive effect of large financial contributions. It's a problem across the country, said Samantha Sanchez, director of the National Institute on Money in State Politics. Sanchez said many states do not require public accounting of inaugural fund-raising.

" 'I think you're looking at a gap which is a common one,' she said. 'And it always comes at a time when the [political] party is about to stage it's biggest event,' said Sanchez. 'Also right before the legislatures meet, which always bothers me.' "

(*The Atlanta Journal-Constitution,* December 30, 2002)

"Amid the chaos of a legislature scrambling to wrap up its two-year session, lawmakers are in the process of quietly exempting themselves and other candidates for state office from filing Internet-ready reports on who's bankrolling their campaigns.

" 'This is a declaration of war on open government,' said Secretary of State J. Kenneth Blackwell. 'It's totally outrageous that this maneuver would be done in the shadows . . . in the 11th hour of a lame-duck session without public debate.' Under a little-noticed provision slipped into an apparently innocuous bill by a House-Senate conference committee Tuesday afternoon, statewide and legislative candidates no longer would be required to file electronic copies of their campaign-finance reports.

"Instead, paper copies—which often stretch hundreds of pages—could be turned over to the secretary of state's office, which would be responsible for having the information entered into a computer.

"That means crucial campaign-finance filings just before the election might not be available on the Internet until after Election Day, Blackwell said. . . .

"The maneuver bucks a national trend toward more disclosure, said Ed Bender, research director for the National Institute on Money in State Politics, based in Montana.

" 'Why they would want to eliminate disclosure and shut information off to voters is kind of mind-boggling,' he said. . . ."

(*Columbus Dispatch* [Ohio], December 5, 2002)

"When it came to lobbying, the Enron Corporation, and Kenneth L. Lay, its former chairman, were about as persistent as anyone had ever seen in California—or Texas, Tennessee, Oregon and Pennsylvania.

"With lavish campaign contributions, a fleet of lobbyists, personal pitches by top Enron executives and even a phone call from George W. Bush, then governor of Texas, to Tom Ridge, then governor of Pennsylvania, Enron was the biggest player in the state legislatures in the late 1990's, pushing its version of energy deregulation.

"Recent attention in the Enron scandal has focused on the company's efforts to influence Congress and the White House. But Enron had been conducting a similar campaign on the state level, with far less visibility and with considerable success.

"The objective was to break up monopoly control of energy markets by local utilities and change the rules so energy would be deregulated. To a large extent that goal was reached—from 1997 to 2000, 24 states adopted some form of energy deregulation, allowing energy companies like Enron to find new markets. . . .

"This lobbying was backed by hefty campaign contributions, $1.9 million to more than 700 candidates in 28 states since 1997, according to the National Institute on Money in State Politics, a nonprofit group. . . .

"Unlike utilities or consumer groups that lobbied for deregulation in one state or a few, Enron took on the issue nationally. Its unique strategy combined a promise of lower electrical costs by ending utility monopolies with old-fashioned statehouse power politics.

" 'In 4 years, energy deregulation passed in 24 states,' said Ed Bender, executive director of the National Institute on Money in State Politics. 'That's amazing. I don't think you can call it a coincidence. They were trying to make something happen.' "

(*The New York Times,* February 9, 2002)

"While the debate rages on in Washington on whether—or how best—to curb the influence of so-called 'soft money' in national political campaigns, two government watchdog organizations are taking a first look at the possible impact of such spending on elections at the state and congressional district levels.

" 'State Secrets' is a joint project of the Center for Public Integrity in Washington, D.C., and the National Institute on Money in State Politics, based in Helena, Mont.

"The groups issued a preliminary report July 26, and promise a full report early next year. The preliminary report shows that political parties registered at the state level raised more than $600 million during the 2000 elections. . . .

"Those who are seeking to outlaw soft money contend they are just a way of circumventing limits on raising and spending money for election campaigns.

"Sponsors of the 'State Secrets' project have compiled data from elections reports for the 1999–2000 cycle submitted by more than 900 political committees in all 50 states, with an effort to eliminate instances in which soft money was inadvertently reported to the federal and state governments.

"When the full report is completed, breakdowns will be available on how Democrats and Republicans fared, as well as lists of the most generous contributors. . . .

" 'Special interests easily evade national scrutiny by pumping huge sums of soft money into the coffers of state political parties,' said Peter Eisner, acting executive director of the Center for Public Integrity, and Samantha Sanchez, co-director of the Institute on Money in State Politics. 'The role of soft money is well-documented in federal elections, but no one has attempted to calculate the vast amount of cash flowing into and out of state and local party committees—until now.' "

(*The New Orleans Times-Picayune,* August 5, 2001)

Insurance Institute for Highway Safety

Established in 1959

DIRECTOR

Brian O'Neill, president. Prior to serving as president, O'Neill was IIHS executive vice-president and was head of the institute's research and communication programs, responsible for developing and implementing programs to reduce losses resulting from motor-vehicle crashes. He was vice chair of the National Safety Council's Committee on Alcohol and Other Drugs and a member of the National Research Council's Committee on Geometric Design Standards for Highway Improvements. He has also served on the advisory committee for the Department of Transportation's National Accident Sampling System.

BOARD OF DIRECTORS

R. Gregory Ator; chair, president, and chief executive officer, Bituminous Insurance Cos.

Jonathan Bennett; senior vice president, Personal Lines Division, Hartford

Charles Chamness; president, National Association of Mutual Insurance Cos.

Paul Condrin; executive vice president, Personal Lines, Liberty Mutual Insurance Co.

Steve George; senior vice president, Property and Casualty Underwriting, USAA

Douglas S. Joyce; president, ALFA Virginia Mutual Insurance

W. G. Jurgensen; chief executive officer, Nationwide Insurance

Mory Katz; chair and chief executive officer, Response Insurance

Daniel Keddie; business support executive, Royal & SunAlliance

Gary Kusumi; chief executive officer, GMAC Insurance Personal Lines

Michael LaRocco; president and chief operating officer, SAFECO Personal Insurance

Edward M. Liddy; chair of the board of directors; chair, president and chief executive officer, Allstate Insurance Co.

Jeffrey A. Ludrof; president and chief executive officer, Erie Insurance Group

James O. Matschulat; senior executive consultant, Middlesex Mutual Assurance Co.

Don McCubbin; executive vice president, Shelter Insurance

Richard R. McLaughlin Jr.; vice president, Amica Mutual Insurance Co.

W. Neal Menefee; president, Rockingham Group

O. M. Nicely; chair, president, and chief executive officer, GEICO Corp.

Frances D. O'Brien; Senior vice president, Worldwide Underwriting manager, Chubb Group of Insurance Cos.

CONTACT INFORMATION

1005 North Glebe Road, Suite 800, Arlington, VA 22201
Phone: (703) 247-1500 • *Fax:* (703) 247-1588
General E-mail: iihs@highwaysafety.org • *Web site:* www.highwaysafety.org

Communications Director: Russ Rader, director, media relations
(703) 247-1500 • rrader@iihs.org
Human Resources Director: Information unavailable

PURPOSE: "The Insurance Institute for Highway Safety is an independent, nonprofit, scientific and educational organization dedicated to reducing the losses—deaths, injuries, and property damage—from crashes on the nation's highways. The Institute is wholly supported by auto insurers."

CURRENT CONCERNS: All factors in motor vehicle crashes (human, vehicular, and environmental) • Interventions that can occur before, during, and after crashes to reduce losses

METHOD OF OPERATION: Performance ratings/Report cards (companies, products, etc.) • Research • Web site

Effectiveness and Political Orientation

"The Insurance Institute for Highway Safety, a research group from Arlington, Va., funded by car insurers, recently conducted side-impact crash tests on a handful of midsized cars. The results were bleak. Only three—the Honda Accord, Toyota Camry and Chevrolet Malibu—passed. And, then, only when equipped with optional side-impact air bags. . . .

"'A wake-up call' is how Adrian K. Lund, chief operating officer for the Insurance Institute, described it. 'For sure, it shows the importance of side-impact air bags.' But most passenger cars are not equipped with these air bags. . . .

"Of course, the National Highway Traffic Safety Administration has said all vehicles pass its stringent standards before being offered for sale. . . . It bangs their bumpers, runs them into walls, hits them in the sides with motorized sleds at 38.5 mph. Officials say this is proof we're safer than we think. Tests conducted by the Insurance Institute are termed 'severe.'

"No offense, but real world collisions . . . are severe. Statistics show this kind of crash claimed 9,600 lives in 2002. . . .

"What the tests illustrated was this, Lund said: the side structures of most passenger cars need to be strengthened. Also shown was that side-impact air bags can reduce fatalities by 10 percent—and with 'side-curtain' bags that cover the window area, they can reduce them 45 percent.

"Over the years, the government has mandated seat belts and front-impact air bags. Now, it is obvious, we need side-impact air bags as standard equipment, too."

(*Newsday* [New York], April 25, 2004)

SCOPE

Members: More than 65 insurance companies
Branches/chapters: None
Affiliates: Highway Loss Data Institute

STAFF

77 total

TAX STATUS

501(c)(3)

FINANCES

2002—$13.37 million
2001—$13.06 million

FUNDING SOURCES

Wholly funded by automobile insurance companies.

PAC

None

EMPLOYMENT

IIHS's Web site provides information about careers in vehicle testing, includes a description of several job training avenues, and lists agencies that run crash-testing facilities. No specific information about employment with the institute is given.

INTERNSHIPS

Information unavailable

NEWSLETTERS

Status Report (10 times per year)

PUBLICATIONS

About Your Airbags
Advancing Vehicle Safety: The Auto Insurers' Commitment
Beginning Teenage Drivers
Crashworthiness Evaluations
Graduated Driver Licensing: Questions & Answers
Injury, Collision & Theft Losses by make and model, 2000–2002 models

"As law enforcement budgets and traffic enforcement squads shrink, the motoring public is becoming much more reckless and aggressive, with less respect for red lights and speed limits.

"An increasing number of jurisdictions across the country, including a few in Georgia, are trying to fill the void with automated camera enforcement.

"So far in Georgia, Decatur, Savannah, Rome, Marietta and Gwinnett County have taken the lead with red light camera enforcement, authorized by the Legislature in 2001. . . .

"Photo speed enforcement is not legal in Georgia, but many observers regard it as an inevitable step if curbing breakneck speed is to become a serious societal goal. . . .

"Hefty fines of $287 per violation have radically changed driver behavior. In 1998, each camera averaged nine violations a day. Last year, that average dropped to two.

"Anne McCartt, senior research associate for the Insurance Institute for Highway Safety, said evidence abounds from 40 years of use in Europe and elsewhere that automated enforcement is a 'cost-effective way to supplement traditional enforcement resources.'

" 'Do red light cameras reduce violations?' she asked. 'There's no question that they do.'

"The institute said 97 American jurisdictions have red light cameras. It rated Georgia's red light camera law, which limits fines to $70 and prohibits vendors from sharing revenues, as 'good,' one of only six so rated. . . .

"Both McCartt and Bell reported a 'halo effect' of changed motorist behavior spreading to intersections without cameras. . . .

"Leslie Blakey, executive director of the National Campaign to Stop Red Light Running, cited a study indicating automated speed enforcement cut crashes by 19 percent overall, 35 percent in urban areas.

"Without use of automated enforcement, she said, motorists will become even more reckless, since most jurisdictions continue to cut traffic patrols.

" 'People simply don't expect they are going to be pulled over and given a ticket,' Blakey said."

(*The Atlanta Journal-Constitution*, April 2, 2004)

"The 2004 Acura TSX and TL sedans and Nissan's 2004 Maxima were singled out for their safety in frontal crash tests recently conducted by an American insurer-funded trade group.

"The three cars earned the 'best pick' designation from the Insurance Institute for Highway Safety, which tests autos hitting a barrier at 65 km/h.

"The '04 Chevy Malibu and '04 Mitsubishi Galant earned 'good' ratings.

"Receiving the Arlington, Va.-based insurer group's highest mark means a driver wearing a seat belt probably will walk away from a crash.

"The Maxima and the Galant have improved from an initial 'poor' grade, the lowest of four grades, when the institute began the tests in 1995. . . .

"The trade group said the air bag failed in the first test of the Verona because of a wiring defect, prompting the Japanese automaker to fix vehicles that had been sold and change production procedures."

(*The Toronto Star* [Canada], March 27, 2004)

"A vehicle's score in a highly publicized insurance industry crash test may not be a good indicator of the chance of survival in a crash, the results of a study out today suggest.

CONFERENCES
Information unavailable

"Occupants in vehicles rated good are three times less likely to die if they hit a vehicle that is rated poor in the Insurance Institute for Highway Safety's crash test. But occupants of vehicles rated anything other than poor have about the same survival chances. . . .

"IIHS says its offset test, so named because a portion of the front end of a vehicle hits a portion of a barrier, mirrors a more common real-world crash than the straight head-on crash test the government does. . . .

"IIHS acknowledged that the link between its test results and a reduction in fatalities was most evident in frontal crashes between similar-sized vehicles.

"David Harless, a Virginia Commonwealth University economist who studies car crashes, says IIHS' study shows its ratings are of only limited use. . . .

" 'To the extent that consumers look to these ratings, they think of them as being a general indicator of safety in a serious crash.'

"Lund acknowledges, 'There are an awful lot of kinds of crashes.' But he says that while the findings don't 'translate directly into other kinds of crashes . . . the additional protection would translate.'

"Automakers, who have redesigned many of their vehicles to do well in the test, have mixed feelings about them.

"Vann Wilber, safety director for the Alliance of Automobile Manufacturers, says the ratings could mislead consumers because they require so many caveats. 'Having said that, it is clear that manufacturers are working to improve their ratings, which should be a good thing for consumers.' "

(*USA Today,* February 5, 2004)

"An alliance of 15 major auto manufacturers and the insurance industry yesterday launched a voluntary pact to make pickup trucks and sport utility vehicles safer by lowering stances and padding interiors with air bags.

"The promise, which is nonbinding, says that by 2007, half of a manufacturer's products must feature side air bags. And by Sept. 1, 2009, 100 percent must be equipped with them. Front air bags are already standard on virtually all vehicles. . . .

"The agreement between the Alliance of Automobile Manufacturers and the nonprofit, industry-funded Insurance Institute for Highway Safety calls for lowering the bumpers of SUVs and pickups, or installing additional 'blockers' below the bumper that will 'fully engage' the passenger-car bumper, according to Robert Strassburger, vice president for safety and harmonization for the auto alliance. The group represents manufacturers on three continents that sell more than 98 percent of all cars sold in the United States. . . .

"Strassburger said at a news conference in Washington yesterday that lower stances could reduce fatalities in collisions between so-called light trucks (vans, SUVs, and pickups) by 16 to 28 percent. Side impact bags, he said, could cut deaths by as much as 45 percent. . . .

"However, critics of the agreement say the industry likely agreed to the plan to avoid facing tougher standards and they also point out the pact does not address the problem of rollovers, which cause 61 percent of deaths in SUV and pickup truck crashes, compared to 23 percent in cars, according to records tracing such fatalities from 1993 through 2002.

"Strassburger denied the announcement was made to avoid regulation, adding that the agreement came about because of 'a challenge by the National Highway Traffic Administration in February.' That's when Jeffrey W. Runge, the NHTSA administrator, caused a huge flap by saying he did not want his children riding in SUVs. . . ."

(*The Boston Globe,* December 5, 2003)

The Interfaith Alliance/
The Interfaith Alliance Foundation

Established in 1994

DIRECTOR

C. Welton Gaddy, president. Author of more than 20 books, the Rev. Dr. Gaddy leads the national nonpartisan grassroots and educational organizations, The Interfaith Alliance and The Interfaith Alliance Foundation, and serves as the Pastor for Preaching and Worship at Northminster (Baptist) Church in Monroe, LA.

BOARD OF DIRECTORS

Gwynne M. Guibord, chair
Sumeet Kaur-Bal, vice chair at large
Marvin Chiles, vice chair at large
Jack Moline, vice chair at large
Alexander Forger, secretary
David J. Gelfand, treasurer
Herbert D. Valentine, founding president
Jane Holmes Dixon, immediate past
    president
W. Mahdi Bray
Amos C. Brown
Joan Brown Campbell
Norma Curtis Cohen
David Currie
Denise Davidoff
Arun Gandhi
Maher Hathout
Leonard B. Jackson, director emeritus
Frederick C. James, director emeritus
T. Kenjitsu Nakagaki
Albert M. Pennybacker, past president
Staccato Powell
Gardner Taylor, director emeritus
William P. Thompson, director emeritus
Foy Valentine, past president
J. Philip Wogaman

SCOPE

Members: 150,000 individuals
Branches/chapters: 47 local alliances
Affiliates: None

STAFF

14 total—12 full-time professional; 2 full-time support; plus 6 interns

TAX STATUS

501(c)(3)

FINANCES

Budget: 2004—$711,221; 2003—$838,976; 2002—$1 million

FUNDING SOURCES

Foundation grants, 68%; individuals, 19%; special events/projects, 8%; other: Internet, 2%; interest, 1%; religious organizations, 2%

PAC

None

CONTACT INFORMATION

1331 H Street, NW, 11th Floor, Washington, DC 20005
Phone: (202) 639-6370 • *Fax:* (202) 639-6375
General E-mail: info@interfaithalliance.org •
Web site: www.interfaithalliance.org

Communications Director: John Lynner Peterson
(202) 639-6370 • jpeterson@interfaithalliance.org
Human Resources Director: Cecelia Smith-Budd, director of finance and administration
(202) 639-6370 • csmith-budd@interfaithalliance.org

PURPOSE: To promote the positive and healing role of religion in public life through encouraging civic participation, facilitating community activism, and challenging religious political extremism.

CURRENT CONCERNS: Religious liberty

METHOD OF OPERATION: Advertisements • Awards program • Conferences/seminars • Congressional testimony • Educational foundation • Internet (databases, electronic bulletin boards, e-mail alerts, and Web site) • Internships • Legislative/regulatory monitoring (federal) • Media outreach • Polling • Speakers program • Mailing lists • Voter registration

SPECIFIC PROGRAMS/INITIATIVES: One Nation, Many Faiths. 2004 Election Year Program

Effectiveness and Political Orientation

"The Interfaith Alliance's 'One Nation, Many Faiths: Vote 2004' kickoff Wednesday brought together leaders of faith-based groups representing Christian, Sikh, Muslim and Unitarian Universalist organizations, among others.

" 'We are registering voters to see that people of faith and goodwill function as an important part of the election, not first and foremost as Democrats, Republicans and independents, but as people of faith and goodwill who care about this nation,' said the Rev. Welton Gaddy, president of the Interfaith Alliance, a religious grass-roots organization. . . ."

(*The Washington Post,* February 7, 2004)

"Even before Sept. 11, 2001, Jawad Khaki was trying to improve communication between people.

"As a Microsoft corporate vice president, he oversees work connecting different computers using the company's Windows operating system.

"After the terrorist attacks, Khaki's 'networking' became a more personal mission.

EMPLOYMENT

Potential applicants can learn about job openings with this organization by consulting the TIA Web site, idealist.org, or *The Washington Post*. This organization offers positions in administration, marketing, communications, organization, policy, and religious affairs. Applicants should send resumes and other materials for employment to Cecelia Smith-Budd, director of finance and administration, 1331 H Street, NW, 11th Floor, Washington DC 20005. Phone: (202) 639-6370. Fax: (202) 639-6375. E-mail: employment @interfaithalliance.org.

INTERNSHIPS

Information about internship opportunities is posted on the Web site, idealist.org, and is available at campus career fairs. Both paid and unpaid positions are offered, and internships last 3 to 4 months. Application deadlines are rolling; at least 20 hours a week are required, with a maximum of 40 per week. Internship areas include communications, development, election year, field, policy, and religious affairs. Current undergraduate or graduate students are eligible. For more information, or to apply, contact Cecelia Smith-Budd, director of finance and administration, 1331 H Street, NW, 11th Floor, Washington DC 20005. Phone: (202) 639-6370. Fax: (202) 639-6375. E-mail: employment@interfaithalliance.org.

NEWSLETTERS

The Light (quarterly)

PUBLICATIONS

Annual Report, www.interfaithalliance.org

CONFERENCES

A Forum on Religion in the 2004 Elections

"As a leader in the Eastside's Muslim community, the Sammamish resident began speaking at forums that sprang up in the wake of the terrorist attacks, met with leaders from other religions and helped to build four homes, all in the name of reaching out to people of different faiths.

" 'I think Sept. 11 kind of became the defining moment. It was a call to action,' the 44-year-old Khaki said. 'I, for one, resolved that I didn't want to let people define who I am.'

"Khaki's work has now earned national recognition with the announcement yesterday that he has won the annual Walter Cronkite Faith and Freedom Award from the Interfaith Alliance Foundation.

"The award salutes people for their work encouraging religious freedom and showing the constructive role of faith in the United States, according to the foundation, an arm of the nonpartisan, Washington, D.C.-based Interfaith Alliance. . . ."

(*The Seattle Times*, April 29, 2003)

"At a vigil last night opposing violence spawned by bigotry, speakers said the need for tolerance takes on additional urgency now that the United States is at war.

"Although American soldiers from this area are dying in Iraq, Muslims here should not be targets of anger and hate, said the Rev. C. Welton Gaddy, president of the Interfaith Alliance Foundation of Washington, D.C. Americans are fighting against the Iraqi government, not the religion of its citizens, he said.

"The Interfaith Alliance Foundation, which encourages clergy to work against hate crimes, and the San Diego Human Relations Commission sponsored the vigil in Balboa Park. About 15 people turned out to listen to the speakers urge tolerance for people of different nationalities, races, religions, genders, sexual orientations and age. . . ."

(*The San Diego Union-Tribune*, March 25, 2003)

"Just this week, I participated in a conference call 'briefing' by Professor Elaine Pagels of Princeton University and the Rev. C. Welton Gaddy, president of the Interfaith Alliance Foundation, on the president's allegedly misguided use of 'religious language.' According to Pagels, a well-known scholar whose work I've long admired, the 'language of good and evil is the language of religious zealots' and of 'children's stories.' 'What [Bush] is actually doing is placing those who disagree with him' in the 'realm of evil,' she asserted.

"When questioned, Pagels acknowledged that the word 'evil' does have some value in describing specific events, such as the 9-11 attacks. But she insisted that Bush was using it too broadly, applying it to entire countries and peoples—a bizarre accusation given the pains the president has taken to single out the Iraqis as victims of Saddam rather than collaborators. . . .

"It is true, to be sure, that Bush uses spiritual and religious language more often than any president in living memory, and that he has developed a vision of the United States as a 'blessed country,' as he said in his State of the Union speech, on a noble mission to crush the forces of darkness. . . .

"Critics such as Pagels and Gaddy cringe at such words, which they consider a barrier to rational discourse. Bush's language, Pagels maintains, 'bypasses the brain and goes straight to the gut.' But does it, really? Isn't the language of moral uplift, with or without religious references, inevitable in any high-stakes political issue such as war and peace? Haven't virtually all of the great political debates and struggles of this nation's history been cast in moral terms—from slavery in the 19th century to civil rights in the 20th, along with dozens of other issues in between?. . ."

(*Rocky Mountain News* [Denver], February 15, 2003)

"Election time often includes a debate of the Godly kind. In a religiously diverse society, public figures walk a fine line between expressing their morality and espousing their religious convictions. How should the candidates handle their religious beliefs in the public sector? In comes the Interfaith Alliance, a nonpartisan, clergy-led organization with more than 150,000 members from more than 50 faiths. The organization interviewed politicians, ministers and consultants to compile a guide for religious political hopefuls. Election-year Guide for Political Candidates was mailed to more than 900 congressional candidates. It can be downloaded at http://www.interfaithalliance.org/programs/ctfd/eygpc.pdf. . . ."

(*St. Petersburg Times* [Florida], October 12, 2002)

Interfaith Center on
Corporate Responsibility

Established in 1971

DIRECTOR

Patricia Wolf, executive director. Wolf, R.S.M., has been a member of the ICCR governing board for eight years and chaired the ICCR board from 1982 to 1984. She has also been a major force behind mobilizing Roman Catholic investment in economic development of low-income and minority communities, founding and serving on boards of directors of several organizations and foundations. Wolf has a Doctor of Humane Letters from Mercy College, Dobbs Ferry, NY, where she completed her undergraduate degree. She has an M.A. from Manhattan College, New York.

BOARD OF DIRECTORS

Will Thomas, chair; Brethren Benefit Trust
Rev. Seamus Finn, vice chair; OMI-Missionary Oblates of Mary Immaculate
Ruth Kuhn, secretary; SC-Region VI Coalition for Responsible Investment
Barbara Aires, treasurer; SC-Sisters of Charity of St. Elizabeth, New Jersey
Vidette Bullock-Mixon; General Board of Pension & Health Benefits, United Methodist Church
Judy Byron; Northwest Coalition for Responsible Investment
John Celichowski; OFM, CAP—Capuchins Francis Coleman, Christian Brothers Investment Services
Margaret Cowden; American Baptist Home Mission Society
Jim Gunning; Unitarian Universalist Service Committee
Mark Regier; Mennonite Mutual Aid
Paul Neuhauser
William Somplatsky-Jarman; Presbyterian Church, USA
Susan Vickers, R.S.M.; Catholic Healthcare West
Margaret Weber; Conference on Corporate Responsibility of Indiana-Michigan

SCOPE

Members: 275 faith-based institutional investors including denominations, religious communities, pension funds, healthcare corporations, foundations and dioceses.
Branches/chapters: None
Affiliates: ICCR is related to the National Council of Churches

STAFF

12 total

TAX STATUS

501(c)(3)

FINANCES

Revenue: 2000—$1.5 million

CONTACT INFORMATION

475 Riverside Drive, Room 550, New York, NY 10115
Phone: (212) 870-2295 • *Fax:* (212) 870-2023
General E-mail: info@iccr.org • *Web site:* www.iccr.org

Communications Director: Julie Wokaty, director of publications and Web site (212) 870-2318 • jwokaty@iccr.org
Human Resources Director: Information unavailable

PURPOSE: "ICCR is a thirty-year-old international coalition of 275 faith-based institutional investors including denominations, religious communities, pension funds, healthcare corporations, foundations and dioceses with combined portfolios worth an estimated $100 billion. As responsible stewards, they merge social values with investment decisions, believing they must achieve more than an acceptable financial return. ICCR members utilize religious investments and other resources to change unjust or harmful corporate policies, working for peace, economic justice and stewardship of the Earth."

CURRENT CONCERNS: Contract suppliers • Corporate governance • Corporate involvement in human rights abuses • Enabling access to capital • Environmental justice • Equal employment opportunity • Foreign military sales • Genetically modified foods • Global warming • International debt forgiveness • Militarism and violence in society • Militarization of outer space • Promoting human rights • Racially offensive logos and ads • Safe, available, and affordable health care • Sweatshops • Tobacco product advertising • Water and food

METHOD OF OPERATION: Coalition forming • Congressional testimony • Dialogue with companies • Divestment of stocks and bonds • Legislative/regulatory monitoring • Library/information clearinghouse • Litigation • Mediation • Prayer vigils • Preparation of Securities and Exchange Commission briefs • Public hearings and investigations • Research • Selective purchasing • Shareholder resolutions (coordinates members' shareholder resolutions, but does not itself own stock and therefore does not act in its own name) • Solicitation

Effectiveness and Political Orientation

"Drug manufacturers have grown accustomed to being attacked over AIDS by irate lefties who accuse them of profiteering. But now they are under fire from a different direction—organised religion.

"A group of religious investors in the US . . . have called on the drugs industry to do more in the fight against AIDS in Africa, including lower prices for the drugs.

"Father Seamus Finn, the group's head and a member of the Roman Catholic Missionary Oblates of Mary Immaculate, said: 'The developers of

FUNDING SOURCES
Institutional memberships, 55%; foundation and individual contributions, 20%; special events, 15%; publications sales, 10%

PAC
None

EMPLOYMENT
Job postings are available at www.iccr.org/employment.php. Postings contain details regarding contact information.

INTERNSHIPS
ICCR offers paid summer internships through the Everett Public Service Internship program. The internships are available to students enrolled in U.S. educational institutions and carry a stipend of $230 per week for ten weeks. Areas of concentration include energy and environment, access to health care, human rights, corporate governance, and militarism and violence. Interns will assist with research on ICCR issues and help organize special events. There are also unpaid internships throughout the year for current students who desire experience in the areas listed above.

Applicants should send a cover letter and resume to conyemelukwe@iccr.org. For more information about the internship program, please check the Everett Internship Web site at www.everettinternships.org. No phone calls; applications are accepted only by e-mail.

NEWSLETTERS
Corporate Examiner (10 times per year)

PUBLICATIONS
The following is a sample list of publications:
A Christian Call to Faith-Based Investing
Blueprint for Change: Corporate Governance for the Future (CD-ROM)
The Proxy Resolutions Book 2004

CONFERENCES
None

these life-saving medicines have an obligation to make these products more accessible.'

"The investors form the AIDS/HIV caucus of a group called the Interfaith Center on Corporate Responsibility, which includes Catholic religious orders, Protestant churches and faith-based pension funds. . . .

"For those surprised by President George W. Bush's decision this year to spend [$15 billion] on AIDS, the ICCR's new campaign provides a clue: AIDS in Africa has become a key issue in US religious circles."

(*Financial Times* [London, England], November 27, 2003)

"Father Michael Crosby, a Capuchin Franciscan living at Milwaukee's St. Benedict the Moor Church, has written a new book, "Rethinking Celibacy, Reclaiming the Church." He writes, "The current crisis around celibacy has made me conclude that this is the moment of grace given us by the Spirit to reclaim the Catholic Church for Jesus Christ and his gospel of liberation from all sinful forms of control. The time is at hand. The reign of God is near. Those who have promoted celibacy as a means of control and exclusivity rather than a mandate of the heart dedicated to wholehearted service must repent." Crosby, 63, has written more than a dozen books. He leads workshops and retreats worldwide on topics from biblical spirituality to socially responsible investing. A leader of the Interfaith Center on Corporate Responsibility, he has a master's degree in economics and a doctorate and licentiate in theology. Journal Sentinel Reporter Tom Heinen interviewed him. . . ."

(*Milwaukee Journal Sentinel* [Wisconsin], November 3, 2003)

"Public opinion is tough enough on chief executives these days, but try being the boss of a utility when some of its own shareholders have labeled it one of the 'Filthy Five' for its copious carbon dioxide emissions.

"That's where James E. Rogers, the president and chief executive of the Cinergy Corporation, finds himself. Cinergy, based in Cincinnati, provides electrical power to about two million customers in Ohio, Indiana and Kentucky. Ninety percent of the electricity it produces comes from its coal-powered plants, which release as much as 70 million tons of carbon dioxide annually. Because of concern about greenhouse gases like carbon dioxide, environmental groups have pressed Cinergy and other utilities to reduce emissions and report on their efforts. Earlier this year, a coalition of shareholders, including the State of Connecticut pension fund and the Interfaith Center on Corporate Responsibility, filed a proxy resolution asking Cinergy to report its climate change risks.

"(Cinergy successfully petitioned the S.E.C. to prevent a vote. But similar ideas have drawn significant support in proxy votes at other electrical utilities—27 percent at American Electric Power and 23 percent at the Southern Company.). . ."

(*The New York Times,* July 6, 2003)

"Nuns and priests are hoping to put the fear of God into the hearts of high-paid executives.

"Faith-based institutional investors—longtime corporate activists on issues like the environment—are taking on CEO pay for the first time at annual shareholders meetings this year.

"At least 21 companies, including the likes of AOL Time Warner, J.P. Morgan Chase and Cisco Systems, face or have faced corporate governance proposals in the current annual meeting season from the Interfaith Center on Corporate Responsibility, the nationwide body that coordinates the efforts of religious groups. Because the ICCR doesn't own stock itself, it must count on its members who do, ranging from orders of sisters and priests to the General Board of Pension and Health Benefits of the United Methodist Church.

"The share ownership allows ICCR members to put their proposals up for a vote at shareholders meetings, most being held this month and next. And in most cases, nuns and priests are leading the charge against lofty CEO pay.

"The sudden interest in executive pay and other governance issues by religious groups is just the latest sign of how corporate scandals have been so deep and disturbing that more investors see it as their business to stop it.

"Top executives appear ready to listen. 'CEOs are afraid to be yelled at by nuns (at the shareholders meetings). It makes (them) look like bad guys,' says Beth Young of the Corporate Library. In fact, drugmaker Pfizer has agreed to begin talking to a group of nuns about ways to reduce pay disparity. . . ."

(*USA Today,* May 20, 2003)

"Shareholder groups filed 862 proposals with companies through early February, up from 802 submitted during all of last year, according to a report by the Investor Responsibility Research Center and the Interfaith Center on Corporate Responsibility. . . ."

(*The Boston Herald,* February 13, 2003)

Investor Responsibility Research Center

Established in 1972

DIRECTOR

Linda Crompton, president and chief executive officer. Crompton has been president and chief executive officer at IRRC since 2001.

BOARD OF DIRECTORS

Edward Whitney, chair
Donald Cassidy, vice chair; Director, Fidelity International Ltd.
Gwenn L. Carr, vice president and secretary; Metropolitan Life Insurance Co.
Maryellen F. Andersen; vice president, Automatic Data Processing, Inc.
Peter C. Clapman; senior vice president and chief counsel, investments, TIAA-CREF
Linda Crompton; president and CEO, IRRC
Charles Elson; visiting professor, Center for Corporate Governance, University of Delaware
Terence Gallagher; CEO, Corporate Governance Associates
James O. Heyworth; former president, Viewer's Choice
Peter M. Igoe; former vice president, corporate operations, Rodale Inc.
Luther Jones
Richard Koppes; official counsel, Jones Day
Nina Lesavoy; consultant
Philip R. Lochner Jr.; former CEO, Time Warner
Paul M. Neuhauser; professor emeritus, Securities Law, University of Iowa
Jonathan A. Small; president, Nonprofit Coordinating Committee of New York

SCOPE

Members: 300 institutional and 200 corporate subscribers
Branches/chapters: None
Affiliates: None

STAFF

80 total

TAX STATUS

Nonprofit organization (not tax-exempt)

FINANCES

Declined to comment

FUNDING SOURCES

Subscriptions, 60%; royalties, investments, and contracts, 30%; foundation grants, 4%; publications sales, 3%; conferences, 3%

PAC

None

EMPLOYMENT

Information on open positions is posted at www.irrc.com/company/employment.htm. Application materials should be mailed to

CONTACT INFORMATION

1350 Connecticut Avenue, NW, Suite 700, Washington, DC 20036-1702
Phone (202) 833-0700 • *Fax:* (202) 833-3555
General E-mail: marketing@irrc.org • *Web site:* www.irrc.org

Communications Director: Michele Soulé
(202) 833-0700 • michele.soule@irrc.org;
Human Resources Director: Not available (e-mail for department is hr@irrc.org.)

PURPOSE: "To conduct impartial research on companies and shareholders worldwide."

CURRENT CONCERNS: Corporate governance • Labor rights • Portfolio screening • Proxy voting guidelines • Shareholder resolutions • Shareholder value • Social responsibility

METHOD OF OPERATION: Conferences/seminars • Information clearinghouse • Internships • Legislative/regulatory monitoring (federal and state) • Research • Web site

Effectiveness and Political Orientation

"When shareholders speak, who really listens? Apple Computer shareholders approved a measure asking the company to expense stock options, but management hasn't adopted it. Same story at scores of major companies these days. Shareholders—who are fighting mad about scandals, outrageous executive compensation and poor corporate performance—have filed 1,069 proposals so far this year, according to the Investor Responsibility Research Center, an independent Washington, D.C.-based research firm. That's up from about 800 last year.

"But who listens? The Council of Institutional Investors counts more than 100 companies this year where shareholders' proposals have passed only to be denied by management. The list reads like a list of Fortune 500 companies: Boeing, ChevronTexaco, Safeway, Sears, Wells Fargo and Xcel Energy. Shareholder proposals are not binding, so management can say no or ignore the issue altogether. A tried-and-true tactic is to employ bureaucracy: 'This committee considered the voting results and requested that review and analysis be done,' U.S. Bancorp vice president Lee Mitau wrote in a letter explaining management's position on three passed shareholder proposals.

"In the end, boards of directors run companies and most shareholders have little power to affect their decisions. When asked to vote for a slate of directors, shareholders typically are given the option to vote 'yes' or 'withhold.' A director with scads of 'withholds' and one 'yes' still can be elected. It's not a democracy, nor should it be. But because most shareholders lack power to

Human Resources, 1350 Connecticut Avenue,
NW, Suite 700, Washington, DC 20036-1702.
Fax: (202) 833-3555. E-mail: hr@irrc.org.

INTERNSHIPS
No information available

NEWSLETTERS
Corporate Social Issues Reporter
    (11 times per year)
Corporate Governance Bulletin (bimonthly)

PUBLICATIONS
*Board Practices/Board Pay 2004: The
    Structure and Compensation of Boards of
    Directors at S&P Super 1,500 Companies*
Corporate Governance State by State
Corporate Takeover Defenses
Stock Plan Dilution 2004

CONFERENCES
None

oust irresponsible directors, the directors needn't worry about any controversy that resonates with shareholders. . . ."

(*The Denver Post,* October 7, 2003)

"Many of the world's largest companies are doing a poor job of preparing for the business impact of global warming, a report issued yesterday by investor, environmental and public interest groups said. Most of the 20 corporate giants discussed, including leaders in the oil, auto and utility industries, are also failing to disclose to investors enough about the financial risks they face from climate change, according to the report, which was prepared by the Investor Responsibility Research Center in Washington.

"None of the companies have produced dollar estimates of the potential costs or benefits of climate change, like more extreme weather, or of the financial impact of changing regulations on carbon emissions, the report said. . . . 'We are not talking about issues that are 50 years out,' said Mindy Luber, executive director of the Coalition for Environmentally Responsible Economies, which commissioned the study. 'We are seeing inadequate board reviews in many, many companies.' . . .

"Dan Cogan, deputy director for social issues at the investor responsibility center, said, 'We gave credit for minimal action, so the relative rankings are more important than the actual scores.' The center advises pension funds and others on corporate governance and social issues affecting companies. With a few notable exceptions, like Alcoa and DuPont, Mr. Cogan said, American companies seem to be discounting the threat of climate change to their businesses more than their overseas competitors.

"While better disclosure will help investors, especially those like pension funds with longtime horizons, it could also stimulate companies to move much faster to reduce carbon dioxide emissions that contribute to climate change, Mr. Cogan said. Emissions of toxic substances plummeted when companies had to start reporting them publicly to the Environmental Protection Agency, he noted. The report is available at www.ceres.org and www.irrc.org."

(*The New York Times,* July 10, 2003)

"Xcel Energy garnered a low score Wednesday in a private group's report showing how companies deal with greenhouse gas disclosures. Xcel, parent of Colorado's largest power utility, received six favorable marks in a checklist of 14 items that measure the degree to which corporations publicize their carbon dioxide emissions. The report was compiled by the Washington, D.C.-based Investor Responsibility Research Center, a group that advises large investors on corporate governance issues.

" 'Despite the fact that Xcel reports emissions data to the Department of Energy, it hasn't reported that data to (Xcel) shareholders,' said Doug Cogan, author of the report and deputy director of social issues for the group. An Xcel official responded that the company takes environmental issues seriously and believes that its reporting to investors is appropriate. 'Xcel Energy believes environmental stewardship is essential to its business,' said spokesman Mark Stutz. 'We're proud of our record to date and continuously strive to improve it.' . . .

"BP received a favorable mark in each of the 14 categories, while IBM was credited in 10 categories. Xcel was given credit in the report for being one of the leading wind-power generators among U.S. utilities. Xcel noted that it has lowered greenhouse gas emissions by retiring several coal-fired power plants and replacing them with natural-gas plants, which emit about 40 percent less carbon dioxide."

(*The Denver Post,* July 10, 2003)

"Shareholders are up in arms about everything from stock options to executive pay. Now more of them are trying to do something about it. With annual meeting season well under way, investors in the post-Enron era are on a record-setting pace in filing shareowner proposals. According to Washington, D.C.-based Investor Responsibility Research Center, this year's proposals totaled 998 as of April 14, well above the record high of 822 in all of 1996. Last year, 802 were filed. . . .

"But the growing number of shareholder proposals underscores . . . how corporate activism has exploded in corporate America. 'Clearly, this has been a year where investors have stood up to be counted,' said Timothy Smith, president of the Social Investment Forum. Coke isn't alone in receiving a record number of proposals. General Electric shareholders, for example, will consider 13 of them at the company's annual meeting next week in Charlotte. Like GE, Coke is one of America's most prominent companies. A look at the proxy of such a company can provide a microcosm of what many activists want. . . .

"Michele Soulé, of the Investor Responsibility Research Center, said some proposals can lead to real action, albeit behind the scenes. Last fall, for example, the AFL-CIO filed a proposal with Coke asking the company to alter an executive retirement plan. Coke agreed, and the AFL-CIO withdrew its proposal. 'They provided some valuable input into what we ultimately did,' Deutsch said. Coke's board reviews the proposals that arrive and, typically, decides to oppose them. A success like the AFL-CIO's is unusual."

(*The Atlanta Journal-Constitution,* April 16, 2003)

"A nasty bear market and a string of corporate scandals have led to a groundswell of shareholder resolutions this year, as angry stockholders take aim at executive pay and corporate governance. At their annual meeting today, Washington Mutual shareholders will vote on measures to rein in pay for management at the rapidly growing bank. And in Federal Way, Weyerhaeuser shareholders will vote on stock options, changing the way directors are elected and limiting management's freedom to prevent the company from being taken over.

"Nationwide, there have been 741 resolutions aimed at improving corporate governance so far this year, up sharply from 529 in all of 2002, according to the Investor Responsibility Research Center, a Washington, D.C., group that monitors corporate-management issues. High executive pay is the target of 316 of this year's proposals. 'There's no question that shareholders are making their voices heard,' said Carol Bowie, a center director. 'The trend is steadily toward more accountability. . . .'

"Though the number of proposals is rising and some have passed, even backers say companies won't change overnight. At Starbucks' annual meeting last month, shareholders nixed labeling food that might have genetically modified ingredients. But shareholders of investment bank Morgan Stanley approved a plan requiring directors to be elected at the same time, rather than in staggered terms. The IRRC's Bowie said the trend is toward more shareholder proposals passing. Last year, a third of proposals that were voted on passed, compared with a quarter the previous year."

(*The Seattle Times,* April 15, 2003)

Izaak Walton League of America

Established in 1922

DIRECTOR

Paul Hansen, executive director. Hansen has worked for the Izaak Walton League of America since 1982 and became executive director in 1995. He formerly headed the IWLA Midwest Office and served as a consultant to the Canadian government on acid rain and other environmental issues of bilateral concern. Hansen is on the board of the Louisiana-Pacific Corporation, the League of Conservation Voters, and the Sport Fishing and Boating Partnership Council and is a professional member of the Boone and Crockett Club and Outdoor Writers Association. He is a graduate of Antioch University and holds a master's degree in natural resources administration.

BOARD OF DIRECTORS

Paul Hansen, executive director
Nathaniel P. Reed Jr., honorary president
Chuck Clayton, president
Raymond J. Koffler Sr., secretary
William R. West, treasurer
Timothy W. Reid, vice president
Stan M. Adams
Charlotte Brooker
Michael Chenoweth
James A. Daniels
James Haring
William H. Kling
Jim A. Madsen
Arlo McDowell
Dawn A. Olson
E. John Trimberger

SCOPE

Members: 40,000 members
Branches/chapters: 330 chapters
Affiliate: Izaak Walton League of America
    Endowment, Inc. (related organization)

STAFF

31 total—25 full-time professional;
9 full-time support

TAX STATUS

501(c)(3)

FINANCES

Budget: 2002—$4.1 million

FUNDING SOURCES

Contributions and grants, 67%; membership dues, 23%; interest income, 3%; sales and other income, 7%

PAC

None

CONTACT INFORMATION

707 Conservation Lane, Gaithersburg, MD 20878-2983
Phone: (301) 548-0150 • *Fax:* (301) 548-9409
General E-mail: general@iwla.org • *Web site:* www.iwla.org

Communications Director: Richard M. Hoppe
(301) 548-0150, ext. 215 • media@iwla.org
Human Resources Director: Mike Lynch
(301) 548-0150 • conserve@iwla.org

PURPOSE: "To conserve, maintain, protect and restore the soil, forest, water and other natural resources of the United States and other lands; to promote means and opportunities for the education of the public with respect to such resources and their enjoyment and wholesome utilization."

CURRENT CONCERNS: American Wetlands Campaign • Fish Kill Network • Midwest Power Plant Campaign • Midwest Wilderness and Public Lands Program • National energy policy • Natural resource conservation • Outdoor ethics • Save Our Streams • Sustainability Education Program

METHOD OF OPERATION: Awards program • Coalition forming • Congressional testimony • Grassroots organizing • Internet (e-mail alerts and Web site) • Legislative/regulatory monitoring (federal and state) • Library/information clearinghouse (open to public) • Litigation • Lobbying (federal, state, and grassroots) • Local and municipal affairs • Media outreach • Participation in regulatory proceedings (federal and state) • Scholarships • Training and technical assistance

Effectiveness and Political Orientation

"A half-dozen national conservation groups sent a letter to President Bush last week urging him to order the release of a federal-state study for restoring Louisiana's coastal wetlands. Army Corps of Engineers and state officials had planned to roll out the Louisiana Coastal Area Ecosystem Restoration Project study, which includes seven statewide restoration alternatives, at a series of meetings in October. However, the plan has gone back and forth between Washington and the state for months. The alternatives are estimated to cost $4.3 billion to $14.7 billion, and would take 30 years to build.

"Now, officials at the White House's Office of Management and Budget, and its Council of Environmental Quality, have placed the plan on hold until more questions are answered about cost and whether the alternatives will work. The conservation groups, however, point out that the study always was considered a first step toward developing a final restoration plan. 'Until a draft plan is released, we cannot work with other interest groups to develop an appropriate response to this economic and environmental catastrophe,' said the letter, which was sent to Bush on Jan. 8.

EMPLOYMENT

Open positions at the Izaak Walton League of America's headquarters and application instructions are posted at www.iwla.org/general/jobs.html. The Izaak Walton League of America is an equal opportunity employer; women and minorities are encouraged to apply. Send resumes to Conservation Director, Izaak Walton League of America, 707 Conservation Lane, Gaithersburg, MD 20878-2983. E-mail: conserve@iwla.org.

INTERNSHIPS

The League offers both paid and unpaid internships. Interns must be willing to work a minimum of 120 hours for the duration of the 15-week internship. Available internships are posted at www.iwla.org. Application materials should be sent to Internship Coordinator, Izaak Walton League of America, 707 Conservation Lane, Gaithersburg, MD 20878-2983. E-mail: conserve@iwla.org.

NEWSLETTERS

Conservation Currents (5 times per year)
League Leader (5 times per year)
Outdoor America (quarterly magazine)
SOS News (biannual)
Sustainability Communicator (quarterly)
Water Courses (semi-annual)

PUBLICATIONS

Air Pollution in Our Parks—1999
Caught in the Treads: Unethical Advertising in the ATV Industry
Caught in the Wake: The Environmental and Human Health Impacts of Personal Watercraft
Closing the Lid on Litter: A Guide to Establishing an Effective Anti-Litter Campaign in Your Community
Going to Market: The Cost of Industrialized Agriculture
Hunting Ethics/Land-Access Project
License to Pollute: Minnesota Coal Plants and the Dirty Power Loophole
Mercury in the Upper Midwest
Passing the Buck: A Comparison of State Fish and Wildlife Agency Funding and the Economic Value of Wildlife-Associated Recreation
Power That Pollutes: A Status Report on Virginia's Outdated Power Plants
Refuge at the Crossroads: The State of the Upper Mississippi River National Wildlife and Fish Refuge
Special Report: Energy Development Stakeholders Summit
Spilling Swill: A Survey of Factory Farm Water Pollution in 1999

CONFERENCES

National convention

"The letter urges Bush to require that 'pilot projects that restore significant amounts of lost wetlands and that demonstrate new restoration techniques are built first.' Signers of the letter to Bush were presidents or directors of the National Wildlife Federation, National Audubon Society, Izaak Walton League of America, Natural Resources Defense Council, Environmental Defense, American Rivers and the Coalition to Restore Coastal Louisiana. . . ."

(*The New Orleans Times-Picayune*, January 15, 2004)

"The Great Plains smack into the Rockies [and] the collision of flatness and verticality results in the Rocky Mountain Front, the only place in the West where large numbers of grizzlies, elk and bighorn sheep . . . on the grassy plain. Seven years ago, the U.S. Forest Service ruled that the Front deserved 'special attention' and halted new oil and gas leasing. Hunters, hikers and assorted lovers of this 100-mile-long stretch of wilderness breathed a collective sigh of relief. A long fight between energy extraction and wildlife protection seemed over. . . .

"But now, with natural gas prices up sharply and with President Bush making domestic energy production a national security priority, the fight over the Front is back on. Although the Forest Service's ban on new leases remains in effect, the Bureau of Land Management is reviewing plans by three companies with existing leases to extract gas from eight wells. . . . The gathering din has begun to worry—and, in some cases, infuriate—America's fishermen and hunters, many of whom are Republicans who voted for Bush. The U.S. Fish and Wildlife Service estimates about 47 million Americans fish or hunt. . . .

"When it comes to politics, a long-standing lament among American sportsmen is that Democrats want your guns and Republicans want your land. Leaders of the country's major fishing and hunting organizations agree that concern about gun-control laws was a key factor in their members' support for Bush in the last election. Yet, with the exception of the National Rifle Association, these leaders say they are hearing from members upset about what the Bush administration is doing to federal land. 'While many of them vote gun rights first and conservation second, many do not,' said Paul Hansen, executive director of the Izaak Walton League, which has 50,000 members, 80 percent of whom describe themselves as Republicans or independents. 'I think the administration is making a big mistake if they are taking this electoral group for granted.'"

(*The Washington Post*, November 4, 2003)

"The Army Corps of Engineers will present a proposal today to spend up to $8.4 billion to help restore the ecosystem of the Upper Mississippi River. At the same time, the corps will lay out options for expanding locks and dams on the river that would cost up to $2.3 billion. These navigation and environmental projects are part of the reconstituted Upper Mississippi River-Illinois Waterway Navigation Study. The results of the study will guide management of the river for the next 50 years. 'It could be big for the region,' corps project manager Denny Lundberg said of the environmental options. 'Obviously, you're not going to restore the river back to its pre-lock-and-dam days. What we tried to do is identify problems that are there now, and try to resolve them going forward.' . . .

"The new proposals, which will be disclosed in a public meeting, include restoring flood plains, building islands and creating backwater pools on the Upper Mississippi. They will be finalized in the spring, after similar meetings in other cities. If approved, the environmental restoration plan would be the second biggest in the nation, second only to the $14 billion plan to save coastal Louisiana and slightly ahead of the mammoth $8 billion Everglades project. The Upper Mississippi plans will ultimately need funding from Congress. . . .

"Some environmentalists are already bracing for a difficult fight over the Upper Mississippi. Richard Moore, Upper Mississippi coordinator for the Izaak Walton League of America, said he thought the navigation case was weak, while environmental improvements were a necessity. The navigation and environmental components should be separate, he said. If it comes down to having both or nothing, Moore said he would not compromise. 'We're not going to be seduced by the promise of restoration money,' he said."

(*St. Louis Post-Dispatch,* October 20, 2003)

"A combination of family planning and health counseling, along with community-based approaches to resource conservation, can pull economies out of the downward spiral of poverty and environmental degradation. This summarizes in a nutshell the conclusions of a week-long study tour to Guatemala undertaken by 12 members of the Izaak Walton League of America in February. . . . For the Maryland-based League, one of the oldest resource conservation organizations in the United States with 400 chapters, the trip marked its first foray into international conservation issues, particularly in the area of educating and advocating against adverse impacts of uncontrolled population growth on an ecosystem.

"According to Jim Baird, director of the League's Sustainability Education Program, the study tour was undertaken to help team members develop a first-hand understanding of the health, population, and economic and environmental challenges facing developing economies. Guatemala was used as a case study. 'We hope that team members will use their insights to educate other league members and the community,' Baird said. 'We hope to marshal enough constituent support to influence decision making at the national level so that more funds will be funneled into family-planning projects in developing economies. . . .

"The 60-strong Elgin chapter, established in 1932, is no stranger to grassroots-oriented, participatory approaches to environmental conservation. Through the years, the chapter has involved local children in its conservation efforts by sponsoring a Boy Scout troop. Every Arbor Day, the chapter and the Scouts focus on promoting environmental consciousness by distributing 2,500 trees to fifth-graders at local schools. . . .

"In addition to helping with resource conservation, Conservation International is also working closely with APROFAM to provide mobile clinics to visit the Peten villages. The mobile clinics help educate villagers on topics ranging from healthy food preparation and storage, the advantages of using natural pesticides in cultivation to the proper use of contraceptives. 'It is a very integrated approach to environmental conservation,' Anderson said. . . ."

(*Chicago Daily Herald,* April 24, 2002)

Joint Center for Political and Economic Studies

Established in 1970

DIRECTOR

Eddie N. Williams, president. Williams founded the Joint Center in 1972. He holds a B.S. from the University of Illinois and an LL.D. from the University of the District of Columbia.

The Center announced in March 2004 that Williams will be stepping down from his post. The organization is currently conducting a nation-wide search for Williams' successor.

BOARD OF DIRECTORS

Elliott S. Hall, chair; partner, Dykema Gossett, PLLC

Norma Ketay Asnes, vice chair; president, Ketay Asnes Productions

W. Frank Fountain, vice chair; senior vice president, DaimlerChrysler Corp.

Hector M. Hyacinthe, treasurer; president, Packard Frank Business and Corporate Interiors, Inc.

Charles U. Daly, secretary

Joyce London Alexander; U.S. Magistrate Judge, U.S. District Court

Larry D. Bailey; president, LDB Consulting

Andrew F. Brimmer; president, Brimmer & Co., Inc.

A. Demetrius Brown; chief executive officer, CMXchange.com

Honorable George L. Brown; senior vice president, L. Robert Kimball and Associates

James P. Comer; Maurice Falk Professor of Child Psychiatry, Yale Child Study Center

Wendell G. Freeland

William M. Freeman

Roderick D. Gillum; vice president, Corporate Responsibility & Diversity, General Motors Corp.

Mirian M. Graddick-Weir; executive vice president, Human Resources, AT&T

Weldon H. Latham; senior partner, Holland & Knight

Thelma Wyatt Cummings Moore; judge, Superior Court of Fulton County, Atlanta Judicial Circuit

Stephen D. Peskoff; president, Underhill Investment Corp.

Charles E. Phillips; executive vice president, Oracle Corp.

Rodney E. Slater; partner, Patton Boggs

Reginald Weaver; president, National Education Association

Eddie N. Williams; president, Joint Center for Political and Economic Studies

SCOPE

Members: None
Branches/chapters: None
Affiliates: None

CONTACT INFORMATION

1090 Vermont Avenue, NW, Suite 1100, Washington, DC 20005-4928
Phone: (202) 789-3500 • *Fax:* (202) 789-6390
General E-mail: info@ced.org • *Web site:* www.jointcenter.org

Communications Director: Liselle Yorke
media@jointcenter.org • (202) 789-6366
Human Resources Director: Not available (e-mail for department is dehr@jointcenter.org.)

PURPOSE: "Informs and illuminates the nation's major public policy debates through research, analysis, and information dissemination in order to improve the socioeconomic status of black Americans and other minorities; expand their effective participation in the political and public policy arenas; and promote communications and relationships across racial and ethnic lines to strengthen the nation's pluralistic society."

CURRENT CONCERNS: Black economic studies and minority economic advancement • Black voter registration and participation • Business development • Civil rights • Democratizing knowledge • Education • Employment and training • Empowering citizens and community leaders • Environmental issues • Health policy • International affairs (particularly Africa) • Minority business • Social security • Welfare and poverty

METHOD OF OPERATION: Coalition forming • Conferences/seminars • Congressional testimony • Congressional voting analysis • Films/video/audiotapes • Grassroots organizing • Information clearinghouse • International activities • Internet (databases, electronic bulletin boards, e-mail alerts, and Web site) • Internships • Legislative/regulatory monitoring (federal) • Library services open to the public • Media outreach • Polling • Research • Speakers program • Telecommunications services (mailing lists) • Training and technical assistance

Effectiveness and Political Orientation

"The number of black elected officials nationwide has reached a record high with African-American women outpacing their male counterparts, a new study found. Over the past three decades, the number of black elected officials rose significantly from 1,469 in 1970 to 9,101 in 2001, according to the study released yesterday by the Joint Center for Political and Economic Studies, a Washington-based think tank that focuses on issues affecting African-Americans. . . .

" 'It's still not clear whether fewer black men are running or whether black women are replacing them in these elections,' said Eddie N. Williams, the center's president. 'What is clear, though, is that black women are coming into their own on the political stage.' The political system is not as male-dominated as it once was, said Minyon Moore, one of the founders of Future PAC, a new

STAFF
43 total—31 full-time professional; 12 full-time support; plus 1 part-time professional; 6 interns

TAX STATUS
501(c)(3)

FINANCES
Budget: 2002—$6.52 million; 2001—$6.29 million; 2000—$6.28 million

FUNDING SOURCES
Government contracts, 36%; corporate donations, 30%; foundation grants, 17%; publications, 13%; individual contributions, 4%

PAC
None

EMPLOYMENT
Information on open positions is posted at www.jointcenter.org/job.html. The Joint Center accepts resumes for posted positions only. Only those selected for interviews will be contacted. Employment ads are generally placed in the *The Washington Post.* Fax: (202) 789-6370. E-mailed to hr@jointcenter.org.

INTERNSHIPS
Available internships are posted at www.jointcenter.org/intern/index.html. Internships are available year-round and are open to juniors, seniors, and graduate students. Internship applications can be sent to Luther Elliott, Joint Center for Political and Economic Studies, 1090 Vermont Avenue, NW, Suite 1100, Washington, DC 20005-4928. Fax: (202) 789-3555.

PUBLICATIONS
The following is a sample list of publications:
African American Officers' Role in the Future Army
The American Workforce in the New Millenium
The Big Picture: Public Policy and Long-term Economic Outlook for African Americans
Building Cultural Competence: A Tool Kit for Workforce Development
Economic Prospectus for African Americans
Effective Minority Supplier Development Programs: Developing Best Practices for the 21st Century
Estimating the Cost of Effective Teen Pregnancy Prevention Programs
Fresh Start: An On-the-Job Survival Guide
Investing In Success: A Supervisor's Guidebook for Supporting and Retaining New Workforce Entrants in Today's Multicultural Workforce
Job Creation Prospects and Strategies
National Costs of Teen Pregnancy and Teen Pregnancy Prevention
The Reproductive Health of African American Adolescents: What We Know and What We Don't Know
Soft Skills and the Minority Workforce: A Guide for Informed Discussion
Soft Skills Training: An Annotated Guide to Selected Programs

national political action committee created to raise money for African-American women candidates. 'It's encouraging. The mystique of it is somehow removed,' Moore said. 'I think more and more women are seeing that they can do it starting at the school board level.'

"David Bositis, a senior research associate at the center, said one reason for the increase is that black women attract a lot of support from female voters, particularly white women. He also said some white voters tend to find black women less threatening than black men, particularly in the South. Overall, the number of black elected officials is expected to increase only slightly as black candidates face more challenges gaining support in racially mixed districts, Bositis said."

(*Newsday* [New York], December 4, 2003)

"Clear 'racial and ideological divides' between African-Americans and whites 'characterize the 2002 political environment,' the Joint Center for Political and Economic Studies concluded from the results of its National Opinion Poll on political issues, which was conducted in September and October and released last week. . . .

"What makes this report remarkable is how this gap has widened since the Joint Center conducted its last poll in 2000. Then, 56% of African-Americans and 57% of whites believed the country was moving in the right direction. Two years later, 40.6% of whites still hew to that belief, but only 23.9% of blacks now agree. . . .

"A slightly higher percentage of blacks than whites said they are better off today because 'it's easier to improve your position when you're starting from a lower income base, as blacks do,' said David Bositis, the Joint Center's senior political analyst, who conducted the poll. This growing sense of economic disparity is likely to stanch the slow ideological shift to the right among African-Americans and produce more pressures from black politicians and civil-rights groups for government action to even out the nation's economic playing field.

"If there is good news in this poll for Republicans who are looking beyond today's elections to the 2004 presidential campaign it is that 50.8% of African-Americans give the president a favorable rating, up from 29% in 2000, when just 10% of the blacks who cast ballots in the presidential election voted for George W. Bush. More revealing is the fact that 80.9% of African-Americans gave former president Bill Clinton a favorable rating in the 2002 poll, down from 91% two years ago. While 38.6% of African-Americans now have an unfavorable view of Bush, only 11.8% said they hold the same view of Clinton. . . ."

(*USA Today,* November 5, 2002)

"An axiom for the midterm political contests this fall: If you know who turns out for the election, you will know how the election turns out. That axiom holds true here in Florida, where black groups are working to bring large numbers of voters to the polls in an effort to defeat the Republican governor, Jeb Bush. It is true in Minnesota, where high voter turnout could catapult an Independent, former Democratic representative Tim Penny, into the governor's office. It is true in Missouri, where a low turnout could throw an appointed senator, Jean Carnahan, a Democrat, out of office.

"Voter turnout is always critical, but its importance is heightened in midterm elections, when fewer voters customarily go to the polls and small swings in participation can have big implications in American politics. In a year where control of the House and the Senate is being determined and where the governors' chairs in the eight biggest states are up for grabs, the emphasis in politics is not on persuasion, but on mobilization. 'The struggle the two parties have is to turn out their partisans,' says David Bositis, senior political analyst for the Joint Center for Political and Economic Studies, which studies issues of concern to African-Americans. 'It is not to convince wavering voters to support one or the other parties.'. . ."

(*The Boston Globe,* October 22, 2002)

"Metro Atlanta is emerging as the new heart of the nation's black middle class, surpassing the traditional center—Washington, D.C.—in many key measures, analysis of census data released today shows. Among major metropolitan areas, Atlanta had the fastest growth in the proportion of black households in the middle-and upper-income brackets during the 1990s, and now boasts the nation's highest percentage of black middle-income households. . . .

"Atlanta has become, in a sense, a modern-day Harlem, a place of opportunity where educated blacks can enjoy the fruits of the post civil rights era economy, said Roderick Harrison, a demographer with the Joint Center for Political and Economic Studies, an African-American think tank in Washington. It's that image that has helped set Atlanta apart from Washington. 'The difference lies less in the numbers and the practical sense than in the imagination,' Harrison said. 'Washington clearly does not capture the imagination in the same way that it used to and in the way that Atlanta does. Something spectacular and historic is occurring there.' . . .

Washington continues to be a prosperous place for blacks. Black households earning middle and upper incomes grew by nearly 23 percent there during the 1990s.

"But many of those residents depend on the federal government for their livelihood, either as federal employees or in work related to government. Harrison, from the Joint Center for Political and Economic Studies, said such an economy is not seen as being as dynamic as Atlanta's, a hub for black small business and a growing center of black culture where numerous African-American athletes and artists choose to maintain homes."

(*The Atlanta Journal-Constitution,* September 25, 2002)

"Colorado had two fewer black elected officials and judges in 2000 than in the previous year, a report by the Joint Center for Political and Economic Studies found. The report by the Washington-based nonpartisan research center said that Colorado had 19 black elected officials. That's one less black elected official—Secretary of State Vikki Buckley, a Republican, died in 1999—and one less black judge—James M. Franklin, who resigned his Colorado Springs judgeship in July 31, 1999—as of Jan. 31, 2000, compared with 1999.

"The 19 matched the number of elected black officials in Colorado at the beginning of 1998. Six were women, the report said. Nationwide the survey by the organization found that there were 9,040 black elected officials in federal, state, county, municipal, education, judicial and law enforcement offices as of Jan. 31, 2000. About 25 percent of black elected officials came into their posts between 1997 and 2000. They moved in as incumbents retired, moved onto higher office or lost re-election bids, the report said.

(*Rocky Mountain News* [Denver], April 1, 2002)

The Keystone Center for Science and Public Policy

Established in 1975

DIRECTOR

Peter S. Adler, president. Prior to his appointment at Keystone, Adler held executive positions with the Hawaii Justice Foundation, the Hawaii Supreme Court's Center for Alternate Dispute Resolution, and the Neighborhood Justice Center. He has served as a Peace Corps volunteer in India, an instructor and associate director of the Hawaii Bound School, and president of the Society of Professionals in Dispute Resolution. He has been awarded the Roberston-Cunninghame Scholar in Residence Fellowship at the University of New England, New South Wales, Australia, a Senior Fellowship at the Western Justice Center, and was a consultant to the U.S. Institute for Environmental Conflict Resolution. Adler has written extensively in the field of mediation and conflict resolution.

BOARD OF TRUSTEES

CONTACT INFORMATION

The Keystone Center, 1628 Sts. John Road, Keystone, CO 80435
Phone: (970) 513-5800 • *Fax:* (970) 262-0152
Washington Office
The Keystone Center, 1020 16th Street, NW, 2nd Floor, Washington, DC 20036
Phone: (202) 452-1590 • *Fax:* (202) 452-1138
General E-mail: tkcspp@keystone.org • *Web site:* www.keystone.org

Communications Director: Helen Littrell, project support coordinator
(970) 513-5800 • hlittrell@keystone.org,
Human Resources Director: Tamara Moses
(970) 513-5800 • tmoses@keystone.org

PURPOSE: "To bring together people from business and industry, environmental and citizen organizations, academia and government to address pressing questions, encourage scientific inquiry, enhance understanding and appreciation of the natural world, and to develop consensus on complex and controversial public policy issues."

CURRENT CONCERNS: Agriculture, food, and nutrition • Biotechnology and genetic resources • Energy • Environmental quality • Health • Natural resources • Science and technology

METHOD OF OPERATION: Facilitation and consulting servers • Mediation • Policy dialogues • Web site

Effectiveness and Political Orientation

"Marilyn Ware, chairman of the Voorhees, N.J.-based American Water Works Company Inc., has received the 2002 Keystone Center Award for Leadership in Industry. . . .

"The Keystone tribute cited Ware, who is a longtime Republican Party activist, as having 'inspired corporate leadership and commitment to public-private cooperation.'

"The Keystone Center is a public policy organization devoted to developing solutions to energy, health and environmental challenges.

"Since 1994, the Keystone awards have recognized environmental, industry, community and government leaders for their leadership, problem-solving skills and efforts 'to promote creative approaches to complex challenges through consensus.'"

(*Lancaster New Era* [Pennsylvania], July 22, 2002)

"Improving public awareness of the growing demand for gas will help build support for expanding the nation's pipeline grid to support a projected 30 Tcf/year market, a group of environmentalists, pipeline industry executives and FERC staff advised in a report released last week.

SCOPE

Members: None
Branches/chapters: None
Affiliates: In addition to SPPP, the Keystone
Center comprises the Science School
Program and the Keystone Symposia on
Molecular and Cellular Biology

STAFF

53 total—35 full-time professional;
18 full-time support

TAX STATUS

501(c)(3)

"The report's list of recommendations was developed through a year-long process with the assistance of the Colorado-based think tank, the Keystone Center. In addition to Office of Energy Projects Director Mark Robinson, participants in the discussions included representatives of the American Gas Assn., the Edison Electric Institute, the Interstate Natural Gas Assn. of America and the National Resources Defense Council.

"Because "public education" is needed to win support for new projects, the group urged the Energy Information Administration to develop more regional supply and demand projections to supplement those studies that look at the country as a whole, explained the NRDC's Patricio Silva at a Washington press briefing April 30.

"The report also advised FERC to facilitate public discussion on infrastructure issues to help assess gas needs in different regions of the country. The commission recently held a conference on gas infrastructure in the Northeast and plans to hold more meetings in other regions (IF, 4 Feb, 4). . . ."

(*Inside F.E.R.C*, May 6, 2002)

"Beginning as a trickle of snowmelt at the Continental Divide, the Snake River swells and flows past ski runs at Keystone, meanders through high-altitude glens and golf courses, and burbles past homes and condos before reaching one of Colorado's biggest fishing holes, Dillon Reservoir.

"Along its short course, the river touches on many of the issues common in many of Colorado's mountain resort communities.

"So, this self-contained corridor has been chosen for intense study by the University of Denver, Keystone Resort and the Keystone Center, teaming as the Snake River Sustainability Laboratory to untangle a knot of growth-related issues.

"The goal is to protect and enhance the Snake River basin by developing a model for planning and decision-making that incorporates environmental, economic and social concerns, said Bruce Hutton, a DU marketing professor.

"The living laboratory grew from an idea provided by John Rutter, Keystone's chief operating officer. 'I started thinking we needed a place to study the concept of sustainability where you could put an umbrella over a geographic area, and where there are a limited number of entities,' he said. . . .

"The issues in the Snake River basin are not unique. Other mountain resort and gateway communities must meet similar challenges in the face of rapid growth—providing housing and social services for the workforce, keeping transportation corridors flowing smoothly, preserving water and air quality, protecting wildlife habitat and maintaining quality of life.

" 'We hope the laboratory will give us a site-specific model that can be applied to other communities,' Rutter said. 'For example, if we build condos, we should understand the relationship of those condos to the natural environment, and what the economic and social implications are. Does each piece of the puzzle sustain itself? Ideally, you come up with a delicate balance,' Rutter said. . . ."

(*The Denver Post*, March 14, 2002)

"A grant from a federal program previously meant to benefit only industrial sites in urban areas has revived an effort to clean the Snake River basin near Keystone.

"The $250,000 from the Environmental Protection Agency marks the first time that a rural hard-rock mining district has tapped into the Brownfields

FINANCES

Revenue: 2002—$4.14 million; 2001—$4 million

FUNDING SOURCES

Private foundations, corporations, international donor organizations, and governmental agencies

PAC

None

EMPLOYMENT

Job openings are posted on the organization's Web site at www.keystone.org/About_Us/Employment/employment.html. Resumes are accepted as an e-mail attachment or mailed to The Keystone Center, Human Resources, 1628 Sts. John Road, Keystone, CO 80435. E-mail: hr@keystone.org.

INTERNSHIPS

Information unavailable

NEWSLETTERS

Consensus (3 times a year)
Discovery (once a year)
Science Schools Field Journal

PUBLICATIONS

The following is a sample of Keystone publications:
Building Trust
Expanding Natural Gas Pipeline Infrastructure to Meet the Growing Demand for Cleaner Power
Keystone Center Dialogue on Global Climate Change
Keystone Center Dialogue on Regional Transmission Organizations
Keystone Center National Policy Dialogue on Trends in Agriculture
National Policy Dialogue on Military Munitions, Final Report

CONFERENCES

Sponsors policy dialogues on various topics.

grant program. The EPA also has provided $85,000 in grants for a University of Colorado water study and to the Keystone Center, a nonprofit organization overseeing the cleanup effort.

"The U.S. Forest Service also has provided $100,000 to survey and mark property boundaries to help delineate mining-claim boundaries.

" 'We're finally building some momentum,' said Mary Davis Hamlin of the Keystone Center. 'I think we are getting to the place where we can start making some choices on on-the-ground projects.'

"The Snake River, which flows from the Continental Divide into Dillon Reservoir—one of Denver's drinking water supplies—is contaminated by heavy metals leaching from abandoned mines.

"Water in the area is so choked with metals and acids that it could qualify for the EPA's Superfund list of the most contaminated sites in the country. . . ."
(*The Associated Press State & Local Wire*, August 6, 2001)

". . . The Assembled Chemical Weapons Assessment (ACWA) program was initiated under the Omnibus Consolidated Appropriations Act, 1997 (Public Law 104-208). As directed within that Public Law, we the Department of Defense, Industry, Federal, State and local leaders as well as affected community members have formed an interactive partnership to identify and demonstrate alternative technologies to the baseline incineration process for the demilitarization of assembled chemical weapons. Congressional direction was based on strong constituent concerns over the health and safety of incineration. In order to address these concerns and define the criteria for an acceptable alternative, public involvement initiatives were set in place to build and maintain a transparent program. The Keystone Center, a neutral third party, was utilized as the facilitator to help build a program based on trust among the stakeholders in reaching consensus of acceptable alternate technologies. . . ."
(*Federal Document Clearing House Congressional Testimony*, April 25, 2001)

Lambda Legal Defense and Education Fund, Inc.

Established in 1973

DIRECTOR
Kevin M. Cathcart, executive director. Cathcart has led Lambda Legal since 1992. Prior to joining Lambda Legal, Cathcart was a staff attorney at the North Shore Children's Law Project and later executive director (1984–1992) of Gay & Lesbian Advocates & Defenders (GLAD) in Boston. Cathcart graduated from Richard Stockton State College in 1976 and the Harvard Graduate School of Education in 1978. He received his J.D. from Northeastern School of Law in 1982.

BOARD OF DIRECTORS
Jamie D. Pedersen, co-chair; Seattle
Martha E. Stark, co-chair; New York
Anthony Timiraos, treasurer; Stamford, CT
Charles MarLett, secretary; Dallas
Jennifer Cast, Seattle
Ann Mei Chang, San Francisco
Ruth Eisenberg, Washington, DC
Victor B. Flatt, Houston
Richard J. Foglia, San Francisco
Mark S. Hamilton, San Francisco
Rand Hoch, West Palm Beach
Cindy Homan, Chicago
Susan Ketcham, Menlo Park, CA
Jon H. Klapper, Atlanta
Chuck Loring, Indianapolis
James McDonough, Chicago
Robert S. Michitarian, San Francisco
Matthew L. Moore, New York
John H. Schwab, Chicago
Lisa Simonetti, Santa Monica, CA
Richard Strulson, Los Angeles
George D. Tuttle, San Francisco
Roy Wesley, Chicago
Claudia Woody, Atlanta
Rick Zbur, Los Angeles
George Zuber, New York

SCOPE
Members: 24,000 individuals
Branches/chapters: regional offices in Los
    Angeles, Chicago, Dallas and Atlanta
Affiliates: None

STAFF
76 total—58 professional; 18 support;
plus 5 volunteers and 10 interns

TAX STATUS
501(c)(3)

FINANCES
Budget: 2003—$10,121,482; 2002—
$8,881,113

FUNDING SOURCES
Individuals, 43%; donated legal services and attorneys fees, 16%; foundations, 16%; bequests, 25%

CONTACT INFORMATION
120 Wall Street, Suite 1500, New York, NY 10005-3904
Phone: (212) 809-8585 • *Fax:* (212) 809-0055
Toll-free: (800) 926-1064
General E-mail: members@lambdalegal.org • *Web site:* www.lambdalegal.org

Communications Director: Eric Ferrero
(212) 809-8585, ext. 227 • eferrero@lambdalegal.org
Human Resources Director: Darren Nimnicht
(212) 809-8585 • dnimnicht@lambdalegal.org

PURPOSE: "Committed to achieving full recognition of the civil rights of lesbians, gay men, bisexuals, the transgendered, and people with HIV or AIDS through impact litigation, education, and public policy work."

CURRENT CONCERNS: Civil rights of lesbians, gay men, bisexuals, the transgendered, and people with HIV/AIDS • Custody, adoption, and visitation rights • Enforcing employment protections • Harassment in schools • Legal rights for lesbian and gay immigrants • Marriage for same-sex couples • Needs of elderly lesbians and gay men

METHOD OF OPERATION: Coalition forming • Conferences/seminars • Demonstrations • Films/video/audiotapes • Information clearinghouse • Internet (e-mail alerts and Web site) • Internships • Legal assistance • Legislative/regulatory monitoring (federal and state) • Litigation • Media outreach • Mediation • Research • Telecommunications services (hotline and mailing lists)

Effectiveness and Political Orientation
"More than a half-century ago, the California Supreme Court became the first in the nation to overturn a law banning interracial marriage, a prohibition that was then widespread and had strong public support. The current battle over same-sex marriage, now before the state's high court, may depend on how the court compares present-day, opposite-sex-only marriage laws with the racially discriminatory laws of an earlier day. It's a point on which the opposing sides disagree sharply.

"The ban on interracial marriage was based on the asserted 'superiority of the white race,' said attorney Jon Davidson of the Lambda Legal Defense and Education Fund, which has joined in the defense of same-sex weddings in San Francisco. At the heart of the current marriage prohibition, he said, is 'an attempt to keep gay people inferior.' John Eastman, a professor at Chapman University School of Law in the city of Orange, countered that the case against same-sex marriage 'is grounded in human nature,' the recognition 'that men and women are different genders.' The old racial laws, he said, derived from 'a failure to recognize the equal humanity of blacks and whites.' . . .

PAC
None

EMPLOYMENT

Information on open positions is posted at www.lambdalegal.org/cgi-bin/iowa/jobs, as well as www.idealist.org. Advertisements are also listed in regional newspapers. Instructions for sending application materials are listed within each posting. Lambda Legal offers administrative, attorney, communications, development, finance, outreach and paralegal positions.

INTERNSHIPS

Summer internships, which are unpaid, are available for second- and third-year law students in both the national and regional offices. "A background in or familiarity with issues, legal and otherwise, that are important to lesbians, gay men, and people with HIV/AIDS will greatly strengthen an application." Internship applications should be mailed to either the national or regional office, as appropriate.

Application materials should be sent to the appropriate regional internship coordinator: New York—Jon Givner, staff attorney, 120 Wall Street, Suite 1500, New York, NY 10005-3904. Phone: (212) 809-8585. Fax: (212) 809-0055. E-mail: jgivner@lambdalegal.org. Chicago—Camilla Taylor, staff attorney, 11 East Adams, Suite 1008, Chicago, IL 60603. Phone: (312) 663-4413. Fax: (312) 663-4307. E-mail: ctaylor@lambdalegal.org. Los Angeles—Stefan Johnson, paralegal, 3325 Wilshire Boulevard; Suite 1300, Los Angeles, CA 90010-1729. Phone: (213) 382-7600. Fax: (213) 351-6050. E-mail: sjohnson@lambdalegal.org. Atlanta—Greg Nevins, staff attorney, 1447 Peachtree Street, NE, Suite 1004, Atlanta, GA 30309-3027. Phone: (404) 897-1880. Fax: (404) 897-1884. E-mail: gnevins@lambdalegal.org. Dallas—Brian Chase, staff attorney, 3500 Oak Lawn Avenue, Suite 500, Dallas, TX 75219-6722. Phone: (214) 219-8585. Fax: (214) 219-4455. E-mail: bchase@lambdalegal.org

Lambda Legal also offers a communications internship, open to students pursuing a career in communications who have an interest in pursuing nonprofit work. An understanding of the issues facing LGBT people and people with HIV and AIDS is also helpful. This position is offered in New York only; apply to Lisa Hardaway, 120 Wall Street, Suite 1500, New York, NY 10005. Phone: (212) 809-8585, ext. 267. E-mail: lhardaway@lambdalegal.org.

NEWSLETTERS

The Lambda Update (3 times a year)

PUBLICATIONS

The following is a list of sample publications:
Adoption by Lesbians and Gay Men: An Overview of the Law in the 50 States
Anti-Gay Initiatives: Pre-Election Challenges to Anti-Gay Ballot Initiatives
Civil Marriage for Lesbians and Gay Men: Organizing in Communities of Faith
Differences Between Real Sex Education & Abstinence-Only Programs

" 'Gays and lesbians do have to deal with discrimination in employment, discrimination in the military, in (child) custody . . . the feelings of inferiority, the feelings of second-class citizenship, the feeling that somebody is going to beat you, shoot you . . . based on how you look,' said Bobbie Wilson, a lawyer for San Francisco in the same-sex marriage case. 'It's hard to compare discriminations,' said Lambda Legal's Davidson. 'The heritage of slavery is something that gay people, other than gay people who are black, don't share. But the reality is that gay people have a history of being under attack in this country.' "

(*The San Francisco Chronicle*, February 29, 2004)

"Church-affiliated social service organizations that receive state funding in Georgia no longer will be able to discriminate in hiring against gays or against applicants who are not of the same faith, under the terms of a lawsuit settled out of court Thursday. The suit, brought last year against the Georgia Department of Human Resources, stemmed from complaints that a Methodist foster home in Decatur fired a female employee because she is gay and refused to hire a therapist because he is Jewish.

"The case ties into Gov. Sonny Perdue's call this week to amend the state constitution because of concerns about legal challenges to government funding of social services provided by faith-based organizations. On Thursday, lawyers for the New York-based Lambda Legal Defense and Education Fund called the out-of-court agreement with the state agency a victory. They said it does not change the law but requires the state to abide by the U.S. Constitution and the Georgia Constitution, both of which forbid state-funded organizations from discriminating in hiring.

" 'A private social service agency subject to the Department of Human Resources can't take government funds and use them to engage in religious programming or to fund positions where there is a religious hiring criteria,' said Susan Sommer, a New York attorney for Lambda. The settlement does not mean 'a Baptist church can't still require that a Baptist minister be Baptist,' Sommer said. It just means that at social service organizations receiving state funding, 'There can't be a sign on the door that says, 'No Jews Allowed.' ' "

(*The Atlanta Journal-Constitution*, October 10, 2003)

"Leaders in the gay and lesbian civil-rights movement are advising same-sex couples jubilant over recent legal victories to stop and consider possible negative consequences of getting married in Canada, such as a loss of insurance benefits or income-tax hassles. They also are discouraging couples from independently filing lawsuits that would seek to have their Canadian marriage recognized in the states where they live. A weak or misguided case, they say, could set back efforts to legalize same-sex marriage in the U.S.

" 'We are cautioning people against filing lawsuits as political acts,' said Jon Davidson, senior counsel of Lambda Legal Defense & Education Fund, a national gay- and lesbian-rights organization. 'We don't think courts would respond well to that.' "

(*The Seattle Times*, July 11, 2003)

"First, the Supreme Court gives Texas a disapproving slap by striking down anti-sodomy legislation. Next, Wal-Mart clambers aboard the equal rights bandwagon to mollify its gay employees. Then there's the blessing recently bestowed on gay men and women by Canada, where non-heterosexual mar-

CONFERENCES
2–3 each year

riage is on the verge of legal codification. It might be a cavalcade of human rights long overdue, but doesn't all this progress signify in Ruth E. Harlow's expert legal opinion that, after 15 years of unrelenting litigation toward gay rights, it finally, really is O.K. to be gay? As a lesbian of long and public standing, Ms. Harlow should be hitching up her low-slung jeans, flinging off those no-nonsense, black-rimmed specs, and turning cartwheels in the privacy of her Brooklyn apartment, should she not?

"But Ms. Harlow is not. She isn't one for spontaneous outbursts. She's a neatnik, so orderly that the crates of documents she hauled home this afternoon from her last day at Lambda Legal Defense and Education Fund are already stacked in her home office below the perfect rows of Matchbox miniatures she collected as a child. She harbors no clutter, be it emotional or decorative. Ms. Harlow—lead counsel in the Supreme Court case in which two Texans, John G. Lawrence and Tyron Garner, took on the state of Texas for jailing and fining them on a 1998 sodomy charge and received vindication on a historic scale on June 26—does not reciprocate with a cute rhymed couplet in response to her visitor's O.K.-to-be-gay question. She barely cracks a polite smile."

(The New York Times, July 8, 2003)

"A day after the Supreme Court struck down Texas' sodomy law, legal scholars and activists predicted the court's broad recognition of privacy rights for gays would bolster future gay-rights cases and could potentially spill over into such areas as doctor-assisted suicide and the fight over legal abortion. 'It certainly puts the wind in our sails to move forward,' said Michael Adams, an attorney for the New York-based Lambda Legal Defense and Education Fund, which represented Houstonians John Lawrence and Tyron Garner in the Texas sodomy case.

"But conservatives opposing the 6–3 ruling also were reinvigorated. 'I'm energized,' said the Rev. Louis Sheldon, chairman of the Traditional Values Coalition. 'This battle is not over. It has just begun.' At the court, which ended its term Friday, the impact of Thursday's ruling was obvious. Citing that decision, which said government has no business dictating what consenting adults, gay or straight, do in their bedrooms, the justices on Friday sent back to Kansas the case of a gay teenager sentenced to 17 years in prison for having sex with another teenage boy.

"Matthew Limon's sentence stems from an incident shortly after he turned 18 when he performed consensual oral sex on a 14-year-old boy at a residential school for developmentally disabled youth where they both lived. If Limon had engaged in oral sex with a 14-year-old girl, his sentence would have been limited to one year because Kansas' 'Romeo and Juliet' law makes consensual sexual relations with a minor a lesser crime if both participants are teens, and if they are opposite-sex partners. . . .

"Adams, of Lambda Legal, said that while the court's decision in the Texas case was 'a ringing declaration in support of the civil rights of gay people,' there is still much work to be done to make gays truly equal in the eyes of the law and society. . . ."

(The Houston Chronicle, June 28, 2003)

Landmark Legal Foundation

Established in 1976

DIRECTOR

Mark R. Levin, president. Prior to his appointment as president, Levin served as Landmark's director of legal policy for more than three years. He worked as an attorney in the private sector and as a top advisor and administrator to several members of former president Ronald Reagan's cabinet. Levin also served as chief of staff to the U.S. attorney general, deputy assistant secretary for elementary and secondary education at the U.S. Education Department, and deputy solicitor at the U.S. Interior Department. He holds a B.A. from Temple University and a J.D. from Temple University School of Law.

BOARD OF DIRECTORS

Lawrence F. Davenport, chair
William K. Hoskins, vice chair
John Richardson, secretary
Edwin Meese III, treasurer; former U.S.
     attorney general
Mark R. Levin
Steve A. Matthews
Gary L. McDowell
W. Bradford Reynolds

SCOPE

Members: None
Branches/chapters: Second office in Kansas
     City, MO
Affiliates: None

STAFF

Declined to comment

TAX STATUS

501(c)(3)

FINANCES

Revenue: 2002—$1.63 million; 2001—$1.47 million

FUNDING SOURCES

Individual contributions, business contributions, and foundation grants

PAC

None

EMPLOYMENT

Declined to comment

INTERNSHIPS

Declined to comment

NEWSLETTERS

Landmark Legal Foundation Newsletter
     (online)

CONTACT INFORMATION

445-B Carlisle Drive, Herndon, Virginia 20170
Phone: (703) 689-2370 • *Fax:* (703) 689-2373
General E-mail: info@landmarklegal.org • *Web site:* www.landmarklegal.org

Communications Director: Eric Christensen, vice president for development and communications
Human Resources Director: Information unavailable

PURPOSE: "Defending the principles of free enterprise, freedom of speech, limited government, and the accountability of public officials."

CURRENT CONCERNS: Education reform and school choice • Internal Revenue Service • Public integrity of public officials

METHOD OF OPERATION: Congressional testimony • Information clearinghouse • Legal assistance • Litigation • Media outreach • Participation in regulatory proceedings (federal and state) • Speakers program • Web site

Effectiveness and Political Orientation

"In response to a Florida Bar complaint, Palm Beach County prosecutors are defending their release of correspondence about plea negotiations with attorneys for radio host Rush Limbaugh. Landmark Legal Foundation filed the ethics complaint against Palm Beach County State Attorney Barry Krischer and his chief assistant for releasing letters with Limbaugh's attorneys.

"Landmark President Mark R. Levin alleged Krischer and Kenneth Selvig misrepresented conversations they had with the state attorney general's office and the bar before deciding to make the letters public. As an elected official, Krischer is not subject to bar regulations.

"According to records released after requests from Landmark and the media, prosecutors rejected a deal suggested by Limbaugh's attorney that called for a drug intervention program rather than charges of illegally obtaining prescription painkillers. Prosecutors wanted Limbaugh to plead guilty to the third-degree felony of 'doctor shopping'—visiting several doctors to receive duplicate prescriptions for a controlled narcotic. . . ."

(*St. Petersburg Times* [Florida], March 7, 2004)

"The Internal Revenue Service has launched an audit of the nation's largest teachers union, bringing holiday joy to conservatives across the country. The charge is that the National Education Association spends its members' dues on political activities, but fails to report the dollars on tax forms. The NEA's leaders promise that they will receive a clean IRS review, just as they did in 1993.

"The difference between then and now is that, then, the Democrats were in charge of the IRS. Now it's a GOP-controlled shop, and no matter how nonpartisan the tax-collecting agency is supposed to be, politics permeates all inside the beltway. To be sure, the complaints that helped spur the IRS inves-

PUBLICATIONS
None

CONFERENCES
None

tigation have political roots. The conservative Landmark Legal Foundation has charged repeatedly that the NEA engages in widespread campaign activity, producing internal strategy documents detailing the group's support for Democratic candidates.

"The issue is not whether the NEA has political interests—anyone who has seen the delegates and signs at Democratic National Conventions would have no doubt on that question. Rather, the issue is whether the union does its political spending in a manner consistent with federal law. Regardless of Landmark's motives, better accountability for the union's political spending is inarguably positive. Dues-payers have every right to know exactly how their money is spent.

"Whether or not the IRS finds wrongdoing at the NEA, the investigation should spur all unions to examine their business practices, and make sure they report fully to government agencies—and to the workers whose money supports them."

(*The Plain Dealer* [Cleveland], December 1, 2003)

"The National Education Association is being audited by the Internal Revenue Service after a complaint about the organization's political spending from a self-described conservative advocacy group. The teachers union confirmed the IRS investigation into a complaint filed by the Landmark Legal Foundation alleging that the association spent millions of dollars in membership dues on political activity and failed to disclose its expenditures.

"The Landmark Legal Foundation, based in Kansas City, Mo., has been filing complaints with federal authorities for at least two years about the political operations of local and national teachers unions, which generally have supported Democratic candidates for office."

(*The Seattle Times,* November 25, 2003)

"A federal judge held the Environmental Protection Agency in contempt Thursday for destroying computer files during the Clinton administration that had been sought by a conservative legal foundation. U.S. District Judge Royce Lamberth also ordered the EPA to pay the Landmark Legal Foundation's legal fees and costs because the agency disobeyed his order to preserve the electronic records of former chief Carol Browner.

"Lamberth ordered the sanctions because he said the EPA had shown 'contumacious conduct'—obstinate resistance to authority. 'This is a major victory for those who believe the EPA has an obligation to comply with the law,' said Landmark President Mark Levin. 'The EPA destroyed vast databases that would have revealed the extent to which Carol Browner and other top officials worked with environmental groups to issue last-minute regulations prior to the end of the Clinton administration,' he said."

(*Deseret Morning News* [Salt Lake City], July 25, 2003)

"A Dane County judge has ordered attorney Ed Garvey to pay nearly $3,000 in legal fees for asking the state Supreme Court to overturn a ruling that Milwaukee's school voucher program is constitutional. Garvey could have ended up paying $65,000. 'I am delighted,' Garvey said at the close of the hearing before Dane County Circuit Judge Michael Nowakowski Friday. The Supreme Court ruled in 1999 that the school voucher program, which allows tax dollars to pay for students' tuition at private schools, was constitutional.

"But Madison Teachers Inc. hired Garvey to fight the decision. Garvey filed a motion in 2002 asking the Supreme Court to overturn the decision. He argued that Justice John Wilcox was biased because voucher supporters helped Wilcox's Supreme Court campaign in 1997. . . .

"The initial bill included fees run up by the Michael Best and Friedrich firm when it represented the state, totaling about $65,000. But state officials said they would seek no more than $14,500. The Landmark Legal Foundation, a pro-voucher group that also was involved in the case, asked for more than $2,200. Nowakowski on Friday awarded the state $2,500 and the Landmark group $407.50. He said the facts of the case meant 'at most, a nominal sanction.'"

(The Associated Press State & Local Wire, May 24, 2003)

Leadership Conference
on Civil Rights, Inc.

Established in 1950

DIRECTOR

Wade Henderson, executive director. In addition to his role as executive director, Henderson is also counsel to the Leadership Conference on Civil Rights Education Fund (LCCREF). Prior to his role with the Leadership Conference, Henderson was the Washington bureau director of the National Association for the Advancement of Colored People (NAACP). He was also previously the associate director of the Washington national office of the American Civil Liberties Union. Henderson serves as the Joseph L. Rauh Jr. Professor of Public Interest Law at the David A. Clarke School of Law, University of the District of Columbia, Washington, DC. He is a graduate of Howard University and the Rutgers University School of Law.

BOARD OF DIRECTORS

Dorothy I. Height, chair; National Council of Negro Women
Antonia Hernandez, vice chair; Mexican American Legal Defense & Education Fund
Judith L. Lichtman, vice chair; National Partnership for Women and Families
William L. Taylor, vice chair; Citizens' Commission on Civil Rights
William D. Novelli, secretary; AARP
Gerald W. McEntee, treasurer; American Federation of State, County & Municipal Employees
Barbara Arnwine; Lawyers' Committee for Civil Rights Under Law
Elizabeth Birch; Human Rights Campaign
Jacqueline Johnson; National Congress of American Indians
Reg Weaver; National Education Association
Christine Chen, Organization of Chinese Americans
Robert W. Edgar; National Council of Churches
Marcia Greenberger; National Women's Law Center
Kim Gandy; National Organization for Women
Kay Maxwell; League of Women Voters
Elaine R. Jones; NAACP Legal Defense & Educational Fund, Inc.
George Kourpias; Alliance for Retired Americans
Leon Lynch; United Steelworkers of America
Kweisi Mfume; NAACP
Laura Murphy; American Civil Liberties Union
Ralph G. Neas; People for the American Way
Mark H. Morial; National Urban League
Nancy Rustad; American Association of University Women
David Saperstein; Union of American Hebrew Congregations
Richard Womack; AFL-CIO
Patrisha Wright; Disability Rights Education and Defense Fund

CONTACT INFORMATION

1629 K Street, NW, 10th Floor, Washington, DC 20006
Phone: (202) 466-3311
General E-mail: Web form available at www.civilrights.org/about/contact_us/ • *Web site:* www.civilrights.org

Communications Director: Shantelle Fowler, (202) 833-9771
Human Resources Director: Lisa M. Haywood, office manager (202) 466-3311

PURPOSE: "To fight discrimination in all its forms, improving intergroup relations, and promoting the full participation of every American in every facet of our nation's life."

CURRENT CONCERNS: Affirmative action • Census 2000 • Civil rights laws • Criminal justice reform • Elementary and Secondary Education Act • Employment Non-Discrimination Act • English-only language legislation • Fair housing • Fair minimum wage • Federal judge appointments • Federal policy against hate crimes • Immigration reform • Religious freedom

METHOD OF OPERATION: Advertisements • Awards program • Coalition forming • Conferences/seminars • Congressional testimony • Congressional voting analysis • Demonstrations • Educational foundation • Grassroots organizing • Information clearinghouse • Internet (e-mail alerts and Web site) • Internships • Legislative/regulatory monitoring (federal and state) • Library/information clearinghouse • Lobbying (federal and grassroots) • Media outreach • Research • Voter registration • Voting records

Effectiveness and Political Orientation

"The Senate dealt another blow to President Bush's proposed tax cut Tuesday, voting to slice it in half. Reversing a position that it took Friday, the Senate voted 51 to 48 for a Democratic amendment that would reduce the cost of the requested reduction from $726 billion to $350 billion. Critics of Bush's proposal were elated. 'The president's reckless tax cut plan is unraveling,' said Wade Henderson, executive director of the Leadership Conference on Civil Rights.

"A few moderate Republicans sided with the Democrats but the White House said the fight is far from over. 'We'll see what the ultimate outcome is, if that vote is the final vote,' presidential spokesman Ari Fleischer said. The vote came on an amendment to the $2.2 trillion budget for next year, and Republicans said they were unlikely to round up enough support to rebuild the tax cut's size before the Senate completes its budget work today."

(*Minneapolis Star-Tribune,* March 26, 2003)

"Dorothy I. Height, chairwoman of the Leadership Conference on Civil Rights, and Wade Henderson, its executive director, recently wrote a letter to

Stephen P. Yokich; International Union, United Automobile Workers of America
Raul Yzaguirre; National Council of La Raza

SCOPE
Members: 185 national organizations
Branches/chapters: None
Affiliates: Leadership Conference Education Fund, a 501(c)(3) organization

STAFF
22 total

TAX STATUS
501(c)(4)

FINANCES
Declined to comment

FUNDING SOURCES
Membership dues and annual fundraiser

PAC
None

EMPLOYMENT
Postings at national civil rights organizations, including those at the LCCR, are available at www.civilrights.org/career_center/index.html#permanent.

INTERNSHIPS
Information about internships can be found at www.civilrights.org/about/lccr/internships.html Applicants should have strong writing skills, a desire and ability to work with diverse groups of people, the ability to work collaboratively, and a high level of personal energy and commitment. Internship application, cover letter, resume, and a short writing sample can sent to intern coordinator, Leadership Conference on Civil Rights/Education Fund, 1629 K Street, NW, 10th Floor, Washington, DC 20006.

NEWSLETTERS
The Civil Rights Monitor (quarterly)

PUBLICATIONS
Publishes brochures, reports, and public service announcements.

CONFERENCES
Hubert H. Humphrey Civil Rights Award Dinner (annual)

Sen. Orrin Hatch (R-Utah) expressing opposition to the nomination of Miguel Estrada to the United States Court of Appeals for the D.C. Circuit. Here are excerpts:

" 'A review of Estrada's record to date indicates that his positions, opinions and legal activities in numerous areas are troublesome and raise serious questions about his commitment to equal justice and civil rights for all Americans. In addition, by refusing to adequately answer numerous questions posed to him at his Sept. 26, 2002, hearing, as well as written questions following the hearing, Estrada has failed to demonstrate a commitment to the continued vigorous enforcement of critical constitutional and statutory rights in the areas of civil rights and civil liberties.

" 'Estrada's nomination has special significance for the communities we represent for a number of reasons, including the unique status of the D.C. Circuit. The U.S. Court of Appeals for the District of Columbia Circuit has a critical role in our federal judicial system and is widely regarded as the second most important court in the United States, after the U.S. Supreme Court. Because of the importance of this court and because several senators have spoken out about the prospects of Estrada being subsequently elevated to the Supreme Court if confirmed, it is important that his nomination be scrutinized.

" 'In our review of Estrada's record made public to date, we are troubled by many of the positions that he has taken in litigation for public and private clients. For example, Estrada has devoted a good deal of time to defending so-called anti-loitering statutes, which have been shown to have a disproportionately negative impact on African-Americans and Latinos.' "

(*The Atlanta Journal-Constitution,* February 10, 2003)

"Civil rights groups are mobilizing to push an ambitious agenda on a broad array of issues—from racial profiling to school spending—that have been given new prominence since Sen. Trent Lott (R-Miss.) plunged the Republican leadership in Congress into a controversy over race. With Republicans eager to demonstrate their sensitivity after racially inflammatory remarks led to Lott's downfall as Senate GOP leader, the Leadership Conference on Civil Rights, Jesse Jackson and others are hoping to pump new life into causes that in many cases have been languishing on Capitol Hill.

"The Leadership Conference, composed of 180 civil rights groups and their labor, religious and other allies, has singled out more than a half-dozen legislative goals that appeared to grow more distant when Republicans solidified their hold on Congress in the November elections and then reemerged after Lott's comments earlier this month. Lott triggered an uproar when he said that the country would have been better off if Strom Thurmond had been elected president in 1948, when Thurmond ran on a pro-segregation platform. Lott resigned under fire from his colleagues as Senate GOP leader Dec. 20 and was replaced by Sen. Bill Frist (R-Tenn.), who will be majority leader when the 108th Congress convenes Jan. 7."

(*The Washington Post,* December 30, 2002)

"On Friday, the same day that Sen. Trent Lott of Mississippi announced his decision to step down as the Senate's top Republican, the Leadership Conference on Civil Rights fired off a five-page letter to President Bush. That missive, much like the words that toppled Lott from power, was rooted in this nation's racial divide.

"The civil rights group presented Bush—who campaigned for the White House as a 'compassionate conservative'—with a shopping list of racially tinged issues. The group hopes Bush will support its views in the wake of Lott's racially insensitive remarks. At the top of the Leadership Conference's list is the Bush administration's as-yet-unspoken position on two cases now before the Supreme Court that challenge the use of affirmative action in the University of Michigan's admission policies for its undergraduate programs and law school.

"The Leadership Conference and other civil rights groups want Bush to back Michigan's policies, which use race as just one of several factors in determining who gets into the school. . . .

"'Your administration can best express its commitment to support progress on matters of civil and human rights by establishing a specific agenda and being responsible for achieving it with sustained, concrete action,' the Leadership Conference said in its letter to Bush, which was signed by its board chairman and its executive director. Whether Bush gives the civil rights group what it wants may ultimately prove less important than the fact that the nation seems—at least for the moment—to have lost its tin ear on race. That's because when it comes to the matter of race, politicians are more likely to follow the national mood, not take the lead in trying to establish it. . . ."

(*USA Today,* December 24, 2002)

"The appointment of conservative 'ideologues' to federal judicial posts, eroded civil liberty protections during the war on terrorism and a Republican tax-cut agenda pose challenges for today's human rights advocates, national civil rights figure Wade Henderson said Friday at the University of New Orleans. In a forum sponsored by UNO's International Project for Nonprofit Leadership, Henderson said that as the 20th century ended, the United States stood out as the last superpower, a nation of vast resources with an enviable democratic government that had made strides in bridging ethnic barriers.

"'Mine was the last generation that was born with one foot planted in (racial) segregation,' said Henderson, executive director of the Leadership Conference on Civil Rights, a coalition of more than 180 groups. 'That transformation was profound, and it shouldn't be ignored.' But President Bush is leading a 'stealth campaign' to undo gains in human and civil rights, Henderson said. He spoke to a diverse crowd of about 150, including veterans of New Orleans' social service and preservation causes.

"Calling Bush 'a very bright individual who is surrounded by people with a hard agenda,' Henderson said the president is appointing, or trying to appoint, conservative activists to judicial posts. Those judges will shape treatment of civil rights issues ranging from affirmative action in college admission offices to proposed job protections for elderly, gay and disabled people, he said."

(*The New Orleans Times-Picayune,* December 7, 2002)

League of Conservation Voters

Established in 1970

DIRECTOR

Deb Callahan, president. Prior to joining LCV in 1996, Callahan was the executive director of the Brainerd Foundation in Seattle. She has also served as the grassroots environmental program director of the W. Alton Jones Foundation and served as both campaign manager and staff for numerous Congressional and presidential campaigns. She holds a B.A. from the University of California, Santa Barbara.

BOARD OF DIRECTORS

Bill Roberts, chair; Beldon Fund
Rodger O. Schlickeisen, vice chair; Defenders of Wildlife
Denis Hayes, treasurer; Bullitt Foundation
Debbie Sease, secretary; Sierra Club
John H. Adams; Natural Resources Defense Council
Brent Blackwelder (honorary); Friends of the Earth
Everett "Brownie" Carson; Natural Resources Council of Maine
Wade Greene; Rockefeller Family & Associates
John "Jay" A. Harris; Changing Horizons Fund
Rampa R. Hormel; Global Environment Project Institute
John Hunting (honorary); Beldon Fund
Tom Kiernan; National Parks Conservation Association
Fred Krupp; Environmental Defense
Martha Marks; Republicans for Environmental Protection (REP America)
William H. Meadows III; Wilderness Society
John D. Podesta; Center for American Progress
Lana Pollack; Michigan Environmental Council
Marie W. Ridder; Trust for Public Lands
Larry Rockefeller; American Conservation Association
Theodore Roosevelt IV (honorary chair); Lehman Brothers, Inc
Donald K. Ross; Rockefeller Family & Associates
Peggy Shepard; West Harlem Environmental Action, Inc.
S. Bruce Smart Jr.; Former Undersecretary of Commerce
Ed Zuckerman; Federation of State Conservation Voter Leagues

SCOPE

Members: Approximately 30,000
Branches/chapters: None
Affiliates: None

STAFF

52 total

CONTACT INFORMATION

1920 L Street, NW, Suite 800, Washington, DC, 20036
Phone: (202) 785-8683 • *Fax:* (202) 835-0491
General E-mail: lcv@lcv.org • *Web site:* www.lcv.org

Communications Director: Chuck Porcari
(202) 785-8683l • cvpress@lcv.org
Human Resources Director: Betsy Loyless, political director
(202) 785-8683

PURPOSE: "To hold members of Congress accountable for their environmental votes and to help elect a pro-environment majority to Congress."

CURRENT CONCERNS: Clean air • Clean water • Climate change • Conservation and environmental protection • Department of Defense readiness and range preservation initiative • Environmental politics • Mercury • Promotion of a pro-conservation majority in Congress • Protecting the Arctic National Wildlife Refuge • Public lands • Toxics

METHOD OF OPERATION: Advertisements • Awards program • Campaign contributions • Congressional voting analysis • Electoral politics • Grassroots organizing • Internet (databases, e-mail alerts, and Web site) • Internships • Legislative/regulatory monitoring (federal) • Media outreach • Polling • Research

Effectiveness and Political Orientation

"A conservation group's annual scorecard that ranks voting records of state lawmakers on environmental issues gave legislators generally low marks for the 2003 legislative session. The non-partisan Wisconsin League of Conservation Voters handed out zeros to 72 legislators, while giving 100% scores to 19 legislators. No lawmakers received zeros in 2002, and 29 received 100% scores that year, said Anne Sayers, spokeswoman for the group.

"The group rated how legislators voted on five key environmental bills in the Assembly and four in the Senate in 2003. 'Given the wide range of issues being scored, we are seeing surprisingly low scores across the board, even from legislators who have tended to do well in the past,' said George Meyer, the group's president and former secretary of the state Department of Natural Resources. Milwaukee-area Assembly members David Cullen, Shirley Krug, Jon Richards, Sheldon Wasserman, Annette Williams and Leon Young—all Democrats—were among those scoring 100%. Sens. Tim Carpenter and Gwen Moore—Democrats from Milwaukee—also received perfect scores."
(*Milwaukee Journal-Sentinel* [Wisconsin], February 4, 2004)

"Marylanders remain committed to protecting the environment, even at the expense of job growth, but they are concerned about the pace of Chesapeake

TAX STATUS
501(c)(4)

FINANCES
Declined to comment.

FUNDING SOURCES
Individual contributions and membership dues, 100%

PAC
League of Conservation Voters Action Fund

PAC CONTRIBUTIONS 2002

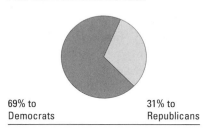

69% to Democrats

31% to Republicans

EMPLOYMENT
Job postings are listed on the LCV Web site, at www.lcv.org/About/AboutList.cfm?c=34.

INTERNSHIPS
Program and development internships are available. Specifics for internships vary by position; details and contact information are available from the postings at the organization's Web site.

NEWSLETTERS
LCV Insider (quarterly)

PUBLICATIONS
Bush and the Environment: A Citizen's Guide to the First 100 Days
Also publishes election candidate scorecards and profiles.

CONFERENCES
Occasional seminars

Bay restoration, according to the poll. The poll found that 59 percent of likely Maryland voters believe the state should 'work hard to protect the environment, even if it might cost some jobs,' while 20 percent believe it is 'more important to grow the economy, even if it hurts the environment.' The response is virtually unchanged over the past four years.

"Even among Republican voters, 46 percent prefer to protect the environment over jobs, compared to 28 percent saying economic growth is more important. 'Protecting the environment has always been a very bipartisan issue, and that's particularly the case in Maryland,' said Susan Brown, executive director of the Maryland League of Conservation Voters. 'This shows Marylanders consistently believe in strong environmental protections and enforcement of those laws, and that is the message the governor and legislature should see from these numbers.'

"Keith Haller, president of the polling company, said Gov. Robert L. Ehrlich Jr. may have gotten the message. 'To come across as a moderate and continue to cross partisan lines,' Haller said, 'he can't ignore a serious commitment to environmental issues, especially the bay.' Ehrlich's legislative agenda for the coming General Assembly session includes several substantive environmental issues, including a proposal for a $2.50 monthly surcharge on users of municipal sewage facilities to help cut pollution into the bay."

(*The Baltimore Sun,* January 11, 2004)

"Robert F. Kennedy Jr., who has made a career out of championing environmental causes, told a Seattle audience yesterday that U.S. Sen. John Kerry, D-Mass., should be the environmental movement's candidate of choice for the Democratic presidential nomination. Calling Kerry 'as much of an environmental champion as Al Gore,' Kennedy boasted to a crowd of about 50 that Kerry holds a 96 percent approval rating with the League of Conservation Voters, has long pushed for 'the Holy Grail' of automobile fuel-efficiency standards, and had a history of activism dating to Kerry's role as a Massachusetts organizer for the first Earth Day in 1970.

"But Kennedy, a Natural Resources Defense Council attorney, vice president for Riverkeeper and president of the Waterkeeper Alliance, reserved the bulk of his 45-minute speech for a wide-ranging critique of President George W. Bush. Bush, he said, has pushed to roll back 200 environmental regulations and has the worst environmental record of any president 'in American history.'. . .

"Cliff Traisman, lobbyist for Washington Conservation Voters, which hosted Kennedy, said among environmentalists, he hears the most talk about Kerry and former Vermont Gov. Howard Dean even though Sen. Joe Lieberman, D-Conn., has the second-highest rating on the League of Conservation Voters report card, at 93 percent. The league rates only candidates with congressional track records, and has not rated Dean. . . ."

(*The Seattle Times,* October 29, 2003)

"When the League of Conservation Voters hosts Democratic presidential hopefuls in a forum tonight, the significance won't be the stands the candidates take on environmental issues. Even close observers see few differences on the subject among the Democrats. For many in the environmental movement, the greater importance of the Los Angeles event will be that it marks the national launch of what could be their biggest campaign effort ever, aimed chiefly at defeating President Bush next year.

"Among the nine announced Democratic challengers, six of whom are planning to participate in the forum, 'All would be better than President Bush when it comes to the environment,' Deb Callahan, president of the League of Conservation Voters, told reporters this week. The purpose of the forum, she said, is mainly to show how the Democrats differ with the Bush administration, which her group portrays as trying to roll back progress on the environment.

"Both the league, which calls itself the political arm of the environmental movement, and the 750,000-member Sierra Club are already hiring political pros, raising funds and planning to dispatch thousands of activists to go door to door in key battleground states."

(*The Atlanta Journal-Constitution,* June 26, 2003)

"Three big conservation groups have endorsed, for the first time, New York City's efforts to build a $1.3 billion plant to filter part of the drinking water supply—bolstering the city's case as it struggles to meet a court deadline by the end of this month to select a site for the project. Leaders of the groups—the Natural Resources Defense Council, Environmental Defense, and the New York League of Conservation Voters—said this week that a 20-page scientific paper commissioned by the Department of Environmental Protection had made a convincing case that filtration was necessary to protect the public health.

"The implications of the endorsements go beyond high-minded science or the sanctity of the city's water. Through most of New York's decade-long struggle over whether, how and where to filter water from the Croton system—which supplies about 10 percent of the city's water from 12 reservoirs in a mostly suburban area north of the city—the debate has been more like a street fight than a scholarly review. And now the conservation groups, by endorsing filtration, have been pulled right into the thick of it, including the most sensitive issue of all, whether the city should be allowed to build the plant where it wants—underneath Mosholu Golf Course in Van Cortlandt Park, which city engineers say is the best, not to mention cheapest, alternative. . . .

(*The New York Times,* May 23, 2003)

League of United Latin American Citizens (LULAC)

Established in 1929

DIRECTOR

Brent Wilkes, national executive director. Wilkes has worked in a variety of capacities for LULAC since 1988. He joined the LULAC National Office in 1996 and assumed the newly created position of executive director in April 1997. Wilkes is a frequent guest on radio and television programs; he is also a regular speaker at rallies and press conferences in support of issues of importance to the Hispanic community. He is a graduate of Dartmouth College.

BOARD OF DIRECTORS

Voting members
Rick Dovalina
Fernando Escabi
Hector M. Flores
Juan B. Garcia
Vera Marquez
Laura Medrano
Manuel Olguin
Frank Ortiz
Desiderio Pesina
Haydee Rivera
David M. Rodriguez
Rosa Rosales
Blanca Vargas
Ray Velarde
Luis Vera
Nonvoting members
Theresa Venegas Filberth
Carolina Muñoz
Luis Nuno-Briones
Roman Palomares
Adrian Rodriguez
Brent Wilkes

SCOPE

Members: 100,000 individuals
Branches/chapters: 600 councils nationwide
Affiliates: LULAC Institute, a 501(c)(3) organization; LULAC Federal Training Institute a 501(c)(3); LULAC National Education Service Centers a 501(c)(3); LULAC National Scholarship Fund a 501(c)(3); and SER-JOBS for Progress, Inc. a 501(c)(3) organization.

STAFF

9 total—7 full-time professional; 2 full-time support; plus 2 part-time staff; 4 interns

TAX STATUS

501(c)(3)

FINANCES

Declined to comment

FUNDING SOURCES

National conference, 40%; membership, 20%; foundation grants, 15%; corporate donations, 15%; federal, state, and local grants, 10%

CONTACT INFORMATION

2000 L Street, NW, Suite 610, Washington, DC 20036
Phone: (202) 833-6130 • *Fax:* (202) 833-6135
Web site: www.lulac.org

Communications Director: Lorraine Quiroga Mullaly
(202) 833-6130 • lquiroga@lulac.org
Human Resources Director: None

PURPOSE: "To advance the economic condition, educational attainment, political influence, health, and civil rights of the Hispanic population of the United States."

CURRENT CONCERNS: Affirmative action • Census • Citizenship • Civil rights • Economic development • Education • Elderly • Employment and training • Environment • Health • Housing • Immigration • Justice • Leadership • Learning English • Political access • Technology • Voter registration and rights • Women • Youth

METHOD OF OPERATION: Advertisements • Awards program • Boycotts • Coalition forming • Conferences/seminars • Congressional testimony • Congressional voting analysis • Demonstrations • Direct action • Film/video/audiotapes • Grantmaking • Grassroots organizing • Initiative/referendum campaigns • International activities • Internships • Legislative/regulatory monitoring (federal and state) • Library/information clearinghouse • Litigation • Lobbying (federal, state, and grassroots) • Local/municipal affairs • Media outreach • Mediation • Participations in regulatory proceedings (federal and state) • Performance ratings • Polling • Professional development services • Research • Scholarships • Speakers program • Telecommunications services • Training • Voter registration • Voting records • Web site

Effectiveness and Political Orientation

"Religious and advocacy groups filed suit Tuesday to block Colorado's new school voucher law, setting up a legal fight that could spill into the nation's classrooms. The suit, filed in Denver District Court, contends that giving taxpayer money to low-income families so their children can attend private school illegally enriches church-run schools. 'Colorado taxpayers should not be asked to subsidize religious indoctrination,' said Jeffrey Sinensky, general counsel of the American Jewish Committee.

"But voucher proponents say Colorado's voucher program gives poor families with children in struggling schools a chance to succeed. They say they are confident it will get legal backing in the state's courts. 'Colorado's low-income families finally will be set free from demonstrably failing schools and empowered to choose the best education for their children,' said Robert

PAC

None

EMPLOYMENT

Available job postings are listed on the LULAC Web site: www.lulac.org/About/Announce .html. LULAC typically offers administrative, policy analysis, development, and communications positions. Applications and resumes should be sent to Brent Wilkes, national executive director, League of United Latin American Citizens, 2000 L Street, NW, Suite 610, Washington, DC 20036. Fax: (202) 833-6135. E-mail: bwilkes@lulac.org.

INTERNSHIPS

Information about unpaid internships is available at www.lulac.org/About/Interns.html. Applicants should have excellent academic records, strong writing and communication skills, and a good knowledge of the Hispanic community and current issues. Applicants should also have a deep sense of commitment to advancing the rights of Hispanic Americans. The ability to write and speak Spanish and English fluently is highly desirable as is extensive experience with using computers.

Internships are available year-round; the duration of programs varies. Applications should be sent to Brent Wilkes, national executive director, League of United Latin American Citizens, 2000 L Street, NW, Suite 610, Washington, DC 20036. Phone: (202) 833-6130. Fax: (202) 833-6135. E-mail: to bwilkes@lulac.org.

NEWSLETTERS

LULAC News (bimonthly)

PUBLICATIONS

LULAC Civil Rights Manual

CONFERENCES

Civil rights summit
Educational summit
National Convention and Exposition (annual)
National Legislative Awards Gala (annual
State conventions (annual)
Women's Conference (annual)

Freedman, attorney for the Washington, D.C.-based Institute for Justice and a voucher supporter.

"Colorado's voucher law was the first passed since the U.S. Supreme Court declared that taxpayer-supported vouchers are constitutional. The decision set the stage for vouchers to be challenged on a state level to determine whether they violate state constitutions, which is why Colorado's effort is gaining national attention. The Colorado PTA, League of United Latin American Citizens, the Interfaith Alliance of Colorado, the Colorado NAACP, former state senators Pat Pascoe and Dorothy Wham, church leaders and a handful of parents were named as plaintiffs.

"The suit also is backed by teachers unions, including the Colorado Education Association and the American Federation of Teachers. Also supporting it are other national organizations, including the American Civil Liberties Union, the American Jewish Committee and Americans United for Separation of Church and State, which see Colorado's experiment in school vouchers as a dangerous blurring of lines separating government and religion."

(*The Denver Post,* May 21, 2003)

"President Bush's nomination of Miguel Estrada for a federal judgeship has exposed sharp divisions among Latinos, who are weighing the possibility of having one of their own on a fast track to the U.S. Supreme Court against a fear that the minority group's interests could be harmed if the Senate confirms the conservative lawyer of Honduran descent. In the divisive intra-ethnic battle, some Latinos have challenged Estrada's allegiance to the Hispanic community, an accusation that others have sharply criticized. Each side has at times accused the other of being anti-Latino. The debate has gotten so nasty on Spanish-language television and over the Internet that this week the National Council of La Raza, a Latino group that says it is neutral on Estrada's nomination, called for both sides to tone down their language.

Estrada's nomination to the Court of Appeals for the District of Columbia has been endorsed by the Hispanic Bar Association, US Hispanic Chamber of Commerce, the Latino Coalition, and the League of United Latin American Citizens, which is comparable to the NAACP. Opposed are the Mexican American Legal Defense and Education Fund, the Puerto Rican Legal Defense and Education Fund, and the Congressional Hispanic Caucus, whose members are Democrats."

(*The Boston Globe,* February 25, 2003)

"The African American and Latino communities in San Antonio and throughout the nation are so inextricably linked by similar histories of oppression and discrimination that coming together to effect major social change is a necessity in the 21st century, community leaders said Monday night. Henry Flores, a political science professor at St. Mary's, and Morris Stribling, a podiatrist and chairman of the Alamo City Chamber of Commerce, told a group of about 30 African American and Latino students gathered at St. Mary's University that as future leaders they had a responsibility to initiate a dialogue that would drive civil rights legislation in years to come.

" 'Nationally, much more so than locally, there has been this movement where African Americans and Latinos pull together to do something about their common situations—poverty, discrimination, oppression,' Flores said. 'There is a need to talk about similarities in our cultures, and that talk needs to begin with your generation,' he said. 'Together, we have more power.'

Stribling, who also is a member of the city's Committee on Integrity and Trust in Local Government, emphasized that a pairing of local African American and Latino organizations, such as the local chapters of the National Association for the Advancement of Colored People and the League of United Latin American Citizens, would make a formidable team for significant change."

(San Antonio Express-News [Texas], February 18, 2003)

"In Anita de Palma's eyes, Hispanic representation in government and society is climbing. It just needs help getting over the mountain top. De Palma, who is president of the Tampa Bay Council of the League of United Latin American Citizens, said the key is encouraging the young generation of Hispanics to take pride in their heritage and to become voters and candidates. 'We still don't have the representation throughout the government and throughout the country,' de Palma said. 'We have enough people; our population count is there. Now we have the education.'

"De Palma and Maltilda Martinez Garcia, a former Florida state director for the League of United Latin American Citizens, were scheduled to speak Saturday afternoon on Hispanic civil rights at the John F. Germany Public Library. In an interview, both women agreed that rights for Hispanics have improved over the years. Martinez Garcia remembers as a young woman going to Clearwater in the 1940s and seeing a sign that read, 'No dogs or Latins allowed.' She also recalled seeing a sign at Redington Beach that read, 'No Jews or Latins allowed.'"

(The Tampa Tribune, September 29, 2002)

"Standing at the podium before some 3,000 NAACP members at their national convention last week, Hector Flores, president of LULAC, the nation's oldest Latino civil rights organization, suddenly seemed inspired. 'Viva NAACP!' he chanted repeatedly at the end of his speech. Soon, the audience was on its feet, in enthusiastic applause. 'Viva LULAC! Viva America!'

"It was the first time in memory that a LULAC leader had spoken before the NAACP convention. As such, Flores' appearance symbolized the relationship between the main civil rights organizations representing the two largest minority groups in the country—there were emotional feelings of unity, but they were based on a particular speech on a particular day, not a full-fledged alliance.

"'So much of our work in our communities depends upon the partnership we celebrate today,' said Flores, who was elected president of the League of United Latin American Citizens last month. 'As long as we continue to work together, our communities will continue to reap great rewards.' According to the 2000 U.S. Census, Latinos have surpassed African-Americans as the largest ethnic group in the country. Buoyed by immigration, the Latino population increased 58 percent in the '90s, to 35.3 million in 2000. During that same period, the black population rose 16 percent, to 34.7 million.

"As the Latino population continues to grow, the role of the NAACP—an organization established to serve 'colored people'—is in question. Who is 'colored,' just African-Americans or others too? Meanwhile, the existence of several Latino civil rights groups—including LULAC, the National Council of La Raza and the Mexican-American Legal Defense and Education Fund—makes creating a unified voice for minority ethnic groups more difficult."

(The Atlanta Journal-Constitution, July 14, 2002)

The League of Women Voters of the United States

Established in 1920

DIRECTOR
Nancy Tate, executive director.

BOARD OF DIRECTORS
Declined to comment

SCOPE
Members: 130,000 individual members and supporters
Branches/chapters: 50 state leagues and leagues in Washington, DC, Hong Kong, and the Virgin Islands; 1,100 local leagues
Affiliate: The League of Women Voters Education Fund (LWVEF), a 501(c)(3) organization

STAFF
Declined to comment

TAX STATUS
501(c)(3), 501(c)(4)

FINANCES
Budget: 2000—$6.5 million;
1999—$2.62 million

FUNDING SOURCES
Member payments, 48%; direct mail contributions, 32%; nationally recruited members, 8%; investment income, 5%; other, 7%

PAC
None

EMPLOYMENT
The League of Women Voters is an Equal Opportunity Employer. The League accepts resumes for posted positions only, which can be found at www.lwv.org/about/jobs/jobs.html. Unsolicited resumes will not be retained. Only those selected for interviews will be contacted.

INTERNSHIPS
Internship opportunities are available in communications, development, operations, and program support. Applicants should submit a cover letter indicating their field of study, desired internship area of focus, internship desired (fall, summer, spring, or winter; full-time or part-time), resume, writing sample, and an unofficial transcript to: Internship Coordinator, The League of Women Voters, 1730 M Street, NW, #1000, Washington, DC 20036-4508. Phone: (202) 429-1965. Fax: (202) 429-0854. E-mail: hr@lwv.org.

NEWSLETTERS
The National Voter (quarterly magazine)

CONTACT INFORMATION
1730 M Street, NW, #1000, Washington, DC 20036
Phone: (202) 429-1965 • *Fax:* (202) 429-0854
General E-mail: lwv@lwv.org • *Web site:* www.lwv.org

Communications Director: Kelly Ceballos
(202) 263-1331 • kceballos@lwv.org
Human Resources Director: Declined to comment

PURPOSE: Encourages the informed and active participation of citizens in government and influences public policy through education and advocacy.

CURRENT CONCERNS: Campaign finance reform • Civil liberties • Election reform • Environment • Reproductive choice • Voting rights

METHOD OF OPERATION: Coalition forming • Educational foundation • Electoral politics • Grassroots organizing • Internet (e-mail alerts and Web site) • Lobbying (federal, state, and grassroots) • Media outreach • Voter registration

Effectiveness and Political Orientation

"A poll conducted by the League of Women Voters of Ohio just prior to the 2002 elections revealed that 83 percent of voters believed that political contributions influence the decisions of judges.

"National polls reflect a similar sad state of affairs.

"For several years, Ohio has been at the center of the national crisis involving contributions to judicial campaigns.

"In 2002, about $13 million was spent to elect two Ohio Supreme Court justices, a substantial portion of which was spent by 'independent committees' that would not name the contributors or disclose their expenditures. That amount is more than was spent on all of the other state Supreme Court elections nationally.

"More than $20 million is expected to be spent in 2004 to elect four justices to the high court. And because 'independent committees' that do not disclose their contributors or their payouts will again spend large sums to influence judicial election outcomes, it is imperative that action be taken now.

"An independent and impartial judiciary is fundamental to a free and democratic society, and Ohioans deserve to have full trust and confidence that the resolution of disputes will be conducted in an environment free of influence of unaccounted and hidden political contributions. The cloak of secrecy must be removed.

"To accomplish this, the Ohio State Bar Association is working with state Sen. Randall Gardner, R-Bowling Green, to enact legislation requiring contributors to judicial campaigns to disclose their contributions.

CONFERENCES

National convention

"The association also took this proposal to the American Bar Association, which overwhelmingly supports this effort and encourages all states and territories to enact similar legislation to protect the integrity of judicial offices. . . ."
(*Columbus Dispatch* [Ohio], March 25, 2004)

"A top state election official said yesterday that county registrars of voters, including San Diego's, pressured the secretary of state to certify a key component of an electronic voting system that was not fully tested and later malfunctioned on election day.

"Marc Carrel, assistant secretary of state for policy and planning, made the remarks during a Board of Supervisors meeting packed by residents, poll workers and representatives of watchdog groups who came to comment on the election.

"Locally, 40 percent of the laptop-like devices that encode the voter cards that call up ballots on touch screens did not boot up properly March 2. As a result, 36 percent of the polling places, or 573 of 1,611, opened late. An undetermined number of voters were turned away. . . .

"Representatives from SAVE-Democracy, San Diego and Imperial counties' chapter of the American Civil Liberties Union and the San Diego County League of Women Voters called for an independent investigation into the election involving outside computer experts and watchdog groups. . . ."
(*The San Diego Union-Tribune,* March 17, 2004)

"The nonpartisan League of Women Voters is complaining that a Republican state House candidate is using information from the League's voter's guide improperly to promote his candidacy.

"Gary Gates of Richmond, who is challenging incumbent District 28 Rep. Glenn Hegar, R-Katy, in the GOP primary, acknowledged using the guide in campaign materials but said he did not intend to mislead voters.

"The League publishes guides that contain candidate biographies and their answers to questions posed by the group. Judy Hollinger, president of the Houston Area League of Women Voters, said Gates' mailer gives the impression that the League has endorsed the GOP candidate.

" 'That has been the bedrock of our organization, to be nonpartisan,' said Hollinger. 'It just distorts the whole idea of what the voter's guide is all about. He's taken it out of context.'. . ."
(*The Houston Chronicle,* March 6, 2004)

"Everyone had served as president five or six times—or was it 65 times?—before they said, 'Enough.'

"When no one else would answer the last call to take over for the six or seven stalwarts, the League of Women Voters of Carroll County voted to disband last June, after 37 years. . . .

"With the demise of the league, no one is sure whether another organization will fill the role of producing the league's local voter's guides, of scheduling candidates forums, launching registration drives and assisting with absentee balloting at nursing homes. . . .

" 'So many people call in here and want to know where the voter's guide is and when it will be printed,' said Patricia K. Matsko, director of the Carroll County Board of Elections. 'I think the public is going to miss that—especially on the local front.'. . .

"The national League of Women Voters began in 1920, six months before women won the right to vote. With a membership that is open to both men and women, the league is nonprofit and nonpartisan—but not tax-deductible because it takes stands on issues, according to its Web site. . . .

"It is not clear whether the state or national groups will provide a voter's guide for the national races, Hanger said.

"Basic information is available on the League of Women Voters of Maryland Web site, including information about voter registration, positions on issues, and how to contact elected representatives. . . .

" 'I think you could say that the League of Women Voters is alive and well,' said state President Judy Morenoff of Rockville, a member for more than 30 years of the Montgomery County chapter, one of the oldest in the nation.

" 'I think, nationwide, it is not a particularly unusual phenomenon,' she said of the Carroll chapter's folding. 'I think the volunteer pool has changed. I think the heart of the volunteer pool years ago was young mothers with hours for community service.' "

(*The Baltimore Sun,* February 24, 2004)

"The USA Patriot Act and the balance between civil liberty and security will be the subjects of a televised forum this week sponsored by the League of Women Voters. . . .

"Scheduled panelists include Paul Perez, U.S. attorney for Florida's Middle District; Carl Whitehead, special agent in the FBI's Tampa office; retired Army Col. Michael Pheneger, treasurer of the American Civil Liberties Union of Florida; and Morris 'Sandy' Weinberg Jr., a lawyer with the firm of Zuckerman Spaeder.

"The League of Women Voters of Hillsborough County and county government television will host the forum from 6 to 7:30 p.m. . . ."

(*Tampa Tribune,* February 24, 2004)

Manhattan Institute for Policy Research

Established in 1977

DIRECTOR
Lawrence J. Mone, president.

BOARD OF DIRECTORS
Dietrich Weissmann, chair; Neuberger & Berman
Byron R. Wien, vice chair; Morgan Stanley & Co.
Roger Hertog, chair emeritus; Alliance Capital Management
Charles H. Brunie, chair emeritus; Brunie Associates
Richard Gilder, chair emeritus; Gilder, Gagnon & Howe
Lawrence J. Mone, president
Robert J. Appel; Appel Associates
Eugene D. Brody; Picanet Partners
Andrew Cader
Timothy G. Dalton Jr.; Dalton Enterprises
Peter M. Flanigan; UBS Warburg
Mark Gerson; Gerson Lehman Group
Maurice R. Greenberg; American International Group
H. Dale Hemmerdinger; ATCO Properties & Management
John W. Holman Jr.; Hintz, Holman & Robillard
Bruce Kovner; Caxton Corp.
William Kristol; *The Weekly Standard*
Frank J. Macchiarola; St. Francis College
Walter Mintz; Cumberland Associates
Rodney W. Nichols
Edward J. Nicoll; Instinet Group, Inc.
Peggy Noonan; author
James Piereson; John M. Olin Foundation
Joseph H. Reich; Beginning With Children Foundation
Richard Reiss Jr.; Georgica Advisors
Joseph L. Rice III; Clayton Dubilier & Rice, Inc.
Robert Rosenkranz; Delphi Financial Group
Nathan E. Saint-Amand, M.D.
Andrew M. Saul; Saul Partners
Robert Skidelsky
Thomas W. Smith; Prescott Investors
William K. Tell Jr.
Thomas K. Tisch; FLF Associates
Walter B. Wriston
Kathryn S. Wylde; New York City Partnership and Chamber of Commerce
Fareed Zakaria; *Newsweek*
Martin E. Zweig; Zweig Cos.

SCOPE
Members: None
Branches/chapters: None
Affiliates: Center for Civic Innovation; Center for Legal Policy

STAFF
39 total—plus interns

CONTACT INFORMATION
52 Vanderbilt Avenue, New York, N.Y. 10017
Phone: (212) 599-7000 • *Fax:* (212) 599-3494
General E-mail: mi@manhattan-institute.org •
Web site: www.manhattan-institute.org

Communications Director: Lindsay M. Young
(212) 599-7000, ext. 315 • lyoung@manhattan-institute.org
Human Resources Director: Information unavailable

PURPOSE: "To develop and disseminate new ideas that foster greater economic choice and individual responsibility."

CURRENT CONCERNS: Barriers to building • Crime reduction • Digital economy • Education reform • Faith-based initiatives • Latin American initiatives • Legal reform • Medical progress • New York City development • Race and ethnicity issues • Safe cities • Social entrepreneurship • Taxes • Urban life • Welfare reform

METHOD OF OPERATION: Conferences/seminars • Fellowship program • Internships • Lecture series • Media outreach • Policy forums • Research • Sponsors debates • Web site

Effectiveness and Political Orientation

"Homeowners and businesses across New York State will pay higher property taxes next year, partly because of inaction in Albany to deal with rising pension costs. The increasing costs that local governments must pay for their employee pension plans is, on average across the state, driving an estimated 15 percent tax increase. 'If governments are coming in less than that amount, they are either cutting services or using up their reserves,' said Edward Farrell, executive director of the New York Conference of Mayors.

"A push for state legislation to lower the costs of the localities fell apart when the State Legislature and Gov. George E. Pataki failed to agree on an assortment of unrelated issues that were expected to bring the lawmakers back to Albany this month for a special session. As a result, the tax bills going out soon to property owners must include higher taxes to help cope with the rising pension costs, Farrell said. Even if lawmakers and Pataki agree, say, in January or February to a pension relief bill, it will be too late, because the tax rates would already have been set for county governments, towns and most cities across New York.

"The failure to enact some quick-fix reforms in December should be a wake-up call to finally impose some dramatic and long-lasting changes on the pension system for state and local government workers, according to the Manhattan Institute, a conservative think tank. The institute claims that taxpayers have been penalized by the leap in pension costs—more than $2.4 billion over the past two years—because of sour Wall Street performance by the pension fund's investments, new benefits for retirees and a system that has become more generous than other public and private pension plans."

(*Buffalo News*, December 23, 2003)

"The racially integrated magnet schools that have sprouted across Connecticut offer attractive educational choices for parents, but cannot by themselves end school segregation, a panel of experts said Tuesday. Despite the opening of dozens of promising, popular magnet schools over the past decade, many children remain in mostly white or mostly black and Latino schools, said panelists at a Courant Key Issues Forum in Hartford. 'I think that the magnet approach that Connecticut is pursuing is a good approach. . . . The trouble is that it's limited . . . [and] it's extremely expensive,' said Jay P. Greene of the Manhattan Institute for Policy Research in New York City.

"Greene, an advocate of tuition vouchers and greater school choice for families, was one of three panelists from outside Connecticut discussing the state's ambitious magnet school effort. Magnet schools have been the state's chief method for complying with a court order in the long-running Sheff vs. O'Neill school desegregation lawsuit. Nearly a year ago, Sheff plaintiffs reached a settlement with the state on how to meet a 1996 state Supreme Court ruling that ordered the state to desegregate Hartford's schools. The settlement calls for an expansion of magnet schools—eight new schools in the Hartford area over the next four years—with cost estimates for construction and operation ranging between $135 million and nearly $250 million."

(*Hartford Courant* [Connecticut], December 3, 2003)

"As the national economy continues to roar forward, New York City officials are maintaining caution until they see stronger signs of a full recovery here. Deputy Mayor Daniel L. Doctoroff said yesterday that while the Bloomberg administration is hopeful the city's economy will show continued improvement, it is not yet ready to roll back the tax increases, or implement additional tax cuts. 'The moment will occur when we feel we are out of the economic woods here,' Doctoroff told a group of business leaders and development officials at a luncheon sponsored by the Manhattan Institute, a conservative think tank. 'But we all agree we want to roll back taxes.'

"The national economy grew by a stunning 8.2 percent in the third quarter, according to statistics announced yesterday. But despite the apparent trend of a national comeback, the city continues to lag, losing 28,400 jobs in the 12 months ending in October. However, economists and other experts do expect the city to follow the national trend of improvement. 'New York City at the very least is approaching the threshold of economic recovery,' said J.P. Morgan/Chase senior regional economist Marc Goloven."

(*Newsday* [New York], November 26, 2003)

"Only two-thirds of Colorado's students graduated from high school in 2001 and a majority were woefully underprepared for college, an educational think tank says in a report released today. The report from the New York-based Manhattan Institute blasted Colorado's educational quality and indicates that the state's minorities are among the worst in the nation when it comes to college readiness. The think tank's graduation rate for Colorado also was nearly 12 percentage points below the state's reported figure.

"Not everyone agreed with what's in the report. 'Obviously, I think a lot of people are going to have a problem with this,' said Deborah Fallin, a spokeswoman for the 37,000-member Colorado Education Association that has battled the Manhattan Institute in the past over school voucher issues. 'You can make numbers say anything you want,' Fallin said. While she and others questioned the group's findings, some school districts and the Colorado Department of Education used the report to renew vows to lessen dropout rates statewide."

(*Rocky Mountain News* [Denver], September 17, 2003)

"Despite consistent financial shortcomings and hefty reliance on inexperienced teachers, charter school students often do better academically than their traditional counterparts, a national study has found. In comparing charter schools with traditional public schools, the authors of the study noted that charter schools tended to serve a disproportionate number of poor, struggling students at risk of dropping out. The authors said, therefore, that it might not be fair to expect charter schools to perform as well on standardized tests as traditional public schools.

"But when measured against those public schools with similar demographic and geographic characteristics, charter schools produced slightly higher gains in math and reading over a one-year period, according to the study, which was conducted by the Manhattan Institute, a national policy research organization. For students with test scores that fall in the middle of the pack, for example, going to a charter school appeared to add an extra two percentile points in reading and three percentile points in math on standardized tests. These gains were relatively modest, the study found, but were large enough to challenge the notion that charter schools suffer academically because they tend to employ so many uncredentialed teachers, as some critics have suggested.

" 'Why do they make greater gains?' said Jay Greene, senior fellow at the Manhattan Institute. 'Charter schools enjoy greater freedom from regulation, and that may give them greater flexibility to meet the needs of their students.' "

(*The New York Times,* July 20, 2003)

Media Access Project

Established in 1971

DIRECTOR

Andrew J. Schwartzman, president and chief executive officer. Schwartzman previous served as MAP's executive director from 1978 to 1996. He is widely published in general, trade, and legal publications. In 1993, Schwartzman received the Everett C. Parker Award for his career contributions to the public interest in communications. Both his undergraduate and law degrees are from the University of Pennsylvania.

BOARD OF DIRECTORS

Peggy Charren; founder, Action for Children's Television

Henry Geller; former assistant secretary of commerce

Kristin Booth Glen; dean, City University of New York School of Law

William E. Kennard; managing director, Telecommunications and Media, Carlyle Group

Albert Kramer; Dickstein, Shapiro, Morin & Oshinsky

Jorge Schement; co-director, Institute for Information Policy, Pennsylvania State University

Jonah Seiger; Connections Media, LLC

Roanne Shaddox Robinson; Privacy Council

Andrew Jay Schwartzman; president and chief executive officer, Media Access Project

SCOPE

Members: None
Branches/chapters: None
Affiliates: None

STAFF

5 total—3 full-time professional; 2 full-time support; plus 1 part-time support

TAX STATUS

501(c)(3)

FINANCES

Revenue: 2002—$677,125; 2001—$632,756; 2000—$513,272

FUNDING SOURCES

Grants, 100%

PAC

None

EMPLOYMENT

Postings are listed at www.mediaaccess.org/employment/. Resumes and other materials should be sent to Cheryl Leanza, deputy director, 1625 K Street, NW, Suite 1000, Washington, DC 20006. E-mail: cleanza@mediaaccess.org.

CONTACT INFORMATION

1625 K Street, NW, Suite 1000, Washington, DC 20006
Phone: (202) 232-4300 • *Fax:* 202) 466-7656
General E-mail: info@mediaaccess.org • *Web site:* www.mediaaccess.org

Communications Director: Harold J. Feld, associate director
(202) 454-5684 • hfeld@mediaaccess.org
Human Resources Director: Amy Zalud, operations manager
(202) 454-5685 • azalud@mediaaccess.org

PURPOSE: Media Access Project is a nonprofit, public interest law firm that promotes the public's First Amendment right to hear and be heard on the electronic media of today and tomorrow.

CURRENT CONCERNS: Broadband access • Civil rights in the media • Diversity in media holdings • Internet governance • Low power radio • Media consolidation • Promoting civic discourse in the media • Protecting free speech • Public interest obligations

METHOD OF OPERATION: Coalition building • Congressional testimony • Internships • Legal assistance • Litigation • Media outreach • Participation in regulatory proceedings (federal) • Web site

Effectiveness and Political Orientation

"The Federal Communications Commission's new media-ownership rules steer a middle course between too much and too little regulation of broadcasters such as Viacom's CBS and publishers such as Tribune Co., said the FCC and Justice Department in a court brief filed yesterday. 'The commission's revised rules are a measured response to the substantial changes in the broadcast industry and the media marketplace in recent years,' the agencies said in a 104-page brief.

"The brief, filed in the 3rd U.S. Circuit Court of Appeals in Philadelphia, responds to filings by consumer groups, broadcasters and publishers that challenge the FCC's rules. Consumer groups said the FCC's June rules went too far in easing restrictions on media acquisitions; networks including CBS and News Corp.'s Fox argued the rules didn't go far enough. FCC Chairman Michael Powell, a Republican, contended that ownership rules should be eased because of the recent proliferation of new media such as the Internet and cable and satellite TV. Consumer groups argued that media consolidation would reduce diversity in news and entertainment.

" 'The industry continues to complain, though they predominately prevailed at the FCC,' said Cheryl Leanza of the nonprofit Media Access Project, a consumer advocacy group that filed a brief challenging the FCC rules. The court temporarily blocked implementation of the six rules in September until it has a chance to review them more thoroughly. The U.S. House voted Monday to tighten one of the new rules by reducing to 39 percent, from 45

INTERNSHIPS
Information on unpaid internships is available at www.mediaaccess.org/employment/ #intern. Resumes, writing samples, and cover letters may be sent to Harold Feld, associate director, 1625 K Street, NW, Suite 1000, Washington, DC 20006. E-mail: hfeld@ mediaaccess.org.

NEWSLETTERS
None

PUBLICATIONS
None

CONFERENCES
None

percent, the limit on the national audience that can be reached by a television network's local stations."

(*The Seattle Times,* December 10, 2003)

"While it can't yet be said the story has a happy ending, it does have a happy middle. Yesterday the Senate Commerce Committee voted against attempts by the Federal Communications Commission to let Big Media grow much, much bigger. The committee, under Chairman John McCain (R-Ariz.), voted to over-turn changes in media ownership rules that had been championed by FCC Chairman Michael Powell, the best friend a media fat cat ever had. The keystone of Powell's plan would have raised the limit on how many broadcast stations one corporation could own—from coverage of 35 percent of U.S. households, the current limit, to a new and dangerous 45 percent maximum. . . .

"Whatever the precise shape of the Senate's bill, it will likely face stubborn opposition on the other side of the Hill from the depressingly powerful Rep. Billy Tauzin (R-La.), chairman of the House Commerce Committee and, so far, a slavish supporter of Powell and his big-media constituency.

"But even Tauzin may be forced to consider what activists are calling a tremendous expression of outrage from the American public—even though the issue got very little coverage on the national networks. People and groups from both the right and left sides of the political spectrum deluged congres-sional offices with complaints about letting gigantic media conglomerates grow ever more gigantic—about sacrificing the principle of media diversity to the corporate god of high profits. . . .

" 'It's an extremely significant step in reversing the FCC agenda,' said Cheryl Leanza, deputy director of the Media Access Project. McCain put icing on the cupcake by introducing an amendment that may eventually require Clear Channel Communications to divest itself of some of the 1,250 radio sta-tions it now controls throughout the country."

(*The Washington Post,* June 20, 2003)

"In June, the Federal Communications Commission is expected to usher in sweeping changes to the information landscape by weakening and perhaps dis-carding several crucial rules limiting media ownership. In an era of corporate giants such as AOL Time Warner, fighting the media consolidation tidal wave might seem like arranging deck chairs on the Titanic. Still, a group of activists—operating with relatively small budgets, very loud voices, and an inexhaustible supply of energy—wage a lonely battle against consolidation in the name of what they say is diversity, fairness, and public interest. Meet four committed Washington outsiders playing an insider's game against long odds.

"Jenny Toomey, rock 'n' roll activist: It's not every day that someone tes-tifying before the Senate Committee on Commerce, Science & Transporta-tion introduces herself as 'a rocker, businesswoman, and an activist.' Toomey, 35, has run an independent record label and has played solo and with the band Tsunami. Now she focuses much of her energy on the job of executive direc-tor of the nonprofit Future of Music Coalition. . . .

"The Media Access Project weighs in on everything from efforts to require broadcasters to provide free airtime to political candidates (it supports that) to the FCC's approval of Comcast's purchase of AT&T's cable systems (it opposes that). A staunch foe of further media deregulation, Schwartman pre-dicts: 'Ultimately, this is going to have to be decided by the Supreme Court.' Schwartzman vows to fight on and leave a legacy more positive than that of another Beltway institution—the hapless basketball team that always lost to the Harlem Globetrotters. 'We're not throwing in the towel,' he says. 'I sometimes joke that we don't want to be the Washington Generals.' "

(*The Boston Globe,* April 30, 2003)

"Privacy and consumer-advocacy groups yesterday asked federal regulators to investigate Amazon.com Inc., claiming that the online retail giant lets children post personal information on its Web site in violation of a federal law. The Electronic Privacy Information Center, the Media Access Project and other groups said Amazon lets children post product reviews, which sometimes include their names, e-mail addresses, or other personal data. A 1998 law, the Children's Online Privacy Protection Act, requires Web sites to get parental consent before allowing children under the age of 13 to post information."

(*The Washington Post,* April 23, 2003)

"Michael K. Powell, chairman of the Federal Communications Commission, said today that he wanted to ease rules that prevent newspapers from owning television or radio stations in the same market. 'It's hard to see how a complete ban on newspapers' owning TV stations serves the public interest,' Mr. Powell said in a speech at a lunch of the Media Institute, a nonprofit group supported by media and communications companies.

"Mr. Powell is one of three commissioners on the FCC to say they favor relaxing a 1975 rule that seeks to prevent a concentration of media power. The five-member commission has tentatively scheduled a meeting on June 2, Mr. Powell said, to adopt new rules on media ownership.

"The federal agency is considering changes to six rules that restrict mergers among newspapers, TV networks and radio stations. Companies like Tribune, the owner of *The Los Angeles Times* and *Chicago Tribune,* and the News Corporation, which owns *The New York Post,* have lobbied to ease the rule. Both companies also own TV stations. 'The rule is as good as dead, though we still don't know whether there will be any limits on cross-ownership and what they will be,' said Blair Levin, an analyst at Legg Mason Wood Walker and a former chief of staff at the FCC.

"Newspapers are now allowed to own TV or radio stations in the same market if they bought them before the 28-year-old rule went into effect, or if the FCC. granted them a waiver. An easing of the rules 'poses a real threat to the democratic process,' said Andrew Schwartzman of the nonprofit Media Access Project, a consumer advocacy group."

(*The New York Times,* March 28, 2003)

Media Research Center

Established in 1987

DIRECTOR

L. Brent Bozell III, chair. Prior to founding the Media Research Center (MRC), Bozell was executive director of the National Conservative Foundation and chair and president of the National Conservative Political Action Committee. Bozell has also served on the board of governors of the Council for National Policy. He graduated from the University of Dallas.

BOARD OF DIRECTORS

L. Brent Bozell, president
Brent Baker, vice president
Darlene Nelson, secretary
Douglas Mills, treasurer
William Rusher; writer
Harold Clark Simmons; former chief
     executive officer, Amalgamated Sugar Co.
Leon J. Weil; Gruntal & Co.
Curtis Windsor

SCOPE

Members: 10,000
Branches/chapters: None
Affiliates: CNSNews.com; Free Market Project (FMP); Parents Television Council (PTC); TimesWatch.org

STAFF

35 total—plus 2 interns

TAX STATUS

501(c)(3)

FINANCES

Revenue: 2002—$5.77 million;
2001—$6.26 million

FUNDING SOURCES

Individuals, 35%; membership/subscriptions, 26%; foundations, 21%; corporations, 15%; royalties, interest, and investments, 3%

PAC

None

EMPLOYMENT

Available job postings are listed at www.mediaresearch.org/jobs/jobs.asp. Application materials can be faxed to Human Resources at (703) 683-9736.

INTERNSHIPS

Internships are available year-round. Postings are listed at www.mediaresearch.org/jobs/jobs.asp#MRCInternships. Application materials should be sent to Douglas Mills, executive director, Media Research Center, 325 South Patrick Street, Alexandria, VA 22314. Fax: (703) 683-9736.

CONTACT INFORMATION

325 South Patrick Street, Alexandria, VA 22314
Phone: (703) 683-9733 • *Fax:* (703) 683-9736
Toll-free: (800) 672-1423
General E-mail: mrc@mediaresearch.org • *Web site:* www.mediaresearch.org

Communications Director: Brent H. Baker
bbaker@mediaresearch.org
Human Resources Director: Douglas Mills
dmills@mediaresearch.org

PURPOSE: "To bring balance and responsibility to the news media."

CURRENT CONCERNS: Abortion • Afghanistan • Arctic National Wildlife Refuge • Business and free enterprise • Campaign Finance Reform • Capital Punishment • Gun rights • Hollywood • Iraq • Kyoto Treaty • Media and politics • Missile defense

METHOD OF OPERATION: Internet (e-mail alerts and Web site,) • Media outreach • Research • Special programs (Conservative Experts, Economic Experts Forum, Montgomery Internship Program)

Effectiveness and Political Orientation

"President Bush has been complaining that the news media act as a filter, keeping good news about the U.S. occupation of Iraq from reaching the public. Does he have a point? Yes, says Brent Baker of the Media Research Center, and the complaining has brought positive results.

"No, says Danny Schechter of MediaChannel. The administration was so successful at selling its viewpoint on Iraq, Schechter says, that Bush can't handle the least bit of independent, skeptical reporting.

"Maybe, says media scholar Stephen Hess of the Brookings Institution, but there's nothing unusual about Bush's complaint. Every recent president has reached a similar point and has complained that the media are treating him unfairly, Hess says."

(*Minneapolis Star Tribune,* November 10, 2003)

"Conservative watchdog groups are turning up the heat on CBS executives over the upcoming miniseries about former President Ronald Reagan. Media Research Center President Brent Bozell said his organization has sent a letter to the 'top 100 corporate advertisers' claiming the movie has 'blatantly distorted the history and is nothing more than a partisan political attack against one of America's most beloved Presidents.'

"The two-part movie stars James Brolin (husband of leading liberal Barbra Streisand) as Reagan and Judy Davis as wife Nancy. While no one outside of CBS has seen the film, leaked portions of the script have turned the project into a pinata for conservative commentators and friends of the Reagans. They have said the movie underplays Reagan's achievements during his eight years in office and unfairly portrays him as insensitive to the AIDS crisis.

"'He's in the last stages of Alzheimer's and a woman who has been sitting by his bedside there holding his hand for nine years—they can't fight back,' said Reagan family friend Merv Griffin on MSNBC's 'Countdown.' But ad-agency executives say it's highly unlikely that protests are going to prompt any sponsors from bailing. 'You know going into a program about a public figure that there are going to be some issues with it,' said one executive at a media-buying firm. . . ."

(*New York Daily News,* October 30, 2003)

"Though *Buffalo Soldiers* has been praised by critics, Miramax studio has weathered a storm of criticism from the public. The conservative Media Research Center calls the film 'flamboyantly unpatriotic' and veterans groups also have complained. Project 21, an African-American leadership network, is offended that the film's title—taken from its source novel—usurps a name given to African-American soldiers when America's military was segregated.

"The first 'buffalo soldiers' served on America's Western frontiers in the 1860s, earning their nickname from Plains Indians for showing the fighting spirit of sacred buffalos. Project 21 has demanded that Miramax rename the film, which the studio has refused to do.

"'When the name 'buffalo soldiers' is uttered, the only thought that anyone has is of those brave men who fought valiantly for all of the people of the United States,' said Project 21 member Michael King. 'This movie would do nothing but tarnish the name of the buffalo soldiers, both past and present, in the minds of the public. The irresponsibility of the filmmakers borders on criminal in my mind.'"

(*The Houston Chronicle,* August 9, 2003)

"Jessica Lynch and the story of her capture and rescue were a blank canvass on which media outlets could paint whatever picture they wanted to about the Iraqi war, women in combat or America, according to a media watchdog group. While Lynch has yet to say anything about her ordeal, media around the world have spun and re-spun her story more times than the rotors on the Black Hawk helicopter that brought her back to her Wirt County home Tuesday.

"'In a story like this, the subject becomes a pawn for competing interests and viewpoints,' said Tim Graham, director of media analysis for the Washington-based Media Research Center. 'I mean, how often do you see a grunt on the cover of Newsweek. This story took on significance and proportions way beyond Jessica Lynch.'

"For instance, here's how the story played in today's London Times: 'For the rest of the world, reality has eroded Private Lynch's heroism. She was not a do-or-die warrior but a teenager from an area of high unemployment who enlisted shortly before a war. Human error and weapons failures contributed to the convoy deaths. But to Americans, she remains a symbol of moral superiority in an ongoing conflict.'

"Graham said much of the reason for the Lynch backlash is the perception among some media outlets that the story benefits the Bush administration and its support of the war. But the spin on the story goes deeper, he said. When Lynch was captured at the beginning of the war while many pundits already were talking about the failure of the American battle plan, Graham said the loss of a female soldier was used to reinforce that conception."

(*Charleston Daily Mail* [West Virginia], July 23, 2003)

"The battlefield isn't the only place journalists are under fire. Back home, news critics are poring over every word reported from Iraq. And they don't like a lot of what they see. Among the mainstream news organizations regularly blasted by supporters of the war who label themselves right-wingers are CNN, NPR and the BBC. And the media watchers critical of the war—some of whom are labeled left-wingers—respond by saying the other side has little to complain about, because it has managed to set the agenda via loud and long complaints about 'the liberal media.'

"Supporters of the war can be found and heard on their Web sites: mediaresearchcenter.com; aim.org; andrewsullivan.com; theamericanprowler .org; nationalreview.com; opinionjournal.com; weeklystandard.com; and freerepublic.com among others. Some of them say coverage of the Iraqi war is too negative. Especially, they say, in light of the relatively easy collapse of Saddam Hussein's regime.

"Others go further: Journalists whose stories don't support the war—or are seen as less than enthusiastic—are left-wingers who are against President George W. Bush and are anti-American. That's the thinking of people like Tim Graham of the Media Research Center. 'I find it appalling when Ted Koppel goes on and says: "We'll try to give you the truth," ' Graham says of the ABC Nightline correspondent. 'I just want to punch him in the face,' says Graham, 'because that's not what they give us.'

"Media Research was founded in 1987 by Brent Bozell, a self-described right-winger whose organization bills itself as the largest conservative media watchdog group in the country. It has taped and transcribed some 20,000 news reports for the purpose of issuing daily alerts 'documenting, exposing and neutralizing liberal media bias.' Critics of the war say the other side is winning its effort to influence reporting—through bigger bank rolls, louder complaints and attempts at intimidation.

"Media Research says it gets about $8 million a year in donations (10 times what the leading liberal group gets) but won't disclose membership. The group operates from Alexandria, Va., and credits itself with helping create the climate that has led to the success of Rush Limbaugh and Fox News. Fox calls itself 'fair and balanced,' but some complain the network is a cheerleader for the war. A Fox News report recently criticized columnist Robert Scheer, who's syndicated by the Chicago Tribune. Scheer observed that during the Revolutionary War, the British said Americans were standing behind trees instead of firing from traditional battlefield formations."

(*St. Louis Post-Dispatch,* April 13, 2003)

Mexican American Legal Defense
and Educational Fund (MALDEF)

Established in 1968

DIRECTOR

Ann Marie Tallman, president and general counsel. Tallman has been involved with MALDEF since 1987. Since 1998, she has been an active MALDEF board member, and has served in leadership capacities as chair of numerous subcommittees. In 1990, as executive director for the Colorado Hispanic League, she spearheaded statewide Hispanic census outreach and was actively involved in reapportionment and political redistricting efforts with MALDEF. Since 1994, Tallman has been an executive with the mortgage lending giant Fannie Mae, and most recently she was senior vice president of Fannie Mae's Single Family Mortgage Business. In 1998–99, she was president and CEO of the nonprofit Fannie Mae Foundation in Washington, DC, where she reengineered the foundation and cultivated collaborative relationships with other foundations and nonprofit organizations. While at the Foundation, Tallman launched the Hispanic Heritage Award Foundation's Youth Awards. Before joining Fannie Mae, Tallman was a deputy director for both the City and County of Denver, in charge of the Planning and Community Development Agency.

BOARD OF DIRECTORS

Antonia Hernández, president and general counsel
Barbara Aldave
Edward J. Avila
Zöe Baird
Mike Baller
Joseph Barish
Carlos Cantu
Gilberto Cardenas
Martin R. Castro
Hector J. Cuellar
Teresa Leger de Fernandez
Bette F. DeGraw
Patricia Diaz Dennis
Rene Diaz
Susana Duarte
Liz Figueroa
Herlinda Garcia
Leo Gomez
Al Gurule
Paul Gutierrez
Frank Herrera
Federico Jimenez
Gregory Luna
Tatcho Mindiola
Gloria Molina
Donald L. Pierce
Matthew J. Piers
Frank J. Quevedo
Guadalupe Rangel
Thomas B. Reston
Maria Saldana
Andrew Segovia

CONTACT INFORMATION

634 S. Spring Street, Los Angeles, CA 90014
Phone: (213) 629-2512 • *Fax:* (213) 629-3120
Washington office
1717 K Street, NW, Suite 311, Washington, DC 20036
Phone: 202) 293-2828 • *Fax:* (202) 293-2849
Web site: www.maldef.org

Communications Director: J. C. Flores
jflores@maldef.org
Human Resources Director: Declined to comment

PURPOSE: "To foster sound public policies, laws and programs to safeguard the civil rights of the 40 million Latinos living in the United States and to empower the Latino community to fully participate in our society."

CURRENT CONCERNS: Education • Employment • Immigrants' rights • Political access • Public resource equity

METHOD OF OPERATION: Awards program • Congressional testimony • Congressional voting analysis • Films/video/audiotapes • Grantmaking • Internet (e-mail alerts and Web site) • Internships • Legal assistance • Legislative/regulatory monitoring (federal and state) • Litigation • Media outreach • Scholarships for Latino law and communications students

Effectiveness and Political Orientation

"Advocates for immigrants urged prosecutors Tuesday to file hate crime charges against five Cherokee High students accused of attacking and robbing two Latino day laborers in Canton. By bragging at school that they had 'robbed some Mexicans,' the boys opened themselves up to charges under Georgia's hate crimes law, said Tisha Tillman, Mexican American Legal Defense and Educational Fund regional counsel.

" 'The violence and hate must be stopped,' Tillman said, 'violence and hate in this instance that has corrupted the minds of five young white high school students and has dehumanized two contributing members of our society.' Tillman said she and others had urged Cobb District Attorney Pat Head to file hate crime charges. 'We believe he needs to be urged further to make sure that a proper and through investigation is done that would support prosecution of these crimes as hate crimes,' she said Tuesday at a news conference on the Marietta Square.

"Head was unavailable for comment Tuesday, but a spokeswoman confirmed he had met Friday with members of the group. In a written statement, Cobb Chief Assistant District Attorney Tom Weathers said: 'We will make our charging decisions based on both the law and evidence in the case.' The hate crime statute, passed in 2000, allows a prosecutor to seek up to five additional years on a conviction if it can be shown that a defendant selected the

Marcia Silverman
Joseph Stern
Ann Marie Wheelock

SCOPE
Members: None
Branches/chapters: Regional offices in
Atlanta, Chicago, Houston, Sacramento,
San Antonio and Washington, DC
Affiliates: None

STAFF
75 total nationwide—50 professional;
25 support; plus 15 interns

TAX STATUS
501(c)(3)

FINANCES
Declined to comment

FUNDING SOURCES
Declined to comment

PAC
None

EMPLOYMENT
Job postings are listed on the MALDEF
Web site, at www.maldef.org/about/
employment.cfm.

INTERNSHIPS
Declined to comment

NEWSLETTERS
Leading Hispanics (2 times a year)
MALDEF (2 times a year)

PUBLICATIONS
Annual report

CONFERENCES
None

victim or vandalized property because of bias or prejudice. The law also requires that prisoners serve at least 90 percent of their sentence prior to parole. . . ."

(*The Atlanta Journal-Constitution*, February 25, 2004)

"Three Latino students rejected by Cal Poly San Luis Obispo have sued the state university, contending that its admission system had illegally discriminated against them by giving undue weight to SAT scores and favoring applicants from the geographic area around the campus. Thomas A. Saenz, a lawyer for the Mexican American Legal Defense and Educational Fund who is representing the students, said Cal Poly's admissions system is discriminatory because Latinos in California score lower on the SAT, on average, than whites. Also, he said, the surrounding areas have fewer Latino and other minorities than the state as a whole.

"Cal Poly's director of public affairs, Leah Kolt, said university officials could not comment because they had not seen the lawsuit, which was filed Wednesday in San Luis Obispo County Superior Court. The League of United Latin American Citizens, an advocacy group, also is a plaintiff. Cal Poly uses a mathematical formula to admit undergraduates. Among other things, the formula awards points to applicants on the basis of their SAT scores. Students from the school's 'service area,' which stretches from Kings County to Lompoc, are awarded extra points. The school is one of several Cal State campuses to consider geography in admissions."

(*The Los Angeles Times,* January 9, 2004)

"Legal challenges mounted this week over the new Republican-sponsored law that redraws Texas congressional districts in order to bring the party more seats in Washington after the elections in 2004. On Tuesday the Mexican American Legal Defense and Educational Fund became the third group to sue the state over the new map since the legislature approved it on Sunday. The fund says the map, approved by Governor Rick Perry on Tuesday, does not accurately reflect Latino voting strength. The map, engineered to shake the Democrats' 17–15 majority in the US House of Representatives, creates up to 22 Republican-leaning districts.

"It has had a dramatic history, featuring five months of bitter debate, two high-profile Democratic walkouts, and $5m in state spending for holding three special sessions over the map. Democrats consider it a transparent power-grab, while Republicans argue that the existing districts do not reflect the state's voter make-up. Such redistricting disputes are common, especially after seats are reapportioned among the states to reflect demographic shifts, following the once-a-decade national census. But the Texas controversy stems from the Republicans' unusual step of redrawing a map agreed upon just two years ago. . . ."

(*Financial Times* [London, England], October 16, 2003)

"There are boxes and boxes of old pictures, documents, history and who knows what else missing from the MALDEF archives and Nina Perales wants them back. Worse, they may not be missing at all. Perales is the regional counsel of the Mexican American Legal Defense and Educational Fund and was involved in coordinating Friday night's 19th Annual Texas Awards Gala at the Westin Hotel. As she was putting the event together, she wanted to present highlights of key events from the past.

"That's when she discovered there may not be any archives. 'I don't know if a box got misplaced or if they were never kept,' Perales said. 'I've called several of the founding members who are still alive and no one seems to have anything.' MALDEF, a national nonprofit organization formed 35 years ago, conducts civil rights legal work. Missing archives notwithstanding, the group can be proud of its many accomplishments over the years.

" 'In Texas, we will file litigation if the new congressional redistricting plan does not fairly reflect the Latino population in this state,' Perales emphasized, as the audience of about 200 applauded and cheered. In Louisiana, she said, 'we stopped the Ouachita Parish School District from requiring an undocumented girl to produce a Social Security number before being allowed to participate in the Gifted and Talented program despite the fact that she had scored over 95 percent on the entrance tests.'

"And Friday, the group filed a settlement of a racial profiling case in Rogers, Ark., 'that will halt the city's practice of targeting Latinos for stops and searches.' "

(*San Antonio Express-News* [Texas], September 27, 2003)

"There's a five-letter fix to the public school funding system under challenge in state court, a Mexican American Legal Defense and Educational Fund lawyer told legislators Tuesday: money. 'There's nothing that's wrong with the system at this point that money can't fix,' MALDEF's Leticia Saucedo told the House Select Committee on Public School Finance. If legislators want wholesale change to the current system, which relies heavily on local property taxes, she added, 'Institute an income tax and then we can all go home.' "

(*San Antonio Express-News* [Texas], June 25, 2003)

Middle East Policy Council

Established in 1981

DIRECTOR

Charles W. Freeman Jr., president. Freeman formerly was assistant secretary of defense for International Security Affairs. He also served as U.S. ambassador to Saudi Arabia; principal deputy assistant secretary of state for African Affairs; deputy chief of mission and chargé d'affaires in the American embassies at both Bangkok and Beijing; director for Chinese affairs at the U.S. Department of State; and principal American interpreter during President Richard Nixon's historic visit to China in 1972. He was elected to the Academy of American Diplomacy in 1995. He is the author of *The Diplomat's Dictionary* and *Arts of Power*. Freeman is also chair of the Board of Projects International, Inc., a Washington-based business development firm that specializes in arranging international joint ventures, acquisitions, and other business operations for its American and foreign clients. He serves as co-chair of the United States-China Policy Foundation and vice chair of the Atlantic Council of the United States. He is a member of the boards of the Institute for Defense Analyses and the Washington World Affairs Council. Freeman earned a certificate in Latin American studies from the National Autonomous University of Mexico, certificates in both the national and Taiwan dialects of Chinese from the former Foreign Service Institute field school in Taiwan, a B.A. from Yale University and a J.D. from the Harvard Law School.

BOARD OF DIRECTORS

Charles W. Freeman Jr., president
Robert D. Bauerlein, vice president; Boeing Co.
Curtis Brand, chair; ExxonMobil, Saudi Arabia, Inc.
Charles W. Brown; U.S. Army, (retired)
William J. Brown; Senior Legal Advisor, EFD, Abu Dhabi Investment Authority
Frank C. Carlucci; chair, Carlyle Group; former U.S. Secretary of Defense
K. V. R. Dey; president and chief executive officer, Liggett Group, Inc. (retired)
Yankel Ginzburg; artist
Najeeb Halaby; attorney at law; former head, Federal Aviation Administration
Omar Kader; president and chief executive officer, Pal-Tech, Inc.
Martha Neff Kessler; consultant, CIA (retired)
George McGovern; UN global ambassador on Hunger; former U.S. senator
Dale F. Nitzschke; chancellor emeritus, Southeast Missouri State University
Talat M. Othman; president, Grove Financial, Inc., Chicago

CONTACT INFORMATION

1730 M Street, NW, Suite 512, Washington, DC 20036
Phone: (202) 296-6767 • *Fax:* (202) 296-5791
General E-mail: info@mepc.org • *Web site:* www.mepc.org

Communications Director: Information unavailable
Human Resources Director: Information unavailable

PURPOSE: "The Middle East Policy Council was founded in 1981 to expand public discussion and understanding of issues affecting U.S. policy in the Middle East."

CURRENT CONCERNS: Broker voting • Corporate governance • Director independence • Executive compensation disclosure • Furthering good pension fund governance • Shareholder approval of stock option plans • Soft dollars

METHOD OF OPERATION: Information unavailable

Effectiveness and Political Orientation

"A former U.S. ambassador to Saudi Arabia is warning that a pending lawsuit against top Saudi government and business figures filed by victims of the Sept. 11, 2001, attacks could jeopardize relations between the two nations and strengthen the hand of anti-American forces in the kingdom's ruling circles.

"If the plaintiffs prevailed, 'it would aid and abet those within the Kingdom, including not a few in the ruling Al-Saud (royal family), who argue that their country should now end its longstanding cooperation with the United States,' former ambassador Chas. W. Freeman Jr. contended in an affidavit. . . .

"Freeman's 15-page statement was filed in federal court in Washington this week by lawyers for Prince Sultan, the Saudi defense minister, as part of a motion to dismiss the lawsuit, which seeks $1 trillion in damages. It alleges that top Saudis financed and promoted the al Qaeda terrorist network; Sultan and the other defendants deny the allegations.

"Freeman, who is paid as an expert witness by Sultan's lawyers, wrote the document on Sultan's behalf, but Sultan's lawyers said the views expressed are not necessarily their client's. In recent weeks, however, Saudi officials have expressed similar views. Last month, Prince Saud Faisal, the Saudi foreign minister, said a congressional report suggesting that the Saudis helped fund al Qaeda is hurting U.S.-Saudi relations.

"Plaintiffs' lawyer Ron Motley cited Freeman's long-standing pro-Saudi views and the fact that an institute he runs, the Middle East Policy Council, has received substantial funds from prominent Saudi business figures. 'He's a flack for the Saudis,' Motley said of Freeman.

"In the affidavit, Freeman said that simply allowing the lawsuit to continue would endanger Saudi counterterrorist cooperation with the United

States and undermine U.S. efforts to sell goods and base U.S. military forces in Saudi Arabia."

(*The Washington Post*, August 14, 2003)

"The Bush administration has been misleading the public about the dangers Iraq poses to the United States and the rest of the world, former Sen. George McGovern said Tuesday.

"McGovern, a Democrat from South Dakota who ran against President Nixon in 1972, spoke at the University of Wyoming College of Education at the invitation of former Sen. Alan Simpson, R-Wyo., and his brother, political science professor emeritus Pete Simpson.

"McGovern said the administration has been unsuccessful in its efforts to show a link between Iraq and the Sept. 11, 2001, terrorist attacks and has also overstated Iraq's arsenal of weapons of mass destruction. . . .

"Since being voted out of the Senate in 1980, McGovern has been a visiting professor at universities including Columbia, Northwestern, Cornell, American University and the University of Berlin.

"He was president of the Middle East Policy Council from 1991–1998. After that, he was appointed by President Clinton as ambassador to the United Nations Food and Agriculture Organization in Rome."

(*Associated Press Newswires*, March 25, 2003)

"If he were still an American diplomat, Charles W. Freeman Jr. says he probably would have resigned in protest by now.

"It's a bleak time for international diplomacy, says the Rhode Island native who was U.S. ambassador to Saudi Arabia during the Gulf War. He sees an administration that's rushing into a preemptive strike against Iraq without the support of the international community and with little justification.

"It's a far cry from the situation 12 years ago when Freeman, now 60 and retired from a decades-long State Department career in the Foreign Service, helped sow the seeds of a broad coalition to fight and finance the war against Iraq.

"He is proud of what was achieved during the Gulf War.

"'I was a strong proponent of military action then because I thought it was justified, it would work and it could improve our position in the region. That's not the case now,' said Freeman, who is still active in the affairs of the Middle East.

"Since 1997, Freeman has been the president of the Middle East Policy Council, a Washington, D.C., think tank."

(*The Providence Journal* [Rhode Island], March 19, 2003)

"Despite the widespread assumption among European, Arab and domestic critics that the Bush administration is targeting Iraq for its oil, not its weapons of mass destruction, it's not at all clear who would benefit if the world's second-largest oil reserves were freed from Saddam Hussein's control.

"Pointing to the close personal and professional ties that President Bush and Vice President Dick Cheney share with the U.S. energy industry, skeptics contend that the White House hopes to secure America's future energy supplies by installing a friendly regime in Baghdad that would hand control of Iraq's oil over to its corporate friends.

"As evidence, critics point to the administration's national energy policy, which was crafted in secret last year with the help of oil industry allies. Among the conclusions of the Cheney-led energy task force: 'The [Persian] Gulf will be a primary focus of U.S. international energy policy. . . .'

"But economics, not politics, are more likely to drive a future Iraqi government's decisions about its oil reserves, experts say.

"Although Iraq sits atop 112 billion barrels of proven oil reserves, its capacity to drill and export that oil is in shambles after 20 years of wars and international sanctions. Thus the next Iraqi government would be best served by opening its oil fields to full international competition and accepting the most lucrative bids, whether they come from Russian, French or American oil companies.

" 'No Iraqi regime that served the interests of North American consumers of energy at the expense of Iraq's national interest and the welfare of the Iraqi people would have any hope of legitimacy at all,' Chas Freeman, president of the Middle East Policy Council and a former U.S. ambassador to Saudi Arabia, testified to a Senate committee last month. 'And, therefore, whatever government is in Baghdad will want to maximize the long-term profit to Iraq of Iraq's energy resources or it will be, by definition, illegitimate.' "

(*Pittsburgh Post-Gazette,* November 24, 2002)

Mothers Against Drunk Driving (MADD)

Established in 1980

DIRECTOR

Bobby Heard, interim executive director. Heard, national director of marketing and development, was interim executive director in spring 2004.

BOARD OF DIRECTORS

Dean Wilkerson, J.D., national executive director
Cynthia S. Roark, chair of the board
Wendy J. Hamilton, national president
Glynn R. Birch, vice president, victim issues
Lynne Goughler, vice president, public policy
Cheyrl L. Jones, vice president, field issues
Stephen E. O'Toole, treasurer
Sammy J. Quintana, secretary
Brenda A. Altman
Michael E. Boland
Raul Caetano
Laura Dean-Mooney
James C. Fell
Paul D. Folkemer
Lelia S. Haddle
Lew Hollinger
Leonard R. Jacob
Chris Johnson
Ruth Ann Lipic
L. Anthony Pace
Glenda Richardson
Linda A. Rothwell
Justin Saint Cyr
Matthew D. Shedd
Theresa Paulette Winn

SCOPE

Members: 2 million members and supporters
Branches/chapters: 600 chapters (including state offices and community action teams)
Affiliates: None

STAFF

Declined to comment

TAX STATUS

501(c)(3)

FINANCES

Budget: 2004—$48 million; 2003—$48.1 million; 2002—$47.4 million

FUNDING SOURCES

Individuals, 43%; government contracts, 20%; corporate donations, 15%; other sources, 18.6%; special events/projects, 1.8%; foundation grants, 1%; membership dues, 0.6%

PAC

None

EMPLOYMENT

MADD often has positions open in both their national and state offices. A list of positions

CONTACT INFORMATION

511 E. John Carpenter Freeway, Suite 700, Irving, TX 75062
Phone: (214) 744-6233 • *Fax:* (972) 869-2206
Web site: www.madd.org

Communications Director: Michelle Parker, acting director of communications
(214) 744-6233 • parker@madd.org
Human Resources Director: Debra Fowler
(214) 744-6233 • fowler@madd.org

PURPOSE: "To stop drunk driving, support victims of this violent crime, and prevent underage drinking."

CURRENT CONCERNS: Child endangerment • Constitutional amendment for victims' rights • Enforcement of seat belt laws • Expanded use of administrative license revocation • Increase beer excise taxes • National enforcement of sobriety checkpoints • National traffic safety fund • Nationwide .08 blood alcohol content (BAC) • Reduce drug- and alcohol-related traffic fatalities • Reinvigorate court-monitoring programs • TEA-21 Reauthorization

METHOD OF OPERATION: Advertisements • Awards program • Coalition forming • Conferences/seminars • Congressional testimony • Films/video/audio tapes • Grassroots organizing • Information clearinghouse • International activities • Internet (e-mail alerts and Web site) • Legislative/regulatory monitoring (federal) • Legislative/regulatory monitoring (state) • Lobbying (federal, state, and grassroots) • Media outreach • Performance rating/Report cards (companies, products, etc.) • Speakers program • Telecommunications services (Hotline: 800-GET-MADD, mailing lists) • Training

Effectiveness and Political Orientation

"Independent, confident teenagers who have good relationships with their parents are more likely to abstain from drugs, alcohol, and sex, according to a national survey conducted by Marlborough-based Students Against Destructive Decisions.

"'How kids define themselves is directly related to the decisions they make,' said Stephen Wallace, chairman of the national SADD organization.

"Teenagers with a strong 'sense of self' are far more likely to avoid 'destructive decision-making,' the survey found.

"Barbara Harrington, executive director of the Massachusetts chapter of Mothers Against Drunk Driving, said many parents wait too long to discuss drugs and alcohol with their children.

"'It's often a case of too little, too late,' she said. 'And many parents don't really understand how serious the consequences can be.'"

(*The Boston Globe,* March 11, 2004)

and contact information for each is available at www.madd.org/aboutus/0,1056, 1648,00.html. Applicants can contact Human Resources, 511 E. John Carpenter Freeway, Suite 700, Irving, TX 75062. Phone: (214) 744-6233. Fax: (972) 869-2206. E-mail: info@madd.org.

INTERNSHIPS

MADD does not have internship opportunities.

NEWSLETTERS

Driven (quarterly)
MADDvocate

PUBLICATIONS

The following is a list of sample publications:
Don't Call Me Lucky
Drunk Driving: An Unacknowledged Form of Child Endangerment
Financial Recovery After a Drunk Driving Crash
Helping Children Cope with Death (English and Spanish)
Impaired Drivers/Child Passengers (English and Spanish)
Monday Mourning
Picking Up the Financial Pieces
Resources that Heal
Selecting a Civil Attorney
Someone You Know Drinks and Drives
Straight Talk About Death for Teenagers
Victim Information Pamphlet (English and Spanish)
Your Grief: You're Not Going Crazy (English and Spanish)
You're Not Alone: MADD Can Help!

CONFERENCES

Law Enforcement Summit
MADD National Conference
State organization meetings
Victim advocacy training

"Records released Wednesday show a wide range of punishments—from suspensions to firings—for government employees caught driving drunk in state-owned vehicles. . . .

"Most of the employees were caught drunk behind the wheel of a state car, but some were punished for driving their own cars under the influence. All references to employees' names and job titles were deleted by the Office of State Employment Relations, which released the records at the request of the Journal Sentinel.

"The lightest punishment was three days without pay. Other than termination, the toughest sanction was 30 days without pay for two employees. One of them, a Department of Corrections supervisor, drove a vehicle with law enforcement plates in November after drinking with underlings.

"Suspensions of five or 10 days simply don't go far enough to punish employees who drive while drunk, said Kari Kinnard, the executive director of Mothers Against Drunk Driving in Wisconsin.

" 'In this state for far too long we have tolerated drunk driving,' she said. 'That (punishment) just furthers the message of tolerance. It is the wrong message to be sending.' "

(*The Milwaukee Journal Sentinel* [Wisconsin], March 11, 2004)

"In the 1980s, Mothers Against Drunk Driving brought the message to Americans, state by state, of the seriousness of this crime. West Virginia was among the states that mandated automatic jail time for those convicted of drunken driving. . . .

"But 20 years later, incarcerating drunken drivers is expensive.

"Not only do these drivers crowd the jails, but the state must supply the indigent ones with a public lawyer. The push to go a little easier on first-time offenders has fiscal appeal. . . .

"Indeed, the Legislature is considering a law requiring offenders to seek treatment-at their own expense-following incarceration.

"Whatever course the law may take, the state should not give up jail time lightly. A night in jail sends the message that the state won't tolerate drinking and driving."

(*Charleston Gazette,* [South Carolina], March 10, 2004)

"Longer liquor hours—what are costs?

"Giving Arizona drinkers an extra hour—until 2 a.m.—to buy alcohol could bring more money into the state, but some say the cost would be too high.

"Extending liquor sales hours would add $3.5 million in sales taxes to Arizona's general fund and would attract more tourists and conventions to the state, the Arizona Tourism Alliance says.

"But a South Side neighborhood group, Tucson Democratic legislators and Mothers Against Drunk Driving of Pima County fear it would send a bad message to young people and increase drunken-driving deaths. Local resort owners, nightclub-goers and managers have mixed viewpoints. . . .

" 'This is going to push everything back an hour,' said Lori Oien, who is on the advisory board of MADD of Pima County. 'You're going to have a conflict of drunks trying to get home versus early-morning workers.' "

(*Arizona Daily Star* [Tucson], March 5, 2004)

"The man who killed Angie Kwiatkowski's 18-year-old daughter six years ago had been arrested for drunken driving just hours before he slammed head-on into the car Karen was riding in.

"He had bailed himself out of jail on an $80 bond, left the police station and, still drunk, picked up his car and turned it into a lethal weapon.

"An Erie County legislator is calling for a law that would force police agencies to impound drunken drivers' cars for at least 12 hours after their arrest—long enough for the driver to sober up and simmer down. . . .

"During a news conference in Erie County Medical Center, legislators and representatives from the Erie County Sheriff's Department, the state police and several DWI prevention programs stood before a tiny blue car that had been mangled in a drunken-driving accident.

"The driver's-side front end had been crumpled in, and a cobweb of cracks reached across the windshield.

"Officials said it serves as a reminder that drunken-driving accidents occur only after a series of deliberate decisions.

" 'MADD doesn't call these accidents anymore,' said Elizabeth Obad, who serves as chairwoman of New York State's Mothers Against Drunk Driving and president of the Erie County chapter. 'Someone makes a choice to drink, and they make a choice to get behind the wheel.' "

(*Buffalo News,* February 28, 2004)

"The Virginia House of Delegates gave preliminary approval Thursday to a set of bills that would give the commonwealth one of the nation's toughest arrays of laws punishing motorists caught drunk.

"The dozen measures approved Thursday include bills that would set mandatory jail time for first-time offenders and increase punishments for those caught a second or third time. The penalties include revocations of driver's licenses. . . .

"Nearly 20 bills against driving under the influence of alcohol and drugs could pass the House by the end of next week. There are another dozen in the Senate. The bills focus largely on toughening penalties or imposing new penalties in three categories: repeat offenders, drivers who are caught with about two times the allowable blood-alcohol level of 0.08, and drivers who refuse to take blood-alcohol tests. . . .

" 'This is the first time that I can remember where there's been this kind of effort by the Virginia General Assembly,' said Jeff Levy, the Virginia state policy liaison for Mothers Against Drunk Driving."

(*The Washington Post,* February 13, 2004)

Mountain States Legal Foundation

Established in 1977

DIRECTOR

William Perry Pendley, president and chief legal officer. Born and raised in Cheyenne, WY, Pendley received B.A. and M.A. degrees in economics and political science from George Washington University in Washington, DC. He served as a captain in the United States Marine Corps, after which he received his J.D. from the University of Wyoming College of Law, where he was senior editor on *Land and Water Law Review.* He served as an attorney to former Sen. Clifford P. Hansen and to the House Interior and Insular Affairs Committee. During the Reagan administration, he served as deputy assistant secretary for energy and minerals of the Department of Interior, where he authored Reagan's National Minerals Policy and Exclusive Economic Zone proclamation. He was also a consultant to the secretary of the Navy and was engaged in the private practice of law in the Washington, DC, area before his return to the West in 1989. He also is admitted to practice law in WY, CO, and VA.

BOARD OF DIRECTORS

William Perry Pendley, president and chief legal officer

L. Jerald Sheffels, chair; Wilbur, Washington

Thomas M. Hauptman, vice-chair; president, KGH Operating Co., Billings, MT

Diemer True, secretary; partner, True Cos., Casper, WY

John F. Kane, treasurer; Kane Cattle Co., Bartlesville, OK

Steven K. Bosley; Louisville, CO

Peter A. Botting; president and chief executive officer, W.A. Botting Co., Woodinville, WA

Stephen M. Brophy; president, Page Land and Cattle Co., Phoenix, AZ

George G. Byers; Lakewood, CO

Cynthia M. Chandley; Ryley Carlock and Applewhite, Phoenix, AZ

Helen Chenoweth-Hage; Tonopah, NV

Scott A. Crozier, Esq.; senior vice president, general counsel and secretary, Petsmart, Inc., Phoenix, AZ

Demar Dahl; Demar Dahl Co., LLC, Fallon, NV

Patrick P. Davison, C.P.A.; Patrick P. Davison, LLC, Billings, MT

Alan Foutz; president, Colorado Farm Bureau, Akron, CO

Dallas P. Horton, D.V.M., M.S.; Horton Feedlot and Research Center, Eaton, CO

Peter W. Hummel; Independent Petroleum Producer, Reno, NV

Jerry D. Jordan; president, Jordan Energy, Inc., Columbus, OH

Karen D. Kennedy; Kennedy Oil, Gillette, WY

CONTACT INFORMATION

2596 South Lewis Way, Lakewood, CO 80227
Phone: (303) 292-2021 • *Fax:* (303) 292-1980
General E-mail: info@mountainstateslegal.org •
Web site: www.mountainstateslegal.com

Communications Director: William Perry Pendley, president and chief legal office
(303) 292-2021 • wpendley@mountainstateslegal.com
Human Resources Director: None

PURPOSE: "Mountain States Legal Foundation, by seeking the proper application of the Constitution and interpretation of the law in the courts, administrative agencies, and other forums, provides a strong and effective voice for freedom of enterprise, the rights of private property ownership, and the multiple use of federal and state resources. It also champions the rights and liberties guaranteed by the Constitution in support of individual and business enterprises and against unwarranted government intrusion."

CURRENT CONCERNS: Access to and use of federal and state lands and resources • Endangered Species Act • Environmental accountability • Freedom of enterprise • Limited and ethical government • Private property rights • Rights and liberties guaranteed by the Constitution • Wetlands

METHOD OF OPERATION: Congressional testimony • Grassroots organizing • Internships • Legal assistance • Litigation • Media outreach • Speakers program • Web site

Effectiveness and Political Orientation

"A coalition of conservation groups moved to intervene in a lawsuit by an anti-environmental law firm aiming to eliminate protection for the Preble's meadow jumping mouse and its Front Range streamside habitat. The Preble's meadow jumping mouse was protected in 1998 under the Endangered Species Act because unmanaged sprawl had devastated riparian ecosystems in Colorado from Colorado Springs to Ft. Collins and northward into southern Wyoming. . . .

"The coalition is seeking to become parties to a lawsuit filed by Mountain States Legal Foundation that claims that the U.S. Fish and Wildlife Service erred when it originally protected the jumping mouse. The conservation groups seek intervenor status to defend the mouse's protected status."

(*U.S. Newswire,* March 9, 2004)

"Without the American Indian Teacher Training Program, Theresa McCann would still be a full-time mom in North Dakota taking night classes.

SCOPE

Members: 70,500 individuals and 4,900 organizations
Branches/chapters: None
Affiliates: None

STAFF

17 total

TAX STATUS

501(c)(3)

FINANCES

Revenue: 2002—$2.3 million; 2001—$2.5 million; 2000—$3.3 million

FUNDING SOURCES

Contributions, program services, and other

PAC

None

EMPLOYMENT

There is no employment information available publicly. Interested applicants can contact William Perry Pendley, president and chief legal office. Phone: (303) 292-2021. E-mail: wpendley@mountainstateslegal.com.

"Instead, the 31-year-old Lakota is a full-time student in Salt Lake City working toward a bachelor's degree at the University of Utah. She hopes to return with her husband and two children to her tribe to teach.

"The federally funded scholarship program paid for her family's move to Utah and also covers their rent. McCann described it as an 'amazing load off a student.'

"But if William Perry Pendley has his way, the program will vanish. 'It flies in the face of the [U.S.] Constitution,' said Pendley, president and chief legal officer of the conservative Denver-based Mountain States Legal Foundation.

"He sent written statements Wednesday to the legal counsels at the University of Utah, California's Humboldt State University, Montana State University and the University of Oregon asserting that the teacher training programs there were unconstitutional.

"In a phone interview, he cited two June decisions by the U.S. Supreme Court that involved the University of Michigan law school and undergraduate admissions policies.

"In one ruling, the court upheld the law school's affirmative-action admissions policy, 5–4. In the second, the court voted 6–3 against the undergraduate admissions policy—which awarded 20 points to applicants if they were black, Latino or American Indian—saying the policy violated the Constitution's equal-protection provisions.

" 'That decision made it clear that setting race as an absolute prerequisite was inadmissible and unconstitutional,' Pendley said."

(*The Salt Lake Tribune*, February 12, 2004)

"Coors is now a major national brand whose heartwarming ads feature a non-notorious family member standing in a field of virgin Colorado snow, while the conservative institutions founded by the old man have also become major brands in their own fields of endeavor.

"Coors was born into a Colorado brewing family that shared the don't-tread-on-me philosophy common in the West, especially among family-owned businesses. Coors himself was just a garden-variety conservative until 1953, when he happened across the book that converted so many merely disgruntled right-wingers into active members of a movement: Russell Kirk's 'Conservative Mind.' In the 1960's, he became an important supporter of Ronald Reagan and served a cantankerous term as regent of the University of Colorado, then boiling with student agitation. He came to the attention of Paul Weyrich, another movement figure who dreamed of establishing a policy institute that could germinate conservative thought as groups like Brookings had long done for liberals. In 1973, Coors gave the organization $250,000, plus another $300,000 for a building. And so the Heritage Foundation was born.

"In 1977, he financed another institution, the Mountain States Legal Foundation. When Reagan was elected president, Coors was identified as a member of his kitchen cabinet; Mountain States' president, James Watt, became secretary of the interior and set off on what environmentalists deemed a reign of terror. As if all that weren't enough, Coors and his brother Bill waged a bitter struggle with workers that ended with the ousting of the company's unions. Joseph Coors was an easy guy to boycott. Bill once described his brother's politics to *The Rocky Mountain News,* not admiringly, as 'far right to Attila the Hun.' "

(*The New York Times,* December 28, 2003)

INTERNSHIPS
For internship information, contact Judy Stoeser. Phone: (303) 292-2021. E-mail: jstoeser@mountainstateslegal.com.

NEWSLETTERS
The Litigator (quarterly)

PUBLICATIONS
It Takes a Hero
War on the West: Government Tyranny on America's Great Frontier

CONFERENCES
None

"The American Antiquities Act of 1906 may sound like an obscure law, but it has played a key role in making America unique. The act gives the president the power to declare national monuments. All but three presidents since the act's passage have used it, and in doing so have preserved about 120 monuments spanning more than 70 million acres. In fact, about half of America's national parks, which can be declared only by Congress, were originally protected by the president under the Antiquities Act.

"The act is not without critics, especially in the West, where the impulse to use and exploit even fragile, beautiful lands is often at odds with the impulse to protect and save the lands.

"For that reason, it is especially important that the U.S. Supreme Court on Monday effectively reinforced the Antiquities Act by refusing to hear a challenge to it. The challenge had been filed by the Mountain States Legal Foundation of Denver, a conservative public interest law firm. The firm argued that then-President Bill Clinton overstepped his authority when he created six new national monuments in the final days of his administration.

"A federal appeals court last year rejected the legal foundation's claim, and the Supreme Court Monday refused to hear an appeal. That ended the case. The repercussions will be felt for decades, if not centuries."

(*Arizona Daily Star* [Tucson], October 9, 2003)

"Wildlife biologists found two lynx kits in a mountainous area of southern Colorado on Wednesday, a milestone of success for the state reintroduction program.

"The tiny kits, their eyes still closed, are tucked into a remote den with their mother somewhere in the eastern part of the lynx core recovery area in the state's southern mountains. . . .

"The lack of documented breeding success had dogged the controversial program, prompting the state agency to release 32 more of the secretive snow cats last winter.

"This year, the Denver-based Mountain States Legal Foundation sued to block the new releases, arguing the presence of lynx would prevent logging programs designed to reduce fire risk. The suit was dismissed."

(*The Denver Post,* May 23, 2003)

MoveOn.org

Established in 1998

DIRECTOR

Peter Schurman, executive director. Schurman previously founded Generation Net, an Internet-based advocacy organization for young people. Peter has 10 years of experience in the nonprofit, public policy, environment, education, and government fields, as a grassroots- and media-organizer, fundraiser, organizational developer, and manager. He has worked on environmental issues for organizations including the Sierra Club and the American Lung Association, on youth organizing with Lead. . . or Leave, and on Capitol Hill for Rep. Gary Ackerman. He believes deeply in broadening the inclusiveness of democratic decision-making through the many-to-many capacity of the Internet. He completed an M.B.A. at Yale University in 2000 and won the Social Entrepreneurship Prize in a business plan competition there. Schurman also holds a B.A. in history from the University of Pennsylvania.

BOARD OF DIRECTORS

Joan Blades
Wes Boyd
Peter Schurman

SCOPE

Members: More than 2,000,000 online
    activists
Branches/chapters: None
Affiliates: None

STAFF

Information unavailable

TAX STATUS

501(c)(4)

FINANCES

Information unavailable

FUNDING SOURCES

Individuals, 97%; other, 3%

PAC

MoveOn.org PAC

PAC CONTRIBUTIONS 2002

100% to   0% to
Democrats   Republicans

CONTACT INFORMATION

Phone: Information unavailable • *Fax:* Information unavailable
General E-mail: info@mepc.org • *Web site:* www.moveon.org

Communications Director: Jessica A. Smith, Fenton Communications, communications contact for MoveOn.org, jessica@fenton.com
Human Resources Director: Information unavailable

PURPOSE: "MoveOn is a catalyst for a new kind of grassroots involvement, supporting busy but concerned citizens in finding their political voice."

CURRENT CONCERNS: Campaign finance • Democratic participation • Environmental and energy issues • Media consolidation • The Iraq war

METHOD OF OPERATION: Advertisements • Boycotts • Direct action • Grassroots organizing • Internet (bulletin boards, e-mail alerts, and Web site) • Legislative/regulatory monitoring (federal) • Lobbying (federal) • Media outreach

Effectiveness and Political Orientation

"When President Bush signed into law the biggest expansion of Medicare in 38 years last December, the moment was widely considered one of unalloyed triumph for the Republicans.

"The legislation was a breakthrough in the long-running partisan dispute over how to deliver prescription drug coverage to the elderly—and a chance for Mr. Bush and Congressional Republicans to begin delivering the first of the new benefits in the midst of an election year. . . .

"On Capitol Hill, Democrats are demanding an investigation into charges that the Bush administration threatened to fire the chief actuary of the Medicare program last year if he gave Congress data on the high cost of the legislation. . . .

"On the campaign trail, Senator John Kerry, the expected Democratic presidential nominee, regularly attacks the new law as a special-interest giveaway 'that does more for drug companies than seniors,' as he put it on Monday. Mr. Kerry added that the administration's efforts to 'silence the truth' about its cost were shocking.

"Other critics of the law are highlighting its flaws in television advertising, mailings and videotapes circulated to 10,000 senior centers and retirement communities in recent weeks. In general, critics assert that the law does little to ease the problem it purports to address: the soaring cost of prescription drugs. . . .

"Families USA outlines these concerns in a videotape narrated by Walter Cronkite, now being distributed to communities with elderly populations around the country. Other opponents are also weighing in, including MoveOn.org Voter Fund, a liberal advocacy group, which has run television ads this year asserting, 'Instead of standing up for seniors, George Bush sided with the drug companies who'd given him huge contributions.'"

(*The New York Times,* March 17, 2004)

"With the Bush-Cheney reelection committee holding a 50-to-1 money advantage over John F. Kerry, Democrats have taken comfort in a series of anti-Bush ads paid for by independent groups such as MoveOn.org and America Coming Together.

"But the Republican Party, along with two senators who led campaign reform effort four years ago—Arizona Republican John McCain and Wisconsin Democrat Russell Feingold—have challenged the legality of these tax-exempt political groups and are urging the Federal Election Commission to halt their activities. . . .

"The McCain-Feingold campaign law, which was enacted in 2002, prohibits members of Congress and political parties from soliciting or spending so-called soft money. . . .

"With the new law in place, soft money donors have been looking for an alternative outlet, which has given rise to groups such as MoveOn.org, America Coming Together, and the Media Fund. These groups have received pledges of up to $10 million each from financier George Soros, Peter Lewis, chairman of the Progressive Corp. insurance company, and other Bush opponents.

" 'We are dedicated to defeating George W. Bush, electing progressives at all levels of government, and mobilizing millions of people to register and vote around the critical issues facing our country,' says the website for ACT, which is led by Ellen Malcolm, also president of EMILY's List, a group that gives financial support to female candidates. Soros himself has declared beating Bush his personal mission."

(*The Boston Globe,* March 16, 2004)

"President Bush comes under attack in two television advertising campaigns being launched today, one by a Democratic-leaning group and the other by a gay Republican organization.

"A $5 million campaign by the Media Fund, run by prominent Democratic consultant Harold Ickes, and the $1 million effort by the Log Cabin Republicans are part of an intensifying political ad war in the week since Sen. John F. Kerry of Massachusetts effectively clinched the Democratic presidential nomination.

"The Bush re-election campaign began running ads late last week touting the president's accomplishments and leadership. The Media Fund and other groups, such as MoveOn.org Voter Fund, are paying for commercials that seek to counter the Bush ads."

(*The Grand Rapids Press* [Michigan], March 10, 2004)

"Has anyone else out there begun to wonder just who these 9/11 'families' are that have been interviewed without end the past week about their 'outrage' over President Bush's TV ads with a quick clip of September 11? Are they all neutral innocents, as depicted, or are they part of an organized anti-Bush opposition. . . ?

"Consider the benignly named September 11th Families for Peaceful Tomorrows. The group has been loudly protesting Mr. Bush's ads, organizing a rally for 'victims' families and firefighters' to condemn the President's 'offensive exploitation' of September 11. Peaceful Tomorrows says its goal is to 'turn our grief into action for peace.' In the *Washington Post*'s coverage this group is 'nonpartisan.' If so, nonpartisan has lost its meaning. . . .

"As for all the media attention, Peaceful Tomorrows has retained the well-known Fenton Communications, a public relations shop that for years has catered to left-wing advocacy groups. The most recent and famous is MoveOn.org, the outfit that had to disavow an ad on its site comparing President Bush to Hitler. A woman at Fenton who works on MoveOn.org's project, Jessica Smith, also works on Peaceful Tomorrow's campaign. Ms. Smith used to work for the Democratic National Committee and for Al Gore's presidential campaign. We are a long way from the land of political innocents."

(*The Wall Street Journal,* March 10, 2004)

"The Berkeley City Council on Tuesday voted to support an activist Web site's proposal to censure President Bush for going to war in Iraq.

"The council approved a resolution, introduced by Councilmember Kriss Worthington, to have Congress censure the president for allegedly misleading Americans on the need to invade Iraq.

"The council voted 8–0, with Councilmember Dona Spring abstaining, to back the proposal, which came from Berkeley-based MoveOn.org."

(*The Oakland Tribune* [California], March 10, 2004)

Moving Ideas Network

Established in 1995

DIRECTOR

Melanie H. Alston-Akers, director. Alston-Akers, who started with Moving Ideas in February 2003, oversees the daily and administrative activities of Moving Ideas including strategic development for future work. Prior to her work at Moving Ideas, Alston-Akers worked for the Academy for Educational Development in Washington, DC. Her principal responsibilities focused on coordinating content and design of the School-to-Work Internet Gateway, a project of the U.S. Departments of Education and Labor and the Web site of the Office of Vocational and Adult Education of the U.S. Department of Education. Alston-Akers has a B.A. from Princeton University and an M.A. in public policy from the University of Michigan.

BOARD OF DIRECTORS

The following are the board of directors for The American Prospect:

Robert Kuttner, president; The American Prospect

Richard Leone, chair; Century Foundation

Paul Starr, vice president; co-editor of *The American Prospect*

Christopher Jencks, treasurer; Kennedy School, Harvard University

Maria Echeveste; Nueva Vista Group, LLC

Danny Goldbert; Artemis Records

Michael J. Johnston; Capital Group Cos.

Randall Kennedy; Harvard Law School

Nancy Mills; AFL-CIO

Robert Reich, co-founder; Brandeis University

Adele Simmons; Chicago Metropolis 2020

Ben Taylor

SCOPE

Members:
Branches/chapters: None
Affiliates: None

STAFF

4 total—plus 1–2 interns

TAX STATUS

501(c)(3)

FINANCES

Moving Ideas Network, as part of The American Prospect, Inc., does not have a separate budget.

FUNDING SOURCES

Foundation grants, 92.3%; membership dues, 7.7%

PAC

None

CONTACT INFORMATION

2000 L Street, NW, Suite 717, Washington DC, 20036
Phone: (202) 776-0730 • *Fax:* (202) 776-0740
General E-mail: movingideas@movingideas.org •
Web site: www.movingideas.org

Communications Director: None
Human Resources Director: None

PURPOSE: "Moving Ideas Network is dedicated to explaining and popularizing complex policy ideas to a broader audience. Our goal is to improve collaboration and dialogue between policy and grassroots organizations, and to promote their work to journalists and legislators. Moving Ideas posts the best ideas and resources from leading progressive research and advocacy institutions, as well as promotes high-quality Web sites and publishes original content. We hope to strengthen democratic participation by providing a more inclusive and intelligible debate about the issues that shape our world."

CURRENT CONCERNS: Culture and media • Economy • GLBT issues • Globalization/trade • Health care policy • Income and wealth • Livable cities • Poverty • Race • Social Security • Working America

METHOD OF OPERATION: Coalition forming • Information clearinghouse • Internships • Media outreach • Research • Web site

Effectiveness and Political Orientation

"Head Start reauthorization should build on the program's strengths, the Moving Ideas Network said today.

"For thirty-eight years, the Head Start program has provided proven, comprehensive services to help disadvantaged pre-school children to successfully perform in school. The House will soon vote on a Head Start Reauthorization bill. According to the Moving Ideas Network, HR 2210 threatens to compromise the program by offering little additional funding, downplaying Head Start's developmental and other non-academic benefits, allowing religious discrimination against employees, and redirecting needed funding to create experimental state-run programs. . . .

"HR 2210 includes a proposal to allow eight states to apply for experimental block grants, which threatens the vitality of Head Start. Remaking this program into a block grant will transfer oversight responsibility from the federal to the state level. With money-strapped states already cutting preschool services, placing Head Start within state budgets jeopardizes the program."

(*U.S. Newswire,* July 19, 2003)

EMPLOYMENT
Information regarding jobs available at Moving Ideas Network and jobs available at member organizations can be found at www.movingideas.org/jobs/. Melanie Alston-Akers, director, Moving Ideas Network, 2000 L Street, NW, Suite 717, Washington, DC 20036. Fax: (202) 776-0740. E-mail: malston-akers@prospect.org. No phone calls.

INTERNSHIPS
Internship information is listed at www.movingideas.org/jobs/internships.html. Applicants must be in undergrad and should have an interest in politics, journalism, and advocacy. Internships are unpaid and cover one semester or summer term. To apply, please mail, fax, or e-mail cover letter, resume, and a letter of recommendation to MIN Internships, The American Prospect, 2000 L Street, NW, Suite 717, Washington, DC 20036. Fax: (202) 776-0740. E-mail: internships@prospect.org. No phone calls.

NEWSLETTERS
Moving Ideas News (weekly)

PUBLICATIONS
In the Flight (online)
On the Hill (online)
Issues in Depth (online)

CONFERENCES
None

"Following is a statement by Moving Ideas Network:

"Legislation to add a prescription drug benefit to Medicare is currently being considered in both the Senate and House. However, neither plan offers the comprehensive drug coverage needed by seniors. Instead, the plans provide minimal monetary relief from rising drug costs while giving a financial windfall to drug companies. In addition, the proposals are scheduled to take effect in 2006, after the 2004 election, allowing Republicans to run for election based on the law's passage and not its effects. Seniors and people with disabilities deserve better. They deserve a drug benefit plan which:

"—Provides a substantial drug coverage benefit

"Although President Bush asserts that these prescription plans are the same that members of Congress enjoy, the truth is that Medicare patients will have to pay more for their drugs, and even more than their Congressional representatives pay. . . .

"—Supports seniors and people with disabilities, not drug and insurance companies: The proposed drug benefit will be delivered by private insurance companies, not Medicare. This strategy undermines the bargaining power of the millions of Medicare patients to negotiate the lowest possible drug prices, as the Veteran's Administration now does. . . .

"—Protects retired workers:

"The Congressional Budget Office estimates these bills could lead employers to drop employer-sponsored prescription drug coverage for 3 million retirees. . . .

"Moving Ideas is a network of more than 125 public interest groups, ranging from large think tanks to grassroots networks. We aim to promote the work of our member groups and allies by supplying essential facts on timely issues. . . .

(*U.S. Newswire*, June 16, 2003)

NAACP Legal Defense
and Educational Fund, Inc. (LDF)

Established 1940

DIRECTOR

Theodore M. Shaw, president and director-counsel. In 1982, Shaw joined LDF, where he directed its education docket and litigated school desegregation, capital punishment, and other civil rights cases in the courts. In 1987, he established LDF's Western Regional Office, where he served as Western regional counsel. In 1990, he left briefly to join the faculty of the University of Michigan Law School, returning to LDF in 1993 as associate director-counsel. Shaw has served as LDF's lead counsel for a group of African American and minority university and high school students in *Gratz v. Bollinger,* the affirmative action admissions case against the University of Michigan undergraduate school. In May 2004, Shaw was named president and director-counsel. He also has extensive international legal experience and is an adjunct professor of law at Columbia Law School. Shaw graduated from Wesleyan University and received his J.D. from Columbia University School of Law in 1979. After graduation, he worked as a trial attorney in the Civil Rights Division of the U.S. Department of Justice in Washington, DC, where he litigated school desegregation and housing discrimination cases.

BOARD OF DIRECTORS

Julius L. Chambers, co-chair
Martin D. Payson, co-chair
Daniel L. Rabinowitz, co-vice chair
Roger W. Wilkins, co-vice chair
James M. Nabrit III, secretary
Eleanor S. Applewhaite, treasurer
Theodore M. Shaw, president and director-counsel
Elaine R. Jones, immediate past president and director-counsel
Billye Suber Aaron, member
Gerald S. Adolph, member
Clarence Avant, member
Mario L. Baeza, member
Mary Frances Berry, member
Johnnie L. Cochran Jr., member
Kenneth C. Edelin, member
Toni G. Fay, member
Gordon G. Greiner, member
Quincy Jones, member
Vernon E. Jordan Jr., member
David E. Kendall, member
Caroline B. Kennedy, member
Tonya Lewis Lee, member
William M. Lewis Jr., member
John D. Maguire, member
Cecilia S. Marshall, member
Richard M. Moss, member
Lawrence Newman, member
C. Carl Randolph, member
Judith T. Saper, member
John W. Walker, member

CONTACT INFORMATION

99 Hudson Street, Suite 1600, New York, NY 10013
Phone: (212) 965-2200 • *Fax:* (212) 226-7592
General E-mail: • *Web site:* www.naacpldf.org

Communications Director: Herschel Johnson
(212) 965-2200
Human Resources Director: Edward Gordon
(212) 965-2200

PURPOSE: To transform the promise of equality into reality for African Americans, other minorities, women, the disabled, the poor and, ultimately, all individuals in areas of education, political participation, economic justice and criminal justice.

CURRENT CONCERNS: Affirmative action in education and the workplace • Civil rights • Environmental justice • Fair employment and welfare reform • Legislative redistricting • Preserving access to health care • School desegregation

METHOD OF OPERATION: Awards program • Coalition forming • Films/video/audio tapes • International activities • Internships • Legal assistance • Legislative/regulatory monitoring (federal) • Litigation • Media outreach • Scholarships • Web site

Effectiveness and Political Orientation

"Five years after 46 people, almost all of them black, were arrested on fabricated drug charges in Tulia, Tex., their ordeal will draw to a close today with the announcement of a $5 million settlement in their civil suit and the disbandment of a federally financed 26-county narcotics task force responsible for the arrests.

"The case attracted national attention because the number of people charged literally decimated the small town's black population. . . .

" 'This is undoubtedly that last major chapter in the Tulia story, and this will conclude the efforts of people in Tulia to get some compensation and justice,' said Jeff Blackburn, a lawyer in Amarillo who represented the people arrested five years ago in the civil suit. . . .

"Mr. Blackburn added that the Panhandle Regional Narcotics Trafficking Task Force failed adequately to supervise the agent, Tom Coleman, in its eagerness to win battles in the war on drugs. . . .

"The settlement will be paid by the City of Amarillo, which had a leading role in running the task force. Marcus W. Norris, the city attorney, said many drug task forces in Texas were poorly organized and governed. That led, he said, to poor supervision of Mr. Coleman in Tulia, a lack of accountability and catastrophic misjudgments. . . .

SCOPE
Members: None
Branch/chapter: Los Angeles and Washington, DC, regional offices
Affiliates: None

STAFF
Declined to comment

TAX STATUS
501(c)(3)

FINANCES
Budget: 2002—$4.5 million

FUNDING SOURCES
Contributions, 84%; court costs/attorney fees awarded, 16%

PAC
None

EMPLOYMENT
LDF offers positions in administrative work, accounting, legal and paralegal work, and data entry. Interested applicants should send resumes and other materials for employment to Edward Gordon, director of human resources, NAACP LDF, 99 Hudson Street, Suite 1600, New York, NY 10013. Phone: (212) 965-2200. Fax: (212) 226-7592.

INTERNSHIPS
Unpaid internships are available to those who have completed at least one year of law school. Internships can last from six weeks to three months. The deadline for summer internships is February 1; fall internships, mid-July; spring internships, mid-November. Interns are expected to work 10 hours per week during fall and spring sessions and 40 hours per week for summer internships. For information, contact Damon Hewitt, assistant counsel, NAACP LDF, 99 Hudson Street, Suite 1600, NY 10013. Phone: (212) 965-2200.

NEWSLETTERS
The Defender (3 times per year)
Equal Justice (quarterly)

PUBLICATIONS
Assembly Line Justice
Bad Times in Tulia, Texas
Death Row USA

CONFERENCES
Annual Institute (May, in New York City)
Sponsors lawyers' training institutes and seminars on civil rights

"Vanita Gupta, a lawyer with the NAACP Legal Defense and Educational Fund, which also represents the plaintiffs along with the Washington firm of Hogan & Hartson, said it was a mistake to focus only on Mr. Coleman's actions.

"'The task force is ultimately culpable for what happened in Tulia,' Ms. Gupta said. 'They hired, supervised and sponsored Tom Coleman's activity in the 18 months he was operating there.'

"'It's not that Tom Coleman was simply a rogue officer,' Ms. Gupta added. 'The problem is that federally funded narcotics task forces operate nationwide as rogue task forces because they are utterly unaccountable to any oversight mechanism.'"

(*The New York Times*, March 11, 2004)

"Paine College students on Wednesday were encouraged to remember the activists who fought for school desegregation and to maintain their battle for a quality education.

"During the college's annual Conference on the Black Experience, two noted scholars recalled the 1954 landmark U.S. Supreme Court decision, *Brown v. Board of Education*. The decision, which celebrates 50 years May 17, overruled the 'separate but equal' doctrine and set in motion the desegregation of the nation's public schools. . . .

"Wednesday's events included lectures by law professor J. Clay Smith and Elaine Jones, who has served as president of the NAACP Legal Defense and Educational Fund since 1993.

"On Wednesday afternoon, Dr. Smith compared the struggle for a good education to a road, urging Paine College students to 'maintain' the road.

"'There is no road for African-American people in this country past *Brown*. It is always going to be a road to *Brown* despite the fact that the Supreme Court decided that case,' said Dr. Smith, who teaches at Howard University School of Law.

"Dr. Smith told Paine students that today's troubled education system must improve.

"He said black people are not continuing their fight for better education with President Bush's No Child Left Behind Act.

"'Where is that enthusiasm?' he asked. 'Don't stand still. Read as much as you can. Debate as much as you can. Criticize as much as you can.'

"'But also, come to the realization of where your road individually is leading. . . . I want them to hear your feet.'"

(*Augusta Chronicle* [Georgia], February 5, 2004)

"Half a century after the Supreme Court ordered the desegregation of American education, schools are almost as segregated as they were when Martin Luther King Jr. was assassinated, according to a new report released by Harvard University researchers.

"The study by the Harvard Civil Rights Project shows that progress toward school desegregation peaked in the late 1980s as courts concluded that the goals of the landmark 1954 Supreme Court decision *Brown v. Board of Education* had largely been achieved. Over the past 15 years, the trend has been in the opposite direction, and most white students now have 'little contact' with minority students in many areas of the country, according to the report. . . .

"'Most schools in this country are overwhelmingly black or overwhelmingly white,' said Elise Boddie, head of the education department of the NAACP Legal Defense and Educational Fund Inc., which litigates civil rights cases. 'We have still not committed ourselves as a country to the mandate of *Brown versus Board of Education*. If these trends are not reversed, we could easily find ourselves back to 1954.'"

(The Washington Post, January 18, 2004)

"Administrators at some of Virginia's historically black colleges and universities said they were pleased with yesterday's Supreme Court decisions on affirmative action in college admissions.

"William R. Harvey, president of Hampton University, called the decisions 'a victory for higher education.'

" 'By allowing race to be considered as part of admissions, the court recognized that diversity is important to the learning environment,' said Marie McDemmond, president of Norfolk State University.

"Both cases came from the University of Michigan. The court upheld the law school's consideration of an applicant's race, but it rejected how the undergraduate-admissions system assigned numerical points to applicants based on race. . . .

"If the court had completely struck down affirmative action in admissions, more black students might have chosen to attend historically black institutions. The NAACP Legal Defense and Educational Fund had expressed concern that enrollment shifts could make the schools all-black and threaten public funding, but McDemmond said she doubts that will happen."

(The Richmond Times-Dispatch [Virginia], June 24, 2003)

"Twenty national civil rights organizations who oppose the nomination of Dennis Shedd to the U.S. Court of Appeals for the 4th Circuit held a press conference today to urge the Senate Judiciary Committee to reject this nomination. Scheduled for a committee vote this Thursday, Oct. 3, Shedd's nomination has drawn strong criticism from groups all over the country who believe that Shedd has demonstrated hostility in civil rights cases involving minorities, women and persons with disabilities.

"Groups opposing the Shedd nomination include the Leadership Conference on Civil Rights (LCCR), National Association for the Advancement of Colored People (NAACP), Alliance for Justice, NAACP Legal Defense and Educational Fund, Mexican American Legal Defense and Educational Fund (MALDEF), American Association of People with Disabilities (AAPD), Bazelon Center for Mental Health Law, the Congressional Black Caucus, NARAL, National Black Caucus of State Legislators, National Partnership for Women and Families, National Urban League, People for the American Way, Planned Parenthood Foundation of America, the California Women's Law Center, the National Bar Association, the National Council of Jewish Women, the North Carolina Academy of Trial Lawyers, Old Dominion Bar Association of Virginia, the South Carolina Progressive Network and the Wisconsin Legislative Black & Hispanic Caucus."

(U.S. Newswire, October 1, 2002)

NARAL Pro-Choice America

Established in 1977

DIRECTOR
Kate Michelman, executive director.

BOARD OF DIRECTORS
Kate Michelman, executive director
Alice Germond, executive president
Elizabeth Cavendish, vice president/legal
   director
Carol Pencke, chair
Nancy Silverman, 1st vice chair
Dagmar Dolby, 2nd vice chair
Richard Gross, member
Michele Hagans, secretary/treasurer
G. Angela Henry, member
Blair Hull, member
Judy Kovler, member
Lisa Perry, member
Anna Quindlen, member
Barbara Silby, member
James Trussell, member
Saundra Whitney, member
Cole Wilbur, member

SCOPE
Members: 500,000 individuals
Branches/chapters: 36 state affiliates
Affiliate: The NARAL Foundation, a 501(c)(3)
   organization

STAFF
Information unavailable

TAX STATUS
501(c)(4)

FINANCES
Revenue: 2002—$19.3 million; 2001—$18.5
million; 2000—$13 million

FUNDING SOURCES
Membership donations and individual
contributions

PAC
NARAL PAC

PAC CONTRIBUTIONS 2002

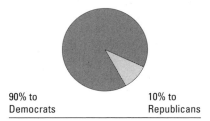

90% to
Democrats

10% to
Republicans

CONTACT INFORMATION
1156 15th Street, NW, Suite 700, Washington, DC 20005
Phone: (202) 973-3000 • *Fax:* (202) 973-3096
General E-mail: See www.prochoiceamerica.org/about/feedback.cfm •
Web site: www.naral.org

Communications Director: David Seldin
(202) 973-3032
Human Resources Director: Information unavailable

PURPOSE: "To protect and preserve the right to choose while promoting policies and programs that improve women's health and make abortion less necessary."

CURRENT CONCERNS: Access to safe abortion services • Comprehensive sexuality education in schools • Opposing coercive reproductive health policies • Protecting women's reproductive freedoms • Working to prevent unintended pregnancy and make abortion less necessary

METHOD OF OPERATION: Advertisements • Awards program • Campaign contributions (federal and state) • Coalition forming • Conferences/seminars • Congressional testimony • Congressional voting analysis • Demonstrations • Films/videos/audiotapes • Grassroots organizing • Internet (e-mail alerts and Web site) • Legislative/regulatory monitoring (federal and state) • Lobbying (federal, state, and grassroots) • Media outreach • Polling • Research • Training • Voting records

Effectiveness and Political Orientation

"Last month, the National Right to Life Committee endorsed Bush for the presidency, as it did in 2000. Carol Tobias, political director for the committee, sees little distinction among the Democratic challengers.

" 'None of them are proposing, or would support, any limits to abortion at all,' she says. 'The Democratic candidates have different positions on the death penalty, gun control, whether we should have gone into Iraq, but on abortion, they're all in lock-step with NARAL and Planned Parenthood and EMILY's List.'

"NARAL is the National Abortion Reproductive Rights Action League. EMILY's List raises funds for Democratic women in favor of abortion rights seeking political office.

"Kate Michelman is president of NARAL Pro-Choice America, which on Tuesday launched a $25 million fund drive called the Choice 2004 Fund. Six Democratic governors, including Jim Doyle of Wisconsin, are spearheading the campaign.

"Michelman says each of the Democratic contenders is strongly in favor of abortion rights and would shun judicial nominees who don't support a woman's constitutional right to privacy.

EMPLOYMENT
Openings are posted on the organization's Web site, at www.prochoiceamerica.org/ about/jobs/index.cfm. Descriptions and contact information is provided for each opening.

INTERNSHIPS
This organization offers internship opportunities. When available, internship openings are posted on the organization's Web site, at www.prochoiceamerica.org/about/jobs/ index.cfm.

NEWSLETTERS
NARAL News (biannual)

PUBLICATIONS
Choices: Women Speak Out About Abortion Who Decides? A State-by-State Review of Abortion and Reproductive Rights, 1998

CONFERENCES
None

" 'We have a Supreme Court that is no more than two justices away from completely overturning *Roe versus Wade,* if new judges are in the mold of the ones President Bush has picked for lower courts,' she says."
(*The Milwaukee Journal Sentinel* [Wisconsin], February 12, 2004)

"Emergency contraceptive pills, now sold only with a doctor's prescription, could soon be available on supermarket and drug store shelves along with aspirin and cough syrup.

"Advisers to the Food and Drug Administration will meet today to consider an application from the major U.S. maker of the 'morning-after pill' to sell the drug, called Plan B, without a doctor's oversight. . . .

"In Massachusetts, where there are an estimated 70,000 unintended pregnancies every year, advocates say women face significant barriers to obtaining the drug that would be eased if it were available over the counter. Half of all hospital emergency rooms refused to provide the morning-after pill to women who asked for it, according to a survey conducted last year by National Abortion and Reproductive Rights Action League Pro-Choice Massachusetts. A quarter of all emergency rooms did not provide the drug to rape victims, the survey found.

"Women able to obtain valid prescriptions have gotten moral lectures from pharmacists when they tried to purchase the drug, added officials at the Planned Parenthood League of Massachusetts. Others were turned away because pharmacies did not keep it in stock. As many as 42 percent of women in Massachusetts may live in areas where it is difficult to get the prescription filled, they said.

" 'Emergency contraception has tremendous potential to reduce unintended pregnancy,' said Melissa Kogut, executive director of NARAL Massachusetts. 'But time is of the essence. Women are more likely to use it if they can get it—without a doctor's visit—at their local drug store.' "
(*The Boston Globe,* December 16, 2003)

"Signaling that abortion might emerge as an important issue in next year's presidential election, a national abortion rights organization began airing a television ad this week targeting President Bush for signing a law that bans one controversial form of the procedure.

"The ad, by NARAL Pro-Choice America, hits Bush for approving a federal law prohibiting a procedure some people call 'partial-birth' abortion. The new law does not allow as an exception the protection of a woman's health.

"The ad began airing Wednesday in Iowa and New Hampshire—the two states holding the first contests of the presidential primary season—and Washington, D.C. The group spent half a million dollars to run their message for a week.

" 'The purpose of running the ads in those states was to model for people engaged in the political process how you confront the president on this issue,' said David Seldin, spokesman for the organization previously known as the National Abortion Rights and Reproductive Rights Action League (NARAL)."
(*Houston Chronicle,* November 8, 2003)

"Responding to pleas from the mother of a woman who was fatally shot in Plainfield 17 months ago, Connecticut lawmakers have adopted new penalties for an assault on a pregnant woman that results in the death of her fetus. . . .

"A similar scenario has begun to play out on the national stage, as fetal rights advocates capitalize on the publicity surrounding the Laci Peterson case to make a renewed push for the Unborn Victims of Violence Act.

"Since 1999, that legislation, which is aimed at punishing anyone who causes the death of an unborn child in the course of committing a federal crime, has twice passed the House, only to languish in the Senate. Last week, however, it was reintroduced with a weighty endorsement from Laci Peterson's family.

"The bill's supporters point to emotionally charged cases such as the Peterson murder, along with evidence that murder is a leading cause of death among pregnant women, as proof that the bill is needed.

"However, Kate Michelman, president of the National Abortion and Reproductive Rights Action League, argued in a written statement Wednesday that the antichoice lawmakers backing the bill are less interested in protecting pregnant women than in 'undermining *Roe v. Wade,* and are even willing to exploit terrible tragedies to do so.' "

(*The Boston Globe,* May 11, 2003)

"She is waging the good fight. Kate Michelman, president of the National Abortion and Reproductive Rights Action League, has won many battles. But in our political system, there are no final victories.

"It has been 30 years since the Supreme Court ruled that women, as part of their constitutional right to privacy, may choose to terminate a pregnancy. . . .

"It is in no small part because of Michelman and her organization that a woman's reproductive freedom is still the law of the land. They have helped elect pro-choice legislators, judges, and executives across this country. NARAL has also provided educational programs and written public policy initiatives. . . .

" 'Kate is that most important of figures in any movement—and especially in the movement for reproductive freedom—a long distance runner,' said feminist Gloria Steinem, founder of Voters for Choice. . . .

"In at least five cases since the 1973 decision, the Supreme Court has upheld the principles of *Roe.* A majority of the American people has consistently supported abortion rights.

"Even so, the pro-choice cause has had setbacks. Over the last eight years, the GOP-controlled Congress has voted 150 times on legislation seeking to restrict a woman's right to choose. The pro-choice cause has lost more than three-fourths of these votes. During this same time, more than 335 anti-choice bills have been passed at the state level.

" 'A woman's right to choose is deeply and gravely imperiled,' Michelman recently noted. 'Only the Constitution stands between women and those who want to take away the right to choose.'

"Michelman and her organization have been effective, with their bipartisan allies in the Senate, in blocking President Bush's anti-choice nominees for the federal bench.

" '*Roe v. Wade* is hanging on by a one-vote majority—with an anti-choice president and Congress eager to install the one justice who could take our freedom away,' Michelman recently noted. 'If *Roe* is overturned, fully half the states would swiftly ban or severely restrict abortion.' "

(*Chicago Sun-Times,* April 30, 2003)

National Association for the Advancement of Colored People (NAACP)

Established in 1909

DIRECTOR

Kweisi Mfume, president and chief executive officer. Mfume became president and chief executive officer of NAACP in 1996. He represented Baltimore in the U.S. House of Representatives and served as chair of the Congressional Black Caucus during the 103rd Congress. Mfume became politically active as a freshman in college, as editor of the school's newspaper, and as head of the Black Student Union. He graduated magna cum laude from Morgan State University and later returned there as an adjunct professor, teaching courses in political science and communications. In 1984, he earned a M.A. in international studies from Johns Hopkins University.

BOARD OF DIRECTORS

Executive officers

Julian Bond, chair; distinguished professor, American University, Washington, DC; professor in history, University of Virginia, Charlottesville, VA

Roslyn Brock, vice chair; director of system fund development, Sisters of Bon Secours Health System, Inc., Marriottsville, MD

Francisco Borges, treasurer; managing director, FGIC Government Services, Simsbury, CT

Carolyn Coleman; special assistant for community affairs to Gov. James B. Hunt Jr., Greensboro, NC

Roy Williams, chair, NAACP Special Contribution Fund; manager of community relations, Chrysler Corp., Detroit, MI

Other members

Richard Allen, Pocola, OK
Melvin Alston, Greensboro, NC
Ben F. Andrews Jr., Hartford, CT
Shieash Averett (youth), Detroit, MI
Ophelia Averitt, Akron, OH
Fred L. Banks Jr., Jackson, MS
Kimberly Bills (youth), Baltimore, MD
Gary Bledsoe, Austin, TX
Cora Breckenridge, Elkhart, IN
Amos Brown, San Francisco, CA
Clayola Brown, New York, NY
Richard Burton, Jacksonville, FL
Clarence Carr, Greendale, MO
William E. Cofield, Frankfort, KY
Babette Colquitt, Fairfax, VA
Denisha Delane (youth), Berkeley, CA
Hazel N. Dukes, New York, NY
Willis Edwards, Los Angeles, CA
Kathrine T. Egland, Gulfport, MS
Myrlie Evers-Williams, Bend, OR
James E. Ghee, Farmville, VA
Nate Gooden, Detroit, MI
William H. Graves, Memphis, TN
Marjorie R. Green, Baltimore, MD
Elaine Harrington, Paterson, NJ
Dorothy Hayden-Watkins, Beverly Hills, CA

CONTACT INFORMATION

4805 Mt. Hope Drive, Baltimore, MD 21215
Phone: (877) NAACP-98 (toll-free) • *Fax:* (410) 486-9257
General E-mail: See www.naacp.org/contact/ •
Web site: www.naacp.org

Communications Director: Office of Communication (410) 486-9227
Human Resources Director: Information unavailable

PURPOSE: "To ensure the political, educational, social and economic equality of minority group citizens; to achieve equality of rights and eliminate race prejudice among citizens of the United States; to remove all barriers of racial and other discrimination through democratic processes."

CURRENT CONCERNS: Affirmative action • Environmental racism • Hate crimes • Human rights in Nigeria • School choice initiatives • Supreme Court

METHOD OF OPERATION: Advertisements • Awards program • Coalition forming • Conferences/seminars • Congressional testimony • Congressional voting analysis • Demonstrations • Grassroots organizing • International activities • Legal assistance • Legislative/regulatory monitoring (federal and state) • Litigation • Lobbying (federal, state, and grassroots) • Local/municipal affairs • Media outreach • Participation in regulatory proceedings (federal) • Research • Scholarships • Television and radio production • Training and technical assistance • Voter registration

Effectiveness and Political Orientation

"Hundreds of thousands of people filled the Mall and marched along Pennsylvania Avenue yesterday to show their support for abortion rights, loudly identifying President Bush as the leading enemy of 'reproductive freedom.'

"Organizers of the March for Women's Lives said they had drawn 1.15 million people, which would make it the largest abortion rights gathering in history. 'This has been the largest march for reproductive rights, the largest march for women's rights and the largest march of any kind in this country,' said Kim Gandy, president of the National Organization for Women.

"Police would not issue an official estimate, but some veteran commanders said the crowd was at least the biggest since the 1995 Million Man March, which independent researchers put at 870,000 people. D.C. Police Chief Charles H. Ramsey would say only that he thought the march had met and perhaps exceeded its organizers' expectations. Their march permit was for as many as 750,000.

"Celebrities, from entertainers to politicians to activists, lent their shine to the event. Actors Cybill Shepherd and Whoopi Goldberg attended, as did singers Ani DiFranco and Moby. Feminist icons Patricia Ireland and Gloria

Alice Huffman, Sacramento, CA
Frank A. Humphrey, Madison, WI
Nancy L. Lane, New York, NY
David Livingston, Decatur, IL
William Lucy, Washington, DC
Annie B. Martin, New York, NY
Michael Nelson, Detroit, MI
Adora Obi Nweze, Miami, FL
Herbert W. Powell, Houston, TX
Demetrius Prather (youth), Atlanta, GA
Mary Ratliff, Columbia, MO
Rupert Richardson, Baton Rouge, LA
Jennifer Rose-Dodd (youth), Colorado
    Springs, CO
Alfred J. Rucks, Las Cruces, NM
Leon Russel, Clearwater, FL
Paula Saizan, Houston, TX
David N. Saperstein, Washington, DC
Morris L. Shearin Sr., Washington, DC
Louise A. Simpson, Freeport, NY
H. H. Singleton II, Conway, SC
Charles E. Smith, Kansas City, MO
Maxine A. Smith, Memphis, TN
Lacy Steele; Bellevue, WA
John Street; mayor, Philadelphia, PA
Jesse H. Turner Jr., Memphis, TN
Menola N. Upshaw, Denver, CO
Rovenia Vaughan, Powhatan, VA
Leroy W. Warren Jr., Silver Spring, MD
Charles Whitehead, Covington, KY
Nicholas Wiggins (youth), East Stroudsburg,
    PA
Richard G. Womack, Washington, DC

SCOPE
Members: 500,000 individuals
Branches/chapters: 1,700 chapters
Affiliates: NAACP/Special Contribution Fund, a
    separate 501(c)(3) organization

STAFF
60 total

TAX STATUS
501(c)(3)

FINANCES
Revenue: 2002—$36.31 million;
2001—$40.66 million

FUNDING SOURCES
Contributions, 71%; program services,
15%; investments, 1.4%; other, 12.5%

PAC
None

EMPLOYMENT
Information unavailable

INTERNSHIPS
Information unavailable

NEWSLETTERS
Crisis magazine (10 times per year)

PUBLICATIONS
None

CONFERENCES
Annual conference

Steinem were there, and so were former secretary of state Madeleine K. Albright and Sen. Barbara Boxer (D-Calif.). Billionaire Ted Turner was there. So was NAACP Chairman Julian Bond. . . .

"About 20 feet back from the front line, a tall, slender man in a linen jacket towered above the women around him, walking with a meditative air. It was NAACP leader Julian Bond. 'Crowds have a calming influence on me,' he said, craning his neck from side to side. 'I've been through a lot of these but never on a pro-choice march. We've supported the pro-choice movement since 1968 but never endorsed something like this.'"

(*The Washington Post*, April 26, 2004)

"Fifty years after the U.S. Supreme Court outlawed school segregation, many public schools are giving graduates 'certificates of attendance rather than meaningful diplomas,' the chief executive of the NAACP told a Minneapolis convention audience Saturday.

"Kweisi Mfume, speaking to the national convention of the American Association of Community Colleges, said the Supreme Court's landmark 1954 ruling promised equal educational opportunity for all. But, he said, poor whites and students of color are still being shortchanged. . . .

"Mfume said that community colleges—of which he is a product—are often 'the only bridge over troubled waters' for blacks, Latinos, Asians, Indians and poor whites, but that 'too many people look over and leap beyond the community colleges when they talk about higher education.'

"Unlike four-year colleges, community colleges 'meet students where they are,' but they face a challenge in trying to retain them. 'I could have been one of those lost and not retained,' he said.

"Mfume, who graduated from Baltimore City College, was a five-term member of Congress before heading the NAACP.

"The Minneapolis convention has brought together community college educators from around the country to talk about issues ranging from student retention to information technology. President Bush will speak to the gathering on Monday.

"Mfume said that at a time of 'hate speech, hate groups, hate radio and hate crimes,' college graduates have a weight on their shoulders that requires them to speak out against all forms of bigotry, which he said 'deplete us as a nation.'"

(*Minneapolis Star Tribune*, April 25, 2004)

"A group of parents concerned that minority students may be receiving unequal treatment in the schools are seeking answers from the Rockdale County school board. . . .

"Among other things, parents asked board members about the qualifications for school resource officers and whether students can be changed from college prep study to the general curriculum without parents being notified.

"The parents asked the board to respond to their questions within three days.

"Lewis Belcher, chairman of the county NAACP's legal redress committee, took the board to task, saying Rockdale's schools have double standards in discipline for black and white students and lack diversity among their faculty, staff and administration. . . ."

(*The Atlanta Journal-Constitution*, April 23, 2004)

"Bernard Croom stands before a group, making a detailed PowerPoint presentation. Executive board members listen intently and nod. The audience is inspired.

"But this is no corporate meeting in a boardroom. The setting is the Richland Correctional Institution activity hall in Mansfield, where a sea of inmates in blue uniforms stretches from wall to wall.

"The 88 men are attending a meeting of the National Association for the Advancement of Colored People.

"Here, the fight for freedom that is the mission of the nation's oldest civil-rights organization takes on a different tone. Liberation from ignorance, addiction and a lifestyle of destruction is seen as the key to ending the cycle of incarceration and recidivism.

"'You need to be about getting it together and getting off these streets,' said Croom, the 34-year-old president of the prison's NAACP chapter. He is serving 15 years to life for murder and drug abuse.

"The Prison Project helps prisoners make a smoother transition back into society by taking advantage of the NAACP's network of support from churches, businesses and other community groups.

"The disproportionate number of blacks in prison motivated the group to focus more on inmates. The Richland chapter was chartered in 2002. . . .

"Sybil Edwards-McNabb, state chairwoman of the NAACP, said the civil-rights movement is about helping people affected by poverty and a lack of education.

"'We have to take the risk of saying to our community, We don't have to allow this and accept it as a lost cause,' she said. 'We are a people of survival. We don't have to be overcome by this.'"

(*Columbus Dispatch* [Ohio], April 11, 2004)

"At It Again: Raynard Lawler, former manager of the Adam's Mark Hotel here, has been fired from his job as interim general manager with HBE Corp.'s Adam's Mark in Buffalo. The firing of the African-American GM will likely cause new headaches for the hotel chain. Harold Crumpton, president of the St. Louis Branch of the NAACP, says his organization will drop the Adam's Mark here from consideration for the organization's Freedom Fund dinner. . . . Tommie Monroe, veep of corporate affairs for the Adam's Mark chain, told the Buffalo News that Lawler was terminated 'because of a difference in opinion over how the hotel should be run and performance issues.' Lawler, who spent 18 years with Hyatt Hotels and two years with the Loew's chain before joining the Adam's Mark, disputes that. But Monroe also told the newspaper: 'Our commitment to diversity has not changed. . . . The decision is not based on race in any form.'. . . Meanwhile, the Buffalo NAACP prez, Frank B. Mesiah, says the group is concerned that the hotel may be discriminating against minorities. If you came in late: Kummer agreed to pay $1.1 million to settle allegations that the Adam's Mark in Daytona Beach, Fla., discriminated against black guests in 1999. And the NAACP began a national boycott of the chain in 2000 and ended it in late 2001. Some local NAACPers and ministers say they are working on plans to picket June Kummer's tony national Home Garden Club convention to protest Lawler's firing. The event is slated to be here this summer. June is half owner in the Adam's Mark hotels."

(*St. Louis Post-Dispatch,* April 8, 2004)

National Association of Manufacturers

Established in 1895

DIRECTOR

Jerry J. Jasinowski, president. Jasinowski became president of the NAM in 1990. Jasinowski joined the U.S. Air Force as an intelligence officer, serving in the Far East in the mid-1960s. He then became assistant professor of economics at the U.S. Air Force Academy. In the early 1970s, Jasinowski managed research and legislative activities for the Joint Economic Committee of Congress. In 1976, he served as director of the Carter administration's economic transition team for the departments of Treasury, Commerce, Labor, the Council of Economic Advisors, and the Federal Reserve. He later was appointed assistant secretary for policy at the U.S. Department of Commerce. Jasinowski received his bachelor's degree in economics from Indiana University and his master's degree in economics from Columbia University. He is a graduate of the Harvard Business School's Advanced Management Program.

BOARD OF DIRECTORS

Arnold A. Allemang; executive vice president, Dow Chemical Co., Midland, MI

Jay Bender; president, Falcon Plastics, Inc., Brookings, SD

James G. Berges; president, EMERSON, St. Louis, MO

John W. Conway; chair of the board, president, and chief executive officer, Crown Cork & Seal Co., Inc., Philadelphia, PA

Richard E. Dauch; co-founder, chair, and chief executive officer, American Axle & Manufacturing, Inc., Detroit, MI

E. Linn Draper Jr.; chair, president, and chief executive officer, American Electric Power, Columbus, OH

Archie W. Dunham; chair of the board, ConocoPhillips, Houston, TX

Ralph F. Hake; chair and chief executive officer, Maytag Corp., Newton, IA

Stephanie Harkness; chair and chief executive officer, Pacific Plastics & Engineering, Soquel, CA

William V. Hickey; president and chief executive officer, Sealed Air Corp., Saddle Brook, NJ

Jerry J. Jasinowski; president, National Association of Manufacturers, Washington, DC

Kendig K. Kneen; chief executive officer/owner, Al-jon, Inc., Ottumwa, IA

Steven F. Leer; president and chief executive officer, Arch Coal, Inc., St. Louis, MO

W. Kirk Liddell; president and chief executive officer, Irex Corp., Lancaster, PA

John A. Luke Jr.; chair and chief executive officer, MeadWestvaco Corp., Stamford, CT

CONTACT INFORMATION

1331 Pennsylvania Avenue, NW, Washington, DC 20004-1790
Phone: (202) 637-3000 • *Fax:* (202) 637-3182
General E-mail: manufacturing@nam.org • *Web site:* www.nam.org

Communications Director: Laura Brown Narvaiz, vice president, communications and media relations
(202) 637-3087 • lnarvaiz@nam.org.
Human Resources Director: Carol Coldren
(202) 637-3016 • ccoldren@nam.org.

PURPOSE: "To enhance the competitiveness of manufacturers and to improve American living standards by shaping a legislative and regulatory environment conducive to U.S. economic growth and to increase understanding among policymakers, the media and the public about the importance of manufacturing to America's economic strength."

CURRENT CONCERNS: Reducing production costs in the U.S. (taxes, health care, tort litigation, regulation, and rising energy prices) • Leveling the international playing field • Promoting innovation, investment, and productivity • Ensuring an adequate supply of skilled workers • Raising awareness that manufacturing is critical to our economy.

METHOD OF OPERATION: Advertisements • Awards program • Coalition forming • Conferences/seminars • Congressional testimony • Congressional voting analysis • Direct action • Educational foundation • Grassroots organizing • Information clearinghouse • Legislative/regulatory monitoring (federal and state) • Litigation • Media outreach • Polling • Product merchandising • Research • Speakers program • Technical assistance and training • Voter registration • Voting records • Web site

Effectiveness and Political Orientation

"New-source review, or N.S.R., involves an obscure and complex set of environmental rules and regulations that most Americans have never heard of, but to people who work in the power industry, few subjects are more crucial. . . .

"The E.P.A. revealed its overhaul of new-source review on Friday, Nov. 22, 2002. For all the buildup, it was a conspicuously low-key debut. President Bush issued no statement about the new guidelines. Christie Whitman declined to attend the news conference, which was run by Jeffrey Holmstead. Cameras were not allowed at the event, which seemed timed to hit the weekly news cycle at its Friday night nadir.

" 'There will be emissions reductions as a result of the final rules that we are adopting today,' Holmstead said. The new rules gave utilities much more maneuverability under N.S.R. The E.P.A. adopted Carol Browner's old 'micro-cap' idea—but abandoned its critical component, the gradual tightening of the cap. Utilities that installed new pollution-control equipment were

SCOPE
Members: 14,000 corporations and businesses
Branches/chapters: 10 offices across the United States
Affiliates: 350 state and local manufacturing, business, and employer associations

STAFF
159 total

TAX STATUS
501(c)(6)

FINANCES
Budget: 2004—$22 million

FUNDING SOURCES
Member dues; nondues member services and products; investments

PAC
None

EMPLOYMENT
Information unavailable

INTERNSHIPS
Information unavailable

PUBLICATIONS
The Facts about Modern Manufacturing
Just-In-Time
NAM Member Focus

given 10-year exemptions from further upgrades. An official with the National Association of Manufacturers called the new rules 'a refreshingly flexible approach to regulation.' The usually staid American Lung Association, in a report issued with a coalition of environmental groups, called the rule changes 'the most harmful and unlawful air-pollution initiative ever undertaken by the federal government.' "

(*The New York Times Magazine,* April 4, 2004)

"U.S. senators from states with toxic waste sites will try this week to move toward reinstatement of a corporate tax to replenish the shrinking Superfund trust fund.

"The fund was created in 1980 to clean up the worst abandoned toxic waste sites in the country. There are 51 such sites in Florida, including the defunct Stauffer phosphate processing plant in Tarpon Springs. . . .

"Opponents of the tax say it is unfair to target all industries because of a minority of irresponsible companies. Keith McCoy, director of environmental quality for the National Association of Manufacturers, said roughly 70 percent of the toxic sites named to a national priority list are cleaned up by the responsible parties.

" 'When you can't find a responsible party, then you have a societal problem,' McCoy said. 'Society as a whole has benefited from the manufacture of these products.'

"Environmental groups say the original intent of the legislation was to use the tax to clean up the worst sites. More importantly, they worry that a dearth of funding is leaving unattended many sites that desperately need to be cleaned up. For instance, the Stauffer site was added to the Superfund list in 1994. It was not until 1998 that the EPA recommended that 50,000 tons of contaminated dirt be consolidated and sealed on the site. The work has not started.

"A recent report by the EPA inspector general said limited funding prevents the agency from 'addressing sites in a manner believed necessary by regional officials and caused projects to be segmented into phases and/or scaled back' "

(*Tampa Tribune,* March 10, 2004)

" 'Manufacturing supported 23 million jobs in the United States last year—15 million manufacturing jobs and another 8 million jobs in other sectors tied to manufacturing,' said Hank Cox, a spokesman for the National Association of Manufacturers in Washington. Members of the association—the country's largest industrial trade association—include GM, Ford Motor Co. and Maytag Corp."

(*The Baltimore Sun,* December 7, 2003)

"Americans are breathing easier and drinking cleaner water than they have in decades, but millions still feel their lungs burn from summer smog and find themselves barred from rivers and lakes too dirty for swimming or fishing.

"That good news/bad news scenario can be found throughout a report card released Monday by the Environmental Protection Agency. The study, commissioned two years ago by outgoing EPA Administrator Christie Whitman, was billed as the federal government's first national assessment of the environment and human health. . . . The report did not involve original research but instead compiled information from more than 30 federal agencies, states, Indian tribes and the private sector.

" 'The EPA's report comes as the Bush administration is weakening the Clean Air and Clean Water acts and slowing down cleanup of toxic waste sites,' said Ed Hopkins of the Sierra Club. 'It is irresponsible to talk about progress made over the last decades while at the same time dismantling the protections that made that progress possible.'

"But a spokesman for the National Association of Manufacturers said the report shows environmental groups are too gloomy and that new environmental protections are unnecessary.

" 'The widely held public perception that U.S. environmental quality is deteriorating, rather than improving, is wildly incorrect,' said Michael Baroody, the group's executive vice president."

(*USA Today,* June 24, 2003)

"Under the Family Time Flexibility Act, an employer can decide to reimburse you for overtime with compensatory (comp) time, rather than with pay. So, if you work eight extra hours, your boss can give you 12 hours of comp time—which you can use or cash out sometime in the next 13 months, at the employer's convenience. . . .

"The Economic Policy Institute—a labor-supported think-tank—opposes the legislation because many low-wage, hourly workers simply cannot live without the extra money they earn working overtime. They also fear employers will discriminate against employees who insist on overtime pay rather than comp time. For these low-wage workers, says Rep. John F. Tierney, D-Mass., the result will be 'less time for their families and less income to support those families.'

"Arlie Hochschild, professor of sociology at UC Berkeley, and author of 'The Second Shift' and 'The Time Bind,' views this legislation as 'a fig leaf covering corporate interests.' The boss, she says, 'will have more incentive to increase overtime and the worker will get an IOU.'

"Not surprisingly, those who support the legislation include the National Association of Manufacturers and other business groups who stand to gain greater flexibility and profit from the bill's passage."

(*The San Francisco Chronicle,* May 1, 2003)

"As President Bush prepared to lead the nation into war, he lost a skirmish Wednesday in a different conflict as the Senate voted against allowing oil exploration in the Arctic National Wildlife Refuge.

"Bush had made the measure a top priority. But Democrats, aided by eight Republicans, won a 52–48 vote, the latest in the 23-year-old political war over the refuge. . . .

"Opponents of drilling in the refuge say it would add an insignificant amount to the energy supply, while damaging an irreplaceable wilderness.

"Jamie Rappaport Clark of the National Wildlife Federation said Wednesday's vote means that 'once again, wildlife has won over wildcatters.'

" 'The message from the Senate is clear. Oil rigs do not belong in the Arctic Wildlife Refuge,' he said. . . .

"The National Association of Manufacturers, which had lobbied for the drilling proposal, said it was 'disappointed by so many senators choosing to ignore the site's potential benefits to our economy.' "

(*The Atlanta Journal-Constitution,* March 20, 2003)

National Audubon Society

Established in 1905

DIRECTOR

John Flicker, president. Flicker assumed the leadership of the National Audubon Society in 1995. Flicker came to Audubon after 21 years with The Nature Conservancy. While in the Midwest, Flicker served as The Nature Conservancy's Great Plains director. A Minnesota native, Flicker graduated from the University of Minnesota and William Mitchell College of Law.

BOARD OF DIRECTORS

John H. Anderson, D.V.M.
Juliet P. Tammenoms Bakker
Steven R. Beissinger
John Bellmon
Gerard A. Bertrand
Carol M. Browner
Leslie Dach
Jack Dempsey
Lynn Dolnick
W. Hardy Eshbaugh
Christopher M. Harte
Vivian Johnson
Charles Kahle
Susannah S. Kent
Tami Longaberger
Allen J. Model
Sarah Muyskens
William W. McQuilkin Jr.
Margery Aylwin Nicolson
David H. Pardoe
Ruth O. Russell
Geoffrey Cobb Ryan
Andrew Sansom
Lloyd Semple
Robert G. Stanton
Michael Stopler
David H. Walsh
Ione Werthman
Alan Wilson
John L. Whitmire
John Whittle
Liz Woedl
William P. Yellowtail
Steven T. Zimmerman

SCOPE

Members: 450,000 individuals
Branches/chapters: 9 regional offices; 508
    chapters throughout the Americas; other
    chapters in Central and South America;
    100 sanctuaries and nature centers
Affiliates: Six affiliates.

STAFF

850 total—650 full-time; 200 part-time;
plus volunteers

TAX STATUS

501(c)(3)

CONTACT INFORMATION

700 Broadway, New York, NY 10003
Phone: (212) 979-3000 • *Fax:* (212) 979-3188
General E-mail: join@audubon.org • *Web site:* www.audubon.org

Communications Director: John Bianchi
(212) 979-3026 • jbianchi@audubon.org.
Human Resources Director: Linda Brooke
(212) 979-3010 • lbrooke@audubon.org

PURPOSE: "To conserve and restore natural ecosystems, focusing on birds and other wildlife, for the benefit of humanity and the earth's biological diversity."

CURRENT CONCERNS: Arctic National Wildlife Refuge • Bird conservation • Changing landscaping practices • Community conservation partnerships • Forest roadless areas • General nature education • Habitat protection • Key place-based conservation (Long Island Sound, Everglades, San Francisco Bay) • Mississippi River • Platte River • Wetland and clean water protections

METHOD OF OPERATION: Advertisements • Awards program • Coalition forming • Congressional testimony • Direct action • Educational foundation • Fax-on-demand • Grassroots organizing • Information clearinghouse • International activities • Internet (databases, electronic bulletin boards, e-mail alerts, and Web site) • Internships • Legislative/ regulatory monitoring (federal and state) • Litigation • Lobbying (federal, state, and grassroots) • Local/municipal affairs • Mailing lists • Media outreach • Mediation • Product merchandising • Research • Shareholder resolutions • Training

Effectiveness and Political Orientation

"President Bush doesn't talk about new-source review very often. In fact, he has mentioned it in a speech to the public only once, in remarks he delivered on Sept. 15, 2003, to a cheering crowd of power-plant workers and executives in Monroe, Mich., about 35 miles south of Detroit. It was an ideal audience for his chosen subject. New-source review, or N.S.R., involves an obscure and complex set of environmental rules and regulations that most Americans have never heard of, but to people who work in the power industry, few subjects are more crucial. . . .

"When I spoke to him recently, Perciasepe, now C.E.O. of the National Audubon Society, put the matter bluntly. The reason new-source review did not get streamlined during the Clinton years, he said, was that the energy companies, utilities and other industries had no interest in any sort of workable reforms. 'In hindsight, maybe we were going after a sort of holy grail,' he told me. 'You were not going to reach agreement with some of these folks,' he

FINANCES
Budget: 2003—$71,267,000;
2002—$70,888,000

FUNDING SOURCES
Individuals, 24%; foundation grants, 15%; publications, 14%; bequests, 14%; investment income, 11%; membership dues, 11%; land sales, 7%; corporate donations, 4%

PAC
None

EMPLOYMENT
Employment opportunities are listed at: www.audubon.org/nas/hr/. Direct questions to the NAS Human Resources Department, 700 Broadway New York, NY 10003. Phone: (212) 979-3000. E-mail: HumanResources@ audubon.org. NAS offers employment in several locations. Resumes and cover letters may be sent to Linda Brooke, vice president, human resources, 700 Broadway, New York, NY 10003. Phone: (212) 979-3010. Fax: (212) 979-3026. E-mail: lbrooke@audubon.org.

INTERNSHIPS
The National Audubon Society offers internships in a number of locations. Internships are handled individually by each program area and location. For more information, fax or e-mail queries. Fax: (651) 731-1330. E-mail: HumanResources@audubon.org.

NEWSLETTERS
Audubon (monthly magazine)

PUBLICATIONS
Audubon's Birds of America
Eye of the Albatross
Audubon House
Audubon Life-List Journal
Giving Back to the Earth: A Teacher's Guide to Project Puffin and Other Seabird Studies
National Audubon Society Birder's Handbook: How to Locate, Observe, Identify, Record, Photograph, and Study Birds
National Audubon Society Book of Wild Birds
National Audubon Society Seafood Lover's Almanac
Project Puffin: How We Brought Puffins Back to Egg Rock
Saving Birds
Wild Bird Photography
Also offers many National Audubon Society Field Guides and computer software items.

CONFERENCES
National convention (biennial)

said, referring to industry representatives, 'because what they really wanted was to not have to do it. . . .'"

(*The New York Times*, April 4, 2004)

"The Audubon Society embarks on a 20-year plan to open nature preserves for inner-city residents

"The National Audubon Society, famous for its preserves far into the wilderness, is reversing a 100-year-old tradition with a plan to open patches of wilderness like this in urban communities. In addition to this preserve just northeast of downtown Los Angeles skyscrapers—and soon-to-be opened parks in Seattle, Philadelphia, and Little Rock, Ark.—the conservation group plans to create 1,000 such oases by 2020.

"The idea behind it is twofold. One is to recognize the long-changed demographic shift of Americans from rural to urban areas. The other is to preserve a unique sense of place and build an ethos of stewardship among the urban poor at an early age. 'How can we expect this country's coming generations to care about a Yellowstone, or Arctic refuge, or rain forests if they can't connect to something natural in the world where they are?' asks John Flicker, president of the National Audubon Society."

(*Christian Science Monitor*, December 30, 2003)

"A look inside the Nature Conservancy reveals a whirring marketing machine that has poured millions into building and protecting the organization's image, laboring to transform the charity into a household name.

"One Conservancy opinion survey measured the Conservancy's name recognition at only 5 percent of Americans concerned about the environment, well below the National Audubon Society's 8 percent, the National Wildlife Federation's 10 percent and Greenpeace's 17 percent.

"Those polled viewed the World Wildlife Fund as more accountable and better at conservation, Audubon and the National Wildlife Fund more successful 'in local areas.'"

(*The Washington Post*, May 4, 2003)

"Within the year, the National Audubon Society wants its Portland group—the country's largest and perhaps most successful Audubon chapter—to merge with it to form a statewide office. The new entity no longer would carry the Portland name. Nor would it answer solely to a Portland board of directors. Nor would it necessarily put Portland-area conservation issues at the top of its to-do list.

"If the Audubon Society of Portland does not agree to a merger, then the National Audubon Society intends to land in the city anyway. It would open a separate office, send out separate fund-raising appeals, work to entice its own new membership and volunteers, and begin to build up to 20 multimillion-dollar educational nature centers around the state.

"In Portland and beyond, a few bird lovers and conservationists coo at the notion, but many more are squawking.

"'The irony is, of course, that they point to us as a national model of how it ought to be done,' says Mike Houck, his voice ruffled with agitation.

"'Well, we agree,' he says. 'We want to maintain that. . . .'

"Intent on vastly expanding the reach of its stagnant, mostly white, upper-middle class, gray-around-the-temples membership, the National Audubon Society in the mid-1990s saw what it needed: change.

"It decided to grow its constituency, fund-raising base and what it calls a nationwide 'culture of conservation' not by investing in existing Audubon chapters, but by opening a new network of professionally run offices and nature centers in key population centers in every state. It wants to woo big-dollar donors. It plans to push hard into diverse ethnic and socioeconomic communities and to try to have its greatest long-term impact by giving children frequent opportunities to learn about nature up close.

"By 2020, National Audubon wants to quintuple its membership to 2.75 million."

(The Oregonian [Portland], May 7, 2002)

National Center
for Educational Accountability

Established in 2001 (National Alliance of Business joined forces with the NCEA in fall 2002)

DIRECTOR

Brad Duggan, president. Duggan has been an active participant in school reform efforts for 30 years and has held leadership positions on more than 20 national and statewide education committees. He has regularly testified before legislative and regulatory bodies on education issues. Previously he was executive director of Just for the Kids, a nonprofit education research and reform organization, for 6 years, after serving as executive director of a state principals' association for 20 years. He was appointed by governors to three statewide commissions and chaired the Texas Advisory Committee on Public Access to Student Achievement Information. He was the 1999 chair of the Texas Society of Association Executives, an organization of 750 professional and trade associations.

BOARD OF DIRECTORS

Tom Luce, chair of the board; counsel, Hughes & Luce

Terry Kelley, vice chair; former chair and chief executive officer, Bank One Regional

John Anderson, member; vice chair, New American Schools

Carolyn Bacon, member; executive director, O'Donnell Foundation

Lee Blitch, member; president, San Francisco Chamber of Commerce

Bill Brock, member; former U.S. secretary of labor, representative, and senator from Tennessee

Barbara Byrd-Bennett, member; chief executive officer, Cleveland Municipal School District

Ken Duberstein, member; president, Duberstein Group, Inc., former chief of staff for President Reagan

James Edgar, member; former governor of Illinois

Tom Engibous, member; chair and chief executive officer, Texas Instruments, Inc.

Larry Faulkner, member; president, University of Texas at Austin

G. Thomas Houlihan, member; executive director, Council of Chief State School Officers

James Hunt Jr., member; former governor of North Carolina

Roberts T. Jones, member; president, Education & Workforce Policy

Manuel J. Justiz, member; dean of College of Education, University of Texas at Austin

Kerry Killinger, member; president, chair and chief executive officer, Washington Mutual

Charles B. Reed, member; chancellor, California State University System

CONTACT INFORMATION

1455 Pennsylvania Avenue, NW, Suite 375, Washington, DC 2000
Phone: (202) 262-2468 • *Web site:* www.nc4ea.org
Toll-free: (800) 787-2848
NCEA Headquarters
4030-2 W. Braker Lane, 2nd Floor, Austin, Texas 78759
Phone: (512) 232-0714 • *Fax:* (512) 232-0777
General E-mail: jftk@just4kids.org • *Web site:* www.nc4ea.org

Communications Director: None
Human Resources Director: None

PURPOSE: "[B]olster the quality of education for students and respond to states' needs as they move forward to implement standards and accountability in the nation's classrooms."

CURRENT CONCERNS: Aligning NCEA efforts with other national business and education groups • Business-led coalitions working on education issues • Providing information on implementing the No Child Left Behind Act

METHOD OF OPERATION: Awards program • Coalition forming • Conferences/seminars • Congressional testimony • Lobbying (federal, state, and grassroots) • Media outreach • Product merchandising • Research • Speakers program • Training and technical assistance

Effectiveness and Political Orientation

"The Chugach School District is one of the strangest in America. Encompassing 22,000 square miles of remote Alaskan wilderness, ranging from the islands of Prince William Sound to isolated "bush" villages, it has only 214 students and barely two dozen teachers on its staff. Unemployment in the area tops 50 percent, and three-fourths of the people—many of them Aleuts—are below the poverty line.

"Yet in seven years, this school district, facing challenges of almost unimaginable scope and complexity, has transformed itself into a national model of education reform whose methods are being copied not only across Alaska, but now in the Seattle public schools as well.

"Last week, the Chugach superintendent, Richard DeLorenzo, stood before a ballroom full of high-powered executives, explaining how little Chugach had won the Malcolm Baldrige National Quality Award, an honor that in the past has gone to companies such as Cadillac and Ritz-Carlton as a signal of their success in providing customer satisfaction. . . .

"But the key to success, DeLorenzo said, was the application of 'Baldrige principles' to the whole process. It began with structured discussions with the 'customers,' the parents and other villagers, local businesses and the students themselves, to identify their needs and goals. The whole system was then redesigned to achieve those results. . . .

SCOPE

Members: None
Branches/chapters: None
Affiliates: None

STAFF

41 total

TAX STATUS

501(c)(3)

FINANCES

Revenue: 2002—$2 million; 2001—$690,000

FUNDING SOURCES

Contributions; government grants; investments; other

PAC

None

EMPLOYMENT

Information unavailable

INTERNSHIPS

Information unavailable

NEWSLETTERS

Work America (monthly)
Workforce Economics (quarterly)
Workforce Trends (bimonthly)

PUBLICATIONS

The following is a sample list of publications:

Aligning Workforce Investment Systems with Employer Demand

Baldrige in Education: Improving Student Performance

Business Coalition Network: Seven Principles of Success

The Formula for Success: A Business Leader's Guide to Supporting Math and Science Achievement

Improving the Quality of Teaching: The Business Role

Linking Workforce Investment with Economic Development

A New Twist: How Employers and Educators Can Work Together to Improve Student Achievement

"This systemic approach to education reform, championed by organizations such as the National Alliance of Business, is being tried in a growing number of districts across the country, and DeLorenzo recently lobbied Secretary of Education Rod Paige to embrace it as the best bet to achieve Bush's goals."

(*Pittsburgh Post-Gazette*, April 15, 2002)

"Wendy Blauvelt attended college on and off for three years, but admits she never quite grasped how important it was for her to complete her education.

"Now, with a full work schedule, two young children and a husband who works second shift, returning to college full time would be nearly impossible, Blauvelt told an audience at the University of Southern Maine in Portland on Wednesday.

"But Blauvelt, who works in customer service for Barber Foods in Portland, is pursuing her dream of higher learning while also keeping her job and spending evenings with her children.

"Blauvelt is one of 18 Barber employees participating in a program called "Pathways to Higher Education" run by Barber, the university and Southern Maine Technical College. The three parties in the partnership touted the program at Wednesday's monthly breakfast meeting of businesspeople in an attempt to draw other companies to participate.

"Under the program, which started last year, faculty from the two schools teach college classes at Barber. The classes consist of two sessions each week with each session lasting two hours. The company and the workers split the cost of the time.

"Maine needs partnerships such as Pathways to stay economically competitive, said Steve McFarland, worksite programs manager at USM. . . .

"McFarland also cited statements by the National Alliance of Business that said investments in employee education and training yield greater returns than investments in technology. 'Think about that,' he urged the audience. 'Where does your business stand on that? Do you have a bigger budget for human development than you do for technology?'"

(*Portland Press Herald,* February 14, 2002)

"A coalition of business leaders and university presidents said yesterday that as the minority population increases, the nation must do more to encourage diversity in education and, ultimately, the workplace. . . .

"The report from the Business-Higher Education Forum said that with more racial and ethnic minorities in the college-age population, universities will be challenged to improve their outreach programs, shore up other policies to promote diversity on campus and press for increased financial aid to make college more accessible.

"Attracting more minority students to classrooms would, in turn, deepen the pool of qualified candidates available to employers, according to the forum, a partnership of the National Alliance of Business and the American Council on Education."

(*The Plain Dealer* [Cleveland], January 11, 2002)

"A distinguished coalition of educators, businesspersons and policymakers announced today the establishment of the National Center for Educational Accountability, a collaborative effort to improve learning through the effective use of school and student data and the identification of best practices.

Rise to the Challenge: A Business Guide to
Creating a Workforce Investment System
That Makes Sense

CONFERENCES
Annual conference

"The National Center for Educational Accountability is a joint venture of Just for the Kids, an Austin, Texas-based nonprofit organization that uses state accountability data to examine and improve school performance; the University of Texas at Austin; and the Education Commission of the States (ECS), an interstate compact that helps state policymakers shape education policies. The collaboration unites a proven education accountability reporting and research model with the research strengths of a major university, and the leadership and policy expertise of a prestigious organization in a joint effort to elevate the quality of public education in this country.

" 'Through this partnership, the lessons learned in many states will serve as a foundation for an innovative research and development program that will influence state and federal education policy,' said Larry R. Faulkner, president of the University of Texas at Austin. 'We expect this to be the country's most influential center working on education accountability.'

"The National Center for Educational Accountability will build on the model of the successful Just for the Kids program begun in Austin in 1995 by attorney and civic leader Tom Luce, who will chair the center's board of directors. After years of research and working with educators, Just for the Kids developed an Internet-based school information system to drive improvement in public schools. The keystone for the program's efforts is academic performance data-facts about student performance that provide the only effective way to identify areas of improvement and low performance."

(*U.S. Newswire,* November 8, 2001)

National Center for Neighborhood Enterprise

Established in 1981

DIRECTOR

Robert L. Woodson Sr., president. Woodson founded the National Center for Neighborhood Enterprise. In the 1960s, Woodson developed and coordinated national and local community development programs. During the 1970s, he directed the National Urban League's Administration of Justice division and then served as a resident fellow at the American Enterprise Institute. In the 1980s, Woodson worked with the House of Umoja, in Philadelphia. He received a John D. and Catherine T. MacArthur Fellowship.

BOARD OF DIRECTORS

Rick Wiederhold, chair; Elizabeth Brinn Foundation.
Michael Baroody; National Association of Manufacturers
Wilhelmina Bell Taylor; Betah Associates
Harold Black; University of Tennessee at Chattanooga
Chloe Coney; Corp. to Develop Communities of Tampa
Clifford Ehrlich; Baruch Fellner, Gibson, Dunn & Crutcher, LLP
Patrick Ford; Burson-Marsteller
Roman Herrera; Victory Fellowship
Myron J. Resnick
Cordelia Taylor; Family House, Inc.
Richard P. Wiederhold
Robert L. Woodson Sr.

SCOPE

Members: None
Branches/chapters: Violence-Free Zone sites in Birmingham, Dallas, Indianapolis, Milwaukee, WI, Washington, DC, and Youngstown, OH
Affiliates: Grassroots organizations in 39 states nationwide

STAFF

14 total—11 full-time professional; 3 full-time support; plus 4 consultants

TAX STATUS

501(c)(3)

FINANCES

Budget: 2002—$2,987,988

FUNDING SOURCES

Foundation grants; corporate donations; government grants; individuals

PAC

None

EMPLOYMENT

Information about employment opportunities may be obtained from Terence Mathis, vice

CONTACT INFORMATION

1424 16th Street, NW, Suite 300, Washington, DC 20036
Phone: (202) 518-6500 • *Fax:* (202) 588-0314
General E-mail: info@ncne.com • *Web site:* www.ncne.com

Communications Director: Heather Humphries, director of development and communications
(202) 518-6500 • info@ncne.com
Human Resources Director: Terence Mathis, vice president
(202) 518-6500 • info@ncne.com

PURPOSE: "To empower neighborhood leaders to promote solutions that reduce crime and violence, restore families, revitalize low-income communities, and create economic enterprise. To accomplish its mission, NCNE provides training, technical assistance, linkages to sources of support, and information for public policy."

CURRENT CONCERNS: Building capacity of faith-based and community organizations • Financial literacy • Rural poverty • Youth violence

METHOD OF OPERATION: Awards program (Annual National Achievement Against the Odds, Regional "Joseph Awards") • Coalition forming • Conferences/seminars • Congressional testimony • Demonstration projects • Documentation of community-based initiatives • Films/video/audiotapes • Grassroots organizing • Media outreach • Participation in regulatory proceedings (federal and state) • Provides linkages to sources of support for grassroots initiatives • Training and technical assistance • Web site

Effectiveness and Political Orientation

"Robert Woodson, founder and president of the National Center for Neighborhood Enterprise and a frequent visitor to Tampa, thinks differently and says out loud what many know but few dare say:

"'Declines in neighborhoods are due in part to the behavior of the people living there. Some of this behavior is a response to economic forces such as unemployment. When neighborhoods experience high crime, dissolution of families, and disintegration of intermediary institutions that represent the core values structures, these things in turn undermine the economic structures.'"

(*Tampa Tribune,* May 18, 2003)

"The drug rehabilitation program at Victory Home is the cornerstone of the ministry. It has been recognized as one of the most effective drug treatment programs in the United States by the National Center for Neighborhood Enterprise, a Washington-based organization that looks for nongovernmental solutions to urban problems."

(*San Antonio Express-News,* July 20, 2003)

president, 1424 Sixteenth Street, NW, Suite 300, Washington, DC 20036. Phone number: (202) 518-6500. Fax: (202) 588-0314. E-mail address: info@ncne.com.

INTERNSHIPS

Hours, duration of internship and types of internships vary. Information about internship opportunities can be obtained from Terence Mathis, vice president, 1424 Sixteenth Street, NW, Suite 300, Washington, DC 20036. Phone number: (202) 518-6500. Fax: (202) 588-0314. E-mail address: info@ncne.com.

NEWSLETTERS

From the Center (quarterly)
eUpdate (monthly e-mail)
In the News (periodic compilation of news clips)

PUBLICATIONS

Applying Market Principles in the Social Economy: An Alternative Giving Strategy
Bridging the Gap: Strategies to Promote Self-Sufficiency Among Low-Income Americans
Empowering Residents of Public Housing: A Resource Guide for Resident Management
Entrepreneurial Enclaves in the African American Experience
Outcry from the Alamo: Ending the Hostility Toward Faith-Based Drug Treatment
Race and Economic Opportunity
The Silent Scandal: Management Abuses in Public Housing
The Triumphs of Joseph: How Today's Community Healers Are Reviving Our Streets and Neighborhoods
Violence-Free Zone Initiatives: Models of Grassroots Youth Crime Intervention Success
Violence-Free Zone Toolkit

CONFERENCES

Occasional

"Six years after gang members in one of the most violent parts of the District called a truce, the survivors of the shootings and neighborhood residents used a quiet church ceremony yesterday to mark the cease-fire's remarkable endurance.

"The truce between gang members in Simple City, as the area around the Benning Terrace public housing complex in Southeast Washington was known, has become city lore. Previous anniversaries have involved marches, church choirs, two-hour ceremonies. Yesterday morning, as a light rain began to fall, about 50 people sank into pews at First Rock Baptist Church and listened to straightforward speeches about the effect of an agreement by a group of young men to stop shooting one another.

"'You have provided the model for programs in at least six other cities to stop violence,' said Robert L. Woodson Sr., director of the National Center for Neighborhood Enterprise, a Washington-based organization that helped negotiate the truce 'There are hundreds of young people across the country who are alive today because of what you did here. . . .'

"Leaders of the National Center for Neighborhood Enterprise and Alliance for Concerned Men pulled gang leaders into a series of tense meetings. Once tempers cooled, the young men on both sides discovered that they were all tired of the conflict. The truce was sealed by a series of hugs.

"The crime rate in the area dropped 28 percent the next year. There has not been a shooting between the crew factions since."

(*The Washington Post,* March 29, 2003)

"When Harry Belafonte called Colin Powell and Condoleezza Rice 'house slaves' for their roles in the Bush administration, we knew the retaliatory strike would be swift and juicy. Stepping up to the mike was one Mr. Robert Woodson, founder of the National Center for Neighborhood Enterprise.

"Woodson led a group of fellow African-Americans in a protest last week outside the Washington Hilton, where Belafonte was being honored at an Africare gala. The protest was 'to express our outrage that this self-appointed king of black America, who is nothing but a bad calypso singer, feels qualified to sit in judgment of the secretary of state and the national security adviser,' Woodson told the *Washington Post.*"

(*St. Louis Post-Dispatch,* October 31, 2002)

"The 'Our Kind of People 800 Register,' set to be published in 2003, will list the 800 wealthiest, best educated and most prominent African-American families in the nation, according to Lawrence Otis Graham, an attorney from upstate New York who conceived the project.

"It is the first attempt to create a national social ranking of black America and may cause controversy.

"Some say the world Graham seeks to quantify in the '800 Register' is an anachronism, rooted in archaic class distinctions that divide black Americans.

"Others express thinly disguised contempt for the idea.

"'I think black people have got a right to be as ridiculous as white people,' said Robert L. Woodson Sr., president of the Washington-based National Center for Neighborhood Enterprise. 'And so, by all means, let's have a social register.'"

(*The Atlanta Journal-Constitution,* March 10, 2002)

National Center for Policy Analysis

Established in 1983

DIRECTOR
John C. Goodman, president. Goodman has served as the center's president since he founded it in 1983. He is the author of numerous studies and several books. Goodman appears on televised debates on such topics as the flat tax, welfare reform, and Social Security privatization. He earned his Ph.D. in economics from Columbia University.

BOARD OF DIRECTORS
John C. Goodman, president
Pete du Pont, chair; Richards, Layton & Finger, former Delaware governor
David L. Brennan, member; chair, White Hat Management, LLC.
Don A. Buchholz, member; chair of the board, SWS Group, Inc.
Dan W. Cook III, member; senior advisor, MHT Partners
Virginia Manheimer, member; trustee, Hickory Foundation
Fred Meyer, member; president and chief executive officer Aladdin Industries, LLC
Henry J. "Bud" Smith, member; chair, Trinity Forum
Thomas W. Smith, member; managing partner, Prescott Investors
James Cleo Thompson Jr., member; chair of the board, Thompson Petroleum Corp.
Jere W. Thompson, member; president, Williamsburg Corp.
Michael L. Whalen, member; president, and chief executive officer, Heart of America Restaurants & Inns

SCOPE
Declined to comment
Branches: Washington, DC office
Affiliates: Declined to comment

STAFF
Declined to comment

TAX STATUS
501(c)(3)

FINANCES
Revenue: 2002—$5.67 million;
2001—$4.77 million

FUNDING SOURCES
Foundations, 61%; corporations, 27%; individuals, 12%

PAC
Declined to comment

EMPLOYMENT
Declined to comment

CONTACT INFORMATION
12770 Coit Road, Suite 800, Dallas, TX 75251
Phone: (972) 386-6272 • *Fax:* (972) 386-0924
General E-mail: ncpa@ncpa.org • *Web site:* www.ncpa.org

Communications Director: Richard Walker
(972) 386-6272 • rwalker@ncpa.org
Human Resources Director: Declined to comment

PURPOSE: The National Center for Policy Analysis (NCPA) is "a nonprofit, nonpartisan public policy research organization. . . . The NCPA's goal is to develop and promote private alternatives to government regulation and control, solving problems by relying on the strength of the competitive, entrepreneurial private sector."

CURRENT CONCERNS: Antitrust • Crime • Economy • Education • Energy • Environmental regulation • Federal spending • Global warming • Government • Health • Immigration • International • Legal • Minimum wage • Privacy • Privatization • Regulation • Security/defense • Social • Social Security • Taxes • Terrorism • Trade • Unions • Welfare • Women in the economy

METHOD OF OPERATION: Declined to comment

Effectiveness and Political Orientation

"Colorado's light hand with labor laws and business regulation and its relatively small government make it one of the most economically free states in the country.

"Economic freedom translates into economic growth, said Devon Herrick, a fellow with the National Center for Policy Analysis in Dallas, one of two free-market think tanks behind the North American Index of Economic Freedom released Tuesday.

" 'If you tie someone's hands and don't let them act economically, you limit growth,' Herrick said.

"Still, the study doesn't explain why Colorado suffered higher job losses and slower growth than other states in the past two years. Herrick said the state's flexibility should help an economic recovery. . . ."

(*The Denver Post,* January 28, 2004)

"You heard it here second. A tax increase is coming in America—and Republicans will be among those who preside over that increase.

"The first place you might have heard about it was, of all places, Reaganite web chat rooms. There, economists have been muttering for a good six months about the prospect of Republican-supervised tax increases. Especially clear has been Bruce Bartlett of the National Center for Policy Analysis, a think-tank in President Bush's own Texas.

"It is not that the less-government types desire tax increases. Far from it. It is just that they totted up the numbers. Taken together, the nation's new Medicare programme and Social Security, its old unreformed pension system, make a tax increase just about inevitable. . . ."

(*Financial Times* [London, England], January 5, 2004)

"The day has arrived, as the 'can't we all just get along?' dreamers hoped and pleaded for, when liberals and conservatives unite, join hands to sing 'Kumbaya'—and in common cause curse the soon-to-be Medicare prescription drug bill.

"Liberals who would forthrightly expand the welfare state, while denouncing pharmaceutical executives as greedy capitalists and parading them through the streets in handcuffed perp-walks, hate the prescription drug bill because it experiments with Medicare competition and with health savings accounts.

"Conservatives who would welcome private-sector competition see this new entitlement as a massive expansion of Medicare with costs that are certain to tumble out of control. Researchers at the Texas-based National Center for Policy Analysis report that of the $395 billion the prescription drug benefit is expected to cost over the next decade, only 6 percent to 7 percent will buy new drugs for seniors. The rest will replace existing drug purchases by insurers and the Medicare population.

"The two extremes, thus, are joined in opposition. Passage is palatable, though, because a Medicare drug benefit has popular political appeal. The gamble for both parties is that they will control the White House and Congress in future years and can expand or kill objectionable provisions. . . ."

(*The Atlanta Journal-Constitution*, November 25, 2003)

"A recent study by the National Center for Policy Analysis (NCPA) finds that Social Security's rate of return—though a miserable investment for all Americans—is especially bad for blacks.

"The average black person is more likely to be completely or heavily reliant on Social Security income than his white counterpart. Cato Institute figures indicate that 75% of blacks rely on Social Security for at least half of their retirement income, while 37% completely depend on Social Security for this income.

"The NCPA study indicates that a white 20-year-old man can expect 47 cents in benefits for each dollar he contributes to Social Security, while a black man of the same age should expect only a 34-cent return for each dollar he contributes. This is because Social Security benefits are inherently tied to life expectancy, which stands at 67.8 years for black men and 73.9 years for white men.

"A similar (though less dramatic) discrepancy exists for women. The NCPA study concludes that blacks would benefit most from Social Security reform and that '[p]ersonal retirement accounts would allow African-Americans the opportunity to earn higher rates of return, save for their own retirement, and accumulate wealth to bequeath to their heirs.'"

(*Human Events*, July 22, 2002)

"'Time to bench team "CAFE,"'" says H. Sterling Burnett, Senior Fellow with the National Center for Policy Analysis. The Corporate Average Fuel Economy [CAFE] standard—a federal mandate that forces auto manufacturers to produce vehicles that meet minimum mileage standards—has three strikes against it. Strike one: CAFE has not realized its intended goal of reducing America's dependence on foreign oil. Imported oil consumption has increased from 35% to 52%; and people doubled their driving mileage in the years since the standard's enactment. Strike two: CAFE will not reduce global warming. With car and light-truck emissions constituting no more than 1.5% of all human-caused greenhouse gas emissions, the less than 0.5% reduction that CAFE standards may contribute to the global warming campaign—a scientifically unfounded effort—is negligible. . . . Strike three: CAFE standards kill. The downsizing of vehicles—a key step toward more fuel economy—has proved to be a death sentence for 46,000 people who have died in car wrecks since CAFE's enactment. . . .

"'Automakers have always been free to produce and market fuel-efficient cars. It's time to let consumers step up to the plate and bat. CAFE's out-and should be retired,' says Burnett."

(*Consumers' Research Magazine,* March 2002)

National Coalition
Against Domestic Violence

Established in 1978

DIRECTOR

Rita Smith, executive director. Smith began working as a crisis line advocate in a shelter for battered women and their children in Colorado in 1981. Since then she has held numerous positions in Colorado and Florida in several local programs and state coalitions, including program supervisor and director. Currently, Smith is the executive director of the National Coalition Against Domestic Violence, where she has been working since late 1992. She also co-authored a legal manual for attorneys working with domestic violence victims in Colorado.

BOARD OF DIRECTORS

Declined to comment

SCOPE

Members: More than 2,000 organizations and individuals
Branches: Public policy office in Washington, DC
Affiliates: Battered/Formerly Battered Women; Women of Color; Lesbian/Bisexual/Transgendered Women; Jewish Women; Child and Youth Advocacy; Rural Women; and Lesbians of Color. Joint projects with FACE TO FACE, Give Back a Smith, S.C.O.R.E.S., American Academy of Facial Plastic and Reconstructive Surgery; American Academy of Facial Dentistry; American Society of Dermatological Surgery

STAFF

7 total—plus 2 part-time; interns and volunteers

TAX STATUS

501(c)(3)

FINANCES

Budget: 2004—$967,500; 2003—$952,213

FUNDING SOURCES

Membership, 30%; product sales, 22%; corporations and foundations, 20%; Combined Federal Campaign, 18%; contributions and miscellaneous, 10%

PAC

None

EMPLOYMENT

Information unavailable

INTERNSHIPS

Information unavailable

CONTACT INFORMATION

P.O. Box 18749, Denver, CO 80218
Mailing address: 119 Constitution Avenue, NE, Washington, DC 20002
Phone: (303) 839-1852 • *Fax:* (303) 831-9251
General E-mail: mainoffice@ncadv.org • *Web site:* www.ncadv.org

Communications Director: Rita Smith, executive director
(303) 839-1852 • rsmith@ncadv.org
Human Resources Director: None

PURPOSE: The National Coalition Against Domestic Violence is "dedicated to the empowerment of battered women and their children and therefore is committed to the elimination of personal and societal violence in the lives of battered women and their children."

CURRENT CONCERNS: "Remember My Name" project • Educational projects and publications • Domestic violence offender gun ban • Welfare reform • Child custody • Battered women's economic security act • Hate crimes act • Violence against women act

METHOD OF OPERATION: Boycotts • Coalition forming • Conferences/seminars • Congressional testimony • Demonstrations • Direct action • Films/video/audiotapes • Grassroots organizing • Initiative/referendum campaigns • International activities • Legislative/regulatory monitoring (federal) • Library/information clearinghouse • Lobbying (federal and grassroots) • Media outreach • Product merchandising • Speakers program • Training and technical assistance

Effectiveness and Political Orientation

"National Domestic Violence Awareness Month grew out of the Day of Unity held by the National Coalition Against Domestic Violence in October 1981.

"The first monthlong observance came in October 1987. Congress set aside the month in 1989 and has done so every year as educational and commemorative activities have grown.

"Reports of family violence have increased in Texas over the last three years. Advocates, noting that crimes of family violence are dramatically underreported, believe the figures show that awareness efforts are working. . . ."
(*San Antonio Express-News,* October 27, 2003)

"Three high profile men, hailing from the entertainment industry, professional sports, and corporate America, gather in Washington, DC on March 5th and 6th to urge the White House and Members of Congress to step up efforts to combat domestic violence. Honoring the 25th anniversary of the National Coalition Against Domestic Violence (NCADV), [Singer-songwriter Michel Bolton, Former NFL quarterback Don McPherson, Verizon

Wireless CEO Denny Strigl] will discuss the vital role men can play in the war to end violence against women.

"Bolton, McPherson and Strigl have a long history supporting this effort. Spurred by thirteen years as a single father to three daughters, Bolton frequently uses his influence to combat domestic violence. McPherson, a former National Football League quarterback, is committed to bringing men and women together to end domestic violence. Strigl's Verizon Wireless HopeLine program has collected more than 750,000 cellular phones for use by domestic violence victims and shelter counselors. . . ."

(*U.S. Newswire,* March 4, 2003)

"Rita Smith has spent the last 20 years working for victims of domestic violence. But it wasn't until last week, when she found herself in sniper-stunned Washington D.C., that she saw life through the eyes of a battered woman.

" 'What became really clear to me was the level of fear I was feeling. It was changing my behavior,' said Smith, executive director of the National Coalition Against Domestic Violence.

"She needed to walk two blocks from her hotel to the subway station. She thought about zigzagging across the street. She thought about whether she even wanted to leave the hotel. And she thought about the women who live their lives in that kind of fear.

" 'The potential was fairly low that I would be hurt that day, but it was real and unpredictable,' she said. 'It's the kind of thing that batterers do: They let you know it will happen, you just don't know when.'

"Knowing they can get help if their abuser confronts them on the street can give battered women some comfort (and, yes, there are some men who are battered by their partners, but 92 percent of the victims are women). So, advocates are working to supply victims with cell phones programmed to dial emergency numbers.

"In observance of Domestic Violence Awareness month, the National Coalition Against Domestic Violence has partnered with The Body Shop to collect used cell phones. The group hopes to collect 30,000 phones, about 3,000 of which will be refurbished and given to victims under the auspices of the Wireless Foundation, a nonprofit formed by the Cellular Telecommunications & Internet Association. The foundation runs the Donate A Phone program."

(*Chicago Sun-Times,* October 23, 2002)

". . . international socialization theories clearly fail to explain the evolution of domestic violence policies in the United States, admittedly a hard case for claims about international socialization. The most important and well-known national-level women's organizations in the fight for federal domestic violence legislation have few transnational contacts and do not make any reference to international norms or U.S. global leadership when discussing domestic violence issues with Congress. As Pat Reuss of the National Organization for Women commented, 'There is a whole giant international movement on domestic violence, but very little connection between them and us. One of our greatest regrets is that we're still not working that closely together with women's groups in other countries. What are there, 215 countries in the world? Women from every one of those countries want to talk to me on how to do it. I just can't, and I do twelve to fourteen hour days.' Most U.S. activists laughed when asked if congressional representatives were concerned with international norms or the country's international image, both requirements for international socialization to work. As Juley Fulcher of the National Coalition Against Domestic Violence said, 'Within Congress there's only a sense of what's coming across their desk, of what's happening right at the moment. Other than efforts to ratify [the UN Convention on the Elimination of All Forms of Discrimination Against Women], which haven't been very successful, there is not much realization of the international arena. There is no real understanding of the connection worldwide.'"

(*Political Science Quarterly,* Summer 2002)

National Coalition for the Homeless

Established in 1984

DIRECTOR

Donald H. Whitehead Jr., executive director. Whitehead spent five years as a homeless person, living with various relatives and on the streets of Cincinnati. In August 1995, he entered a six-month treatment program at the Drop Inn Center. He was then hired as the outreach coordinator, which led to his creating a public radio program, a community access cable television show, and a newspaper focused on homelessness. Whitehead also founded "The Homeless Think Tank" to help Cincinnati develop its strategy for providing services to the homeless population. When he became the executive director of The National Coalition for the Homeless, he was the first African American and formerly homeless person to be appointed to that position—as well as the youngest. He serves on numerous boards and is a frequent speaker on the national level about homelessness. Whitehead attended the University of Cincinnati and the City College of Chicago. He also served in the U.S. Navy.

BOARD OF DIRECTORS

Executive Committee

Barbara Anderson; chair, Southern Indiana Housing Initiative, Jeffersonville, IN

Anita Beaty; executive director, Metro Atlanta Task Force for the Homeless, Atlanta, GA

Michael D. Chesser; executive director, Upstate Homeless Coalition of South Carolina, Greenville, SC

Brian Davis; North East Ohio Coalition for the Homeless, Cleveland, OH

Bob Erlenbusch; executive director, L.A. Coalition to End Hunger & Homelessness, Los Angeles, CA

Phillip Pappas; Community Human Services, Pittsburgh, PA

Sue Watlov Phillips; Elim Transitional Housing, Inc., Minneapolis, MN

Jim Cain; executive director, Iowa Coalition for Housing & the Homeless, Des Moines, IA

Ellen Dailey; National Consumer Advisory Board, Boston HCH Program, Roxbury, MA

Lynn Lewis; New York, NY

John Parvensky; president, Colorado Coalition for the Homeless, Denver, CO

Delena Stephens; Diocese of Saint Augustine Office of Justice & Peace, Jacksonville, FL

Julia Tripp; University of Massachusetts Boston, McCormick Institute, Boston, MA

CONTACT INFORMATION

1012 14th Street, NW, Suite 600, Washington, DC 20005-3471
Phone: (202) 737-6444 • *Fax:* (202) 737-6445
General E-mail: info@nationalhomeless.org •
Web site: www.nationalhomeless.org

Communications Director: Donald H. Whitehead Jr., executive director (202) 737-6444, ext. 14 • dwhitehead@nationalhomeless.org
Human Resources Director: None

PURPOSE: "To end homelessness. We focus our work in the following four areas: housing justice, economic justice, health care justice, and civil and voting rights."

CURRENT CONCERNS: Chronic homelessness initiative • Civil rights • Educating children and youth in homeless situations • Families, children, and homelessness • Health care access • Illegal to be homeless initiative • National housing trust fund • Universal living wage • Voter registration

METHOD OF OPERATION: Advocacy • Awards program • Coalition forming • Conferences/seminars • Congressional testimony • Congressional voting analysis • Grassroots organizing • Information clearinghouse • Internet (databases, e-mail alerts, and Web site) • Internships • Legislative/regulatory monitoring (federal and state) • Library/information clearinghouse • Lobbying (federal, state, and grassroots) • Media outreach • Partnerships • Policy advocacy • Public education • Research • Technical assistance • Training and technical assistance • Voter registration

Effectiveness and Political Orientation

"The objective of *Street Sense* [a Washington, D.C. newspaper written, produced, and distributed by the homeless] is twofold: to help homeless people earn income and reenter the working world and to educate the public about homelessness and poverty.

" 'We want to empower homeless people—build their self-esteem by helping them earn a living and encouraging them to take on more leadership,' says Donald Whitehead, executive director of the National Coalition for the Homeless, which is housing and supporting the Washington paper. 'Just the mere contact with the rest of the world gets (homeless) people excited in bigger and brighter things.'

"Mr. Whitehead, who today sports a blazer, light purple button-down shirt, and a trim and tidy goatee, would know—he was once homeless himself, selling the street paper in Cincinnati.

"Like many of the approximately 50 'homeless' papers in the U.S. and the 60 or so more across the globe, the D.C. paper will be sold for $1 by homeless people who then keep most of the profits. Vendors typically get their first

SCOPE

Members: 400 dues-paying, plus network of more than 21,000 organization members
Branches/chapters: None
Affiliates: None

STAFF

6 total—3 full-time staff; 2 full-time contractors; 1 fellow; plus 3 interns and 1 senior volunteer

TAX STATUS

501(c)(3)

FINANCES

Budget: 2004—$615,000; 2003—$756,000; 2002—$1.5 million

FUNDING SOURCES

Individual donations, 51%; foundation grants, 20%; corporate donations, 12%; membership dues, 11%; publications, 3%; conferences, 3%

PAC

None

EMPLOYMENT

Job announcements are posted online at http://www.nationalhomeless.org/jobannouncements.html. Openings at member organizations are also posted. Applications and resumes can be mailed to Donald H. Whitehead Jr., executive director, National Coalition for the Homeless, 1012 14th Street, NW, Suite 600, Washington, DC 20005-3471. Fax: (202) 737-6445. E-mail: dwhitehead@nationalhomesless.org.

INTERNSHIPS

Unpaid internships in the issue areas of civil rights, health, affordable housing and income (living wage/welfare reform), media/publications, and grassroots organizing are available. Internships last from 3 weeks to 6 months. Applicants should send a cover letter, resume, and short (no more than 3 pages) writing sample on any topic to Donald H. Whitehead Jr., executive director, National Coalition for the Homeless, 1012 14th Street, NW, Suite 600, Washington, DC 20005-3471. Fax: (202) 737-6445. E-mail: dwhitehead@nationalhomeless.org. Individuals interested in volunteering are also encouraged to apply.

NEWSLETTERS

Safety Network (quarterly, also online)

PUBLICATIONS

The following is a sample list of publications:
America's Homeless Children and Youth: An Educational Reader for High School Students
America's Homeless Children: An Educational Reader for Elementary School Students
America's Homeless Children: An Educational Reader for Middle School Students
America's Homeless Children: Word Cards for Preschool and Kindergarten Students
Educational Resources on Homelessness for Elementary School Students and Teachers

10 papers free, and then pay some small percentage—usually 10 to 30 cents—back to the paper for production costs. . . .

"There are approximately 14,000 homeless people in the Washington area, yet only a dozen people showed up at the orientation meetings to express interest in hawking the paper. Fred Anderson, who coordinates the vendors, says this is typical at the beginning, and he is not worried. 'We think there will be a snowball effect.'

" 'Homeless people,' explains August Mallory, a *Street Sense* writer, 'are not visionaries. They don't have too many dreams of greatness. But when they get pointed in the right direction they get into it.' "

(*Christian Science Monitor,* November 17, 2003)

"In theory, removing the chronic homeless from shelters should free more beds. But Donald Whitehead, the executive director of the National Coalition for the Homeless, thinks the rest of the homeless need an initiative too. He recommends the Bringing America Home Act, an omnibus bill that includes everything from building more affordable housing units to raising the minimum wage.

"This is unlikely to find much favour in Congress. Even leftish economists would query the idea that the government should start building lots of subsidised housing, especially during a housing bubble. Increasing the minimum wage can increase unemployment.

"All the same, the lack of cheap housing certainly has an effect on the number of homeless. In 1970, there were 6.5m low-cost rental units and roughly 6.2m low-income renters; now there are 7.9m low-cost rental units and some 9.9m low-income renters, according to a new report from the Joint Centre for Housing Studies of Harvard University. The report also says that three in ten American households—some 14.3 million—spend more than half their income on housing. . . ."

(*Economist,* August 23, 2003)

". . . the oldest and largest advocacy group on [the homeless] issue. . . ."

(*Time,* January 20, 2003)

"Under greater pressure from the federal government to identify and educate homeless children, a group of about 800 educators, advocates, and providers of services to the homeless gathered here from across the country to discuss ways to comply with the new requirements.

"The 2001 reauthorization of the McKinney-Vento Homeless Assistance Act, which was passed as part of the 'No Child Left Behind' Act, more clearly defines how schools should determine if a child is homeless. It also mandates that school districts each have a liaison responsible for making sure students living in homeless or transitional situations are enrolled in school and receiving additional services if needed.

" 'This is a major change,' Barbara Duffield, the education director of the Washington-based National Coalition for the Homeless, said here at the annual conference of the National Association for the Education of Homeless Children and Youth. 'We're no longer waiting for children to identify themselves.' "

(*Education Week,* October 16, 2002)

Educational Resources on Homelessness for High School Students and Teachers
Educational Resources on Homelessness for Middle School Students and Teachers
Lesson Plans on Family Homelessness for Elementary School
Lesson Plans on Family Homelessness for High School
Lesson Plans on Family Homelessness for Middle School
Lesson Plans on Family Homelessness for Preschool and Kindergarten
What You Can Do to Help Children and Families Who Are Homeless
Also publishes fact sheets and reports on specific issues.

CONFERENCES
Conferences on various issues related to homelessness at the national and the local level.

Also sponsors such events as Walk-a-Mile, candidate forums, get-out-the-vote drives, and National Hunger & Homelessness Awareness Week.

"But despite its success, [Thomas J. Pappas School, one of the more than 30 schools exclusively for homeless children] and other schools for homeless students have been under fire by the Department of Education and even other homeless organizations, such as the National Coalition for the Homeless. These groups have successfully argued that homeless schools were unconstitutional, that they promoted segregation and that they resulted in inferior education. . . ."

(*USA Today,* September 3, 2002)

National Committee
for Responsive Philanthropy

Established in 1976

DIRECTOR

Rick Cohen, executive director. Before joining NCRP in March, 1999, Cohen worked for nearly 7 years at the national office of the Local Initiatives Support Corporation (LISC). At LISC in New York City, he was vice president for strategic planning, in charge of conducting strategic reassessments of LISC programs throughout the nation. He also served as vice president of the Enterprise Foundation, where he oversaw most of Enterprise's community development technical assistance services. In the public sector, Cohen spent four years as the director of the Jersey City Department of Housing and Economic Development. He is the author or co-author of several books, journal articles, and monographs. He was named one of the *NonProfit Times Power and Influence Top 50* in 2002 and 2003. He received a B.A. in political science from Boston University in 1972 and a Master's in city planning from the University of Pennsylvania in 1975.

BOARD OF DIRECTORS

James Abernathy, member; Environmental Support Center, Washington, DC

Christine Ahn, member; Institute for Food & Development Policy, Oakland, CA

Gary Bass, member; OMB Watch, Washington, DC

Paul S. Castro, member; Jewish Family Service of Los Angeles, Los Angeles, CA

Lana Cowell, member; Greater Community Shares/Cleveland, Cleveland, OH

Louis Delgado, member; Philanthropy & Nonprofit Sector, Loyola University, Chicago, IL

Mike Doyle, member; Public Interest Fund of Illinois, Champaign, IL

Pablo Eisenberg, member; Georgetown University, Public Policy Institute, Washington, DC

Angel Falcon, member; PRLDEF Institute for Puerto Rican Policy, New York, NY

Richard Farias, member; Tejano Center for Community Concerns, Houston, TX

Margaret Fung, member; Asian American Legal Defense & Education Fund, New York, NY

Robert Gnaizda, member; Greenlining Institute, San Francisco, CA

Laura Harris, member; Americans for Indian Opportunity, Bernalillo, NM

David R. Jones, member; Community Service Society, New York, NY

Rhonda Karpatkin, member; Consumers Union, New York, NY

Larry Kressley, member; Public Welfare Foundation, Washington, DC

Julianne Malveaux, member; Last Word Productions, Inc., Washington, DC

CONTACT INFORMATION

2001 S Street, NW, Suite 620, Washington, DC 20009
Phone: (202) 387-9177 • *Fax:* (202) 332-5084
General E-mail: info@ncrp.org • *Web site:* www.ncrp.org

Communications Director: Michelle Abrenilla, chief operating officer
(202) 387-9177, ext. 14 • michelle@ncrp.org
Human Resources Director: Michelle Abrenilla, chief operating officer
(202) 387-9177, ext. 14 • michelle@ncrp.org

PURPOSE: The National Committee for Responsive Philanthropy (NCRP) is an independent nonprofit organization that works to strengthen and preserve the nonprofit sector and improve the sector's ability to represent and serve politically, economically, or socially disadvantaged populations and constituencies, by promoting greater philanthropic openness and accountability, and responsiveness to these individuals.

CURRENT CONCERNS: Advocacy for a new philanthropy • Alternative funds assistance program • Communications and outreach • Corporate grantmaking project • Democracy and philanthropy program • Enhancing philanthropic accountability

METHOD OF OPERATION: Coalition forming • Grassroots organizing • Information clearinghouse • Internet (databases, e-mail alerts, and Web site) • Internships • Lobbying (federal and grassroots) • Media outreach • Research • Speakers program

Effectiveness and Political Orientation

". . . a liberal Washington, D.C., group that tracks conservative foundations. . . ."

(*The Wichita Eagle* [Kansas], March 5, 2004)

"A company, union, or wealthy individual can often gain access to elected power brokers by giving money to their favorite charities. In gratitude, the elected official might listen to the donor's concerns, or even do a favor, such as vote for a certain bill.

"This kind of mutual back-scratching is currently legal, and being used by a number of elected Republicans and Democrats. And what's more, the donor's identity can be kept secret under tax rules governing nonprofits.

"But the National Committee for Responsive Philanthropy wants to change this dubious practice. It has asked the IRS to remove the tax-exempt status of a charity set up by House majority leader Tom DeLay who's using the nonprofit to channel access to himself and other GOP leaders.

"Mr. Delay's charity, Celebrations for Children, was started last September to help troubled youth, a cause he and his wife say they have long sup-

Pete Manzo, member; Center for Nonprofit Management, Los Angeles, CA

William Merritt, member; National Black United Fund, Newark, NJ

Nadia Moritz, member; The Young Women's Project, Washington, DC

Terry Odendahl, member; Institute for Collaborative Change, Santa Fe, NM

Linda Richardson, member; Black United Fund of Pennsylvania, Philadelphia, PA

Greg Truog, member; Community Shares USA, CO

Bill Watanabe, member; Little Tokyo Service Center, Los Angeles, CA

SCOPE
300 total (individuals, 62%; organizations, 38%)
Branches/chapters: Washington, DC
Affiliates: None

STAFF
8 total—7 full-time professional; 1 full-time support; plus 1 part-time professional; 3 interns

TAX STATUS
501(c)(3)

FINANCES
Budget: 2004—$1.5 million; 2003—$1.5 million; 2002—$1.3 million

FUNDING SOURCES
Foundation grants, 79%; membership dues, 9%; church grants, 4%; contracts/service agreements, 3%; miscellaneous, 2.5%; corporate donations, 1.5%; publications, 0.5%; interest, 0.5%

PAC
None

EMPLOYMENT
NCRP posts job openings online on its Web site at www.ncrp.org, and at www.monster.com and washingtondc.craigslists.org. Recipients of NCRP's e-mail alerts also receive notices of openings. Most hiring is in the areas of research, finance, communications, and development. Resumes and cover letters can be sent to Michelle Abrenilla, chief operating officer, 2001 S. Street, NW, Suite 620, Washington, DC 20009. Fax: (202) 332-5084. E-mail: michlle@ncrp.org.

INTERNSHIPS
Paid internships of 25 hours per week during the academic year and 35 hours per week during the summer are available and are posted online at www.ncrp.org and at www.monster.com and washingtondc.craigslists.org. Internships are for a minimum of 3 months with the deadline for summer interns April 1; other deadlines depend on availability. Applicants should have at least two completed years of college course work in public policy, political science, or related fields; a basic knowledge of the nonprofit and philanthropic sector; experience in conducting policy-related research, both quantitatively and qualitatively;

ported. But the charity is asking for donations between $10,000 and $500,000 for fundraisers at the 2004 GOP convention in New York. Donors will receive box seats to the Republican National Convention, tickets to Broadway shows, slots in a golf tournament, and time with DeLay and other lawmakers on a yacht or at a dinner, depending on the donation. . . ."

(*Christian Science Monitor*, February 4, 2004)

"Are . . . repeated revelations of mismanagement and wrongdoing taking a toll on employee giving? While official numbers are hard to come by, anecdotal evidence suggests the answer is yes. 'Nonprofit organizations used to have spotless reputations, but with the recent epidemic of philanthropy scandals, suspicion has run rampant,' says Craig Wichner, president and chief executive officer of KindMark, a Mill Valley, California-based company that automates workplace-giving programs. 'The sad result is that people have become less likely to give because they are so disillusioned.'

"Employees aren't the only ones who are becoming more cautious. Some employers are reconsidering long-standing relationships with their partners in workplace-giving programs. The United Way's management troubles in Washington, D.C., for example, convinced the leaders of the Combined Federal Campaign of the National Capital Area, the largest federal workplace-giving program, to select a non-United Way campaign partner for the first time since the 1970s.

"The National Committee for Responsive Philanthropy hopes that such moves will reshape the practices of charities and third-party vendors in the philanthropic field, highlighting 'the importance of accountability and transparency throughout the philanthropic and charitable sector,' says Rick Cohen, executive director of the committee. . . ."

(*Workforce*, July 2003)

"Private foundations can increase their giving by billions of dollars and still stay in business, concludes a study released last week that gives a boost to proposed legislation on the subject.

"The findings of the National Committee for Responsive Philanthropy, a Washington-based foundation-watchdog group, support a measure that would require philanthropies to up their annual giving, a move that others say could spell the end for some foundations.

"Currently, private foundations—including many that support education-related nonprofit organizations—are required by law to donate 5 percent of their total assets each year to charities to retain tax-exempt status. But in tallying that distribution, they are allowed to include administrative costs.

"The proposed Charitable Giving Act of 2003, introduced in the House last month, would no longer allow such costs to count toward foundations' charitable-giving totals. Sponsored by Rep. Roy Blunt, R-Mo., the bill has not been the subject of hearings, nor has a companion measure been introduced in the Senate.

"Such a change would infuse an additional $2 billion to $4.3 billion annually into the country's nonprofit sector, including groups that support K-12 education. In 2002, giving by U.S. foundations totaled approximately $30 billion, according to the New York City-based Foundation Center.

" 'Research shows that this is a modest and reasonable tax reform that would help charities with billions of dollars in new grants, while still sustain-

strong verbal and written communication skills with an analytical eye for detail; strong computer skills; proficiency with Internet research; and strong commitment to NCRP's vision of philanthropy.

Applications can be mailed to Jeff Krehely, deputy director, 2001 S Street, NW, Suite 620, Washington, DC 20009. Fax: (202) 332-5084. E-mail: jeff@ncrp.orgs.

NEWSLETTERS
Responsive Philanthropy (quarterly)

PUBLICATIONS
$1 Billion for Ideas: Conservative Think Tanks in the 1990s
A Billion Here, a Billion There: The Empirical Data Add Up
Advocacy for Social Change in Metropolitan Washington
Axis of Ideology: Conservative Foundations and Public Policy
Closing the Loophole: Removing Foundation Overhead Costs from Payout
Giving at Work 2003
Helping Charities, Sustaining Foundations: Reasonable Tax Reform Would Aid America's Charities, Preserve Foundation Perpetuity and Enhance Foundation Effectiveness and Efficiency
The Core of the Matter
Understanding Social Justice Philanthropy

CONFERENCES
None

ing foundations in the long term and encouraging foundation efficiency,' said Sloan C. Wiesen, a spokesman for the responsive-philanthropy group. . . ."

(*Education Week*, June 18, 2003)

National Conference of Catholic Bishops/United States Catholic Conference

DIRECTOR
Reverend Monsignor William P. Fay, general secretary.

BOARD OF DIRECTORS
Wilton D. Gregory, president
William S. Skylstad, vice president
James P. Keleher, treasurer
William B. Friend, secretary
William P. Fay, general secretary
Bruce E. Egnew, associate general secretary
David J. Malloy
Lourdes Sheehan, RSM

SCOPE
Members: 290 active and retired U.S. Catholic bishops
Branches/chapters: Office of Film and Broadcasting in New York City and a branch office of Migration and Refugee Services in Miami
Affiliates: None

STAFF
More than 350 lay people, priests, and religious

TAX STATUS
501(c)(3)

FINANCES
Budget: 1999—$20 million

FUNDING SOURCES
Financial support from U.S. dioceses on a per capita basis

PAC
None

EMPLOYMENT
Current job openings with this organization are posted on their Web site at www.usccb.org/hr/index.htm. Clergy/religious candidates must request written approval from their diocesan bishop or religious superior before an application can be considered. Diocesan lay employees must also request approval from the local bishop. Minorities are encouraged to apply. Competitive starting salaries with excellent work environment and fringe benefit package including free parking. Please submit a resume with a cover letter indicating the position you are interested in and salary requirements to Office of Human Resources, United States Conference of Catholic Bishops, 3211 Fourth Street, NE, Washington, DC 20017-1194.
Fax: (202) 541-3412. E-mail: resumes@usccb.org. No phone calls please.

Established in 1966

CONTACT INFORMATION
3211 4th Street NE, Washington, DC 20017
Phone: (202) 541-3000 • *Fax:* (202) 541-3322
Web site: www.usccb.org

Communications Director: Msgr. Francis J. Maniscalco
(202) 541-3200
Human Resources Director: Linda D. Hunt
(202) 541-3000

PURPOSE: The National Conference of Catholic Bishops/United States Catholic Conference promotes the greater good that the Church offers humankind, especially through forms and programs of the apostolate fittingly adapted to the circumstances of time and place. This purpose is drawn from the universal law of the Church and applies to the episcopal conferences that are established all over the world for the same purpose.

CURRENT CONCERNS: Agriculture • Capital punishment • Catholic doctrine, worship, evangelization, and religious education • Disabled persons • Economic justice • Elderly • Energy • Health • Hispanics • Human rights • Immigration reform • Poverty • Pro-life support • Women in society and in the Church • Workers' rights

METHOD OF OPERATION: Awards programs • Congressional testimony • Educational and catechetical ministry • Films/video/audiotapes • Grantmaking • Grassroots organizing • International activities • Legislative/regulatory monitoring (federal) • Library/information clearinghouse • Litigation • Lobbying (federal) • Media outreach • Movie and television reviews • Participation in regulatory proceedings (federal) • Pastoral letters • Refugee resettlement • Television and radio production • Voluntary relief services • Web site

Effectiveness and Political Orientation

"The leadership of the U.S. Conference of Catholic Bishops has rejected the recommendation by a panel of prominent Roman Catholic lay people that it immediately authorize a second round of independent audits of sex abuse procedures in dioceses across the country.

"Last year, teams of auditors, mainly former FBI agents, were hired by the church to visit all 195 U.S. dioceses and determine whether they were complying with the charter on sex abuse that the bishops adopted in June 2002 under the glare of a national scandal.

"The audits were a cornerstone of the bishops' response to the scandal, allowing an unprecedented degree of outside scrutiny of how bishops run their dioceses. Many church officials, victims' groups and lay Catholic organizations assumed that the audits would be an automatic, annual process. But it now appears that may not be the case.

"At a meeting in Washington of the Administrative Committee of the bishops conference March 23 to 25, the National Review Board, a panel of 13 lay Catholic leaders appointed by the bishops, recommended that the church 'immediately go ahead with another round of audits, as we believe the charter requires,' said the board's chairman, Anne M. Burke. . . .

"But several members of the bishops' conference, including Cardinal Edward M. Egan of New York and Bishop Fabian W. Bruskewitz of Lincoln, Neb., wrote letters urging the 48-member Administrative Committee to postpone any decision on audits until the next regular business meeting of the 300 active U.S. bishops, which will take place in November."

(*The Washington Post,* April 7, 2004)

"A statement by Pope John Paul II that health care providers are morally obliged to provide food and water to patients in persistent vegetative states has left church officials uncertain what impact it would have at the nation's more than 600 Catholic hospitals.

"The statement, made March 20 but translated into English on Thursday, raised major questions in the church's decades-long debate over how far health care providers should go to keep alive people who have been in deep comas for long periods.

"Among them: How might the pope's stance affect a patient who has made an advanced directive ordering physicians to remove feeding tubes after he or she has slipped into an irreversible coma?

"Catholic officials said it could be months or longer before the United States Conference of Catholic Bishops—the American church's governing body—or the Vatican provided clarification on how Catholic hospitals should apply the pope's words.

" 'We are waiting for an analysis from our moral theologians, who will look at every angle,' said Cardinal William H. Keeler, who oversees the six Catholic hospitals in the Archdiocese of Baltimore. 'As to its full implications, I'm really not clear yet.' "

(*The Baltimore Sun,* April 3, 2004)

"America has always been a difficult fit for the Roman Catholic Church. Here is a country founded by Protestant sectarians who thought the Anglican church was a little too Roman, a country where religious pluralism is the law and individual rights are celebrated. Then there's the Church of Rome, the hierarchical 'one true faith' where priests stand between God and man.

"Now comes Raymond L. Burke, archbishop of St. Louis, to suggest that America's 'hedonistic culture'—the individual pursuit of pleasure—is the most significant cause of the church's priest sexual abuse crisis. Bombarded by permissiveness, some priests not only ignore their vows of celibacy, but the laws governing the sexual abuse of children.

"A reach? Shaquille O'Neal should have such a reach.

"Archbishop Burke made his remarks Friday in reaction to the release of 52 years worth of statistics about priest sex abuse. The study, commissioned by the National Conference of Catholic Bishops, suggested that at least 4 percent of American priests in the past five decades were involved in child sex abuse. For priests ordained in the early 1970s, the percentage runs as high as 10 percent. . . .

"Archbishop Burke has argued that the sex abuse crisis—and indeed, most of the church's problems—can be solved with return to traditional teachings. Conservatives, Archbishop Burke among them, were more comfortable when there was no such thing as 'primacy of conscience' for Catholics. You went to Mass on Sunday, made your Easter obligation, ate fish on Friday, sent your kids (of which you had a lot, because the Rhythm Method didn't work) to the nuns for education and—this above all—obeyed the priest."

(*St. Louis Post-Dispatch,* March 2, 2004)

"Milwaukee Archbishop Timothy M. Dolan, a firm supporter of sanctity-of-life teachings and a friend of La Crosse Bishop Raymond L. Burke, is happy that Burke's disciplining of Catholic politicians who support abortion 'front-burnered' that issue.

"But Dolan, who was installed as archbishop a year and a half ago, is waiting for a task force from the U.S. Conference of Catholic Bishops to propose guidelines for bishops this fall before deciding whether he will emulate Burke. . . ."

(*Milwaukee Journal Sentinel* [Wisconsin], January 25, 2004)

"The U.S. Conference of Catholic Bishops approved a document Wednesday that condemns same-sex unions and reaffirms church teaching that homosexuality is sinful and unnatural.

"The seven-page report, presented by Bishop J. Kevin Boland of Savannah, was approved as the nation's Catholic bishops met in Washington during an annual meeting that ends today.

"Boland, chairman of the Committee on Marriage and Family Life, called for the church to take a public stand against a growing movement to legalize same-sex unions.

"Boland said many Americans are becoming ambivalent about viewing marriage as an institution that should be confined to a man and a woman. The document passed 234–3. . . ."

(*The Atlanta Journal-Constitution,* November 13, 2003)

National Conference of State Legislatures

Established in 1975

DIRECTOR

William T. Pound, executive director. Pound has been with the Conference since its founding in 1975 and has been instrumental in the development of many of its innovative programs and services designed for legislators, legislative leaders, and legislative staff. He has been executive director since September 1987. He makes numerous television and radio appearances, has had many articles published, and speaks on topics of state government fiscal condition, education and public policy issues, and on the activities of state legislatures and federalism. Pound served as chair of the Academy for State and Local Government and the Big Seven state and local organizations in 1997–1998 and 2002-2003. He currently has oversight responsibilities for the State and Local Legal Center. He was educated at the University of Colorado, University of Denver, and University of Wisconsin. He taught political science and public policy at three universities.

BOARD OF DIRECTORS

Martin Stephens, president; speaker, UT
John Hurson, president-elect; delegate, MD
Steven Rauschenberger, vice president; senator, IL
Angela Monson, immediate past president and president, NCSL Foundation; senator, OK
Max Arinder, staff chair; executive director, Legislative PEER Committee, MS
James Greenwalt, staff vice chair; director senate information systems and administrative services department, MN
Gary Olson, immediate past staff chair and secretary/treasurer, NCSL Foundation; director, Senate Fiscal Agency, MI

SCOPE

Members: 7,382 state legislators and an estimated 30,000 state legislative staff.
Branches/chapters: All 50 state legislatures, as well as those in the commonwealths and territories.
Affiliates: None

STAFF

157 total—123 full-time professional; 34 full-time support; plus 18 part-time professional; 4 part-time support; and 21 interns

TAX STATUS

170(c)(1)

FINANCES

Finances: 2001—$14.4 million; 2000—$13.7 million

CONTACT INFORMATION

7700 East First Place, Denver, CO 80230
Phone: (303) 364-7700 • *Fax:* (303) 364-7800
General E-mail: info@ncsl.org • *Web site:* www.ncsl.org

Communications Director: Gene Rose, public affairs director
(303) 856-1518 • gene.rose@ncsl.org
Human Resources Director: Annette Durlam
(303) 856-1383 • annette.durlam@ncsl.org

PURPOSE: The National Conference of State Legislatures is the bipartisan organization that serves the legislators and staffs of the states, commonwealths, and territories. The conference hopes to improve the quality and effectiveness of state legislatures, promote policy innovation and communication among state legislatures, and ensure state legislatures a strong, cohesive voice in the federal system. NCSL provides research, technical assistance and opportunities for policymakers to exchange ideas on the most pressing state issues and is an effective and respected advocate for the interests of the states in the American federal system.

CURRENT CONCERNS: Federal mandates • No Child Left Behind • Streamline • Sales tax • Fiscal issues • Welfare reform • Health care • Energy • Environment • Legislative management • Criminal justice • Information technology

METHOD OF OPERATION: Advertisements • Awards program • Coalition forming • Conferences/seminars • Congressional testimony • Educational foundation • Films/video/audiotapes • Information clearinghouse • International activities • Internet (databases, electronic bulletin boards, e-mail alerts, and Web site) • Internships • Legal assistance • Legislative/regulatory monitoring (federal and state) • Library services for members only • Lobbying (federal) • Media outreach • Participation in regulatory proceedings (federal) • Polling • Product merchandising • Professional development services • Research • Technical assistance • Telecommunications services (mailing lists) • Training

SPECIFIC PROGRAMS/INITIATIVES: Trust for Representative Democracy, a civic education initiative

Effectiveness and Political Orientation

"A federal appeals court here has upheld methods used by more than half the states to control the cost of prescription medicines bought for Medicaid recipients and other low-income people.

"In its ruling, on Friday, the court rejected a challenge by the pharmaceutical industry, which had attacked Michigan's strategy for encouraging low-income patients to use lower-cost medicines.

FUNDING SOURCES
Grants and contracts, 36%; publications, meetings, and other income, 32%; state dues, 32%

PAC
None

EMPLOYMENT
Job openings are available on the NCSL Web site at http://www.ncsl.org/public/joblegis.htm. Positions offered include those in policy, research, accounting, administrative, public affairs, publications, and marketing. Applicants should send resumes and other materials for employment to Annette Durlam, human resources director, 7700 East First Place, Denver, CO 80230. Phone: (303) 364-7700. Fax: (303) 364-7800. E-mail: annette.durlam@ncsl.org.

INTERNSHIPS
Both paid and unpaid internships are offered. Internships usually last one semester, sometimes longer depending on project or program. Internship areas include public policy and public affairs. Application deadlines, eligibility requirements, and required hours vary. Postings and requirements are available on the NCSL Web site at http://www.ncsl.org/public/joblegis.htm. Annette Durlam, human resources director, 7700 East First Place, Denver, CO 80230. Phone: (303) 364-7700. Fax: (303) 364-7800. E-mail: annette.durlam@ncsl.org.

NEWSLETTERS
LegisBrief

PUBLICATIONS
State Legislatures Directory On-line
State Health Notes
State Legislatures Magazine

CONFERENCES
Annual Meeting, various locations, usually one week between mid-July and mid-August
Leader to Leader Meeting, DC, usually held in February or March
Spring Forum in Washington, DC, usually in April
Fall Forum in various cities, usually in early December
Education Finance Seminar, various cities, usually in early February
Skills Seminar for Legislative Staff, various cities, usually in August
Senior Fiscal Professional Development Seminar for legislative staff, various cities, fall
Information Technology Professional Development Seminar for legislative staff, various cities, fall
Legal Services Professional Development Seminar for legislative staff, various cities, fall
Public Information and Media Relations Professional Development Seminar for legislative staff, various cities, fall
Services and Security Professional Development Seminar for legislative staff, various cities, fall

"The decision is significant because a rapidly growing number of states have adopted 'preferred drug lists' like Michigan's as a way to control soaring drug costs. The National Conference of State Legislatures says that 26 states are using such lists and that 10 others have enacted laws authorizing their use. . . ."

(*The New York Times,* April 6, 2004)

"With the media's political Doppler radar fixed squarely on this November's presidential showdown, a less-obvious political battle is taking place that, in several ways, will have a more direct impact on the lives of Americans.

"The outcome also could more accurately reflect where voters stand on a spate of domestic issues, from gay marriage to abortion and taxes.

"The battle for party control over state legislatures, say experts, is more intense than at any point in recent political memory.

"Of the more than 7,000 legislative seats in the U.S., the GOP holds a slim 60-seat advantage. And of the 50 states, 25 have legislative chambers that could switch party control with a shift of just three seats or less.

"In Maine and Colorado, a switch of one seat could reverse longtime party dominance of both legislative and executive branches. While in North Carolina, South Carolina and Georgia, a change in three seats could significantly reshape the political path of the South's fastest-growing states.

"Several of the nation's key battleground states—Missouri, Oklahoma, Oregon, and Washington—could solidify political alliances for years to come.

" 'This is a far bigger election year for state legislatures than most,' says Tim Story, election analyst for the National Conference of State Legislatures. 'Because there are so many close votes which could shift party control of legislative chambers, it will likely have an impact on every issue before state government from civil unions to transportation, education, and health care.' "

(*Christian Science Monitor,* March 30, 2004)

"This could mark society's next forward step as it moves from the information age to the bioscience era.

"One important catalyst of this movement is stem-cell research—a controversial, new scientific field that analyzes the building blocks of life. Some people even envision an entire new medical field—which would involve thousands of jobs that could not be easily outsourced.

"Seeing this potential, a number of states are beginning a race to fund the stem-cell field. Yesterday, the governor of New Jersey, in his budget proposal, said he wanted to spend $6.5 million a year over five years. Wisconsin, which considers itself a leader in the field, is already paying salaries and funding laboratories. A group is trying to get a ballot initiative in California that would commit the state to spend almost $300 million a year on such research.

" 'In 20 years, you can't imagine a major university without a stem-cell program,' says Andrew Cohn, a spokesman for the WiCell Research Institute, a research organization associated with the University of Wisconsin.

" 'The field is growing so fast that last year there were 71 bills introduced in 29 states that could potentially affect embryonic or fetal stem-cell research,' says Alissa Johnson, a senior policy specialist at the National Conference of State Legislatures in Washington. 'Only five bills were actually enacted, but there are 34 bills being carried over in 13 states. So far this year, 11 new bills have been introduced in six states,' she says.

" 'At this point most states are looking to regulate embryonic research via cloning,' she says. . . ."

(*Christian Science Monitor*, February 25, 2004)

"Sen. Richard Moore (D-Uxbridge) asked the head of the state police yesterday to consider joining a controversial information-sharing system that allows law-enforcement agencies to rapidly search billions of personal records.

"The database—known as the Multi-State Anti-Terrorism Information Exchange, or 'Matrix'—has taken heat recently from privacy advocates who are concerned about its massive scope.

"But Moore said the Matrix only contains information that's already available to law enforcement agencies. The Matrix, however, significantly increases the speed at which police can get data from other jurisdictions, Moore said.

" 'All of that information is already available,' Moore said. 'It's just that they're putting it together quicker. The time saves lives and saves money.'

"Moore said he sent information about the program yesterday to Col. Thomas Foley, head of the state police. The state's involvement will likely be determined by Gov. Mitt Romney's Executive Office of Public Safety, the state police's parent agency, Moore said.

"A Matrix fact sheet by the National Conference of State Legislatures shows the program could cost states up to $1.5 million a year to participate in it once federal grant money runs out later this year. . . ."

(*The Boston Herald*, February 24, 2004)

"In response to revelations of lavish gift-giving to Colorado lottery staff, lawmakers are mulling a plan that would limit the kinds of gifts and the circumstances under which state employees are permitted to accept them.

"We're not against such legislation per se, although we're not persuaded it's that necessary. Administrators have ample power to end abuses in their departments if they determine action is needed. Indeed, Director of Revenue M. Michael Cooke, who oversees the lottery, moved quickly to clarify policies on giving and receiving gifts when news of problems surfaced. Similarly strict policies were adopted for the entire Department of Revenue.

"If the legislature does decide to wade into this issue, we urge it to look beyond the lottery and adopt consistent policies for all state agencies. As *News* reporter Burt Hubbard discovered, the policies are all over the map, and there's no good reason for it.

"As we see it, the more valuable the freebie the tighter the restriction. Or as described by Peggy Kerns, director of the Center for Ethics in Government at the National Conference of State Legislatures, the most effective rule is to allow no gifts or only those 'of such low value that it's some item you wouldn't want anyway.'

"Coffee mugs. Ball-point pens. Tote bags. These are unlikely to sway anyone's vote on a major contract. We would also include in this category food and drink, like coffee and a bagel or breakfast at an event state employees are expected to attend as part of their job. In the work-a-day world, such exchanges are as typical as the trading of business cards. . . ."

(*Rocky Mountain News* [Denver], February 16, 2004)

National Congress of American Indians

Established in 1944

DIRECTOR
Jacqueline Johnson, executive director.

BOARD OF DIRECTORS
Tex G. Hall, president; Mandan, Hidatsa and Arikara Nation, New Town, ND

Joel A. Garcia, first vice president; San Juan Pueblo, San Juan Pueblo, NM

Juana Majel/Dixon, secretary; Pauma-Yuima, Escundido, CA

W. Ron Allen, treasurer; Jamestown S'Klallam Tribe, Sequim, WA

STAFF
13 total—10 full-time professional; 3 full-time support; plus 1 part-time professional; 1 part-time support; 1 intern

TAX STATUS
501(c)(3)

FINANCES
Revenue: 2002—$914,865; 2001—$640,635

FUNDING SOURCES
Conferences, 35%; government contracts, 20%; tribal donations, 20%; corporate donations, 15%; membership, 10%

SCOPE
Members: More than 250 tribes and 4,000 individuals
Branches/chapters: None
Affiliates: None

PAC
Information unavailable

EMPLOYMENT
Information unavailable

INTERNSHIPS
NCAI internships are available for summer or semester periods to students enrolled in institutions of higher learning. Fellowships are for an 11-month period, for students who have completed their undergraduate degrees. Fellows will receive a stipend of approximately $16,500 to cover their living expenses over the course of the 11-month period they serve, as well as coverage under NCAI's health insurance plan. Semester and summer internships are unpaid, but NCAI encourages interns to work with their tribes or local organizations to sponsor their housing or other costs. Specific duties for each intern or fellow will vary, depending on the nature of the legislative issues being addressed, their experience each brings to the position, and individual working style. Responsibilities will include legislative, administrative, and grassroots outreach work; advocacy; research; and writing.

CONTACT INFORMATION
1301 Connecticut Avenue, NW, Suite 200, Washington, DC 20036
Phone: (202) 466-7767 • *Fax:* (202) 466-7797
General E-mail: ncai@ncai.org • *Web site:* www.ncai.org

Communications Director: Jason McCarty, public relations jmccarty@ncai.org.
Human Resources Director: Information unavailable

PURPOSE: NCAI's mission is to protect and advance the rights of American Indians and Alaskan Natives and to inform the public and the federal government on tribal self-government, treaty rights, and a broad range of federal policy issues affecting tribal governments.

CURRENT CONCERNS: Defending tribal sovereignty • Economic development • Education • Environmental protection • Gaming • Health care • Housing • Interior appropriations • Native American mascots • Nuclear waste • Religious, cultural, and human rights • Transportation • Welfare reform

METHOD OF OPERATION: Coalition forming • Conferences/seminars • Congressional testimony • Congressional voting analysis • Direct action • Grassroots organizing • International activities • Internet (Web site) • Legislative/regulatory monitoring (federal and state) • Lobbying (federal) • Media outreach • Participation in regulatory proceedings (federal and state) • Technical assistance and training

Effectiveness and Political Orientation

"Right on the heels of the Janet Jackson Super Bowl incident, several Native American groups are demanding an apology after a performance by OutKast at Sunday night's 46th Grammy Awards ceremony.

"The performance of OutKast's 'Hey Ya!' featuring Andre 'Andre 3000' Benjamin featured a Native American-themed dance and actor Jack Black reciting a monologue with a Navajo 'Beauty Way' song playing in the background.

"A flying tepee came down on the stage amid a group of women wearing green buckskin-like skirts and fringed halter tops. Benjamin sported an Indian brave-themed costume. Many Native Americans also say the lyric 'Hey ya' sounds similar to chants in powwow songs.

"For the past week, American Indian communities around the country have been saying the performance portrayed Native Americans in poor taste.

"Now a national Native American newspaper and other American Indian groups are issuing an ultimatum to the Grammy organizers: Apologize publicly or face a discrimination lawsuit. . . .

"The newspaper, the National Congress of American Indians and the National Indian Gaming Association are drafting letters to the Federal Com-

More information regarding NCAI internships, including applications, is available online at www.ncai.org/main/pages/ncai_profile/internship.asp. The NCAI internship contact person is Aura Kanegis. Phone:(202) 466-7767. E-mail: akangegis @ncai.org.

NEWSLETTERS
NCAI Sentinel (quarterly)

PUBLICATIONS
None

CONFERENCES
Annual convention (fall)
Executive Council Session (every February in Washington, DC)
Mid-Year Conference (summer, usually June)

munications Commission (FCC) and the National Academy of Recording Arts and Sciences, which produces the Grammys.

" 'The recording academy should be held responsible for what happened. We're looking at who's ultimately responsible for approving the performances,' said King, a member of the Rosebud Sioux tribe. . . ."

(*The Seattle Times,* February 14, 2004)

"For much of his professional career, William G. Myers III has been a lawyer and lobbyist for mining, grazing and cattle interests and a severe critic of environmentalists.

"Now, Myers, 48, has been nominated by President Bush to the San Francisco-based U.S. 9th Circuit Court of Appeals, which reviews federal court decisions from nine western states, including California, and considers more significant environmental cases than any other federal appeals court.

"Myers, an attorney in Boise, Idaho, faces a tough confirmation battle as nearly 100 environmental, tribal, civil rights, labor and women's organizations have mounted a major campaign to defeat him in the Senate. Myers' first hearing will be today in the Senate Judiciary Committee.

"The Coalition for a Fair and Independent Judiciary has called Myers 'an ideologue who would use his position on the court to promote his personal agenda of attacking safeguards for tribal rights and the environment in order to favor' the industries he has represented.

"Jackie Johnson, spokeswoman for the National Congress of American Indians, which represents about 250 tribes, said this is the first time the organization has formally opposed a judicial nominee during the Bush administration. Johnson criticized Myers' role as the Interior Department's chief lawyer during the first two years of the Bush administration.

" 'Myers was the architect of a rollback of protections for sacred native sites on public lands that are central to the free exercise of religion for many Native American people,' she said. . . ."

(*The Los Angeles Times,* February 5, 2004)

"The estimated 1.5 million American Indian voters nationwide is a tiny fraction of the more than 100 million U.S. registered voters, but the concentration of American Indians in three states with Democratic presidential contests on Tuesday—Arizona, New Mexico, and Oklahoma—gives them a chance to demonstrate their growing political clout.

"Recognizing the opportunity to both showcase and boost their political strength this year, tribal leaders recently launched 'Native Vote 2004' in an effort to persuade more American Indians to vote while keeping them apprised of the latest campaign developments. The National Congress of American Indians has pledged to mobilize one million American Indian voters this fall in eight states with significant American Indian populations: Alaska, Arizona, California, Michigan, Minnesota, New Mexico, Oklahoma and South Dakota. . . ."

(*Pittsburgh Post-Gazette,* February 1, 2004)

"U.S. Sen. Ben Nighthorse Campbell's plan to deregulate gas drilling, power plants and other energy projects on American Indian land has sparked a heated debate in Indian country about the federal government's obligations to tribes.

"Campbell, the only American Indian in the Senate, said his proposal would bring badly needed jobs and development to severely depressed reservation economies. The proposal is backed by the Bush administration, Colorado's Southern Ute Indian Tribe and the staff of a leading Indian energy group, the Council of Energy Resource Tribes.

"The plan would allow tribes to develop their own environmental regulations, which would have to be approved by the Interior Department.

"Once approved, tribes wouldn't have to wait for the federal government to do environmental impact statements—which take a year or more and cost hundreds of thousands of dollars—to do energy projects.

"But the nation's biggest tribe, the Navajo Nation, is leading a host of others in a fight against the proposal, comparing it to the Navajos' disastrous entry into uranium mining during the Cold War. The mining sickened thousands of Indian miners and scarred Navajo lands with abandoned mine shafts.

"Navajo President Joe Shirley Jr. says Campbell's plan would let the federal government out of its legal 'trust' obligation to look out for the interests of tribes.

"'I view the trust relationship between the Navajo and the U.S. government as a sacred relationship,' Shirley said in an interview. 'This is an issue resounding through Navajo Country.'

"Another leading group, the National Congress of American Indians, is in the middle, expressing 'concern' that the relationship between tribes and the federal government would be reduced. . . ."

(*The Denver Post,* July 28, 2003)

National Consumers League

Established in 1899

DIRECTOR

Linda F. Golodner, president and chief executive officer. Before joining the National Consumers League in 1983, Golodner was president of her own public affairs firm. She also worked for U.S. Representative James F. O'Hara of Michigan. Golodner chairs the National Council on Patient Information and Education, and the Alliance Against Fraud in Telemarketing and Electronic Commerce. Golodner serves on the board of directors of the National Patient Safety Foundation, the Patient Safety Institute, the Union Community Fund, and the American National Standards Institute, where she chairs the Consumer Interest Forum and has represented ANSI on the U.S. delegation to ISO-COPOLCO. She is on the executive board of the Conference for Food Protection, the Interstate Shellfish Sanitation Conference, the Advisory Council of the Joint Institute for Food Safety and Applied Nutrition, and the Steering Committee of the Centers for Education and Research on Therapeutics. In addition, she co-chairs the Verizon Consumer Advisory Board and is a member of the Water Quality Health Council and the Underwriters Laboratories Consumer Advisory Council. Golodner is a founding member of, and co-chairs, the Child Labor Coalition, and she serves on the board of directors of the International Cocoa Initiative. She co-chaired the White House Apparel Industry Partnership and serves on the board of directors of its successor organization, the Fair Labor Association. Golodner is a former commissioner and chair of the Fairfax County Commission for Women. She graduated summa cum laude from the University of Maryland in 1975.

BOARD OF DIRECTORS

Samuel A. Simon, chair; Issue Dynamics, Inc.
Evelyn Dubrow, honorary chair; UNITE!
Jane King, vice chair; AARP
Esther Shapiro, vice chair
Pastor Herrera Jr., secretary; Los Angeles
    County Department of Consumer Affairs
Dolores Langford Bridgette, treasurer;
    University of the District of Columbia
    Community Outreach & Extension Services
Linda Golodner, president; National
    Consumers League
Erma Angevine, honorary president
Jack Blum, counsel; Lobel, Novins & Lamont
Judy M. Asazawa; Asian Pacific Community
    Fund
Morton Bahr; Communications Workers of
    America
Debra Berlyn; Consumer Policy Consulting
Alan Bosch
Jim Conran; Consumers First

CONTACT INFORMATION

1701 K Street, NW, Suite 1200, Washington, DC 20006
Phone: (202) 835-3323 • *Fax:* (202) 835-0747
General E-mail: info@nclnet.org • *Web site:* www.nclnet.org

Communications Director: Carol McKay
(202) 835-3323 • carolm@nclnet.org
Human Resources Director: Sara Cooper, executive vice president
(202) 835-3323 • sarac@nclnet.org

PURPOSE: Works to identify, protect, represent, and advance the economic and social interests of consumers and workers. The National Consumers League is a private, nonprofit advocacy group representing consumers on marketplace and workplace issues. NCL provides government, businesses, and other organizations with the consumer's perspective on concerns including child labor, privacy, food safety, and medication information.

CURRENT CONCERNS: Child labor • Consumer education • Consumer fraud • Consumer product safety • Direct-to-consumer advertising of pharmaceuticals • Environment • Labor standards • Managed care-impact on consumers • Patient information • Privacy • Telecommunications and technology • Truth-in-labeling of consumer products

METHOD OF OPERATION: Advertisements • Awards program • Coalition forming • Conferences/seminars • Congressional testimony • Demonstrations • Direct action • Films/video/audiotapes • Grassroots organizing • Information clearinghouse • International activities • Internet (electronic bulletin boards, e-mail, and Web site) • Internships • Legislative/regulatory monitoring (federal and state) • Media outreach • Participation in regulatory proceedings (federal, state) • Polling • Research • Scholarships

SPECIFIC PROGRAMS/INITIATIVES: Alliance Against Fraud in Telemarketing and Electronic Commerce Coalition • Child Labor Coalition • National Fraud Information Center • Internet Fraud Watch • LifeSmarts • SOS Rx Coalition

Effectiveness and Political Orientation

"Legalizing the importation of U.S.-made drugs from other countries, while not a long-term solution to the problem of high-priced prescription drugs, is an important first step in making medicines more affordable, consumer advocates told a government task force Friday.

"Surgeon General Richard H. Carmona opened the first of six 'listening sessions' by acknowledging that 'the eyes of the nation are on this task force.' The Bush administration is under increasing political pressure from lawmak-

SCOPE

Members: 5,000 individuals and organizations
Branches/chapters: None
Affiliates: Consumers League of Ohio;
    Consumers League of New Jersey;
    National Consumers League Student
    Organization at South Dakota University

STAFF

18 total—13 full-time professional; 5 full-time
support; plus 2 part-time professional

TAX STATUS

501(c)(3)

FINANCES

Revenue: 2002—$2 million;
2001—$1.7 million

FUNDING SOURCES

Foundation grants/corporate donations,
77%; government contracts, 2%; publications,
1%; membership dues, 11%; special events/
projects, 9%

PAC

None

EMPLOYMENT

Potential applicants can learn about job openings with this organization through
http://www.nclnet.org/staffpositions.html.
This organization offers positions in adminis-

ers, governors, mayors and millions of Americans who buy their drugs from
Canada illegally to legalize such imports.

"Reflecting the administration's anti-importation stance, Carmona, chairman of the 13-member panel, said his job is to 'protect the American people,'
who 'must understand that the government has no way to certify' that
imported drugs are safe.

"The advocates, who represented groups ranging from the Minnesota
Senior Federation, which runs a drug-importation program for 6,000 people,
to the 35 million-member AARP, also spoke of safety.

" 'Drugs that are not affordable are neither safe nor effective,' said Alison
Rein of the National Consumers League.

" 'There is a growing recognition that not being able to afford needed prescription drugs is a threat to the health of the American people,' said Gail
Shearer, director of health policy analysis for Consumers Union. 'There are
tens of thousands of deaths a year because people are not getting the needed
drugs.' "

(*The Los Angeles Times,* March 20, 2004)

"Question: what do grapes, sulphur dioxide, tartaric acid, tannin, yeast, yeast
nutrient (diammonium phosphate), carbon dioxide, nitrogen, pectolytic
enzymes and egg albumin have in common? Answer: they're all listed among
the ingredients of the rather enjoyable Underworld Shiraz Viognier 2001
(pounds 6.99, Co-Op). And another question: do you want to know that all
this stuff has gone into the wine you are drinking? Answer: I can't speak for
you or for anyone else, but I can say for certain that I am deeply and unequiv-
ocally of two minds on the subject.

"One thing's for certain: where the Co-Op has led, others will follow. In
the US, they may have to follow by a law if two eminently worthy organisations get their way. The National Consumers League and the Center for
Science in the Public Interest have proposed the introduction of a uniform
'alcohol facts' label which would go on all bottles containing the demon drink.
This would give standardised information on alcohol content, serving size,
calories and ingredients, so that consumers could see what they were getting
and compare like with like.

"I support clear, detailed labelling as a matter of principle. But in this case,
it's a little hard to see who will benefit. Do some people really want to compare the calorie content of a Napa Valley Cabernet with that of Bud Lite before
they decide which to buy? Of course, those suffering from food allergies will
benefit. So, in their own enchanting way, would the far greater numbers who
believe they suffer from food allergies. They'll have a whole new set of facts
and figures to worry about. . . ."

(*Independent on Sunday* [London, England], January 11, 2004)

"Federal regulators said yesterday that they had issued the first citation for violations of the national do-not-call list.

"The Federal Communications Commission cited but did not fine CPM
Funding of Irvine, Calif., which does business as California Pacific Mortgage.

"The agency said in a statement that it had received consumer complaints
of unwanted sales solicitations from the company. Further violations could
result in fines of as much as $11,000 for each violation.

"United States residents have added 55.4 million phone numbers to the
do-not-call registry since it was established in June, according to the Federal

tration, public policy (food, health, fair labor, fraud, teen consumer education, consumer issues, consumer protection, and child labor), communications, consumer service counseling, and event planning. Applicants should send resumes and other materials for employment to Sara Cooper, executive vice president, 1701 K Street, NW, Suite 1200, Washington, DC 20006. Phone: (202) 835-3323. Fax: (202) 835-0747. E-mail: sarac@nclnet.org.

INTERNSHIPS
Information regarding internships is available at www.nclnet.org/staffpositions.html. Positions are unpaid, and internships last a minimum of 8 weeks. Application deadlines are open; interns are required to work a minimum of 20 hours per week. Internship areas include public policy and communications. For more information, or to apply, contact Sara Cooper, executive vice president, 1701 K Street, NW, Suite 1200, Washington, DC 20006. Phone: (202) 835-3323. Fax: (202) 835-0747. E-mail: sarac@nclnet.org.

NEWSLETTERS
Child Labor Monitor (quarterly)
Focus on Fraud (quarterly)
NCL Bulletin (bimonthly)

PUBLICATIONS
The following is a sample list of publications:
Alcohol: How It All Adds Up
Alternative Health Care: New Promise, New Pitfalls
Bacterial Resistance: When Antibiotics Don't Work
Bottled Water: What You Should Know
Consumer Credit Series
Consumer Guide to Dietary Supplements
Consumer Guide to Generic Drugs
Consumer Guide to Home Fire Safety
The Earth's Future is in Your Shopping Cart
First Annual Report by Non-Governmental Organizations on the ILO Convention 182
Food Irradiation . . . What You Need to Know
From Market to Mealtime: What You Should Know About Meat, Poultry and Seafood
Mammograms—A Consumer Guide to Breast Cancer Detection
Online E-ssentials: Consumer Guide to Internet Safety, Privacy, and Security
Protecting Your Eyes from the Sun
Putting the Financial Pieces Together: Solving the Financial Puzzle
Taking Care of Headaches
Your Health is in Your (Clean) Hands—a Consumer Guide to Hand Hygiene

CONFERENCES
No regularly scheduled conferences

Trade Commission. The trade commission is administering the list and jointly enforcing it with the F.C.C. A spokesman for the trade commission, Mitchell Katz, said his agency had not yet issued any enforcement actions under the list.

"Susan Grant, vice president of the National Consumers League, applauded the enforcement action. 'It's good news that they have started,' she said. 'It takes a while to get complaints and look into them and determine to your agency's satisfaction that you think someone has violated the law.'"

(*The New York Times*, December 19, 2003)

"There has been fear and confusion since the government announced 17 months ago that it was halting its study of a hormone-replacement drug commonly prescribed to women during menopause.

"Add to that, cranky days, sleepless nights and too many miserably warm moments.

"'Most people were just freaked out,' said Dr. Patricia Smith, an obstetrician-gynecologist who practices in Katy. 'Either they stopped cold turkey, or their doctors told them to quit right away.'

"Now, she said, many women want to return to hormone-replacement therapy, while others continue to search for solutions that seem safer.

"A recent survey of Houston women found that more than two-thirds of women experiencing menopause symptoms said their symptoms have made them uncomfortable or embarrassed. But 20 percent said they haven't talked to their doctors about the impact their symptoms have had upon their lives, and more than one-third said they don't understand all of the potential treatment options.

"The survey, commissioned by the National Consumers League for a Web-based campaign on menopause, was conducted by J.D. Power and Associates.

"The campaign is designed to help women evaluate their symptoms and prepare for discussing them with their doctors. (For more information, check out www.nclnet.org/menopause.). . ."

(*The Houston Chronicle*, December 9, 2003)

"From coverage areas, to pricing, to cell phone safety and etiquette, there's a lot to know, and lots of ways to get tripped up when shopping for mobile phone service. The Federal Communications Commission provides tips at www.fcc.gov, as does the National Consumers League at www.nclnet.org. The NCL also offers a free consumer brochure available by calling 202-835-3323. . . ."

(*Pittsburgh Post-Gazette*, August 24, 2003)

National Council of La Raza

Established in 1968

DIRECTOR

Raul Yzaguirre, president and chief executive officer. Yzaguirre has spent the last two decades as the president of the National Council of La Raza. He was the first Hispanic recipient of the Rockefeller Public Service Award. In 1989, he was awarded a fellowship to the Institute of Politics at Harvard's John F. Kennedy School of Government, and in 1994 he received the Aguila Azteca, (Aztec Eagle) the highest honor that is given to a noncitizen from the Government of Mexico. From 1993 to 1995, he served as chair of the Independent Sector, a coalition of more than 850 voluntary, community, and philanthropic organizations. He also served as chair of the Presidential Commission on Educational Excellence for Hispanic Americans. He currently serves on the boards of the Sears, Roebuck, and Co., the Enterprise Foundation, and is a member of the Council on Foreign Relations. Yzaguirre is the recipient of five honorary doctorates.

BOARD OF DIRECTORS

Jose Villarreal, chair; partner, Akin, Gump, Strauss, Hauer, & Feld, L.L.P., San Antonio, TX

Raymond Lozano, first vice chair; principal account executive, DTE Energy, Detroit, MI

Mónica Lozano, second vice chair; president, *La Opinión,* Los Angeles, CA

Kenneth I. Trujillo, secretary/treasurer; Trujillo Rodriguez & Richards, L.L.C., Philadelphia, PA

Salvador Balcorta, executive committee; executive director, Centro de Salud Familiar, La Fe, El Paso, TX

Andrea Bazán-Manson, executive committee; executive director, El Pueblo, Inc., Raleigh, NC

Phyllis Gutiérrez Kenney, executive committee; representative, Seattle, WA

Antonia Jiménez, executive committee; chief administrative officer, executive office of health & human services, Boston, MA

Horace Deets; retired executive director, AARP

Patricia Fennell; executive director, Latino Community Development Agency, Oklahoma City, OK

Irma Flores Gonzáles; consultant, Santa Fe, NM

Robert W. Gary; retired president, Allstate Insurance, Avon, CO

W. Roger Haughton; chairman & chief executive officer, PMI Group, Inc., Walnut Creek, CA

Linda Lehrer; consultant, East Hampton, NY

Arabella Martínez; chief executive officer, Spanish Speaking Unity Council, Oakland, CA

CONTACT INFORMATION

1111 19th Street, NW, Suite 1000, Washington, DC 20036
Phone: (202) 785-1670 • *Fax:* (202) 776-1792
General E-mail: info@nclr.org • *Web site:* www.nclr.org

Communications Director: Lisa Navarrete, vice president, office of public information
(202) 776-1744 • lnavarrete@nclr.org
Human Resources Director: Julie Perez
(202) 776-1780 • jperez@nclr.org

PURPOSE: "To reduce poverty and discrimination, and improve life opportunities for Hispanic Americans of all nationality groups in all regions of the country."

CURRENT CONCERNS: Civil rights • Education • Health • Economic issues (jobs, taxes, social security, and assets development) • Housing and community development • Workforce development • Immigration • Media and telecommunications issues • Voting

METHOD OF OPERATION: Coalition forming • Conferences/seminars • Congressional testimony • Congressional voting analysis • Information clearinghouse • International activities • Internet (databases, electronic bulletin boards, e-mail alerts, and Web site) • Internships • Legislative/regulatory monitoring (federal, state) • Lobbying (federal, state, grassroots) • Mailing lists • Media outreach • Participation in regulatory proceedings (federal, state) • Performance ratings/Report cards (companies, products, etc.) • Research • Telecommunications services • Technical assistance • Training • Voter registration

SPECIFIC PROGRAMS/INITIATIVE: Technology Initiatives Program • Institute for Hispanic Health • Center for Community Educational Excellence • Center for Emerging Latino Leadership • Center for Latino Economic Opportunities • Afro-Latino Initiative

Effectiveness and Political Orientation

"Spanish-language radio, once considered a tame alternative to its English counterpart, is becoming known for shows with language and jokes racy enough to make Howard Stern blush.

"Recently, for example, the most popular Spanish-language radio show among young people in South Florida, El Vacilon de la Manana on WXDJ-FM, broadcast the voices of a masturbating priest and a pot-smoking welfare recipient. In another of their pranks, they called Haitian President Jean-Bertrand Aristide's office, and when they couldn't get through, they called his secretary gay. . . .

SCOPE

Members: 35,000 dues-paying individual associates.

Branches/chapters: 5 field offices in Phoenix, Arizona; Los Angeles; Chicago; San Antonio; and San Juan, Puerto Rico

Affiliates: 302 independent community-based organizations in 37 states, Puerto Rico, and DC

STAFF

115 total—82 full-time professional; 33 full-time support; plus 2 part-time support and 2 volunteers

TAX STATUS

501(c)(3)

FINANCES

Budget: 2004—$27.2 million; 2003—$27.77 million; 2002—$23.88 million

FUNDING SOURCES

Foundation grants, 35%; corporate donations, 16%; government contracts, 21%; individuals, 1%; conferences, 16%; other sources, 11%

"The rise of the Spanish shock jocks in markets with large Latino populations has raised a chorus of complaints from Hispanic leaders, programming watchdogs and politicians who warn the medium is too explicit and largely unregulated.

" 'The standard by which we judge radio has been shattered. The level of acrimony that is there, the crude language, it's inappropriate for public hearing,' said Raul Yzaguirre, president of the Washington-based National Council of La Raza. 'Spanish-language radio is raunchier than English. And there is no accountability whatsoever.'

"Of the 20 investigators in the FCC's obscenity enforcement bureau, only one speaks Spanish, officials at the commission say. So when complaints about Spanish radio come in, they are farmed out to a private company that turns the tapes into English transcripts, which are then reviewed by FCC staff. . . ."

(*The Houston Chronicle*, February 29, 2004)

"A 'road map' to courting the Latino vote released by the nation's largest Hispanic civil rights organization offers no wide-open highways but stops at several key issues for a disparate and complex group.

"The 59-page State of Hispanic America 2004, released Tuesday by the Washington, D.C.-based National Council of La Raza, says candidates can't expect to win votes from the country's 35 million Hispanics by focusing on immigration, or floating Spanish phrases from the stump.

"Raul Yzaguirre, executive director of La Raza, said at a news conference Tuesday that only a comprehensive approach on issues from education and health, to employment and home ownership would inspire the many Latinos in big electoral states such as New York to support a candidate. Other issues, such as immigration, counterterrorism, criminal justice and workers' rights were on the agenda but not as unifying to Latinos, he said.

" 'There's something that happens in this country that doesn't happen in our countries of origin,' Yzaguirre said, pointing out that voter participation in nations like Mexico and Puerto Rico commonly reaches above 80 percent. 'What is it? My experience tells me that a lot of Latinos feel that participating in elections doesn't make a difference in their lives. What we're trying to do is say that these are the issues that will galvanize Latinos. . . .' "

(*Newsday* [New York], February 27, 2004)

"It's an election year, and the odor of campaign politics is in the air. And after President Bush's immigration reform proposal last Wednesday, the odor is one of empty promises, catchy phrases and little substance.

"Raul Yzaguirre, president of the National Council of La Raza, the largest Latino rights group in the U.S., summed up the feelings of thousands of people—many of them voters—about the President's proposals.

" 'The more we hear, the less enchanted we are,' Yzaguirre said immediately after watching the Washington press conference.

"He was right on target.

"Because despite the hype, there is not much to be enchanted about in the plan, which would revolve on a new temporary worker program. Any similarities to President Franklin Roosevelt's disastrous Bracero Program [are] not pure coincidence.

"Like FDR's guest worker program, Bush's proposed 'immigration reform' seems to be just another way to bring in immigrant workers to feed U.S. industry's insatiable appetite for cheap labor. . . ."

(*New York Daily News*, January 11, 2004)

PAC
None

EMPLOYMENT

Potential applicants can learn about job openings with this organization by consulting the Web site, media postings, and Web postings on sites such as craigslist.org, idealist.org, and nonprofitjobs.org. This organization offers positions in the areas of programming, policy, administrative, health, accounting, human resources, marketing, resource development, education, information technology, and public relations. Applicants should send resumes and other materials for employment to Julie Perez, human resources manager, 1111 19th Street, NW, Suite 1000. Phone: (202) 776-1780. Fax: (202) 776-1775. E-mail: jperez@nclr.org.

INTERNSHIPS

This organization offers both paid and unpaid internships. For information regarding internship opportunities, consult the organization's Web site, craigslist.org, idealist.org, and nonprofitjobs.org. The duration of internships varies, application deadlines are rolling, and hours required varies. All areas have internship opportunities; candidates must be college student or above to be eligible. For more information, or to apply, contact Pamela Rodriguez, 1111 19th Street, NW, Suite 1000. Phone: (202) 785-1670. Fax: (202) 776-1792. E-mail: prodriguez@nclr.org.

NEWSLETTERS

Agenda (quarterly)

PUBLICATIONS

The following is a list of selected publications:
Beyond the Census: Hispanics and An American Agenda
The Hispanic Community and Diabetes: Uniting for Action
A Hispanic Perspective on Employment Discrimination in the Federal Workplace
Locked Out: Hispanic Underrepresentation in Federally-Assisted Housing Programs
Moving Toward an Immigrant Integration Agenda
Social Security, Hispanic Americans, and Proposed Reform
Testimony on Election Reform
Testimony on Latinos and the Equal Employment Opportunity Commission
Testimony on Latinos and Police Brutality
Testimony on Terrorism, Immigration, and Civil Rights
The Socioeconomic Status of Latino Children: A Review of Key Issues
U.S. Latino Children: A Status Report
Untapped Potential: A Look at Hispanic Women in the U.S.
Voter Registration "How-To" Packet for Community-Based Organizations
Also publishes issue briefs, curricula, fact sheets, policy statements, and congressional testimony on specific issues.

CONFERENCES

Capital Awards Dinner, February or March; Annual Conference, July

"President Bush's immigration reform proposal faces major obstacles in Congress and drew immediate fire Wednesday from both sides of the immigration debate.

"Democrats and immigrant advocates said it offers too little to immigrants. Republican critics branded it as a form of amnesty that would reward people who violate immigration laws.

"An estimated 8 million to 10 million illegal workers in the United States would be, in the president's words, allowed to come out of the "shadows of American life" and obtain three-year temporary residency visas.

"American businesses, which have long pressed for a larger supply of foreign labor, would be able to hire large numbers of temporary foreign workers, either from here or abroad, if they can demonstrate that they cannot find Americans to fill the positions.

"The swift, sharp reaction to the plan, which was laid out Wednesday at the White House, indicates that passage will be problematic, especially in the partisan atmosphere of an election year.

"Cecilia Munoz, vice president of the National Council of La Raza, an immigrant advocacy group, said the plan was a step backward from 2001, when the president first suggested legalization of those who are in the country without permission.

" 'He's creating a proposal that asks people to sign up for temporary worker status that effectively promises no permanent status,' she said. 'People would essentially be at the mercy of their employers. Their ability to remain in the United States would depend entirely on the goodwill of their employers.' "

(*The Atlanta Journal-Constitution*, January 8, 2004)

"The Departments of Justice and Homeland Security are unlawfully using a national crime database to get local police departments to enforce civil immigration laws, lawyers who have assembled a federal class-action lawsuit against the practice said yesterday.

"The lawsuit, which they plan to file today in Federal District Court in Brooklyn, is the first to challenge the addition of civil information about thousands of noncitizens to the National Criminal Information Center database, which the F.B.I. uses to notify law enforcement agencies about people wanted for crimes.

"Congress has neither authorized nor required local police agencies to routinely arrest people for such violations, and a bill that would do so has drawn unexpectedly strong opposition from many police departments, including those in New York, Los Angeles, Miami, Houston, Denver, Boston and Chicago. Advocates for immigrants argue that it would undermine local crime-fighting by making immigrants even more fearful of reporting crimes or helping with police investigations.

"The plaintiffs in the lawsuit—the National Council of La Raza, the New York Immigration Coalition, the American-Arab Anti-Discrimination Committee, the Latin American Workers Project and Unite—contend that Attorney General John Ashcroft, Homeland Security and the F.B.I. are misusing the database."

(*The New York Times*, December 17, 2003)

National Council of the Churches of Christ in the U.S.A.

Established in 1950

DIRECTOR

Bob Edgar, general secretary. Edgar has been general secretary since 2000. An ordained elder in the United Methodist Church, he came to the council from Claremont Theological School, Claremont, CA, where he was president from 1990 to 2000. He also served six terms in the U.S. House of Representatives from Pennsylvania. Among other appointments, he served as chair of the Congressional Clearinghouse on the Future (1982–1986) and as a member of the Select Committee on Assassinations. His wide-ranging career has also included pastorates at United Methodist congregations and stints as a teacher, college chaplain, community organizer, and director of a think tank on national security issues. Edgar serves on the board of directors of Independent Sector, an alliance of national organizations interested in fostering the not-for-profit contribution in society, and of the National Coalition on Health Care. He is a member of the board of trustees of the National Religious Partnership for the Environment and the board of directors of the Environmental and Energy Study Institute, an independent, nonprofit organization that is a principal resource for Congress on environmental and energy issues. He received a B.A. from Lycoming College, Williamsport, Pa., and the master of divinity degree from the Theological School of Drew University, Madison, N.J. He holds four honorary doctoral degrees.

BOARD OF DIRECTORS

Thomas L. Hoyt Jr., president; bishop, Fourth Episcopal District, Christian Methodist Episcopal Church (Mississippi and Louisiana), Shreveport, LA

Robert W. Edgar, general secretary; United Methodist, New York, NY

Michael E. Livingston, president-elect; executive director, International Council of Community Churches, Trenton, NJ

Clare J. Chapman, vice president; executive director of finance and administration, General Commission on Christian Unity and Interreligious Concerns, United Methodist Church, New York, NY

Betty Voskuil, vice president; coordinator for diaconal ministries, Hunger Education and Reformed Church World Service, Reformed Church in America; chair, Church World Service Board of Directors, Grand Rapids, MI

Randall R. Lee, vice president at large; assistant to the bishop and director, Department for Ecumenical Affairs, Evangelical Lutheran Church in America, Chicago, IL

CONTACT INFORMATION

475 Riverside Drive, Suite 880, New York, NY 10115
Phone: (212) 870-2227 • *Fax:* (212) 870-2030
General E-mail: news@ncccusa.org • *Web site:* www.ncccusa.org

Communications Director: Wesley M. Pattillo
wpattillo@ncccusa.org • (212) 870-2048
Human Resources Director: Joan Gardner
(212) 870-2258 • jgardner@ncccusa.org

PURPOSE: "To be a community through which churches can make visible their unity given in Christ and can work together responsibly in witness and service."

CURRENT CONCERNS: Access to healthcare for all • AIDS crisis in Africa • Building hospitable community • Environmental justice • Foreign assistance • Gun violence • Hunger relief act • International justice and human rights • Jubilee 2000 Debt Relief Campaign • Justice for women • Minimum wage/living wage standards • Peace with justice • Pillars of peace for the 21st century • Public schools advocacy • Public witness/legislative advocacy • Racial justice and reconciliation

METHOD OF OPERATION: Advertisements • Coalition forming • Conferences/seminars • Congressional testimony • Films/video/audiotapes • International activities • Internet (Web site) • Legal assistance • Legislative/regulatory monitoring (federal) • Litigation (amicus briefs) • Media outreach • Mediation • Research • Shareholder resolutions • Television and radio production • Training and technical assistance

Effectiveness and Political Orientation

"It was a page from a familiar script: Recruit some star power to bring attention to a social cause. Find a symbolic locale in the nation's capital and let the cameras roll.

"The cause this time was the prisoners at the U.S. naval base at Guantanamo Bay, Cuba, arrested in the war in Afghanistan. So on a chilly and windy day yesterday, using the Supreme Court as a backdrop, a dozen people, including actress Vanessa Redgrave, representatives of various human rights and religious organizations and a few family members of those imprisoned, railed against the Bush administration and the lack of access to the detainees.

" 'We don't know who among them may be guilty or innocent,' said the Rev. Robert W. Edgar, general secretary of the National Council of Churches. 'But due process of law is being held prisoner on Guantanamo Bay.' "

(*The Washington Post,* March 9, 2004)

"In a sparsely furnished apartment in Pyongyang, the capital of North Korea, the woman stood and offered her song of faith. In deep tones of conviction

Thelma Chambers-Young, vice president at large; director of Christian Education, Holy Temple Baptist Church, Progressive National Baptist Convention, Inc.; immediate past president, PNBC Women's Department, Oklahoma City, OK

Vicken Aykazian, secretary; diocesan legate and ecumenical officer, Diocese of the Armenian Orthodox Church of America, Washington, DC

Elenie K. Huszagh, immediate past president; Greek Orthodox laywoman, Nehalem, OR

SCOPE

Members: 36 Protestant, Anglican and Orthodox member denominations
Branches/chapters: Offices in Baltimore, Maryland; Elkhart, Indiana; and Miami; 25 Church World Service/CROP offices across the United States; several regional representatives overseas
Affiliates: None

STAFF

350 total

TAX STATUS

501(c)(3)

FINANCES

Budget: 2000-$60 million

FUNDING SOURCES

Public and community appeals, 40%; member contributions, 20%; refugee resettlement contracts with the U.S. government and federal disaster relief funds, 15%; individuals and corporations, 11%; sales, royalties, and other income, 10%; U.S. government contract for AmeriCorps program, 4%

PAC

None

EMPLOYMENT

See the Employment Opportunities Web site at www.ncccusa.org/jobs/jobshome.html for current NCC open job postings.

INTERNSHIPS

Information unavailable

NEWSLETTERS

Mark-Up (newsletter of the NCC Washington office)
EcuLink (quarterly)

PUBLICATIONS

The following is a list of selected publications:
God Is One: The Way of Islam
Families Valued
First, We Must Listen
Moments in Time
Mythmakers
Children's World Series
World Map: Peters Projection
Yearbook of American and Canadian Churches (annual)
Also publishes books, pamphlets, videos, and other resources

that touched the listening visitors seated on the floor, she sang of 'the sorrows that like sea billows roll,' yet 'it is well with my soul.'

"Other members of the small house church shared in prayer, singing, and conversation as they met by special dispensation of the government with an ecumenical delegation of Christians from America.

"While the North Korean government arranged the gathering, 'what it couldn't orchestrate is the genuineness of the spirituality, which was very evident,' says the Rev. John McCullough, executive director of Church World Service (CWS), the humanitarian agency of 36 Christian denominations.

"During a five-day visit to North Korea in November, the U.S. delegation from CWS and the National Council of Churches (NCC) met with local congregations and the Korean Christians Federation (KCF), and delivered 420 metric tons of flour to help assuage the country's severe food shortage. Part of a year-long joint initiative by U.S. and Korean ecumenical groups to support a peaceful resolution to the tense political and humanitarian crises, the trip also involved sessions with North and South Korean officials. . . ."

(*Christian Science Monitor,* January 7, 2004)

"The year 2003 dawned with war clouds gathering over the Iraqi skies as President Bush, against the counsel of most religious leaders, prepared for a preemptive strike to dislodge Saddam Hussein.

"Catholic and mainline Protestant church leaders rallied opposition to a war they said was unjust, while evangelical and some Jewish leaders stood by the White House.

" 'This war is wrong; it is sinful; it is killing,' said Catholic Bishop Thomas Gumbleton of Detroit before he was led away in plastic handcuffs at a March 26 protest outside the White House. 'It is against the law of God.'

"Bush largely ignored the protests from the pulpits and the sidewalks, refusing to meet with bishops from his own denomination, the 8.3 million-member United Methodist Church. The president reluctantly accepted an envoy sent by Pope John Paul II before the bombs started to fall March 19.

"After the war was won in record time, U.S. casualties mounted and the prospects for a lasting Iraqi peace seemed uncertain—even with the Dec. 13 capture of Saddam Hussein. It was, war opponents say, a vindication of their prophecies.

" 'The churches were right,' said the Rev. Bob Edgar, general secretary of the National Council of Churches, a staunch opponent of the war. 'We always knew the U.S. could win militarily. . . . But I think the churches' instinct on the moral ground was exactly right, that winning the peace was more important than winning the war.' "

(*The Washington Post,* December 27, 2003)

"Representatives of 11 denominations and faith groups that oversee the Interfaith Conference of Greater Milwaukee have voted to admit the city's Islamic Society to full membership, the first addition in three decades, conference officials said Tuesday.

"Coming the same week as Thanksgiving and the Eid al-Fitr, or feast of fast breaking, the announcement was a symbol of how Muslim-Americans are trying to get more involved in and be better understood by society.

" 'The Muslim community used to be isolated,' Mequon physician Waleed Najeeb said Tuesday as an estimated record crowd of 4,000 to 5,000 Muslims flowed in and out of the Milwaukee County Sports Complex in

CONFERENCES
Ecumenical Young Adult Ministry Event
General Assembly (annual)
Sponsors frequent issue consultations dealing
with specific issues such as families, refugee
resettlement, theological dialogue, racism,
and economic development.

Franklin. 'Now, almost every week we have interfaith functions. Either we go out, or they come to the Islamic Center, all faiths—Judaism, Christianity, Islam.'

"The Milwaukee decision reflects a trend since Sept. 11, 2001, in New York, Chicago and other cities to include Muslims and other faiths, said the Rev. Shanta Premawardhana, National Council of Churches associate general secretary for interfaith relations.

" 'Where there are hate crimes, there have been more attempts to bring people together because suddenly they have come to realize in communities across the country how important these relationships are,' Premawardhana said. 'We are trying to build such relationships before the hate crime happens.' "
(*Milwaukee Journal Sentinel* [Wisconsin], November 26, 2003)

"Progressive clergy who marshaled opposition to the Vietnam War and support for the civil rights movement a generation ago re-emerged yesterday to counter what they call the "partisan God" proclaimed by the Bush White House.

"Organizers of the Clergy Leadership Network, a loose-knit alliance of liberal clergy, promised to be a "coalition of conscience" in opposition to President Bush's economic and foreign policies.

" 'In a democracy, the way to change the policy is to change the policymakers,' said the Rev. Joan Brown Campbell, former general secretary of the National Council of Churches. 'Does that make us partisan? That is yours to decide.' "
(*The San Diego Union-Tribune,* November 22, 2003)

"The National Rifle Association has an enemies list. One way or another, you're probably on it.

"By name? No. Fewer than 300 celebrities, national figures and journalists rate individual billing on its Web site. (Having failed to make Nixon's list, I am chagrined at not being on the NRA's either. Maybe this will fix that.)

"But the likelihood is high that you, like me, belong to or support at least one of the 142 organizations that the NRA faults as 'anti-gun.' Among them: The AARP. The AFL-CIO. The American Medical Association. The American Bar Association. Common Cause. The League of Women Voters of the United States. The National Education Association. The National Council of the Churches of Christ in the U.S.A. The National Council of La Raza. The National Council of Negro Women. The National Council of Jewish Women. The Southern Christian Leadership Conference. The Unitarian Universalist Association. The U.S. Catholic Conference. The YMCA of the U.S.A. . . ."
(*St. Petersburg Times* [Florida], November 16, 2003)

National Council on the Aging

Established in 1950

DIRECTOR

James P. Firman, president and chief executive officer. Prior to joining NCOA in January 1995, Firman was, for 10 years, president and chief executive officer of the United Seniors Health Cooperative (USHC), a nonprofit consumers organization that he founded with other leaders in the field. From 1981 to 1984, he served as a senior program officer at The Robert Wood Johnson Foundation, where he helped develop initiatives in aging and health care finance, as well as the model Interfaith Volunteer Caregivers program. He is a co-founder of Grantmakers in Aging. He has written several books and many articles on issues in aging, for consumers as well as professionals. Firman holds M.B.A. and Ed.D. degrees from Columbia University.

BOARD OF DIRECTORS

James P. Firman, president and chief executive officer, National Council on the Aging, Washington, DC

Sandra King, chair; Jewish Family Service of Los Angeles, CA

Ronald W. Schoeffler, chair-elect; Senior Citizens Council of Greater Augusta & the CSRA, Georgia, Inc., Augusta, GA

Molly Mettler, past chair; Healthwise, Inc., Boise, ID

Josselyn Bennett, secretary; Evangelical Lutheran Church in America, Chicago, IL

Ken Oliver, treasurer; Assisted Care Solutions, LLC, Birmingham, AL

Yung-Ping "Bing" Chen; University of Massachusetts Boston, Boston, MA

Rutherford "Jack" Brice; Decatur, GA

Kristin Duke; CENLA AAA, Alexandria, LA

Sharron Dreyer; Fairfax Department of Housing and Community Development, Fairfax, VA

Timothy Foley; Harrison Township, MI

Jorge Lambrinos; Edward R. Roybal Institute for Applied Gerontology, California State University, Los Angeles

Jonathan Lavin; Suburban Area Agency on Aging, Oak Park, IL

E. Craig MacBean; Prime Dynamics, LLC, Richmond, VA

Jan Nestler; Elder and Adult Day Services, Bellevue, WA

John B. Rentz; Employer Group Benefits Resources, McLean, VA

Howard L. Rodgers; New Orleans Council on Aging, New Orleans, LA

Janet Sainer; Brookdale Foundation Group, New York, NY

Skip Schlenk; Aurora, CO

Cyndee Rice Sims; Senior Neighbors of Chattanooga, Chattanooga, TN

Jane Stenson; Catholic Charities USA, Alexandria, VA

CONTACT INFORMATION

300 D Street S.W., Suite 801, Washington, DC 20024
Phone: (202) 479-1200 • *Fax:* (202) 479-0735
TDD: (202) 479-6674
General E-mail: info@ncoa.org • *Web site:* www.ncoa.org

Communications Director: Scott L. Parkin
scott.parkin@ncoa.org
Human Resources Director: Wanda R. Baker
wanda.baker@ncoa.org

PURPOSE: "dedicated to improving the health and independence of older persons; increasing their continuing contributions to communities, society and future generations; and building caring communities."

CURRENT CONCERNS: Arts and humanities programs for older adults • Employment options for older workers • Equitable access to health care, including long-term services • Housing needs of older Americans • Interdependence of children, youth, families, and the elderly • Literacy • Midlife and retirement planning • Services for older persons • Social Security income

METHOD OF OPERATION: Advertisements • Awards program (Achievement Award, Civic Commitment Award, Community Service Award, and Distinguished Achievement Award) • Coalition forming • Congressional testimony • Fellowship program • Films/video/audiotapes • International activities • Internet (Web site) • Legislative/regulatory monitoring (federal and state) • Library/information clearinghouse • Lobbying (federal) • Media outreach • Research • Telecommunications services (mailing lists) • Training and technical assistance

Effectiveness and Political Orientation

"Yvette Huyghue-Pannell, director of the senior center, was a little surprised about a request for belly dancing. Because about a dozen seniors expressed interest in learning it, a class was formed.

"Turns out the belly dancing was harder than it looked, and the class lasted only eight weeks. But the Bloomfield Senior Center's responsiveness to its clientele, and the variety of classes offered at the center are two of the reasons the center has earned national accreditation from the National Institute of Senior Centers, a unit of the National Council on the Aging.

"Though there are thousands of senior centers nationwide, fewer than 100 have received the accreditation, which the council began bestowing in 1998. The Bloomfield center is the second in Connecticut to receive the distinction; the Newington Senior Center was accredited last year.

" 'It was a validation,' said M. Virginia Hallisey, a member and former chairman of Bloomfield's Commission on Aging. 'We're very excited about it.'

David Turner; Salt Lake County Aging Services, Salt Lake City, UT

Satya Verma; Pennsylvania College of Optometry, Elkins Park, PA

William Wasch; William Wasch Associates, Middletown, CT

Lawrence J. Weiss; Sanford Center on Aging, Reno, NV

Stephen M. Wing; CVS Pharmacy, Twinsburg, OH

Peter Wyckoff; Minnesota Senior Federation, St. Paul, MN

Carol S. Zernial; Bexar AAA, San Antonio, TX

SCOPE

Members: 3,800 members include senior centers, adult day service centers, area agencies on aging, faith congregations, senior housing facilities, employment services, and other consumer organizations. NCOA also includes a voluntary network of more than 14,000 leaders from academia, business and labor who support our mission and work.

Branches/chapters: None

Affiliates: Health Promotion Institute, National Association of Older Worker Employment Services, National Adult Day Services Association, National Center on Rural Aging, National Institute of Senior Centers, National Institute of Senior Housing, National Institute on Community-based Long-term Care, National Institute on Financial Issues and Services for Elders, National Interfaith Coalition on Aging

STAFF

90 total

TAX STATUS

501(c)(3)

FINANCES

Revenue: 2002—$48.82 million; 2001—$48.53 million; 2000—$47.43 million

FUNDING SOURCES

Government contracts, 93%; foundation and corporate grants, 3%; memberships, publications sales, and other services, 4%

PAC

None

EMPLOYMENT

NCOA maintains an online "Jobs board," available as a link from www.ncoa.org, under "Find a job" (www.ncoa.org/content.cfm ?sectionID=206), where they place their own job postings, as well as those of other organizations. For inquiries, contact Wanda R. Baker, director for human resources, wanda.baker@ ncoa.org.

INTERNSHIPS

Information unavailable

NEWSLETTERS

Vital Aging Report (quarterly)

" 'It's like the Good Housekeeping Seal of Approval,' Huyghue-Pannell said.

"The process took two years, beginning with a self-evaluation, which took stock of the center's programs and services. . . ."

(*Hartford Courant* [Connecticut], January 20, 2004)

"In a break with party leaders, centrist Democrats proposed today that Medicare provide drug benefits immediately to people who have low incomes or high prescription drug expenses.

"Members of both parties said Congress could eventually embrace such a plan if lawmakers could not agree on more ambitious proposals to pay drug costs for all Medicare beneficiaries, regardless of income.

"The new proposal was offered by Representatives Cal Dooley of California and Rahm Emanuel of Illinois, with support from 16 other House members who call themselves New Democrats.

" 'Our proposal is fiscally and politically realistic,' said Mr. Dooley, a House member for 12 years. It would, he said, provide drug benefits to people with the greatest financial needs. . . .

"Howard J. Bedlin, vice president of the National Council on the Aging, a research and advocacy group, said, 'This is not the ultimate solution, but it would be a good start, a potential compromise, that could attract bipartisan support if we find there's not enough money to provide more comprehensive drug benefits.' "

(*The New York Times,* April 2, 2003)

"Good news this week for older people who find it hard to afford the drugs they need: A public-private partnership led by the National Council on the Aging (NCOA) has launched an Internet service that reveals whether a particular person is likely to qualify for any of more than 240 prescription discount programs operated by drug companies, government agencies and other parties. These programs offer nearly 800 prescription drugs for free or at reduced rates."

(*The Washington Post,* January 28, 2003)

"More than 25 years ago, the National Council on Aging did a study of the prevailing attitudes about aging in an attempt to debunk some myths and misconceptions.

"This year the council commissioned a follow-up study to see how things have changed. Many of the questions asked were identical to those used a quarter-century ago. Some were designed to explore new issues.

"The number of older people who answered "yes" to the question of whether money, health, loneliness or crime was a serious problem for them dropped, compared with 1974. Also, fewer people reported that these things seemed to be a general problem for people over 65.

"People in the study said they look forward to living a long time. But when asked what worried them about living a long time, the most common answer was memory loss, followed by suffering from uncontrollable pain. Financial issues such as not being able to pay for long-term care or outliving their pension were mentioned less frequently. . . .

"So what makes for a vital and meaningful later life? Most people think it's a close relationship with family and friends and taking care of your health,

PUBLICATIONS
None

CONFERENCES
Annual meeting
Co-sponsors a variety of institutes, workshops,
    and meetings on issues dealing with the
    elderly.
Teleconferences

the survey reported. Next comes a rich spiritual life, being involved in your community and having new learning experiences, it said.

"People in the survey said that to prepare for a good old age they should prepare a living will and build up their savings. To lesser extents, their goals are to develop hobbies, change their health habits and purchase long-term care insurance, the survey showed. . . ."

(*The New Orleans Times-Picayune,* June 23, 2002)

"Nancy Speir was searching the Internet for health insurance for her 84-year-old father when she found the Western Reserve Area Agency on Aging in Cleveland.

"Or so she thought.

"What she heard when she called was an enticement for phone sex—'raw, uncensored conversations with local babes.'

"The agency provides home health care, home-delivered meals and other senior services in five Northeast Ohio counties.

" 'It has nothing to do with young girls,' said Ron Hill with a laugh. Hill, the agency's executive director, hadn't heard about the phone number glitch before yesterday.

"The number was provided by a popular Internet site called www. benefitscheckup.org, run by the National Council on the Aging.

"Senior advocacy groups across the nation praised the site when it was launched last June as one-stop shopping for government services, including homemaker services, food stamps, assistance in paying for Medicare and even an offer of volunteer opportunities.

"It cost $2 million to develop and has attracted another $2.5 million in foundation support. . . .

" 'It is embarrassing, and for older people especially,' said Scott Parkin at the National Council on the Aging, who said no one had complained about the problem.

"It may be difficult to find the wrong number today, though.

"Yesterday, Parkin alerted the computer programmers at America Online, which hosts the site.

" 'They're fixing it as we speak,' he said. . . ."

(*The Plain Dealer* [Cleveland], February 27, 2002)

National Federation of Independent Business

Established in 1943

DIRECTOR

Jack Faris, president and chief executive officer. Faris has served as president and chief executive officer of NFIB since April 1992. For 12 years, Faris owned his own marketing and management consulting firm, working primarily with small and independent businesses. Faris served as campaign finance director for Tennessee govenor Lamar Alexander in 1978 and as executive director of the Republican National Finance Committee from 1978 to 1981. He also has worked in the banking industry and for the international construction firm of Joe M. Rodgers and Associates. Faris serves on the President's Export Council and represents the United States on the executive and steering committees of the International Small Business Congress. He is past president of the Nashville Rotary Club and has served on numerous civic boards, including the American Cancer Society, the Fellowship of Christian Athletes and the Nashville Symphony. Faris graduated from David Lipscomb University in Nashville, TN.

BOARD OF DIRECTORS

Tom Musser, chair
Susan Andrews
Kevin Clark
Noelle Clark
Tim Clayton
Don Cogman
Brad Eiffert
Lloyd Falconer
Jack Faris
Lu Ann Walker Maddox
Ruth Lopez Novodor
Sunder Ramani
Richard Reinhardt
Henry Van De Putte Jr.

SCOPE

Members: 600,000 business owners
Branches/chapters: Legislative offices in 50 states
Affiliates: NFIB Education Foundation, NFIB Legal Foundation, 501(c)(3) organizations

STAFF

1,000 total

TAX STATUS

501(c)(6)

FINANCES

Budget: 2004—$85 million; 2003—$81 million; 2002—$80 million

FUNDING SOURCES

Membership dues, 100%

CONTACT INFORMATION

1201 F Street, NW, Suite 200, Washington, DC 20004-1221
Phone: (202) 554-9000 • *Fax:* (202) 554-0496
Web site: www.nfib.com

Communications Director: Mindi Boyagian, director of media relations (202) 554-9000 • mindi.boyagian@NFIB.org
Human Resources Director: Therese Arbuckle, national employment manager (615) 872-5800 • therese.arbuckle@NFIB.org

PURPOSE: "To impact public policy at the state and federal level and be a key business resource for small and independent business in America."

CURRENT CONCERNS: Balancing the federal budget • Death tax repeal • Government mandates • Health care reform • Legal reform • OSHA reform • Product liability • Regulatory reform • Superfund reform • Tax relief and simplification • Wage reform

METHOD OF OPERATION: Awards programs (Guardian of Small Business Awards) • Campaign contributions • Coalition forming • Conferences/seminars • Congressional testimony • Congressional voting analysis • Educational foundation • Grassroots organizing • International activities • Legislative/regulatory monitoring (federal and state) • Lobbying (federal, state, and grassroots) • Media outreach • Participation in regulatory proceedings (federal and state) • Research

Effectiveness and Political Orientation

"Minnesota's minimum wage, frozen at the federal rate of $5.15 an hour for the past seven years, would rise to $6.65 over the next 16 months under a bill sent to the Senate floor Wednesday.

"A party-line vote of eight DFLers in favor and six Republicans opposed in the Jobs, Energy and Community Development Committee produced one of the rare legislative movements on the state's wage floor since it was increased from $4.75 per hour in 1997.

"But the bill, sponsored by Sen. Ellen Anderson, DFL-St. Paul, has far to go before it could become law. No hearings have been scheduled in the Republican-controlled House, and when representatives of Republican Gov. Tim Pawlenty's administration were invited to comment on the bill for the Senate panel Wednesday, they declined.

"As usual when it comes to a minimum-wage increase, religious groups, unions and advocates for women, children and the poor testified in its favor Wednesday, while business representatives spoke against it.

" 'There's no place in Minnesota where somebody can make it on $5.15 an hour,' said Tarryl Clark of the Minnesota Community Action Association.

PAC
NFIB Safe Trust Political Action Committee

PAC CONTRIBUTIONS 2002

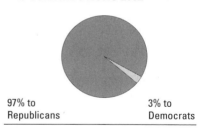

97% to
Republicans

3% to
Democrats

EMPLOYMENT

Openings with this organization are posted at www.nfib.com. Applicants should send resumes and other materials for employment to NFIB, Attention: Therese Arbuckle, national employment manager, 53 Century Boulevard, Suite 250, Nashville, TN 37214. Phone: (615) 872-5800.

INTERNSHIPS

Internship opportunities are posted on the organization's Web site, under the Education Foundation link. Summer internships require 35 hours per week, and they include the Institute's seven-week curriculum, which consists of two three-credit courses examining the history and philosophy of government regulation. In order to be eligible, interns will have completed at least two semesters of study at an accredited college or university before the start of the program. An application for admission is required (available at www.dcinternships.org), along with two letters of recommendation, an official transcript, typed one-page resume, and a 300–500 word essay.

The contact person for NFIB internships is Therese Arbuckle, national employment manager, 53 Century Boulevard, Suite 250, Nashville, TN 37214. Phone: (615) 872-5800.

NEWSLETTERS

Capitol Coverage Newsletter (several times per year)
MyBusiness Magazine (6 times per year)
MyBusiness Minute Newsletter (weekly)
NFIB Member Ballot (state and federal ballots sent three times per year)
VOICE email Newsletter (biweekly)
NFIB's E-News (daily newsletter)

PUBLICATIONS

How Congress Voted
NFIB Grassroots Power Manual
InPolitics
Small Business Focus
Small Business Economic Trends

CONFERENCES

Congressional Small Business Summit (biennial)
National Leadership Conference

" 'If the minimum wage is raised,' replied Mike Hickey of the National Federation of Independent Business, 'job loss is going to occur. The question is how much and where.'

"Under questioning, however, he said he had no evidence that Minnesota lost jobs when the minimum wage was raised in 1997 along with the federal rate. Hickey and other business spokesmen said Minnesota should not get ahead of the federal rate, which also has stayed at $5.15."

(*Minneapolis Star Tribune,* March 11, 2004)

"Just one year after she opened a custom drapery shop, Birdie Godlock is looking at an unusual location for expansion—the self-storage unit next door.

"Godlock, a 40-year veteran of the apparel and furniture industry, opened shop about a year ago at the Shurgard Self Storage Center in Pineville, N.C., a place better known for storing furniture than incubating businesses.

"Orders for drapes and bedspreads are coming in so fast to her living-room-size unit that she is already thinking about leasing more space and getting help. 'It's like a snowball,' said Godlock, 58.

"The ranks of entrepreneurs such as Godlock have grown as companies downsized in the economic downturn. And if the Shurgard center is an indication, more of them are turning to these low-cost, inconspicuous units, and some are so confident they're talking about hiring their first employees.

"The government does not break out estimates of hiring by small businesses, but it is widely acknowledged they create the bulk of new jobs in the economy, particularly in the early stages of a recovery.

"Small-business hiring plans hit their highest level in December since 1999, itself a record year, according to a survey by the National Federation of Independent Business. . . ."

(*Milwaukee Journal Sentinel* [Wisconsin], March 8, 2004)

"Over coffee and bagels Friday morning, Jim Noon explained to a group of fellow small-business owners why Colorado lawmakers ought to look at revamping the state's property tax system.

"The current system, he said, will increasingly place an unfair share of the burden of Colorado's property tax bill on businesses. Keeping and attracting companies will become more and more difficult for the state. . . .

"Voters last fall soundly rejected a proposal that would have repealed the Gallagher Amendment, a 1982 measure that holds down residential property taxes. Many businesses, both large and small, lobbied to put the proposal, known as Amendment 32, on the ballot.

"Noon, who owns Centennial Container Inc., a seller of boxes and shipping supplies, said the proposal was poorly written. He said legislators ought to look at including a repeal of Gallagher in a plan to undo constitutional restraints on Colorado's budget this session. . . .

" 'They voted against the first line,' which said their residential property tax assessment rate would rise to 8 percent and be frozen there, he said. It was expected to decline to 7.96 percent this year, after steadily falling over the years from 21 percent in 1983.

"The business sector rate is 29 percent. . . ."

(*Rocky Mountain News* [Denver], February 28, 2004)

"In economic terms, spring may finally be arriving for small business—a little sooner, it seems, than for corporate America.

" 'Because data collection and analysis can take at least a year, there are no hard statistics about the state of small business today,' said Chad Moutray, chief economist for the Office of Advocacy of the Small Business Administration.

"And economic observers are wary about predicting growth after a series of false starts followed the 2001 recession.

" 'Nevertheless, a general sense of optimism seems to prevail among small-business owners, one that is far greater than a year ago,' said William C. Dunkelberg, chief economist for the National Federation of Independent Business, a small-business advocacy group in Washington that conducts a monthly survey measuring such things.

"Moreover, Mr. Dunkelberg said, many small businesses—defined by the Small Business Administration as those that employ fewer than 500 workers—also reported plans for increased capital spending and investment in inventories.

"Perhaps even more significant is that job growth among small businesses is 'strong in every industry, including manufacturing,' Mr. Dunkelberg said, although federal payroll statistics show overall job creation to be anemic at best. But those statistics do not always pick up hiring at small businesses and start-ups at the beginning of business upswings, economists say. . . ."

(*The New York Times,* February 24, 2004)

"When President Bush urged Congress during his State of the Union address to give small businesses more freedom to 'band together' to negotiate lower health insurance rates, some lobbyists rejoiced while others were distressed.

"Such arrangements, called association health plans, have been around for years, but operating under state insurance regulations, which in many places require insurers to cover a variety of conditions and treatments that self-insured plans, offered by many large employers, exclude to cut costs.

"By paying most medical costs out of pocket, self-insurers not only avoid paying for an insurance company's profit, they also get a break from federal law. The 1974 Employee Retirement Income Security Act exempts them from state insurance regulation, giving them considerable freedom to decide which medical conditions they will cover and which they will not.

"It's a benefit that many smaller companies would like to have.

"A federal preemption of state rules would cut costs by eliminating state requirements and by allowing association plans to offer standardized coverage across more than one state, proponents say. These efficiencies would allow businesses that now can't afford coverage to obtain it for their workers, according to backers.

" 'It's a fairness issue,' said Jack Faris, president of the National Federation of Independent Business, a strong supporter of the plans. When the small-business employee 'in a pickup truck can't get insurance and the employee working [for a big company] on the assembly line can, it's just not fair—and the president understands it,' Faris said."

(*The Washington Post,* January 22, 2004)

National Gay and
Lesbian Task Force and Policy Institute

Established in 1973

DIRECTOR

Matt Foreman, executive director. Foreman has worked for gay, lesbian, bisexual and transgender rights for 25 years. Foreman began his tenure as executive director of the National Gay and Lesbian Task Force in May 2003. Previously, he was executive director of the Empire State Pride Agenda from 1997 to 2003. From 1990 to 1996, Foreman served as executive director of New York City Gay and Lesbian Anti-Violence Project (AVP), building it into the nation's leading GLBT crime victim assistance agency. Prior to joining AVP, Foreman worked in prison policy and administration for 10 years, including service as assistant commissioner of the West Virginia Department of Corrections, executive assistant to the New York City correction commissioner, and as director of a medium/minimum security facility on Rikers Island. Foreman is also a founder of Heritage of Pride, and in 2002 he was appointed to the New York City Commission on Human Rights. He graduated from West Virginia Wesleyan College in 1976 and New York University School of Law in 1982.

BOARD OF DIRECTORS

Loren Ostrow, co-chair
Beth Zemsky, co-chair
Marsha Botzer, treasurer
Alan Acosta
Maureen Burnley
Glenn Carlson
Candy Cox
Susan Culligan
Danny Gibson
Craig Hoffman
Ernest Hopkins
Yosenio Lewis
Mary Morten
Ken Ranftle
Mark Sexton
Calpernia Addams
Jerry Clark
Jody Laine
Paula Redd Zeman

SCOPE

Members: 20,000 individuals and organizations
Branches/chapters: None, however there are offices in Los Angeles, Cambridge, and New York
Affiliates: Task Force Policy Institute, a separate 501(c)(3) organization

CONTACT INFORMATION

1325 Massachusetts Avenue, Suite 600, Washington, DC 20005
Phone: (202) 393-5177 • *Fax:* (202) 393-2241
General E-mail: TheTaskForce@TheTaskForce.org •
Web site: www.TheTaskForce.org

Communications Director: Sheri A. Lunn
(202) 393-5177 • slunn@thetaskforce.org
Human Resources Director: None

PURPOSE: "Founded in 1973, the National Gay and Lesbian Task Force was the first national lesbian, gay, bisexual and transgender (LGBT) civil rights and advocacy organization and remains the movement's leading voice for freedom, justice, and equality. We work to build the grassroots political strength of our community by training state and local activists and leaders and organizing broad-based campaigns to defeat anti-LGBT referenda and advance pro-LGBT legislation. Our Policy Institute, the community's premiere think tank, provides research and policy analysis to support the struggle for complete equality. As part of a broader social justice movement, we work to create a world that respects and makes visible the diversity of human expression and identity where all people may fully participate in society."

CURRENT CONCERNS: Anti-gay legislative and ballot measures • Anti-gay violence • Countering the Right Wing • Discrimination against the gay community • Ex-gay movement • Family issues • Gay rights movement • Government response to HIV • HIV/AIDS crisis • Medicaid reform • Repeal of sodomy laws • Youth issues

METHOD OF OPERATION: Advertisements • Awards program • Boycotts • Coalition forming • Conferences/seminars • Congressional testimony • Demonstrations • Direct action • Films/video/audiotapes • Grassroots organizing assistance • Initiative/referendum campaigns • International activities • Internet (databases, e-mail alerts, and Web site) • Legislative/regulatory monitoring (federal and state) • Library/information clearinghouse • Lobbying (federal, state, and grassroots) • Media outreach • Polling • Research • Training and technical assistance

SPECIFIC PROGRAMS/INITIATIVES: Policy Institute • Organizing & Training • Creating Change Conference • Transgender Civil Rights Project

Effectiveness and Political Orientation

"The Democrats running for president are more supportive of gay rights than any previous primary ticket, but most are not quite pro-gay enough for the National Gay and Lesbian Task Force Policy Institute.

"The group issued a report Wednesday that says most of the Democratic candidates do not fully support its political positions, instead adopting a stance consistent with U.S. public opinion polls.

"'Most of these candidates are very much on safe ground on all of the positions they are taking on gay issues and aren't risking a whole lot,' said Matt Foreman, the group's executive director.

"Former Illinois Sen. Carol Moseley Braun is the only candidate who supports all 11 of the group's issues, including the right for gay couples to marry. Gay marriage is the most divisive issue among the Democratic hopefuls. The only three who support it are long shots—Braun, Al Sharpton and Rep. Dennis Kucinich of Ohio. . . .

"Graham spokesman Jamal Simmons said Graham supports equal opportunity and legal protection for gays and has a much stronger record than President Bush.

"'I'm sure there will be some groups that differ with this position or that one,' Simmons said. 'But you stack any one of us against George Bush and it's a clear choice for that community.'

"Foreman said gays have been a reliable Democratic voting bloc, but noted that a quarter of gays who voted in the 2000 election chose President Bush, up from the 14 percent who voted for his father in 1992.

"'There is some percentage of the gay vote that is up for grabs and the Democrats shouldn't take it for granted,' he said."

(*Associated Press State & Local Wire,* May 28, 2003)

"John D'Emilio, the honoree for this year's [Lambda Literary Foundation's] Editor's Choice Award, has been active in making gay studies a recognized part of the university curriculum. He is a scholar and activist. His 1983 title, *Sexual Politics, Sexual Communities,* helped create the field of gay history. He was the founding director of the National Gay and Lesbian Task Force's Policy Institute. D'Emilio is professor of history and director of the Gender and Women's Studies Program at the University of Illinois at Chicago. . . ."

(*Lambda Book Report,* January 2003)

"Sometimes it takes despair to provoke action. And for despair, AIDS was unbeatable. Until the epidemic, lesbian and gay activists had been the usual motley crew: artsy-lefty types who didn't want to belong to the mainstream anyway or folks who'd been so bashed, blackmailed or ostracized that they felt they had little to lose (and self-respect to gain) by stamping 'homo' on their resumes. And until AIDS, lesbians and gay men, like girls and boys at a junior high school dance, kept their political distance: Girls were feminists who worked on issues such as rape or battering or Central America or nuclear disarmament while boys touted (and practiced) sexual freedom. AIDS flushed out passable white gay men, men 'for whom gay liberation had meant they could have better party lives—I'm serious!' says John D'Emilio, history professor at the University of Illinois at Chicago and founding director of the National Gay and Lesbian Task Force Policy Institute, 'but who wouldn't have thought of going to a gay pride march or a Lambda fundraiser.' The prospect of early death concentrated such minds wonderfully. Abruptly, these men's high-level Rolodexes, disposable incomes and insider skills went to work building organizations and lobbying policy makers. Women, meanwhile, started bringing two decades of feminist analysis and women's health organizing to the epidemic. For the first time, they were welcomed instead of driven away by misogyny. . . ."

(*The American Prospect,* October 21, 2002)

"By the end of the year the city could begin granting rights to domestic partners who originally registered in other cities, states, and countries, under a bill being considered in the city council's committee on general welfare. . . .

"Currently domestic partners—both same sex and male-female—can register with the city clerk after they have lived together for a year. According to the city clerk, Victor Robles, at least 17,140 couples have registered with the city as domestic partners since the program began in 1989. The couples pay $20 for a certificate that grants them the right to visit their partners in hospitals, claim the bodies of their deceased partners, receive spousal health insurance benefits, and many other advantages normally reserved for married couples.

"Under current law, couples who register as domestic partners in other localities and then move to New York are still required to live together for a year in New York before they can register with the city and be granted the rights afforded locally to domestic partners.

"The bill under consideration would automatically extend these rights and privileges to domestic partners who registered elsewhere. Newcomers would not need to register again with the city, for the certificate they received elsewhere would be valid in New York. . . .

"A research fellow at the National Gay and Lesbian Task Force Policy Institute, Brian Cahill, said the measure before the city council was 'good public policy, good business, good politics.' Mr. Cahill said the bill, if passed, might alleviate the fears of gay business leaders who are hesitant about moving to New York from such states as California, which has generous domestic partner legislation. . . ."

(*The New York Sun,* June 26, 2002)

"Barriers of society and institutional oppression constantly stump us, but we educate ourselves and learn along the way. When I came out about nine years ago I began my life's mission for equality. In college I started a lesbian, gay, bisexual and transgender (LGBT) social group and club. Since then I have worked for numerous organizations to promote gay rights, and now I head the Racial and Economic Justice Initiative at the National Gay and Lesbian Task Force and Policy Institute. This initiative seeks to add economic and racial-justice priorities to the agendas of mainstream LGBT organizations and to educate non-gay civil rights groups working on race and poverty about their LGBT constituencies. I will continue to work in any capacity to ensure that my family, young and old LGBT people and society in general are free from all types of oppression. I strive to show my family the importance of linking all struggles and discriminatory acts. With time comes change and, at times, understanding. Society has a long way to go in the struggle for LGBT human rights and it has made some accomplishments. Until we can realize the connections and how oppressions work to conquer and divide society, we will never be a united liberated front. . . ."

(*Ebony,* March 2001)

National Governors Association

Established in 1908

DIRECTOR
Raymond C. Scheppach Jr., executive director.

BOARD OF DIRECTORS
Information unavailable

SCOPE
Members: "The members of NGA are the governors of the 50 states, the territories of American Samoa, Guam, and the Virgin Islands, and the commonwealths of the Northern Mariana Islands and Puerto Rico."
Branches/chapters: None
Affiliates: None

STAFF
96 total—80 full-time professional; 16 full-time support; plus 1 part-time professional; 2 part-time support; 5–10 interns

TAX STATUS
501(c)(3)

FINANCES
Budget: 2001—$15.9 million

FUNDING SOURCES
Membership dues, 30%; government contracts, 24%; foundation grants, 23%; corporate donations, 9%; conferences, 4%; investment income, 7%; EVT subscriptions, 3%

PAC
None

EMPLOYMENT
The NGA offers opportunities in a variety of state public policy issues. All open positions are listed on the NGA Web site. The NGA only accepts resumes in specific application to posted positions: all vacant positions have an identifying number (available on job posting) that must be referenced in application material. Apply to Human Resource Management, National Governors Association, Position #, 444 North Capitol Street, NW, Suite 267, Washington, DC 20001. Fax: (202) 624-7870. E-mail: webmaster@nga.org.

INTERNSHIPS
The NGA offers a limited number of unpaid and paid internships. Applications for internships should be submitted directly to the hiring department. Instructions for applicants are contained in the text of the posting.

NEWSLETTERS
Governors' Bulletin (biweekly)

CONTACT INFORMATION
444 N. Capitol Street, NW, Suite 267, Washington, DC 20001
Phone: (202) 624-5300 • *Fax:* (202) 624-5313
General E-mail: webmaster@nga.org • *Web site:* www.nga.org

Communications Director: Christine LaPaille
(202) 624-5300 • clapaille@nga.org
Human Resources Director: Kaye Habetler
(202) 624-5300

PURPOSE: "To help shape and implement national policy and solve state problems."

CURRENT CONCERNS: Crime and public safety • Economic development • Education • Environment • Federalism • Health care • Transportation • Welfare • Workforce development

METHOD OF OPERATION: Awards program • Conferences/seminars • Congressional testimony • Information clearinghouse • Internet (electronic bulletin boards, e-mail alerts, and Web site) • Internships • Legislative/regulatory monitoring (federal and state) • Lobbying (federal) • Media outreach • Participation in regulatory proceedings (federal) • Research • Technical assistance and training

Effectiveness and Political Orientation

"The nation's governors assembled here Saturday with an agenda that underscored the gap between what they say their fiscally strapped states need and what they can expect to get from the Bush administration and Congress, even in an election year.

"The governors asked for an ambitious, six-year highway bill at a time when some in Congress are eyeing a stripped-down measure, and President Bush is threatening to veto the bill if it gets too pricey.

"State leaders also complained about soaring healthcare costs, even as Bush is seeking to curb federal Medicaid spending.

"And they urged more flexibility and funding to carry out Bush's cornerstone education initiative, the No Child Left Behind Act, at a time when federal funding is being squeezed all around and the White House is increasingly sensitive to the growing budget deficit. . . .

"Another area of bipartisan—and perennial—concern is the cost of healthcare and of Medicaid, the federal-state program for the poor. States got some relief under last year's Medicare prescription drug bill, which calls for the federal government to pay more of the drug costs of the elderly poor who qualify for both Medicare and Medicaid.

"But Raymond Scheppach, executive director of the governors association, said state leaders would continue to push the federal government to do more for those people and to oppose efforts to cut payments and impose tighter regulations.

"In general, Scheppach said, the underlying problem in current federal-state relations is that neither level of government is swimming in money.

" 'You get pushing and shoving in terms of how do I push my costs off to another level of government,' Scheppach said. 'It's clear that things are going to be tight, and they are going to be tight for the next five years.' "

(The Los Angeles Times, February 22, 2004)

"On top of his busy schedule announcing myriad proposals for Minnesota, Gov. Tim Pawlenty also is proving to be something of a joiner when it comes to various national boards and commissions. . . .

"The chairman of the National Governors Association (NGA), Dirk Kempthorne of Idaho (part of the group of governors who went to Iraq with Pawlenty, all selected by the Defense Department) named him to be one of four lead governors on federal budget issues.

"Pawlenty also serves on NGA committees dealing with education and legal affairs, and is generally considered a lead governor on the prescription drug issue. . . ."

(Minneapolis Star Tribune, February 22, 2004)

"The latest report from National Governors Association (NGA) shows the states are modestly trimming their huge budget overhangs after recovering from their spending sprees of the roaring late '90s.

"While some particularly profligate states such as California are still digging themselves out of deep budget holes, many are seeing the benefits of their spending restraint as well as a rising economy.

"The question now is whether all states have learned this lesson from the long boom of the last decade: Save for rainy days. Or, even better, have a constitutional provision mandating restraint. . . .

"The report projects just a 0.2 percent increase in state spending in fiscal 2004 over 2003—the smallest since 1979. That marks some of the first good news for states since their revenues dropped precipitously in 2001. And the NGA predicts tax collections will rise again—by a modest 5.1 percent in fiscal 2004. (States saw their tax revenues rise an average 5.9 percent in September.)

"Unlike the federal government, nearly all states are required by law to balance their budgets. To achieve that, they've had to raise taxes and fees by $20 billion, and cut spending by $25 billion.

"Beyond their own choices in spending, states have been walloped by federal mandates for spending in education and healthcare, a potentially unconstitutional form of taxation without representation. . . ."

(Christian Science Monitor, December 10, 2003)

"Thanks to a few senators fronting for state and local tax collectors, the effort to enact a permanent ban on Internet-access taxes stalled in the Senate Tuesday for a second time this month. A temporary moratorium on the tax expired Nov. 1, so consumers ought to start worrying about a future of taxes levied on everything from dial-up access to e-mail.

"The culprits are the National Governors Association, National Conference of State Legislatures and a gallery of greedy states and municipalities, whose allies in Congress warn that a permanent extension of the moratorium would rob them of tax revenue. What they hope to do is circumvent the federal Tax Nondiscrimination Act with legislation that labels as much Internet activity as possible as 'telecommunications services.' That would enable state and local governments to apply existing phone taxes to the Internet by fiat, without any debate or vote. . . ."

(*Rocky Mountain News* [Denver], November 30, 2003)

"The national moratorium on Internet taxes has been a virtual virtue—in most instances. But it's time to end the glaring unfairness to states that rely on ordinary retail sales tax.

"Sen. Ron Wyden, D-Ore., has sponsored legislation to extend a prohibition on those taxes that unfairly single out Web-based sales such as an Internet access tax, which amounts to double taxation. But Internet retailers who escape sales taxes that others pay have an unfair advantage that should be curbed.

"The National Governors Association estimates that sales taxes make up roughly one-third of states' revenue in those states where sales taxes apply. Together with major retailers, the governors have asked Congress to consider a simplified sales tax proposal that would help level the playing field between the tax-free-wheeling world of online shopping and the disadvantage faced by on-site retailers in their states. . . ."

(*The Oregonian* [Portland], September 30, 2003)

National League of Cities

Established in 1924

DIRECTOR

Donald J. Borut, executive director. Donald Borut has more than 35 years' experience in municipal government and organizational leadership in the public interest sector. Prior to his NLC appointment in 1990, he was deputy executive director of the International City Management Association (ICMA), the nation's preeminent organization representing professional administrators in local governments. Borut began working in city government in 1964 as a staff assistant in the office of the city administrator in Ann Arbor, MI. He advanced to the post of assistant city administrator of Ann Arbor before leaving the city to join the ICMA staff in 1971. Borut has served on numerous advisory boards, editorial boards, and other committees in the public interest sector, including serving as chair of the board of Public Technology, Inc. In 1992, he was elected to the National Academy of Public Administration. He currently holds the post of secretary general of the North American Section of the International Union of Local Authorities (IULA). He is a graduate of Oberlin College, with a master's degree in public administration from the University of Michigan.

BOARD OF DIRECTORS

Charles Lyons, president; selectman, Arlington; Shawsheen Valley Technical High School, Billerica, MA

Anthony A. Williams, first vice president; mayor, Washington, DC

Jim Hunt, second vice president; council member, Clarksburg, WV

John DeStefano Jr., immediate past president; mayor, New Haven, CT

Karen Anderson, past president; mayor, Minnetonka, MN

Clarence Anthony, past president; mayor, South Bay, FL

William H. Hudnut III, past president; vice mayor, Chevy Chase, MD; senior resident fellow, Urban Land Institute

Sharpe James, past president; mayor, Newark, NJ

Brian J. O'Neill, past president; councilman, Philadelphia, PA

Lorraine Anderson; council member, Arvada, CO

Ronald Bates; mayor pro tem, Los Alamitos, CA

Phil Bazemore; mayor pro tem, Monroe, NC

Daniel Beardsley Jr.; executive director, Rhode Island League of Cities and Towns, Providence, RI

Conrad W. Bowers; mayor, Bridgeton, MO

Rozelle Boyd; councilor, Indianapolis, IN

Kenneth Bueche; executive director, Colorado Municipal League, Denver, CO

CONTACT INFORMATION

1301 Pennsylvania Avenue, NW, Washington, DC 20004-1763
Phone: (202) 626-3000 • *Fax:* (202) 626-3043
General E-mail: None • *Web site:* www.nlc.org

Communications Director: Michael Reinemer
(202) 626-3003 • reinemer@nlc.org
Human Resources Director: Liz McClain
(202) 626-3070 • mcclain@nlc.org

PURPOSE: The league's mission is to strengthen cities as centers of opportunity, leadership, and governance.

CURRENT CONCERNS: Homeland security • Public safety • Affordable housing • Transportation • Children and families • Preservation of local authority • Civil rights

METHOD OF OPERATION: Awards program • Coalition forming • Conferences/seminars • Congressional testimony • Grassroots organizing • International activities • Internet (Web site) • Internships • Legislative/regulatory monitoring (federal) • Litigation • Lobbying (federal and grassroots) • Local/municipal affairs • Media outreach • Participation in regulatory proceedings (federal) • Polling • Professional development services • Research • Technical assistance • Training

SPECIFIC PROGRAMS/INITIATIVES: The National League of Cities operates numerous programs ranging from affordable housing to racial justice. See Programs section of the NLC Web site: www.nlc.org.

Effectiveness and Political Orientation

"Ralston is one of 12 U.S. cities to receive help in developing a long-range plan to improve the lives of children from birth to age 5.

"The help will come in the form of technical assistance from the National League of Cities' Institute for Youth, Education and Families. That group is working with the Freddie Mac Foundation to promote early care and education for children.

"Ralston's plan will address parent education, health, safety, quality child care and school readiness.

"A staff member from the league's institute will review the plan and make sure it has no gaps, Ralston Mayor Don Groesser said. The plan should be ready to implement by June, he said. . . ."

(*Omaha World Herald* [Nebraska], March 24, 2004)

"Hartford is one of five cities selected to receive technical assistance from the National League of Cities to expand options and innovations in high school education. . . .

Leo V. Chaney Jr.; councilman, Dallas, TX
Roger C. Claar; mayor, Bolingbrook, IL
Roosevelt Coats; councilman, Cleveland, OH
Lisa Dooley; executive director, West Virginia Municipal League, Charleston, WV
C. Virginia Fields; Manhattan Borough President, New York, NY
Clay Ford Jr.; mayor pro tem, Gulf Breeze, FL
Del Haag; council member, Buffalo, MN
S. Ellis Hankins; executive director, North Carolina League of Municipalities, Raleigh, NC
Ken Harward; executive director, Association of Idaho Cities, Boise, ID
Lester Heitke; mayor, Willmar, MN
Ruth Hopkins; council member, Prairie Village, KS
Ted Jennings; mayor, Brewton, AL
Willa Johnson; councilwoman, Oklahoma City, OK
Helen Kawagoe; city clerk, Carson, CA
Joseph Maestas; councilor, Española, NM
Cynthia McCollum; council member, Madison, AL
Rudolph McCollum Jr.; mayor, Richmond, VA
Don Moler; executive director, League of Kansas Municipalities, Topeka, KS
Carlton Moore; commissioner, Fort Lauderdale, FL
Joe Moore; alderman, Chicago, IL
Nancy Nathanson; councilor, Eugene, OR
Kathleen M. Novak; mayor, Northglenn, CO
Alex Padilla; council president, Los Angeles, CA
Bart Peterson; mayor, Indianapolis, IN
Margaret Peterson; council member at large, West Valley City, UT
Terry Riley; council member, Kansas City, MO
John Russo; city attorney, Oakland, CA
Jeanie E. Smith; executive director, Mississippi Municipal League, Jackson, MS
Shep Stahel; deputy mayor pro tem, Plano, TX
Liberato Silva; vice mayor, Flagstaff, AZ
Ted Tedesco; mayor, Ames, IA
Dan Thompson; executive director, League of Wisconsin Municipalities, Madison, WI
Dick Traini; assembly chair, Anchorage, AK

SCOPE

Members: 1,800 direct member cities, towns, and villages
Branches/chapters: None
Affiliates: 49 state municipal leagues

STAFF

101 total—70 full-time professional; 31 full-time support

TAX STATUS

501(c)(3)

FINANCES

Budget: 2004—$15.7 million; 2003—$14.6 million; 2002—$14.7 million

FUNDING SOURCES

Foundation grants, 13%; government contracts, 1%; publications, 5%; membership:

"Over two years, officials from the National League of Cities' Institute for Youth, Education and Families will work with city and school officials to identify ways to strengthen the public high schools. Mayor Eddie A. Perez said the initiative will complement his recently announced Higher Education Initiative that aims to increase the number of city graduates who go on to four-year colleges.

"The National League of Cities' program is funded by the Bill & Melinda Gates Foundation, although Hartford will not directly receive a monetary grant, officials said. . . ."

(*Hartford Courant* [Connecticut], March 10, 2004)

"When Columbus Mayor Michael B. Coleman unveiled his proposed 2004 budget—including 88 layoffs—he took care to note that things are much worse in Cleveland and Pittsburgh.

"Cleveland has laid off 254 police officers, 70 firefighters and 180 other city employees and will close city cemeteries on Mondays to help narrow a $61 million budget gap.

"Last month, Pennsylvania declared Pittsburgh financially distressed, giving the city the authority to levy taxes without state approval. Pittsburgh, with a projected $42 million deficit, has laid off 640 workers.

"The two industrial cities have lost half their populations over the past 50 years, eating away at their tax bases.

"The situation is largely the same nationwide: The recession has pummeled many cities and their budgets.

"Results of a 328-city survey by the National League of Cities showed in November that 81 percent of those cities' finance directors were unable to meet their financial needs compared with the previous year.

"Nearly half increased fees in 2003. Thirty percent cut workers, 29 percent imposed new fees, and 11 percent cut services. . . ."

(*Columbus Dispatch* [Ohio], January 18, 2004)

"Life is busy when you're a school superintendent. And it can be even more demanding if you're also a selectman and your town is struggling to overcome a looming deficit. Add to this workload the leadership responsibilities for a national lobbying group and you can guess what it's like to walk in Charlie Lyons's shoes.

"Lyons, 50, a Springfield native and longtime Arlington resident, manages a schedule that would challenge the stamina of a marathon runner. Already superintendent of the Shawsheen Valley Technical School District and an Arlington selectman, he became president of the Washington, D.C.-based National League of Cities at its annual conference in Nashville last month. The post requires him to be on the road at least 50 days, traveling to some of the member cities and towns spread out across the United States. . . .

"Lyons has already served a one-year term as the NLC's first vice president, a job that also required a lot of travel, so he is accustomed to the demands of the new office. Last year, he spent close to 40 days on the road, he said. . . .

"The National League of Cities represents municipal governments throughout the United States. According to its Web site, its mission is to strengthen and promote cities as centers of opportunity, leadership, and governance, and to serve as a national resource to and advocate for the more than 18,000 cities and towns it represents. . . ."

(*The Boston Globe*, January 8, 2004)

36%; conferences, 22%; service fees, 12%;
rental and investments, 8%; education and
training, 3%

PAC
None

EMPLOYMENT
Potential applicants can learn about job openings with this organization through its Web
site at www.nlc.org, by consulting the job hotline: (202) 626-3199, and from the classified
section of *Nation's Cities Weekly*. This organization offers positions in advocacy, legislative,
research, program management, communications, membership, event planning, financial
management, and administration. Applicants
should send resumes and other materials for
employment to Director, Human Resources,
1301 Pennsylvania Avenue, NW, Washington,
DC 20004-1763. Phone: (202) 626-3070. Fax:
(202) 628-8360.

INTERNSHIPS
This organization offers internships; potential
applicants can learn about internship opportunities through the Policy and Federal Relations
Center. To apply, send a cover letter and
resume to Human Resources, National League
of Cities, 1301 Pennsylvania Ave, NW,
Washington, DC 20004.

NEWSLETTERS
None

PUBLICATIONS
Primary publication: *Nation's Cities Weekly,* a
tabloid newspaper

CONFERENCES
Annual Congressional City Conference, (every
March in Washington, DC)
Annual Congress of Cities (every December)

"When Hiram McCrary donated land for right of way in the 1880s, it brought the railroad to Crawford County in Middle Georgia. A city soon grew around the train depot, and it was named Roberta in honor of McCrary's daughter.

"Today, Roberta, west of Macon, has a mayor and a five-member City Council, but none of the politicians who run this town named in honor of a woman has a name that sounds even remotely feminine.

"There's an Ervin and an Ephraim, a Robert, a David, a Wincel and an Oscar. Not a woman in the group—and none will be challenging the male leadership when municipal elections are held Nov. 4.

"In fact, there hasn't been a woman in Roberta's city government for more than 20 years. That's true in a lot of cities in Georgia and across the nation.

"City councils have gotten older and more ethnically diverse in the past two decades, mirroring the nation's shifting demographics. But the percent-age of women mayors and council members has declined, from 32 percent to 28 percent, according to a recent study by the National League of Cities based on once-a-decade surveys.

"In Georgia, the situation is bleaker for women: They hold fewer than 23 percent of the City Council and mayoral seats.

"Nationally, the numbers improve in big cities. That's the case in Atlanta, which has a majority-female council and Mayor Shirley Franklin, but it's not true in the rest of Georgia. Of the 20 largest cities in the state, seven have no women in elected positions and all but Atlanta are majority male. . . ."

(*The Atlanta Journal-Constitution*, October 13, 2003)

National Legal Center for the Public Interest

Established in 1975

DIRECTOR
Ernest B. Hueter, president.

BOARD OF DIRECTORS
Joan D. Aikens; Government Relations, Eastwood & Azia

Craig Barrett; president and chief executive officer, Triple Creek Ranch

Griffin B. Bell; King & Spalding

K. David Boyer Jr.; MetroStar Systems

Carolyn S. Chambers; chair and chief executive officer, Chambers Communications Corp

David Davenport, Esq.; School of Public Policy; Pepperdine University

Arnaud de Borchgrave; senior advisor, Center for Strategic International Studies

Fred F. Fielding; Wiley, Rein & Fielding

Stephen F. Gates; senior vice president and general counsel, ConocoPhillips

Vincent A. Gierer Jr.; chair, president and chief executive officer, UST Inc.

Glen A. Holden; managing partner, Holden Co.

Dean R. Kleckner

Douglas W. Kmiec; professor of constitutional law; Pepperdine University School of Law

Howard J. Krongard, counsel, Freshfields Bruckhaus Deringer

Charles T. Manatt; Manatt, Phelps & Phillips, LLP

Kenneth R. Masterson, executive vice president; general counsel, and secretary, FedEx Corp.

Dwight D. Opperman; chair, Key Investment, Inc.

Raymond P. Shafer; governor

Peter G. Skinner; executive vice president and general counsel; Dow Jones & Co.

N. David Thompson

William H. Webster; Milbank, Tweed, Hadley & McCloy

Caspar W. Weinberger; chair, FORBES, Inc.

Walter E. Williams; professor, Department of Economics, George Mason University

James I. Wyer; of counsel, St. John & Wayne

SCOPE
Members: None
Branches/chapters: None
Affiliates: None

STAFF
4 total—3 full-time professional; 1 full-time support; plus 1 part-time professional; 1–2 interns

TAX STATUS
501(c)(3)

CONTACT INFORMATION
1600 K Street, NW, Suite 800, Washington, DC 20006
Phone: (202) 466-9360 • *Fax:* (202) 466-9366
General E-mail: info@nlcpi.org • *Web site:* www.nlcpi.org

Communications Director: Irene A. Jacoby, senior vice president
(202) 466-9360 • ijacoby@nlcpi.org
Human Resources Director: None

PURPOSE: To foster knowledge about law and the administration of justice, and by so doing to promote our society's commitment to individual rights, free enterprise, private ownership of property, limited government, and a fair and efficient system for the administration of justice.

CURRENT CONCERNS: Developments in the legislative, judiciary, and executive branches that affect law and legal policy

METHOD OF OPERATION: Conferences/seminars • Educational foundation • Internet (databases) • Internships • Legislative/regulatory monitoring (federal) • Media outreach • Research • Speakers program

Effectiveness and Political Orientation

"The Supreme Court agreed on Monday to settle one of the most disputed questions in civil rights law: how to win an age discrimination case in the absence of proof that an employer deliberately singled out older workers for unfavorable treatment.

"The issue in a case brought by a group of older police officers in Jackson, Miss., is whether the federal law against age discrimination covers policies that do not relate directly to age but that have a disparate impact on older workers.

"In this case, the older officers are trying to show that new wage scales, intended to make the pay for more recently hired officers more competitive with other police departments in the region, had the effect of giving proportionately smaller increases to the more senior officers. . . .

"Both the Federal District Court in Jackson and the United States Court of Appeals for the Fifth Circuit, in New Orleans, ruled for the city on the ground that the law requires proof of 'disparate treatment,' meaning intentional discrimination. . . .

"For more than 20 years, the Equal Employment Opportunity Commission has had a regulation on its books that adopts the broader 'disparate impact' interpretation of the law. But when the issue was before the Supreme Court two years ago, the Bush administration did not defend the regulation and filed no brief in the case.

"Its reticence no doubt reflected the fact that across the entire range of employment discrimination law, the ability of judges to impose remedies when plaintiffs have not proven deliberate discrimination is under sustained attack from employer groups and conservative legal organizations. When the

FINANCES

Budget: 2004—$1.3 million;
2003—$1.3 million; 2002—$1.3 million

FUNDING SOURCES

Foundation grants, 18%; corporate donations, 57%; individuals, 3%; special events/projects, 15%; other sources, 7% (includes conferences)

PAC

None

EMPLOYMENT

Potential applicants can learn about job openings with this organization through the organization's Web site. This organization offers administrative positions. Applicants should send resumes and other materials for employment to Irene A. Jacoby, senior vice president, 1600 K Street, NW, Suite 800, Washington, DC 20006. Phone: (202) 466-9360. Fax: (202) 466-9366. E-mail: ijacoby@nlcpi.org.

INTERNSHIPS

Potential applicants can learn about internship opportunities through the organization's Web site and through school listings. Positions are unpaid and usually last one semester. Application deadlines are ongoing and hours are flexible. Interns working for the Center assist in monitoring decisions of the Supreme Court and other courts, act as research assistants to senior staff members, write for Center publications, and conduct research projects of their own that will contribute to future activities of the Center. Interns are usually in law school or graduate school but university seniors also are considered. Interested individuals should contact Irene A. Jacoby, senior vice president, 1600 K Street, NW, Suite 800, Washington, DC 20006. Phone: (202) 466-9360. Fax: (202) 466-9366. E-mail: ijacoby@nlcpi.org.

NEWSLETTERS

Briefly+Perspectives on Legislation, Regulation and Litigation (monthly)
Judicial/Legislative Watch Report (monthly)
National Legal Center News (semiannually)
White Papers (periodic)

PUBLICATIONS

The following is a list of sample publications:
Abolition of Diversity Jurisdiction: An Idea Whose Time Has Come?
American Enterprise, the Law, and the Commercial Use of Space
Antitrust Contribution and Claim Reduction: An Objective Assessment
Civil Rights and the Disabled: The Legislative Twilight Zone
Corporate Criminal Liability: Is It Time for a New Look?
Employers' Rights and Responsibilities
Ergonomics: OSHA's Strange Campaign to Run American Business
Ethics in the Courts: Policing Behavior in the Federal Judiciary
Federal Product Liability Law—It Should Be Enacted Now!
Institutional Investors, Social Investing, and Corporate Governance

earlier case was pending, one prominent conservative group, the National Legal Center for the Public Interest, published a study of discrimination law that said that the disparate-impact approach 'deserves to be attacked at every opportunity.'"

(*The New York Times*, March 30, 2004)

"The mistrial of Frank Quattrone, banker to the internet, could prove a legal milestone of the post-Enron era in America. But that was not the only thing that made it newsworthy last week. Mr Quattrone is famous for having financially sired such new-age companies as Amazon.com and Netscape. But his fame was eclipsed last week by a far more mundane form of parentage: a juror in his trial had a baby.

"This was the first really big show trial of the internet era, and the fact that it ended in mistrial must give other white collar celebrities hope that they too will escape the public's vengeance. But the trial was more than that: it was a sort of cultural soap opera, where the personal lives of jurors were a central feature.

"One became a father, another suffered sudden illness of an ailing parent, a third had to complete a house purchase. Deliberations were delayed as a result: suddenly wives, children, mothers and estate agents of the jury seemed an obstacle to the impartial administration of justice.

"But the bigger message was: American justice depends on the welfare of hoi polloi. Jurors are people too and, increasingly, they are the common people.

"According to a recent study from the National Legal Centre for the Public Interest, a think-tank, the American jury is increasingly composed of unemployed and retired persons—because the rest of us manage to avoid jury duty altogether. So the fate of everyone from Mr Quattrone to the Washington, DC, sniper depends on the ability of courts to communicate basic principles of justice to the lowest common denominator of juror...."

(*Financial Times* [London, England], October 27, 2003)

"Each year, the National Legal Center for the Public Interest holds a General Counsel Briefing covering issues of concern to corporate counsel. This year's General Counsel Briefing will be held June 9 and 10 at The National Press Club and the Willard Hotel, Washington, DC. There is a charge of $700, with reductions for more than one from the same organization. CLE credit, including ethics, is available.

"The Program will include the following panel discussions: Homeland Security: Everybody's Business: officers' and directors' responsibilities after September 11, emergency preparedness, the legal significance of information assurance standards, cooperation with law enforcement, new risks and new responsibilities for international corporations after September 11. The moderator is John L. Howard, senior vice-president and general counsel, W. W. Grainger, Inc...."

(*The Metropolitan Corporate Counsel*, May 2003)

"In reviewing the trend toward expansion of international trade on the part of Republicans and moderate Democrats in Congress, the Judicial/Legislative Watch newsletter notes that legislation enhancing business dealings with Cuba is moving ahead without consideration of whether that country is supporting terrorists. The newsletter, published by the National Legal Center for the

CONFERENCES

Public Interest, suggests that if trade enhancement were tied to proof that the Castro regime is supporting terrorists, business could be mighty slow.

"Cuban Premier Fidel Castro would fail the test due to his 'history of support for guerrilla movements in Colombia [the Revolutionary Armed Forces of Columbia and the National Liberation Army], Spain [Basque ETA terrorists], the United Kingdom [Irish Republican Army], Peru [Shining Path], Panama, Venezuela, Puerto Rico, Nicaragua, El Salvador and elsewhere.' Additionally, Castro would flunk on grounds of 'his continuing heavy support for narcoterrorism and his increasingly publicized involvement with Osama bin Laden and international terrorist movements,' the newsletter notes. . . ."

(*Insight on the News,* March 25, 2002)

"The National Legal Center for the Public Interest in Washington, DC has introduced a year-long series of public service announcements under the title Supreme Court Briefs.

"The program will consist of three segments of 20 announcements each. Segments will be released at four-month intervals for a total of 60 different announcements to be broadcast over a 12-month period. . . .

"The texts of the one-minute announcements initially will deal with vignettes of the Supreme Court: its make-up, modus operandi, history, and facts about justices. . . .

"The texts of Supreme Court Briefs can be found on the National Legal Center Web site at www.nlcpi.org."

(*The Metropolitan Corporate Counsel,* February 2002)

National Organization for Women (NOW)

Established in 1966

DIRECTOR

Kim Gandy, president. Gandy was elected president of NOW in 2001, after serving as executive vice president since 1991. Gandy was responsible for NOW's legislative agenda and litigation docket. Prior to taking on a national post at NOW, Gandy had been active in women's rights in Louisiana for more than a decade, using her skills as an organizer and an attorney to advance issues of importance to women. Gandy graduated from Louisiana Tech University in 1973 with a B.S. in mathematics, and she received her law degree in 1978 from Loyola University School of Law, where she was a member of the Loyola Law Review.

BOARD OF DIRECTORS

Kim Gandy, president
Karen Johnson, vice president—executive
Terry O'Neill, vice president—membership
Olga Vives, vice president—action

SCOPE

Members: 500,000 individuals
Branches/chapters: 550 chapters
Affiliates: NOW Foundation, Inc., a 501(c)(3) organization

STAFF

30 total—plus 15 interns; 20 volunteers

TAX STATUS

501(c)(4)

FINANCES

Information unavailable

FUNDING SOURCES

Membership dues, 74%; contributions, 17%; sales and royalties, 6%; conferences and other, 4%

PAC

NOW/PAC and NOW Equality PAC

PAC CONTRIBUTIONS 2002

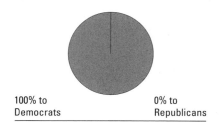

100% to Democrats   0% to Republicans

EMPLOYMENT

Position openings at NOW are posted on the Web site at www.now.org/organization/work.html. Details regarding the position, as

CONTACT INFORMATION

733 15th Street, NW, 2nd Floor, Washington, DC 20005
Phone: (202) 628-8669 • *Fax:* (202) 785-8576
TTY: (202) 331-9002
General E-mail: now@now.org • *Web site:* www.now.org

Communications Director: Lisa Bennett
(202) 628-8669, ext. 123 • communications@now.org.
Human Resources Director: Information unavailable

PURPOSE: NOW acts "to bring about equality for all women. NOW works to eliminate discrimination and harassment in the workplace, schools, the justice system, and all other sectors of society; secure abortion, birth control and reproductive rights for all women; end all forms of violence against women; eradicate racism, sexism and homophobia; and promote equality and justice in our society."

CURRENT CONCERNS: Economic equality for women • Abortion rights, reproductive freedom and other women's health issues • Civil rights for all and opposing racism • Opposing bigotry against lesbians and gays • Ending violence against women

METHOD OF OPERATION: Advertisements • Awards program • Boycotts • Campaign contributions • Coalition forming • Conferences/seminars • Congressional testimony • Demonstrations • Direct action • Electoral politics • Films/video/audiotapes • Grassroots organizing • Initiative/referendum campaigns • International activities • Internet (Web site) • Legislative/regulatory monitoring (federal and state) • Litigation • Lobbying (federal, state, and grassroots) • Local/municipal affairs • Media outreach • Participation in regulatory proceedings (federal and state) • Product merchandising • Research • Speakers program • Telecommunications services • Training and technical assistance • Voter registration • Voting records

Effectiveness and Political Orientation

"There was a time when the abortion debate focused on the right of a woman to choose whether to end her pregnancy without the threat of criminal penalties or government harassment. How far this debate has moved from there was evident in a courthouse in Salt Lake City this month.

"Melissa Ann Rowland stands accused of refusing to have a Caesarean section to save the lives of twins she was carrying. According to doctors and nurses at a hospital there, Rowland refused the C-section because of the scar that would result and allegedly stated she would rather 'lose one of the babies than be cut like that.' Rowland has been charged with murder after one baby was stillborn and the other barely survived.

INTERNSHIPS

NOW offers internship opportunities (both full- and part-time) throughout the year. A minimum of 3 days per week is required. College credit can be arranged. Details and applications for NOW internships are available at www.now .org/organization/intern.html. Prospective interns should be hardworking, enthusiastic and flexible individuals who possess or seek a working knowledge of women's issues and feminist organizing. Interns should also be committed to continuing to struggle for equality and justice once they leave the internship program. Interns work with one of the following teams: Government Relations/Public Policy Team, Field Organizing Team, Membership Team, Direct Mail and Fundraising Team, Communications Team, Web Team, and Political Action Committee.

Interested applicants should send a cover letter that expresses why they want to intern for NOW and that details their ability to work in a fast-paced feminist environment; a current resume; a completed application form, and two letters of recommendation. For further questions, contact Karen Johnson, executive vice president, National Organization for Women, 733 15th Street, NW, 2nd Floor, Washington, DC 20005. Phone: (202) 628-8669, ext. 125. E-mail: nowinterns@aol.com.

NEWSLETTERS

National NOW Times (5 times per year)

PUBLICATIONS

Publishes various books, brochures, videos, and NOW merchandise.

CONFERENCES

Sponsors an annual national conference, regional and state conferences, and issue conferences as appropriate.

"The president of the National Organization for Women, Kim Gandy, proclaimed that she was 'aghast' that Rowland had been charged criminally and insisted that charges would never have been brought if Rowland were a 'soccer mom,' rather than a drug user with a checkered past. Other groups have called the charges an attack on motherhood or a conspiracy of anti-abortion advocates.

"For my part as a pro-choice law professor, the only thing more shocking than the alleged indifference shown to these babies by Rowland is the equal indifference shown by pro-choice groups in blindly embracing this cause. . . ."
(*Milwaukee Journal Sentinel* [Wisconsin], March 29, 2004)

"Virgin Atlantic Airways Friday scrapped plans to install bright-red urinals shaped like women's open lips at New York's John F. Kennedy International Airport, saying it had received complaints they were offensive. . . .

" 'Virgin Atlantic was very sorry to hear of people's concerns about the design of the "Kisses" urinals to be fitted into our clubhouse at JFK Airport. We can assure everyone who complained to us that no offense was ever intended,' Virgin spokesman John Riordan said in a statement.

"Riordan said the British company received several dozen complaints from people and groups including the National Organization for Women after its plans for the urinals had been made public. NOW had posted a message on its Web site urging members to complain to Virgin chief Richard Branson.

" 'I don't know many men who think it's cool to pee in a woman's mouth, even a porcelain one,' said NOW President Kim Gandy on the Web site. . . ."
(*Toronto Sun* [Canada], March 22, 2004)

"Supreme Court Justice Ruth Bader Ginsburg on Friday defended her involvement with the liberal NOW Legal Defense and Education Fund, and said justices should not 'lightly recuse' themselves over possible conflicts of interest.

"Responding to questions from law students at the University of Connecticut in Hartford, Ginsburg said she did not see a problem in her lending her name and presence to an annual lecture series that the fund co-sponsors with the Assn. of the Bar of the City of New York.

"In a Los Angeles Times article this week, some legal experts said Ginsburg should not be affiliated with the legal defense fund because it often is involved in cases before the Supreme Court.

"In January, for instance, Ginsburg took the side of the legal defense fund in a medical screening case. Two weeks later, the justice made her latest speaking appearance for the lecture series.

"Ginsburg said Friday that the lecture series 'is not a money-making enterprise.'

" 'I think and thought and still think it's a lovely thing. Let the lecture speak for itself,' she said. . . ."
(*The Los Angeles Times,* March 13, 2004)

"The U.S. Department of Education is exactly right to relax the coeducation rules for schools.

"Proposed new federal regulations could encourage the creation of more same-sex public schools and allow coed schools to provide separate classes for boys and girls. This is not some dastardly plot to turn the clock back to the discriminatory days of separate-but-equal schooling. Nor do the changes signal a return to the days when schooling was considered to be a waste of time for females. To the contrary, the changes could help ensure that even more girls get a quality education.

"Although research on same-sex schools has been inconclusive, anecdotal evidence suggests students focus more on academics when there are no distractions caused by the opposite sex. Those distractions become more pronounced in the upper grades with the onset of puberty.

"Several studies do indicate, however, that girls and boys learn differently and that some students actually do better when separated from the opposite sex. This appears to be fairly prevalent among younger girls, many of whom are intimidated by aggressive boys.

"Kim Gandy, president of the National Organization for Women, contends that single-sex education is inherently discriminatory and demeaning. She claims that it enhances negative stereotypes and makes things even tougher for men to accept women as equals in the workplace.

"The salient issue is whether schools should have the freedom to do what they believe is in the best interests of their students. The feds are not trying to impose anything. These proposed changes, which will undergo months of public hearings and a comprehensive review, are voluntary. . . ."

(*The San Diego Union-Tribune,* March 8, 2004)

"A group of University of Colorado students will hold a rally Monday to voice their concerns about an independent panel that will investigate football recruiting practices.

"They say students and someone with sexual assault prevention experience should serve on the panel.

" 'Students definitely need to be part of this panel,' said Megan Irby, 21, a senior majoring in psychology and sociology. 'Students are very much affected, and they should be protecting students, not just athletes. We don't have any power over this panel. That's why we're asking for a reconsideration of the panel.'

"Irby is a member of SAFE-T (Students Advocating for Fair and Equal Treatment), which is holding the noon rally at the University Memorial Center fountain on the Boulder campus.

"Also scheduled to speak are representatives of several advocacy groups, including the National Organization for Women.

"Members of SAFE-T are circulating petitions, asking the CU Board of Regents to reconsider the panel's makeup. . . ."

(*Rocky Mountain News* [Denver], February 21, 2004)

National Organization on Disability

Established in 1982

DIRECTOR

Alan A. Reich, president. Before founding the National Organization on Disability (N.O.D.), Reich served as president of its predecessor, the U.S. Council for the International Year of Disabled Persons (1981). Previously, he was an executive with the Polaroid Corp. and deputy assistant secretary of state for educational and cultural affairs. Reich is past chair of the People-to-People Committee on Disability and the Paralysis Cure Research Foundation. He is chair of the World Committee on Disability. He has a B.A. from Dartmouth College, an M.A. from Middlebury College Russian School, and an M.B.A. from Harvard University.

BOARD OF DIRECTORS

George H. W. Bush, honorary chair; former president
Michael R. Deland, chair; former chair, White House Council on Environmental Quality
Christopher Reeve, vice chair; actor
Alan A. Reich, president
Arlene E. Anns; former publisher, McGraw-Hill Cos., Inc.
Phillip E. Beekman; retired chief executive officer, Hook SupeRx, Inc.
Henry B. Betts, M.D.; past president/medical director, Rehabilitation Institute of Chicago
Peter D. Blanck; professor and director of the Law, Health Policy & Disability Center, University of Iowa College of Law
Bertram S. Brown, M.D.; Forensic Medical Advisory Services
John M. Derrick Jr.; chair and chief executive officer, Potomac Electric Power Co.
Richard M. DeVos Sr.; N.O.D. founding chair; retired president, Amway Corp.
Brooke Ellison; author and disability advocate
Stephen L. Feinberg; chair and chief executive officer, Dorsar Investment Co., Inc.
John D. Firestone; partner, Secor Group
Bruce Gelb; former ambassador to Belgium
Robert David Hall; actor and disability advocate
Stephen L. Hammerman; deputy commissioner of legal matters, New York City
Louis J. Hutchinson III; chief executive officer, Crunchy Technologies
I. King Jordan, Ph.D.; president, Gallaudet University
Peter B. Kovler; director, Marjorie Kovler Fund
William P. Kupper Jr.; president and publisher, *BusinessWeek*
Len Lauer; president, Sprint PCS

CONTACT INFORMATION

910 16th Street, NW, Suite 600, Washington, DC 20006-2988
Phone: (202) 293-5960 • *Fax:* (202) 293-7999
TTY: (202) 293-5968
General E-mail: ability@nod.org • *Web site:* www.nod.org

Communications Director: Brewster Thackeray
(202) 293-5960 • brewster@nod.org
Human Resources Director: Paul Stilpp
(202) 293-5960 • stilpp@nod.org

PURPOSE: The mission of the National Organization on Disability is to expand the participation and contribution of America's 54 million men, women, and children with disabilities in all aspects of life.

CURRENT CONCERNS: Community accessibility • Emergency preparedness • Employment of people with disabilities • Health care access • Housing access • Public awareness of disability issues • Transportation access

METHOD OF OPERATION: Advertisements • Awards program • Conferences/seminars • Grassroots organizing • International activities • Internet (Web site) • Information clearinghouse • International activities • Internships • Lobbying (federal) • Media outreach • Polling • Research

SPECIFIC PROGRAMS/INITIATIVES: CEO Council • Community Partnership Program (CPP) • Emergency Preparedness Initiative • National Partnership Program (NPP) • Religion and Disability Program

Effectiveness and Political Orientation

"A settlement of a federal class-action lawsuit will over the next three years make every city polling place accessible to people who are blind or use wheelchairs.

"U.S. District Judge John R. Padova on Wednesday approved the settlement between the city and the National Organization on Disability and nine residents.

"Under the agreement, each of the 1,682 city polling places will have at least one electronic voting machine by the beginning of 2006 that blind or visually impaired voters can use.

"The city will also create a panel to evaluate the 800 or so polling places that are not accessible to people who use wheelchairs, and modifications to make them accessible must be completed by May 2006."

(*Associated Press Newswires,* November 20, 2003)

"Los Angeles Mayor James K. Hahn on Friday rescinded and replaced a questionnaire sent out to the city's 300 city commissioners asking whether they are gay, lesbian or disabled, after privacy and discrimination concerns were raised.

SCOPE
Members: None
Branches/chapters: None
Affiliates: None

STAFF
17 total

TAX STATUS
501(c)(3)

FINANCES
Budget: 2004—$2 million; 2003—$2 million; 2002—$1.8 million

FUNDING SOURCES
Corporate donations, 50%; individuals, 29%; foundation grants, 20%; publications, 1%

PAC
None

EMPLOYMENT
Declined to comment

INTERNSHIPS
Interns at N.O.D. (up to three per semester) are college students or graduates who are interested in disability issues generally or a specific part of N.O.D.'s agenda, and work with the directors of the program to which they are assigned. Recent interns have focused on legislative issues, communications and publicity, N.O.D.'s Web page, and community and business outreach. In addition, the Start on Success (SOS) Program offers part-time paid internships to high school students with physical, mental, or sensory disabilities. SOS candidates are selected by teachers on the basis of interest and aptitude. Current program locations are: Alabama, Baltimore, Ohio, Philadelphia, Pittsburgh. Job sites and responsibilities vary. Details for each program location are available at the SOS Program Web site: www.startonsuccess.org. The SOS program consultant is Tracey McDade, 910 16th Street,

"Some city officials saw the original questionnaire as improperly mandating that personal information be provided. Hahn's office sent out a new form that clearly says giving the information is voluntary and the information will not be made public. . . .

"A spokeswoman for Hahn said the information would help gauge whether city panels reflected the city's diversity.

"Still, some advocates for the disabled voiced concern over the city's requesting such personal information.

" 'If it's not relevant to their job, people have a right to question why they are being asked,' said Brewster Thackeray, a spokesman for the National Organization on Disabilities."

(*The Los Angeles Times,* November 1, 2003)

"According to a 2000 survey by the National Organization on Disability and Harris Interactive, only 3 out of 10 disabled persons, aged 18 to 64 hold either full- or part-time jobs. That compares with 8 out of 10 people without disabilities who said they were working.

"Brewster Thackeray, vice president of communications for the NOD, said increased availability of telecommuting should help improve the employment numbers of disabled.

" 'We need more employers to think outside the box and look at alternatives to traditional employment arrangements,' Thackeray said. 'While we strongly advocate integrating disabled persons in the mainstream work force, that can't work for everyone. Technology is making it possible to be a lot more creative.' "

(*Buffalo News,* August 11, 2003)

"Internet use by people with disabilities is increasing at twice the pace of other Americans, but this population still is catching up, according to a poll conducted by Harris Interactive for the National Organization on Disability. In 2001, about 38 percent of adults with disabilities used the Internet at home, compared with 7 percent in 1998. For the general population, the percentage of Internet users increased from 26 to 56 in the same period. The National Organization on Disability, http://www.nod.org, credits technological advances—such as screen readers, instant messaging and voice-recognition technology—for widening the disabled community's access to the Internet."

(*The San Diego Union-Tribune,* February 11, 2002)

"Almost four years after it was dedicated, the memorial to President Franklin D. Roosevelt gets a controversial addition today as President Clinton unveils a statue of the 32nd president in a wheelchair.

" 'This dedication represents a great victory for people with disabilities,' said Alan Reich, president of the National Organization on Disability, which led the effort to add the wheelchair statue.

" 'FDR's memorial finally will acknowledge his significant disability experience, which forged his leadership qualities—courage, determination and compassion—that enabled him to successfully lead the nation through the worst crises of the 20th Century,' Reich said.

"The new statue, and a new 'room' to house it, are part of the 7.5-acre memorial, which includes other outdoor 'rooms,' each dedicated to one of his four terms in office from 1933 to 1945. The life-size bronze sculpture by Robert Graham depicts Roosevelt sitting in a wheelchair gazing upward. . . ."

(*The Palm Beach Post* [Florida], January 10, 2001)

NW, Washington, DC 20006. Phone: (813) 223-9698. Fax: (813) 223-9558. E-mail: mcdade@nod.org.

NEWSLETTERS
N.O.D. E-newsletter (online biweekly)

PUBLICATIONS
From Barriers to Bridges
Emergency Preparedness Initiative Guide for Emergency Managers, Planners & Responders
Loving Justice
Money and Ideas: Creative Approaches to Congregational Access
That All May Worship
2000 N.O.D./Harris Survey of Community Participation
2004 N.O.D./Harris Survey of Americans with Disabilities

CONFERENCES
Community Partnership Program Statewide Conference (various states during the year)
Emergency Preparedness Initiative Conference, Sept. 2004
That All May Worship Conferences (held throughout the year across the nation)

"Slight improvements in quality of life for people with disabilities over the last four years have still left them far behind most other Americans, says a survey released Thursday by the National Organization on Disability. The gap between the disabled and others shrank in five areas: employment, high school graduation, attendance at religious services, eating out and satisfaction with life. Both progress by those with disabilities and slippage by others played a part in closing the gap. However, there was little change in how far those with disabilities lag behind others in health care, socializing, transportation and income."

(*The Atlanta Journal and Constitution,* June 25, 2004)

National Parks Conservation Association

Established in 1919

DIRECTOR

Thomas C. Kiernan, president. Kiernan became chief executive officer of the National Parks Conservation Association in January 1998 following three years as president of the Audubon Society of New Hampshire. He applied his expertise in clean air and water to prior positions as well, including the Oregon Department of Environmental Quality, EPA Office of Air and Radiation, and Arthur Andersen & Co. Kiernan was co-founder of the Rocky Mountain Outdoor Center, CO. He holds an M.B.A from Stanford University and a B.A. in environmental computer modeling from Dartmouth College.

BOARD OF DIRECTORS

Gretchen Long, chair; Wilson, WY
Steven A. Denning, vice chair; Greenwich, CT
Thomas F. Secunda, vice chair; Croton-on-Hudson, NY
H. William Walter, vice chair; Minneapolis, MN
Robert B. Keiter, secretary; Salt Lake City, UT
Dwight C. Minton, treasurer; Princeton, NJ
William G. Watson, past chair; Wichita, KS
Susan Babcock; Pasadena, CA
James E. Bostic Jr.; Atlanta, GA
Jessica H. Catto; San Antonio, TX
David M. Doyle; Newport Coast, CA
Michael V. Finley; Atlanta, GA
Denis P. Galvin; McLean, VA
Vincent E. Hoenigman; San Francisco, CA
Mary H. Johnson; Gray, TN
Dennis Takahashi Kelso; Capitola, CA
Karl Komatsu; Fort Worth, TX
Michael J. Kowalski; Butler, NJ
Robert Leggett; Great Falls, VA
Pamela A. Matson; Palo Alto, CA
Glenn Padnick; Beverly Hills, CA
Audrey Peterman; Atlanta, GA
L. E. Simmons; Houston, TX
Dolph C. Simons Jr.; Lawrence, KS
Theodore M. Smith; Cambridge, MA
Gene T. Sykes; Los Angeles, CA
W. Richard West; Washington, DC

SCOPE

Members: 300,000
Branches/chapters: NPCA works in communities and national parks through seven regional offices and four field offices, in addition to the national office in Washington, DC: Alaska Regional Office in Anchorage, AK; Mid-Atlantic Regional Office in Washington, DC; Northern Rockies Regional Office in Helena, MT; Glacier Field Office in Whitefish, MT; Grand Teton Field Office in Jackson, WY; Pacific Northwest Regional Office in Seattle, WA; Pacific Regional Office in

CONTACT INFORMATION

1300 19th Street, NW, Suite 300
Washington, DC 20036
Phone: (202) 223-6722 • *Fax:* (202) 659-0650
Toll-free: (800) 628-7275
General E-mail: npca@npca.org • *Web site:* www.eparks.org

Communications Director: Linda M. Rancourt
(202) 223-6722
Human Resources Director: Karen Allen
(202) 223-6722 • kallen@npca.org

PURPOSE: Founded in 1919, the nonpartisan National Parks Conservation Association is America's only private, nonprofit advocacy organization dedicated solely to protecting, preserving, and enhancing the National Park System for present and future generations.

CURRENT CONCERNS: Air pollution in parks • Park funding and management • Park-related legislation and policies • Protection of park wildlife • Transportation

METHOD OF OPERATION: Awards program • Coalition forming • Congressional testimony • Congressional voting analysis • Direct action • E-mail alerts • Grassroots organizing • Information clearinghouse • Internet (electronic bulletin boards and Web site) • Internships • Legislative/regulatory monitoring (federal) • Litigation • Lobbying (federal, grassroots) • Media outreach • Participation in regulatory proceedings (federal) • Performance ratings/report cards • Polling

SPECIFIC PROGRAMS/INITIATIVES: State of the Parks® • Business Plan Initiative

Effectiveness and Political Orientation

"Olympic National Park is so pressed for cash that officials plan to close the visitors center in Forks and eliminate most seasonal rangers this summer, and they agreed to keep the popular Hurricane Ridge Road open in April only after the city of Port Angeles promised to help foot the snowplow bill.

"The plans were brought to light by the National Parks and Conservation Association (NPCA), a national-parks advocacy group, which is releasing a report today suggesting that chronic money shortages and rising expenses are forcing park superintendents across the country to make painful decisions on how to spend their money this year.

"The report contends that officials overseeing the nation's 387 parks or historic sites are freezing jobs and cutting programs and asking staffers to make do with less a trend some parks officials in Washington state reluctantly con-

Oakland, CA; Central Valley Field Office in Fresno, CA; California Desert Field Office in Joshua Tree, CA; Southeast Regional Office in Knoxville, TN; and Sun Coast Regional Office in Hollywood, FL
Affiliates: None

STAFF
88 total—72 professional; 16 support; plus 2 part-time professional; 4 interns

TAX STATUS
501(c)(3)

FINANCES
Budget: 2003—$20.7 million; 2002—$21.4 million

FUNDING SOURCES
Contributions, 63%; grants, 15%; special events, 5%; marketing income, 5%; bequests, 5%; membership dues, 4%; investment and other income, 3%

PAC
None

EMPLOYMENT
Job opportunities are listed at NPCA's Web site (www.eparks.org/jobs) and the MELDI (Minority Environmental Leadership Development Institute) Web site (sitemaker.umich.edu/meldi/employment_opportunities). Positions are offered in the areas of administration, government relations, accounting, customer service, grassroots organizing, communications, and other fields. NPCA accepts resumes and applications only in response to specific openings; contact information for application materials varies by position.

INTERNSHIPS
Paid and unpaid internships are offered in communications, government affairs, development, and programs. Duration of internships, hours required, and eligibility requirements vary by position. Internship opportunities are posted at NPCA's Web site (www.eparks.org.jobs), appropriate trade Web sites, and colleges and universities. Application deadlines are rolling. The internship coordinator is Karen Allen, senior director, Human Resources, 1300 19th Street, NW, Suite 300, Washington, DC 20036. Phone: (202) 223-6722. Fax: (202) 659-0650. E-mail: kallen@npca.org.

NEWSLETTERS
National Parks (quarterly magazine)
ParkLines (weekly E-mail)

PUBLICATIONS
Alaska's National Parks: Conflict, Controversy, and Congress
Analysis and Recommendations for the National Park Service in Response to Vision Statement
Biodiversity in the National Parks: Looming Threats to America's Most Valued Plants and Animals

firmed seeing here. They're hoping visitors won't notice much of a difference this year. . . .

"NPCA doesn't dispute that the parks' loss of buying power has occurred over time. The group claims in its new report that the agency is losing valuable personnel. The number of full-time rangers nationwide dropped 16 percent from 1980 to about 1,539 in 2001 even as 60 million more people visited national parks. Since 1999, it has lost 172 interpreters.

"The group has been critical of President Bush, who made national parks a priority during his 2000 campaign and promised to put more money toward a multibillion-dollar backlog in park maintenance. The administration has, but the agency still struggles with operational issues."

(*The Seattle Times*, March 16, 2004)

"Citing a trio of common themes, the National Parks Conservation Association is releasing today its sixth annual list of the 10 most endangered national parks in the country.

"Inadequate funding, air pollution and policy decisions—including those allowing the use of snowmobiles and all-terrain vehicles—are the key issues facing the parks on this year's list, said Joy Oakes, mid-Atlantic regional director of the NPCA, an advocacy group.

" 'Funding is a critical and chronic issue throughout the national parks system,' she said. 'Its impacts ripple throughout the individual park and throughout the park system.'

"For every dollar the parks system needs to run smoothly, Oakes said, it receives about 67 cents from the federal government. It would take about $600 million annually to bridge the gap between what the system gets—its fiscal 2004 appropriation is $1.6 billion—and what it needs to maintain 388 national parks, Oakes said."

(*The Washington Post*, January 14, 2004)

"A coalition of environmental groups criticized Gov. Jeb Bush Thursday for the environmental achievement it once praised, the one he touts the most in his re-election campaign: restoration of the Everglades.

"Just two years ago, the Everglades Coalition gave Bush and his environmental chief, David Struhs, a Steward of the Everglades award.

"Now, the coalition says Bush is jeopardizing the $7.8-billion restoration plan. They say the state has refused to write tight rules to ensure that water goes to natural systems before it is used for agriculture and growth.

"The coalition includes 43 environmental groups, including the National Wildlife Federation, the Sierra Club, the National Audubon Society and the World Wildlife Fund.

" 'We'd like to give Gov. Bush a better grade for this,' said Mary Munson, director of the Suncoast region of the National Parks Conservation Association. 'It's not too late for him to be an environmental hero.' "

(*St. Petersburg Times* [Florida], October 11, 2002)

"In this fragile swath of the Everglades, the Bush administration delighted Florida environmentalists two weeks ago by backing a National Park Service plan to restrict access for swamp buggies and other off-road vehicles.

"In Yellowstone National Park, by contrast, the administration has infuriated environmentalists and many park rangers by abandoning a Park Service plan to ban snowmobiles. . . .

CONFERENCES

None

" 'Snowmobiles in Yellowstone arouse the interest of a national environmental audience, but they are not a defining political issue in states or regions near the park,' said Ron Tipton, senior vice president of the National Parks Conservation Association, a group chartered by Congress to advocate park preservation. 'Florida and the Everglades are different. It has taken the administration nearly a year, but they seem to have figured out the politics of environmentalism in South Florida.' "

(*The New York Times,* April 3, 2002)

"When President Bush rolls out the new federal budget a week from Monday, he'll be laying the ground work for a grassroots lobbying campaign in Colorado and a number of other states where national parks are highly popular.

"It's part of an aggressive plan developed in recent weeks by a coalition led by the National Parks Conservation Association. The organization is one of the few big environmental groups that didn't oppose Gale Norton's bid to become interior secretary.

"Now, it's using some of the chips it gained with that maneuver to pressure Bush to make good on his promise to boost spending for parks. And Colorado, home to the highly popular Rocky Mountain National Park, is one of the states that the coalition has selected as a battleground to pressure lawmakers to come to the aid of the park system.

"It's not a cause that's unpopular either at the White House or in Congress. Indeed, as Ronald J. Tipton, senior vice president of the parks conservation association recalled last week, the president has said he wants to spend upwards of $5 billion over the next five years to reduce the backlog of needed improvements to national parks. 'They will not ask for less money,' he said.

"What Tipton wants to do is make certain that lawmakers share in Bush's enthusiasm for parks. The coalition—'not just a bunch of green organizations,' as Tipton puts it—has targeted about 50 lawmakers, many of them conservative Western Republicans, to press their call for a $280 million increase in park operating funds this year."

(*The Denver Post,* January 27, 2002)

National Partnership for Women & Families

Established in 1971

DIRECTOR

Debra L. Ness, president. For more than two decades, Ness has been an ardent advocate for the principles of fairness and social justice. As executive vice president of the National Partnership for Women & Families for 13 years, Ness played a leading role in positioning the organization as a powerful and effective advocate for today's women and families. Ness is a former national field director for NARAL Pro-Choice America. She currently serves on the board of directors for a number of health quality organizations and commissions, including the National Committee for Quality Assurance (NCQA), the National Quality Forum (NQF) and the Leapfrog Group. She earned a B.S. degree from Drew University and a M.S. at the Columbia University School of Social Work.

BOARD OF DIRECTORS

Debra L. Ness, president, Washington, DC
Ellen R. Malcolm, chair; president, EMILY's List, Washington, DC
Pauline A. Schneider, vice chair; Hunton & Williams, Washington, DC
Nikki Heidepriem, secretary; Heidepriem & Mager, Washington, DC
Chris Sale, treasurer; Inter-American Development Bank, Washington, DC
Linda A. Bergthold; Watson Wyatt Worldwide, Los Angeles, CA
Nancy L. Buc; Buc & Beardsley, Washington, DC
Lisa Caputo; Women & Co., NY
Ranny Cooper; Weber Shandwick, Washington, DC
Linda D. Fienberg; NASD Dispute Resolution, Inc., Washington, DC
Vincent Kerr; Uniprise, UnitedHealth Group, Hartford, CT
Patricia King; Georgetown University Law Center, Washington, DC
R. May Lee; NY
Robin A. Lenhardt; Georgetown University Law Center, Washington, DC
Cheryl D. Mills; New York University, NY
Arnold Milstein; William M. Mercer, Inc., San Francisco, CA
Richard North Patterson; San Francisco, CA
Sheli Z. Rosenberg; Equity Group Investment, Chicago, IL
Judith Scott; SEIU, Washington, DC
Sally Susman; Estee Lauder Cos., New York, NY
Kay Kahler Vose; Porter Novelli, Washington, DC

SCOPE

Members: 2,500
Branches/chapters: None
Affiliates: None

CONTACT INFORMATION

1875 Connecticut Avenue, NW, Suite 650, Washington, DC 20009
Phone: (202) 986-2600 • *Fax:* (202) 986-2539
General E-mail: info@nationalpartnership.org •
Web site: www.nationalpartnership.org

Communications Director: Myra Clark-Siegel
(202) 986-2600 • info@nationalpartnership.org
Human Resources Director: Information unavailable

PURPOSE: "Dedicated to improving the lives of women and families through public education and advocacy, the National Partnership promotes fairness in the workplace, quality health care, and policies that help women and men meet the dual demands of work and family."

CURRENT CONCERNS: Affirmative action • Caregiving • Civil rights • Equal Employment Opportunity enforcement • Equal pay • Family/medical leave • Genetic discrimination • Health care and health insurance • Medical privacy • Paid leave/family leave benefits • Patient's rights • Pregnancy discrimination • Reproductive rights • Sexual harassment • Welfare/low-income workers

METHOD OF OPERATION: Coalition forming • Conferences/seminars • Congressional testimony • Internet (E-mail alerts and Web site) • Legislative/regulatory monitoring (federal and state) • Library/information clearinghouse • Litigation • Lobbying (federal, state, and grassroots) • Media outreach • Participation in regulatory proceedings (federal) • Research • Speakers program

Effectiveness and Political Orientation

"With the economy uncertain and many companies looking to keep down costs and pare their employment rolls, growing numbers of workers are filing charges of pregnancy discrimination.

"Lawyers specializing in labor law as well as leaders of women's advocacy groups around the country say they have detected an increase in pregnancy discrimination cases in recent years. And at the federal level, claims of discriminatory treatment during pregnancy filed with the Equal Employment Opportunity Commission have increased 39 percent over the last 10 years, to 4,714 in 2002. That is a tiny fraction of the number of working women, but Jocelyn C. Frye, director of legal and public policy for the National Partnership for Women and Families, a nonprofit advocacy group for women in the workplace, said that this was because pregnancy discrimination cases rarely reach the federal level. Many complaints are handled by state agencies, settled or simply dropped.

" 'Most women are not inclined to go to court, especially with a baby coming,' she said. Even so, the number of women calling her organization for

STAFF
29 total

TAX STATUS
501(c)(3)

FINANCES
Revenue: 2002—$3.6 million

FUNDING SOURCES
Foundations, 54%; individuals, 23%; corporate donations, 4%; special events and other, 19%

PAC
None

EMPLOYMENT
Open positions are posted at www.national-partnership.org.

INTERNSHIPS
Information about internships and fellowships is available at www.nationalpartnership.org. Responsibilities, candidate qualifications, and application deadlines vary by position. Internships are available in the areas of Action Council and membership, annual luncheon, work and family, workplace fairness, and communications. Internships are unpaid but available for course credit. Fall and spring interns work 10 to 20 hours per week; summer interns generally work full-time. To apply, submit letter of interest, resume, writing sample, transcripts, and references to National Partnership for Women & Families, Volunteer Internship Program, 1875 Connecticut Avenue, NW, Suite 650, Washington, DC 20009. Specify internship area(s) of interest.

Unpaid Law clerk internships are also available in the Work and Family Program, Workplace Fairness Program, and Health Care Program. Students may receive course credit or are encouraged to seek fellowship funding from their school. Fall and spring internships are available; summer interns generally work full-time for 8 to 10 weeks. Application deadlines are March 15th for summer, July 15th for fall, and November 15th for spring. Submit letter of interest, resume, writing sample, transcripts, and references to National Partnership, Law Clerk Internship Program, 1875 Connecticut Avenue, NW, Suite 650, Washington, DC 20009. Specify internship area(s) of interest.

NEWSLETTERS
National Partnership News

PUBLICATIONS
Ask Your Candidates About Work/Family Issues
Balancing Acts: Work/Family Issues on Prime-Time TV
Detours on the Road to Employment: Obstacles Facing Low Income Women
Family Leave Benefits: A Menu of Policy Models for State and Local Policy Leaders
Guide to the Family & Medical Leave Act: Questions and Answers

information on how to handle discrimination has increased over the last two years, she said."

(*The New York Times,* September 14, 2003)

"The U.S. Supreme Court last week ruled that nearly 5 million state government workers are protected by a federal law that guarantees they won't lose their jobs if they take limited time off to deal with family medical emergencies. This 'is a tremendous victory for working families and a welcome affirmation that Congress has the power to outlaw gender bias,' says Judith Lichtman of the National Partnership for Women & Families."

(*U.S. News and World Report,* June 9, 2003)

"It was the Labor Department's 1996 ruling that counted the common cold, flu, earaches, headaches and other routine ailments as 'serious health conditions' that put many employers in a swivet over benefits offered under the Family and Medical Leave Act.

"The business community, fearing employees would be absent from work for minor ailments, geared up almost immediately to press Congress and the Labor Department for 'technical corrections' to the rules.

"The law, passed a decade ago, provides workers at companies with more than 50 employees up to 12 weeks of unpaid leave and job protection for the birth or adoption of a child, to care for an immediate family member, or to tend to a serious health condition. Businesses felt so strongly about the need to 'fix' some of the rules that they created the FMLA Technical Corrections Coalition in 1997, and about 300 companies and trade associations joined. . . . The Clinton administration, which viewed the law as a signature piece of legislation, was not disposed to change the rules. In surveys done for the Labor Department, Clinton regulators insisted that companies were not finding it onerous to comply. A Labor survey in 2000, for example, said millions of workers have taken the leave, using it 'infrequently and for relatively short periods of time.'

"The Bush administration has been more receptive to industry complaints and is talking to business groups, AARP, unions and women's advocacy groups about what works and doesn't work with the regulations. . . .

"Judith L. Lichtman, president of the National Partnership for Women & Families, said the problems employers are complaining about are of 'questionable merit.'

" 'If the Bush administration wants to think of itself as family-friendly, it should put its policies where its rhetoric is—expand on existing FMLA rights,' Lichtman said."

(*The Washington Post,* February 4, 2003)

"The National Partnership for Women & Families, a national nonprofit organization that promotes workplace flexibility, says leave provisions that made elder care more manageable for busy workers have become increasingly important. According to the group, 25 percent of all U.S. households currently provide informal care for an older relative, and those numbers are expected to increase significantly."

(*The Boston Globe,* June 23, 2002)

CONFERENCES
National Partnership Luncheon (annual luncheon usually held in June, Washington, DC)

"The Bush administration is pressing ahead with a plan to cover unborn children under a public health-insurance program, a move that abortion-rights groups say is designed to set a legal precedent for defining fetuses as people.

"The Department of Health and Human Services plans to propose a regulation in coming weeks allowing states to extend coverage under the State Children's Health Insurance Program to 'children not yet born.' HHS officials said the program is meant to cover more prenatal care immediately, nothing more.

"S-CHIP, as it is known, covers low-income children under age 19 whose families aren't eligible for Medicaid, the state-federal health-insurance program for the poor. Almost 11 million women of child-bearing age lack health insurance, HHS estimates.

"Opponents of the change said it is unnecessary. States can expand S-CHIP to cover prenatal care by applying for a federal waiver, as New Jersey and Rhode Island have done. In addition, states can offer prenatal care for low-income women through Medicaid. 'There is no reason to do it in this way if the goal is to cover pregnant women,' said Laurie Rubiner of the National Partnership for Women and Families, a nonprofit advocacy group based here."

(*The Wall Street Journal*, February 1, 2002)

National People's Action (NPA)

Established in 1971

DIRECTOR

Inez Killingsworth, Brenda LaBlanc, and **Emira Palacios,** co-chairs. Killingsworth became involved with community groups on Cleveland's East Side in the early 1970s, including being named president of the East Side Organizing Project. In July 2002 she helped bring about an historic Community Reinvestment Agreement with Charter One Bank, after a recent national study had found that Cleveland-based Charter One was making only 7% of its loans in minority census tracts. She is a national spokesperson for NPA on predatory lending.

LaBlanc has worked with the Des Moines Citizens for Community and NPA for decades to make banks accountable to neighborhood residents, and to strengthen and preserve the Community Reinvestment Act. Over the years, she has built strong relationships with bankers, regulators and community residents. She was instrumental in making Des Moines one of the first cities in the nation to have its own CRA agreement, and her efforts have helped secure more than 70 million dollars in home loans in Des Moines low-income neighborhoods.

Palacios has been involved as a community leader with Wichita, Kansas' Sunflower Community Action since October 2000. Since then, Palacios has become a tireless advocate for immigrants' rights and community improvement. On the national level she is leading the fight for the Student Adjustment Act, a piece of federal legislation that would give undocumented students access to higher education.

BOARD OF DIRECTORS
None

SCOPE
Members: NPA is a coalition of 302 grassroots neighborhood groups from across the country.
Branches/chapters: None
Affiliates: None

STAFF
Volunteer organization

TAX STATUS
501(c)3

FINANCES
None

FUNDING SOURCES
Information unavailable

PAC
None

CONTACT INFORMATION

810 North Milwaukee Avenue, Chicago, IL 60622
Phone: (312) 243-3038 • *Fax:* (312) 243-7044
General E-mail: npa@npa-us.org • *Web site:* www.npa-us.org

Communications Director: Tracy Van Slyke
(312) 243-3038
Human Resources Director: None

PURPOSE: "National People's Action is a multiracial/ethnic, inter-generational, nonpartisan coalition of hundreds of local community organizations that volunteer their time to make communities throughout the U.S. safer, healthier and more stable environments."

CURRENT CONCERNS: Affordable housing • Community Reinvestment Act • Education • Family farm issues • Immigrant rights • Job training and employment • Neighborhood safety • Predatory lending • Youth

METHOD OF OPERATION: Coalition forming • Conferences/seminars • Congressional testimony • Demonstrations • Direct action • Grassroots organizing • Internet (Web site) • Legislative monitoring (federal and state) • Lobbying (federal and state) • Local/municipal affairs • Media outreach • Participation in regulatory proceedings (federal and state)

Effectiveness and Political Orientation

"Springtime in the nation's capital brings cherry blossoms, tourists, and this year, swarms of protesters to the home of White House adviser Karl Rove.

" 'We don't wait around, we go straight to the people in power,' said Tracy Van Slyke, communications officer for National People's Action, an advocacy group based in Chicago.

"The group visits Washington each year for its national conference, where members meet with lawmakers and agency officials and stage demonstrations to call attention to their issues. . . .

"More than a dozen yellow school buses filled with demonstrators paid a house call to Rove on Sunday afternoon. The boisterous group gathered in the yard of his tony northwest Washington home and sent a delegate to knock on the door.

"They were there to highlight what they termed Bush administration foot-dragging on the Development, Relief and Education for Alien Minors Act, or DREAM. The bill, now languishing in the Senate, would allow young immigrants who have lived at least five years in this country to apply for legal residency after they graduate from high school."

(*The Houston Chronicle,* March 30, 2004)

"Citing excessive default rates on government-insured home loans—particularly in low-income and minority urban neighborhoods—a coalition of housing advocates is demanding that the Department of Housing and Urban Development turn up the heat on lenders who put people in homes they can't afford, and don't do enough to keep them there.

"Despite its responsibility to borrowers, the Federal Housing Administration 'continues to do business' with the worst lenders, with the result that too many families lose their homes, National People's Action alleged when it released a study it says documents high default rates in 22 major cities.

" 'We need HUD to truly enforce' its system for monitoring and terminating lenders with inordinately high default rates, said the NPA's chairwoman, Inez Killingsworth.

"NPA also called for similar programs to monitor real estate agents and appraisers who are associated with a high level of defaults and who are part of what it terms 'the three-headed monster' that persuades buyers to purchase poorly maintained houses with inflated values.

"The study was done by the National Training and Information Center, a nonprofit resource center in Chicago for grassroots community groups. It found that, between 1996 and 2000, default rates were higher in the low-income census tracts of 21 of the 22 cities surveyed than in middle-income tracts.

"It also found that defaults were greater in minority census tracts than in white census tracts in 19 cities."

(*The Boston Globe,* June 9, 2002)

"Emboldened by the newly empowered Democratic majority in the Senate, the family farm movement has launched a national campaign to block the confirmation of President Bush's nominee for the Agriculture Department's undersecretary for rural development because of his advocacy of corporate megafarms.

"Thomas C. Dorr, a prominent Republican fundraiser, farmer and business executive in western Iowa, had already come under fire last month from black lawmakers and civil rights groups for comments that seemed to suggest a link between the economic success of three Iowa farm counties and their lack of ethnic and religious diversity.

"Now more than 160 farm groups and their allies in the labor, environmental, civil rights and consumer movements have petitioned Sen. Tom Harkin (D-Iowa), the new chairman of the Senate Agriculture Committee, to block Dorr's confirmation. They say Dorr should be rejected not only because of his controversial statements about ethnic uniformity and prosperity but also because he has advocated a farm system that favors huge corporate agribusinesses at the expense of family farms. . . .

"The coalition petitioning Harkin includes FARM AID, United Farm Workers of America, the National Campaign for Sustainable Agriculture, National Farmers Organization, National Catholic Rural Life Conference and National People's Action."

(*The Washington Post,* June 15, 2001)

" 'The numbers are astounding,' said Judy Ramirez of East Side PRIDE, a coalition of block clubs and community groups. 'What we have is an abandoned building crisis in Buffalo.'

"A recent survey by the coalition found hundreds of abandoned buildings in the vicinity of eight schools on the East Side. . . .

"While most of the houses are boarded up, dozens of others are open and accessible. And with that comes the danger of young children wandering in and getting hurt—or worse, a stranger pulling them in. . . .

"National People's Action, a Chicago-based neighborhood advocacy group, has followed the abandoned housing issue nationwide and believes Buffalo has one of the most serious problems in the country.

" 'I've talked to people in other cities and even they are surprised by the large number of abandoned houses in Buffalo,' said Kim Harman of National People's Action."

(Buffalo News, January 17, 2001)

National Rifle Association of America (NRA)

Established in 1871

DIRECTOR

Wayne R. LaPierre Jr., executive vice president. Prior to being named executive vice president of the National Rifle Association (NRA) in 1991, LaPierre was executive director of the NRA Institute for Legislative Action, the NRA's lobbying arm. He served in this position from 1986 to 1991. LaPierre began his career with the NRA in 1978 as a state liaison and was named director of state and local affairs in 1979. In 1980 he became director of federal affairs.

BOARD OF DIRECTORS

Kayne B. Robinson, president
Sandra S. Froman, 1st vice president
John C Sigler, 2nd vice president
Wayne LaPierre, executive vice president
Chris W. Cox, executive director, Institute for Legislative Action
Craig D. Sandler, executive director, General Operations
Edward J. Land, secretary
Wilson H. Phillips, treasurer
Plus 76 additional board members

SCOPE

Members: 4 million
Branches/chapters: None
Affiliates: NRA Foundation, a 501(c)(3) organization, and NRA Institute for Legislative Action (NRA-ILA)

STAFF

Information unavailable

TAX STATUS

501(c)(4)

FINANCES

Information unavailable

FUNDING SOURCES

Contributions; membership dues; publication sales

PAC

Political Victory Fund

PAC CONTRIBUTIONS 2002

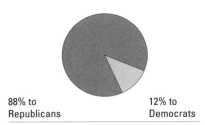

88% to Republicans

12% to Democrats

CONTACT INFORMATION

11250 Waples Mill Road, Fairfax, VA 22030
Phone: (703) 267-1000 • *Fax:* (703) 267-3918
General E-mail: ila-contact@nrahq.org •
Web site: www.nra.org and www.nraila.org

Communications Director: Kelly Hobbs, public affairs
(703) 267-1000 • KHobbs@nrahq.org
Human Resources Director: Information unavailable

PURPOSE: "The purpose and objectives of the NRA are: (1) to protect and defend the Constitution of the United States, especially with reference to the inalienable right of the individual American citizen guaranteed by such Constitution to acquire, possess, transport, carry, transfer ownership of, and enjoy the right to use arms, in order that the people may always be in a position to exercise their legitimate individual rights of self-preservation and defense of family, person, and property, as well as to serve effectively in the appropriate militia for the common defense of the Republic and individual liberty of its citizens; 2) to promote public safety, law and order, and the national defense; 3) to train members of law enforcement agencies, the armed forces, the militia, and people of good repute in marksmanship and in the safe handling and efficient use of small arms; 4) to foster and promote the shooting sports, including the advancement of amateur competitions in marksmanship at the local, state, regional, national, and international levels; and 5) to promote hunter safety, and to promote and defend hunting as a shooting sport and as a viable necessary method of fostering the propagation, growth, conservation, and wise use of our renewable wildlife resources."

CURRENT CONCERNS: Federal, state, and local legislation protecting the rights of law-abiding gun owners • Hunting restrictions • National campaign of firearms safety and training • Sportsmen's issues • Wilderness and park hunting

METHOD OF OPERATION: Advertisements • Awards program • Campaign contributions • Coalition forming • Conferences/seminars • Congressional testimony • Congressional voting analysis • Demonstrations • Direct action • Electoral politics • Films/video/audiotapes • Grantmaking • Grassroots organizing • Information clearinghouse • Initiative/referendum campaigns • International activities • Internet (e-mail alerts and Web site) • Legal assistance • Legislative/regulatory monitoring (federal and state) • Litigation • Lobbying (federal, state, and grassroots) • Local/municipal affairs • Media outreach • Participation in regulatory proceedings (federal and state) • Performance ratings • Polling • Product merchandising • Research • Scholarships • Shareholder resolutions • Speakers program • Television and radio production • Training and technical assistance • Voter registration

Open positions are posted at www.nrahq.org/
careers/jobs.asp. E-mail resumes, cover letters, and salary requirements to careers@
nrahq.org; fax to (703) 267-3938; or mail to
NRA, 11250 Waples Mills Road, Fairfax, VA
22030, Attn: Human Resources.

Resumes are entered into our database.
Due to the volume of resumes that we receive,
we are unable to respond personally to each
one individually. Representatives from human
resources will contact candidates whose skills
are a match for open positions.

Job seekers who would like to work for
National Rifle Association but do not see positions that match their skills are encouraged to
send their resumes. The National Rifle
Association is an employment-at-will
employer.

INTERNSHIPS
Information unavailable

NEWSLETTERS
ILA Grassroots Alert (online weekly)

PUBLICATIONS
American Hunter (monthly)
American Rifleman (monthly)
America's First Freedom (monthly)
NRA InSights (monthly)
Shooting Illustrated (monthly)
Shooting Sports USA (monthly)
Woman's Outlook (monthly)

CONFERENCES
NRA Annual Meetings & Exhibits
Local meetings and training sessions on gun
  use and safety

Effectiveness and Political Orientation

"An effort to pass a bill in the Senate that would have shielded gun makers and sellers from lawsuits related to gun violence collapsed Tuesday after gun-control advocates loaded the measure with two amendments that turned the bill's sponsors against it.

"The bill was a top priority for the National Rifle Assn. But before the final vote, gun control advocates successfully proposed amendments to extend the federal ban on assault weapons and to tighten background checks for sales at gun shows.

"Just before the final vote, the NRA told its Senate allies that it could no longer support the bill, which had 54 sponsors as the day began. The chief sponsor, Sen. Larry E. Craig (R-Idaho), then stunned colleagues by urging them to vote against his own bill.

"With both sides of the issue now opposed to the bill, the vote to kill it was 90 to 8. 'I've never seen anything quite like this,' said an amazed Sen. John McCain (R-Ariz.) after the final vote. Sen. Charles E. Schumer (D-N.Y.), a leader of the gun control forces, joked that the vote would jeopardize his 0% favorability rating from the NRA.

"In a joint statement, Wayne R. LaPierre, the NRA's executive vice president, and Chris W. Cox, the NRA's chief lobbyist: 'While we will continue to work to save the U.S. firearms industry, we have said from the start that we would not allow this bill to become a vehicle for added restrictions on the law-abiding people of America.' "

(*The Los Angeles Times,* March 3, 2004)

"Costly legal, legislative and political battles in the last decade have left the National Rifle Association with a $100 million deficit, reopening a bitter debate within the group about how it manages its money.

"In the past decade the group's efforts have helped Republicans win the White House and Congress and led to laws in more than 30 states banning lawsuits against gun manufacturers. In the last year the N.R.A. helped pay for a losing legal battle against campaign finance legislation, which the Supreme Court upheld this month.

"But through many of those years, according to Internal Revenue Service and N.R.A. records, the organization spent more than it took in.

"Even in 2000, when gun owners helped elect George W. Bush as president, pushing N.R.A. membership to a 10-year high, expenses outstripped revenues by $20.4 million, according to I.R.S. filings.

" 'The victories we have delivered have been costly, cutting deeply into the N.R.A.'s budgets,' Wayne R. LaPierre Jr., the group's executive vice president and chief executive, wrote in an N.R.A. magazine, *America's 1st Freedom,* in October. 'Winning takes millions of dollars beyond what individual members' dues cover. Today, if we were faced with a full-blown legislative assault, we simply would not have the war chest.' "

(*The New York Times,* December 21, 2003)

"It's not every day the National Rifle Association and the American Civil Liberties Union are outraged by the same Supreme Court decision.

"The two organizations are often used to represent opposite poles of American politics, the gun-toting right and the liberal left. But both groups hated yesterday's unexpectedly broad ruling by the court to uphold the major provisions of the McCain-Feingold campaign finance law. . . .

"Under the ruling, groups wishing to use television ads to criticize—or even mention—federal candidates in the decisive months of an election year must comply with an array of regulations before they can say their piece. . . .

"Wayne LaPierre, head of the NRA, called the ruling 'the most significant change in the First Amendment since the Alien and Sedition Acts of 1798, which tried to make it a crime to criticize a member of Congress.'

" 'This whole thing from the start has been an inside deal among politicians to stop criticism, whether it comes from us or from the Sierra Club,' LaPierre said.

" 'Well, we're going to be heard,' he added, 'and they're going to be surprised how loud we're going to be heard.' "

(*The Washington Post,* December 11, 2003)

"The National Rifle Association's newest publication, a 75-page magazine written for its growing female membership, has been such a hit since it premiered last January within the organization that Wal-Mart began carrying it on nearly 10 percent of its newsstands nationwide this month. And over the next two months the nation's largest retailer will expand its sales, featuring *Outlook* in more than half of their 2,900 stores. . . .

"NRA officials say *Outlook* grew out of a demand by its female membership, a population that is growing, although the organization says it has no exact statistics. . . .

"There are four million dues-paying members of the NRA in the United States (annual membership cost $35). . . . Encouraging women to become active participants is part of a strategy of investing in its future. . . .

"The magazine runs on advertising from companies like Winchester Ammunition, Kimber pistols, and Taurus revolvers—companies that signed on before they knew the magazine could have exponential reach outside the new membership of the NRA. Wal-Mart is the world's largest single newsstand, and 70 percent of the magazines the chain sells are bought by women. Suddenly, the newsstand price of $3.59 could mean a nice bump in profits for the publishing wing of the NRA."

(*The Boston Globe,* November 28, 2003)

"It's hard to imagine a more motley crew: the National Rifle Association, the National Organization of Women, the U.S. Conference of Catholic Bishops and dozens of other groups of all stripes and political persuasion. Time was, the only thing they could all agree on was that the sky is blue. Then along came an issue with remarkable powers to get them all working together: the prospect of big media companies growing even bigger.

"Their forceful opposition to Big Media persuaded the House of Representatives last week to, in effect, overturn a recent ruling by the Federal Communications Commission that would have relaxed media ownership rules, allowing companies like Viacom and News Corp. to own TV stations that reach 45 percent of the national audience, up from 35 percent. If the House's vote becomes law, it could mean Viacom and News Corp. will have to sell some stations to get back under the cap."

(*Newsweek,* August 4, 2003)

National Right to Life Committee

Established in 1973

DIRECTOR
Wanda Franz, president. Franz is professor emerita in the West Virginia University Department of Child Development & Family Studies. She holds a B.A. from the University of Washington; an M.S. from West Virginia University, and a Ph.D. from West Virginia University.

BOARD OF DIRECTORS
Geline B. Williams, chair

SCOPE
Members: Information unavailable
Branches/chapters: More than 3,000 local chapters
Affiliates: National Right to Life Committee Educational Trust Fund (501(c)(3)); National Right to Life Conventions, Inc.; Horatio R. Storer Foundation, Inc.; 50 state affiliates

STAFF
53 total

TAX STATUS
501(c)(4)

FINANCES
Revenue: 2002—$15 million

FUNDING SOURCES
Direct public support, 97%; program service revenue, 1%; interest on savings and temporary cash investments, 1%; other, 1%

PAC
NRL Political Action Committee

PAC CONTRIBUTIONS 2002

98% to
Republicans

2% to
Democrats

EMPLOYMENT
Information unavailable

INTERNSHIPS
NRLC offers college student internships throughout the academic year and through the NRLC Summer Internship Program. Positions are available within several departments of NRLC. To request an application, send e-mail to students@nrlc.org.

CONTACT INFORMATION
512 10th Street, NW, Washington, DC 20004
Phone: (202) 626-8800
General E-mail: nrlc@nrlc.org • *Web site:* www.nrlc.org

Communications Director: Kristi Hayes, assistant to media relations (202) 626-8825 • khayes@nrlc.org
Human Resources Director: Information unavailable

PURPOSE: "The ultimate goal of the National Right to Life Committee is to restore legal protection to innocent human life. The primary interest of the National Right to Life Committee and its members has been the abortion controversy; however, it is also concerned with related matters of medical ethics which relate to the right to life issues of euthanasia and infanticide."

CURRENT CONCERNS: Abortion • Assisted suicide • Euthanasia • Human cloning • Medicare • Partial-birth abortion • RU-486

METHOD OF OPERATION: Advertisements • Awards program • Campaign contributions • Conferences/seminars • Congressional testimony • Congressional voting analysis • Demonstrations • Electoral politics • Internet (e-mail alerts and Web site) • Grassroots organizing • Information clearinghouse • Legislative/regulatory monitoring (federal and state) • Litigation • Lobbying (federal and state) • Media outreach • Polling • Voting records

Effectiveness and Political Orientation

"Even before President Bush signs into law the first federal ban on an abortion procedure in 30 years, social conservatives are moving on several other legislative and political fronts in their decades-long campaign to establish what they call the unborn's right to life.

"Their agenda for the next year: pass more bills to protect fetuses, stop human cloning and hinder abortions; confirm pending nominees who are sympathetic to the antiabortion movement to federal trial and appellate courts; and, with an eye to potential future Supreme Court vacancies, reelect Bush and expand the slender Republican Senate majority.

" 'We're on the offensive,' said Carol Tobias, political director for the National Right to Life Committee. 'I've been saying for many years that we're eventually going to win this battle and protect unborn children.'. . .

"Kate Michelman, president of NARAL Pro-Choice America, said antiabortion activists had seized the opportunity created this year by unified Republican rule in Washington.

" 'It's very rare that they have the presidency, the House and the Senate all under their control at the same time,' Michelman said. 'That's why they will push hard to continue to make legislative gains. If they remain in control of all three institutions, including the presidency, for the next five years, on

NEWSLETTERS
National Right to Life News (monthly)

PUBLICATIONS
None

CONFERENCES
NRLC Convention (annual)

the judicial front they will make enormous gains, and on the legislative front, it's open season.'"

(*The Los Angeles Times,* October 26, 2003)

". . . the nation's largest anti-abortion group."

(*The Houston Chronicle,* July 6, 2003)

"As the National Right to Life Committee's president kicked off the group's 30th annual convention Thursday morning, she alluded to a historic St. Louis legal case that represents the darkest period in the nation's history.

"Wanda Franz noted that the same institution that legalized abortion in 1973 had upheld the right to own slaves in the famous case of Dred Scott more than 100 years earlier. One day, she told the more than 300 people gathered in the ballroom of the Hyatt Regency St. Louis at Union Station, the nation will look back on the U.S. Supreme Court's acceptance of abortion with the same disbelief and shame that it feels when it reflects on its earlier approval of slavery.

"But as Franz and others in the anti-abortion movement compare the nation's current acceptance of abortion with that of slavery, the lack of African-Americans and other minorities among its ranks is glaring.

"Statistically, no group is more tied to abortion than the nation's minorities. A study by the Alan Guttmacher Institute in Washington shows that nearly 60 percent of all abortions performed annually are done on African-American, Hispanic and Asian women. Moreover, the abortion rates among African-American women are more than four times that of white women, and the rates among Hispanic and Asian women are more than twice that of white women.

"Franz and others at the convention say those numbers reflect plans by Planned Parenthood and other abortion providers to target minorities so as to limit their population. Planned Parenthood has said repeatedly that it does not target any particular race or ethnicity."

(*St. Louis Post-Dispatch,* July 4, 2003)

"Sequestered behind anonymous, locked doors, two powerhouse organizations located just blocks apart in downtown Washington have been engaged in a profound struggle over the nation's abortion laws for the past three decades. They have raised millions of dollars and signed up thousands of supporters, all moved by passion.

"As the landmark Supreme Court decision *Roe vs. Wade* turns 30 on Wednesday, the National Right to Life Committee and NARAL Pro-Choice America have become multimillion-dollar operations dedicated to either reversing or preserving the court's decision.

"'These national groups have been critical in helping to shape how Americans think about the issue of reproductive rights,' said Debra Dodson, a political scientist at the Center for American Women and Politics at Rutgers University in New Jersey. . . .

"It is difficult to discern the precise membership and budget of NARAL and National Right to Life, because each is an interlocking array of state and local chapters, non-profit educational groups, political action committees and other units. . . .

"National Right to Life is even more decentralized than NARAL; great power and money reside with its 50 state affiliates and 3,000 local chapters.

The group says it took in a total of about $15 million last year, spending $3.8 million on contributions to candidates."

(*Chicago Tribune,* January 22, 2003)

"President Bush, calling human life a 'sacred gift from our creator,' announced last night he would allow taxpayers' dollars to pay for limited research into stem cells, but he rejected a call from scientists for broader experimentation with human embryos. . . .

"Bush will permit federal money to finance research into a small number of existing stem-cell clusters. Such cell 'lines' have already been extracted from embryos and can regenerate indefinitely. However, Bush said, he will not allow federal money to pay for the study of stem cells derived from new embryos— even those created in fertility clinics that will otherwise be discarded. . . .

" 'While National Right to Life mourns the loss of life for those embryos from whom stem cell lines have already been derived, nothing the National Right to Life Committee or President Bush can do can restore the lives of those embryos who have already died,' said Laura Echevarria, a spokeswoman for the group."

(*The San Francisco Chronicle,* August 10, 2001)

National Taxpayers Union

Established in 1969

DIRECTOR

John Berthoud, president. Berthoud is former vice president of the Alexis de Tocqueville Institution and former legislative director for Tax and Fiscal Policy at American Legislative Exchange Council. He is currently a lecturer at George Washington University. He received a B.A. from Georgetown University, an M.A. in international affairs from Columbia University, and a Ph.D. in political economy from Yale University.

BOARD OF DIRECTORS

John Berthoud, president, National Taxpayers Union
David M. Stanley, chair, National Taxpayers Union and Iowans for Tax Relief
Edward D. Failor Sr., vice chair, National Taxpayers Union; president, Iowans for Tax Relief
James Dale Davidson, founder and chair emeritus, National Taxpayers Union; London-Washington Pub.
Jeff Boeyink, secretary, National Taxpayers Union; executive vice-president, Iowans for Tax Relief
Barbara Anderson; executive director, Citizens for Limited Taxation
Michael Aronstein; president, Commercial Materials, L.L.C.
J. Kenneth Blackwell; Ohio secretary of state
James Buchanan; professor, Center for the Study of Public Choice
James Clark; former Maryland state senator
Sol Erdman
Steve Forbes; Forbes Inc.
David Keating; senior counselor, National Taxpayers Union
Mike Riley; Taxpayers Network Inc.
Cloyd Robinson; vice chair, Iowans for Tax Relief
Jean Leu Stanley
John S. Thomas; E.A. Morris Charitable Foundation
Richard Vedder; Ohio University
Herbert A. Wilson
Curtin Winsor; Columbia Partners

SCOPE

Members: 350,000 individuals and small businesses
Branches/chapters: Allied with more than 500 independent state and local taxpayer groups across the country and affiliated with three groups: Iowans for Tax Relief, Nebraska Taxpayers for Freedom, and Arlington County (VA) Taxpayers Association. These three groups were formed and operate independently of NTU.

CONTACT INFORMATION

108 North Alfred Street, Alexandria, VA 22314
Phone: (703) 683-5700 • *Fax:* (703) 683-5722
General E-mail: ntu@ntu.org • *Web site:* www.ntu.org

Communications Director: Pete Sepp
(703) 683-5700, pressguy@ntu.org
Human Resources Director: Douglas Frank, vice president for membership; (703) 683-5700, dfrank@ntu.org

PURPOSE: National Taxpayers Union (NTU) is a nonprofit, nonpartisan citizen group founded in 1969 to work for lower taxes, less wasteful spending, taxpayer rights, and accountable government at all levels. The NTU Foundation is the NTU's research and educational arm.

CURRENT CONCERNS: Alternative Minimum Tax reform/elimination • Balanced budget and tax limitation amendments to U.S. Constitution • Constitutional spending limits/voter approval requirements for tax increases at the state level • Entitlement reform, including personal savings accounts • Internet taxation • Litigation reform • Making permanent the 2001 and 2003 federal tax relief laws • Private/state alternatives to federal transportation policies • Reforming congressional pay and perks • Replacement of current tax system with single-rate consumption tax

METHOD OF OPERATION: Advertisements • Awards program • Coalition forming • Conferences/seminars • Congressional testimony • Congressional voting analysis • Demonstrations • Direct action • Educational foundation • Films/video/audiotapes • Grassroots organizing • Information clearinghouse • Initiative/referendum campaigns • International activities • Internet (databases, e-mail alerts, and Web site) • Internships • Legislative regulatory monitoring (federal and state) • Library services open to the public • Litigation • Lobbying (federal, state, and grassroots) • Local/municipal affairs • Media outreach • Participation in regulatory proceedings (federal and state) • Performance ratings • Polling • Research • Speakers program • Voting records

SPECIFIC PROGRAMS/INITIATIVES: Federal legislative campaigns for tax and spending reform • State campaigns against tax increases or in favor of tax limits

Effectiveness and Political Orientation

". . . a nonprofit organization committed to eliminating wasteful government spending. . . ."

(*St. Petersburg Times* [Florida], February 10, 2004)

Affiliates: National Taxpayers Union Foundation, the nonpartisan research arm of NTU [501(c)(3)].

STAFF

13 total—8 full-time professional (duties split with NTU Foundation); 5 full-time support; plus 1 part-time professional; 2–5 interns; volunteers

TAX STATUS

501(c)(4)

FINANCES

Budget: 2004—Approximately $3.5 million; 2003—Approximately $3.5 million; 2002—$3.2 million

FUNDING SOURCES

Donations from individuals, businesses, and private foundations, approximately 90%; rent, interest on investments, mailing list rental, and caging services, approximately 10%

PAC

National Taxpayers Union Campaign Fund

PAC CONTRIBUTIONS 2002

100% to Republicans

0% to Democrats

EMPLOYMENT

Administrative, policy analysis, and research positions are posted at the "Jobs" section of www.ntu.org. Check the details of each particular position for information on submitting resumes and other application materials.

INTERNSHIPS

Internships are offered in the areas of policy analysis, legislative research, basic media placement, and basic lobbying. Internships are paid, unless taken for academic credit. The duration of internship positions is flexible, although a minimum of six weeks is required. Hours are flexible; part-time hours are possible. Applicants must have at least one year of college completed, good research and writing skills, and interest in fiscal policy. Application deadlines are flexible, year-round. The internship coordinator is Jeff Dircksen, director of congressional analysis, NTU Foundation, 108 North Alfred Street, Alexandria, VA 22314. Phone: (703) 683-5700. Fax: (703) 683-5722. E-mail: ntu@ntu.org.

NEWSLETTERS

Capital Ideas (NTU Foundation's newsletter) (six times per year)
Dollars & Sense (NTU's member newsletter) (six times per year)

"Conservatives and other limited-government types are furious at President George W. Bush for his big-spending ways. . . .

"Those who dislike the trend have been vocal in their opposition. On Jan. 15, six right-leaning groups—including the Club for Growth, the National Taxpayers Union and Citizens Against Government Waste—announced that they had made a 'major break' with the Bush White House and the Republican-controlled Congress in response to budgeting that had driven discretionary spending up 27 percent in Bush's first three years in office."

(*The Washington Post*, February 8, 2004)

"Conservative groups yesterday delivered a scathing indictment of legislation to create a prescription drug benefit for elderly Americans, saying the bill was not only bad policy but politically dangerous for the Republicans who crafted the bill.

"Calling on Republican leaders and President George W. Bush to rethink their backing for the plan, a powerful coalition of 42 conservative groups said the bill did not do enough to curtail future spending on Medicare, the federal health insurance plan covering 40m people aged 65 years and over.

"The blast from the right came as House and Senate Republican leaders raced to put the finishing touches on the legislation, hoping to rush it to the floors of both chambers and trying to outrun the avalanche of criticism that has grown since the Medicare deal was reached last weekend.

" 'Congress is on the verge of making its most monumental fiscal mistake in a generation,' said John Berthoud, president of the National Taxpayers Union, a leading conservative group that assembled the coalition in less than two days."

(*Financial Times* [London, England], November 21, 2003)

"Various government watchdog groups are urging Congress to re-evaluate the Pentagon's plans to lease 100 Boeing 767 jetliners for $16 billion, calling the deal a prime example of corporate welfare while the company is under investigation for possible misconduct in other government contracts.

"In a show of solidarity, seven nonprofit groups signed a letter dated June 10 asking the chairmen of key defense committees to review the deal, which must be approved by Congress.

"The modified airplanes would be leased from Boeing to replace part of the Air Force's fleet of tanker planes that are used to refuel aircraft in flight. Pentagon officials and advocates of the deal contend that the current fleet of KC-135 Stratotankers are four decades old and must be replaced. If the Pentagon buys the planes at the end of the lease, the deal would cost $20 billion.

"The price tag, the Pentagon's unwillingness to consider alternatives, and revelations that Boeing is under investigation for allegedly acquiring proprietary information from some of its competitors have put the deal firmly in the sights of a variety of advocacy groups.

" 'As numerous independent assessments have confirmed, the proposed financing scheme appears to be a profligate waste of taxpayer dollars,' according to the letter signed by Taxpayers for Common Sense, Public Citizen, National Taxpayers Union, Council for a Livable World, National Law and Policy Center, Project on Government Oversight, and Citizens Against Government Waste."

(*The Boston Globe*, June 10, 2003)

Tax Savings Report (tax law advisory newsletter) (ten times per year)

PUBLICATIONS

Chartbook on Entitlements and the Aging of America
How to Fight Property Taxes
Standing Together: How to Form a State or Local Taxpayer Group
Plus numerous policy papers, issue briefs, video interviews, and studies on fiscal issues.

CONFERENCES

National Taxpayers Conference, a three-day policy forum/training session for state and local activists; location and frequency vary, but generally Washington, DC, every two years. Other seminars for policy experts, Congressional staff, and the public are held infrequently.

"In 2001, Minnesota Reps. Jim Ramstad and Martin Sabo each sent more than 800,000 pieces of mass mail to their constituents, ranking them among the 15 most frequent mass mailers in the House.

"The National Taxpayers Union—a fiscal watchdog group that compiled the numbers—says many members essentially use such mailings as campaign literature at taxpayers' expense.

"Pete Sepp, a spokesman for the group, said the mailings can't be explicitly partisan. But he said the mailings—which are paid for out of a member's office budget and often are in the form of a newsletter—can present the member in a favorable light.

" 'They can plant self-congratulatory messages that their opponents have to pay money to counter,' Sepp said."

(*Minneapolis Star Tribune*, April 18, 2003)

"St. Louis-area residents will be targeted over the next couple of weeks by an advertising campaign against union violence launched by a national taxpayers group.

"The National Taxpayers Union has chosen St. Louis along with Washington, Pittsburgh, Memphis, Rapid City, S.D., and Columbus, Ohio, for ads on television and radio and in newspapers.

"The ads will last a week or two, with the overall cost about $500,000, said John Berthoud, president of the taxpayers' union, a conservative advocacy group that wants federal racketeering laws to apply to cases of union violence.

"The 335,000-member taxpayers group hopes to put pressure on House Minority Leader Richard Gephardt, D-Mo., to address the issue. Thursday, a House panel on employee-employer relations will examine workplace violence, including the union role."

(*St. Louis Post-Dispatch*, September 24, 2002)

National Training and Information Center (NTIC)

Established in 1972

DIRECTOR

Joseph Mariano, executive director. Mariano's work with grassroots community organizations and neighborhood issues encompassed a wide variety of experiences at the local, statewide and national levels. In 1994, Mariano became the NTIC training director. In the late 1980s, he was the director of the Logan Square Neighborhood Association. He started his career in community organizing in 1974, working for the social justice agency of the Diocese of Cleveland, Ohio—the Catholic Commission for Community Action. He was one of the founding staff organizers with Project Interface, which was an organizing project on Cleveland's racially tense east side that successfully brought African Americans and white ethnic groups together in an issue-based neighborhood organization. The project evolved into the Buckeye Woodland Community Congress and Mariano became that organization's executive director.

BOARD OF DIRECTORS

Marilyn Evans, president; Working in Neighborhoods, Cincinnati, OH

Bruce Gottschall, secretary/treasurer; Neighborhoods Housing Services of Chicago, Inc., Chicago, IL

Paul Battle; Affordable Housing Network of New Jersey, Newark, NJ

Calvin Bradford; Bradford & Associates, Williamsburg, VA

Tommy T. C. Calvert; Neighborhoods First Alliance, San Antonio, TX

Roger Coughlin; Catholic Charities, Chicago, IL

Joe Fagan; Iowa Citizens for Community Improvement, Des Moines, IA

Inez Killingsworth; co-chair, National People's Action; East Side Organizing Project, Cleveland, OH

Brenda LaBlanc; co-chair, National People's Action; Des Moines Citizens for Community Improvement, Des Moines, IA

Joseph Mariano; NTIC executive director

John McNight; Institute for Policy Research, Evanston, IL

Emira Palacios; co-chair, National People's Action; Sunflower Community Action, Wichita, KS

Shel Trapp; co-founder of National Training and Information Center, Chicago, IL

SCOPE

Members: NTIC is a resource center providing training, technical assistance, and consulting to approximately 100 community organizations nationwide.
Branches/chapters: None
Affiliates: None

CONTACT INFORMATION

810 North Milwaukee Avenue, Chicago, IL 60622
Phone: (312) 243-3035 • *Fax:* (312) 243-7044
General E-mail: ntic@ntic-us.org • *Web site:* www.ntic-us.org

Communications Director: Emily Severson
(312) 243-3035 • emily@ntic-us.org
Human Resources Director: Kimberly Roberts, organizing director
(312) 243-3035 • kimberly@ntic-us.org

PURPOSE: "NTIC's mission is to build grassroots leadership and strengthen neighborhoods through issue-based community organizing."

CURRENT CONCERNS: Affordable utilities • Community reinvestment • Education • FHA policies • Immigrants' rights • Job development • Neighborhood safety (anticrime and antidrug organizing) • Predatory subprime mortgage lending • Subsidized housing (creation and preservation of affordable rental units) • Youth organizing

METHOD OF OPERATION: Coalition forming • Conferences/seminars • Grantmaking • Grassroots organizing • Internet (Web site) • Legislative monitoring (federal and state) • Local/municipal affairs • Media outreach • Participation in regulatory proceedings (federal and state) • Research • Training and technical assistance

Effectiveness and Political Orientation

"CitiFinancial, the consumer finance arm of Citigroup, has signed an agreement with a community organizing group that had been among its harshest critics to improve its lending procedures for people with impaired credit.

"The pact announced Tuesday with the National Training and Information Center, a Chicago-based nonprofit that coordinates National Peoples [sic] Action neighborhood groups, ends more than 2½ years of sparring over CitiFinancial's subprime lending practices.

"Inez Killingsworth, an NTIC board member and co-chair of National Peoples [sic] Action, said the agreement would benefit consumers who have impaired loans or face foreclosure on their homes. . . .

"Discord with community groups such as National Peoples [sic] Action began when Citigroup, the nation's largest financial institution, announced that it was buying Associates First Capital Corp., one of the nation's largest lenders to high-risk borrowers. . . .

"Prodded by community groups, CitiFinancial has initiated a series of reforms, including the elimination of single-premium credit insurance, which is a high-cost add on for low-income borrowers; severed relations with many of the brokers who had fed clients to Associates, and pledged a special review process for all potential foreclosures."

(Associated Press Newswires, May 13, 2003)

STAFF
17 total—15 professional; 2 support; plus volunteers and interns

TAX STATUS
501(c)4

FINANCES
Budget: 2002—$2.5 million

FUNDING SOURCES
Government grants, 53%; contributions, 45%; investments and other, 2%.

PAC
None

EMPLOYMENT
For information about open positions, check www.ntic-us.org. Resumes and other application materials should be sent to Kimberly Roberts, organizing director, National Training and Information Center, 810 North Milwaukee Avenue, Chicago, IL 60622. Phone: (312) 243-3035

INTERNSHIPS
Internships are available; hours, duration, and application deadlines vary depending on NTIC's needs. Job responsibilities may include assisting with research, media, or organizing. Internships are generally unpaid. Potential applicants should contact Amalia Nieto Gomez for information, (312) 243-3035.

NEWSLETTERS
Disclosure (6 times per year)
NTIC Reports (4 times per year)

PUBLICATIONS
Asset Forfeiture: Getting a Piece of the Pie
Basics of Organizing
Blessed Be the Fighters
A Challenge for Change
Citigroup: Reinventing Redlining (NTIC study)
Devil's in the Details: Analysis of FHA Default Concentration and Lender (NTIC study)
Dynamics of Organizing: Building Power by Developing the Human Spirit
FHA: Families HUD Abandoned (NTIC study)
Outside the Law: How Lenders Dodge Community Reinvestment (NTIC study)
Preying on Neighborhoods: Subprime Mortgage Lending and Chicagoland Foreclosures (NTIC study)
Slash and Burn Financing (NTIC study)
Strategies for Developing a Drug Free Zone
Taking Our Neighborhoods Back
This Old Reg: The Community Reinvestment Act Needs Renovation (NTIC study)
Who, Me a Researcher? Yes You!

CONFERENCES
Organizer's Conference (November)
Leadership Meeting (January)
Leadership Summit (March)
National Neighborhoods Conference (Spring or Summer)
Youth Strategy Conference (Summer)

"Charter One Financial Inc. yesterday announced that Fannie Mae has agreed to buy up to $2.5 million in mortgage loans it makes to low- and moderate-income home buyers in Cleveland.

"The program is part of a $1 billion affordable housing agreement struck a year ago by the Cleveland banking company and the Federal National Mortgage Association, better known as Fannie Mae.

"The Low Down Payment Home Mortgage program will enable qualifying borrowers to buy homes in Cleveland with the lesser of $500 or 1 percent of the home purchase price. . . .

"National Training and Information Center, a community advocate in Chicago, and its local affiliate, the East Side Organizing Project, helped to develop the program. It is being adopted in several cities."

(*The Plain Dealer* [Cleveland], May 13, 2003)

"A national citizens group Monday accused Citigroup of using predatory lending practices to steer low-income borrowers to overpriced mortgages and home equity loans in 17 cities nationwide, including Buffalo.

"The National Training and Information Center, a Chicago-based group that previously unveiled problems in the Federal Housing Administration loan program, said the banking giant offers lower-rate loans through numerous branches in a limited number of cities.

"Yet the report said Citigroup pushes high-rate loans on many inner cities through its affiliated operations, CitiFinancial and The Associates.

"The findings echo the claims in a Federal Trade Commission lawsuit filed against Citigroup last year, accusing the company of deceptive lending practices in Georgia."

(*Buffalo News,* June 4, 2002)

"Gaps in federal law make it impossible to know whether residents in economically disadvantaged areas of Cincinnati and other cities are being unfairly given high-interest home-mortgage loans, a new study concludes.

"The study, released today, looked at lending patterns in Cincinnati and nine other cities to determine whether quality loans are being made available to low- and moderate-income neighborhoods.

"Banks are required under the Community Reinvestment Act to get more loans into such communities. But critics say predatory lenders are filling the gaps banks have left in many poor communities. . . .

"Subprime loans are made at a higher interest rate to borrowers who, because of bad credit or other reasons, don't qualify for regular loans. Yet it is impossible to measure the quality of subprime loans in Cincinnati because lenders aren't required to disclose interest rates attached to such loans, said the study by the National Training and Information Center, which trains grassroots organizations across the country."

(*The Cincinnati Post,* March 6, 2002)

"Illinois residents with poor credit histories would receive more protection from unscrupulous lenders under state regulations approved recently by a legislative panel.

"The rules, proposed by Gov. George Ryan and fought by the powerful banking and lending industry, were adopted in response to widely publicized increases in home foreclosures and lending abuses in the Chicago area.

"But activists say downstate communities will benefit from the plan because their residents aren't immune from predatory lending.

"The new rules may 'put some of these crooks out of business,' said Gail Cincotta, executive director of the National Training and Information Center, a not-for-profit consumer advocacy group based in Chicago."

(*The San Diego Union-Tribune,* April 29, 2001)

National Trust for Historic Preservation

Established in 1949

DIRECTOR

Richard Moe, president. Before becoming president of the National Trust in 1993, Moe worked in private law practice. Previously he was an assistant to Walter F. Mondale, first in the Senate and later as Vice President Mondale's chief of staff. Moe also has held positions in city and state government and chaired the Minnesota Democratic-Farmer-Labor Party. He is a graduate of Williams College and received his law degree from the University of Minnesota.

BOARD OF DIRECTORS

William B. Hart, chair; South Berwick, ME
Jonathan Kemper, vice chair; Kansas City, MO
Aida Alvarez; Piedmont, CA
Michael A. Andrews; Washington, DC
Adele Chatfield-Taylor; New York, NY
Mary Moragne Cooke; Honolulu, HI
Spencer R. Crew; Cincinnati, OH
Julia Jones Daniels; Raleigh, NC
Mary Werner DeNadai; Chaddsford, PA
Susan Guthrie Dunham; Oklahoma City, OK
Jennifer Emerson; Seattle, WA
Elinor K. Farquhar; Washington, DC
Harvey B. Gantt; Charlotte, NC
R. Anthony Goldman; New York, NY
William W. Grant III; Denver, CO
Bradley Hale; Atlanta, GA
Dealey Decherd Herndon; Austin, TX
J. Clifford Hudson; Oklahoma City, OK
Daniel P. Jordan; Charlottesville, VA
Bruce D. Judd; San Francisco; CA
Gordon F. Kingsley; Wellesley, MA
Mark J. Kington; Alexandria, VA
Karl A. Komatsu; Fort Worth, TX
Judy O'Bannon; Indianapolis, IN
Louise Bryant Potter; Locust Grove, VA
John F. W. Rogers; New York, NY
Ellen Ramsey Sanger; San Francisco, CA
Robert A. M. Stern; New York, NY
John H. Welborne; Los Angeles, CA
W. Richard West; Washington, DC
Robert White; Salt Lake City, UT
Mtamanika Youngblood; Atlanta, GA

SCOPE

Members: Over 200,000
Branches/chapters: 6 regional offices; 2 field offices
Affiliates: Owns 25 historic sites

STAFF

308 total—177 full-time professional; 131 full-time support; plus 12 part-time professional; 16 part-time support; 3,000–4,000 volunteers

TAX STATUS

501(c)(3)

CONTACT INFORMATION

1785 Massachusetts Avenue, NW, Washington, DC 20036-2117
Phone: (202) 588-6000 • *Fax:* (202) 588-6038 • *Web site:* www.nthp.org

Communications Director: Katie Callahan, public relations manager
(202) 588-6218 • Katie_Callahan@nthp.org
Human Resources Director: Information unavailable

PURPOSE: "The National Trust for Historic Preservation is a privately funded nonprofit organization that provides leadership, education and advocacy to save America's diverse historic places and revitalize our communities."

CURRENT CONCERNS: Community revitalization • Public policy on preservation • Rural preservation • Stewardship of historic sites

METHOD OF OPERATION: Advertisements • Awards program • Coalition forming • Conferences/seminars • Congressional testimony • Films/video/audiotapes • Grantmaking • Grassroots organizing • Internet (Web site) • Internships • Legal assistance • Legislative/regulatory monitoring (federal and state) • Litigation • Lobbying (federal, state, grassroots) • Local/municipal affairs • Media outreach • Participation in regulatory proceedings (federal and state) • Product merchandising • Research • Scholarships • Training and technical assistance

SPECIFIC PROGRAMS/INITIATIVES: Associate Sites Program (national network of historic sites grouped by theme and region) • BARN AGAIN! • Heritage Tourism Program • National Main Street Center • Save America's Treasures (with the National Park Service) • Rural Heritage Program • Statewide and Local Partnerships Program

Effectiveness and Political Orientation

"The architectural landscape of Eastern Massachusetts, dominated in so many communities by church steeples and bell towers, is at risk of being diminished as the region's largest religious denomination, the Roman Catholic Archdiocese of Boston, prepares to shutter a significant number of parishes, preservationists say.

"Preservation groups, who have had an often unhappy history with Catholic church leaders in Boston, have begun quietly meeting with church officials and with government agencies in an effort to prevent the destruction of church buildings that they say have come to define many neighborhoods, and that in some cases are of historical or architectural significance. The preservationists, seeking to avoid confrontation with the archdiocese, say that they understand and respect the archdiocese's need and right to close churches, but that they want to help the church preserve buildings associated with parishes that do close.

FINANCES
Revenue: 2002—$44.4 million

FUNDING SOURCES
Contributions, 35%; investment income, 16%; contract services, article sales, and advertising, 13%; grants, 11%; membership dues, 9%; admissions and special events, 9%; miscellaneous, 6%, rental income, 2%

PAC
None

EMPLOYMENT
Job openings in the Washington, DC office, regional offices, and historic sites are posted at www.nthp.org. Positions available may be in the areas of: development, programs, communications, policy, community revitalization. To apply for a position, send a cover letter, resume, and salary requirements to: Office of Human Resources, 1785 Massachusetts Avenue, NW, Washington, DC 20036. Fax: (202) 588-6059. E-mail: jobs@nthp.org.

INTERNSHIPS
NTHP offers a 10-week summer internship program in its Washington, DC office. Between 15 and 20 interns work on individual projects and may attend weekly educational sessions on topics relating to preservation, Trust programs, and nonprofit management. A limited number of internships are available at other times or at other locations, such as NTHP's regional offices and historic sites. Intern responsibilities may include researching and compiling case studies on preservation-related topics; developing architectural and collections databases; marketing the annual conference and other workshops; promoting cultural diversity programs; researching community revitalization projects; helping develop resources for statewide and local partners; improving program Web sites; and working on fundraising, membership development, communications, and marketing. Some openings require graduate study or previous experience in preservation, urban planning or historic site management, while others offer entry-level opportunities.

Internships are unpaid. Schedules are generally flexible for interns who are not able to volunteer on a full-time basis. Students may be eligible for academic credit through their individual schools. Funding for some projects is available through the Everett Public Service Internship Program (everettinternships.org). Deadlines and more information are posted at www.nthp.org. To apply for an internship, send a cover letter and resume to Office of Human Resources, 1785 Massachusetts Avenue, NW, Washington, DC 20036. Fax: (202) 588-6059. E-mail: jobs@nthp.org (if applying by e-mail, specify "Internships" in the subject line).

NEWSLETTERS
Forum Journal (quarterly)
Forum News (bimonthly)
Main Street News (monthly)
Preservation (bimonthly)

" 'We have seen, on a national basis, a burgeoning trend of historic religious properties being abandoned because of shrinking congregations, flight to the suburbs, and declining clergy, especially in the Catholic Church,' said Marilyn M. Fenollosa, senior program officer at the National Trust for Historic Preservation's Northeast office. 'These buildings have stood as community landmarks from the time they were built, and many of them deserve to be preserved because they are important architecturally, historically, and from a community perspective.'. . .

"The leading preservation groups in Massachusetts, including Preservation Mass, the National Trust for Historic Preservation, the Boston Preservation Alliance, the Lowell Historic Board, Historic Salem Inc., Historic Boston Inc., the Boston Landmarks Commission, and the Cambridge Historical Commission, have formed a coalition to attempt to preserve Catholic church buildings. The coalition, which has begun meeting weekly, is trying to decide how best to reduce the likelihood that significant buildings will be torn down."

(*The Boston Globe*, March 28, 2004)

"A debate with few precedents in American historic preservation—what are the meaningful physical remnants of a place that was all but destroyed?—has turned into a confrontation between preservationists and state officials.

"Yesterday, the National Trust for Historic Preservation called on the Lower Manhattan Development Corporation to let the keeper of the National Register of Historic Places determine which remnants of the World Trade Center deserved heightened scrutiny; for example, the severed cast-iron PATH tubes or the smoke-scarred ruins of an underground parking garage.

" 'Those smoke scars would be analogous to the strafing marks in the concrete at Pearl Harbor, which are considered highly significant physical remains from the 1941 attack,' Elizabeth S. Merritt and Marilyn Fenollosa of the trust wrote in a letter criticizing the development corporation's findings. 'Yet these smoke scars appear to be dismissed as lacking in significance without any analysis whatsoever.' "

(*The New York Times*, March 6, 2004)

" 'Heritage tourism' is a lucrative but largely untapped source of new tourism dollars within the $525.8 billion U.S. travel industry, speakers at the seventh annual Colorado Preservation Inc. conference said Friday. . . .

" 'Defined as travel to a location where both the site and activities represent authentic slices of people and the past, heritage tourism is growing at more than twice the 5.6 percent growth rate of travel overall,' said Amy Webb, who directs the National Trust for Historic Preservation's heritage tourism program from Boulder.

" 'That translates to a 13 percent increase for heritage tourism between 1996 and 2002,' she said."

(*The Denver Post*, February 9, 2004)

"Farnsworth House, the seminal modernist structure of architect Ludwig Mies van der Rohe, sold for more than $7.5 million during a cliffhanger auction Friday at Sotheby's, with preservationists prevailing over private bidders who many feared would dismantle and move the 'floating' glass house.

" 'This is a happy day for all of us, because I just signed the title for the Farnsworth House,' said Richard Moe, president of the National Trust for Historic Preservation, which paid more than it ever has for a historic site. Moe

CONFERENCES

National Preservation Conference (annual)

Town Meeting on Main Street (annual)

spoke at a post-auction news conference, where the announcement of the identity of the winning bidder brought a round of applause.

"Farnsworth House became an icon of modernism, and a signature work of the German immigrant architect known simply as Mies. It is but a small glass house, slightly more than 2,000 square feet, built of steel beam construction five feet above the ground along the Fox River in Plano, Ill., outside Chicago. It seems to levitate within its wooded environment in a way that critics have described as poetic, magical and breathtaking. . . .

"Farnsworth's fate gripped many in the art world, who feared that what is widely considered a national treasure would vanish from view.

"'As the dawn came to New York this morning, we did not have the resources to do what we did,' said John Bryan, former chair and chief executive officer of the Chicago-based Sara Lee Corp. and president of Friends of the Farnsworth House, which also raised money.

"But a story broadcast Friday on National Public Radio about the future of Farnsworth helped smoke out some crucial donors. The National Trust received several substantial monetary infusions Friday morning, Moe said, pushing the preservationists over the top."

(*The Washington Post,* December 13, 2003)

"You can still spend the night at the Grand Hotel on Michigan's Mackinac Island, the Sir Francis Drake in San Francisco or the Waldorf-Astoria in New York City.

"If you've got the money, you can stay at any of the 168 historic hotels listed in the new annual directory issued by the National Trust for Historic Preservation, except one:

"'In Memoriam, Mapes Hotel, Reno, Nevada, Built 1947—Demolished 2000.'

"Nearly a year after it was blown up on Super Bowl Sunday and its bricks were sold as $1 souvenirs, the former hotel-casino is being honored with a special tribute on the back page of the 2001 Historic Hotels of America guide.

"It's part of an effort by preservationists to make the most of their worst defeat in more than a decade, to declare that 'never again' shall a historic treasure like the Mapes be lost to the wrecking ball.

"'If it could happen to the Mapes, it could happen to other places,' said Richard Moe, president of the nonprofit trust based in Washington.

"'It has been a sobering experience for a lot of preservationists because we have been so successful at staving off these kinds of threats,' he said. 'But maybe we needed that.'"

(*The Los Angeles Times,* January 28, 2001)

National Urban League

Established in 1910

DIRECTOR

Marc H. Morial, president and chief executive officer. Morial served as mayor of New Orleans from 1994–2002. He was president of the United States Conference of Mayors in 2001 and 2002. He also served two years in the Louisiana state senate where he was recognized as conservationist senator of the year, education senator of the year and legislative rookie of the year for his accomplishments. Prior to his elected service, he was a lawyer in private practice; the Louisiana Bar Association honored him in 1988 with its Pro Bono Publico Award. He earned a law degree from the Georgetown University Law Center in 1983 and also earned a B.A. in Economics and African American Studies from the University of Pennsylvania in 1980.

BOARD OF DIRECTORS

Information not available.

SCOPE

Members: Approximately 50,000
Branches/chapters: None
Affiliates: 115 local affiliates in 34 states and the District of Columbia

STAFF

107 total

TAX STATUS

501(c)(3)

FINANCES

Revenue: 2002—$39.4 million

FUNDING SOURCES

Grants and contracts from government agencies, 56%; contributions, 17%; donated materials and services, 9%; program service fees, 6%; affiliate dues, 4%; interest, dividends, and gain on investments, 3%; special events, 2%; other, 3%

PAC

None

EMPLOYMENT

Job openings are posted at the "Career Center" section of the National Urban League's Web site (www.nul.org). Resumes should be sent to recruitment@nul.org or faxed to (212) 558-5497.

INTERNSHIPS

The National Urban League offers a six-week paid summer internship program (second week of June through the end of July) for college sophomores or juniors. Interns are assigned to national office departments, based on the interest of the student and department need.

CONTACT INFORMATION

120 Wall Street, New York, NY 10005
Phone: (212) 558-5300 • *Fax:* (212) 344-5332
General E-mail: info@nul.org • *Web site:* www.nul.org

Communications Director: Chatarra Jenkins, media relations assistant (212) 558-5300, cjenkins@nul.org
Human Resources Director: Information unavailable

PURPOSE: "The mission of the Urban League movement is to enable African Americans to secure economic self-reliance, parity and power and civil rights."

CURRENT CONCERNS: Civil rights • Economic self-sufficiency through good jobs, homeownership, entrepreneurship and wealth accumulation • Education and career development • Employment and job training • Youth and family development

METHOD OF OPERATION: Awards program • Coalition forming • Conferences/ seminars • Congressional testimony • Internet (Web site) • Internships • Job bank • Legislative/regulatory monitoring (federal) • Media outreach • Product merchandising • Research • Scholarships • Training • Voter registration

Effectiveness and Political Orientation

"More than 200 years after the Constitution stopped counting each African-American as three-fifths of a person, the overall well-being of blacks is still about three-quarters that of whites, according to a broad new survey released here yesterday by the National Urban League.

"Most strikingly, African-Americans' economic health is barely half that of whites,' the data show. The nation's 34.6 million blacks also have poorer health, receive lower-quality educations and are granted fewer social justice protections than whites.

" 'While we have gained much ground in the past 40 years since the historic civil rights era, the ground on which we stand today is precarious and shaky,' said Marc H. Morial, president of the New York-based Urban League, speaking from the National Press Club in downtown Washington. 'There's good news and there's bad news.'

"In the last half-century, the black middle class has quadrupled, poverty has shrunk by half and there are more African-American elected officials than ever, Morial said.

"But despite those gains, such progress is outweighed by persistent and stark inequality, the data show."

(*Newsday* [New York], March 25, 2004)

Applicants must have demonstrated academic achievement, strong interpersonal and communication skills, enthusiasm and eagerness to learn about the National Urban League, involvement in academic, extracurricular and community-related activities.

Applicants must submit a current academic transcript (minimum 2.7 GPA), resume, two academic letters of recommendation, and a one-page essay expressing interest in the program. The application deadline is in April; check the "Career Center" section of www.nul.org for the exact date and other details about the internship. Submit all application materials in one packet to National Urban League Internship Program, Human Resources Department, 120 Wall Street, New York, NY 10005. Phone: (212) 558-5402. Fax: (212) 558-5497. E-mail: recruitment@nul.org.

NEWSLETTERS
Opportunity Journal (quarterly)
To Be Equal (weekly column)

PUBLICATIONS
State of Black America (annual)
In addition, The National Urban League Institute for Opportunity & Equality produces a number of reports, studies, statements, and articles.

CONFERENCES
Annual conference
Black Executive Exchange Program (annual)
Equality Opportunity Day (EOD) Awards Dinner (annual)
NULITES Youth Leadership Summit (during annual conference)

"On his way to repositioning himself as a centrist for the 2004 campaign, President Bush last week made a rare appearance before the National Urban League, the nation's oldest African-American organization.

"But when Bush stood before the group's national conference in Pittsburgh, he may have been speaking as much to white, suburban swing voters as he was to black business leaders and activists.

"In the coming election, the real fight is going to be over white moderates rather than the historically Democrat-leaning African-Americans. To fortify his base, Bush needs to soften his image and remind voters of what he calls his 'compassionate conservatism.'

"'It's his way of saying, "I am president of all the people, and I do want to have lines out to everybody,"' said Stephen Hess, presidential scholar at the Washington-based Brookings Institution. 'It has a certain effect on others who are concerned that he has much too little support in (the African-American) community.'

"In 2000, Bush won only 9 percent of the black vote. Although his political handlers have since targeted African-Americans as a key area for improvement, Bush's schedule has largely overlooked such large, established black organizations.

"For three years in a row, Bush has declined to meet with the National Association for the Advancement of Colored People, a group he spoke to during his first campaign. Bush also has not met with the leadership of the Urban League or the Leadership Conference on Civil Rights. . . .

"Hess noted that the business-oriented and generally more centrist Urban League was no random choice for Bush, who declined an invitation last year to address the more liberal and civil-rights-oriented NAACP at its national conference in Houston."

(*Houston Chronicle*, August 4, 2003)

"The 2003 National Urban League conference concluded yesterday on a note of encouragement and motivation, as nearly 10,000 visitors headed home to continue their work for justice, civil rights and the advancement of black families.

"'It's been a great conference,' said Marc Morial, new president of the National Urban League. 'I believe Pittsburgh surprised people. They were warmly embraced here.'

"More than 2,500 registered guests and 7,000 others hit the David L. Lawrence Convention Center last Thursday for a week of activities geared toward motivating youths and young professionals and discussing everything from affirmative action to AIDS awareness.

"The conference heard from President Bush and seven of the nine Democrats who would like to have his job, as well as authors, community experts, business leaders and celebrities who provided a mix of information and entertainment in a riverfront venue that gave Pittsburgh a chance to shine. . . .

"Now comes the work. Morial laid out national goals to attack the crisis of unemployment and incarceration that plagues young black men, and called for national summits on education and health.

"'Affiliates have a desire to work with the process,' he said."

(*Pittsburgh Post-Gazette*, July 31, 2003)

"Marc Morial, New Orleans' ambitious and charismatic former mayor who failed to translate his popularity into a third term, was named president of The National Urban League on Thursday, making him one of the most prominent African-American leaders in the country.

"Despite the third-term defeat, Morial remained a powerful figure when he left the mayor's post last May. But his reputation in New Orleans has suffered some since Mayor Ray Nagin began focusing his anti-patronage spotlight on some of the contracts Morial awarded to close associates.

"A 45-year-old Democrat, Morial is the latest in a long line of power brokers to lead the civil rights organization, which was created in 1910 to empower African-Americans to enter the social and economic mainstream. Morial succeeds Hugh Price, a Yale-educated lawyer who stepped down last year. Among other notables who have led the organization are Vernon Jordan, one of President Clinton's closest confidants, and John Jacob, a senior vice president of Anheuser-Busch.

"Morial, who has coveted a spot on the national stage since he entered politics a dozen years ago, beat out more than 450 other applicants for the job, including current and former members of Congress, other former big-city mayors and corporate foundation executives, said Charles Hamilton Jr., chairman of the Urban League's search committee. . . .

"Morial did not return calls Thursday, but told the Associated Press that his first priority as president will be to raise the Urban League's profile."

(*The New Orleans Times-Picayune,* May 16, 2003)

"The Capitol Hill campaign to make home mortgage insurance premiums tax-deductible has taken a giant step with the introduction of a bipartisan bill co-sponsored by key members of the tax-writing House Ways and Means Committee. . . .

"The bill (H.R. 1336) would affect the mortgages of an estimated 12 million-plus American homeowners, and reverse a decades-old IRS prohibition against write-offs of mortgage insurance payments. Co-sponsored by Reps. Paul D. Ryan, R-Wis., and William J. Jefferson, D-La., the bill would apply to home loans with private mortgage insurance, Federal Housing Administration insurance, veterans guaranty coverage and Rural Housing Service mortgages.

"Besides the co-sponsorship of six other tax committee members, the measure has drawn endorsements from an unusual collection of 21 interest groups ranging from the National Urban League to the National Conference of Black Mayors, the National Taxpayers Union, the National Education Association, the National League of Cities, the Consumer Federation of America and the Mortgage Bankers Association of America.

"Minority housing advocacy groups support the measure because mortgage insurance in its various forms covers an estimated 57 percent of all home purchase loans made to African-American and Hispanic borrowers."

(*The San Diego Union-Tribune,* March 30, 2003)

National Wildlife Federation

Established in 1936

DIRECTOR

Larry J. Schweiger, president and chief executive officer. Schweiger has had a distinguished career in wildlife conservation. He previously served for eight years as president and chief executive officer of the Western Pennsylvania Conservancy. From 1981 to 1995 he served in several positions at NWF, including publisher of the organization's award winning magazines, senior vice president for constituent development and conservation action, and vice president of NWF's affiliate and regional programs department. He has received many awards for his efforts in conservation including the Distinguished Service Award for Special Conservation Achievement from NWF in June 1995. He was selected as Pennsylvania's environmental professional of the year in 2002.

BOARD OF DIRECTORS

Rebecca L. Scheibelhut, chair
Jerome C. Ringo, chair-elect
Stephen E. Petron, vice chair, Eastern Region
Spencer Tomb, vice chair, Central Region
Craig D. Thompson, vice chair, Western Region
Paul Beaudette, Region 1 director
Stephen K. Allinger, Region 2 director
Andrew C. Brack, Region 3 director
J. Stephen O'Hara Jr., Region 4 director
David Carruth, Region 5 director
Daniel J. Deeb, Region 6 director
James L. Baldock, Region 7 director
Earl B. Matthew, Region 8 director
Gene T. Oglesby, Region 9 director
Charles E. Olmsted III, Region 10 director
Thea Levkovitz, Region 11 director
Gerald H. Meral, Region 12 director
Kathleen Hadley, Region 13 director
Lyvier Conss, at-large director
Michael Dombeck, at-large director
Faith Gemmill, at-large director
Thomas Gonzales, at-large director
Levi Holt, at-large director
James T. Martin, at-large director
Rodolfo Ogarrio, at-large director
Christine Thompson, at-large director
J. David Wimberly, at-large director
Bryan Pritchett, past chair

SCOPE

Members: More than 4 million members and supporters
Branches/chapters: 11 field offices nationwide
Affiliates: 46 state and territorial affiliates

STAFF

564 total—564 full-time; plus 52 part-time; 20 interns; 120 volunteers

CONTACT INFORMATION

11100 Wildlife Center Drive, Reston, VA 20190-5362
Phone: (703) 438-6000 • *Fax:* (703) 438-3570
Toll-free: (800) 822-9919
General E-mail: info@nwf.org • *Web site:* www.nwf.org

Communications Director: Mary Burnette
(703) 438-6097 • burnette@nwf.org
Human Resources Director: Information unavailable

PURPOSE: "To educate, inspire, and assist individuals and organizations of diverse cultures to conserve wildlife and other natural resources and to protect the earth's environment in order to achieve a peaceful, equitable, and sustainable future."

CURRENT CONCERNS: Clean water • Conservation education • Conservation funding • Endangered species/biodiversity/habitats • Land stewardship • Public/private lands • Sustainable communities • Water quality • Wetlands

METHOD OF OPERATION: Advertisements • Awards program (National Conservation Achievement Awards) • Coalition formation • Conferences/seminars • Congressional/state legislative testimony • Curriculum materials • Films/video/audiotapes • Grassroots organizing • Internet (e-mail alerts and Web site) • Internships • Legislative/regulatory monitoring (federal and state) • Litigation • Local/municipal affairs • Media outreach • Participation in regulatory proceedings (federal and state) • Product merchandising • Research • Telecommunications services (Environmental Hotline: (202) 797-6655)

Effectiveness and Political Orientation

"The Bush administration is about to dramatically loosen an upcoming regulation that would reduce mercury pollution from coal-fired power plants, according to federal documents obtained by environmental activist groups.

"The Bush administration, under a Dec. 15 deadline, will regulate mercury—a powerful neurotoxin that affects children and pregnant women—for the first time ever, new U.S. Environmental Protection Agency Administrator Michael Leavitt said yesterday.

" 'We will be regulating mercury as a source from power plants,' Leavitt said. 'We want to be able to reduce it.'

"But those cuts would appear to be several times weaker than what the Clean Air Act would require, according to a speech two years ago by then-EPA chief Christie Whitman.

"Officials at the Natural Resources Defense Council and National Wildlife Federation, who obtained the documents, said the current proposals called for reducing power plant mercury emissions to 34 tons a year from 48 tons a year by 2007.

TAX STATUS
501(c)(3)

FINANCES
Budget: 2004—$120 million;
2002—$115 million

FUNDING SOURCES
Nature education materials, 43%; individuals, 33%; publications and films, 17%; foundation grants/corporate donations, 4%; other, 3%

PAC
None

EMPLOYMENT
Positions at NWF's headquarters and field offices are posted at NWF's Web site. Positions may be available in the areas of communications, education, administration, and training. A cover letter and resume should be submitted with the online application form at www.nwf.org, by mail to National Wildlife Federation, Attn: Human Resources (Job #), 11100 Wildlife Center Drive, Reston, VA 20190-5362. Fax: (703) 438-6039. E-mail: jobopp@nwf.org.

INTERNSHIPS
Internships are available in the conservation, education, fundraising, communications, and legal and publications departments. Positions are posted at www.nwf.org. Undergraduate juniors or seniors, recent graduates, and graduate students from all fields of study may apply. Internships are paid, but special attention will be given to applicants who can secure their own funding. Applicants are selected based on a variety of measures, including professional goals, course work, job experience, resume and cover letter, GPA, and professional/academic references. Applications should be submitted via the online form at www.nwf.org; deadlines are rolling.

Candidates should demonstrate commitment to and experience working with multicultural communities, environmental justice and diversity. Medical, dental, and health benefits are available to interns who work a minimum of 20 hours per week and expect to complete a 24-week internship. Occasionally, some departments substitute a paid salary with college credit. For-credit interns are not eligible for benefits. Internship coordinator information is not available.

NEWSLETTERS
EnviroAction (monthly)
National Wildlife (bimonthly magazine)
Ranger Rick (monthly publication for ages 6–12)
Wild Animal Baby (monthly publication for ages 1–3)
Wildlife Online (monthly E-newsletter)
Your Big Backyard (monthly publication for preschoolers)

PUBLICATIONS
Attracting Birds, Butterflies and Other Backyard Wildlife
Conservation Directory (annual)

"But Whitman's December 2001 speech to the Edison Electric Institute indicated that current provisions under the Clean Air Act would require reducing those emissions to about 5 tons by 2007."

(*The San Diego Union-Tribune,* December 3, 2003)

"Bush administration officials have drafted a rule that would significantly narrow the scope of the Clean Water Act, stripping many wetlands and streams of federal pollution controls and making them available to being filled for commercial development.

"The rule, spelled out in an internal document provided to *The Times* by a senior government official, says that Clean Water Act protection would no longer be provided to 'ephemeral washes or streams' that do not have groundwater as a source. Streams that flow for less than six months a year would also lose protection, as would many wetlands, according to the document.

"State and federal officials have estimated that up to 20 million acres of wetlands, 20% of the wetlands outside of Alaska, could lose protection under a new rule like the one in the draft. The effect would be greater in California and other parts of the arid West, where many streams flow only seasonally or after rain or snowmelts.

"Julie Sibbing, a wetlands policy expert at the National Wildlife Federation, said, 'It's like writing off the entire Southwest from the Clean Water Act, where water is more precious than in any other region of the country. Up to 80% to 90% of streams in the Southwest would not fall under the Clean Water Act if this rule were to go forward.'"

(*The Los Angeles Times,* November 6, 2003)

"A pair of lawsuits filed by environmental groups Thursday accuse federal officials of allowing developers and miners to destroy crucial habitat for the endangered Florida panther.

"One lawsuit challenges a permit approved by the Army Corps of Engineers and the U.S. Fish and Wildlife Service that allows Florida Rock Industries to open a 6,000-acre limestone mine in Fort Myers in panther habitat. In exchange, Florida Rock will set aside 800 acres for preservation.

"The other suit filed by the National Wildlife Federation and two other groups targets blanket permits issued by the Corps of Engineers for some types of development without individual environmental reviews. The permits are intended to be used when there will be minimal impact on the environment. The groups say they have been used for development in Lee and Collier counties that has been harmful to panthers.

"The Florida panther is one of the most endangered mammals in the world."

(*St. Petersburg Times* [Florida], June 27, 2003)

"Mercury in the rainwater of several Southeastern and Gulf Coast states exceeds the safe level for lake water, as established by the Environmental Protection Agency, by as much as 96 times, an environmental group reported Thursday.

"The National Wildlife Federation said EPA sampling stations in Georgia and seven other Southern states showed mercury levels that would make fish toxic to humans who ate them. Mercury found in contaminated fish destroys nerve cells and easily crosses the placenta into unborn babies, researchers say.

CONFERENCES
NWF annual meeting (held in March)
Also sponsors workshops, seminars, special
events, and "outdoor discovery and
recreation" events.

The National Academy of Sciences has warned that consumption of contaminated fish by pregnant women can lead to children with learning disabilities.

"The National Wildlife Federation, the largest environmental organization in the United States, called on the EPA to crack down on the sources of mercury in the atmosphere, especially coal-burning electric power plants."
(*The Atlanta Journal-Constitution*, May 30, 2003)

"A federal judge on Wednesday ruled that the government's plan to restore salmon in much of the Pacific Northwest violates the Endangered Species Act, a decision that could have sweeping economic and social consequences for the region.

"Unless the decision by U.S. District Court Judge James Redden in Oregon is overturned, the federal government will have to overhaul its plan. The new proposal could include changes in how the Columbia and Snake rivers are regulated by a series of hydropower dams.

"Redden's ruling revived hopes among environmentalists for a plan to breach, or partially tear down, four federal dams on the lower Snake River in eastern Washington state. Many scientists view the dams as the most important factor in the long decline of salmon and steelhead—ocean-going trout—that migrate to and from the Pacific Ocean.

"A dozen populations of salmon and steelhead that rely on the two rivers are now listed as either endangered or threatened. . . .

"Environmentalists hailed the ruling. 'They need to put dam breaching back on the table,' said Jan Hasselman, counsel for the Seattle office of the National Wildlife Federation, one of 13 conservation and sportsmen's groups that challenged the plan. 'The science is clear . . . that removal of the four lower Snake dams is the surest way to recover these species.' "
(*USA Today*, May 8, 2003)

"The Arctic National Wildlife Refuge in Alaska is a pristine spot where herds of caribou migrate to give birth, but it is also 'believed to be able to produce more oil than the entire state of Texas,' Interior Secretary Gale A. Norton said yesterday in a speech here at the annual meeting of the National Wildlife Federation.

"As Norton endorsed the Bush administration's plans to drill for oil in Alaska, members of the nation's largest wildlife preservation group listened politely. Afterward, they formed 20-person lines behind two microphones to pepper her with questions about protecting the arctic and other reserves.

" 'We would apply the most stringent environmental standards ever applied anywhere' if Congress were to allow drilling in the refuge, Norton said. She said her department also wants to 'heal our landscapes and restore health to our national forests.'. . .

"But wildlife federation organizers greeted her message with skepticism.

" 'It was good of her to come,' said Jamie Rappaport Clark, the group's senior vice president for conservation programs. 'But the speech was overarching, message spinning. She has to support the administration's position, and the administration's position is not positive for the environment.' "
(*The Washington Post*, March 30, 2003)

National Women's Political Caucus

Established in 1971

DIRECTOR

Roselyn O'Connell, president. O'Connell was the director of public affairs at Planned Parenthood of central and northern Arizona where she was responsible for public policy development, legislative affairs, advocacy, and grassroots organizing since 1997. She has also served as precinct committee person for District 18 in north-central Phoenix, the New York Life Women's Advisory Board, and Soroptomists International. O'Connell graduated with honors in geography and political science from Western Oregon State College in Monmouth, OR.

BOARD OF DIRECTORS

Roselyn O'Connell, president
Llenda Jackson-Leslie, vice president, communications, first vice president
Dolores Mitchell, vice president, political planning
Lori Durbin, vice president, membership
Tina Sheinbein, vice president, development
Marguerite Cooper, vice president, education and training
Lulu Flores, vice president, diversity and outreach
Julie Hoff, secretary
Barbara Davidson, treasurer

SCOPE

Members: 50,000
Branches/chapters: 300 state and local caucuses
Affiliate: NWPC Leadership, Development, Education, and Research Fund, a 501(c)(3) organization

STAFF

7 total

TAX STATUS

501(c)(4)

FINANCES

Information unavailable

FUNDING SOURCES

Membership dues, 40%; special events, 23%; direct mail solicitations, 20%; preconvention, 10%; other, 7%

PAC

NWPC Campaign Support Committee

CONTACT INFORMATION

1634 Eye Street, NW, Suite 310, Washington, DC 20006
Phone: (202) 785-1100 • *Fax:* (202) 785-3605
General E-mail: info@nwpc.org • *Web site:* www.nwpc.org

Communications Director: Tressa Feher, external affairs director
(202) 785-1100 • feher@nwpc.org
Human Resources Director: None

PURPOSE: "The purpose of the National Women's Political Caucus is to increase women's participation in the political process and to identify, recruit, train and support pro-choice women for election and appointment to public office."

CURRENT CONCERNS: Equality for all women • Eradicate sexism, racism, anti-Semitism, ageism, ableism, violence, poverty, and discrimination on the basis of religion or sexual orientation • Reproductive freedom

METHOD OF OPERATION: Awards program • Campaign contributions • Campaign skills training • Coalition forming • Conferences/seminars • Electoral politics • Grassroots organizing • Internet (e-mail alerts and Web site) • Lobbying (federal, state, and grassroots) • Local/municipal affairs • Media outreach • Research • Technical assistance

Effectiveness and Political Orientation

"Saying she was proud of 'breaking new ground' in her presidential campaign, Carol Moseley Braun yesterday ended her long-shot candidacy for the Democratic nomination and threw her support to former Vermont governor Howard Dean. . . .

"Braun, 56, the first black woman elected to the U.S. Senate, said she decided to quit after realizing that her 'nontraditional campaign' could not overcome disadvantages in funding and organization. . . .

"Braun jumped into the presidential race in September, pledging to remain in the contest 'until people are voting.' She won the support of two major women's groups, the National Organization for Women and the National Women's Political Caucus. But she failed to draw much financial support."

(*The Washington Post*, January 16, 2004)

"Protesters staged several Bay Area rallies Friday to criticize Republican gubernatorial candidate Arnold Schwarzenegger for admittedly behaving 'badly' toward women and for a 1975 interview in which he expressed admiration for Adolf Hitler.

"The National Women's Political Caucus, Alameda North held a noon news conference outside the Alameda County Administration Building in

PAC CONTRIBUTIONS 2002

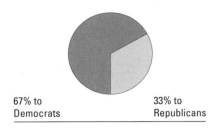

67% to
Democrats

33% to
Republicans

EMPLOYMENT
Information unavailable

INTERNSHIPS
Information unavailable

NEWSLETTERS
NWPC Weekly Political Report (e-mail)

PUBLICATIONS
None

CONFERENCES
Biennial convention
Campaign conferences and trainings are held
by state and local caucuses

Oakland to urge ANG Newspapers to retract its Sept. 28 endorsement of Schwarzenegger."

(*The Oakland Tribune* [CA], October 4, 2003)

"Though the major parties are vigorously wooing women's votes, this campaign season has not been easy for some leading feminist groups.

"When the National Organization for Women sponsored one of the first forums for Democratic presidential candidates, only one of the top contenders showed up. In the latest blow, *The New York Times*—a longtime champion of women's rights—dismissed as 'silly' NOW's decision to endorse the lone woman in the Democratic race.

"'We have become a target,' said Roselyn O'Connell, president of the National Women's Political Caucus, which joined NOW in endorsing former Illinois Sen. Carol Moseley Braun.

"'There is a movement coming from a number of different places to marginalize and discredit the feminist movement,' O'Connell said. 'The parties and candidates want women's votes, but they expect us to capitulate on the things that are important to us.'

"NOW and the political caucus were infuriated by Sunday's editorial in the *Times,* which said the endorsement of Braun—a longshot candidate—'trivialized the important role women will play in the coming election.'"

(*Associated Press Newswires,* September 17, 2003)

"Democratic presidential candidate Carol Moseley Braun won the backing Tuesday of two major women's groups and said their support 'guarantees' the formal launch of her campaign next month.

"The National Organization for Women's Political Action Committee, or NOW/PAC, and the National Women's Political Caucus made the unusual early endorsements as they cited Braun for her long-standing support for their issues.

"Although the feminist leaders offered no objections to the other eight Democratic candidates, they made no apologies for making the only woman, who is also a decided long shot, their favorite. . . .

"As of the end of June, the campaign had just $22,000 in the bank. Even so, her backers note that she has ranked higher than some better-financed competitors in some public opinion polls and is ahead in her home state.

"The endorsements are no guarantee of an influx of cash. Political action committees can donate no more than $5,000. However, leaders of the women's groups said they would encourage members to donate to Braun's campaign.

"Braun, speaking at the National Press Club here, credited the "powerful encouragement" from the women's groups for her decision to officially announce her candidacy on Sept. 22."

(*The Atlanta Journal-Constitution,* August 27, 2003)

"Valerie Brown, Sonoma County's first female supervisor since 1991, has appealed to the local chapter of the National Women's Political Caucus to reconsider its decision not to endorse her—and will appeal to the national level, if necessary.

"Brown, 56, who was mayor of the city of Sonoma from 1990–1991 and a state Assemblywoman from 1992–1998, was appointed by Gov. Gray Davis in August to the 1st District seat vacated by Mike Cale, who retired for health reasons.

"She is running for the seat in the Nov. 5 election, facing Edward Kenny, 75, director for the Valley of the Moon Water District and a World War II veteran.

"Despite Brown's experience and support for women's issues that surfaced during her interview with caucus members, on Sept. 16 the 70-member caucus voted against endorsing her.

"The caucus declined to comment on its vote, saying the reasons for their decisions are confidential. But some insiders have suggested that, although Brown has the experience, local knowledge and feminist views that the caucus seeks, they balked because of Brown's two consulting jobs, in Sacramento and Los Angeles, which they claimed would distract her from her supervisorial duties. . . .

"Brown pointed out Cale owned a small winery while he was a supervisor and said the caucus is creating a "glass ceiling" by imposing a different standard for women. Brown wrote that she will issue an appeal to the national level, if necessary. . . .

" 'I cannot talk about it because that (e-mail) memo is supposed to go to members,' said Anne-Therese Ageson, president of the 70-member caucus. 'It is a still a confidential issue.' "

(*The San Francisco Chronicle,* October 5, 2002)

Natural Resources Defense Council

Established in 1970

DIRECTOR

John H. Adams, president. Adams served as NRDC's executive director from its inception in 1970 until he was named NRDC president in 1998, a tenure unparalleled by the leader of any other environmental organization. Prior to his work at NRDC, he served as assistant U.S. attorney for the Southern District of New York. Adams is chair of the board of the Open Space Institute and sits on the boards of numerous other environmental organizations. He has also served on governmental advisory committees, including President Clinton's Council for Sustainable Development. Adams is a graduate of Michigan State University and the Duke University School of Law.

BOARD OF DIRECTORS

Frederick A. O. Schwarz Jr., Esq., chair; senior counsel, Cravath, Swaine & Moore

Adrian W. DeWind, chair emeritus; of counsel, Paul, Weiss, Rifkind, Wharton & Garrison

Adam Albright, vice chair; private investor; environmentalist

Patricia Bauman, vice chair; co-director, Bauman Foundation

Robert J. Fisher, vice chair; board member, Sun Microsystems, GAP Inc.

Alan Horn, vice chair; president and chief operating officer, Warner Brothers

Daniel R. Tishman, vice chair; chair and chief executive officer, Tishman Construction Corp. of New York

Henry R. Breck, treasurer; chair, Ark Asset Management Co., Inc.

Richard E. Ayres; Ayres Law Group

Laurie David; producer, activist

Sharon Saul Davis; philanthropist, conservationist

Leonardo DiCaprio; actor, environmentalist

John E. Echohawk; executive director, Native American Rights Fund

Robert Epstein; co-founder, Sybase, Inc., Colorado Microdisplay, and Britton-Lee

Michael C. Finnegan; managing director, J.P. Morgan Securities

Michel Gelobter, Ph.D.; executive director, Redefining Progress

David Hahn-Baker; president, Inside/Out Political Consultants

Jill Tate Higgins; private investor; general partner, Lakeside Enterprises, L.P.

Charles E. Koob; partner, Simpson, Thacher & Bartlett

Philip B. Korsant; member, Ziff Brothers Investments

Ruben Kraiem; partner, Paul, Weiss, Rifkind, Wharton & Garrison

Jonathan Z. Larsen; journalist

Nicole Lederer; co-founder, Environmental Entrepreneurs

CONTACT INFORMATION

40 West 20th Street, New York, NY 10011
Phone: (212) 727-2700 • *Fax:* (212) 727-1773
General E-mail: nrdcinfo@nrdc.org • *Web site:* www.nrdc.org

Communications Director: Alan Metrick
(212) 727-4467 • ametrick@nrdc.org
Human Resources Director: None

PURPOSE: The Natural Resources Defense Council's purpose is to safeguard the Earth: its people, its plants and animals and the natural systems on which all life depends.

CURRENT CONCERNS: Cities and green living • Clean air and energy • Clean water and oceans • Environmental legislation • Global warming • Nuclear weapons and waste • Parks, forests and wildlands • Toxic chemicals and health • Wildlife and fish

METHOD OF OPERATION: Advertisements • Coalition forming • Conferences/seminars • Congressional testimony • Grassroots organizing • Information clearinghouse • International activities • Internet (e-mail alerts and Web site) • Internships • Legal assistance • Legislative/regulatory monitoring (federal and state) • Litigation • Lobbying (federal, state, and grassroots) • Local/municipal affairs • Media outreach • Participation in regulatory proceedings (federal and state) • Research • Technical assistance

Effectiveness and Political Orientation

"After a decade of battling environmentalists, Caltrans agreed in court Wednesday to install pollution controls on state highways to reduce the flow of toxic storm water into streams, rivers and the ocean.

"The pact, reached after a year of negotiation with the Natural Resources Defense Council and Santa Monica BayKeeper, was filed in U.S. District Court in Los Angeles, where the two groups sued the state transportation department in 1993.

"It sets the stage for installation of filtering devices that Caltrans once considered ineffective and too costly for its 15,000-mile highway system. Hundreds of projects, including new freeways and major improvements to older roads, could be affected.

" 'This is a major step toward a cleaner ocean, not only in Southern California, but throughout the state,' said David Beckman, an NRDC attorney based in Santa Monica. 'One of the strongest opponents of cleaning up runoff is now committing to a progressive program that will reduce polluted storm water from highways by as much as 80%.'

"Caltrans officials heralded the agreement, which could settle the lawsuit, as a sign that the giant transportation agency was willing to form new alliances with environmentalists to combat storm-water pollution. Recent studies

SCOPE

Members: More than 1 million individuals
Branches/chapters: 3 branch offices in Los Angeles, San Francisco, and Washington, DC
Affiliates: NRDC is the parent organization of the NRDC Action Fund, a 501(c)(4) organization.

STAFF

234 total—175 full-time professional/administrative; 59 full-time support; plus 14 part-time; 10 interns

TAX STATUS

501(c)(3)

FINANCES

Budget: 2004—$48.0 million; 2003—$52.8 million

FUNDING SOURCES

Membership and individual contributions, 78%; foundations and other grants, 18%; fees, contracts, and other revenues, 4%

PAC

None

EMPLOYMENT

Declined to comment

INTERNSHIPS

Declined to comment

showing the practicality of storm-water controls have persuaded the agency to try to resolve the case."

(*The Los Angeles Times*, April 8, 2004)

"A federal judge ruled Thursday that the Bush administration must release thousands of pages of documents related to a White House task force that met behind closed doors to develop a national energy policy.

"The ruling, by Judge Paul L. Friedman of Federal District Court here, was a victory for the Natural Resources Defense Council, an environmental lobbying group, and Judicial Watch, a conservative legal group. The two organizations have been trying to find out whether the task force, headed by Vice President Dick Cheney, was heavily influenced by energy executives and lobbyists."

(*The New York Times*, April 2, 2004)

"Blasted for its 'deplorable' treatment of local residents and feeble attempts to curb air and water pollution, the Port of Houston scored an F in a review released Monday by a nationwide environmental advocacy group. It was the lowest grade given to any of the nation's 10 largest ports.

" 'There is a severe lack of effort on their part to control their pollution. They had to have a gun to their head to do something about air pollution at their terminals,' said Diane Bailey, a scientist with the Natural Resources Defense Council, which authored the report.

"Of the 10 ports surveyed, the Port of Houston—specifically the 11 publicly owned container terminals operated by the Port of Houston Authority— ranked worst, with an F. That grade corresponds to a 'reckless lack of concern for public health and the environment,' according to the NRDC.

"A Port Authority spokeswoman called the report inaccurate and flawed and said it was another attempt by the environmental community to derail the $1.2 billion Bayport project.

"Chief among the report's criticisms was the authority's plan to construct a new container terminal in Bayport on an undeveloped parcel of land and over local residents' objections. The NRDC recommends the Port Authority use an alternative site."

(*Houston Chronicle*, March 23, 2004)

"Environmental groups sued yesterday to block the Bush administration from opening millions more acres in the National Petroleum Reserve in Alaska to oil and natural gas drilling.

"The Interior Department last month finalized a plan to make the vast majority of an 8.8 million-acre portion in the northwest area of the reserve available for drilling.

"However, a coalition of groups—including the National Audubon Society, Wilderness Society, Natural Resources Defense Council, Alaska Wilderness League and Sierra Club—filed a lawsuit in federal district court in Alaska to stop the drilling.

"The groups said the administration ignored several federal laws intended to protect key wildlife areas in the reserve for polar bears, caribou, wolves, grizzly bears and migrating birds, and did not adequately study the likely harm that drilling will cause."

(*The Washington Post*, February 18, 2004)

"Gov. Gray Davis, escalating the state's war with the Bush administration over the environment, announced a lawsuit Friday challenging the federal government's refusal to regulate tailpipe emissions of greenhouse gases.

"California and other states plan to argue that the U.S. Environmental Protection Agency was wrong when it declared in August that it lacks authority to limit emissions of carbon dioxide and other gases implicated in global warming, state officials said. . . .

"The Natural Resources Defense Council and the Sierra Club endorsed the suit. NRDC attorney Gail Feuer said the EPA's finding that greenhouse gases aren't pollutants 'makes a mockery of the English language.' "

(*The San Francisco Chronicle,* October 4, 2003)

The Nature Conservancy

Established in 1951

DIRECTOR

Steve McCormick, president and chief executive officer. McCormick arrived at The Nature Conservancy soon after graduating from law school in 1976 and rose through the ranks to spend 16 years as executive director of the California state program. He also chaired the committee that created Conservation by Design, the scientific framework for setting priorities and taking action that now guides the Conservancy's work in 28 countries. McCormick has a B.S. in agricultural economics from the University of California at Berkeley (1973) and a J.D. from the University of California Hastings College of Law (1976). He also attended the Stanford Executive Program in 1993.

BOARD OF DIRECTORS

Henry M. Paulson Jr., chair
Steven J. McCormick, president and chief
    executive officer
Philip J. James, vice chair
Leigh H. Perkins Jr., vice chair
Jan V. Portman, secretary
John P. Morgridge, treasurer
Executive Committee
D. Correll Jr.
John W. Fitzpatrick
Philip J. James
Steven J. McCormick
John P. Morgridge
Roger Milliken Jr.
Henry M. Paulson Jr.
Leigh H. Perkins Jr.
Jan V. Portman
Joseph W. Prueher
Shirley Young
Members
Catherine G. Abbott
Alfred R. Berkeley III
Joel E. Cohen
Gordon Crawford
Edward E. Crutchfield
Edward N. Dayton
Carol E. Dinkins
E. Linn Draper Jr.
Christopher H. Foreman Jr.
Anthony P. Grassi
Harry Groome
John S. Hendricks
William L. Horton
Frances C. James
Glenn C. Janss
Yolanda Kakabadse N.
Meredith Meiling
James C. Morgan
William W. Murdoch
Daniel M. Neidich
John P. Sall
Christine M. Scott
John F. Smith Jr.

CONTACT INFORMATION

4245 N. Fairfax Dr., Suite 100, Arlington, VA 22203-1606
Phone: (703) 841-5300 • *Fax:* (703) 841-1283
General E-mail: comment@tnc.org • *Web site:* www.nature.org

Communications Director: Jim Petterson, associate director of marketing-communications
(303) 541-0369 • jpetterson@tnc.org
Human Resources Director: Darryl Varnado
(703) 841-7493 • dvarnado@tnc.org

PURPOSE: "To preserve plants, animals, and natural communities that represent the diversity of life on Earth by protecting the land and waters they need to survive."

CURRENT CONCERNS: The loss, alteration and conversion of natural areas and wildlife habitat that imperils the plants, animals and natural communities that represent the diversity of life on Earth.

METHOD OF OPERATION: Congressional testimony • Initiative/referendum campaigns • International activities • Internet (Web site) • Lobbying (federal, state, and grassroots) • Media outreach • Research • Technical assistance

SPECIFIC PROGRAMS/INITIATIVES: Climate Change • Invasive Species • Freshwater • Marine • Fire

Effectiveness and Political Orientation

"A section of the country's largest dairy farm will be set aside for conservation of four rare prairie species under a federal agreement, Interior Secretary Gale A. Norton announced Saturday.

"The agreement with Threemile Canyon Farms, a 94,000-acre operation with 45,000 head of cattle in the high desert east of Boardman, will protect the burrowing Washington ground squirrel, which has lost most of its habitat to agriculture. . . .

"Under the agreement, Threemile Canyon Farms, owned by R.D. Offutt Co. of Fargo, N.D., the world's largest potato producer, will pay the Nature Conservancy $130,000 annually to monitor the protected land. Much of the rest of the property will remain a farm.

"Conservation groups criticized the Bush administration for taking credit for their work to protect the land. The groups sued Offutt four years ago and forced it to set aside 23,000 acres and reduce withdrawals from a salmon stream flowing into the Columbia River. Offutt also agreed to contribute $1.25 million to buy water rights in the Columbia basin to protect flows for salmon. . . ."

(*The Washington Post*, April 26, 2004)

Douglas W. Walker
Georgia Welles
Joy B. Zedler

SCOPE
Members: 1 million
Branches/chapter: 400 offices in all 50 states
and in 27 other countries
Affiliates: Nature Conservancy Action Fund
501(c)4

STAFF
2,710 total—2,710 full-time; plus 287 part-time; 58 temporary full-time; 13 temporary part-time; 22 interns

TAX STATUS
501(c)(3)

FINANCES
Revenue: 2003—$840,961,000;
2002—$923,010,000

FUNDING SOURCES
Foundation grants, 25%, corporate donations, 8%, individuals, 55%, other, 12%

PAC
None

EMPLOYMENT
Potential applicants can learn about job openings within this organization by consulting the Web site at nature.org. This organization offers the following types of positions: administrative, marketing, legal, science, membership, cartography, government relations. See job postings for contact information or send e-mail to careers@tnc.org.

INTERNSHIPS
Both paid and unpaid internship opportunities are posted at nature.org. The duration of internships varies, as do application deadlines and hours. Internships are offered in a variety of areas and eligibility requirements vary. See individual postings for contact information. Contact information depends on department and chapter offering the program.

NEWSLETTERS
Nature Conservancy Magazine
Great Places E-newsletter
Chapter newsletters

PUBLICATIONS
Rivers of Life

CONFERENCES
Annual meeting

"The Nature Conservancy, a worldwide land preservation group that has protected more than 1-million acres in Florida from development, wants to give Hernando County some land.

"Since 1974, the conservancy has been steward of the 320-acre Janet Butterfield Brooks Preserve, on the east side of Citrus Way just south of Centralia Road, in northwest Hernando County. But the group's main focus is protecting larger ecosystems, such as the 6,300-acre Apalachicola Bluffs and Ravines Preserve.

"Smaller, far-flung holdings such as the Brooks preserve tax the conservancy's resources.

"For members of the county Environmentally Sensitive Lands Committee, to whom the conservancy made its overture, the acquisition makes sense in several ways. It would connect to land the county already manages and open up the now-closed preserve to the public. But concerns remain about whether the county has the means to manage the site.

"'We are hopeful and cautiously optimistic,' said committee chairman Eugene Kelly, 'and just need a little bit more information to make a well-considered decision.'

"The Brooks preserve is a living island of Florida's natural history, undisturbed by progress. . . ."

(*St. Petersburg Times* [Florida], April 19, 2004)

"Office Depot yesterday announced a Dollars 2.2m initiative with three international conservation organisations aimed at advancing more environmentally-friendly practices.

"The number two US office supply retailer has formed the Forest & Biodiversity Conservation Alliance in co-operation with The Nature Conservancy, NatureServe and Conservation International. . . .

"Office Depot in January severed business with Asia Pulp & Paper of Singapore, which has been criticised for its logging practices in Indonesia. Office Depot's main supplier is Weyerhaeuser, the Washington-based lumber company. Mr Nelson added: 'The activities of this alliance will . . . provide Office Depot with the information and tools we need to incorporate conservation science into our procurement decisions.' Funding over the next five years will be spent on identifying and managing threatened forests, developing methods to keep track of biological species and training forest managers and scientists. Projects are expected to focus on forests in Canada and Brazil. . . .

"Brian Levine, spokesperson, said Office Depot aimed to be a leader in 'issues of environmental concern.' The company planned to focus on recycling and pollution reduction, forest and biodiversity conservation and developing the market for environmentally-friendly products.

"Steve McCormick, chief executive of The Nature Conservancy, said: 'The Alliance hopes actively to influence conservation decisions made on the ground, at the forest landscape level.

"'We will use our expertise to help integrate scientific knowledge and leading edge biodiversity conservation planning into forest management decision-making.'"

(*Financial Times* [London, England], March 23, 2004)

"The expansion of Great Sand Dunes National Monument into a national park has stalled because of a lawsuit over the San Luis Valley's water.

"When Congress approved the monument in 1932, scientists didn't understand the complex water, geological and biological systems that surround and sustain the dunes. So in 2000, Congress voted to include the entire ecosystem in the expanded national park. But it's not a done deal, because old feuds keep surfacing.

"To complete the new park, Uncle Sam needs to buy the Baca Ranch. Nestled northwest of the dunes, the 150-square-mile spread has breathtaking scenery, critical wildlife habitat—and huge underground water reserves. The water, crucial ecologically, also fuels political and legal wars.

"In 1985, American Water Development Inc. bought the Baca, and in 1986 it applied for underground water rights. Alarmed that AWDI would drain their valley, San Luis Valley residents rallied to oppose the project. AWDI lost a big legal battle in 1991 and had to pay its opponents $2.7 million. The water export plan appeared dead. Nope.

"In 1995, The Nature Conservancy (one of the world's premier conservation groups) tried to buy the Baca and preserve the ranch's waters and landscapes.

"Sadly, it was outbid by a private company, Cabeza de Vaca, which pursued the water project with vigor. Cabeza's backers included Yale University, through a California-based investment firm, Farallon Capital Management. Importantly, Cabeza's operating agreement said the project had to be done by 1999 or the deal was dead, according to state court documents."

(*The Denver Post*, March 4, 2004)

"At a time when efforts to reform the corporate world are getting all of the attention, there is another group of chief executives who remain insulated from the effects of scandals at Tyco, WorldCom and the like. They are America's not-for-profit profiteers: the executives who cash in at universities, foundations and other tax-exempt organizations.

"A review of media accounts and public information reveals that many of the same questionable transactions detailed in the corporate scandals are occurring in the world of non-profits. University and foundation presidents are using tax-free dollars for luxury apartments and cars, personal loans and other perks. These abuses occur because non-profits are getting a pass from some promising corporate-accounting and conflict-of-interest reforms.

"Recently, the Nature Conservancy, the world's largest environmental organization with nearly $3.3 billion in land and investments, was accused in a series of *Washington Post* articles of violations ranging from hiding the personal income of employees to sweetheart land deals for favored parties to using not-for-profit funds to give a $1.5 million loan to a board member. Congress is looking into the transactions, and the IRS took the rare step of announcing that it will physically move into the headquarters of the charity for a long-term audit. . . ."

(*USA Today*, February 12, 2004)

9to5, National Association of Working Women

Established in 1973

DIRECTOR

Ellen Bravo, national director. Bravo has been with 9to5 since 1982, when she helped start the Milwaukee chapter. She has taught several courses on women and work, including graduate seminars on sexual harassment and on work/family issues. Bravo has served on a number of state and federal bodies, including the bipartisan Commission on Leave appointed by Congress to study the impact of the Family and Medical Leave Act. In 1997, she was the recipient of a "Women of Vision" award from the Ms. Foundation.

BOARD OF DIRECTORS

E. Marie Barnum-Hill
Beth Blair, executive committee
Kathy Dean
Cathy Deppe, executive committee
Patsy Gibson
Burgena Mitchell
KiKi Peppard
Renee Ray

SCOPE

Members: 10,000 individuals
Branches/chapters: 3 National staffed offices, 25 unstaffed chapters
Affiliates: 9to5, Working Women Education Fund (501c3); 9to5, Poverty Network Initiative (501c3) under WWEF.

STAFF

15 total—12 professional; 3 support; plus 2 interns; volunteers

TAX STATUS

501(c)(5)

FINANCES

Budget: 2004—$816,500; 2003—$905,050; 2002—$898,000

FUNDING SOURCES

Conferences, corporate donations, foundation grants, individuals, membership dues, publications, training, and speaking

PAC

None

EMPLOYMENT

Information on open positions can be obtained from the Web site: www.9to5.org and on the National Organizers Alliance site: http://www.noacentral.org. The organization offers positions in organizing, administrative, and managerial areas. Potential applicants may send resumes and other materials for employment to Linda Garcia-Barnard, director of administration, 152 W. Wisconsin Avenue, Suite 408, Milwaukee, WI, 53203. Phone: (414)

CONTACT INFORMATION

152 W. Wisconsin Avenue, Suite 408, Milwaukee, WI, 53203
Phone: (414) 274-0925 • *Fax:* (414) 272-2870.
General E-mail: 9to5@9to5.org • *Web site:* www.9to5.org

Communications Director: Sangita Nayak
(414) 274-0926 • pr@9to5.org
Human Resources Director: Linda Garcia-Barnard, director of administration
(414) 274-0933 • lindagb@9to5.org

PURPOSE: "To strengthen women's ability to win economic justice."

CURRENT CONCERNS: Antidiscrimination (sex, race, and sexual orientation) • Equity for nonstandard jobs • Family and medical leave benefits • Family-friendly policies for low-wage women • Work/family policies

METHOD OF OPERATION: Awards program • Coalition forming • Conferences/seminars • Congressional testimony • Demonstrations • Direct action • Grassroots organizing • Information clearinghouse • Internet (e-mail alerts and Web site) • Internships • Legislative/regulatory monitoring (federal) • Lobbying (grassroots) • Media outreach • Performance ratings/Report cards • Research • Speakers program • Telecommunications (toll-free hotline) • Training • Voter registration

Effectiveness and Political Orientation

"To headline Lowell's women's week, Ellen Bravo, head of the National Association of Working Women for the last decade, will speak March 2 in two free lectures about women working in this economy. She is the author of 'The 9to5 Guide to Combating Sexual Harassment' and 'The Job Family Challenge: Not for Women Only,' and is frequently quoted in The New York Times, The Wall Street Journal, Parenting magazine, and other national publications."

(*The Boston Globe*, February 29, 2004)

"A snapshot of Georgia's program for uninsured children shows that it's packed with kids of Wal-Mart employees.

"A state survey found 10,261 of the 166,000 children covered by Georgia's PeachCare for Kids health insurance in September 2002 had a parent working for Wal-Mart Stores. . . .

"The survey findings surface as Wal-Mart's pay, benefits and corporate policies have come under fire nationally. Labor unions and other critics have denounced the Arkansas-based retail giant for what they call low-wage, low-benefit jobs. And unions fear the influence Wal-Mart practices could have on employee benefits in all industries. . . .

" 'Most employees who make $7 to $8 an hour can't afford health insurance,' said Cindia Cameron, organizing director of 9to5, National Association

274-0933. Fax: (414) 272-2870. E-mail:
lindagb@9to5.org.

INTERNSHIPS

Unpaid internships in the areas of organizing, administration, and media are offered. See www.9to5.org for internship opportunities. Internships is generally cover 2–4 months. Application deadlines and hours vary. Contact Linda Garcia-Barnard, director of administration, 152 W. Wisconsin Avenue, Suite 408, Milwaukee, WI 53203. Phone: (414) 274-0933. Fax: (414) 272-2870. E-mail: lindagb@9to5.org.

NEWSLETTERS

The 9to5 Newsline for individuals
    (5 times per year)
The 9to5 Newsline for institutions
    (5 times per year)

PUBLICATIONS

9to5 Guide to Combating Sexual Harassment
The Job/Family Challenge: Not for Women Only
Publishes research reports on various issues
Wage Replacement for Family Leave: Is It Feasible?
Welfare As We Know It: The Case For Reforming TANF
Women at Work

CONFERENCES

Annual Leadership Training Conference;
    Washington DC, early June.

of Working Women. 'When a very wealthy employer passes off to taxpayers what is rightfully a labor force cost, that's a serious public policy problem.' "
(*The Atlanta Journal-Constitution*, February 27, 2004)

"Now that the federal Family and Medical Leave Act is 10 years old, both its supporters and critics in Congress seem to be saying, 'It's a great thing. Let's change it. . . .'

"Because FMLA leave is unpaid, 'Many people who need it the most can't afford to take it, so the law gives them nothing,' said Ellen Bravo, co-director of 9to5, National Association of Working Women. . . ."
(*The Boston Herald*, May 5, 2003)

"A bill introduced in the state Senate aims at restricting the use of staffing agencies to replace striking workers.

"The proposal, from Sen. Tim Carpenter (D-Milwaukee), stems from complaints by striking sausage makers who are entering their 12th month of picketing at the Tyson pepperoni plant in Jefferson.

" 'I felt it was very unfair to use temporary workers against the Tyson workers,' Carpenter said. He said that especially in a difficult labor market, temporary workers shouldn't have to choose between not earning a paycheck and crossing a picket line. 'It's pitting good people against good people,' Carpenter said.

"Ellen Bravo, national director of Milwaukee-based 9to5, National Association of Working Women, agreed.

" 'I think the Tyson's strike reminds us that the problem of replacement workers is a difficult one for any group of workers trying to improve their situation,' Bravo said."
(*Milwaukee Journal Sentinel* [Wisconsin], January 28, 2004)

"With the economy uncertain and many companies looking to keep down costs and pare their employment rolls, growing numbers of workers are filing charges of pregnancy discrimination. . . .

"Ellen Bravo, the director of 9to5 National Association of Working Women in Milwaukee, said, 'Pregnancy discrimination is still alive and well and escalating.' She attributed some of the increase in complaints to corporate downsizing, but said a heightened awareness of women's rights at work also played a role. . . .

"Ms. Bravo of 9to5 says she believes that pregnancy discrimination cases are undercounted because many women are afraid to make waves. Some accept demotions because they are happy to have a job and others believe that a lawsuit could be career suicide."
(*The New York Times*, September 14, 2003)

"Without a hint of melodrama, moms say their most important job is raising children, but that gets short shrift from policymakers and corporate America. Women are made to decide between children and career. Although it's not over, women who choose children are penalized for their decision.

"Experts in the field call children the 'human capital' produced by parents. Women suffer, children suffer and, ultimately, society suffers.

" 'We have this big contradiction,' said Ellen Bravo, director of 9to5, the National Association of Working Women. 'We say we care about early childhood development and how important it is for the future, but we pay day care workers so little, and we don't value the women who stay home to take care of their children.

" 'That's what we really think of mothers. . . .'

" 'We need to challenge the stereotypes about this work,' said Bravo of 9to5. 'It marginalizes women and what they do. Raising children is women's work, or so the argument goes. It's what women do. Therefore, it's considered less important. . . .'

"Technology has provided at-home moms a chance at both worlds. With Internet-connected computers, cell phones and fax machines, thousands of women now telecommute to jobs or work as consultants or independent contractors, said Marie Bailey of BlueSuitMom.com, who does so herself.

"But this doesn't always work out as planned, Bravo said.

" 'The problem is that most people underestimate what it takes to be a caretaker,' she said. 'So they wind up working at midnight, figuring they'd squeeze stuff in during the day. So if you work at home, sometimes you have to get child care anyway.'

"Bailey, in her book 'The Women's Home-Based Business Book of Answers,' interviewed 40 women who worked out of their home while taking care of children and found Bravo's assessment to be accurate."

(*San Antonio Express-News* [Texas], September 6, 2003)

The Ocean Conservancy

Established in 1972

DIRECTOR

Roger T. Rufe Jr., president and chief executive officer. He joined The Ocean Conservancy after a 34-year career in the U.S. Coast Guard. While in the Coast Guard, Admiral Rufe served as captain of five ships, as chief of congressional affairs, and as U.S. delegate to the Marine Environment Protection Committee of the International Maritime Organization in London. Rufe leads The Ocean Conservancy's strategic initiatives to expand the organization's capacity regionally and nationally to clean America's oceans, protect marine wildlife, conserve and restore marine fish populations, and protect ocean ecosystems. Rufe is a member of the Pew Oceans Commission, an independent group of American leaders from science, fishing, conservation, business, and government conducting the first review of national ocean policies in more than 30 years. He also serves on the Executive Committee of the World Conservation Union's Species Survival Commission. Rufe earned a B.S. in Engineering from the U.S. Coast Guard Academy and a M.A. in public administration from New York University. He is a graduate of the Naval War College and the National War College.

BOARD OF DIRECTORS

Robert N. Allen Jr.
John Bierwirth
Janet Bohlen
Paul K. Dayton
Sylvia A. Earle
Debra Erickson
James L. Ferman Jr.
Philip M. Gresh
David P. Hunt
Gale Anne Hurd
Chris Kuebler
Thomas Joseph Lucey
Caroline Macomber
Cecily Majerus
Susan P. Martin
J. Thomas McMurray
Steven Miller
H. Edward Muendel
John C. Ogden
R. Dana Ono
Feodor Pitcairn
Shari Sant Plummer
Robert S. Shulman
Barbara Sweet
John R. Twiss Jr.
George M. Woodwell

SCOPE

Members: 155,000 members; 600,000 volunteers and activists
Branches/chapters: Regional offices in AK, CA, FL, and ME

CONTACT INFORMATION

1725 DeSales Street, NW, Suite 600, Washington, DC 20036
Phone: (202) 429-5609 • *Fax:* (202) 872-0619
General E-mail: ocean@oceanconservancy.org •
Web site: www.oceanconservancy.org

Communications Director: Stephanie Drea
(202) 857-1682 • sdrea@oceanconservancy.org
Human Resources Director: Denise Thomas-Toliver
(202) 429-5609 • dtoliver@oceanconservancy.org

PURPOSE: "The Ocean Conservancy strives to be the world's foremost advocate for the oceans. Through research, education, and science-based advocacy, we inform, inspire and empower people to speak and act for the oceans."

CURRENT CONCERNS: Promoting the health, diversity and resilience of coastal and ocean ecosystems

METHOD OF OPERATION: Advertisements • Coalition forming • Conferences/seminars • Congressional testimony • Grassroots organizing • Internet (databases, e-mail alerts, and Web site) • Internships • Legislative/regulatory monitoring (federal and state) • Litigation • Lobbying (federal, state, and grassroots) • Media outreach • Polling • Product merchandising • Research

SPECIFIC PROGRAMS/INITIATIVES: Clean Oceans program (to restore and protect clean ocean and coastal waters) • Education and outreach to inspire an ocean ethic in everyone • Fish program (to ensure healthy, abundant marine fish populations and responsible fishing) • The International Coastal Cleanup • Marine wildlife program (to conserve and restore marine wildlife and the habitats that sustain them)

Effectiveness and Political Orientation

"More than 40,000 volunteers are expected to turn out Saturday to comb 340 tons of trash from California's marine areas in an annual event that the 'Guinness Book of World Records' has hailed as the world's largest garbage collection.

"The 18th Annual California Coastal Cleanup Day, held in concert with the Ocean Conservancy's international event, will take place from 9 a.m. to noon at dozens of locations around the Bay Area. . . .

"Information about the kinds of trash and where it was found will be entered into the Ocean Conservancy's international database, which is used to figure out pollution solutions.

"For example, last year, more than 297,000 cigarette butts were plucked from California's shores.

Field offices in Santa Cruz and Santa Barbara, CA; Key West, FL, St. John, Virgin Islands Office of Pollution Prevention and Monitoring, Virginia Beach, VA
Affiliates: None

STAFF
109 total—84 full-time professional; 25 full-time support; plus 1 support part-time, 600,000 volunteers; and 2 interns

TAX STATUS
501(c)(3)

FINANCES
Budget: 2004—$12 million; 2003—$12 million; 2002—$12 million

FUNDING SOURCES
Contributions, grants, and bequests, 88%; investment income, 6%; federal financial assistance, 4%; program income, royalties, and other, 2%

PAC
None

EMPLOYMENT
Potential applicants can learn about job openings with this organization through postings on its Web site at www.oceanconservancy.org. This organization offers positions as administrators, accountants, scientists, fundraisers, legislative and media specialists, information technology and web specialists, writers and editors, grassroots and advocacy organizers, program directors, and counsels. Applicants should send resumes and other materials for employment to Julie Burritt, human resources generalist, 1725 DeSales Street, NW, Suite 600, Washington, DC 20036. Phone: (202) 429-5609. Fax: (202) 872-0619. E-mail: jobs@oceanservancy.org.

INTERNSHIPS
This organization offers internship opportunities. Potential applicants can learn about paid and unpaid internships from the organization's Web site at www.oceanconservancy.org. Duration of internships and hours per week can vary depending on the internship and the availability of the applicant; application deadlines are posted with the internship opportunity. Internships may become available at any of Ocean Conservancy's offices. Applicants must be either an undergraduate or graduate student.

The internship coordinator at this organization is Julie Burritt, human resources generalist, 1725 DeSales Street, NW, Suite 600, Washington, DC 20036. Phone: (202) 429-5609. Fax: (202) 872-0619. E-mail: jobs@oceanservancy.org.

NEWSLETTERS
Blue Planet Quarterly Magazine
Coastal Connection Newsletter
   (3 times per year)

"Since the program's inception in 1985, more than 506,000 Californians have removed more than 7.5 million pounds of trash and recyclables from the states' marine areas, according to program literature.

"Nationwide last year, more than 745,000 people hauled away more than 12.5 million pounds of trash in one day.

"And this year, more than 100 countries are expected to participate in the international cleanup event."

(*The San Francisco Chronicle,* September 19, 2002)

"Luxury cruise ships that carry millions of passengers each year to the world's most remote beauty spots are endangering marine life with a trail of pollution, a new study has warned.

"The new generation of super-liners—some of which can carry as many as 2,500 passengers and 1,200 crew—are daily pumping thousands of gallons of sewage, oily water, garbage and chemicals into the sea with potentially disastrous effects for delicately balanced ecosystems such as coral reefs.

"The report by the American conservation group the Ocean Conservancy comes as the leading cruise firms in Britain, P&O, Cunard and Fred Olsen, plan to expand their fleets.

"Last month, Cunard laid the keel for its new Pounds 600m flagship, the Queen Mary 2, which will be [the] largest and most expensive passenger ship ever built when it enters service in 2004. The ship will carry 2,620 passengers and 1,254 crew.

"The vessel is, however, just one of many new ships. 'These cruise holidays are increasingly popular but the ships are like floating cities without any rules on sewage and waste disposal,' said Roger Rufe of the Ocean Conservancy.

"The study found the amount of waste generated by each cruise passenger was far greater than it would be if they holidayed on land. A typical ship's daily waste output would include:

"37,000 gallons of oily bilge water; 30,000 gallons of sewage; 255,000 gallons of waste water—from showers, laundries and galleys; 15 gallons of toxic waste from photo-processing, dry cleaning and painting; seven tons of rubbish.

"The report adds that the number of ships is surging. In 2000 about 240 cruise liners carried 10m people to and through some of the world's most vulnerable wildlife areas, including the glacial bays of Alaska, coral reefs and islands in the Caribbean and the historic coasts of the Mediterranean."

(*Sunday Times* [London, England], July 21, 2002)

"The world's oceans are in failing health today, mostly the result of years of overfishing, according to a report by the Ocean Conservancy, a Washington, D.C.-based environmental group.

"Overfishing is proving to be even more damaging than pollution or global warming, said Roger Rufe, president of the Ocean Conservancy and a retired Coast Guard vice admiral. 'It has had a more profoundly negative effect on ocean ecosystems than all other human impacts,' he said.

"Dozens of species of fish are so vulnerable that without immediate action—including an overhaul of the way fisheries are managed—they face extinction, the report warned. . . .

"The Ocean Conservancy is recommending that the national fisheries service adopt a plan for sustaining entire underwater ecosystems, rather than take a species-by-species, crisis-management approach. It also proposes a national agency to oversee the oceans."

(*Milwaukee Journal Sentinel* [Wisconsin], July 14, 2002)

"Two environmental groups filed a lawsuit Monday that accused the National Oceanic and Atmospheric Administration and the National Marine Fisheries Service of failing to halt overfishing of large coastal sharks.

"The suit, filed in federal court in Tampa, is part of an ongoing dispute between environmental groups like the Audubon Society and Ocean Conservancy and fishermen over how many pounds of shark should be caught in the Gulf of Mexico and along the Atlantic coast each year.

"The latest suit claimed that the government agencies have failed to rebuild large coastal shark populations and that the National Marine Fisheries Service has 'short-circuited public participation in fisheries management by illegally eliminating opportunity for comment and allowing key management decisions to be made through secret negotiations and by outside parties. . . .'

"The suit centers on the government quota on shark fishing in coastal waters. In 1997, the quota was 1,284 tons per year. In 1998, the marine service released a controversial report that suggested the shark population would fall below sustainable levels if the quota wasn't lowered. In 1999, the quota was lowered to 816 tons per year but never instituted, as lawsuits and other disputes quickly followed. Fishermen are currently working under the 1997 quota.

"Monday's lawsuit calls for the marine service to reinstitute the 1999 quota. The suit alleges that the marine service caved in to the fishermen. The marine service called for the 1998 study to be peer reviewed. After receiving the opinion of the four review panel members, two of whom had no shark experience, the marine service allowed the 1997 quota to stand, the suit stated. . . ."

(*St. Petersburg Times* [Florida], January 30, 2002)

"About 2,000 Western New Yorkers combed the shorelines of Lake Erie, Lake Ontario and many other waterways Saturday during an international cleanup effort.

"Volunteers representing 55 organizations turned out for the 13th annual Great Lakes Beach Sweep, part of the International Coastal Cleanup of the Ocean Conservancy.

"The cleanup is billed as the largest environmental volunteer project in the world, with 90 countries and all 50 states participating.

"The local effort also targeted shoreline of waterways in Erie, Chautauqua, Cattaraugus and Niagara counties.

"From Wilson to Dunkirk Harbor, area residents filled hundreds of bags with shoreline debris.

"Volunteers worked two hours, walking beaches and shorelines, where they found litter as large as beds and doors. . . ."

(*Buffalo News,* September 16, 2001)

OMB Watch

Established in 1983

DIRECTOR

Gary D. Bass, founder and executive director. Bass has testified before Congress, appeared on national television, addressed groups across the country, and written extensively on federal budgetary, program management, regulatory, and information policy issues. Previously, he created in 1989 the Right-to-Know Network (RTK NET), a free online computer service to provide community groups with access to government data, such as data on toxic chemicals, censuses, housing demographics, home mortgage activity, and campaign finances. Bass also served as president of the Human Services Information Center. He received a combined doctorate in psychology and education from the University of Michigan.

BOARD OF DIRECTORS

Nancy Amidei, vice-chair; University of WA School of Social Work

Gary Bass, executive director, OMB Watch

Barbara Chow; executive director, National Geographic Society, Education Foundation

Lynn R. Goldman; professor, Johns Hopkins University, Bloomberg School of Public Health

Kristine Jacobs; executive director, Jobs Now Coalition

Ed Jayne; associate director of Legislation, AFSCME

Bob Lawrence, treasurer; consultant

Mark Lloyd; director, Civil Rights Forum on Comm. Policy

Paul Marchand; director of governmental affairs, The Arc

J. Michael McCloskey

Ellen Miller; publisher, TomPaine.com

David C. Rice

Mark Rosenman, chair; distinguished public service professor, vice president for social responsibility, Union Institute

Margaret Seminario; director, Occupational Safety & Health Dept., AFL-CIO

Barbara Somson; deputy legislative director, United Auto Workers

Jim Weill; president, Food Research and Action Center

SCOPE

Members: Listservs contain more than 10,000 e-mail addresses from individuals, nonprofit organizations, business, and government entities

Branches/chapters: None

Affiliates: None

STAFF

15 total—12 full-time professional; 3 full-time support; plus 1 part-time support

CONTACT INFORMATION

1742 Connecticut Avenue, NW, Washington, DC 20009

Phone: (202) 234-8494 • *Fax:* (202) 234-8584

General E-mail: ombwatch@ombwatch.org • *Web site:* www.ombwatch.org

Communications Director: Information unavailable

Human Resources Director: Barbara Western, director of operations (202) 234-8494, westernb@ombwatch.org

PURPOSE: OMB Watch is a nonprofit research and advocacy organization dedicated to promoting government accountability and citizen participation in public policy decisions. This mission centers on four main areas: the federal budget; regulatory policy; public access to government information; and policy participation by nonprofit organizations. OMB Watch was founded in 1983 to lift the veil of secrecy shrouding the powerful White House Office of Management and Budget (OMB). The organization has since expanded its focus to include the substantive areas that OMB oversees.

CURRENT CONCERNS: Environmental regulation • Estate tax • Information policy • Nonprofit advocacy rights • Right-to-know • Secrecy • Social investment

METHOD OF OPERATION: Awards program • Coalition forming • Conferences/ seminars • Congressional testimony • Grassroots organizing • Information clearinghouse • Initiative/referendum campaigns • Internet (databases, electronic bulletin boards, e-mail alerts, and Web site) • Legislative/ regulatory monitoring (federal) • Lobbying (federal and grassroots) • Mailing lists • Media outreach • Participation in regulatory proceedings (federal) • Polling • Research • Speakers program • Technical assistance • Training

SPECIFIC PROGRAMS/INITIATIVES: Americans for a Fair Estate Tax • Citizens for Sensible Safeguard • Let America Speak, rtknet.org • Social Investment Initiative

Effectiveness and Political Orientation

"Responding to a chorus of criticism from science advocacy and citizen groups, the White House Office of Management and Budget yesterday released a revised version of proposed guidelines aimed at standardizing the way federal agencies release and use scientific information.

"The revisions mark a partial retreat in what proponents—led by OMB chief of regulatory affairs John Graham—have said was a central strategy in the war against 'junk science.' The 'peer review' guidelines set strict criteria that must be met before scientific information may be released through agency Web sites or other channels, especially if that information is to be used in the crafting of significant regulations.

TAX STATUS
501(c)(3)

FINANCES
Budget: 2004—$1.6 million;
2003—$1.4 million

FUNDING SOURCES
Foundation grants, 88%; corporate donations, 5%; individuals, 3%; publications, 1%; other (technical assistance/reimbursements), 3%

PAC
None

EMPLOYMENT
Current openings are available on the Web site: www.idealist.org. Applications may be sent to Barbara Western, director of operations, 1742 Connecticut Avenue, NW, Washington, DC 20009. Phone: (202) 234-8494. Fax: (202) 234-8584. E-mail: ombwatch@ombwatch.org.

INTERNSHIPS
OMB Watch offers unpaid internships. Information can be found on the Web site or at www.craiglist.org. Application deadline varies. Internship are available in the areas of the federal budget, information policy, non-profit advocacy, and regulatory policy. For more information, contact Barbara Western, director of operations, 1742 Connecticut Avenue, NW, Washington, DC 20009. Phone: (202) 234-8494. Fax: (202) 234-8584. E-mail: ombwatch@ombwatch.org.

NEWSLETTERS
OMB Watcher
Executive Report

PUBLICATIONS
The following is a sample list of publications:
An Attack on Nonprofit Speech: Death By a Thousand Cuts
Citizen's Platform for Right-to-Know
Democracy at Work: Nonprofit Use of Technology for Public Policy Purposes
Handcuffing America's Charities: Case Examples of Organizations Affected by the Istook Amendment
The Nonprofit Agenda: Recommendations to President George W. Bush to Strengthen the Nonprofit Sector
Nonprofit America: Summary of Findings and Outcomes
Plugged in, Tuning up: An Assessment of State Legislative Websites
Results and Findings: Survey of Nonprofits On Government Grants
So You Want to Make A Difference: Advocacy is the Key
Speaking up in the Internet Age: Use and Value of Constituent E-Mail and Congressional Web Sites
Strengthening Nonprofit Advocacy— Preliminary Report
Through the Corridors of Power: A Guide to Federal Rulemaking

"Industry had generally supported the initial version of the proposed guidelines, saying it would help keep shoddy science from shaping federal policies. Among the groups that had written in support were the National Association of Manufacturers, the National Petrochemical and Refiners Association and the American Chemistry Council.

"But critics saw the guidelines as an attempt by the executive branch to gain control over the federal flow of scientific information and slow the implementation of regulations that would be costly to industry. Some advocacy groups and even the Department of Health and Human Services had said the proposal was so slanted against the public interest that it ought to be withdrawn and rethought from scratch.

"'We listened to the scientific community and made revisions designed to make the peer-review policy more objective and workable,' Graham said yesterday.

"The new version, which is now open for an additional 30 days of outside comments, adopts several of the suggestions that were submitted to OMB by 187 outside individuals and groups and by various federal agencies during a comment period that closed in January. . . .

"'These are pretty complex federal rules, and you can't rush this through,' said Gary Bass, executive director of OMB Watch, a Washington-based watchdog group.

"Bass said the guidelines are misguided because they centralize scientific review in an executive office lacking any particular scientific expertise, thus undermining, he said, the federal agencies that have that expertise and subverting the oversight role of Congress. . . ."

(*The Washington Post*, April 16, 2004)

"As the nation stepped up security yesterday with extra police on the streets and fighter jets in the sky, a broad range of specialists warned that the color-coded terrorism alert system should be replaced because it frightens people and wastes public resources even in those cities not mentioned as possible targets in intelligence reports. . . .

"Keith Ashdown of Taxpayers for Common Sense said the across-the-board display of security contributed to an endemic problem of homeland security policy: a funding mechanism that spreads most federal assistance across the country equally rather than giving a disproportionate number of grants to higher-risk targets, such as New York City and Washington, D.C.

"Sean Moulton, a senior policy analyst at OMB Watch, said a related problem has been the failure of the US government to conduct a comprehensive survey measuring exactly how much it costs the nation for each day spent at 'orange' rather than at 'yellow' alert. Specialists say it's a lot, but can't be precise.

"'Normally, the OMB [Office of Management and Budget] would be screaming about doing a cost-benefit analysts,' he said. 'It would make the decision easier if we knew that every time the alert status changed, it cost the nation, say, a billion dollars. Then maybe that would create pressure for a geographic system.'"

(*The Boston Globe*, December 23, 2003)

"Anne Henry, staff attorney at the Minnesota Disability Law Center, was among 12 people selected for a new 'Public Interest Hall of Fame,' created by a public interest advocacy group in Washington, D.C.

"The hall of fame was launched this year by OMB Watch, an organization that was formed 20 years ago to monitor the U.S. Office of Management and Budget but now focuses on broader government accountability as well.

" 'We were looking for unsung heroes, for people who have shown a huge commitment to protecting and promoting the public interest, ' said Gary D. Bass, OMB Watch executive director. . . ."

(*Minneapolis Star Tribune,* October 7, 2003)

"In a move touted as the most significant review of regulations since the Reagan administration, the White House is scrutinizing hundreds of federal rules that industry leaders and others say are too costly and burdensome.

"The review could affect everyday life for millions of Americans by changing such requirements as energy efficiency standards for washing machines and the labeling of genetically modified foods.

"President Bush's opponents say the administration is trying not just to put its imprint on regulations, but to roll back rules crafted by past Congresses and presidents on issues ranging from the environment to workplace safety.

" 'In the Reagan administration, they waged an ideological war on regulation. That war was targeted at health, safety, environmental and civil rights rules,' said Gary Bass, executive director of OMB Watch, a consumer group that tracks the Office of Management and Budget. 'Maybe what (Bush officials) are trying to say, in code, is that they will reinvigorate that same ideological war.' "

(*The San Francisco Chronicle,* December 22, 2002)

"Removing information from Web sites became more of a government interest after Sept. 11, as agencies took down information they thought might be useful to terrorists.

"A nonprofit group in Washington called OMB Watch is trying to assess just how much information agencies removed from public Web sites under the new directives. The group sent requests under the Freedom of Information Act to a dozen agencies in January. So far, only the Environmental Protection Agency has sent back a list.

"According to OMB Watch, E.P.A. officials have restored much of the information that they withdrew from its Web sites last fall, including pages dealing with watersheds in New York City and the Envirofacts database, which allows users to retrieve information about air pollution, chemicals at government and business installations, water pollution and grants.

"Responses to the group's inquiry indicate that other agencies may have removed a significant amount of information from the Web. The Energy Department, according to OMB Watch, reported that it had stacks of information waiting to be organized before it could be sent.

" 'We have nothing we can nail them down on, and we have no index of what they had in the past,' said Sean Moulton, a senior policy analyst with OMB Watch. He said the directives to remove data and the new data-quality guidelines were part of 'an overarching mosaic that is about restricting information and removing information from public access.'

" 'Unfortunately,' Mr. Moulton said, 'Sept. 11 is being utilized as a pivot point for industry to push an agenda they already had.'

"OMB Watch has advocated creation of an office that would oversee what data agencies publish online and the security measures they use. . . ."

(*The New York Times,* June 3, 2002)

Operation Save America

Established in 1988

DIRECTOR

Rev. Philip "Flip" Benham, national director. Benham co-founded Operation Save America in 1988 (then known as Operation Rescue) and has served as its national director since 1994. He earned B.A. degrees in political science and international relations from Florida State University and holds a master of divinity degree from Asbury Theological Seminary.

BOARD OF DIRECTORS

Philip "Flip" Benham, national director

SCOPE

Members: None
Branches/chapters: Chapters in some states
Affiliates: None

STAFF

10 total

TAX STATUS

Nonprofit (not tax-exempt)

FINANCES

Information unavailable

FUNDING SOURCES

Donations

PAC

None

EMPLOYMENT

Information unavailable

INTERNSHIPS

Information unavailable

NEWSLETTERS

Monthly newsletter

PUBLICATIONS

The following is a sample list of brochures:
9/11—Will We Connect the Dots?
Abortion, Islam, and Homosexuality: What Do These Three Have in Common?
Abortion, Who Is Most Responsible?
Are Christians Terrorists?
Does God Still Judge the Nations?
Would Jesus Carry Such Graphic Pictures?
Homosexuality vs. Christianity: Should We Build Bridges or Storm the Gates?

CONFERENCES

Holy Week Conference
national conference in January
summer conference

CONTACT INFORMATION

P.O. Box 740066, Dallas, TX 75374
Phone: (972) 240-9370 • *Fax:* (972) 240-9789
General E-mail: osa@operationsaveamerica.org •
Web site: www.operationsaveamerica.org

Communications Director: Information unavailable
Human Resources Director: Information unavailable

PURPOSE: To "take up the cause of preborn children in the name of Jesus Christ. . . . Jesus Christ is the only answer to the abortion holocaust. It is upon our activist repentance at abortion mills, abortionists' homes, churches, and practices that the Gospel is visibly lived out. We become to the church, to our city, and to our nation living parables which rightly represent God's heart toward His helpless children."

CURRENT CONCERNS: Abortion • Homosexuality • Pornography

METHOD OF OPERATION: Boycotts • Demonstrations • Direct action • Films/video/audiotapes • Grassroots organizing • Initiative/referendum campaigns • Litigation • Media outreach

Effectiveness and Political Orientation

"Members of a local pro-life chapter Wednesday conducted what could be the first of many protests against a planned medical office in the Town of Tonawanda that may include abortion services.

"Toting anti-abortion placards, about two dozen members of Operation Save America Buffalo gathered at 3834 Delaware Ave. to demonstrate against pregnancy terminations in general and the possibility of abortion services at this facility in particular.

"'We're here to warn the neighborhood of what's coming their way,' said the Rev. Robert Behn, an organizer of the protest.

"'One of the problems is that people are all worked up over this, but the same thing is happening in offices on Main Street, Sweet Home Road and in private doctors' offices in the Buffalo area. The location is immaterial. The location has nothing to do with it. Abortion is abortion, and it continues on a large scale.'

"'We are trying to wake up the community, anybody, to stand up for these little babies,' said Behn's wife, Bonnie. . . ."

(*Buffalo News,* March 14, 2002)

"Two pastors—Daniel Thompson, 39, and Kevin Stanfield, 44—were arrested in Wichita, Kan., Saturday morning as they knelt in the street after the final march of a weeklong anti-abortion protest. Coordinated by Operation Save

America, the anti-abortion Summer of Mercy renewal campaign targeted one of the few clinics in the nation that perform late-term abortions. . . ."

(*The Atlanta Journal-Constitution,* July 22, 2001)

"Twenty-eight years after *Roe vs. Wade,* antagonists in the abortion wars chose Cleveland to stage a weekend of bitter words, dueling placards and megaphones raised against hymns.

"Operation Save America, formerly Operation Rescue, brought its road show here, picketing yesterday along several blocks of Euclid Ave. bordering Case Western Reserve University and University Hospitals. Christian children bused in from Pittsburgh held posters of mangled, dead fetuses.

"All the while, students from CWRU and Cleveland State and Ohio State universities who support abortion rights maneuvered to block the signs, shouting challenges and profanity at pickets.

" 'Pro-life men, who are you kidding? You kill doctors and terrorize women,' CWRU student David M. Johnson, 19, chanted into a megaphone. His words mingled with the singing of youths from the Living Hope Church near Pittsburgh, who harmonized on 'Everything That Has Breath Praises the Lord' as their own exhaling made puffs in the cold air. . . .

" 'Take the Gospel of Jesus Christ to the gates of hell and what happens? God shows up,' said the Rev. Philip 'Flip' Benham, executive director of Operation Save America in Dallas. 'I've seen it happen. We can close down these abortion mills in Cleveland in eight months. God has made a promise the gates of hell cannot prevail against him. Goliath, you are comin' down!'

"Benham said his group has forced more than 500 clinics offering abortions to close and expects success in Cleveland. He challenged about 25 pastors at Church on the Rise in Westlake yesterday: 'If they were taking 4-year-olds out of your church and slaughtering them in a building next door, would you be writing a letter to Congress?'. . ."

(*The Plain Dealer* [Cleveland], January 20, 2001)

"When you come to Wichita, bring a flower, or a fetus. It all depends on your perspective. Mayor Bob Knight, an abortion foe, says he has a 'real problem' with antiabortion protesters who displayed graphic posters of abortions around town last week. 'I believe it inflicts deep pain,' he says. 'I'd rather see pictures of roses and neighbors holding hands in support of each other.' But Troy Newman, head of the West Coast arm of the radical antiabortion group Operation Save America, just upped the antics. On Thursday, he orchestrated a 'memorial' service for 'Mark,' an aborted fetus preserved in a glass jar filled with formaldehyde. 'This is blood guilt. . . . It infects the land,' Newman told a crowd of about 200 antiabortion activists.

"The stunt underscored how desperate Operation Save America (previously Operation Rescue) is to recapture what it considers the magic of 1991. That year, 30,000 protesters converged on this city for a 46-day 'Summer of Mercy.' They blockaded abortion clinics and stuck glue in clinic locks. By the time it ended, there had been 2,700 arrests and the city had an $800,000 tab. Ten years later, new federal and state laws have severely curtailed Operation Save America's protest options. Withering 106-degree temperatures kept the numbers down and forced abortion foes to parade in their air-conditioned cars in the afternoon."

(*U.S. News & World Report,* July 30, 2001)

"On the day in 1994 that he says God commanded him to kill an abortion doctor, Paul Hill rose at 4 a.m. and prayed fervently as he clutched his Bible. He drove to a women's clinic in Pensacola, Fla., where he regularly brandished a sign with the exhortation [to] execute murderers, abortionists, accessories. When Dr. John Britton arrived at 7:30 a.m. with his bodyguard and his wife, Hill approached them, raised his shotgun and killed both men. He then laid down his weapon and awaited arrest. At his subsequent trial, Hill, now 49, tried to argue that his act was 'justifiable homicide'—imperative to protect the unborn. When the judge barred that defense, Hill remained silent and unrepentant for the rest of the trial, until a jury convicted him and sentenced him to death. . . .

"Until now, most had assumed that the abortion battle's bloodiest days had passed. After the 1998 killing of an abortion doctor (there have been seven abortion-related murders and 17 attempted ones so far, according to Saporta), Attorney General Janet Reno established a task force to combat such violence, and it abated. Tough laws enacted in the mid-1990s curbed protesters who tried to block access to clinics. The legal crackdown persuaded many to migrate from the streets to the legislatures, where they've become potent lobbying forces. They've struggled to insulate their cause from any association with Hill's fanaticism. Even those still in the streets mostly draw the line at nonviolent civil disobedience—like Flip Benham, director of Operation Save America, who says he's urged members not 'to join that circus' in Florida. . . ."

(*Newsweek,* September 8, 2003)

Pacific Legal Foundation

Established in 1973

DIRECTOR

Robert K. Best, president and chief executive officer. Best previously served as chief of the environmental and land use sections and as deputy director of the Pacific Legal Foundation. He has held several positions in California state government, most recently as director of the department of transportation under Gov. George Deukmejian. His background includes military service and private legal practice. Best served as an adjunct professor at the University of the Pacific's McGeorge School of Law and as a faculty associate with the Lincoln Institute of Land Policy in Cambridge, MA.

BOARD OF TRUSTEES

Richard R. Albrecht; counsel, Perkins Coie LLP, Seattle, WA

Thomas G. Bost; professor of law, Pepperdine University School of Law, Malibu, CA

James J. Busby; president, owner, Security Owners Corp., Martinez, CA

John A. Campbell; president, Lachlan Investments LLC, Fortuna, CA

James L. Cloud; executive vice president, Wells Fargo Bank Alaska, N.A., Anchorage, AK

Greg M. Evans; president and general manager, Evans Management Services, Santa Cruz, CA

Leonard S. Frank; senior vice president, Governmental Affairs, Pardee Homes, Los Angeles, CA

Timothy R. Hall; owner, T. R. Hall Land & Cattle Co., Firebaugh, CA

John C. Harris, chair and chief executive officer, Harris Farms, Inc., Coalinga, CA

Wade L. Hopping; Hopping, Green & Sams, Tallahassee, FL

Thomas C. Leppert; chair and chief executive officer, Turner Corp., Dallas, TX

Warner C. Lusardi; chair of the board, Lusardi Construction Co., San Marcos, CA

Robert E. McCarthy; McCarthy & Rubright, Walnut Creek, CA

April J. Morris; management consultant, Anaheim, CA

Mark S. Pulliam; Latham & Watkins, San Diego, CA

Jerry W. P. Schauffler, president (retired); W.S.I. Builders, Inc., Lafayette, CA

Richard T. Thieriot, chair; Parrott Investment Co., San Francisco, CA

Jeffrey T. Thomas; Gibson, Dunn & Crutcher LLP, Irvine, CA

Charles W. Trainor; Trainor Robertson, Sacramento, CA

Ronald E. van Buskirk; Pillsbury Winthrop LLP, San Francisco, CA

CONTACT INFORMATION

3900 Lennane Drive, Sacramento, CA 95834
Phone: (916) 419-7111 • *Fax:* (916) 419-7747
General E-mail: plf@pacificlegal.org • *Web site:* www.pacificlegal.org

Communications Director: Sigfredo Cabrera
(916) 362-2833 • plf@pacificlegal.org
Human Resources Director: Brenda Beltran
(916) 362-2833 • blb@pacificlegal.org,

PURPOSE: "To utilize the judicial system to influence the law, regulatory environment, and public policy in ways that support the constitutional rights of individuals, the sanctity of property rights, and limits on government authority."

CURRENT CONCERNS: Discrimination • Education reform • Environmental regulation • Government regulation • Judicial responsibility • Land use • Limited government • Private property rights • Rent control • Taxpayer rights • Tort reform • Victims' rights

METHOD OF OPERATION: College of Public Interest Law (postgraduate fellowships) • Conferences/ seminars • Congressional testimony • Legal assistance • Legislative/regulatory monitoring (federal and state) • Library/ information clearinghouse • Litigation • Media outreach • Mediation • Participation in regulatory proceedings (federal) • Research • Speakers program • Training and technical assistance

Effectiveness and Political Orientation

"The Bush administration's plan to alter the Northwest's salmon-saving strategy was met with outrage Thursday by conservation groups claiming that decades and billions of dollars of effort that provided endangered species protection would unravel.

" 'It's totally inverting the way that we view the criteria for success in dealing with the region's salmon problem,' said Jason Miner, conservation director for Oregon Trout, a Portland-based nonprofit group leading restoration projects across the state.

"Miner was referring to the plan's directive to count hatchery fish as part of the total salmon population estimates. . . .

"But many details remain unclear.

"Foremost: Whether the policy will lead to the removal of federal protection from any of the 26 stocks of Pacific salmon now listed as threatened or endangered by the National Oceanic and Atmospheric Administration Fisheries, also known as NOAA Fisheries.

" 'There are still loopholes that NOAA Fisheries could pursue,' said Russ Brooks, an attorney with the Pacific Legal Foundation. The California-based

Richard D. Williams; Williams, Smyth &
Jacks LLP, Los Angeles, CA
Donald J. Willis; Schwabe, Williamson &
Wyatt, Portland, OR

SCOPE

Members: 25,000 supporters
Branches/chapters: Anchorage, AK; Coral
Gables, FL; Honolulu, HI; Bellevue, WA
Affiliates: None

STAFF

42 total

TAX STATUS

501(c)(3)

FINANCES

Revenue: 2002—$7.34 million;
2001—$9.00 million

FUNDING SOURCES

Information unavailable

PAC

None

EMPLOYMENT

Offers law clerk positions to second-, third-,
and fourth-year law school students. Fellowships are also available. See Web site for
more information: http://www.pacificlegal.
org/Employment.asp.

INTERNSHIP OPPORTUNITIES

Information unavailable

NEWSLETTERS

Action Reports (weekly)
At Issue (monthly)
Guide Post (quarterly)

PUBLICATIONS

*A Commonsense Policy to Protect the
Environment*
*Enforcing the California Civil Rights Initiative:
PLF Takes Government Lawbreakers to
Court*
*Environmental Activists Subvert National
Forest Policy*
*Lose Your Property, Lose Your Freedom: A
Wake Up Call for America*
*A Positive Force: The Involvement of Religious
Organizations in Charter Schools*

CONFERENCES

Sponsors or co-sponsors 5–6 annual
conferences on such topics as land use,
rent control, wetlands, and endangered
species

foundation, representing farmers and home builders, brought the lawsuit that forced the government to reconsider the role of hatchery salmon.

"The property owners Brooks represents argue that salmon protections have illegally restricted their use of water and land. They maintain that the fish don't merit federal protection when abundant hatchery fish can readily prevent extinction. Pacific Legal Foundation has filed lawsuits seeking the removal of several stocks from the endangered list.

"Brooks said the government's new approach 'certainly helps us out.' But he said, 'It remains to be seen in the coming year, how this will play out.'"

(*The Oregonian* [Portland], April 30, 2004)

"Services will be held Monday for James L. Wanvig of San Francisco, founder of the Pacific Legal Foundation, the nation's first public interest law firm specializing in property rights. . . .

"He worked for more than 40 years with the San Francisco law firm of Pillsbury Madison & Sutro and founded the Pacific Legal Foundation in 1973, a legacy he may be best remembered for. The foundation, the first to fight for individual property rights, has grown to be the largest and most influential of its type in the country. . . .

"Prompted by what he viewed as the government's increasing infringement of property rights, in 1973 Mr. Wanvig formulated the idea of a public interest law firm that would fight for the rights of private property owners. With the help of several other leading law firms and supporters, he established the foundation in Sacramento and became its first vice chairman.

"'He was one of the original movers and shakers and pulled the foundation together 30 years ago,' said Bob Best, incumbent president of the Pacific Legal Foundation. 'It was a totally new idea to have a foundation of this type. He took the ball and ran with it and turned it into a working idea for this foundation.'

"The foundation has since argued cases before the U.S. Supreme Court, including a case in 1987 that overturned a California Coastal Commission requirement on coastal property owners. . . ."

(*The San Francisco Chronicle,* April 17, 2004)

"The U.S. Fish and Wildlife Service on Monday took the first step toward removing the Western snowy plover from the list of endangered species, a move that could end more than a decade of beach restrictions and other government efforts to keep the shorebird from going extinct.

"The action, which begins a 12-month timetable for scientific study and review, was prompted by petitions from the city of Morro Bay and a citizens group in Lompoc, upset that sections of their beaches have been fenced off during the plover's lengthy nesting season.

"The tiny gray-brown and white plover has emerged as a bird that developers and off-road vehicle drivers love to hate. A popular bumper sticker reads 'Eat Plover.'

"State and federal restrictions to protect the plovers that nest on prime real estate—sandy beaches near the ocean—have thwarted some construction, put popular beaches off-limits to sunbathers and reduced the size of a sandy playground set aside for off-roaders near Pismo Beach.

"'It would be bad enough to close beaches for a bird that is endangered or threatened; it's a crime to do it for a bird that's not,' said Greg Broderick, a Pacific Legal Foundation attorney who filed a lawsuit to force the delisting

question. Broderick maintains that the government relied on 'junk science' to list the plover as threatened under the Endangered Species Act. . . ."

(The Los Angeles Times, March 23, 2004)

"One of the nation's largest conservative public interest law firms has come to the defense of a Hillsborough limousine company owner accused of charging his fares too little.

"The Pacific Legal Foundation, a nonprofit law group based in California, says the county agency that regulates cars for hire is trampling Daniel Steiner's constitutional rights by imposing unfair regulations on him that make it impossible for him to make a living.

"Steiner has been on six months' probation since Oct. 8, when the Hillsborough Public Transportation Commission ruled that he was charging too little for limousine rides.

"The agency ordered him to stop charging his customers less than the required minimum $40 each for rides. PTC regulators said his business threatened the cabbie industry by undercutting the mileage-based fares they must charge.

"A lawyer for the Pacific Legal Foundation—sometimes described as the ACLU of the right—appeared before the PTC Wednesday seeking to have Steiner's punitive probation lifted.

"The PTC denied the request in a 4–0 vote. . . .

"Alicia Rause, a Pacific foundation lawyer based in Coral Gables, accused the commission of concocting a bogus interpretation of its own rules, and threatening to put Steiner out of business to benefit cab companies. . . .

" 'We're not saying they don't have the right to regulate,' Rause said. 'But not to the point where he no longer has the right to work.' "

(St. Petersburg Times [Florida], December 11, 2003)

"A legal challenge from a taxpayer group is likely to delay the first of nearly $15 billion worth of long-term bond sales needed to balance the new state budget, raising the possibility that the plan could begin to unravel.

"State Treasurer Phil Angelides said yesterday that it will be 'very difficult' to sell $1.9 billion in bonds in time to make a scheduled $550 million payment to the state employee retirement system Oct. 1.

"The Legislature, deadlocked between Republicans who oppose tax increases and Democrats who oppose deep spending cuts, took the unprecedented step of using long-term bonds to close much of the $38 billion budget gap.

"However, the bonds are being challenged by the Howard Jarvis Taxpayers Association and the conservative Pacific Legal Foundation, which contend that the state's constitution requires long-term debt to be approved by voters. . . ."

(The San Diego Union-Tribune, August 23, 2003)

Pacific Research Institute for Public Policy

Established in 1979

DIRECTOR

Sally C. Pipes, president and chief executive officer. Before becoming president of the Pacific Research Institute (PRI) in 1991, Pipes was assistant director of the Fraser Institute in Vancouver, Canada. She previously worked for the Financial Institutions Commission of British Columbia and was a member of the Vancouver City Planning Commission. Pipes writes a bimonthly column in *Chief Executive Magazine.*

BOARD OF DIRECTORS

Lisa Gable, chair; Guillermin Group
Sally C. Pipes, president & chief executive officer, Pacific Research Institute
F. Christian Wignall, vice chair; Capstan, LLC
Thomas C. Magowan, secretary/treasurer; Club Minibar, Inc.
Katherine H. Alden; Woodside Hotels & Resorts
Frank E. Baxter; Jefferies & Co., Inc.
Katherine E. Boyd
Michael Carpenter; Altria Group
Robert J. Ernst III; attorney at law
James T. Farrell; Fremont Group
Peter C. Farrell; ResMed
Mark B. Hoffman; Commerce One
Samuel H. Husbands Jr.
Clark S. Judge; White House Writers Group
David H. Keyston, emeritus
Francis A. O'Connell, emeritus
Daniel Oliver; former chair, Federal Trade Commission
Brian S. Tracy; Brian Tracy International
Richard A. Wallace; Freedom Communications, Inc
Jean R. Wente; Wente Vineyards

SCOPE

Members: None
Branches/chapters: Sacramento, California, office
Affiliates: None

STAFF

15 total

TAX STATUS

501(c)(3)

FINANCES

Revenue: 2002—$3.15 million; 2001—$4.42 million; 2000—$4.34 million

FUNDING SOURCES

Foundation grants, 75%; individual donations, 18%; corporate donations, 7%

PAC

None

CONTACT INFORMATION

755 Sansome Street, Suite 450, San Francisco, CA 94111
Phone: (415) 989-0833 • *Fax:* (415) 989-2411
Sacramento Office
1414 K Street, Suite 200, Sacramento, CA 95814
Phone: (916) 448-1926 • *Fax:* (916) 448-3856
General E-mail: info@pacificresearch.org • *Web site:* www.pacificresearch.org

Communications Director: Susan Martin, public relations associate
(415) 955-6120 • smartin@pacificresearch.org
Human Resources Director: Information unavailable

PURPOSE: "Promotes the principles of individual freedom and personal responsibility. The Institute believes these principles are best encouraged through policies that emphasize a free economy, private initiative, and limited government."

CURRENT CONCERNS: Children's issues • Civil rights • Education • Environmental studies • Health care reform • Legal reform • Privatization • Regulation of the Internet • Urban studies

METHOD OF OPERATION: Awards program • Conferences/seminars • Congressional testimony • Educational foundation • Internet (Web site) • Legislative/regulatory monitoring (federal and state) • Library/information clearinghouse • Media outreach • Research • Scholarships • Speakers program

Effectiveness and Political Orientation

"A feud over telecommunications policy has erupted among leading conservatives that paints Grover Norquist, an informal adviser to the Bush administration, as a friend of telecommunications regulation and puts others in the unusual position of siding with Democratic senators.

"A dozen conservative scholars yesterday wrote a letter to Norquist assailing him for what they charge is his wrongheaded approach to telecommunications regulation. The letter alleges that Norquist has abandoned his free-market roots when it comes to issues such as implementation of a national broadband policy.

"Conservatives and major industry groups have vigorously advocated a national broadband policy that would include deregulating key aspects of the industry. But they've been frustrated by their lack of progress at a time when the White House and Congress are both in Republican hands. Some have blamed Norquist, who they say has been hesitant to embrace deregulatory measures in telecom.

"'Your position on telecommunications deregulation is contrary to the views of the vast majority of free-market economists and policy analysts,' the letter states. 'Your continuing advocacy of the pro-regulation position is destruc-

INTERNSHIPS

Summer unpaid policy internships are available within PRI's four research centers: education, entrepreneurship, the environment, and technology. Applicants for the education internship must be willing to work in PRI's Sacramento office; the other positions are based in San Francisco. Job responsibilities include research assistance and some administrative duties, as well as the opportunity to write op-eds and/or short policy briefings for possible publication. A background in economics or political science is helpful but not required. Internships typically begin in early June and conclude in late August. Send a resume and cover letter to Lisa MacLellan, vice president of public policy, 755 Sansome Street, Suite 450, San Francisco, CA 94111. Fax: (415) 989-2411. E-mail: lmaclellan@pacificresearch.org.

NEWSLETTERS

Action Alerts (periodic)
Capital Ideas (weekly)
The Contrarian (bimonthly)
Impact (monthly)

PUBLICATIONS

The following is a sample list of publications:
The Age of Reagan: The Fall of the Old Liberal Order 1964–1980
Foreign Entanglements: An Institutional Critique of U.S. Foreign Policy
Free The Universities: Reforming Higher Education To Keep Pace With The Information Age
Lead Astray: Inside an EPA Superfund Disaster
School Reform: The Critical Issues
Telecrisis: How Regulation Stifles High-Speed Internet Access
They Have Overcome: High-Poverty, High-Performing Schools in California

CONFERENCES

Annual Privatization Dinner
Breakfasts, lunches, receptions, and policy forums

tive to the cause of limited government. To the extent your efforts are successful, the effect will be to reduce capital formation, slow job creation, impede productivity growth and stifle individual liberty and economic freedom.'

"The presidents of the Progress and Freedom Foundation, the Pacific Research Institute and the Competitive Enterprise Institute as well as scholars at the Hoover Institution and the Manhattan Institute all signed the letter."

(*The Washington Post,* February 26, 2004)

"In 'Prey,' Michael Crichton's latest novel, to be released this week, the master of technology run amok sets his sights on nanotechnology and describes a horde of bacterium size machines that break out of a lab and evolve into flesh eating, self reproducing predators. While even experts in nanotechnology consider it 'so new that it barely exists,' the science already sparks widespread alarm among environmentalists and disarmament proponents, not to mention science fiction writers.

"Over the summer, the Action Group on Erosion, Technology and Concentration, in Winnipeg, Manitoba, called on world leaders to declare an immediate moratorium on the commercial production of nano materials. In the August issue of 'Disarmament Diplomacy,' Editor Sean Howard made an appeal for an 'inner space' treaty 'to protect the planet from devastation caused accidentally, or by terrorists, or in open conflict by artificial atomic and molecular structures capable of destroying environments and life forms from within.'

"Last week, to counter the growing negative publicity and promote a policy environment more conducive to nanotechnology, the Pacific Research Institute for Public Policy released a report examining several regulatory alternatives. PRI added nanotechnology to its studies last year when it discovered that cautionary tales of unchecked nanotechnology were not relegated to technophobes."

(*eWeek,* November 25, 2002)

"Environmental quality continues to make dramatic improvements in the US, according to the 2002 Index of Leading Economic Indicators recently released by the Pacific Research Institute (PRI).

"The study used government data to examine long-term air and water quality trends, toxic chemicals and land use, as well as biodiversity issues. . . ."

(*Environmental Design & Construction,* May 2002)

"When there's evidence that a traditional form of teaching works well, California educrats are swift to act. Alas, acting means writing a letter that takes umbrage at the notion that traditional pedagogy can work.

"Last month, the San Francisco libertarian think-tank Pacific Research Institute released a survey that blasted California State University, which trains more than half of California's teachers, for cleaving to 'student-centered' instruction. (Harvard education professor Jeanne Chall described the 'student-centered' philosophy as fearing that direct teaching 'may inhibit the learner, diminishing curiosity and deflating creativity.') The institute cited research that found 'teacher-centered' instruction—where the teacher uses lesson plans, drills and lectures—to be more effective, especially for poor kids. The institute also found that CSU education schools are knee-deep in the student-centered muck.

"The survey was not peer-reviewed. One researcher cited in the survey complained to a CSU dean that PRI selectively (if accurately) reported pro-teacher-centered findings, but not contrary information. . . ."

(*The San Francisco Chronicle,* May 31, 2001)

"With cleaner water and air and reduced toxic emissions in the United States since the first Earth Day in 1970—according to the Pacific Research Institute's 'Index of Leading Environmental Indicators'—efforts to curtail planetary defilement obviously are succeeding in some measure. Less clear is what or who should get credit for the progress that has been made. Such considerations will figure into how nations deal with continuing pollution problems.

"In touting environmental progress, PRI maintains that wealthy nations are more able to battle pollution, which is an argument for economic policies that let business thrive. Those policies, in turn, favor the goals of the Summit of the Americas, which began Friday in Quebec to hammer out agreements among 34 nations to abolish tariffs within the Western Hemisphere, creating a Free-Trade Area of the Americas and bringing competition and wealth in its wake. . . ."

(*The Houston Chronicle,* April 22, 2001)

Peace Action

Established in 1957

DIRECTOR

Kevin Martin, executive director. Martin became executive director of Peace Action and Peace Action Education Fund in September 2001. Martin previously served as director of Project Abolition from August 1999 through August 2001. He came to Project Abolition after ten years in Chicago as executive director of Illinois Peace Action. Prior to his decade-long stint in Chicago, Kevin directed the community outreach canvass for Peace Action (then called Sane/Freeze) in Washington, DC. He started his career with SANE (prior to the merger with The Nuclear Freeze) in 1985 as a door-to-door canvasser in Washington, Boston, and Pittsburgh. Martin received a B.A. in international politics from Pennsylvania State University in 1984.

BOARD OF DIRECTORS

Information unavailable

STAFF

19 total—15 full-time professional; 4 full-time support; plus 6 part-time support; 20 volunteers; 4 interns

TAX STATUS

Peace Action is 501(c)(4)

FINANCES

Budget: 2004—$1.1 million; 2003—$1.2 million; 2002—$802,000

FUNDING SOURCES

Foundation grants, 5%; membership dues, 85%; special events/projects, 10%

SCOPE

Members: 103,000
Branches/chapters: 28 state affiliates
　　100 chapters
Affiliates: Peace Action Education Fund is
　　501(c)(3)

PAC

Peace Action PAC

PAC CONTRIBUTIONS 2002

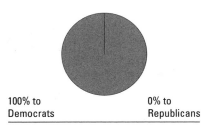

100% to
Democrats

0% to
Republicans

CONTACT INFORMATION

1100 Wayne Ave, Suite 1020, Silver Spring, MD 20910
Phone: (301) 565-4050 • *Fax:* (301) 565-0850
Web site: www.peace-action.org

Communications Director: Scott Lynch
(301) 565-4050x330 • slynch@peace-action.org
Human Resources Director: Information unavailable

PURPOSE: (the merger of SANE and The Nuclear Freeze movement) is committed to educating and organizing at the grassroots level to produce the political will to achieve nuclear disarmament, a reduction of the Pentagon's piece of the Federal discretionary budget from the current 52% to 25%, an end to the international arms trade and the building of a foreign policy based on American democratic values, the rule of law, human rights and international cooperation.

CURRENT CONCERNS: Arms trade • Federal budget • Foreign policy • National security • Nuclear weapons • Patriot Act • Preemptive war policy (President Bush's) • Star wars missile defense

METHOD OF OPERATION: Advertisements • Campaign contributions • Congressional voting analysis • Demonstrations • Direct action • Educational foundation • Electoral politics • Films/video/audio tapes • Grantmaking • Grassroots organizing • Information clearinghouse • Initiative/referendum campaigns • International activities • Internet (databases, e-mail alerts, and Web site) • Internships • Legislative/regulatory monitoring (federal) • Legislative/regulatory monitoring (state) • Litigation • Lobbying (federal, state, and grassroots) • Local/municipal affairs • Mailing lists • Media outreach • Participation in regulatory proceedings (federal) • Polling • Product merchandising • Professional development services • Speakers program • Training • Voter registration • Voting records

SPECIFIC PROGRAMS/INITIATIVES: Campaign for a New Foreign Policy

Effectiveness and Political Orientation

"Recognizing that the occupation of Iraq by multinational corporations will continue, and further recognizing that to change the economic structure of a country by an occupying power is a violation of both the Hague Resolutions and the U.S. Army's Law of Land Warfare, which both protect property rights embodied in a country's basic laws, Peace Action, the nation's largest grassroots peace and justice organization, approved resolutions at its national congress in November, calling for the following actions:

- Congressional hearings to investigate the activities and influence of war profiteers.

EMPLOYMENT

Current openings are available on the Web site. Send materials to Peter Deccy, development director, 1100 Wayne Ave, Suite 1020, Silver Spring, MD 20910. Phone: (301) 565-4050, ext. 330. Fax: (301) 565-0850. E-mail: pdeccy@peace-action.org.

INTERNSHIPS

Offers paid and unpaid internships during summer, fall, and spring. Application deadline is ongoing. Interns are required to work 20–30 hours per week. Internship areas include communications, organizing, and development. Interns must have strong written and verbal communication skills. For additional information, contact Carrie Benzschawel, program associate. Phone: (301) 565-4050, ext. 314. E-mail: cbenzschawel@peace-action.org.

NEWSLETTERS

Action Report (quarterly)

PUBLICATIONS

International Cooperation
Nuclear Weapons
Real Solutions for a Safer World (fact sheet)
Throwing Money at the Pentagon (fact sheet)
US and Iraq
US Arms Sales

CONFERENCES

Peace Action National Congress organizational governance; location varies; once a year

- Congressional action to curb war profiteering through an 'excess profits' tax, as has been done in prior wars.
- An end to the corporate takeover of Iraq's industry and resources, and their immediate return to the Iraqi people. . . ."

(*Chicago Sun-Times,* December 17, 2003)

"The Smithsonian Institution's planned exhibit of the restored Enola Gay, the B-29 that dropped the first atomic bomb on Hiroshima, Japan, during World War II, will be vigorously protested next month, members of the Western New York Peace Center were told Thursday evening.

"Kevin Martin, executive director of the 91,000-member group Peace Action, spoke to 250 people attending the Peace Center's 37th annual dinner in the Buffalo Convention Center.

" 'U.S. militarism is deeply entrenched,' Martin said, citing the Smithsonian's plans to feature the Enola Gay when opening the new annex to its Air & Space Museum near Dulles International Airport in Virginia. The exhibit opens Dec. 15 amid the holiday season. . . .

" 'I have been to Hiroshima and Nagasaki, and I know people who survived the bombs,' Martin said.

"The director of the new annex says the Enola Gay shouldn't stir controversy because its purpose is to celebrate the role of the B-29 in World War II, not the destruction of the two Japanese cities.

" 'If that were true, they could restore any old B-29,' Martin said. 'There darned well is going to be controversy. We will be there with a 78-year-old survivor who has cancer, who is going to see the plane that dropped the bomb on his city. We're in solidarity with them.'

"Martin said a coalition of groups in the nation's capital asked the Smithsonian to show a more balanced exhibit, but 'we know they won't—and then we'll take the appropriate steps as our counsels call us to take.'. . ."

(*Buffalo News,* October 31, 2003)

"When streets in San Francisco and elsewhere swelled with anti-war demonstrators last winter, activists predicted that President Bush would feel the wrath as Americans marched into the voting booth in 2004.

"Those promises, however, sounded hollow as mass demonstrations dwindled after the war started. The suburbanites and first-time marchers whom activist leaders touted as the base of a new movement retreated to the apolitical cocoon of the carpool, and the rest splintered back into their interest groups.

"Now, with hostilities lingering in Iraq, no weapons of mass destruction having been found, Bush's approval rating dropping and the presidential election season fast approaching, anti-war leaders are trying to rekindle the movement's embers with an unofficial mantra: 'We were right.'

"From an ad featuring a 1983 photo of Defense Secretary Donald Rumsfeld shaking hands with Saddam Hussein that appeared last week on BART, to a TV commercial that began airing in major markets, some peace movement coalitions are trying to reunite their diverse followers by appealing to one of the few things they have in common—their loathing of the Bush administration.

" 'Once the war started, a lot of first-time marchers felt it would be unpatriotic to protest their government and a lot of people went home to lick their wounds,' said Michael Kieschnick, president of Working Assets, a San Francisco long-distance company that donates to liberal causes.

"With polls showing increasing skepticism about the human and economic cost of the war, however, some anti-war groups are seizing the moment. . . .

"California Peace Action, a Berkeley group, rolled out its Rumsfeld-Hussein ads last week on transit systems in Chicago, Washington, DC, and the Bay Area as a way to coax candidates of all stripes to talk about foreign policy—traditionally not a mouth-watering subject for voters."

(*The San Francisco Chronicle,* July 17, 2003)

"Direct Action to Stop the War led hundreds of protesters into the streets to shut down 'business as usual' here in the days after the war started. The anti-war group's mass civil disobedience snarled traffic, forced companies to send workers home and led to more than 2,000 arrests.

"The price to organize all that disruption? Less than $5,000, the group says.

" 'We could do more with more money, and we're definitely trying to get more financial support,' Direct Action organizer Patrick Reinsborough says. 'But we've done a great deal with pretty much no money. We'll take people power over money any day.'

"The anti-war movement runs on more than a shoestring, but it doesn't have deep pockets. Most of the money for marches and demonstrations comes from thousands of donations under $50. Volunteers supply most of the labor to organize, publicize and manage protests. . . .

"Just as the anti-war movement relies on the Internet to recruit followers and coordinate protests, it also increasingly depends on the Web for fundraising. Several groups seek donations on their Web sites.

"National anti-war groups are trying to use celebrities to promote their cause and help raise funds. Many artists contribute money to anti-war efforts, although at this point Hollywood is not a large source of cash, organizers say.

"Groups say they must limit expenses and seek donated office space and phone lines. Pay is often low. But organizers say they sense financial support growing.

" 'People have been coming out of the woodwork,' says Kevin Martin, executive director of Peace Action in Washington. Comedians and a few bands offered Peace Action the proceeds from a recent Los Angeles fundraiser. 'We did almost no work and raised over $8,000 in a one-night benefit at the Roxy,' he says. . . ."

(*USA Today,* March 31, 2003)

People for the American Way

Established in 1984

DIRECTOR

Ralph G. Neas, president. Prior to joining People for the American Way, Neas served as the executive director of the Leadership Conference on Civil Rights. He began his career as chief legislative assistant to U.S. senators Edward W. Brooke (R-MA) and Dave Durenberger (R-MN). During that period, he became the senior Senate staffer on civil rights issues. He drafted the first Women's Economic Equity Act and had a hand in legislation involving civil rights, campaign finance reform, consumer rights, education, environment, ethics reform, health care, and reproductive rights. Neas has also directed national campaigns that have produced landmark legislation such as the Civil Rights Act of 1991, the 1990 Americans with Disabilities Act, the Civil Rights Restoration Act of 1988, the 1988 Fair Housing Acts Amendments, the Japanese Americans Civil Liberties Act, and the 1982 Voting Rights Extension. Neas earned his B.A. from the University of Notre Dame and his J.D. from the University of Chicago Law School.

BOARD OF DIRECTORS

David E. Altschul, chair
James A. Autry
Alec Baldwin
Arthur Bellinzoni
Marilyn Bergman
Lara Bergthold
Mary Frances Berry
Hon. John H. Buchanan Jr.
Father Robert Drinan
Maria Echaveste
Michael Gartner
James Hormel
Dolores Huerta
Michael B. Keegan
Howard Klein
Norman Lear
Rev. Timothy McDonald
Jack Melamed
Ralph G. Neas
John Payton
Anthony T. Podesta
David S. Rose
Joshua Sapan
Carole Shields
Clyde Shorey
Margery Tabankin
Reg Weaver
Geraldine Day Zurn

SCOPE

Members: More than 300,000
Branches/chapters: 5 regional office in Los Angeles, CA; Tallahassee, FL; Chicago, IL; New York, NY; and Houston, TX
Affiliates: People for the American Way Action Foundation, a 501(c)(3) organization

CONTACT INFORMATION

2000 M Street, NW, Suite 400, Washington, DC 20036
Phone: (202) 467-4999 • *Fax:* (202) 293-2672
Toll-free: (800) 326-7329
General E-mail: pfaw@pfaw.org • *Web site:* www.pfaw.org

Communications Director: Peter Montgomery, vice president of communications
(202) 467-4999 • media@pfaw.org.
Human Resources Director: Dibby Johnson
(202) 467-4999 • hr@pfaw.org.

PURPOSE: People for the American Way works to "preserve a climate in which every citizen has the right to believe, worship, think and speak freely." The organization is "dedicated to defending civil rights and liberties, freedom of expression and religion, and to promoting respect for diversity, equal justice, and a sense of community."

CURRENT CONCERNS: Artistic freedom • Building democracy • Censorship • Civil liberties • Civil rights • Education • First Amendment rights • Judicial nominations • Race relations • Regulation of the Internet • Religious expression • Religious Right

METHOD OF OPERATION: Advertisements • Citizen action • Coalition forming • Curriculum development • Extremist activities monitoring • Films/video/audiotapes • Grassroots organizing • Internet • Library/information clearinghouse • Litigation • Media outreach • Polling • Research • Speakers program • Televangelist monitoring

Effectiveness and Political Orientation

"Hundreds of non-profit groups and their members are flooding the Federal Election Commission with objections to new regulations that they fear could limit their election-year advocacy activities.

"Protests are coming from the whole political spectrum, from the National Right to Life Committee to the Sierra Club. They worry that proposed new rules restricting the fundraising of independent political groups could also hamper the ability of non-profit issue groups to criticize federal officeholders during election season, or to mobilize their supporters to vote.

"'This could devastate non-profit advocacy,' said Ralph Neas, president of People for the American Way, a liberal organization. . . ."

(*USA Today,* April 7, 2004)

"A federal appeals court has ruled unconstitutional a Virginia law aimed at preventing juveniles from accessing 'sexually explicit' material on the Internet.

"In a 2 to 1 decision, a panel of the U.S. Court of Appeals for the 4th Circuit this week upheld a lower court ruling that the statute violates First

STAFF
88 total—64 full-time professional; 24 full-time support; plus 2 part-time professional; 4 volunteers; 15 interns

TAX STATUS
501(c)(4)

FINANCES
Budget: 2004—$6.64 million; 2003—$5.45 million; 2002—$5.24 million

FUNDING SOURCES
Individuals, 38%; membership dues, 40%; special events/projects, 11%; other sources, associations, 7%; other, 4%

PAC
People for the American Way Voters Alliance PAC

PAC CONTRIBUTIONS 2002

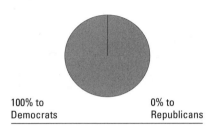

100% to Democrats   0% to Republicans

EMPLOYMENT
The national office in Washington, DC, and five regional offices offer positions such as political organizers, legislative and media representatives, research analysts, writers, and administrative personnel. Openings are posted on the Web site. Interested applicants should send a cover letter and resume to Dibby Johnson, director of human resources, People For the American Way, 2000 M Street, NW, Suite 400, Washington, DC 20036. Fax: (202) 293-2672. E-mail: hr@pfaw.org.

INTERNSHIPS
Several of the departments have paid and unpaid internships available throughout the year, usually covering a semester or during the summer. Interns work with staff in public policy, field, research, education policy, online strategies, and communications departments to track legislation, monitor congressional hearings, assist with grassroots organizing, and help with current research and writing projects, as well as some support duties. These internships, when available, are posted on our Web site. The application deadline varies; however, the application deadline for summer is April 1. Interns work 15–40 hours per week. Prospective interns should have an interest in advocacy and progressive issues and a willingness to learn. Other requirements vary by department. Additional information is available online at: http://www.pfaw.org/pfaw/general/default.aspx?oid=2790.

Interested applicants should send a cover letter and resume to Dibby Johnson, director of human resources, People For the American

Amendment freedoms. Although the state has a 'compelling' interest in protecting minors from potentially harmful online material, the court said, it is impossible to do so in the unfettered, global realm of the Internet without keeping the same material from adults. . . .

"Since 1985, Virginia has barred stores from putting pornographic materials, such as magazines, where minors can see them. In 1999, the law was amended to make it a crime to use the Internet to sell, rent or lend pictures or written narratives that depict 'sexual excitement, sexual conduct or sado-masochistic abuse' to juveniles.

"Several plaintiffs, including PSINet Inc., which was purchased by Washington, D.C.-based Cogent Communications Group Inc. after it filed for bankruptcy, and the nonprofit group People for the American Way, challenged the law. U.S. District Judge James H. Michael Jr. ruled the statute unconstitutional in 2001, and the state appealed.

"Elliot M. Mincberg, legal director for People for the American Way, yesterday hailed the decision as a victory for free speech. Similar laws in New York, New Mexico and Michigan also have been declared unconstitutional, he said. He said he sees the addition of Virginia to that list as particularly significant.

" 'The 4th Circuit Court, by reputation, is probably the most conservative court in the country,' Mincberg said. 'Having the 4th Circuit agree with other courts that have heard this question is a very important step.'

"Restricting Internet use by children, he said, is a decision best left to parents. . . ."

(*The Washington Post*, March 27, 2004)

"States may exclude students majoring in theology from college scholarship programs without running afoul of the Constitution, the Supreme Court ruled Wednesday.

" 'Training someone to lead a congregation is an essentially religious endeavor,' Chief Justice William H. Rehnquist wrote in an opinion for the court's 7–2 majority. 'Indeed, majoring in devotional theology is akin to a religious calling as well as an academic pursuit.'

"Experts said the ruling likely will mean more fights in state legislatures over whether to use taxpayers' money to help parents send children to private, church-based schools. In a 2002 ruling, the high court allowed greater state involvement in religious education, but the justices appeared to draw back with Wednesday's ruling.

"Groups that support separation of church and state hailed the ruling, while those that favor a closer relationship were disappointed.

" 'No state should be compelled by the federal government to fund religious instruction,' said Ralph G. Neas, president of People for the American Way Foundation. 'The Supreme Court reaffirmed this principle and, in the process, strengthened the foundation of religious liberty.' "

(*Hartford Courant* [Connecticut], February 26, 2004)

"A top aide to Senate majority leader Bill Frist, Republican of Tennessee, said yesterday that he is resigning amid an investigation into GOP surveillance of private memos of Democrats on the Senate Judiciary Committee.

"Manuel Miranda, who advised Frist in the bitter partisan warfare over judicial nominees, confirmed yesterday that he intends to officially announce

Way, 2000 M Street, NW, Suite 400,
Washington, DC 20036. Fax: (202) 293-2672.
E-mail: hr@pfaw.org.

NEWSLETTERS
People for the American Way News (quarterly)

PUBLICATIONS
Congressional Handbook
*Dereliction of Duty: Florida's Failed Education
    Policy*
Janice Rogers Brown: In Her Own Words
Upper Brackets: The Right's Tax Cut Boosters
*Who Gets the Credit? Who Pays the
    Consequences? The Illinois Tuition Tax
    Credit*

CONFERENCES
Sponsors conferences periodically

his resignation early next week. News of his intent was first reported yesterday by *The Hill*, a Washington-based newspaper that covers congressional affairs.

"Miranda had been on leave pending the outcome of an investigation into how more than a dozen internal Democratic files detailing strategy for blocking certain nominees were obtained by *The Wall Street Journal*'s editorial page in November. The memos showed the influence of outside interest groups, like the NAACP and People for the American Way, in Democratic decisions about which nominees to fight. . . ."

(*The Boston Globe*, February 6, 2004)

"The U.S. Senate Judiciary Committee is scheduled to meet today to take up the nomination of Janice Rogers Brown to the U.S. Circuit Court of Appeals in the District of Columbia. The appearance is certain to be too little and too late to correct a well-orchestrated campaign of misinformation.

"Left-wing political groups like the NAACP, the Black Congressional Caucus and the misnamed People for the American Way have been working for months to create a strong negative impression of this nominee, suggesting that Brown, though female and black, has turned her back on their interests and on Americans in general.

"It is difficult to blame these groups for their reliance on what is a proven smear technique. They know that if they can successfully tarnish someone's reputation before they make their first and only appearance before the appropriate Senate committee, their dirty work will be difficult, if not impossible, to correct.

"Sure enough, since Brown was nominated by President Bush, little or nothing has been done by the administration to support her.

"Should her committee hearing be televised, it is likely that just a tiny portion of the American public will be able to hear her testimony without media filters.

"Most Americans will never have a chance to hear a detailed discussion of her judicial record. They will only hear secondhand reports in which that record is repeatedly characterized as extreme, insensitive and uncaring."

(*The Denver Post*, October 22, 2003)

People for the Ethical Treatment of Animals (PETA)

Established in 1980

DIRECTOR
Ingrid Newkirk, president. Before helping found People for the Ethical Treatment of Animals (PETA), Newkirk was a deputy sheriff, a Maryland state law enforcement officer, and chief of Animal Disease Control for the District of Columbia's Commission on Public Health. She has written numerous articles and books and has appeared on many national radio and television programs.

BOARD OF DIRECTORS
Michael Rodman, chair
Ingrid Newkirk, secretary
Jeanne Roush

SCOPE
Members: 800,000
Branches/chapters: Declined to comment
Affiliates: (all are nonprofits) People for the Ethical Treatment of Animals India; PETA Deutschland (Stuttgart); Research and Education Foundation; PETA Europe, Ltd. (London); Stichting PETA Nederlands (Amsterdam)

STAFF
201 total—144 full-time professional; 57 full-time support; plus 4 part-time professional; 2 part-time support; 15 volunteers; 6 interns

TAX STATUS
501(c)(3)

FINANCES
Budget: 2004—$22.91 million (estimate); 2003—$21.48 million; 2002—$16.41 million

FUNDING SOURCES
Donations, 94%; merchandise sales, 4%; interest and dividends, 2%

PAC
None

EMPLOYMENT
Employment opportunities are listed on the Web site. Ads are listed in various newspapers throughout the country and with hundreds of colleges and universities. Positions are available in the areas of policy, communications, media, audiovisual, domestic animal issues/casework/fieldwork, humane education, marketing, outreach/grassroots campaigning, writing, research and investigations, captive animal issues/casework, wildlife issues/casework, library, print production, advertising, publications, Web design, legal, finance, information technology, operations, customer service, development, fundraising, membership services, planned giving, and human resources.

CONTACT INFORMATION
501 Front Street, Norfolk, VA 23510
Phone: (757) 622-7382 • *Fax:* (757) 622-0457
General E-mail: peta@peta.org • *Web site:* www.peta.org

Communications Director: Lisa Lange, president of communications
(757) 622-7382, ext. 8284 • peta@peta.org
Human Resources Director: Vicki Carey
(757) 622-7382 • peta@peta.org

PURPOSE: People for the Ethical Treatment of Animals (PETA), with more than 800,000 members, is the largest animal rights organization in the world. Founded in 1980, PETA is dedicated to establishing and protecting the rights of all animals. PETA operates under the simple principle that animals are not to eat, wear, experiment on, or use for entertainment. PETA focuses its attention on the four areas in which the largest numbers of animals suffer the most intensely for the longest periods of time: on factory farms, in laboratories, in the fur trade, and in the entertainment industry. It also works on a variety of other issues, including the cruel killing of beavers, birds, and other "pests," and the abuse of backyard dogs. PETA works through public education, cruelty investigations, research, animal rescue, legislation, special events, celebrity involvement, and direct action.

CURRENT CONCERNS: Abusive animal laboratories • Animals used for entertainment (circuses, rodeos) • Cruelty-free consumer products • Dissection of animals in schools • Factory farming of animals • Hunting and fishing • Product testing on animals • Puppy mills • Trapping and ranching of animals for fur • Treatment of animals in leather trade • Vegetarianism

METHOD OF OPERATION: Advertisements • Awards program • Boycotts • Campaign contributions • Coalition forming • Conferences/seminars • Congressional testimony • Demonstrations • Direct action • Educational foundation • Films/video/audiotapes • Grassroots organizing • International activities • Internet (databases, electronic bulletin boards, e-mail alerts, and Web site) • Internships • Legislative/regulatory monitoring (federal and state) • Library services open to the public • Litigation • Media outreach • Participation in regulatory proceedings (federal) • Performance rating/Report cards (companies and products) • Product merchandising • Research • Shareholder resolutions • Speakers program • Telecommunications services (Hotline: (757) 662-7382) • Technical assistance • Training

Effectiveness and Political Orientation

"Rumor had it that among the personalized bricks purchased by folks at San Diego's new Petco Park, one contained a subtle criticism from the People for Ethical Treatment of Animals (PETA).

"True, says snopes.com, investigator of urban myths.

For further information regarding open positions, call Human Resources at (757) 622-7382. You may send your resume with a cover letter to PETA, ATTN: Human Resource Dept., 501 Front Street, Norfolk, VA 23510. Fax: (757) 628-0789. E-mail: jobopenings@peta.org.

INTERNSHIPS

Internships are open to persons 18 or older. Prospective interns must have a genuine desire to protect animals. Internships are unpaid, but interns receive a food stipend. Length of internships vary and generally last about three months. Applications are accepted all year long. Assignments are flexible and based on the needs of the organization and the skills and interests of the intern. Interns can help with grassroots outreach activities, including demonstrations and tabling events; counsel students and activists about animal issues; conduct library and online research; correspond with members; and deal with local, national, and international media to communicate the animal rights message. Interns also do clerical work, prepare mailings, create props for demonstrations, and help with local outreach.

For more information on the internship program, review the Web site: http://www.peta.org/about/i-faq.asp. Interested applicants should send the intern application form (available on the Web site), a resume, a two-page, double-spaced essay, and three letters of recommendation. Send application package to Melynda DuVal, Human Resource Specialist, 501 Front Street, Norfolk, VA 23510. Phone: (757) 622-7382. Fax: (757) 628-0789. E-mail: MelyndaD@peta.org.

NEWSLETTERS

GRRR! (Kids magazine, three times a year)
PETA's Animal Times (five times a year)

PUBLICATIONS

The Compassionate Cook
Cooking with PETA
Cruelty Free Shopping Guide
Guide to Compassionate Living
PETA Case Reports
PETA Fact Sheets
Shopping Guide for Caring Consumers
Also publishes videos and other marketing material.

CONFERENCES

None

"PETA, which has long complained about conditions at Petco stores, first tried to display a message directly condemning the pet chain but was rebuffed. So, snopes.com said, the group reverted to an acrostic—a message spelled out by the first letters of a series of words.

"In this case it was: 'Break Open Your Cold Ones! Toast The Padres!

"Enjoy This Championship Organization!'

"(Translation: Boycott you-know-what). . . ."

(*The Los Angeles Times,* May 1, 2004)

"Comedian Bill Maher thinks Columbia University's up to something politically incorrect.

"The sharp-tongued stand-up this week spammed nearly 1,800 faculty and staff with an e-mail lambasting the school for its experiments on primates, saying 'wasting money to . . . disfigure and terrorize animals puts Columbia in an ugly and embarrassing position.'

"The university responded by defending its research practices and saying its academics are committed to the highest standards of animal care.

"In his letter, Maher, an animal rights advocate, says one Columbia experiment has pregnant baboons being injected with nicotine and morphine while their fetuses are operated on in utero.

"He says a university veterinarian called People for the Ethical Treatment of Animals to report her colleagues' work habits after seeing experimenters remove a monkey's eyeball to induce a stroke.

"'Even Poe, in a morphine-induced nightmare, couldn't have dreamed up anything as scary as this,' Maher says, in directing staffers to a Web site, www.columbiacruelty.com.

"A Columbia University official would not comment on the group's spam tactic, but defended university practices. . . .

"A PETA spokesman said the group acquired the nearly 1,800 e-mail addresses by cutting and pasting them from departmental Web sites."

(*Newsday* [New York], April 29, 2004)

"Saturday's soggy weather may have dampened many weekend plans, but one Orange County animal lover was particularly vexed.

"'I woke up, looked out the window and went right back to sleep, hoping that it was just a bad dream,' said Ashly Smith, who had planned to spend the morning demonstrating at Huntington Beach's popular Dog Beach.

"When Smith, who helped organize the protest, finally pushed herself to drive to Dog Beach with Peanut, her basset hound, the place was nearly deserted. She headed back home.

"The People for the Ethical Treatment of Animals had hoped to stage a 'snarl in' to protest the alleged mistreatment of animals by a major pet food manufacturer and a billboard company's refusal to let PETA put its claims on an outdoor sign in Orange County. . . .

"PETA alleges that it has uncovered animal abuse by a research lab operated by the Iams Co. of Dayton, Ohio. But when the organization tried to advertise its alleged findings on an Orange County billboard, the sign's owner, New York-based Viacom Outdoor, refused to accept the ad.

"'We have tried to place several other billboards, and we're really very surprised at the reaction we're getting,' said Allison Ezell, national coordinator of PETA's anti-Iams campaign. 'The billboard companies are very scared of going up against Proctor & Gamble, the parent company of Iams.'

"A spokesman for Iams on Friday denied that the company had mistreated animals. 'Their allegations conflict with the basic principles Iams uses in conducting feeding studies,' Kurt Iverson, manager of external relations, said regarding the PETA campaign. The charges, he said, 'are absolutely not true—that's the best way to put it.'"

(*The Los Angeles Times,* April 18, 2004)

"It was only 9C in Toronto yesterday but it felt much hotter at Nathan Phillips Square as a young couple from PETA got down and dirty to promote the vegetarian lifestyle.

"The boyfriend and girlfriend—who hail from the U.S.—set up an air mattress on the sidewalk, crawled under a blanket in their skivvies and locked lips for a one-hour love session dubbed the 'live make-out tour.'

"'We wanted to exemplify what most people already know, which is that vegetarians make better lovers,' a shivering Ravi Chand, 24, said of the passionate People for the Ethical Treatment of Animals demonstration.

"'They tend to be sexier, slimmer, and have more endurance in and out of the bedroom,' added Chand, the PETA campaign co-ordinator, a native of Norfolk, Va. . . ."

(*The Toronto Sun* [Canada], April 15, 2004)

"Nearly naked, painted in tiger stripes and kneeling in cages, activists from People for the Ethical Treatment of Animals took their traveling protest to the Boardwalk on Friday, railing against forthcoming shows by the Ringling Brothers and Barnum & Bailey circus. Two protesters handed out pamphlets, played a video that they said showed abusive circus trainers and appealed to passers-by to boycott the circus. . . ."

(*The New York Times,* April 12, 2004)

"Singer and actress Beyonce Knowles has been attacked by animal-rights activists for continually wearing fur.

"The powerful US lobby group People For The Ethical Treatment of Animals (PETA) will tomorrow launch a campaign against the Grammy award-winning Destiny's Child frontwoman.

"The campaign will begin with a full-page advertisement in the music magazine Billboard, slamming her appearances in animal pelts which, it says, sets a shocking example.

"It features a chilling picture of a pet dog killed by a trap set for animals whose skins are used in fashion.

"'Dear Beyonce: Your many fans at PETA are saddened you have ignored repeated appeals calling your attention to the way minks, foxes and chinchillas are gassed, strangled and electrocuted on fur farms for your wardrobe,' the advertisement reads. . . .

"PETA has also been attacking fast-food giant KFC for its allegedly cruel treatment of chickens."

(*The Sunday Telegraph* [Sydney, Australia], April 11, 2004)

Pesticide Action Network (PANNA) North America Regional Center

Established in 1984

DIRECTOR

Monica Moore, co-director and program director; and **Stephen Scholl-Buckwald**, co-director and managing director. As co-director, Moore oversees all PANNA programs and represents PAN North America to PAN International. She has worked on pesticide issues since 1980, including working with non-governmental organizations. She serves as an advisor or board member for many local, national, and international organizations, has been active in international consultations on preservation of biodiversity and genetic resources, and serves on the Executive Committee of Californians for Pesticide Reform, a coalition of more than 160 organizations.

As co-director of PANNA, Scholl-Buckwald since 1991 has been responsible for coordinating administration, finances, and development. He is also treasurer and grants manager for Californians for Pesticide Reform, of which PANNA is the primary fiscal sponsor. He has served previously as treasurer on the boards of the Institute for Food and Development Policy (Food First) and Earth Share of California. Scholl-Buckwald taught and then served as a dean at colleges in Ohio and California from 1969 to 1985. He also from 1985 to 1991, co-owned a restaurant in Davis, CA, with his partner, and worked in restaurants and organic foods retailing in the Bay Area.

BOARD OF DIRECTORS

Rajiv Bhatia; Department of Public Health, City and County of San Francisco
Dick Bunce; Golden Gate National Parks Conservancy
Ignacio H. Chapela; College of Natural Resources, University of California, Berkeley
Sandra "J. D." Doliner; Opus 4
John Harrington, treasurer, Harrington Investments, Inc.
Reggie James; Consumers Union
María Elena Martínez-Torrez; International Network of Women's Funds
Michelle Mascarenhas; Food and Society Policy Fellow
José R. Padilla; California Rural Legal Assistance, Inc.
Patricia Scott; Public Radio International
Amy C. Shannon; Enlaces America, Heartland Alliance
Kay Treakle; board vice-president, C.S. Mott Foundation

SCOPE

Members: None
Branches/chapters: PANNA is one of five autonomous regional centers (with Africa,

CONTACT INFORMATION

49 Powell Street, Suite 500, San Francisco, CA 94102
Phone: (415) 981-1771 • *Fax:* (415) 981-1991
General E-mail: panna@panna.org • *Web site:* www.panna.org

Communications Director: Kelly Campbell
(415) 981-1771 • kcampbell@panna.org
Human Resources Director: Angelica Barrera
(415) 981-1771 • angelica@panna.org

PURPOSE: "Pesticide Action Network (PAN) North America works to replace pesticide use with ecologically sound and socially just alternatives. As one of five PAN Regional Centers worldwide, we link local and international consumer, labor, health, environment and agriculture groups into an international citizens' action network. This network challenges the global proliferation of pesticides, defends basic rights to health and environmental quality, and works to insure the transition to a just and viable society."

CURRENT CONCERNS: Community organizing/empowerment • Corporate/government accountability • Environmental health • Genetic engineering • Pesticide reform

METHOD OF OPERATION: Coalition forming • Conferences/seminars • Grassroots organizing • Information clearinghouse • Initiative/referendum campaigns • International activities • Internet (databases, e-mail alerts, and Web site) • Internships • Legislative/regulatory monitoring (federal and state) • Library (open to public) • Lobbying (federal, state, and grassroots) • Local/municipal affairs • Media outreach • Participation in regulatory proceedings (federal and state) • Research • Technical assistance

Effectiveness and Political Orientation

"According to the Pesticide Action Network, 60 million pounds of pesticides a year are used in California, 6 million to 10 million of them sulfur, depending on how wet the year was. In a report called 'Fields of Poison: California Farmworkers and Pesticides,' the network, along with California Rural Legal Assistance and the United Farm Workers, concluded that 'agricultural workers face greater threat of suffering from pesticide-related illnesses—including acute poisonings and long-term effects such as cancer and birth defects—than any other sector of society. . . . Grapes continue to rank first in reported illnesses, attributed in part to frequent high-level applications of sulfur.'

"They would be spraying sulfur in Keegan every 10 days, and Rally every 16 days, until the end of June, after which they had to stop to be sure there wasn't the stinky-egg smell of hydrogen sulfide on the harvested grapes. They sprayed all day and would spray again that night, working from midnight on, after the wind died down and they could control the coverage without its blowing all over creation. Sulfur's tendency to be carried into areas beyond the

Asia/Pacific, Europe, and Latin America) of PAN Regional Centers, an international coalition of more than 600 independent, nongovernmental citizen organizations working for pesticide reform in more than 60 countries

Affiliates: More than 140 organizations (http://www.panna.org/about/affiliates.html)

STAFF

21 total—15 full-time; 6 part-time; plus 10 others

TAX STATUS

501(c)(3)

FINANCES

Budget: 2004—$1.81 million
Revenue: 2003—$464,637;
2002—$1.37 million

FUNDING SOURCES

Grants, 73%; fees, contracts, and other, 11%; donations, 10%; contributions, 6%

PAC

None

EMPLOYMENT

Employment opportunities are listed on the PANNA Web site: http://www.panna.org/about/jobs.html as well as the following sites: www.panna.org, www.idealist.org, www.craigslist.org, and www.opportunitynocs.org. Resumes and other materials for employment can be sent to Angelica Barrera, human resources/office manager, 49 Powell Street, Suite 502, San Francisco, CA 94102. Phone: (415) 981-1771. Fax: (415) 981-1991. E-mail: angelica@panna.org or panna@panna.org.

INTERNSHIPS

PANNA seeks people who share a commitment to environmental and social justice issues and a special interest in pesticide reform. Internships are unpaid, although local transportation is reimbursed. The duration of the internship and the hours are flexible. Applications are accepted all year long. For more information see the following Web sites: http://www.panna.org/howHelp/currentInternships.dv.html. For more information, contact Angelica Barrera, human resources/office manager, 49 Powell Street, Suite 502, San Francisco, CA 94102. Phone: (415) 981-1771. Fax: (415) 981-1991. E-mail: angelica@panna.org or panna@panna.org.

NEWSLETTERS

Global Pesticide Campaigner (3 times per year)
Partners Update (quarterly)
Pesticide Action Network Updates (online periodical)
Pesticide Research Updates (online newsletter 3 times per year)

PUBLICATIONS

The following is a sample list of publications:
Bayer Corporate Fact Sheet

vineyard was what made it so threatening. People who lived near vineyards told the Pesticide Action Network that the sulfur gave them headaches, sore throats and respiratory and skin irritations. Nobody had studied these low-dose exposures, said Susan Kegley, a scientist with the network. 'They are doing experiments on humans, there's just no one to look at the results,' she said. The Environmental Protection Agency considers sulfur to be organic. There were many regulations covering its use—you had, for example, to clean and flush your equipment every day, and provide workers with protective equipment—but there were no restrictions. . . ."

(*The San Francisco Chronicle*, April 20, 2004)

"Two major drift cases in Kern County contributed to almost doubling the number of the state's pesticide illnesses in 2002.

"The state investigated 1,859 potential cases of pesticide illness in 2002, compared with 979 the previous year, according to the Department of Pesticide Regulation's annual pesticide-illness report made public Thursday.

"The number of pesticide cases in the central San Joaquin Valley counties of Fresno, Kings, Madera and Tulare declined by 21% in 2002 compared with 2001.

"State officials said the Kern County cases—which accounted for 373 suspected or confirmed illnesses—stem from two incidents involving the accidental release of the potent fumigant metam sodium. . . .

"Environmentalists are pleased that the county and state appear to be placing a high priority on enforcement, but they say the Kern County cases point to the continued dangers of fumigants.

" 'Year after year, fumigants cause the majority of poisoning cases in the state,' said Margaret Reeves, staff scientist for the Pesticide Action Network in San Francisco. 'And the 2002 numbers can't illustrate that any better.' "

(*Fresno Bee* [California], February 27, 2004)

"Two major incidents of drifting farm chemicals in Kern County contributed to pesticide-related illnesses more than doubling in California from 2001 to 2002, according to state figures released Thursday.

"Pesticides were considered at least a possible factor in 1,316 illnesses reported in 2002, compared to 616 in 2001, the California Department of Pesticide Regulation's annual summary shows.

"Agriculture was the cause of 53 percent of the state's cases in 2002, compared with 31 percent in 2001 and 37 percent in 2000.

"Pesticide-related illnesses in the Northern San Joaquin Valley rose to 119 in 2002, an increase from 65 in 2001. About half of the cases, 58, were attributed to agriculture uses.

"The statistics include illnesses related to agricultural, occupational and home pesticide uses.

" 'The increase in pesticide illnesses is an ongoing problem due to soil fumigants, because of drift,' said Dr. Margaret Reeves, staff scientist with Pesticide Action Network North America. 'Two-thirds of the cases in 2002 were related to drift. It doesn't include the unreported cases.'

"Reeves and other health advocates say the demographics of California farmworkers—often single, male and working illegally—leads to underreporting.

CONFERENCES

Conferences on pesticide reform, in the Bay Area, every 2–3 years

Taking Back Our Food, Farms and Playgrounds, trinational conference

Topical workshops as campaigns require

" 'Because many workers don't have the proper knowledge, they don't realize their illness may be tied to pesticides, and they don't appear in the data,' Reeves said. . . ."

(Modesto Bee [California], February 27, 2004)

Physicians for Social Responsibility

Established in 1961

DIRECTOR

Robert K. Musil, chief executive officer and executive director. Musil has served as chief executive officer and executive director since 1995 after holding the position of PSR's director of policy and programs from 1992 to 1995. Musil came to Physicians for Social Responsibility after serving from 1988 to 1992 as executive director of the Professionals' Coalition for Nuclear Arms Control, Washington, DC. Musil is a former Army captain and instructor in communications at the Defense Information School, Ft. Benjamin Harrison, IN, and former director of the Military Affairs Project of the Center for National Security Studies, Washington, DC. Musil has taught American studies, government, and communications, as well as courses on nuclear arms control and war/peace issues at Northwestern, Temple, LaSalle, and St. Joseph's Universities. He is a graduate of Yale, Northwestern, and Johns Hopkins Universities.

BOARD OF DIRECTORS

Sid Alexander, M.D.
Ira Helfand, M.D.
John Pastore, M.D.
Dorothy Anderson, M.D.
Robert Bernstein, M.D.
Alan Lockwood, M.D.
Cathey Falvo, M.D.
Cynthia Bearer, M.D., Ph.D.
Andrew Harris, M.D.
Joel Chinitz, M.D.
Michael McCally, M.D., Ph.D.
Mark Hilty
Louis Borgenicht, M.D.
Clara Michael, M.D.
Evan Kanter, M.D., Ph.D.
Dave Hall, M.D.
Jim Trombold, M.D.
Lisa Jacobson
Jeff Patterson, D.O.
Mary Zupanc

SCOPE

Members: 30,000 health care professionals and concerned citizens
Branches/chapters: 51 chapters
Affiliates: International Physicians for the Prevention of Nuclear War (nonprofit 501(c)(3)—includes 58 IPPNW affiliates worldwide

STAFF

21 total—17 full-time professional; 4 full-time support; plus 5 interns

TAX STATUS

501(c)(3)

CONTACT INFORMATION

1875 Connecticut Avenue, Suite 1012, Washington, DC 20009
Phone: (202) 667-4260 • *Fax:* (202) 898-4201
General E-mail: psrnatl@psr.org • *Web site:* www.psr.org

Communications Director: James Snyder
(202) 667-4260, ext. 215 • jsnyder@psr.org
Human Resources Director: Madeline Riley, office manager
(202) 667-4260, ext. 210 • mriley@psr.org

PURPOSE: "Physicians for Social Responsibility combines the power of an active and concerned citizenry with the credibility of physicians and other health professionals to promote public policies that protect human health from the threats of nuclear war and other weapons of mass destruction, global environmental degradation, and the epidemic of gun violence in our society today."

CURRENT CONCERNS: Atomic legacies • Climate change • Emissions • Environmental health • Firearm regulation • International security • Mercury • Nuclear weapons • Terrorism • Testing • Toxics • Violence prevention • Weapons of mass destruction

METHOD OF OPERATION: Coalition building • Conferences • Congressional testimony • Demonstrations • Direct action • Electoral politics • Films/video/audio tapes • Grassroots organizing • Information clearinghouse • International activities • Internet (e-mail alerts and Web site) • Internships • Legislative/regulatory monitoring (federal and state) • Lobbying (federal, state, and grassroots) • Local/municipal affairs • Media outreach • Participation in regulatory proceedings (federal and state) • Performance ratings/report cards • Polling • Research • Shareholder resolutions • Training • Voter registration • Voting records

Effectiveness and Political Orientation

"Concerned that the administration may not meet its target for reducing mercury emissions by 2018, Environmental Protection Agency Administrator Mike Leavitt has ordered additional studies to see how it might tighten the proposed rule.

"The move followed revelations that the EPA had short-circuited the traditional rulemaking process and had adopted some industry recommendations verbatim. Although some environmental groups welcomed the policy shift, they argued the administration is still not doing enough to curb harmful emissions from power plants. . . .

" 'A few sandbags to stem the tide of this public outrage is not sufficient,' said Susan West Marmagas, environment and health program director for

FINANCES
Budget: 2004—$3,455,140;
2003—$3,299,680; 2002—$3,506,646

FUNDING SOURCES
Individuals, 42%; membership dues, 26%; foundation grants, 26%; government contracts, 6%

PAC
None

EMPLOYMENT
Positions are advertised in *Roll Call, The Hill,* www.idealist.org, and http://www.psr.org/ home.cfm?id=employment. PSR offers positions in public health and advocacy. Applicants should send cover letters and resumes to Madeline Riley, office manager, 1875 Connecticut Avenue, NW, Suite 1012, Washington, DC 20009. Phone: (202) 667-4260, ext. 215. Fax: (202) 667-4201. E-mail: mriley@psr.org.

INTERNSHIPS
Full-time internships are available. Internships are advertised in *Roll Call, The Hill,* www.idealist.org, www.psr.org, and www.everettinternship.org. Most internships are paid. Durations and application deadlines vary. Everett Internships are 10 weeks in duration and have an application deadline of April 15. Internships are in the areas of security, environment and health, violence prevention, and development. Applicants must be university student or recent graduates. Interested applicants should contact Madeline Riley, office manager, 1875 Connecticut Avenue, NW, Suite 1012, Washington, DC 20009. Phone: (202) 667-4260, ext. 215. Fax: (202) 667-4201. E-mail: mriley@psr.org.

NEWSLETTERS
PSR Reports (membership newsletter, quarterly)

PUBLICATIONS
Cancer and the Environment
Degrees of Danger/Breath of Fresh Air: State Reports on Public Health Dangers of Climate Change and Toxic Emissions
Emerging Links: Periodic Update on Emerging Links to Disease
A False Sense of Security: Critical Examination of Missile Defense in Counterproliferation Doctrine
Using Indicators to Measure Progress on Children's Environmental Health
What Wrongs Our Arms May Do: Examination of U.S. counterproliferation policy

CONFERENCES
National PSR Conference; Emerging Links, Public health conference on emerging links to disease, Washington, Annual

Physicians for Social Responsibility, an advocacy group that seeks tighter mercury limits."

(*The Washington Post,* March 17, 2004)

"American jets killed Iraqi troops with firebombs—similar to the controversial napalm used in the Vietnam War—in March and April as Marines battled toward Baghdad. . . .

"During the war, Pentagon spokesmen disputed reports that napalm was being used, saying the Pentagon's stockpile had been destroyed two years ago.

"Apparently the spokesmen were drawing a distinction between the terms 'firebomb' and 'napalm.' If reporters had asked about firebombs, officials said yesterday they would have confirmed their use.

"What the Marines dropped, the spokesmen said yesterday, were 'Mark 77 firebombs.' They acknowledged those are incendiary devices with a function 'remarkably similar' to napalm weapons. . . .

" 'Incendiaries create burns that are difficult to treat,' said Robert Musil, executive director of Physicians for Social Responsibility, a Washington group that opposes the use of weapons of mass destruction.

"Musil described the Pentagon's distinction between napalm and Mark 77 firebombs as 'pretty outrageous.'

" 'That's clearly Orwellian,' he added."

(*The San Diego Union-Tribune,* August 5, 2003)

"Many scientists and physicians say children are more vulnerable than adults to chemical exposures because of their size, metabolism and behavior. Others admit that because little is known about the dangers to children from pesticide exposure, therein lies the problem.

" 'Even at low levels, pesticides can affect adversely a child's neurological, respiratory, immune and endocrine system,' according to a statement from Physicians for Social Responsibility.

" 'Of the 48 most commonly used pesticides in schools, a majority threaten health,' the statement continues"

(*The Seattle Times,* October 20, 2002)

"For the first time since the height of the cold war, the US is seriously contemplating the use of nuclear weapons. But this time they would not be used, as they would have been then, against another nuclear power. The proposal is that they would be used against countries developing weapons of mass destruction—chemical and biological as well as nuclear weapons. . . .

"The Washington-based Physicians for Social Responsibility (PSR), which campaigns for nuclear disarmament, says that an attack on Saddam Hussein's presidential bunker in Baghdad with a B61-11 bomb, for example, 'could cause upwards of 20,000 deaths.' "

(*The Guardian* [London, England], August 6, 2002)

"Anti-nuclear groups such as the Union of Concerned Scientists and Physicians for Social Responsibility argue that the United States helps legitimize the building and possible use of nuclear weapons by refusing to give up its own."

(*Pittsburgh Post-Gazette,* June 9, 2002)

"In 1989 when the Berlin Wall collapsed and one by one eastern European countries rolled their Communist leaders out of power, the peace movement around the world packed its collective bags and went home.

"It seems incredibly naive of a movement that had become so battle-hardened and influential in such a short time, but many reasoned that if the Soviet bloc was gone, so was the threat of nuclear war.

"Dr Helen Caldicott thought as much. She had toured the world in the 80s preaching the anti-nuclear message, was nominated for a Nobel peace prize and co-founded the 23,000-member 'Physicians for Social Responsibility,' which won the peace prize in 1985.

"She became the scourge of right-wing politicians the world round, dismissed as 'irresponsible and extreme' by groups such as the powerful Washington think-tank the National Centre for Public Policy but adored by peace and green groups. . . .

"(S)he's back on the lecture circuit and back in print, with a new book titled *The New Nuclear Danger,* written to update her famous 1984 book *Missile Envy.*"

(*The New Zealand Herald* [Auckland, New Zealand], June 8, 2002)

Planned Parenthood Federation of America, Inc.

Established in 1916

DIRECTOR

Gloria Feldt, president. Feldt taught in the Head Start program and was active in the civil rights movement. She joined Planned Parenthood in 1974. Feldt was a Planned Parenthood affiliate chief executive, first in West Texas and later in Arizona. She became president of the Planned Parenthood Federation of America (PPFA) in 1996. She is also president of the Planned Parenthood Action Fund, the organization's political arm. She is the author of two books: *The War on Choice: The Right-Wing Attack on Women's Rights and How to Fight Back,* and *Behind Every Choice Is a Story.*

BOARD OF DIRECTORS

La Don Love, chair
Lucy J. Karl, vice chair
James D. Young, treasurer
Jill Vinjamuri-Gettman, secretary
Liz Accles
Cindy Ashley
Jennifer A. Barefoot
Mark Bigelow
Tracey L. Braun
Suzanne Cluett
Mary Cruz
Audrey Bracey Deegan
Anita Perez Ferguson
Marcia Ann Gillespie
Cynthia A. Gomez
Patricio Gonzales
Joanne E. Howard
Carolina Jimenez-Hogg
Jill June
Sally Beauchamp Kagerer
Melisa Lindamood
Stephen J. Mather
Glenn McGee
Frederick A. B. Meyerson
Karen Pearl
Joseph Rauh
William Stanley III
Judy Tabar
Alfredo Vigil (honorary)
Esperanza Garcia Walters
Leslie Walton
Calvin L. Warren
Jon T. Wilcox

SCOPE

Members: None
Branches/chapters: 125 affiliates
    (with 866 clinic sites)
Affiliate: Planned Parenthood Action Fund, a
    501(c)(4) organization

STAFF

Approximately 5,000 full-time; 5,000 part-time; 10,000 volunteers

CONTACT INFORMATION

1780 Massachusetts Avenue, NW, Washington, DC 20036
Phone: (202) 785-3351 • *Fax:* (202) 293-4349
New York Office
434 West 33rd Street, New York, NY 10001
Phone: (212) 541-7800 • *Fax:* (212) 245-1845
General E-mail: communications@ppfa.org • *Web site:* www.ppfa.org

Communications Director: Elizabeth Toledo, vice president, communications
elizabeth.toledo@ppfa.org
Human Resources Director: Information unavailable

PURPOSE: "To provide comprehensive reproductive and complementary health care services in settings which preserve and protect the essential privacy and rights of each individual; to advocate public policies which guarantee these rights and ensure access to such services; to provide educational programs which enhance understanding of individual and societal implications of human sexuality; to promote research and the advancement of technology in reproductive health care and encourage understanding of their inherent bioethical, behavioral, and social implications."

CURRENT CONCERNS: Abortion • Adolescent services • Censorship and First Amendment rights • Early pregnancy detection • International family planning • Patients' rights • Population • Reproductive freedom • Sexuality education • Universal access to services • Voluntary sterilization • Women's rights

METHOD OF OPERATION: Advertisements • Awards program • Coalition forming • Conferences/seminars • Congressional testimony • Congressional voting analysis • Electoral politics • Films/video/audiotapes • Grassroots organizing • Health care services • Initiative/referendum campaigns • International activities • Internet (databases, e-mail alerts, and Web site) • Internships • Legislative/regulatory monitoring (federal and state) • Library services open to the public • Litigation • Lobbying (federal, state, and grassroots) • Local/municipal affairs • Media outreach • Medical services via clinics throughout the United States • Polling • Polling • Speakers program • Telecommunications services (Hotline: (800) 230-PLAN) • Voter registration • Voting records

Effectiveness and Political Orientation

"Courts in three states are scheduled to hear legal challenges today to the Partial-Birth Abortion Ban Act, with opponents arguing that it is unconstitutional and overly broad.

" 'My heart is in my throat; this is an extraordinary challenge to a terrible law for women's health and rights,' Gloria Feldt, president of Planned Parent-

TAX STATUS
501(c)(3)

FINANCES
Budget: 2003—$730 million

FUNDING SOURCES
Clinic income, 36%; government grants, 33%; private contributions, 30%; Alan Guttmacher Institute and Other, 1%

PAC
Planned Parenthood Political Action Fund Inc. Political Action Committee

PAC CONTRIBUTIONS 2002

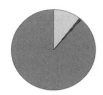

| 87% to | 12% to | 1% to |
| Democrats | Republicans | Other |

EMPLOYMENT
Open positions are advertised on the Web site: www.plannedparenthood.org/about/jobs/index.html. Each of the 125 Planned Parenthood affiliates recruits for its own vacancies. Affiliate contact information is maintained on the www.ppfa.org Web site. For national office positions, interested applicants should contact: Manager-Employment and Staffing, Planned Parenthood Federation of America, 434 West 33 Street, New York, NY 10001. Fax: (212) 868-4695. E-mail: resumes@ppfa.org.

INTERNSHIPS
Information unavailable

NEWSLETTERS
Clergy Voices
Educators Update
E-mail Newsletter
teenwire.com E Newsletter

PUBLICATIONS
The following is a sample list of publications:
AIDS & HIV: Questions and Answers
Birth Control Choices for Teens
Emergency Contraception
Having Your Period
HPV & Cervical Cancer: Questions & Answers
Human Sexuality—What Children Should Know and When They Should Know It
Sexually Transmitted Infections: The Facts
Teensex? It's OK to Say No Way!
The Facts of Life—A Guide for Teens and Their Families
The Gynecological Visit and Exam: Your Key to Good Health
Tus Alternativas Anticonceptivas
A Young Man's Guide to Sexuality
Your Contraceptive Choices

hood Federation of America, said in an interview on Friday. 'This law is bad medicine. It basically puts politicians in the examining room.' "

(*The New York Times*, March 29, 2004)

"The Girl Scout movement in President George W Bush's Texan heartland is in crisis because of a row over sex education. One troop has been disbanded and the other has dwindled to only two members.

"The turmoil engulfing the normally placid world of girl scouting—as guiding is known in America—has broken out in Crawford, the small conservative town where Mr Bush has built his family ranch.

"John Pisciotta, the director of Pro-Life Waco, a local anti-abortion group, was outraged when he discovered that the district girl scout council had endorsed Planned Parenthood, a liberal lobby group that teaches birth control. . . .

"The group is also a prominent supporter of a woman's right to choose on abortion."

(*Sunday Telegraph* [London, England], March 7, 2004)

"With the Food and Drug Administration considering two expert committees' recommendations to make the 'morning after' birth-control pill available over the counter, the public debate continues. . . . Opponents fear that greater access to this method of contraception after the fact will lessen motivation to use condoms, especially among teens, and increase the spread of sexually transmitted diseases.

" 'Saying it's going to promote unprotected sex is a backward way of looking at it,' says Susan Yolen, vice president for public affairs at Planned Parenthood of Connecticut. 'What if you realize the diaphragm had a hole in it or the condom broke, not to mention date rape. Not having to find a doctor and pay a co-pay, and especially over a holiday or while you're on vacation, is all to the good. Imagine yourself on a Friday night. It's now midnight; you're scared to death. It's the weekend before Christmas. Who do you call? You're terrified.

" 'I don't think it'll largely be teens who use the morning-after pill. Unintended pregnancies among 40-year-olds are almost at the same level as teenagers.' "

(*Hartford Courant* [Connecticut], December 23, 2003)

"One week before a new state abortion law goes into effect, clinics that will be required to adhere to it say they are confused about how to implement it and are critical of what they see as the state Health Department's deliberate foot-dragging in giving them guidance. . . .

"Planned Parenthood indicated that it will comply with most of the law but will not be providing information required in the statute that it considers medically or scientifically inaccurate, setting the stage for another possible showdown.

"The division reflects the volcanic nature of abortion politics and may be a signal of continuing friction between the administration of Gov. Tim Pawlenty, which opposes abortion, and organizations such as Planned Parenthood, which lobby against abortion restrictions but also act as health care agencies that provide abortions."

(*Minneapolis Star Tribune*, June 23, 2003)

Also offers a selection of educational booklets and other marketing material.

CONFERENCES
Annual conference

"Planned Parenthood and its sex education programs could be coming soon to a church or synagogue near you.

"In a turn-the-tables maneuver aimed squarely at religious conservatives, the group known for its liberal posture on reproductive issues is reaching out to places of worship in the Milwaukee area.

"Crafted to answer Planned Parenthood's critics, the effort to find new audiences of young people is called a 'faith-based initiative'—a not-so-subtle reference to President Bush's move to fund socially active religious groups."

(*Milwaukee Journal Sentinel* [Wisconsin], July 6, 2002)

Population Connection

Established in 1968

DIRECTOR

Peter H. Kostmayer, president. Kostmayer served in the U.S. House of Representatives for 14 years. From 1994 to 1995 he served as regional administrator of the Environmental Protection Agency in the Middle Atlantic states. Kostmayer is a graduate of Columbia University and was a fellow at the University of Pennsylvania's Institute for Environmental Studies.

BOARD OF DIRECTORS

John Lazuras, president; owner, Retail Resources, Inc., San Francisco, CA

Joe E. Bailey; president, Monticello Software, Mineral, VA

Michael F. Burke; associate director, Environmental Protection Agency, Region 3, Washington, DC

Patricia Burke; home health nurse, Adventist Home Health Services, Vienna, VA

Sachu Constantine; international program manager, Alliance to Save Energy, Washington, DC

Dianne Dillon-Ridgley; consultant, New York, NY

Blake Eisenhart; vice president, Unisys Corp., Blue Bell, PA

Mark Grayson Sr.; director, Communications, PHARMA, Stamford, CT

Kerry L. Haynie; assistant. professor, Rutgers University, New Brunswick, NJ

Tom Kim; corporate attorney, Latham & Watkins, Washington, DC

Eugene Kutscher; district science chair, Roslyn, New York Public Schools, Roslyn, NY

Tyrone Malloy; obstetrician/gynecologist

April Osajima; director of public policy, Girls Inc., New York, NY

Herb Sambol; New York, NY

Lara Bonham Tabac; city research scientist, NY City Dept. of Health & Mental Hygiene, New York, NY

David Weiss; executive director, Energy Solutions Center, Washington, DC

Rosamond Reed; Wulsin

SCOPE

Members: 71,000 individuals
Branches/chapters: 14 chapters
Affiliates: (information not located)

STAFF

40 total—plus 4 fellowships per semester; 8–10 volunteers

TAX STATUS

501(c)(3)

CONTACT INFORMATION

1400 16th Street, NW, Suite 320, Washington, DC 20036
Phone: (202) 332-2200
Toll-free: (800) 767-1956 • *Fax:* (202) 332-2302
General E-mail: info@populationconnection.org •
Web site: www.populationconnection.org

Communications Director: Tim Cline
tcline@populationconnection.org
Human Resources Director: Pat Parker, director of administration
pparker@populationconnection.org

PURPOSE: "To mobilize broad public support for a sustainable balance of the earth's people, environment, and resources, as well as informing the public on matters related to population, environment, the status of women, and the quality of life for all people."

CURRENT CONCERNS: Abortion access • Family planning • Education • Foreign aid assistance • Immigration and population • International development • Population stabilization • Prochoice • Sustainable development • Teen births and pregnancy • Women's empowerment

METHOD OF OPERATION: Advertisements • Awards program • Coalition forming • Conferences/seminars • Congressional testimony • Congressional voting analysis • Direct action • Education and outreach • Films/videos/audiotapes • Grassroots organizing • Information clearinghouse • Internet (e-mail alerts and Web site) • Internships • Legislative/regulatory monitoring (federal and state) • Lobbying (federal, state, and grassroots) • Media outreach • Product merchandising • Research • Speakers program • Telecommunications services • Training • Voting records

Effectiveness and Political Orientation

"South Korea is the 9th most kid-friendly nation in the world, according to a report by Population Connection, a U.S. grassroots organization. The group studied the overall living conditions for children in 81 countries with populations over 10 million in its Kid-Friendly Countries Report Card released on the Internet. South Korea took 9th place on the list—first among Asian countries—by receiving an overall 'A' in indexes such as health, education, economics and environment.

"The nation's high ranking was regarded as rather unexpected by some, considering the fact that most Korean children are exposed to fierce competition in school in order to get into a good college or university. The most kid-friendly nation in the world was Belgium, followed by the Netherlands, Australia and France. The four countries received an overall grade of 'A+' in the report. Britain, Portugal, United States, Spain and Italy ranked between

FINANCES
Budget: 2003—Declined to comment;
2002—$4 million

FUNDING SOURCES
Individual contributions, 83%; foundation
grants, 15%; other, 2%

PAC
None

EMPLOYMENT
Postings are listed at http://www.population-
connection.org/Employment/. All application
materials should be sent to Population
Connection, 1400 16th Street, NW, Suite 320,
Washington, DC 20036.

INTERNSHIPS
Paid and unpaid internships are available in
the following areas: field and outreach, government relations, media and communications,
and population education. Application materials should be mailed to Jay Keller, Population
Connection, 1400 16th Street, NW, Suite 320,
Washington, DC 20036.

NEWSLETTERS
The Reporter (quarterly)

PUBLICATIONS
*Counting on People: Elementary Population
    and Environmental Activities*
Earth Matters: Studies for Our Global Future
*In Growth We Trust: Sprawl, Smart Growth
    and Rapid Population Growth*
*Living a Quality Future—Kid-Friendly Cities
    Report Card 2001* (annual)
*Multiplying People, Dividing Resources:
    Global Math Activities*
*Nuestro Mundo, Nuestro Futuro (Our World,
    Our Future)*
*People and the Planet: Lessons for a
    Sustainable Future*
Sharing a Small World
World Population (video)
Also publishes activist kits and fact sheets.

CONFERENCES
None

5th and 10th in the report, after being graded an 'A' together with South Korea. . . .

"But the country [South Korea] received a relatively low grade in environment-related indexes, with 92 percent of the population granted access to improved drinking water facilities and only 63 percent able to use improved sanitation facilities. Population Connection, an organization based in Washington D.C., advocates campaigns to stabilize population growth, viewing it to be one of the key factors threatening the quality of life around the globe. Critics pointed out that as the survey is centered on demography-related fields, the report failed to cover all areas concerning children's well-being."

(*Korea Times* [Seoul, South Korea], January 6, 2004)

"It wasn't that Denise Perez ever made a conscious choice not to have children, she has just prioritized other things in the past 25 years of her life: school, travel, work and more school. While she said she loves children, she can't really picture herself having any of her own. 'My hope someday is to meet someone who has children,' said Perez, 40, an aide to Denver City Councilwoman Rosemary Rodriguez. 'I think that would be ideal.' . . .

"Among all women of childbearing age in the U.S., 44 percent don't have kids. That number is up from 35 percent in 1976, numbers show. Women in the same age group, on average, had 1.9 children in 2002, compared with the 1976 average of 3.1 children. 'I think people sometimes feel sorry for us,' said Kelli Fritts, a 37-year-old lobbyist for AARP. 'They wonder, 'What's wrong? Doesn't she want a child?' I think it works for some, and not others.' The number of childless women between the ages of 35 and 39 also increased dramatically. In 1980, 12 percent of women in that age group were without kids. In 2002, the number was 20 percent. . . .

"Some experts say the census report is proof that women now view motherhood not as an expectation but as an option. 'It shows that personal choices are finally able to be reflected,' said Tim Cline, who works at Population Connection, a Washington-based advocacy group for population limits. 'Our feeling is if you give women education, reproductive health care options and economic opportunity, then they'll make their own decision. In our studies, these options usually mean the number of children they have goes down,' he said."

(*The Denver Post*, October 24, 2003)

"In a major blow to President George W. Bush's foreign aid policy, the US Senate voted late Wednesday to repeal his ban on assistance to international family planning groups that fight for the availability of abortion. By a vote of 53-43, senators rejected a motion to kill an amendment by Democrat Barbara Boxer of California that strikes down the so-called Mexico City Policy, an anti-abortion measure reaffirmed by Bush on his second day in office. The Boxer amendment, which has thus been allowed to stand, is attached to a 27-billion-dollar State Department foreign aid bill being debated by the chamber.

"The Mexico City Policy, often referred to as 'the global gag rule,' bars the US government from providing assistance to organizations that advocate abortion as one of family planning tools and openly counsel women about abortion services. 'These organizations face two choices, they can either refuse US assistance or give up the right to speak freely,' an elated Boxer said in a statement. She said 'the global gag rule' would be unconstitutional if it applied to family planning groups in the United States. 'How can we export a policy that denies free speech and still say we support democracy?' the lawmaker asked. . . .

"Bush, eager to shore up his conservative political base, reinstated the funding ban on January 22, 2001, in a memorandum sent to the head of the US Agency for International Development. 'It is my conviction that taxpayer funds should not be used to pay for abortions or advocate or actively promote abortion, either here or abroad,' the president said in that document. But even after the Senate vote, the tug-of-war over population control was expected to continue. . . .

" 'The Bush administration's global gag rule has made family-planning services—which reduce the need for abortion—harder for the world's poorest women to access,' said Kate Michelman, president of NARAL Pro-Choice America. Population Connection President Peter Kostmayer said he believed the White House policy also violated the First Amendment to the US Constitution, which guarantees free speech. 'Even if you are against abortion, the fact that we have been dictating reproductive health policies for women in developing countries, without regard to their laws or customs, should demonstrate just how wrong this policy was,' he said."

(*Agence France Presse* [news service], July 10, 2003)

"When it comes to its children, Nevada is a negligent parent, study after study has found. In more than 50 of the most recent national surveys of children's issues by government agencies, nonprofit foundations and trade associations, most involving data that is no more than 3 years old, Nevada had far more negative than positive rankings. The state ranks among the nation's worst in per-pupil spending, high school dropout rate, the number of children without health insurance, the tally of linguistically challenged children, child protective service caseloads and cash benefits for needy families. . . .

"Taking care of children is even more pressing in Nevada because it has such a large percentage of children and because so many of them are younger than 5. Nevada is the 35th most populous state, but it has the 21st highest percentage of children. For children younger than age 5, Nevada's percentage ranks only behind Utah's. Not all the rankings are bad. The state has far fewer children living in poverty than most states, fewer disabled children than the norm and among the best-built schools in the nation. Single mothers in Nevada rank eighth and single fathers rank 13th respectively in median income compared with their peers nationwide. But Nevada's negative rankings overwhelm the positives. . . .

"Jay Keller, national field director for Population Connection, a Washington, D.C.-based nonprofit group that advocates slow population growth, says Nevada's communities must manage their populations better because rapid growth makes it difficult to resolve issues in which children rank poorly. 'They have to look at what kind of growth they can actually handle and what that growth means,' Keller said. 'The problem with growth is the stretching of resources. If you're not doing a good enough job now, you're not going to do better by adding 10,000 or 50,000 people.'. . ."

(*Las Vegas Sun,* May 28, 2003)

The Progress & Freedom Foundation

Established in 1993

DIRECTOR

Raymond L. Gifford, president. Before joining the foundation in 2003, Gifford served as chair of the Colorado Public Utilities Commission for four years. Before joining the commission, Gifford served as first assistant attorney general. From 1993 to 1996, he worked for two national law firms: Kirkland & Ellis and Baker & Hostetler. Gifford earned his law degree from the University of Chicago. He began his legal career as a law clerk to the Hon. Richard P. Matsch of the U.S. District Court for the District of Colorado. Gifford earned a Bachelor's degree from St. John's College in Annapolis, MD.

BOARD OF DIRECTORS

George Keyworth, chair, The Progress & Freedom Foundation

Jeffrey Eisenach, vice chair; CapAnalysis Group, LLC

Larry Harlow; president, Timmons & Company

William Roesing

Peter Harter; consultant, Farrington Group

Mark Grady; dean, George Mason University School of Law

SCOPE

Members: None
Branches/chapters: None
Affiliates: Center for the Study of Digital Property; Institute for Regulatory Law and Economics.

STAFF

15 total—10 full-time professional; 5 full-time support; plus 1 intern

TAX STATUS

501(c)(3)

FINANCES

Budget: 2004—$2.7 million; 2003—$2.0 million; 2002—$1.8 million

FUNDING SOURCES

Corporate donations, 90%; conferences, 5%; foundation grants, 3%; publications, 1%; individual contributions, 1%

PAC

None

EMPLOYMENT

Positions are advertised at www.pff.org and in local Washington, DC, media. The Progress & Freedom Foundation hires scholars as well as positions in administrative, communications, clerical, and research areas. Applicants should send cover letters and resumes to Human Resources/PFF, 1401 H Street, NW, Suite

CONTACT INFORMATION

1401 H Street, NW, Suite 1075, Washington, DC 20005-2110
Phone: (202) 289-8928 • *Fax:* (202) 289-6079
General E-mail: mail@pff.org • *Web Site:* www.pff.org

Communications Director: David M. Fish, vice president for communications and external affairs
(202) 289-8928 • dfish@pff.org
Human Resources Director: Jane T. Creel, director of finance and operations
(202) 289-8928 • jcreel@pff.org

PURPOSE: "The Progress & Freedom Foundation is a market-oriented think tank that studies the digital revolution and its implications for public policy. Its mission is to educate policymakers, opinion leaders and the public about issues associated with technological change, based on a philosophy of limited government, free markets and individual sovereignty."

CURRENT CONCERNS: Communications • Intellectual property • Internet • E-commerce • Energy and competition

METHOD OF OPERATION: Conferences/seminars • Congressional testimony • Educational foundation • Fellowships • Information clearinghouse • Internet (electronic bulletin boards, e-mail alerts, and Web site) • Legislative/regulatory monitoring (federal and state) • Media outreach • Participation in regulatory proceedings (federal and state) • Research • Speakers program

Effectiveness and Political Orientation

"The Justice Department filed an antitrust lawsuit to stop Oracle Corp.'s $9.4 billion takeover bid for business software rival PeopleSoft Inc. . . .

"Thomas Lenard, an economist at the Progress and Freedom Foundation, a conservative research group, was an outspoken supporter of the Justice Department's effort to break up Microsoft. But he believes the government should stay out of this takeover fight."

(*The Atlanta Journal-Constitution*, February 27, 2004)

" 'The marketplace pressures in the competition will ultimately protect consumers and give them the services they want,' said Randolph May, senior fellow and director of communications policy studies at the Progress & Freedom Foundation, a technology think tank with backers that include phone and cable companies."

(*The Sunday Oregonian* [Portland], January 4, 2004)

"Critics are outraged that an official state Web page on regulatory reform offers links only to six conservative organizations. . . .

"Wade Buchanan, president of the liberal Bell Policy Center in Denver, also criticized the links to conservative groups.

1075, Washington, DC 20005. Fax: (202) 289-8928. E-mail: mail@pff.org.

INTERNSHIPS

Internships are advertised at www.pff.org. Durations of internships are for a minimum of three months. Working hours are about 30 hours per week. Internships are available in the areas of communications and public policy. Applicants must have completed some undergraduate work in a relevant field of study. Interested applicants should contact Human Resources/PFF, 1401 H Street, NW, Suite 1075, Washington, DC 20005. Fax: (202) 289-8928. E-mail: mail@pff.org.

NEWSLETTERS

None

PUBLICATIONS

Cities Online: Urban Development & the Internet
Communications Deregulation and FCC Reform
Competition, Innovation and the Microsoft Monopoly: Antitrust in the Digital Marketplace
Deregulating Electricity: The Federal Role
The Digital Economy Fact Book
Periodic Commentaries on the Policy Debate
Privacy and the Commercial Use of Personal Information
Privacy and the Digital State: Balancing Public Information and Personal Privacy
Privacy Online: A Report on the Information Practices and Policies of Commercial Web Sites

CONFERENCES

The Aspen Summit (Aspen, CO, annually in August)
DC policy lunches (numerous topics, several per year)
Congressional Seminars (numerous topics, Capitol Hill, approximately one per month)
CEO Lunches (numerous topics, downtown DC, 6 to 8 per year)
Miscellaneous conferences (numerous topics, primarily in DC)

" 'I'm concerned when the state has links to only one kind of policy organization,' he said.

"The state offers links to the following groups: The Heritage Foundation, The Cato Institute, Privatization Center, Progress & Freedom Foundation, Reason Public Policy Institute and the Milken Institute."

(*Rocky Mountain News* [Denver], December 3, 2003)

"Ray Gifford, former chairman of the Colorado Public Utilities Commission and now executive director of the Progress and Freedom Foundation, a Washington, D.C.-based think tank, said he doesn't think bricks-and-mortar retailers are completely without justification in wanting tax equity.

"But Gifford said that the multistate compact smacks of a tax cartel and an effort to keep in place a 'high-tax regime.'

"Philosophically, Gifford's group believes the fewer taxes the better. And if you think something is good, such as the Internet, then 'your insight should be not to increase the tax burden.' "

(*Rocky Mountain News* [Denver], October 27, 2003)

"Aspen's population of big brains swelled last week, when The Progress & Freedom Foundation, a conservative think tank, hosted its annual summit at the Hotel St. Regis. Among those on the agenda were Federal Communications Commission Chairman Michael Powell and Viacom President Mel Karmazin."

(*The Denver Post*, August 24, 2003)

"The F.T.C. chairman, Timothy J. Muris, told an audience at the annual Aspen Summit of the Progress and Freedom Foundation, a free-market-oriented group, that 'no one should expect any new law to make a substantial difference by itself.' Some proposed measures, like a national do-not-spam registry that would resemble the wildly popular national do-not-call list, would be impossible to enforce, he said."

(*The New York Times*, August 22, 2003)

"The 10-year-old Progress & Freedom Foundation announced a change in leadership yesterday, naming Republican lawyer Raymond L. Gifford, the chair of the Colorado Public Utilities Commission, as its next president.

" 'I will probably start by playing to my strengths, which are telecom and electricity regulation, and by looking to the state side of that equation, which is very important and often overlooked, ' said Gifford, 35, an expert on regulatory law and economics—and a protege of Gale A. Norton, the interior secretary and former Colorado attorney general. . . .

"PFF's low point came in the mid-1990s, when it was implicated in the House ethics committee investigation into then-House Speaker Newt Gingrich (R-Ga.). After a three-year inquiry, the IRS cleared PFF, but the tank had suffered financially.

"The foundation survived, focusing more narrowly on digital and telecommunication issues, and founding the well-regarded Aspen Summit, an annual conference on cyberspace policy. Its annual budget is about $2 million per year, all of which is raised from corporations."

(*The Washington Post*, December 17, 2002)

Project Vote Smart

Established in 1992

DIRECTOR
Richard Kimball, president. Before joining Project Vote Smart, Kimball worked as an educator.

BOARD OF DIRECTORS
Information unavailable

SCOPE
Members: Information unavailable
Branches/chapters: Satellite offices in Boston and Tucson
Affiliates: None

STAFF
Information unavailable

TAX STATUS
501(c)(3)

FINANCES
Budget: 2000—$1.9 million

FUNDING SOURCES
Individual memberships, 70%; foundation grants, 30%

PAC
None

EMPLOYMENT
The Project maintains a modest staff primarily composed of recent college graduates dedicated to the PVS mission of voter education and candidate accountability. All staff commit to work through the next general election, at a minimal salary. The Project Vote Smart pledge, signed by all staff, commits individuals to absolute impartiality, respect, and deference toward all citizens and professional integrity in refusing any kind of financial gain resulting from association with PVS. All of our positions start at $14,500 annually and increase to $17,000 after six months. PVS provides medical and dental benefits.

Interested applicants should send a cover letter, resume, and three references to the address below, or e-mail them (as Microsoft Word or rich text attachments) to jobs@vote-smart.org. Information on current openings can be found at http://www.vote-smart.org/program_jobs.php. For further information, contact the Human and Office Resources Director, Project Vote Smart, One Common Ground, Philipsburg, MT 59858. E-mail: jobs@vote-smart.org.

INTERNSHIPS
National interns work full-time as temporary staff members. They may be assigned to a specific department or may work on special projects in several departments, as needed.

CONTACT INFORMATION
One Common Ground, Philipsburg, MT 59858
Phone: (406) 859-8683 • *Fax:* (406) 859-8675
General E-mail: commments@vote-smart.org •
Web site: http://www.vote-smart.org

Communications Director: Lindsay Siler, media director
lindsay@vote-smart.org
Human Resources Director: Information unavailable

PURPOSE: "To give all citizens free, instant access to abundant factual information about candidates and elected officials from a nonpartisan source."

CURRENT CONCERNS: Giving all citizens free access to relevant factual information about more than 13,000 candidates and elected officials at the federal and state levels

METHOD OF OPERATION: Internet (databases and Web site) • Library services open to the public • Media outreach • Research • Telecommunications services • Voting records • Voter registration

Effectiveness and Political Orientation

"Let's take it as a given that politicians should take stands on issues.

"The problem is that many don't want to. They would rather mouth platitudes and rely on canned TV messages to project an image of the person they would like voters to think they are.

"Project Vote Smart is a bipartisan effort to get politicians on the record about issues that are important to voters.

"All candidates for national office and state legislatures, and some governors, are sent a form called the National Political Awareness Test, and asked to fill it out. The questions have been reviewed by journalists, political scientists and others in an effort to keep them fair and impartial.

"But in the past 10 years, the answers from politicians have been fewer each year. The rate of participation has dropped from 60 percent to 30 percent or less and one of the lowest rates is in Florida, project officials say.

"A number of politicians have candidly told Project Vote Smart's people that leaders of both major parties have told them to shun the test and avoid taking a position in writing.

"Apparently what the party leaders fear is that opponents will use the test for opposition research, and base their attacks on their opponent's statements. Actual quote: 'Don't cooperate with Project Vote Smart. Your opponent will use it to see what you think about issues and might use it against you.'"

(*The Florida Times-Union* [Jacksonville], January 26, 2004)

The overriding qualification for securing an internship position at Project Vote Smart is a willingness to commit 100% to the project's goals and mission. Internships cover 10 weeks. Applicants must submit a completed application form, resume, cover letter, and a minimum of three references. Those desiring scholarship assistance must also complete a Scholarship Request Form. All application materials must be submitted together. Applicants must specify for which term they are applying. Applications can be found on the back of brochures, on the links above, or by calling the toll-free hotline (888) 868-3762. Financial assistance is often made available to students to help with expenses while interning with Project Vote Smart. In Montana, students receive free room and board at the Great Divide Ranch. There are also some other small scholarships available.

For additional information, contact the Internship Director, One Common Ground, Philipsburg, MT 59858. Phone: (406) 859-8683. E-mail: intern@vote-smart.org.

NEWSLETTERS
On Common Ground (biannual)

PUBLICATIONS
The Reporter's Sourcebook
U.S. Government: Owner's Manual
Voter's Self-Defense Manual
Vote Smart Web Yellow Pages (online)

CONFERENCES
Press conferences when the results of the National Political Awareness Test are available.

"Of the major candidates for president, only two refused to take Project Vote Smart's 2004 National Political Awareness Test—President George W. Bush and Democratic front-runner Howard Dean.

"The nonprofit citizens' organization for years has asked candidates for state and federal offices to submit their positions on the issues people care about. . . .

"The two front-runners apparently didn't want to give their opponents any more ammunition, but their decision deprives voters of the chance to better understand their views.

"The test, designed by political scientists, politicians and journalists, covers 17 issue areas."

(*Tampa Tribune,* January 19, 2004)

"MTV: Music Television today announced the official launch of the 'Choose or Lose 2004' campaign to help mobilize more than 20 million young adults aged 18 to 30 to vote in the 2004 election. Dubbed '20 Million Loud,' this call to action has been adopted as an achievable goal by MTV's 'Choose or Lose 2004' and a diverse coalition of innovative youth organizations, including Rock the Vote, Hip-Hop Team Vote, Smack Down Your Vote, New Voters Project, Declare Yourself, and more than 100 organizations in the Youth Vote Coalition. . . .

"MTV's 'Choose or Lose 2004' will strategically partner with a number of organizations to achieve the shared goal of '20 Million Loud.' Partners include the Youth Vote Coalition, the Hip Hop Summit Action Network, Smack Down the Vote, Meetup.com, Project Vote Smart, National Council of La Raza, Black Youth Vote, Youth Service America, the New Voters Project, Youth Venture, CIRCLE Research, the NAACP, Harvard University Institute of Politics, and a diverse group of more than 100 other youth voting organizations. Also, MTV and Rock the Vote's long-standing partnership will continue this year with Rock the Vote serving as the online and primary grassroots voter registration partner for the 'Choose or Lose 2004' campaign."

(*PR Newswire,* January 14, 2004)

"Every election season you're bombarded by political advertising laced with double talk or dirty laundry. And it's getting worse all the time. Enter Project Vote Smart, at www.vote-smart.org, to clear the way to finding out who's who and where they stand. This site has comprehensive campaign information that includes profile information for federal elected officials and candidates available in five categories. There is also information on the state level. If you're not registered to vote, you can do so from the site. Just in case you suspect a lack of diversity among the members of PVS, you might be interested in knowing that the organization was inaugurated in 1992 by former Presidents Carter and Ford, former U.S. Sens. Barry Goldwater and George McGovern, and former U.S. Reps. Newt Gingrich and Geraldine Ferraro."

(*Houston Chronicle,* November 3, 2003)

"Everybody talks about making American campaigns more substantive, less shallow.

"More substantive, meaning more issue-oriented. Less shallow, meaning less packaged, less ridden with simple slogans and attack ads.

"The candidates say they're for it. The news media brass say they're for it. The voters say they want it. If only candidates would talk about issues, voters would care more about elections and re-engage in politics.

"That it doesn't happen election after election is always someone else's fault. So do we really want that? And if we do, is anyone doing anything about it?

"Project Vote Smart is trying. The Montana-based organization has an equal distribution of Republicans and Democrats, liberals and conservatives on its board (both Newt Gingrich and George McGovern, for example). It thinks if it gives voters hard information about candidates—positions on issues, voting records, campaign finance reports—that voters will respond. If voters have an alternative to hype and 'hit pieces,' they'll demand more substance.

"And it just might work if the candidates bothered to fill out the issues questionnaire sent out by Vote Smart (www.vote-smart.org). Aaron Brock, the group's news director, said the percentage of candidates responding to the National Political Awareness Test has dropped from nearly 75 percent in 1996 to less than 50 percent this year.

"Our candidates ignored the questionnaire more than most. Of the nine congressional winners, just three—U.S. Reps. Jim McDermott (D-Seattle), Richard 'Doc' Hastings (R-Pasco) and Jennifer Dunn (R-Bellevue)—bothered with it."

(*The News Tribune* [Tacoma, Wash.], December 12, 2002)

Property and
Environment Research Center

Established in 1980 (formerly Political Economy Research Center)

DIRECTOR

Terry L. Anderson, executive director. Anderson is also a senior fellow at the Hoover Institution. Anderson is the author or editor of 30 books. Anderson is professor emeritus of economics at Montana State University. He received his Ph.D. in economics from the University of Washington in 1972 and was awarded a Fulbright Research Fellowship to Canterbury University.

BOARD OF DIRECTORS

David R. Atkinson; Palmer Square Partners
Thomas E. Beach; Beach Investment Counsel, Inc.
David W. Brady; Stanford University Graduate School of Business
Thomas J. Bray; columnist, *Detroit News*
Jean A. Briggs; assistant managing editor, *Forbes*
David G. Cameron; Dana Ranch Co.
William A. Dunn; chair, Dunn Capital Management
Joseph N. Ignat; managing director, Blackburn Consultants, LLC
Paul J. Ingrassia; president, Dow Jones Newswires
Andrew S. Martzloff; managing director, Bitterroot Capital Advisors, LLC
E. Wayne Nordberg; chair, Hollow Brook Associates, LLC
George F. Ohrstrom; president, Ohrstrom Foundation, Inc.
Leigh Perkins; chair, Orvis Co.
Vernon L. Smith; Interdisciplinary Center for Economic Science, George Mason University

SCOPE

Members: None
Branches/chapters: None
Affiliates: None

STAFF

13 total—8 full-time professional; 3 full-time support; plus 2 part-time professional; 9 affiliated scholars

TAX STATUS

501(c)(3)

FINANCES

Budget: 2004—$2.05 million; 2003—$1.85 million; 2002—$2.26 million

FUNDING SOURCES

Foundation grants, 91%; individual contributions, 6%; corporate donations, 3%

PAC

None

CONTACT INFORMATION

2048 Analysis Drive, Suite A, Bozeman MT 59718
Phone: (406) 587-9591 • *Fax:* (406) 586-7555
General E-mail: perc@perc.org • *Web site:* www.perc.org

Communications Director: Jane S. Shaw, outreach director
(406) 587-9591 • perc@perc.org
Human Resources Director: Monica L. Guenther, administrative director
(406) 587-9591 • perc@perc.org

PURPOSE: "PERC is dedicated to improving environmental quality through property rights and markets."

CURRENT CONCERNS: Agriculture and the environment • Conservation easements • Environmental education • Environmental entrepreneurship • Environmental stewardship • Fisheries management • Forestry • Land trusts • National and state parks • Native American economies • Recycling • Water marketing • Wildlife management

METHOD OF OPERATION: Conferences/seminars • Congressional testimony • Information clearinghouse • Internet (electronic bulletin boards, e-mail alerts, and Web site) • Internships • Media outreach • Performance ratings/report cards • Research • Speakers program

Effectiveness and Political Orientation

"With the annual event known as Earth Day approaching it is reasonable to ask: Are the taxpayers getting their money's worth from the Endangered Species Act?

"As luck would have it, someone has asked. Randy Simmons and Kimberly Frost did a paper for the Property and Environment Research Center on the topic.

"They contend accounting of the cost of that legislation done by the U.S. Fish and Wildlife Service is flawed, and substantially underestimates the actual amount.

"Many costs are either ignored or underestimated by the government, the researchers say."

(*The Florida Times-Union* [Jacksonville], April 19, 2004)

"The League of Conservation Voters—the most politically aggressive national environmental group—has launched new television ads in politically important markets, such as Los Angeles, blasting Bush's record. 'The Bush administration's approach to the environment demonstrates a clear bias toward the interests of the oil industry, the utility industry, and other corporate contributors at the expense of the health and safety of the public,' the group said last week in its presidential report card.

EMPLOYMENT
Job openings are advertised on www.perc.org. The organization offers positions in the area of environmental economics research. Interested applicants should send cover letters and resumes to Monica L. Guenther, administrative director, 2048 Analysis Drive, Suite A, Bozeman MT 59718. Phone: (406) 587-9591. Fax: (406) 586-7555. E-mail: perc@perc.org.

INTERNSHIP OPPORTUNITIES
Paid, full-time internships in the area of natural resource issues are available. Internships last three months. Deadlines for application are February 13 for summer, June 30 for fall, and October 29 for spring. PERC advertises internships at www.perc.org/education/fellowships.php?s=4. Applicants must be law students or graduate students. Interested applicants should contact Daniel K. Benjamin, graduate fellowship director, 2048 Analysis Drive, Suite A, Bozeman MT 59718. Phone: (406) 587-9591. Fax: (406) 586-7555. E-mail: perc@perc.org.

NEWSLETTERS
PERC Policy Series (3–4 times per year)
PERC Reports (quarterly)

PUBLICATIONS
The following is a sample list of publications:
A Blueprint for Environmental Education
Ecological Agrarian: Agriculture's First Evolution in 10,000 Years
Enviro-Capitalists: Doing Good While Doing Well
Environment and the Economy: EcoDetectives
Facts, Not Fear: Teaching Children About the Environment
Fencing the Fishery: A Primer on Ending the Race for Fish
Free Market Environmentalism, Revised Edition
A Guide to Smart Growth
Political Environmentalism: Going Behind the Green Curtain
Property Rights: A Practical Guide to Freedom
Saving Our Streams Through Water Markets
Sovereign Nations or Reservations? An Economic History of American Indians
The Greening of U.S. Foreign Policy
Water Markets: Priming the Invisible Pump
What Everyone Should Know About Economics and the Environment

CONFERENCES
Conference for Journalists (annual)
Kinship Conservation Institute for Environmental Leaders (annual)
Legislative briefings and seminars
Liberty Fund colloquia for scholars
Liberty Fund Colloquium for Business Executives (annual)
Political Economy Forum (annual)
Student Seminar on Free Market Environmentalism (annual)

"At the same time, some key conservative groups are voicing disappointment with Bush as well. The Political Economy Research Center—the leading free-market advocacy group, whose experts have advised the White House—gives Bush a C-minus on how well he conducted environmental policy during his first two years.

"'President Bush's administration is moving away from the principles of free-market environmentalism, when we thought he would be moving toward it,' says Bruce Yandle, senior associate with the Bozeman, Mont.-based research center."

(*Christian Science Monitor,* July 3, 2003)

"While struggling with one of the worst droughts in history, planners from across the West gathered here Friday to hear Interior Secretary Gale A. Norton announce a grand new initiative called Water 2025. . . .

"Ms. Norton encouraged the formation of a 'water bank' in the Klamath basin allowing farmers to be paid for relinquishing water to conservationists. That solution was in keeping with the scholarly work she did two decades ago at the Political Economy Research Center, a hub of free-market environmentalism in Montana. But her former colleagues there say that otherwise she has generally put little of her theories into practice. Her midterm report card from the research center contained mainly C's and faulted her for leaving most land-use decisions up to bureaucrats rather than using auctions and other market mechanisms."

(*The New York Times,* June 9, 2003)

"A strong farm lobby gets its way almost as much as the defense industry does, said Terry Anderson, director of the Political Economy Research Center, an economic think tank in Bozeman. The subsidies prop up land values and are supported by big corporations selling farm equipment and backing mortgages, he said.

"'Their business depends on these subsidies as much as the farmers do,' Anderson said. 'Financial markets don't want to be left holding the bag when farmers aren't doing well.'"

(*Associated Press State & Local Wire,* December 18, 2002)

"An advocate of limited federal regulation and proponent of private sector solutions to environmental problems will carry out the Bush administration's new 'healthy forests' initiative, a signal the president's strategy may hinge on the economic rather than the ecological value of western lands.

"By naming Allan K. Fitzsimmons wildland fuels coordinator this week, Interior Secretary Gale Norton put him in charge of President Bush's 'common sense' management plan for fire-prone western wildlands. . . .

"An environmental consultant who served as a political appointee in the Reagan and former Bush administrations, Fitzsimmons has been an intense critic of federal attempts to apply safeguards across broad ecosystems such as the forests of the Northwest.

"Attempts to manage ecosystems elevates 'environmental protection above the pursuit of human welfare,' he wrote in a 1994 analysis for the Cato Institute, a libertarian think tank. Balanced policies 'and greater reliance on market forces, rather than . . . intrusions of the government into land-use decisions, should guide federal actions. . . .'

"In announcing the appointment, Norton made no mention of Fitzsimmons' strident stands on environmental topics. Instead, she said, Fitzsimmons 'has a proven reputation as a problem-solver.'

" 'There's no question that will include some logging where it makes sense,' said Terry Anderson of the Political Economy Research Center in Bozeman, Mont., where Fitzsimmons has done research. 'He's going to look at managing resources to take maximum advantage of the value, whether it's timber or recreation or something else.' "

(*The Oregonian* [Portland], August 30, 2002)

Public Citizen, Inc.

Established in 1971

DIRECTOR

Joan Claybrook, president. Claybrook became president of Public Citizen Inc., in 1982. She was administrator of the National Highway Traffic Safety Administration from 1977 to 1981. Claybrook, who began her association with Ralph Nader projects in 1970, founded Public Citizen's Congress Watch in 1973, and served as its director until 1977. Claybrook has written numerous articles and frequently testifies before congressional committees. She earned a law degree from Georgetown University Law Center.

BOARD OF DIRECTORS

Joan Claybrook
Howard Metzenbaum
Joseph Page
Adolph L. Reed

SCOPE

Members: 160,000
Branches/chapters: Six divisions and two state offices (CA and TX)
Affiliate: Public Citizen Foundation, Inc., a 501(c)(3) organization (Public Citizen, Inc. is an umbrella organization for six projects: Buyers Up, Congress Watch, Critical Mass Energy Project, the Health Research Group, Litigation Group, and Global Trade Watch)

STAFF

113 total

TAX STATUS

501(c)(4)–Public Citizen, Inc.
501(c)(3)–Public Citizen Foundation, Inc.

FINANCES

Budget: 2002—$4.7 million;
2001—$3.6 million

FUNDING SOURCES

Membership dues, contributions, foundation grants, and sales of publications—does not accept government or corporate contributions

PAC

None

EMPLOYMENT

Information on employment opportunities can be found on Public Citizen's Web site: www.citizen.org/jobs/. Interested applicants should send resumes and other materials for employment to Human Resources, Public Citizen, 1600 20th Street, NW, Washington, DC 20009.

CONTACT INFORMATION

1600 20th Street, NW, Washington, DC 20009
Phone: (202) 588-1000 • *Fax:* (202) 588-7799
General E-mail: member@citizen.org • *Web site:* www.citizen.org

Communications Director: Booth Gunter
(202) 588-1000 • bgunter@citizen.org
Human Resources Director: Declined to comment

PURPOSE: Public Citizen is a national, nonprofit consumer advocacy organization founded in 1971 to represent consumer interests in Congress, the executive branch and the courts. This organization fights for openness and democratic accountability in government, for the right of consumers to seek redress in the courts; for clean, safe and sustainable energy sources; for social and economic justice in trade policies; for strong health, safety and environmental protections; and for safe, effective and affordable prescription drugs and health care.

CURRENT CONCERNS: Auto safety • Campaign finance reform • Citizen empowerment • Clean and safe energy sources • Consumer rights in the marketplace • Corporate and government accountability • Drug and food safety • Environment • Fair trade policies • Freedom of information and open government • Health care delivery • Healthful environment and workplace • Insurance reform • Nuclear safety • Occupational health • Product liability • Regulatory reform • Safe products

METHOD OF OPERATION: Coalition forming • Conferences/seminars • Congressional testimony • Congressional voting analysis • Grassroots organizing • Information clearinghouse • International activities • Internet (databases, e-mail alerts, and Web site) • Legislative/regulatory monitoring (federal) • Legislative/regulatory monitoring (state) • Litigation • Lobbying (federal) • Media outreach • Participation in regulatory proceedings (federal) • Research

Effectiveness and Political Orientation

"The Bush administration on Thursday strongly opposed Senate legislation that would set strict deadlines for it to require automakers to strengthen car roofs, protect passengers from ejection and implement other safety measures.

"The legislation approved by the Commerce Committee, chaired by Arizona Republican John McCain, proposes the most sweeping auto safety mandate since landmark legislation in 2000 that followed a massive recall of Firestone tires linked to deadly blowouts and vehicle rollovers.

"Major consumer groups are frustrated with years of delay in getting the government to set a crush-resistance standard for car roofs, and they enthusiastically back the Senate bill, which would set deadlines no later than 2008 for imposing its safety requirements.

" 'Congress now needs to pass legislation that will establish rollover prevention and protection standards, anti-ejection standards and long-overdue safeguards,' said Joan Claybrook, president of the Public Citizen consumer group and a former NHTSA administrator.

"Claybrook and others said agency historically makes meaningful progress only when forced to take action."

(*Reuters News,* March 18, 2004)

"The share of new prescriptions written for the cholesterol-lowering drug Lipitor surged during the past week as the Pfizer Inc. blockbuster got a boost from a big study showing it was better than Bristol-Myers Squibb Co.'s Pravachol in preventing heart attacks.

"But Lipitor's gains came not at the expense of Pravachol, but of AstraZeneca PLC's Crestor, the latest and most potent contender in the global $22 billion market for cholesterol pills called statins. . . .

"The shift in market share may also have been influenced by the advocacy group Public Citizen, which issued a call on March 4 for the Food and Drug Administration to withdraw Crestor from the market because of potentially life-threatening side effects."

(*The Wall Street Journal,* March 18, 2004)

"Pharmaceutical giant GlaxoSmithKline PLC launched an advertising campaign yesterday touting the company's research and its scientists, and attempting to explain to increasingly frustrated consumers why prescription drugs cost so much. . . .

"Frank Clemente of consumer advocacy group Public Citizen, which has been critical of pharmaceutical companies and has called on Congress to push for reform, was doubtful the ads would change any minds.

" 'Next to the tobacco industry, the drug industry has the biggest public relations problem,' Clemente said. 'There's so much direct evidence of Americans getting price-gouged on medications that it's going to take a lot to convince them of anything otherwise.'

"He suggested that the ads could really be geared toward lawmakers. The Bush administration and Republican congressional leaders are being forced to take a hard new look at the idea of importing cheaper prescription drugs from foreign countries as an election-year clamor grows for removing prohibitions."

(*Pittsburgh Post-Gazette,* March 16, 2004)

"Gary Putman is an accomplished mechanic with bills to pay and a business to grow.

"Yet more and more these days, he's forced to wave customers away from his popular shop in West Seattle. He literally can't crack the computer code he needs to diagnose and fix an assortment of maladies ranging from climate systems to brakes to electrical glitches that commonly strike late-model cars.

" 'If you don't have the code, you lose the job. They have to go to the dealers. It's an illegal monopoly, in my opinion. It happens enough that it's a real problem,' said Putman, who owns Westside Import Repair. . . .

"The grumbling has gotten so loud that Congress is stepping in. Bills have been introduced in both the House and Senate that would require the automakers to provide the data to anyone who needs it. It would apply to any make of car sold in the United States.

" 'You don't want technology to destroy competitiveness,' said Sen. Lindsey Graham, R-S.C., who offered one of the bills. 'There's no reason you shouldn't be able to take your car to anyone you want rather than there being only one option.'

"The effort is also backed by an improbable coalition that includes Public Citizen, the consumer watchdog founded by Ralph Nader; major auto parts retailers, including NAPA and Carquest; independent mechanics such as Putman; AAA; and the powerful National Federation of Independent Business."

(*Seattle Post-Intelligencer,* March 15, 2004)

"Freddie Mac ousted its chief lobbyist amid an investigation into allegations that he broke federal election laws in raising money for Republican members of Congress. . . .

"Freddie Mac last year hired the law firm Covington & Burling to examine allegations by a nonprofit watchdog group, Public Citizen, to the Federal Election Commission. Public Citizen alleged that Mr. Delk didn't properly account for dozens of fund-raising dinners at Washington's posh Galileo Restaurant and elsewhere for a long list of Republican politicians, including House Majority Leader Tom DeLay, House Speaker Dennis Hastert, House Financial Services Chairman Michael Oxley, and Sen. Richard Shelby, chair of the Senate Banking Committee."

(*The Wall Street Journal,* March 12, 2004)

Public Knowledge

Established in 2001

DIRECTOR

Gigi B. Sohn, president and co-founder. An internationally known communications policy attorney, Sohn seeks to apply her constituency-building and advocacy expertise to intellectual property policy. From 1999 to 2001, she served as a project specialist in the Ford Foundation's Media, Arts and Culture unit. In that capacity, she oversaw grantmaking in the Foundation's media policy and technology portfolio and advised the Foundation on the future direction of the portfolio. Prior to joining the Ford Foundation, Gigi served as executive director of the Media Access Project (MAP), a Washington, D.C.–based public interest telecommunications law firm. Gigi also served as a member of his Advisory Committee on the Public Interest Obligations of Digital Television Broadcasters ("Gore Commission") in October 1997. Gigi is an adjunct professor at Georgetown University and a senior fellow at the University of Melbourne Faculty of Law in Melbourne, Australia. In 2001, she was an adjunct professor at the Benjamin N. Cardozo School of Law, Yeshiva University, in New York City.

Sohn holds a B.S. in broadcasting and film, summa cum laude, from the Boston University College of Communication and a J.D. from the University of Pennsylvania Law School.

BOARD OF DIRECTORS

Gigi B. Sohn, president
Hal Abelson, member; professor, Massachusetts Institute of Technology, Cambridge, MA
David Bollier, member; writer and activist, Amherst, MA
Hon. Reed Hundt, member; senior advisor, McKinsey and Co., Washington, DC
Lawrence Lessig, member; professor, Stanford Law School, Palo Alto, CA
Laurie Racine, member; president, Center for the Public Domain, Chapel Hill, NC

SCOPE

Members: Information unavailable
Branches/chapters: None
Affiliates: None

STAFF

5 total

TAX STATUS

501(c)(3)

FINANCES

Revenue: 2002—$1 million

FUNDING SOURCES

Individual contributions, 99.9%; investments and other, 0.1%

CONTACT INFORMATION

1875 Connecticut Avenue, NW, Suite 650, Washington, DC 20009
Phone: (202) 518-0020 • *Fax:* (202) 986-2539
General E-mail: pk@publicknowledge.org •
Web site: www.publicknowledge.org

Communications Director: Art Brodsky
(202) 518-0020, ext 103 • abrodsky@publicknowledge.org
Human Resources Director: Information unavailable

PURPOSE: "Public Knowledge is a new public-interest advocacy organization dedicated to fortifying and defending a vibrant information commons. This Washington, DC based group works with wide spectrum of stakeholders—libraries, educators, scientists, artists, musicians, journalists, consumers, software programmers, civic groups and enlightened businesses—to promote the core conviction that some fundamental democratic principles and cultural values—openness, access, and the capacity to create and compete—must be given new embodiment in the digital age."

CURRENT CONCERNS: Copyright term extension • Database legislation • Digital rights management • FCC broadcast flag • Open access • Peer-to-peer networks • RIAA amnesty • Super DMCAs

METHOD OF OPERATION: Grassroots organizing • Information clearinghouse • Internet (Web site) • Legislative/regulatory monitoring (federal) • Litigation • Media outreach

Effectiveness and Political Orientation

"A federal appeals panel Friday handed a victory to privacy advocates and a costly setback to the major record labels, outlawing a technique that the music industry had used to identify—so it could then sue—people accused of pirating music.

"The decision by the U.S. Court of Appeals for the District of Columbia is the latest in a series of rulings that may embolden music fans to share songs online and download them illegally. But Cary Sherman, president of the Recording Industry Assn. of America, stressed that the appeals court's decision wouldn't stop the labels from filing lawsuits; it would simply make the process more cumbersome and expensive.

" 'This is a very big step,' said Gigi Sohn, president of Public Knowledge, an advocacy group for more limited copyright laws, calling the decision 'an early holiday gift from the court to Internet users.' "

(*The Los Angeles Times,* December 20, 2003)

"The Federal Communications Commission yesterday approved the first-ever requirement that some personal computers and other consumer electronic

PAC
None

EMPLOYMENT
Employment information can be found at http://www.publicknowledge.org/about-us/jobs-internships.

INTERNSHIPS
Public Knowledge offers unpaid legal internships during the school year and summer. Internships last 8–10 weeks and are either full-time or part-time (10–20 hours per week). An internship with Public Knowledge is an opportunity to work on the latest intellectual property issues and technology policy developments. Applicants should direct questions to Nathan Mitchler at nmitchler@publicknowledge.org. Additional information can be found at http://www.publicknowledge.org/about-us/jobs-internships.

NEWSLETTERS
None

PUBLICATIONS
Information unavailable

CONFERENCES
Information unavailable

devices be equipped with technology to help block Internet piracy of digital entertainment.

"The move is a victory for the movie industry, which has lobbied hard for regulations aimed at stemming the tide of copying and online trading of movies and television shows.

"But consumer advocates warned that the scheme could force people to buy new equipment and lead to ongoing regulation of how computers are built. And they worry that the new rules would potentially hinder the copying of programming not entitled to industry protection, such as shows that are no longer covered by copyright. . . .

" 'Having just given big media companies more control over what consumers can see on their TV sets by lifting media ownership limits, the FCC has now given these same companies more control over what users can do with that content, leaving consumers as two-time losers,' said Gigi B. Sohn, president of Public Knowledge.

"Sohn and others say the plan will not stop Internet distribution, because programs copied onto video cassettes can easily be re-copied in digital form and sent online. Blocking that, they said, would require wholesale equipment changes."

(*The Washington Post,* November 5, 2003)

"Two students at the Massachusetts Institute of Technology have developed a system for sharing music within their campus community that they say can avoid the copyright battles that have pitted the music industry against many customers. . .

"The students say the system, which they plan to officially announce today, falls within the time-honored licensing and royalty system under which the music industry allows broadcasters and others to play recordings for a public audience. Major music industry groups are reserving comment, while some legal experts say the M.I.T. system mainly demonstrates how unwieldy copyright laws have become. A novel approach to serving up music on demand from one of the nation's leading technical institutions is only fitting, admirers of the project say. The music industry's woes started on college campuses, where fast Internet connections and a population of music lovers with time on their hands sparked a file-sharing revolution.

" 'It's kind of brilliant,' said Mike Godwin, the senior technology counsel at Public Knowledge, a policy group in Washington that focuses on intellectual property issues. If the legal theories hold up, he said, 'they've sidestepped the stonewall that the music companies have tried to put up between campus users and music sharing.' "

(*The New York Times,* October 27, 2003)

Rainforest Action Network

Established in 1985

DIRECTOR

Michael Brune, executive director. Brune joined Rainforest Action Network (RAN) in 1998 to work on the Home Depot campaign. At that time, "old growth free" and "endangered forest free" were far from household terms in America. One year later, Home Depot, the world's largest home improvement retailer, became the world's first to make a public commitment to stop sourcing wood from old growth forests. Subsequently, Brune negotiated old growth free agreements with lumber retailers, including Lowe's and Menards and homebuilders, including Centex Homes and KB Home. After his promotion to campaign director, he became the driving force behind RAN's campaigns to lead more companies such as Kinko's and Boise Cascade out of old growth and endangered forests. His leadership has helped support the rights of indigenous communities from South America to Southeast Asia, preserve the Great Bear Rainforest of British Columbia and stop Citigroup from funding rainforest destruction. Prior to joining RAN, Brune worked as a campaigner for the Coast Rainforest Coalition and public outreach director for Greenpeace in San Francisco. He received a B.S. in accounting and finance from Westchester University.

BOARD OF DIRECTORS

James Gollin, chair
Randall Hayes, president and secretary
Scott Price, treasurer
Andre Carothers, member
Nancy Harris Dalwin, member
Martha Rynham Di Sario, member
Allan Hunt-Badiner, member
Michael Klein, member
Jodie Evans, member
Idelisse Malave, member
Stephen Stevick, member
Pamela Wellner, member

SCOPE

Members: 30,000
Branches/chapters: None
Affiliates: There are more than 150 Rainforest Action Groups (RAGs) based in the United States and Europe that are informally associated with the Rainforest Action Network. They receive support materials, but no funding.

STAFF

23 total—21 full-time professional; 2 part-time professional; plus 15 volunteers; 25 interns

TAX STATUS

501(c)(3)

CONTACT INFORMATION

221 Pine Street, Suite 500, San Francisco, CA 94104
Phone: (415) 398-4404 • *Fax:* (415) 398-2732
General E-mail: rainforest@ran.org • *Web site:* www.ran.org
Communications Director: Paul West
(415) 398-4404, ext. 319 • media@ran.org
Human Resources Director: Stephanie Viviano, director of finance and operations
(415) 398-4404, ext. 317 • rainforest@ran.org

PURPOSE: Rainforest Action Network works to protect the Earth's rainforests and support the rights of their inhabitants through education, grassroots organizing, and nonviolent direct action.

CURRENT CONCERNS: Certified logging • Climate change • Consumption reduction • Global forest protection • Sustainable economic development • Transformation of government and corporate policy

METHOD OF OPERATION: Campaign contributions • Coalition forming • Direct action • Grantmaking • Grassroots organizing • Internet (e-mail alerts and Web site) • Media outreach

Effectiveness and Political Orientation

"Rainforest Action Network today sent letters to 'The Liquidators,' ten of the most environmentally destructive US-based banks, issuing an Earth Day deadline to meet or beat new industry best practices set by Citigroup's recently announced environmental initiatives. The letter follows the release of a secret Pentagon report confirming that catastrophic climate change is a greater national security threat than terrorism and a World Bank report recommending it phase out funding for fossil fuel projects by 2008. . . .

"In a March 10, 2004 letter, Rainforest Action Network executive director Michael Brune proposed that the banks take immediate first steps to phase out all funding and investment for extractive industries (oil, gas, mining, logging) in endangered ecosystems; commit to support the right of indigenous and local populations to have free and prior informed consent to projects on their lands; commit to independent third party chain-of-custody certification in regions where over 50 percent of logging is illegal; prioritize funding for sustainable alternatives, such as Forest Stewardship Council certified logging projects and clean energy sources such as solar and wind power; provide and promote retail financial products including energy efficient and energy improvement mortgages to encourage mainstream adoption of clean energy sources; and commit to reduce investments in greenhouse gas producing industries, beginning with an immediate ban in new funding for coal. . . .

FINANCES
Budget: 2004—$2.4 million;
2003—$2 million; 2002—$2 million

FUNDING SOURCES
Individual contributions, 39%; foundation
grants, 33%; membership, 20%; special
events/projects, 8%

PAC
None

EMPLOYMENT
Information on employment opportunities can
be found at craigslist.org, *Opportunitynocs,
Idealist,* and *Environmental Career.*

INTERNSHIPS
For information on internships, applicants
should contact Internship Committee, 221 Pine
Street, Suite 500, San Francisco, CA 94104.
Phone: (415) 398-4404. Fax: (415) 398-2732.
E-mail: rainforest@ran.org. Internships and
volunteer opportunities are unpaid and located
in the San Francisco office.

NEWSLETTERS
Rainforest Action Alert (bimonthly)
World Rainforest Report (biannual)

PUBLICATIONS
Amazonia: Voices from the Rainforest
Cut Waste Not Trees
*Drilling to the Ends of the Earth: The
	Ecological, Social, and Climate Imperative
	for Ending Petroleum Exploration*
*Guide to Tree-Free, Recycled, and Certified
	Papers*
Importing Destruction
Mitsubishi Campaign Organizer's Manual
Southeast Asia Directory
Treasures of the Rainforest
Wood Users Guide
World Rainforest Report
World Rainforest Week Organizer's Packet
Also publishes brochures and fact sheets.

CONFERENCES
Declined to comment

"Rainforest Action Network works to protect the Earth's rainforests and support the rights of their inhabitants through education, grassroots organizing, and non-violent direct action."

(*Ascribe News,* March 11, 2004)

"Forest activists who helped persuade building giants Home Depot and Lowe's to stop buying products made of wood from some old-growth forests have set their sights on a new target in Seattle's back yard: Weyerhaeuser.

"Citing a breakdown in talks with the Federal Way timber giant over its forest practices primarily in Canada a group of environmental activists climbed a construction crane in Seattle's Belltown neighborhood for five hours yesterday, hanging a 50-by-50-foot banner that read: 'Wake up Weyerhaeuser, Protect Forests Now.'

"The Rainforest Action Network, based in San Francisco, and the Forest Action Network, based in Canada, claimed responsibility for the spectacle, which led to the arrests of the five women on suspicion of reckless endangerment and criminal trespass, both misdemeanors, police said. . . .

" 'They haven't moved off the dime. They're talking to us as if it were still the mid-1980s and they didn't have to respond, but the reality is the market has changed,' said Michael Brune, executive director of the Rainforest group. 'In the public consciousness, old-growth forests are now as fundamental as baseball, apple pie and Derek Jeter. Areas that have escaped industrial logging to date should remain off-limits.' "

(*The Seattle Times,* February 20, 2004)

"Rainforest Action Network and Citigroup today announced that Citigroup has adopted a comprehensive environmental policy that sets a new standard for the financial services industry. The policy provides a long-term framework for Citigroup to promote higher environmental standards through its business practices.

"The policy sets standards related to endangered ecosystems, illegal logging, ecologically sustainable development and climate change.

" 'Today, Citigroup has articulated the strongest environmental policies yet of any private financial institution in the world,' said Michael Brune, executive director of Rainforest Action Network. 'With this move, Citigroup joins a growing family of leading companies that are working to transform humanity's greatest challenges into new opportunities for a sustainable future. This moment marks a milestone in worldwide movement to stop global warming and deforestation. We can not overstate the importance of changing such a vast enterprise and look forward to working together with Citigroup in the coming years.' "

(*PR Newswire,* January 22, 2004)

Reason Foundation

Established in 1978

DIRECTOR
David C. Nott, president and chief executive officer. Nott came to this position in 2001 after serving as president of two of the country's leading free-market institutions: the Institute for Humane Studies (IHS) and the Mercatus Center, both at George Mason University in Virginia. While there, he dramatically expanded both organizations, conceiving several new programs, recruiting new, high-profile staff, and dramatically expanding the organizations' operating budgets and fundraising bases. He also worked as a petroleum engineer for Shell Western Exploration & Production Inc. in Bakersfield, CA, where he did business planning, economic analysis, and reservoir engineering. Nott is an engineer by training, receiving his bachelor degrees in economics and engineering, from Stanford University. He remains a registered professional engineer in CA.

BOARD OF DIRECTORS
Harry Teasley Jr., chair of the board, Tampa, FL
William A. Dunn, chair-elect; DUNN Capital Management, Stuart, FL
Robert W. Poole Jr., founder
David Nott, president
Nicholas Gillespie, vice president, magazine
Adrian Moore, vice president, research
Murielle Schulze, treasurer
Donald Heath, secretary
Thomas E. Beach, member; Beach Investment Counsel, Inc., Radnor, PA
David Fleming, member; Latham & Watkins, Universal City, CA
C. Boyden Gray, member; Wilmer, Cutler & Pickering, Washington, DC
James D. Jameson, member; Rancho Santa Fe, CA
Manuel S. Klausner, member; Law Offices of Manuel S. Klausner, Los Angeles, CA
David H. Koch, member; Koch Industries, New York, NY
James Lintott, member; Sterling Foundation Management, LLC, Great Falls, VA
Stephen Modzelewski, member; Maple Engine, LLC, Princeton, NJ
Sara A. O'Dowd, member; Heller Ehrman White & McAuliffe, Palo Alto, CA
Randall Smith, member; InSite MediaCom, LLC, Beverly Hills, CA
Al H. St. Clair, member; Procter & Gamble, Cincinnati, OH

SCOPE
Members: None
Branches/chapters: None
Affiliates: Reason Public Policy Institute (policy research division) and *Reason* magazine (current affairs commentary division).

CONTACT INFORMATION
3415 South Sepulveda Boulevard, Suite 400, Los Angeles, CA 90034
Phone: (310) 391-2245 • *Fax:* (310) 391-4395
General E-mail: info@reason.org • *Web site:* www.reason.org
Washington Office
1001 Pennsylvania Avenue, NW, Suite 200 South, Washington, DC 20004

Communications Director: Chris Mitchell, director of media relations
(310) 391-2245, ext. 3037 • chris.mitchell@reason.org
Human Resources Director: Information unavailable

PURPOSE: "The mission of Reason Foundation is to advance a free society by developing, applying, and promoting libertarian principles, including free markets, individual liberty, and the rule of law."

CURRENT CONCERNS: Biotechnology • Culture • Education (competitive contracting, private practice teaching, and school choice) • Environment (deregulation, hazardous waste, risk assessment, and solid waste disposal) • Government reform • Privatization (competitive government, public/private partnerships, and volunteerism) • Transportation • Urban policy (housing, land use, and sprawl)

METHOD OF OPERATION: Conferences/seminars • Information clearinghouse • Internet (databases, e-mail alerts, and Web site) • Media outreach • Research • Telecommunications services (mailing lists)

Effectiveness and Political Orientation

"Washington got it all wrong on airport security policy, the Reason Foundation opines. A new analysis by the think tank avers that 'by devoting equal resources to every passenger and every piece of luggage, [the U.S.] spends too much on people who are no threat and too little on the few who might be.' The Reason study calls for a risk-based decision-making airport security system that would focus on identifying 'potentially bad people,' not finding 'bad objects.' . . . Reason wants passengers who are more likely to be terrorists singled out. . . ."

(Aviation Week & Space Technology, June 2, 2003)

"The idea of high-occupancy toll lanes, where variable congestion pricing and occupancy requirements are used to manage traffic volume, is speeding up throughout the U.S. In an era of tight budgets and increasing congestion, state transportation departments, federal agencies and private firms could implement more HOT lane projects in the next few years.

"'HOT lanes are one flavor of managed-lane options and will be part of the future of transportation solutions,' says Benjamin G. Perez, senior professional associate for PB Consult, New York City. Perez and colleague Gian-Claudia Sciara co-authored a new report on HOT lanes, available at http://ops.fhwa.dot.gov/Travel/. The Reason Foundation, a Los Angeles-based think tank, publicly advocated HOT lanes in a conference this month. . . ."

(*Engineering News-Record,* March 17, 2003)

"Local commuters don't want car-pool lanes and would benefit more if Orange and Los Angeles Counties converted diamond lanes into toll lanes, according to a report released Tuesday.

"A study by the Los Angeles-based transportation group Reason Foundation suggests that toll operations like the 91 Express Lanes should be used as models of success. . .

" 'This is a way out of the funding crisis as far as transportation is concerned for L.A. and Orange County,' said Robert Poole, the report's co-author and Reason Foundation director. . . .

"The report has drawn some interest in Washington, D.C., where Poole plans to brief a committee that approves federal transportation spending."

(*The Orange County Register,* [California] February 26, 2003)

"As Americans continue to flirt with ways to reduce waste while managing disposal capacity, recent reports note that the nation's overall recovery rate is increasing. This may be thanks, in part, to some communities' love affair with variable-rate waste management, also known as pay-as-you-throw [PAYT], programs.

"According to the Los Angeles-based Reason Foundation's recent study, 'Variable-Rate or "Pay-as-You-Throw" Waste Management: Answers to Frequently Asked Questions,' PAYT is proving to be a powerful source reduction tool. In fact, on average it has helped more than 5,000 communities to reduce their overall refuse tonnage by nearly 17 percent.

"The majority of communities across the United States adhere to a flat-rate system—collected through a portion of property taxes or a fixed bill amount. However, 'putting a price on the waste stream creates incentives for people to separate [recyclables] out and makes them more suitable for re-marketing as recycled goods,' says Kenneth Green, chief scientist for the Reason Foundation, a nonprofit research and education organization.

" 'The most surprising finding of the study is the sheer magnitude of the waste that can be avoided [with PAYT],' Green says. 'I don't think that many people have an idea that through changing the incentives and the pricing mechanism that you can have such [an] effect on the end outcome.'. . .

"According to the Reason Foundation's study, PAYT can be implemented via several collection systems. . .

" 'Virtually any community can find [a method] suitable for their lifestyle,' Green says. 'It's not imposed by a one-size-fits-all approach based on municipal government.' "

(*Waste Age,* November 2002)

"Intercity highway lanes that are dedicated to trucking—paid for with public bonds and repaid by assessing tolls against the truckers that use them—would reduce accidents between cars and trucks and could cut motor carriers' costs by up to $40 billion a year.

"That proposal emerged from a recent study conducted by the Reason Foundation, a West Coast research group.

" 'Toll truckways would be freeways-within-the-freeway and provide a system geared toward safer, more productive trucks,' said Robert Poole, director

School-Facilities Crunch through Public-Private Partnerships

Urban Growth Boundaries and Housing Affordability: Lessons from Portland

Also publishes an annual report and policy studies.

CONFERENCES

Frequent presentations and seminars with nonprofit groups, corporations, and governmental organizations

of transportation studies at the Reason Foundation and co-author of the report, in a press release. Poole said the specialized lanes, which would be added to existing interstate highways and divided from other lanes with Jersey barriers, would reduce accidents and allow carriers to operate larger trucks. 'Trucking companies will be willing to pay tolls to use the lanes,' he suggested, 'because they will significantly cut costs by delivering larger loads faster and with greater reliability.' . . ."

(*Logistics Management,* July 1, 2002)

Resources for the Future (RFF)

Established in 1952

DIRECTOR

Paul R. Portney, president. Portney was named president of RFF in 1995. An economist by training, he joined the research staff in 1972. Portney then became a senior fellow and directed two of RFF's research divisions—the Quality of the Environment Division and the Center for Risk Management. He became vice president in 1989. From 1979 to 1980, Portney took leave from RFF to be chief economist at the Council on Environmental Quality in the Executive Office of the President. He has held teaching positions at the University of California-Berkeley and Princeton University. He also chaired the Environmental Economics Advisory Committee of the U.S. Environmental Protection Agency's Science Advisory Board and was a member of the its executive committee. In 2001, he was chair of the National Research Council's committee on the future of the Corporate Average Fuel Economy program. He received his bachelor's degree in economics from Alma College in 1967, and his Ph.D. in economics from Northwestern University in 1973.

BOARD OF DIRECTORS

Robert E. Grady, chair; partner and managing director, Carlyle Group
Frank E. Loy, vice-chair; Washington, DC
Paul R. Portney, president; president and senior fellow, Resources for the Future
Edward F. Hand, vice president, external affairs
Lesli A. Creedon, vice president, external affairs
Catherine G. Abbott, member; McLean, VA
Vicky A. Bailey, member; Johnston and Associates, LLP
Joan Z. Bernstein, member; Counsel Bryan Cave, LLP
Julia Carabias Lillo, member; Universidad Nacional Autónomia de México México D.F., México
Norman L. Christensen Jr., member; Nicholas School of the Environment, Duke University
Maureen L. Cropper, member; lead economist, World Bank Group
W. Bowman Cutter, member; managing director, Warburg Pincus
John M. Deutch, member; institute professor, Department of Chemistry, Massachusetts Institute of Technology
E. Linn Draper Jr., member; chair of the board, president, and chief executive officer, American Electric Power Co., Inc.
Mohamed T. El-Ashry, member; former chair and chief executive officer, Global Environmental Facility
Dod A. Fraser, member; Sackett Partners Incorporated, White Plains, NY

CONTACT INFORMATION

1616 P Street, NW, Washington, DC 20036
Phone: (202) 328-5000 • *Fax:* (202) 939-3460
General E-mail:, info@rff.org • *Web site:* www.rff.org

Communications Director: Stanley N. Wellborn
(202) 328-5026 • wellborn@rff.org
Human Resources Director: Helen Marie Streich
(202) 328-5053 • streich@rff.org

PURPOSE: Resources for the Future improves environmental and natural resource policymaking worldwide through objective social science research of the highest caliber.

CURRENT CONCERNS: Energy, electricity and climate change • Environment and development • Environmental management • Food and agriculture • Fundamental research studies • Natural and biological resources • Public health and the environment • Technology and the environment • Urban complexities

METHOD OF OPERATION: Advertisements • Awards programs • Conferences/seminars • Congressional testimony • Films/video/audiotapes • International activities • Internet (databases, electronic bulletin boards, e-mail alerts, and Web site) • Internships • Library services for members only • Media outreach • Other (book publishing) • Participation in regulatory proceedings (federal) • Research • Speakers program • Telecommunications services (mailing lists) • Technical assistance • Training

Effectiveness and Political Orientation

"Sen. Lieberman will be the first speaker in a new series of public policy leadership forums hosted by Resources For the Future (RFF) that will feature national lawmakers and policy experts. . . .

"RFF is an independent environmental, energy, and natural resource policy research center, located in Washington, DC. Through a half-century of scholarship, RFF has built a reputation for reasoned analysis of important problems and for developing innovative solutions to environmental challenges.

"Energy policy has been, and will continue to be, central to the economic and environmental well-being of the nation. From its founding conference in 1952, RFF has provided an ongoing public forum where scholars, lawmakers, business leaders, and environmental advocates debate important policy issues."
(*U.S. Newswire*, May 5, 2003)

"How much will it cost to finish cleaning-up the most contaminated sites in the US? Despite many estimates since the early 1980s, the answer remains elusive.

SCOPE
Members: None
Branches/chapters: None
Affiliates: None

STAFF
81 total—55 full-time professional staff; 12 full-time support staff; 13 part-time professional; 1 part-time support; plus 1 volunteer

TAX STATUS
501(c)(3)

FINANCES
Budget: 2004—$11.3 million; 2003—$12.4 million; 2002—$12.6 million

FUNDING SOURCES
Government contracts, 31%; investments and real estate income, 20%; corporate donations, 17%; foundation grants, 11%; other sources, 11%; publications, 7%; individuals, 3%

PAC
None

EMPLOYMENT
Information on employment opportunities is located at www.rff.org/rff/About/Employment_Opportunities/Index.cfm. To apply online, e-mail a resume and cover letter to John Mankin, human resources assistant, RFF, 1616 P Street NW, Washington, DC 20036. Phone: (202) 328-5000. Fax: (202) 939-3460. E-mail: mankin@rff.org.

"In July last year, a study requested by the US Congress revealed the difficulties inherent in any prediction. The study by Resources for the Future (RFF), entitled Superfund's Future: What Will It Cost?, examined the Superfund programme and in particular, the National Priorities List (NPL), which is frequently referred to as the list of the most contaminated sites in the US.

"RFF estimated the number of sites that would be added to the NPL in fiscal years 2000 to 2009 (that is, October 1, 1999, to September 30, 2009) and the cost of cleaning them up.

"RFF reported that the US Environmental Protection Agency (EPA) does not necessarily list sites on the NPL because they are the most contaminated sites in the US. The decision to list a site is affected by many factors, including the money available to the EPA from the Superfund programme. . . .

"RFF based its projections, which it emphasised were surrounded by uncertainty, on the EPA adding 35 sites, including two mega sites, to the NPL each year. That assumption was based on the EPA having added 36 sites including two mega-sites, in fiscal year 2000, the large number of eligible sites and the EPA's continued discovery of seriously contaminated sites (known colloquially as 'pop ups').

"RFF considered that even if no more sites were added to the NPL, the cost of the Superfund programme, which was $1.54bn in fiscal year 1999, would not decrease until fiscal year 2004. RFF further considered that the annual cost would not fall below $1.4bn until fiscal year 2008."

(*Insurance Day*, May 9, 2002)

"Resources for the Future (RFF) is proud to announce the appointment of Margaret Glavin. As a visiting scholar at RFF, she will play a leadership role in the continued development and management of the independent research institute's food safety program. . . .

"RFF's food safety program focuses on improving regulatory decision making and the allocation of government food safety resources to reduce the risk of food-borne disease. RFF is currently collaborating with the University of Maryland School of Medicine, the Iowa State University College of Agriculture, and the Milbank Memorial Fund to develop the decision tools required to manage a more science- and risk-based food safety system.

"RFF is an independent, non-profit research institute dedicated to environmental and natural resource scholarship of the highest caliber. For 50 years, RFF researchers have examined critical issues facing our country and world, including biodiversity, energy security and reliability, land use and conservation, antibiotic resistance, international development, climate change, electric utility restructuring, space technologies, food safety, and sustainable forestry. RFF prides itself on putting forth realistic policy options for the consideration of key leaders and decision makers."

(*U.S. Newswire*, April 26, 2002)

"Why do so many Colorado ski resorts want to slow economic growth and choke off the very prosperity on which they depend? That's a trick question, of course, since ski resorts don't consciously favor stagnation. A number of them do, however, support a controversial proposal that would damage the economy.

"The evidence is a letter sent last week from more than 35 ski areas across the United States, including a dozen in Colorado, to Sens. John McCain and Joe Lieberman indicating support for the senators' Climate Stewardship Act.

INTERNSHIPS

RFF offers a variety of professional internships and academic fellowships and internships to about 12–15 people every year. Academic programs at RFF promote research and policy analysis in RFF's discipline fields by supporting work at colleges, universities, and other institutions, both in the United States and elsewhere, and by bringing researchers to RFF to contribute to projects underway and to the formulation of new lines of inquiry. Academic fellowships and internships include fellowships in environmental regulatory implementation, the Joseph L. Fisher Doctoral Dissertation Fellowships, the Gilbert F. White Postdoctoral Fellowship Program, the Walter O. Spofford Jr. Memorial Internship Program, and paid summer internship programs. Internships last for 10 weeks during the summer and many are funded. Interns are required to work 35 hours a week. Deadline for applications is March 15. Additional information about these and other available internship opportunities is located at http://www.rff.org/rff/About/Fellowships_and _Internships/Index.cfm.

NEWSLETTERS

Resources (quarterly)

PUBLICATIONS

The following is a sample list of publications:
Climate Change
Controlling Ozone and Fine Particulates
Economic Growth and the Scarcity of Natural Resources
Economics and Policy Setting of Renewable Energy
Evolution of Hazardous Waste Programs: Lessons from Eight Countries
Footing the Bill for Superfund Cleanups: Who Pays and How?
Measuring Marginal Congestion Costs of Urban Transportation
Pollution Control in the United States: Evaluating the System
Productivity in Natural Resource Industries: Improvement through Innovation
Public Policies for Environmental Protection
The RFF Reader in Environmental and Resource Management
Science and Technology Advice for Congress
Science at EPA: Information in the Regulatory Process
Sustainability of Temperate Forests
Unleashing the Clean Water Act
A Vision for the U.S. Forest Service
When Are No Fishing Zones the Best Management Practice?

CONFERENCES

The RFF Seminar Series (Weekly)
Policy Leadership Forum
Hans Landsberg Memorial Lecture (Annual)
RFF Council (semiannual)
Numerous other conferences and academic seminars scheduled throughout the year.

The good news is that this bill was also defeated last week by a vote of 55-43, so for the time being the ski resorts' lobbying failed. But we'd hope they'd reconsider their position before Congress takes up some version of this idea again, as it almost certainly will.

"The Climate Stewardship Act is a so-called 'cap and trade' bill that would have required most sectors of the American economy to reduce their levels of greenhouse-gas emissions to 2000 levels by 2010. The law would create a market in emission allowances with the total supply set at that level, and businesses subject to the law—commercial, industrial, transportation and electrical power—would be required to purchase enough allowances to cover their emissions.

Nobody knows how much this would cost the economy, although the regulatory apparatus alone would have to be huge. Resources for the Future, a green group that actually supports the idea, cites figures that a more draconian standard dropped from the original bill—1990 levels by 2016—would add about 13 cents to the price of a gallon of gas and 77 cents to the price of a thousand cubic feet of natural gas. But the group also blithely acknowledges that the Environmental Protection Agency says it could be a tenth of that, or 10 times as much."

(*Denver Rocky Mountain News,* November 11, 2003)

The Rockford Institute

Established in 1976

DIRECTOR

Thomas J. Fleming, president. Fleming is also editor of *Chronicles: A Magazine of American Culture* and author of *The Politics of Human Nature* and *The Conservative Movement*. He received his Ph.D. in classics from the University of North Carolina.

SCOPE

Members: None
Branches/chapters: None
Affiliates: Center for International Affairs

STAFF

10 total

TAX STATUS

501(c)(3)

FINANCES

Revenue: 2002—$845,195;
2001—$1.17 million

FUNDING SOURCES

Individuals, 35%; publications, 35%; foundations/corporations, 20%; other, 10%

PAC

None

EMPLOYMENT

Information unavailable

INTERNSHIPS

Information unavailable

CONTACT INFORMATION

928 North Main Street, Rockford, IL 61103
Phone: (815) 964-5053 • *Fax:* (815) 964-9403
General E-mail: info@rockfordinstitute.org •
Web site: www.chroniclesmagazine.org/TRI/About.htm

Communications Director: Christopher J. Check, executive vice president (815) 964-5053 • execvp@rockfordinstitute.org.
Human Resources Director: Information unavailable

PURPOSE: "The Institute grounds its work in the promotion of liberty, the defense of natural family, the affirmation of Scriptural Truth, the promotion of self reliance and decentralization in politics and economics, and the celebration of moral and artistic excellence in culture. In the broadest sense, we strive to contribute to the renewal of Christendom in this time and place."

CURRENT CONCERNS: Campaign finance reform • Crime and punishment • Drug war • Gay rights • Home schooling • Immigration • Judicial tyranny • Neoconservatism • New world order • Public education • States' rights • Teaching the classics • Term limits

METHOD OF OPERATION: Awards program (the Ingersoll Prizes) • Coalition forming • Commissioned studies • Conferences/seminars • Congressional testimony • Films/video/audiotapes • International activities • Internet • Library/information clearinghouse • Media outreach • Speakers program • Telecommunications services (mailing lists)

Effectiveness and Political Orientation

"Even viewed through the time warp of Australian parliamentary politics, it's obvious that neoconservatism as a world view is in the ascendant. Tony Blair's reinvention of himself and most of the British Labour Party along Thatcherite lines is the starkest evidence of that paradigm shift. Blair's triumph, in dragging his party into the coalition of the willing, was emblematic of an ideological argument comprehensively won. Politically, economically and socially conservative policy (with—or preferably without—futuristic window-dressing) actually works.

"As with the fall of the Berlin Wall, our local intelligentsia can be expected to remain pretty much in denial about this unheard-of fit between what most people want and policies that deliver it for about a decade. Coincidentally, 10–15 years seems to me to be roughly the shelf-life of neoconservatism as a dominant paradigm because no triumph or reverse, however complete it seems, is permanent and when people are on a good thing they all too seldom stick to it.

"Curiously, it was the Iraq war that, as Rachel Alexander put it, 'brought out a deep division' within the American Right's thinking. 'As the first decade of the

2000s progresses, it is becoming increasingly clear that the two types of conservatism that will define the decade are neoconservatism and palaeoconservatism.'

"Palaeoconservatism is at the very least a useful corrective to neocon trumphalism. The American Heritage Dictionary definition is: 'Extremely stubborn or stubbornly conservative in politics.' According to Alexander, the term 'actually originated in the Rockford Institute's *Chronicles* magazine as a reaction to what was seen as increasingly neocon encroachment into conservatism. Palaeocons claim that their brand is the descendant of conservative thought of the 1950s and 1960s. Palaeocons prefer an isolationist foreign policy and accuse neocons of being interventionist and soft on big government programs.'"

(*The Weekend Australian* [Australia], June 28, 2003)

"From the very beginning of the War on Terror, there has been dissent, and as the war has proceeded to Iraq, the dissent has grown more radical and more vociferous. Perhaps that was to be expected. But here is what never could have been: Some of the leading figures in this antiwar movement call themselves 'conservatives.'

"These conservatives are relatively few in number, but their ambitions are large. They aspire to reinvent conservative ideology: to junk the 50-year-old conservative commitment to defend American interests and values throughout the world—the commitment that inspired the founding of this magazine—in favor of a fearful policy of ignoring threats and appeasing enemies. . . .

"You may know the names of these antiwar conservatives. Some are famous: Patrick Buchanan and Robert Novak. Others are not: Llewellyn Rockwell, Samuel Francis, Thomas Fleming, Scott McConnell, Justin Raimondo, Joe Sobran, Charley Reese, Jude Wanniski, Eric Margolis, and Taki Theodoracopulos. . . .

"The writers I quote call themselves 'paleoconservatives,' implying that they are somehow the inheritors of an older, purer conservatism than that upheld by their impostor rivals. . . . Frustrated ambition is not a propitious foundation for an intellectual movement. 'Jobs for the lads' may be an effective slogan for a trade union, but the paleos needed to develop a more idealistic explanation for their resentments, if they were to have any hope of influencing the main body of the conservative movement. They needed an ideology of their own.

"Developing such an ideology was not going to be an easy task. There was no shortage of disaffected right-wingers. . . .

"Yet the job had to be done—and thanks to a lucky accident, there was a place to do it. In the 1970s, Leopold Tyrmand, an emigre Polish Jew who had survived the death camps, scraped together some money to found a magazine he hoped would serve as a conservative alternative to *The New York Review of Books*. He called it *Chronicles of Culture*. . . .

"So, *Chronicles* advocated protectionism for American industry and restrictions on nonwhite immigration. It defended minimum-wage laws and attacked corporations that moved operations off-shore. And it championed the Southern Confederacy of the 1860s and the anti-civil rights resistance of the 1960s.

"The decisive year for both the magazine and paleoconservatism was 1989. Until then, *Chronicles* had managed to coexist with most of the rest of the conservative community. This coexistence was symbolized by the Rockford Institute, which sponsored not only *Chronicles* but also the Center for

Religion and Society in New York, headed by Richard John Neuhaus, a Lutheran minister who had been involved in both the civil rights movement and the anti-Vietnam protests."

(National Review, April 7, 2003)

"The West worried at first that Russian President Vladimir Putin would kill reform and restart the Cold War. After all, Putin was a Communist Party member, an apparatchik and a spy. But who does the West want to run Eastern Europe? Party members, apparatchiks and spies. Ex-communists today are the preferred rulers of the former Warsaw Pact. Ex-anti-communists are the new enemy. . . . Today's ruling class is full of yesterday's radicals. . . . Such roots help explain the fondness of Western officials for people like Zoran Djindjic, prime minister of Serbia. In his younger years, Djindjic ran with a radical crowd that hated Yugoslavia's pro-Western brand of socialism. . . . By contrast, Vojislav Kostunica, Serbia's president, was a conservative, Christian, pro-Western anti-communist. A constitutional scholar, he translated 'The Federalist Papers' into Serbian. Kostunica also condemned NATO's bombing of Serbia, so Western diplomats and journalists tagged him a nationalist. 'When they call someone a nationalist, it's the kiss of death,' said Srdja Trifkovic, once an adviser to Kostunica, now at the Rockford Institute in Illinois. 'That person is no longer invited to diplomatic cocktail parties, and U.S. money for political purposes will go elsewhere.' "

(Investor's Business Daily, June 25, 2002)

Rutherford Institute

Established in 1982

DIRECTOR

John W. Whitehead, president and founder. In 1982, Whitehead established The Rutherford Institute, a nonprofit civil liberties and human rights organization whose international headquarters are located in Charlottesville, VA. The author of numerous books, Whitehead has written for numerous magazines and journals and produced many pamphlets and brochures providing legal information to the general public. His law reviews have been published widely. He earned a B.A. from the University of Arkansas in 1969 and a J.D. degree from the University of Arkansas School of Law in 1974. He served as an officer in the U.S. Army from 1969 to 1971.

BOARD OF DIRECTORS

John W. Whitehead, president and chief executive officer
Michael Masters, M.D., vice president
Donovan Campbell Jr., treasurer
Alexis I. Crow, Secretary
Linda McGuire, member

SCOPE

Members: None
Branches/chapters: Offices in Bolivia, United Kingdom, and Hungary; student chapters on law school campuses
Affiliates: None

STAFF

501 total

TAX STATUS

501(c)(3)

FINANCES

Revenue: 2003—$2 million;
2002—$2.1 million; 2001—$2.5 million

FUNDING SOURCES

Individual contributions, 95.5%; program services, 2.4%; sales and other, 2.1%

PAC

None

EMPLOYMENT

Information unavailable

INTERNSHIPS

The Rutherford Institute offers a Summer Internship Program, open to qualified law students interested in receiving a grounding in critical areas of law impacting civil liberties and religious freedom. The program's intensive lectures and course work are coupled with practical assignments related to the ongoing work of The Rutherford Institute. Admission decisions for second and third year law stu-

CONTACT INFORMATION

P.O. Box 7482, Charlottesville, VA 22906
Phone: (804) 978-3888 • *Fax:* (804) 978-1789
General E-mail: tristaff@rutherford.org • *Web site:* www.rutherford.org

Communications Director: Nisha Mohammed
(804) 978-3888 • nisha@rutherford.org
Human Resources Director: Information unavailable

PURPOSE: "The Institute's mission is twofold: to provide legal services in the defense of religious and civil liberties and to educate the public on important issues affecting their constitutional freedoms."

CURRENT CONCERNS: Churches, parochial schools, home schools • Civil liberties • Free speech • Human rights and justice • International religious persecution • Parental rights and family autonomy • Peaceful protest • Religious freedom • Sanctity of life • Sexual harassment • Students' rights

METHOD OF OPERATION: Conferences/seminars • Films/video/audio tapes • International activities • Internet (Web site) • Internships • Legal assistance • Legislative/regulatory monitoring (federal) • Litigation • Media outreach • Research • Speakers program

Effectiveness and Political Orientation

"The U.S. Supreme Court will not review the case of a New Jersey student who was prohibited by his public school district from distributing pencils and candy canes with religious messages.

"The justices announced last week that they would not hear an appeal filed by the family of Daniel Walz. He was a 5-year-old pre-kindergarten student when Egg Harbor Township school officials prevented him from giving the items to classmates at holiday parties in 1998.

"His family claimed he was a victim of religious discrimination and the Rutherford Institute, a Charlottesville, Va.–based civil liberties organization, sued on his behalf. But a federal judge ruled that school officials acted properly, and that decision was upheld last August by a three-judge panel of the 3rd U.S. Circuit Court of Appeals."

(*Associated Press*, April 2, 2004)

"A killer set to be executed Thursday has asked state officials to honor his religious beliefs by not performing an autopsy on his body after his death.

"Brian Lee Cherrix made the request in letters to Gov. Mark R. Warner, Attorney General Jerry W. Kilgore and Chief Medical Examiner Marcella F. Fierro, according to the Rutherford Institute and a spokeswoman for the Virginia Capital Representation Resource Center.

"Cherrix was sentenced to death in 1998 for the murder of Tessa Van Hart, 23, a pizza-delivery woman who was sodomized and shot on Chinco-

dents are made during November, and decisions for first year law students are made during February preceding the summer program. Early application is strongly recommended. The Institute also offers Work Study, Independent Research, and Externship Programs. These programs provide law students with the opportunity to gain procedural and substantive knowledge through legal research and writing. Applicants to the programs should send a cover letter, resume, writing sample (under 20 pages), and two references to Joel Whitehead, internship program coordinator, The Rutherford Institute, P.O. Box 7482, Charlottesville, VA 22906-7482. Phone: (434) 978-3888. Fax: (434) 978-1789. E-mail: internships@rutherford.org.

NEWSLETTERS

ACTION Newsletter (monthly)
Litigation Report (monthly)
oddSpeak Magazine (online)
Parakletos (bimonthly)
Rutherford Newsletter (quarterly)

PUBLICATIONS

The following is a sample list of publications:
Are Sincere Killings Okay?
Arresting Abortion
Censored on the Job: Your Religious Rights
Christians Involved in the Political Process
Church vs. State
Civil Disobedience: A Judeo-Christian Perspective
Freedom of Religious Expression
Home Education: Rights and Reasons
Parents' Rights
Pocket Constitution
Politically Correct: Censorship in American Culture
Prayer at Graduation Ceremonies
Public School Religious Clubs
Sexual Harassment: How to Prevent and Remedy Sexual Harassment in the Workplace
The Silent Tragedy of Partial-Birth Abortion
Teachers' Rights in Public Education
The Truth about the Wall of Separation
Women's Rights and the Law
Also publishes videos, audiotapes, and other resources.

CONFERENCES

Annual conference

teague Island in January 1994. Cherrix believes an autopsy would violate his Christian belief against mutilating the human body, which is God's temple, according to the Rutherford Institute of Charlottesville, a nonprofit civil-liberties organization that works to defend constitutional and human rights.

"Executed inmates are routinely autopsied, as are all persons who die while in state custody.

"The Corrections Department has told Cherrix that state law requires the autopsy to protect the government from being sued should it be alleged he was injured or killed by means other than execution.

"John W. Whitehead, president of the Rutherford Institute, disagrees.

"'Even if Virginia law required an autopsy in these circumstances, which it doesn't, Brian Lee Cherrix's right to have his sincerely held religious belief protected should outweigh any interest the commonwealth has in performing an autopsy on him after his execution,' Whitehead said in a statement."
(*Richmond Times Dispatch* [Virginia], March 14, 2004)

"Heard about the little girl bounced from her Georgia classroom for carrying a Tweety Bird wallet attached to a 10-inch chain? How about the 13-year-old Gwinnett County middle-schooler suspended nine days for "pretending" to drink wine (her mother said it was grape juice)?

"Now there's the one about the creative writer whose private musings—justly or unjustly—have landed her in hot water. Rachel Boim, 14, is one of the latest students to be disciplined under a policy that makes no exception for conduct that threatens the security of students, teachers or administrators.

"It is called zero tolerance, and it ensnared Boim, a Roswell High School freshman, because she wrote a fictional tale of a student who dreams she kills a teacher.

"It is also a kind of policy that has critics calling it 'political correctness run amok,' according to John Whitehead, who has fought zero-tolerance policies in court as president of the Rutherford Institute, a Virginia-based conservative religious organization. . . ."
(*The Atlanta Journal-Constitution,* October 27, 2003)

Sea Shepherd Conservation Society

Established in 1977

DIRECTOR
Paul Watson, president and founder. Captain Watson began his career at sea in 1968 with the Norwegian merchant marine, leaving to spend two years with the Canadian Coast Guard in the early 1970s. In 1972, he joined with other members of the Sierra Club in founding the Greenpeace Foundation and served as first officer on all Greenpeace voyages against whaling until 1977. Watson left Greenpeace in 1977 to found the Sea Shepherd Conservation Society. He is a professor of ecology at Pasadena College of Design.

BOARD OF DIRECTORS
Richard Dean Anderson, member
Jerry Vlasak, member
Paul Watson, founder and president
Ben Zuckerman, member

SCOPE
Members: 42,000 worldwide
Branches/chapters: Branches in the United
 Kingdom, Singapore, Netherlands, Brazil,
 Australia, Canada, and two regional
 offices in CA
Affiliates: None

STAFF
5 total

TAX STATUS
501(c)(3)

FINANCES
Revenue: 2002—$991,234; 2001—$1 million

FUNDING SOURCES
Contributions, nearly 100%

PAC
None

EMPLOYMENT
Information unavailable

INTERNSHIPS
Information unavailable

PUBLICATIONS
None

NEWSLETTERS
Ocean Realm Magazine (quarterly)

CONFERENCES
None

CONTACT INFORMATION
P.O. Box 2616, Friday Harbor, Washington 98250
Phone: (360) 370-5650 • *Fax:* (360) 370-5651
General E-mail: info@seashepherd.org • *Web site:* www.seashepherd.org

Communications Director: Jared Rubin
media@seashepherd.org
Human Resources Director: Lori Pye, director of operations
(310) 456-1141 • lori@seashepherd.org

PURPOSE: "Involved with the investigation and documentation of violations of international laws, regulations, and treaties protecting marine wildlife species. Also involved with the enforcement of these laws when there is no enforcement by national governments or international regulatory organizations due to absence of jurisdiction or lack of political will."

CURRENT CONCERNS: Illegal sealing • Illegal worldwide whaling • Marine mammal conservation worldwide

METHOD OF OPERATION: Advertisements • Demonstrations • Direct action • Films/video/audio tapes • Grassroots organizing • International activities • Media outreach • Participation in regulatory proceedings (federal) • Participation in regulatory proceedings (state) • Product merchandising • Speakers program • Telecommunications services (mailing lists) • Undercover documentation

Effectiveness and Political Orientation

"Paul Watson is as close as you can get to a 21st-century pirate of the high seas.

"As the self-proclaimed 'captain' and founder of Sea Shepherd Conservation Society, he has rammed ships, sunk them and been jailed by foreign nations, all in the name of saving the lives of marine animals. Watson is now trying to take over the national Sierra Club to further his cause.

"He makes no apologies. He claims that the 10 ships his group sank between 1979 and 1998 were illegally hunting for whales.

" 'It's no different than policemen apprehending bank robbers,' Watson explains. 'You have to ram the car to stop them.'

"Now the outspoken—blustering, some say—Watson is coming to San Diego to raise money for his next mission: saving seals off Newfoundland.

"Depending on whom you talk to, he is either an environmental hero or an eco-terrorist; few see him as anything in between. . . .

"Watson co-founded Greenpeace, but he and the group parted ways over his aggressive tactics.

"He went on to found Sea Shepherd in 1977.

" 'The best way to understand Sea Shepherd is to view it as a more radical Greenpeace,' said Rik Scarce, author of the book 'Eco-Warriors: Understanding the Radical Environmental Movement.' "

(*The San Diego Union-Tribune,* January 10, 2004)

"A Canadian photographer describes the slaughter of dolphins for food in Japan as 'shocking' and 'surreal.'

"Brooke McDonald was volunteering with the Sea Shepherd Conservation Society when she took the photos in Taiji, Japan, three weeks ago.

"The controversial anti-whaling group released the images of bloodstained inlets and speared dolphins in a bid to embarrass the Japanese government into stopping the hunt.

"The hunt, locals say, has been part of Taiji's culture for at least 400 years.

"Using nets and sonar to confuse the animals, fishermen corral pods of striped dolphins into sheltered bays. They are then speared before being hauled aboard small boats.

"McDonald, 29, and her British colleague, cameraman Morgan Whorwood, spent five nights hiding in the woods above one of the Taiji bays, waiting for their chance to photograph the hunt in which 60 dolphins were killed on Oct. 6.

" 'It was the most shocking thing I've ever seen in my life,' McDonald, a native of Vancouver, said yesterday in a telephone interview from Britain. . . ."

(*The Toronto Star* [Canada], October 30, 2003)

"At first, the comparison seems right:

"Documentary filmmaker Rob Stewart is a modern-day Ulysses fighting perils valiantly on the sea to return home, undoubtedly enriched by his experiences. But in speaking with Stewart, one realizes that his home is not the transitory residences that he establishes in Montreal and Toronto. His true home is the sea. It is the perils above water that he must combat to return to the deep blue sanctuaries of the world, where his chosen companions—sharks—always await him.

"The shark, the perfect predator swimming ceaselessly in the depths of our oceans' great unknown, has become the synthesis of our fears. But for Stewart, the shark defines truth and beauty. It is an unusual affinity, although perhaps a necessary one. For without human intervention, Stewart claims, sharks may be on a fast track to extinction. . . .

"Last spring, Stewart began shooting the first two documentaries in the Sharkwater series with the assistance of the Sea Shepherd Conservation Society, an international nonprofit organization committed to ending illegal-fishing activities. Stewart departed from Los Angeles with a small crew and Panasonic's AJ-HDC27 camera aboard Sea Shepherd's boat, *Ocean Warrior.*

"Their quest was straightforward: By invitation, Sea Shepherd would travel to Costa Rica, sign an agreement with the Costa Rican president allowing them to enforce fishing laws at Cocos Island, and then move on to Galapagos where they would similarly help Galapagos National Park fight poachers. Stewart would get ample footage on land and on the boat documenting Sea Shepherd activities, while also spending much of his time shooting footage of sharks underwater."

(*Video Systems,* December 2002)

"The scene is part Steven Spielberg, part Sam Peckinpah. It features Chinese newlyweds strolling dreamily into a wedding banquet, unaware of the carnage around them: The hem of the bride's gown is soaked with blood, and mutilated sharks lie everywhere. The gory image is one of a series of wedding scenes appearing on hundreds of thousands of free postcards printed and distributed in Asia by the Singapore chapter of the Sea Shepherd Conservation Society, based in Malibu, Calif. The group is working to halt the rapid decline in numbers of sharks worldwide by discouraging Asians from eating shark fin soup. Real sharks were used to produce the photographs. 'We have to hit people as hard as we can,' says Grant Pereira, a Singaporean of Portuguese descent who heads the chapter there. 'If they eat it as a status symbol, we have to attack that.'

"Shark fin soup is a Chinese delicacy and is de rigueur at Chinese banquets. Top-quality soup with an entire fin intact can cost $100 per person. Sea Shepherd estimates that up to 40 sharks are killed to produce soup for a 500-guest wedding. The group's biggest concern is 'finning,' where fisherman merely hack off the fin and throw the rest of the shark overboard to bleed to death."

(*Business Week,* July 29, 2002)

"The most vocal group of animal rights opponents, the Sea Shepherd Conservation Society, has sent its boats to Neah Bay to record the death struggles and cries of any whale that is hunted in order to prove that, contrary to the Makah belief, whales do not give themselves willingly to death. . . ."

(*Hypatia-A Journal of Feminist Philosophy,* Winter 2001)

Servicemembers Legal Defense Network

Established in 1993

DIRECTOR

C. Dixon Osburn, executive director. Osburn is a lawyer who received his J.D./M.B.A. degree from Georgetown University and his A.B. from Stanford University. He has been honored by gay lawyers' groups in Washington, DC, and Boston for his leadership. He has appeared on "Nightline" and written extensively on "Don't Ask, Don't Tell, Don't Pursue."

BOARD OF DIRECTORS

Thomas T. Carpenter, captain, USMC (1970–1980); co-chair; Los Angeles, CA
Jody Hoenninger, lieutenant., USAF (1978–1980); co-chair; San Francisco, CA
Jean Albright, master sergeant, USAF (retired); member; Chicago, IL
CDR Thomas C. Clark, USNR (retired); member; New York, NY
Prof. Kathleen Clark; St. Louis, MO
Col. Amy S. Courter; captain, South Lyon, MI
Anna M. Curren; San Diego, CA
The Honorable Romulo L. Diaz Jr.; Philadelphia, PA
Joe Tom Easley; Miami, FL & New York, NY
G. Christopher Hammet, M.D.; San Antonio, TX
Arthur J. Kelleher, M.D.; San Diego, CA
Linda Netsch, major, USAF (1984–1998); member, Mount Pleasant, SC
Antonious L. K. Porch; Brooklyn, NY

SCOPE

Members: None
Branches: None
Affiliates: None

STAFF

14 total

TAX STATUS

501(c)(3)

FINANCES

Budget: 2002—$2.3 million; 2001—$1.3 million; 2000—$1.3 million

FUNDING SOURCES

Individuals and foundation grants, 51%; special charitable bequests, 33%; special events/projects, 10%; other sources, 6%

PAC

None

EMPLOYMENT

Employment opportunities are located at http://www.sldn.org/templates/opportunities/index.html?section=46. Information

CONTACT INFORMATION

P.O. Box 65301, Washington, DC 20035-5301
Phone: (202) 328-3244 • *Fax:* (202) 797-1635
General E-mail: sldn@sldn.org • *Web site:* www.sldn.org

Communications Director: Steve Ralls
Human Resources Director: Vibha Bhatia, staff associate for operations

PURPOSE: "Servicemembers Legal Defense Network (SLDN) is a national, nonprofit legal services, watchdog and policy organization dedicated to ending discrimination against and harassment of military personnel affected by 'Don't Ask, Don't Tell' and related forms of intolerance."

CURRENT CONCERNS: Don't Ask, Don't Tell, Don't Pursue • Ensure proper implementation of DOD recommendations against antigay harassment and intrusive investigations • Stop the selective use of criminal charges to threaten, coerce, and imprison gay service members • Stop witch hunts of service members accused as gay, lesbian, or bisexual • Uphold privacy of conversations between service members and their doctors

METHOD OF OPERATION: Advertisements • Conferences/seminars • Congressional testimony • Grassroots organizing • Information clearinghouse • Internet (e-mail alerts and Web site) • Internships • Legal assistance • Litigation • Media outreach • Performance ratings/Report cards • Research • Speakers program • Training

Effectiveness and Political Orientation

"In the decade since President Bill Clinton and Congress adopted a policy allowing gays to serve in the armed forces as long as they kept their sexual orientation to themselves, about 10,000 service members have been discharged on the ground of failing to do so, said a report released Wednesday by a gay rights group.

"The study, by the Servicemembers Legal Defense Network, says such discharges have continued at a rate of one or two a day.

"The group's report was its 10th annual survey examining the effects of the 'don't ask, don't tell' policy, an approach that fell far short of Clinton's initial pledge to allow gays to serve openly.

"Under the policy, a compromise that resulted from the furious resistance of the Joint Chiefs of Staff to Clinton's effort to carry out his promise, the total of such discharges last year was 787, the lowest number since 1995. There were 906 such discharges in 2002 and 1,273 in 2001.

" 'Gay discharge numbers have dropped every time America has entered a war,' the report said, 'from Korea to Vietnam to the Persian Gulf to present conflicts.'

"The number of gays dismissed from the military under the Pentagon's 'don't-ask, don't tell' policy has dropped to its lowest level in nine years as U.S.

regarding where to send resume and supporting materials is listed within each job description.

INTERNSHIPS

Information on internships can is listed at http://www.sldn.org/templates/opportunities/index.html?section=46. Interested applicants can fax or send e-mail. Fax: (202) 797-1635. E-mail: hr@sldn.org.

NEWSLETTERS

Annual and quarterly reports

PUBLICATIONS

Conduct Unbecoming (annual report)
Legal Update
Survival Guide: How To Survive Under "Don't Ask, Don't Tell, Don't Pursue"

CONFERENCES

Cooperating Attorney Training Program
(various locations, ongoing)
Service Member Training Seminars (various locations, ongoing)

forces fought in Afghanistan and Iraq, according to a report by an advocacy group."

(*The International Herald Tribune* [Paris, France], March 25, 2004)

"The military discharged 787 gays and lesbians last year, according to the Servicemembers Legal Defense Network, which attributed the decline to the importance of U.S. operations in Afghanistan and Iraq.

"The figure marks a 17 percent decrease from 2002 and a 39 percent drop from 2001, just before the conflicts began in Afghanistan and Iraq.

" 'You have to ask yourself, and you have to ask the Pentagon, why are the discharges going down?' said C. Dixon Osburn, executive director of the advocacy group and one of the report's authors. 'When they need people, they keep them. When they don't, they implement their policy of discrimination with greater force.' "

(*The Washington Post,* March 23, 2004)

"Three retired military officers, two generals and an admiral who have been among the most senior uniformed officers to criticize the 'don't ask, don't tell' policy for homosexuals in the military, disclosed on Tuesday that they are gay. . . .

"They are the highest-ranking military officers to acknowledge that they are gay. Col. Margarethe Cammermeyer was discharged from the Washington State National Guard in 1992 for being a lesbian. She was later reinstated.

"Ten years after the Clinton administration instituted the policy of 'don't ask, don't tell,' it remains contentious and has fallen far short of President Bill Clinton's vow to allow gays to serve openly. The officers hope to spur a dialogue, in Washington and in the military, about changing the policy.

"Nearly 10,000 service members have been discharged for being gay under the policy, which was signed into law by Mr. Clinton on Nov. 30, 1993, according to the Servicemembers Legal Defense Network, a gay rights group that monitors military justice. The group made the officers available to *The New York Times* as part of a campaign to mark the anniversary of the policy's official inception."

(*The New York Times,* December 10, 2003)

Sierra Club

Established in 1892

DIRECTOR

Carl Pope, executive director. Before becoming executive director in 1992, Pope held other positions in the Sierra Club, including political director and conservation director. His background also includes service in the Peace Corps. Pope has served on the boards of many organizations, including the California League of Conservation Voters, Public Voice, National Clean Air Coalition, and Zero Population Growth. He is a graduate of Harvard College.

BOARD OF DIRECTORS

Larry Fahn, president
Bernie Zaleha, vice president
Ed Dobson, secretary
Jan O'Connell, treasurer
Jim Catlin, member
Nick Aumen, member
Robbie Cox, member
Jennifer Ferenstein, member
Lisa Force, member
Marcia Hanscom, member
Doug La Follette, member
Chuck McGrady, member
Paul Watson
David Wells
Ben Zuckerman

SCOPE

Members: 700,000 individuals
Branches/chapters: 65 chapters, including 396 groups; 28 field offices
Affiliates: Sierra Club Foundation, a 501(c)(3) organization

STAFF

150 total

TAX STATUS

501(c)(4)

FINANCES

Budget: 2003—$95 million

FUNDING SOURCES

Membership; contributions and grants; book sales; advertising; outings; reimbursement; royalties

PAC

Sierra Club Political Committee

CONTACT INFORMATION

408 C Street NE, Washington, DC 20002
Phone: (202) 547-1141 • *Fax:* (202) 547-6009
General E-mail: information@sierraclub.org • *Web site:* www.sierraclub.org

Communications Director: Kerri Glover, national media director
media.team@sierraclub.org
Human Resources Director: Information unavailable

PURPOSE: "To explore, enjoy, and protect the wild places of the earth; to practice and promote the responsible use of the earth's ecosystems and resources; to educate and enlist humanity to protect and restore the quality of the natural and human environment; and to use all lawful means to carry out these objectives."

CURRENT CONCERNS: Ancient forests • Clean air • End commercial logging on federal lands • International campaigns (green trade, global warming, population and human rights, and the environment) • Protect water quality • Responsible trade • Stop sprawl

METHOD OF OPERATION: Advertisements • Boycotts • Campaign contributions • Coalition forming • Congressional testimony • Congressional voting analysis • Demonstrations • Electoral politics • Films/video/audio tapes • Grassroots organizing • Initiative/referendum campaigns • International activities • Internet (Web site) • Legal assistance • Legislative/regulatory monitoring (federal and state) • Information clearinghouse • Litigation • Lobbying (federal, state, and grassroots) • Local/municipal affairs • Media outreach • Other (Outings Program; national program of more than 350 outings annually; chapters and groups offer more than 8,000 outings annually, including Inner City Outings) • Participation in regulatory proceedings (federal and state) • Polling • Product merchandising • Research • Telecommunications services (hotline: (202) 675-2394)

Effectiveness and Political Orientation

"The Southern Poverty Law Center is known for fighting hate groups but is not usually a player in environmental politics. Neither is the neo-Nazi group White Politics Inc. But in the Sierra Club's current board elections, they are just two of a potpourri of groups seeking to influence the outcome of a contest that could radically reshape the 112-year-old organization.

"On one level, the battle for control of the Sierra Club board is a dispute over the impact on ecological concerns of population pressures fueled by immigration. More broadly, however, it is a tale of how the organization, buoyed by a rich treasury and a savvy grass-roots outreach effort, has become enmeshed in a bitter fight over how to best leverage the nonprofit's influence in national politics.

PAC CONTRIBUTIONS 2002

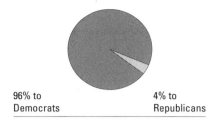

96% to
Democrats

4% to
Republicans

EMPLOYMENT
Current Sierra Club job opportunities are listed at http://www.sierraclub.org/jobs/. Chapter offices handle their own recruitment efforts and should be contacted directly for current job opportunities. Unless otherwise indicated in the job description, apply to San Francisco office. E-mail resumes are preferred. Applicants should specify which job they are applying for in the subject line. Cover letters and resumes should be sent as attachments (MS Word/Adobe Acrobat) unless otherwise requested. Cover letters requested. Due to the large volume of resumes that the HR Department receives, the Sierra Club is no longer able to acknowledge receipt of the resumes. Sierra Club Human Resources Department, 85 Second Street, 2nd Floor, San Francisco, CA 94105. Fax: (415) 977-5796. E-mail: resumes@sierraclub.org.

INTERNSHIPS
Information unavailable

NEWSLETTERS
The Planet (bimonthly magazine)
Sierra (bimonthly magazine)
Sierra Club Bulletin
All chapters and many groups regularly publish newsletters reporting local environmental news and Club events

PUBLICATIONS
The following is a sample list of publications:
Alaska: Images of the Country
An Appalachian Tragedy
The Art of Adventure
Aurora: The Mysterious Northern Lights
The Case Against the Global Economy
Clearcut: The Tragedy of Industrial Forestry
Ecological Medicine: Healing the Earth, Healing Ourselves
Ecopsychology
Endangered Mexico
Fifty Classic Climbs of North America
Global Warming
Lessons of the Rainforest
Living with Wildlife
Mother Nature: Animal Parents and Their Young
The Plundered Seas
The Sierra Club Guide to Planting in Nature
The Sierra Club Naturalist's Guide to the Deserts of the Southeast
Understanding Forests
Woman and Nature
Your Land and Mine

"The stakes are high: Bolstered by anonymous gifts totaling more than $100 million, the group founded by John Muir, himself an immigrant from Scotland, now boasts an annual budget of $83 million and a membership of 750,000.

"'The Sierra Club is the most prominent and influential group in America in terms of environmentalism,' said Mark Potok, editor of the Southern Poverty Law Center's Intelligence Report, who said the center got involved because it discovered hate groups were urging followers to vote in the board election. 'That's why it's seen as a prize. The aim is to hijack the credibility, the reputation, the membership and the finances of a very important political player.'"

(The Washington Post, March 22, 2004)

"A national environmental group has filed a protest petition with the U.S. Environmental Protection Agency over a Sauget waste incinerator, claiming that the plant constitutes a health hazard to minority residents in East St. Louis.

"The group, the Sierra Club, has been monitoring the state's effort to grant a new air permit to Onyx Environmental Services and has mobilized opposition and local activists who are against the plant. It claims the state's actions have been deficient so far.

"New federal rules imposed in the mid-1990s required states to review and issue more comprehensive permits to all major pollution sources by 1998. Illinois and other states did not meet that deadline for all their industries, such as Onyx.

"The new permits establish better record-keeping and monitoring programs for each source of pollution.

"Sierra Club's petition asks the U.S. Environmental Protection Agency to review alleged inadequacies in the proposed permit, and perhaps take over the permitting process from the state."

(St. Louis Post-Dispatch, March 8, 2004)

"An unusual alliance of anti-immigration advocates and animal-rights activists is attempting to take over the leadership of the Sierra Club, America's oldest national environmental group, in what is emerging as a bitter fight over the future of the 112-year-old organization founded by Scottish immigrant John Muir.

"Leaders of a faction that failed to persuade the club to take a stand against immigration in 1998 are seeking to win majority control of the group's 15-member governing board in a spring election—this time, as part of a broader coalition that includes vegetarians, who want the club to denounce hunting, fishing and raising animals for human consumption.

"In response, 11 former Sierra Club presidents have written a letter expressing 'extreme concern for the continuing viability of the club,' protesting what they see as a concerted effort by outside organizations to hijack the mainstream conservationist group and its $95-million annual budget.

"Some of the insurgent candidates vying for the five available seats on the governing board only recently joined the Sierra Club. If they win, they will control eight of the 15 seats. Members will vote in the board elections in March, with the results tallied in April. People who join the club by the end of January should be able to vote.

Also publishes Adventure Travel Guides, Guides to the National Parks, Guides to the Natural Areas of the United States, and totebooks.

CONFERENCES
National Campaigns & Training/Planning
  Retreat

"The election has attracted the interest of anti-immigration groups, which are encouraging their members to join the club to help elect the insurgent candidates.

" 'What has outraged Sierra Club leaders is that external organizations would attempt to interfere and manipulate our election to advance their own agendas,' said Robert Cox, a past Sierra Club president."

(*The Los Angeles Times,* January 18, 2004)

"Under fire from Wisconsin Republicans, Sen. Russ Feingold has called on the Wisconsin Sierra Club to cease running a television ad that criticizes state Sen. Bob Welch, one of the men trying to unseat him.

"The Wisconsin Sierra Club ad began running this week on cable stations in Milwaukee, Madison, Racine and Kenosha and says: 'Extremists in the Legislature like Senator Bob Welch want to open up our rivers and lakes to destruction.'

"The ad refers to a Senate bill Welch has sponsored that the Wisconsin Wildlife Federation says would lower standards designed to protect fish and wildlife habitat. The ad also suggests that the bill was written by developer lobbyists and claims that big polluters and developers gave Welch's campaign almost $300,000. . . .

"Brett Hulsey, senior Midwest representative for the Sierra Club, defended the ads, saying that they dealt not with the Senate race, but rather the legislation Republicans are negotiating with Gov. Jim Doyle. Hulsey said analysis of the bill's impact on the environment was done by the Wisconsin Wildlife Federation, which he stressed is not considered 'liberal.' "

(*Milwaukee Journal Sentinel* [Wisconsin], December 4, 2003)

Southern Poverty Law Center

Established in 1971

DIRECTOR

Richard Cohen, president and chief executive officer. Cohen, formerly the center's general counsel and vice president for programs, became president and chief executive officer, in November 2003. Cohen came to the Center in 1986 as its legal director. In 1999, he was a finalist for the national Trial Lawyer of the Year Award for his work on *Macedonia Baptist Church v. Christian Knights of the Ku Klux Klan.* In recent years, Cohen has served as the center's vice president for programs, providing oversight of the center's programmatic activities, including its tolerance education projects. He is a graduate of Columbia University and the University of Virginia School of Law.

BOARD OF DIRECTORS

James McElroy
Patricia Clark; Fellowship of Reconciliation
Lloyd "Vic" Hackley
Howard Mandell
Julian Bond; NAACP
Joe Levin, SPLC president emeritus

SCOPE

Members: 500,000 (mostly individuals)
Branches/chapters: None
Affiliates: None

STAFF

114 total—47 full-time professional; 60 full-time support; 7 part-time support; plus 3 interns

TAX STATUS

501(c)(3)

FINANCES

Budget: 2004—$25.3 million; 2003—$21.9 million; 2002—$21.5 million

FUNDING SOURCES

Individual contributions, 92%; foundation grants, 5%; investment income, 2%; list rental 1%

PAC

None

EMPLOYMENT

Employment opportunities are advertised on the Center's Web site, www.splcenter.org and on job search Web sites such as www.idealist.org. The center hires attorneys, writers, graphic designers, accountants, protective service officers, and research fellows. Applicants may send cover letters and resumes to Human Resources Specialist, 400 Washington Avenue, Montgomery, AL 36104. Phone: (334)

CONTACT INFORMATION

400 Washington Avenue, Montgomery, AL 36104
Phone: (334) 956-8200 • *Fax:* (334) 956-8481
General E-mail: info@splcenter.org • *Web site:* www.splcenter.org

Communications Director: Penny Weaver, community affairs director
(334) 956-8314 • penny@splcenter.org
Human Resources Director: Sam Whalum
(334) 956-8351 • swhalum@splcenter.org

PURPOSE: "To combat hate, intolerance and discrimination through education and litigation."

CURRENT CONCERNS: Civil rights litigation • Monitoring hate group activity • Tolerance education

METHOD OF OPERATION: Advertisements • Educational foundation • Civil Rights Memorial • Films/video/audiotapes • Grantmaking • Information clearinghouse • Initiative/referendum campaign • Internet (e-mail alerts and Web site) • Internships • Legal assistance • Litigation • Media outreach • Research • Speakers program

Effectiveness and Political Orientation

"(T)he Southern Poverty Law Centre (is) a well-respected U.S. civil rights organization that tracks hate groups and fights them in the courts."
(*Ottawa Citizen* [Canada], January 7, 2004)

"Alabama Chief Justice Roy Moore, who became a hero to religious conservatives for refusing to remove his Ten Commandments monument from the state courthouse, was thrown off the bench yesterday by a judicial ethics panel for having 'placed himself above the law.'

"Richard Cohen, president of the Southern Poverty Law Centre, one of three groups that sued Moore over the monument, said the court and the Alabama attorney-general, who prosecuted the case, were courageous. . . .

" 'They stood up to a popular political figure and said no one is above the law. We intend now to file a complaint with the Alabama State Bar Association asking that Moore be disbarred,' he said."
(*The Toronto Star* [Canada], November 14, 2003)

"(T)he Southern Poverty Law Center, which keeps tabs on right-wing groups, identified 706 active hate groups in the United States in 2002, listing 48 in Texas. The center said the American Knights of the Ku Klux Klan and Blood and Honour, a neo-Nazi group, have chapters in San Antonio.

"Daniel Levitas, author of 'The Terrorist Next Door: The Militia Movement and the Radical Right' cautioned that not all of the 706 are domes-

956-8396. Fax: (334) 956-8481. E-mail:
humanresources@splcenter.org.

INTERNSHIPS

Full-time, paid summer internships are available. The application deadline is November 30. Internships are in the legal department. Applicants are exceptional second-year law students who possess strong academic backgrounds, excellent research and writing skills, and a commitment to public interest law. Internship inquiries may be sent to Legal Department Employment Coordinator, P.O. Box 2087, Montgomery, AL 36102-2087. Phone: (334) 956-8200. Fax: (334) 956-8481. E-mail: legal@splcenter.org.

NEWSLETTERS

Intelligence Report (quarterly)
SPLC Report (quarterly)
Teaching Tolerance (semiannual)

PUBLICATIONS

Free at Last
Mighty Times: The Legacy of Rosa Parks (film)
101 Tools for Tolerance
A Place at the Table
Responding to Hate at School
Starting Small
Ten Ways to Fight Hate
10 Ways to Fight Hate on Campus
A Time for Justice (film)
The Ku Klux Klan: A History of Racism and Violence
The Shadow of Hate (film)
Us and Them

CONFERENCES

The Center does not usually host conferences or seminars.

---

tic terrorist groups, but he said many are 'devoted to criminal violence' and some are 'truly committed to a terroristic agenda.'

"As for the patriot or militia movement, the Southern Poverty Law Center identified 143 such domestic groups in 2002, 21 in Texas, which usually ranks high for militia activity, along with California and Florida, said Mark Potok of the center.

" 'The militia movement began in 1994, peaked in 1996 with 856 groups and has diminished every year since then,' Potok said. 'It is a pale shadow of its former self.'

"But he warned the decline in the number of such groups shouldn't mean authorities have to drop their guard."

(*San Antonio Express-News* [Texas], January 11, 2004)

"Armed federal agents slipped silently into place around Byron Calvert Cecchini's Leesburg home. They pounded on the door, rousing the self-described white supremacist from bed. For several hours, the agents scoured the house, loading his computer, Rolodex and files into a Ryder truck.

"The FBI began investigating Cecchini because of his ties to one of the largest neo-Nazi groups in the United States. In an affidavit seeking a warrant for the pre-dawn raid this year, an agent wrote that Cecchini had a 'violent criminal history' and probably owned weapons. . . .

" 'The radical right from coast to coast is in near-hysteria over the arrests,' said Mark Potok, who tracks extremist groups for the Southern Poverty Law Center."

(*The Washington Post,* May 19, 2003)

" 'There is some convergence of interests ideologically,' between radical Middle Eastern Muslims and radical black American Muslims, said Mark Potok of the Southern Poverty Law Center, best known for its legal battles against the Ku Klux Klan.

" 'If any kind of operational alliance happens between radical Islamists and Americans, the Black Muslims will be involved.' "

(*The Houston Chronicle,* October 16, 2002)

"In recent decades the KKK has been a mere shadow of its dreadful former self—more derided than feared. But since September 11 civil liberties organisations have noticed an increase in support for the KKK and other neo-Nazi groups.

"The intelligence project at the Southern Poverty Law Centre, a civil rights organisation that tracks right-wing hate groups, counted a 12 percent increase in their number in the US last year from 602 in 2000 to 676. The centre estimates that there were about 50,000 race-hate incidents in the same time. The FBI has recorded about 30,000."

(*The Times* [London, England], May 25, 2002)

Traditional Values Coalition

Established in 1981

DIRECTOR
Andrea Sheldon Lafferty, executive director. Laffety, a former Reagan Administration official, directs the day-to-day lobbying in Washington. She works regularly with members of the House and Senate and their staffs on behalf of the member churches of the Traditional Values Coalition (TVC).

BOARD OF DIRECTORS
Andrea Sheldon Lafferty, executive director

SCOPE
Members: 43,000 churches
Branches/chapters: None
Affiliate: Traditional Values Coalition
    Education and Legal Institute

STAFF
Declined to comment

TAX STATUS
501(c)(4)

FINANCES
Declined to comment

FUNDING SOURCES
Membership dues; donations; publications

PAC
Traditional Values Coalition PAC

PAC CONTRIBUTIONS 2002

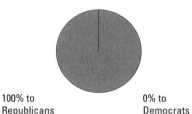

100% to
Republicans

0% to
Democrats

EMPLOYMENT
Individuals seeking employment opportunities with this organization should contact the organization by phone for details.

INTERNSHIPS
TVC offers paid internships throughout the year. Appointments normally last 2 to 3 months (or longer, depending on intern). Interns are required to work 40 hours per week during summer internships. Applicants should send a resume and cover letter stating why they are interested in interning at TVC; a writing sample regarding a current event (no more than 3 pages); a letter of recommendation from a professor; and a letter of recommenda-

CONTACT INFORMATION
139 C Street, SE, Washington, DC 20003
Phone: (202) 547-8570 • *Fax:* (202) 546-6403

California Office
100 South Anaheim Blvd., Suite 350, Anaheim, CA 92805
Phone: (714) 520-0300 • *Fax:* (714) 520-9602
General E-mail: tvcwashdc@traditionalvalues.org •
Web site: www.traditionalvalues.org

Communications Director: Amy Skeen
(202) 547-8570
Human Resources Director: None

PURPOSE: "To fight the increasing attacks on our Judeo-Christian heritage."

CURRENT CONCERNS: Abortion • Education • Family tax relief • Homosexual advocacy • Marriage • Parental empowerment • Pornography • Religious freedom

METHOD OF OPERATION: Coalition forming • Conferences/seminars • Congressional testimony • Congressional voting analysis • Films/video/audiotapes • Grassroots organizing • Internet (e-mail alerts and Web site) • Internships • Lobbying (federal, state, and grassroots) • Media outreach

Effectiveness and Political Orientation

"After complaints from Republican congressional staff members and conservative groups such as the Traditional Values Coalition, Bush administration officials have decided to withhold money for an international health conference that opponents say promotes abortion.

"The Department of Health and Human Services, which has given hundreds of thousands of dollars to the Global Health Council over the past few years, backed off plans to contribute $170,000 for the June conference because it appeared the money could be used for lobbying, HHS spokesman Bill Pierce said.

"Conservative activists, however, took credit last night for persuading the administration to abandon a conference the federal government has supported for 30 years.

" 'Obviously this conference does not reflect the administration policies,' said Andrea Lafferty, executive director of the Traditional Values Coalition. Initial reports that the liberal MoveOn.org would participate demonstrated a 'clearly political agenda' that was not 'in sync' with the Republican administration, she added. . . ."

(*The Washington Post,* April 27, 2004)

tion from the applicant's pastor. TVC will work with students and universities to meet credit requirements. Onsite housing is generally available as part of the internship. Applications for internships at TVC headquarters in Anaheim, CA, should be sent by mail or facsimile to Beverly Sheldon, 100 S. Anaheim Blvd., Suite 350, Anaheim, CA 92805. Fax: (714) 520-9602. Applications for internships at TVC's Washington, DC, office should be sent by mail or facsimile to April Waugh, chief of staff, 139 C Street, SE, Washington, DC 20003. Fax: (202) 547-8570.

NEWSLETTERS
Traditional Values Report (bimonthly)
TVC Talking Points (addresses specific issues)

PUBLICATIONS
Various reports and bulletins are available for download from the TVC Web site

CONFERENCES
National conference held annually (Washington, DC)
Several regional conferences throughout the year

"A corporate governance watchdog group will make its case today that twice a year Union Pacific Corp. should report its political contributions to shareholders.

"A company spokeswoman said the Center for Political Accountability mischaracterized U.P.'s 2002 political contributions in an effort to sway shareholders before the company's annual meeting in Salt Lake City.

"The Washington, D.C.–based center distributed information this week reporting that U.P. made $1,032,022 in corporate contributions in the 2002 election cycle and that the company 'gave to conduits that, in turn, contributed to controversial groups' such as Texans for a Republican Majority and the Traditional Values Coalition. The latter opposes gay rights, abortion rights and the teaching of evolution in public schools. . . ."
(*Omaha World Herald* [Nebraska], April 16, 2004)

"Responding to criticism from conservatives, the director of the National Institutes of Health has told lawmakers the government should continue to pay for studies of sexual behavior because they could have a powerful impact on public health.

"Last fall, the Traditional Values Coalition accused the institutes of paying for 'smarmy projects' and studies of 'bizarre sexual practices with little or no bearing on public health.' The group asked Representative Billy Tauzin, a Louisiana Republican who is chairman of the House Energy and Commerce Committee, to investigate.

"Among the projects were a study of truckers, prostitutes, drug use and sexually transmitted diseases, and studies of sexual behavior in older men, sexual risk-taking and sexual dysfunction. . . ."
(*The New York Times,* January 30, 2004)

"A coalition of religious leaders recently announced the formation of a new political advocacy organization designed to mobilize voters in opposition to Bush administration policies.

"The group, Clergy Leadership Network, will operate from an expressly religious, expressly partisan view. It promises to 'bring about sweeping changes in our nation's political leadership,' providing a counterpoint to 'failing public policies.'

"My first reaction, upon hearing this announcement, was: Amen. It's high time liberal clergy unite to counter groups like the Christian Coalition, Family Research Council and the Traditional Values Coalition. For decades now, these and similar groups have been busily shaping how Americans think about such issues as school prayer, lesbian and gay civil rights, sex education, and even the war on terrorism. They've injected a right-wing Christian perspective into myriad public debates and have done so in increasingly sophisticated ways, rarely using overtly religious language but nonetheless expressing religious beliefs that are not universally held.

"But my excitement was tempered when I read the fine print and learned that this new clergy advocacy group will steer away from discussing a range of social issues—so-called hot-button topics including abortion and gay marriage. 'Our key issues,' a spokesman said, 'are people without jobs, people who are hungry, people burying children killed in Iraq. These are real issues that override flashy talk about sexual orientation.' "
(*Newsday* [New York], December 10, 2003)

"Fearing that Massachusetts could be the first gay marriage domino to fall, conservative groups around the country are setting their sights on the Bay State for a major political stand against same-sex marriage here.

" 'Massachusetts is our Iwo Jima. For us, it's our last stand. We're going to raise the flag,' said the Rev. Louis Sheldon, chairman of the Traditional Values Coalition, based in Washington, D.C.

"Sheldon said the Supreme Judicial Court's landmark finding that gays and lesbians have the right to wed could cast the institution of marriage into turmoil nationally. His group is asking its members across the country to call and write Massachusetts legislators and urge them to get behind an effort to amend the state's constitution to ban same-sex marriage. . . ."

(*The Boston Herald,* November 21, 2003)

TransAfrica/TransAfrica Forum

DIRECTOR

Bill Fletcher, president. Fletcher was formerly the vice president for international trade union development programs for the George Meany Center/National Labor College of the AFL-CIO. Prior to his service at the Meany Center, Fletcher served as education director and assistant to the president of the AFL-CIO. He has authored numerous articles and co-wrote the pictorial booklet, *The Indispensable Ally: Black Workers and the Formation of the Congress of Industrial Organizations, 1934–1941*. Fletcher is a graduate of Harvard University.

BOARD OF DIRECTORS

Danny Glover, chair; international human rights activist/actor, San Francisco, CA
James L. Davis; Washington, DC
Manthia Diawara; director, Institute of African-American Affairs; university professor, New York University, NY
Patricia A. Ford; executive vice president, Service Employees International Union, Washington, DC
Sylvia Hill; professor of Urban Affairs, University of the DC, Washington, DC
Julianne Malveaux; president and chief executive officer, Last Word Productions, Inc., Washington, DC
Walter Mosley; author, New York, NY
Charles J. Ogletree Jr.; professor of law and associate dean, Harvard Law School, Cambridge, MA

SCOPE

Members: More than 40,000 supporters
Branches/chapters: None
Affiliates: TransAfrica Forum
(research institute)

STAFF

9 total

TAX STATUS

501(c)(4)

FINANCES

Revenue: 2002—$2.8 million
2001—$275,606

FUNDING SOURCES

Membership dues; annual benefit dinner; direct mail campaign

PAC

None

EMPLOYMENT

Declined to comment

CONTACT INFORMATION

1426 21st Street, NW, Second Floor, Washington, DC 20036
Phone: (202) 223-1960 • *Fax:* (202) 223-1966
General E-mail: info@transafricaforum.org •
Web site: www.transafricaforum.org

Communications Director: Mwiza Munthali, director of information
(202) 223-1960, ext. 137 • mmunthali@transafricaforum.org
Human Resources Director: Selena Mendy Singleton, executive vice president

PURPOSE: "TransAfrica Forum is a nonprofit organization dedicated to educating the general public—particularly African Americans—on the economic, political and moral ramifications of U.S. foreign policy as it affects Africa and the Diaspora in the Caribbean and Latin America. TransAfrica Forum serves as a major research, educational, and organizing institution for the African-American community. Acting in concert with likeminded organizations and individuals, we sponsor seminars, conferences, community awareness projects, and training programs that promote U.S. policies that are supportive of human rights, democracy, and sustainable economic development."

CURRENT CONCERNS: Debt relief for Africa • U.S.-Cuba relations embargo • U.S. foreign policy vis-à-vis Africa and the Caribbean

METHOD OF OPERATION: Boycotts • Coalition forming • Conferences/seminars • Congressional testimony • Congressional voting analysis • Demonstrations • Direct action • Grassroots organizing • Internet (Web site) • Library/information clearinghouse • Lobbying (federal and grassroots)

SPECIFIC PROGRAMS/INITIATIVES: One Standard! (campaign for a fair and just U.S. policy toward Haitian refugees) • Globalization Monitor (focused on reparations for Africa) • TransAfrica Youth and Student Network (promoting activism among young people) • Scholars' Council (provides African World perspectives on health, education, labor, women, economics, and sustainable development) • Arthur R. Ashe Jr. Foreign Policy Library Seminars and Public Forums (provide opportunities for greater awareness of the forces shaping the Africa)

Effectiveness and Political Orientation

"The sports media spoke in a unified voice of praise in January when Joe Gibbs was named new coach of the National Football League's Washington Redskins. Gibbs is a Hall of Fame coach who led the Washington franchise to three Super Bowl titles in the '80s and '90s. Many headlines enthused his return would mark a 'New Era For the Redskins.'

"The paradox of that idea is striking: In the 21st Century an NFL team is still known by an ethnic slur crafted during the nation's frontier days. The

Information about the organization's internship opportunities is found on the Web site. Students are selected based on their individual interests and backgrounds in conjunction with organizational needs. Interns must put in a minimum of 16 hours per week at TransAfrica Forum; a minimum of 24 hours per week is required in the summer. Most students arrange to receive academic credit as well as financial assistance at their educational institutions (ranging from high school to graduate school). There are no paid internship positions. Interns should have excellent writing skills, strong organizational skills, competency on IBM/PC, and good knowledge of MS Word. It is preferred that interns have an academic background in international studies, African studies, Caribbean studies, Latin American studies, history, political science, economics/business, or communications.

Interested applicants should submit a letter of intent that indicates what the student would like to gain from an internship; a current resume; a brief writing sample (maximum 5 pages); and the completed application form. Applications and further information can be obtained by contacting Mwiza Munthali, TransAfrica/TransAfrica Forum, 1426 21st Street, NW, Second Floor, Washington, DC 20036. Phone: (202) 223-1960. Fax: (202) 223-1966. E-mail: info@transafricaforum.org.

NEWSLETTERS
None

PUBLICATIONS
African Country Comparison to the United States
The Case for Black Reparations
Child Soldiers in Africa: The Problem and the Solutions
The Consequences of the U.S. Economic Embargo on Afro-Cubans
Female Genital Mutilation in Africa
Forty Years of Hostility: Consequences of the United States Economic Embargo on Cuba
Report of the Fact-Finding Delegation to Haiti
The Sub-Saharan Africa Debt Burden

CONFERENCES
Various panels throughout the year. Conference on June 11 and 12, 2004

term 'Redskins' derives from an old, genocidal practice in this country of scalping Native Americans to earn a bounty. A bounty hunter could prove he had killed a native by turning in a scalp, which often were bloody and called 'redskins.' This bit of etymology was part of a July 2000 editorial in Maine's *Portland Press Herald* explaining why it banned the team name from its sports pages. . . .

"What I find mystifying, however, is the civil rights community's lack of attention to this issue. One would shudder to think what the NAACP would do with a sports team named the Chicago Jigaboos. We saw how angry many black groups became when the rapper Nelly announced he was marketing something called 'Pimp Juice.'

"African Americans know the difficulty of holding America accountable for the errors of its past, so we should be leading the way in correcting the ongoing error of demeaning mascots. That's why I was happy to see Bill Fletcher Jr. of TransAfrica Forum make the call for other black groups to get involved in the fight to change the name of the Washington Redskins. I join Fletcher in his call and expand it to retire all Native American mascots to the dustbin of discarded stereotypes."

(*In These Times*, February 16, 2004)

"Too many African-American leaders seem to have a two-faced approach when it comes to human rights violations, repression and corruption in Africa and the Caribbean.

"Last June, the TransAfrica Forum, a progressive African-American organization, released a letter condemning the ongoing repression orchestrated by President Robert Mugabe in Zimbabwe, arguing that 'Black American(s) cannot afford to romanticize African leaders if they hope to remain relevant to the struggles on the continent. They must be willing to condemn wrongdoing, even if that means criticizing some revered leaders.' That was very well put, but what about Haiti?

"In its May 16, 2003 report, TransAfrica argued for the release of frozen foreign aid to Haiti. But it was silent about the deteriorating state of the government. How can Bill Fletcher Jr., president of TransAfrica, explain his organization's unquestioning support for the regime of Jean-Bertrand Aristide while taking on Mugabe? . . .

"How can the Congressional Black Caucus, TransAfrica and other groups like these ignore the murder of Haiti's most prominent journalist, Jean Dominique, the lack of cooperation by the government in investigating the murder, the ensuing silencing of Radio Haiti Inter, his radio station, and the fact that his widow, like the police chief, has had to flee to the United States after she shut the station down?

"When Jean Bertrand Aristide was ousted in a coup, only a few months after his election in 1991, supporters of democracy in Haiti from around the world rallied to his cause. The Congressional Black Caucus, along with TransAfrica, were in the forefront of the efforts that led to Aristide's return three years later.

"Since then Aristide's performance as a leader has fallen far short of expectations. . . ."

(*Newsday* [New York], November 13, 2003)

"On Saturday morning, Damu Smith and two busloads of mostly African-American peace activists will trek from Washington to New York City to rally near the United Nations for world peace. They will be among thousands expected there on a day that some say will be the world's largest mobilization for peace: Rallies, marches and protests are planned in at least 350 cities around the globe.

"The presence of African-American leaders at the New York rally is significant. United for Peace and Justice, the rally's sponsor, is co-chaired by Bill Fletcher, president of Washington-based TransAfrica Forum. Like Smith, who founded Black Voices for Peace, Fletcher is committed to making sure African-Americans are heard as part of the peace movement. . . .

"It is easy to support peace when world conflicts are not imminent. How can today's peace activists maintain their views as the terrorism alert rises to orange and the FBI and CIA say that another attack by al-Qaeda is likely to happen soon?

" 'I believe that the Bush administration's policies are exacerbating conditions that give rise to people wanting to attack us,' Smith says. 'If we attack Iraq, we will be more vulnerable to retaliation. Our best path to security [is developing] policies that support human rights and negotiation, not confrontation.'

"People around the globe are mobilizing to make that very point. Our entire world would be a safer place if we would shrug off the rhetoric of confrontation and negotiate instead of attempt to annihilate. Smith, Fletcher and thousands more are planning to gather in New York in the best of African-American traditions: raising our voices for peace."

(*USA Today*, February 14, 2003)

"San Franciscan Danny Glover, the 'actor-activist' unafraid to take outspoken political positions, has found himself a nifty national platform to raise some radical Cain.

"The soft-spoken, 55-year-old Glover is now chairman of TransAfrica Forum, a 25-year-old group that was in the forefront of protesting South Africa's now-departed apartheid regime but ran into serious financial problems in the 1990s.

" 'We were confronted with something new and daunting—it's called change,' said Glover, who was in Washington this week to help TransAfrica open its new rented 5,500-square-foot headquarters. Until last year, the group was housed in much grander quarters, but it sold the building for $5.2 million, money it is using to help reinvigorate itself.

" 'We were very close to shutting the doors,' said Glover's alter ego at TransAfrica, group President Bill Fletcher Jr. 'We were facing very difficult times, and he came through for us.'

"The actor injected more than $1 million into saving the group, became chairman last year and helped recruit a high-powered new board whose members include Harry Belafonte, author Walter Mosley and Julianne Malveaux, another San Francisco native who is an economist and writer.

"Glover also has tried to attract college students to the cause and altered the group's focus to include a whole range of new issues, such as the negative aftermath of colonialism on African nations and the effort in the United States to win support for reparations for slavery.

"TransAfrica's leaders also are outspoken in their opposition to a possible war against Iraq and President Bush's new national security plan. . . ."

(*The San Francisco Chronicle*, November 15, 2002)

Trial Lawyers for Public Justice

Established in 1982

DIRECTOR

Arthur H. Bryant, executive director. Bryant has been executive director since 1987. He has won major victories and established new precedents in several areas of the law, including constitutional law, civil rights, consumer protection, and mass torts. As part of his work, Bryant has been involved in airbag and preemption litigation for more than 16 years. In 2001, he was selected by The National Law Journal as one of the 100 Most Influential Lawyers in America. In January 2003, the Board of Governors of the Consumer Attorneys of Los Angeles named him as the recipient of the George Moscone Memorial Award for Outstanding Public Service. In August 2003, Bryant received the "Pursuit of Justice Award" from the Tort Trial and Insurance Practice Section of the American Bar Association for his work in promoting justice and access to the courtroom. Bryant is a graduate of Swarthmore College and Harvard Law School.

BOARD OF DIRECTORS

Executive Committee

J. Gary Gwilliam, president; Gwilliam, Ivary, Chiosso, Cavalli & Brewer, Oakland, CA

Jeffrey M. Goldberg, president-elect; Jeffrey M. Goldberg Law Offices Chicago, IL

Thomas M. Dempsey, vice president; Law Offices of Thomas M. Dempsey, Los Angeles, CA

Alan R. Brayton, treasurer; Brayton v Purcell, Novato, CA

Sandra H. Robinson, secretary; Jack Olender & Associates, Washington, DC

Harry G. Deitzler, executive committee member; Hill, Peterson, Carper, Bee & Deitzler, Charleston, WV

Gerson H. Smoger, executive committee member; Smoger & Associates, P.C., Dallas, TX

Mona Lisa Wallace, executive committee member; Wallace & Graham, P.A., Salisbury, NC

Paul L. Stritmatter, immediate past president; Stritmatter Kessler Whelan Withey Coluccio, Hoquiam, WA

George W. Shadoan, president, TLPJ, P.C.; Shadoan & Michael, Rockville, MD

Diane L. Abraham, CA
Roberta E. Ashkin, NY
Danielle Banks, PA
Esther E. Berezofsky, NJ
Robert J. Bonsignore, MA
Raymond P. Boucher, CA
Robert E. Cartwright Jr., CA
Michael V. Ciresi, MN
Joan B. Claybrook, DC
Gerri R. Colton, CA
Linda M. Correia, DC
Tracey D. Conwell, TX

CONTACT INFORMATION

1717 Massachusetts Avenue, NW, Suite 800, Washington, DC 20036-2001
Phone: (202) 797-8600 • *Fax:* (202) 232-7203
General E-mail: tlpj@tlpj.org • *Web site:* www.tlpj.org

Communications Director: Jonathan Hutson
(202) 797-8600, ext. 246 • jhutson@tlpj.org
Human Resources Director: Barbara Reeves, administration and finance director
(202) 797-8600, ext. 238

PURPOSE: "Trial Lawyers for Public Justice is a national public interest law firm that marshals the skills and resources of trial lawyers to create a more just society. Through creative litigation, public education, and innovative work with the broader public interest community, we: protect people and the environment; hold accountable those who abuse power; challenge governmental, corporate and individual wrongdoing; increase access to the courts; combat threats to our justice system; and inspire lawyers and others to serve the public interest."

CURRENT CONCERNS: Auto safety and airbag litigation • Civil rights and civil liberties • Class action abuse • Consumer safety • Discrimination • Environmental protection • Equal rights for female intercollegiate athletes • Federal preemption • Lead paint • Mandatory arbitration abuse • Pesticides • Product safety • Protective orders and court secrecy • Toxic torts

METHOD OF OPERATION: Awards program (Trial Lawyer of the Year Award) • Conferences/seminars • Information clearinghouse (Class Action Abuse Prevention Project, Federal Preemption Project, Federal Rules Project, Lead Paint Litigation Clearinghouse, Mandatory Arbitration Abuse Prevention Project, and Project ACCESS) • Internet (Web site) • Internships • Legal assistance • Litigation • Research • Training and technical assistance (Environmental Enforcement Project)

Effectiveness and Political Orientation

"Internal government documents show that officials from a variety of agencies unsuccessfully criticized the Bush administration's effort to let coal miners continue the practice of 'mountaintop removal' mining—the leveling of mountain peaks to extract coal—in Appalachia.

"At issue is a draft environmental impact statement analyzing the effects of the widely practiced technique on streams, wildlife and forests and proposing three approaches for regulation.

"Although the administration said all three approaches would improve environmental protections, the U.S. Fish and Wildlife Service said the administration's alternatives to regulate mountaintop removal mining 'cannot be

Harry G. Deitzler, WV
Mike Eidson, FL
Steven E. Fineman, NY
Grover G. Hankins, TX
Steve Baughman Jensen, TX
Rosalind Fuchsberg Kaufman, NY
Althea T. Kippes, CA
Jack Landskroner, OH
Roger L. Mandel, TX
Stanley J. Marks, AZ
Jerry J. McKernan, LA
S. C. "Buster" Middlebrooks, AL
Richard H. Middleton Jr., GA
Mark R. Mueller, TX
Barry J. Nace, DC
Jack H. Olender, DC
Stuart A. Ollanik, CO
Robert L. Parks, FL
Albert M. Pearson III, GA
Kieron F. Quinn, MD
Brent Rosenthal, TX
Anthony Z. Roisman, VT
John F. Romano, FL
William A. Rossbach, MT
Ronald H. Rouda, CA
Leonard W. Schroeter, WA
Bernard W. Smalley Sr., PA
Stephen Smith, VA
Christine D. Spagnoli, CA
James Sturdevant, CA
Ernie F. Teitell, CT
C. Tab Turner, AR
Sharon L. Van Dyck, MN
James W. Vititoe, CA
Henry H. Wallace, PA
Simon Walton, MD
Mikal C. Watts, TX
Harvey Weitz, NY
Perry Weitz, NY
Martha K. Wivell, MN
Stephen I. Zetterberg, CA

SCOPE
Members: 2,000 attorneys and other
    individuals
Branches/chapters: Office in Oakland, CA
Affiliate: Trial Lawyers for Public Justice is a
    project of the TLPJ Foundation

STAFF
22 total—16 full-time professional; 6 full-time
support; plus 2 part-time professional;
2 interns

TAX STATUS
Professional corporation with bylaws requiring
all revenues be used for public interest litigation.

FINANCES
Budget: 2000—$3 million (includes TLPJ
Foundation)

FUNDING SOURCES
Membership fees; foundations fees; legal fees

PAC
None

interpreted as ensuring any improved environmental protection,' according to a document obtained through a Freedom of Information Act request.

"The agency had advocated that one alternative would minimize the impact on streams, fish and wildlife, according to the document, which was released along with others by Trial Lawyers for Public Justice, a Washington-based public-interest law firm that submitted the FOIA request. . . .

"The administration 'eliminated all environmentally protective alternatives from consideration. That's not scientifically or intellectually honest,' said Jim Hecker, environmental enforcement director at Trial Lawyers for Public Justice. 'People within the agencies are very disappointed. Scientists who worked on [the environmental impact statement] were furious that the other options were not considered.'

"The Fish and Wildlife Service commented that the administration's approaches 'belie four years of work and accumulated evidence of environmental harm, and would substitute permit process tinkering for meaningful and measurable change,' Hecker said."

(*The Los Angeles Times,* January 7, 2004)

"Seattle police who arrested World Trade Organization protesters by the bus-load four years ago had no probable cause to do so, a federal judge has ruled, possibly leaving the city vulnerable to damages from a class-action lawsuit. . . .

"Lawyers for the protesters contended that the city violated their clients' First Amendment and Fourth Amendment rights with the arrests, according to Victoria Ni, an attorney with Trial Lawyers for Public Justice. . . .

"According to Ni, the protesters and onlookers were trapped, herded and arrested by the Seattle Police Department outside of an area that had been established as a no-protest zone during the convention. . . .

"The class-action lawsuit originally was filed in October 2000 on behalf of about 600 people. The claims of most of the original plaintiffs were dismissed in fall 2001 when U.S. District Court Judge Barbara Rothstein ruled the city had the right to create and enforce a no-protest zone during a state of emergency. City officials created the zone after some protesters clogged the streets and damaged some property.

"But that ruling did not affect the claims of the 157 current plaintiffs, who were outside the no-protest zone at the time of their arrest, according to an assistant to Steve Berman, the protesters' lead attorney, who was brought in by Trial Lawyers for Public Justice. . . .

"A trial is scheduled for next month, when protesters will have to prove the arrests were part of an official city policy, Ni said.

" 'We're going to show that the arrests were ratified and approved by the mayor or the chief of police,' she said."

(*The Seattle Times,* December 31, 2003)

"A Maryland state judge has knocked down a class-action settlement involving late fees on telephone bills, saying the attorneys' request for $13 million in legal fees was excessive, considering that affected consumers would each get only a $6 refund.

"In a decision written last week but made public yesterday, Judge Steven I. Platt of the Prince George's County Circuit Court said the attorneys' fees 'are not justified by the small benefit' received by consumers, either individually or collectively. He said the request for $13 million was 'based on phantom numbers and calculations.'

EMPLOYMENT

Potential applicants can learn about job openings with this organization by consulting the web site at www.tlpj.org/jobs.htm.

INTERNSHIPS

Potential applicants can learn about internship opportunities with this organization by consulting the web site at www.tlpj.org/jobs.htm. Internships are unpaid.

NEWSLETTERS

Public Justice (quarterly)

PUBLICATIONS

In the News (annual)
Membership Directory (annual)
Trial Lawyers Doing Public Justice (annual)

CONFERENCES

Public Interest Coalition Conferences

"The settlement in the four-year-old lawsuit against Bell Atlantic-Maryland, which is now Verizon Maryland, was opposed by the Trial Lawyers for Public Justice, a public-interest law firm. Last spring, the organization challenged the size of the attorney fees as well as the fact that they were not disclosed in the bill inserts sent to more than 2 million customers notifying them of the settlement.

"'Virtually all of the money on the table would have gone to the lawyers, and only a very small share would have gone to the class members themselves,' said Michael J. Quirk, a staff attorney for the group. Quirk said that although more than 2 million Maryland customers may have been eligible for the $6 refund (or more if they had documents to prove they were due more), only 18,000 submitted claims, making the settlement worth less than $200,000. That was far less than the $51.9 million that Verizon had put aside, Quirk said."

(*The Washington Post*, November 18, 2003)

"When Robert Gibson of Bath, Ohio, bought a Land Rover Discovery last fall in Akron, he got a four-wheel-drive but lost the grip on his legal rights.

"Gibson says he didn't read the back of the sales contract and wound up forfeiting his right to sue the dealer if something went wrong.

"'It is terrible. They point out all the good points, but not that clause,' Gibson said.

"An increasing number of car dealers nationwide are trying to get their customers to surrender their day in court in favor of arbitration, in which an arbitrator—not a judge or jury—makes the decision, said Paul Bland, a senior staff lawyer with the Trial Lawyers for Public Justice, a consumer advocacy group in Washington. . . ."

(*The New Orleans Times-Picayune*, August 11, 2002)

"Crown Central Petroleum Corp. has agreed to settle for $1.6 million a lawsuit alleging pollution violations at its Pasadena refinery.

"The action, filed in 1997, was the first citizen suit against a corporate polluter in Texas under the federal Clean Air Act. The settlement, filed Friday, requires federal court approval. . . .

"The lawsuit accused the company of more than 15,000 hours of pollution violations at its Pasadena refinery. The Clean Air Act allows citizens to sue polluters when state regulators fail to enforce environmental laws, but no previous citizen suit had ever been successfully prosecuted in Texas under the statute.

"The settlement will force Crown to pay more if monitoring shows it violates pollution laws again. . . .

"The deal was announced by the groups that brought the action, including the Trial Lawyers for Public Justice. It filed suit on behalf of such environmental groups as Texans United, the Sierra Club and the Natural Resource Defense Council, as well as people living near the refinery.

"'This is a major victory for citizen enforcement of the federal Clean Air Act,' Jim Hecker of the trial lawyers group said in a written statement."

(*The Houston Chronicle*, February 10, 2001)

U.S. Chamber of Commerce

Established in 1912

DIRECTOR

Thomas J. Donohue, president and chief executive officer. Donohue was a group vice president of the U.S. Chamber of Commerce for 8 years before becoming president and chief executive officer in 1997. Previously he was president and chief executive office of the American Trucking Association. Donohue earned a bachelor's degree from St. John's University and an M.B.A. from Adelphi University.

BOARD OF DIRECTORS

Thomas J. Donohue, president and chief executive officer

Jeffrey C. Crowe Jr., chair; chair and chief executive officer, Landstar System, Inc., Jacksonville, FL

John W. Bachmann, vice chair; director, AMR Corp., Fort Worth, TX

Larry A. Liebenow, immediate past chair and chair of the executive committee; president, chair and chief executive officer, Quaker Fabric Corp., Fall River, MA

William G. Little, treasurer; director, Crown Holdings, Inc., Philadelphia, PA

Maura W. Donahue, Southeast regional vice chair; vice president, Donahue/Favret Contractors, Inc., Mandeville, LA

Craig L. Fuller, Central East regional vice chair; president and chief executive officer, National Association of Chain Drug Stores, Alexandria, VA

Erle A. Nye, South Central vice regional chair; chair of the board and chief executive officer, TXU Corp., Dallas, TX

John Ruan III, North Central vice regional chair; chair and chief executive officer, Ruan Transportation Management Systems, Des Moines, IA

Paul S. Speranza, Northeast regional vice chair; senior vice president, general counsel, and secretary, Wegmans Food Markets, Rochester, NY

Frank L. VanderSloot, West regional vice chair; president, and chief executive officer, Melaleuca, Inc., Idaho Falls, ID

SCOPE

Members: 3 million businesses; 830 business associations; 96 American chambers of commerce overseas

Branches/chapters: 2,800 state and local chapters

Affiliates: National Chamber Foundation, a 501(c)(3) organization; Center for Workforce Preparation, a 501(c)(3) organization

STAFF

Information unavailable

CONTACT INFORMATION

1615 H Street, NW, Washington, DC 20062-2000L

Phone: (202) 659-6000

Toll-free: (800) 638-6582 • *Fax:* (202) 463-5800

General E-mail: chambers@uschamber.com • *Web site:* www.uschamber.org

Communications Director: Linda Rozett
(202) 463-5682

Human Resources Director: Information unavailable

PURPOSE: "To advance human progress through an economic, political and social system based on individual freedom, incentive, initiative, opportunity, and responsibility."

CURRENT CONCERNS: Biennial budgeting • Biotechnology • Brownfields • Business development • Clean air quality standards • Competition • Fast-track trade negotiating authority • Internet taxation and privacy • Labor law reform • Networking • Open markets • Regulation • Taxes • Telecommunications infrastructure

METHOD OF OPERATION: Advertisements • Awards program • Coalition forming • Conferences/seminars • Congressional testimony • Congressional voting analysis • Direct action • Educational foundation • Electoral politics • Grassroots organizing • Information clearinghouse • International activities • Internet (e-mail alerts and Web site) • Internships • Legal assistance • Legislative/regulatory monitoring (federal and state) • Litigation • Lobbying (federal and grassroots) • Media outreach • Participation in regulatory proceedings (federal) • Professional development services • Telecommunications services • Voting records

Effectiveness and Political Orientation

"The top business lobby in the United States vowed yesterday to fight any attempts to restrict the exporting of jobs overseas, warning that the country will pay a 'tremendous heavy price' if proposals to curb outsourcing are adopted. The U.S. Chamber of Commerce, representing 3 million businesses, said it takes exception to assertions by politicians that American companies are 'selling out' the nation's future by moving jobs abroad. 'The chamber's message is clear: The U.S. must be able to source around the world to stay competitive in the global economy, and the business community will fight any attempts by our government to restrict outsourcing,' Thomas J. Donohue, the chamber's president, said at a news conference.

"Outsourcing, particularly moving high-tech jobs to low-wage Asian and Latin American countries, has become a key subject of debate between President Bush and Democratic challenger Sen. John Kerry. Kerry has promised that if elected president, he would make the most sweeping reform of international tax law in four decades to stem the flow of U.S. jobs overseas. His

TAX STATUS
501(c)(6)

FINANCES
Declined to comment

FUNDING SOURCES

PAC
USChamberPAC (NCAP)

PAC CONTRIBUTIONS 2002

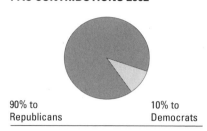

90% to
Republicans

10% to
Democrats

EMPLOYMENT
Postings are listed at https://secure.recruiting-center.net/clients/uschamber/PublicJobs/Can viewjobs.cfm? Submission of applications online is encouraged, but application materials may be mailed to Human Resources Department, U.S. Chamber of Commerce, 1615 H Street, NW, Washington, DC 20062-2000.

INTERNSHIPS
Internships are available for juniors and seniors in college. Candidates must be proficient in Microsoft Windows and Word, be deadline-oriented, and possess excellent oral and written communication skills. Students majoring in political science, government, international business, or communications are especially encouraged to apply. A cover letter, resume, writing sample, and letter of recommendation from an instructor are required. Materials may be sent to the attention of the internship coordinator, Human Resources Department, U.S. Chamber of Commerce, 1615 H Street, NW, Washington, DC 20062-2000.

NEWSLETTERS
Uschamber.com (monthly)
U.S. Chamber Daily (daily e-mail)

PUBLICATIONS
Building an Effective Government Affairs
Program
Chamber of Commerce Bylaws: A Guideline
for Working and Format
Congressional Handbook (annual)
Congressional Issues (annual)
Developing a Chamber of Commerce:
Personnel and Procedures Manual
Developing a Program of Work
Directory of American Chambers of Commerce
Abroad
Directory of State Chambers of Commerce
Employee Benefits (annual)
Get Out the Vote Education Packet
Grassroots Handbook
How They Voted (annual)
National Business Agenda (biannual)

plan would eliminate tax breaks that encourage companies to move jobs overseas and use the savings to encourage companies to create jobs in the United States.

"Donohue expressed concern yesterday that about 80 proposed state and federal bills designed to stop outsourcing are being prepared. He said the nation will 'pay a tremendous economic price' if such legislation is enacted. He said a study on outsourcing conducted by the chamber found that it is not the major threat to American workers that it has been made out to be. 'While there are various estimates on the number of jobs moved overseas, it remains, by all accounts, a small percentage of our economy,' he said."

(*The Baltimore Sun*, April 15, 2004)

"The debate over shareholders' rights to nominate corporate directors heated up Wednesday as the U.S. Chamber of Commerce threatened to sue regulators if the Securities and Exchange Commission adopts a controversial new rule on the issue. "If the commission proceeds with this proposal, we will challenge it in court,' chamber President Thomas Donohue warned in a statement to SEC commissioners during a roundtable discussion in Washington. Shareholders and business officials are debating SEC proposals that would give pension funds and other investors the right to place candidates for board elections directly on proxy materials.

"But to do so, shareholders who nominate candidates must hold at least 1% of a company's stock, or more than 35% of the votes cast by shareholders must be withheld from a director. Some shareholders contend those thresholds are too high. Corporate leaders argued that the SEC proposals, if adopted, would jeopardize state laws that already govern business practices. 'When you give stockholders that right and take it away from directors, you're creating a massive change in the structure of state corporate law,' said attorney Robert Todd Lang for the Business Roundtable trade group.

"In 1990, the Business Roundtable won a federal lawsuit that challenged whether the SEC had more legal authority than states on the issue of shareholder votes. Several legal experts disagreed with the business officials. Law professor John Coffee at Columbia University said the SEC has the legal authority to adopt rules that would allow shareholders to nominate directors. Beyond broad-based SEC rules that would cover all publicly traded companies, legal experts suggested alternatives to give shareholders more power in board elections."

(*USA Today*, March 11, 2004)

"Madison County has once again given Illinois one of the most anti-business legal climates in America, with the state dropping from 38th to 44th in an annual study of litigation fairness, the nation's largest business organization said Monday. 'Illinois' legal system is one of the most unfair (in America)' for corporate lawsuit defendants, said Thomas J. Donohue, president of the U.S. Chamber of Commerce. He said that was the reason the group chose Illinois on Monday to unveil a million-dollar national advertising campaign calling for restrictions on suits. 'One of the chief reasons Illinois is ranked so poorly is because of a single county: Madison County, Illinois,' Donohue said."

(*St. Louis Post-Dispatch*, March 9, 2004)

"An accelerating economic recovery in the United States is expected to finally reduce unemployment there by year end, according to a prominent forecaster with the U.S. Chamber of Commerce. That and other influences should help backstop a return to stronger growth in Canada. Martin Regalia, the U.S. Chamber's vice-president and chief economist, told the Global Business Forum in Banff, Alta., that although the U.S. economy has been growing for seven quarters, 2.3 million jobs have been lost south of the border.

"Nonetheless, he expects positive job figures to appear in the next month and the stubbornly high U.S. unemployment rate to start falling by early next year. 'I think we're going to see an acceleration in this economy in the second half,' Regalia said, adding that 'the third-quarter growth rate looks like it's going to be five percent or more.' The unemployment situation is among several factors that is constraining the outlook for the U.S., particularly in light of the high levels of consumer debt many Americans are carrying.

" 'As the economy picks up and as interest rates inexorably begin to rise, the debt levels will become more restrictive and more restrictive,' Regalia said. 'I think these debt levels are going to restrain consumption once the interest rates pick up.' After a strong spurt of expansion in the second half, Regalia sees overall growth for 2003 in the U.S. of about 3.5 percent, with a slight increase to 3.8 percent in 2004. Those figures were somewhat stronger than a forecast released by the Bank of Nova Scotia yesterday that pegged real growth this year in the U.S. at 2.7 percent and 3.5 percent in 2004."

(*The Gazette* [Montreal, Canada], September 26, 2003)

"With more than 207,900 part-time troops rebuilding war-torn Iraq and involved in the war on terrorism, two national military organizations have urged the U.S. Chamber of Commerce to lead the way toward changing how employers treat workers who are in the Reserves and National Guard. During a meeting in New Orleans last week, the Reserve Officers Association and the National Committee for the Employer Support of the Guard and Reserve called on Thomas Donohue, president and chief executive of the U.S. Chamber, to convene meetings of government officials and business leaders who are affected when reservists and Guard members are called to active duty.

"The need for enhanced military-business relations is clear, military officials said, because Reserve mobilizations have rippling effects through society. When service members are called to active duty, they are pulled away from civilian life; families are left to manage households and navigate military bureaucracy alone; and employers are forced to fill manpower voids. And in most cases, families are left in a financial lurch because civilian employers pay more than the military.

" 'Every time you mobilize one soldier, you're going to upset that person's family, you're going to touch his economics, you're going to touch his employer,' said Army Reserve Col. David Davenport, Reserve Officers Association national president. 'If he's a college student, you're going to touch a university or a school somewhere.' ESGR and Reserve Officers Association representatives said they hope that combining forces will give them a louder voice to push national issues, such as encouraging the U.S. Chamber to help make the lives of reservists and National Guard members easier when called to active duty. That includes having companies make up the difference between military employees' civilian income and that provided by the military."

(*The New Orleans Times-Picayune,* June 29, 2003)

U.S. ENGLISH, Inc.

Established in 1983

DIRECTOR

Mauro E. Mujica, chair of the board and chief executive officer. Mujica has led U.S. English since 1993. Previously he was an architect with his own practice for 28 years. Born in Chile, Mujica emigrated to the United States in 1965 and became a naturalized citizen in 1970. He holds bachelor's and master's degrees from Columbia University.

BOARD OF DIRECTORS

Mauro E. Mujica, chair, Washington, DC
Jacques Barzun; author and professor, Columbia University, New York, NY
Saul Bellow; writer, Boston, MA
Edward A. Capano; publisher, New York, NY
Denton Cooley; surgeon, Houston, TX
Midge Decter; writer, New York, NY
Jorge Delgado; agronomist, San Juan, Puerto Rico
Dinesh Desai
Mrs. Richard DeVos
Andre Emmerich; art dealer and writer, New York, NY
George Gilder; economist, New York, NY
Harry Glassman; M.D.
Nathan Glazer; sociologist, Cambridge, MA
Charles Gogolak
Charlton Heston; actor, Beverly Hills, CA
Lee Majors; actor, Ft. Lauderdale, FL
Sen. Eugene J. McCarthy; Woodville, VA
Laura McKenzie; author, Los Angeles, CA
Harvey Meyerhoff
Jerry M. Mosier; advertising executive, East Hanover, NJ
Barbara Mujica; professor, Georgetown University, Washington, DC
Alex Olmedo
Arnold Palmer; Youngstown, PA
Margie Petersen
Norman Podhoretz; writer and editor, New York, NY
Hubertus-Georg Renner
Donald M. Ross
Randolph Rowland; insurance executive, Burlington, VT
James Schlesinger; economist, Washington, DC
Arnold Schwarzenegger; governor of California, Sacramento, CA
Charles E. Scripps; newspaper publisher, Cincinnati, OH
Norman D. Shumway; former U.S. representative, San Francisco, CA
Togo Tanaka
Alex Trebek; television game show host, Los Angeles, CA
George W. Wilson
Rosalyn Yalow; biophysicist, Bronx, NY

CONTACT INFORMATION

1747 Pennsylvania Avenue, NW, Suite 1050, Washington, DC 20006
Phone: (202) 833-0100 • *Fax:* (202) 833-0108
Toll-free: (800) 873-4547
General E-mail: info@usenglish.org • *Web site:* www.usenglish.org

Communications Director: Rob Toonkel
(202) 833-9771 • rtoonkel@usenglish.org
Human Resources Director: Information unavailable

PURPOSE: "U.S. English is the nation's largest citizen's action group dedicated to preserving the unifying role of a common language in the United States. Through the passage of official English legislation at the state and federal levels, U.S. English is committed to ensuring unity within our nation and giving newcomers a chance at the American Dream."

CURRENT CONCERNS: Bilingual education • Multilingualism in government

METHOD OF OPERATION: Advertisements • Coalition forming • Congressional testimony • Educational foundation • Grantmaking • Grassroots organizing • Initiative/referendum campaigns • Internet (e-mail alerts and Web site) • Internships • Legislative/regulatory monitoring (federal and state) • Lobbying (federal, state, and grassroots) • Media outreach • Polling • Research

Effectiveness and Political Orientation

"The era of forced multilingual ballots 'hit a new low' when the town of Briny Breezes, Fla., was forced to print election notices in Spanish despite the fact everybody understands English. Furthermore, federal law required leaders of the tiny oceanfront retirement community to provide bilingual election information to residents—even though there was no election to hold. 'This is the epitome of government multilingualism gone amok,' says U.S. English Chairman Mauro E. Mujica, whose office is one block from the White House. 'How many communities will have to throw away precious tax dollars to fund unnecessary multilingual services?'

"Mr. Mujica, who immigrated to the United States from Chile, says Briny Breezes 'has gotten caught up in the ugly tentacles of the Voting Rights Act,' which requires all towns within a county to print ballots in foreign languages when the number of foreign language speakers in that county rises above a certain threshold. Two years ago, tony Palm Beach County was informed that more than 5 percent of its voters were Spanish-speaking, forcing each of its 37 municipalities to print ballots in Spanish and provide bilingual poll workers.

"But U.S. census statistics show that 99 percent of Briny Breezes' population of 411, 98 percent of whom are U.S. citizens, speak English 'very well.' And talk about being U.S. citizens for a long time, the town's median age is 70, double the U.S. average of 35 years. Nevertheless, the town was required

SCOPE

Members: 1.8 million individuals
Branches/chapters: None
Affiliates: U.S. English Foundation, a 501(c)(3)
organization

STAFF

8 total—7 full-time; 1 part-time

TAX STATUS

501(c)(4)

FINANCES

Budget: 2003—$3 million

FUNDING SOURCES

Individual donations, 100%

PAC

None

EMPLOYMENT

Job openings can be found on the U.S. English
Web site at http://www.usenglish.org/inc/
about/jobs.asp. Applications and resumes
should be sent to Mauro E. Mujica, chair of
the board, 1747 Pennsylvania Avenue, NW,
Suite 1050, Washington, DC 20006. Fax: (202)
833-0108. E-mail: info@usenglish.org.

INTERNSHIPS

Paid internships are available. Information
about internships can be found at http://www.
usenglish.org/inc/about/jobs.asp. Students
must be enrolled in or have graduated from
college and will have opportunities to work
with many of the day-to-day operations,
including communications, research, government relations, and marketing. Internship
applications should be sent to Rob Toonkel,
director of communications and research, 1747
Pennsylvania Avenue, NW, Suite 1050,
Washington DC 20006. Fax: (202) 833-0108.
E-mail: info@usenglish.org.

NEWSLETTERS

The U.S. English Report (quarterly e-mail
newsletter)

PUBLICATIONS

Various fact sheets and issue briefings

CONFERENCES

None

to print a double-sided notice—one side in English, the other in Spanish—to inform residents that there would be no election."

(*The Washington Times,* February 25, 2004)

"They were the go-to people when customers needed advice in Spanish about eyeshadow or perfume. But when Hispanic employees wanted to speak Spanish to one another, they say it was forbidden—even on lunch breaks. Five women who worked for the cosmetics store Sephora in New York filed complaints, and the Equal Employment Opportunity Commission (EEOC) sued last fall on their behalf. They argue the policy is too restrictive and amounts to national-origin discrimination, which is illegal under the Civil Rights Act of 1964.

"'All of the [women say] how hurtful it is to be told that you can't speak your own language,' says EEOC attorney Raechel Adams. 'Language is so closely tied to their culture and their ethnicity. [Ironically,] they were expected to assist Spanish-speaking customers.'. . .

"For bilingual people, suppressing the tendency to talk in both languages can be difficult. They may know enough English to get by in their jobs, but to talk about family or other topics with friends, their primary language offers them a much richer vocabulary. . . .

"But when conversations are restricted, 'there's almost an issue of dehumanization.' says Karl Krahnke, a linguistics professor at Colorado State University. 'They are not being viewed as humans with the same social needs as anybody else.' Some insist those complexities shouldn't keep employers from creating a language policy if they think it's good for business. 'I speak four languages . . . but a business has the right to establish rules for whatever reason—it could be safety, it could be social . . . so other [workers] won't feel insulted,' says Mauro E. Mujica, chairman of U.S. English in Washington, D.C. His organization promotes official-English policies, which exist in 27 states and apply only to government, not the private sector. But workplace policies, he says, should not extend to people's personal time. . . ."

(*Christian Science Monitor,* January 26, 2004)

"As President Bush unveiled a new plan this week to temporarily legalize the status of millions of immigrants, Maria Garcia, of Salt Lake City, listened intently. The developments in Washington could dramatically affect her life here as an undocumented worker. Bush's plan would allow illegal immigrants to have their status legalized for renewable three-year terms if they can be matched to willing employers in the United States. 'The [existing] system is not working,' Bush said. 'Our nation needs an immigration system that serves the American economy and reflects the American dream.'. . .

"Raul Yzaguirre, president of the Washington-based National Council of La Raza, said the Bush plan 'appears to offer the business community full access to the immigrant workers it needs while providing very little to the workers themselves.' Mauro Mujica, chairman of U.S. English, the Washington organization behind the English-as-the-official-language ballot initiative that Utah voters supported by a two-to-one margin in 2000, said the Bush proposal would create a 'two-faced method of dealing with visitors to our nation—fingerprints and procedures for those who announce their arrival, amnesty for those who dash across the border.' "

(*Salt Lake Tribune,* January 8, 2004)

"Arnold Schwarzenegger swept through Fresno, hometown of leading Democratic rival Lt Gov Cruz Bustamante, as the candidate for the position of California governor fended off criticism for ties to a controversial group. Schwarzenegger, running as a Republican, was called on by the League of United Latin American Citizens, the nation's oldest Hispanic civil rights group, to resign from the advisory board of US English, which seeks to make English the official language of the US. The Austrian-born actor refused."

(*Sunday Mail* [Johannesburg, South Africa], August 31, 2003)

"As members of this week's Think Tank showed, there appears to be little middle ground on whether the government should offer multilingual ballots. As naturalized citizens, two of the participants—Zheya Gai and Munir Chavla—offered unique perspectives. In spite of their shared backgrounds as immigrants, they differ on the law that offers ballots in the native tongues of non-English-speaking voters. Unlike other immigrants, they arrived in the United States speaking English.

"Like Gai and Chavla, Mauro E. Mujica is an immigrant-turned-citizen. He arrived here in 1965 from Chile and spoke little English. Today he is chairman of U.S. English, whose mission is to preserve the 'unifying role of the English language in the United States.' The group also backs federal legislation that would make English the official language. The law would apply only to federal and state government and functions. So it probably comes as no surprise that the Washington, D.C.-based group opposes multilingual ballots.

"First of all, Mujica expressed serious doubts about the translation process. How does a person who doesn't speak English know the translation is accurate, Mujica asked? As someone who speaks four languages and is learning a fifth, he understands the nuances occurring in different tongues. What if a translator has a bias? Because of those concerns, he believes multilingual balloting is ripe for manipulation and abuse of those who don't know English.

"Furthermore, voting is far more complex than simply translating ballots. There's a lot leading up to casting that vote—candidate debates, reading newspaper articles and understanding referendums to name a few. Voting is the last part, Mujica said. Not knowing the language traps non-English-speaking immigrants in a linguist slavery, Mujica said. He compared it to the control exercised over American slaves when they were prohibited from learning to read and write."

(*Pittsburgh Post-Gazette,* November 24, 2002)

U.S. Term Limits

Established in 1992

DIRECTOR
Howard S. Rich, president.

BOARD OF DIRECTORS
Howard S. Rich, president
Peter Ackerman
Travis Anderson
Steven Baer
Terence Considine
Edward Crane
Cora Fields
Mike G. Ford
Blair M. Hull
Sally Reed Impastato
Paul Jacob
Ken Langone
Paul Raynault
Joseph Stillwell
Donna Weaver
William Wilson

SCOPE
Members: 177,000 individuals
Branches/chapters: None
Affiliates: None

STAFF
9 total—6 professional; 3 support;
plus 3 interns

TAX STATUS
501(c)(3)

FINANCES
Declined to comment

FUNDING SOURCES
Individual contributions; foundation grants

PAC
None

EMPLOYMENT
Information unavailable

INTERNSHIPS
Internships are available for undergraduates, recent graduates, and graduate students. Information is posted at http://www.termlimits.org/Get_Involved/interns.html. Responsibilities include research assistance to the political staff, assistance to the director of operations, and some clerical chores including preparing mass mailings. Applications should be sent to Ryan Ellis, U.S. Term Limits, 10 G Street, NE, Suite 410, Washington, DC 20002. E-mail: rellis@ustermlimits.org.

NEWSLETTERS
No Uncertain Terms (10 times per year; available online)

CONTACT INFORMATION
10 G Street, NE, Suite 410, Washington, DC 20002
Phone: (202) 379-3000 • *Fax:* (202) 379-3010
Toll free: (800) 733-6440
General E-mail: admin@termlimits.org • *Web site:* www.termlimits.org

Communications Director: Kurt A. Gardinier
(202) 379-3000, ext. 109 • kagardinier@ustermlimits.org
Human Resources Director: Information unavailable

PURPOSE: "To rally Americans to restore citizen control of government by limiting the terms of politicians at the local, state and congressional levels."

CURRENT CONCERNS: Congressional, state, and local term limits on elected officials

METHOD OF OPERATION: Coalition forming • Direct action • Education foundation • Films/videos/audiotapes • Grassroots organizing • Initiative/referendum campaigns • Internet (e-mail alerts and Web site) • Internships • Legal assistance • Litigation • Media outreach • Polling • Research • Speakers program

Effectiveness and Political Orientation

"Now that the Wyoming Supreme Court has heard arguments in a lawsuit challenging the state's term limits law, Wyoming Secretary of State Joe Meyer felt free Friday to express his thoughts. 'I don't think term limits make any sense whatsoever,' Meyer said. 'You're getting rid of someone with 12 years of experience and replacing them with someone who can't find the bathroom.' The bottom line, he said, lies in the answer to one question: How is Wyoming better off with term limits than without them?

"Meyer said he has watched the Legislature at work. 'I've been there,' he said. 'I know those people. I know those 11 people who are going to be leaving. Every one of them has an expertise. After 12 years, ask yourself why now you say the world is a better place because those people won't be here.' But Paul Jacobs of the U.S. Term Limits Foundation said, 'I have never heard of a legislator who, after two years, said, "I haven't figured it out yet." '

"Jacobs said George Washington provided one of the best examples for term limits. When there was talk of making him king, he resigned his military commission. After he was elected president, he stepped down after serving two terms. 'It's part of the American ideal that you hold the power, and then you turn it back,' he said."

(*Wyoming Tribune-Eagle* [Cheyenne], April 3, 2004)

"Arkansas's largest business group will head a broad coalition to amend the state constitution to give legislators longer terms, its president said Monday. The state Chamber of Commerce-Associated Industries of Arkansas is organizing groups to back a legislative proposal to amend Amendment 73. Passed by voters in 1992, Amendment 73 limits state representatives to three two-year terms and state senators to two four-year terms. Proposed Amendment 1, referred by the legislature to the November general election ballot, would allow House members to serve six two-year terms and state senators to serve three four-year terms.

" 'We're part of a coalition that is going to head up that effort,' Chamber president Ron Russell said. 'It will be one of the broadest-based coalitions that this state has ever had, and it'll just be a grassroots campaign.'

"Among the supporters of proposed Amendment 1 is the Arkansas Farm Bureau, which has a long-standing policy favoring longer terms for legislators. Farm Bureau spokesman Stanley Hill said extending lawmakers' terms would benefit the organization's rural, agricultural base. Having short terms 'tends to concentrate power in urban areas. That's been a drawback. It hurts our influence.' Tim Jacob, a business machines salesman from Little Rock and a local leader of the 1992 term limits drive financed largely by Washington-based U.S. Term Limits Inc., criticized this year's effort to extend term limits."

(*The Commercial Appeal* [Memphis, Tenn.], March 30, 2004)

"Three years ago, no one paid much mind to the quixotic idea of a couple of lawmakers from rural North Florida who were sick of seeing the state's Constitution peppered with special-interest ballot measures like net bans or bullet trains. Republican Rep. Joe Pickens and Democratic Sen. Rod Smith were freshmen legislators without much clout. And their issue—making it harder to amend the state Constitution—didn't lend itself to snappy sound bites. . . .

"Voters will likely be asked to require a 60 percent majority to pass a citizen initiative, instead of a simple majority, and to give the Florida Supreme Court more power to kill initiatives that don't seem to belong in the Constitution. The Legislature doesn't know when it will ask voters these questions. . . . The debate has raised the ire of the liberal People for the American Way and the Ballot Initiative Strategy Center, a labor-backed pro-initiative group out of Washington, D.C., that is pushing a November ballot measure that would raise Florida's minimum wage. It has also drawn the attention of the voters-rights group Citizens in Charge, a pro-initiative Washington, D.C., group run by Paul Jacob, who helped launch the term-limits revolution nationwide.

" 'What they're asking is for voters to give up their right to keep them accountable,' said Philip Blumel, who, along with fellow registered independent voter Rick Shepherd, led a successful eight-year term-limit initiative in 2002 in Palm Beach County. The two this week launched a new group, the Florida Initiative League, with Citizens in Charge's help to oppose the Legislature's plan. 'The question here is, 'Who's the boss?' I thought we'd answered that question many times in this country,' said Jacob, president of Citizens in Charge and founder of U.S. Term Limits, the Washington group that supported term limit initiatives across the country. . . ."

(*St. Petersburg Times* [Florida], March 24, 2004)

"Sen. Chris Beutler of Lincoln is offering an alternative to replace term limits put on state lawmakers by voters in 2000. Beutler introduced a proposed constitutional amendment Tuesday that would ask voters to do away with term limits but allow them to recall a lawmaker from office after eight years. 'To the extent that some people would prefer not to choose between having term limits and not having term limits, this is a modified solution,' Beutler said. Under the two-term limit, Beutler and 19 other senators now in office—or nearly 40 percent of Nebraska's 49-member unicameral Legislature—will have to leave by 2006. Another 24 senators would leave by 2008 if re-elected in 2004, meaning 44 of 49 current lawmakers would be gone in five years.

"Opponents say term limits will increasingly allow legislative rookies to be outmaneuvered by lobbyists and bureaucrats with more experience—especially in Nebraska's one-house Legislature. Supporters argue term limits eliminate the 'good ol' boy' system they say is rife with back-room deals and open to corruption. Seventeen states now have term limits, according to the National Conference of State Legislatures. The Legislature's Executive Board last year killed two proposed constitutional amendments regarding term limits. The Nebraska Term Limits Committee spent more than $380,000 to help get the constitutional amendment passed.

"The group was bankrolled by the Washington-based U.S. Term Limits, which promotes term limits nationwide. Term limits opponents, Nebraskans Against Outside Influence, spent just $66,000. Paul Jacob, of U.S. Term Limits, called Beutler's proposal 'silly.' 'I think a lot of voters in Nebraska will like recalls, but they sure are not going to trade it for term limits.' "

(*Omaha World Herald* [Nebraska], January 14, 2004)

"America's statehouses are not the male bastion they used to be, but women's progress in winning legislative seats stalled in the early 1990s and has not recovered. A major culprit, according to lawmakers and academic researchers, is the legislative term limits adopted in 17 states. Washington state, with no such limits, has the largest percentage of women 36.7 percent.

"The topic of women's progress in the nation's statehouses was on the minds of women attending the annual National Conference of State Legislatures last month. In seminars, luncheons and workshops, women asked why they have seen so little progress in winning state legislative seats since the watershed year of 1992. If anything, political scientists said, the momentum that brought gains for women lawmakers in the 1970s and '80s is dwindling.

" 'The pipeline is not any fuller in terms of the number of women,' said Cindy Simon-Rosenthal, associate director of the Carl Albert Congressional Research and Studies Center at the University of Oklahoma. One consolation might be that female legislators are continuing to make strides within their institutions. Women are winning an increasing number of leadership positions that make them powerful figures in their states. In four states, women hold the top spot in the Senate. In four other states, members of the lower chamber seek recognition from 'Madame Speaker.'

"Oklahoma Sen. Angela Monson, . . . like several other legislators at the conference, said the drive in the early 1990s to impose term limits on legislators might be curtailing women's progress. . . .

"Advocates of term limits disagree, contending that they are only now kicking in and haven't been given a chance to prove their value for women and minorities. 'Term limits are blamed by those in power for anything they don't like,' said Stacie Rumenap, executive director of U.S. Term Limits, a national organization that promotes term limits for politicians at the local, state and congressional levels."

(*The Seattle Times,* August 17, 2003)

Union of Concerned Scientists

Established in 1969

DIRECTOR

Kevin Knobloch, president. Knobloch first worked at UCS from 1989 to 1992 as legislative director for arms control and national security. He returned in January 2000 and was named president in December 2003. He holds a master's degree in public administration from the John F. Kennedy School of Government at Harvard University, and a bachelor's degree from the University of Massachusetts at Amherst.

BOARD OF DIRECTORS

Kurt Gottfried, chair; professor emeritus, Cornell University, Ithaca, NY
Peter A. Bradford, vice chair; visiting lecturer, Yale School of Forestry and Environmental Studies, New Haven, CT
James S. Hoyte, treasurer; lecturer, Environmental Sciences and Public Policy Program, Harvard University, Cambridge, MA
Thomas Eisner; professor, Cornell University, Ithaca, NY
James A. Fay; board member emeritus; professor emeritus, Massachusetts Institute of Technology, Cambridge, MA
Richard L. Garwin; scientist and author, New York, NY
Geoffrey M. Heal; professor, Graduate School of Business, Columbia University, New York, NY
Anne R. Kapuscincki; professor, University of Minnesota and director, Institute for Social, Economic and Ecological Sustainability at the University of Minnesota, Minneapolis, MN
James J. McCarthy; professor, Harvard University, Cambridge, MA
Mario J. Molina; professor, Massachusetts Institute of Technology, Cambridge, MA
Stuart L. Pimm; professor, Duke University, Durham, NC
Adele Simmons; senior associate, Center for International Studies, University of Chicago, Chicago, IL
Nancy Stephens; actress, Los Angeles, CA
Thomas H. Stone; chair and chief executive officer, Stone Capital Group
Ellyn R. Weiss; artist, Boston, MA

SCOPE

Members: 50,000 individuals
Branches/chapters: Regional offices in Washington, DC and Berkeley, CA
Affiliates: None

STAFF

59 total—50 professional; 9 support; plus interns and volunteers

CONTACT INFORMATION

2 Brattle Square, Cambridge, MA 02238-9105L
Phone: (617) 547-5552 • *Fax:* (617) 864-9405
Web site: www.uscusa.org

Communications Director: Suzanne Shaw
(617) 547-5552
Human Resources Director: Information unavailable

PURPOSE: The Union of Concerned Scientists (UCS) is a nonprofit partnership of scientists and citizens combining rigorous scientific analysis, innovative policy development and effective citizen advocacy to achieve practical environmental solutions.

CURRENT CONCERNS: Advanced (hybrid) vehicles • Antibiotic resistance • Auto pollution standards • Biotechnology • Cars and SUVs • Clean Energy Act • Climate control • Federal restructuring proposals • Forests • Global warming • Higher fuel economy standards • International conflict • International cooperation • Invasive species • Missile defense • Monarchs and toxin pollen • National missile defense • Nuclear safety • Nuclear terrorism • Renewable energy • Restoring scientific integrity • Space weapons • Sustainable agriculture • Trucks and buses • U.S.-China relations

METHOD OF OPERATION: Congressional testimony • Films/video/audiotapes • Grassroots organizing • Internet (Web site) • Legislative/regulatory monitoring (federal and state) • Lobbying (federal, state, and grassroots) • Media outreach • Participation in regulatory proceedings (federal and state) • Policy analysis • Research • Speakers program

Effectiveness and Political Orientation

"A leading environmental group will release a report today that says the technology already exists for automakers to significantly curb emissions of global warming gases. The Union of Concerned Scientists will contend that the amount of carbon dioxide produced by cars and trucks in California will double by 2040 without state restrictions on greenhouse gas emissions. The report comes as the California Air Resources Board is scheduled to hold a hearing Tuesday on the greenhouse gas issue in Sacramento in advance of proposing new emission rules in May.

"A 2002 state law requires the air board to develop what would be the nation's first plan to slash automotive emissions of carbon dioxide and other gases that can trap heat in the atmosphere, contributing to the condition known as global warming. 'The auto industry is expected to fight stricter standards tooth and nail, just as they have every new environmental or safety standard for the past three decades,' said report author Louise Bedsworth, a senior analyst with the group's clean-car program in Berkeley. Her report suggests

TAX STATUS
501(c)(3)

FINANCES
Revenue: 2002—$8.11 million;
2001—$8.83 million; 2000—$7.77 million

FUNDING SOURCES
Foundations, 49%; general support, 18%;
capital campaign, 17%; major donors, 10%;
other, 6%

PAC
None

EMPLOYMENT
Postings are available at http://www.ucsusa.
org/ucs/about/page.cfm?pageID=888. Application materials should be sent to the appropriate office listed in the posting.

INTERNSHIPS
UCS offers paid internships in the Clean
Energy, Clean Vehicles, and Global
Environment programs. More information
about internship programs can be found on the
Web site: http://www.ucsusa.org/ucs/about/
page.cfm?pageID=1027. General e-mail correspondence concerning internships should be
sent to internship@ucsusa.org. Instructions
for applicants can be found here: http://www.
ucsusa.org/ucs/about/page.cfm?pageID=
1027#howtoapply. Materials should be sent to
the internship coordinator at the office where
the internship is offered: Union of Concerned
Scientists, 2 Brattle Square, Cambridge, MA
02238-9105, or Union of Concerned Scientists,
1707 H Street, NW, Suite 600, Washington,
DC 20006-3962.

NEWSLETTERS
earthwise (quarterly)

PUBLICATIONS
The following is a sample list of publications:
*Automaker Rankings: The Environmental
    Performance of Car Companies*
Biotechnology and the Environment
*Building a Better SUV: A Blueprint for Saving
    Lives, Money, and Gasoline*
*Common Sense on Climate Change: Practical
    Solutions to Global Warming*
*Communicating Ecosystem Services: Tools for
    Scientists to Engage the Public*
*Diesel Passenger Vehicles and the
    Environment*
*Energy Security: Solutions to Protect
    America's Power Supply and Reduce Oil
    Dependence*
*Gone to Seed: Transgenic Contaminants in the
    Traditional Seed Supply*
*Greener SUVs: A Blueprint for Cleaner, More
    Efficient Light Trucks*
*Logging Off: Mechanisms to Stop or Prevent
    Industrial Logging in Forests of High
    Conservation Value*
*Money Down the Pipeline: Uncovering the
    Hidden Subsidies to the Oil Industry*
Nature and the Marketplace
*A New Road: The Technology and Potential of
    Hybrid Vehicles*

several existing technologies that can be used to lower greenhouse gas emissions without adding much to the cost of a car."

(*The Los Angeles Times*, April 19, 2004)

"The White House issued a detailed rebuttal yesterday to accusations by an
advocacy group and 60 prominent scientists that the Bush administration had
distorted or suppressed scientific information to suit its politics. In a letter to
Congress, which had requested a White House response, Dr. John H. Marburger III, science adviser to President Bush, said most of the accusations were
false and in some cases 'preposterous.'

"In February, the advocacy group, the Union of Concerned Scientists,
which has long criticized administration policies on issues like biotechnology,
global warming and nuclear power, released a 38-page report, finding, 'There
is significant evidence that the scope and scale of the manipulation, suppres-
sion and misrepresentation of science by the Bush administration is unprecedented.' The report was endorsed by 60 influential scientists, including 20
Nobel laureates and people who had served in past Republican administrations.

"Yesterday, Dr. Marburger rejected almost every point. 'The accusations
in the document are inaccurate, and certainly do not justify the sweeping conclusions of either the document or the accompanying statement,' he wrote. In
a few places, he said, the administration had erred, but he added that the mistakes had nothing to do with a lack of scientific integrity. For instance, he
agreed that the Environmental Protection Agency had included text from a
document prepared by lawyers for the utilities industry in the preamble of a
proposed rule restricting power-plant pollution. But that text, he said, had no
bearing 'on the integrity of the science used by E.P.A.'"

(*The New York Times*, April 3, 2004)

"A coalition of nuclear-industry companies plans to commit more than $35
million to apply jointly for the first new nuclear power plant license in decades.
With electricity demand on the rise, natural gas prices soaring and concern
growing over the environmental effects of carbon emissions from coal and natural gas, utilities are trying to pave the way to eventually replace aging nuclear
plants with new nuclear facilities. Energy experts and utility executives say
advanced designs of nuclear plants offer promising potential for nuclear
energy—improved safety, stable fuel prices, lower production costs and less of
an environmental impact than other fuels used to generate electricity.

" 'We all have a common goal in that we want to preserve the nuclear
option,' said Marilyn Kray, vice president of project development for Exelon
Nuclear, a subsidiary of one of the consortium's members and the company
taking the lead for the consortium. Critics of the effort point out the obvious
dangers of accidents or terrorism associated with nuclear plants. They worry
that existing plants—many of which have been operating for 30 years or
more—are unsafe and new designs are unproven.

" 'It would not be prudent at this time to place undue reliance on a risky
technology with unproven safety performance,' said David Lochbaum, a nuclear safety engineer for the Union of Concerned Scientists, a Cambridge,
Mass.-based Nuclear watchdog organization. 'Nuclear experiments belong in
the laboratory, not within the U.S. electricity marketplace.' The 103 nuclear
plants now operating in 31 states provide 20 percent of the nation's power,
but no company has applied to build a new plant since 1973, when conserva-

CONFERENCES
None

tion efforts helped slow growth in power demand and utilities began favoring natural gas-fired plants."

(*The Houston Chronicle,* April 1, 2004)

"Ford Motor will use some technology from Toyota's hybrid engine for its hybrid Escape sport-utility vehicle, set to hit dealers this fall, the two automakers said Tuesday. Ford says it will modify about 20 of the 370 patents that Toyota holds for its gas/electric hybrid technology, used in the Prius car. The patents Ford is buying involve software that controls, among other things, whether the gas engine or electric motor is used. In hybrid vehicles, power to the wheels shifts from the gas engine to the electric motor depending on demand to save fuel.

"Ford becomes the second automaker to tap Toyota's hybrid technology. Nissan reached an agreement with Toyota last year to use all its patents. The Nissan hybrid could go on sale as early as 2006. Neither Nissan nor Ford will buy parts from Toyota. They will get blueprints. Toyota hopes to get other automakers to use its technology. If successful, that should speed efforts to bring hybrids to market. 'It's a good opportunity for automakers to learn what Toyota has developed,' says David Friedman, research director for the clean vehicle program at the Union of Concerned Scientists.

"Toyota has refused to say how much the company invested to develop its hybrid technology. When Prius initially went on sale, analysts estimated Toyota was spending about $40,000 to build each one while selling the car for about $20,000 to get consumers familiar with the technology. Prius has since become profitable, says Toyota spokeswoman Nancy Hubbell. Toyota has been selling Prius in Japan since 1997 and in the USA since 2000. The car uses a four-cylinder gas engine and a 50-kilowatt electric motor. The government estimates it gets 55 mpg in combined city/highway driving. . . ."

(*USA Today,* March 10, 2004)

"Traditional varieties of three major U.S. food crops—corn, soybeans and canola—are 'pervasively contaminated' with low levels of genetically modified material, new research shows. The Union of Concerned Scientists says the spread of bits of genetically engineered DNA in the seed supply, if unchecked, could disrupt global agricultural trade and allow material from so-called transgenic crops engineered to produce drugs, vaccines and plastics to seep into the food supply. 'This study shatters the presumption that at least one portion of the seed supply—traditional varieties of crops—is truly free of genetically engineered elements,' said Margaret Mellon, director of the group's food and environment program.

" 'Seed contamination is the back door to the food supply,' she warned. 'And that door is wide open, and any of the hundreds of genetic varieties that are being grown or tested can move through it—right to the breakfast table. No one wants this kind of contamination in their corn flakes.' Genetically modified crops have spread rapidly in recent years. U.S. farmers last year planted more than 100 million acres of genetically modified corn, soybeans, canola and cotton. With wheat and rice poised for approval in the next few years, worldwide plantings of genetically engineered crops are expected to soar to 250 million acres in the next five years. . . ."

(*The Atlanta Journal-Constitution,* February 24, 2004)

United States Conference of Mayors

Established in 1932

DIRECTOR

J. Thomas Cochran, executive director. Cochran has worked with the U.S. Conference of Mayors since 1971. Previously he was a legislative representative for the National League of Cities. He holds a bachelor's and a J.D. degree from the University of Georgia.

BOARD OF TRUSTEES

Mayor Elizabeth G. 'Betty' Flores, Laredo, TX
Mayor Michael A. Guido, Dearborn, MI
Mayor Patrick Henry Hays, North Little Rock, AR
Mayor Sharpe James, Newark, NJ
Mayor William A. Johnson Jr., Rochester, NY
Mayor Scott L. King, Gary, IN
Mayor Dannel P. Malloy, Stamford, CT
Mayor Arlene J. Mulder, Arlington Heights, IL
Mayor Rita L. Mullins, Palatine, IL
Mayor Meyera E. Oberndorf, Virginia Beach, VA
Mayor Douglas H. Palmer, Trenton, NJ
Mayor Bill Purcell, Nashville, TN
Mayor David W. Smith, Newark, CA
Mayor Greg Sparrow, DeKalb, IL

SCOPE

Members: 1,300 mayors
Branches/chapters: None
Affiliates: None

STAFF

50 total—25 professional; 25 support

TAX STATUS

501(c)(3)

FINANCES

Declined to comment

FUNDING SOURCES

Declined to comment

PAC

None

EMPLOYMENT

Information unavailable

INTERNSHIPS

Information unavailable

NEWSLETTERS

US Mayor Newspaper (biweekly)

PUBLICATIONS

Affordable Housing Crisis Recommendations
Best Practices: Anti-Terrorism
Best Practices: Cancer Prevention

CONTACT INFORMATION

1620 Eye Street, NW, Washington, DC 20006
Phone: (202) 293-7330 • *Fax:* (202) 293-2352
General E-mail: info@usmayors.org • *Web site:* www.usmayors.org

Communications Director: Rhonda Spears, press contact
(202) 861-6766 • rspears@usmayors.org
Human Resources Director: Information unavailable

PURPOSE: "To provide a policy development and legislative action force in federal-city relationships to ensure that federal policy meets urban needs, and to assist in the capacity building of mayors and their cities."

CURRENT CONCERNS: Affirmative action • AIDS prevention • Antiterrorism efforts • Brownfields • City livability • Civil Rights laws • Criminal justice reform • Drug abuse and treatment • Elementary and Secondary Education Act • Employment Non-Discrimination Act • English-only language legislation • Fair housing • Fair minimum wage • Federal judge appointments • Federal policy against hate crimes • Immigration reform • Job creation and training • Municipal solid waste • Recycling • Religious freedom • Sports franchises • Taxes • Telecommunications

METHOD OF OPERATION: Awards program • Coalition forming • Conferences/seminars • Congressional testimony • Grantmaking • Information clearinghouse • International activities • Internet (Web site) • Legislative/regulatory monitoring (federal) • Lobbying (federal) • Local/municipal affairs • Media outreach • Product merchandising • Research

Effectiveness and Political Orientation

"The U.S. Conference of Mayors on Thursday blasted the Bush administration's homeland security grants system, charging that the fire, police and rescue agencies in 75 percent of the nation's cities have received zero help. 'The money comes to the states by Federal Express, but the cities get the money by pony express,' said conference president James A. Garner, mayor of Hempstead.

"Out of the more than $20 million in homeland security grants announced for Buffalo by Washington officials, including Sen. Charles E. Schumer, D-N.Y., in the last 18 months, Buffalo has so far received only $900,000. That was two weeks ago. Garner said the conference will renew its call that federal homeland security money be sent directly to the cities and not routed through the states. A bill doing just that was proposed by Sen. Hillary Rodham Clinton, D-N.Y., but was quashed by the Senate's Republican majority.

"Buffalo Mayor Anthony M. Masiello said in an interview that the state-based process is the result of partisan politics, where the Republican Bush administration favors governors who are predominantly Republican. Masiello, who is attending the conference, said this builds unfortunate delays into the system. But Masiello said Buffalo in one way may be better off than most. 'We have a format where we work out allocations with the Erie County government,' Masiello said, adding that it could serve as a model for the country."

(*Buffalo News,* January 23, 2004)

"Two and a half years after Sept. 11, 2001, three of four U.S. cities, many of them cash-strapped like Pittsburgh, have not received money from the homeland security program that is supposed to help local police and fire officials prevent or respond to a terrorist attack. One by one yesterday, an angry array of city leaders attending the annual U.S. Conference of Mayors meeting complained that the money appropriated by Congress is being distributed through the states and that bureaucratic red tape has kept most of them from getting a penny under the highly touted first-responder program.

"A survey of 215 cities in all 50 states and Puerto Rico found that cities are paying for increased security by tightening already-overstretched belts in other areas and are not happy about it. The study, done for the mayors with funds provided by a security software firm called SentryPoints, found that 76 percent of 215 cities surveyed have received no money at all for improving their first response in the event of an attack or protecting 'critical infrastructures,' although Congress appropriated $1.5 billion."

(*Pittsburgh Post-Gazette,* January 23, 2004)

"Homelessness and hunger among low-income, working families are spreading so dramatically that many major U.S. cities, including San Antonio, can't keep up with the growing demand for basic needs, according to a new report. A new survey of 25 large cities by the U.S. Conference of Mayors found that emergency food requests rose an average of 17 percent last year, while the demand for emergency shelter jumped 13 percent. And only a third of the eligible low-income households were served by assisted housing. Comparatively, San Antonio saw a 7 percent increase in emergency food requests and an 8 percent increase in demand for shelter. The city offered assisted housing to only 19 percent of those who needed it.

" 'This survey underscores the impact the economy has had on everyday Americans,' said James Garner, president of the conference and the mayor of Hempstead, N.Y. 'We don't expect it to get any better next year.' The Conference of Mayors annually surveys the 25 cities whose mayors serve on its Task Force on Hunger and Homelessness. San Antonio Mayor Ed Garza is a member. The report cited a large percentage of the homeless who couldn't find any assistance for food and shelter during the year.

"Across the country, 30 percent of requests for emergency shelter went unmet, as did 14 percent of requests for food assistance, the survey shows. In San Antonio, about 12 percent of people seeking emergency shelter were turned away, and 14 percent of the hungry were not fed, according to the survey. Bob Martindale, executive director of SAMMinistries, one of the city's largest homeless service charities, said the working poor can't make ends meet. . . .

"Garner said funding additional services for the homeless is difficult for cities struggling to recover from budget shortfalls and state cutbacks in social service programs. . . ."

(*San Antonio Express-News* [Texas], December 27, 2003)

"At a time when more people are finding themselves homeless, the Bush administration is spending more in an effort to eradicate the problem. Locally, that will result in significantly more money being made available for both emergency shelters and for programs designed to help people get into stable housing. 'It's more [money] than it has been in the past,' said Hempstead Village Mayor James Garner, president of the U.S. Conference of Mayors. 'But it's not sufficient.'

"On Friday, Roy Bernardi, assistant secretary of the Department of Housing and Urban Development, said the Bush administration will give almost $1.3 billion in grants to groups and agencies to help the homeless. On Long Island, Nassau agencies will get $6.6 million, 15.2 percent more than last year. Suffolk agencies will get $3.9 million, a 6.6 percent increase. Most of the money will go to nonprofit groups that provide temporary housing and other services such as job training, drug treatment and domestic violence counseling, to help alleviate problems associated with homelessness, Bernardi said during a telephone news conference on Friday. 'That's the way it should be, because they know their communities best,' he said of the local groups."

(*Newsday* [New York], December 23, 2003)

"The US Conference of Mayors painted a dismal picture yesterday of growing homelessness and hunger among low-income, working families and reported a dramatic decrease in 2003 in the ability of most of the nation's 25 major cities to meet these basic needs. 'This survey underscores the impact the economy has had on everyday Americans,' said conference president James A. Garner, the mayor of Hempstead, N.Y. Garner said a recovering economy will not immediately solve state and local budget shortfalls or reverse cutbacks in social-service programs. 'We don't expect it to get any better next year.'

"The conference's annual survey found that in nearly all the cities, requests for emergency food assistance have increased by an average of 17 percent over last year, and the demand for emergency shelter rose by an average of 13 percent. More than half of the cities surveyed reported that emergency food assistance facilities had to either turn people away or limit the groceries families could receive on each visit. Of those requesting food help, 59 percent were families and 39 percent were employed, the report said.

"In 84 percent of the cities surveyed, shelters reported turning away homeless families because of too few beds and other resources. Officials estimated that 30 percent of requests for shelter by homeless people, and 33 percent of the requests by homeless families were unmet, according to the Conference of Mayors report. Philip Mangano, an advocate for the homeless in Boston before he became the Bush administration's point person on the issue last year, said the pattern of growing needs, reported year after year by the Conference of Mayors, shows the 'insanity' of traditional strategies for temporarily sheltering the homeless. He called for a new approach based on permanent housing and directed social services. . . ."

(*The Boston Globe,* December 19, 2003)

United States Public Interest Research Group (USPIRG)

Established in 1983

DIRECTOR

Gene Karpinski, executive director. Karpinski has been executive director of the U.S. Public Interest Research Group since 1984. Previously he was the field director for People for the American Way. He has also been director of the Colorado Public Interest Research Group (CoPIRG), and field director for Public Citizen's Congress Watch. He is a 1974 graduate of Brown University and a 1977 graduate of the Georgetown University Law Center.

BOARD OF DIRECTORS

Information unavailable

SCOPE

Members: USPIRG serves as "the national lobbying office for state Public Interest Research Groups (PIRGs), which are nonprofit . . . organizations." Its membership is the aggregate of the various state PIRGs.

Branches/chapters: Regional field offices in Boston, Atlanta, New Orleans, and Salt Lake City; 35 state PIRGs

Affiliates: U.S. PIRG Education Fund, a 501(c)(3) organization

STAFF

25 total—plus interns

TAX STATUS

501(c)(4)

FINANCES

Revenue: 2003—$5.19 million; 2002—$7.38 million; 2001—$4.8 million

FUNDING SOURCES

Primarily individual donations

PAC

None

EMPLOYMENT

Job postings at USPIRG and state PIRGs can be found at http://www.pirg.org/jobs/. An application form is available at http://www.pirg.org/jobs/application/Index.html; online submission of application materials is encouraged. Potential candidates can send e-mail to jobs@pirg.org for further information.

INTERNSHIPS

Information about internships can be found at http://www.pirg.org/jobs/internships/graduate/index.html. "Most PIRG interns are graduate students in law, public policy or environmental studies, but students in any area of study may apply. Intern supervisors provide ongoing training. Previous campaign and/or advocacy experience is a plus." Cover

CONTACT INFORMATION

218 D Street, SE, Washington, DC 20003
Phone: (202) 546-9707 • *Fax:* (202) 546-2461
General E-mail: uspirg@pirg.org • *Web site:* www.uspirg.org

Communications Director: Elizabeth Hitchcock
(202) 546-9707 • lizh@pirg.org
Human Resources Director: Rick Trilsch
(202) 546-9707 • rick@pirg.org or jobs@pirg.org

PURPOSE: "U.S. PIRG's mission is to deliver persistent, result-oriented public interest activism that protects our environment, encourages a fair, sustainable economy, and fosters responsive, democratic government."

CURRENT CONCERNS: Arctic drilling • Arctic wilderness • Arsenic standards • Bank and ATM fees • Campaign finance reform • Clean air • Clean water • Election Reform • Endangered species • Energy • Environmental protection • Forests protection • Genetically modified foods • Global warming • Health care • Media ownership • Oceans • Playground safety • Polluter pork • Power plants • Privacy and ID theft • Public lands • Student aid • Superfund • Supreme Court decisions • Toxics • Toy safety

METHOD OF OPERATION: Coalition forming • Congressional voting analysis • Grassroots organizing • Internet • Legislative/regulatory monitoring (federal) • Lobbying (federal) • Media outreach • Research • Voter registration

Effectiveness and Political Orientation

"Environmentalists will again descend on BP's annual general meeting next week, demanding that the oil giant stay out of 'protected and sensitive areas.' Campaigners, who have bought BP shares, have put down a special resolution that will be put to the vote at the event, to be held in London on Thursday.

"Activists, led by US Public Interest Research Group (US Pirg), are particularly concerned about BP's stated interest in the Arctic Wildlife Refuge in Alaska. The resolution, if passed, would force BP to produce a report on the 'risks to shareholder value from operating in protected and sensitive environments.' According to US Pirg, BP is in danger of falling behind some of its competitors if it does not adopt a 'no-go' policy for such areas.

"A BP spokesman said the issue of opening up the Arctic Wildlife Refuge was 'a decision for the American people.' The company has recommended voting against the resolution. It has told shareholders: 'Rather than operate a blanket no-go policy, we assess each potential site for investment case-by-case, thoroughly examining the risks of development.'"

(*The Independent* [London, England], April 10, 2004)

"More employers are replacing traditional paychecks with payroll cards, a new type of system that allows employees to get money out of cash machines instead

letters can be sent to Amy Perry, hiring director, 29 Temple Place, Boston, MA 02111. Fax: (617) 292-8057.

NEWSLETTERS
Citizen Agenda (quarterly)

PUBLICATIONS
None

CONFERENCES
Twice per year-an eastern and western PIRG organizational conference

of cashing checks. Instead of getting a paycheck, employees can opt to get cards that are credited each pay period with their wages. Workers can use the cards to withdraw money from ATMs or they can use them like a debit card to make purchases. Some users have to pay a transaction fee or monthly charge for the cards; in other cases, fees are waived. Employees who use the payroll cards often get a paper or electronic pay stub with wage and tax information.

"The use of such cards is expected to grow quickly. Over the next year, about 50% of employers plan to evaluate the benefits of payroll cards for their companies, according to a survey by the American Payroll Association. Already, major employers such as Sears, McDonald's, Blockbuster and Domino's use payroll cards. But some critics say the cards are bad for employees, because workers may be charged fees for accessing cash. Some say such cards don't give users the chance to save as they might with a bank account. The cards also may not have the same consumer protections as other debit or credit cards if an unauthorized user gets hold of them.

" 'We see payroll cards contributing to a second-class system of consumers,' says Ed Mierzwinski at consumer advocacy group U.S. Public Interest Research Group. 'The companies are just trying to save money. Companies ought to leverage their power to force banks to offer affordable accounts.' "

(*USA Today,* February 16, 2004)

"A coalition of environmental and consumer groups suspects the White House is directing policy in favor of 'black hydrogen' as it pursues President Bush's vision of a future based on the clean fuel. Black hydrogen, say members of the Green Hydrogen Coalition, is produced from coal, oil, natural gas or nuclear power—the same fuels many environmentalists think cause so many problems today. 'Green hydrogen,' by contrast, would be generated by renewable energy sources.

" 'We have the potential in this country to generate at least four times our energy needs from renewable sources—and that does not include solar,' said Katherine Morrison, an attorney with the U.S. Public Interest Research Group. But, she said, the administration this year supported a national energy policy bill that would have spent enormous sums subsidizing research to find ways of extracting hydrogen from coal and other fossil fuels. The bill is stalled in the Senate for reasons not related to hydrogen fuel.

" 'They're just wrong,' said Energy Department spokesman Joe Davis. 'This administration supports clean energy through our hydrogen economy program.' He said the department is funding research on taking hydrogen from renewable sources, as well as fossil fuels and nuclear power. When hydrogen is fed into a fuel cell, similar to a large battery, it produces electricity, heat and pure water. The exhaust contains no carbon dioxide, the gas scientists believe is heating up the atmosphere and causing the Earth's climate to change."

(*The Atlanta Journal-Constitution,* December 7, 2003)

"Environmentalists and their congressional allies are pushing for legislation that would require oil refineries to stop using a chemical the critics claim threatens the health and safety of residents near the facilities. The U.S. Public Interest Research Group wants Congress to require refinery operators to stop using hydrofluoric acid in favor of alternative chemicals that would pose less risk if released by accident or during a terrorist attack.

"Industry officials say they have safety measures in place to prevent accidents involving the chemical, which is used to help refine gasoline. According to a report released by the group Tuesday, more than 15 million people live near facilities that store large amounts of hydrofluoric acid used in the refining process. Texas has 12 refineries that store hydrofluoric acid, and more than 1 million people live nearby.

"The group urged Congress to approve a bill by Rep. Frank Pallone, D-N.J., and supported by Rep. Sheila Jackson Lee, D-Houston, that would require federal agencies to identify facilities that pose the greatest risk to area residents, then recommend security and safety improvements. 'If there is a cost-effective, safer technology available to meet the same end product, companies should be using these technologies in order to reduce the risk to the public,' Pallone said."

(*The Houston Chronicle,* October 15, 2003)

"Cable TV deregulation has failed consumers in its promise to boost competition and lower prices, according to a report released this week by the U.S. Public Interest Research Group. In the Pittsburgh region, for instance, the consumer advocacy group calculated that cable rates have jumped 11 percent annually from 1999 through 2002. 'Since deregulation seven years ago, the cable industry has price-gouged consumers by raising its prices more than 50 percent,' said Ed Mierzwinski, consumer program director for U.S. Pirg. It blamed industry consolidation for stifling competition and limiting choices."

(*Pittsburgh Post-Gazette,* August 15, 2003)

"Although uninsured New Orleanians pay less for commonly prescribed medications than their counterparts in any other city in a new national survey, they still pay substantially more than the best available price, pollsters found. In a survey of 26 cities, researchers for U.S. PIRG found New Orleanians without health coverage paid 56 percent more than the best price the federal government can negotiate for people such as veterans and government employees and retirees. Using that as a baseline, analysts found that local prescription prices for uninsured New Orleans ranged from 12 percent higher for Lanoxin, which strengthens and regulates the heartbeat, to 90 percent higher for the ulcer drug Prilosec.

" 'We were at the low end of the prices that our survey found, which I think is fantastic, but it's still pretty high,' said Aaron Viles, the organization's field director for this part of the United States. A spokeswoman for Blue Cross Blue Shield of Louisiana called it 'a case of simple economics.' 'A group has more purchasing power than an individual,' Dianne Eysink said. 'If you don't have that kind of advocate, you pay more.' The report, "Paying the Price: A 19-State Survey of the High Cost of Prescription Drugs," 'dramatically underscores the fact that patients need coverage,' said Jeff Trewhitt, a spokesman for the Pharmaceutical Research and Manufacturers of America, a Washington-based trade group."

(*The New Orleans Times-Picayune,* July 16, 2003)

The Urban Institute

Established in 1968

DIRECTOR

Robert D. Reischauer, president. Before joining the Urban Institute, Reischauer was the director of the Congressional Budget office.

BOARD OF DIRECTORS

Joel L. Fleishman, chair
Robert M. Solow, vice chair
Dick Thornburgh, vice chair
Robert D. Reischauer, president
Michael Beschloss
John M. Deutch
Richard C. Green Jr.
Richard B. Fisher
Fernando A. Guerra
Robert S. McNamara
Charles L. Mee Jr.
Robert C. Miller
Robert E. Price
Louis A. Simpson
Judy Woodruff

SCOPE

Members: None
Branches/chapters: None
Affiliates: None

STAFF

379 total—329 full-time professional;
50 full-time support

TAX STATUS

501(c)(3)

FINANCES

Budget: 2004—$74 million;
2003—$75.5 million; 2002—$65.6 million

FUNDING SOURCES

Foundation grants, 30%; government contracts, 68%; state, local, and private individuals, 2%

PAC

None

EMPLOYMENT

Potential applicants can learn about job openings with this organization from its website at www.urban.org and from www.washington-jobs.com. This organization offers positions in the areas of research, communication, accounting, human resources, and administration. Applicants should send resumes and other materials for employment to Human Resources Department/Urban Institute, 2100 M Street, NW, Washington, DC. 20007. E-mail: ddangel@ui.urban.org.

INTERNSHIPS

Paid internships are offered by this organization. Potential applicants can learn about

CONTACT INFORMATION

2100 M Street, NW, Washington, DC 20037
Phone: (202) 833-7200 • *Fax:* (202) 728-0232
General E-mail: paffairs@ui.urban.org • *Web site:* www.urban.org

Communications Director: Kathleen Courrier, vice president for communication
(202) 261-5730 • kcourrie@ui.urban.org
Human Resources Director: Deb Hoover
dhoover@ui.urban.org

PURPOSE: "To sharpen thinking about society's problems and efforts to solve them, improve government decisions and their implementation, and increase citizens' awareness about important public choices."

CURRENT CONCERNS: Reflected by the Urban Institute's policy centers: • Assessing the New Federalism (cross-center project) • Education • Health policy • Justice policy • Income and benefits policy • International activities • Labor, human services, and population • Nonprofits and philanthropy • Retirement project • Tax policy

METHOD OF OPERATION: Conferences/seminars • Congressional testimony • International activities • Internet (databases, e-mail alerts, and Web site) • Internships • Media outreach • Research • Technical assistance

Effectiveness and Political Orientation

"Companies should treat their low-wage workers better—for the companies' own good.

"That was the conclusion of a corporate-funded study released Thursday that described the precarious existence of many hourly-wage earners.

"The study highlighted 15 programs—ranging from subsidized child care at Bank of America to emergency loans available at Levi Strauss & Co.—that improved workers' lot while bettering their employers' bottom lines.

"Along with two other reports on low-wage workers also released Thursday, the study illustrates the increasing attention being paid to these employees, who account for a growing percentage of the American workforce.

" 'Anything that increases employee satisfaction and morale, and basically makes it easier for [low-wage workers] to show up for work every day, can have a tremendous impact on employee engagement, customer service and productivity,' said Donna Klein, chief executive of Corporate Voices for Working Families, which sponsored the study conducted by the Boston College Center for Work and Family. Corporate Voices, founded by Marriott Hotels in 2001, has 47 members. . . .

"The two other reports released Thursday, one by the Urban Institute and the other by two leading researchers of low-wage labor, underscored low-wage

internship opportunities from the organization's website at www.urban.org and from www.washingtonjobs.com. The duration of internships varies; most positions are for the summer months. Internship areas include research and communications. Applicants should send queries to Human Resources Office/Urban Institute, 2100 M Street, NW, Washington DC 20037. E-mail: ddangel@ui.urban.org.

NEWSLETTERS

Several e-mail newsletters and discussion lists:
UI Update
ANF Hot Off the Press
Health Policy Center
Justice Policy Center
National Center for Charitable Statistics (NCCS)
National Neighborhood Indicators Partnership (NNIP) News
Metropolitan Housing and Communities
Research for Our Region
Tax Policy Center

PUBLICATIONS

The following is a sample list of publications:
Contemporary U.S. Tax Policy
The Gay and Lesbian Atlas
Exploring Organizations and Advocacy: Governance and Accountability
Federalism and Health Policy
Kinship Care
Prisoners Once Removed: The Impacts of Incarceration and Reentry on Children, Families, and Communities
Performance Management: Getting Results
State Responses to the 2004 Budget Crisis
Trends in Naturalization

CONFERENCES

Sponsors 20–25 annually

workers' difficulties in an age of changing technology, globalization and pressure from Wall Street for short-term earnings.

"For example, by analyzing data from a 2002 survey of 40,000 households, the Urban Institute documented that 41% of all parents earning as much as twice the federal poverty level didn't receive paid sick leave, vacation days or other forms of compensated leave.

"Of those with higher earnings, 84% had some form of paid leave, the Urban Institute found. . . ."

(*The Los Angeles Times,* April 23, 2004)

"In a remarkable opinion poll released this week, as Americans were filing their Form 1040s, some two-thirds of respondents told the Associated Press that their federal taxes have gone up or remained the same during the last three years.

"Domestic advisers at the White House must be spitting tacks. Three historic tax bills, proposed by President Bush and passed by Congress in 2001, 2002 and 2003, have delivered the biggest federal tax cut since Ronald Reagan took office more than 20 years ago. The federal tax burden today, measured as a share of national income, has sunk to its lowest level since 1950. Don't taxpayers know what's good for them?

"Actually, they do. For the tax packages passed by Congress these last three years have overwhelmingly handed out tax relief to the rich, with only hit-and-miss benefits for the middle class.

"The Center on Budget and Policy Priorities, a Washington think tank, estimated this week that households in the middle of the income distribution will get an average tax cut of $647 this year, while those in the top 1 percent will get a tax cut of almost $35,000. The Urban Institute-Brookings Institution Tax Policy Center, a nonpartisan research group, says that someone who earned $35,000 last year and happened to be single and childless got a tax cut of $350, while a married couple with two children and income of $100,000 got over $3,400. . . ."

(*Minneapolis Star Tribune,* April 15, 2004)

"Optimally, the debt to society incurred by a convicted felon ought to be considered fully discharged at the completion of his sentence. However, ex-cons face many obstacles, one of the toughest being landing a job. Unemployment greases the slide back into the criminal life. Public distrust of one-time criminals makes it harder still for them to get jobs and keep to the straight and narrow path.

"A recent study, 'A Portrait of Prisoner Re-entry in Texas,' a research project by the nonpartisan Urban Institute in Washington, D.C., shed some light on what the typical ex-convict is up against here. In 2001, the study found, an astounding 26 percent of inmates returned to Harris County on supervised parole were turned loose in only a handful of communities: Alief, East Houston, Third Ward-MacGregor, Kashmere Gardens, East Little York-Homestead and Trinity-Houston Gardens.

"The distribution was not a conspiracy to dump prisoners on poor neighborhoods, but the natural inclination of newly freed men and women to head for home, the place where, if you go there, they pretty much have to take you in. Unfortunately, the old neighborhood also is the place where the fresh-out-of-the-joint felon is likely to fall back in with the bad crowd that landed him behind bars. . . ."

(*The Houston Chronicle,* March 24, 2004)

"Among those watching to see if anything new would emerge from Mexican President Vicente Fox's meetings with President Bush, none had more interest than the growing community of undocumented Mexicans—and the employers who knowingly violate the law by hiring them.

"Both Bush and Fox have focused on fixing immigration, but many more people now have a direct stake in the matter. The population of undocumented Mexicans in the United States grew 165 percent between 1990 and 2002, says Jeffrey Passel of the Urban Institute, and they are no longer concentrated in a few states.

"Their employers are as quiet as they are diverse, ranging from homemakers who hire domestics to the small construction contractors who hire skilled craftsmen to eateries that take on kitchen help.

"But there are also large corporations, some in the Fortune 500, that often use contractors to distance themselves from the law to hire workers for salaries and conditions most Americans reject. . . ."

(San Antonio Express-News [Texas], March 7, 2004)

"The U.S. Senate is set to debate a bill today that would put a $250,000 limit on pain-and-suffering awards for patients who successfully sue their obstetricians for botched deliveries or prenatal care.

"The goal of the measure, some say, is twofold: to assist medical specialists who have witnessed the sharpest increases in malpractice insurance in recent years, and to force opponents such as Sen. Patty Murray, D-Wash., to take a vote that later could be spun by political opponents as anti-physician and anti-family.

"While medical-malpractice insurance reform has been a hot issue on Capitol Hill for years, the language and tactics are getting sharper.

"And now a doctors group is targeting Washington state and its two U.S. senators in a multi-million-dollar national campaign that says physicians are leaving the state, and patients are suffering, because of high malpractice-insurance costs.

"The campaign singles out Murray and fellow Democratic Sen. Maria Cantwell, claiming the two lawmakers are forcing doctors out of business because they oppose caps on damage awards.

"Observers say the medical-malpractice debate is deeply infused with partisan politics that pits Democrats, whose campaigns are largely supported by trial lawyers, against Republicans, who receive contributions from doctors and insurance groups.

"When it comes to health care, policy has taken a distant back seat to politics, said Robert Berenson, a medical doctor and senior fellow at the Urban Institute, a Washington, D.C.-based think tank.

" 'This (issue) absolutely lines up with who's giving to which party,' he said. 'This is all being done for political ends.' "

(The Seattle Times, February 23, 2004)

The Washington Institute for Near East Policy

Established in 1985

DIRECTOR

Dennis Ross, director. For more than 12 years, Ambassador Ross played a leading role in shaping U.S. involvement in the Middle East peace process and in dealing directly with the parties in negotiations. A highly skilled diplomat, Ross assisted the peace process in both the George H. W. Bush and Bill Clinton administrations. He was instrumental in assisting Israelis and Palestinians in reaching the 1995 Interim Agreement; he also successfully brokered the Hebron Accord in 1997, facilitated the 1994 Israel-Jordan peace treaty, and intensively worked to bring Israel and Syria together. A scholar and diplomat with more than two decades of experience in Soviet and Middle East policy, Ross worked closely with Secretaries of State James Baker, Warren Christopher, and Madeleine Albright and served as director of the State Department's Policy Planning office in the first Bush administration. During the Reagan administration, he served as director of Near East and South Asian affairs on the National Security Council staff and as deputy director of the Pentagon's Office of Net Assessment. Ambassador Ross was awarded the Presidential Medal for Distinguished Federal Civilian Service by President Clinton. From 1984 to 1986, he served as executive director of the Berkeley-Stanford program on Soviet International Behavior. Ross has published articles extensively on the former Soviet Union, arms control, and the greater Middle East. He is a 1970 graduate of UCLA and has received honorary doctorates from the Jewish Theological Seminary and Syracuse University.

BOARD OF ADVISORS

Warren Christopher
Lawrence S. Eagleburger
Alexander Haig
Max M. Kampelman
Jeane Kirkpatrick
Samuel W. Lewis
Edward Luttwak
Michael Mandelbaum
Robert McFarlane
Martin Peretz
Richard Perle
George P. Shultz
R. James Woolsey
Mortimer Zuckerman

SCOPE

Members: None
Branches/chapters: None
Affiliates: None

STAFF

47 total—plus 6 research interns; 6 visiting fellows

CONTACT INFORMATION

1828 L Street, NW, Suite 1050, Washington, DC 20036
Phone: (202) 452-0650 • *Fax:* (202) 223-5364
General E-mail: info@washingtoninstitute.org •
Web site: www.washingtoninstitute.org

Communications Director: Information unavailable
Human Resources Director: Information unavailable

PURPOSE: "To develop and advance a balanced and realistic understanding of U.S. national interest in the Near East."

CURRENT CONCERNS: U.S. interests in the Middle East

METHOD OF OPERATION: Research • Telecommunication services
(Fax broadcasts: PeaceWatch and PolicyWatch)

Effectiveness and Political Orientation

"Jonathan Schanzer of the Washington Institute for Near East Policy spent January and February in Iraq and is writing a book on Al-Qaida affiliates. Although he sees tactical mistakes, Schanzer broadly supports the Bush administration policy and says, 'We're doing as good a job as we can in Iraq.'

"Since the collapse of the Baathist regime, violent opposition to the U.S. program has come from four elements that occupy what Schanzer calls 'concentric and overlapping circles.'. . .

"Schanzer rejects the idea that support for Al-Sadr is widespread among the Shiites. Most Shiites with whom he spoke in Iraq this winter agreed with the U.S. goal of establishing a relatively secular democracy in Iraq, he said. Their frustration was that it wasn't happening fast enough.

"Some of the attacks on U.S. troops last week appeared to involve collaboration, for the first time, between Sunni and Shiite elements of the resistance. The good news, Schanzer said half-jokingly, is that the danger of a Sunni-vs.-Shiite civil war was declining. The bad news is that it seems more likely now that Sunni and Shiite opposition groups are making common cause against the United States."

(*Minneapolis Star Tribune,* April 11, 2004)

"Just when the British embassy (and most of Washington) assumed that the quicksands of Iraq had swallowed them up, the neocons are back with a vengeance. Bush's 'Democracy for the middle east' speech came from the latest neocon recruit to the White House team, David Wurmser, who along with Richard Perle in 1996 wrote the celebrated 'A clean break' strategy document for incoming Israeli premier Binyamin Netanyahu. In September, Wurmser was promoted from a mid-ranking job on the staff of the state department's token neocon John Bolton to running the middle east desk in vice-president Dick Cheney's personal national security council. . . . Wurmser was formerly

TAX STATUS
501(c)(3)

FINANCES
Revenue: 2002—$3.8 million;
2001—$4.86 million

FUNDING SOURCES
Private donations; publication sales; foundation grants

PAC
None

EMPLOYMENT
Information unavailable

INTERNSHIPS
This organization offers research internship opportunities, which are listed on their web site at http://www.washingtoninstitute.org. Research internships are part- or full-time positions open to current undergraduates as well as recent graduates. Interns provide administrative and research support for Institute staff. Interested applicants should send a cover letter and resume to Patrick Clawson, deputy director, The Washington Institute for Near East Policy. This organization has also sponsored a fundraising internship. For more information on this internship, contact Laura Milstein, director of development, The Washington Institute for Near East Policy, 1828 L Street, NW, Suite 1050, Washington, DC 20036.

NEWSLETTERS
None

PUBLICATIONS
The following is a sample list of publications:
Covering the Intifada: How the Media Reported the Palestinian Uprising
'Fight on All Fronts': Hizballah, the War on Terror, and the War in Iraq
Dancing with Saddam: The Strategic Tango of Jordanian-Iraqi Relations
International Military Intervention: A Detour on the Road to Israeli-Palestinian Peace
The New Pillar: Conservative Arab Gulf States and U.S. Strategy
The West Bank Fence: A Vital Component in Israel's Strategy of Defense
Also publishes audiotapes, conference proceedings, policy papers, and monographs.

CONFERENCES
Annual Weinberg Founders Conference (fall)
Soref Symposium (spring)

with the American Enterprise Institute and the strongly pro-Israel Washington Institute for Near East Policy. . . ."

(Prospect, November 20, 2003)

"Wednesday's events in the Middle East provide a ray of hope—for the first time in years—that progress can be made to end the violent standoff between Israelis and Palestinians.

"In embracing the American 'road map' aimed at resolving the conflict, Palestinian Prime Minister Mahmoud Abbas and Israeli Prime Minister Ariel Sharon said all the right things, say analysts, who also point to the unexpectedly energetic involvement of President George W. Bush in the just-ended summit in Jordan.

" 'Guarded optimism is a good expression,' said Jeffrey White, who spent 34 years with the Defense Intelligence Agency and other intelligence groups, mostly as an analyst on the Middle East, before going last fall to the Washington Institute for Near East Policy.

" 'I spend so long looking at these things that I tend to be pessimistic. But clearly the fact that this meeting occurred, that Abbas and Sharon said some pretty good things, that's useful.'

"In dramatic statements, the Israelis agreed to dismantle settlements built since the fall of 2001, support a provisional Palestinian state and make significant military pullbacks, while the Palestinians committed to end terrorism aimed at Israel and work to get militant groups to lay down their weapons. . . ."

(St. Louis Post-Dispatch, June 5, 2003)

"The Bush administration should recruit representatives from a wide array of countries to help run postwar Iraq and not rule Iraq alone or solely with U.S. military allies, a Washington think tank asserts in a report to be released today.

"A broad-based authority, which should include people from Iraq and neighboring Arab countries, is the best way to win public support and establish the legitimacy of the U.S.-led project to build democracy, said the Washington Institute for Near East Policy. To encourage fresh Iraqi leadership and prevent a concentration of power among Iraqis, two advisory councils should be established, with membership spread widely and considerable responsibility delegated to provincial officials. Chairmanship of the executive council, one of the two bodies, should rotate, the report said.

"Iraqis should also lead the reconstruction effort, the better to convince skeptics that the war was not waged for oil, it said. Decisions about international oil companies doing business in Iraq should be made by Iraqis, wrote the authors, Patrick Clawson, David Makovsky and Matthew Levitt.

" 'America's endeavor in Iraq will ultimately fail if the United States attempts to remake Iraq in its own image,' the report said. The United States must make a long-term commitment or risk a setback that would 'impede all our other Middle East endeavors for many years to come.'. . .

"The institute's approach, edited by former Middle East negotiator Dennis Ross, contends that authoritarian governments in the region pose a greater threat to U.S. interests than would an effort to spread liberal democracy and free-market economics. . . ."

(The Washington Post, April 9, 2003)

"America's top Middle East diplomat, Dennis Ross, will join the Washington Institute for Near East Policy think tank after he steps down as US special

Middle East envoy this month, sources close to Ross told *The Jerusalem Post.*

"The institute, a prominent educational foundation in Washington that carries out scholarly research on the Middle East, plans to make the announcement on Tuesday. . . ."

(The Jerusalem Post [Jerusalem, Israel], January 14, 2001)

Washington Legal Foundation

Established in 1977

DIRECTOR

Daniel J. Popeo, chair and general counsel. Before founding the Washington Legal Foundation (WLF) in 1977, Popeo was a federal trial attorney for the Interior Department. Formerly he was on the staff of the U.S. Attorney General and on the White House legal staff under Presidents Nixon and Ford.

BOARD OF DIRECTORS

Dick Thornburgh, chair; Kirkpatrick & Lockhart LLP, Washington, DC

Frank J. Fahrenkopf Jr., chair emeritus; Hogan & Hartson LLP., Washington, DC

Ernest Gellhorn, chair emeritus; George Mason University Foundation Professor of Law, Washington, DC

Richard K. Willard, chair emeritus; senior vice president, and general counsel, Gillette Co.

Joseph A. Artabane; Artabane & Belden, P.C., Washington, DC

Mary Azcuenaga; Heller Ehrman White & McAuliffe, Washington, DC

Thomas E. Baker; Florida International College of Law, Miami, FL

Haley Barbour; governor of Mississippi, Jackson, MS

Randy E. Barnett; professor, Boston University School of Law, Boston, MA

Thomas Hale Boggs Jr.; Patton Boggs LLP, Washington, DC

Gary B. Born; Wilmer, Cutler & Pickering, London, England

M. Jane Brady; attorney general, State of Delaware, Dover, DE

Michael K. Brown; Reed Smith, Los Angeles, California

James H. Burnley IV; Venable LLP, Washington, DC

Arnold Burns; Arnhold & S. Bleichroeder, Inc., New York, NY

Tom Campbell; dean, Haas School of Business, University of California at Berkeley, CA

Michael A. Carvin; Jones Day, Washington, DC

Alan F. Coffey Jr.; McLean, VA

Charles Cooper; Cooper & Kirk, Washington, DC

Joseph E. diGenova; diGenova & Toensing, Washington, DC

William A. Donohue; New York, New York

Richard Duesenberg; former senior vice president and general counsel, Monsanto Co., St. Louis, MO

Harold Furtchgott-Roth; American Enterprise Institute, Washington, DC

Kenneth S. Geller; Mayer, Brown, Rowe & Maw, Washington, DC

Stuart M. Gerson; Epstein Becker & Green, P.C., Washington, DC

CONTACT INFORMATION

2009 Massachusetts Avenue, NW, Washington, DC 20036
Phone: (202) 588-0302 • *Fax:* (202) 588-0386
General E-mail: info@wlf.org • *Web site:* www.wlf.org

Communications Director: Glenn Lammi, chief counsel, Legal Studies Division (202) 588-0302 • glammi@wlf.org
Human Resources Director: None

PURPOSE: The Washington Legal Foundation (WLF) defends and promotes the principles of free enterprise and individual rights through an effective combination of precedent-setting litigation; publishes in seven free-standing, distinct formats; and conducts extensive communications and educational outreach.

CURRENT CONCERNS: Administrative law • Business civil liberties • Civil justice reform • Class action reform • Commercial free speech • Constitutional law • Environmental law • Food and drug law • National security and defense • Product liability • Property rights law • Punitive damages

METHOD OF OPERATION: Advertisements • Direct action • Educational foundation • Internet (Web site) • Internships • Legal assistance • Legislative/regulatory monitoring (federal and state) • Litigation • Local/municipal affairs • Media outreach • Participation in regulatory proceedings (federal and state) • Research • Speakers program

Effectiveness and Political Orientation

"The US Supreme Court heard arguments yesterday in what could prove a landmark antitrust case involving two telecommunications giants and their duty to help each other compete in providing telephone service. The case arises out of the much-disputed Telecommunications Act of 1996, which imposed duties on monopoly carriers to share their facilities at discounted rates with competitors. Because it is being brought as an antitrust suit, however, it could have implications far beyond the telecom industry.

"In a 'friend of the court' brief, the US government said it could affect 'the entire national economy.' The court is being asked to decide whether a lawsuit can proceed against Verizon over charges that it refused to give rival AT&T access to its local telephone network in New York, as required under the Telecoms Act. AT&T and Verizon had settled that dispute; but now Curtis Trinko, a law firm that is one of AT&T's customers, is suing on behalf of itself and other customers who claim service suffered because of Verizon's actions.

" 'This has the potential to be a landmark antitrust opinion,' says Stephen Bradbury of Kirkland & Ellis, who wrote a brief on the case for the Washington Legal Foundation, a think-tank. The case could be decided on several different grounds, almost all of which could have broad implications. The jus-

SCOPE

Members: None
Branches/chapters: None
Affiliates: None

STAFF

18 total—11 full-time professional; 7 full-time support; plus 4 part-time; 3 interns

TAX STATUS

501(c)(3)

tices could decide that customers, such as Mr Trinko's law firm, are not allowed to sue under the antitrust laws because they are only indirectly harmed by the actions of a monopolist like Verizon. The justices spent most of their time yesterday examining this issue."

(*Financial Times* [London, England], October 15, 2003)

"An advocacy group for terminally ill patients sued the Food and Drug Administration in U.S. District Court yesterday in an attempt to get more experimental anti-cancer drugs into the hands of people who want to try promising new remedies. The Abigail Alliance for Better Access to Developmental Drugs, based in Arlington, sued the FDA and Department of Health and Human Services, arguing that the government's slow approval process for drugs violates the constitutional rights of people who are not responding to approved drugs and are expected to die.

"Alliance founder Frank Burroughs said that the average length of time it takes the agency to approve such drugs—6.9 years—is too long, and drug companies make room for only a tiny fraction of patients in their clinical trials when seeking drug approval. The group is named after his daughter Abigail, who died of head and neck cancer two years ago at the age of 21. She had been trying to get two experimental drugs, Erbitux and Iressa, during her illness. 'We're trying to solve the problem that Abigail had and that hundreds of thousands of people have: They run out of options to save their own lives,' said Burroughs. An FDA spokesperson said the agency had not yet seen the suit and could not comment until reviewing it.

"The complaint, filed by the Washington Legal Foundation on behalf of the Alliance, says FDA policy violates patients' rights to privacy and liberty. The lawsuit also enumerates the struggle of four Alliance patients who were urged by their physicians to try experimental drugs because traditional drugs and remedies were not working. None of the four could get into the drug companies' clinical trials."

(*The Washington Post*, July 29, 2003)

"In a ruling that will protect more than $200 million a year in legal aid for the poor, a divided Supreme Court sharply limited yesterday the right of legal clients to collect interest earned on money they leave in escrow with their lawyers. The 5–4 decision upheld laws now in effect in all 50 states that take money deposited with lawyers to pay for fees or other legal costs and pool those funds in a bank account that earns interest. The earnings are then used to finance legal aid for individuals who cannot afford their own counsel.

"The accrued interest, which exceeds $200 million a year nationwide, has grown in importance, because conservative lawmakers in Congress have succeeded in repeated attacks on direct government funding of legal aid. A conservative legal advocacy group, the Washington Legal Foundation, has been campaigning for years to force states to pay to legal clients the interest earned on their pooled funds left with lawyers. The court ruled five years ago that the interest was clients' private property, but it did not settle whether the state had to pay compensation to offset the transfer of that interest to legal aid organizations. The new decision said that compensation is not required."

(*The Boston Globe*, March 27, 2003)

"A 1993 EPA report saying second-hand tobacco smoke causes cancer was upheld by a federal appeals court in Richmond yesterday. A lower court had

FINANCES
Budget: 2004—4.5 million;
2003—$4 million; 2002—$4 million

FUNDING SOURCES
Foundation grants, 42%; corporate donations, 37%; individual donations, 15%;
investments, 6%

PAC
None

EMPLOYMENT
Postings are available at www.wlf.org
/Resources/Employment/. Letters of
interest and resumes can be e-mailed to
administration@wlf.org or sent to Constance
C. Larcher, president and executive director,
Washington Legal Foundation, 2009 Massa-
chusetts Avenue, NW, Washington, DC 20036.

INTERNSHIPS
Paid and unpaid internships are available.
Internship opportunities at the WLF "expose
the student to a broad range of legal and policy issues, enhance research, writing and networking skills, and offer the benefits of
working closely with supervisors in a small,
collegial office. Applicants should be ambitious self-starters with excellent research,
writing and communication skills, and an interest in the intersection between law and public
policy." All available internships are posted at
http://www.wlf.org/Resources/Employment/.
Letters of interest, resumes, and current writing samples should be sent to Constance C.
Larcher, president and executive director.

NEWSLETTERS
None

PUBLICATIONS
The following is a sample list of publications:
*Altering Patent Suit Proof Burden Would Chill
    Innovation*
*Better Late Than Sorry: Medicare Reform
    Ushers in New Rules on Generic Drugs*
*Coming to Terms with America's Criminal
    Alien Crisis*
*Deciding the Rules for Detainees: Wars Are
    Not Criminal Prosecutions*
*Engineering Legal Risk Management into
    Agricultural Biotechnology*
*"Informal" EPA Waste Regulation Treads on
    Due Process Protections*
*Lawyers, Other Corporate Advisers Face
    Exposure to Securities Claims*
*New State Law Permits Private Bounty Hunter
    Suits Against California Employers*
*Petitions Seek Investigations of Asbestos
    Plaintiff Recruitment*
*Self-Evaluative Privilege Would Benefit
    Insurers and Their Customers*
*The Seven Myths of Highly Effective Plaintiffs'
    Lawyers*

CONFERENCES
Media press briefings, Washington, DC
    (irregular)

invalidated the report. But the three-judge panel of the 4th U.S. Circuit Court of Appeals that made yesterday's ruling in the long-running case gave the Big Tobacco plaintiffs 30 days to file an appeal to the U.S. Supreme Court. Paul Kamenar, senior executive counsel for the Washington Legal Foundation, which filed a brief on the side of the tobacco companies, said the opinion finds that the EPA report was not the type of government agency action that any court can review.

"Other agencies have imposed restrictions on indoor smoking based in part on the report, Kamenar said, but 'the report itself does not impose any legal obligations on anyone.' If it did, the courts might have standing to review it in a legal action. 'I think the decision is erroneous,' said Kamenar, 'and I don't know why it took $3\frac{1}{2}$ years to render a decision.' The case started after the U.S. Environmental Protection Agency published a report, under the Radon Gas and Indoor Air Quality Research Act, that classified environmental tobacco smoke as a known human carcinogen. The report was formally issued in January 1993. . . ."

(*Richmond Times Dispatch* [Virginia], December 12, 2002)

"A Georgia foundation that hands out about $5 million a year to legal programs that help the poor could be in jeopardy because of a case considered Monday by the U.S. Supreme Court. The court heard arguments about whether states can allow the short-term interest earned on escrow accounts used by lawyers to be used to help pay for legal services for the poor. The accounts, known as IOLTAs, are set up to handle law clients' real estate transactions and other deals. Lawyers say it is cheaper and easier to combine money in large trust accounts than to set up individual accounts for each client.

"About $160 million nationwide is collected each year. In Georgia, the IOLTA money is administered by the Georgia Bar Foundation, which gave out $5.1 million in grants during its last fiscal year. A conservative public interest law firm, the Washington Legal Foundation, has been challenging the funds since 1990. It won the first round at the Supreme Court in 1998, with a 5–4 ruling that the interest earned from those IOLTA trust accounts are the private property of the clients.

"In this latest challenge in a case out of Washington state, justices are being asked to decide whether the states' use of the money violates the Fifth Amendment, which says property shall not be taken for public use without fair compensation. 'I'm very concerned about this attack on IOLTA because thousands of Georgians are depending on IOLTA dollars for help,' the foundation's executive director, C. Len Horton, said in an interview Monday. 'A lot of this money makes a significant impact on very serious problems.'"

(*The Atlanta Journal-Constitution,* December 10, 2002)

Weidenbaum Center

Established in 1975

DIRECTOR

Steven S. Smith, director. Smith is the Kate M. Gregg professor of social sciences and professor of political science at Washington University. He has worked on Capitol Hill in several capacities and has served as a senior fellow at the Brookings Institution. He has authored or coauthored six books on congressional politics and recently a book on the formation of the Russian State Duma. He received his Ph.D. from the University of Minnesota in 1980.

BOARD OF DIRECTORS

Steven S. Smith, director

Murray Weidenbaum, honorary chair; Mallinckrodt Distinguished University Professor, Washington University, St. Louis, MO

Gloria Lucy; assistant director, Washington University, St. Louis, MO

Richard J. Mahoney; distinguished executive in residence, Washington University, St. Louis, MO

Russell Roberts; director, Weidenbaum Center Media Retreat, Washington University, St. Louis, MO

Paul Rothstein; associate director; Associate professor of economics, Washington University, St. Louis, MO

Melinda Warren; director, Weidenbaum Center Forum, Washington University, St. Louis, MO

SCOPE

Members: None
Branches/chapters: None
Affiliates: None

STAFF

9 total—plus interns and adjunct scholars

TAX STATUS

501(c)(3)

FINANCES

Declined to comment

FUNDING SOURCES

Corporate donations, 31%; foundation grants, 18%; individual donations, 10%; other 41%

PAC

None

EMPLOYMENT

Information unavailable

INTERNSHIPS

Information unavailable

CONTACT INFORMATION

Campus Box 1027, Washington University, St. Louis, MO 63130-4899
Phone: (314) 935-5630 • *Fax:* (314) 935-5688
General E-mail: moseley@wc.wustl.edu • *Web site:* wc.wustl.edu

Communications Director: None
Human Resources Director: None

PURPOSE: "The Weidenbaum Center at Washington University in St. Louis supports scholarly research, public affairs programs, and other activities in the fields of economics, government, and public policy."

CURRENT CONCERNS: City and local government • Education • Global competition • Management issues • Regulatory and environmental tax policy

METHOD OF OPERATION: Conferences/seminars • Congressional testimony • Internet (Web site) • Internships • Media outreach • Participation in regulatory proceedings (federal) • Research • Scholarships • Speakers program

Effectiveness and Political Orientation

"Are you more or less free in your economic life than you were 20 years ago? The question is not trivial because economic freedom is highly correlated with real per capita income and is a necessary component of fundamental liberty.

"Government taxing, spending and regulating erode economic freedom. There are those who argue that, at least in the United States, total government taxing and spending has not grown as a share of gross domestic product [GDP] over the last 40 years [it has fluctuated between approximately 28 percent and 33 percent of GDP], and so we need not worry. . . . Unfortunately, governments in almost all countries are taxing and spending well above the growth and general welfare maximizing rates.

"Even more disturbing is the fact government regulation is growing rapidly in virtually every country. A recent study by the Mercatus Institute of George Mason University and the Weidenbaum Center at the Washington University in St. Louis found direct federal government regulatory spending had grown to $30.1 billion in 2002, but the total cost of regulations on the economy is estimated to be $843 billion (or almost a third of direct federal outlays)."

(The Washington Times, September 26, 2003)

"Voters get one choice, take it or leave it. Ballot-box stuffing is widespread. Ballots aren't secret, and vote totals may not be disclosed for weeks. While that may sound like a horror story from a Third World dictatorship, it's also the way elections work today in corporate America. But the Securities and Exchange Commission is studying changes that may bring a bigger dose of democracy to the boardroom.

"Some big pension funds and other shareholder advocates say that investors should have the right to nominate candidates for the board of directors, without going through an expensive proxy fight. It would be simple, they say, for companies to list shareholders' nominees on the ballot right beside the candidates chosen by the board's nominating committee. Companies like ExxonMobil and Intel don't like that idea. They told the SEC that the process would become unwieldy and that special-interest groups would use board elections as a soapbox to preach about labor or environmental issues.

" 'The worry is that it will scare off a lot of good people who don't want to engage in a campaign,' said Murray Weidenbaum, founder of the Weidenbaum Center at Washington University. 'We're describing a more politicized corporate governance process.' "

(*St. Louis Post-Dispatch,* June 29, 2003)

"Harried taxpayers scrambling to meet today's (Tuesday, April 15) filing deadline can expect to hear a sympathetic message from President Bush as he attempts to exploit their frustrations to advance his own political agenda. Executing a quick pivot from the war in Iraq, Bush plans to use the White House Rose Garden as the setting to pitch his tax-cut plan at a moment when Americans are likely to be the most fed up with paying their annual levy to the federal taxman. . . .

"With many economists arguing that the Bush Administration is running short on time to accelerate the economy's growth rate, the president is redoubling his efforts to convince voters that his 10 year, $726 billion tax cut plan is the right tonic for reversing a net erosion in job creation that has occurred on his watch. . . .

"Aided by the GOP's slender majorities in both the House and Senate, the administration strategy may involve an attempt to eke out more votes from conservative Democrats in districts and states carried by Bush in 2000. Bush himself apparently will lend a hand in the launching the grass-roots campaign. On Wednesday, he plans to visit a Boeing factory in St. Louis to talk about the economy and his budget in addition to the war's progress in Iraq. In contrast to his first year in office when he traveled the country frequently to tout his tax-cutting blueprint for the White House, Bush has in recent months remained largely focused on the war.

"That may be about to change. 'He is risk-averse at this stage,' said Steve Smith, director of the Weidenbaum Center on the Economy, Government and Public Policy at St. Louis' Washington University. 'Given his father's experience he knows that military victory doesn't guarantee electoral success.' "

(*Copley News Service,* April 14, 2003)

"The United States has deployed more than 1,000 warplanes, hundreds of tanks and thousands of bombs to fight the war in Iraq. The navy is ordering more Tomahawk cruise missiles. Military equipment is the only category of durable goods orders that's rising. The benefit to the economy? Modest at best, economists say. The main reason: The U.S. economy is much larger now than during past wars, when a surge in defence spending made a difference. The U.S. also entered the Iraq conflict well-stocked with hardware. Technology now allows attacks from a greater distance, reducing weapon loss and the need for replacement gear.

"In short, the Iraq war isn't spurring an expansion of the U.S. industrial base to meet military needs. 'Today's situation is fundamentally different,' said Murray Weidenbaum, a former assistant Treasury secretary and former chair-

man of former president Ronald Reagan's Council of Economic Advisers. The Second World War, the Korean War and the Vietnam War, by contrast, 'had a tremendous economic impact,' said Mr. Weidenbaum, who is now honorary chairman of the Weidenbaum Center at Washington University in St. Louis."
(*Ottawa Citizen* [Canada], April 5, 2003)

"In the 1980s, the fledgling shareholder-rights movement crusaded against entrenched executives who were concerned only with preserving their jobs. The company answer was to pay managers with stock options. The theory: The bosses would do well only if shareholders did well. But an options-enriched executive isn't necessarily an enlightened one. Instead of building shareholder wealth over the long run, the stock-options system seems to encourage executives to pump up the stock price by any means possible, for at least as long as it takes the executive to cash in.

"It's naive to assume that shareholders and executives always are playing on the same team. Each option that's issued to an executive dilutes the ownership interest of other shareholders. A survey by Mercer Human Resource Consulting shows that the overhang of existing options amounts to 15 percent of total company shares. Options have gotten out of hand partly because companies don't have to show them as expenses in financial statements. 'It's like off-budget items for the government,' said Murray Weidenbaum, economist and founder of the Weidenbaum Center at Washington University. 'If it's off-budget, you don't pay as much attention to it.'

"Weidenbaum, who has served on several corporate boards over the last three decades, says that options can be a good motivator but that boards have been too generous. He says companies should have to calculate the cost of options and show it on the income statement. 'It's a message to the board that this is not play money; this is serious money.'"
(*St. Louis Post-Dispatch,* July 3, 2002)

"The days are long gone, thank goodness, when being on a corporate board was all about belonging to the right clubs and currying favor with the chief executive. At most companies today, directors take their responsibilities seriously, poring over audit reports, questioning management and demanding changes when anything is amiss. But in too many crises, from Enron Corp. to Adelphia Communications Corp., the board has been asleep at the switch or far too close to management.

"Now the New York Stock Exchange has proposed a set of rules that should make boardrooms far less clubby. The rules would require boards to have a majority of independent directors, would put independent directors in charge of selecting new board members and would let shareholders vote on all stock-option plans. . . .

"The NYSE rules won't start for two years, but quite a few companies might have to revamp their boards to comply if the reforms are enforced. At St. Louis' Stifel Financial Corp., for example, four of 11 directors are insiders, one is affiliated with the company's law firm and two work for Gateway Venture Partners, in which Stifel is an investor. . . . Murray Weidenbaum, economist and founder of the Weidenbaum Center at Washington University, has served on various corporate boards. He likes the proposed rules and suggests that U.S. companies adopt one more idea, this one from Britain. There, he said, most boards are led by an independent director, not by the chief executive."
(*Ventura County Star* [California], June 13, 2002)

The Wilderness Society

Established in 1935

DIRECTOR

William H. Meadows III, president. Before joining The Wilderness Society in 1996, Meadows was director of the Sierra Club's Centennial Campaign. He also served as vice chair of Sierra Club's Tennessee chapter and was on the board of the Tennessee Environmental Council. Meadows has extensive experience in higher education and has been Vanderbilt University's executive director of alumni relations, Sweet Briar College's vice president for college relations, and the district director of the Council for Advancement and Support of Education. He received his B.A. and M.Ed. from Vanderbilt University.

BOARD OF DIRECTORS

Rebecca L. Rom, chair
Theodore Roosevelt IV, vice chair
Brenda S. Davis, vice chair
David Bonderman, treasurer
Doug Walker, secretary

SCOPE

Members: 247,000 members and supporters
Branches/chapters: Anchorage, AK; Seattle, WA; San Francisco, CA; Boise, ID; Bozeman, MT; Denver, CO; Boston, MA; Atlanta, GA; and The Wilderness Support Center-Durango, CO
Affiliates: None

STAFF

138 total

TAX STATUS

501(c)(3)

FINANCES

Budget: 2004—$20 million

FUNDING SOURCES

Foundation grants, 9%; individuals, 70%; bequests, 13%; miscellaneous, 8%

PAC

None

EMPLOYMENT

Potential applicants can learn about job openings with The Wilderness Society through its web site, www.wilderness.org. This organization offers positions for economists, ecologists, writers, lawyers, accountants, fundraisers, and others. Applicants should send resumes and other materials for employment to Kelly White, director of human resources, 1615 M Street, NW, Washington, DC 20037. No phone calls please. Fax: (202) 454-2546. E-mail: kelly_white@tws.org.

CONTACT INFORMATION

1615 M Street, NW, Washington, DC 20036
Phone: (202) 833-2300 • *Fax:* (202) 429-3958 or (202) 429-8443
General E-mail: member@tws.org • *Web site:* www.wilderness.org

Communications Director: Betsy Garside
(202) 429-2626 • betsy_garside@tws.org
Human Resources Director: Kelly White
(202) 429-8447 • kelly_white@tws.org

PURPOSE: The Wilderness Society (TWS) works to protect America's wilderness and to develop a national network of wild lands through public education, scientific analysis and advocacy. The goal of TWS is to ensure that future generations will enjoy the clean air and water, wildlife, natural beauty, opportunities for recreation and spiritual renewal that pristine forests, rivers, deserts and mountains provide.

CURRENT CONCERNS: America's national monuments • Arctic National Wildlife Refuge • Land and water conservation • National forests/roadless area protection • Off-road vehicle damage control • Oil and gas drilling in the Rockies • Wilderness • Wildfire policy

METHOD OF OPERATION: Awards program • Coalition forming • Conferences/seminars • Congressional testimony • Demonstrations • Films/videos/audiotapes • Grassroots organizing • Information clearinghouse • Internet (Web site) • Legislative/regulatory monitoring (federal and state) • Litigation • Lobbying (federal and grassroots) • Media outreach • Polling • Remote sensing • Research

Effectiveness and Political Orientation

"Environmental groups sued yesterday to block the Bush administration from opening millions more acres in the National Petroleum Reserve in Alaska to oil and natural gas drilling.

"The Interior Department last month finalized a plan to make the vast majority of an 8.8 million-acre portion in the northwest area of the reserve available for drilling.

"However, a coalition of groups—including the National Audubon Society, Wilderness Society, Natural Resources Defense Council, Alaska Wilderness League and Sierra Club—filed a lawsuit in federal district court in Alaska to stop the drilling.

"The groups said the administration ignored several federal laws intended to protect key wildlife areas in the reserve for polar bears, caribou, wolves, grizzly bears and migrating birds, and did not adequately study the likely harm that drilling will cause."

(The Washington Post, February 18, 2004)

INTERNSHIPS
Internship opportunities with The Wilderness Society can be found on the Web site: www.wilderness.org. Positions are both paid and unpaid. Internships can last up to 6 months; 37.5 hours per week are required. Internship areas include development; communications; public policy; mid-Atlantic program; four corners, and off-road vehicles. The internship coordinator at TWS is Louise Tucker, intern coordinator, 1615 M Street, NW, Washington, DC 20036. Phone: (202) 429-2665. Fax: (202) 429-3945. E-mail: louise_tucker@tws.org.

NEWSLETTERS
America's Wilderness (three times per year)
Wilderness Magazine (annual)

PUBLICATIONS
Alaska National Interest Lands Conservation Act
America's Bounty: Our National Lands
Broken Promises: Oil Development in Alaska
Economic Values of Protecting Roadless Areas in the United States
Land Ethic Toolbox
Nature's Services in Eastern Forests
Restoring Balance to Wildland Fire Policy
Virginia's Mountain Treasures
Wildlands for Wildlife

CONFERENCES
None

"Colorado's wildfire season is creeping up, and a diverse group of conservationists, federal scientists and community officials want the public to understand how it affects lives and pocketbooks.

"So they are hosting a forum, 'What Every Westerner Should Know About Wildfire,' aimed not only at those who live on the outskirts of national forests but also at the shop owner and suburbanites, said Lisa Smith, of the Southern Rockies Conservation Alliance.

"'Definitely this is something happening in everyone's backyard,' said Smith.

"Panelists include the Sierra Club's Ramon Ajero; Merrill Kaufmann of the U.S. Forest Service, Rocky Mountain Research Station; Dan Kashian, postdoctoral fellow at Colorado State University; Tony Cheng, assistant professor at Colorado State University; Tom Fry, wildland fire program coordinator with The Wilderness Society; Mike Babler, district forester with the Colorado State Forest Service; and Tony Simons, Larimer County wildfire safety specialist. . . ."

(*The Denver Post,* February 17, 2004)

"A federal appeals court said Tuesday that national wildlife rules bar the stocking of salmon in a protected Alaskan lake, even if little harm comes from the activity.

"For nearly 20 years, the Alaska Department of Fish and Game has incubated salmon eggs and released millions of young fish into the Tustumena Lake in the Kenai refuge, a protected wildlife area.

"The Wilderness Society and the Alaska Center for the Environment sued over the stocking, saying it violated the U.S. Wilderness Act, which bars commercial activity in wildlife areas. The 9th Circuit Court of Appeals based in San Francisco agreed and voted 11 to 0 to reverse a lower court ruling.

"The en banc panel of judges found that there could be worse things than stocking fish in a lake, but still held it was not permissible under the Wilderness Act. . . ."

(*The Los Angeles Times,* December 31, 2003)

"Natural-gas supplies are tight. The solution: drill more, or conserve more?

"Energy officials, politicians and environmentalists debated the issue Monday as a congressional task force sought answers at a hearing in Golden.

"Natural-gas prices have more than doubled in the past year, and speakers agreed that the hike is caused by flat production and low supplies.

"But agreement ended there.

"The hot-button issues of access to federal lands, government review of drilling permits and environmental impact of gas production triggered heated exchanges between a Wilderness Society official and two Republican members of Congress.

"Peter Morton, a resource economist with the Wilderness Society, said natural gas demand has been flat over the past six years. Morton added that adequate amounts of gas can be produced without expediting new drilling permits on federal lands.

"'Lack of access is not a problem,' he said. 'Industry has plenty of access to public land—perhaps too much.'

"Morton testified that the nation's energy demand can be met with less gas drilling, more use of renewable energy, increased conservation and efficiency, and importation of cheaper natural gas from overseas.

"Rep. Barbara Cubin, R-Wyo., peppered Morton with questions about his testimony, particularly his suggestions for less domestic drilling and more imports.

" 'We have the strongest environmental protections in the world,' Cubin said. 'But you would rather import energy from countries where there are no environmental protections?'

"Rep. C. L. 'Butch' Otter, R-Idaho, criticized Morton for suggesting that Americans should lessen their demand for natural gas with conservation. . . ."

(*The Denver Post,* August 26, 2003)

"The Bush administration has directed federal land managers to begin removing obstacles to oil and gas development in parts of five Rocky Mountain states.

"Directives issued last week to state directors of the Bureau of Land Management give them the tools to put into effect the administration's long-standing goal of opening the Rocky Mountain West to increased oil and gas development. Offices in Colorado, Montana, New Mexico, Utah and Wyoming, have until Dec. 31 to decide on removing the limits.

" 'Our overall objective is to ensure the timely development of these critical energy resources in an environmentally sound manner,' the director of the bureau, Kathleen Clarke, said in a statement.

"Environmentalists say the policies are another step in White House efforts to give energy development priority over conservation.

" 'This policy shifts the land management equation in favor of drilling and automatically assumes that oil and gas production is the top value of public lands,' said Dr. Pete Morton, a resource economist with the Wilderness Society. . . ."

(*The New York Times,* August 9, 2003)

"You couldn't tell the protesters from the dinner guests outside the Women's University Club Monday night. There were no shouted slogans, no rude cat calls, no hand-painted signs. It was the politest, most civil, best-dressed demonstration in years.

"Members of the Sierra Club and the Wilderness Society stood in pairs on the Sixth Avenue sidewalk. They were handing out greeting-card-sized 'ballots.'

"Target of the protest was the dinner's featured speaker, newly minted Alaska Sen. Lisa Murkowski, 45. She was appointed last December by her father, newly elected Alaska Gov. Frank Murkowski, to serve his unexpired Senate term. The Murkowskis have taken heat for this nepotism, but pols say the new Republican senator is bright, capable and refreshingly moderate.

"Except for one thing: Sen. Murkowski defends drilling for oil in the Arctic National Wildlife Refuge. Discarding a prepared speech, Murkowski approached the issue head-on during the dinner, sponsored by the University of Washington's Center for Women & Democracy. . . .

"At the end of the evening, demonstrators dispersed. They'd spoken to Murkowski when she arrived, asking her to follow the lead of Washington's senators and oppose drilling in the preserve.

"Did the speech or the protest change anyone's mind? Probably not. But both sides showed class. . . ."

(*The Seattle Times,* April 23, 2003)

Women's Campaign Fund

Established in 1974

DIRECTOR

Susan Medalie, executive director. Prior to becoming executive director at WCF, Medalie served as deputy finance director of a presidential campaign, deputy director of the U.S. Holocaust Memorial Council, assistant dean at the George Washington National Law Center, and a consultant. She has a B.A. from Sarah Lawrence, a M.A. from George Washington University, and a J.D. from American University Law School.

BOARD OF DIRECTORS

Terese Colling, co-chair; Colling, Murphy, Swift, Hynes, & Selfridge, Washington, DC
Doreen Frasca, co-chair; president, Frasca and Associates, New York, NY

SCOPE

Members: None
Branches/chapters: None
Affiliates: Women's Campaign Research Fund

STAFF

6 total—plus 3 interns

TAX STATUS

501(c)(4)

FINANCES

Declined to comment

FUNDING SOURCES

Individual contributions, 75%; corporate and PAC donations, 25%

PAC

Women's Campaign Fund Inc.

PAC CONTRIBUTIONS 2002

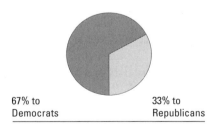

67% to Democrats

33% to Republicans

EMPLOYMENT

Information unavailable

INTERNSHIPS

Information unavailable

NEWSLETTERS

Women's Campaign Fund Newsletter
(irregular)

CONTACT INFORMATION

734 15th Street, NW, Suite 500, Washington, DC 20005
Phone: (202) 393-8164
Toll-free: (800) 446-8170 • *Fax:* (202) 393-0649
General E-mail: deputy@wcfonline.org • *Web site:* www.wcfonline.org

Communications Director: None
Human Resources Director: None

PURPOSE: The goal of the Women's Campaign Fund is to "provide prochoice women of all parties with the resources they need to win—not just money, but strategic consulting, fundraising, networking, field campaigning and get-out-the-vote assistance."

CURRENT CONCERNS: Electing prochoice women to political office • Financial and technical campaign support • Preserving access to reproductive choice

METHOD OF OPERATION: Assistance for campaigns • Campaign contributions • Coalition forming • Conferences/seminars • Electoral politics • Information clearinghouse • Internet (e-mail alerts and Web site) • Internships • Media outreach • Speakers program • Technical assistance and training

Effectiveness and Political Orientation

"Excerpts from a Monitor breakfast on unmarried women voters: . . . Celinda Lake is president of Lake Snell Perry, a national political research firm. She holds an undergraduate degree from Smith College, and a masters in political science and survey research from the University of Michigan. She has served as political director of the Women's Campaign Fund and Research Director at the Institute for Social Research in Ann Arbor. . . .

"On impact if unmarried women voted at the same rate as the rest of [voters in a given] state: (Lake) 'If you look at unmarried women. . . . you can see the tremendous numbers of these women in key states like 184,000 in Ohio, 125,000 in Michigan, 167,000 in Pennsylvania, 202,000 in Florida. These women exist in the battleground states.' On key concerns of unmarried women voters: (Lake) 'Low income . . . is a very marked characteristic of this group. Not surprisingly then, when you look at their top concerns it is money, money, money. Concern about rising costs, concern about health care, concern about not being able to afford retirement, not being able to afford a college education. What is interesting is that these economic concerns start even younger among unmarried women. So among unmarried women they are starting to worry dramatically about retirement even at the age of 30 where among married women it usually tends to be 45 or older before you really start to worry about retirement.'

"On why unmarried women voters have not been targeted before: (Lake) 'There has been this sense that they don't all live in one neighborhood, you

PUBLICATIONS
None

CONFERENCES
Parties of Your Choice, twice a year in Washington, DC, and New York

can't spot them right away. And I think politicians do tend to target themselves. And politicians also tend to target who is already voting.'"
(*Christian Science Monitor,* December 17, 2003)

"No woman has won the presidency—or vice presidency, for that matter—but the election of Rep. Nancy Pelosi, California Democrat, as the party's House leader is being cheered as an 'about time.' Susan Medalie, executive director of the Women's Campaign Fund, says Mrs. Pelosi's election as Democratic minority leader, replacing Rep. Richard A. Gephardt of Missouri, is excellent news for the women of this country and for citizens nationwide [earlier this fall, Mrs. Pelosi was honored with WCF's Woman of the Year Award].

"After this month's midterm election, women will make up 13 percent of the Senate and 13 percent of the House. There also will be six women governors for the first time. . . ."
(*The Washington Times,* November 18, 2002)

"Michigan Democrat John Dingell had not faced a serious primary challenger since being elected to Congress in 1955. It is why Dingell's struggle this summer to beat fellow incumbent Lynn Rivers seemed so odd. Redistricting forced Dingell and Rivers into a primary fight, a skirmish fueled by EMILY's List, the fund-raising organization devoted to helping Democratic women who favor abortion rights. The group not only endorsed Rivers but also funded ads attacking Dingell.

"Dingell won anyway, by a margin of 18 percentage points. But EMILY's List's pointed attacks on the veteran congressman and on other prominent Democratic men this year prompted some party insiders to fume about the group's rough tactics. 'There's nothing new in this,' scoffs Ellen Malcolm, president and founder of EMILY's List, which has been backing Democratic women for 17 years. 'What is different is that we ran against [former Clinton aide] Rahm Emanuel and John Dingell, and they both have a lot of friends in Washington.'. . .

"Democrats are concerned that the group's attacks will weaken Democratic candidates and give Republicans ideas. But EMILY's List isn't apologizing for playing hard. 'Our job is to bring newcomers into politics, which is the toughest job there is,' Malcolm said. 'We'll all work together in the general election. We're a major ally for Democrats in their fight to control Congress.' Susan Medalie, executive director of the Women's Campaign Fund, the 28-year-old nonpartisan pro-abortion rights fund-raising group for women, said the attacks on EMILY's List this year have been unfair because the group acted no differently from other political advocacy groups.

" 'I just think [the attacks] are wrong,' Medalie said. 'EMILY's List has a great function. They've done the best they can to help women candidates.' "
(*The Atlanta Journal-Constitution,* September 15, 2002)

"On the last Sunday in September, Rep. Pam Jochum, D-Dubuque, will bring together a small group of like-minded legislators to put on a political fund-raiser at Clarke College. But this fund-raiser will be unlike most held before. The legislators all are women, and the money they raise will be used only to help get female Democrats elected to the Iowa General Assembly. . . .

"Jochum said she's taken on the fund-raisers because she believes women can use a hand up. 'Women don't have a more difficult time fund-raising, but it is different,' Jochum said. 'Women have been raised to be "givers" rather than "takers." They don't have the comfort level yet for asking for contributions.' Women know how to raise money, Jochum said, but 'It's a different experience when you're asking for money for yourself.'. . .

"Since she went to the state house 10 years ago, the cost of campaigning has far outpaced inflation, Jochum said. While a few thousand dollars was enough then, 'Candidates today can't think about running for state house for less than $35,000.' Rep. Andra Atteberry, D-Manchester, also feels that fund raising for women is 'not more difficult, just different.' 'I don't see that people tend to give more to men than women,' Atteberry said. 'If you ask me, it's as difficult for (men) to raise money as it is for me.'. . .

"To become a floor leader, a person has to be able to attract large contributors, and Jochum's opposition to abortion puts her in conflict to national Democratic political action committees such as EMILY's List. An acronym for 'Early Money Is Like Yeast' (it helps the 'dough' rise), EMILY's List is devoted to helping elect female Democrats who support abortion rights. Women's Campaign Fund, another major PAC, is dedicated to electing Republican, Democratic and Independent women who support abortion rights, as is The National Women's Political Caucus. . . ."

(*Telegraph Herald* [Dubuque, Iowa], September 9, 2002)

"Senate Majority Leader Beverly Daggett's success as a lawmaker may be one of the reasons why Maine ranks among states with the most women serving in legislatures. Since the late 1980s, Daggett advanced from a seat in the state House of Representatives to a leadership position in the Senate. She also saw the number of women senators increase along the way, from nine the year she was elected to 15 today. 'Once you have a critical mass of women in a group, women can relate to that, as opposed to any organization that is predominantly male,' Daggett said. 'Other women see women (politicians) who are successful and they begin to say, 'I can do that, too.'"

"Maine ranks 10th in percentage of women state legislators, according to the Center for American Women and Politics, a branch of the Eagleton Institute of Politics at Rutgers State University of New Jersey. Roughly 30 percent are women—15 of 35 in the Senate and 41 of 151 in the House. . . .

"Political experts and women candidates say Maine's 63 years with at least one woman in the U.S. Senate has contributed to a legislative body where nearly one-third of the members are women. . . .

"Susan Medalie, executive director of the Political Action Committee Women's Campaign Fund, says only California and Washington state have two women serving as their state's U.S. senators. Medalie says her PAC exists to help women starting out in politics. It has found many women start on their city councils, then run for the state legislature to gain more political experience. 'It's the way women are able to get the experience and the name recognition, then go on to run for Congress, or governor, or all the way to the president of the United States,' she said."

(*Portland Press Herald* [Maine], July 5, 2002)

World Resources Institute

Established in 1982

DIRECTOR

Jonathan Lash, president. Lash has served on or chaired the boards of many environmental and natural resources organization, including the President's Council on Sustainable Development, the National Commission on Superfund, and the Earth Council. He previously directed the environmental law and policy program of the Vermont Law School and held positions in Vermont state government. Lash's background includes work in the Peace Corps, as a federal prosecutor and as an attorney for the Natural Resources Defense Council. He received a B.A. from Harvard and an M.A. and J.D. from Catholic University.

BOARD OF DIRECTORS

William D. Ruckelshaus, chair; strategic director, Madrona Venture Group

Julia Marton-Lefèvre, vice chair; executive director, Leadership for Environment & Development International, United Kingdom

Agatha "Gay" S. Barclay; secretary-treasurer, PAVA Foundation

Frances G. Beinecke; executive director, Natural Resources Defense Council

David T. Buzzelli; retired vice president and director, Dow Chemical Co.

Deb Callahan; president, League of Conservation Voters

Leslie Dach; vice-chair, Edelman Worldwide

Michael R. Deland; chair, National Organization on Disability

Alice "Tish" F. Emerson; senior advisor, Mellon Foundation

José-Maria Figueres; managing director, Center for the Global Agenda, World Economic Forum, Costa Rica

David Gergen; professor of public service and director of the Center for Public Leadership at the Kennedy School of Government, Harvard University

John H. Gibbons; former assistant to the president for science and technology; former director, Office of Science and Technology Policy

Paul Gorman; executive director, National Religious Partnership for the Environment

James A. Harmon; former president of the Export Import Bank

Denis Hayes; president, Bullitt Foundation

Cynthia R. Helms; former chair of WorldWIDE (World Women in the Environment)

Samuel C. Johnson; chair emeritus, S.C. Johnson and Son, Inc.

Yolanda Kakabadse; president, World Conservation Union; executive president, Fundacion Futuro Latinoamericano, Ecuador

CONTACT INFORMATION

10 G Street, NE, Suite 800, Washington, DC 20002
Phone: (202) 729-7600 • *Fax:* (202) 729-7610
General E-mail: lauralee@wri.org • *Web site:* www.wri.org

Communications Director: Adlai Amor, director of media relations
(202) 729-7736 • aamor@wri.org
Human Resources Director: Vivian Fong
(202) 729-7692 • vivianf@wri.org

PURPOSE: "To move human society to live in ways that protect Earth's environment and its capacity to provide for the needs and aspirations of current and future generations."

CURRENT CONCERNS: Agriculture • Biological resources • Climate change • Coastal and marine ecosystems • Forests/grasslands/drylands • Global warming • Governance and institutions • Population • Sustainable enterprise • Water resources

METHOD OF OPERATION: Congressional testimony • International activities • Internet • Legislative/regulatory monitoring (federal) • Library/information clearinghouse (open to public by appointment) • Media outreach • Research

Effectiveness and Political Orientation

"Talks aimed at preventing a breakdown of the Montreal Protocol on the ozone layer, usually seen as the world's most successful environmental treaty, start today in Montreal. The meeting will attempt to break the deadlock over a US request to continue widespread use of methyl bromide, a powerful ozone-depleting fumigant. A conference intended to resolve the issue ended in stalemate last November.

"Failure to reach agreement could prompt the US to violate the treaty, which could deepen the rift between the US and the European Union over other environmental issues. . . . Concern about the outcome of this week's meeting has been heightened by a US request last month for some additional exemptions of methyl bromide, suggesting it was moving further away from a reasonable compromise, said David Doniger, Climate Center Policy Director at the Natural Resources Defense Council, an environmental group. Mr Doniger said that an uncompromising approach by all sides presented a 'colossal threat' to the Montreal Protocol. Greenhouse gas emissions have risen 11 percent in the 10 years since ratification of the UN framework convention on climate change, according to the World Resources Institute, the US environment group. The 10th anniversary of the treaty's ratification on Sunday prompted calls for more political commitment and international co-operation on the issue of climate change.

" 'We have not made significant progress in curbing global warming in the last decade. In fact, the latest scientific reports indicate that global warming is

SCOPE

Members: None
Branches/chapters: None
Affiliates: Network of advisors, collaborators, international fellows and partner institutions in 63 countries

STAFF

135 total—plus interns

TAX STATUS

501(c)(3)

FINANCES

Budget: 2002—$25.33 million; Revenue: 2001—$15.18 million

FUNDING SOURCES

Private foundations; governmental and inter-governmental institutions; corporations; individual donations

PAC

None

EMPLOYMENT

Postings are listed at http://joblist.wri.org/. Cover letters, and curriculum vitae or resumes should be directed to the individual or office listed in each posting. WRI only accepts resumes for current vacancies.

worsening,' said Jonathan Pershing of the WRI. 'We are quickly moving to the point where the damage will be irreversible.' "

(*Financial Times* [London, England], March 24, 2004)

"Indications Russia will reject the Kyoto pact on greenhouse gas reduction have participants at a United Nations conference worried the global treaty might never get off the ground. When organizers began planning for the conference, which begins today in Milan, many hoped Russia would have joined the protocol. The treaty, negotiated in 1997 in Kyoto, Japan, sets a target of cutting greenhouse gas emissions by eight percent below 1990 levels by 2012. . . .

"After U.S. president George W. Bush rejected the treaty's pollution reductions in 2001 as too harmful to the economy, Russia's support was needed to meet the 55-percent requirement. But in October, Russian president Vladimir Putin said the pact would fail to reverse climate change, 'even with 100 percent compliance.' His economic adviser, Andrei Illarionov, said the protocol would 'doom Russia to poverty, weakness and backwardness.' Putin later told Prime Minister Jean Chretien he does plan to ratify the treaty.

"Under the pact, if a country exceeds its emissions levels, it can be forced to cut back industrial production. Since the United States is the world's largest polluter, its refusal to join Kyoto is already 'a big drag' on the battle to fight global warming, said Jonathan Pershing, a geologist heading the delegation of the World Resources Institute, a Washington environmental think tank. A rejection by Russia will present a dilemma to countries that have embraced the treaty, participants said.

" 'There's a number of forks in the road,' Pershing said. 'Those countries who have said 'yes' go forward without a formal international treaty. But how do you do that?' Environment Minister David Anderson has said Canada will implement the pact even if Russia decides to back out."

(*The Gazette* [Montreal, Canada], December 1, 2003)

"How much do fireplaces and wood stoves contribute to global warming? What about the burning of garden waste? A. In the United States, more heat-trapping greenhouse gas is absorbed by the regrowth of forests and other plants than is released by burning wood, said Kevin Baumert, a researcher at the World Resources Institute, an environmental research group. Burning of garden waste makes a negligible contribution to the greenhouse gas burden, he added. Green plants use the greenhouse gas carbon dioxide for photosynthesis as they grow, and it is recycled to the atmosphere when they die.

"In the United States, the major greenhouse emissions are carbon dioxide from the burning of fossil fuel and methane from agriculture, Mr. Baumert said. Forest fires and deforestation in the tropics are an entirely different situation, he said. In countries like Brazil and Indonesia, emissions from deforestation are a huge source of carbon dioxide, and such emissions are even larger than carbon dioxide emissions from the burning of fossil fuel in many tropical countries.

" 'When trees are cut down there is an assumption that they will be burned or rot, with carbon dioxide emitted at some point,' Mr. Baumert said. 'It doesn't matter whether it burns in a fireplace or rots in the forest.' "

(*The New York Times,* November 18, 2003)

"World oil and gas supplies are headed for a 'production crunch' sometime between 2010 and 2020 when they cannot meet supply, because global re-

INTERNSHIPS
Internships in a variety of WRI programs are available. Postings are listed at http://joblist.wri.org/.

NEWSLETTERS
Special Bulletin (irregular)
Working Paper (irregular)

PUBLICATIONS
The following is a sample list of publications:
Aligning Commitments: Public Participation, International Decision-Making, and the Environment
Beyond Grey Pinstripes 2003: Preparing MBAs for Social and Environmental Stewardship
Corporate Accountability Movement: Lessons and Opportunities
Ecosystems and Human Well-being: A Framework for Assessment
Environmental Stories to Watch in 2004
Gaining the Air Quality and Climate Benefit for Telework
The Greenhouse Gas Protocol
Highlighting Coral Reefs in Coastal Planning and Management in Sabah, Malaysia
Journalist Guide to World Resources 2002–2004
Making Participation Work: Lessons from Civil Society Engagement in the WSSD
Mining and Critical Ecosystems: Mapping the Risks
Outcomes of Johannesburg: Assessing the World Summit on Sustainable Development
TerraViva! World Resources
What Works: Serving the Poor, Profitably
Working 9 to 5 on Climate Change: An Office Guide
World Resources 2002–2004: Decisions for the Earth: Balance, Voice, and Power

CONFERENCES
Sustainable Enterprise Summit (annual)

serves are 80 percent smaller than had been thought, new forecasts suggest. Research presented this week at the University of Uppsala in Sweden claims that oil supplies will peak soon after 2010, and gas supplies not long afterwards, making the price of petrol and other fuels rocket, with potentially disastrous economic consequences unless people have moved to alternatives to fossil fuels.

"While forecasters have always known that such a date lies ahead, they have previously put it around 2050, and estimated that there would be time to shift energy use over to renewables and other non-fossil sources. But Kjell Aleklett, one of a team of geologists who prepared the estimate, said earlier estimates that the world's entire reserve amounts to 18,000 billion barrels of oil and gas—of which about 1,000 billion has been used up so far—are 'completely unrealistic.' He, Anders Sivertsson and Colin Campbell told New Scientist magazine that less than 3,500 billion barrels of oil and gas remain in total.

"Dr James McKenzie, senior assistant on the climate change program at the World Resources Institute in Washington, DC, said: 'We won't run out of oil—but what will happen is that production will decline, and that's when all hell will break loose.' . . .

"Dr McKenzie said that on this topic the argument splits between economists and geologists: 'The economists think it will just force the price of oil up, which will mean it will become economic to extract it from all sorts of unusual places, such as tarry sands or deposits which are 90 percent rock and 10 percent oil. But the geologists say—you tell us where the deposits are and we'll find them. We've looked and we can't.'"

(*The Independent* [London, England], October 2, 2003)

"Efforts to rebuild Iraq must contend with severe pollution and other environmental problems, the results of more than two decades of war, international sanctions and mismanagement by Saddam Hussein, environmental groups said. 'Many environmental problems in Iraq are so alarming that an immediate assessment and a cleanup plan are needed urgently,' said Pekka Haavisto, chairman of a preliminary study by the U.N. Environmental Program.

"Environmentalists acknowledged the three-week war that toppled Saddam's regime did not trigger the natural catastrophe envisioned by many, including burning oil fields, demolition of dams and the use of chemical and biological weapons. Nor did battlefield maneuvers by tanks and other heavy vehicles appear to damage large areas of fragile desert and river basins. But they warned the accumulation of physical damage to Iraq's environmental infrastructure and warfare debris are major threats to public health and the nation's redevelopment.

" 'In terms of how people live from day to day, the environmental pieces are important. There are things that can be fixed cheaply and quickly by engineers,' said Jonathan Lash, president of World Resources Institute, a Washington-based advocacy group. The United Nations and other agencies are preparing to conduct field assessments in Iraq. But any inquiry would require the permission of the U.S. military administration supervising Iraq's reconstruction. Lash said despite diplomatic difficulties, the U.N. Environmental Program should evaluate Iraq. The agency has previously studied the effects of war on Afghanistan, the Balkans and Palestinian territories."

(*The Associated Press State & Local Wire,* April 24, 2003)

World Wildlife Fund (WWF)

Established in 1948

DIRECTOR

Kathryn S. Fuller, president and chief executive officer. Fuller has served as president and chief executive officer of World Wildlife Fund since 1989. Trained as a lawyer and marine ecologist, Fuller joined WWF in 1983 after heading the Wildlife and Marine Resources Section of the U.S. Justice Department. Fuller received a B.A. from Brown University and a J.D. from the University of Texas. She pursued graduate studies in marine, estuarine, and environmental science at the University of Maryland and is the recipient of several honorary degrees.

BOARD OF DIRECTORS

William K. Reilly, chair; president, and chief executive officer, Aqua International Partners, L.P., San Francisco, CA

Edward P. Bass, vice chair; chair, Fine Line, Inc., Fort Worth, TX

Kathryn S. Fuller, president

William T. Lake, treasurer; partner, Wilmer, Cutler, & Pickering, Washington, DC

Alison Richard, secretary; vice-chancellor, Cambridge University, Cambridge, UK

Nancy Abraham; senior vice president, UBS Financial Services Inc., New York, NY

Bruce E. Babbitt; Latham & Watkins, Washington, DC

Richard Blum; chair, Blum Corporate Partners, San Francisco, CA

David Bonderman; principal, general partner, and founder, Texas Pacific Group, Fort Worth, TX

Julia Carabias; Universidad Nacional Autonoma de Mexico, Mexico City, Mexico

Lavinia Currier; president, Sacharuna Foundation, The Plains, VA

Brenda S. Davis; vice president, Technical Resources, Johnson & Johnson, New Brunswick, NJ

Jared M. Diamond; professor of geography, University of California at Los Angeles, CA

Pamela Ebsworth; Bellevue, WA

Lynn A. Foster; senior vice president, Ashbridge Investment Management, New York, NY

Wolcott Henry; president, Curtis and Edith Munson Foundation, Washington, DC

Jeremy Jackson; professor of oceanography, Scripps Institution of Oceanography, La Jolla, CA

S. Curtis Johnson; president, JohnsonDiversey, Inc., Sturtevant, WI

Shelly Lazarus; chair and chief executive officer, Ogilvy & Mather Worldwide, New York, NY

Lawrence H. Linden; advisory director, Goldman Sachs, New York, NY

CONTACT INFORMATION

1250 24th Street, NW, Washington, DC 20037-1175
Phone: (202) 293-4800 • *Fax:* (202) 293-9211
General E-mail: Not available • *Web site:* www.wwfus.org

Communications Director: Phil Kavits
(202) 778-9540 • phil.kavits@wwfus.org
Human Resources Director: Information unavailable

PURPOSE: WWF is "dedicated to protecting the world's wildlife and wildlands. . . . WWF directs its conservation efforts toward three global goals: protecting endangered spaces, saving endangered species, and addressing global threats."

CURRENT CONCERNS: Agriculture and aquaculture • Climate change • Community outreach • Conservation and development • Education • Endangered habitats • Endangered species • Forests • Global threats • International environmental policy • Ocean rescue • Toxic chemicals • Tropical rain forest destruction • U.S. environmental policy • Wildlife conservation • Wildlife trade

METHOD OF OPERATION: Congressional testimony • Direct action • Films, video, audiotapes • Grantmaking • International activities • Internet (e-mail alerts and Web site) • Legislative/regulatory monitoring (federal and state) • Media outreach • Participation in regulatory proceedings (federal) • Product merchandising • Research • Training and technical assistance

Effectiveness and Political Orientation

"The Sumatran tiger is on the brink of extinction because illegal poaching and logging is destroying its natural habitat, the World Wildlife Fund and Traffic, the British-based wildlife-trade monitor, report. Only about 500 to 600 Sumatran tigers still live in the wild, and poaching is reducing the number by 50 a year. Sue Lieberman, director of the W.W.F. species program, said the tiger could be saved if Indonesia enforced bans on poaching and trade in animal parts, and if international donors helped villagers find alternative means of earning a living. Two Indonesian tigers have died out: the Bali tiger in the 1940's and the Java tiger in the 1980's."

(*The New York Times*, March 16, 2004)

"The mainland's national school curriculum is about to get a lot greener in what has been touted as a major breakthrough in education policy. The Ministry of Education has launched new guidelines making environmental education a compulsory part of the curriculum taught to some 197 million children. The guidelines were developed in co-operation with the World Wildlife Fund (WWF). Zhu Muju, deputy director of basic education at the

SCOPE

Members: 1.2 million

Branches/chapters: Offices in AK, FL, OR, and TX

Affiliates: International affiliates in more than 30 countries

STAFF

345 total—276 professional; 69 support; plus interns

TAX STATUS

501(c)(3)

FINANCES

Budget: 2003—$102.13 million
Revenue: 2002—$93.23 million

FUNDING SOURCES

Contributions, 67%; government grants and contracts, 16%; in-kind and other earned revenues, 10%; WWF Network revenues, 7%

PAC

None

EMPLOYMENT

Open positions are available at www.resourcehire.com/clients/worldwildlifefund/publicjobs/. Online submission of applications and resumes is encouraged.

INTERNSHIPS

Paid internships are available. See www.resourcehire.com/clients/worldwildlifefund/publicjobs/ for further information.

Ministry of Education, said the guidelines would 'lay the foundations for the nation's sustainable growth strategy.'

"They provide for the incorporation of 'environmental education elements' into already existing subjects on the curriculum, such as biology and geography. 'It's not a separate class,' said Ms. Zhu. 'It just wasn't practical to set up a special subject for environmental education. But we hope the guidelines will help students develop an overall awareness of environmental issues,' she said. James Harkness, chief representative of WWF China, said the guidelines aimed to emphasise not only the development of environmental knowledge, 'but also students' skills, attitudes and values, as well as their commitment to building a sustainable future.'"

(*South China Morning Post* [Hong Kong], November 3, 2003)

"Just one little piece of coral is all it takes to land you in the slammer. That's one of the messages the U.S. Fish and Wildlife Service and the World Wildlife Fund hope to get out this winter to the growing number of vacationers who are jetting home from the Caribbean with souvenirs made from coral, turtle shells and other contraband. 'It's a significant and growing problem,' says Craig Hoover of the World Wildlife Fund, which has joined with the federal agency to issue an updated guide to forbidden items. Buyer Beware, which arrives at border crossings and travel agencies this month, highlights illegal animal and plant material such as coral, turtle shells and crocodile skins that border agents increasingly are finding packed in tourist bags.

"Most of the products are banned because they come from animals that are endangered. In a few cases, the animals or animal parts pose a health risk. Agents nabbed nearly 4,000 travelers last year hauling forbidden animal and plant material from the Caribbean. A few were trying to smuggle live animals. (Seized: 105 live parrots.) They face up to a year in jail and $25,000 in fines. 'I had one man who tried to smuggle in a toucan taped on his back,' says Hoover, a former Fish and Wildlife agent. 'We also had a woman who tried to get a small monkey past us in her hair.'"

(*USA Today,* October 17, 2003)

"The label said the package shipped from Singapore contained magazines and books. But U.S. Customs inspectors decided that was a lie. When they opened it, they found 198 Fly River turtles, 25 Indian star tortoises and three Timor monitor lizards, all protected by international law. Authorities arrested Lawrence Wee Soon Chye, 38, of Singapore, whom they identified as the shipper and receiver. In July, Chye was indicted on conspiracy and smuggling charges. He pleaded guilty Sept. 25 to three violations in a plea agreement that could net him 37 months in prison when he is sentenced this year, likely in December. Chye, who remains jailed in Orlando, faced up to 15 years in prison and $750,000 in fines.

"'The courts are taking these cases a lot more seriously,' says Craig Hoover, deputy director of a World Wildlife Fund unit that monitors the animal trade. While they don't have numbers, authorities say wildlife smuggling is growing. The rewards are enough to entice those involved to take the risks associated with supplying rare animals and their remains as food, fashion and fancy pets. Tom MacKenzie, a spokesman for the U.S. Fish and Wildlife Service in Atlanta, says Chye's cache would have been worth $155,000 on the pet trade's black market. 'It's flat-out all about money,' MacKenzie says. 'We believe wildlife smuggling is No. 3 in the black market, behind drugs and arms.'"

(*Tampa Tribune* [Florida], October 14, 2003)

"During 50 years of Communist rule in former Yugoslavia, the Croatian island of Vis remained an inaccessible naval base lost in the middle of the Adriatic. The islanders eked out a living from fishing and services for the Yugoslav military. Tourism, which in today's Croatia generates about $5.5 billion in revenue a year, came much later to the island than it did elsewhere on the Adriatic coast. . . . The island has only four small hotels. The place looks more like an early 20th century fishermen's settlement. With luck, it may stay that way.

"The World Wildlife Fund (WWF) has designated Vis as one of the 10 last paradises on the Mediterranean and is taking steps to preserve its pristine beauty and wildlife, while giving locals a chance to make some money in the process. The WWF estimates that by 2020, some 350 million vacationers a year—or 22 percent of all tourists worldwide—will be flocking to the Mediterranean basin, up from the current 220 million. It also believes that Croatia is likely to become one of the leading tourist destinations in the region, and that the growth in tourism, if unchecked, may irreversibly destroy its nature.

"WWF marine biologist Paolo Guglielmi says that some parts of the Mediterranean, such as most of the Middle East and the Spanish and Italian coasts, 'are already lost forever. But we have identified 10 last paradises that are still remarkable for their biodiversity and are worth huge efforts to save,' he says. Among them are Vis and two other southern Croatian islands—Lastovo and Mljet—where tourism, although on a steady rise, has so far had a low impact on the environment. . . ."

(*The Toronto Star* [Canada], July 26, 2003)

"Newly released satellite images show that the Amazon rain forest is disappearing at an increasing rate, with about 10,000 square miles lost mainly to pasture land, soybean plantations and illegal logging in the 12-month period that ended last August. The government said on Thursday that the area represented a 40 percent rise in deforestation compared with a year earlier, when about 7,000 square miles of rain forest were lost. It was the fastest acceleration in the loss in the Amazon forest, the world's largest continuous area of rain forest, since the same 12-month period in 1994 and 1995, environmentalists said.

"'It is terribly serious,' said Luis Meneses, coordinator of the World Wildlife Fund's Amazon project in Brasilia. 'Our fear is that the period for 2002–2003 could be even worse.' The environmental group Greenpeace has warned that the rain forest could be wiped out in 80 years if deforestation rates are not slowed. Scientists say about a fifth of the Amazon has already vanished, helping to accelerate global warming. Brazil's new, left-leaning government, which has publicly embraced environmental issues, pledged to act immediately. The environment minister, Marina Silva, called the new data 'highly worrying' and promised 'emergency action,' although no specific proposals were offered.

"Despite years of lobbying, the World Wildlife Fund says that of the six states with rain forest on their territory, only one, Acre, which contains less than 10 percent of the Amazon area, has put laws into effect to promote sustainable development through controlled logging and modern farming technology. . . ."

(*The New York Times*, June 28, 2003)

Worldwatch Institute

Established in 1974

DIRECTOR

Christopher Flavin, president. Flavin became president of Worldwatch in September 2000. He was a participant in the Earth Summit in Rio de Janeiro in 1992, the Climate Change Conference in Kyoto Japan in 1997, and the World Summit on Sustainable Development in Johannesburg in 2002. He is a founding member of the board of directors of the Business Council for Sustainable Energy and is a member of the National Academy of Sciences Board on Energy and Environmental Systems, the Climate Institute, and the Environmental and Energy Study Institute. Flavin graduated cum laude from Williams College.

BOARD OF DIRECTORS

Oystein Dahle, chair; chair, Touring Association of Norway, Slependen, Norway

Tom Crain, vice chair, treasurer; managing director (retired), Scudder Stevens and Clark, Cincinnati, OH

Larry Minear, secretary; director, Humanitarianism & War Project, Feinstein International Famine Center, Tufts University, Medford, MA

Christopher Flavin; president, Worldwatch Institute, Washington, DC

Geeta B. Aiyer; president, Boston Common Asset Management, LLC, Boston, MA

Adam Albright; president, The ARIA Foundation, Richmond, MA

Cathy Crain; vice president/Senior Portfolio manager (retired), Scudder Stevens and Clark, Cincinnati, OH

James Dehlsen; chair and chief executive officer, Clipper Windpower, Inc., Goleta, CA

Lynne Gallagher; president, Telecom/Telematique, Inc., Washington, DC

Satu Hassi; member of Parliament and leader of Green Parliamentary Group, former environment minister and development minister, Helsinki, Finland

John McBride; chief executive officer, Aspen Airport Business Center, Aspen, CO

Izaak van Melle; former president, Van Melle Organization, Breda, Netherlands

Akio Morishima; chair, Institute for Global Environmental Strategies, Kanagawa, Japan

Wren Wirth; president, Winslow Foundation, Washington, DC

SCOPE

Members: 150 partner organizations in 40 countries
Branches/chapters: None
Affiliates: None

CONTACT INFORMATION

1776 Massachusetts Avenue, NW, Washington, DC 20036-1904L
Phone: (202) 452-1999 • *Fax:* (202) 296-7365
General E-mail: worldwatch@worldwatch.org •
Web site: www.worldwatch.org

Communications Director: Susan Finkelpearl
(202) 452-1992, ext. 517 • sfinkelpear@worldwatch.org
Human Resources Director: None

PURPOSE: "Dedicated to fostering the evolution of an environmentally sustainable society, one in which human needs are met in ways that do not threaten the health of the natural environment or the prospects of future generations."

CURRENT CONCERNS: Agriculture • Biodiversity • Bioinvasion • Climate change • Consumption • Degradation of oceans • Depletion of the ozone layer • Ecological and human health • Economics, institutions, and security • Food and water shortages • Forests • Freshwater ecosystems • Gender • Globalization • Governance • Health and diseases • Information technology • Loss of biological diversity • Natural disasters • Oceans • Pollution • Renewable energy • Population growth • Security • Sustainability • Urbanization • Water

METHOD OF OPERATION: Internet (e-mail alerts and Web site) • Internships • Media outreach • Product merchandising • Research • Voter registration • Voting records

Effectiveness and Political Orientation

"In Shanghai this month, bicyclists found themselves banned from certain portions of main thoroughfares. By next year, this ubiquitous two-wheel mode of transportation will have been kicked off such roads altogether. Why? To make way for all the new cars—11,000 more every week—pouring onto Chinese streets and highways. A sure sign of growing affluence in the developing world? Without a doubt. A consumer trend portending a better world? That depends on one's point of view.

" 'Rising consumption has helped meet basic needs and create jobs,' says Christopher Flavin, president of the Worldwatch Institute, a Washington, D.C., think tank. 'But as we enter a new century, this unprecedented consumer appetite is undermining the natural systems we all depend on, and making it even harder for the world's poor to meet their basic needs.' That's the message underlying Worldwatch's annual 'State of the World' report, an influential book-length collection of data-packed chapters that has been used by supporters as ammunition and by critics as a pincushion since 1984.

"This year's report focuses on the growing global 'consumer class'— defined as individuals whose 'purchasing power parity' in local currency is

STAFF
23 total—20 full-time; 3 part-time

TAX STATUS
501(c)(3)

FINANCES
Revenue: 2002—$1.8 million;
2001—$2.53 million

FUNDING SOURCES
Foundation grants, 50%; sales of publications, 50%

PAC
None

EMPLOYMENT
Available postings are listed on the institute's Web site at www.worldwatch.org/about/jobs/, and at www.idealist.org. Typically positions in administration, development, communications, and research are offered. Interested applicants should note that Worldwatch only accepts resumes for current vacancies. Letters of interest and resumes can be sent to Worldwatch Institute, 1776 Massachusetts Avenue, NW, Washington, DC 20036-1904. E-mail: jobs@worldwatch.org.

INTERNSHIPS
The Institute offers unpaid internships in research and communications. Available positions are listed at www.worldwatch.org/about/jobs/. Interns are typically asked to work 10–20 hours per week. The duration of internships is flexible, and deadlines for applications are rolling. Applicants should have exemplary academic records, solid research and computer skills, and strong backgrounds in environmental studies. International experience and excellent writing skills are desirable. Application materials should be sent to 1776 Massachusetts Avenue, NW, Suite 800, Washington, DC 20036.

NEWSLETTERS
World Watch Magazine (bimonthly magazine)

PUBLICATIONS
The following is a sample list of publications:
The Anatomy of Resource Wars
City Limits: Putting the Brakes on Sprawl
Climate of Hope: New Strategies for Stabilizing the World's Atmosphere
Correcting Gender Myopia: Gender Equity, Women's Welfare, And The Environment
Deep Trouble: The Hidden Threat of Groundwater Pollution
Hydrogen Futures: Toward a Sustainable Energy System
Invoking the Spirit: Religion and Spirituality in the Quest for a Sustainable World
Micropower: The Next Electrical Era
Reading the Weathervane: Climate Policy from Rio To Johannesburg
Safeguarding the Health of Oceans
Signposts (annual)
State of the World (annual)
Traveling Light: New Paths for International Tourism

more than $7,000 a year (roughly the poverty level in Western Europe). As economies expand—accelerated by globalization that has opened up markets, greater efficiency in manufacturing, and advancing technologies—that consumer class has grown rapidly. It's the main reason there are more than 1 billion cellphones in the world today. The consumer class now includes more than 1.7 billion people. High percentages in North America, Western Europe, and Japan (85 to 90 percent) are no surprise.

"But nearly half of all consumers now are in developing nations. China and India alone account for 362 million of those shoppers, more than in all of Western Europe. . . ."

(*Christian Science Monitor*, January 22, 2004)

"The one principle of feng shui which doesn't seem total hooey is that broken objects are a real downer. The burnt-out toaster, the jammed video, the silent state-of-the-art CD system fill us with fury and frustration in the face of their almost mystical unfathomability. I must be an old-fashioned girl, because my instinct when faced with a broken object is to have it mended. But no one fixes kettles any more, or (with few exceptions) toasters, or many videos or even smaller hi-fis. Many come in impenetrable sealed units, parts are unavailable and it wasn't even worth the cost of labour to fix my 120 Dualit kettle.

"Better to chuck it away, buy a spanking new one. You might think we'd gain pleasure from perpetually restocking our homes with the latest stuff. Not so, according to the Worldwatch Institute, whose annual State of the World report was published this week. It found that while Americans have more cars, luxury goods and bigger houses, they were no happier than in 1957 when they were half as wealthy. For the 1950s consumer, domestic machines were shiny, modern miracles, eliminating drudgery, freeing lives for leisure. There was pride in ownership. But now a dishwasher or fridge is designed to last seven years. A washing machine will probably drop dead at three if heavily used."

(*The Times* [London, England], January 10, 2004)

"Maybe you can wolf down those chocolates you got for Christmas with a clear conscience after all. For, though they may do your waistline no good, they might just help to save the world. Most of the chocolate that comes from Brazil, a major producer and exporter—and some from other nations—is helping to preserve endangered rainforest, a new report published here reveals. And, the report says, with proper development, 'forest chocolate' could rescue one of the world's most crucial and most threatened wildlife areas.

"The area is Brazil's Atlantic Forest, which runs along the country's coast, from its eastern-most point near Recife to close to the Uruguayan border. It is among the richest ecosystems on the planet: 476 tree species have been found in a single hectare of the forest, compared to a typical 15 or 20 in temperate woodlands such as those in Britain or North America. The Worldwatch Institute, which produced the report, says that parts of the forest boast 'the highest level of tree species diversity ever recorded anywhere on earth.' . . .

Only about seven percent of its original extent remains, and it has been reduced to a green archipelago of forest fragments. Cocoa—the main ingredient of chocolate—is one of its last remaining causes for hope, the report says. It is ideal for growing in the rainforest, as it needs constant water and flourishes in the shade of big trees.

" 'Farmers do not have to clear all their forest in order to make a living with it,' says the institute. 'It can be grown profitably under forest canopy and

CONFERENCES

None

can, in effect, help to pay for rainforest conservation.' The report adds that 'most Brazilian coffee' is grown in this way, under a system called 'cabruca.' This is not virgin rainforest; the bushes and smaller trees have largely been replaced by cacao trees—which grow the melon-sized fruit packed with cocoa beans—and the larger trees have been thinned out. 'But its value for conservation is considerable because so little undisturbed forest remains,' the report says. 'It still supports an extraordinary array of wildlife.'

(*Independent on Sunday* [London, England], December 28, 2003)

"America might be fatter than almost every other country, but the rest of the world is catching up to us. For the first time in history, as many people are overweight as underweight, according to a study by the Worldwatch Institute. 'Often, nations have simply traded hunger for obesity,' said study co-author Brian Halweil. There were more than 300 million obese adults in the world in 2000, a 50 percent increase over 1995. Global obesity 'threatens to overwhelm both developed and developing countries,' the World Health Organization said.

"With the exception of a few small countries such as Samoa, the United States has the world's highest-reported adult-obesity rate. Among the democratic, free-market members of the Organization for Economic Cooperation and Development, the United States is the fattest, by far, with a 31 percent obesity rate. But obesity rates have increased in all 30 OECD countries during the past 20 years. In most countries, people typically underestimate their weight when surveyed by researchers. In U.S. surveys, by contrast, volunteers are weighed by health professionals. The U.S. method provides higher but more accurate rates. So countries that rely on self-reporting might have obesity rates closer to the United States than statistics indicate."

(*The Chicago Sun-Times,* July 2, 2003)

"Concerned about dying babies and hurting mothers, a team of Russian doctors recently visited Atlanta as part of a unique initiative to improve maternal and infant health care in their country. Dubbed the Balashikha Project, the privately financed project allows the doctors to shadow their U.S. counterparts for several weeks. While in Atlanta, the three Russian physicians visited maternity and neonatal wards to observe patient care at Grady and Crawford Long hospitals and were given a peek at some of the latest technology used to treat premature babies and at-risk pregnancies. The foreign doctors also met officials of the Emory University schools of medicine, nursing, law and public health and visited the Centers for Disease Control and Prevention.

"Four out of five maternal deaths worldwide are the result of complications related to pregnancy and childbirth such as bleeding, prolonged or obstructed labor, and infection, according to the Washington-based Worldwatch Institute, which tracks global environmental, social and economic trends. 'In the last 15 years, we physicians are noticing a decrease in the health of the general population [in Russia],' said Dr. Yury Ermilov, director of the Balashikha Maternity Hospital. 'Therefore the health of mothers and children is no exception.'. . ."

(*The Atlanta Journal-Constitution,* May 28, 2003)

State Index

Name Index

Johnson, Richard, 1
Johnson, Ronald S., 16, 17
Johnson, S. Curtis, 713
Johnson, Samuel C., 710
Johnson, Stefan, 434
Johnson, Vivian, 489
Johnson, Willa, 540
Johnson, William A., Jr., 686
Johnston, Kelly, 231
Johnston, Michael J., 475
Johnston, Robert, 154
Jones, Camara Phyllis, 59
Jones, Cheryl L., 466
Jones, David R., 506
Jones, Elaine R., 439, 477, 478
Jones, Ingrid Saunders, 273
Jones, James R., 35
Jones, Jim, 209
Jones, Ken, 385
Jones, Landon, 61
Jones, Luther, 422
Jones, Nancy E., 273
Jones, Napoleon, Jr., 30
Jones, Patricia, 64, 315
Jones, Quincy, 477
Jones, Roberts T., 492
Jones, Samuel Shepard, Jr., 4
Jontz, Jim, 66
Jordan, Amos A., 183
Jordan, Ann Dibble, 109, 129
Jordan, Charles R., 233
Jordan, Daniel P., 572
Jordan, I. King, 548
Jordan, Jerry D., 469
Jordan, Michael H., 74, 109
Jordan, Ruth, 519
Jordan, Vernon E., Jr., 477, 577
Joseph, Joshua, 317
Joyce, Douglas S., 412
Joyner, Tom, 144
Judd, Bruce D., 572
Judge, Clark S., 605
June, Jill, 623
Junéja, Tika, 10
Jung, Andrea, 129
Jurgensen, W. G., 412
Justiz, Manuel J., 492

Kaden, Lewis B., 304
Kader, Omar, 463
Kagerer, Sally Beauchamp, 623
Kahle, Brewster, 288
Kahle, Charles, 489
Kahn, David V., 53
Kakabadse, Yolanda, 587, 710
Kaller, Keith, 443
Kamenar, Paul, 700
Kami, Nancy S., 340
Kampelman, Max M., 695
Kane, John F., 469
Kane, Robert, 3
Kanegis, Aura, 516
Kanoute, Amadou, 245
Kanter, Arnold, 364
Kanter, Evan, 620
Kaplan, Diane, 273
Kaplan, Elaine D., 5

Kaplan, Jerome, 53
Kaplan, Joel S., 102
Kapoor, Aditi C., 711
Kapuscincki, Anne R., 683
Karas, Barry, 375
Karl, Lucy J., 623
Karliner, Joshua, 251, 253
Karmazin, Mel, 630
Karp, Roberta, 112
Karpatkin, Rhoda, 506
Karpinski, Gene, 689
Karzai, Hamid, 365
Kashian, Dan, 705
Kasputys, Joseph E., 254
Katen, Karen, 129, 401
Kathwari, Farooq, 364
Katz, Elliot M., 329, 387, 389
Katz, Mitchell, 520
Katz, Mory, 412
Katzen, Sally, 148
Kauffman, Amy, 373, 374
Kaufman, Rosalind Fuchsberg, 672
Kaufmann, Merrill, 705
Kaur-Bal, Sumeet, 415
Kavits, Phil, 713
Kawagoe, Helen, 540
Kay, Alan F., 145
Kay, Laura, 400
Kazmir, Munr, 53
Keating, David, 566
Keating-Edh, Barbara, 238
Keck, W. M., II, 401
Keddie, Daniel, 412
Keefe, Diane, 249
Keegan, Lisa Graham, 297
Keegan, Michael B., 611
Keeler, William H., 510
Keenan, Nancy, 155
Keene, David A., 31, 32
Keest, Kathleen, 92
Kegley, Susan, 618
Keiter, Robert B., 551
Keleher, James P., 509
Kelleher, Arthur J., 658
Keller, Jay, 627, 628
Keller, Ric, 218–219
Kelley, A. Benjamin, 137
Kelley, Peter, 61
Kelley, Terry, 492
Kellogg, David, 269
Kelly, Eugene, 588
Kelly, Michael, 151
Kelso, Dennis Takahashi, 551
Kemp, Jack F., 211, 297, 298
Kemper, Jonathan, 572
Kempthorne, Dirk, 537
Kendall, David E., 477
Kendall, Kathryn, 74
Kennard, Donald Ray, 56
Kennard, William E., 454
Kennedy, Caroline B., 477
Kennedy, David B., 404
Kennedy, Donald, 126
Kennedy, Edward M., 60, 325, 369
Kennedy, Karen D., 469
Kennedy, Margaret A., 384
Kennedy, Quentin J., 96

Kennedy, Randall, 475
Kennedy, Robert F., Jr., 187, 443
Kennedy, Susan, 45, 46
Kennedy, Victoria Reggie, 107
Kenney, Phyllis Gutierrez, 169
Kenny, Edward, 583
Kenny, Luella, 157
Kent, Susannah S., 489
Kerlikowske, Gil, 80
Kerns, Peggy, 514
Kerr, Vincent, 554
Kerr, Walter, 121
Kerrey, Bob, 226
Kerrigan, Karen, 116
Kerry, John, 11, 21, 51, 107, 144, 164, 167, 176, 402, 443, 472, 473, 674
Kerry, Teresa. *See* Heinz, Teresa
Kessler, Martha Neff, 463
Kesster, David, 246
Kest, Steven, 91
Ketcham, Susan, 433
Keyston, David H., 605
Keyworth, George, 629
Khairallah, David, 25
Khaki, Jawad, 415, 416
Khama, S. K. I., 235
Khanachet, Samer, 25
Khanna, Sri Ram, 243
Khor, Martin, 251
Khoury, George Majeed, 25
Kiernan, Thomas C., 442, 551
Kieschnick, Michael, 609
Kiley, Brad, 134
Kilgore, Jerry W., 653
Killinger, Kerry, 492
Killingsworth, Inez, 557, 569
Kim, Jinsoo H., 88
Kim, Tom, 626
Kimball, Michele, 3
Kimball, Richard, 631
Kimmelman, Gene, 246, 247, 248
Kindler, Jeffrey B., 96
King, Gwendolyn S., 255
King, Jane, 518
King, Martin Luther, Jr., 151, 478
King, Maxwell, 273
King, Michael, 458
King, Patricia, 554
King, Sandra, 527
King, Scott L., 686
King, Susan R., 255
King, William Russell, 116
Kingfisher, Pame, 157
Kingo, Lise, 112
Kingsley, Gordon F., 572
Kington, Mark J., 572
Kinnan, Chris, 200
Kinnard, Kari, 467
Kinsey, Christopher M., 116
Kipp, Barbara H., 315
Kipper, David A., 53
Kippes, Althea T., 672
Kipps, Clarence T., Jr., 699
Kirk, Roger, 93
Kirk, Russell, 470
Kirkegaard, Jacob, 402
Kirkley-Bey, Marie, 142

Kirkpatrick, Jeane J., 133, 297, 312, 695
Kirsch, Peter A., 104
Kirschenbaum, Malcolm R., 349
Kiser, Anthony C. M., 218
Kissinger, Henry A., 182
Klaassens, Paul J., 312, 372, 398
Klapper, Jon H., 433
Klausner, Manuel S., 644
Kleckner, Dean R., 542
Klein, Arnold W., 45
Klein, Dennis F., 53
Klein, Donna, 692
Klein, Howard, 611
Klein, Michael, 194, 642
Klein, Naomi, 41
Kleinschmidt, Lea, 267, 268
Klepner, Jerry, 338
Kleweno, Phil, 358
Kline, Phill, 699
Klinetobe, Lee M., 367
Kling, William H., 424
Klingensmith, Michael J., 45
Klose, Kevin, 394
Kmiec, Douglas W., 542
Kneen, Kendig K., 486
Knight, Robert, 224, 600
Knight, Scott E., 247
Knobloch, Kevin, 206, 683
Knowles, Beyonce, 616
Knowles, Marie L., 109
Knox, John A., 286
Knudsen, Thomas, 200
Knuth, Kathy, 397
Koch, David H., 131, 644
Koenig, Thomas H., 160
Koffel, Martin M., 40
Koffler, Raymond J., Sr., 424
Kogut, Melissa, 481
Kohler, Mary, 650
Kohr, Howard, 48, 50
Kokolj, Nancy, 358
Kolb, Charles M., 212, 213, 214, 215
Kolesnik, Kris J., 5
Kolt, Leah, 461
Komatsu, Karl A., 551, 572
Kommers, Nathan, 173
Koob, Charles E., 584
Koppel, Ted, 459
Koppelman, Murray, 82
Koppes, Richard, 422
Korb, Lawrence, 391
Kormos, Rebecca, 236
Korn, Joel, 235
Kornblatt, Tracy, 213
Korologos, Ann McLaughlin, 233
Korsant, Philip B., 584
Kostmayer, Peter Houston, 626
Kostunica, Vojislav, 652
Kourpias, George J., 23, 439
Kovler, Judy, 480
Kovler, Peter B., 10, 166, 548
Kovner, Bruce, 40, 451
Kowalski, Michael J., 551
Kraemer, Harry M. J., Jr., 228
Krahnke, Karl, 678
Kraiem, Ruben, 584
Kramer, Albert H., 454

Lee, Randall R., 524
Lee, Sheila Jackson, 691
Lee, Tonya Lewis, 477
Leeds, Roger, 364
Leer, Steven F., 486
Leeth, Toni Rhodes, 59
Lefrak, Stephen, 171
Leggett, Dee, 61
Leggett, Robert N., Jr., 551
Legum, Doug, 352
Legvold, Robert, 126
Lehrer, Linda, 521
Lemley, Ann, 2
Lenard, Thomas, 629
Lenhardt, Robin A., 554
Leno, Jay, 370
Leon, Rachel, 216
Leonard, Jerris, 4
Leone, Richard, 134, 475
Lepore, Dawn Gould, 129
Leppert, Thomas C., 602
Leppin, Betty, 240
Lerner, Al, 351
Lesavoy, Nina, 422
Lescano, Maria, 358
Lessig, Lawrence, 288, 640
Lessner, Richard, 31, 33
LeTien, Jean, 106, 107
Leuschen, David M., 61
Leven, Charles, 1
Levi, Robin, 275
Levin, Joe, 663
Levin, Mark R., 436, 437
Levine, Arnold J., 45
Levine, Brian, 588
Levine, Felice J., 430
Levine, Jacqueline, 53
Levine, James, 321
Levine, Murray, 157
Levitas, Daniel, 663
Levitt, Arthur, Jr., 228
Levitt, Matthew, 696
Levkovitz, Thea, 578
Levy, Jay A., 45
Levy, Jeff, 468
Levy, Leon, 430
Levy, Robert, 404
Lewis, Charles, 172
Lewis, Edwin L., 96
Lewis, Elise Carlson, 269
Lewis, Lynn, 503
Lewis, Nancy, 406
Lewis, Peter, 134, 473
Lewis, Samuel W., 695
Lewis, Stephen R., Jr., 126
Lewis, William M., Jr., 477
Lewis, Yosenio, 533
Leyba, Glenn, 28
Liberatore, Robert G., 255
Lichter, Linda S., 163
Lichter, S. Robert, 163
Lichtman, Judith L., 439, 555
Liddell, W. Kirk, 486
Liddy, Edward M., 118, 129, 412
Liebeler, Susan W., 699
Liebenow, Larry A., 674
Lieberman, Gerald, 430

Lieberman, Joseph I., 49, 144, 443, 648
Lieberman, Marty, 375
Lieberman, Sue, 713
Liggio, Leonard, 221
Light, Paul C., 255
Ligon, Duke R., 470
Likens, Gene E., 303
Limbaugh, Rush, 436, 459
Lin, Maya, 585
Lind, William, 348
Lindamood, Melisa, 623
Linden, Lawrence H., 648, 713
Lindsay, James M., 269
Lindsey, Lawrence, 211
Ling, Sin Yen, 88–89
Linsky, Andy, 375
Lintott, James, 404, 644
Lipic, Ruth Ann, 466
Lipman, Ira A., 140
Lipper, Kenneth, 255
Lippman, Harley, 53
List, Robert, 116
Litman, Roslyn, 28
Little, Julian, 352
Little, William G., 116, 674
Littrell, Helen, 430
Liu, Eric, 215
Livingston, David, 484
Livingston, Michael E., 524
Lloyd, Mark, 148, 596
Lo, Nancy, 89
Loanzon, Cora, 39
Lochbaum, David, 684
Lochner, Philip R., Jr., 422
Locke, R. Christopher, 307
Lockwood, Alan, 620
Lodal, Jan M., 93
Loe, Cheryl, 340
Loewenberg, Susan, 172
Logan, Justin, 132
London, Herbert I., 372
Lonergan, Pierce J., 116
Lonergan, Robert A., 96
Long, Gretchen, 551
Long, Michael, 31
Longaberger, Tami, 489
Lopez, Oscar M., 235
Lopez, Ralph, 107
Lord, Betty Bao, 349
Lorenz, Eugene W., 381
Loring, Chuck, 433
Lott, John, 133, 156
Lott, Trent, 3, 440, 441
Love, L. Don, 623
Lowe, Rolland C., 273
Lowenthal, Abraham, 269
Lowery, Elizabeth, 431
Loy, Frank E., 304, 364, 402, 647
Loyless, Betsy, 442
Lozano, Mónica C., 521
Lozano, Raymond, 521
Lubber, Mindy, 206, 207, 208
Lubchenco, Jane, 304
Luber, Mindy, 422
Lucas, Donald L., 35
Lucas, Kate, 289
Luce, Tom, 492, 494

McMurray, J. Thomas, 593
McNamara, Robert S., 692
McNeill, Michele V., 45
McNight, John, 569
McPeake, Ellen, 361
McPhee, Gerald T., 116
McPhee, Penelope, 273
McPherson, Don, 500
McPherson, Peter, 235
McQuilkin, William W., Jr., 489
Meacher, Michael, 353
Meadows, Tashee, 355
Meadows, William H., 442, 704
Medalie, Susan, 707, 708, 709
Medina, David, 375
Medrano, Laura, 445
Mee, Charles L., Jr., 692
Meek, Kendrick, 169
Meeks, James, 106, 107
Meese, Edwin, III, 124, 436
Mehler, I. Barry, 82
Meiling, Meredith, 587
Meiners, Roger, 238
Meisinger, Susan R., 315, 316
Melamed, Bill, 45
Melamed, Jack, 611
Meléndez, Sara E., 315
Mellon, Margaret, 685
Mellor, William H., 404
Melmed, Matthew E., 338
Melnicke, Meir, 53
Meltzer, Ronni, 82
Mendelsohn, Janet, 140
Mendoza, Charles J., 1
Menefee, W. Neal, 412
Meneses, Luis, 715
Menino, Thomas M., 9, 89, 549
Meral, Gerald H., 578
Merchant, Kathryn E., 273
Merck, Josephine A., 585
Merkerson, S. Epatha, 121
Merritt, Elizabeth S., 573
Merritt, Jack N., 93
Merritt, William, 507
Mertz, Delores, 56
Mesiah, Frank B., 485
Metrick, Alan, 584
Mettler, Molly, 527
Metzenbaum, Howard, 637
Metzner, Richard H., 45
Meyer, Fred, 497
Meyer, George, 442
Meyer, Joe, 680
Meyer, Judy L., 61
Meyer, Katherine A., 137, 277
Meyer, Paulette J., 143
Meyerhoff, Harvey M., 226, 677
Meyers, Ellie, 146
Meyers, Michael, 28
Meyers, Robert M., 146
Meyerson, Frederick A. B., 623
Meza, Roberto H. Murray, 112
Mfume, Kweisi, 439, 483, 484
Michael, Clara, 620
Michael, James H., Jr., 612
Michelman, Kate, 480, 482, 563
Michitarian, Robert S., 433

Middendorf, William J., 367
Middlebrooks, S. C. "Buster," 672
Middleton, Richard H., Jr., 672
Mierzwinski, Ed, 690, 691
Mies van der Rohe, Ludwig, 573
Mikva, Abner J., 175
Miller, E. Ethelbert, 406
Miller, Ellen S., 175, 596
Miller, Henry I., 37
Miller, Judith, 79
Miller, Lawrence, 82
Miller, Nodine, 58
Miller, Patricia Howell, 320
Miller, Paul S., 53
Miller, Preston R., 711
Miller, Robert C., 692
Miller, Steven, 593
Miller, Thomas V. Mike, 173–174, 262
Milleron, Laura, 185
Milligan, Lisa, 385
Milliken, Roger, Jr., 587
Milling, Rob, 362
Mills, Cheryl, 134, 554
Mills, Douglas, 457
Mills, Kim, 376
Mills, Nancy, 475
Milstein, Arnold, 554
Milstein, Laura, 696
Mincberg, Elliot M., 612
Mindiola, Tatcho, Jr., 460
Minear, Larry, 716
Miner, Jason, 602
Mineta, Norman Y., 15
Minge, David, 209
Minnery, Tom, 71, 337
Minton, Dwight C., 551
Minton Beddoes, Zanny, 126
Mintz, Walter, 451
Miranda, Manuel, 612, 613
Mitau, Lee, 421
Mitchell, Burgena, 590
Mitchell, Chris, 644
Mitchell, Cleta, 31
Mitchell, Dave, 106
Mitchell, Dolores, 581
Mitchell, George J., 269
Mitchell, Larry, 519
Mitchler, Nathan, 641
Mittermeier, Russell A., 235
Mix, Wes, 263
Mixon, Vidette Bullock, 206
Mlambo-Ngcuka, Phumzile, 353
Mobley, Stacey J., 487
Moby, 483
Model, Allen J., 489
Modzelewski, Stephen W., 404, 644
Moe, Richard, 572
Moebius, Wanda, 171
Moghissi, A. Alan, 37
Mohammed, Nisha, 653
Mokhiber, Albert, 25
Moler, Don, 540
Molina, Gloria, 460
Molina, Mario, 683
Moline, Jack, 415
Moncrief, Dawn, 329, 330
Mone, Lawrence J., 451

Pollard, Arnold, 54
Pollard, William, 413
Pollock, Richard, 131
Poole, Robert W., Jr., 644, 645, 646
Pope, Carl, 660
Pope, James Arthur, 32
Popeo, Daniel J., 124, 698
Popper, Andrew F., 160
Porcari, Chuck, 442
Porch, Antonious L. K., 658
Porter, Andrew, 297
Porter, John Edward, 109
Porter, Michael E., 267
Portman, Jan V., 587
Portney, Paul R., 647
Potok, Mark, 661, 664
Potter, Louise Bryant, 572
Potter, Trevor, 375
Potts, Stephen D., 315
Poulard, Othello, 151
Pound, William T., 512
Powell, Alma J., 74
Powell, Burnele Venable, 246
Powell, Colin, 74, 75, 115, 126, 269, 270, 371, 373, 496
Powell, Herbert W., 484
Powell, Michael K., 217, 454, 456, 630
Powell, Staccato, 415
Power, J. D., 520
Powers, Melanie, 384
Powers, Nina, 100
Poynter, Pete, 56
Pozen, Robert C., 228
Prager, Kenneth M., 37
Prahalad, C. K., 711
Prather, Demetrius, 484
Pratt, Harold A., 431
Premawardhana, Shanta, 526
Presser, Stephen B., 699
Prettner, Yvonne, 195
Price, Hugh, 577
Price, Robert E., 692
Price, Scott, 642
Price, Sol, 191
Prichard, Peter S., 349
Prickett, Glenn, 431
Priest, George L., 699
Priest, Mark, 303
Priestly, Frank S., 470
Principe, Sarah, 256
Pritchett, Bryan, 578
Pritzker, Nicholas J., 236
Pritzker, Robert A., 40
Probst, Marian, 355
Prueher, Joseph W., 587
Pryce, Deborah, 2
Pryor, William H., Jr., 20, 164
Pulitzer, Joseph, IV, 146
Pulliam, H. Ronald, 277
Pulliam, Mark S., 602
Purcell, Bill, 686
Pusey, Allen, 172
Putin, Vladimir, 652, 711
Putman, Gary, 638
Putnam, Howard D., 140
Pye, Lori, 655

Qian Yi, 711

Quattrone, Frank, 543
Quevedo, Frank J., 460
Quindlen, Anna, 320, 480
Quinn, Jack, 119–120
Quinn, Kieron F., 672
Quintana, Sammy J., 466
Quintero, Sofia, 10
Quirk, Michael J., 673

Rabb, George, 277
Rabinovitz, Jeremy, 49
Rabinowitz, Daniel L., 477
Rabinowitz, Leonard, 46
Racicot, Marc, 377
Racine, Laurie, 640
Rader, Russ, 412
Rafeedie, Ramiz, 26
Rahe, Mary, 372
Rahn, Richard W., 35
Raimondo, Justin, 651
Raines, Franklin D., 118
Raisian, John, 370
Ralls, Steve, 658
Ramage, Patrick, 384
Ramani, Sunder, 530
Ramey, Thomas C., 385
Ramirez, Jack, 413
Ramirez, Judy, 558
Ramsey, Charles H., 483
Ramsey, Joe, 381
Ramsey, Stephen, 431
Ramstad, Jim, 568
Rancourt, Linda M., 551
Randall, Lewis E., 131
Randolph, C. Carl, 477
Rands, Tim, 286
Ranftle, Ken, 533
Rangel, Guadalupe, 460
Ranieri, Lewis S., 304
Rankin, Singleton, 714
Ranney, George A., Jr., 233
Ransom, Curt, 383
Ransom, David M., 464
Rapoport, Miles, 169
Rapson, Cal, 519
Rasmussen, Arthur E., 398
Rathour, Amric Singh, 52
Ratliff, Mary, 484
Ratner, Gary, 54
Rattner, Steven, 109, 226
Rauh, Joseph, 623
Rauschenberger, Steven, 512
Rause, Alicia, 604
Raven, Peter H., 711
Ray, David, 265, 332
Ray, Renee, 590
Raymar, Robert, 54
Raymond, Lee R., 40
Raymont, Victoria, 375
Raymont, Wendy Marcus, 215
Raynault, Paul, 680
Read, Patricia, 395
Read, Robin, 522
Reagan, Ronald, 21, 255, 298, 373, 457, 470, 693
Redden, James, 580
Redford, Robert, 585
Redgate, William T., 140

Robin, Henry, 375
Robinson, Alexia, 343
Robinson, Barbara Paul, 129
Robinson, Cloyd, 566
Robinson, Davis R., 464
Robinson, Kayne B., 560
Robinson, Mark, 431
Robinson, Roanne Shaddox, 454
Robinson, Roger W., Jr., 180
Robinson, Ron, 32
Robinson, Sandra H., 671
Robles, Victor, 535
Rochkind, Matt, 309
Rockefeller, David, 402
Rockefeller, Laurance, 442, 585
Rockefeller, Nelson A., Jr., 233
Rockoff, Alvin J., 82
Rockwell, Llewellyn, 651
Rockwood, John M., 146
Rodgers, Carla, 332, 333
Rodgers, Howard L., 527
Rodin, Judith, 110, 129
Rodman, Michael, 614
Rodman, Veronique, 40
Rodriguez, Adrian, 445
Rodriguez, Arturo S., 522
Rodriguez, David M., 445
Rodriguez, Maria, 243
Rodriguez, Pamela, 523
Rodriguez, Pedro, 519
Rodriguez, Rosemary, 627
Roemer, Tim, 166
Roesing, William, 629
Rogers, Gary L., 487
Rogers, James E., 419
Rogers, John F. W., 572
Rogers, Julie L., 273
Rogers, Robert B., 74
Rogstad, Barry K., 35
Rohatyn, Felix G., 182
Rohe, John, 332
Roisman, Anthony Z., 672
Roizman, Israel, 54
Rolike, Rose, 39
Rolle, Scott L., 31
Rollins, Kevin B., 40
Rom, Rebecca L., 704
Roman, George C., 464
Roman, Kenneth, 549
Romano, John F., 672
Romero, Anthony D., 28
Romney, Mitt, 376, 514
Roop, Robert, 381
Roosevelt, David A., 549
Roosevelt, Franklin D., 522, 549
Roosevelt, Theodore, IV, 442, 704, 711
Roque, Atila, 251
Rosales, Henry, 375
Rosales, Rosa, 445
Rose, David S., 611
Rose, Gene, 512
Rose, Jeffrey O., 381
Rose, Jonathan F. P., 585
Rose, Pat, 390
Rose-Dodd, Jennifer, 484
Rosen, Christine, 313
Rosen, Howard F., 168

Rosen, Jack, 54
Rosen, Joseph, 54
Rosenberg, Ernie, 307
Rosenberg, Mark, 106, 107
Rosenberg, Norman, 19
Rosenberg, Sheli Z., 554
Rosenblatt, Melissa, 324
Rosenblum, Lya Dym, 54
Rosenfeld, Carol, 358
Rosenfield, Allan, 45
Rosenkranz, Robert, 451
Rosenman, Mark, 596
Rosenthal, Brent, 672
Rosenthal, John, 106, 107
Rosenwald, E. John, Jr., 304, 549
Ross, Bernard, 105
Ross, Dennis, 695, 696, 697
Ross, Donald K., 442
Ross, Donald M., 677
Ross, James D., 381
Ross, Robert K., 340
Rossbach, William A., 672
Rotenberg, Marc, 291, 292, 293
Roth, Allen, 32
Roth, Kenneth, 378
Rothstein, Barbara, 672
Rothstein, Paul, 701
Rothstein, Renee, 48
Rothwell, Linda A., 466
Rotner, Philip R., 215
Rotterman, Marc E., 31
Rouda, Ronald H., 672
Rouse, James J., 116
Roush, Jeanne, 614
Roush, Thomas W., 585
Roux, David J., 304
Rove, Karl, 68, 69, 371, 557
Rovig, David B., 470
Rowe, Audrey, 191
Rowe, John W., 40
Rowe, Mark, 140
Rowland, Melissa Ann, 545, 546
Rowland, Randolph, 677
Rowley, Diane L., 59
Royer, Patricia, 519
Rozett, Linda, 674
Ruan, John R., III, 674
Rubenfeld, Abby, 375
Rubenstein, David M., 402
Rubin, Alan A., 549
Rubin, Jared, 655
Rubin, Robert E., 209, 226, 269
Rubiner, Laurie, 556
Rubinger, Michael, 394
Rucci, Anthony J., 140
Ruckelshaus, William D., 35, 710
Rucks, Alfred J., 484
Rudd, Cari, 309
Ruddock, Joan, 354
Rudie, Sheryl, 225
Rudman, Warren B., 226, 227, 269
Rufe, Roger T., Jr., 593, 594
Ruggiero, Renato, 402
Ruhl, B. Suzi, 306
Ruhl, Suzi, 157
Rule, Charles F. "Rick," 699
Rumenap, Stacie, 682

Somson, Barbara, 596
Sonego, John, 358, 359
Sorensen, Theodore C., 270
Soros, George, 270, 294, 402, 473
Sorrell, Martin, 229
Sosman, Martha B., 336
Soukup, Jeff, 358
Soulé, Michele, 421, 423
Soundarrajan, Raj, 38
Souter, David H., 4
Spagnoli, Christine D., 672
Spalt, Allen, 100
Spangler, Scott M., 711
Sparks, Don L., 470
Sparrow, Greg, 686
Speakman, Willard A., III, 390
Spears, Rhonda, 686
Speir, Nancy, 529
Spencer, Alonzo, 157
Spencer, Steve R., 116
Speranza, Paul S., 674
Spero, Joan E., 270
Speth, James Gustave, 585, 711
Spielberg, Steven, 657
Spivey, Paul, 272
Sport, Lynne, 126
Sposato, Steve, 106, 107
Sprague, Daniel M., 260
Spring, Dona, 474
Stachelberg, Winnie, 375, 377
Stahel, Shep, 540
Staheli, Donald L., 75
Staley, Peter R., 45
Staley, Warren R., 487
Stallman, Bob, 35
Stamatos, Cleo Manuel, 519
Standish, Marion, 338
Stanfield, Kevin, 599
Stanford, Michael R., 116
Stang, Robert, 307
Stanley, David M., 566
Stanley, Jean Leu, 566
Stanley, William, III, 623
Stanton, Glenn, 335
Stanton, Robert G., 307, 489
Stark, Martha E., 433
Starr, Adele E., 146
Starr, Kenneth W., 699
Starr, Paul, 475
Starrett, Cam, 129
Stata, Ray, 267
Stauber, Karl, 273
Staunton, Marshall, 197
Stavins, Robert N., 648
Stavropoulos, William S., 41
Steedman, Doria, 352
Steel, Lewis M., 406
Steel, Shawn, 265
Steele, Lacy, 484
Steele, Shari, 288, 289
Steele, W. Fletcher, 487
Stein, Daniel A., 332, 333, 334
Stein, Elliot, 343
Stein, Michael, 251
Steinberg, Alan W., 277
Steinberg, Lillian, 54
Steinbrook, William R., Jr., 154

Steinbruner, Maureen S., 166, 167
Steinem, Gloria, 482, 483
Steiner, Daniel, 604
Steiner, Jerry, 431
Steinhauser, Lesley, 13
Steinmann, David P., 180
Stempler, Gerald, 82
Stenberg, Don, 699
Stengel, Sue, 83
Stennis, John, 349
Stenson, Jane, 527
Stephens, Delena, 503
Stephens, Martin, 512
Stephens, Nancy, 683
Stephenson, Richard, 200
Stern, Joseph, 461
Stern, Marc, 54, 55
Stern, Paula, 93
Stern, Robert A. M., 572
Stern, Sarah, 54
Stern, Walter P., 373
Sternberg, Stephen S., 37
Stevick, Stephen, 642
Stewart, Ben, 361
Stewart, Colin, 326
Stewart, Don, 215
Stewart, Donald M., 394
Stewart, Rob, 656
Stewart, Walter J., 381
Stier, Jeff, 37, 38, 39
Stiglitz, Joseph E., 648
Stillwell, Joseph, 680
Stilp, Gene, 160–161
Stilpp, Paul, 548
Stipanovich, Coleman, 257
Stitle, Stephen A., 373
Stochaj, Ricki, 519
Stockman, David A., 209, 211
Stone, Alan J., 338
Stone, Gail, 257
Stone, Judith Lee, 13, 15
Stone, Linda, 714
Stone, Thomas H., 683
Stopler, Michael, 489
Storms, Clifford B., 97
Stout, Janette, 132
Stout, Susan, 338
Strassburger, Robert, 414
Straub, Terrence D., 166
Straus, Philip A., Jr., 146
Strauss, David, 231
Strauss, Mark A., 35
Strauss, Robert S., 183, 699
Street, John, 484
Streich, Helen Marie, 647
Streisand, Barbra, 457
Strharsky, Harry, 275
Stribling, Morris, 446
Strigl, Denny, 501
Stritmatter, Paul L., 671
Strohbehn, Edward L., Jr., 648
Strong, Maurice F., 381
Strossen, Nadine, 28
Struhs, David, 552
Struhsacker, Debra W., 470
Strulson, Richard, 433
Stuart, Robert D., Jr., 163

Subject Index

Bold entries indicate coverage of principal public interest groups.

AARP, 1–3
Abortion issue, 199, 295, 480–483, 545–546, 563–565, 599–601, 623–625
Abstinence, sexual, 45–46
Accuracy in Media, Inc., 4–6
ACLU. *See* American Civil Liberties Union
ACORN. *See* Association of Community Organizations for Reform Now
Action on Smoking and Health, 7–9
ACUS. *See* The Atlantic Council of the United States
ADA. *See* Americans for Democratic Action
Adam's Mark Hotel, 485
Advertising. *See* Marketing
   presidential candidates. *See* Presidential race
Advocacy Institute, 10–12
Advocates for Highway and Auto Safety, 13–15
Affirmative action in university admissions, 51, 298
Afghanistan
   civilian casualties, 378
   democracy in, 270
   postwar contracts in, 173
   U.S. nuclear power plants, intelligence about, 363
   U.S. plan in, 365–366
Africa
   civil wars, 380
   energy policy, 353–354
   HIV/AIDS crisis, 184
   promotion of education about, 668–670
   wildlife, 236
African Americans, 163. *See also* Civil rights
   advancement of, 483–485, 575–577, 668–670
   economic issues, 575
   education, 478, 484
   getting out the vote, 379, 428
   infant deaths among, 195–196
   legal defense, 477–479
   media treatment of, 458
   politics, 427–429
   presidential campaign, 576, 581
   prisoners, 485
   protests, 496
   social register of, 496
   Social Security benefits, 498
Agriculture. *See also* Animals; Food and nutrition
   subsidies, 311
Agriculture Department, U.S., 558
AIDS. *See* HIV/AIDS
AIDS Action, 16–18
AIPAC. *See* American Israel Public Affairs Committee
Air travel
   audio available to passengers, 161
   pets in transit, 64–65
   privacy issues, 289–290, 291
   screening and security issues, 79, 149, 644
Alabama, 197–198, 201, 202
Alaska, 277–278, 492, 585, 704
Alcoholic beverages
   advertising, 178–179
   drunk drivers. *See* Substance abuse
   labeling, 519

Alliance for Justice, 19–21
Alliance for Retired Americans, 22–24
al Qaeda, 463, 695. *See also* Afghanistan
Altria, 122, 396
Amazon, 456, 715
American-Arab Anti-Discrimination Committee, 25–27
American Civil Liberties Union (ACLU), 28–30
American Conservative Union, 31–33
American Council for Capital Formation, 34–36
American Council on Science and Health, 37–39
American Enterprise Institute for Public Policy Research, 40–42, 133
American Family Association, 43–44
American Foundation for AIDS Research (amfAR), 45–47
American Indians, 469–470, 515–516, 668–669
American Israel Public Affairs Committee (AIPAC), 48–50
American Jewish Committee, 51–52
American Jewish Congress, 53–55
American Legislative Exchange Council, 56–57
American Public Health Association, 59–60
American Red Cross, 99
American Rivers, 61–63
Americans Coming Together, 294
Americans for Democratic Action (ADA), 66–67
Americans for Tax Reform, 68–70
American Society for the Prevention of Cruelty to Animals (ASPCA), 64–65
Americans United for Separation of Church and State, 71–73
America's Promise—The Alliance for Youth, 74–75
amfAR. *See* American Foundation for AIDS Research
Amnesty International USA, 76–78
Anheuser-Busch Company, 234
Animals. *See also* Endangered species; Marine resources; Wildlife
   abuse of, 381–386, 614–616
   advocacy groups, 355–357, 381–389, 614–616
   air travel by, 64–65
   chimpanzees, 65, 236
   cockfighting, 383
   dogfighting, 383
   farm animals, 329–331, 587
   feral cats, 368
   fraternities abusing, 382
   protection of, 64–65
   research using, 615
   rights of, 124, 355–357, 369
   shelters, 381
ANSER Institute for Homeland Security, 79–81
Anti-Defamation League, 82–83
Anti-Semitism, 25, 54, 82–84, 102–103, 318
Antitrust law, 698–699
Arab American Institute, 85–87
Arab Americans, 25–27, 85–87, 151, 199, 263–265, 416
Arbitration, 673
Arctic National Wildlife Refuge, 300, 488, 580, 689, 706
Arkansas, 680–681
Armed forces. *See* Military
Army Corps of Engineers, 62, 63, 425, 579
Asian American Legal Defense and Education Fund, 88–90
Asian Americans, 88–90
ASPCA. *See* American Society for the Prevention of Cruelty to Animals

Center on Budget and Policy Priorities, 191–193, 693
Central American Free Trade Agreement, 402
CERES. *See* Coalition for Environmentally Responsible Economies
Charities and charitable societies. *See also* Nonprofit organizations;
	Philanthropy
	boards, 349
	decreases in donations, 341, 507
	donations in return for political favors, 506
	evaluation of, 98–99
	false pretenses and misuse, 272–273, 507, 589
	promotion of, 393–395
	solicitation methods, 362, 394–395
Charleston's Promise, 74
Chesapeake Bay, 442–443
Children and youth, 74–75. *See also* Families
	advocacy groups, 194–196
	brand-name product selection, 39
	character building, 74
	custody issues, 280–281, 399
	day care, 320–321
	divorce and, 399
	food and nutrition, 178
	health care, 195–196
	homeless, 504
	Internet access, 150, 611–612
	movie ratings, 336
	pesticides and, 621
	quality of life, 539
	rights of, 280
	safety of, 242
	school breakfast programs, 338
	smoking, 121–123
	violence and, 82
	vision problems, 75
	welfare issues, 280–281
Children's Defense Fund, 194–196
Chimp Haven Inc., 65
China
	environmental education, 714
	HIV/AIDS, 47
	importing of genetically modified crops and food, 362
	military, 94
	Taiwan and, 95
	transportation plans vs. environment, 716
Christian Coalition of America, 197–199
Christian conservatives, 43–44, 197–199, 335–337, 650–652,
	665–667
Christianity, 312, 524–526, 665–667
Chumbawamba, 253
Church and state, 20, 29, 30, 44, 52, 55, 71–73, 405, 416, 612, 663
Church burnings, 151–152
CIA, 81
Cinergy Corporation, 419
Cingular Wireless, 246
Citicorp, 569
Cities. *See also* Local government
	abandoned buildings, 558–559
	advancement of, 539–541
	economic issues, 452, 540, 687
	educational issues, 539–540
	nature preserves, 490
Citigroup Inc., 643
Citizens for a Sound Economy, 200–202
Citizens for Tax Justice, 203–205
Citizenship, 557
Civil rights. *See also* Hispanics
	affirmative action in university admissions, 51, 298

African Americans, 195
Arab Americans, 25–27, 263–265
Asian Americans, 89–90
conservative agenda for, 299
digital age, 288–290
discrimination, 25–27
gays and lesbians, 30, 44, 376, 405, 434–435
prisoners held in war on terrorism, 29–30, 77–78
protection of, 25–27, 151–153, 439–441, 653–655, 663–665
Cleveland, Ohio, 540
Climate change. *See* Environmental issues
**Coalition for Environmentally Responsible Economies
(CERES), 206–208**
Colleges. *See* Universities and colleges
Colorado, 72, 189, 278, 429, 445–446, 452, 497, 531, 705
Columbia University, 615
Comcast Co., 241, 247, 257
Committee for a Responsible Federal Budget, 209–211
Committee for Economic Development, 212–214
Common Cause, 215–217
Common Good, 186, 218–220
Community empowerment, 142–144, 495–496, 569–571
Community Reinvestment Act, 570
Community Technology Foundation of California, 275
Competitive Enterprise Institute, 221–223
Competitiveness, economic, 266–268
Computer industry. *See also* Technology
	outsourcing, 402–403
Concerned Women for America, 224–225
Concord Coalition, 226–227
The Conference Board, Inc., 228–230
Conflict of interest, 104, 215–216, 393–394, 506
Congress. *See also* Government; State government
	budget, 70
	entitlements, 226–227
	funding for staff, equipment, etc., 232
	Iraq war and, 231
	monitoring groups, 231–232
	protectionism, 167–168
	race relations, 440
	retirements from, 67
	women in, 708
Congressional Management Foundation, 231–232
Congressional nominees
	conservative issues, 32
	pro-business, 115–117
Connecticut, 452, 481–482
Conservation, 233–234, 286–287, 424–426, 442–445, 587–589,
	593–595. *See also* Natural resources, conservation of
Conservation Fund, 233–234
Conservation International, 235–237
Conservatism. *See also* Christian conservatives
	congressional nominees, 31–32
	on role of government, 33
	presidential nominees, 32, 69
	promotion of, 31–33, 40–42, 131–133, 297–299, 346–348,
	367–369
Conservative Political Action Conference, 69
Constitution, U.S.
	First Amendment rights, 611. *See also* Free speech
	Marriage Amendment, proposal for, 44, 224, 297, 327,
	335–336, 358, 373, 375–376, 398
	privacy rights. *See* Privacy, right of
	religious freedom, 54
Consumer Alert, 238–239
Consumer confidence polls, 229
Consumer Federation of America, 240–242

disabled citizens, 548
discrimination at polls, 89–90
environmental issues, 662
fairness, 188–190
getting out the vote, 255, 294, 379, 428, 632
Hispanic vote, 522
instant runoff system, 188–190
judicial, 213–214
malfunctioning voting machines, 449
multilingual ballots, 89
pro-choice candidates, 581–583
redistricting, 189–190, 461
religious practices and, 110
soft money, 173, 411
state campaign finance reform, 409–411
state legislatures, 189–190, 513
tax initiatives, 200–201
term limits, 680–682
union endorsements, 11, 21
voter guides, 199, 449
voter outreach, 631–633
voter registration. *See* Voter registration
women, 581–583, 707–710
Electronic Frontier Foundation, 288–290
Electronic media. *See* Media
Electronic Privacy Information Center (EPIC), 291–293
Eli Lily and Company, 248
E-mail. *See* Internet
EMILY's List, 294–296
Emissions control. *See* Environmental issues
Employment. *See also* Workplace issues
    age discrimination, 542–543
    disabled, 549
    ex-cons, 693
    gays and lesbians, 434
    jobs creation, 229
    lawsuits, toxic chemical, 39
    layoffs, 230
    minimum wage, 530–531
    minorities, 485
    outsourcing, 249, 402–403, 674–675
    pregnancy discrimination, 554, 591
    undocumented workers. *See* Immigration
    unemployment, 192, 675–676
    volunteer programs, participation in, 113
    women, 129–130, 590–592
Empower America, 297–299
Endangered species
    lynx, 278–279, 471
    protection of, 62, 277–279, 469, 634, 713–715
    snowy plover, 603
    Sumatran tigers, 713
Endangered Species Act, 62, 469, 580, 634
Energy policy, 167, 204, 238–239, 300–302, 585, 647–649, 704
    Africa, 353–354
    American Indian lands, 516–517
    Arctic drilling, 300, 488, 580, 689, 706
    biobased products, 301
    Canada, 344
    Iraq, 406, 464–465
    land conservation and, 425
    natural gas, 705
    pipeline, 430–431
Energy rates, 239
    gas prices, 343–344
English, as official language, 676–679
Enola Gay, 609

Enron, 317, 410–411
Environmental and Energy Study Institute, 300–302
Environmental Defense, 303–305
Environmental issues. *See also* Natural resources, conservation of;
        Pollution
    advocates for, 157–159, 206–209, 233–237, 283–287, 300–305,
        352–354, 361–363, 430–432, 442–445, 584–586,
        620–622, 634–636, 642–643, 647–649, 660–662,
        683–685, 704–707, 710–712, 716–718
    air pollution. *See* Pollution
    bank lending and, 249
    business and, 35–36
    citizen suits, 673
    Congress and, 41
    consumers and, 206–207
    corporations, 58, 236–237, 250, 253, 307, 422, 588
    dry cleaning, 38–39
    ecoterrorism, 57
    education about, 713
    election issues, 662
    emissions control, 222, 300–301, 419, 486–487, 489, 578–579,
        620–621, 649, 683–684
    global warming, 207, 221, 303–304, 642, 683–684, 711
    "green" products, 250
    landfills, 159
    mining waste, 671–672
    pesticides. *See* Pesticides
    protesters, 283–285, 361, 706
    public utilities, 208
    quality of, 606, 607
    recycling programs, 157, 354
    river protection, 61–63
    state laws, 442
    Superfund, 487, 648
    sustainable development, 626–628, 690, 716–718
    toxics, 311
    trade and, 97
    waste disposal, 645, 661
    wetlands, 424
    wolf control, 277
Environmental Law Institute, 306–308
Environmental Protection Agency (EPA), 223
    air pollution, 486–487, 579, 620–621
    clean-up efforts, 487–488
    dry cleaning regulations, 38–39
    pesticides, 100–101, 310
    sanctions against, 437
    second-hand smoke dangers, 699–700
    waste permitting, 661
    water pollution, 579–580
Environmental Working Group, 309–311
Estate tax, 34–35, 394
Ethics. *See also* Moral issues
    Congress, 215–216
    corporations, 140–141, 258, 316–317
    promotion of, 140–141, 312–317
    state government, 216, 514
Ethics and Public Policy Center, 312–314
Ethics Resource Center, 315–317
Eugenics, 312–313
Everglades, 552
Extradition treaty, 379
ExxonMobil, 35–36

Fairness & Accuracy in Reporting (FAIR), 318–319
Fair trade, 77
Faith-based initiatives, 52, 54, 55, 71, 124, 337, 625

Families. *See also* Children and youth
    advocacy groups, 320–322, 326–328, 335–337, 398–400, 554–556
    family leave, 555, 591
Families and Work Institute, 320–322
Families USA Foundation, 323–325, 472
Family and Medical Leave Act of 1993, 555, 591
Family planning. *See* Reproductive health
Family Research Council, 44, 326–328, 377
FARM (Farm Animal Reform Movement), 329–331
Farnsworth House, 573–574
Fatah, 180
Federal Aviation Administration (FAA), 64
Federal Communications Commission (FCC), 173, 217, 454–456, 519, 562, 640
Federal Elections Commission (FEC), 611
Federal Housing Administration (FHA), 570
Federal Trade Commission (FTC), 292
Federation for American Immigration Reform, 332–334
Financial Accounting Standards Board (FASB), 258
Financial services. *See also* Investments
    auto loans, 241
    credit and credit cards, 242, 293, 569
    environmental lending, 249
    lending practices, 569
    mortgage loans. *See* Mortgage industry
    privacy of personal information, 66–67
Firearms. *See also* Gun control
    advocacy groups, 560–562
    concealed weapons, 107–108
    women and, 562
Firestone Tires, 139
FirstEnergy, 177
Fish and fisheries, 61
    dolphins, 656
    habitat protection, 62, 655–657
    lobsters, 384–385
    salmon, 38, 309–310, 580, 602–603, 705
    sharks, 304–305, 595, 656
    shrimp, 235
    tuna, 286, 287
Fish and Wildlife Service, U.S., 356–357, 671, 714
"527" groups. *See* Taxation
Florida
    constitution, 681
    elections, 190
    Everglades, 552
    land conservation, 588
    limousine rates, 604
    panthers, 579
    telephone rates, 216
Focus on the Family, 72, 335–337
Food and Drug Administration (FDA)
    experimental drug approvals, 699
    morning-after pill, 224–225, 481, 624
    tobacco, 122
Food and nutrition
    advocacy groups, 178–179, 329–331
    beef, 179, 304, 330, 382
    children, 178
    "Fair Trade Certified," 77
    farm animals and, 329–331, 382
    fast food, 178
    foie gras, 368–369
    food labeling, 37–38, 519
    genetically modified crops and food, 238, 244–245, 352–353, 362, 685

hunger and, 338–339, 688
    ice cream, 179
    lawsuits, 218
    low carbohydrate diet plans, 38
    organic food, 77, 310
    pesticide use and, 617–618
    poultry, 304
    research, 338–339
    salt, 60
    school breakfast program, 338
    vegetarianism, 330–331, 616
Food Research and Action Center (FRAC), 338–339
Ford Foundation, 274
Ford Motor Company, 685
Foreign relations
    intelligence information, 21
    Middle East, 85
    understanding of, 93–95, 269–271
Forest and forestry. *See also* Logging industry
    protection of, 287
    rain forests, 642–643, 717
The Foundation Center, 340–342
Foundation on Economic Trends, 343–345
Foundations, 272–274, 349, 395, 506–508. *See also* Charities and charitable societies; Philanthropy
France and anti-Semitism, 54
Fraud
    charities. *See* Charities and charitable societies
    identity, 149, 333–334
Freddie Mac, 639
Free Congress Research and Education Foundation (FCF), 66, 346–348
Freedom Forum, 349–351
Freedom of Information Act, 278, 598, 672
Freedom Ride 2004, 195
Free enterprise advocacy, 221–223, 644–646
Freeport-McMoRan Copper & God Inc., 251
Free speech
    marketing and sales, 44
    promotion of, 349–351, 611–613
Friends of the Earth (FoE), 352–354
The Fund for Animals, 355–357

Gambling, 185–186, 298
Gangs, 496
Gay and Lesbian Alliance Against Defamation (GLAAD), 358–360
Gay and lesbian rights
    advocacy groups, 358–360, 375–377, 433–435, 533–535
    Boy Scouts ban, 30
    Catholic Church position, 511
    civil rights, 30, 44, 376, 405
    domestic partnership bills, 535
    employment discrimination, 434
    media and, 318–319
    military service issues, 658–659
    political clout of, 377
    presidential candidates on, 533–534
    same-sex marriage, 43–44, 224, 281, 297, 326–327, 335, 360, 370, 375–376, 398, 433, 667
    state laws, 225, 281, 376, 405, 434–435
    TV characters, 359
    university courses, 534
General Motors Corporation, 252
Genetically modified crops and food. *See* Food and nutrition
Genetic engineering, 312–313

Georgia, 434
Girl Scouts, 624
GlaxoSmithKline PLC, 638
Globalization, 170, 252, 268, 401–403
    boycotts and protests against, 407–408
Government. *See also* Congress; Local government; State government
    accountability, 172–174, 215–217, 436–439
    citizen participation in, 254–256
    continuity operation in case of attack, 181
    contracts, 173
    minority role in, 447
    salaries, 58
    spending, 33, 132, 167, 202, 226, 282, 367–368, 567
    term limits, 680–682
Governors, 260, 536–538
Grammy Awards ceremony, 515
Great Sand Dunes National Monument, 588
Greenhouse gases, 222, 300–301, 303–304, 422–423, 586, 649, 683–684, 711
Greenpeace USA, 35–36, 361–363
Guantanamo Bay prisoners, 29–30, 77–78, 380, 524
Gun control, 106–108. *See also* Firearms
    high school alliance against guns, 20
    lawsuits against manufacturers, 561
    legislation, 561

Haiti, 269–270, 669
H&R Block Inc., 91
Hate groups and crimes, 82–84, 151, 661
    anti-Semitism, 82–84
    identification of groups, 663–664
    Latinos as victims, 460
Health care. *See also specific diseases*
    advocacy groups, 169–171, 178–179, 323–325, 620–622
    bioterrorism, 60
    blood pressure, 60
    businesses, 261–262
    Catholic hospitals, 510
    children, 195–196
    cholesterol-lowering drugs, 638
    counseling, 169
    drug abuse. *See* Substance abuse
    drug price reduction, 23–24
    elderly, 323–324
    HIV/AIDS, 16–17
    infant deaths, 195–196
    managed care plans, 214
    medical malpractice, 160, 161–162, 219, 694
    mental health, 261
    obesity. *See* Obesity
    pregnancy, 556, 718
    prescription drugs. *See* Pharmaceutical industry; Prescription drugs
    reproductive. *See* Reproductive health
    research standards for government regulations, 59–60, 96
    SARS, 24
    small businesses, 532
    smoking. *See* Smoking
    stem-cell research, 513, 565
    uninsured, 325
    vision problems, 75
    women, 520, 590–592, 718
Healthy Families, 196
Henry L. Stimson Center, 364–366
The Heritage Foundation, 135, 367–369
Heritage tourism, 573
Highway safety. *See* Automobiles

Hispanics
    advocates for, 445–447, 521–523
    civil rights, 447, 460–462
    media, 521–522
    voting, 522
Historic preservation, 572–574
HIV/AIDS, 16–17
    drugs for, 46, 418–419
    epidemic, 46, 184
    gay rights and, 534–535
    lawsuits, 18
Holocaust, 84, 181
Home Depot, 643
Homeland security, 79–81. *See also* Air travel; Terrorism, war on
    business and, 268
    citizen's perspective, 254
    closed public records for purposes of, 351
    immigration security, 86
Homeland Security Department, 80, 86, 148
Homelessness, 12, 503–505, 688
Homosexuals. *See* Gay and lesbian rights
Honduras, 125
Hooker Chemical & Plastics, 157
Hoover Institution on War, Revolution, and Peace, 370–371
Household International Inc., 92
Housing
    affordable housing, 143, 557–558
    mortgage loans, 92, 143, 570, 577
Housing and Urban Development Department, 558
Houston, Texas, 585
Hudson Institute, 372–374
Human rights, promotion of, 76–78, 378–379
Human Rights Campaign (HRC), 375–377
Human Rights Watch, 378–380
The Humane Society of the United States, 381–383
Hunting
    African wildlife, 236
    anti-hunting advocates, 355–356, 385
    seals, 385
    traps, 386
    walrus, 385
    wolves, 277–278

Iams Co., 615–616
IBM, 39
Identity theft and fraud, 149, 333–334
IFAW (International Fund for Animal Welfare), 384–386
Illinois, 675
Immigration
    anti-immigration sentiment, 332–334
    minors and citizenship, 557
    policies, 76, 86–87, 88–89, 315
    reform, 334, 523
    registration of Arab males, 86–87, 88–89, 264–265
    terrorism issues and, 347–348, 523
    undocumented workers, 332–333, 678, 694
In Defense of Animals, 387–389
The Independent Institute, 390–392
Independent Sector, 393–395
India
    HIV/AIDS, 47
    Pakistan dispute with, 271
INFACT, 396–397
Infant deaths, 195–196
Information access
    closed public records for security purposes, 351
    data mining, 292–293

Mad cow disease, 179
MADD. *See* Mothers Against Drunk Driving
Malaria Project, 187
MALDEF. *See* Mexican American Legal Defense and Educational Fund
Manhattan Institute for Policy Research, 451–453
Manufacturing industries, 486–488
Marine resources. *See also* Fish and fisheries
    coral reefs, 714
    protection of, 593–595, 655–657
    whales, 657
Marketing, 11
    alcoholic beverages, 178
    anti-smoking campaigns, 121–122
    gay advocates enlisting sponsors to withdraw from conservative talk show, 359
    media issues, 163
    Medicare prescription drug coverage, 22–23
    obscenity in, 44
    telemarketing, 291
Marriage, 43–44, 224, 326–328, 370, 399–400. *See also* Gay and lesbian rights
Maryland, 442–443
Massachusetts, 260–261, 376, 572, 667
Massachusetts Institute of Technology, 641
Mayors, 686–688
McDonald's Corporation, 11–12, 304
Media. *See also* Television
    accuracy of, 5–6, 318–319
    advocacy groups, 454–459
    broadcast regulations, 173
    First Amendment rights and, 454–456
    gays and lesbians, 318–319
    Hispanics, 521–522
    Iraq war, 319, 457, 458–459
    liberal bias, 407
    mergers and acquisitions, 217, 455
    ownership rules, 454–456, 562
    partisanship, 457
    politics and government coverage, 165, 254–255, 374
    public service announcements about U.S. Supreme Court, 544
    quality of, 163–165, 318–319
Media Access Project, 454–456
Media Research Center, 457–459
Medicaid, 556
Medical care. *See* Health care
Medical malpractice, 160, 161–162, 219, 694
Medicare
    prescription drug coverage, 2–3, 22–23, 324, 368, 476, 528, 567
    spending, 367–368, 472–473, 498
Mental health, 261
Mercury emissions, 578–579, 620–621
Mergers, 217, 246, 257, 569, 629
Mexican American Legal Defense and Educational Fund (MALDEF), 460–462
Mexican Americans. *See* Hispanics
Mexico, 127, 267, 286
Michigan, 512–513
Microsoft, 292
Middle East
    democracy in, 40
    Palestinians, 48, 85
    suicide bombers, 180, 199
    understanding of issues, 463–465, 695–697
Middle East Policy Council, 463–465
Midwest states, 261
Military

defense, 94, 145–147, 180–181
gays and lesbians, 658–659
illegal immigrants in, 334
land mines, 379
missile defense system, 94, 147
personnel shortage, 390
religious observances, 73
spending, 392
women in, 225
Million Mom March, 106–108
Mines and mining, 234, 353–354, 671–672
Minnesota, 194, 204, 252, 530, 537
Minorities. *See also specific minority groups*
    abortion issues, 564
    economic advancement, 427–429
    employment, 163–164, 485, 548–549
Missile defense program, 94, 147
Mississippi River, 425
Modern Red SchoolHouse Institute, 373
Moral issues. *See* Ethics; Religion
Mortgage industry, 92, 143, 570, 577
Mothers Against Drunk Driving (MADD), 466–468
Motorcycle accident statistics, 15
Motor vehicles. *See* Automobiles
Mountain States Legal Foundation, 469–471
MoveOn.org, 472–474
Moving Ideas Network, 475–476
Ms. Foundation, 321
Multilateralism, 128
Museums
    closure of Jewish museum, 103
    Newseum, 350
    Smithsonian Institution, 609
Muslims, 263–265, 415–416, 664. *See also* Islam
    discrimination against, 151
    war on terrorism and, 54–55

NAACP. *See* National Association for the Advancement of Colored People
NAACP Legal Defense and Educational Fund, Inc., 477–479
NAFTA. *See* North American Free Trade Agreement
NARAL Pro-Choice America, 480–482, 563, 564
National Academy of Sciences, 63, 580
National Association for the Advancement of Colored People, 447, **483–485**
National Association of Manufacturers, 486–488
National Audubon Society, 489–491
National Center for Educational Accountability, 492–494
National Center for Neighborhood Enterprise, 495–496
National Center for Policy Analysis, 497–499
National Coalition Against Domestic Violence, 500–502
National Coalition for the Homeless, 503–505
National Committee for Responsive Philanthropy, 506–508
National Conference of Catholic Bishops/United States Catholic Conference, 509–511
National Conference of Editorial Writers, 330
National Conference of State Legislatures, 512–514
National Congress of American Indians, 515–517
National Consumers League, 518–520
National Council of Churches, 314
National Council of La Raza, 521–523
National Council of the Churches of Christ in the U.S.A., 524–526
National Council on the Aging, 527–529
National Education Association, 436–437
National Federation of Independent Business, 530–532
National Gay and Lesbian Task Force and Policy Institute, 44, **533–535**

Telephone industry
    cellular phones, 173, 520
    mergers and acquisitions, 246
    number-portability, 173, 247
    rate hikes, 216
    telemarketing, 291, 519
Television. *See also* Media
    gay characters, 359
    portrayal of pubic officials, 83–84
    unauthorized recordings, 290
Ten Commandments, 20–21, 30, 72, 663
Term limits, 680–682
Terrorism. *See also* Homeland security
    alerts, 80
    drinking water and, 306–307
    lawsuits against countries supporting, 93
    prisoners, rights of, 29–30
    September 11 attacks, 282, 473
Terrorism, war on
    airport security, 149
    American Muslims and, 54–55, 264
    bioterrorism, 60
    budget analysis of, 597
    Cuba, 543–544
    government policies, 181
    immigration and, 347–348, 523
    Iraq linked to, 372
    misinformation about, 350–351
Texas
    gay rights, 405
    redistricting, 190, 461
    state legislature, 190
Thimerosal, 248
Think tanks. *See individual organizations*
Tobacco industry. *See also* Smoking
    anti-tobacco activities, 121–123
    boycotts of, 396–397
    children and, 121–123
Tourism, 573, 715
    cruise ships, 594
    ecotourism, 235–236
Toxic substances. *See also* Pesticides
    employee lawsuits, 39
    PBDEs, 311
Toyota, 685
Trade. *See also* World Trade Organization
    barriers, 244
    China, 362
    environmental issues, 97
    free trade, 402
    Mexico, 127, 267
    NAFTA, 127
    protectionism, 132, 167–168
Traditional Values Coalition, 44, 665–667
Traffic. *See* Automobiles; Transportation issues
TransAfrica/TransAfrica Forum, 668–670
Transportation issues
    commuting, 347, 644–645
    drunk driving, 466–468
    environmental issues, 716
    light-rail systems, 347
    limousine rates, 604
    traffic congestion, 348
Trial Lawyers for Public Justice, 671–673

Union of Concerned Scientists, 683–685

Union Pacific Corp., 666
Unions
    endorsement of political candidates, 11, 21
    retiree membership, 24
    violence, 568
United Airways, 79
United Kingdom, 352–353, 361, 379
United Nations, 207
    weapons inspection program, 126–127
United Nations Foundation, 125
United States
    leadership, 365
United States Conference of Mayors, 686–688
United States Public Interest Research Group, 689–691
Universities and colleges
    affirmative action, 51, 298
    black universities and colleges, 479
    business education, 258
    business partnership with, 493
    Catholic, 54
    discrimination, 461
    fraternities and animals, 382
    gay rights, 534
    promiscuity on campus, 399
    religious freedom, 44, 54
    SAT scores, 90, 156, 461
    sports recruiting policies, 547
    teacher education, 606
University of Colorado, 547
University of North Carolina, 44
Urban areas. *See* Cities
The Urban Institute, 692–694
U.S. Chamber of Commerce, 674–676
U.S. ENGLISH, Inc., 677–679
U.S. Term Limits, 680–682
Utah, 370

Verizon, 698–699
Vinson & Elkins, 374
Violence. *See also* Gun control
    domestic violence, 500–502
    high school alliance against guns, 20
    youth, 82
Virgin Atlantic Airlines, 546
Virginia, 69, 201, 203, 468, 479, 611–612
Vis, 715
Volunteerism, 113
Voter registration, 198, 264, 415, 516
Voting rights, 188–190, 448–450

Wal-Mart Stores, 376, 590–591
Walt Disney Co., 257
War. *See* Afghanistan; Iraq
War on terrorism. *See* Terrorism, war on
War reporting, 5–6
The Washington Institute for Near East Policy, 695–697
Washington Legal Foundation, 698–700
Water. *See also* Rivers
    cleanup of California coast, 593
    pollution, 306–307, 444, 579–580
    protection of, 584
    quality, 306–307, 444
Watercraft in national parks, 287
Weapons. *See also* Firearms; Gun control; Nuclear weapons
    biological, 126, 146
    chemical, 126, 432